D0225385

SIXTH EDITION

Foundations *of* Physiological Psychology

Neil R. Carlson
University of Massachusetts, Amherst

PEARSON

Boston | New York | San Francisco
Mexico City | Montreal | Toronto | London | Madrid | Munich | Paris
Hong Kong | Singapore | Tokyo | Cape Town | Sydney

Series Editor: Kelly May
Series Editorial Assistant: Adam Whitehurst
Marketing Manager: Karen Natale
Composition and Prepress Buyer: Linda Cox
Cover Administrator: Linda Knowles
Editorial-Production Coordinator: Mary Beth Finch
Photo Researcher: Helane Manditch-Prottas
Editorial-Production Service: Barbara Gracia
Text Designer: Carol Somberg
Copyeditor: Barbara Willette
Illustrator: Jay Alexander
Electronic Composition: Omegatype Typography, Inc.

Copyright © 2005, 2002, 1999, 1995,1992, 1988 Pearson Education, Inc.

Internet: www.ablongman.com

All rights reserved. No part of the material protected by this copyright notice may be reproduced or utilized in any form or by any means, electronic or mechanical, including photocopying, recording, or by any information storage and retrieval system, without written permission from the copyright owner.

To obtain permission(s) to use material from this work, please submit a written request to Allyn and Bacon, Permissions Department, 75 Arlington Street, Boston, MA 02116 or fax your request to 617-848-7320.

Between the time Web site information is gathered and published, some sites may have closed. Also the transcription of URLs can result in typographical errors. The publisher would appreciate notification where these occur so that they may be corrected in subsequent editions.

Library of Congress Cataloging-in-Publication Data
Carlson, Neil R.,
Foundations of physiological psychology / Neil R. Carlson.—6th ed.
p. cm
Includes bibliographical references and index.
ISBN 0-205-42723-5
1. Psychophysiology. I. Title
QP360.C35 2005
612.8—dc26 2004044764

Photo Credits: p. 1, Martin Harvey/Peter Arnold, Inc.; p. 2, © Rachel Epstein, PhotoEdit; p. 6, photo courtesy of Neil R. Carlson; p. 17, © Michael Schwarz/The Image Works; p. 26, Jim Karageorge/Taxi/© GettyImages, Inc.; p. 39, © Clay Wiseman/Animals Animals; p. 51, © R. Kuiter/Animals Animals; p. 61, Ray Massey/Image Bank/ © GettyImages, Inc.; p. 75, © John Eastcott/Yva Momatiuk/ The Image Works; p. 80, © Myrleen Ferguson Cate/PhotoEdit; p. 83, Mike Powell/Allsport Photography/© GettyImages, Inc.; p. 94, Catherine Ledner/Stone/© GettyImages, Inc.; p. 107, © Leonard Lee Rue, III/Earth Scenes; p. 109, © Tom Prettyman/PhotoEdit; p. 122, © B. Daemmrich/ The Image Works; p. 147, © Denis MacDonald/PhotoEdit; p. 150, © Michael Schwarz/The Image Works; p. 154, Anthony Cassidy/Stone/© GettyImages, Inc.; p. 157, © Carson Baldwin. Jr./Animals Animals; p. 164, © Richard Kolar/ Animals Animals; p. 181, © Amwell/Stone/GettyImages, Inc.; p. 188, Gandee Vasan/Image Bank/© GettyImages, Inc.; p. 198, © Michael Newman/PhotoEdit; p. 209, © Michael Newman/PhotoEdit; p. 221, © Tom Prettyman/PhotoEdit; p. 226, White Packert/Image Bank/© GettyImages, Inc.; p.236, © Tom Brakefield/The Image Works; p. 256, Kaz Chiba/Taxi/© GettyImages, Inc.; p. 260, Daly & Newton/ Stone/© GettyImages, Inc.; p. 273, © David Joel/Stone; p. 292, Jonathan Skow/Taxi/© GettyImages, Inc.; p. 299, © Gerald Lacz/Animals Animals; p. 304, © B. Daemmrich/ The Image Works; p. 311, © Robert Brenner/PhotoEdit; p. 321, Alexandra Grablewski/FoodPix/GettyImages, Inc.; p. 333, © Lawrence Migdale/Stone; p. 349, © Earl Dotter; p. 356, Art Montes de Oca/Taxi/© GettyImages, Inc.; p. 371, © Elizabeth Crews/The Image Works; p. 376, Denis Boissavy/Taxi/ © GettyImages, Inc.; p. 385, Elyse Lewin/ Image Bank/© GettyImages, Inc.; p. 398, Hideki Fujii/ Image Bank/© GettyImages, Inc.; p. 401, © Spencer Grant/PhotoEdit; p. 416, © B. Daemmrich/The Image Works; p. 422, © Cameramann/The Image Works; p. 432, © James Shaffer/PhotoEdit; p. 438, © Paul Conklin/ PhotoEdit; p. 444, © Ellen Senisi/The Image Works; p. 460, Color Day Production/Image Bank/© GettyImages, Inc.; p. 467, © Robert Brenner/PhotoEdit; p. 475, © 1993 Eric Nelson/Custom Medical Stock Photo; p. 484, © Photo Researchers, Inc.; p. 495, Kamil Vojnar/Taxi/ © GettyImages, Inc.; p. 497, © Eastcott/Momatiuk/The Image Works; p. 507, © Paul Conklin/PhotoEdit; p. 520, © Cindy Charles/PhotoEdit; p. 522, Uwe Krejci/Stone Allstock/© GettyImages, Inc.

Printed in the United States of America

10 9 8 7 6 5 4 3 2 1 VHP 08 07 06 05 04

in memory of
Paul Wayne Johnson

BRIEF CONTENTS

CONTENTS

CHAPTER 6

CHAPTER 7

CHAPTER 8

Sleep and Biological Rhythms 226

CHAPTER 9

Reproductive Behavior 260

CHAPTER 10

Emotion 292

PREFACE

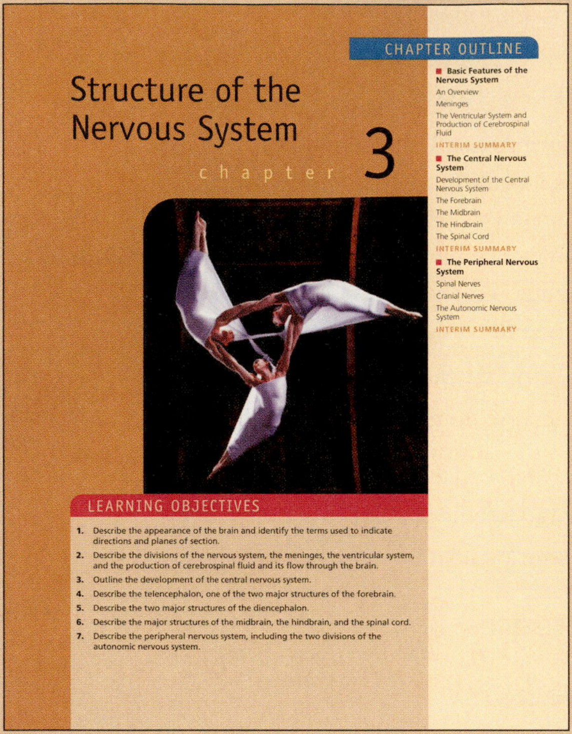
Structure of the Nervous System

chapter 3

CHAPTER OUTLINE

- **Basic Features of the Nervous System**
  - An Overview
  - Meninges
  - The Ventricular System and Production of Cerebrospinal Fluid
  - INTERIM SUMMARY
- **The Central Nervous System**
  - Development of the Central Nervous System
  - The Forebrain
  - The Midbrain
  - The Hindbrain
  - The Spinal Cord
  - INTERIM SUMMARY
- **The Peripheral Nervous System**
  - Spinal Nerves
  - Cranial Nerves
  - The Autonomic Nervous System
  - INTERIM SUMMARY

LEARNING OBJECTIVES

1. Describe the appearance of the brain and identify the terms used to indicate directions and planes of section.
2. Describe the divisions of the nervous system, the meninges, the ventricular system, and the production of cerebrospinal fluid and its flow through the brain.
3. Outline the development of the central nervous system.
4. Describe the telencephalon, one of the two major structures of the forebrain.
5. Describe the two major structures of the diencephalon.
6. Describe the major structures of the midbrain, the hindbrain, and the spinal cord.
7. Describe the peripheral nervous system, including the two divisions of the autonomic nervous system.

All my life I have wanted to know how things work. When I was a boy, I took apart alarm clocks, radios, my mother's sewing machine, and other interesting gadgets, to see what was inside. Much to my parents' relief, I outgrew that habit (or at least got better at putting things back together), but my curiosity is still with me. Since my college days, I have been trying to find out all I can about the workings of the most intricate piece of machinery that we know of: the human brain.

The field of neuroscience research is a very busy and productive one today. A large number of scientists are trying to understand the physiology of behavior, using more and more advanced methods, yielding more and more interesting results. Their findings provide me with much to write about. I admire their dedication and hard work, and I thank them for giving me something to say. Without their efforts I could not have written this book.

I wrote the first edition of this book at the request of my colleagues who teach the course, and who wanted a briefer version of *Physiology of Behavior* with more emphasis on research related to humans. The first part of this book is concerned with foundations: the history of the field, the structure and functions of neurons, neuroanatomy, psychopharmacology, and methods of research. The second part is concerned with inputs: the sensory systems. The third part deals with what might be called "motivated" behavior: sleep, reproduction, emotion, and ingestion. The fourth part deals with learning and with verbal communication. The final part deals with neurological and mental disorders.

Content Changes

Of course, all chapters in this book have been revised. My colleagues keep me busy by providing me with interesting research results to describe in my book. The problem is always to include the interesting new material without letting the length of the book get out of hand. Like the previous editions, this edition contains a chapter on neurological disorders, which is not found in *Physiology of Behavior.*

The following list includes some of the information that is new to this edition:

- Functional imaging studies on perception of form from motion
- New research on the role of outer hair cells in amplification of vibrations of the basilar membrane
- New research on the presence of dorsal and ventral streams in the auditory system
- New research on the capsaicin nociceptor in knockout mice
- "Olfactotopic" representation in olfactory cortex
- Deep brain stimulation for Parkinson's disease
- The discovery that narcolepsy is a neurodegenerative disease of hypocretinergic neurons
- New research on the role of adenosine as a sleep-promoting chemical
- The discovery of two families of pheromone receptor proteins
- New research on the effects of estradiol on women's sexual interest
- New research on the human amygdala and emotional memory
- New research on the role of the prefrontal cortex in decision making and moral judgments

- The role of serotonin in functions of prefrontal cortex: relevance to anger and aggression
- New research on the mechanisms of long-term potentiation and its role in learning
- The role of place cells in spatial memory
- Functional imaging studies of the human hippocampus
- A new section on the bilingual brain
- The role of languages with irregular orthography in the prevalence of developmental dyslexia
- Evidence for loss of cerebral gray matter in schizophrenia
- New research on the interactions between prefrontal cortex, ventral tegmental area, and nucleus accumbens in the development of schizophrenia
- Evidence that depression may result from hyperactivity of the amygdala and orbitofrontal cortex and hypoactivity of the subgenual prefrontal cortex
- Lack of a fusiform face area in the brains of autistic adults
- A new section on attention-deficit/hyperactivity disorder
- The role of increased sensitivity of brain glucocorticoid receptors in posttraumatic stress disorder
- The role of basolateral amygdala in classically conditioned drug craving
- Evidence that the orbitofrontal cortex and anterior cingulate cortex are involved in drug craving
- Evidence that stress early in life can increase susceptibility to drug addiction

There are some important differences between this book and *Physiology of Behavior.* The text of this book is not simply a shorter and denser version of its predecessor. I kept the illustrative examples, especially those dealing with human disorders, and added explanations of phenomena to be sure that students without much background in biology could understand what I was saying. Although I have simplified some of the detailed explanations I have retained the important principles.

Strategies for Learning

This theme, which runs throughout the book, was created to help apply physiological psychology to daily life. You will find a "Strategies for Learning" heading in Chapter 1, and a chapter entitled "Methods and Strategies of Research." This chapter does not contain a bewildering list of research methods; instead, the reader is led through a set of hypothetical investigations organized the way that a research project might proceed. Each step illustrates a particular procedure in the context in which it would be applied in an ongoing program.

- **Learning Objectives.** Each chapter begins with a list of learning objectives, which also serve as the framework for the study guide that accompanies this text.
- **Prologue.** A Prologue, which contains the description of an episode involving a neurological disorder or an issue in neuroscience, opens each chapter.
- **Epilogue.** An Epilogue at the end of the chapter resolves the issues raised in the prologue, discussing them in terms of what the reader has learned in the chapter, or introduces a related topic.
- **Interim Summary** follows each major section of the book. They not only provide useful reviews, but also break each chapter into manageable chunks.
- **Thought Questions** follow most interim summaries, and provide an opportunity to think about what has been learned in the previous section.
- **Definitions of Key Terms** are printed in the margin near the places where the terms are first discussed. Pronunciation guides for terms that might be difficult to pronounce are also found there.
- **Key Concepts.** Each chapter ends with key concepts, which provide a quick review. A list of **Suggested Readings** and **Suggested Web Sites** provide more information about the topics discussed in the chapter.

Full-Color Art

The illustrations in this book were prepared by Jay Alexander, of I-Hua Graphics. Jay also works in the Psychology Department at the University of Massachusetts, and he and I have been working together on my books for several years. I think the result of our collaboration is a set of clear, consistent, and attractive illustrations.

Strategies for Learning Supplements

I have prepared a revised CD-ROM, which contains the *Neuroscience Animations* and the *Computerized Study Guide.* The animations demonstrate some of the most important principles of neuroscience through movement and interaction. The animations have been substantially revised and expanded from the previous version. They include modules on neurophysiology (Neural Communication,

The Action Potential, Synapses, and Postsynaptic Potentials), neuroanatomy (The Rotatable Brain, Brain Slices, and Meninges and CSF), psychopharmacology, research methods, audition, memory, and verbal communication. The modules on research methods include three new videos demonstrating histological methods, autoradiography, and implantation of an intracranial cannula. The interactive *Computerized Study Guide,* accessible through the same menu, contains a set of self-tests that include multiple-choice questions and an on-line review of terms and definitions. The questions and list of terms and definitions present questions and keep track of your progress, presenting missed items until you have answered all of them correctly. The computerized study guide also includes interactive figures and diagrams from the book that will help students learn terms and concepts. This CD-ROM is included free with the purchase of a new book.

A *Study Guide,* which my wife and I wrote, is also available. This workbook provides a framework for guiding study behavior. It promotes a thorough understanding of the principles of physiological psychology through active participation in the learning process. The study guide contains a set of Concept Cards. An important part of learning about physiological psychology is acquiring a new vocabulary, and the concept cards will help with this task. Terms are printed on one side of these cards, and definitions are printed on the other.

The publisher of this book, Allyn & Bacon, hosts a companion Web site for this text: **www.ablongman.com/carlson6e**. This site contains additional multiple-choice test questions for students, organized by chapter. This forum allows you to further practice exam taking. The Web site also provides hot links to other relevant sites of interest and research updates, provided by Paul Wellman, Professor of Psychology at Texas A&M.

Supplements for Instructors

Several supplements are available for instructors who adopt this book.

- **Instructor's Manual.** Written by Bill Meil, Indiana University of Pennsylvania, this is an excellent tool for classroom preparation and management. Each chapter includes an At-A-Glance Grid, with detailed pedagogical information linking to other available supplements, teaching objectives, lecture material, demonstrations and activities, and an updated list of video, media, suggested readings, and web resources. In addition, the appendix includes a comprehensive list of student handouts.
- **Test Bank.** Written by Paul Wellman, Texas A&M University, this resource is filled with challenging questions that target key concepts. Each chapter has approximately 100 questions, including multiple-choice, true/false, short answer, and essay, each with an answer justification, page references, a difficulty rating, and type designation. In addition, the appendix includes a sample open-book quiz. This product is also available in TestGen 5.5 computerized version, for use in creating tests in the classroom.
- **Powerpoint Presentation.** An interactive tool for use in the classroom, was created by Grant McLaren, Edinboro University of Pennsylvania. Each chapter includes images from the textbook, with demonstrations. In addition, the CD-ROM contains the electronic Instructor's Manual files.
- **Transparencies for Physiological Psychology, © 2005.** Completely updated. There are approximately 100 full-color acetates to enhance classroom lecture and discussion. This package includes images from Allyn and Bacon's major physiological psychology texts.
- **Digital Media Archive for Physiological Psychology, © 2004.** This is a comprehensive source for video and animation; text images, including charts, graphs, tables, and figures; and PowerPoint lecture presentations, all from Allyn and Bacon's major physiological psychology texts. It is a powerful tool for customized classroom presentation.
- **Physiological Psychology VideoWorkshop, Instructor's Teaching Guide.** A CD-ROM includes 10 video modules that offer many useful ideas for integrating VideoWorkshop into your course. It also includes correlation grids for individual physiological psychology texts, summaries for each video clip, critical thinking questions, multiple-choice questions, web links, and an answer key for the Student Learning Guide. For your review, the CD-ROM and Student Learning Guide is also included in the Teaching Guide, giving you the complete program in one easy reference.
- **CourseCompass.** Powered by Blackboard, this course management system uses a powerful suite of tools so instructors can create an online presence for any course.

In Conclusion

Trying to keep up with the rapid progress being made in neuroscience research poses a challenge for teachers and textbook writers. If a student simply memorizes what we believe at the time to be facts, he or she is left with knowledge that quickly becomes obsolete. In this book I have tried to provide enough background material and enough knowledge of basic physiological processes so that the reader can revise what he or she has learned when research provides us with new information.

I designed this text to be interesting and informative. I have endeavored to provide a solid foundation for further study. Students who will not take subsequent courses in this or related fields should receive the satisfaction of a much better understanding of their own behavior. Also, they will have a greater appreciation for the forthcoming advances in medical practices related to disorders that affect a person's perception, mood, or behavior. I hope that people who carefully read this book will henceforth perceive human behavior in a new light.

Acknowledgements

Although I must accept the blame for any shortcomings of the book, I want to thank colleagues who helped me. I thank Bill Meil for his work on the instructor's manual and Paul Wellman for his work on the test bank. I want to thank colleagues who helped me with the present edition of this book and the latest edition of *Physiology of Behavior* by sending reprints of their work, suggesting topics that I should cover, sending photographs that have been reproduced in this book, and pointing out deficiencies in the previous edition. I thank the following reviewers for their comments on this edition:

Adriana Alcantara, University of Texas at Austin
Janis L. Anderson, University of New Mexico
John F. Axelson, Holy Cross College
Norris R. Bancroft, Weber State University
Mark E. Basham, Metro State College of Denver
Jon E. Grahe, Monmouth College

I also want to thank the people at Allyn and Bacon. Kelly May, my editor, provided assistance, support, and encouragement, and Adam Whitehurst, editorial assistant, who helped to gather comments and suggestions from colleagues who have read the book. Erin Liedel oversaw the production of the ancillary material: study guide, Animation CD-ROM, instructor's manual, transparencies, Videoworkshop, PowerPoint, and digital media archive. Mary Beth Finch, the production editor, assembled the team that designed and produced the book. Carol Somberg designed the book—which looks pretty good, I think. Barbara Gracia, of Woodstock Publishers' Services, demonstrated her masterful skills of organization in managing the book's production. She got everything done on time, despite an extremely tight schedule. Few people realize what a difficult, demanding, and time-consuming job a production editor has with a project such as this, with hundreds of illustrations and an author who tends to procrastinate, but I do, and I thank her for all she has done. Barbara Willette served as copy editor. She gave me a chance to fix my errors before anyone else saw them in print.

I must also thank my wife Mary for her support. Writing is a lonely pursuit, because one must be alone with one's thoughts for many hours of the day. I thank her for giving me the time to read, reflect, and write without feeling that I was neglecting her too much.

To the Reader

I hope that in reading this book you will come not only to learn more about the brain but also to appreciate it for the marvelous organ it is. The brain is wonderfully complex, and perhaps the most remarkable thing is that we are able to use it in our attempt to understand it.

While working on this book, I imagined myself talking with students, telling them interesting stories about the findings of clinicians and research scientists. Imagining your presence made the task of writing a little less lonely. I hope that the dialogue will continue. Please write to me and tell me what you like and dislike about the book. My address is: Department of Psychology, Tobin Hall, University of Massachusetts, Amherst, Massachusetts 01003. My e-mail address is *nrc@psych.umass.edu.* If you write to me (or send me an e-mail), we can make the conversation a two-way exchange.

NRC

Origins of Physiological Psychology

chapter 1

CHAPTER OUTLINE

LEARNING OBJECTIVES

1. Describe the behavior of people with split brains and explain what this phenomenon contributes to our understanding of self-awareness.
2. Describe the goals of scientific research.
3. Describe the biological roots of physiological psychology.
4. Describe the role of natural selection in the evolution of behavioral traits.
5. Describe the evolution of the human species.
6. Discuss the value of research with animals and ethical issues concerning their care.
7. Describe career opportunities in neuroscience.
8. Outline the strategies that will help you learn as much as possible from this book.

PROLOGUE

René's Inspiration

René, a lonely and intelligent young man of eighteen years, had secluded himself in Saint-Germain, a village to the west of Paris. He had recently suffered a nervous breakdown and chose the retreat to recover. Even before coming to Saint-Germain, he had heard of the fabulous royal gardens built for Henri IV and Marie de Médicis, and one sunny day he decided to visit them. The guard stopped him at the gate, but when he identified himself as a student at the King's School at La Flèche, he was permitted to enter. The gardens consisted of a series of six large terraces overlooking the Seine, planted in the symmetrical, orderly fashion so loved by the French. Grottoes were cut into the limestone hillside at the end of each terrace; René entered one of them. He heard eerie music accompanied by the gurgling of water but at first could see nothing in the darkness. As his eyes became accustomed to the gloom, he could make out a figure illuminated by a flickering torch. He approached the figure, which he soon recognized as that of a young woman. As he drew closer, he saw that she was actually a bronze statue of Diana, bathing in a pool of water. Suddenly, the Greek goddess fled and hid behind a bronze rosebush. As René pursued her, an imposing statue of Neptune rose in front of him, barring the way with his trident.

René was delighted. He had heard about the hydraulically operated mechanical organs and the moving statues, but he had not expected such realism. As he walked back toward the entrance to the grotto, he saw the plates buried in the ground that controlled the valves operating the machinery. He spent the rest of the afternoon wandering through the grottoes, listening to the music and being entertained by the statues.

During his stay in Saint-Germain, René visited the royal gardens again and again. He had been thinking about the relationship between the movements of animate and inanimate objects, which had concerned philosophers for some time. He thought he saw in the apparently purposeful, but obviously inanimate, movements of the statues an answer to some important questions about the relationship between the mind and the body. Even after he left Saint-Germain, René Descartes revisited the grottoes in his memory; and he went so far as to name his daughter Francine after their designers, the Francini brothers of Florence.

The last frontier in this world—and perhaps the greatest one—lies within us. The human nervous system makes possible all that we can do, all that we can know, and all that we can experience. Its complexity is immense, and the task of studying it and understanding it dwarfs all previous explorations our species has undertaken.

Most physiological psychologists believe that by understanding the workings of the nervous system we eventually will understand how we think, remember, and act—and will even understand the nature of our own self-awareness.

One of the most universal of all human characteristics is curiosity. We want to explain what makes things happen. In ancient times, people believed that natural phenomena were caused by animating spirits. All moving objects—animals, the wind and tides, the sun, moon, and stars—were assumed to have spirits that caused them to move. For example, stones fell when they were dropped because their animating spirits wanted to be reunited with Mother Earth. As our ancestors became more sophisticated and learned more about nature, they abandoned this approach (which we call *animism*) in favor of physical explanations for inanimate moving objects. But they still used spirits to explain human behavior.

From the earliest historical times, people have believed that they possessed something intangible that animated them—a mind, a soul, or a spirit. This belief stems from the fact that each of us is aware of his or her own existence. When we think or act, we feel as though something inside us is thinking or deciding to act. But what is the nature of the human mind? We have physical bodies with muscles that move them and sensory organs such as eyes and ears that perceive information about the world around us. Within our bodies the nervous system plays a central role, receiving information from the sensory organs and controlling the movements of the muscles. But what is the mind, and what role does it play? Does it *control* the nervous system? Is it a *part of* the nervous system? Is it physical and tangible, like the rest of the body, or is it a spirit that will always remain hidden?

Physiological psychologists take an empirical and practical approach to the study of human nature. Most of us believe that the mind is a phenomenon produced by the activity of the nervous system. We believe that once we understand the workings of the human body—in particular, the workings of the nervous system—we will be able to explain how we perceive, how we think, how we remember, and how we act. We will even be able to explain the nature of our own self-awareness. Of course, we are far from understanding the workings of the nervous system, so only time will tell whether this belief is justified.

Figure 1.1

Will the human brain ever completely understand its own workings? A sixteenth-century woodcut from the first edition of *De humani corporis fabrica (On the Workings of the Human Body)* by Andreas Vesalius.

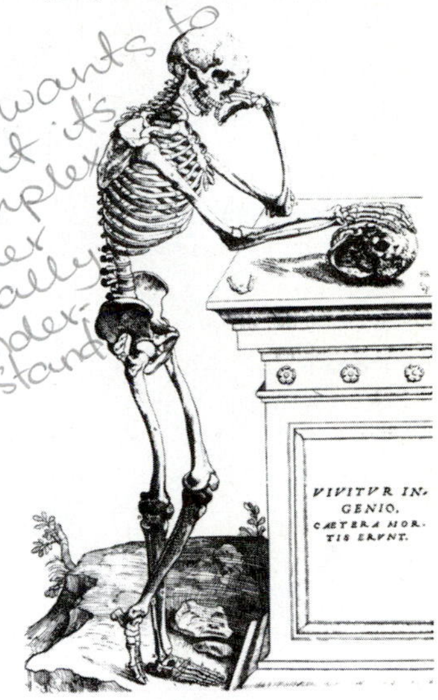

Courtesy of National Library of Medicine.

Understanding Human Consciousness: A Physiological Approach

How can physiological psychologists study human consciousness? First, let's define our terms. The word *consciousness* can be used to refer to a variety of concepts, including simple wakefulness. Thus, a researcher may write about an experiment using "conscious rats," referring to the fact that the rats were awake and not anesthetized. By *consciousness,* I am referring to something else: the fact that we humans are aware of—and can tell others about—our thoughts, perceptions, memories, and feelings.

We know that brain damage or drugs can profoundly affect consciousness. Because consciousness can be altered by changes in the structure or chemistry of the brain, we may hypothesize that consciousness is a physiological function, just as behavior is. We can even speculate about the origins of this self-awareness. Consciousness and the ability to communicate seem to go hand in hand. Our species, with its complex social structure and enormous capacity for learning, is well served by our ability to communicate: to express intentions to one another and to make requests of one another. Verbal communication makes cooperation possible and permits us to establish customs and laws of behavior. Perhaps the evolution of this ability is what has given rise to the phenomenon of consciousness. That is, our ability to send and receive messages with other people enables us to send and receive our own messages—in other words, to think and to be aware of our own existence. (See ***Figure 1.1.***)

Split Brains

Studies of humans who have undergone a particular surgical procedure demonstrate dramatically how disconnecting parts of the brain that are involved with perceptions from parts that are involved with verbal behavior also disconnects them from consciousness. These results suggest that the parts of the brain involved in verbal behavior may be the ones responsible for consciousness.

The surgical procedure is one that has been used for people with very severe epilepsy that cannot be controlled by drugs. In these people, nerve cells in one side of the brain become overactive, and the overactivity is transmitted to the other side of the brain by a structure called the corpus callosum. The **corpus callosum** is a large bundle of nerve fibers that connect corresponding parts of one side of the brain with those of the other. Both sides of the brain then engage in wild activity and stimulate each other, causing a generalized epileptic seizure. These seizures can occur many times each day, preventing the person from leading a normal life. Neurosurgeons

corpus callosum (***core*** *pus ka* ***low*** *sum*) A large bundle of nerve fibers that connect corresponding parts of one side of the brain with those of the other.

Figure 1.2

The split-brain operation. A "window" has been opened in the side of the brain so that we can see the corpus callosum being cut at the midline of the brain.

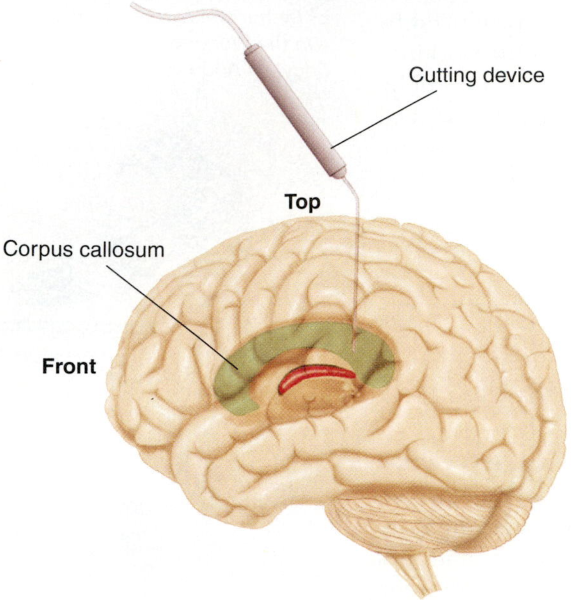

discovered that cutting the corpus callosum (the **split-brain operation**) greatly reduced the frequency of the epileptic seizures.

Figure 1.2 shows a drawing of the split-brain operation. We see the brain being sliced down the middle, from front to back, dividing it into its two symmetrical halves. A "window" has been opened in the left side of the brain so that we can see the corpus callosum being cut by the neurosurgeon's special knife. (See ***Figure 1.2.***)

Sperry (1966) and Gazzaniga and his associates (Gazzaniga, 1970; Gazzaniga and LeDoux, 1978) have studied these patients extensively. The largest part of the brain consists of two symmetrical parts, called the **cerebral hemispheres,** which receive sensory information from the opposite sides of the body. They also control movements of the opposite sides. The corpus callosum enables the two hemispheres to share information so that each side knows what the other side is perceiving and doing. After the split-brain operation is performed, the two hemispheres are disconnected and operate independently. Their sensory mechanisms, memories, and motor systems can no longer exchange information. The effects of these disconnections are not obvious to the casual observer, for the simple reason that only one hemisphere—in most people, the left—controls speech. The right hemisphere of an epileptic person with a split brain appears to be able to understand verbal instructions reasonably well, but it is incapable of producing speech.

Because only one side of the brain can talk about what it is experiencing, people who speak with a person with a split brain are conversing with only one hemisphere: the left. The operations of the right hemisphere are more difficult to detect. Even the patient's left hemisphere has to learn about the independent existence of the right hemisphere. One of the first things that these patients say they notice after the operation is that their left hand seems to have a "mind of its own." For example, patients may find themselves putting down a book held in the left hand, even if they have been reading it with great interest. This conflict occurs because the right hemisphere, which controls the left hand, cannot read and therefore finds the book boring. At other times, these patients surprise themselves by making obscene gestures (with the left hand) when they had not intended to. A psychologist once reported that a man with a split brain had attempted to beat his wife with one hand and protect her with the other. Did he *really* want to hurt her? Yes and no, I guess.

One exception to the crossed representation of sensory information is the olfactory system. That is, when a person sniffs a flower through the left nostril, only the left brain receives a sensation of the odor. Thus, if the right nostril of a patient with a split brain is closed, leaving only the left nostril open, the patient will be able to tell us what the odors are (Gordon and Sperry, 1969). However, if the odor enters the right nostril, the patient will say that he or she smells nothing. But, in fact, the right brain *has* perceived the odor and *can* identify it. To show that this is so, we ask the patient to smell an odor with the right nostril and then reach for some objects that are hidden from view by a partition. If asked to use the left hand, controlled by the hemisphere that detected the smell, the patient will select the object that corresponds to the odor—a plastic flower for a floral odor, a toy fish for a fishy odor, a model tree for the odor of pine, and so forth. But if asked to use the right hand, the patient fails the test because the right hand is connected to the left hemisphere, which did not smell the odor. (See ***Figure 1.3.***)

The effects of cutting the corpus callosum reinforce the conclusion that we become conscious of something only if information about it is able to reach the parts

Interesting

split-brain operation Brain surgery that is occasionally performed to treat a form of epilepsy; the surgeon cuts the corpus callosum, which connects the two hemispheres of the brain.

cerebral hemispheres The two symmetrical halves of the brain; constitute the major part of the brain.

Figure 1.3

Identification of an object in response to an olfactory stimulus by a person with a split brain.

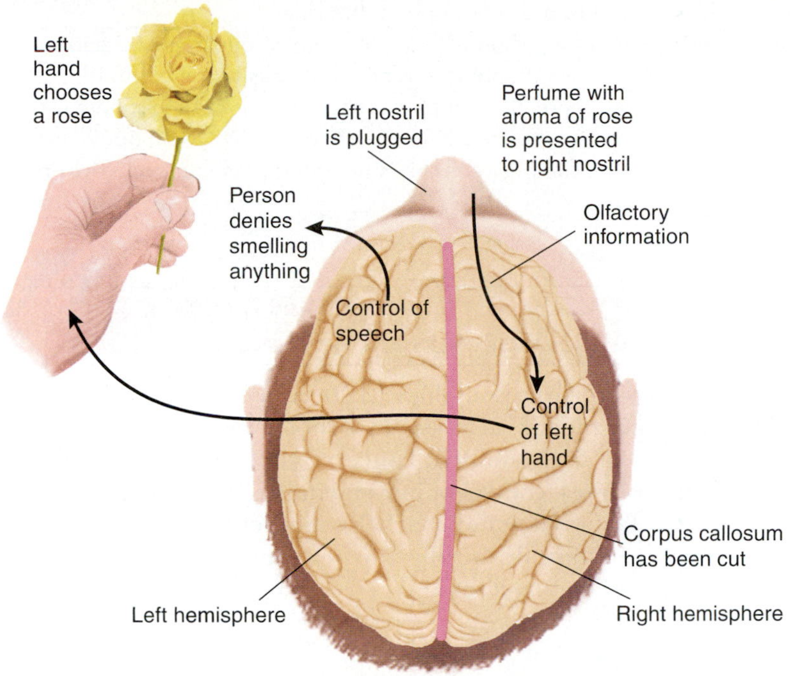
Left
hand
chooses
a rose
Left nostril
is plugged
Perfume with
aroma of rose
is presented
to right nostril
Person
denies
smelling
anything
Olfactory
information
Control of
speech
Control
of left
hand
Corpus callosum
has been cut
Left hemisphere
Right hemisphere

of the brain responsible for verbal communication, which are located in the left hemisphere. If the information does not reach these parts of the brain, then that information does not reach the consciousness associated with these mechanisms. We still know very little about the physiology of consciousness, but studies of people with brain damage are beginning to provide us with some useful insights. This issue is discussed in later chapters.

INTERIM SUMMARY

Understanding Human Consciousness: A Psychological Approach

The concept of the mind has been with us for a long time—probably from the earliest history of our species. Modern science has adopted a belief that the world consists of matter and energy and that what we call the mind can be explained by the same laws that govern all other natural phenomena. Studies of the functions of the human nervous system tend to support this position, as the specific example of the split brain shows. Brain damage, by disconnecting brain functions from the speech mechanisms in the left hemisphere, reveals that the mind does not have direct access to all brain functions.

When sensory information about a particular object is presented to the right hemisphere of a person who has had a split-brain operation, the person is not aware of the object but can, nevertheless, indicate by movements of the left hand that the object has been perceived. This phenomenon suggests that consciousness involves operations of the verbal mechanisms of the left hemisphere. Indeed, consciousness may be, in large part, a matter of our "talking to ourselves." Thus, once we understand the language functions of the brain, we may have gone a long way to understanding how the brain can be conscious of its own existence.

THOUGHT QUESTIONS

1. Could a sufficiently large and complex computer ever be programmed to be aware of itself? Suppose that someone someday claims to have done just that. What kind of evidence would you need to prove or disprove this claim?
2. Clearly, the left hemisphere of a person with a split brain is conscious of the information it receives and of its own thoughts. It is not conscious of the mental processes of the right hemisphere. But is it possible that the right hemisphere is conscious, too, but is just unable to talk to us? How could we possibly find out whether it is? Do you see some similarities between this issue and the one raised in the first question?

The Nature of Physiological Psychology

The modern history of physiological psychology has been written by psychologists who have combined the experimental methods of psychology with those of physiology and have applied them to the issues that concern all psychologists. Thus, we have studied perceptual processes, control of movement, sleep and waking, reproductive behaviors, ingestive behaviors, emotional behaviors, learning, and language. In recent years we have begun to study the physiology of human pathological conditions, such as addictions and mental disorders.

The Goals of Research

The goal of all scientists is to explain the phenomena they study. But what do we mean by *explain*? Scientific explanation takes two forms: generalization and reduction. Most psychologists deal with **generalization.** They explain particular instances of behavior as examples of general laws, which they deduce from their experiments. For instance, most psychologists would explain a pathologically strong fear of dogs as an example of a particular form of learning called *classical conditioning*. Presumably, the person was frightened earlier in life by a dog. An unpleasant stimulus was paired with the sight of the animal (perhaps the person was knocked down by an exuberant dog or was attacked by a vicious one), and the subsequent sight of dogs evokes the earlier response: fear.

Most physiologists deal with **reduction.** They explain complex phenomena in terms of simpler ones. For example, they may explain the movement of a muscle in terms of the changes in the membranes of muscle cells, the entry of particular chemicals, and the interactions among protein molecules within these cells. By contrast, a molecular biologist would explain these events in terms of forces that bind various molecules together and cause various parts of the molecules to be attracted to one another. In turn, the job of an atomic physicist is to describe matter and energy themselves and to account for the various forces found in nature. Practitioners of each branch of science use reduction to call on sets of more elementary generalizations to explain the phenomena they study.

Studies of people with brain damage have given us insights into the brain mechanisms involved in reading and writing.

The task of the physiological psychologist is to explain behavior in physiological terms. But physiological psychologists cannot simply be reductionists. It is not enough to observe behaviors and correlate them with physiological events that occur at the same time. Identical behaviors may occur for different reasons and thus may be initiated by different physiological mechanisms. Therefore, we must understand "psychologically" why a particular behavior occurs before we can understand what physiological events made it occur.

Let me provide a specific example: Mice, like many other mammals, often build nests. Behavioral observations show that mice will build nests under two conditions: when the air temperature is low and when the animal is pregnant. A nonpregnant mouse will build a nest only if the weather is cool, whereas a pregnant mouse will build one regardless of the temperature. The same behavior occurs for different reasons. In fact, nest-building behavior is controlled by two different physiological mechanisms. Nest building can be studied as a behavior related to the process of temperature regulation, or it can be studied in the context of parental behavior.

In practice, the research efforts of physiological psychologists involve both forms of explanation: generalization and reduction. Ideas for experiments are stimulated by the investigator's knowledge both of psychological generalizations about behavior and of physiological mechanisms. A good physiological psychologist must therefore be both a good psychologist *and* a good physiologist.

Biological Roots of Physiological Psychology

Study of (or speculations about) the physiology of behavior has its roots in antiquity. Because its movement is necessary for life, and because emotions cause it to beat more strongly, many ancient cultures, including the Egyptian, Indian, and Chinese, considered the heart to be the seat of thought and emotions. The ancient Greeks did, too, but Hippocrates (460–370 B.C.) concluded that this role should be assigned to the brain.

Not all ancient Greek scholars agreed with Hippocrates. Aristotle did not; he thought the brain served to cool the passions of the heart. But Galen (A.D. 130–200), who had the greatest respect for Aristotle, concluded that Aristotle's role for the brain was "utterly absurd, since in that case Nature would not have placed the encephalon [brain] so far from the heart, . . . and she would not have attached the sources of all the senses [the sensory nerves] to it (Galen, 1968 translation, p. 387). Galen thought enough of the brain to dissect and study the brains of cattle, sheep, pigs, cats, dogs, weasels, monkeys, and apes (Finger, 1994).

René Descartes, a seventeenth-century French philosopher and mathematician, has been called the father of modern philosophy. Although he was not a biologist, his speculations about the roles of the mind and brain in the control of behavior provide a good starting point in the history of physiological psychology. Descartes assumed that the world was a purely mechanical entity that, once having been set in motion by God, ran its course without divine interference. Thus, to understand the world, one had only to understand how it was constructed. To Descartes, animals were mechanical devices; their behavior was controlled by environmental stimuli. His view of the human body was much the same: It was a machine. As Descartes observed, some movements of the human body were automatic and involuntary. For example, if a person's finger touched a hot object, the arm would immediately withdraw from the source of stimulation. Reactions like this did not require participation of the mind; they occurred automatically. Descartes called these actions **reflexes** (from the Latin *reflectere,* "to bend back upon itself"). Energy coming from the outside source would be reflected back through the nervous system to the muscles, which would contract. The term is still in use today, but of course we explain the operation of a reflex differently.

Like most philosophers of his time, Descartes was a dualist; he believed that each person possesses a mind—a uniquely human attribute that is not subject to the laws of the universe. But his thinking differed from that of his predecessors in one important way: He was the first to suggest that a link exists between the human mind and its purely physical housing, the brain. He believed that the mind controls the

generalization Type of scientific explanation; a general conclusion based on many observations of similar phenomena.

reduction Type of scientific explanation; a phenomenon is described in terms of the more elementary processes that underlie it.

reflex An automatic, stereotyped movement produced as the direct result of a stimulus.

Figure 1.4

A woodcut from *De homine* by René Descartes, published in 1662. Descartes believed that the "soul" (what we would today call the *mind*) controls the movements of the muscles through its influence on the pineal body. His explanation is modeled on the mechanism that animated statues in the royal gardens. According to his theory, the eyes sent visual information to the brain, where it could be examined by the soul. When the soul decided to act, it would tilt the pineal body (labeled H in the diagram), which would divert pressurized fluid through nerves to the appropriate muscles.

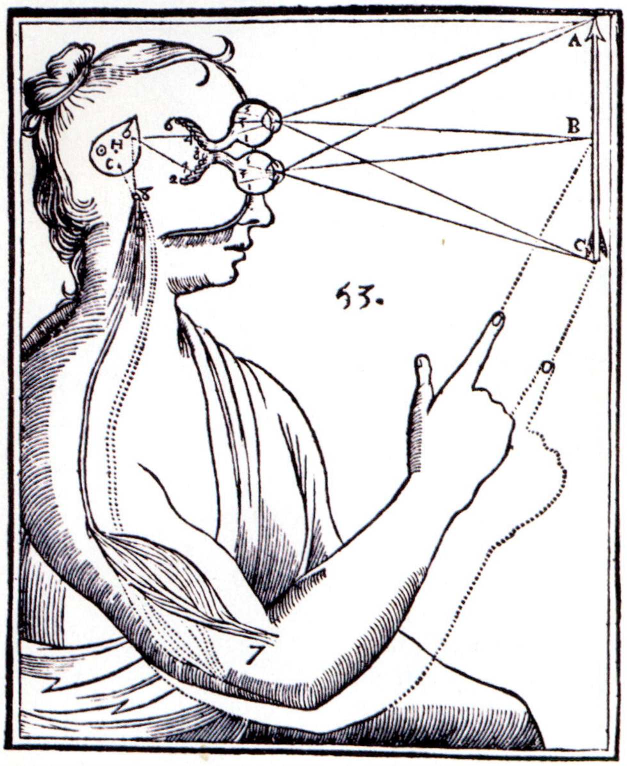

movements of the body, while the body, through its sense organs, supplies the mind with information about what is happening in the environment. In particular, he hypothesized that this interaction takes place in the pineal body, a small organ situated on top of the brain stem, buried beneath the cerebral hemispheres. He noted that the brain contains hollow chambers (the *ventricles*) that are filled with fluid, and he hypothesized that this fluid is under pressure. In his theory, when the mind decides to perform an action, it tilts the pineal body in a particular direction like a little joystick, causing fluid to flow from the brain into the appropriate set of nerves. This flow of fluid causes the same muscles to inflate and move. (See ***Figure 1.4***.)

As we saw in the prologue, the young René Descartes was greatly impressed by the moving statues in the royal gardens (Jaynes, 1970). These devices served as models for Descartes in theorizing about how the body worked. The pressurized water of the moving statues was replaced by pressurized fluid in the ventricles; the pipes were replaced by nerves; the cylinders by muscles; and finally, the hidden valves by the pineal body. This story illustrates one of the first times that a technological device was used as a model for explaining how the nervous system works. In science, a **model** is a relatively simple system that works on known principles and is able to do at least some of the things that a more complex system can do. For example, when scientists discovered that elements of the nervous system communicate by means of electrical impulses, researchers developed models of the brain based upon telephone switchboards and, more recently, computers. Abstract models, which are completely mathematical in their properties, have also been developed.

Descartes's model was useful because, unlike purely philosophical speculations, it could be tested experimentally. In fact, it did not take long for biologists to prove that Descartes was wrong. For example, Luigi Galvani, a seventeenth-century Italian physiologist, found that electrical stimulation of a frog's nerve caused contraction of the muscle to which it was attached. Contraction occurred even when the nerve and muscle were detached from the rest of the body, so the ability of the muscle to contract and the ability of the nerve to send a message to the muscle were characteristics of these tissues themselves. Thus, the brain did not inflate muscles by directing pressurized fluid through the nerve. Galvani's experiment prompted others to study the nature of the message transmitted by the nerve and the means by which muscles contracted. The results of these efforts gave rise to an accumulation of knowledge about the physiology of behavior.

One of the most important figures in the development of experimental physiology was Johannes Müller, a nineteenth-century German physiologist. (See ***Figure 1.5***.) Müller was a forceful advocate of the application of experimental techniques to physiology. Previously, the activities of most natural scientists were limited to observation and classification. Although these activities are essential, Müller insisted that major advances in our understanding of the workings of the body would be achieved only by experimentally removing or isolating animals' organs, testing their responses to various chemicals, and otherwise altering the environment to see how the organs responded. His most important contribution to the study of the physiology of behavior was his **doctrine of specific nerve energies.** Müller observed that although all nerves carry the same basic message, an electrical impulse, we perceive the messages of dif-

model A mathematical or physical analogy for a physiological process; for example, computers have been used as models for various functions of the brain.

doctrine of specific nerve energies Müller's conclusion that because all nerve fibers carry the same type of message, sensory information must be specified by the particular nerve fibers that are active.

experimental ablation The research method in which the function of a part of the brain is inferred by observing the behaviors an animal can no longer perform after that part is damaged.

ferent nerves in different ways. For example, messages carried by the optic nerves produce sensations of visual images, and those carried by the auditory nerves produce sensations of sounds. How can different sensations arise from the same basic message?

The answer is that the messages occur in different channels. The portion of the brain that receives messages from the optic nerves interprets the activity as visual stimulation, even if the nerves are actually stimulated mechanically. (For example, when we rub our eyes, we see flashes of light.) Because different parts of the brain receive messages from different nerves, the brain must be functionally divided: Some parts perform some functions, while other parts perform others.

Müller's advocacy of experimentation and the logical deductions from his doctrine of specific nerve energies set the stage for performing experiments directly on the brain. Indeed, Pierre Flourens, a nineteenth-century French physiologist, did just that. Flourens removed various parts of animals' brains and observed their behavior. By seeing what the animal could no longer do, he could infer the function of the missing portion of the brain. This method is called **experimental ablation** (from the Latin *ablatus,* "carried away"). Flourens claimed to have discovered the regions of the brain that control heart rate and breathing, purposeful movements, and visual and auditory reflexes.

Figure 1.5

Johannes Müller (1801–1858).

Courtesy of National Library of Medicine.

Soon after Flourens performed his experiments, Paul Broca, a French surgeon, applied the principle of experimental ablation to the human brain. Of course, he did not intentionally remove parts of human brains to see how they worked. Instead, he observed the behavior of people whose brains had been damaged by strokes. In 1861 he performed an autopsy on the brain of a man who had had a stroke that resulted in the loss of the ability to speak. Broca's observations led him to conclude that a portion of the cerebral cortex on the left side of the brain performs functions necessary for speech. (See ***Figure 1.6.***) Other physicians soon obtained evidence supporting his conclusions. As you will learn in Chapter 13, the control of speech is not localized in a particular region of the brain. Indeed, speech requires many different functions, which are organized throughout the brain. Nonetheless, the method of experimental ablation remains important to our understanding of the brains of both humans and laboratory animals.

As I mentioned earlier, Luigi Galvani used electricity to demonstrate that muscles contain the source of the energy that powers their contractions. In 1870, German physiologists Gustav Fritsch and Eduard Hitzig used electrical stimulation as a tool for understanding the physiology of the brain. They applied weak electrical current to the exposed surface of a dog's brain and observed the effects of the stimulation. They found that stimulation of different portions of a specific region of the brain caused contraction of specific muscles on the opposite side of the body. We now refer to this region as the *primary motor cortex,* and we know that nerve cells there communicate directly with those that cause muscular contractions. We also know that other regions of the brain communicate with the primary motor cortex and thus control behaviors. For example, the region that Broca found necessary for speech communicates with, and controls, the portion of the primary motor cortex that controls the muscles of the lips, tongue, and throat, which we use to speak.

Figure 1.6

Broca's area, a region of the brain named for French surgeon Paul Broca. Broca discovered that damage to a part of the left side of the brain disrupted a person's ability to speak.

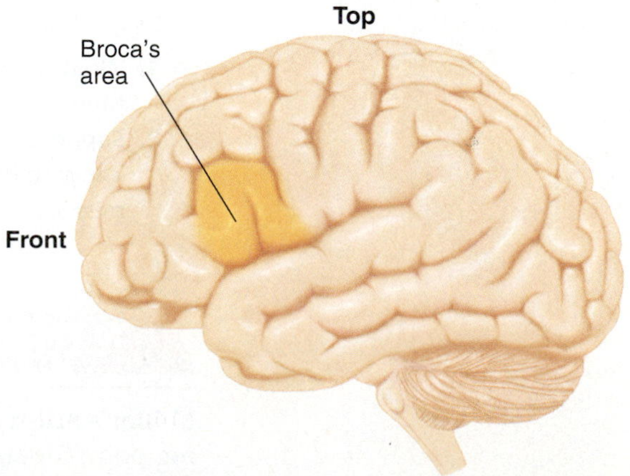

One of the most brilliant contributors to nineteenth-century science was the German physicist and physiologist Hermann von Helmholtz. Helmholtz devised a mathematical formulation of the law of conservation of energy, invented the ophthalmoscope (used to examine the retina of the eye), devised an important and influential theory of color vision and color blindness, and studied audition, music, and many physiological processes. Although Helmholtz had studied under Müller, he opposed Müller's belief that human organs are endowed with a vital nonmaterial force that coordinates their operations. Helmholtz believed that all aspects of physiology are mechanistic, subject to experimental investigation.

Helmholtz was also the first scientist to attempt to measure the speed of conduction through nerves. Scientists had previously believed that such conduction was identical to the conduction that occurs in wires, traveling at approximately the speed of light. But Helmholtz found that neural conduction was much slower—only about 90 feet per second. This measurement proved that neural conduction was more than a simple electrical message, as we will see in Chapter 2.

Twentieth-century developments in experimental physiology include many important inventions, such as sensitive amplifiers to detect weak electrical signals, neurochemical techniques to analyze chemical changes within and between cells, and histological techniques to see cells and their constituents. Because these developments belong to the modern era, they are discussed in detail in subsequent chapters.

INTERIM SUMMARY

The Nature of Physiological Psychology

All scientists hope to explain natural phenomena. In this context, the term *explanation* has two basic meanings: generalization and reduction. Generalization refers to the classification of phenomena according to their essential features so that general laws can be formulated. For example, observing that gravitational attraction is related to the mass of two bodies and to the distance between them helps to explain the movement of planets. Reduction refers to the description of phenomena in terms of more basic physical processes. For example, gravitation can be explained in terms of forces and subatomic particles.

Physiological psychologists use both generalization and reduction to explain behavior. In large part, generalizations use the traditional methods of psychology. Reduction explains behaviors in terms of physiological events within the body—primarily within the nervous system. Thus, physiological psychology builds upon the tradition of both experimental psychology and experimental physiology.

The physiological psychology of today is rooted in important developments of the past. René Descartes proposed a model of the brain based on hydraulically activated statues. His model stimulated observations that produced important discoveries. The results of Galvani's experiments eventually led to an understanding of the nature of the message transmitted by nerves between the brain and the sensory organs and the muscles. Müller's doctrine of specific nerve energies paved the way for study of the functions of specific parts of the brain through the methods of experimental ablation and electrical stimulation.

THOUGHT QUESTIONS

1. What is the value of studying the history of physiological psychology? Is it a waste of time?
2. Suppose we studied just the latest research and ignored explanations that we now know to be incorrect. Would we be spending our time more profitably, or might we miss something?

Natural Selection and Evolution

Müller's insistence that biology must be an experimental science provided the starting point for an important tradition. However, other biologists continued to observe, classify, and think about what they saw, and some of them arrived at valuable conclusions. The most important of these scientists was Charles Darwin. (See *Figure 1.7.*) Darwin formulated the principles of *natural selection* and *evolution,* which revolutionized biology.

Functionalism and the Inheritance of Traits

Darwin's theory emphasized that all of an organism's characteristics—its structure, its coloration, its behavior—have functional significance. For example, their strong talons and sharp beaks permit eagles to catch and eat prey. Most caterpillars that eat green leaves are themselves green, and their color makes it difficult for birds to see them against their usual background. Mother mice construct nests, which keep their offspring warm and out of harm's way. Obviously, the behavior itself is not inherited—how can it be? What *is* inherited is a brain that causes the behavior to occur. Thus, Darwin's theory gave rise to **functionalism,** a belief that characteristics of living organisms perform useful functions. So, to understand the physiological basis of various behaviors, we must first understand what these behaviors accomplish. We must therefore understand something about the natural history of the species being studied so that the behaviors can be seen in context.

To understand the workings of a complex piece of machinery, we should know what its functions are. This principle is just as true for a living organism as it is for a mechanical device. However, an important difference exists between machines and organisms: Machines have inventors who had a purpose when they designed them, whereas organisms are the result of a long series of accidents. Thus, strictly speaking, we cannot say that any physiological mechanisms of living organisms have a *purpose.* But they do have *functions,* and these we can try to determine. For example, the forelimbs shown in Figure 1.8 are adapted for different uses in different species of mammals. (See *Figure 1.8.*)

A good example of the functional analysis of an adaptive trait was demonstrated in an experiment by Blest (1957). Certain species of moths and butterflies have spots

Figure 1.7

Charles Darwin (1809–1882). His theory of evolution revolutionized biology and strongly influenced early psychologists.

North Wind Picture Archives.

functionalism The principle that the best way to understand a biological phenomenon (a behavior or a physiological structure) is to try to understand its useful functions for the organism.

Figure 1.8

Bones of the forelimb: (a) human, (b) bat, (c) whale, (d) dog. Through the process of natural selection, these bones have been adapted to suit many different functions.

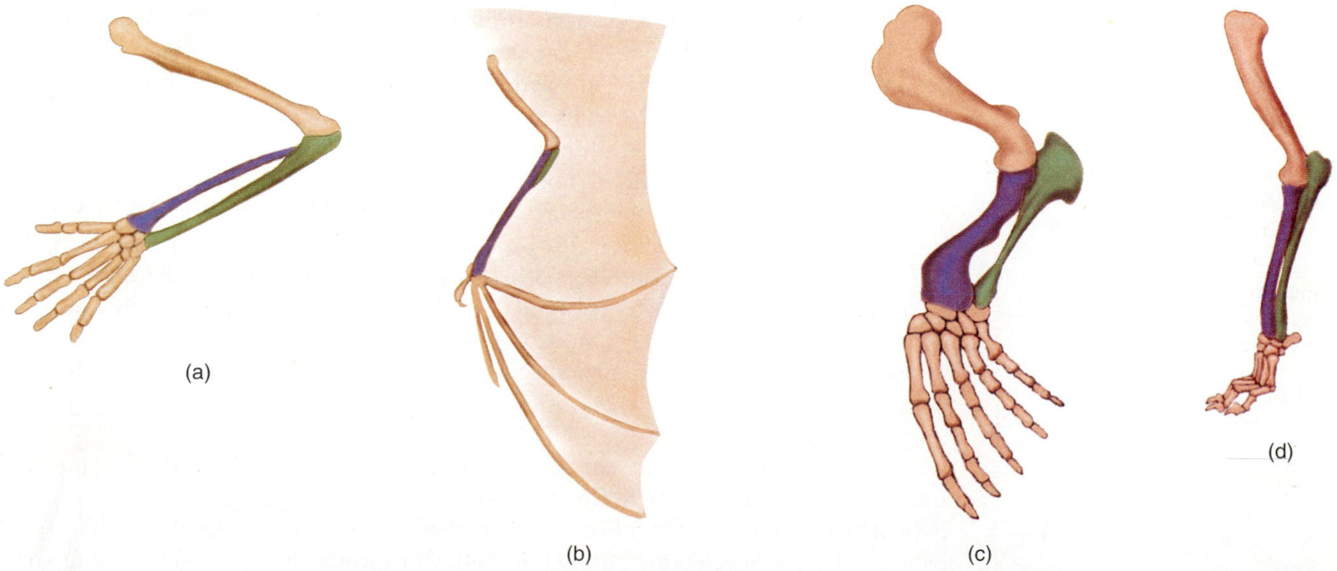

Figure 1.9

The owl butterfly. This butterfly displays its eyespots when approached by a bird. The bird usually will fly away.

Cosmos/Photo Researchers, Inc.

on their wings that resemble eyes—particularly the eyes of predators such as owls. (See ***Figure 1.9.***) These insects normally rely on camouflage for protection; the backs of their wings, when folded, are colored like the bark of a tree. However, when a bird approaches, the insect's wings flip open, and the hidden eyespots are suddenly displayed. The bird then tends to fly away, rather than eat the insect. Blest performed an experiment to see whether the eyespots on a moth's or butterfly's wings really disturbed birds that saw them. He placed mealworms on different backgrounds and counted how many worms the birds ate. Indeed, when the worms were placed on a background that contained eyespots, the birds tended to avoid them.

Darwin formulated his theory of evolution to explain the means by which species acquired their adaptive characteristics. The cornerstone of this theory is the principle of **natural selection.** Darwin noted that members of a species were not all identical and that some of the differences they exhibited were inherited by their offspring. If an individual's characteristics permit it to reproduce more successfully, some of the individual's offspring will inherit the favorable characteristics and will themselves produce more offspring. As a result, the characteristics will become more prevalent in that species. He observed that animal breeders were able to develop strains that possessed particular traits by mating together only animals that possessed the desired traits. If *artificial selection,* controlled by animal breeders, could produce so many varieties of dogs, cats, and livestock, perhaps *natural selection* could be responsible for the development of species. Of course, it was the natural environment, not the hand of the animal breeder, that shaped the process of evolution.

Darwin and his fellow scientists knew nothing about the mechanism by which the principle of natural selection works. In fact, the principles of molecular genetics were not discovered until the middle of the twentieth century. Briefly, here is how the process works: Every sexually reproducing multicellular organism consists of a large number of cells, each of which contains chromosomes. Chromosomes are large, complex molecules that contain the recipes for producing the proteins that cells need to grow and to perform their functions. In essence, the chromosomes contain the blueprints for the construction (that is, the embryological development) of a particular member of a particular species. If the plans are altered, a different organism is produced.

The plans do get altered; mutations occur from time to time. **Mutations** are accidental changes in the chromosomes of sperms or eggs that join together and develop into new organisms. For example, cosmic radiation might strike a chromosome in a cell of an animal's testis or ovary, thus producing a mutation that affects that animal's offspring. Most mutations are deleterious; the offspring either fails to survive or survives with some sort of deficit. (See ***Figure 1.10.***) However, a small percentage of mutations are beneficial and confer a **selective advantage** to the organism that possesses them. That is, the animal is more likely than other members of its species to live long enough to reproduce and hence to pass on its chromosomes to its own offspring. Many different kinds of traits can confer a selective advantage: resistance to a particular disease, the ability to digest new kinds of food, more effective weapons for defense or for procurement of prey, and even a more attractive appearance to members of the opposite sex (after all, one must reproduce to pass on one's chromosomes).

Naturally, the traits that can be altered by mutations are physical ones; chromosomes make proteins, which affect the structure and chemistry of cells. But the *effects* of these physical alterations can be seen in an animal's behavior. Thus, the process of natural selection can act on behavior indirectly. For example, if a partic-

natural selection The process by which inherited traits that confer a selective advantage (increase an animal's likelihood to live and reproduce) become more prevalent in the population.

mutation A change in the genetic information contained in the chromosomes of sperms or eggs, which can be passed on to an organism's offspring; provides genetic variability.

selective advantage A characteristic of an organism that permits it to produce more than the average number of offspring of its species.

ular mutation results in changes in the brain that cause a small animal to stop moving and freeze when it perceives a novel stimulus, that animal is more likely to escape undetected when a predator passes nearby. This tendency makes the animal more likely to survive and produce offspring, thus passing on its genes to future generations.

Other mutations are not immediately favorable, but because they do not put their possessors at a disadvantage, they are inherited by at least some members of the species. As a result of thousands of such mutations, the members of a particular species possess a variety of genes and are all at least somewhat different from one another. Variety is a definite advantage for a species. Different environments provide optimal habitats for different kinds of organisms. When the environment changes, species must adapt or run the risk of becoming extinct. If some members of the species possess assortments of genes that provide characteristics permitting them to adapt to the new environment, their offspring will survive, and the species will continue.

Figure 1.10

An example of a maladaptive trait. An albino alligator would have difficulty sneaking up on its prey and would probably not survive in the wild. Most mutations do not produce selective advantages, but those that do are passed on to future generations.

J. H. Robinson/Animals Animals.

Evolution of the Human Species

To *evolve* means to develop gradually (from the Latin *evolvere,* "to unroll"). The process of **evolution** is a gradual change in the structure and physiology of plant and animal species as a result of natural selection. New species evolve when organisms develop novel characteristics that can take advantage of unexploited opportunities in the environment.

The first vertebrates to emerge from the sea—some 360 million years ago—were amphibians. In fact, amphibians have not entirely left the sea; they still lay their eggs in water, and the larvae that hatch from them have gills and only later transform into adults with air-breathing lungs. Seventy million years later, the first reptiles appeared. Reptiles had a considerable advantage over amphibians: Their eggs, enclosed in a shell just porous enough to permit the developing embryo to breathe, could be laid on land. Thus, reptiles could inhabit regions away from bodies of water, and they could bury their eggs where predators would be less likely to find them. Reptiles soon divided into three lines: the *anapsids,* the ancestors of today's turtles; the *diapsids,* the ancestors of dinosaurs, birds, lizards, crocodiles, and snakes; and the *synapsids,* the ancestors of today's mammals. One group of synapsids, the *therapsids,* became the dominant land animal during the Permian period. Then, about 248 million years ago, the end of the Permian period was marked by a mass extinction. Dust from a catastrophic series of volcanic eruptions in present-day Siberia darkened the sky, cooled the earth, and wiped out approximately 95 percent of all animal species. Among those that survived was a small therapsid known as a *cynodont*—the direct ancestor of the mammal, which first appeared about 220 million years ago. (See ***Figure 1.11.***)

Mammals (and the other warm-blooded animals, birds) were only a modest success for many millions of years. Dinosaurs ruled, and mammals had to remain small and inconspicuous to avoid the large variety of agile and voracious predators. Then, around 65 million years ago, another mass extinction occurred. An enormous meteorite struck the Yucatan peninsula of present-day Mexico, producing a cloud of dust that destroyed many species, including the dinosaurs. Small, nocturnal mammals survived the cold and dark because they were equipped with insulating fur and a mechanism for maintaining their body temperature. The void left by the extinction of so many large herbivores and carnivores provided the opportunity for mammals to expand into new ecological niches, and expand they did.

evolution A gradual change in the structure and physiology of plant and animal species—generally producing more complex organisms—as a result of natural selection.

Figure 1.11

Evolution of vertebrate species.

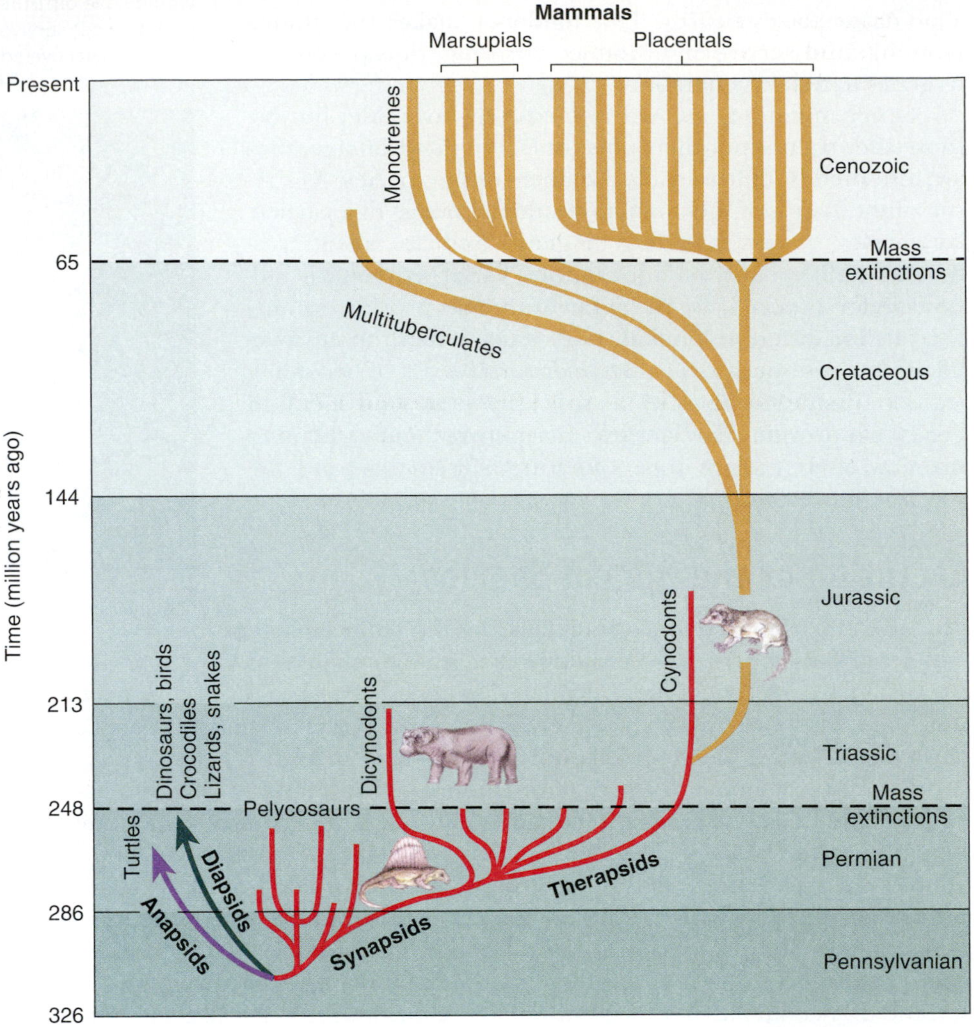

Redrawn with permission from Carroll, R. *Vertebrate Paleontology and Evolution.* New York: W. H. Freeman, 1988.

The climate of the early Cenozoic period, which followed the mass extinction at the end of the Cretaceous period, was much warmer than it is today. Tropical forests covered much of the land areas, and in these forests our most direct ancestors, the primates, evolved. The first primates, like the first mammals, were small and preyed on insects and small cold-blooded vertebrates such as lizards and frogs. They had grasping hands that permitted them to climb about in small branches of the forest. Over time, larger species developed, with larger, forward-facing eyes (and the brains to analyze what the eyes saw), which facilitated arboreal locomotion and the capture of prey. As fruit-bearing plants evolved, primates began to exploit this energy-rich source of food, and the evolution of color vision enabled them to easily distinguish ripe and unripe fruit.

The first *hominids* (humanlike apes) appeared in Africa. They appeared not in dense tropical forests, but in drier woodlands and in the savanna—vast areas of grasslands studded with clumps of trees and populated by large herbivorous animals and the carnivores that preyed on them. Our fruit-eating ancestors continued to eat fruit, of course, but they evolved characteristics that enabled them to gather roots and tubers as well, to hunt and kill game, and to defend themselves against other predators. They made tools that could be used to hunt, produce clothing, and construct dwellings; they discovered the many uses of fire; they domesticated dogs, which greatly increased their ability to hunt and helped warn of attacks by predators; and they developed the ability to communicate symbolically, by means of spoken words.

Our closest living relatives—the only hominids besides ourselves who have survived—are the chimpanzees, gorillas, and orangutans. DNA analysis shows that genetically there is very little difference between these four species. For example, humans and chimpanzees share 98.8 percent of their DNA. (See ***Figure 1.12.***)

Figure 1.12

A pyramid illustrating the percentage differences in DNA among the four major species of hominids.

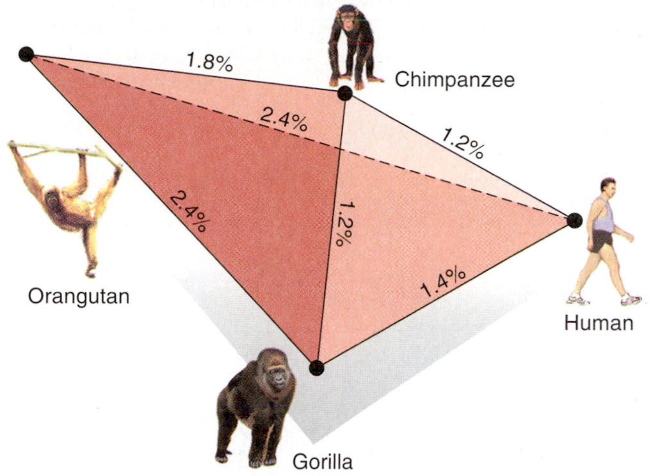

Redrawn with permission from Lewin, R. *Human Evolution: An Illustrated Introduction.* Boston: Blackwell Scientific Publications, 1984.

The first hominid to leave Africa did so around 1.7 million years ago. This species, *Homo erectus* ("upright man"), scattered across Europe and Asia. One branch of *Homo erectus* appears to be the ancestor of *Homo neanderthalis,* which inhabited Western Europe between 120,000 and 30,000 years ago. Neanderthals resembled modern humans. They made tools out of stone and wood and discovered the use of fire. Our own species, *Homo sapiens,* evolved in East Africa around 100,000 years ago. They migrated to other parts of Africa, and out of Africa to Asia, Polynesia, Australia, Europe, and the Americas. They encountered the Neanderthals in Europe around 40,000 years ago and coexisted with them for approximately 10,000 years. Eventually, the Neanderthals disappeared—perhaps through interbreeding with *Homo sapiens,* perhaps through competition for resources. Scientists have not found evidence for warlike conflict between the two species.

Evolution of Large Brains

Humans possessed several characteristics that enabled them to compete with other species. Their agile hands enabled them to make and use tools. Their excellent color vision helped them to spot ripe fruit, game animals, and dangerous predators. Their mastery of fire enabled them to cook food, provide warmth, and frighten nocturnal predators. Their upright posture and bipedalism made it possible for them to walk long distances efficiently, with their eyes far enough from the ground to see long distances across the plains. Bipedalism also permitted them to carry tools and food with them, which meant that they could bring fruit, roots, and pieces of meat back to their tribe. Their linguistic abilities enabled them to combine the collective knowledge of all the members of the tribe, to make plans, to pass information on to subsequent generations, and to form complex civilizations that established their status as the dominant species. All of these characteristics required a larger brain.

A large brain requires a large skull, and an upright posture limits the size of a woman's birth canal. A newborn baby's head is about as large as it can be. As it is, the birth of a baby is much more arduous than the birth of mammals with proportionally smaller heads, including those of our closest primate relatives. Because a baby's brain is not large or complex enough to perform the physical and intellectual abilities of an adult, it must continue to grow after the baby is born. In fact, all mammals (and all birds, for that matter) require parental care for a period of time while the nervous system develops. The fact that young mammals (and, particularly, young humans) are guaranteed to be exposed to the adults who care for them

Figure 1.13

Neoteny in evolution of the human skull. The skulls of fetal humans and chimpanzees are much more similar than those of the adults are. The grid lines show the pattern of growth, indicating much less change in the human skull from birth to adulthood.

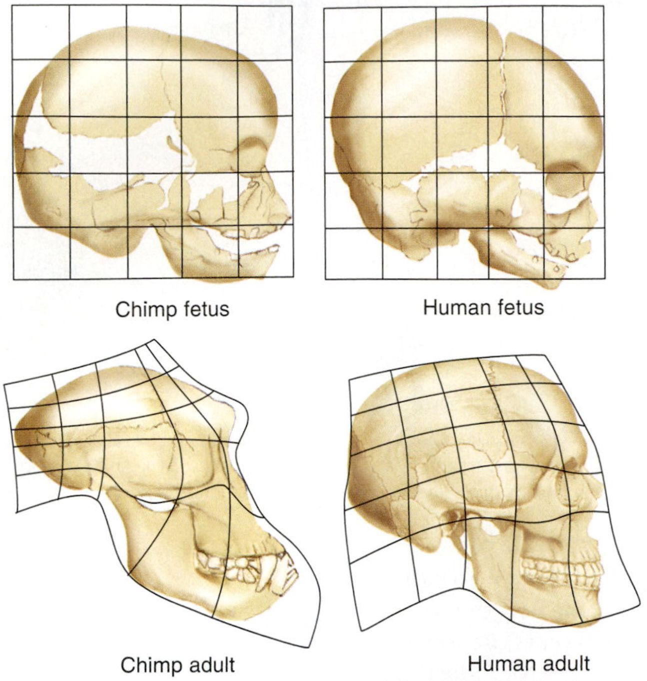

Redrawn with permission from Lewin, R. *Human Evolution: An Illustrated Introduction,* 3rd ed. Boston: Blackwell Scientific Publications, 1993.

means that a period of apprenticeship is possible. Consequently, the evolutionary process did not have to produce a brain with specialized circuits that performed specialized tasks. Instead, it could simply produce a larger brain with an abundance of neural circuits that could be modified by experience. Adults would nourish and protect their offspring and provide them with the skills they would need as adults. Some specialized circuits were necessary, of course (for example, those involved in analyzing the complex sounds we use for speech), but by and large, the brain is a general-purpose, programmable computer.

What types of genetic changes are required to produce a larger brain? This question will be addressed in more detail in Chapter 3, but the most important principle appears to be a slowing of the process of maturation, allowing more time for growth. This phenomenon is known as **neoteny** (roughly translated as "extended youth"). The brains of newborn mammals are larger than those of humans, relative to their body weight. After birth the body grows proportionally faster than the brain. However, the mature human head and brain retain some infantile characteristics, including their disproportionate size. Figure 1.13 shows fetal and adult skulls of chimpanzees and humans. As you can see, the fetal skulls are much more similar than those of the adults. The grid lines show the pattern of growth, indicating much less change in the human skull from birth to adulthood. (See ***Figure 1.13.***)

INTERIM SUMMARY

Natural Selection and Evolution

Darwin's theory of evolution, which was based on the concept of natural selection, provided an important contribution to modern physiological psychology. The theory asserts that we must understand the functions performed by an organ or body part or by a behavior. Through random mutations, changes in an individual's genetic material cause different proteins to be produced, which results in the alteration of some physical characteristics. If the changes confer a selective advantage on the individual, the new genes will be transmitted to more and more members of the species. Even behaviors can evolve, through the selective advantage of alterations in the structure of the nervous system.

Amphibians emerged from the sea 360 million years ago. One branch, the therapsids, became the dominant land animal until a catastrophic series of volcanic eruptions wiped out most animal species. A small therapsid, the cynodont, survived the disaster and became the ancestor of the mammals. The earliest mammals were small, nocturnal insectivores who lived in trees. They remained small and inconspicuous until the extinction of the dinosaurs, which occurred around 65 million years ago. The vacant ecological niches were quickly filled by mammals. Primates also began as small, nocturnal, tree-dwelling insectivores. Larger fruit-eating primates, with forward-facing eyes and larger brains, eventually evolved.

The first hominids appeared in Africa around 25 million years ago, eventually evolving into four major species: orangutans, gorillas, chimpanzees, and humans. Our ancestors acquired bipedalism around 3.7 million years ago and discovered toolmaking around 2.5 million years ago. The first hominids to leave Africa, *Homo erectus,* did so around 1.7 million

neoteny A slowing of the process of maturation, allowing more time for growth; an important factor in the development of large brains.

years ago and scattered across Europe and Asia. *Homo neanderthalis* evolved in Western Europe, eventually to be replaced by *Homo sapiens,* which evolved in Africa around 100,000 years and spread throughout the world. By 30,000 years ago *Homo sapiens* had replaced *Homo neanderthalis.*

The evolution of large brains made possible the development of toolmaking, fire building, and language, which in turn permitted the development of complex social structures. Large brains also provided a large memory capacity and the abilities to recognize patterns of events in the past and to plan for the future. Because an upright posture limits the size of a woman's birth canal and therefore the size of the head that passes through it, much of the brain's growth must take place after birth, which means that children require an extended period of parental care. This period of apprenticeship enabled the developing brain to be modified by experience.

Although human DNA differs from that of chimpanzees by only 1.2 percent, our brains are more than three times larger, which means that a small number of genes is responsible for the increase in the size of our brains. As we will see in Chapter 3, these genes appear to retard the events that stop brain development, resulting in a phenomenon known as neoteny.

THOUGHT QUESTIONS

1. What useful functions are provided by the fact that a human can be self-aware? How was this trait selected for during the evolution of our species?
2. Are you surprised that the difference in the DNA of humans and chimpanzees is only 1.2 percent? How do you feel about this fact?
3. If our species continues to evolve, what kinds of changes do you think might occur?

Ethical Issues in Research with Animals

Most of the research described in this book involves experimentation on living animals. Any time we use another species of animals for our own purposes, we should be sure that what we are doing is both humane and worthwhile. I believe that a good case can be made that research on the physiology of behavior qualifies on both counts. Humane treatment is a matter of procedure. We know how to maintain laboratory animals in good health in comfortable, sanitary conditions. We know how to administer anesthetics and analgesics so that animals do not suffer during or after surgery, and we know how to prevent infections with proper surgical procedures and the use of antibiotics. Most industrially developed societies have very strict regulations about the care of animals and require approval of the experimental procedures used on them. There is no excuse for mistreating animals in our care. In fact, the vast majority of laboratory animals *are* treated humanely.

Unlike pet owners, scientists who use animals in their research must follow stringent regulations designed to ensure that the animals are properly cared for.

We use animals for many purposes. We eat their meat and eggs, and we drink their milk; we turn their hides into leather; we extract insulin and other hormones from their organs to treat people's diseases; we train them to do useful work on farms or to entertain us. Even having a pet is a form of exploitation; it is we—not they—who decide that they will live in our homes. The fact is, we have been using other animals throughout the history of our species.

Pet owning causes much more suffering among animals than scientific research does. As Miller (1983) notes, pet owners are not required to receive permission from a board of experts that includes a veterinarian to house their pets, nor are they subject to periodic inspections to be sure that their homes are clean and sanitary, that their pets have enough space to exercise properly, or that their pets' diets are appropriate. Scientific researchers are. Miller also notes that fifty times more dogs and cats are killed by humane societies each year because they have been abandoned by former pet owners than are used in scientific research.

If a person believes that it is wrong to use another animal in any way, regardless of the benefits to humans, there is nothing anyone can say to convince him or her of the value of scientific research with animals. For this person the issue is closed from the very beginning. Moral absolutes cannot be settled logically; like religious beliefs, they can be accepted or rejected, but they cannot be proved or disproved. My arguments in support of scientific research with animals are based on an evaluation of the benefits the research has to humans. (We should also remember that research with animals often helps *other animals;* procedures used by veterinarians, as well as those used by physicians, come from such research.)

Before describing the advantages of research with animals, let me point out that the use of animals in research and teaching is a special target of animal rights activists. Nicholl and Russell (1990) examined twenty-one books written by such activists and counted the number of pages devoted to concern for different uses of animals. Next, they compared the relative concern the authors showed for these uses to the numbers of animals actually involved in each of these categories. The results indicate that the authors showed relatively little concern for animals used for food, hunting, or furs, or for those killed in pounds. In contrast, although only 0.3 percent of the animals are used for research and education, 63.3 percent of the pages were devoted to criticizing this use. In terms of pages per million animals used, the authors devoted 0.08 to food, 0.23 to hunting, 1.27 to furs, 1.44 to killing in pounds—and 53.2 to research and education. The authors showed 665 times more concern for research and education than for food and 231 times more than for hunting. Even the use of animals for furs (which consumes two-thirds as many animals as research and education) attracted 41.9 times less attention per animal.

The disproportionate amount of concern that animal rights activists show toward the use of animals in research and education is puzzling, particularly because this is the one *indispensable* use of animals. We *can* survive without eating animals, we *can* live without hunting, we *can* do without furs. But without using animals for research and for training future researchers, we *cannot* make progress in understanding and treating diseases. In not too many years our scientists will probably have developed a vaccine that will prevent the further spread of AIDS. Some animal rights activists believe that preventing the deaths of laboratory animals in the pursuit of such a vaccine is a more worthy goal than preventing the deaths of millions of humans that will occur as a result of the disease if a vaccine is not found. Even diseases that we have already conquered would take new victims if drug companies could no longer use animals. If they were deprived of animals, these companies could no longer extract hormones used to treat human diseases, and they could not prepare many of the vaccines that we now use to prevent them.

Our species is beset by medical, mental, and behavioral problems, many of which can be solved only through biological research. Let us consider some of the major neurological disorders. Strokes, caused by bleeding or occlusion of a blood vessel within the brain, often leave people partly paralyzed, unable to read, write, or converse with their friends and family. Basic research on the means by which nerve cells communicate with each other has led to important discoveries about the causes of the death of brain cells. This research was not directed toward a specific practical goal; the potential benefits actually came as a surprise to the investigators.

Experiments based on these results have shown that if a blood vessel leading to the brain is blocked for a few minutes, the part of the brain that is nourished by that vessel will die. However, the brain damage can be prevented by first administering a drug that interferes with a particular kind of neural communication. This research is important, because it may lead to medical treatments that can help to reduce the brain damage caused by strokes. But it involves operating on a laboratory animal such as a rat and pinching off a blood vessel. (The animals are anesthetized, of course.) Some of the animals will sustain brain damage, and all will be killed so that their brains can be examined. However, you will probably agree that research like this is just as legitimate as using animals for food.

As you will learn later in this book, research with laboratory animals has produced important discoveries about the possible causes or potential treatments of neurological and mental disorders, including Parkinson's disease, schizophrenia, manic-depressive illness, anxiety disorders, obsessive-compulsive disorders, anorexia nervosa, obesity, and drug addictions. Although much progress has been made, these problems are still with us, and they cause much human suffering. Unless we continue our research with laboratory animals, the problems will not be solved. Some people have suggested that instead of using laboratory animals in our research, we could use tissue cultures or computers. Unfortunately, neither tissue cultures nor computers are substitutes for living organisms. We have no way to study behavioral problems such as addictions in tissue cultures, nor can we program a computer to simulate the workings of an animal's nervous system. (If we could, that would mean that we already had all the answers.)

This book will discuss some of the many important discoveries that have helped to reduce human suffering. For example, the discovery of a vaccine for polio, a serious disease of the nervous system, involved the use of rhesus monkeys. As you will learn in Chapter 4, Parkinson's disease, an incurable, progressive neurological disorder, has been treated for years with a drug called L-DOPA, discovered through animal research. Now, because of research with rats, mice, rabbits, and monkeys stimulated by the accidental poisoning of several young people with a contaminated batch of synthetic heroin, patients are being treated with a drug that may actually slow down the rate of brain degeneration. Researchers have hopes that a drug will be found to prevent the brain degeneration altogether.

The easiest way to justify research with animals is to point to actual and potential benefits to human health, as I have just done. However, we can also justify this research with a less practical, but perhaps equally important, argument. One of the things that characterize our species is a quest for an understanding of our world. For example, astronomers study the universe and try to uncover its mysteries. Even if their discoveries never lead to practical benefits such as better drugs or faster methods of transportation, the fact that they enrich our understanding of the beginning and the fate of our universe justifies their efforts. The pursuit of knowledge is itself a worthwhile endeavor. Surely, the attempt to understand the universe within us—our nervous system, which is responsible for all that we are or can be—is also valuable.

Careers in Neuroscience

What is physiological psychology, and what do physiological psychologists do? By the time you finish this book, you will have as complete an answer as I can give to these questions, but perhaps it is worthwhile for me to describe the field and careers that are open to those who specialize in it before we begin our study in earnest.

Physiological psychologists study all behavioral phenomena that can be observed in nonhuman animals. They attempt to understand the physiology of behavior: the role of the nervous system, interacting with the rest of the body (especially the endocrine system, which secretes hormones), in controlling behavior. They study such topics as sensory processes, sleep, emotional behavior, ingestive behavior, aggressive behavior, sexual behavior, parental behavior, and learning and memory.

physiological psychologist A scientist who studies the physiology of behavior, primarily by performing physiological and behavioral experiments with laboratory animals.

They also study animal models of disorders that afflict humans, such as anxiety, depression, obsessions and compulsions, phobias, psychosomatic illnesses, and schizophrenia.

Although physiological psychology is the original name for this field, several other terms are now in general use, such as *biological psychology, biopsychology, psychobiology,* and *behavioral neuroscience.* Most professional physiological psychologists have received a Ph.D. from a graduate program in psychology or from an interdisciplinary program. (My own university awards a Ph.D. in Neuroscience and Behavior. The program includes faculty members from the departments of psychology, biology, biochemistry, exercise science, and computer science.)

Physiological psychology belongs to the larger field of *neuroscience.* Neuroscientists concern themselves with all aspects of the nervous system: its anatomy, chemistry, physiology, development, and functioning. The research of neuroscientists ranges from the study of molecular genetics to the study of social behavior. The field has grown enormously in the last few years; meetings of the Society for Neuroscience are attended by well over twenty thousand members and graduate students.

Most professional physiological psychologists are employed by colleges and universities, where they are engaged in teaching and research. Others are employed by institutions devoted to research—for example, laboratories owned and operated by national governments or by private philanthropic organizations. A few work in industry, usually for pharmaceutical companies that are interested in assessing the effects of drugs on behavior. To become a professor or independent researcher, one must receive a doctorate—usually a Ph.D., although some people turn to research after receiving an M.D. Nowadays, most physiological psychologists spend two years in a temporary postdoctoral position, working in the laboratory of a senior scientist to gain more research experience. During this time, they write articles describing their research findings and submit them for publication in scientific journals. These publications are an important factor in obtaining a permanent position.

Two other fields often overlap with that of physiological psychology: *neurology* and *experimental neuropsychology.* Neurologists are physicians involved in the diagnosis and treatment of diseases of the nervous system. Most neurologists are solely involved in the practice of medicine, but a few engage in research devoted to advancing our understanding of the physiology of behavior. They study the behavior of people whose brains have been damaged by natural causes, using advanced brain-scanning devices to study the activity of various regions of the brain as a subject participates in various behaviors. This research is also carried out by experimental neuropsychologists—scientists with a Ph.D. in psychology and specialized training in the principles and procedures of neurology.

Not all people who are engaged in neuroscience research have doctoral degrees. Many research technicians perform essential—and intellectually rewarding—services for the scientists with whom they work. Some of these technicians gain enough experience and education on the job to enable them to collaborate with their employers on their research projects rather than simply work for them.

INTERIM SUMMARY

Ethical Issues in Research with Animals

Research on the physiology of behavior necessarily involves the use of laboratory animals. It is incumbent on all scientists using these animals to see that they are housed comfortably and treated humanely, and laws have been enacted to ensure that they are. Such research has already produced many benefits to humankind and promises to continue to do so.

Physiological psychology (also called biological psychology, biopsychology, psychobiology, and behavioral neuroscience) is a field devoted to our understanding of the physiology of behavior. Physiological psychologists are allied with other scientists in the broader field of neuroscience. To pursue a career in physiological psychology (or in the sister field of experimental neuropsychology), one must obtain a graduate degree and (usually) serve two years or more as a "postdoc"—a scientist pursuing further training.

THOUGHT QUESTION

Why do you think some people are apparently more upset about using animals for research and teaching than about using them for other purposes?

Strategies for Learning

The brain is a complicated organ. After all, it is responsible for all our abilities and all our complexities. Scientists have been studying this organ for a good many years and (especially in recent years) have been learning a lot about how it works. It is impossible to summarize this progress in a few simple sentences; therefore, this book contains a lot of information. I have tried to organize this information logically, telling you what you need to know in the order you need to know it. (After all, to understand some things, you need to understand other things first.) I have also tried to write as clearly as possible, making my examples as simple and as vivid as I can. Still, you cannot expect to master the information in this book by simply giving it a passive read; you will have to do some work.

Learning about the physiology of behavior involves much more than memorizing facts. Of course, there *are* facts to be memorized: names of parts of the nervous system, names of chemicals and drugs, scientific terms for particular phenomena and procedures used to investigate them, and so on. But the quest for information is nowhere near completed; we know only a small fraction of what we have to learn. And almost certainly, many of the "facts" that we now accept will someday be shown to be incorrect. If all you do is learn facts, where will you be when these facts are revised?

The antidote to obsolescence is knowledge of the process by which facts are obtained. In science, facts are the conclusions scientists make about their observations. If you learn only the conclusions, obsolescence is almost guaranteed. You will have to remember which conclusions are overturned and what the new conclusions are, and that kind of rote learning is hard to do. But if you learn about the research strategies the scientists use, the observations they make, and the reasoning that leads to the conclusions, you will develop an understanding that is easily revised when new observations (and new "facts") emerge. If you understand what lies behind the conclusions, then you can incorporate new information into what you already know and revise these conclusions yourself.

In recognition of these realities about learning, knowledge, and the scientific method, this book presents not just a collection of facts, but also a description of the procedures, experiments, and logical reasoning that scientists have used in their attempt to understand the physiology of behavior. If, in the interest of expediency, you focus on the conclusions and ignore the process that leads to them, you run the risk of acquiring information that will quickly become obsolete. On the other hand, if you try to understand the experiments and see how the conclusions follow from the results, you will acquire knowledge that lives and grows.

Now let me offer some practical advice about studying. You have been studying throughout your academic career, and you have undoubtedly learned some useful strategies along the way. Even if you have developed efficient and effective study skills, at least consider the possibility that there might be some ways to improve them.

If possible, the first reading of the assignment should be as uninterrupted as you can make it; that is, read the chapter without worrying much about remembering details. Next, after the first class meeting devoted to the topic, read the assignment again in earnest. Use a pen or pencil as you go, making notes. *Don't use a highlighter.* Sweeping the felt tip of a highlighter across some words on a page provides some instant gratification; you can even imagine that the highlighted words are somehow being transferred to your knowledge base. You have selected what is important, and when you review the reading assignment you have only to read the highlighted words. But this is an illusion.

Be active, not passive. Force yourself to write down whole words and phrases. The act of putting the information into your own words will not only give you something to study shortly before the next exam but also put something into your head (which is helpful at exam time). Using a highlighter puts off the learning until a later date; rephrasing the information in your own words starts the learning process *right then.*

A good way to get yourself to put the information into your own words (and thus into your own brain) is to answer the questions in the study guide. If you cannot answer a question, look up the answer in the book, *close the book,* and write the answer down. The phrase *close the book* is important. If you *copy* the answer, you will get very little out of the exercise. However, if you make yourself remember the information long enough to write it down, you have a good chance of remembering it later. The importance of the study guide is *not* to have a set of short answers in your own handwriting that you can study before the quiz. The behaviors that lead to long-term learning are doing enough thinking about the material to summarize it in your own words, then going through the mechanics of writing those words down.

Before you begin reading the next chapter, let me say a few things about the design of the book that might help you with your studies. The text and illustrations are integrated as closely as possible. In my experience, one of the most annoying aspects of reading some books is not knowing when to look at an illustration. Therefore, in this book you will find figure references in boldfaced italics (like this: ***Figure 5.6***), which means "stop reading and look at the figure." These references appear in locations I think will be optimal. If you look away from the text then, you will be assured that you will not be interrupting a line of reasoning in a crucial place and will not have to reread several sentences to get going again. You will find sections like this: "Figure 4.1 shows an alligator and a human. This alligator is certainly laid out in a linear fashion; we can draw a straight line that starts between its eyes and continues down the center of its spinal cord. (See ***Figure 4.1.***)" This particular example is a trivial one and will give you no problems no matter when you look at the figure. But in other cases the material is more complex, and you will have less trouble if you know what to look for before you stop reading and examine the illustration.

You will notice that some words in the text are *italicized* and others are printed in **boldface.** Italics mean one of two things: Either the word is being stressed for emphasis and is not a new term, or I am pointing out a new term that is not necessary for you to learn. On the other hand, a word in boldface is a new term that you should try to learn. Most of the boldfaced terms in the text are part of the vocabulary of the physiological psychologist. Often, they will be used again in a later chapter. As an aid to your studying, definitions of these terms are printed in the margin of the page, along with pronunciation guides for those terms whose pronunciation is not obvious. In addition, a comprehensive index at the end of the book provides a list of terms and topics, with page references.

At the end of each major section (there are usually three to five of them in a chapter) you will find an *Interim Summary,* which provides a place for you to stop and think again about what you have just read to make sure that you understand the direction in which the discussion has gone. Many interim summaries are followed by some thought questions, which may serve to stimulate your thoughts about what you have learned and apply them to questions that have not yet been answered. Taken together, these sections provide a detailed summary of the information introduced in the chapter. My students tell me that they review the interim summaries just before taking a test.

Okay, the preliminaries are over. The next chapter starts with something you can sink your (metaphorical) teeth into: the structure and functions of neurons, the most important elements of the nervous system.

EPILOGUE

Models of Brain Functions

René Descartes had no way to study the operations of the nervous system. He did, however, understand how the statues in the Royal Gardens at Saint-Germain were powered and controlled, which led him to view the body as a complicated piece of plumbing. Many scientists have followed Descartes's example, using technological devices that were fashionable at the time to explain how the brain worked.

What motivates people to use artificial devices to explain the workings of the brain? The most important reason, I suppose, is that the brain is enormously complicated. Even the most complex human inventions are many times simpler than the brain, and because they have been designed and made by people, people can understand them. If an artificial device can do some of the things that the brain does, then perhaps both the brain and the device accomplish their tasks in the same way.

Most models of brain function developed in the last half of the twentieth century have been based on the modern, general-purpose digital computer. Actually, they have been based not on the computers themselves but on computer *programs.* Computers can be programmed to store any kind of information that can be coded in numbers or words, can solve any logical problem that can be explicitly described, and can compute any mathematical equations that can be written. Therefore, in principle at least, they can be programmed to do the things we do: perceive, remember, make deductions, solve problems.

The construction of computer programs that simulate human brain functions can help to clarify the nature of these functions. For instance, to construct a program and simulate, say, perception and classification of certain types of patterns, the investigator is forced to specify precisely what is required by the task of pattern perception. If the program fails to recognize the patterns, then the investigator knows that something is wrong with the model or with the way it has been implemented in the program. The investigator revises the model, tries again, and keeps working until it finally works (or until he or she gives up the task as being too ambitious).

Ideally, this task tells the investigator the kinds of processes the brain must perform. However, there is usually more than one way to accomplish a particular goal; critics of computer modeling have pointed out that it is possible to write a program that performs a task that the human brain performs and comes up with exactly the same results but does the task in an entirely different way. In fact, some say, given the way that computers work and what we know about the structure of the human brain, the computer program is *guaranteed* to work differently.

When we base a model of brain functions on a physical device with which we are familiar, we enjoy the advantage of being able to think concretely about something that is difficult to observe. However, if the brain does not work like a computer, then our models will not tell us very much about the brain. Such models are *constrained* ("restricted") by the computer metaphor; they will be able to do things only the way that computers can do them. If the brain can actually do some different sorts of things that computers cannot do, the models will never contain these features.

In fact, computers and brains are fundamentally different. Modern computers are *serial devices;* they work one step at a time. (*Serial,* from the Latin *sererei* "to join," refers to events that occur in order, one after the other.) Programs consist of a set of instructions stored in the computer's memory. The computer follows these instructions, one at a time. Because each of these steps takes time, a complicated program will take more time to execute. But we do some things extremely quickly that computers take a very long time to do. The best example is visual perception. We can recognize a complex figure about as quickly as a simple one; for example, it takes about the same amount of time to recognize a friend's face as it does to identify a simple triangle. The same is not true at all for a serial computer. A computer must "examine" the scene through an input device something like a television camera. Information about the brightness of each point of the picture must be converted into a number and stored in a memory location. Then the program examines each memory location, one at a time, and does calculations that determine the locations of lines, edges, textures, and shapes; finally, it tries to determine what these shapes represent. Recognizing a face takes *much* longer than recognizing a triangle. In fact, even the best computer programs do a terrible job in recognizing faces.

Unlike serial computers, the brain is a *parallel processor,* in which many different modules (collections of circuits of neurons) work simultaneously at different tasks. A complex task is broken down into many smaller ones, and separate modules work on each of them. Because the brain consists of many billions of neurons, it can afford to devote different clusters of neurons to different tasks. With so many things happening at the same time, the task gets done quickly.

Very recently, researchers have turned the tables and have begun developing models of *computers* that resemble the *nervous system.* The elements of these computers are based on nerve cells, and the rules that govern the way they interact are based on the rules you will learn about in Chapter 2. Furthermore, instead of programming these models to perform a function, researchers give them information that permits them to learn, just as a real brain does. Someday, we may even see organic computers, using materials similar to those found in the body; scientists are developing polymers (special organic compounds) that can take over the functions of the silicon chips used in the integrated circuits that make up present-day computers.

KEY CONCEPTS

UNDERSTANDING HUMAN CONSCIOUSNESS: A PHYSIOLOGICAL APPROACH

1. Physiological psychologists believe that the mind is a function performed by the brain.
2. Study of human brain functions has helped us gain some insight into the nature of human consciousness, which appears to be related to the language functions of the brain. This chapter described one example, the effects of the split-brain operation.

THE NATURE OF PHYSIOLOGICAL PSYCHOLOGY

3. Scientists attempt to explain natural phenomena by means of generalization and reduction. Because physiological psychologists use the methods of psychology and physiology, they employ both types of explanations.
4. Descartes developed the first model to explain how the brain controls movement, based on the animated statues in the royal gardens. Subsequently, investigators tested their ideas with scientific experiments.

NATURAL SELECTION AND EVOLUTION

5. Darwin's theory of evolution, with its emphasis on function, helps physiological psychologists discover the relations between brain mechanisms, behaviors, and an organism's adaptation to its environment.
6. We owe our status as the dominant species to our bipedal stance, our agile hands, our excellent vision, and the behavioral and cognitive abilities provided by our large, complex brains, which enable us to adapt to a wide variety of environments, exploit a wide variety of resources, and, with the development of language, form large, complex communities.

ETHICAL ISSUES IN RESEARCH WITH ANIMALS

7. Scientific research with animals has taught us most of what we know about the functions of the body, including that of the nervous system. This knowledge is essential in developing ways to prevent and treat neurological and mental disorders.

CAREERS IN NEUROSCIENCE

8. Physiological psychologists study the physiology of behavior by performing research with animals. They use the research methods and findings of other neuroscientists in pursuit of their particular interests.

SUGGESTED READINGS

Allman, J. M. *Evolving Brains.* New York: Scientific American Library, 1999.

Butterfield, H. *The Origins of Modern Science: 1300–1800.* New York: Macmillan, 1959.

Damasio, A. R. *Descartes's Error: Emotion, Reason, and the Human Brain.* New York: G. P. Putnam, 1994.

Finger, S. *Origins of Neuroscience: A History of Explorations into Brain Function.* New York: Oxford University Press, 1994.

Schultz, D., and Schultz, S. E. *A History of Modern Psychology.* New York: Academic Press, 1996.

SUGGESTED WEB SITES

Brain and Behavior Course

www.nyu.edu/classes/azmitia/lectures/

The Brain and Behavior site contains a series of 22 online lectures developed at New York University, including two lectures devoted to the history of neuroscience. The site also contains sample quizzes as well as links to other neuroscience sites.

Broca's Classic Paper on the Patient Tan

www.yorku.ca/dept/psych/classics/Broca/pert-e.htm

In 1861, Pierre Paul Broca published a case report relating the loss of language to damage to the left anterior hemisphere of the brain. This site provides a translation of Broca's report.

The Descent of Man by Charles Darwin

www.yorku.ca/dept/psych/classics/Darwin/Descent/index.htm

This site provides access to seven of the chapters published by Charles Darwin in his book *The Descent of Man* (1871) in which he lays out his view on the evolution of humans.

Mendel's Garden

www.unb.ca/web/units/psych/likely/mendel/call_mgarden.htm

This site will link students to a demonstration of the principles of genetic determination as examined by Gregor Mendel in his garden.

Split-Brain Syndrome

www.uwm.edu/~johnchay/sb.htm

An online demonstration of the study of split-brain patients is the focus of this site.

Split-Brain Consciousness

www.macalester.edu/~psych/whathap/UBNRP/Split_Brain/Split_Brain_Consciousness.html

This site provides a series of modules relating to the study of the split-brain including essays on consciousness, the history of the split-brain operation, and the behavior of split-brain patients.

Structure and Functions of Cells of the Nervous System

chapter 2

CHAPTER OUTLINE

LEARNING OBJECTIVES

1. Name and describe the parts of a neuron and explain their functions.
2. Describe the supporting cells of the central and peripheral nervous systems and describe and explain the importance of the blood–brain barrier.
3. Briefly describe the neural circuitry responsible for a withdrawal reflex and its inhibition by neurons in the brain.
4. Describe the measurement of the action potential and explain how the balance between the forces of diffusion and electrostatic pressure is responsible for the membrane potential.
5. Describe the role of ion channels in action potentials and explain the all-or-none law and the rate law.
6. Describe the structure of synapses, the release of neurotransmitter, and the activation of postsynaptic receptors.
7. Describe postsynaptic potentials: the ionic movements that cause them, the processes that terminate them, and their integration.
8. Describe the role of autoreceptors and axoaxonic synapses in synaptic communication and describe the role of neuromodulators and hormones in nonsynaptic communication.

PROLOGUE

Unresponsive Muscles

Kathryn D. was getting desperate. All her life she had been healthy and active, eating wisely and keeping fit with sports and regular exercise. She went to her health club almost every day for a session of low-impact aerobics, followed by a swim. But several months ago, she began having trouble keeping up with her usual schedule. At first, she found herself getting tired toward the end of her aerobics class. Her arms, particularly, seemed to get heavy. Then when she entered the pool and started swimming, she found that it was hard to lift her arms over her head; she abandoned the crawl and the backstroke and did the sidestroke and breaststroke instead. She did not have any flulike symptoms, so she told herself that she needed more sleep and perhaps she should eat a little more.

Over the next few weeks, however, things only got worse. Aerobics classes were becoming an ordeal. Her instructor became concerned and suggested that Kathryn see her doctor. She did so, but he could find nothing wrong with her. She was not anemic, showed no signs of an infection, and seemed to be well nourished. He asked how things were going at work.

"Well, lately I've been under some pressure," she said. "The head of my department quit a few weeks ago, and I've taken over his job temporarily. I think I have a chance of getting the job permanently, but I feel as if my bosses are watching me to see whether I'm good enough for the job." Kathryn and her physician agreed that increased stress could be the cause of her problem. "I'd prefer not to give you any medication at this time," he said, "but if you don't feel better soon we'll have a closer look at you."

She *did* feel better for a while, but then all of a sudden her symptoms got worse. She quit going to the health club and found that she even had difficulty finishing a day's work. She was certain that people were noticing that she was no longer her lively self, and she was afraid that her chances for the promotion were slipping away. One afternoon she tried to look up at the clock on the wall and realized that she could hardly see—her eyelids were drooping, and her head felt as if it weighed a hundred pounds. Just then, one of her supervisors came over to her desk, sat down, and asked her to fill him in on the progress she had been making on a new project. As she talked, she found herself getting weaker and weaker. Her jaw was getting tired, even her tongue was getting tired, and her voice was getting weaker. With a sudden feeling of fright she realized that the act of breathing seemed to take a lot of effort. She managed to finish the interview, but immediately afterward she packed up her briefcase and left for home, saying that she had a bad headache.

She telephoned her physician, who immediately arranged for her to go to the hospital to be seen by Dr. T., a neurologist. Dr. T. listened to a description of her symptoms and examined her briefly. She said to Kathryn, "I think I know what may be causing your symptoms. I'd like to give you an injection and watch your reaction." She gave some orders to the nurse, who left the room and came back with a syringe. Dr. T. took it, swabbed Kathryn's arm, and injected the drug. She started questioning Kathryn about her job. Kathryn answered slowly, her voice almost a whisper. As the questions continued, she realized that it was getting easier and easier to talk. She straightened her back and took a deep breath. Yes, she was sure. Her strength was returning! She stood up and raised her arms above her head. "Look," she said, her excitement growing. "I can do this again. I've got my strength back! What was that you gave me? Am I cured?"

The brain is the organ that moves the muscles. That might sound simplistic, but ultimately, movement—or, more accurately, behavior—is the primary function of the nervous system. To make useful movements, the brain must know what is happening outside, in the environment. Thus, the body also contains cells that are specialized for detecting environmental events. Of course, complex animals such as we do not react automatically to events in our environment; our brains are flexible enough that we behave in different ways, according to present circumstances and those we experienced in the past. Besides perceiving and acting, we can remember and decide. All these abilities are made possible by the billions of cells found in the nervous system or controlled by them.

This chapter describes the structure and functions of the most important cells of the nervous system. Information, in the form of light, sound waves, odors, tastes, or contact with objects, is gathered from the environment by specialized cells called **sensory neurons.** Movements are accomplished by the contraction of muscles, which are controlled by **motor neurons.** (The term *motor* is used here in its original sense to refer to movement, not to a mechanical engine.) And in between sensory neurons and motor neurons come the **interneurons**—neurons that lie entirely within the central

sensory neuron A neuron that detects changes in the external or internal environment and sends information about these changes to the central nervous system.

motor neuron A neuron located within the central nervous system that controls the contraction of a muscle or the secretion of a gland.

interneuron A neuron located entirely within the central nervous system.

nervous system. *Local interneurons* form circuits with nearby neurons and analyze small pieces of information *Relay interneurons* connect circuits of local interneurons in one region of the brain with those in other regions. Through these connections, circuits of neurons throughout the brain perform functions essential to tasks such as perceiving, learning, remembering, deciding, and controlling complex behaviors. How many neurons are there in the human nervous system? I have seen estimates of between 100 billion and 1000 billion, but no one has counted them yet.

To understand how the nervous system controls behavior, we must first understand its parts—the cells that compose it. Because this chapter deals with cells, you need not be familiar with the structure of the nervous system, which is presented in Chapter 3. However, you need to know that the nervous system consists of two basic divisions: the central nervous system and the peripheral nervous system. The **central nervous system (CNS)** consists of the parts that are encased by the bones of the skull and spinal column: the brain and the spinal cord. The **peripheral nervous system (PNS)** is found outside these bones and consists of the nerves and most of the sensory organs.

Cells of the Nervous System

The first part of this chapter is devoted to a description of the most important cells of the nervous system—neurons and their supporting cells—and to the blood–brain barrier, which provides neurons in the central nervous system with chemical isolation from the rest of the body.

Neurons

Basic Structure

See Animation 2.1, Neurons and Supporting Cells, for an interactive tutorial on the information presented in the following section.

The neuron (nerve cell) is the information-processing and information-transmitting element of the nervous system. Neurons come in many shapes and varieties, according to the specialized jobs they perform. Most neurons have, in one form or another, the following four structures or regions: (1) cell body, or soma; (2) dendrites; (3) axon; and (4) terminal buttons. (See ***Animation 2.1, Neurons and Supporting Cells.***)

Soma. The **soma** (cell body) contains the nucleus and much of the machinery that provides for the life processes of the cell. (See ***Figure 2.1.***) Its shape varies considerably in different kinds of neurons.

Dendrites. *Dendron* is the Greek word for tree, and the **dendrites** of the neuron look very much like trees. (See ***Figure 2.1.***) Neurons "converse" with one another, and dendrites serve as important recipients of these messages. The messages that pass from neuron to neuron are transmitted across the **synapse,** a junction between the terminal buttons (described later) of the sending cell and a portion of the somatic or dendritic membrane of the receiving cell. (The word *synapse* derives from the Greek *sunaptein,* "to join together.") Communication at a synapse proceeds in one direction: from the terminal button to the membrane of the other cell. (Like many general rules, this one has some exceptions. As we will see in Chapter 4, some synapses pass information in both directions.)

Axon. The **axon** is a long, slender tube, often covered by a *myelin sheath.* (The myelin sheath is described later.) The axon carries information from the cell body to the terminal buttons. (See ***Figure 2.1.***) The basic message it carries is called an *action potential.* This function is an important one and will be described in more detail

central nervous system (CNS) The brain and spinal cord.

peripheral nervous system (PNS) The part of the nervous system outside the brain and spinal cord, including the nerves attached to the brain and spinal cord.

soma The cell body of a neuron, which contains the nucleus.

dendrite A branched, treelike structure attached to the soma of a neuron; receives information from the terminal buttons of other neurons.

synapse A junction between the terminal button of an axon and the membrane of another neuron.

axon The long, thin, cylindrical structure that conveys information from the soma of a neuron to its terminal buttons.

Figure 2.1

The principal parts of a multipolar neuron.

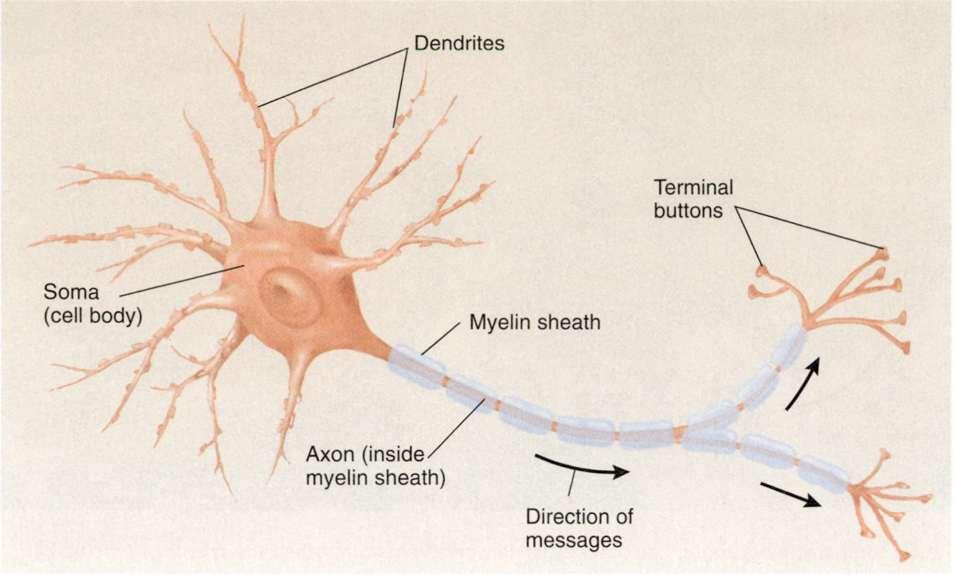

multipolar neuron A neuron with one axon and many dendrites attached to its soma.

bipolar neuron A neuron with one axon and one dendrite attached to its soma.

unipolar neuron A neuron with one axon attached to its soma; the axon divides, with one branch receiving sensory information and the other sending the information into the central nervous system.

later in the chapter. For now, it suffices to say that an action potential is a brief electrical/chemical event that starts at the end of the axon next to the cell body and travels toward the terminal buttons. The action potential is like a brief pulse; in a given axon the action potential is always of the same size and duration. When it reaches a point where the axon branches, it splits but does not diminish in size. Each branch receives a *full-strength* action potential.

Like dendrites, axons and their branches come in different shapes. In fact, the three principal types of neurons are classified according to the way in which their axons and dendrites leave the soma. The neuron depicted in Figure 2.1 is the most common type found in the central nervous system; it is a **multipolar neuron.** In this type of neuron the somatic membrane gives rise to one axon but to the trunks of many dendritic trees.

Bipolar neurons give rise to one axon and one dendritic tree, at opposite ends of the soma. (See ***Figure 2.2a.***) Bipolar neurons are usually sensory; that is, their dendrites detect events occurring in the environment and communicate information about these events to the central nervous system.

The third type of nerve cell is the **unipolar neuron.** It has only one stalk, which leaves the soma and divides into two branches a short distance away. (See ***Figure 2.2b.***) Unipolar neurons, like bipolar neurons, transmit sensory information from the environment to the CNS. The treelike branches outside the CNS are dendrites that detect sensory information. The branches on the end of the axon within the CNS end in terminal buttons. The dendrites of most unipolar neurons detect touch, temperature changes,

Figure 2.2

Neurons. (a) A bipolar neuron, primarily found in sensory systems (for example, vision and audition). (b) A unipolar neuron, found in the somatosensory system (touch, pain, and the like).

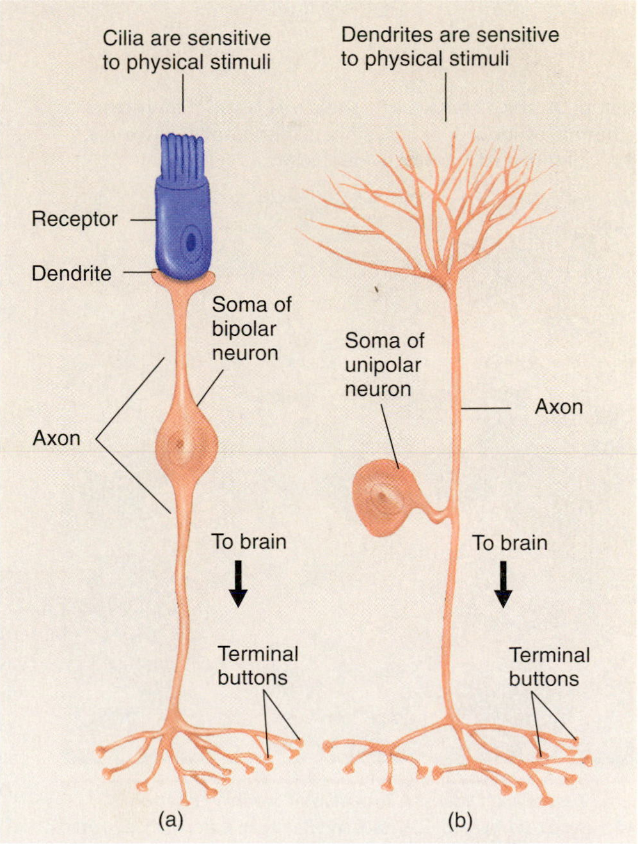

Touch, temperature changes, pain, and other sensory events that affect the skin are detected by the dendrites of unipolar neurons.

terminal button The bud at the end of a branch of an axon; forms synapses with another neuron; sends information to that neuron.

neurotransmitter A chemical that is released by a terminal button; has an excitatory or inhibitory effect on another neuron.

membrane A structure consisting principally of lipid molecules that defines the outer boundaries of a cell and also constitutes many of the cell organelles.

cytoplasm The viscous, semiliquid substance contained in the interior of a cell.

and other sensory events that affect the skin. Other unipolar neurons detect events in our joints, muscles, and internal organs.

The central nervous system communicates with the rest of the body through nerves attached to the brain and to the spinal cord. Nerves are bundles of many thousands of individual fibers, all wrapped in a tough, protective membrane. Under a microscope nerves look something like telephone cables, with their bundles of wires. (See ***Figure 2.3.***) Like the individual wires in a telephone cable, nerve fibers transmit messages through the nerve, from a sense organ to the brain or from the brain to a muscle or gland.

Figure 2.3

Nerves. A nerve consists of a sheath of tissue that encases a bundle of individual nerve fibers (also known as axons). BV = blood vessel; A = individual axons.

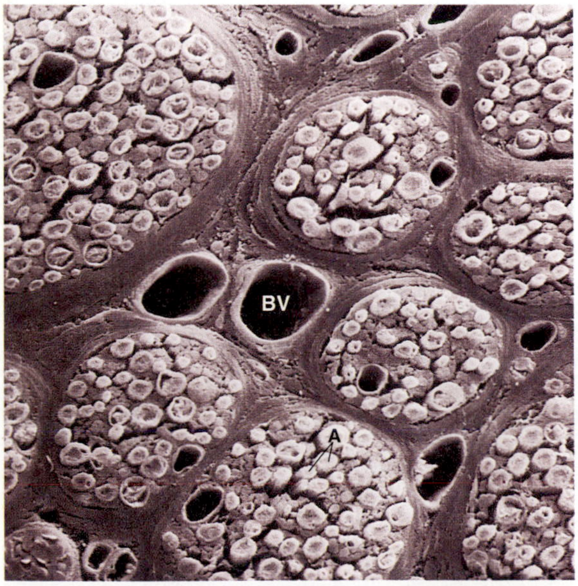

From *Tissues and Organs: A Text-Atlas of Scanning Electron Microscopy,* by Richard G. Kessel and Randy H. Kardon. Copyright © 1979 by W. H. Freeman and Co. Reprinted by permission.

Terminal Buttons. Most axons divide and branch many times. At the ends of the twigs are found little knobs called **terminal buttons.** (Some neuroscientists prefer the original French word *bouton,* and others simply refer to them as *terminals.*) Terminal buttons have a very special function: When an action potential traveling down the axon reaches them, they secrete a chemical called a **neurotransmitter.** This chemical (there are many different ones in the CNS) either excites or inhibits the receiving cell and thus helps to determine whether an action potential occurs in its axon. Details of this process will be described later in this chapter.

An individual neuron receives information from the terminal buttons of axons of other neurons, and the terminal buttons of *its* axons form synapses with other neurons. A neuron may receive information from dozens or even hundreds of other neurons, each of which can form a large number of synaptic connections with it. Figure 2.4 illustrates the nature of these connections. As you can see, terminal buttons can form synapses on the membrane of the dendrites or the soma. (See ***Figure 2.4.***)

Figure 2.4

An overview of the synaptic connections between neurons. The arrows represent the directions of the flow of information.

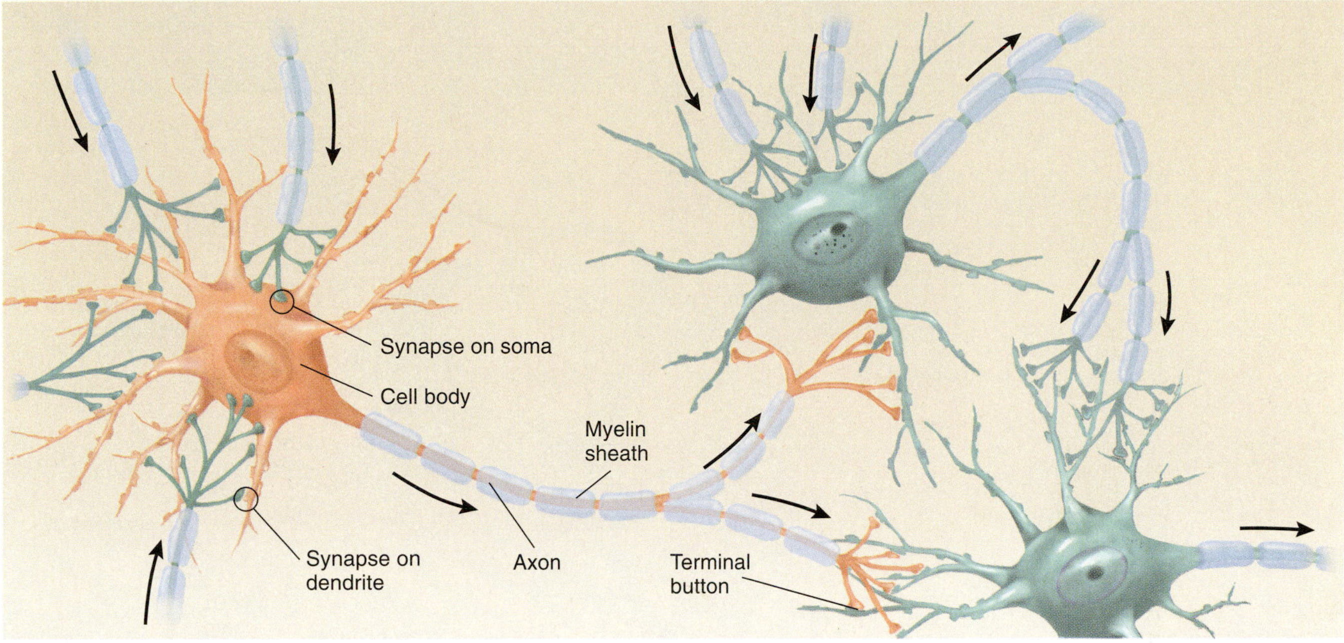

Internal Structure

Figure 2.5 illustrates the internal structure of a typical multipolar neuron. (See *Figure 2.5.*) The **membrane** defines the boundary of the cell. It consists of a double layer of lipid (fatlike) molecules. Embedded in the membrane are a variety of protein molecules that have special functions. Some proteins detect substances outside the cell (such as hormones) and pass information about the presence of these substances to the interior of the cell. Other proteins control access to the interior of the cell, permitting some substances to enter but barring others. Still other proteins act as transporters, actively carrying certain molecules into or out of the cell. Because the proteins that are found in the membrane of the neuron are especially important in the transmission of information, their characteristics will be discussed in more detail later in this chapter.

The cell is filled with **cytoplasm,** a jellylike substance that contains small specialized structures, just as the body contains specialized organs. Among these structures are **mitochondria,** which break down nutrients such as glucose and provide the cell with energy to perform its functions. Mitochondria produce a chemical called **adenosine triphosphate (ATP),** which can be used throughout the cell as an energy source. Many eons ago mitochondria were free-living organisms that came to "infect" larger cells. Because the mitochondria could extract energy more efficiently than their hosts, they became useful to them and eventually became a permanent part of them. Mitochondria still contain their own genetic information and multiply independently of the cells in which they live. We inherit our mitochondria from our mothers; fathers' sperms do not contribute any mitochondria to the ova they fertilize.

Deep inside the cell is the **nucleus** (from the Latin word for "nut"). The nucleus contains the chromosomes. **Chromosomes,** as you have probably already learned, consist of long strands of **deoxyribonucleic acid (DNA).** The chromosomes have an important function: They contain the recipes for making proteins. Portions of the chromosomes, called **genes,** contain the recipes for individual proteins.

mitochondria An organelle that is responsible for extracting energy from nutrients.

adenosine triphosphate (ATP) (*ah* ***den*** *o seen*) A molecule of prime importance to cellular energy metabolism; its breakdown liberates energy.

nucleus A structure in the central region of a cell, containing the chromosomes.

chromosome A strand of DNA, with associated proteins, found in the nucleus; carries genetic information.

deoxyribonucleic acid (DNA) (*dee ox ee* ***ry*** *bo new* ***clay*** *ik*) A long, complex macromolecule consisting of two interconnected helical strands; along with associated proteins, strands of DNA constitute the chromosomes.

gene The functional unit of the chromosome, which directs synthesis of one or more proteins.

Figure 2.5

The principal internal structures of a multipolar neuron.

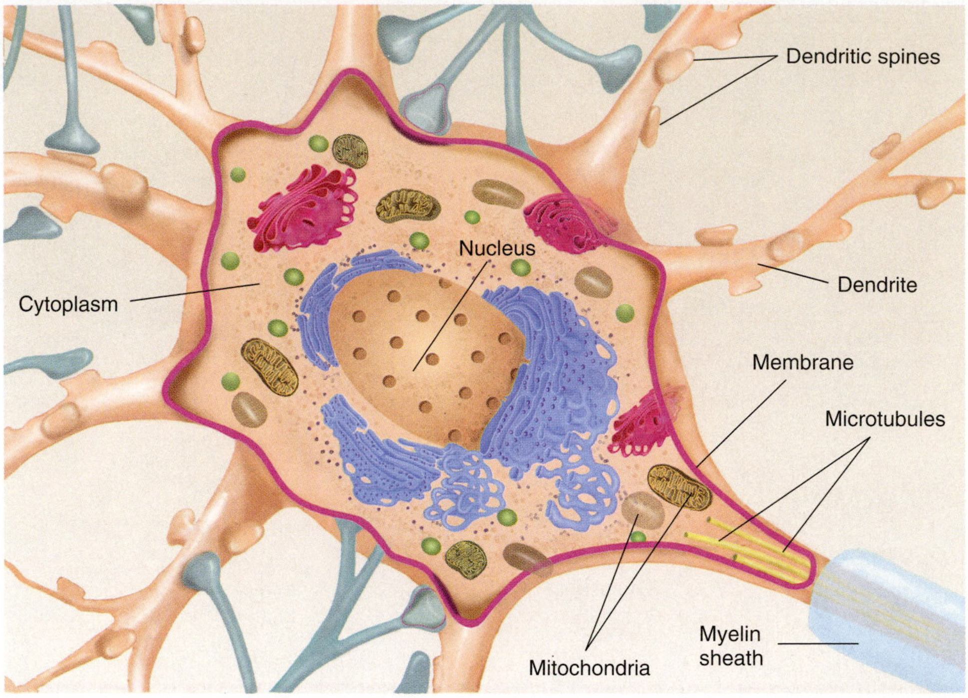

cytoskeleton Formed of microtubules and other protein fibers, linked to each other and forming a cohesive mass that gives a cell its shape.

enzyme A molecule that controls a chemical reaction, combining two substances or breaking a substance into two parts.

axoplasmic transport An active process by which substances are propelled along microtubules that run the length of the axon.

microtubule (*my kro* ***too*** *byool*) A long strand of bundles of protein filaments arranged around a hollow core; part of the cytoskeleton and involved in transporting substances from place to place within the cell.

Animation 2.1, Neurons and Supporting Cells, provides more information about the internal structure of neurons.

Proteins are important in cell functions. If a neuron grown in a tissue culture is exposed to a detergent, the lipid membrane and much of the interior of the cell dissolve away, leaving a matrix of insoluble strands of protein. This matrix, called the **cytoskeleton,** gives the neuron its shape. The cytoskeleton is made of various kinds of protein strands, linked to each other and forming a cohesive mass.

Besides providing structure, proteins serve as enzymes. **Enzymes** are the cell's marriage brokers or divorce judges: They cause particular molecules to join together or split apart. Thus, enzymes determine what gets made from the raw materials contained in the cell, and they determine which molecules remain intact.

Proteins are also involved in transporting substances within the cell. Axons can be extremely long, relative to their diameter and the size of the soma. For example, the longest axon in a human stretches from the foot to a region located in the base of the brain. Because terminal buttons need some items that can be produced only in the soma, there must be a system that can transport these items rapidly and efficiently through the axoplasm (that is, the cytoplasm of the axon). This system, **axoplasmic transport,** is an active process that propels substances from one end of the axon to the other. This transport is accomplished by long protein strands called **microtubules,** bundles of thirteen filaments arranged around a hollow core. Microtubules serve as railroad tracks, guiding the progress of the substances being transported. Movement from the soma to the terminal buttons is called *anterograde* axoplasmic transport. (*Antero-* means "toward the front.") *Retrograde* axoplasmic transport carries substances from the terminal buttons back to the soma. (*Retro-* means "toward the back.") Anterograde axoplasmic transport is remarkably fast: up to 500 mm per day. Retrograde axoplasmic transport is about half as fast. Energy for both forms of transport is supplied by ATP, produced by the mitochondria. (See ***Animation 2.1, Neurons and Supporting Cells.***)

Supporting Cells

Neurons constitute only about half the volume of the CNS. The rest consists of a variety of supporting cells. Because neurons have a very high rate of metabolism but have no means of storing nutrients, they must constantly be supplied with nutrients and oxygen or they will quickly die. Thus, the role played by the cells that support and protect neurons is very important to our existence.

Glia

The most important supporting cells of the central nervous system are the *neuroglia,* or "nerve glue." **Glia** (also called *glial cells*) do indeed glue the CNS together, but they do much more than that. Neurons lead a very sheltered existence; they are buffered physically and chemically from the rest of the body by the glial cells. Glial cells surround neurons and hold them in place, controlling their supply of nutrients and some of the chemicals they need to exchange messages with other neurons; they insulate neurons from one another so that neural messages do not get scrambled; and they even act as housekeepers, destroying and removing the carcasses of neurons that are killed by disease or injury.

There are several types of glial cells, each of which plays a special role in the CNS. The three most important types are *astrocytes, oligodendrocytes,* and *microglia.* **Astrocyte** means "star cell," and this name accurately describes the shape of these cells. Astrocytes (or *astroglia*) provide physical support to neurons and clean up debris within the brain. They produce some chemicals that neurons need to fulfill their functions. They help to control the chemical composition of the fluid surrounding neurons by actively taking up or releasing substances whose concentrations must be kept within critical levels. Finally, astrocytes are involved in providing nourishment to neurons.

Some of the astrocyte's processes (the arms of the star) are wrapped around blood vessels. Other processes are wrapped around parts of neurons, so the somatic and dendritic membranes of neurons are largely surrounded by astrocytes. Recent evidence suggests that astrocytes receive nutrients from the capillaries, store them, and release them to neurons when needed (Tsacopoulos and Magistretti, 1996; Magistretti et al., 1999). Besides having a role in transporting chemicals to neurons, astrocytes serve as the matrix that holds neurons in place. These cells also surround and isolate synapses, limiting the dispersion of neurotransmitters that are released by the terminal buttons. (See ***Figure 2.6.***)

When neurons die, certain kinds of astrocytes take up the task of cleaning away the debris. These cells are able to travel around the CNS; they extend and retract their processes (*pseudopodia,* or "false feet") and glide about the way amoebas do. When these astrocytes contact a piece of debris from a dead neuron, they push themselves against it, finally engulfing and digesting it. We call this process **phagocytosis** (*phagein,* "to eat"; *kutos,* "cell"). If there is a considerable amount of injured tissue to be cleaned up, astrocytes will divide and produce enough new cells to do the task. Once the dead tissue is broken down, a framework of astrocytes will be left to fill in the vacant area, and a specialized kind of astrocyte will form scar tissue, walling off the area.

The principal function of **oligodendrocytes** is to provide support to axons and to produce the **myelin sheath,**

Figure 2.6

Structure and location of astrocytes, whose processes surround capillaries and neurons of the central nervous system.

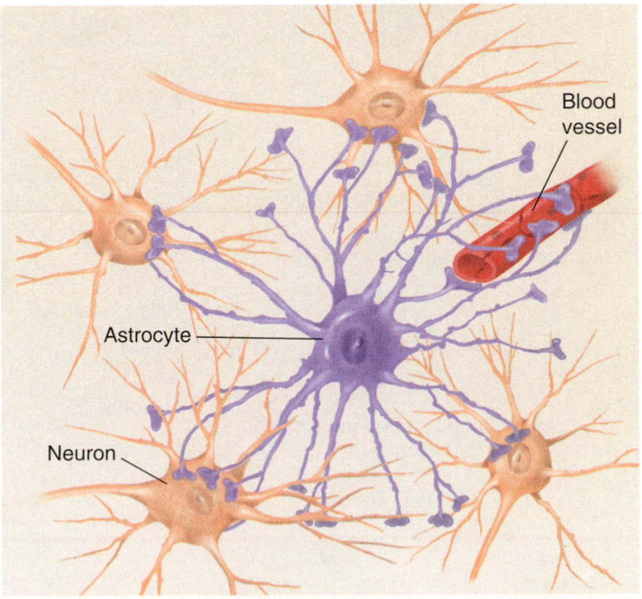

glia (***glee*** *ah*) The supporting cells of the central nervous system.

astrocyte A glial cell that provides support for neurons of the central nervous system, provides nutrients and other substances, and regulates the chemical composition of the extracellular fluid.

phagocytosis (***fagg*** *o sy* ***toe*** *sis*) The process by which cells engulf and digest other cells or debris caused by cellular degeneration.

oligodendrocyte (*oh li go* ***den*** *droh site*) A type of glial cell in the central nervous system that forms myelin sheaths.

myelin sheath (***my*** *a lin*) A sheath that surrounds axons and insulates them, preventing messages from spreading between adjacent axons.

which insulates most axons from one another. (Some axons are not myelinated and lack this sheath.) Myelin, 80 percent lipid and 20 percent protein, is produced by the oligodendrocytes in the form of a tube surrounding the axon. This tube does not form a continuous sheath; rather, it consists of a series of segments, each approximately 1 mm long, with a small (1–2 μm) portion of uncoated axon between the segments. (A *micrometer,* abbreviated μm, is one-millionth of a meter, or one-thousandth of a millimeter.) The bare portion of axon is called a **node of Ranvier,** after its discoverer. The myelinated axon, then, resembles a string of elongated beads. (Actually, the beads are *very much* elongated—their length is approximately 80 times their width.)

A given oligodendrocyte produces up to fifty segments of myelin. During the development of the CNS, oligodendrocytes form processes shaped something like canoe paddles. Each of these paddle-shaped processes then wraps itself many times around a segment of an axon and, while doing so, produces layers of myelin. Each paddle thus becomes a segment of an axon's myelin sheath. (See ***Figures 2.7*** and ***2.8a.***)

As their name indicates, **microglia** are the smallest of the glial cells. Like some types of astrocytes, they act as phagocytes, engulfing and breaking down dead and dying neurons. But in addition, they serve as one of the representatives of the immune system in the brain, protecting the brain from invading microorganisms. They are primarily responsible for the inflammatory reaction in response to brain damage.

Schwann Cells

In the central nervous system the oligodendrocytes support axons and produce myelin. In the peripheral nervous system the **Schwann cells** perform the same functions. Most axons in the PNS are myelinated. The myelin sheath occurs in segments, as it does in the CNS; each segment consists of a single Schwann cell, wrapped many times around the axon. In the CNS the oligodendrocytes grow a number of paddle-shaped processes that wrap around a number of axons. In the PNS a Schwann cell

Figure 2.7

An oligodendrocyte, which forms the myelin that surrounds many axons in the central nervous system. Each cell forms one segment of myelin for several adjacent axons.

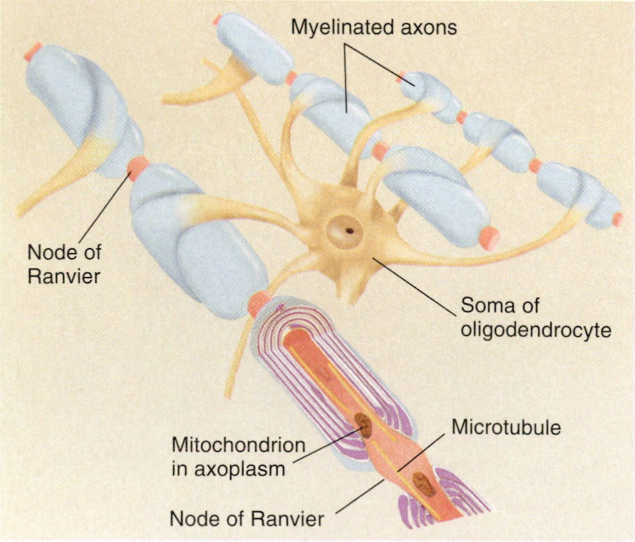

Figure 2.8

Formation of myelin. During development a process of an oligodendrocyte or an entire Schwann cell tightly wraps itself many times around an individual axon and forms one segment of the myelin sheath. (a) Oligodendrocyte. (b) Schwann cell.

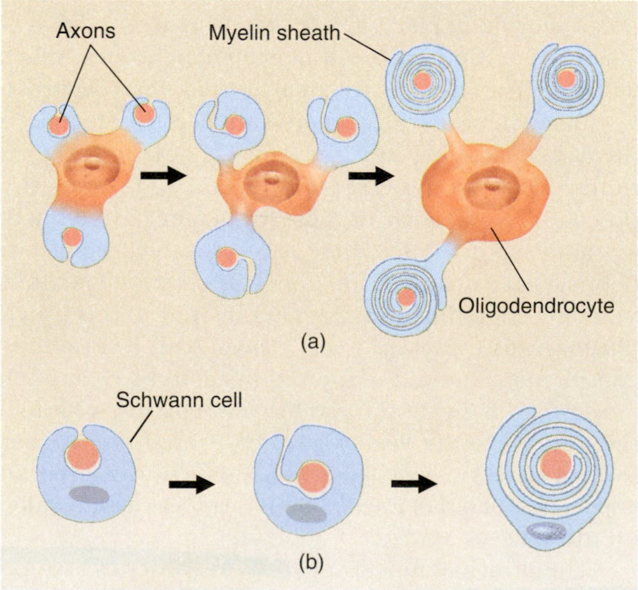

provides myelin for only one axon, and the entire Schwann cell—not merely a part of it—surrounds the axon. (See ***Figure 2.8b.***)

The Blood–Brain Barrier

Over one hundred years ago, Paul Ehrlich discovered that if a blue dye is injected into an animal's bloodstream, all tissues except the brain and spinal cord will be tinted blue. However, if the same dye is injected into the fluid-filled ventricles of the brain, the blue color will spread throughout the CNS (Bradbury, 1979). This experiment demonstrates that a barrier exists between the blood and the fluid that surrounds the cells of the brain—the **blood–brain barrier.**

Some substances can cross the blood–brain barrier; others cannot. Thus, it is *selectively permeable* (*per,* "through"; *meare,* "to pass"). In most of the body the cells that line the capillaries do not fit together absolutely tightly. Small gaps are found between them that permit the free exchange of most substances between the blood plasma and the fluid outside the capillaries that surrounds the cells of the body. In the central nervous system the capillaries lack these gaps; therefore, many substances cannot leave the blood. Thus, the walls of the capillaries in the brain constitute the blood–brain barrier. (See ***Figure 2.9.***) Other substances must be actively transported through the capillary walls by special proteins. For example, glucose transporters bring the brain its fuel, and other transporters rid the brain of toxic waste products (Rubin and Staddon, 1999).

Figure 2.9

The blood–brain barrier. (a) The cells that form the walls of the capillaries in the body outside the brain have gaps that permit the free passage of substances into and out of the blood. (b) The cells that form the walls of the capillaries in the brain are tightly joined.

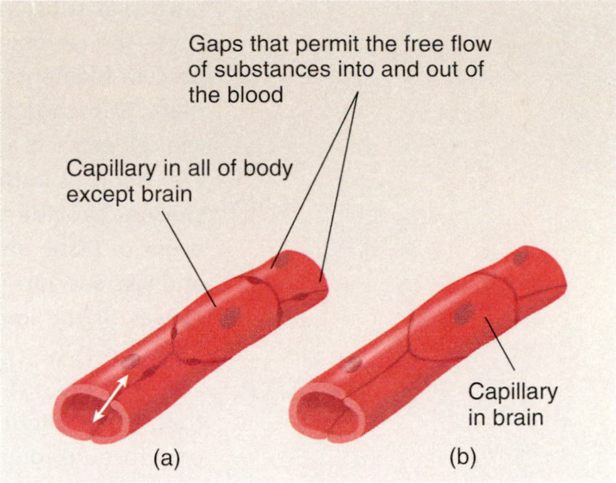

What is the function of the blood–brain barrier? As we will see, transmission of messages from place to place in the brain depends on a delicate balance between substances within neurons and in the extracellular fluid that surrounds them. If the composition of the extracellular fluid is changed even slightly, the transmission of these messages will be disrupted, which means that brain functions will be disrupted. The presence of the blood–brain barrier makes it easier to regulate the composition of this fluid. In addition, many of the foods that we eat contain chemicals that would interfere with the transmission of information between neurons. The blood–brain barrier prevents these chemicals from reaching the brain.

The blood–brain barrier is not uniform throughout the nervous system. In several places the barrier is relatively permeable, allowing substances that are excluded elsewhere to cross freely. For example, the **area postrema** is a part of the brain that controls vomiting. The blood–brain barrier is much weaker there, permitting neurons in this region to detect the presence of toxic substances in the blood. A poison that enters the circulatory system from the stomach can thus stimulate this area to initiate vomiting. If the organism is lucky, the poison can be expelled from the stomach before it causes too much damage.

node of Ranvier (***raw*** *vee ay*) A naked portion of a myelinated axon, between adjacent oligodendroglia or Schwann cells.

microglia The smallest of glial cells; act as phagocytes and protect the brain from invading microorganisms.

Schwann cell A cell in the peripheral nervous system that is wrapped around a myelinated axon, providing one segment of its myelin sheath.

blood–brain barrier A semipermeable barrier between the blood and the brain produced by the cells in the walls of the brain's capillaries.

area postrema (*poss* ***tree*** *ma*) A region of the medulla where the blood–brain barrier is weak; poisons can be detected there and can initiate vomiting.

INTERIM SUMMARY

Cells of the Nervous System

Neurons are the most important cells of the nervous system. The central nervous system (CNS) includes the brain and spinal cord; the peripheral nervous system (PNS) includes nerves and some sensory organs.

Neurons have four principal parts: soma (cell body), dendrites, axon, and terminal buttons. They communicate by means of synapses, located at the ends of the axons. When an action potential travels down an axon, the terminal buttons secrete a chemical that has either an excitatory or an inhibitory effect on the neuron with which it communicates. The interactions of circuits of neurons, with their excitatory and inhibitory synapses, are responsible for all of our perceptions, memories, thoughts, and behavior.

Neurons contain a quantity of clear cytoplasm, enclosed in a membrane. Embedded in the membrane are protein molecules that have special functions, such as the transport of particular substances into and out of the cell. The nucleus contains the genetic information—the recipes for the all the proteins that the body can make. Microtubules and other protein filaments compose the cytoskeleton and help to transport chemicals from place to place. Mitochondria serve as the location for most of the chemical reactions through which the cell extracts energy from nutrients.

Neurons in the central nervous system are supported by glial cells. Within the CNS, astrocytes provide the primary support and also remove debris and form scar tissue in the event of tissue damage. Oligodendrocytes form myelin, the substance that insulates axons, and also support unmyelinated axons. Microglia are phagocytes that serve as the representatives of the immune system. Within the PNS, support and myelin are provided by the Schwann cells.

In most organs, molecules freely move between the blood within the capillaries that serve them and the extracellular fluid that bathes their cells. The molecules pass through gaps between the cells that line the capillaries. The walls of the capillaries of the CNS lack these gaps and thus form a barrier between the blood and the brain. As a consequence, fewer substances can enter or leave the brain across the blood–brain barrier.

THOUGHT QUESTION

The fact that the mitochondria in our cells were originally microorganisms that infected our very remote ancestors points out that evolution can involve interactions between two or more species. Many species have other organisms living inside them; in fact, the bacteria in our intestines are necessary for our good health. Some microorganisms can exchange genetic information, so adaptive mutations developed in one species can be adopted by another. Is it possible that some of the features of the cells of our nervous system were bequeathed to our ancestors from other species?

Communication Within a Neuron

This section describes the nature of communication *within* a neuron—the way an action potential is sent from the cell body down the axon to the terminal buttons, informing them to release some neurotransmitter. The details of synaptic transmission—the communication between neurons—will be described in the next section. As we will see in this section, an action potential consists of a series of alterations in the membrane of the axon that permit various substances to move between the interior of the axon and the fluid surrounding it. These exchanges produce electrical currents. (See ***Animation 2.2, The Action Potential.***)

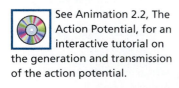

See Animation 2.2, The Action Potential, for an interactive tutorial on the generation and transmission of the action potential.

Neural Communication: An Overview

Before I begin my discussion of the action potential, let's step back and see how neurons can interact to produce a useful behavior. We begin by examining a simple assembly of three neurons and a muscle that control a withdrawal reflex. In the next two figures (and in subsequent figures that illustrate simple neural circuits), multipolar neurons are depicted in shorthand fashion as several-sided stars. The points of these stars represent dendrites, and only one or two terminal buttons are shown at the end of the axon. The sensory neuron in this example detects painful stimuli. When its dendrites are stimulated by a noxious stimulus (such as contact with a hot object), it sends messages down the axon to the terminal buttons, which are located in the spinal cord. (You will recognize this cell as a unipolar neuron; see ***Figure 2.10.***) The terminal buttons of the sensory neuron release a neurotransmitter that excites the interneuron, causing it to send messages down its axon. The terminal buttons of the interneuron release a neurotransmitter that excites the motor neuron, which sends messages down its axon. The axon of the motor neuron joins a nerve and travels to a muscle. When the terminal buttons of the motor neuron release their neurotransmitter, the muscle cells contract, causing the hand to move away from the hot object. (See ***Figure 2.10.***)

So far, all of the synapses have had excitatory effects. Now let us complicate matters a bit to see the effect of inhibitory synapses. Suppose you have removed a hot casserole from the oven. As you start walking over to the table to put it down, the heat begins to penetrate the rather thin potholders you are using. The pain caused by the hot casserole triggers a withdrawal reflex that tends to make you drop it. Yet you manage to keep hold of it long enough to get to the table and put it down. What prevented your withdrawal reflex from making you drop the casserole on the floor?

The pain from the hot casserole increases the activity of excitatory synapses on the motor neurons, which tends to cause the hand to pull away from the casserole. However, this excitation is counteracted by *inhibition*, supplied by another source: the brain. The brain contains neural circuits that recognize what a disaster it would be if you dropped the casserole on the floor. These neural circuits send information to the spinal cord that prevents the withdrawal reflex from making you drop the dish.

Figure 2.11 shows how this information reaches the spinal cord. As you can see, an axon from a neuron in the brain reaches the spinal cord, where its terminal buttons form synapses with an inhibitory interneuron. When the neuron in the brain becomes active, its terminal buttons excite this inhibitory interneuron. The interneuron releases an inhibitory neurotransmitter, which *decreases* the activity of the motor neuron, blocking the withdrawal reflex. This circuit provides an example of a contest between two competing tendencies: to drop the casserole and to hold onto it. (See ***Figure 2.11.***)

Figure 2.10

A withdrawal reflex, a simple example of a useful function of the nervous system. The painful stimulus causes the hand to pull away from the hot iron.

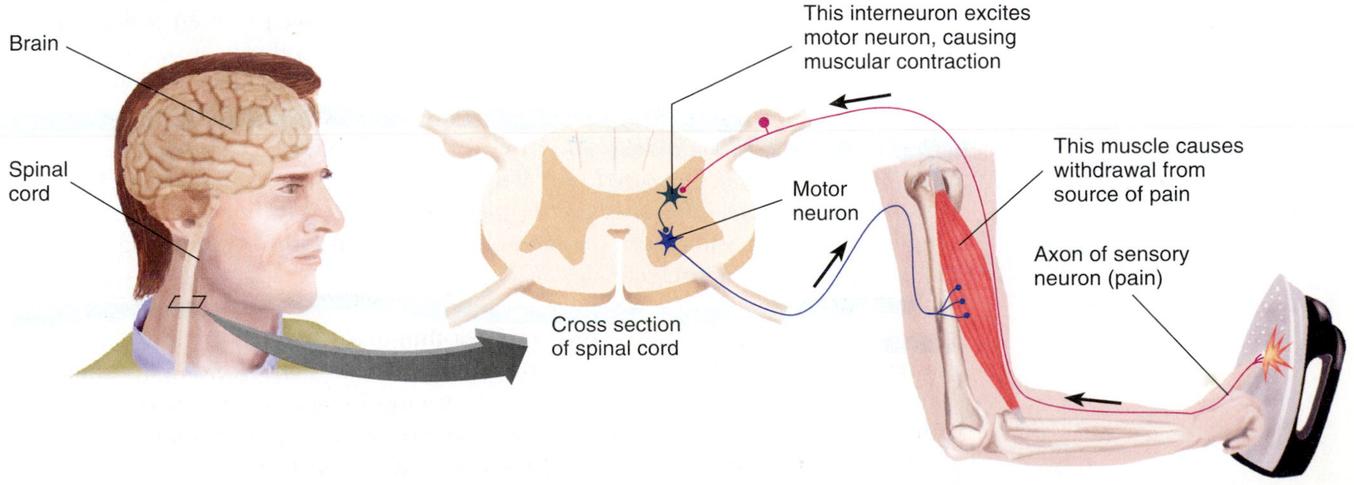

Figure 2.11

The role of inhibition. Inhibitory signals arising from the brain can prevent the withdrawal reflex from causing the person to drop the casserole.

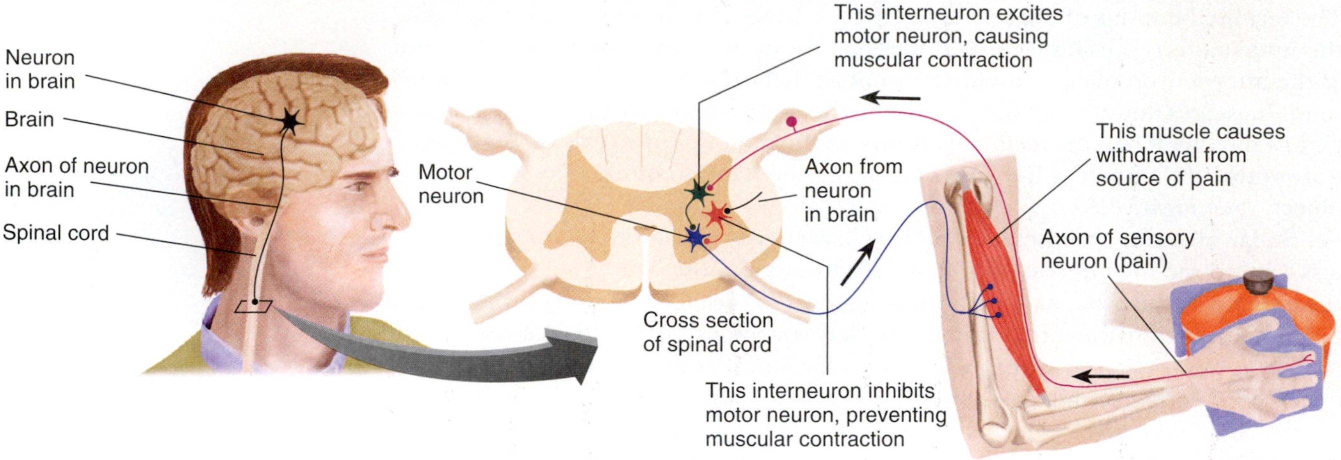

Of course, reflexes are more complicated than this description, and the mechanisms that inhibit them are even more so. And thousands of neurons are involved in this process. The five neurons shown in Figure 2.11 represent many others: Dozens of sensory neurons detect the hot object, hundreds of interneurons are stimulated by their activity, hundreds of motor neurons produce the contraction—and thousands of neurons in the brain must become active if the reflex is to be inhibited. Yet this simple model provides an overview of the process of neural communication, which is described in more detail later in this chapter.

Measuring Electrical Potentials of Axons

Let's examine the nature of the message that is conducted along the axon. To do so, we obtain an axon that is large enough to work with. Fortunately, nature has provided the neuroscientist with the giant squid axon (the giant axon of a squid, not the axon of a giant squid!). This axon is about 0.5 mm in diameter, which is hundreds of times larger than the largest mammalian axon. (This large axon controls an emergency response: sudden contraction of the mantle, which squirts water through a jet and propels the squid away from a source of danger.) We place an isolated giant squid axon in a dish of seawater, in which it can exist for a day or two.

To measure the electrical charges generated by an axon, we will need to use a pair of electrodes. **Electrodes** are electrical conductors that provide a path for electricity to enter or leave a medium. One of the electrodes is a simple wire that we place in the seawater. The other one, which we use to record the message from the axon, has to be special. Because even a giant squid axon is rather small, we must use a tiny electrode that will record the membrane potential without damaging the axon. To do so, we use a microelectrode.

A **microelectrode** is simply a very small electrode, which can be made of metal or glass. In this case we will use one made of thin glass tubing, which is heated and drawn down to an exceedingly fine point, less than a thousandth of a millimeter in diameter. Because glass will not conduct electricity, the glass microelectrode is filled with a liquid that conducts electricity, such as a solution of potassium chloride.

We place the wire electrode in the seawater and insert the microelectrode into the axon. (See ***Figure 2.12a.***) As soon as we do so, we discover that the inside of the axon is negatively charged with respect to the outside; the difference in charge be-

electrode A conductive medium that can be used to apply electrical stimulation or to record electrical potentials.

microelectrode A very fine electrode, generally used to record activity of individual neurons.

membrane potential The electrical charge across a cell membrane; the difference in electrical potential inside and outside the cell.

oscilloscope A laboratory instrument that is capable of displaying a graph of voltage as a function of time on the face of a cathode ray tube.

resting potential The membrane potential of a neuron when it is not being altered by excitatory or inhibitory postsynaptic potentials; approximately –70 mV in the giant squid axon.

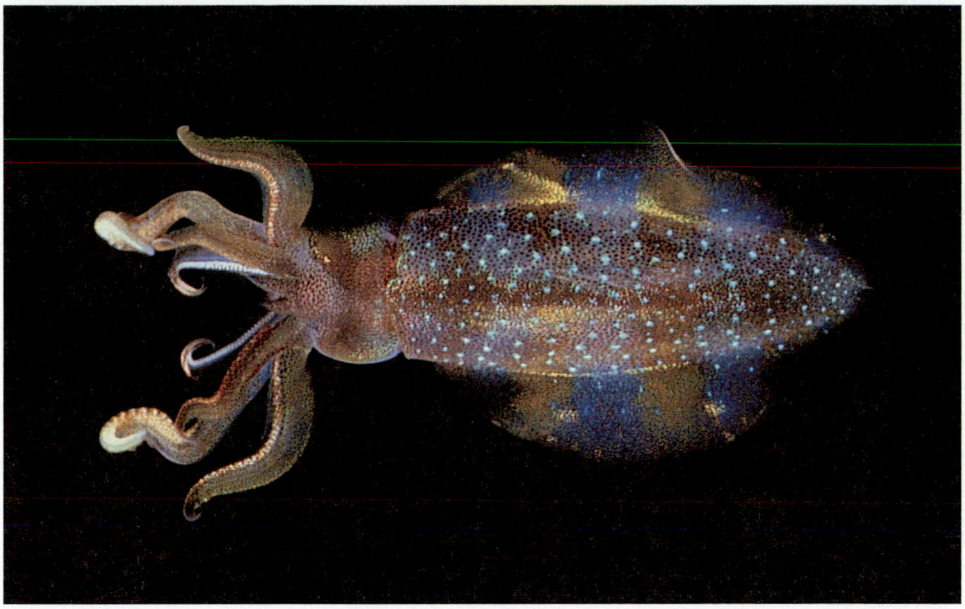

Using the giant axon of the squid, researchers discovered the nature of the message carried by axons.

ing 70 mV (millivolts, or thousandths of a volt). Thus, the inside of the membrane is –70 mV. This electrical charge is called the **membrane potential.** The term *potential* refers to a stored-up source of energy—in this case, electrical energy. For example, a flashlight battery that is not connected to an electrical circuit has a *potential* charge of 1.5 V between its terminals. If we connect a light bulb to the terminals, the potential energy is tapped and converted into radiant energy (light). (See ***Figure 2.12b.***) Similarly, if we connect our electrodes—one inside the axon and one outside it—to a very sensitive voltmeter, we will convert the potential energy to movement of the meter's needle. Of course, the potential electrical energy of the axonal membrane is very weak in comparison with that of a flashlight battery.

As we will see, the message that is conducted down the axon consists of a brief change in the membrane potential. However, this change occurs very rapidly—too rapidly for us to see if we were using a voltmeter. Therefore, to study the message, we will use an **oscilloscope.** This device, like a voltmeter, measures voltages, but it also produces a record of these voltages, graphing them as a function of time. These graphs are displayed on a screen, much like the one found in a television. The vertical axis represents voltage, and the horizontal axis represents time, going from left to right.

Once we insert our microelectrode into the axon, the oscilloscope draws a straight horizontal line at –70 mV, as long as the axon is not disturbed. This electrical charge across the membrane is called the **resting potential**—the membrane potential measured while the membrane is at rest.

Now let's disturb the resting potential and see what happens. To do so, we will use another device—an electrical stimulator that allows us to alter the membrane

Figure 2.12

Measuring electrical charge. (a) A voltmeter detecting the charge across a membrane of an axon. (b) A light bulb detecting the charge across the terminals of a battery.

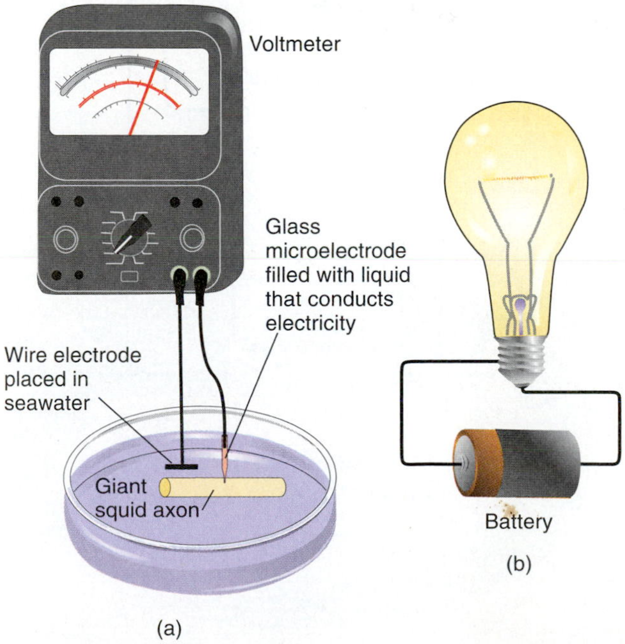

potential at a specific location. (See ***Figure 2.13.***) The stimulator can pass current through another microelectrode that we have inserted into the axon. Because the inside of the axon is negative, a positive charge applied to the inside of the membrane produces a **depolarization.** That is, it takes away some of the electrical charge across the membrane near the electrode, reducing the membrane potential.

Let's see what happens to an axon when we artificially change the membrane potential at one point. Figure 2.14 shows a graph drawn by an oscilloscope that has been monitoring the effects of brief depolarizing stimuli. The graphs of the effects of these separate stimuli are superimposed on the same drawing so that we can compare them. We deliver a series of depolarizing stimuli, starting with a very weak stimulus (number 1) and gradually increasing their strength. Each stimulus briefly depolarizes the membrane potential a little more. Finally, after we present depolarization number 4, the membrane potential suddenly reverses itself, so that the inside becomes *positive* (and the outside becomes negative). The membrane potential quickly returns to normal, but first it overshoots the resting potential, becoming **hyperpolarized**—more polarized than normal—for a short time. The whole process takes about 2 msec (milliseconds). (See ***Figure 2.14.***)

This phenomenon, a very rapid reversal of the membrane potential, is called the **action potential.** It constitutes the message carried by the axon from the cell body to the terminal buttons. The voltage level that triggers an action potential—which was achieved only by depolarizing shock number 4—is called the **threshold of excitation.**

Figure 2.13

The means by which an axon can be stimulated while its membrane potential is being recorded.

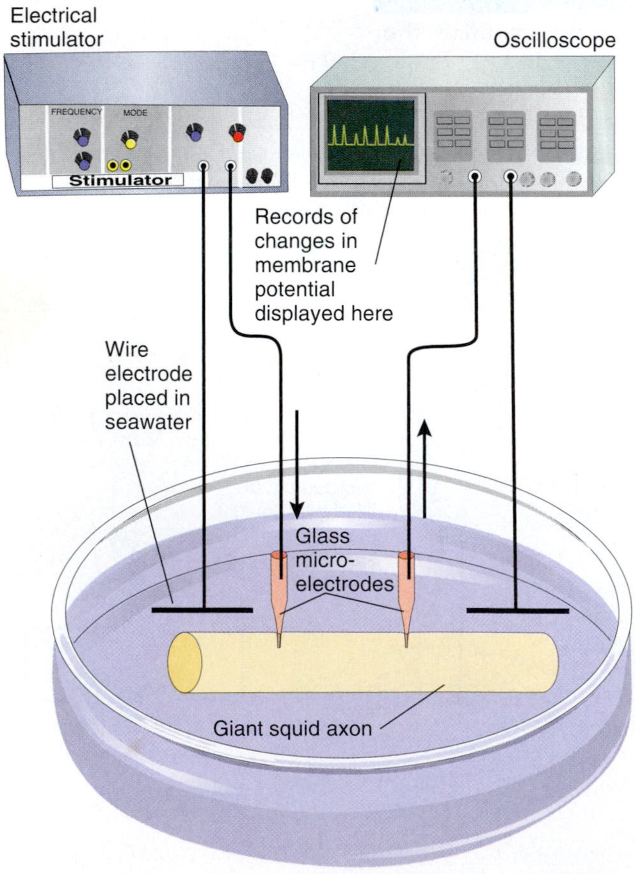

Figure 2.14

An action potential. These results would be seen on an oscilloscope screen if depolarizing stimuli of varying intensities were delivered to the axon shown in Figure 2.13.

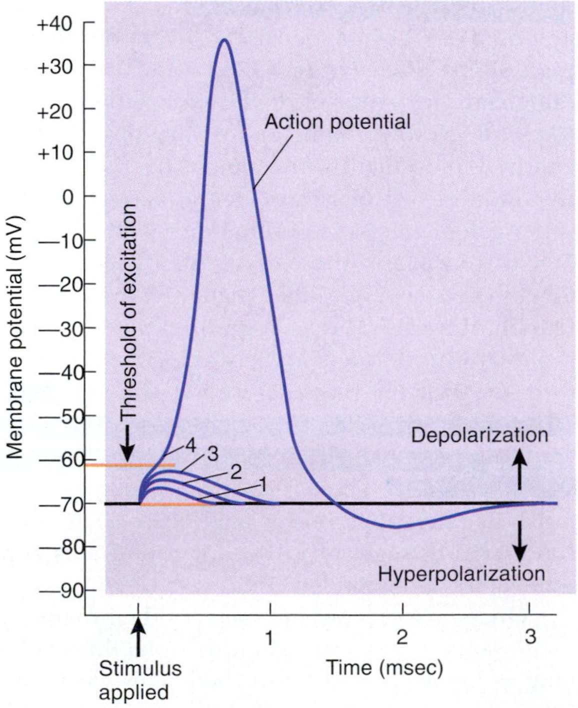

The Membrane Potential: Balance of Two Forces

To understand what causes the action potential to occur, we must first understand the reasons for the existence of the membrane potential. As we will see, this electrical charge is the result of a balance between two opposing forces: diffusion and electrostatic pressure.

The Force of Diffusion

When a spoonful of sugar is carefully poured into a container of water, it settles to the bottom. After a time the sugar dissolves, but it remains close to the bottom of the container. After a much longer time (probably several days), the molecules of sugar distribute themselves evenly throughout the water, even if no one stirs the liquid. The process whereby molecules distribute themselves evenly throughout the medium in which they are dissolved is called **diffusion.**

When there are no forces or barriers to prevent them from doing so, molecules will diffuse from regions of high concentration to regions of low concentration. Molecules are constantly in motion, and their rate of movement is proportional to the temperature. Only at absolute zero [0 K (kelvin) = −273.15°C = −459.7°F] do molecules cease their random movement. At all other temperatures they move about, colliding and veering off in different directions, thus pushing one another away. The result of these collisions in the example of sugar and water is to force sugar molecules upward (and to force water molecules downward), away from the regions in which they are most concentrated.

The Force of Electrostatic Pressure

When some substances are dissolved in water, they split into two parts, each with an opposing electrical charge. Substances with this property are called **electrolytes**; the charged particles into which they decompose are called **ions.** Ions are of two basic types: *Cations* have a positive charge, and *anions* have a negative charge. For example, when sodium chloride (NaCl, table salt) is dissolved in water, many of the molecules split into sodium cations (Na^+) and chloride anions (Cl^-). (I find that the easiest way to keep the terms *cation* and *anion* straight is to think of the cation's plus sign as a cross, and remember the superstition of a black *cat* crossing your path.)

As you have undoubtedly learned, particles with the same kind of charge repel each other (+ repels +, and – repels –), but particles with different charges are attracted to each other (+ and – attract). Thus, anions repel anions, cations repel cations, but anions and cations attract each other. The force exerted by this attraction or repulsion is called **electrostatic pressure.** Just as the force of diffusion moves molecules from regions of high concentration to regions of low concentration, electrostatic pressure moves ions from place to place: Cations are pushed away from regions with an excess of cations, and anions are pushed away from regions with an excess of anions.

Ions in the Extracellular and Intracellular Fluid

The fluid within cells (**intracellular fluid**) and the fluid surrounding them (**extracellular fluid**) contain different ions. The forces of diffusion and electrostatic pressure contributed by these ions give rise to the membrane potential. Because the membrane potential is produced by a balance between the forces of diffusion and electrostatic pressures, understanding what produces this potential requires that we know the concentration of the various ions in the extracellular and intracellular fluids.

There are several important ions in these fluids. I will discuss four of them here: organic anions (symbolized by A^-), chloride ions (Cl^-), sodium ions (Na^+), and potassium ions (K^+). The Latin words for sodium and potassium are *natrium* and *kalium;*

depolarization Reduction (toward zero) of the membrane potential of a cell from its normal resting potential.

hyperpolarization An increase in the membrane potential of a cell, relative to the normal resting potential.

action potential The brief electrical impulse that provides the basis for conduction of information along an axon.

threshold of excitation The value of the membrane potential that must be reached to produce an action potential.

diffusion Movement of molecules from regions of high concentration to regions of low concentration.

electrolyte An aqueous solution of a material that ionizes—namely, a soluble acid, base, or salt.

ion A charged molecule. *Cations* are positively charged, and *anions* are negatively charged.

electrostatic pressure The attractive force between atomic particles charged with opposite signs or the repulsive force between atomic particles charged with the same sign.

intracellular fluid The fluid contained within cells.

extracellular fluid Body fluids located outside of cells.

Figure 2.15

The relative concentration of some important ions inside and outside the neuron and the forces acting on them.

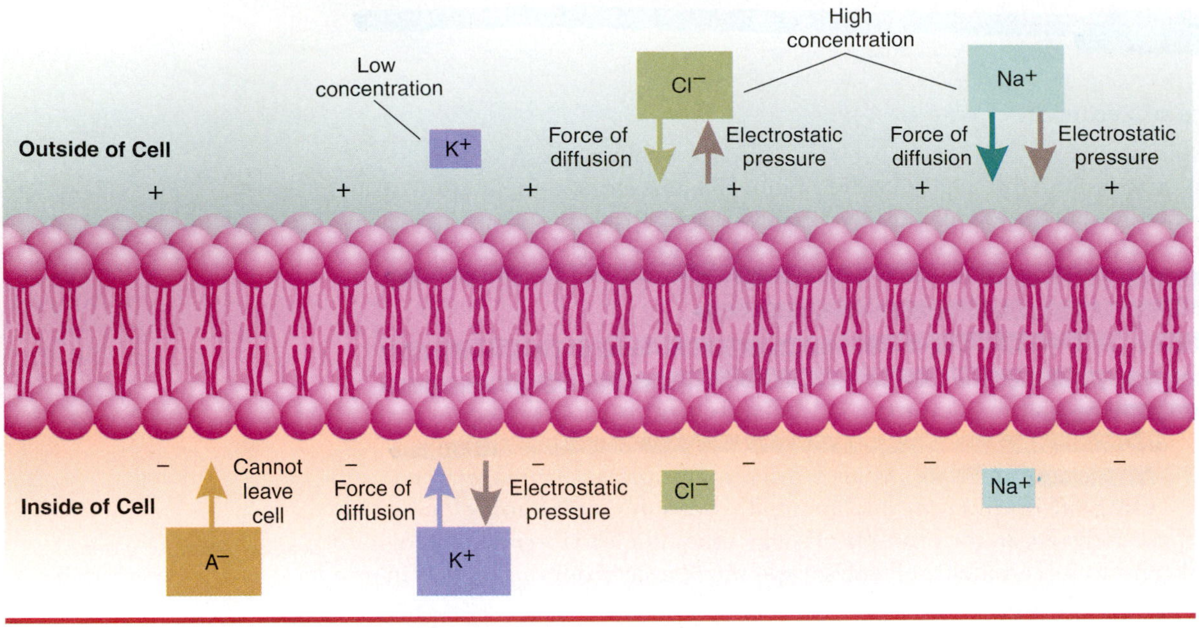

hence, they are abbreviated *Na* and *K*, respectively. Organic anions—negatively charged proteins and intermediate products of the cell's metabolic processes—are found only in the intracellular fluid. Although the other three ions are found in both the intracellular and extracellular fluids, K^+ is found predominantly in the intracellular fluid, whereas Na^+ and Cl^- are found predominantly in the extracellular fluid. The sizes of the boxes in Figure 2.15 indicate the relative concentrations of these four ions. (See ***Figure 2.15.***) The easiest way to remember which ion is found where is to recall that the fluid that surrounds our cells is similar to seawater, which is predominantly a solution of salt, NaCl. The primitive ancestors of our cells lived in the ocean; thus, the seawater was their extracellular fluid. Our extracellular fluid thus resembles seawater, produced and maintained by regulatory mechanisms that are described in Chapter 11.

Let us consider the ions in Figure 2.15, examining the forces of diffusion and electrostatic pressure exerted on each and reasoning why each is located where it is. A^-, the organic anion, is unable to pass through the membrane of the axon; therefore, although the presence of this ion within the cell contributes to the membrane potential, it is located where it is because the membrane is impermeable to it.

The potassium ion K^+ is concentrated within the axon; thus, the force of diffusion tends to push it out of the cell. However, the outside of the cell is charged positively with respect to the inside, so electrostatic pressure tends to force the cation inside. Thus, the two opposing forces balance, and potassium ions tend to remain where they are. (See ***Figure 2.15.***)

The chloride ion Cl^- is in greatest concentration outside the axon. The force of diffusion pushes this ion inward. However, because the inside of the axon is negatively charged, electrostatic pressure pushes the anion outward. Again, two opposing forces balance each other. (See ***Figure 2.15.***)

The sodium ion Na^+ is also in greatest concentration outside the axon, so it, like Cl^-, is pushed into the cell by the force of diffusion. But unlike chloride, the sodium ion is *positively* charged. Therefore, electrostatic pressure does *not* prevent Na^+ from entering the cell; indeed, the negative charge inside the axon *attracts* Na^+. (See ***Figure 2.15.***)

How can Na^+ remain in greatest concentration in the extracellular fluid, despite the fact that both forces (diffusion and electrostatic pressure) tend to push it inside? The answer is this: Another force, provided by the *sodium-potassium pump,* continuously pushes Na^+ out of the axon. The sodium-potassium pump consists of a large number of protein molecules embedded in the membrane, driven by energy provided by molecules of ATP produced by the mitochondria. These molecules, known as **sodium-potassium transporters,** exchange Na^+ for K^+, pushing three sodium ions out for every two potassium ions they push in. (See ***Figure 2.16.***)

Figure 2.16

A sodium-potassium transporter, situated in the cell membrane.

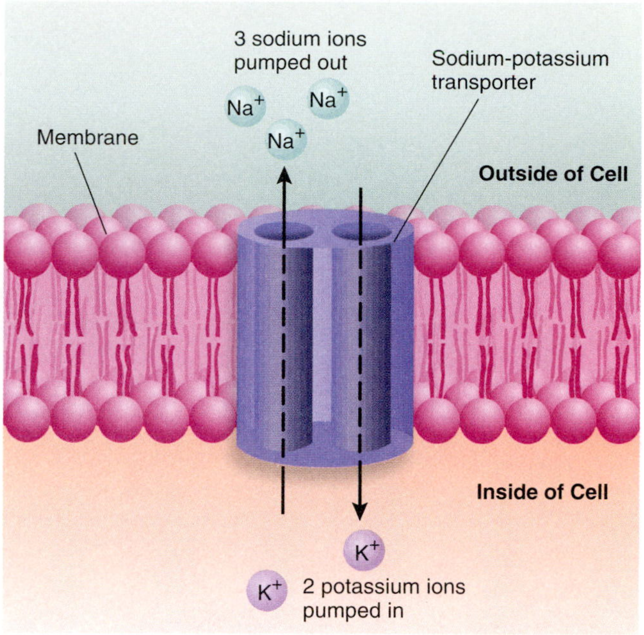

Because the membrane is not very permeable to Na^+, sodium-potassium transporters very effectively keep the intracellular concentration of Na^+ low. By transporting K^+ into the cell, they also produce a small increase in the intracellular concentration of K^+. The membrane is approximately 100 times more permeable to K^+ than to Na^+, so the increase is slight; but as we will see when we study the process of neural inhibition later in this chapter, it is very important. The transporters that make up the sodium-potassium pump use considerable energy: Up to 40 percent of a neuron's metabolic resources are used to operate them. Neurons, muscle cells, glia—in fact, most cells of the body—have sodium-potassium transporters in their membrane.

The Action Potential

As we saw, the forces of both diffusion and electrostatic pressure tend to push Na^+ into the cell. However, the membrane is not very permeable to this ion, and sodium-potassium transporters continuously pump out Na^+, keeping the intracellular level of Na^+ low. But imagine what would happen if the membrane suddenly became permeable to Na^+. The forces of diffusion and electrostatic pressure would cause Na^+ to rush into the cell. This sudden influx (inflow) of positively charged ions would drastically change the membrane potential. Indeed, experiments have shown that this mechanism is precisely what causes the action potential: A brief increase in the permeability of the membrane to Na^+ (allowing these ions to rush into the cell) is immediately followed by a transient increase in the permeability of the membrane to K^+ (allowing these ions to rush out of the cell). What is responsible for these transient increases in permeability?

We already saw that one type of protein molecule embedded in the membrane—the sodium-potassium transporter—actively pumps sodium ions out of the cell and pumps potassium ions into it. Another type of protein molecule provides an opening that permits ions to enter or leave the cells. These molecules provide **ion channels,** which contain passages ("pores") that can open or close. When an ion channel is open, a particular type of ion can flow through the pore and thus can enter or leave the cell. (See ***Figure 2.17.***) Neural membranes contain many thousands of ion channels. For example, the giant squid axon contains several hundred sodium channels in each square micrometer of membrane. (There are one million square micrometers in a square millimeter; thus, a patch of axonal membrane the size of a lowercase letter "o" in this book would contain several hundred million sodium channels.) Each sodium channel can admit up to 100 million ions per second when

sodium-potassium transporter A protein found in the membrane of all cells that extrudes sodium ions from and transports potassium ions into the cell.

ion channel A specialized protein molecule that permits specific ions to enter or leave cells.

Figure 2.17

Ion channels. When they are open, ions can pass through them, entering or leaving the cell.

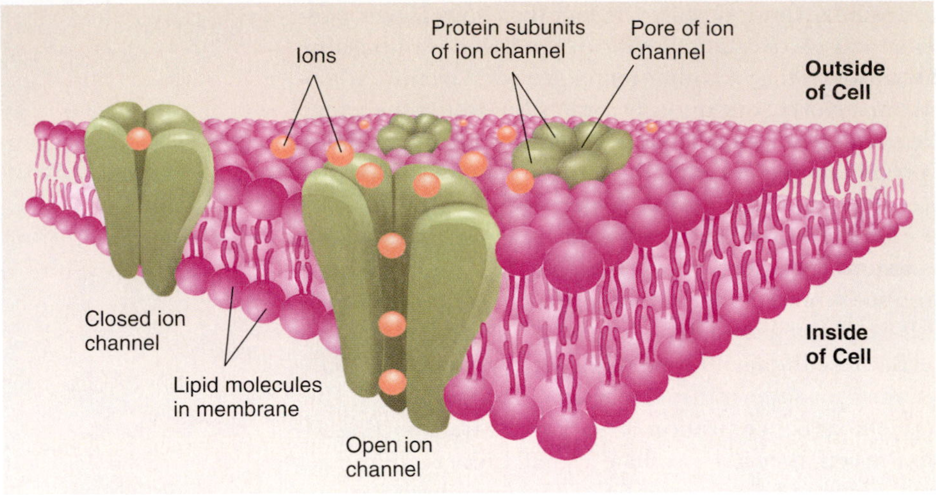

Figure 2.18

The movements of ions during the action potential. The diagram at the top shows the opening of sodium channels at the threshold of excitation, their refractory condition at the peak of the action potential, and their resetting when the membrane potential returns to normal.

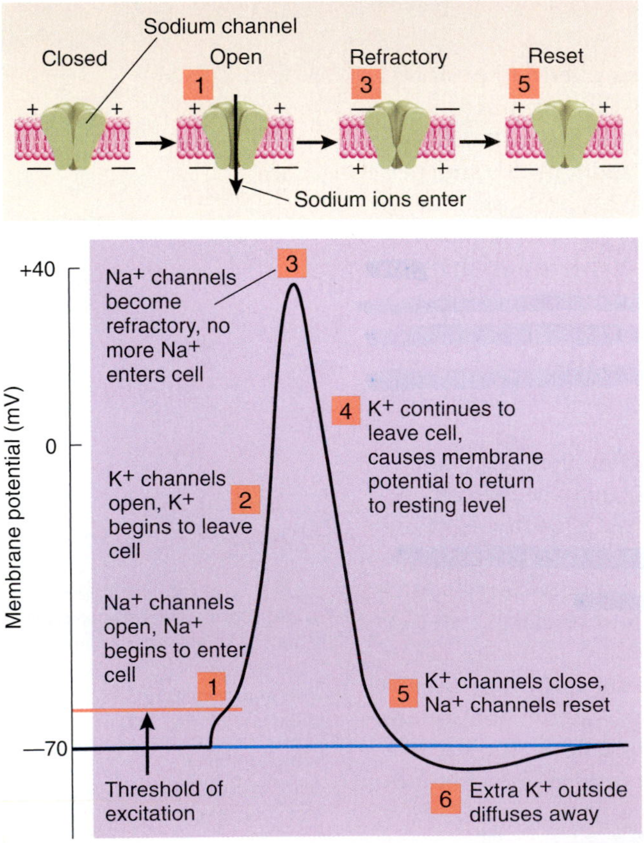

it is open. Thus, the permeability of a membrane to a particular ion at a given moment is determined by the number of ion channels that are open.

The following numbered paragraphs describe the movements of ions through the membrane during the action potential. The numbers on the figure correspond to the numbers of the paragraphs that follow. (See ***Figure 2.18.***)

1. As soon as the threshold of excitation is reached, the sodium channels in the membrane open and Na^+ rushes in, propelled by the forces of diffusion and electrostatic pressure. The opening of these channels is triggered by reduction of the membrane potential (depolarization); they open at the point at which an action potential begins: the threshold of excitation. Because these channels are opened by changes in the membrane potential, they are called **voltage-dependent ion channels.** The influx of positively charged sodium ions produces a rapid change in the membrane potential, from –70 mV to +40 mV.
2. The membrane of the axon contains voltage-dependent potassium channels, but these channels are less sensitive than voltage-dependent sodium channels. That is, they require a greater level of depolarization before they begin to open. Thus, they begin to open later than the sodium channels.
3. At about the time the action potential reaches its peak (in approximately 1 msec), the sodium channels become *refractory*—the channels become blocked and cannot open again until the membrane once more reaches the resting potential. At this time, then, no more Na^+ can enter the cell.

4. By now, the voltage-dependent potassium channels in the membrane are open, letting K^+ ions move freely through the membrane. At this time, the inside of the axon is *positively* charged, so K^+ is driven out of the cell by diffusion and by electrostatic pressure. This outflow of cations causes the membrane potential to return toward its normal value. As it does so, the potassium channels begin to close again.
5. Once the membrane potential returns to normal, the potassium channels are closed, and no more potassium leaves the cell. At around this time, the sodium channels reset so that another depolarization can cause them to open again.
6. The membrane actually overshoots its resting value (–70 mV) and only gradually returns to normal. The accumulation of K^+ ions outside the membrane are responsible for this temporary hyperpolarization. The extra ions K^+ soon diffuse away, and the membrane potential returns to –70 mV. Eventually, sodium-potassium transporters remove the Na^+ ions that leaked in and retrieve the K^+ ions that leaked out.

voltage-dependent ion channel An ion channel that opens or closes according to the value of the membrane potential.

all-or-none law The principle that once an action potential is triggered in an axon, it is propagated, without decrement, to the end of the fiber.

Experiments have shown that an action potential temporarily increases the number of Na^+ ions inside the giant squid axon by 0.0003 percent. Although the concentration just inside the membrane is high, the total number of ions entering the cell is very small relative to the number already there. This means that on a short-term basis, sodium-potassium transporters are not very important. The few Na^+ ions that manage to leak in diffuse into the rest of the axoplasm, and the slight increase in Na^+ concentration is hardly noticeable. However, sodium-potassium transporters are important on a *long-term* basis. Without the activity of sodium-potassium transporters, the concentration of sodium ions in the axoplasm would eventually increase enough that the axon would no longer be able to function.

Conduction of the Action Potential

Now that we have a basic understanding of the resting membrane potential and the production of the action potential, we can consider the movement of the message down the axon, or *conduction of the action potential.* To study this phenomenon, we again make use of the giant squid axon. We attach an electrical stimulator to an electrode at one end of the axon and place recording electrodes, attached to oscilloscopes, at different distances from the stimulating electrode. Then we apply a depolarizing stimulus to the end of the axon and trigger an action potential. We record the action potential from each of the electrodes, one after the other. Thus, we see that the action potential is conducted down the axon. As the action potential travels, it remains constant in size. (See ***Figure 2.19***.)

This experiment establishes a basic law of axonal conduction: the **all-or-none law.** This law states that an action potential either occurs or does not occur; and once triggered, it is transmitted down the axon to its end. An action potential always remains the same size, without growing or diminishing. When an action potential reaches a point where the axon branches, it splits but does not diminish in size. An axon will

Figure 2.19

Conduction of the action potential. When an action potential is triggered, its size remains undiminished as it travels down the axon. The speed of conduction can be calculated from the delay between the stimulus and the action potential.

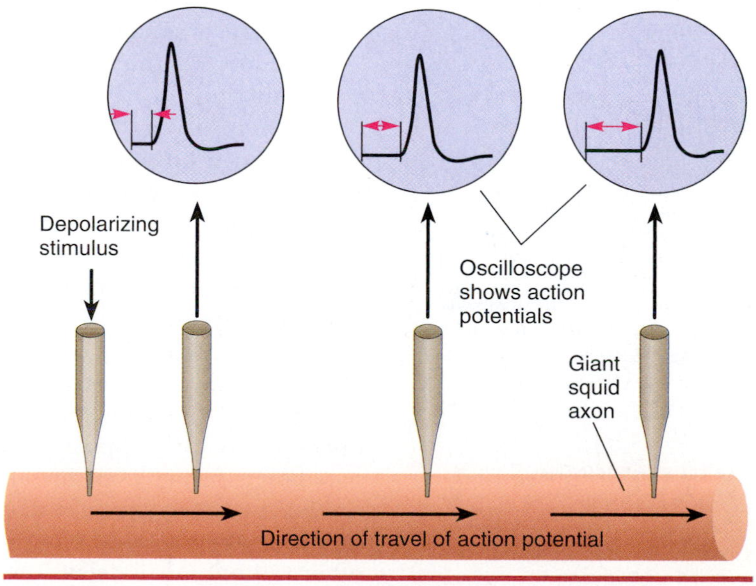

Figure 2.20

The rate law. The strength of a stimulus is represented by the rate of firing of an axon. The size of each action potential is always constant.

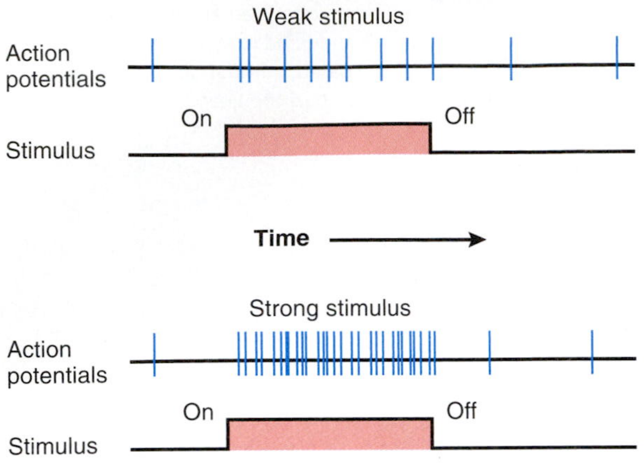

transmit an action potential in either direction, or even in both directions if it is started in the middle of the axon's length. However, because action potentials in living animals always start at the end attached to the soma, axons normally carry one-way traffic.

As you know, the strength of a muscular contraction can vary from very weak to very forceful, and the strength of a stimulus can vary from barely detectable to very intense. We know that the occurrence of action potentials in axons controls the strength of muscular contractions and represents the intensity of a physical stimulus. But if the action potential is an all-or-none event, how can it represent information that can vary in a continuous fashion? The answer is simple: A single action potential is not the basic element of information; rather, variable information is represented by an axon's *rate of firing.* (In this context, *firing* refers to the production of action potentials.) A high rate of firing causes a strong muscular contraction, and a strong stimulus (such as a bright light) causes a high rate of firing in axons that serve the eyes. Thus, the all-or-none law is supplemented by the **rate law.** (See ***Figure 2.20.***)

Recall that all but the smallest axons in mammalian nervous systems are myelinated; segments of the axons are covered by a myelin sheath produced by the oligodendrocytes of the CNS or the Schwann cells of the PNS. These segments are separated by portions of naked axon, the nodes of Ranvier. Conduction of an action potential in a myelinated axon is somewhat different from conduction in an unmyelinated axon.

Schwann cells and the oligodendrocytes of the CNS wrap tightly around the axon, leaving no measurable extracellular fluid between them and the axon. The only place where a myelinated axon comes into contact with the extracellular fluid is at a node of Ranvier, where the axon is naked. In the myelinated areas there can be no inward flow of Na^+ when the sodium channels open, because there *is* no extracellular sodium. The axon conducts the electrical disturbance from the action potential to the next node of Ranvier. The disturbance is conducted passively, the way an electrical signal is conducted through an insulated cable. The disturbance gets smaller as it passes down the axon, but it is still large enough to trigger a new action potential at the next node. The action potential gets retriggered, or repeated, at each node of Ranvier, and the electrical disturbance that results is conducted along the myelinated area to the next node. Such conduction, hopping from node to node, is called **saltatory conduction,** from the Latin *saltare,* "to dance." (See ***Figure 2.21.***)

Saltatory conduction confers two advantages. The first is economic. Sodium-potassium transporters must expend energy to get rid of the excess Na^+ that enters the axon during the action potential. Sodium-potassium transporters must be located along an unmyelinated axon because Na^+ enters everywhere. However, because Na^+ can enter a myelinated axon only at the nodes of Ranvier, much less gets in, and consequently, much less has to be pumped out again. Therefore, a myelinated axon expends much less energy to maintain its sodium balance.

The second advantage to myelin is speed. Conduction of an action potential is faster in a myelinated axon because the transmission between the nodes is very fast. Increased speed enables an animal to react faster and (undoubtedly) to think faster. One of the ways to increase the speed of conduction is to increase size. Because it is so large, the unmyelinated squid axon, with a diameter of 500 µm, achieves a conduction velocity of approximately 35 m/sec (meters per second). However, a myelinated cat axon achieves the same speed with a diameter of a mere 6 µm. The fastest myelinated axon, 20 µm in diameter, can conduct action potentials at a speedy 120 m/sec, or 432 km/h. At that speed, a signal can get from one end of an axon to the other without much delay.

rate law The principle that variations in the intensity of a stimulus or other information being transmitted in an axon are represented by variations in the rate at which that axon fires.

saltatory conduction Conduction of action potentials by myelinated axons. The action potential appears to jump from one node of Ranvier to the next.

Figure 2.21

Saltatory conduction, showing propagation of an action potential down a myelinated axon.

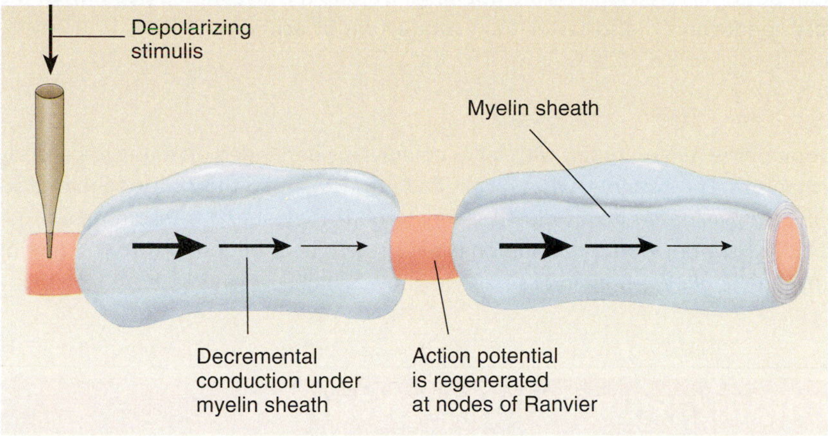

INTERIM SUMMARY

Communication Within a Neuron

The withdrawal reflex illustrates how neurons can be connected to accomplish useful behaviors. The circuit responsible for this reflex consists of three sets of neurons: sensory neurons, interneurons, and motor neurons. The reflex can be suppressed when neurons in the brain activate inhibitory interneurons that form synapses with the motor neurons.

The message conducted down an axon is called an action potential. The membranes of all cells of the body are electrically charged, but only axons can produce action potentials. The resting membrane potential occurs because various ions are located in different concentrations in the fluid inside and outside the cell. The extracellular fluid (like seawater) is rich in Na^+ and Cl^-, and the intracellular fluid is rich in K^+ and various organic anions, designated as A^-.

The cell membrane is freely permeable to water, but its permeability to various ions—in particular, Na^+ and K^+—is regulated by ion channels. When the membrane potential is at its resting value (–70 mV), the voltage-dependent sodium and potassium channels are closed. The experiment with radioactive seawater showed us that some Na^+ continuously leaks into the axon but is promptly forced out of the cell again by the sodium-potassium transporters (which also pump potassium *into* the axon). When an electrical stimulator depolarizes the membrane of the axon so that its potential reaches the threshold of excitation, voltage-dependent sodium channels open, and Na^+ rushes into the cell, driven by the force of diffusion and by electrostatic pressure. The entry of the positively charged ions further reduces the membrane potential and, indeed, causes it to reverse, so the inside becomes positive. The opening of the sodium channels is temporary; they soon close again. The depolarization caused by the influx of Na^+ activates voltage-dependent potassium channels, and K^+ leaves the axon, traveling down its concentration gradient. This efflux (outflow) of K^+ quickly brings the membrane potential back to its resting value.

Because an action potential of a given axon is an all-or-none phenomenon, neurons represent intensity by their rate of firing. The action potential normally begins at one end of the axon, where the axon attaches to the soma. The action potential travels continuously down unmyelinated axons, remaining constant in size, until it reaches the terminal buttons. (If the axon divides, an action potential continues down each branch.) In myelinated axons ions can flow through the membrane only at the nodes of Ranvier, because the axons are covered everywhere else with myelin, which isolates them from the extracellular fluid. Thus, the action potential is conducted passively from one node of Ranvier to the next. When the electrical message reaches a node, voltage-dependent sodium channels open, and the action potential reaches full strength again. This mechanism saves a considerable amount of energy because sodium-potassium transporters are not needed along the myelinated portions of the axon. Saltatory conduction is also faster than conduction of action potentials in unmyelinated axons.

THOUGHT QUESTION

The evolution of the human brain, with all its complexity, depended on many apparently trivial mechanisms. For example, what if cells had not developed the ability to manufacture myelin? Unmyelinated axons must be very large if they are to transmit action potentials rapidly. How big would the human brain have to be if oligodendrocytes did not produce myelin? *Could* the human brain as we know it have evolved without myelin?

Communication Between Neurons

Now that you know about the basic structure of neurons and the nature of the action potential, it is time to describe the ways in which neurons can communicate with each other. These communications make it possible for circuits of neurons to gather sensory information, make plans, and initiate behaviors.

The primary means of communication between neurons is *synaptic transmission*—the transmission of messages from one neuron to another through a synapse. As we saw, these messages are carried by neurotransmitters, released by terminal buttons. These chemicals diffuse across the fluid-filled gap between the terminal buttons and the membranes of the neurons with which they form synapses. As we will see in this section, neurotransmitters produce **postsynaptic potentials**—brief depolarizations or hyperpolarizations—that increase or decrease the rate of firing of the axon of the postsynaptic neuron.

Neurotransmitters exert their effects on cells by attaching to a particular region of a receptor molecule called the **binding site.** A molecule of the chemical fits into the binding site the way a key fits into a lock: The shape of the binding site and the shape of the molecule of the neurotransmitter are complementary. A chemical that attaches to a binding site is called a **ligand,** from *ligare,* "to bind." Neurotransmitters are natural ligands, produced and released by neurons. But other chemicals found in nature (primarily in plants or in the poisonous venoms of animals) can serve as ligands, too. In addition, artificial ligands can be produced in the laboratory. These chemicals are discussed in Chapter 4, which deals with drugs and their effects.

postsynaptic potential Alterations in the membrane potential of a postsynaptic neuron, produced by liberation of neurotransmitter at the synapse.

binding site The location on a receptor protein to which a ligand binds.

ligand (***ligh** gand* or ***ligg** and*) A chemical that binds with the binding site of a receptor.

dendritic spine A small bud on the surface of a dendrite, with which a terminal button of another neuron forms a synapse.

presynaptic membrane The membrane of a terminal button that lies adjacent to the postsynaptic membrane and through which the neurotransmitter is released.

postsynaptic membrane The cell membrane opposite the terminal button in a synapse; the membrane of the cell that receives the message.

synaptic cleft The space between the presynaptic membrane and the postsynaptic membrane.

synaptic vesicle (***vess** i kul*) A small, hollow, beadlike structure found in terminal buttons; contains molecules of a neurotransmitter.

Structure of Synapses

As you have already learned, synapses are junctions between the terminal buttons at the ends of the axonal branches of one neuron and the membrane of another. Synapses can occur in three places: on dendrites, on the soma, and on other axons. These synapses are referred to as *axodendritic, axosomatic,* and *axoaxonic.* Axodendritic synapses can occur on the smooth surface of a dendrite or on **dendritic spines**—small protrusions that stud the dendrites of several types of large neurons in the brain. (See ***Figure 2.22.***)

Figure 2.23 illustrates a synapse. The **presynaptic membrane,** located at the end of the terminal button, faces the **postsynaptic membrane,** located on the neuron that receives the message (the *postsynaptic* neuron). These two membranes face each other across the **synaptic cleft,** a gap that varies in size from synapse to synapse but is usually around 20 nm wide. (A nanometer (nm) is one billionth of a meter.) The synaptic cleft contains extracellular fluid, through which the neurotransmitter dif-

Figure 2.22

Types of synapses. Axodendritic synapses can occur on the smooth surface of a dendrite (a) or on dendritic spines (b). Axosomatic synapses occur on somatic membrane (c). Axoaxonic synapses consist of synapses between two terminal buttons (d).

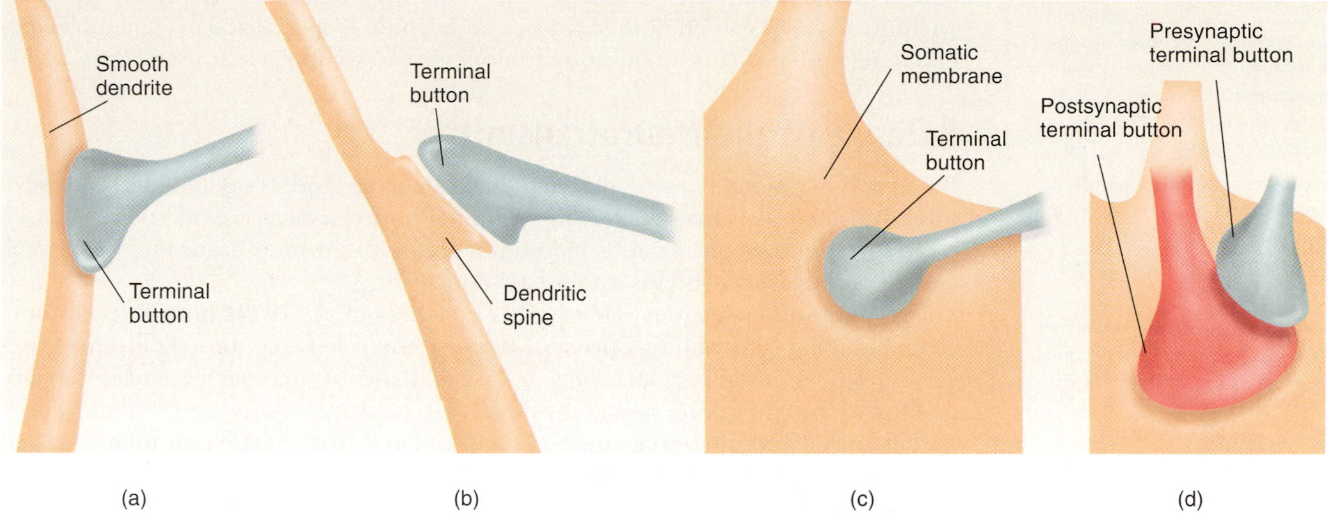

fuses. A meshwork of filaments crosses the synaptic cleft and keeps the presynaptic and postsynaptic membranes in alignment. (See ***Figure 2.23.***)

As you might have noticed in Figure 2.23, the cytoplasm of the terminal button contains **synaptic vesicles,** small, rounded objects in the shape of spheres or ovoids. (The term *vesicle* means "little bladder.") These vesicles are found in greatest numbers around the part of the presynaptic membrane that faces the synaptic cleft—next

Figure 2.23

Details of a synapse.

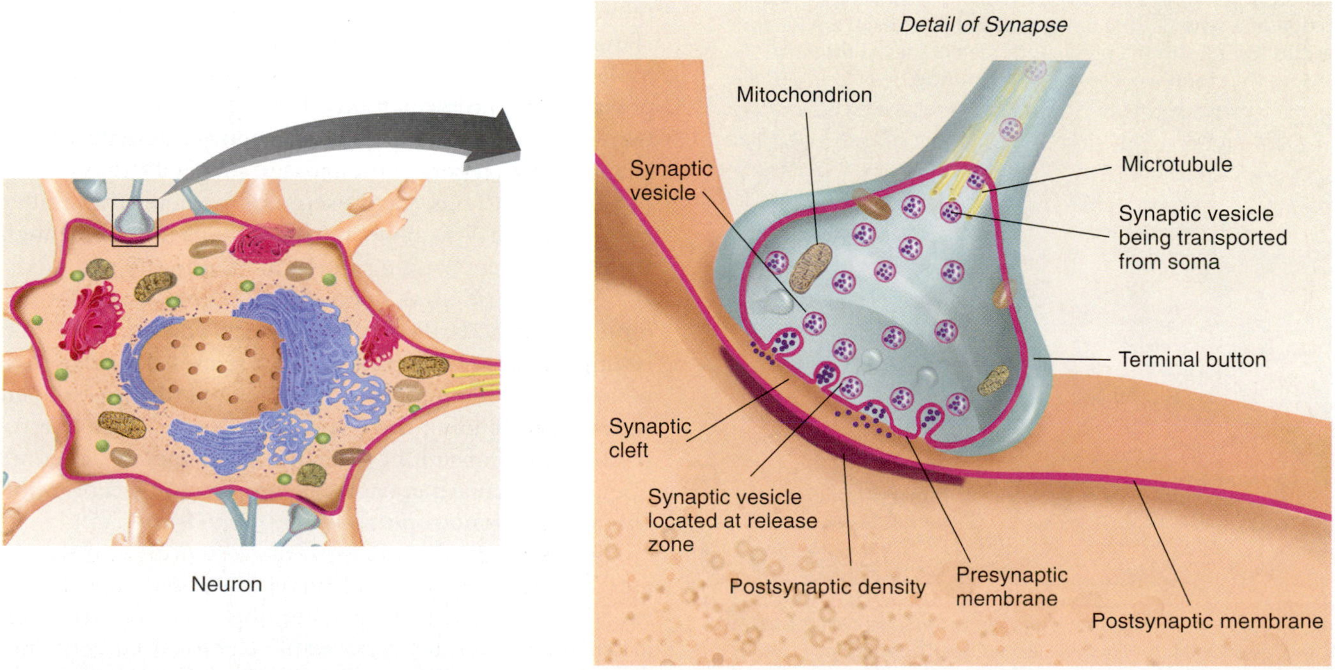

release zone A region of the interior of the presynaptic membrane of a synapse to which synaptic vesicles attach and release their neurotransmitter into the synaptic cleft.

postsynaptic receptor A receptor molecule in the postsynaptic membrane of a synapse that contains a binding site for a neurotransmitter.

neurotransmitter-dependent ion channel An ion channel that opens when a molecule of a neurotransmitter binds with a postsynaptic receptor.

ionotropic receptor (*eye on oh **trow** pik*) A receptor that contains a binding site for a neurotransmitter and an ion channel that opens when a molecule of the neurotransmitter attaches to the binding site.

to the **release zone,** the region from which neurotransmitter is released. Synaptic vesicles are produced in the soma and are carried by fast axoplasmic transport to the terminal button. (See ***Figure 2.23.***)

In an electron micrograph the postsynaptic membrane under the terminal button appears somewhat thicker and more dense than the membrane elsewhere. This postsynaptic density is caused by the presence of receptors—specialized protein molecules that detect the presence of neurotransmitters in the synaptic cleft. (See ***Figure 2.23.***)

Release of the Neurotransmitter

When action potentials are conducted down an axon (and down all of its branches), something happens inside all of the terminal buttons: Several synaptic vesicles located just inside the presynaptic membrane fuse with the membrane and then break open, spilling their contents into the synaptic cleft.

Heuser and colleagues (Heuser, 1977; Heuser et al., 1979) obtained photomicrographs that illustrate this process. Because the release of neurotransmitter is a very rapid event, taking only a few milliseconds to occur, special procedures are needed to stop the action so that the details can be studied. The experimenters electrically stimulated the nerve attached to an isolated frog muscle and then dropped the muscle against a block of pure copper that had been cooled to 4 K (approximately –453°F). Contact with the supercooled metal froze the outer layer of tissue in 2 msec or less. The ice held the components of the terminal buttons in place until they could be chemically stabilized and examined with an electron microscope. Figure 2.24 shows a portion of the synapse in cross section; note the vesicles that appear to be fused with the presynaptic membrane, forming the shape of an omega (Ω). (See ***Figure 2.24.***)

See Animation 2.3, Synapses, for more detailed information about the structure of synapses and the release of neurotransmitters.

For more detailed information about the structure of synapses and release of the neurotransmitter, see ***Animation 2.3, Synapses.***

Figure 2.24

A photograph from an electron microscope, showing a cross section of a synapse. The omega-shaped figures (Ω) are synaptic vesicles fusing with the presynaptic membranes of terminal buttons that form synapses with frog muscle.

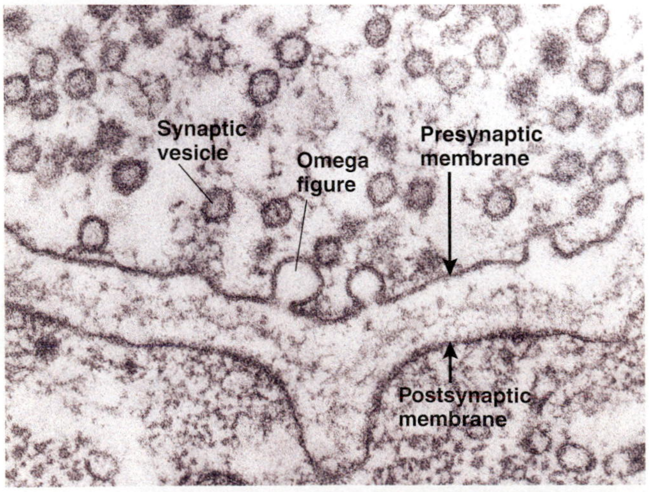

From Heuser, J. E., in *Society for Neuroscience Symposia,* Vol. II, edited by W. M. Cowan and J. A. Ferrendelli. Bethesda, MD: Society for Neuroscience, 1977.

Activation of Receptors

How do molecules of the neurotransmitter produce a depolarization or hyperpolarization in the postsynaptic membrane? They do so by diffusing across the synaptic cleft and attaching to the binding sites of special protein molecules located in the postsynaptic membrane, called **postsynaptic receptors.** Once binding occurs, the postsynaptic receptors open **neurotransmitter-dependent ion channels,** which permit the passage of specific ions into or out of the cell. Thus, the presence of the neurotransmitter in the synaptic cleft allows particular ions to pass through the membrane, changing the local membrane potential.

Neurotransmitters open ion channels by at least two different methods, direct and indirect. The direct method is simpler, so I will describe it first. Figure 2.25 illustrates a neurotransmitter-dependent ion channel that is equipped with its own binding site. When a molecule of the appropriate neurotransmitter attaches to it, the ion channel opens. The formal name for this combination receptor/ion channel is an **ionotropic receptor.** (See ***Figure 2.25.***)

Ionotropic receptors were first discovered in the organ that produces electrical current in *Torpedo,* the electric ray, where they occur in great number. (The electric ray is a fish that generates a powerful electrical current, not some kind of Star Wars weapon.) These receptors, which are sensitive to a neurotransmitter called *acetylcholine,* contain sodium channels. When these channels are open, sodium ions enter the cell and depolarize the membrane.

The indirect method is more complicated. Some receptors do not open ion channels directly but instead start a chain of chemical events. These receptors are called **metabotropic receptors** because they involve steps that require that the cell expend metabolic energy. Metabotropic receptors are located in close proximity to another protein attached to the membrane—a **G protein.** When a molecule of the neurotransmitter binds with the receptor, the receptor activates a G protein situated inside the membrane next to the receptor. When activated, the G protein activates an enzyme that stimulates the production of a chemical called a **second messenger.** (The neurotransmitter is the first messenger.) Molecules of the second messenger travel through the cytoplasm, attach themselves to nearby ion channels, and cause them to open. Compared with postsynaptic potentials produced by ionotropic receptors, those produced by metabotropic receptors take longer to begin and last longer. (See ***Figure 2.26.***)

The first second messenger to be discovered was *cyclic AMP,* a chemical that is synthesized from ATP. Since then, several other second messengers have been discovered. As you will see in later chapters, second messengers play an important role in both synaptic and nonsynaptic communication. And they can do more than open ion channels. For example, they can travel to the nucleus or other regions of the neuron and initiate biochemical changes that affect the functions of the cell. They can even turn specific genes on or off, thus initiating or terminating production of particular proteins.

Figure 2.25

Ionotropic receptors. The ion channel opens when a molecule of neurotransmitter attaches to the binding site. For purposes of clarity the drawing is schematic; molecules of neurotransmitter are actually much larger than individual ions.

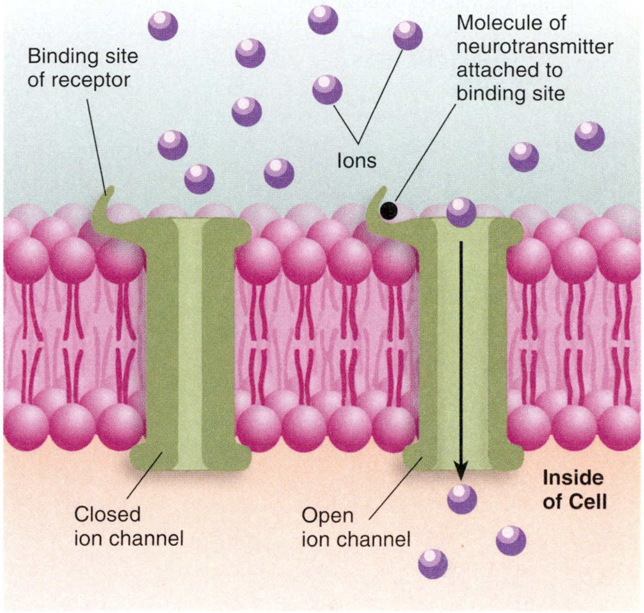

Postsynaptic Potentials

Postsynaptic potentials can be either depolarizing (excitatory) or hyperpolarizing (inhibitory). What determines the nature of the postsynaptic potential at a particular synapse is not the neurotransmitter itself. Instead, it is determined by the

The skin of *Torpedo,* the electric ray, contains large numbers of ionotropic receptors with sodium channels. The flow of sodium through these channels produces an electric current.

metabotropic receptor (*meh tab oh **trow** pik*) A receptor that contains a binding site for a neurotransmitter; activates an enzyme that begins a series of events that opens an ion channel elsewhere in the membrane of the cell when a molecule of the neurotransmitter attaches to the binding site.

G protein A protein coupled to a metabotropic receptor; conveys messages to other molecules when a ligand binds with and activates the receptor.

second messenger A chemical produced when a G protein activates an enzyme; carries a signal that results in the opening of the ion channel or causes other events to occur in the cell.

Figure 2.26

Metabotropic receptors. When a molecule of neurotransmitter binds with a receptor, a second messenger is produced that opens nearby ion channels.

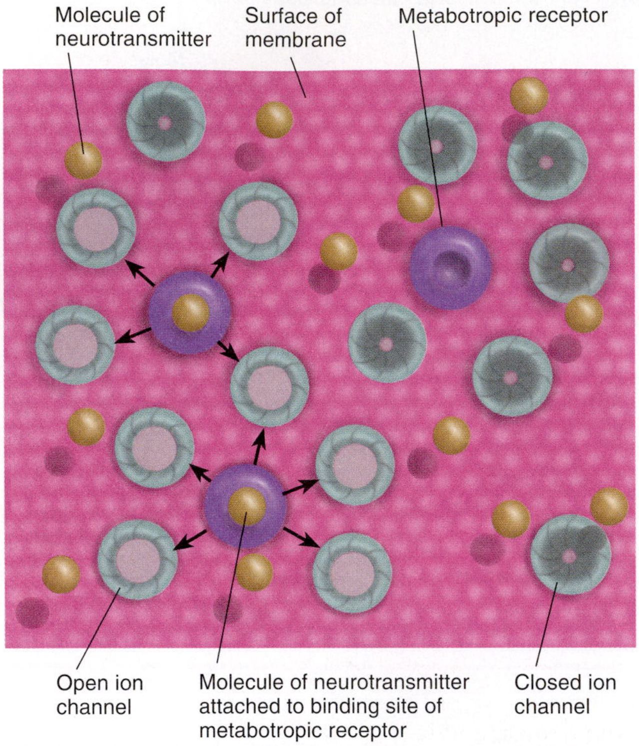

characteristics of the postsynaptic receptors—in particular, *by the particular type of ion channel they open.* In different parts of the brain, a particular neurotransmitter may bind with different types of ion channels, each of which may have a different effect. (By analogy, a particular key might open several different doors, which open up to very different types of rooms.)

As Figure 2.27 shows, three major types of neurotransmitter-dependent ion channels are found in the postsynaptic membrane: sodium (Na^+), potassium (K^+), and chloride (Cl^-). Although the figure depicts only directly activated (ionotropic) ion channels, you should realize that many ion channels are activated indirectly, by metabotropic receptors coupled to G proteins.

The neurotransmitter-dependent sodium channel is the most important source of excitatory postsynaptic potentials. As we saw, sodium-potassium transporters keep sodium outside the cell, waiting for the forces of diffusion and electrostatic pressure to push it in. When sodium channels are opened, sodium rushes in and causes a depolarization—an **excitatory postsynaptic potential (EPSP).** (See ***Figure 2.27a.***)

Earlier, we saw that sodium-potassium transporters maintain a small surplus of potassium ions inside the cell. If potassium channels open, some of these cations will follow this gradient and leave the cell. Because K^+ is positively charged, its outflow will hyperpolarize the membrane, producing an **inhibitory postsynaptic potential** (IPSP). (See ***Figure 2.27b.***)

At many synapses, inhibitory neurotransmitters open the chloride channels, instead of (or in addition to) potassium channels. The effect of opening chloride channels depends on the membrane potential of the neuron.

Figure 2.27

Ionic movements during postsynaptic potentials.

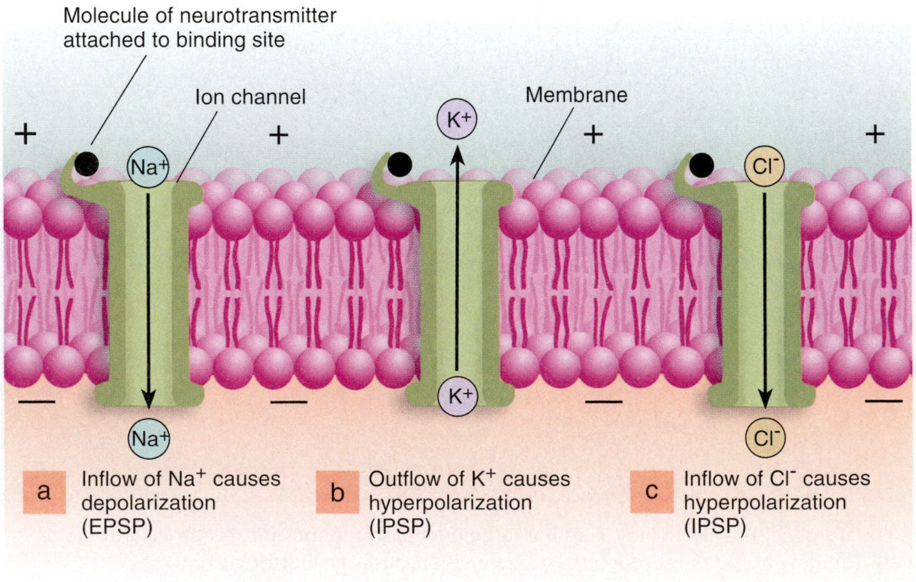

If the membrane is at the resting potential, nothing happens, because (as we saw earlier) the forces of diffusion and electrostatic pressure balance perfectly for the chloride ion. However, if the membrane potential has already been depolarized by the activity of excitatory synapses located nearby, then the opening of chloride channels will permit Cl^- to enter the cell. The inflow of anions will bring the membrane potential back to its normal resting condition. Thus, the opening of chloride channels serves to neutralize EPSPs. (See ***Figure 2.27c.***)

Termination of Postsynaptic Potentials

Postsynaptic potentials are brief depolarizations or hyperpolarizations caused by the activation of postsynaptic receptors with molecules of a neurotransmitter. They are kept brief by two mechanisms: reuptake and enzymatic deactivation.

The postsynaptic potentials produced by almost all neurotransmitters are terminated by **reuptake.** This process is simply an extremely rapid removal of neurotransmitter from the synaptic cleft by the terminal button. The membrane of the terminal button contains special transporter molecules that draw on the cell's energy reserves to force molecules of the neurotransmitter from the synaptic cleft directly into the cytoplasm—just as sodium-potassium transporters move Na^+ and K^+ across the membrane. When an action potential arrives, the terminal button releases a small amount of neurotransmitter into the synaptic cleft and then takes it back, giving the postsynaptic receptors only a brief exposure to the neurotransmitter. (See ***Figure 2.28.***)

excitatory postsynaptic potential (EPSP) An excitatory depolarization of the postsynaptic membrane of a synapse caused by the liberation of a neurotransmitter by the terminal button.

inhibitory postsynaptic potential (IPSP) An inhibitory hyperpolarization of the postsynaptic membrane of a synapse caused by the liberation of a neurotransmitter by the terminal button.

reuptake The reentry of a neurotransmitter just liberated by a terminal button back through its membrane, thus terminating the postsynaptic potential.

Figure 2.28

Reuptake. Molecules of a neurotransmitter that has been released into the synaptic cleft are transported back into the terminal button.

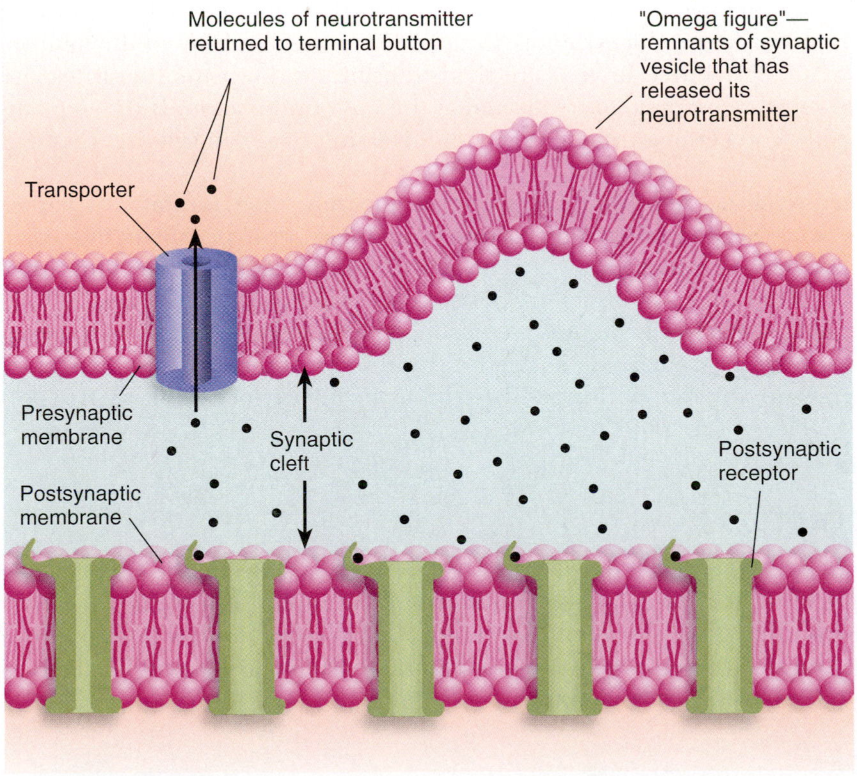

Enzymatic deactivation is accomplished by an enzyme that destroys molecules of the neurotransmitter. As far as we know, postsynaptic potentials are terminated in this way for only one neurotransmitter: **acetylcholine (ACh).** Transmission at synapses on muscle fibers and at some synapses between neurons in the central nervous system is mediated by ACh. Postsynaptic potentials produced by ACh are short-lived because the postsynaptic membrane at these synapses contains an enzyme called **acetylcholinesterase (AChE).** AChE destroys ACh by cleaving it into its constituents: choline and acetate. Because neither of these substances is capable of activating postsynaptic receptors, the postsynaptic potential is terminated once the molecules of ACh are broken apart. AChE is an extremely energetic destroyer of ACh; one molecule of AChE will chop apart more than five thousand molecules of ACh each second.

Effects of Postsynaptic Potentials: Neural Integration

We have seen how neurons are interconnected by means of synapses, how action potentials trigger the release of neurotransmitters, and how these chemicals initiate excitatory or inhibitory postsynaptic potentials. Excitatory postsynaptic potentials increase the likelihood that the postsynaptic neuron will fire; inhibitory postsynaptic potentials decrease this likelihood. (Remember, "firing" refers to the occurrence of an action potential.) Thus, the rate at which an axon fires is determined by the relative activity of the excitatory and inhibitory synapses on the soma and dendrites of that cell. If there are no active excitatory synapses or if the activity of inhibitory synapses is particularly high, that rate could be close to zero.

See Animation 2.4, Postsynaptic Potentials, for more detailed information on the production and integration of excitatory and inhibitory postsynaptic potentials.

Let us look at the elements of this process. (See ***Animation 2.4, Postsynaptic Potentials.***) The interaction of the effects of excitatory and inhibitory synapses on a particular neuron is called **neural integration.** (*Integration* means "to make whole," in the sense of combining two or more functions.) Figure 2.29 illustrates the effects of excitatory and inhibitory synapses on a postsynaptic neuron. Figure 2.29(a) shows what happens when several excitatory synapses become active. The release of the neurotransmitter produces depolarizing EPSPs in the dendrites of the neuron. These EPSPs (represented in red) are then transmitted down the dendrites and across the soma to the *axon hillock* located at the base of the axon. If the depolarization is still strong enough when it reaches this point, the axon will fire. (See ***Figure 2.29a.***)

Now let's consider what would happen if, at the same time, inhibitory synapses also become active. Inhibitory postsynaptic potentials are hyperpolarizing—they bring the membrane potential away from the threshold of excitation. Thus, they tend to cancel the effects of excitatory postsynaptic potentials. (See ***Figure 2.29b.***)

The rate at which a neuron fires is controlled by the relative activity of the excitatory and inhibitory synapses on its dendrites and soma. If the activity of excitatory synapses goes up, the rate of firing will go up. If the activity of inhibitory synapses goes up, the rate of firing will go down.

Autoreceptors

Postsynaptic receptors detect the presence of a neurotransmitter in the synaptic cleft and initiate excitatory or inhibitory postsynaptic potentials. But the postsynaptic membrane is not the only location of receptors that respond to neurotransmitters. Many neurons also possess receptors that respond to the neurotransmitter that *they themselves* release, called **autoreceptors.**

enzymatic deactivation The destruction of a neurotransmitter by an enzyme after its release—for example, the destruction of acetylcholine by acetylcholinesterase.

acetylcholine (ACh) (*a see tul **koh** leen*) A neurotransmitter found in the brain, spinal cord, and parts of the peripheral nervous system; responsible for muscular contraction.

acetylcholinesterase (AChE) (*a see tul koh lin **ess** ter ace*) The enzyme that destroys acetylcholine soon after it is liberated by the terminal buttons, thus terminating the postsynaptic potential.

neural integration The process by which inhibitory and excitatory postsynaptic potentials summate and control the rate of firing of a neuron.

autoreceptor A receptor molecule located on a neuron that responds to the neurotransmitter released by that neuron.

Figure 2.29

Neural integration. (a) If several excitatory synapses are active at the same time, the EPSPs they produce (shown in red) summate as they travel toward the axon, and the axon fires. (b) If several inhibitory synapses are active at the same time, the IPSPs they produce (shown in blue) diminish the size of the EPSPs and prevent the axon from firing.

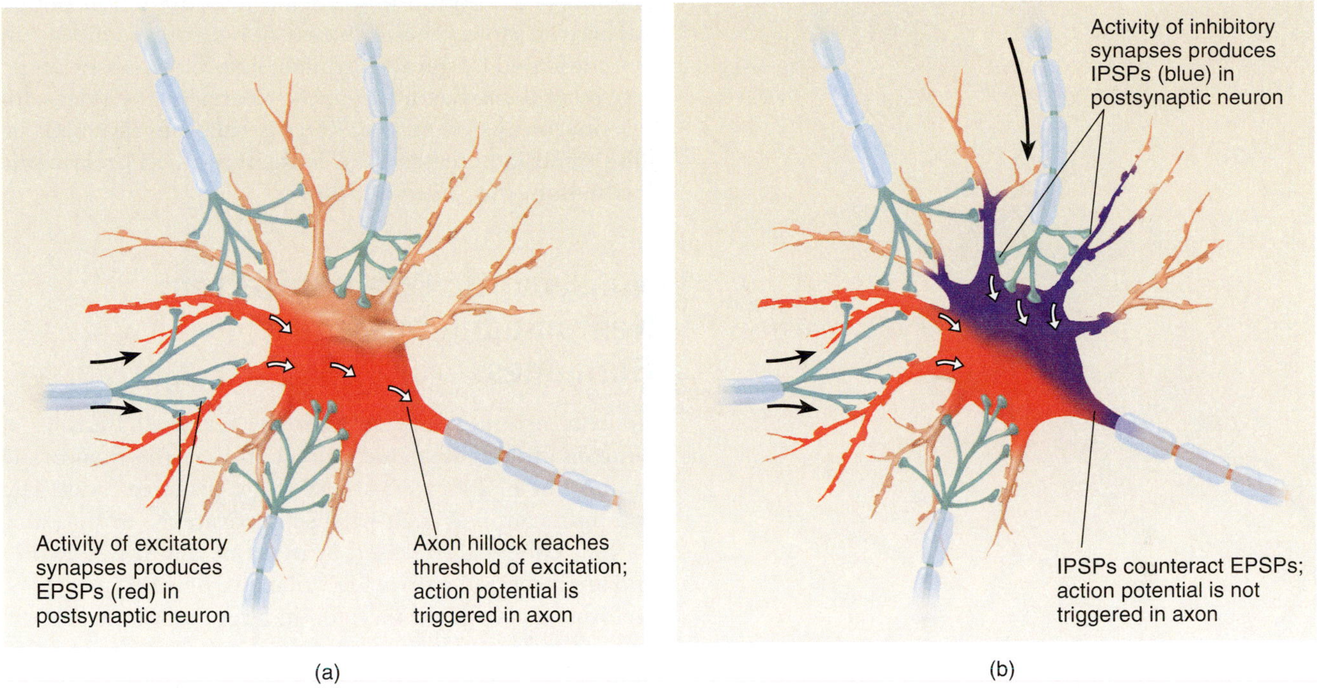
Activity of excitatory synapses produces EPSPs (red) in postsynaptic neuron
Axon hillock reaches threshold of excitation; action potential is triggered in axon
(a)
Activity of inhibitory synapses produces IPSPs (blue) in postsynaptic neuron
IPSPs counteract EPSPs; action potential is not triggered in axon
(b)

Autoreceptors can be located on the membrane of any part of the cell, but in this discussion we will consider those located on the terminal button. In most cases these autoreceptors do not control ion channels. Thus, when stimulated by a molecule of the neurotransmitter, autoreceptors do not produce changes in the membrane potential of the terminal button. Instead, they control internal processes, including the synthesis and release of the neurotransmitter. (As you may have guessed, autoreceptors are metabotropic; the control they exert on these processes is accomplished through G proteins and second messengers.) In most cases the effects of autoreceptor activation are inhibitory; that is, the presence of the neurotransmitter in the extracellular fluid in the vicinity of the neuron causes a decrease in the rate of synthesis or release of the neurotransmitter. Most investigators believe that autoreceptors are part of a regulatory system that controls the amount of neurotransmitter that is released. If too much is released, the autoreceptors inhibit both production and release; if not enough is released, the rates of production and release go up.

Axoaxonic Synapses

As we saw in Figure 2.22, the central nervous system contains three types of synapses. Activity of the first two types, axodendritic and axosomatic synapses, causes postsynaptic excitation or inhibition. The third type, axoaxonic synapses, does not contribute directly to neural integration. Instead, the activity of these synapses alters the amount of neurotransmitter released by the terminal buttons of the postsynaptic

Figure 2.30

An axoaxonic synapse. The activity of terminal button A can increase or decrease the amount of neurotransmitter released by terminal button B.

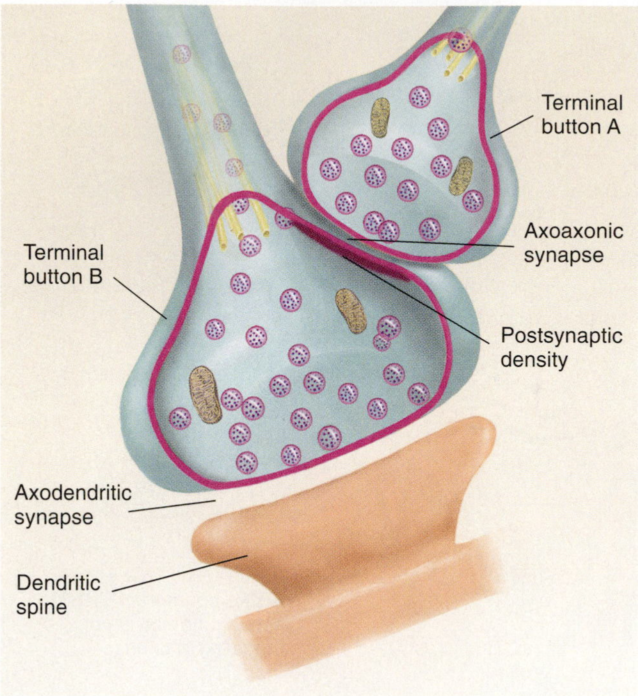

axon. These synapses can produce presynaptic modulation: presynaptic inhibition or presynaptic facilitation.

As you know, the release of a neurotransmitter by a terminal button is initiated by an action potential. Normally, a particular terminal button releases a fixed amount of neurotransmitter each time an action potential arrives. However, the release of neurotransmitter can be modulated by the activity of axoaxonic synapses. If the activity of the axoaxonic synapse decreases the release of the neurotransmitter, the effect is called **presynaptic inhibition.** If it increases the release, it is called **presynaptic facilitation.** (See *Figure 2.30.*)

Nonsynaptic Communication: Neuromodulators and Hormones

Neurotransmitters are released by terminal buttons of neurons and are detected by receptors in the membrane of another cell located a very short distance away. The communication at each synapse is private. Neuromodulators are chemicals released by neurons that travel farther and are dispersed more widely than are neurotransmitters. **Neuromodulators** are secreted in larger amounts and diffuse for longer distances, modulating the activity of many neurons in a particular part of the brain. For example, neuromodulators affect general behavioral states such as vigilance, fearfulness, and sensitivity to pain. Most neuromodulators are composed of proteinlike molecules called *peptides,* which are described in Chapter 4.

Most **hormones** are produced in cells located in the **endocrine glands** (from the Greek *endo-,* "within," and *krinein,* "to secrete"). Others are produced by specialized cells located in various organs, such as the stomach, the intestines, the kidneys, and the brain. Cells that secrete hormones release these chemicals into the extracellular fluid. The hormones are then distributed to the rest of the body through the bloodstream. Hormones affect the activity of cells (including neurons) that contain specialized receptors located either on the surface of their membrane or deep within their nuclei. Cells that contain receptors for a particular hormone are referred to as **target cells** for that hormone; only these cells respond to its presence. Many neurons contain hormone receptors, and hormones are able to affect behavior by stimulating the receptors and changing the activity of these neurons. For example, a sex hormone, testosterone, increases the aggressiveness of most male mammals.

INTERIM SUMMARY

Communication Between Neurons

Synapses consist of junctions between the terminal buttons of one neuron and the membrane—usually the somatic or dendritic membrane—of another. When an action potential is transmitted down an axon, the terminal buttons at the end release a neurotransmitter, a chemical that produces either depolarizations (EPSPs) or hyperpolarizations (IPSPs) of the postsynaptic membrane. The rate of firing of the axon of the postsynaptic cell is determined by the relative activity of the excitatory and inhibitory synapses on the membrane of its dendrites and soma—a phenomenon known as *neural integration*.

Terminal buttons contains synaptic vesicles, mostly clustered around the release zone of the presynaptic membrane. When an action potential reaches a terminal button, it causes the release of the neurotransmitter: Synaptic vesicles that are located at the release zone fuse with the presynaptic membrane of the terminal button, break open, and release their neurotransmitter into the synaptic cleft.

The activation of postsynaptic receptors by molecules of a neurotransmitter causes neurotransmitter-dependent ion channels to open, resulting in postsynaptic potentials. Ionotropic receptors contain ion channels, which are directly opened when a ligand attaches to the binding site. Metabotropic receptors are linked to G proteins, which, when activated, open ion channels by producing a chemical called a second messenger.

The nature of the postsynaptic potential depends on the type of ion channel that is opened by the postsynaptic receptors at a particular synapse. Excitatory postsynaptic potentials occur when Na^+ enters the cell. Inhibitory postsynaptic potentials are produced by the opening of K^+ channels or Cl^- channels.

Postsynaptic potentials are normally brief. They are terminated by two means. The most common mechanism is reuptake: retrieval of molecules of the neurotransmitter from the synaptic cleft by means of transporters located in the presynaptic membrane, which transport the molecules back into the cytoplasm. Acetylcholine is deactivated by the enzyme acetylcholinesterase.

The presynaptic membrane, as well as the postsynaptic membrane, contains receptors that detect the presence of a neurotransmitter. Presynaptic receptors, also called autoreceptors, monitor the quantity of neurotransmitter that a neuron releases and apparently regulate the amount that is synthesized or released. Axoaxonic synapses produce presynaptic inhibition or presynaptic facilitation, reducing or enhancing the amount of neurotransmitter that is released.

Neuromodulators and hormones, like neurotransmitters, act on cells by attaching to the binding sites of receptors and initiating electrical or chemical changes in these cells. However, whereas the action of neurotransmitters is localized, neuromodulators and hormones have much more widespread effects.

presynaptic inhibition The action of a presynaptic terminal button in an axoaxonic synapse; reduces the amount of neurotransmitter released by the postsynaptic terminal button.

presynaptic facilitation The action of a presynaptic terminal button in an axoaxonic synapse; increases the amount of neurotransmitter released by the postsynaptic terminal button.

neuromodulator A naturally secreted substance that acts like a neurotransmitter except that it is not restricted to the synaptic cleft but diffuses through the extracellular fluid.

hormone A chemical that is released by an endocrine gland and that has effects on target cells in other organs.

endocrine gland A gland that liberates its secretions into the extracellular fluid around capillaries and hence into the bloodstream.

target cell The type of cell that contains receptor for a particular hormone and is affected by that hormone.

THOUGHT QUESTIONS

1. Why does synaptic transmission involve the release of chemicals? Direct electrical coupling of neurons is far simpler, so why do our neurons not use it more extensively? (A tiny percentage of synaptic connections in the human brain do use electrical coupling.) Normally, nature uses the simplest means possible to a given end, so there must be some advantages to chemical transmission. What do you think they are?
2. Consider the control of the withdrawal reflex illustrated in Figure 2.11. Could you design a circuit using electrical synapses that would accomplish the same tasks?

EPILOGUE

Myasthenia Gravis

"Am I cured?" asked Kathryn.

Dr. T. smiled ruefully. "I wish it were so simple!" she said. "No, I'm afraid you aren't cured, but now we know what is causing your weakness. There *is* a treatment," she hastened to add, seeing Kathryn's disappointment. "You have a condition called *myasthenia gravis*. The injection I gave you lasts only for a few minutes, but I can give you some pills that have effects that last much longer." Indeed, as she was talking, Kathryn felt herself weakening, and she sat down again.

Myasthenia gravis was first described in 1672 by Thomas Willis, an English physician. The term literally means "grave muscle weakness." It is not a very common disorder, but most experts believe that many cases—much milder than Kathryn's, of course—go undiagnosed. Kathryn's disease involved her face, neck, arm, and trunk muscles, but sometimes only the eye muscles are involved. Before the 1930s, Kathryn would have become bedridden and almost certainly would have died within a few years, probably of pneumonia resulting from difficulty in breathing and coughing. But fortunately, Kathryn's future is not so bleak. The cause of myasthenia gravis is well understood, and it can be treated, if not cured.

The hallmark of myasthenia gravis is *fatigability.* That is, a patient has reasonable strength when rested but becomes very weak after moving for a little while. For many years, researchers have realized that the weakness occurs in the synapses on the muscles, not in the nervous system or the muscles themselves. In the late nineteenth century, a physician placed electrodes on the skin of a person with myasthenia gravis and electrically stimulated a nerve leading to a muscle. The muscle contracted each time he stimulated the nerve, but the contractions became progressively weaker. However, when he placed the electrodes above the muscle and stimulated it directly, the contractions showed no signs of fatigue. Later, with the development of techniques of electrical recording, researchers found that the action potentials in the nerves of people with myasthenia gravis were completely normal. If nerve conduction and muscular contraction were normal, then the problem had to lie in the synapses.

In 1934, Dr. Mary Walker remarked that the symptoms of myasthenia gravis resembled the effects of curare, a poison that blocks neural transmission at the synapses on muscles. The antidote for curare poisoning was a drug called *physostigmine,* which deactivates acetylcholinesterase (AChE). As you learned in this chapter, AChE is an enzyme that destroys the neurotransmitter acetylcholine (ACh) and terminates the postsynaptic potentials it produces. By deactivating AChE, physostigmine greatly increases and prolongs the effects of ACh on the postsynaptic membrane. Thus, it increases the strength of synaptic transmission at the synapses on muscles and reverses the effects of curare. (Chapter 4 will say more about both curare and physostigmine.)

Dr. Walker reasoned that if physostigmine reversed the effects of curare poisoning, perhaps it would also reverse the symptoms of myasthenia gravis. She tried it, and it did within a matter of a few minutes. Subsequently, pharmaceutical companies discovered drugs that could be taken orally and that produced longer-lasting effects. Nowadays, an injectable drug is used to make the diagnosis, and an oral drug is used to treat it.

Researchers turned their efforts to understanding the cause of myasthenia gravis (MG). They made several interesting observations. First, people with MG usually had tumors or other abnormalities in their thymus gland; if the gland was removed, their symptoms often got better. (Kathryn's neurologist might recommend that this step be taken.) Second, microscopic examination of tissue taken from the muscles of MG patients showed damage localized to the region around the synapses, and this region showed an infiltration of white blood cells. These two facts suggested that the immune system was involved; white blood cells are responsible for the immune reaction, and the thymus gland is one of the sources of these cells.

In fact, MG is an *autoimmune disease.* Normally, the immune system protects us from infections by being alert for proteins that are present on invading microorganisms. The immune system produces antibodies that attack these foreign proteins, and the microorganisms are killed. However, sometimes the immune system makes a mistake and becomes sensitized against one of the proteins that are normally present in our bodies. As researchers have found, the blood of patients with MG contains antibodies against the protein that makes up acetylcholine receptors. Thus, myasthenia gravis is an autoimmune disease in which the immune system attacks and destroys many of the person's ACh receptors, which are necessary for synaptic transmission.

Recently, researchers have succeeded in developing an animal model of MG. An *animal model* is a disease that can be produced in laboratory animals and that closely resembles a human disease. The course of the disease can then be studied, and possible treatments or cures can be tested. In this case, the disease is produced by extracting ACh-receptor protein from electric rays (*Torpedo*) and injecting it into laboratory animals. The animals' immune systems become sensitized to the protein and develop antibodies that attack their own ACh receptors. The animals exhibit the same muscular fatigability shown by people with MG, and they become stronger after receiving an injection of a drug such as physostigmine.

One promising result that has emerged from studies with the animal model of MG is the finding that an animal's immune system can be *desensitized* so that it will not produce antibodies that destroy ACh receptors. If ACh-receptor proteins are modified and then injected into laboratory animals, their immune systems develop an antibody against the altered protein. This antibody does not attack the animals' own ACh receptors. Later, if they are given the pure ACh-receptor protein, they do *not* develop MG. Apparently, the pure protein is so similar to the one to which the animals were previously sensitized that the immune system does not bother to produce another antibody. Perhaps a vaccine can be developed that can be used to arrest MG in its early stages by inducing the person's immune system to produce the harmless antibody rather than the one that attacks acetylcholine receptors.

Even with the drugs that are available to physicians today, myasthenia gravis remains a serious disease. The drugs do not restore a person's strength to normal, and they can have serious side effects. But the progress made in the laboratory in recent years gives us hope for a brighter future for people like Kathryn.

KEY CONCEPTS

CELLS OF THE NERVOUS SYSTEM

1. Neurons have a soma, dendrites, an axon, and terminal buttons. Circuits of interconnected neurons are responsible for the functions performed by the nervous system. Neurons are supported by glia and by Schwann cells, which provide myelin sheaths, housekeeping services, and physical support. The blood–brain barrier helps to regulate the chemicals that reach the brain.

COMMUNICATION WITHIN A NEURON

2. The action potential occurs when the membrane potential of an axon reaches the threshold of excitation. Although the action potential is electrical, it is caused by the flow of sodium and potassium ions through voltage-dependent ion channels in the membrane. Saltatory conduction, which takes place in myelinated axons, is faster and more efficient than conduction in unmyelinated axons.

COMMUNICATION BETWEEN NEURONS

3. Neurons communicate by means of synapses, which enable the presynaptic neuron to produce excitatory or inhibitory effects on the postsynaptic neuron. These effects increase or decrease the rate at which the axon of the postsynaptic neuron sends action potentials down to its terminal buttons.
4. When an action potential reaches the end of an axon, it causes some synaptic vesicles to release a neurotransmitter into the synaptic cleft. Molecules of the neurotransmitter attach themselves to receptors in the postsynaptic membrane.
5. When they become activated by molecules of the neurotransmitters, postsynaptic receptors produce either excitatory or inhibitory postsynaptic potentials by opening voltage-controlled sodium, potassium, or chloride ion channels.
6. The postsynaptic potential is terminated by the destruction of the neurotransmitter or by its reuptake into the terminal button.
7. Autoreceptors help to regulate the amount of neurotransmitter that is released.
8. Axoaxonic synapses consist of junctions between two terminal buttons. Release of neurotransmitter by the first terminal button increases or decreases the amount of neurotransmitter released by the second.
9. Neuromodulators and hormones have actions similar to those of neurotransmitters: They bind with and activate receptors on their target cells.

SUGGESTED READINGS

Aidley, D. J. *The Physiology of Excitable Cells,* 4th ed. Cambridge, England: Cambridge University Press, 1998.

Cowan, W. M., Südhof, T. C., and Stevens, C. F. *Synapses.* Baltimore, MD: Johns Hopkins University Press, 2001.

Kandel, E. R., Schwartz, J. H., and Jessell, T. M. *Principles of Neural Science,* 4th ed. New York: McGraw-Hill, 2000.

Nicholls, J. G., Martin, A. R., Fuchs, P. A., and Wallace, B. G. *From Neuron to Brain,* 4th ed. Sunderland, MA: Sinauer, 2001.

SUGGESTED WEB SITES

Acion Potential Animation

www.fiu.edu/orgs/psych/psb_4003/figures/a_p.htm

This site provides a colorful animation of the ionic events that occur during an action potential.

Tutorial on the Action Potential

http://pavlov.psyc.queensu.ca/~symonsl/brains/actpot.html

A tutorial with an animation of the action potential is the focus of this site.

Action Potential Simulator

www.phypc.med.wayne.edu/jeffram.axon3.htm

This site provides a powerful simulation program of the ionic and electrical events that occur during an action potential. The simulator allows the instructor to demonstrate EPSPs, IPSPs, and the effects of toxins such as TTX and TEA on the membrane potential.

Synapse Web

http://synapses.bu.edu/

This site is devoted to the anatomy of synapses and includes images of synaptic connections as well as links to other sites relating to synapses.

Cell Membrane Animations

www.emile-21.com/VRML/membPotO.html

This site provides a series of animations relating to the cell membrane potential. The animations require the installation of a VRML plug-in.

Structure of the Nervous System

chapter 3

LEARNING OBJECTIVES

1. Describe the appearance of the brain and identify the terms used to indicate directions and planes of section.
2. Describe the divisions of the nervous system, the meninges, the ventricular system, and the production of cerebrospinal fluid and its flow through the brain.
3. Outline the development of the central nervous system.
4. Describe the telencephalon, one of the two major structures of the forebrain.
5. Describe the two major structures of the diencephalon.
6. Describe the major structures of the midbrain, the hindbrain, and the spinal cord.
7. Describe the peripheral nervous system, including the two divisions of the autonomic nervous system.

CHAPTER OUTLINE

PROLOGUE

The Left Is Gone

Miss S. was a sixty-year-old woman with a history of high blood pressure, which was not responding well to the medication she was taking. One evening she was sitting in her reclining chair reading the newspaper when the phone rang. She got out of her chair and walked to the phone. As she did, she began feeling giddy and stopped to hold onto the kitchen table. She has no memory of what happened after that.

The next morning, a neighbor, who usually stopped by to have coffee with Miss S., found her lying on the floor, mumbling incoherently. The neighbor called an ambulance, which took Miss S. to a hospital.

Two days after her admission, I visited her in her room, along with a group of people being led by the chief of neurology. The neurological resident in charge of her case had already told us that she had had a stroke in the back part of the right side of the brain. He had attached a CT scan to an illuminated viewer mounted on the wall and had showed us a white spot caused by the accumulation of blood in a particular region of her brain. (You can look at the scan yourself if you like; it is shown in Figure 5.17.)

About a dozen of us entered Miss S.'s room. She was awake but seemed a little confused. The resident greeted her and asked how she was feeling. "Fine, I guess," she said. "I still don't know why I'm here."

"Can you see the other people in the room?"

"Why, sure."

"How many are there?"

She turned her head to the right and began counting. She stopped when she had counted the people at the foot of her bed. "Seven," she reported. "What about us?" asked a voice from the left of her bed. "What?" she said, looking at the people she had already counted. "Here, to your left. No, toward your left!" the voice repeated. Slowly, rather reluctantly, she began turning her head to the left. The voice kept insisting, and finally, she saw who was talking. "Oh," she said, "I guess there are more of you."

The resident approached the left side of her bed and touched her left arm. "What is this?" he asked. "Where?" she said. "Here," he answered, holding up her arm and moving it gently in front of her face.

"Oh, that's an arm."

"An arm? Whose arm?"

"I don't know. . . . I guess it must be yours."

"No, it's yours. Look, it's a part of you." He traced with his fingers from her arm to her shoulder.

"Well, if you say so," she said, still sounding unconvinced.

When we returned to the residents' lounge, the chief of neurology said that we had seen a classic example of unilateral neglect, caused by damage to a particular part of the brain. "I've seen many cases like this," he explained. "People can still perceive sensations from the left side of their body, but they just don't pay attention to them. A woman will put makeup on only the right side of her face, and a man will shave only half of his beard. When they put on a shirt or a coat, they will use their left hand to slip it over their right arm and shoulder, but then they'll just forget about their left arm and let the garment hang from one shoulder. They also don't look at things located toward the left or even the left halves of things. Once I saw a man who had just finished eating breakfast. He was sitting in his bed, with a tray in front of him. There was half of a pancake on his plate. 'Are you all done?' I asked. 'Sure,' he said. I turned the plate around so that the uneaten part was on his right. He gave a startled look and said, 'Where the hell did that come from?'"

The exercise on the CD-ROM for Chapter 3 entitled "Figures and Diagrams" will help you learn the names and locations of the major structures of the nervous system.

The goal of neuroscience research is to understand how the brain works. To understand the results of this research, you must be acquainted with the basic structure of the nervous system. The number of terms introduced in this chapter is kept to a minimum (but as you will see, the minimum is still a rather large number). (See ***Chapter 3 Animations: Figures and Diagrams.***) With the framework you will receive from this chapter and from the animations, you should have no trouble learning the material presented in subsequent chapters.

Basic Features of the Nervous System

Before beginning a description of the nervous system, I want to discuss the terms that are used to describe it. The gross anatomy of the brain was described long ago, and everything that could be seen without the aid of a microscope was given a name. Early anatomists named most brain structures according to their similarity to commonplace objects: amygdala, or "almond-shaped object"; hippocampus, or "sea horse"; genu, or "knee"; cortex, or "bark"; pons, or "bridge"; uncus, or "hook," to give a few examples. Throughout this book I will translate the names of anatomical terms as I introduce them, because the translation makes the terms more memorable. For example, knowing that *cortex* means "bark" (like the bark of a tree) will help you to remember that the cortex is the outer layer of the brain.

When describing features of a structure as complex as the brain, we need to use terms denoting directions. Directions in the nervous system are normally described relative to the **neuraxis,** an imaginary line drawn through the spinal cord up to the front of the brain. For simplicity's sake, let's consider an animal with a straight neuraxis. Figure 3.1 shows an alligator and two humans. This alligator is certainly laid out in a linear fashion; we can draw a straight line that starts between its eyes and continues down the center of its spinal cord. (See ***Figure 3.1.***) The front end is **anterior,** and the tail is **posterior.** The terms **rostral** (toward the

neuraxis An imaginary line drawn through the center of the length of the central nervous system, from the bottom of the spinal cord to the front of the forebrain.

anterior With respect to the central nervous system, located near or toward the head.

posterior With respect to the central nervous system, located near or toward the tail.

rostral "Toward the beak"; with respect to the central nervous system, in a direction along the neuraxis toward the front of the face.

Figure 3.1

Side and frontal views of alligator and human, showing the terms used to denote anatomical directions.

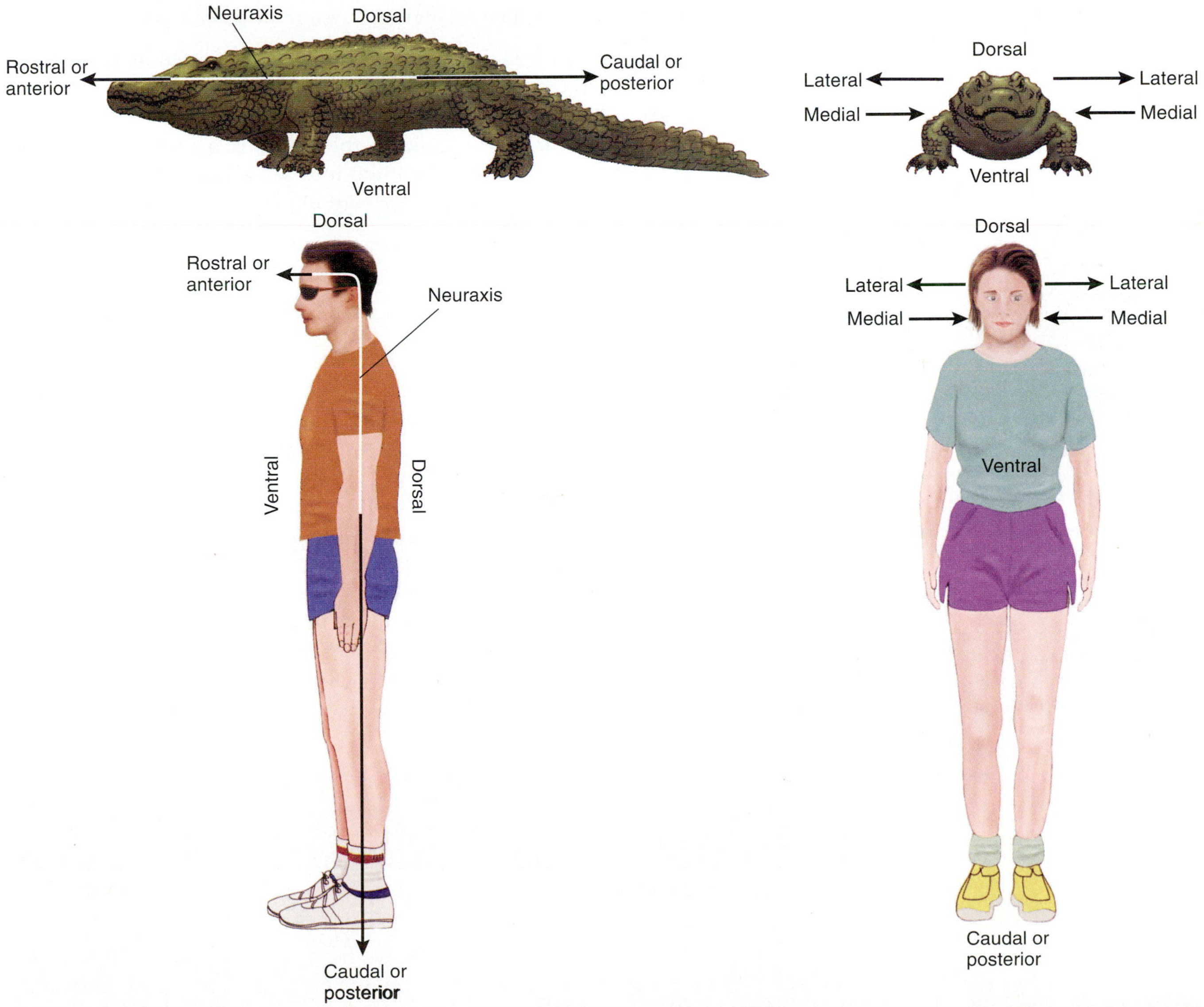

beak) and **caudal** (toward the tail) are also employed, especially when referring specifically to the brain. The top of the head and the back are part of the **dorsal** surface, while the **ventral** (front) surface faces the ground. (*Dorsum* means "back," and *ventrum* means "belly.") These directions are somewhat more complicated in the human; because we stand upright, our neuraxis bends, so the top of the head is perpendicular to the back. (You will also encounter the terms *superior* and *inferior*. In referring to the brain, *superior* means "above," and *inferior* means "below." For example, the *superior colliculi* are located above the *inferior colliculi*.) The frontal views of both the alligator and the human illustrate the terms **lateral** and **medial:** toward the side and toward the midline, respectively. (See ***Figure 3.1.***)

Two other useful terms are *ipsilateral* and *contralateral*. **Ipsilateral** refers to structures on the same side of the body. If we say that the olfactory bulb sends axons to the *ipsilateral* hemisphere, we mean that the left olfactory bulb sends axons to the left hemisphere and the right olfactory bulb sends axons to the right hemisphere. **Contralateral** refers to structures on opposite sides of the body. If we say that a particular region of the left cerebral cortex controls movements of the *contralateral* hand, we mean that the region controls movements of the right hand.

To see what is in the nervous system, we have to cut it open; to be able to convey information about what we find, we slice it in a standard way. Figure 3.2 shows a human nervous system. We can slice the nervous system in three ways:

1. Transversely, like a salami, giving us **cross sections** (also known as **frontal sections** when referring to the brain)
2. Parallel to the ground, giving us **horizontal sections**
3. Perpendicular to the ground and parallel to the neuraxis, giving us **sagittal sections.** The **midsagittal plane** divides the brain into two symmetrical halves. The sagittal section in Figure 3.2 lies in the midsagittal plane.

Note that because of our upright posture, cross sections of the spinal cord are parallel to the ground. (See ***Figure 3.2.***)

caudal "Toward the tail"; with respect to the central nervous system, in a direction along the neuraxis away from the front of the face.

dorsal "Toward the back"; with respect to the central nervous system, in a direction perpendicular to the neuraxis toward the top of the head or the back.

ventral "Toward the belly"; with respect to the central nervous system, in a direction perpendicular to the neuraxis toward the bottom of the skull or the front surface of the body.

lateral Toward the side of the body, away from the middle.

medial Toward the middle of the body, away from the side.

ipsilateral Located on the same side of the body.

contralateral Located on the opposite side of the body.

cross section With respect to the central nervous system, a slice taken at right angles to the neuraxis.

frontal section A slice through the brain parallel to the forehead.

horizontal section A slice through the brain parallel to the ground.

sagittal section (***sadj** i tul*) A slice through the brain parallel to the neuraxis and perpendicular to the ground.

midsagittal plane The plane through the neuraxis perpendicular to the ground; divides the brain into two symmetrical halves.

An Overview

The nervous system consists of the brain and spinal cord, which make up the *central nervous system (CNS)*, and the cranial nerves, spinal nerves, and peripheral ganglia, which constitute the *peripheral nervous system (PNS)*. The CNS is encased in bone: The brain is covered by the skull, and the spinal cord is encased by the vertebral column. (See ***Table 3.1.***)

Figure 3.3 shows the relation of the brain and spinal cord to the rest of the body. Do not be concerned with unfamiliar labels on this figure; these structures will be described later. (See ***Figure 3.3*** on page 66.) The brain is a large mass of neurons, glia, and other supporting cells. It is the most protected organ of the body, encased in a tough, bony skull and floating in a pool of cerebrospinal fluid. The brain receives a copious supply of blood and is chemically guarded by the blood–brain barrier.

Table 3.1

The Major Divisions of the Nervous System

Central Nervous System (CNS)	Peripheral Nervous System (PNS)
Brain	Nerves
Spinal cord	Peripheral ganglia

Figure 3.2

Planes of section as they pertain to the human central nervous system.

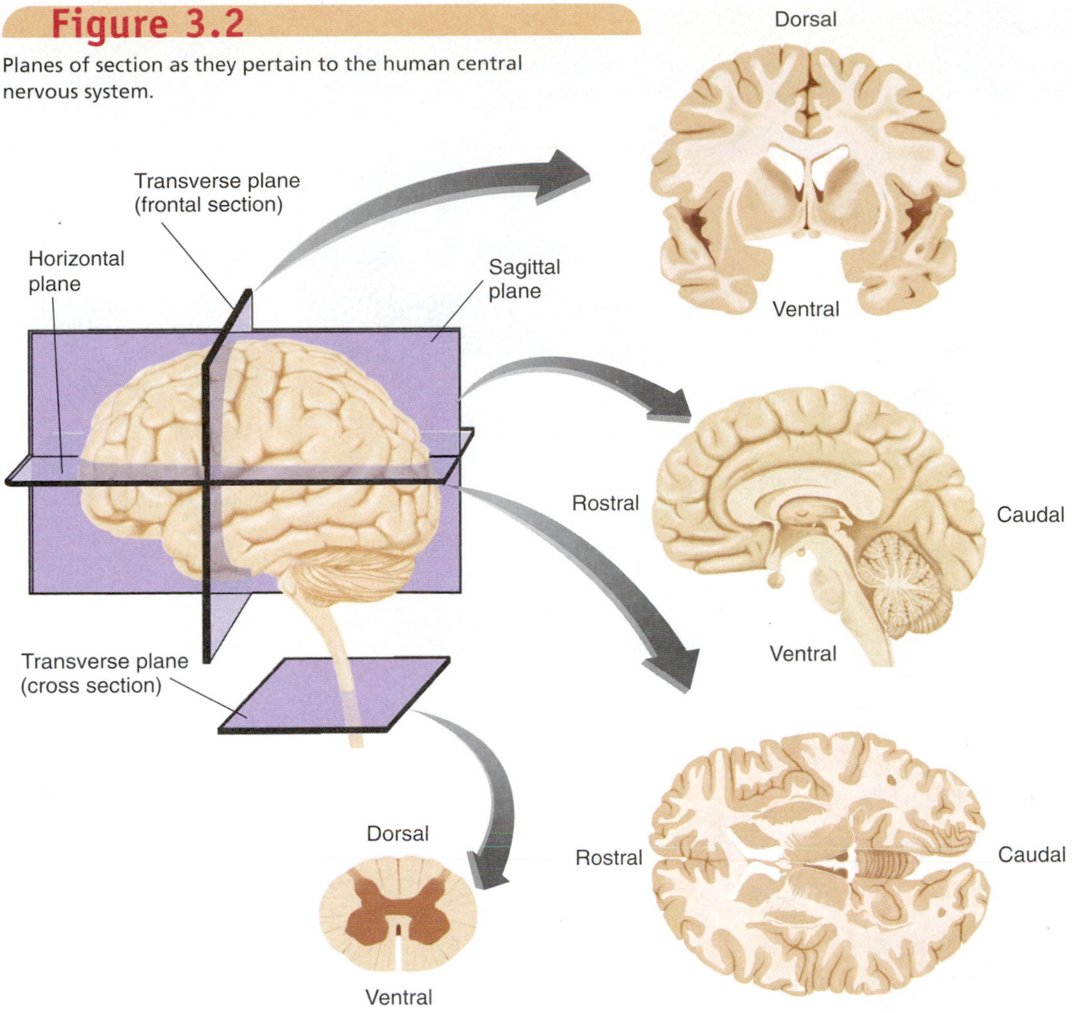

Meninges

The entire nervous system—brain, spinal cord, cranial and spinal nerves, and peripheral ganglia—is covered by tough connective tissue. The protective sheaths around the brain and spinal cord are referred to as the **meninges** (singular: *meninx*). The meninges consist of three layers, which are shown in Figure 3.3. The outer layer is thick, tough, and flexible but unstretchable; its name, **dura mater,** means "hard mother." The middle layer of the meninges, the **arachnoid membrane,** gets its name from the weblike appearance of the *arachnoid trabeculae* that protrude from it (from the Greek *arachne,* meaning "spider"; *trabecula* means "track"). The arachnoid membrane, soft and spongy, lies beneath the dura mater. Closely attached to the brain and spinal cord, and following every surface convolution, is the **pia mater** ("pious mother"). The smaller surface blood vessels of the brain and spinal cord are contained within this layer. Between the pia mater and the arachnoid membrane is a gap called the **subarachnoid space.** This space is filled with a liquid called **cerebrospinal fluid (CSF).** (See ***Figure 3.3.***)

The peripheral nervous system (PNS) is covered with two layers of meninges. The middle layer (arachnoid membrane), with its associated pool of CSF, covers only the brain and spinal cord. Outside the central nervous system, the outer and inner layers (dura mater and pia mater) fuse and form a sheath that covers the spinal and cranial nerves and the peripheral ganglia.

meninges (singular: **meninx**) (*men **in** jees*) The three layers of tissue that encase the central nervous system: the dura mater, arachnoid membrane, and pia mater.

dura mater The outermost of the meninges; tough and flexible.

arachnoid membrane (*a **rak** noyd*) The middle layer of the meninges, located between the outer dura mater and inner pia mater.

pia mater The layer of the meninges that clings to the surface of the brain; thin and delicate.

subarachnoid space The fluid-filled space that cushions the brain; located between the arachnoid membrane and the pia mater.

cerebrospinal fluid (CSF) A clear fluid, similar to blood plasma, that fills the ventricular system of the brain and the subarachnoid space surrounding the brain and spinal cord.

Figure 3.3

(a) The relation of the nervous system to the rest of the body. (b) Detail of the meninges that cover the central nervous system. (c) A closer view of the lower spinal cord and cauda equina.

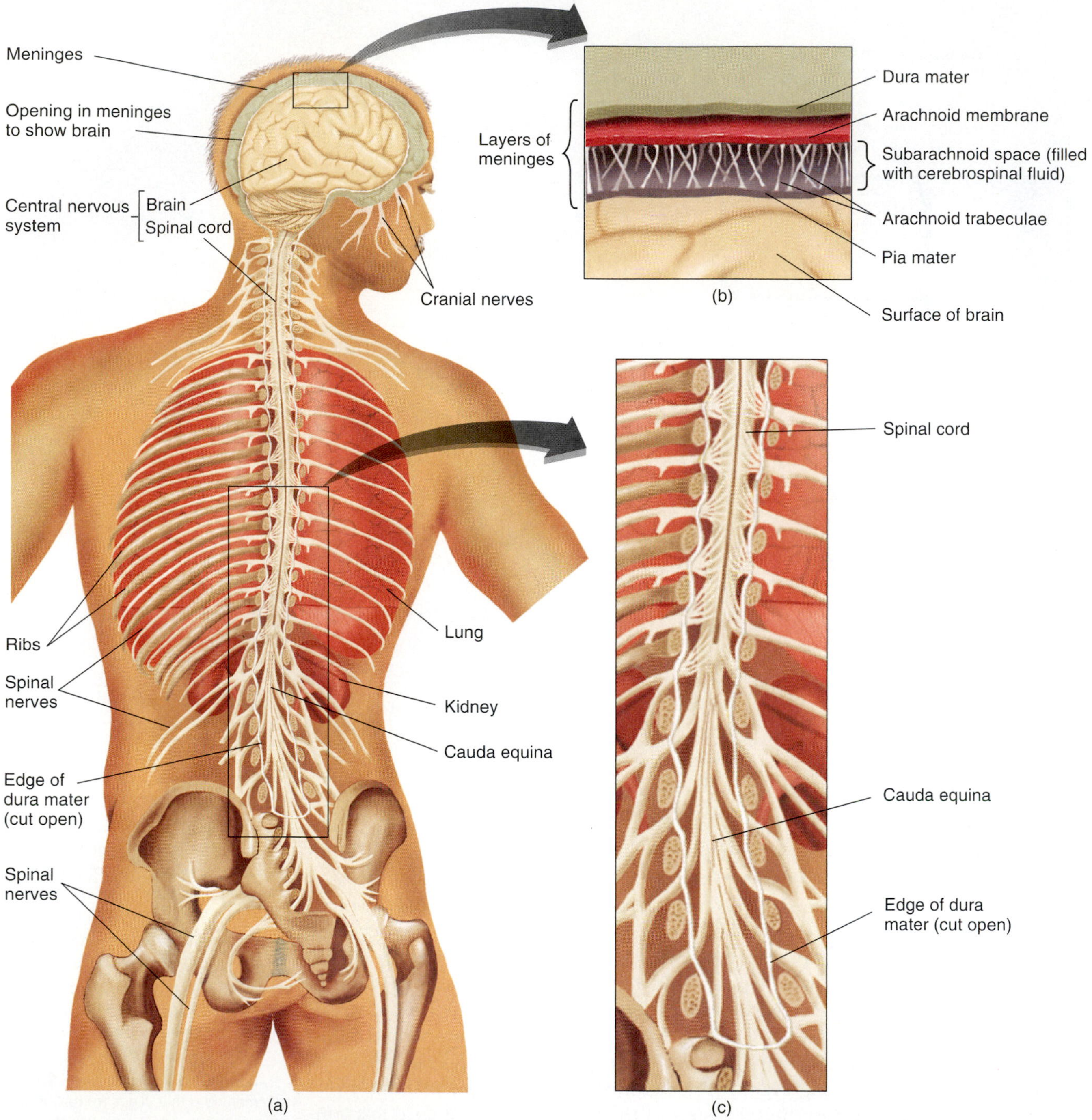

The Ventricular System and Production of Cerebrospinal Fluid

The brain is very soft and jellylike. The considerable weight of a human brain (approximately 1400 g), along with its delicate construction, necessitates that it be protected from shock. A human brain cannot even support its own weight well; it is

Figure 3.4

The ventricular system of the brain. (a) Lateral view of the left side of the brain. (b) Frontal view.

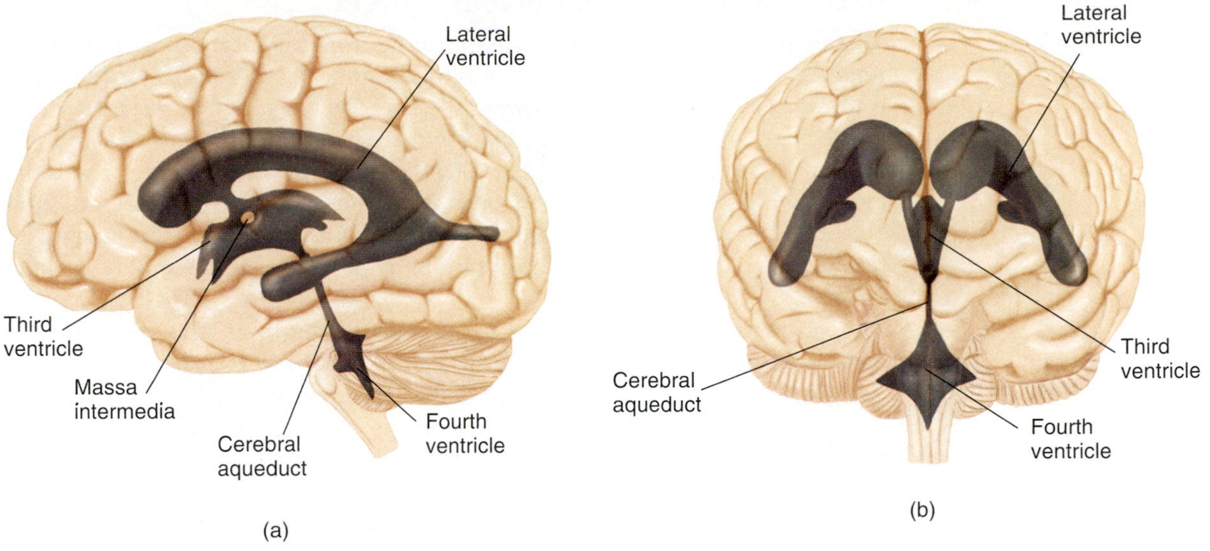

difficult to remove and handle a fresh brain from a recently deceased human without damaging it.

Fortunately, the intact brain within a living human is well protected. It floats in a bath of CSF contained within the subarachnoid space. Because the brain is completely immersed in liquid, its net weight is reduced to approximately 80 g; thus, pressure on the base of the brain is considerably diminished. The CSF surrounding the brain and spinal cord also reduces the shock to the central nervous system that would be caused by sudden head movement.

The brain contains a series of hollow, interconnected chambers called **ventricles** ("little bellies"), which are filled with CSF. (See ***Figure 3.4.***) The largest chambers are the **lateral ventricles,** which are connected to the **third ventricle.** The third ventricle is located at the midline of the brain; its walls divide the surrounding part of the brain into symmetrical halves. A bridge of neural tissue called the *massa intermedia* crosses through the middle of the third ventricle and serves as a convenient reference point. The **cerebral aqueduct,** a long tube, connects the third ventricle to the **fourth ventricle.** The lateral ventricles constitute the first and second ventricles, but they are never referred to as such. (See ***Figure 3.4.***)

Cerebrospinal fluid is extracted from the blood and resembles blood plasma in its composition. It is manufactured by special tissue with an especially rich blood supply called the **choroid plexus,** which protrudes into all four of the ventricles. CSF is produced continuously; the total volume of CSF is approximately 125 ml, and the half-life (the time it takes for half of the CSF present in the ventricular system to be replaced by fresh fluid) is about 3 hours. Therefore, several times this amount is produced by the choroid plexus each day.

Cerebrospinal fluid is produced by the choroid plexus of the lateral ventricles and flows into the third ventricle. More CSF is produced in this ventricle, which then flows through the cerebral aqueduct to the fourth ventricle, where still more CSF is produced. The CSF leaves the fourth ventricle through small openings that connect with the subarachnoid space surrounding the brain. The CSF then flows through the subarachnoid space around the central nervous system, where it is reabsorbed into the blood supply. (See ***Animation 3.1, Meninges and CSF.***)

ventricle (***ven*** *trik ul*) One of the hollow spaces within the brain, filled with cerebrospinal fluid.

lateral ventricle One of the two ventricles located in the center of the telencephalon.

third ventricle The ventricle located in the center of the diencephalon.

cerebral aqueduct A narrow tube interconnecting the third and fourth ventricles of the brain, located in the center of the mesencephalon.

fourth ventricle The ventricle located between the cerebellum and the dorsal pons, in the center of the metencephalon.

choroid plexus The highly vascular tissue that protrudes into the ventricles and produces cerebrospinal fluid.

See Animation 3.1, Meninges and CSF, for an interactive tutorial on the meninges, the ventricular system, and the production, circulation, and reabsorption of CSF.

INTERIM SUMMARY

Basic Features of the Nervous System

Anatomists have adopted a set of terms to describe the locations of parts of the body. *Anterior* is toward the head, *posterior* is toward the tail, *lateral* is toward the side, *medial* is toward the middle, *dorsal* is toward the back, and *ventral* is toward the front surface of the body. In the special case of the nervous system, *rostral* means toward the beak (or nose), and *caudal* means toward the tail. *Ipsilateral* means "same side," and *contralateral* means "other side." A cross section (or, in the case of the brain, a frontal section) slices the nervous system at right angles to the neuraxis, a horizontal section slices the brain parallel to the ground, and a sagittal section slices it perpendicular to the ground, parallel to the neuraxis.

The central nervous system (CNS) consists of the brain and spinal cord, and the peripheral nervous system (PNS) consists of the spinal and cranial nerves and peripheral ganglia. The CNS is covered with the meninges: dura mater, arachnoid membrane, and pia mater. The space under the arachnoid membrane is filled with cerebrospinal fluid, in which the brain floats. The PNS is covered with only the dura mater and pia mater. Cerebrospinal fluid is produced in the choroid plexus of the lateral, third, and fourth ventricles. It flows from the two lateral ventricles into the third ventricle, through the cerebral aqueduct into the fourth ventricle, then into the subarachnoid space, and finally back into the blood supply.

The Central Nervous System

Although the brain is exceedingly complicated, an understanding of the basic features of brain development makes it easier to learn and remember the location of the most important structures. With that end in mind, I introduce these features here in the context of development of the central nervous system. Two animations will help you learn and remember the structure of the brain. ***Animation 3.2, The Rotatable Brain*** is just what the title implies: a drawing of the human brain that you can rotate in three dimensions. You can choose whether to see some internal structures or see specialized regions of the cerebral cortex. ***Animation 3.3, Brain Slices*** is even more comprehensive. It consists of two sets of photographs of human brain slices, taken in the transverse (frontal) and horizontal planes. As you move the cursor across each slice, brain regions are outlined, and their names appear. If you want to know how to pronounce these names, you can click on the region. You can also see magnified views of the slices and move them around by clicking and dragging. Finally, you can test yourself: The computer will present names of the regions shown in each slice, and you try to click on the correct region.

See Animation 3.2, The Rotatable Brain, for an interactive examination of the human brain.

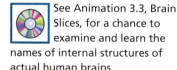

See Animation 3.3, Brain Slices, for a chance to examine and learn the names of internal structures of actual human brains.

Development of the Central Nervous System

The central nervous system begins early in embryonic life as a hollow tube, and it maintains this basic shape even after it is fully developed. During development, parts of the tube elongate, pockets and folds form, and the tissue around the tube thickens until the brain reaches its final form.

An Overview of Brain Development

Development of the nervous system begins around the eighteenth day after conception. Part of the *ectoderm* (outer layer) of the back of the embryo thickens and

Figure 3.5

A schematic outline of brain development, showing its relation to the ventricles. (a) and (c) Early development. (b) and (d) Later in development. (e) A lateral view of the left side of a semitransparent human brain, showing the brain stem "ghosted in." The colors of all figures denote corresponding regions.

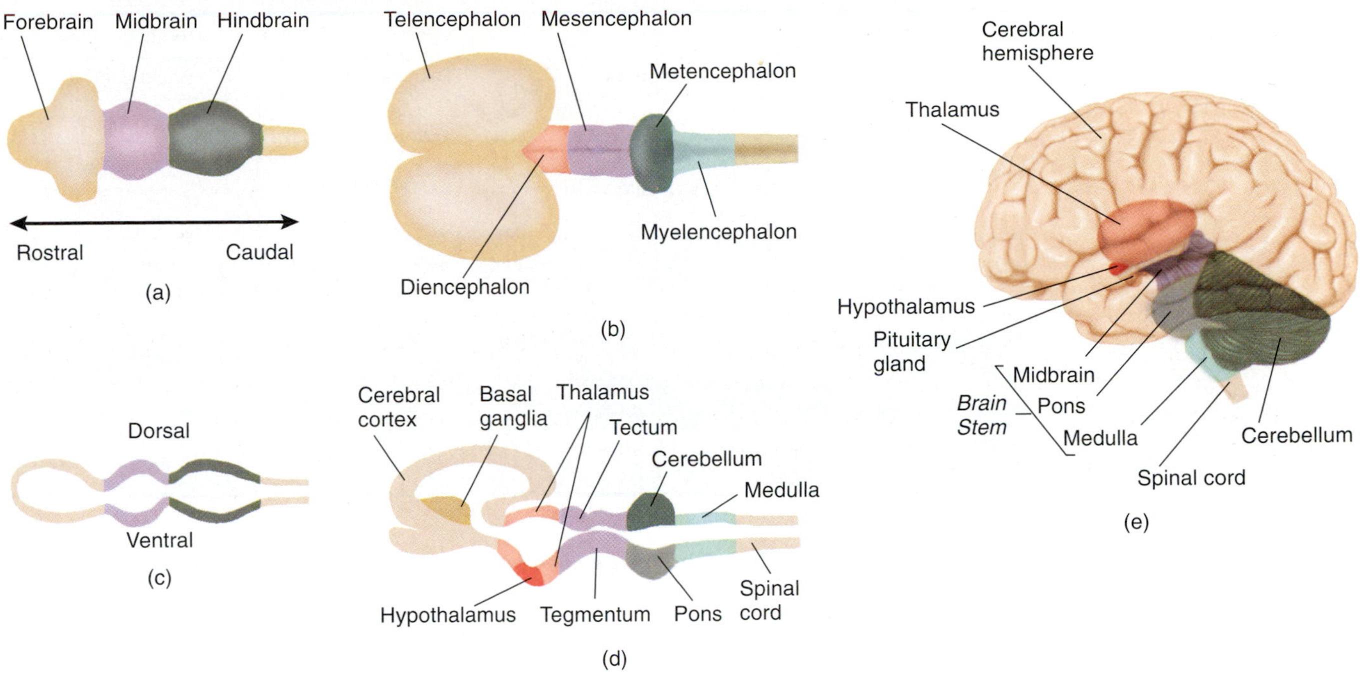

forms a plate. The edges of this plate form ridges that curl toward each other along a longitudinal line, running in a rostral–caudal direction. By the twenty-first day these ridges touch each other and fuse together, forming a tube—the **neural tube**—that gives rise to the brain and spinal cord.

By the twenty-eighth day of development the neural tube is closed, and its rostral end has developed three interconnected chambers. These chambers become ventricles, and the tissue that surrounds them becomes the three major parts of the brain: the forebrain, the midbrain, and the hindbrain. (See ***Figures 3.5a*** and ***3.5c.***) As development progresses, the rostral chamber (the forebrain) divides into three separate parts, which become the two lateral ventricles and the third ventricle. The region around the lateral ventricles becomes the telencephalon ("end brain"), and the region around the third ventricle becomes the diencephalon ("interbrain"). (See ***Figures 3.5b*** and ***3.5d.***) In its final form, the chamber inside the midbrain (mesencephalon) becomes narrow, forming the cerebral aqueduct, and two structures develop in the hindbrain: the metencephalon ("afterbrain") and the myelencephalon ("marrowbrain"). (See ***Figure 3.5e.***)

Table 3.2 summarizes the terms I have introduced here and mentions some of the major structures found in each part of the brain. The colors in the table match those in Figure 3.5. These structures will be described in the remainder of the chapter, in the order in which they are listed in Table 3.2. (See ***Table 3.2.***)

Details of Brain Development

Brain development begins with a thin tube and ends with a structure weighing approximately 1400 g (about 3 lb) and consisting of several hundreds of billions of cells. Where do these cells come from, and what controls their growth?

neural tube A hollow tube, closed at the rostral end, that forms from ectodermal tissue early in embryonic development; serves as the origin of the central nervous system.

Table 3.2

Anatomical Subdivisions of the Brain

Major Division	Ventricle	Subdivision	Principal Structures
Forebrain	Lateral	Telencephalon	Cerebral cortex
			Basal ganglia
			Limbic system
	Third	Diencephalon	Thalamus
			Hypothalamus
Midbrain	Cerebral aqueduct	Mesencephalon	Tectum Tegmentum
Hindbrain	Fourth	Metencephalon	Cerebellum
			Pons
		Myelencephalon	Medulla oblongata

The cells that line the inside of the neural tube—the **ventricular zone**—give rise to the cells of the central nervous system. These cells divide, producing neurons and glia, which then migrate away from the center. Ten weeks after conception the brain of the human fetus is about 1.25 cm (0.5 in.) long and, in cross section, is mostly ventricle—in other words, hollow space. By 20 weeks the brain is about 5 cm (2 in.) long and has the basic shape of the mature brain. In cross section we see more brain tissue than ventricle.

Let's consider the development of the cerebral cortex, about which most is known. *Cortex* means "bark," and the **cerebral cortex**, approximately 3 mm thick, surrounds the cerebral hemispheres like the bark of a tree. Corrected for body size, the cerebral cortex is larger in humans than in any other species. As we will see, circuits of neurons in the cerebral cortex play a vital role in cognition and control of movement.

The cerebral cortex develops from the inside out. That is, the first cells to be produced by the ventricular zone migrate a short distance and establish the first layer. The next cells pass through the first layer and form the second one. The last cells to be produced must pass through all the ones born before them.

What guides neurons to their final resting place? Rakic (1972, 1988) discovered that a special form of glial cell provides pathways that neurons follow during their migration. These cells, **radial glia,** extended fibers radially outward from the ventricular zone, like spokes in a wheel. These fibers end in cuplike feet that attach to the surface of the cortex, and as the cortex grows thicker, these fibers grow along with it.

The cells in the ventricular zone that give rise to neurons are known as **founder cells.** During the first phase of development, founder cells divide, making new founder cells and increasing the size of the ventricular zone. This phase is referred to as **symmetrical division,** because the division of each founder cell produces two identical cells. Then, seven weeks after conception, founder cells receive a signal to begin a period of **asymmetrical division.** During this phase founder cells divide asymmetrically, producing another founder cell, which remains in place, and a neuron, which travels outward into the cerebral cortex, guided by the fiber of a radial glial cell. Neurons crawl along radial fibers like amoebas, pushing their way through neurons that were born earlier and finally coming to rest. (See ***Figure 3.6.***)

ventricular zone A layer of cells that line the inside of the neural tube; contains founder cells that divide and give rise to cells of the central nervous system.

cerebral cortex The outermost layer of gray matter of the cerebral hemispheres.

radial glia Special glia with fibers that grow radially outward from the ventricular zone to the surface of the cortex; provide guidance for neurons migrating outward during brain development.

founder cells Cells of the ventricular zone that divide and give rise to cells of the central nervous system.

symmetrical division Division of a founder cell that gives rise to two identical founder cells; increases the size of the ventricular zone and hence the brain that develops from it.

asymmetrical division Division of a founder cell that gives rise to another founder cell and a neuron, which migrates away from the ventricular zone toward its final resting place in the brain.

Figure 3.6

A cross section through the nervous system early in its development. Radially oriented glial cells help to guide the migration of newly formed neurons.

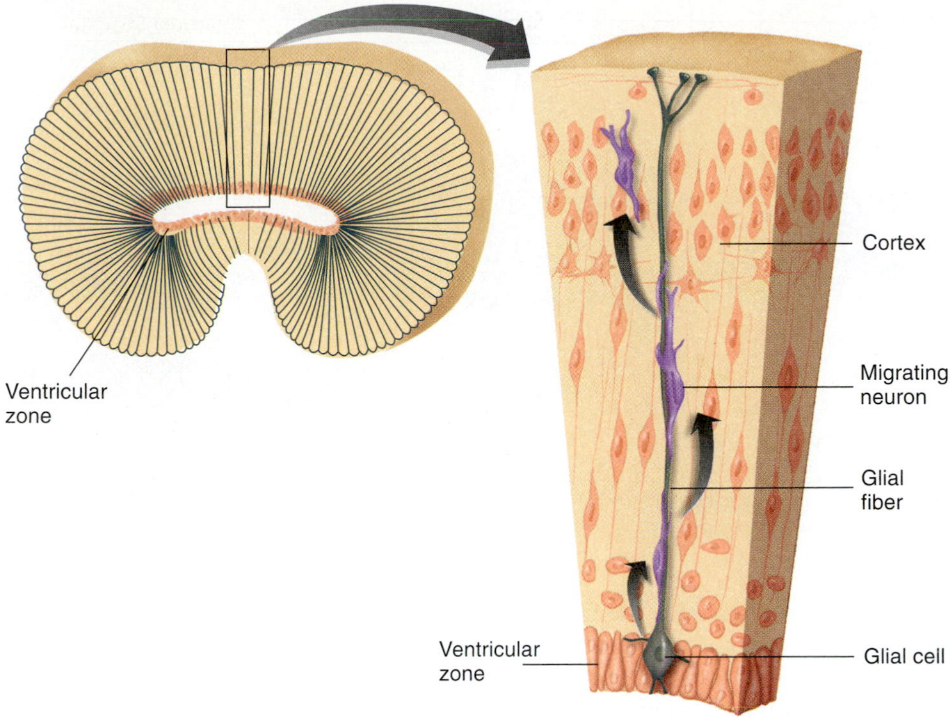

Adapted from Rakic, P. A small step for the cell, a giant leap for mankind: A hypothesis of neocortical expansion during evolution. *Trends in Neuroscience,* 1995, *18,* 383–388.

The period of asymmetrical division lasts about three months. Because the human cerebral cortex contains about 100 billion neurons, there are about one billion neurons migrating along radial glial fibers on a given day. The migration path of the earliest neurons is the shortest and takes about one day. The last neurons have the longest distance to go, because the cortex is thicker by then. Their migration takes about two weeks. The end of cortical development occurs when the founder cells receive a chemical signal that causes them to die—a phenomenon known as **apoptosis** (literally, a "falling away"). Molecules of the chemical that conveys this signal bind with receptors that activate killer genes within the cells. (All cells have these genes, but only certain cells respond to the chemical signal that turns them on.) Once neurons have migrated to their final locations, they begin forming connections with other neurons. They grow dendrites, which receive the terminal buttons from the axons of other neurons, and they grow axons of their own.

The ventricular zone gives rise to more neurons than are needed. In fact, these neurons must compete to survive. The axons of approximately 50 percent of these neurons do not find vacant postsynaptic cells of the right type with which to form synaptic connections, so they die by apoptosis. This phenomenon, too, involves a chemical signal; when a presynaptic neuron establishes synaptic connections, it receives a signal from the postsynaptic cell that permits it to survive. The neurons that come too late do not find any available space and therefore do not receive this life-sustaining signal. This scheme might seem wasteful, but apparently the evolutionary process found that the safest strategy was to produce too many neurons and let them fight to establish synaptic connections rather than try to produce exactly the right number of each type of neuron.

apoptosis (*ay po* ***toe*** *sis*) Death of a cell caused by a chemical signal that activates a genetic mechanism inside the cell.

Figure 3.7

Evidence of neurogenesis. (a) A section through a part of the hippocampus, showing cells containing DNA labeled with a radioactive nucleotide. (b) A magnified view of part of the same section.

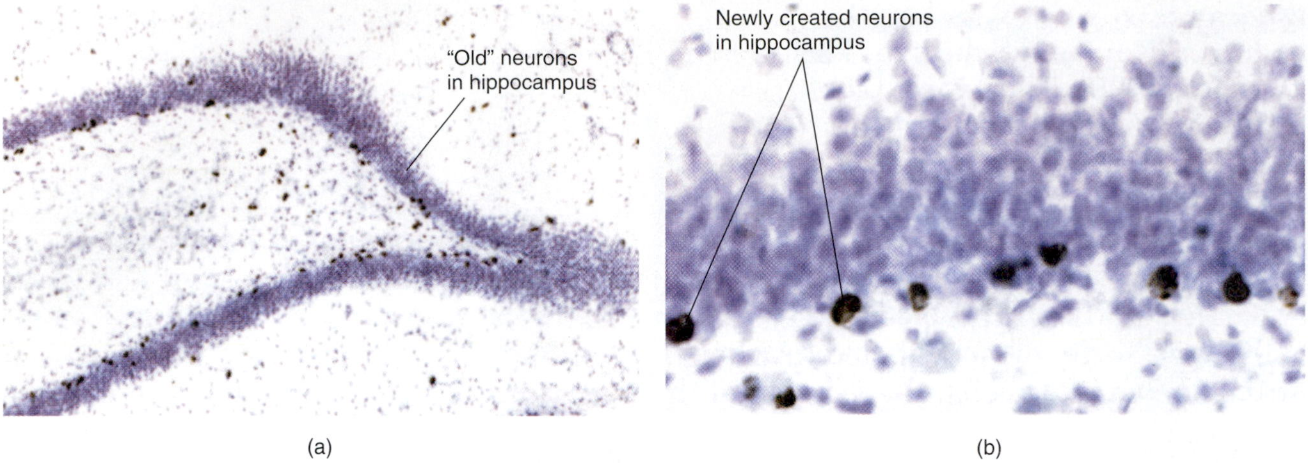

From Cameron, H. A. and McKay, R. D. G. *Journal of Comparative Neurology,* 2001, *435,* 406–417. Copyright © 2001. Reprinted by permission of Wiley-Liss, Inc., a subsidiary of John Wiley & Sons, Inc.

During development, thousands of different pathways—groups of axons that connect one brain region with another—develop in the brain. Within many of these pathways the connections are orderly and systematic. For example, the axons of sensory neurons from the skin form orderly connections in the brain; axons from the little finger form synapses in one region, those of the ring finger form synapses in a neighboring region, and so on. In fact, the surface of the body is "mapped" on the surface of the brain. Similarly, the surface of the retina of the eye is "mapped" on another region of the surface of the brain.

For many years researchers have believed that *neurogenesis* (production of new neurons) does not take place in the fully developed brain. However, recent studies have shown this belief to be incorrect—the adult brain contains some stem cells (similar to the founder cells that give rise to the cells of the developing brain) that can divide and produce neurons. Detection of newly produced cells is done by administering a small amount of a radioactive form of one of the nucleotide bases that cells use to produce the DNA that is needed for neurogenesis. The next day the animals' brains are removed and examined with methods described in Chapter 5. Such studies have found evidence for neurogenesis in the adult brain (Cameron and McKay, 2001.) (See ***Figure 3.7.***) However, although the mature brain can produce new neurons, there is no evidence yet that indicates that these neurons can establish connections to replace neural circuits that have been destroyed through injury, stroke, or disease (Horner and Gage, 2000).

Evolution of the Human Brain

The brains of the earliest vertebrates were smaller than those of later animals; they were simpler as well. The evolutionary process brought about genetic changes that were responsible for the development of more complex brains, with more parts and more interconnections.

The human brain is larger than that of any other primate when corrected for body size—more than three times larger than that of a chimpanzee, our closest relative. What types of genetic changes are required to produce a large brain? Considering that the difference between the genes of humans and those of chimpanzees is only 1.2 percent, the number of genes responsible for the differences between the chimpanzee brain and the human brain must be small. After all, only a small percentage of the 1.2 percent is devoted to brain development. In fact, Rakic (1988) suggests that the size differences between these two brains could be caused by a very simple process.

We just saw that the size of the ventricular zone increases during symmetrical division of the founder cells located there. The ultimate size of the brain is determined by the size of the ventricular zone. As Rakic notes, each symmetrical division doubles the number of founder cells and thus doubles the size of the brain. The human brain is ten times larger than that of a rhesus macaque monkey. Thus, between three and four additional symmetrical divisions of founder cells would account for the difference in the size of these two brains. In fact, the stage of symmetrical division lasts about two days longer in humans, which provides enough time for three more divisions. The period of asymmetrical division is longer, too, which accounts for the fact that the human cortex is 15 percent thicker. Thus, delays in the termination of the symmetrical and asymmetrical periods of development could be responsible for the increased size of the human brain. A few simple mutations of the genes that control the timing of brain development could be responsible for these delays.

The Forebrain

As we saw, the **forebrain** surrounds the rostral end of the neural tube. Its two major components are the telencephalon and the diencephalon.

Telencephalon

The telencephalon includes most of the two symmetrical **cerebral hemispheres** that make up the cerebrum. The cerebral hemispheres are covered by the cerebral cortex and contain the limbic system and the basal ganglia. The latter two sets of structures are primarily in the **subcortical regions** of the brain—those located deep within it, beneath the cerebral cortex.

Cerebral Cortex. As we saw, *cortex* means "bark," and the cerebral cortex surrounds the cerebral hemispheres like the bark of a tree. In humans the cerebral cortex is greatly convoluted. These convolutions, consisting of **sulci** (small grooves), **fissures** (large grooves), and **gyri** (bulges between adjacent sulci or fissures), greatly enlarge the surface area of the cortex, compared with a smooth brain of the same size. In fact, two-thirds of the surface of the cortex is hidden in the grooves; thus, the presence of gyri and sulci triples the area of the cerebral cortex. The total surface area is approximately 2360 cm^2 (2.5 ft^2), and the thickness is approximately 3 mm.

The cerebral cortex consists mostly of glia and the cell bodies, dendrites, and interconnecting axons of neurons. Because cells predominate, the cerebral cortex has a grayish brown appearance, and it is called *gray matter.* (See ***Figure 3.8.***) Millions of axons run beneath the cerebral cortex and connect its neurons with those located elsewhere in the brain. The large concentration of myelin around these axons gives this tissue an opaque white appearance—hence the term *white matter.*

Different regions of the cerebral cortex perform different functions. Three regions receive information from the sensory organs. The **primary visual cortex,** which receives visual information, is located at the back of the brain, on the inner surfaces of the cerebral hemispheres—primarily on the upper and lower banks of the **calcarine fissure.** (*Calcarine* means "spur-shaped." See ***Figure 3.9.***) The **primary auditory cortex,** which receives auditory information, is located on the upper surface of a deep fissure in the side of the brain—the **lateral fissure.** (See inset, ***Figure 3.9.***) The **primary somatosensory cortex,** a vertical strip of cortex just caudal to the **central sulcus,** receives information from the body senses. As Figure 3.9 shows, different regions of the primary somatosensory cortex receive information from different regions of the body. In addition, the base of the somatosensory cortex receives information concerning taste. (See ***Figure 3.9.***)

forebrain The most rostral of the three major divisions of the brain; includes the telencephalon and diencephalon.

cerebral hemisphere (*sa **ree** brul*) One of the two major portions of the forebrain, covered by the cerebral cortex.

subcortical region The region located within the brain, beneath the cortical surface.

sulcus (plural: sulci) (***sul** kus, **sul** sigh*) A groove in the surface of the cerebral hemisphere, smaller than a fissure.

fissure A major groove in the surface of the brain, larger than a sulcus.

gyrus (plural: gyri) (***jye** russ, **jye** rye*) A convolution of the cortex of the cerebral hemispheres, separated by sulci or fissures.

primary visual cortex The region of the posterior occipital lobe whose primary input is from the visual system.

calcarine fissure (***kal** ka rine*) A fissure located in the occipital lobe on the medial surface of the brain; most of the primary visual cortex is located along its upper and lower banks.

primary auditory cortex The region of the superior temporal lobe whose primary input is from the auditory system.

lateral fissure The fissure that separates the temporal lobe from the overlying frontal and parietal lobes.

primary somatosensory cortex The region of the anterior parietal lobe whose primary input is from the somatosensory system.

central sulcus (***sul** kus*) The sulcus that separates the frontal lobe from the parietal lobe.

Figure 3.8

A slice of a human brain showing fissures and gyri and the layer of cerebral cortex that follows these convolutions.

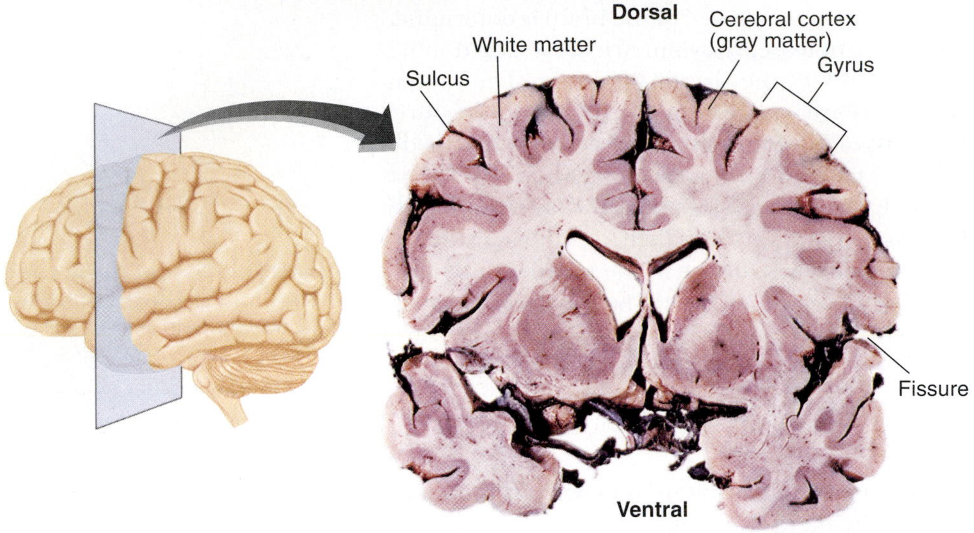

Figure 3.9

A lateral view of the left side of a human brain and part of the inner surface of the right side. The inset shows a cutaway of part of the frontal lobe of the left hemisphere, permitting us to see the primary auditory cortex on the dorsal surface of the temporal lobe, which forms the ventral bank of the lateral fissure.

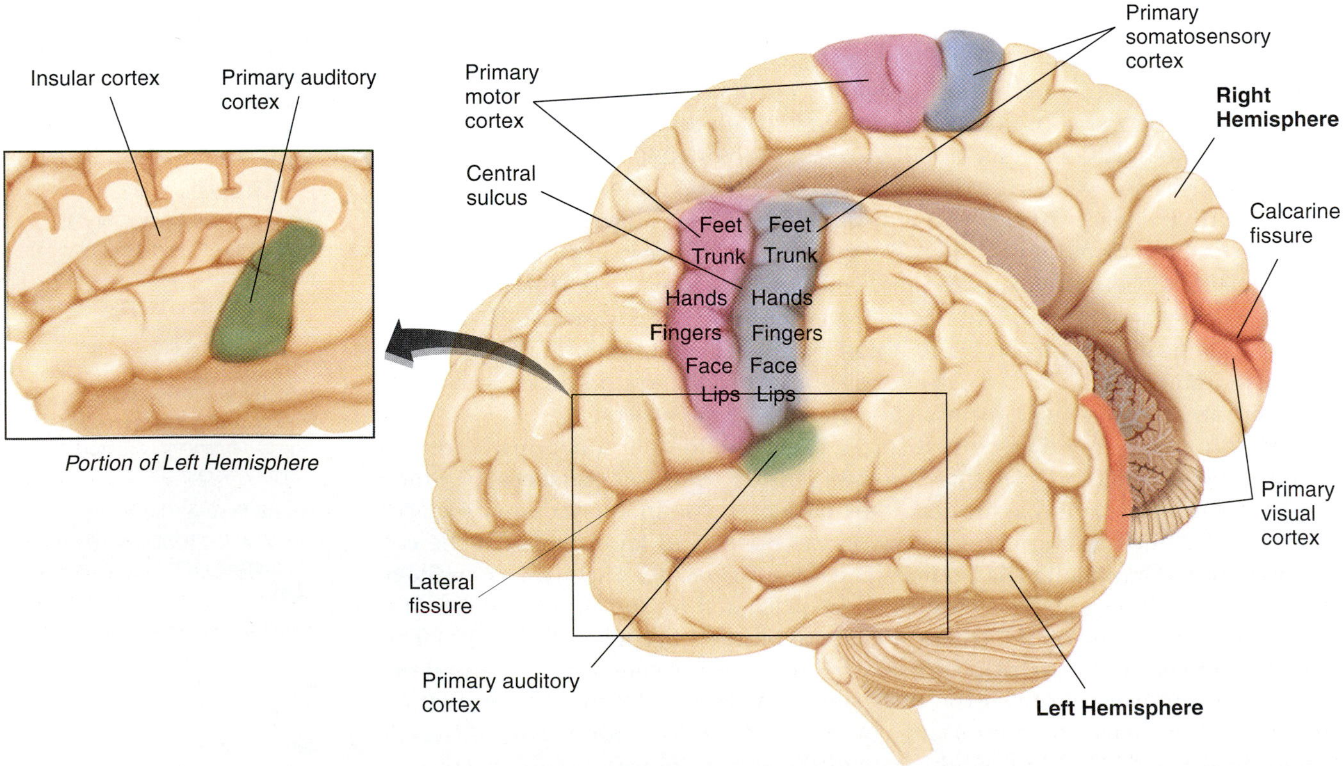

With the exception of olfaction and gustation (taste), sensory information from the body or the environment is sent to primary sensory cortex of the contralateral hemisphere. Thus, the primary somatosensory cortex of the left hemisphere learns what the right hand is holding, the left primary visual cortex learns what is happening toward the person's right, and so on.

The region of the cerebral cortex that is most directly involved in the control of movement is the **primary motor cortex,** located just in front of the primary somatosensory cortex. Neurons in different parts of the primary motor cortex are connected to muscles in different parts of the body. The connections, like those of the sensory regions of the cerebral cortex, are contralateral; the left primary motor cortex controls the right side of the body and vice versa. Thus, if a surgeon places an electrode on the surface of the primary motor cortex and stimulates the neurons there with a weak electrical current, the result will be movement of a particular part of the body. Moving the electrode to a different spot will cause a different part of the body to move. (See ***Figure 3.9.***) I like to think of the strip of primary motor cortex as the keyboard of a piano, with each key controlling a different movement. (We will see shortly who the "player" of this piano is.)

The ability to navigate depends heavily on circuits of neurons in the parietal lobe.

The regions of primary sensory and motor cortex occupy only a small part of the cerebral cortex. The rest of the cerebral cortex accomplishes what is done between sensation and action: perceiving, learning and remembering, planning, and acting. These processes take place in the *association areas* of the cerebral cortex. The central sulcus provides an important dividing line between the rostral and caudal regions of the cerebral cortex. (See ***Figure 3.9.***) The rostral region is involved in movement-related activities, such as planning and executing behaviors. The caudal region is involved in perceiving and learning.

Discussing the various regions of the cerebral cortex is easier if we have names for them. In fact, the cerebral cortex is divided into four areas, or *lobes,* named for the bones of the skull that cover them: the frontal lobe, parietal lobe, temporal lobe, and occipital lobe. Of course, the brain contains two of each lobe, one in each hemisphere. The **frontal lobe** (the "front") includes everything in front of the central sulcus. The **parietal lobe** (the "wall") is located on the side of the cerebral hemisphere, just behind the central sulcus, caudal to the frontal lobe. The **temporal lobe** (the "temple") juts forward from the base of the brain, ventral to the frontal and parietal lobes. The **occipital lobe** (from the Latin *ob,* "in back of," and *caput,* "head") lies at the very back of the brain, caudal to the parietal and temporal lobes. Figure 3.10 shows these lobes in three views of the cerebral hemispheres: a ventral view (a view from the bottom), a midsagittal view (a view of the inner surface of the right hemisphere after the left hemisphere has been removed), and a lateral view. (See ***Figure 3.10.***)

Each primary sensory area of the cerebral cortex sends information to adjacent regions, called the **sensory association cortex.** Circuits of neurons in the sensory association cortex analyze the information received from the primary sensory cortex; perception takes place there, and memories are stored there. The regions of the sensory association cortex located closest to the primary sensory areas receive information from only one sensory system. For example, the region closest to the primary visual cortex analyzes visual information and stores visual memories. Regions of the sensory association cortex located far from the primary sensory areas receive

primary motor cortex The region of the posterior frontal lobe that contains neurons that control movements of skeletal muscles.

frontal lobe The anterior portion of the cerebral cortex, rostral to the parietal lobe and dorsal to the temporal lobe.

parietal lobe (*pa **rye** i tul*) The region of the cerebral cortex caudal to the frontal lobe and dorsal to the temporal lobe.

temporal lobe (***tem** por ul*) The region of the cerebral cortex rostral to the occipital lobe and ventral to the parietal and frontal lobes.

occipital lobe (*ok **sip** i tul*) The region of the cerebral cortex caudal to the parietal and temporal lobes.

sensory association cortex Those regions of the cerebral cortex that receive information from the regions of primary sensory cortex.

Figure 3.10

The four lobes of the cerebral cortex, the primary sensory and motor cortex, and the association cortex. (a) Ventral view, from the base of the brain. (b) Midsagittal view, with the cerebellum and brain stem removed. (c) Lateral view.

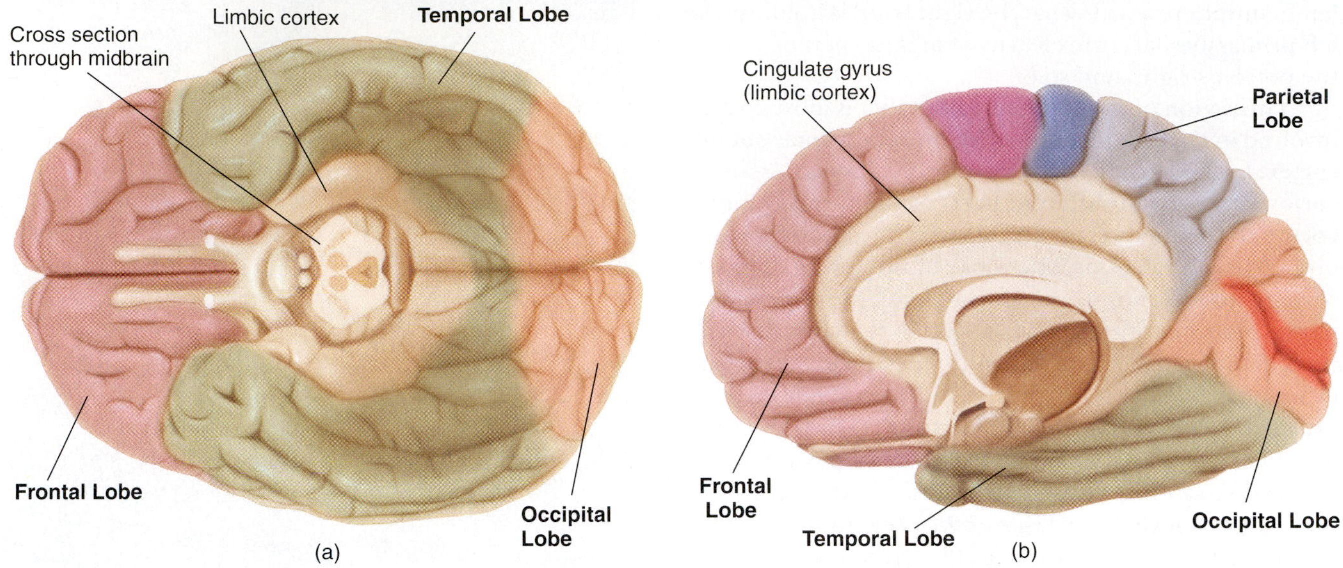

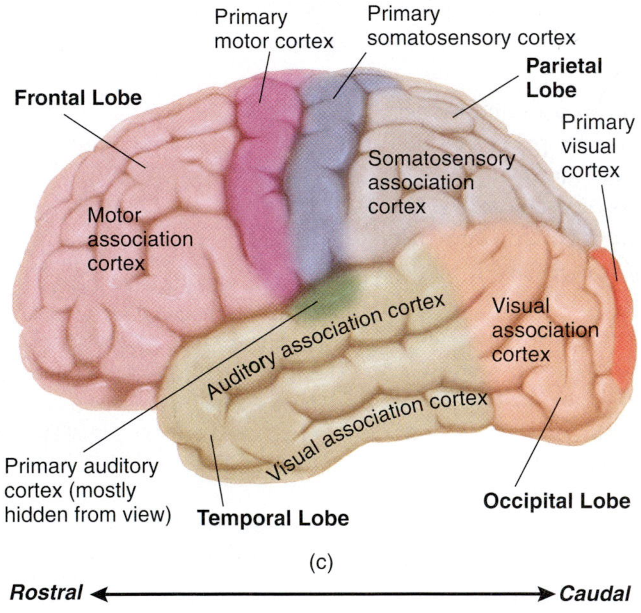

information from more than one sensory system; thus, they are involved in several kinds of perceptions and memories. These regions make it possible to integrate information from more than one sensory system. For example, we can learn the connection between the sight of a particular face and the sound of a particular voice. (See ***Figure 3.10.***)

If people sustain damage to the somatosensory association cortex, their deficits are related to somatosensation and to the environment in general; for example, they may have difficulty perceiving the shapes of objects that they can touch but not see, they may be unable to name parts of their bodies (see the case below), or they may have trouble drawing maps or following them. Destruction of the primary visual cortex causes blindness. However, although people who sustain damage to the visual association cortex will not become blind, they may be unable to recognize objects by sight. People who sustain damage to the auditory association cortex may have difficulty perceiving speech or even producing meaningful speech of their own. People who sustain damage to regions of the association cortex at the junction of the three posterior lobes, where the somatosensory, visual, and auditory functions overlap, may have difficulty reading or writing.

Just as regions of the sensory association cortex of the posterior part of the brain are involved in perceiving and remembering, the frontal association cortex is involved in the planning and execution of movements. The **motor association cortex** (also known as the *premotor cortex*) is located just rostral to the primary motor cortex. This region controls the primary motor cortex; thus, it directly controls behavior. If the primary motor cortex is the keyboard of the piano, then the motor association cortex is the piano player. The rest of the frontal lobe, rostral to the motor associa-

motor association cortex The region of the frontal lobe rostral to the primary motor cortex; also known as the premotor cortex.

tion cortex, is known as the **prefrontal cortex.** This region of the brain is less involved with the control of movement and more involved in formulating plans and strategies.

Although the two cerebral hemispheres cooperate with each other, they do not perform identical functions. Some functions are *lateralized*—located primarily on one side of the brain. In general, the left hemisphere participates in the *analysis* of information—the extraction of the elements that make up the whole of an experience. This ability makes the left hemisphere particularly good at recognizing *serial events*—events whose elements occur one after the other—and controlling sequences of behavior. (In a few people the functions of the left and right hemispheres are reversed.) The serial functions that are performed by the left hemisphere include verbal activities, such as talking, understanding the speech of other people, reading, and writing. These abilities are disrupted by damage to the various regions of the left hemisphere. (I will say more about language and the brain in Chapter 13.)

In contrast, the right hemisphere is specialized for *synthesis;* it is particularly good at putting isolated elements together to perceive things as a whole. For example, our ability to draw sketches (especially of three-dimensional objects), read maps, and construct complex objects out of smaller elements depends heavily on circuits of neurons that are located in the right hemisphere. Damage to the right hemisphere disrupts these abilities.

We are not aware of the fact that each hemisphere perceives the world differently. Although the two cerebral hemispheres perform somewhat different functions, our perceptions and our memories are unified. This unity is accomplished by the **corpus callosum,** a large band of axons that connects corresponding parts of the association cortex of the left and right hemispheres: The left and right temporal lobes are connected, the left and right parietal lobes are connected, and so on. Because of the corpus callosum, each region of the association cortex knows what is happening in the corresponding region of the opposite side of the brain.

Figure 3.11 shows a *midsagittal* view of the brain. The brain (and part of the spinal cord) has been sliced down the middle, dividing it into its two symmetrical halves. The left half has been removed, so we see the inner surface of the right half. The cerebral cortex that covers most of the surface of the cerebral hemispheres (including the frontal, parietal, occipital, and temporal lobes) is called the **neocortex** ("new" cortex, because it is of relatively recent evolutionary origin). Another form of cerebral cortex, the **limbic cortex,** is located around the medial edge of the cerebral hemispheres (*limbus* means "border"). The **cingulate gyrus,** an important region of the limbic cortex, can be seen in this figure. (See ***Figure 3.11.***) In addition, if you look back at the top two drawings in Figure 3.10, you will see that the limbic cortex occupies the regions that have not been colored in. (Refer to ***Figure 3.10.***)

Figure 3.11 also shows the corpus callosum. To slice the brain into its two symmetrical halves, one must slice through the middle of the corpus callosum. (Recall that I described the split-brain operation, in which the corpus callosum is severed, in Chapter 1.) (See ***Figure 3.11.***)

As I mentioned earlier, one of the Chapter 3 animations on the CD-ROM will permit you to view the brain from various angles and see the locations of the specialized regions of the cerebral cortex. (See ***Animation 3.2, The Rotatable Brain.***)

Limbic System. A neuroanatomist, Papez (1937), suggested that a set of interconnected brain structures formed a circuit whose primary function was motivation and emotion. This system included several regions of the limbic cortex (already described) and a set of interconnected structures surrounding the core of the forebrain. A physiologist, MacLean (1949), expanded the system to include other structures and coined the term **limbic system.** Besides the limbic cortex, the most important parts of the limbic system are the **hippocampus** ("sea horse") and the **amygdala** ("almond"), located next to the lateral ventricle in the temporal lobe. The

prefrontal cortex The region of the frontal lobe rostral to the motor association cortex.

corpus callosum (*ka **loh** sum*) A large bundle of axons that interconnects corresponding regions of the association cortex on each side of the brain.

neocortex The phylogenetically newest cortex, including the primary sensory cortex, primary motor cortex, and association cortex.

limbic cortex Phylogenetically old cortex, located at the medial edge ("limbus") of the cerebral hemispheres; part of the limbic system.

cingulate gyrus (***sing** yew lett*) A strip of limbic cortex lying along the lateral walls of the groove separating the cerebral hemispheres, just above the corpus callosum.

limbic system A group of brain regions including the anterior thalamic nuclei, amygdala, hippocampus, limbic cortex, and parts of the hypothalamus, as well as their interconnecting fiber bundles.

hippocampus A forebrain structure of the temporal lobe, constituting an important part of the limbic system; includes the hippocampus proper (Ammon's horn), dentate gyrus, and subiculum.

amygdala (*a **mig** da la*) A structure in the interior of the rostral temporal lobe, containing a set of nuclei; part of the limbic system.

See Animation 3.2, The Rotatable Brain, for an interactive examination of the human brain.

Figure 3.11

A midsagittal view of the brain and part of the spinal cord.

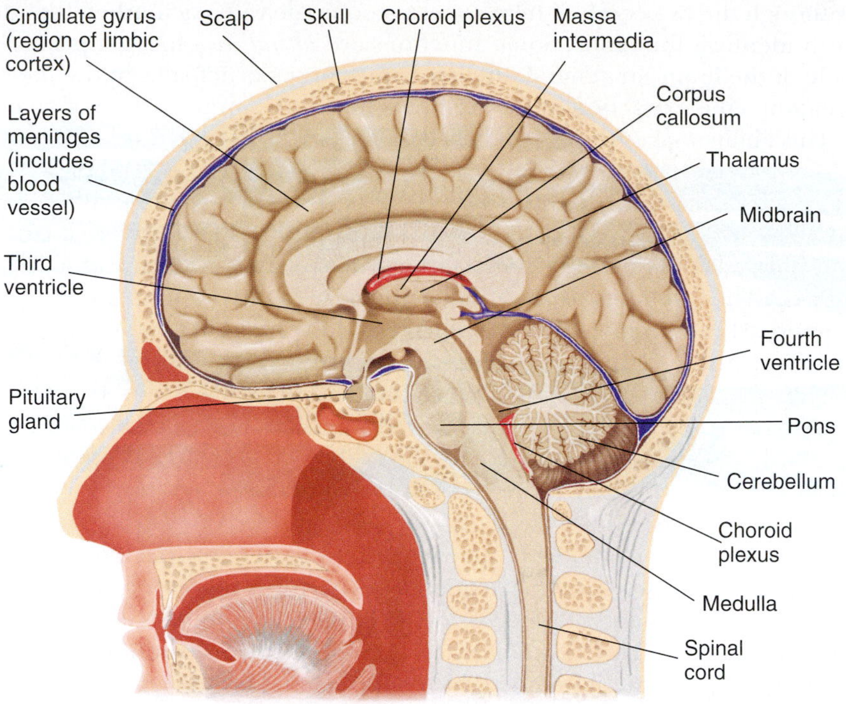

fornix ("arch") is a bundle of axons that connects the hippocampus with other regions of the brain, including the **mammillary** ("breast-shaped") **bodies,** protrusions on the base of the brain that contain parts of the hypothalamus. (See ***Figure 3.12.***)

MacLean noted that the evolution of this system, which includes the first and simplest form of cerebral cortex, appears to have coincided with the development of emotional responses. As you will see in Chapter 14, we now know that parts of the limbic system (notably, the hippocampal formation and the region of limbic cortex that surrounds it) are involved in learning and memory. The amygdala and some regions of limbic cortex are specifically involved in emotions: feelings and expressions of emotions, emotional memories, and recognition of the signs of emotions in other people.

Figure 3.12

The major components of the limbic system. All of the left hemisphere except for the limbic system has been removed.

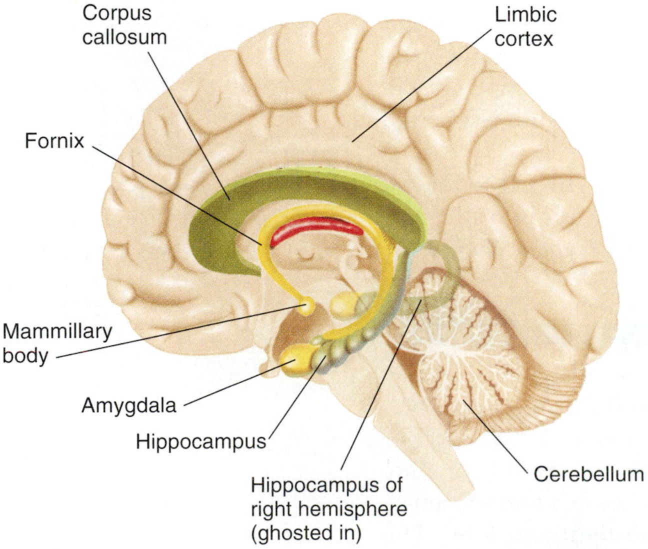

Basal Ganglia. The **basal ganglia** are a collection of subcortical nuclei in the forebrain that lie beneath the anterior portion of the lateral ventricles. **Nuclei** are groups of neurons of similar shape. (The word *nucleus,* from the Greek word for "nut," can refer to the inner portion of an atom, to the structure of a cell that contains the chromosomes, and—as in this case—to a collection of neurons located within the brain.) The major parts of the basal ganglia are the *caudate nucleus,* the *putamen,* and the *globus pallidus* (the "nucleus with a tail," the "shell," and the "pale globe"). (See ***Figure 3.13***). The basal ganglia are involved in the control of movement. For example, Parkinson's disease is caused by degeneration of certain neurons located in the midbrain that

Figure 3.13

The location of the basal ganglia and diencephalon, ghosted in to a semitransparent brain.

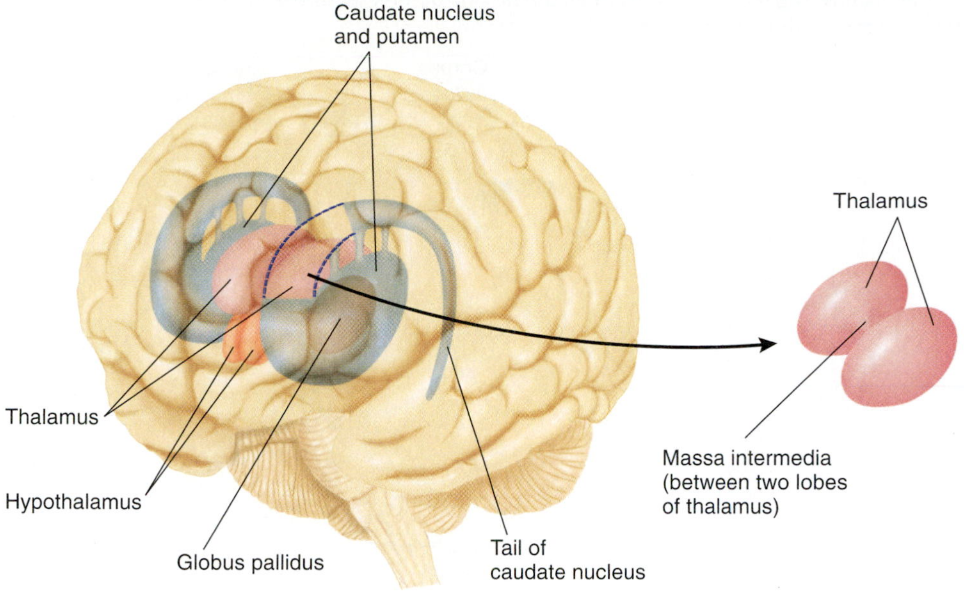

send axons to the caudate nucleus and the putamen. The symptoms of this disease are of weakness, tremors, rigidity of the limbs, poor balance, and difficulty in initiating movements.

Diencephalon

The second major division of the forebrain, the **diencephalon,** is situated between the telencephalon and the mesencephalon; it surrounds the third ventricle. Its two most important structures are the thalamus and the hypothalamus. (See ***Figure 3.13.***)

Thalamus. The **thalamus** (from the Greek *thalamos,* "inner chamber") makes up the dorsal part of the diencephalon. It is situated near the middle of the cerebral hemispheres, immediately medial and caudal to the basal ganglia. The thalamus has two lobes, connected by a bridge of gray matter called the *massa intermedia,* which pierces the middle of the third ventricle. (See ***Figure 3.13.***) The massa intermedia is probably not an important structure, because it is absent in the brains of many people. However, it serves as a useful reference point in looking at diagrams of the brain; it appears in Figures 3.4, 3.11, 3.13, and 3.14.

Most neural input to the cerebral cortex is received from the thalamus; indeed, much of the cortical surface can be divided into regions that receive projections from specific parts of the thalamus. **Projection fibers** are sets of axons that arise from cell bodies located in one region of the brain and synapse on neurons located within another region (that is, they *project to* these regions).

The thalamus is divided into several nuclei. Some thalamic nuclei receive sensory information from the sensory systems. The neurons in these nuclei then relay the sensory information to specific sensory projection areas of the cerebral cortex. For example, the **lateral geniculate nucleus** receives information from the eye and sends axons to the primary visual cortex, and the **medial geniculate nucleus** receives information from the inner ear and sends axons to the primary auditory cortex. Other thalamic nuclei project to specific regions of the cerebral cortex, but they do not relay sensory information. For example, the **ventrolateral nucleus** receives

fornix A fiber bundle that connects the hippocampus with other parts of the brain, including the mammillary bodies of the hypothalamus; part of the limbic system.

mammillary bodies (***mam*** *i lair ee*) A protrusion of the bottom of the brain at the posterior end of the hypothalamus, containing some hypothalamic nuclei; part of the limbic system.

basal ganglia A group of subcortical nuclei in the telencephalon, the caudate nucleus, the globus pallidus, and the putamen; important parts of the motor system.

nucleus (plural: nuclei) An identifiable group of neural cell bodies in the central nervous system.

diencephalon (*dy en* ***seff*** *a lahn*) A region of the forebrain surrounding the third ventricle; includes the thalamus and the hypothalamus.

thalamus The largest portion of the diencephalon, located above the hypothalamus; contains nuclei that project information to specific regions of the cerebral cortex and receive information from it.

projection fiber An axon of a neuron in one region of the brain whose terminals form synapses with neurons in another region.

lateral geniculate nucleus A group of cell bodies within the lateral geniculate body of the thalamus that receives fibers from the retina and projects fibers to the primary visual cortex.

medial geniculate nucleus A group of cell bodies within the medial geniculate body of the thalamus; receives fibers from the auditory system and projects fibers to the primary auditory cortex.

ventrolateral nucleus A nucleus of the thalamus that receives inputs from the cerebellum and sends axons to the primary motor cortex.

Figure 3.14

A midsagittal view of part of the brain, showing some of the nuclei of the hypothalamus. The nuclei are situated on the far side of the wall of the third ventricle, inside the right hemisphere.

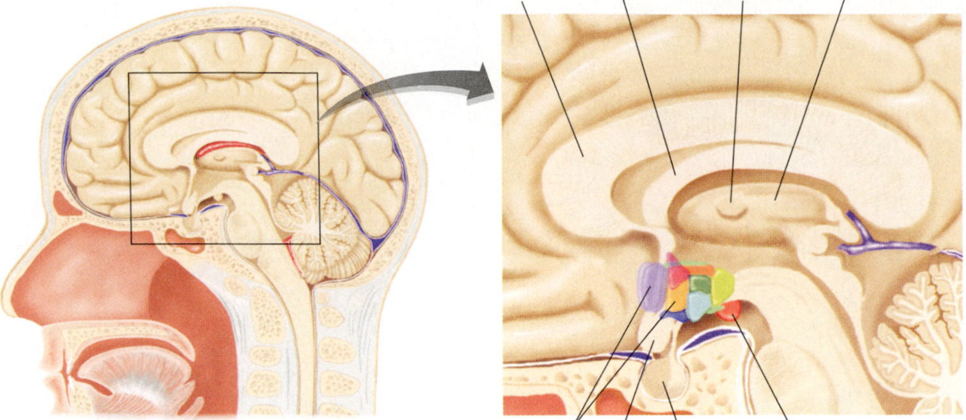

hypothalamus The group of nuclei of the diencephalon situated beneath the thalamus; involved in regulation of the autonomic nervous system, control of the anterior and posterior pituitary glands, and integration of species-typical behaviors.

optic chiasm (***kye*** *az'm*) An X-shaped connection between the optic nerves, located below the base of the brain, just anterior to the pituitary gland.

anterior pituitary gland The anterior part of the pituitary gland; an endocrine gland whose secretions are controlled by the hypothalamic hormones.

neurosecretory cell A neuron that secretes a hormone or hormonelike substance.

information from the cerebellum and projects it to the primary motor cortex. And as we will see in Chapter 9, several nuclei are involved in controlling the general excitability of the cerebral cortex. To accomplish this task, these nuclei have widespread projections to all cortical regions.

Hypothalamus. As its name implies, the **hypothalamus** lies at the base of the brain, under the thalamus. Although the hypothalamus is a relatively small structure, it is an important one. It controls the autonomic nervous system and the endocrine system and organizes behaviors related to survival of the species—the so-called four F's: fighting, feeding, fleeing, and mating.

The hypothalamus is situated on both sides of the ventral portion of the third ventricle. The hypothalamus is a complex structure, containing many nuclei and fiber tracts. Figure 3.14 indicates its location and size. Note that the pituitary gland is attached to the base of the hypothalamus via the pituitary stalk. Just in front of the pituitary stalk is the **optic chiasm,** where half of the axons in the optic nerves (from the eyes) cross from one side of the brain to the other. (See ***Figure 3.14.***) The role of the hypothalamus in the control of the four F's (and other behaviors, such as drinking and sleeping) will be considered in several chapters later in this book.

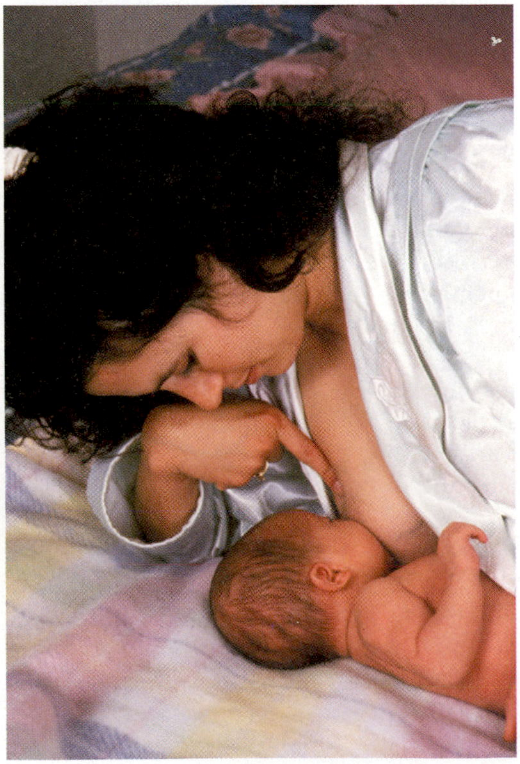

Prolactin, a hormone produced by the anterior pituitary gland, stimulates milk production in a nursing mother. Oxytocin, a hormone released by the posterior pituitary gland, stimulates the ejection of milk when the baby sucks on a nipple.

Much of the endocrine system is controlled by hormones produced by cells in the hypothalamus. A special system of blood vessels directly connects the hypothalamus with the **anterior pituitary gland.** (See ***Figure 3.15.***) The hypothalamic hormones are secreted by specialized neurons called **neurosecretory cells,** located near the base of the pituitary stalk.

Figure 3.15

The pituitary gland. Hormones released by the neurosecretory cells in the hypothalamus enter capillaries and are conveyed to the anterior pituitary gland, where they control its secretion of hormones. The hormones of the posterior pituitary gland are produced in the hypothalamus and carried there in vesicles by means of axoplasmic transport.

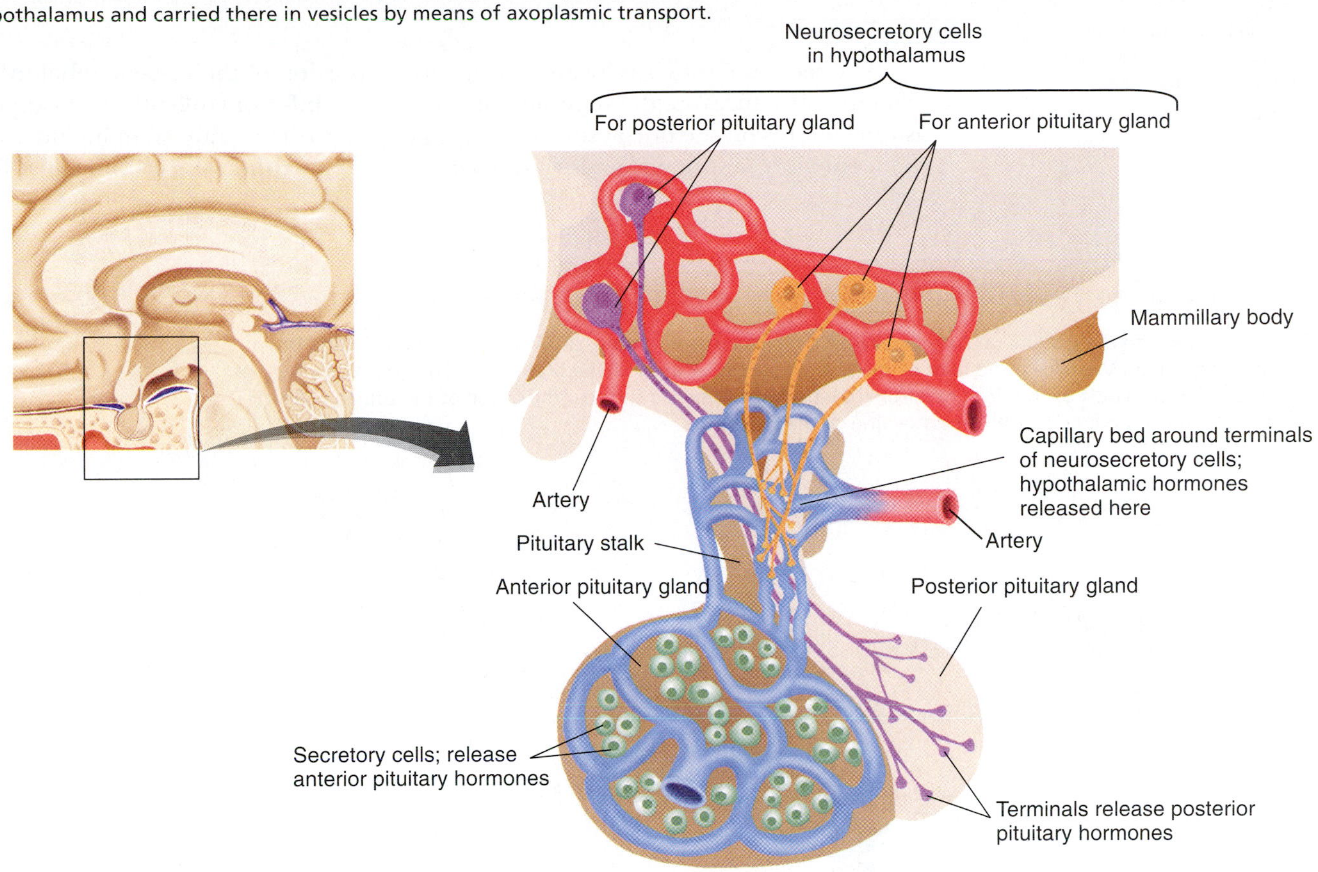

These hormones stimulate the anterior pituitary gland to secrete its hormones. For example, *gonadotropin-releasing hormone* causes the anterior pituitary gland to secrete the *gonadotropic hormones,* which play a role in reproductive physiology and behavior.

Most of the hormones secreted by the anterior pituitary gland control other endocrine glands. Because of this function, the anterior pituitary gland has been called the body's "master gland." For example, the gonadotropic hormones stimulate the gonads (ovaries and testes) to release male or female sex hormones. These hormones affect cells throughout the body, including some in the brain. Two other anterior pituitary hormones—prolactin and somatotropic hormone (growth hormone)—do not control other glands but act as the final messenger. The behavioral effects of many of the anterior pituitary hormones are discussed in later chapters.

The **posterior pituitary gland** is in many ways an extension of the hypothalamus. The hypothalamus produces the posterior pituitary hormones and directly controls their secretion. These hormones include oxytocin, which stimulates ejection of milk and uterine contractions at the time of childbirth, and vasopressin, which regulates urine output by the kidneys. They are produced by two different sets of neurons in the hypothalamus whose axons travel down the pituitary stalk and terminate in the posterior pituitary gland. The hormones are carried in vesicles through the axoplasm of these neurons and collect in the terminal buttons in the posterior pituitary gland. When these axons fire, the hormone contained within their terminal buttons is liberated and enters the circulatory system.

posterior pituitary gland The posterior part of the pituitary gland; an endocrine gland that contains hormone-secreting terminal buttons of axons whose cell bodies lie within the hypothalamus.

midbrain The mesencephalon; the central of the three major divisions of the brain.

mesencephalon (*mezz en **seff** a lahn*) The midbrain; a region of the brain that surrounds the cerebral aqueduct; includes the tectum and the tegmentum.

tectum The dorsal part of the midbrain; includes the superior and inferior colliculi.

The Midbrain

The **midbrain** (also called the **mesencephalon**) surrounds the cerebral aqueduct and consists of two major parts: the tectum and the tegmentum.

Tectum

The **tectum** ("roof") is located in the dorsal portion of the mesencephalon. Its principal structures are the **superior colliculi** and the **inferior colliculi,** which appear as four bumps on the dorsal surface of the **brain stem.** The brain stem includes the diencephalon, midbrain, and hindbrain; it is so called because it looks just like

Figure 3.16

The cerebellum and brain stem. (a) Lateral view of a semitransparent brain, showing the cerebellum and brain stem ghosted in. (b) View from the back of the brain. (c) A dorsal view of the brain stem. The left hemisphere of the cerebellum and part of the right hemisphere have been removed to show the inside of the fourth ventricle and the cerebellar peduncles. (d) A cross section of the midbrain.

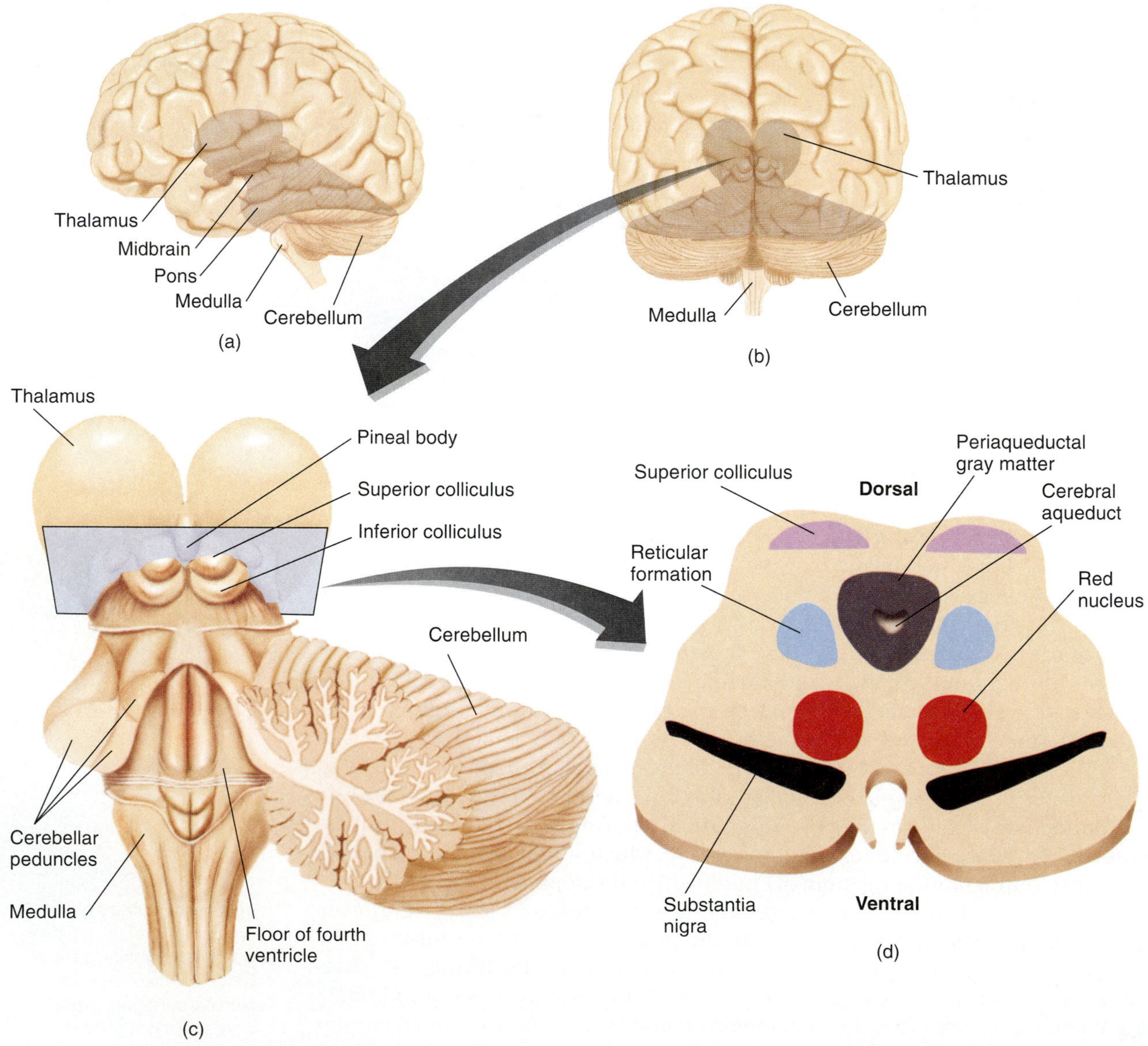

that—a stem. Figure 3.16 shows several views of the brain stem: lateral and posterior views of the brain stem inside a semitransparent brain, an enlarged view of the brain stem with part of the cerebellum cut away to reveal the inside of the fourth ventricle, and a cross section through the midbrain. (See ***Figure 3.16.***) The inferior colliculi are a part of the auditory system. The superior colliculi are part of the visual system. In mammals they are primarily involved in visual reflexes and reactions to moving stimuli.

superior colliculi (*ka **lik** yew lee*) Protrusions on top of the midbrain; part of the visual system.

inferior colliculi Protrusions on top of the midbrain; part of the auditory system.

brain stem The "stem" of the brain, from the medulla to the diencephalon, excluding the cerebellum.

tegmentum The ventral part of the midbrain; includes the periaqueductal gray matter, reticular formation, red nucleus, and substantia nigra.

reticular formation A large network of neural tissue located in the central region of the brain stem, from the medulla to the diencephalon.

periaqueductal gray matter The region of the midbrain surrounding the cerebral aqueduct; contains neural circuits involved in species-typical behaviors.

red nucleus A large nucleus of the midbrain that receives inputs from the cerebellum and motor cortex and sends axons to motor neurons in the spinal cord.

substantia nigra A darkly stained region of the tegmentum that contains neurons that communicate with the caudate nucleus and putamen in the basal ganglia.

Tegmentum

The **tegmentum** ("covering") consists of the portion of the mesencephalon beneath the tectum. It includes the rostral end of the reticular formation, several nuclei controlling eye movements, the periaqueductal gray matter, the red nucleus, the substantia nigra, and the ventral tegmental area. (See ***Figure 3.16d.***)

The **reticular formation** is a large structure consisting of many nuclei (over ninety in all). It is also characterized by a diffuse, interconnected network of neurons with complex dendritic and axonal processes. (Indeed, *reticulum* means "little net"; early anatomists were struck by the netlike appearance of the reticular formation.) The reticular formation occupies the core of the brain stem, from the lower border of the medulla to the upper border of the midbrain. (See ***Figure 3.16d.***) The reticular formation receives sensory information by means of various pathways and projects axons to the cerebral cortex, thalamus, and spinal cord. It plays a role in sleep and arousal, attention, muscle tonus, movement, and various vital reflexes. Its functions will be described more fully in later chapters.

The **periaqueductal gray matter** is so called because it consists mostly of cell bodies of neurons ("gray matter," as contrasted with the "white matter" of axon bundles) that surround the cerebral aqueduct as it travels from the third to the fourth ventricle. The periaqueductal gray matter contains neural circuits that control sequences of movements that constitute species-typical behaviors, such as fighting and mating. As we will see in Chapter 7, opiates such as morphine decrease an organism's sensitivity to pain by stimulating receptors on neurons located in this region.

The **red nucleus** and **substantia nigra** ("black substance") are important components of the motor system. A bundle of axons that arises from the red nucleus constitutes one of the two major fiber systems that bring motor information from the cerebral cortex and cerebellum to the spinal cord. The substantia nigra contains neurons whose axons project to the caudate nucleus and putamen, parts of the basal ganglia. As we will see in Chapter 4, degeneration of these neurons causes Parkinson's disease.

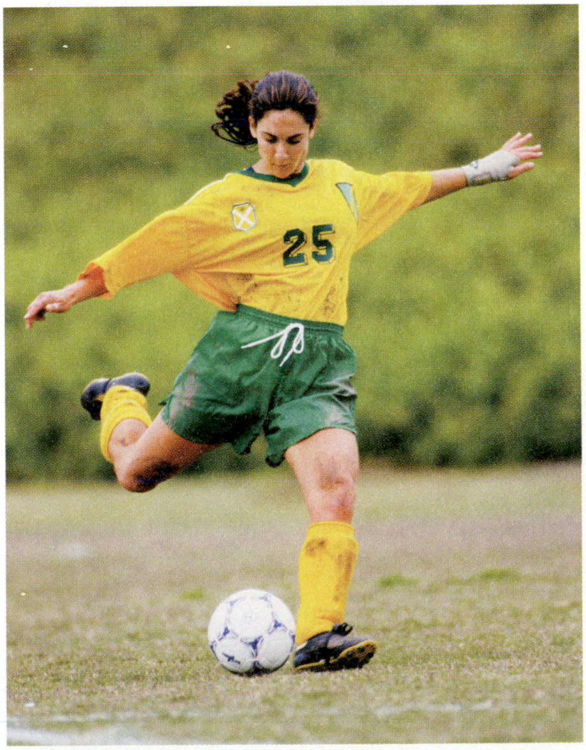

The cerebellum plays an important role in coordinating skilled movements.

The Hindbrain

The **hindbrain,** which surrounds the fourth ventricle, consists of two major divisions: the metencephalon and the myelencephalon.

Metencephalon

The metencephalon consists of the pons and the cerebellum.

Cerebellum. The **cerebellum** ("little brain"), with its two hemispheres, resembles a miniature version of the cerebrum. It is covered by the **cerebellar cortex** and has a set of **deep cerebellar nuclei**. These nuclei receive projections from the cerebellar cortex and themselves send projections out of the cerebellum to

hindbrain The most caudal of the three major divisions of the brain; includes the metencephalon and myelencephalon.

cerebellum (*sair a **bell** um*) A major part of the brain located dorsal to the pons, containing the two cerebellar hemispheres, covered with the cerebellar cortex; an important component of the motor system.

cerebellar cortex The cortex that covers the surface of the cerebellum.

deep cerebellar nuclei Nuclei located within the cerebellar hemispheres; receive projections from the cerebellar cortex and send projections out of the cerebellum to other parts of the brain.

cerebellar peduncle (***pee** dun kul*) One of three bundles of axons that attach each cerebellar hemisphere to the dorsal pons.

other parts of the brain. Each hemisphere of the cerebellum is attached to the dorsal surface of the pons by bundles of axons: the superior, middle, and inferior **cerebellar peduncles** ("little feet"). (See ***Figure 3.16c.***)

Damage to the cerebellum impairs standing, walking, or performance of coordinated movements. (A virtuoso pianist or other performing musician owes much to his or her cerebellum.) The cerebellum receives visual, auditory, vestibular, and somatosensory information, and it also receives information about individual muscle movements being directed by the brain. The cerebellum integrates this information and modifies the motor outflow, exerting a coordinating and smoothing effect on the movements. Cerebellar damage results in jerky, poorly coordinated, exaggerated movements; extensive cerebellar damage makes it impossible even to stand.

Pons. The **pons,** a large bulge in the brain stem, lies between the mesencephalon and medulla oblongata, immediately ventral to the cerebellum. *Pons* means "bridge," but it does not really look like one. (Refer to ***Figures 3.11*** and ***3.16a.***) The pons contains, in its core, a portion of the reticular formation, including some nuclei that appear to be important in sleep and arousal. It also contains a large nucleus that relays information from the cerebral cortex to the cerebellum.

Myelencephalon

The myelencephalon contains one major structure, the **medulla oblongata** (literally, "oblong marrow"), usually just called the *medulla.* This structure is the most caudal portion of the brain stem; its lower border is the rostral end of the spinal cord. (Refer to ***Figures 3.11*** and ***3.16a.***) The medulla contains part of the reticular formation, including nuclei that control vital functions such as regulation of the cardiovascular system, respiration, and skeletal muscle tonus.

Figure 3.17

A ventral view of the human spinal column, with details showing the anatomy of the vertebrae.

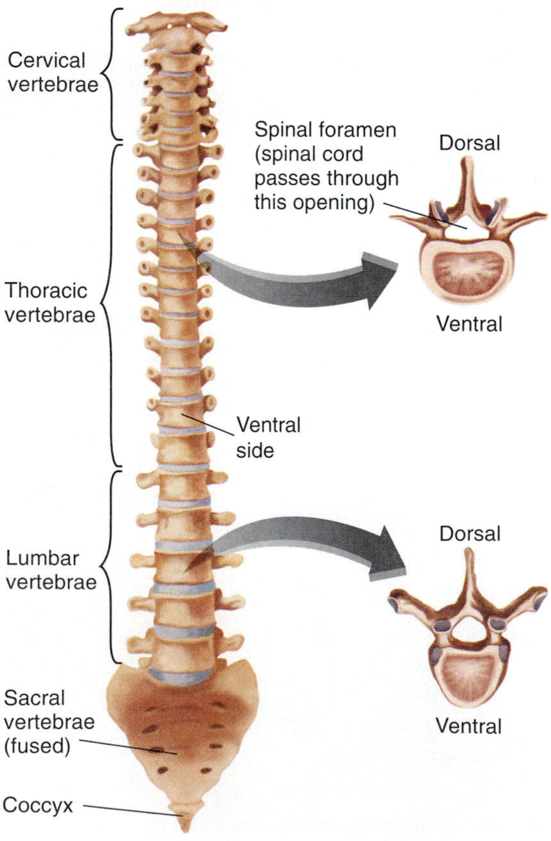

The Spinal Cord

The **spinal cord** is a long, conical structure, approximately as thick as an adult's little finger. The principal function of the spinal cord is to distribute motor fibers to the effector organs of the body (glands and muscles) and to collect somatosensory information to be passed on to the brain. The spinal cord also has a certain degree of autonomy from the brain; various reflexive control circuits (some of which are described in Chapter 8) are located there.

The spinal cord is protected by the vertebral column, which is composed of twenty-four individual vertebrae of the *cervical* (neck), *thoracic* (chest), and *lumbar* (lower back) regions and the fused vertebrae making up the *sacral* and *coccygeal* portions of the column (located in the pelvic region). The spinal cord passes through a hole in each of the vertebrae (the *spinal foramens*). Figure 3.17 illustrates the divisions and structures of the spinal cord and vertebral column. (See ***Figure 3.17.***) Note that the spinal cord is only about two-thirds as long as the vertebral column; the rest of the space is filled by a mass of **spinal roots** composing the **cauda equina** ("horse's tail"). (Refer to ***Figure 3.3c.***)

Early in embryological development the vertebral column and spinal cord are the same length. As development progresses, the vertebral column grows faster than the spinal cord.

This differential growth rate causes the spinal roots to be displaced downward; the most caudal roots travel the farthest before they emerge through openings between the vertebrae and thus compose the cauda equina. To produce the **caudal block** that is sometimes used in pelvic surgery or childbirth, a local anesthetic can be injected into the CSF contained within the sac of dura mater surrounding the cauda equina. The drug blocks conduction in the axons of the cauda equina.

Figure 3.18(a) shows a portion of the spinal cord, with the layers of the meninges that wrap it. Small bundles of fibers emerge from each side of the spinal cord in two straight lines along its dorsolateral and ventrolateral surfaces. Groups of these bundles fuse together and become the thirty-one paired sets of **dorsal roots** and **ventral roots.** The dorsal and ventral roots join together as they pass through the intervertebral foramens and become spinal nerves. (See ***Figure 3.18a.***)

Figure 3.18(b) shows a cross section of the spinal cord. Like the brain, the spinal cord consists of white matter and gray matter. Unlike the brain's, its white matter (consisting of ascending and descending bundles of myelinated axons) is on the outside; the gray matter (mostly neural cell bodies and short, unmyelinated axons) is on the inside. In Figure 3.18(b), ascending tracts are indicated in blue; descending tracts are indicated in red. (See ***Figure 3.18b.***)

pons The region of the metencephalon rostral to the medulla, caudal to the midbrain, and ventral to the cerebellum.

medulla oblongata (*me* ***doo*** *la*) The most caudal portion of the brain; located in the myelencephalon, immediately rostral to the spinal cord.

spinal cord The cord of nervous tissue that extends caudally from the medulla.

spinal root A bundle of axons surrounded by connective tissue that occurs in pairs, which fuse and form a spinal nerve.

cauda equina (*ee* ***kwye*** *na*) A bundle of spinal roots located caudal to the end of the spinal cord.

caudal block The anesthesia and paralysis of the lower part of the body produced by injection of a local anesthetic into the cerebrospinal fluid surrounding the cauda equina.

dorsal root The spinal root that contains incoming (afferent) sensory fibers.

ventral root The spinal root that contains outgoing (efferent) motor fibers.

Figure 3.18

The spinal cord. (a) A portion of the spinal cord, showing the layers of the meninges and the relation of the spinal cord to the vertebral column. (b) A cross section through the spinal cord. Ascending tracts are shown in blue; descending tracts are shown in red.

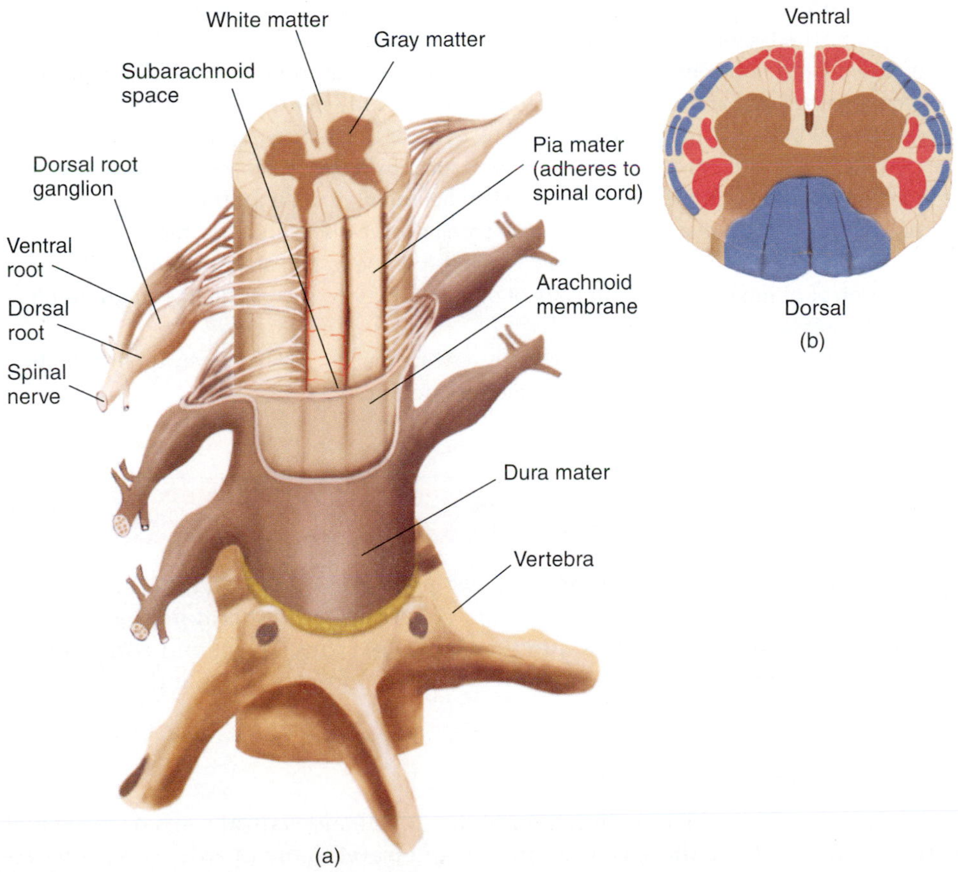

INTERIM SUMMARY

The Central Nervous System

The brain consists of three major divisions, organized around the three chambers of the tube that develops early in embryonic life: the forebrain, the midbrain, and the hindbrain. The development of the neural tube into the mature central nervous system is illustrated in Figure 3.6, and Table 3.2 outlines the major divisions and subdivisions of the brain.

During the first phase of brain development, symmetrical division of the founder cells of the ventricular zone, which lines the neural tube, increases its size. During the second phase, asymmetrical division of these cells gives rise to neurons, which migrate up the fibers of radial glial cells to their final resting places. There, neurons develop dendrites and axons and establish synaptic connections with other neurons. Later, neurons that fail to develop a sufficient number of synaptic connections are killed through apoptosis. The large size of the human brain, relative to the brains of other primates, appears to be accomplished primarily by lengthening the first and second periods of brain development.

The forebrain, which surrounds the lateral and third ventricles, consists of the telencephalon and diencephalon. The telencephalon contains the cerebral cortex, the limbic system, and the basal ganglia. The cerebral cortex is organized into the frontal, parietal, temporal, and occipital lobes. The central sulcus divides the frontal lobe, which deals specifically with movement and the planning of movement, from the other three lobes, which deal primarily with perceiving and learning. The limbic system, which includes the limbic cortex, the hippocampus, and the amygdala, is involved in emotion, motivation, and learning. The basal ganglia participate in the control of movement. The diencephalon consists of the thalamus, which directs information to and from the cerebral cortex, and the hypothalamus, which controls the endocrine system and modulates species-typical behaviors.

The midbrain, which surrounds the cerebral aqueduct, consists of the tectum and tegmentum. The tectum is involved in audition and the control of visual reflexes and reactions to moving stimuli. The tegmentum contains the reticular formation, which is important in sleep, arousal, and movement; the periaqueductal gray matter, which controls various species-typical behaviors; and the red nucleus and the substantia nigra, both of which are parts of the motor system. The hindbrain, which surrounds the fourth ventricle, contains the cerebellum, the pons, and the medulla. The cerebellum plays an important role in integrating and coordinating movements. The pons contains some nuclei that are important in sleep and arousal. The medulla oblongata, too, is involved in sleep and arousal, but it also plays a role in control of movement and in control of vital functions such as heart rate, breathing, and blood pressure.

The outer part of the spinal cord consists of white matter: axons conveying information up or down. The central gray matter contains cell bodies.

The Peripheral Nervous System

The brain and spinal cord communicate with the rest of the body via the cranial nerves and spinal nerves. These nerves are part of the peripheral nervous system, which conveys sensory information to the central nervous system and conveys messages from the central nervous system to the body's muscles and glands.

Spinal Nerves

The **spinal nerves** begin at the junction of the dorsal and ventral roots of the spinal cord. The nerves leave the vertebral column and travel to the muscles or sensory receptors they innervate, branching repeatedly as they go. Branches of spinal nerves

spinal nerve A peripheral nerve attached to the spinal cord.

Figure 3.19

A cross section of the spinal cord, showing the route taken by afferent and efferent axons through the dorsal and ventral roots.

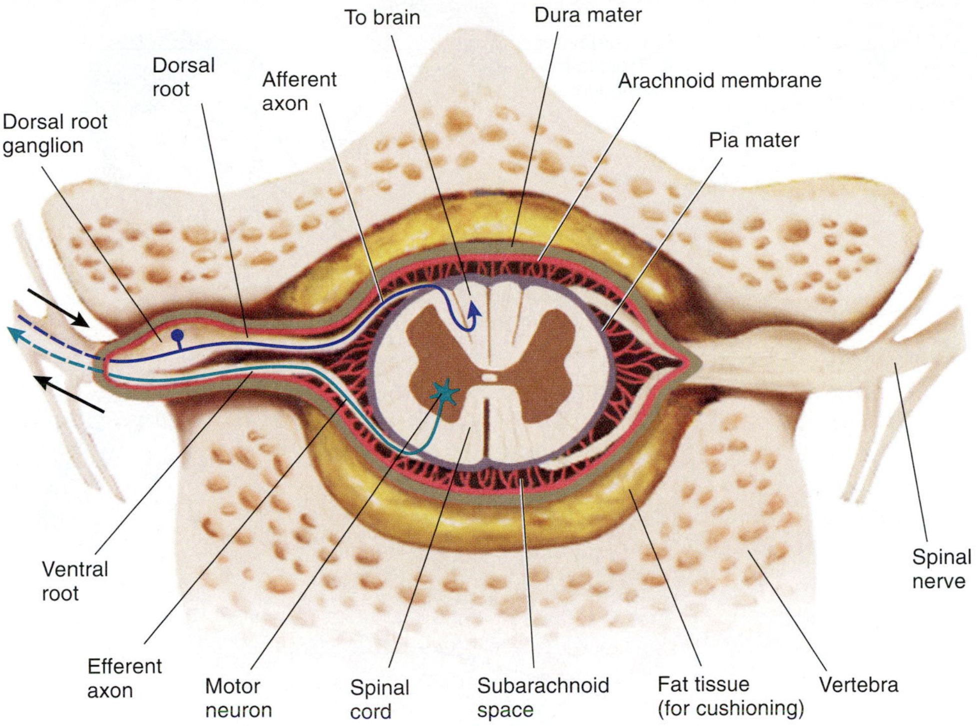

often follow blood vessels, especially those branches that innervate skeletal muscles. (Refer to ***Figure 3.3.***)

Now let us consider the pathways by which sensory information enters the spinal cord and motor information leaves it. The cell bodies of all axons that bring sensory information into the brain and spinal cord are located outside the CNS. (The sole exception is the visual system; the retina of the eye is actually a part of the brain.) These incoming axons are referred to as **afferent axons** because they "bear toward" the CNS. The cell bodies that give rise to the axons that bring somatosensory information to the spinal cord reside in the **dorsal root ganglia,** rounded swellings of the dorsal root. (See ***Figure 3.19.***) These neurons are of the unipolar type (described in Chapter 2). The axonal stalk divides close to the cell body, sending one limb into the spinal cord and the other limb out to the sensory organ. Note that all of the axons in the dorsal root convey somatosensory information.

Cell bodies that give rise to the ventral root are located within the gray matter of the spinal cord. The axons of these multipolar neurons leave the spinal cord via a ventral root, which joins a dorsal root to make a spinal nerve. The axons that leave the spinal cord through the ventral roots control muscles and glands. They are referred to as **efferent axons** because they "bear away from" the CNS. (See ***Figure 3.19.***)

Cranial Nerves

Twelve pairs of **cranial nerves** are attached to the ventral surface of the brain. Most of these nerves serve sensory and motor functions of the head and neck region. One of them, the *tenth,* or **vagus nerve,** regulates the functions of organs in the thoracic

afferent axon An axon directed toward the central nervous system, conveying sensory information.

dorsal root ganglion A nodule on a dorsal root that contains cell bodies of afferent spinal nerve neurons.

efferent axon (***eff*** *ur ent*) An axon directed away from the central nervous system, conveying motor commands to muscles and glands.

cranial nerve A peripheral nerve attached directly to the brain.

vagus nerve The largest of the cranial nerves, conveying efferent fibers of the parasympathetic division of the autonomic nervous system to organs of the thoracic and abdominal cavities.

Figure 3.20

The twelve pairs of cranial nerves and the regions and functions they serve. Red lines denote axons that control muscles or glands; blue lines denote sensory axons.

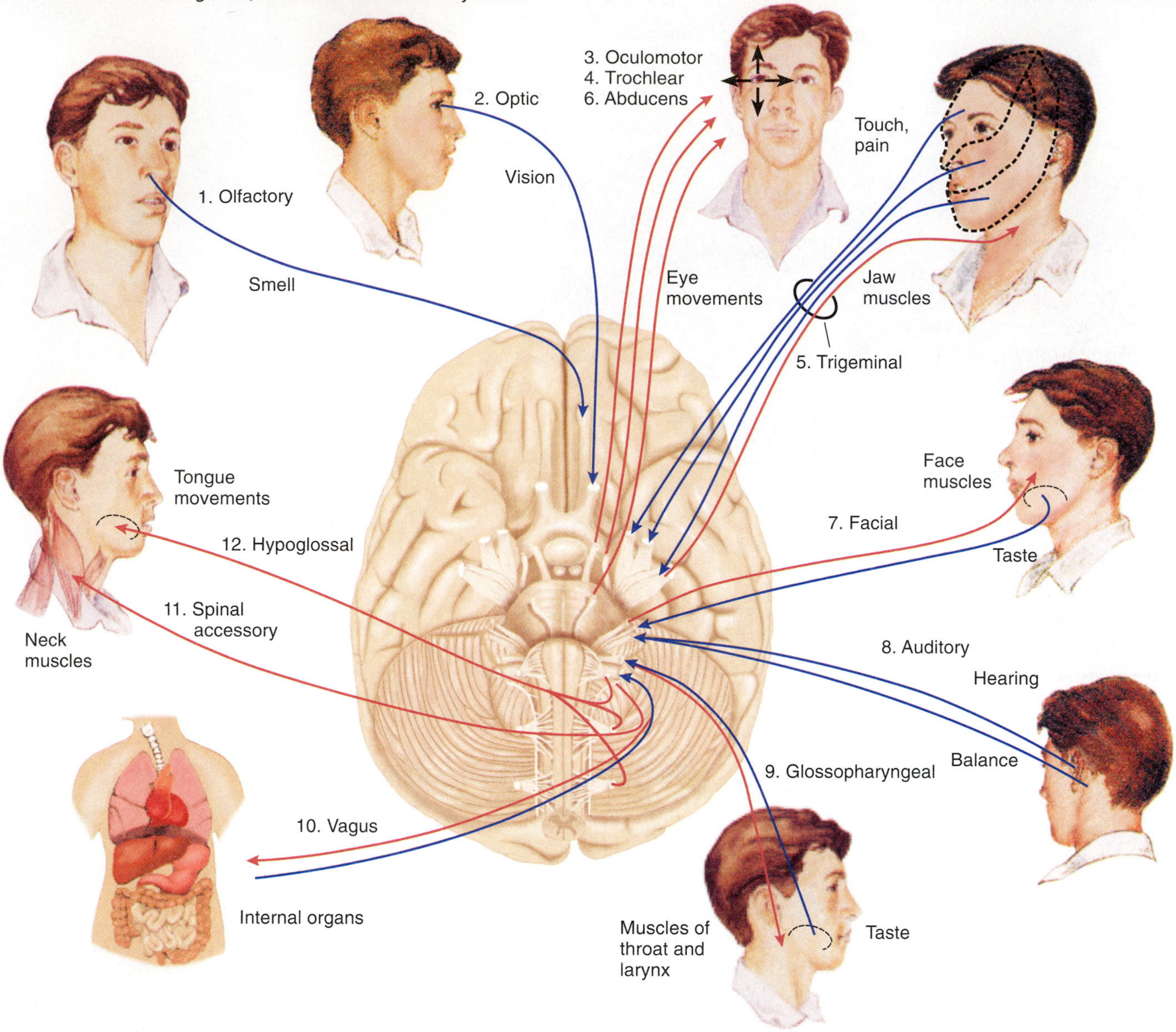

olfactory bulb The protrusion at the end of the olfactory nerve; receives input from the olfactory receptors.

and abdominal cavities. It is called the *vagus* ("wandering") nerve because its branches wander throughout the thoracic and abdominal cavities. (The word *vagabond* has the same root.) Figure 3.20 presents a view of the base of the brain and illustrates the cranial nerves and the structures they serve. Note that efferent (motor) fibers are drawn in red and that afferent (sensory) fibers are drawn in blue. (See ***Figure 3.20.***)

As I mentioned in the previous section, cell bodies of sensory nerve fibers that enter the brain and spinal cord (except for the visual system) are located outside the central nervous system. Somatosensory information (and the sense of taste) is received, via the cranial nerves, from unipolar neurons. Auditory, vestibular, and visual information is received via fibers of bipolar neurons (described in Chapter 2). Olfactory information is received via the **olfactory bulbs,** which receive information from the olfactory receptors in the nose. The olfactory bulbs are complex structures containing a considerable amount of neural circuitry; actually, they are part of the brain. Sensory mechanisms are described in more detail in Chapters 6 and 7.

The Autonomic Nervous System

The part of the peripheral nervous system that I have discussed so far—which receives sensory information from the sensory organs and that controls movements of the skeletal muscles—is called the **somatic nervous system.** The other branch of the peripheral nervous system—the **autonomic nervous system (ANS)**—is concerned with regulation of smooth muscle, cardiac muscle, and glands. (*Autonomic* means "self-governing.") Smooth muscle is found in the skin (associated with hair follicles), in blood vessels, in the eyes (controlling pupil size and accommodation of the lens), and in the walls and sphincters of the gut, gallbladder, and urinary bladder. Merely describing the organs that are innervated by the autonomic nervous system suggests the function of this system: regulation of "vegetative processes" in the body.

The ANS consists of two anatomically separate systems: the *sympathetic division* and the *parasympathetic division.* With few exceptions organs of the body are innervated by both of these subdivisions, and each has a different effect. For example, the sympathetic division speeds the heart rate, whereas the parasympathetic division slows it.

Sympathetic Division of the ANS

The **sympathetic division** is most involved in activities associated with expenditure of energy from reserves that are stored in the body. For example, when an organism is excited, the sympathetic nervous system increases blood flow to skeletal muscles, stimulates the secretion of epinephrine (resulting in increased heart rate and a rise in blood sugar level), and causes piloerection (erection of fur in mammals that have it and production of "goose bumps" in humans).

The cell bodies of sympathetic motor neurons are located in the gray matter of the thoracic and lumbar regions of the spinal cord (hence the sympathetic nervous system is also known as the *thoracolumbar system*). The fibers of these neurons exit via the ventral roots. After joining the spinal nerves, the fibers branch off and pass into **sympathetic ganglia** (not to be confused with the dorsal root ganglia). Figure 3.21 shows the relation of these ganglia to the spinal cord. Note that individual sympathetic ganglia are connected to the neighboring ganglia above and below, thus forming the **sympathetic ganglion chain.** (See ***Figure 3.21.***)

The axons that leave the spinal cord through the ventral root belong to the **preganglionic neurons.** With one exception, all sympathetic preganglionic axons enter the ganglia of the sympathetic chain, but not all of them form synapses there. (The exception is the medulla of the adrenal gland, described in Chapter 10.) Some axons leave and travel to one of the other sympathetic ganglia, located among the internal organs. All sympathetic preganglionic axons form synapses with neurons located in one of the ganglia. The neurons with which they form synapses are called **postganglionic neurons.** In turn, the postganglionic neurons send axons to the target organs, such as the intestines, stomach, kidneys, or sweat glands. (See ***Figure 3.21.***)

Parasympathetic Division of the ANS

The **parasympathetic division** of the autonomic nervous system supports activities that are involved with increases in the body's supply of stored energy. These activities include salivation, gastric and intestinal motility, secretion of digestive juices, and increased blood flow to the gastrointestinal system.

Cell bodies that give rise to preganglionic axons in the parasympathetic nervous system are located in two regions: the nuclei of some of the cranial nerves (especially the vagus nerve) and the intermediate horn of the gray matter in the sacral region

somatic nervous system The part of the peripheral nervous system that controls the movement of skeletal muscles or transmits somatosensory information to the central nervous system.

autonomic nervous system (ANS) The portion of the peripheral nervous system that controls the body's vegetative functions.

sympathetic division The portion of the autonomic nervous system that controls functions that accompany arousal and expenditure of energy.

sympathetic ganglia Nodules that contain synapses between preganglionic and postganglionic neurons of the sympathetic nervous system.

sympathetic ganglion chain One of a pair of groups of sympathetic ganglia that lie ventrolateral to the vertebral column.

preganglionic neuron The efferent neuron of the autonomic nervous system whose cell body is located in a cranial nerve nucleus or in the intermediate horn of the spinal gray matter and whose terminal buttons synapse upon postganglionic neurons in the autonomic ganglia.

postganglionic neuron Neurons of the autonomic nervous system that form synapses directly with their target organ.

parasympathetic division The portion of the autonomic nervous system that controls functions that occur during a relaxed state.

Figure 3.21

The autonomic nervous system and the target organs and functions served by the sympathetic and parasympathetic branches.

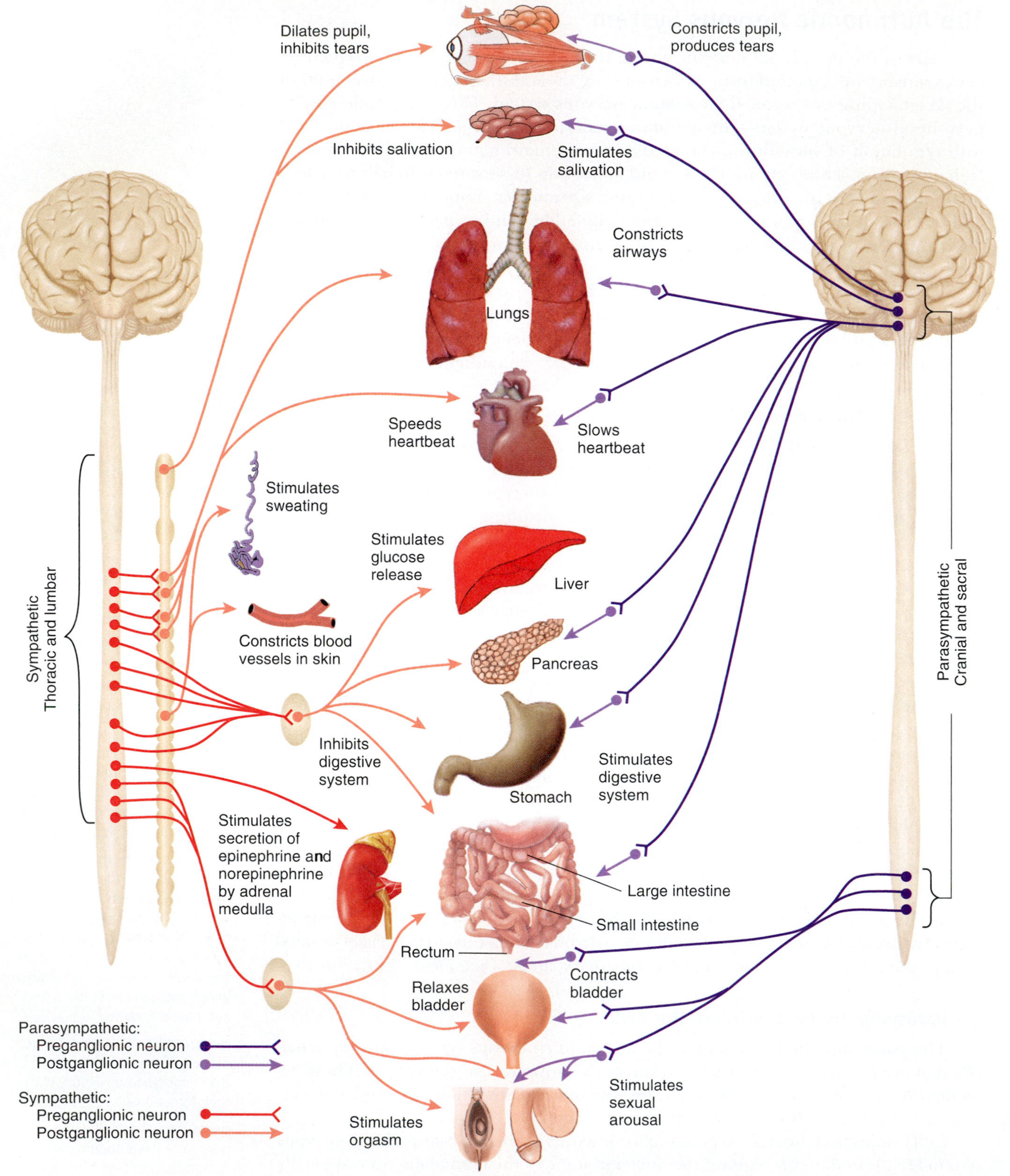

Table 3.3

The Major Divisions of the Peripheral Nervous System

Somatic Nervous System	Autonomic Nervous System (ANS)
SPINAL NERVES	SYMPATHETIC BRANCH
Afferents from sense organs	Spinal nerves (from thoracic and lumbar regions)
Efferents to muscles	Sympathetic ganglia
CRANIAL NERVES	PARASYMPATHETIC BRANCH
Afferents from sense organs	Cranial nerves (3rd, 7th, 9th, and 10th)
Efferents to muscles	Spinal nerves (from sacral region)
	Parasympathetic ganglia (adjacent to target organs)

of the spinal cord. Thus, the parasympathetic division of the ANS has often been referred to as the *craniosacral system.* Parasympathetic ganglia are located in the immediate vicinity of the target organs; the postganglionic fibers are therefore relatively short. The terminal buttons of both preganglionic and postganglionic neurons in the parasympathetic nervous system secrete acetylcholine.

Table 3.3 summarizes the major divisions of the peripheral nervous system.

INTERIM SUMMARY

The Peripheral Nervous System

The spinal nerves and the cranial nerves convey sensory axons into the central nervous system and motor axons out from it. Spinal nerves are formed by the junctions of the dorsal roots, which contain incoming (afferent) axons, and the ventral roots, which contain outgoing (efferent) axons. The autonomic nervous system consists of two divisions: the sympathetic division, which controls activities that occur during excitement or exertion, such as increased heart rate; and the parasympathetic division, which controls activities that occur during relaxation, such as decreased heart rate and increased activity of the digestive system. The pathways of the autonomic nervous system contain preganglionic axons, from the brain or spinal cord to the sympathetic or parasympathetic ganglia, and postganglionic axons, from the ganglia to the target organ.

EPILOGUE

Unilateral Neglect

When we see people like Miss S., the woman with unilateral neglect, we realize that perception and attention are somewhat independent. The perceptual mechanisms of our brain provide the information, and the mechanisms involved in attention determine whether we become conscious of this information.

Unilateral neglect occurs when the right parietal lobe is damaged. The parietal lobe contains the primary somatosensory cortex. It receives information from the skin, the muscles, the joints, the internal organs, and the part of the inner ear that is concerned with balance. Thus, it is concerned with the body and its position. But that is not all; the association cortex of the parietal lobe also receives auditory and visual information from the association cortex of the occipital and temporal lobes. Its most important function seems to be to put together information about the movements and location of the parts of the body with the locations of objects in space around us. The right and left parietal lobes each handle somewhat different tasks; the left concerns itself with the position of the parts of the body, and the right concerns itself with the three-dimensional space around the body and the contents of that space. (The left parietal lobe is also involved in language abilities, but they will be discussed later, in Chapter 13.)

If unilateral neglect simply consisted of blindness in the left side of the visual field and anesthesia of the left side of the body, it would not be nearly as interesting. Individuals with pure unilateral neglect are neither half blind nor half numb. Under the proper circumstances they *can* see things located to their left, and they *can* tell when someone touches the left side of their bodies. But normally, they ignore such stimuli and act as if the left side of the world and of their bodies did not exist.

Volpe, LeDoux, and Gazzaniga (1979) presented pairs of visual stimuli to people with unilateral neglect—one stimulus in the left visual field and one stimulus in the right. Invariably, the people reported seeing only the right-hand stimulus. But when the investigators asked the people to say whether or not the two stimuli were identical, they answered correctly—*even though they said that they were unaware of the left-hand stimulus.*

If you think about the story that the chief of neurology told about the man who ate only the right half of a pancake, you will realize that people with unilateral neglect *must* be able to perceive more than the right visual field. Remember that people with unilateral neglect fail to notice not only things to their left but also the *left halves* of things. But to distinguish between the left and right halves of an object, you first have to perceive the entire object—otherwise, how would you know where the middle was?

People with unilateral neglect also demonstrate their unawareness of the left half of things when they draw pictures. For example, when asked to draw a clock, they almost always successfully draw a circle; but then when they fill in the numbers, they scrunch them all in on the right side. Sometimes they simply stop after reaching 6 or 7, and sometimes they write the rest of the numbers underneath the circle. When asked to draw a daisy, they begin with a stem and a leaf or two and then draw all the petals to the right. When asked to draw a bicycle, they draw wheels and then put in spokes, but only on the right halves of the wheels.

Bisiach and Luzzatti (1978) demonstrated a similar phenomenon, which suggests that unilateral neglect extends even to a person's own visual imagery. The investigators asked two patients with unilateral neglect to describe the Piazza del Duomo, a well-known landmark in Milan, the city in which they and the patients lived. They asked the patients to imagine that they were standing at the north end of the piazza and to tell them what they saw. The patients duly named the buildings, but only those on the west, to their right. Then the investigators asked the patients to imagine themselves at the south end of the piazza. This time, they named the buildings on the east—again, to their right. Obviously, they knew about *all* of the buildings and their locations, but they visualized them only when the buildings were located in the right side of their (imaginary) visual field.

You might wonder whether damage to the *left* parietal lobe causes unilateral *right* neglect. The answer is yes, but it is very slight, it is difficult to detect, and it seems to be temporary. For all practical purposes, then, there is no right neglect. But why not? The answer is still a mystery. To be sure, people have suggested some possible explanations, but they are still quite speculative. Not until we know a lot more about the brain mechanisms of attention we will be able to understand this discrepancy.

KEY CONCEPTS

BASIC FEATURES OF THE NERVOUS SYSTEM

1. The central nervous system consists of the brain and spinal cord; it is covered with the meninges and floats in cerebrospinal fluid.

THE CENTRAL NERVOUS SYSTEM

2. The nervous system develops first as a tube, which thickens and forms pockets and folds as cells are produced. The tube becomes the ventricular system.
3. The primary cause of the difference between the human brain and that of other primates is a slightly extended period of symmetrical and asymmetrical division of founder cells located in the ventricular zone.
4. The forebrain, surrounding the lateral and third ventricles, consists of the telencephalon (cerebral cortex, limbic system, and basal ganglia) and diencephalon (thalamus and hypothalamus).
5. The midbrain, which surrounds the cerebral aqueduct, consists of the tectum and tegmentum.
6. The hindbrain, which surrounds the fourth ventricle, contains the cerebellum, the pons, and the medulla.

THE PERIPHERAL NERVOUS SYSTEM

7. The spinal and cranial nerves connect the central nervous system with the rest of the body. The autonomic nervous system consists of two divisions, sympathetic and parasympathetic.

SUGGESTED READINGS

Diamond, M. C., Scheibel, A. B., and Elson, L. M. *The Human Brain Coloring Book.* New York: Barnes & Noble, 1985.

Gluhbegovic, N., and Williams, T. H. *The Human Brain: A Photographic Guide.* New York: Harper & Row, 1980.

Heimer, L. *The Human Brain and Spinal Cord: Functional Neuroanatomy and Dissection Guide,* 2nd ed. New York: Springer-Verlag, 1995.

Nauta, W. J. H., and Feirtag, M. *Fundamental Neuroanatomy.* New York: W. H. Freeman, 1986.

Netter, F. H. *The CIBA Collection of Medical Illustrations. Vol. 1: Nervous System. Part 1: Anatomy and Physiology.* Summit, NJ: CIBA Pharmaceutical Products Co., 1991.

Woolsey, T. A., Hanaway, J., and Gado, M. H. *The Brain Atlas: A Guide to the Human Central Nervous System,* 2nd ed. Hoboken, NJ: John Wiley & Sons, 2003.

SUGGESTED WEB SITES

Neuroscience Images

http://synergy.mcg.edu/pt/PT413/images/image.html

Color images of the external surface of the human brain are provided by this site.

The Global Spinal Cord

http://www.anatomy.wisc.edu/sc97/text/SC/contents.htm

The ascending and descending fibers of the spinal cord are the focus of this Web site.

Harvard Brain Atlas

http://www.med.harvard.edu/AANLIB/home.html

This link provides access to the Whole Brain Atlas page that provides images of normal as well as damaged human brains.

Insights from a Broken Brain

http://science-education.nih.gov/nihHTML/ose/snapshots/multimedia/ritn/Gage/Broken_brain1.html

Phineas Gage is the subject of this Web site. The site briefly describes the accident that resulted in damage to his frontal lobes and the personality changes that followed the accident. The site contains several graphics and a description of two recent imaging techniques (PET and MRI).

Medical Neuroscience

http://www.indiana.edu/~m555/

This Web site provides a large number of sections of human brain. Each section can be viewed in either a labeled or unlabeled mode. A unique feature of the site relates to a series of clinical cases relating brain damage to function.

Psychopharmacology

chapter 4

CHAPTER OUTLINE

LEARNING OBJECTIVES

1. Describe the routes of administration of drugs and their subsequent distribution within the body.
2. Describe drug effectiveness, the effects of repeated administration of drugs, and the placebo effect.
3. Describe the effects of drugs on synaptic activity.
4. Review the general role of neurotransmitters and neuromodulators, and describe the acetylcholinergic pathways in the brain and the drugs that affect these neurons.
5. Describe the monoaminergic pathways in the brain and the drugs that affect these neurons.
6. Review the role of neurons that release amino acid neurotransmitters and describe drugs that affect these neurons.
7. Describe the effects of peptides, lipids, nucleosides, and soluble gases released by neurons.

PROLOGUE

A Contaminated Drug

In July 1982 some people in northern California began showing up at neurology clinics displaying dramatic, severe symptoms (Langston, Ballard, Tetrud, and Irwin, 1983). The most severely affected patients were almost totally paralyzed. They were unable to speak intelligibly, they drooled constantly, and their eyes were open with a fixed stare. Others, less severely affected, walked with a slow, shuffling gait and moved slowly and with great difficulty. The symptoms looked like those of Parkinson's disease, but that disorder has a very gradual onset. In addition, it rarely strikes people before late middle age, and the patients were all in their twenties or early thirties.

The common factor linking these patients was intravenous drug use; all of them had been taking a "new heroin," a synthetic opiate related to meperidine (Demerol). Because the symptoms looked like those of Parkinson's disease, the patients were given L-DOPA, the drug used to treat this disease, and they all showed significant improvement in their symptoms. But even with this treatment the symptoms were debilitating. In normal cases of Parkinson's disease, L-DOPA therapy works for a time, but as the degeneration of dopamine-secreting neurons continues, the drug loses its effectiveness. This pattern of response also appears to have occurred in the young patients (Langston and Ballard, 1984).

Some detective work revealed that the chemical that caused the neurological symptoms was not the synthetic opiate itself but another chemical with which it was contaminated. According to researcher William Langston, the mini-epidemic appears to have started "when a young man in Silicon Valley was sloppy in his synthesis of synthetic heroin. That sloppiness led to the presence of MPTP, which by an extraordinary trick of fate is highly toxic to the very same neurons that are lost in Parkinson's disease" (Lewin, 1989, p. 467). Because of the research that followed up on that "trick of fate," patients with Parkinson's disease are now receiving a drug that appears to slow the rate of degeneration of their dopamine-secreting neurons. There is hope that new drugs may even halt the degeneration, giving patients many more years of useful, productive lives and preventing others from ever developing the disease.

Chapter 2 introduced you to the cells of the nervous system, and Chapter 3 described its basic structure. Now it is time to build on this information by introducing the field of psychopharmacology. **Psychopharmacology** is the study of the effects of drugs on the nervous system and (of course) on behavior. (*Pharmakon* is the Greek word for "drug.")

As we will see in this chapter, drugs have *effects* and *sites of action*. **Drug effects** are the changes we can observe in an animal's's physiological processes and behavior. For example, the effects of morphine, heroin, and other opiates include decreased sensitivity to pain, slowing of the digestive system, sedation, muscular relaxation, constriction of the pupils, and euphoria. The **sites of action** of drugs are the points at which molecules of drugs interact with molecules located on or in cells of the body, thus affecting some biochemical processes of these cells. For example, the sites of action of the opiates are specialized receptors situated in the membrane of certain neurons. When molecules of opiates attach to and activate these receptors, the drugs alter the activity of these neurons and produce their effects. This chapter considers both the effects of drugs and their sites of action.

Psychopharmacology is an important field of neuroscience. It has been responsible for the development of psychotherapeutic drugs, which are used to treat psychological and behavioral disorders. It has also provided tools that have enabled other investigators to study the functions of cells of the nervous system and the behaviors controlled by particular neural circuits.

psychopharmacology The study of the effects of drugs on the nervous system and on behavior.

drug effect The changes a drug produces in an animal's physiological processes and behavior.

sites of action The locations at which molecules of drugs interact with molecules located on or in cells of the body, thus affecting some biochemical processes of these cells.

Principles of Psychopharmacology

This chapter begins with a description of the basic principles of psychopharmacology: the routes of administration of drugs and their fate in the body. The second section discusses the sites of drug actions. The final section discusses specific neurotransmitters and neuromodulators and the physiological and behavioral effects of specific drugs that interact with them.

Pharmacokinetics

To be effective, a drug must reach its sites of action. To do so, molecules of the drug must enter the body and then enter the bloodstream so that they can be carried to the organ (or organs) they act on. Once there, they must leave the bloodstream and come into contact with the molecules with which they interact. For almost all of the drugs we are interested in, this means that the molecules of the drug must enter the central nervous system. Some behaviorally active drugs exert their effects on the peripheral nervous system, but these drugs are less important to us than those that affect cells of the CNS.

Molecules of drugs must cross several barriers to enter the body and find their way to their sites of action. Some molecules pass through these barriers easily and quickly; others do so very slowly. And once molecules of drugs enter the body, they begin to be metabolized—broken down by enzymes—or excreted in the urine (or both). In time, the molecules either disappear or are transformed into inactive fragments. The process by which drugs are absorbed, distributed within the body, metabolized, and excreted is referred to as **pharmacokinetics** ("movements of drugs").

Routes of Administration

First, let's consider the routes by which drugs can be administered. For laboratory animals the most common route is injection. The drug is dissolved in a liquid (or, in some cases, suspended in a liquid in the form of fine particles) and injected through a hypodermic needle. The fastest route is **intravenous (IV) injection**—injection into a vein. The drug immediately enters the bloodstream, and it reaches the brain within a few seconds. The disadvantages of IV injections are the increased care and skill they require in comparison to most other forms of injection and the fact that the entire dose reaches the bloodstream at once. If an animal is especially sensitive to the drug, there may be little time to administer another drug to counteract its effects.

An **intraperitoneal (IP) injection** is rapid, but not as rapid as an IV injection. The drug is injected through the abdominal wall into the *peritoneal cavity*—the space that surrounds the stomach, intestines, liver, and other abdominal organs. IP injections are the most common route for administering drugs to small laboratory animals. An **intramuscular (IM) injection** is made directly into a large muscle, such as those found in the upper arm, thigh, or buttocks. The drug is absorbed into the bloodstream through the capillaries that supply the muscle. If very slow absorption is desirable, the drug can be mixed with another drug (such as ephedrine) that constricts blood vessels and retards the flow of blood through the muscle.

A drug can also be injected into the space beneath the skin, by means of a **subcutaneous (SC) injection.** A subcutaneous injection is useful only if small amounts of drug need to be administered, because large amounts would be painful. Some fat-soluble drugs can be dissolved in vegetable oil and administered subcutaneously. In this case, molecules of the drug will slowly leave the deposit of oil over a period of several days. If *very* slow and prolonged absorption of a drug is desired, the drug can be formed into a dry pellet or placed in a sealed silicone rubber capsule and implanted beneath the skin.

Oral administration is the most common form of administering medicinal drugs to humans. Because of the difficulty of getting laboratory animals to eat something that does not taste good to them, researchers seldom use this route. Some chemicals cannot be administered orally because they will be destroyed by stomach acid or di-

pharmacokinetics The process by which drugs are absorbed, distributed within the body, metabolized, and excreted.

intravenous (IV) injection Injection of a substance directly into a vein.

intraperitoneal (IP) injection (*in tra pair i toe **nee** ul*) Injection of a substance into the *peritoneal cavity*—the space that surrounds the stomach, intestines, liver, and other abdominal organs.

intramuscular (IM) injection Injection of a substance into a muscle.

subcutaneous (SC) injection Injection of a substance into the space beneath the skin.

oral administration Administration of a substance into the mouth, so that it is swallowed.

gestive enzymes or because they are not absorbed from the digestive system into the bloodstream. For example, insulin, a peptide hormone, must be injected. **Sublingual administration** of certain drugs can be accomplished by placing them beneath the tongue. The drug is absorbed into the bloodstream by the capillaries that supply the mucous membrane that lines the mouth. (Obviously, this method works only with humans, who can cooperate and leave the capsule beneath their tongue.) Nitroglycerine, a drug that causes blood vessels to dilate, is taken sublingually by people who suffer the pains of angina pectoris, caused by obstructions in the coronary arteries.

Drugs can also be administered at the opposite end of the digestive tract, in the form of suppositories. **Intrarectal administration** is rarely used to give drugs to experimental animals. For obvious reasons this process would be difficult with a small animal. In addition, when agitated, small animals such as rats tend to defecate, which would mean that the drug would not remain in place long enough to be absorbed. And I'm not sure I would want to try to administer a rectal suppository to a large animal. Rectal suppositories are most commonly used to administer drugs that might upset a person's stomach.

The lungs provide another route for drug administration: **inhalation.** Nicotine, freebase cocaine, and marijuana are usually smoked. In addition, drugs used to treat lung disorders are often inhaled in the form of a vapor or fine mist. The route from the lungs to the brain is very short, and drugs administered this way have very rapid effects.

Some drugs can be absorbed directly through the skin, so they can be given by means of **topical administration.** Natural or artificial steroid hormones can be administered this way, as can nicotine (as a treatment to make it easier for a person to stop smoking). The mucous membrane lining the nasal passages also provides a route for topical administration. Commonly abused drugs such as cocaine hydrochloride are often sniffed so that they come into contact with the nasal mucosa. This route delivers the drug to the brain very rapidly. (The technical, rarely used name for this route is *insufflation.* And note that sniffing is not the same as inhalation; when powdered cocaine is sniffed, it ends up in the mucous membrane of the nasal passages, not in the lungs.)

Finally, drugs can be administered directly into the brain. As we saw in Chapter 2, the blood–brain barrier prevents certain chemicals from leaving capillaries and entering the brain. Some drugs cannot cross the blood–brain barrier. If these drugs are to reach the brain, they must be injected directly into the brain or into the cerebrospinal fluid in the brain's ventricular system. To study the effects of a drug in a specific region of the brain (for example, in a particular nucleus of the hypothalamus), a researcher will inject a very small amount of the drug directly into the brain. This procedure, known as **intracerebral administration,** is described in more detail in Chapter 5. To achieve a widespread distribution of a drug in the brain, a researcher will get past the blood–brain barrier by injecting the drug into a cerebral ventricle. The drug is then absorbed into the brain tissue, where it can exert its effects. This route, **intracerebroventricular (ICV) administration,** is used very rarely in humans—primarily to deliver antibiotics directly to the brain to treat certain types of infections.

Figure 4.1 shows the time course of blood levels of a commonly abused drug, cocaine, after intravenous injection, inhalation, sniffing, and oral administration. The amounts received were not identical, but the graph illustrates the relative rapidity with which the drug reaches the blood. (See ***Figure 4.1.***)

sublingual administration (*sub ling wul*) Administration of a substance by placing it beneath the tongue.

intrarectal administration Administration of a substance into the rectum.

inhalation Administration of a vaporous substance into the lungs.

topical administration Administration of a substance directly onto the skin or mucous membrane.

intracerebral administration Administration of a substance directly into the brain.

intracerebroventricular (ICV) administration Administration of a substance into one of the cerebral ventricles.

Figure 4.1

The concentration of cocaine in blood plasma after intravenous injection, inhalation, sniffing, and oral administration.

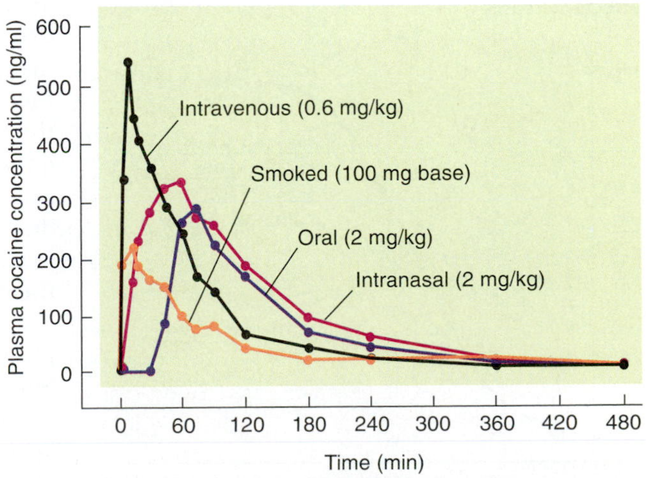

Adapted from Feldman, Meyer, and Quenzer, 1997; after Jones, 1990.

Distribution of Drugs Within the Body

As we saw, drugs exert their effects only when they reach their sites of action. In the case of drugs that affect behavior, most of these sites are located on or in particular cells in the central nervous system. The previous section described the routes by which drugs can be introduced into the body. With the exception of intracerebral or intracerebroventricular administration the differences in the routes of drug administration vary only in the rate at which a drug reaches the blood plasma (that is, the liquid part of the blood). But what happens next? All the sites of action of drugs that are of interest to psychopharmacologists lie outside the blood vessels.

Several factors determine the rate at which a drug in the bloodstream reaches sites of action within the brain. The first is lipid solubility. The blood–brain barrier is a barrier only for water-soluble molecules. Molecules that are soluble in lipids pass through the cells that line the capillaries in the central nervous system, and they rapidly distribute themselves throughout the brain. For example, diacetylmorphine (more commonly known as heroin) is more lipid soluble than morphine is. Thus, an intravenous injection of heroin produces more rapid effects than does one of morphine. Even though the molecules of the two drugs are equally effective when they reach their sites of action in the brain, the fact that heroin molecules get there faster means that they produce a more intense "rush" and thus explains why drug addicts prefer heroin to morphine.

Inactivation and Excretion

Drugs do not remain in the body indefinitely. Many are deactivated by enzymes, and all are eventually excreted, primarily by the kidneys. The liver plays an especially active role in enzymatic deactivation of drugs, but some deactivating enzymes are also found in the blood. The brain also contains enzymes that destroy some drugs. In some cases enzymes transform molecules of a drug into other forms that themselves are biologically active. Occasionally, the transformed molecules is *even more* active than the one that is administered. In such cases the effects of a drug can have a very long duration.

Figure 4.2

A dose-response curve. Increasingly stronger doses of the drug produce increasingly larger effects until the maximum effect is reached. After that point, increments in the dose do not produce any increments in the drug's effect. However, the risk of adverse side effects increases.

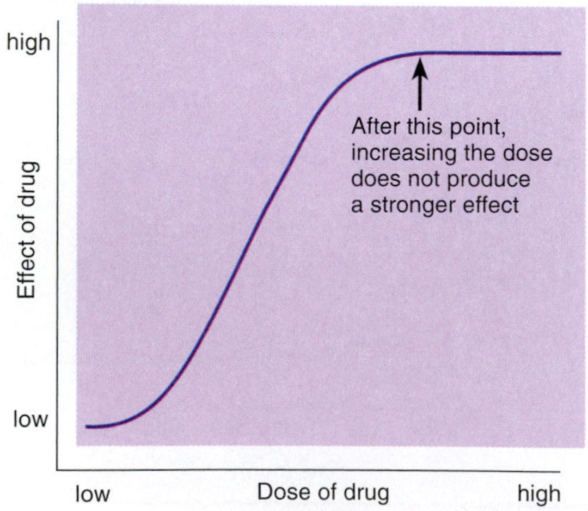

Drug Effectiveness

Drugs vary widely in their effectiveness. A small dose of a relatively effective drug can equal or exceed the effects of larger amounts of a relatively ineffective drug. The best way to measure the effectiveness of a drug is to plot a **dose-response curve.** To do this, subjects are given various doses of a drug, usually defined as milligrams of drug per kilogram of a subject's body weight, and the effects of the drug are plotted. Because the molecules of most drugs distribute themselves throughout the blood and then throughout the rest of the body, a heavier subject (human or laboratory animal) will require a larger quantity of a drug to achieve the same concentration as a smaller subject. As Figure 4.2 shows, increasingly stronger doses of a drug cause increasingly larger effects, until the point of maximum effect is reached. At this point, increasing the dose of the drug does not produce any more effect. (See ***Figure 4.2.***)

Most drugs have more than one effect. Opiates such as morphine and codeine produce analgesia (reduced sensitivity to pain), but they also depress the activity of neurons in the medulla that control heart rate and respiration. A physician who prescribes an opiate to relieve a patient's pain wants to administer a dose that is large enough to produce analgesia but not enough to depress heart rate and respiration—effects that could be fatal. Figure 4.3 shows two dose-response curves, one for the analgesic effects of a painkiller and one for the drug's depressant effects on respiration. The difference between these curves indicates the drug's margin of safety. Obviously, the most desirable drugs have a large margin of safety. (See ***Figure 4.3.***)

One measure of a drug's margin of safety is its **therapeutic index.** This measure is obtained by administering varying doses of the drug to a group of laboratory animals such as mice. Two numbers are obtained: the dose that produces the desired effects in 50 percent of the animals and the dose that produces toxic effects in 50 percent of the animals. The therapeutic index is the ratio of these two numbers. For example, if the toxic dose is five times higher than the effective dose, then the therapeutic index is 5.0. The lower the therapeutic index, the more care must be taken in prescribing the drug. For example, barbiturates have relatively low therapeutic indexes—as low as 2 or 3. In contrast, tranquilizers such as Librium or Valium have therapeutic indexes of well over 100. As a consequence, an accidental overdose of a barbiturate is much more likely to have tragic effects than a similar overdose of Librium or Valium.

Figure 4.3

Dose-response curves for the analgesic effect of morphine and for the drug's adverse side effects, its depressant effect on respiration. A drug's margin of safety is reflected by the difference between the dose-response curve for its therapeutic effects and that for its adverse side effects.

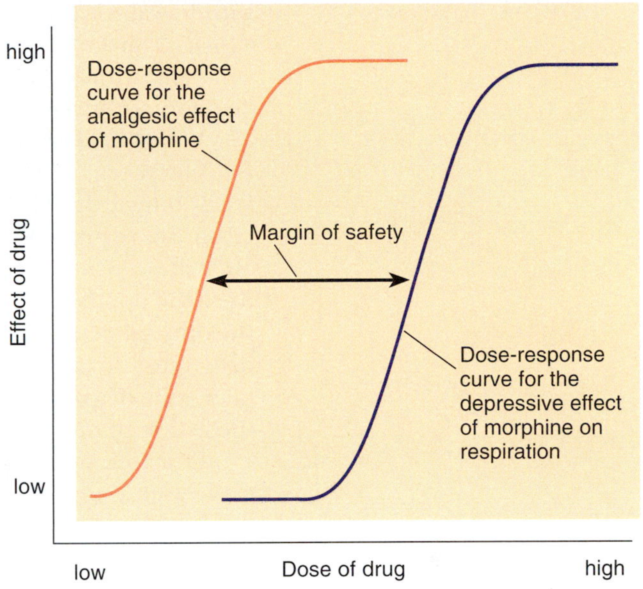

Why do drugs vary in their effectiveness? There are two reasons. First, different drugs—even those with the same behavioral effects—may have different sites of action. For example, both morphine and aspirin have analgesic effects, but morphine suppresses the activity of neurons in the spinal cord and brain that are involved in pain perception, whereas aspirin reduces the production of a chemical involved in transmitting information from damaged tissue to pain-sensitive neurons. Because the drugs act very differently, a given dose of morphine (expressed in terms of milligrams of drug per kilogram of body weight) produces much more pain reduction than the same dose of aspirin.

The second reason that drugs vary in their effectiveness has to do with the affinity of the drug with its site of action. As we will see in the next major section of this chapter, most drugs of interest to psychopharmacologists exert their effects by binding with other molecules located in the central nervous system—with presynaptic or postsynaptic receptors, with transporter molecules, or with enzymes involved in the production or deactivation of neurotransmitters. Drugs vary widely in their **affinity** for the molecules to which they attach—the readiness with which the two molecules join together. A drug with a high affinity will produce effects at a relatively low concentration, whereas one with a low affinity must be administered in relatively high doses. Thus, even two drugs with identical sites of action can vary widely in their effectiveness if they have different affinities for their binding sites. In addition, because most drugs have multiple effects, a drug can have high affinities for some of its sites of action and low affinities for others. The most desirable drug has a high affinity for sites of action that produce therapeutic effects and a low affinity for sites of action that produce toxic side effects. One of the goals of research by drug companies is to find chemicals with just this pattern of effects.

Effects of Repeated Administration

Often, when a drug is administered repeatedly, its effects will not remain constant. In most cases its effects will diminish—a phenomenon known as **tolerance.** In other cases a drug becomes more and more effective—a phenomenon known as **sensitization.**

dose-response curve A graph of the magnitude of an effect of a drug as a function of the amount of drug administered.

therapeutic index The ratio between the dose that produces the desired effect in 50 percent of the animals and the dose that produces toxic effects in 50 percent of the animals.

affinity The readiness with which two molecules join together.

tolerance A decrease in the effectiveness of a drug that is administered repeatedly.

sensitization An increase in the effectiveness of a drug that is administered repeatedly.

Let's consider tolerance first. Tolerance is seen in many drugs that are commonly abused. For example, a regular user of heroin must take larger and larger amounts of the drug for it to be effective. And once a person has taken an opiate regularly enough to develop tolerance, that individual will suffer **withdrawal symptoms** if he or she suddenly stops taking the drug. Withdrawal symptoms are primarily the opposite of the effects of the drug itself. For example, heroin produces euphoria; withdrawal from it produces *dysphoria*—a feeling of anxious misery. (*Euphoria* and *dysphoria* mean "easy to bear" and "hard to bear," respectively.) Heroin produces constipation; withdrawal from it produces nausea and cramping. Heroin produces relaxation; withdrawal from it produces agitation.

Withdrawal symptoms are caused by the same mechanisms that are responsible for tolerance. Tolerance is the result of the body's attempt to compensate for the effects of the drug. That is, most systems of the body, including those controlled by the brain, are regulated so that they stay at an optimal value. When the effects of a drug alter these systems for a prolonged time, compensatory mechanisms begin to produce the opposite reaction, at least partially compensating for the disturbance from the optimal value. These mechanisms account for the fact that more and more of the drug must be taken to achieve a given level of effects. Then, when the person stops taking the drug, the compensatory mechanisms make themselves felt, unopposed by the action of the drug.

Research suggests that there are several types of compensatory mechanisms. As we will see, many drugs that affect the brain do so by binding with receptors and activating them. The first compensatory mechanism involves a decrease in the effectiveness of such binding. Either the receptors become less sensitive to the drug (that is, their affinity for the drug decreases) or the receptors decrease in number. The second compensatory mechanism involves the process that couples the receptors to ion channels in the membrane or to the production of second messengers. After prolonged stimulation of the receptors, one or more steps in the coupling process become less effective. (Of course, *both* effects can occur.) The details of these compensatory mechanisms are described in Chapter 16, which discusses the causes and effects of drug abuse.

As we have seen, many drugs have several different sites of action and thus produce several different effects. This means that some of the effects of a drug may show tolerance but others may not. For example, barbiturates cause sedation and also depress neurons that control respiration. The sedative effects show tolerance, but the respiratory depression does not. This means that if larger and larger doses of a barbiturate are taken to achieve the same level of sedation, the person begins to run the risk of taking a dangerously large dose of the drug.

Sensitization is, of course, the exact opposite of tolerance: Repeated doses of a drug produce larger and larger effects. Because compensatory mechanisms tend to correct for deviations away from the optimal values of physiological processes, sensitization is less common than tolerance. And some of the effects of a drug may show sensitization while others show tolerance. For example, repeated injections of cocaine become more and more likely to produce movement disorders and convulsions, whereas the euphoric effects of the drug do not show sensitization—and may even show tolerance.

Placebo Effects

A **placebo** is an innocuous substance that has no specific physiological effect. The word comes from the Latin *placere,* "to please." A physician may sometimes give a placebo to anxious patients to placate them. (You can see that *placate* also has the same root.) But although placebos have no *specific* physiological effect, it is incorrect to say that they have *no* effect. If a person thinks that a placebo has a physiological effect, then administration of the placebo may actually produce that effect.

withdrawal symptom The appearance of symptoms opposite to those produced by a drug when the drug is administered repeatedly and then suddenly no longer taken.

placebo (*pla **see** boh*) An inert substance that is given to an organism in lieu of a physiologically active drug; used experimentally to control for the effects of mere administration of a drug.

When experimenters want to investigate the behavioral effects of drugs in humans, they must use control groups whose members receive placebos, or they cannot be sure that the behavioral effects they observe were caused by specific effects of the drug. Studies with laboratory animals must also use placebos, even though we need not worry about the animals' "beliefs" about the effects of the drugs we give them. Consider what you must do to give a rat an intraperitoneal injection of a drug. You reach into the animal's cage, pick the animal up, hold it in such a way that its abdomen is exposed and its head is positioned to prevent it from biting you, insert a hypodermic needle through its abdominal wall, press the plunger of the syringe, and replace the animal in its cage, being sure to let go of it quickly so that it cannot turn and bite you. Even if the substance you inject is innocuous, the experience of receiving the injection would activate the animal's autonomic nervous system, cause the secretion of stress hormones, and have other physiological effects. If we want to know what the behavioral effects of a drug are, we must compare the drug-treated animals with other animals who receive a placebo, administered in exactly the same way as the drug. (By the way, a skilled and experienced researcher can handle a rat so gently that it shows very little reaction to a hypodermic injection.)

INTERIM SUMMARY

Principles of Psychopharmacology

Psychopharmacology is the study of the effects of drugs on the nervous system and behavior. Drugs are exogenous chemicals that are not necessary for normal cellular functioning that significantly alter the functions of certain cells of the body when taken in relatively low doses. Drugs have *effects,* physiological and behavioral, and they have *sites of action*—molecules with which they interact to produce these effects.

Pharmacokinetics is the fate of a drug as it is absorbed into the body, circulates throughout the body, and reaches its sites of action. Drugs may be administered by intravenous, intraperitoneal, intramuscular, and subcutaneous injection; they may be administered orally, sublingually, intrarectally, by inhalation, and topically (on skin or mucous membrane); and they may be injected intracerebrally or intracerebroventricularly. Lipid-soluble drugs easily pass through the blood–brain barrier, whereas others pass this barrier slowly or not at all.

The dose-response curve represents a drug's effectiveness; it relates the amount administered (usually in milligrams per kilogram of the subject's body weight) to the resulting effect. Most drugs have more than one site of action and therefore more than one effect. The safety of a drug is measured by the difference between doses that produce desirable effects and those that produce toxic side effects. Drugs vary in their effectiveness because of the nature of their sites of actions and the affinity between molecules of the drug and these sites of action.

Repeated administration of a drug can cause either tolerance, often resulting in withdrawal symptoms, or sensitization. Tolerance can be caused by decreased affinity of a drug with its receptors, by decreased numbers of receptors, or by decreased coupling of receptors with the biochemical steps it controls. Some of the effects of a drug may show tolerance, while others may not—or may even show sensitization.

Sites of Drug Action

Throughout the history of our species, people have discovered that plants—and a few animals—produce chemicals that act on synapses. (Of course, the people who discovered these chemicals knew nothing about neurons and synapses.) Some of these chemicals have been used for their pleasurable effects; others have been used to treat illness, reduce pain, or poison other animals (or enemies). More recently, scientists have learned to produce completely artificial drugs, some with potencies far greater than those of the naturally occurring ones. The traditional uses of drugs remain, but in addition, they can be used in research laboratories to investigate the operations of the nervous system. Most drugs that affect behavior do so by affecting synaptic transmission. Drugs that affect synaptic transmission are classified into two general categories. Those that block or inhibit the postsynaptic effects are called **antagonists.** Those that facilitate them are called **agonists.** (The Greek word *agon* means "contest." Thus, an *agonist* is one who takes part in the contest.)

This section will describe the basic effects of drugs on synaptic activity. Recall from Chapter 2 and Animation 2.3 that the sequence of synaptic activity goes like this: Neurotransmitters are synthesized and stored in synaptic vesicles. The synaptic vesicles travel to the presynaptic membrane, where they become docked. When an axon fires, voltage-dependent calcium channels in the presynaptic membrane open, permitting the entry of calcium ions. The calcium ions initiate the release of the neurotransmitters into the synaptic cleft. Molecules of the neurotransmitter bind with postsynaptic receptors, causing particular ion channels to open, which produces excitatory or inhibitory postsynaptic potentials. The effects of the neurotransmitter are kept relatively brief by their reuptake by transporter molecules in the presynaptic membrane or by their destruction by enzymes. In addition, the stimulation of presynaptic autoreceptors regulates the synthesis and release of the neurotransmitter. The discussion of the effects of drugs in this section follows the same basic sequence. All of the effects I will describe are summarized in Figure 4.4, with some details shown in additional figures. I should warn you that some of the effects are complex, so the discussion that follows bears careful reading. I recommend that you study ***Animation 4.1, Actions of Drugs,*** which reviews this material.

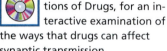

See Animation 4.1, Actions of Drugs, for an interactive examination of the ways that drugs can affect synaptic transmission.

Effects on Production of Neurotransmitters

The first step is the synthesis of the neurotransmitter from its precursors. In some cases the rate of synthesis and release of a neurotransmitter is increased when a precursor is administered; in these cases the precursor itself serves as an agonist. (See step 1 in ***Figure 4.4.***)

The steps in the synthesis of neurotransmitters are controlled by enzymes. Therefore, if a drug inactivates one of these enzymes, it will prevent the neurotransmitter from being produced. Such a drug serves as an antagonist. (See step 2 in ***Figure 4.4.***)

Effects on Storage and Release of Neurotransmitters

Neurotransmitters are stored in synaptic vesicles, which are transported to the presynaptic membrane, where the chemicals are released. The storage of neurotransmitters in vesicles is accomplished by the same kind of transporter molecules that are responsible for reuptake of a neurotransmitter into a terminal button. The transporter molecules are located in the membrane of synaptic vesicles, and their action is to pump molecules of the neurotransmitter across the membrane, filling the vesicles. Some of the transporter molecules that fill synaptic vesicles are capable of being blocked by a drug. Molecules of the drug bind with a particular site on the transporter and inactivate it. Because the synaptic vesicles remain empty, nothing is released when the vesicles eventually rupture against the presynaptic membrane. The drug serves as an antagonist. (See step 3 in ***Figure 4.4.***)

antagonist A drug that opposes or inhibits the effects of a particular neurotransmitter on the postsynaptic cell.

agonist A drug that facilitates the effects of a particular neurotransmitter on the postsynaptic cell.

Some drugs act as antagonists by preventing the release of neurotransmitters from the terminal button. They do so by deactivating the proteins that cause synap-

Figure 4.4

A summary of the ways in which drugs can affect the synaptic transmission (AGO = agonist; ANT = antagonist; NT = neurotransmitter). Drugs that act as agonists are marked in blue; drugs that act as antagonists are marked in red.

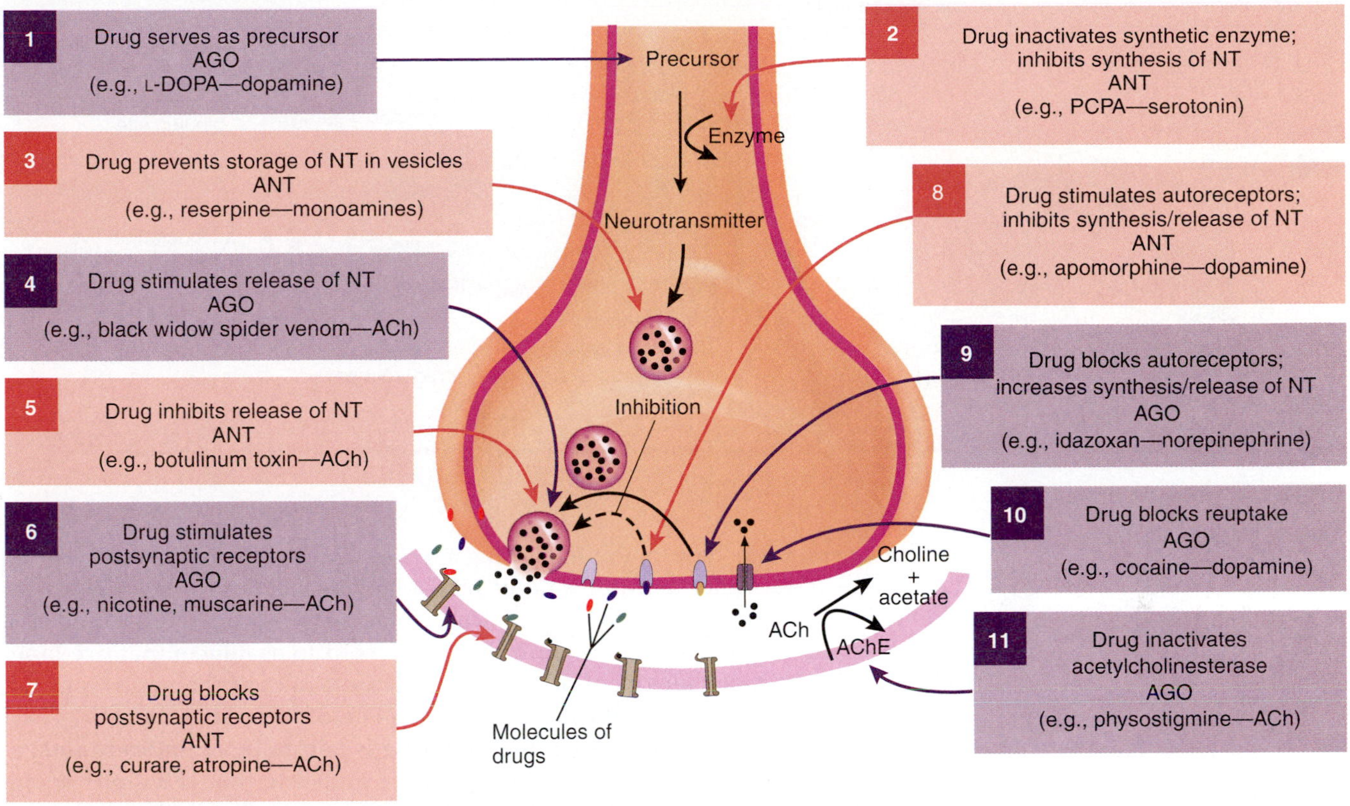

tic vesicles to fuse with the presynaptic membrane and expel their contents into the synaptic cleft. Other drugs have just the opposite effect: They act as agonists by binding with these proteins and directly triggering release of the neurotransmitter. (See steps 4 and 5 in *Figure 4.4.*)

Effects on Receptors

The most important—and most complex—site of action of drugs in the nervous system is on receptors, both presynaptic and postsynaptic. Let's consider postsynaptic receptors first. (Here is where the careful reading should begin.) Once a neurotransmitter is released, it must stimulate the postsynaptic receptors. Some drugs bind with these receptors, just as the neurotransmitter does. Once a drug has bound with the receptor, it can serve as either an agonist or an antagonist.

A drug that mimics the effects of a neurotransmitter acts as a **direct agonist.** Molecules of the drug attach to the binding site to which the neurotransmitter normally attaches. This binding causes ion channels controlled by the receptor to open, just as they do when the neurotransmitter is present. Ions then pass through these channels and produce postsynaptic potentials. (See step 6 in *Figure 4.4.*)

Drugs that bind with postsynaptic receptors can also serve as antagonists. Molecules of such drugs bind with the receptors but do not open the ion channel. Because they occupy the receptor's binding site, they prevent the neurotransmitter from opening the ion channel. These drugs are called **receptor blockers** or **direct antagonists.** (See step 7 in *Figure 4.4.*)

direct agonist A drug that binds with and activates a receptor.

receptor blocker A drug that binds with a receptor but does not activate it; prevents the natural ligand from binding with the receptor.

direct antagonist A synonym for receptor blocker.

Figure 4.5

Actions of drugs at binding sites on receptors. (a) Competitive binding. Direct agonists and antagonists act directly on the neurotransmitter binding site. (b) Noncompetitive binding. Indirect agonists and antagonists act on an alternative binding site and modify the effects of the neurotransmitter on opening of the ion channel.

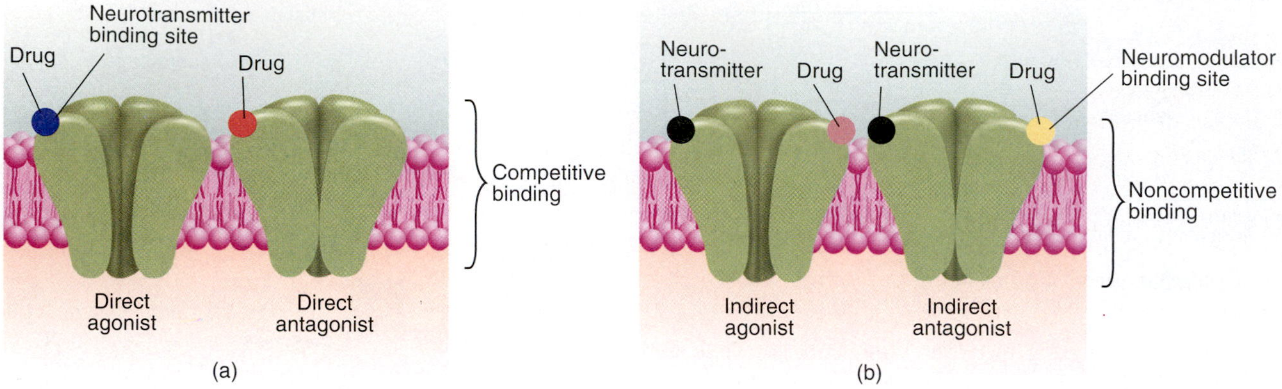

Some receptors have multiple binding sites, to which different ligands can attach. Molecules of the neurotransmitter bind with one site, and other substances (such as neuromodulators and various drugs) bind with the others. Binding of a molecule with one of these alternative sites is referred to as **noncompetitive binding,** because the molecule does not compete with molecules of the neurotransmitter for the same binding site. If a drug attaches to one of these alternative sites and prevents the ion channel from opening, the drug is said to be an **indirect antagonist.** The ultimate *effect* of an indirect antagonist is similar to that of a direct antagonist, but its site of action is different. If a drug attaches to one of the alternative sites and *facilitates* the opening of the ion channel, it is said to be an **indirect agonist.** (See ***Figure 4.5.***)

As we saw in Chapter 2, the presynaptic membranes of some neurons contain autoreceptors that regulate the amount of neurotransmitter that is released. Because stimulation of these receptors causes less neurotransmitter to be released, drugs that selectively activate presynaptic receptors act as antagonists. Drugs that *block* presynaptic autoreceptors have the opposite effect: They *increase* the release of the neurotransmitter, acting as agonists. (Refer to steps 8 and 9 in ***Figure 4.4.***)

noncompetitive binding Binding of a drug to a site on a receptor; does not interfere with the binding site for the principal ligand.

indirect antagonist A drug that attaches to a binding site on a receptor and interferes with the action of the receptor; does not interfere with the binding site for the principal ligand.

indirect agonist A drug that attaches to a binding site on a receptor and facilitates the action of the receptor; does not interfere with the binding site for the principal ligand.

Effects on Reuptake or Destruction of Neurotransmitter

The next step after stimulation of the postsynaptic receptor is termination of the postsynaptic potential. Two processes accomplish that task: Molecules of the neurotransmitter are taken back into the terminal button through the process of reuptake, or they are destroyed by an enzyme. Drugs can interfere with either of these processes. In the first case molecules of the drug attach to the transporter molecules that are responsible for reuptake and inactivate them, thus blocking reuptake. In the second case molecules of the drug bind with the enzyme that normally destroys the neurotransmitter and prevents the enzymes from working. The most important example of such an enzyme is acetylcholinesterase, which destroys acetylcholine. Because both types of drugs prolong the presence of the neurotransmitter in the synaptic cleft (and hence in a location where they can stimulate postsynaptic receptors), they serve as *agonists.* (Refer to steps 10 and 11 in ***Figure 4.4.***)

INTERIM SUMMARY

Sites of Drug Action

The process of synaptic transmission entails the synthesis of the neurotransmitter, its storage in synaptic vesicles, its release into the synaptic cleft, its interaction with postsynaptic receptors, and the consequent opening of ion channels in the postsynaptic membrane. The effects of the neurotransmitter are then terminated by reuptake into the terminal button or by enzymatic deactivation.

Each of the steps necessary for synaptic transmission can be interfered with by drugs that serve as *antagonists,* and a few of these steps can be stimulated by drugs that serve as *agonists.* In particular, drugs can increase the pool of available precursor, block a biosynthetic enzyme, prevent the storage of neurotransmitter in the synaptic vesicles, stimulate or block the release of the neurotransmitter, stimulate or block presynaptic or postsynaptic receptors, retard reuptake, or deactivate enzymes that destroy the neurotransmitter postsynaptically or presynaptically. A drug that activates postsynaptic receptors serves as an agonist, whereas one that activates presynaptic autoreceptors serves as an antagonist. A drug that blocks postsynaptic receptors serves as an antagonist, whereas one that blocks autoreceptors serves as an agonist.

Neurotransmitters and Neuromodulators

Because neurotransmitters have two general effects on postsynaptic membranes—depolarization (EPSP) or hyperpolarization (IPSP)—one might expect that there would be two kinds of neurotransmitters, excitatory and inhibitory. Instead, there are many different kinds—several dozen, at least. In the brain most synaptic communication is accomplished by two neurotransmitters: one with excitatory effects (glutamate) and one with inhibitory effects (GABA). (Another inhibitory neurotransmitter, glycine, is found in the spinal cord and lower brain stem.) Most of the activity of local circuits of neurons involves balances between the excitatory and inhibitory effects of these chemicals, which are responsible for most of the information transmitted from place to place within the brain. In fact, there are probably no neurons in the brain that do not receive excitatory input from glutamate-secreting terminal buttons and inhibitory input from neurons that secrete either GABA or glycine. And with the exception of neurons that detect painful stimuli, all sensory organs transmit information to the brain through axons whose terminals release glutamate. (Pain-detecting neurons secrete a peptide.)

What do all the other neurotransmitters do? In general, they have modulating effects rather than information-transmitting effects. That is, the release of neurotransmitters other than glutamate and GABA tends to activate or inhibit entire circuits of neurons that are involved in particular brain functions. For example, secretion of acetylcholine activates the cerebral cortex and facilitates learning, but the information that is learned and remembered is transmitted by neurons that secrete glutamate and GABA. Secretion of norepinephrine increases vigilance and enhances readiness to act when a signal is detected. Secretion of serotonin suppresses certain categories of species-typical behaviors and reduces the likelihood that the animal acts impulsively. Secretion of dopamine in some regions of the brain generally activates voluntary movements but does not specify which movements will occur. In other regions secretion of dopamine reinforces ongoing behaviors and makes them more likely to occur at a later time. Because particular drugs can selectively affect neurons that secrete particular neurotransmitters, they can have specific effects on behavior.

acetyl-CoA (*a* ***see*** *tul*) A cofactor that supplies acetate for the synthesis of acetylcholine.

choline acetyltransferase (ChAT) (***koh*** *leen a see tul* ***trans*** *fer ace*) The enzyme that transfers the acetate ion from acetyl coenzyme A to choline, producing the neurotransmitter acetylcholine.

botulinum toxin (*bot you* ***lin*** *um*) An acetylcholine antagonist; prevents release by terminal buttons.

black widow spider venom A poison produced by the black widow spider that triggers the release of acetylcholine.

neostigmine (*nee o* ***stig*** *meen*) A drug that inhibits the activity of acetylcholinesterase.

nicotinic receptor An ionotropic acetylcholine receptor that is stimulated by nicotine and blocked by curare.

muscarinic receptor (*muss ka* ***rin*** *ic*) A metabotropic acetylcholine receptor that is stimulated by muscarine and blocked by atropine.

This section introduces the most important neurotransmitters, discusses some of their behavioral functions, and describes the drugs that interact with them. As we saw in the previous section of this chapter, drugs have many different sites of action. Fortunately for your information-processing capacity (and perhaps your sanity), not all types of neurons are affected by all types of drugs. As you will see, that still leaves a good number of drugs to be mentioned by name. Obviously, some are more important than others. Those whose effects I describe in some detail are more important than those I mention in passing. If you want to learn more details about these drugs (and many others), you should consult an up-to-date psychopharmacology text.

Acetylcholine

Acetylcholine is the primary neurotransmitter secreted by efferent axons of the central nervous system. All muscular movement is accomplished by the release of acetylcholine, and ACh is also found in the ganglia of the autonomic nervous system and at the target organs of the parasympathetic branch of the ANS. Because ACh is found outside the central nervous system in locations that are easy to study, this neurotransmitter was the first to be discovered, and it has received much attention from neuroscientists. Some terminology: These synapses are said to be *acetylcholinergic. Ergon* is the Greek word for "work." Thus, *dopaminergic* synapses release dopamine, *serotonergic* synapses release serotonin, and so on. (The suffix *-ergic* is pronounced "***ur*** *jik.*")

The axons and terminal buttons of acetylcholinergic neurons are distributed widely throughout the brain. Three systems have received the most attention from neuroscientists: those originating in the dorsolateral pons, the basal forebrain, and the medial septum. The effects of ACh released in the brain are generally facilitatory. The acetylcholinergic neurons located in the dorsolateral pons are responsible for eliciting most of the characteristics of REM sleep (the phase of sleep during which dreaming occurs). Those located in the basal forebrain are involved in activating the cerebral cortex and facilitating learning, especially perceptual learning. Those located in the medial septum control the electrical rhythms of the hippocampus and modulate its functions, which include the formation of particular kinds of memories.

Acetylcholine is composed of two components: *choline,* a substance derived from the breakdown of lipids, and *acetate,* the anion found in vinegar, also called acetic acid. Acetate cannot be attached directly to choline; instead, it is transferred from a molecule of *acetyl-CoA*. CoA (coenzyme A) is a complex molecule, consisting in part of the vitamin pantothenic acid (one of the B vitamins). CoA is produced by the mitochondria, and it takes part in many reactions in the body. **Acetyl-CoA** is simply CoA with an acetate ion attached to it. ACh is produced by the following reaction: In the presence of the enzyme **choline acetyltransferase (ChAT),** the acetate ion is transferred from the acetyl-CoA molecule to the choline molecule, yielding a molecule of ACh and one of ordinary CoA. (See ***Figure 4.6.***)

Figure 4.6

The biosynthesis of acetylcholine.

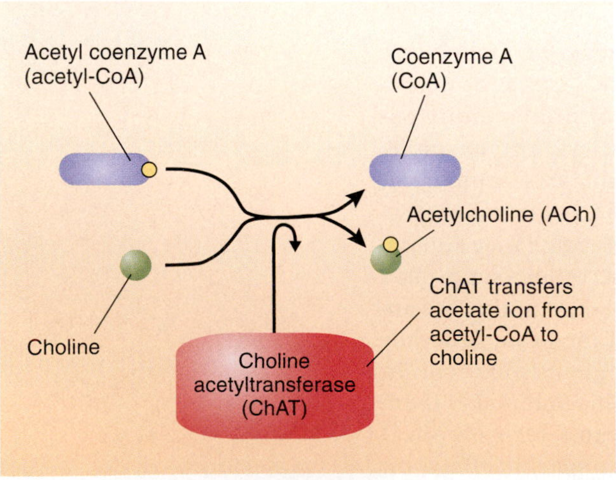

A simple analogy will illustrate the role of coenzymes in chemical reactions. Think of acetate as a hot dog and choline as a bun. The task of the person (enzyme) who operates the hot dog vending stand is to put a hot dog into the bun (make acetylcholine). To do so, the vendor needs a fork (coenzyme) to remove the hot dog from the boiling water. The vendor inserts the fork into the hot dog (attaches acetate to CoA) and transfers the hot dog from fork to bun.

Two drugs, botulinum toxin and the venom of the black widow spider, affect the release of acetylcholine. **Botulinum toxin** is produced by *clostridium botulinum,* a bacterium that can grow in improperly canned food. This drug prevents the release of ACh (step 5 of Figure 4.4). The drug is an extremely potent poison; someone once calculated that a teaspoonful of pure botulinum toxin could kill the world's entire human population. You undoubtedly know that *botox* treatment has become fashionable. A dilute (obviously!) solution of botulinum toxin is injected into people's facial muscles to stop muscular contractions that are causing wrinkles. In contrast, **black widow spider venom** has the opposite effect: It stimulates the release of ACh (step 4 of Figure 4.4). Although the effects of black widow spider venom can also be fatal, the venom is much less toxic than botulinum toxin. In fact, most healthy adults would have to receive several bites, but infants or frail, elderly people would be more susceptible.

You will recall from Chapter 2 that after being released by the terminal button, ACh is deactivated by the enzyme acetylcholinesterase (AChE), which is present in the postsynaptic membrane. (See ***Figure 4.7.***)

Figure 4.7

The destruction of acetylcholine by acetylcholinesterase.

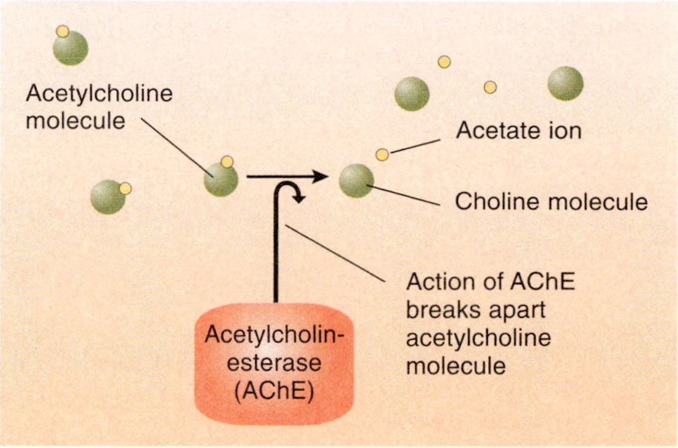

Drugs that deactivate AChE (step 11 of Figure 4.4) are used for several purposes. Some are used as insecticides. These drugs readily kill insects but not humans and other mammals, because our blood contains enzymes that destroy them. (Insects lack the enzyme.) Other AChE inhibitors are used medically. For example, a hereditary disorder called *myasthenia gravis* is caused by an attack of a person's immune system against acetylcholine receptors located on skeletal muscles. The person becomes weaker and weaker as the muscles become less responsive to the neurotransmitter. If the person is given an AChE inhibitor such as **neostigmine,** the person will regain some strength, because the acetylcholine that is released has a more prolonged effect on the remaining receptors. (Fortunately, neostigmine cannot cross the blood–brain barrier, so it does not affect the AChE found in the central nervous system.)

There are two different types of ACh receptors—one ionotropic and one metabotropic. These receptors were identified when investigators discovered that different drugs activated them (step 6 of Figure 4.4). The ionotropic ACh receptor is stimulated by nicotine, a drug found in tobacco leaves. (The Latin name of the plant is *Nicotiniana tabacum.*) The metabotropic ACh receptor is stimulated by muscarine, a drug found in the poison mushroom *Amanita muscaria.* Consequently, these two ACh receptors are referred to as **nicotinic receptors** and **muscarinic receptors,** respectively. Because muscle fibers must be able to contract rapidly, they contain the rapid, ionotropic nicotinic receptors.

Amanita muscaria, a colorful mushroom, is the source of muscarine, a drug that stimulates muscarinic acetylcholine receptors.

Because muscarinic receptors are metabotropic in nature and thus control ion channels through the production of second messengers, their actions are slower and more prolonged than those of nicotinic receptors. The central nervous system contains both kinds of ACh receptors, but muscarinic receptors predominate. Some nicotinic receptors are found at axoaxonic synapses in the brain, where they produce presynaptic facilitation.

Just as two different drugs stimulate the two classes of acetylcholine receptors, two different drugs *block* them (step 7 of Figure 4.4). Both drugs were discovered in nature long ago, and both are still used by modern medicine. The first,

atropine (*a* tro peen) A drug that blocks muscarinic acetylcholine receptors.

curare (*kew* **rahr** *ee*) A drug that blocks nicotinic acetylcholine receptors.

monoamine (**mahn** *o a meen*) A class of amines that includes indolamines such as serotonin and catecholamines such as dopamine, norepinephrine, and epinephrine.

catecholamine (*cat a* **kohl** *a meen*) A class of amines that includes the neurotransmitters dopamine, norepinephrine, and epinephrine.

dopamine (DA) (**dope** *a meen*) A neurotransmitter; one of the catecholamines.

L-DOPA (*ell* **dope** *a*) The levorotatory form of DOPA; the precursor of the catecholamines; often used to treat Parkinson's disease because of its effect as a dopamine agonist.

nigrostriatal system (*nigh grow stry* **ay** *tul*) A system of neurons originating in the substantia nigra and terminating in the neostriatum (caudate nucleus and putamen).

mesolimbic system (*mee zo* **lim** *bik*) A system of dopaminergic neurons originating in the ventral tegmental area and terminating in the nucleus accumbens, amygdala, and hippocampus.

mesocortical system (*mee zo* **kor** *ti kul*) A system of dopaminergic neurons originating in the ventral tegmental area and terminating in the prefrontal cortex.

Parkinson's disease A neurological disease characterized by tremors, rigidity of the limbs, poor balance, and difficulty in initiating movements; caused by degeneration of the nigrostriatal system.

atropine, blocks muscarinic receptors. The drug is named after Atropos, the Greek fate who cut the thread of life (which a sufficient dose of atropine will certainly do). Atropine is one of several *belladonna alkaloids* extracted from a plant called the deadly nightshade, and therein lies a tale. Many years ago, women who wanted to increase their attractiveness to men put drops containing belladonna alkaloids into their eyes. In fact, *belladonna* means "pretty lady." Why was the drug used this way? One of the unconscious responses that occurs when we are interested in something is dilation of our pupils. By blocking the effects of acetylcholine on the pupil, belladonna alkaloids such as atropine make the pupils dilate. This change makes a woman appear more interested in a man when she looks at him, and, of course, this apparent sign of interest makes him regard her as more attractive.

Another drug, **curare,** blocks nicotinic receptors. Because these receptors are the ones found on muscles, curare, like botulinum toxin, causes paralysis. However, the effects of curare are much faster. The drug is extracted from several different species of plants found in South America, where it was discovered long ago by people who used it to coat the tips of arrows and darts. Within minutes of being struck by one of these points, an animal collapses, ceases breathing, and dies. Nowadays, curare (and other drugs with the same site of action) are used to paralyze patients who are to undergo surgery so that their muscles will relax completely and not contract when they are cut with a scalpel. An anesthetic must also be used, because a person who receives only curare will remain perfectly conscious and sensitive to pain, even though paralyzed. And, of course, a respirator must be used to supply air to the lungs.

The Monoamines

Epinephrine, norepinephrine, dopamine, and serotonin are four chemicals that belong to a family of compounds called **monoamines.** Because the molecular structures of these substances are similar, some drugs affect the activity of all of them to some degree. The first three—epinephrine, norepinephrine, and dopamine—belong to a subclass of monoamines called **catecholamines.** It is worthwhile learning the terms in Table 4.1, because they will be used many times throughout the rest of this book. (See ***Table 4.1.***)

The monoamines are produced by several systems of neurons in the brain. Most of these systems consist of a relatively small number of cell bodies located in the brain stem, whose axons branch repeatedly and give rise to an enormous number of terminal buttons distributed throughout many regions of the brain. Monoaminergic neurons thus serve to modulate the function of widespread regions of the brain, increasing or decreasing the activities of particular brain functions.

Dopamine

The first catecholamine in Table 4.1, **dopamine (DA),** produces both excitatory and inhibitory postsynaptic potentials, depending on the postsynaptic receptor. Dopamine is one of the more interesting neurotransmitters because it has been implicated in several important functions, including movement, attention, learning, and the reinforcing effects of drugs that people tend to abuse; therefore, it is discussed in Chapters 12, 14, 15, and 16.

Table 4.1

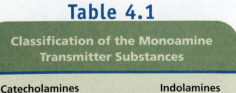

Classification of the Monoamine Transmitter Substances

Catecholamines	Indolamines
Dopamine	Serotonin
Norepinephrine	
Epinephrine	

The synthesis of the catecholamines is somewhat more complicated than that of ACh, but each step is a simple one. The precursor molecule is modified slightly, step by step, until it achieves its final shape. Each step is controlled by a different enzyme, which causes a small part to be added or taken off. The precursor for the two major catecholamine neurotransmitters (dopamine and norepinephrine) is *tyrosine,* an essential amino acid that we must obtain from our diet. An enzyme converts tyrosine into **L-DOPA.** Another enzyme converts L-DOPA into dopamine. In dopaminergic neurons, that conversion

Amines found in foods such as cheese would be toxic, but they are deactivated by the monoamine oxidase found in the blood.

is the last step, but in noradrenergic neurons, dopamine is converted into norepinephrine. These reactions are shown in ***Figure 4.8.***

The brain contains several systems of dopaminergic neurons. The three most important of these originate in the midbrain. The cell bodies of neurons of the **nigrostriatal system** are located in the substantia nigra and project their axons to the neostriatum: the caudate nucleus and the putamen. The neostriatum is an important part of the basal ganglia, involved in the control of movement. The cell bodies of neurons of the **mesolimbic system** are located in the ventral tegmental area and project their axons to several parts of the limbic system, including the nucleus accumbens, amygdala, and hippocampus. (The term *meso-* refers to the midbrain, or mesencephalon.) The nucleus accumbens plays an important role in the reinforcing (rewarding) effects of certain categories of stimuli, including those of drugs that people abuse. The cell bodies of neurons of the **mesocortical system** are also located in the ventral tegmental area. Their axons project to the prefrontal cortex. These neurons have an excitatory effect on the frontal cortex and thus affect such functions as formation of short-term memories, planning, and strategy preparation for problem solving. (See ***Table 4.2.***)

Degeneration of dopaminergic neurons that connect the substantia nigra with the caudate nucleus causes **Parkinson's disease,** a movement disorder characterized by tremors, rigidity of the limbs, poor balance, and difficulty in initiating movements. The cell bodies of these neurons are located in a region of the brain called the *substantia nigra* ("black substance"). This region is normally stained black with melanin, the substance that gives color to skin. This compound is produced by the breakdown of dopamine. (The brain damage that causes Parkinson's disease was discovered by pathologists who observed that the substantia nigra of a deceased person who had had this disorder was pale rather than black.) People with Parkinson's disease are given L-DOPA, the precursor to dopamine. Although dopamine cannot cross the blood–brain barrier, L-DOPA can. Once L-DOPA reaches the brain, it is taken up by dopaminergic neurons and is converted to dopamine (step 1

Figure 4.8

Biosynthesis of the catecholamines.

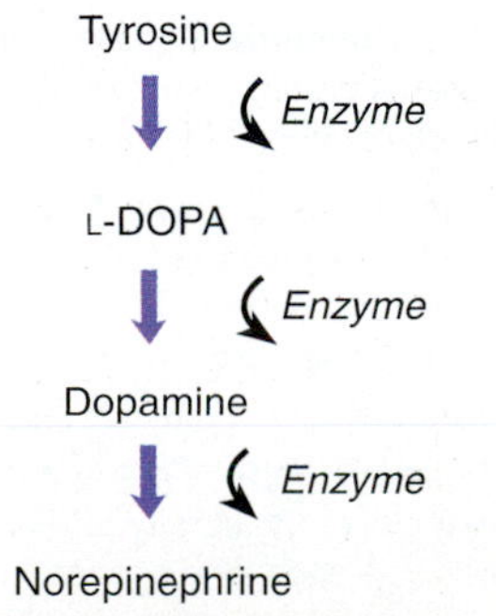

Table 4.2

The Three Major Dopaminergic Pathways

Name	Origin (Location of Cell Bodies)	Location of Terminal Buttons	Behavioral Effects
Nigrostriatal system	Substantia nigra	Neostriatum (caudate nucleus and putamen)	Control of movement
Mesolimbic system	Ventral tegmental area	Nucleus accumbens and amygdala	Reinforcement, effects of addictive drugs
Mesocortical system	Ventral tegmental area	Prefrontal cortex	Short-term memories, planning, strategies for problem solving

of Figure 4.4). The increased synthesis of dopamine causes more dopamine to be released by the surviving dopaminergic neurons in patients with Parkinson's disease. As a consequence, the patients' symptoms are alleviated.

Another drug, **AMPT** (or α-methyl-*p*-tyrosine), inactivates tyrosine hydroxylase, the enzyme that converts tyrosine to L-DOPA (step 2 of Figure 4.4). Because this drug interferes with the synthesis of dopamine (and of norepinephrine, as well), it serves as a catecholamine antagonist. The drug is not normally used medically, but it has been used as a research tool in laboratory animals.

The drug **reserpine** prevents the storage of monoamines in synaptic vesicles by blocking the transporters in the membrane that pump monoamines into the vesicles (step 3 of Figure 4.4). Because the synaptic vesicles remain empty, no neurotransmitter is released when an action potential reaches the terminal button. Reserpine, then, is a monoamine antagonist. The drug, which comes from the root of a shrub, was discovered over three thousand years ago in India, where it was found to be useful in treating snakebite and seemed to have a calming effect. Pieces of the root are still sold in markets in rural areas of India. In Western medicine reserpine was previously used to treat high blood pressure, but it has been replaced by drugs with fewer side effects.

Several different types of dopamine receptors have been identified, all metabotropic. Of these, two are the most common: *D_1 dopamine receptors* and *D_2 dopamine receptors*. It appears that D_1 receptors are exclusively postsynaptic, whereas D_2 receptors are found both presynaptically and postsynaptically in the brain. Several drugs stimulate or block specific types of dopamine receptors.

Several drugs inhibit the reuptake of dopamine, thus serving as potent dopamine agonists (step 10 of Figure 4.4). The best known of these drugs are amphetamine, cocaine, and methylphenidate. Amphetamine has an interesting effect: It causes the release of both dopamine and norepinephrine by causing the transporters for these neurotransmitters to run in reverse, propelling DA and NE into the synaptic cleft. Of course, this action also blocks reuptake of these neurotransmitters. Cocaine and **methylphenidate** simply block dopamine reuptake. Because cocaine also blocks voltage-dependent sodium channels, it is sometimes used as a topical anesthetic, especially in the form of eye drops for eye surgery. Methylphenidate (Ritalin) is used to treat children with attention deficit disorder.

The production of the catecholamines is regulated by an enzyme called **monoamine oxidase (MAO).** This enzyme is found within monoaminergic terminal buttons, where it destroys excessive amounts of neurotransmitter. A drug called **deprenyl** destroys the particular form of monoamine oxidase (MAO-B) that is found

AMPT A drug that blocks the activity of tyrosine hydroxylase and thus interferes with the synthesis of the catecholamines.

reserpine (*ree **sur** peen*) A drug that interferes with the storage of monoamines in synaptic vesicles.

methylphenidate (*meth ul **fen** i date*) A drug that inhibits the reuptake of dopamine.

monoamine oxidase (MAO) (***mahn** o a meen*) A class of enzymes that destroy the monoamines: dopamine, norepinephrine, and serotonin.

deprenyl (***depp** ra nil*) A drug that blocks the activity of MAO-B; acts as a dopamine agonist.

Figure 4.9

The role of monoamine oxidase in dopaminergic terminal buttons and the action of deprenyl.

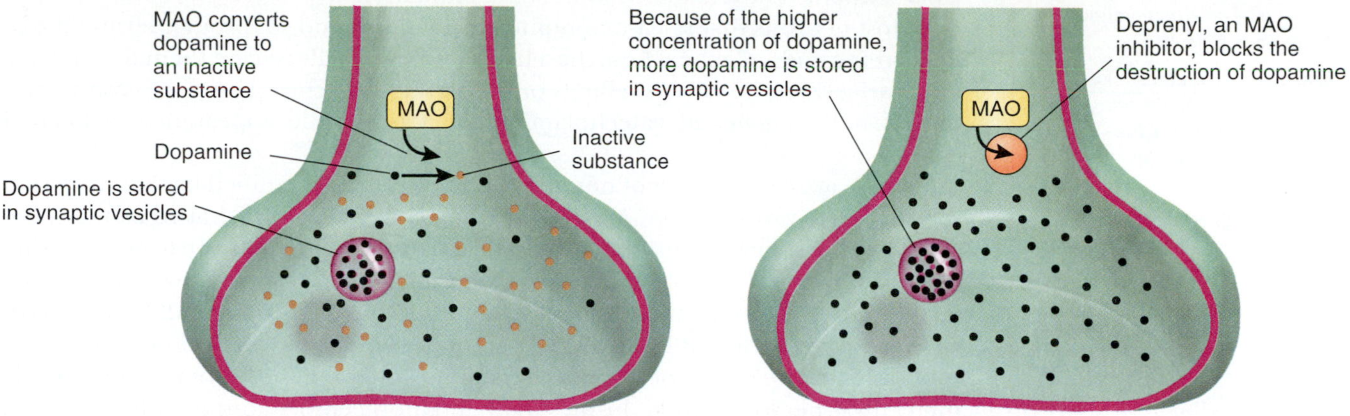

in dopaminergic terminal buttons. Because deprenyl prevents the destruction of dopamine, more dopamine is released when an action potential reaches the terminal button. Thus, deprenyl serves as a dopamine agonist. (See ***Figure 4.9.***)

MAO is also found in the blood, where it deactivates amines that are present in foods such as chocolate and cheese; without such deactivation these amines could cause dangerous increases in blood pressure.

Dopamine has been implicated as a neurotransmitter that might be involved in schizophrenia, a serious mental disorder whose symptoms include hallucinations, delusions, and disruption of normal, logical thought processes. Drugs such as **chlorpromazine,** which block D_2 receptors, alleviate these symptoms (step 7 of Figure 4.4). Hence, investigators have speculated that schizophrenia is produced by overactivity of dopaminergic neurons. More recently discovered drugs, such as **clozapine,** may exert their therapeutic effects by blocking D_4 receptors. The physiology of schizophrenia is discussed in Chapter 15.

Norepinephrine

Because **norepinephrine (NE),** like ACh, is found in neurons in the autonomic nervous system, this neurotransmitter has received much experimental attention. I should note that the terms *Adrenalin* and *epinephrine* are synonymous, as are *noradrenalin* and *norepinephrine.* Let me explain why. **Epinephrine** is a hormone produced by the adrenal medulla, the central core of the adrenal glands, located just above the kidneys. Epinephrine also serves as a neurotransmitter in the brain, but it is of minor importance compared with norepinephrine. *Ad renal* is Latin for "toward kidney." In Greek, one would say *epi nephron* ("upon the kidney"), hence the term *epinephrine.* The latter term has been adopted by pharmacologists, probably because the word *Adrenalin* was appropriated by a drug company as a proprietary name; therefore, to be consistent with general usage, I will refer to the neurotransmitter as *norepinephrine.* The accepted adjectival form is *noradrenergic;* I suppose that *norepinephrinergic* never caught on because it takes so long to pronounce.

We have already seen the biosynthetic pathway for norepinephrine in Figure 4.8. The drug **fusaric acid,** which prevents the conversion of dopamine to norepinephrine, blocks the production of NE.

Almost every region of the brain receives input from noradrenergic neurons. The cell bodies of most of these neurons are located in seven regions of the pons and medulla and one region of the thalamus. The cell bodies of the most important noradrenergic system begin in the **locus coeruleus,** a nucleus located in the dorsal

chlorpromazine (*klor* ***proh*** *ma zeen*) A drug that reduces the symptoms of schizophrenia by blocking dopamine D_2 receptors.

clozapine (***kloz*** *a peen*) A drug that reduces the symptoms of schizophrenia, apparently by blocking dopamine D_4 receptors.

norepinephrine (NE) (*nor epp i* ***neff*** *rin*) One of the catecholamines; a neurotransmitter found in the brain and in the sympathetic division of the autonomic nervous system.

epinephrine (*epp i* ***neff*** *rin*) One of the catecholamines; a hormone secreted by the adrenal medulla; serves also as a neurotransmitter in the brain.

fusaric acid (*few* ***sahr*** *ik*) A drug that inhibits the activity of the enzyme dopamine-β-hydroxylase and thus blocks the production of norepinephrine.

locus coeruleus (*sur* ***oo*** *lee us*) A dark-colored group of noradrenergic cell bodies located in the pons near the rostral end of the floor of the fourth ventricle.

axonal varicosity An enlarged region along the length of an axon that contains synaptic vesicles and releases a neurotransmitter or neuromodulator.

idazoxan A drug that blocks presynaptic noradrenergic α_2 receptors and hence acts as an agonist, stimulating the synthesis and release of NE.

serotonin (5-HT) (*sair a* ***toe*** *nin*) An indolamine neurotransmitter; also called 5-hydroxytryptamine.

PCPA A drug that inhibits the activity of tryptophan hydroxylase and thus interferes with the synthesis of 5-HT.

fluoxetine (*floo* ***ox*** *i teen*) A drug that inhibits the reuptake of 5-HT.

fenfluramine (*fen* ***fluor*** *i meen*) A drug that stimulates the release of 5-HT.

LSD A drug that stimulates 5-HT_{2A} receptors.

pons. The axons of these neurons project to widespread regions of the brain. As we will see in Chapter 8, one effect of activation of these neurons is an increase in vigilance—attentiveness to events in the environment.

Most neurons that release norepinephrine do not do so through terminal buttons on the ends of axonal branches. Instead, they usually release them through **axonal varicosities,** beadlike swellings of the axonal branches. These varicosities give the axonal branches of catecholaminergic neurons the appearance of beaded chains.

There are several types of noradrenergic receptors, identified by their differing sensitivities to various drugs. Actually, these receptors are usually called *adrenergic* receptors rather than *noradrenergic* receptors, because they are sensitive to epinephrine (Adrenalin) as well as norepinephrine. Neurons in the central nervous system contain β_1- and β_2-*adrenergic receptors* and α_1- and α_2-*adrenergic receptors.* All four kinds of receptors are also found in various organs of the body besides the brain and are responsible for the effects of the catecholamines when they act as hormones outside the central nervous system. In the brain all autoreceptors appear to be of the α_2 type. The drug **idazoxan** blocks α_2 autoreceptors and hence acts as an agonist. All adrenergic receptors are metabotropic, coupled to G proteins that control the production of second messengers.

Serotonin

The third monoamine neurotransmitter, **serotonin** (also called **5-HT,** or 5-hydroxytryptamine), has also received much experimental attention. Its behavioral effects are complex. Serotonin plays a role in the regulation of mood; in the control of eating, sleep, and arousal; and in the regulation of pain. Serotonergic neurons are involved somehow in the control of dreaming.

The precursor for serotonin is the amino acid *tryptophan.* An enzyme converts tryptophan to *5-HTP* (5-hydroxytryptophan). Another enzyme converts 5-HTP to 5-HT (serotonin). (See ***Figure 4.10.***) The drug **PCPA** (*p*-chlorophenylalanine) blocks the conversion of tryptophan to 5-HTP and thus serves as a serotonergic antagonist.

The cell bodies of serotonergic neurons are found in nine clusters, most of which are located in the raphe nuclei of the midbrain, pons, and medulla. The two most important clusters are found in the dorsal and medial raphe nuclei, and I will restrict my discussion to these clusters. The word *raphe* means "seam" or "crease" and refers to the fact that most of the raphe nuclei are found at or near the midline of the brain stem. Both the dorsal and median raphe nuclei project axons to the cerebral cortex. In addition, neurons in the dorsal raphe innervate the basal ganglia, and those in the median raphe innervate the dentate gyrus, a part of the hippocampal formation.

Investigators have identified at least nine different types of serotonin receptors, and pharmacologists have discovered drugs that serve as agonists or antagonists for many, of the types of 5-HT receptors.

Drugs that inhibit the reuptake of serotonin have found a very important place in the treatment of mental disorders. The best known of these, **fluoxetine** (Prozac), is used to treat depression, some forms of anxiety disorders, and obsessive-compulsive disorder. These disorders—and their treatment—are discussed in Chapters 15 and 16. Another drug, **fenfluramine,** which causes the release of serotonin as well as inhibits its reuptake, is used as an appetite suppressant in the treatment of obesity. Chapter 12 discusses the topic of obesity and its control by means of drugs.

Several hallucinogenic drugs appear to produce their effects by interacting with serotonergic transmission. **LSD** (lysergic acid diethylamide) produces distortions of visual perceptions that some people find awesome and fascinating but that simply frighten other people. This drug, which is effective in extremely small doses, is a direct agonist for postsynaptic 5-HT_{2A} receptors in the forebrain. Another drug,

Figure 4.10

Biosynthesis of serotonin (5-hydroxytryptamine, or 5-HT).

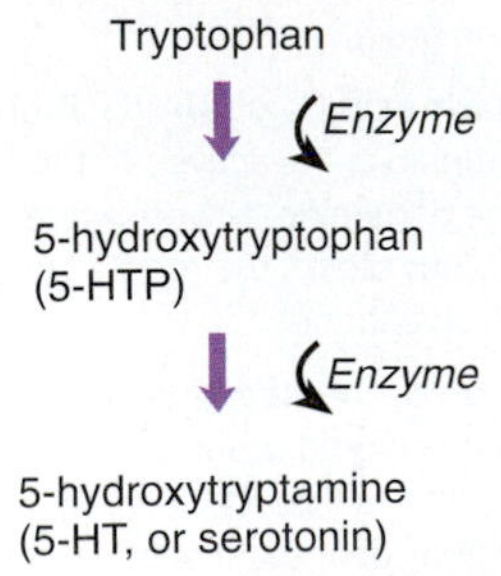

MDMA (methylenedioxymethamphetamine), is both a noradrenergic and serotonergic agonist and has both excitatory and hallucinogenic effects. Like its relative amphetamine, MDMA (popularly called "ecstasy") causes noradrenergic transporters to run backwards, this causing the release of NE and inhibiting its reuptake. This site of action is apparently responsible for the drug's excitatory effect. MDMA also causes serotonergic transporters to run backwards, and this site of action is apparently responsible for the drug's hallucinogenic effects. Unfortunately, research indicates that MDMA can damage serotonergic neurons and cause cognitive deficits.

Amino Acids

So far, all of the neurotransmitters I have described are synthesized within neurons: acetylcholine from choline, the catecholamines from the amino acid tyrosine, and serotonin from the amino acid tryptophan. Some neurons secrete simple amino acids as neurotransmitters. Because amino acids are used for protein synthesis by all cells of the brain, it is difficult to prove that a particular amino acid is a neurotransmitter. However, investigators suspect that at least eight amino acids may serve as neurotransmitters in the mammalian central nervous system. As we saw in the introduction to this section, three of them are especially important because they are the most common neurotransmitters in the CNS: glutamate, gamma-aminobutyric acid (GABA), and glycine.

Glutamate

Because **glutamate** (also called *glutamic acid*) and GABA are found in very simple organisms, many investigators believe that these neurotransmitters are the first to have evolved. Besides producing postsynaptic potentials by activating postsynaptic receptors, they also have direct excitatory effects (glutamic acid) and inhibitory effects (GABA) on axons; they raise or lower the threshold of excitation, thus affecting the rate at which action potentials occur. These direct effects suggest that these substances had a general modulating role even before the evolutionary development of specific receptor molecules.

Glutamate is the principal excitatory neurotransmitter in the brain and spinal cord. It is produced in abundance by the cells' metabolic processes. There is no effective way to prevent its synthesis without disrupting other activities of the cell.

Investigators have discovered four types of glutamate receptors. Three of these receptors are ionotropic and are named after the artificial ligands that stimulate them: the **NMDA receptor,** the **AMPA receptor,** and the **kainate receptor.** The other glutamate receptor—the **metabotropic glutamate receptor**—is (obviously!) metabotropic. Actually, there appear to be at least seven different metabotropic glutamate receptors, but little is known about their functions except that some of them serve as presynaptic autoreceptors. The AMPA receptor is the most common glutamate receptor. It controls a sodium channel, so when glutamate attaches to the binding site, it produces EPSPs. The kainate receptor, which is stimulated by the drug kainic acid, has similar effects.

The NMDA receptor has some special—and very important—characteristics. It contains at least six different binding sites: four located on the exterior of the receptor and two located deep within the ion channel. When it is open, the ion channel controlled by the NMDA receptor permits both sodium and calcium ions to enter the cell. The influx of both of these ions causes a depolarization, of course, but the entry of calcium (Ca^{2+}) is especially important. Calcium serves as a second messenger, binding with—and activating—various enzymes within the cell. These enzymes have profound effects on the biochemical and structural properties of the cell. As we shall see, one important result is alteration in the characteristics of the synapse that provide one of the building blocks of a newly formed memory. These

MDMA A drug that serves as a noradrenergic and serotonergic agonist, also known as "ecstasy"; has excitatory and hallucinogenic effects.

glutamate An amino acid; the most important excitatory neurotransmitter in the brain.

NMDA receptor A specialized ionotropic glutamate receptor that controls a calcium channel that is normally blocked by Mg^{2+} ions; has several other binding sites.

AMPA receptor An ionotropic glutamate receptor that controls a sodium channel; stimulated by AMPA.

kainate receptor (***kay*** *in ate*) An ionotropic glutamate receptor that controls a sodium channel; stimulated by kainic acid.

metabotropic glutamate receptor (*meh tab a* ***troh*** *pik*) A category of metabotropic receptors that are sensitive to glutamate.

Figure 4.11

A schematic illustration of an NMDA receptor, with its binding sites.

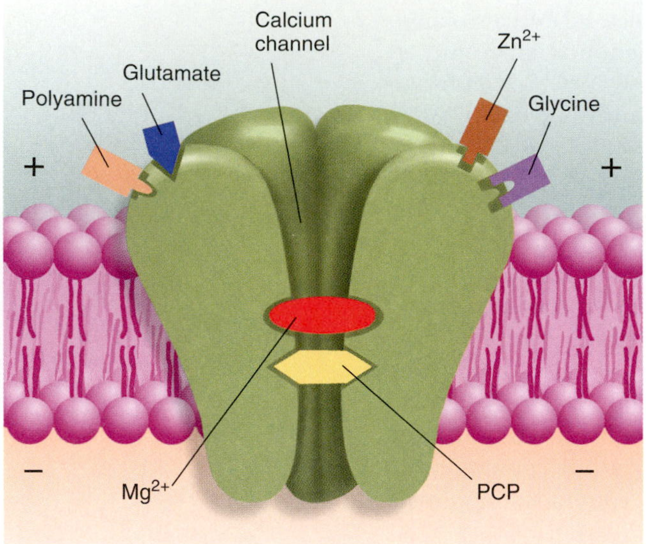

effects of NMDA receptors will be discussed in much more detail in Chapter 12. The drug **AP5** (2-amino-5-phosphonopentanoate) blocks the glutamate binding site on the NMDA receptor and impairs synaptic plasticity and certain forms of learning.

Figure 4.11 presents a schematic diagram of an NMDA receptor and its binding sites. Obviously, glutamate binds with one of these sites, or we would not call it a glutamate receptor. However, glutamate by itself cannot open the calcium channel. For that to happen, a molecule of glycine must be attached to the glycine binding site, located on the outside of the receptor. (We do not yet understand why glycine—which also serves as an inhibitory neurotransmitter in some parts of the central nervous system—is required for this ion channel to open.) (See ***Figure 4.11.***)

One of the six binding sites on the NMDA receptor is sensitive to alcohol. In fact, as we will see in Chapter 14, researchers believe that this binding site is responsible for the dangerous convulsions that can be caused by sudden withdrawal from heavy, long-term alcohol abuse. Another binding site is sensitive to a hallucinogenic drug, **PCP** (phencyclidine, also known as "angel dust"). PCP serves as an indirect antagonist; when it attaches to its binding site, calcium ions cannot pass through the ion channel. PCP is a synthetic drug and is not produced by the brain. Thus, it is not the natural ligand of the PCP binding site. What that ligand is and what useful functions it serves are not yet known.

Several drugs affect glutamatergic synapses. As you already know, NMDA, AMPA, and kainate serve as direct agonists at the receptors named after them.

GABA

GABA (gamma-aminobutyric acid) is produced from glutamic acid by the action of an enzyme (glutamic acid decarboxylase, or GAD) that removes a carboxyl group. The drug **allylglycine** inactivates GAD and thus prevents the synthesis of GABA (step 2 of Figure 4.4). GABA is an inhibitory neurotransmitter, and it appears to have a widespread distribution throughout the brain and spinal cord. Two GABA receptors have been identified: $GABA_A$ and $GABA_B$. The $GABA_A$ receptor is ionotropic and controls a chloride channel; the $GABA_B$ receptor is metabotropic and controls a potassium channel.

As you know, neurons in the brain are greatly interconnected. Without the activity of inhibitory synapses these interconnections would make the brain unstable. That is, through excitatory synapses neurons would excite their neighbors, which would then excite *their* neighbors, which would then excite the originally active neurons, and so on, until most of the neurons in the brain would be firing uncontrollably. In fact, this event does sometimes occur, and we refer to it as a *seizure.* (*Epilepsy* is a neurological disorder characterized by the presence of seizures.) Normally, an inhibitory influence is supplied by GABA-secreting neurons, which are present in large numbers in the brain. Some investigators believe that one of the causes of epilepsy is an abnormality in the biochemistry of GABA-secreting neurons or in GABA receptors.

Like NMDA receptors, $GABA_A$ receptors are complex; they contain at least five different binding sites. The primary binding site is, of course, for GABA. The drug **muscimol** (derived from the ACh agonist, muscarine) serves as a direct agonist for this site (step 6 of Figure 4.4). Another drug, **bicuculline,** blocks this GABA binding

AP5 (2-amino-5-phosphonopentanoate) A drug that blocks the glutamate binding site on NMDA receptors.

PCP Phencyclidine; a drug that binds with the PCP binding site of the NMDA receptor and serves as an indirect antagonist.

GABA An amino acid; the most important inhibitory neurotransmitter in the brain.

allylglycine A drug that inhibits the activity of GAD and thus blocks the synthesis of GABA.

muscimol (***musk*** *i mawl*) A direct agonist for the GABA binding site on the $GABA_A$ receptor.

bicuculline (*by* ***kew*** *kew leen*) A direct antagonist for the GABA binding site on the $GABA_A$ receptor.

site, serving as a direct antagonist (step 7 of Figure 4.4). A second site on the $GABA_A$ receptor binds with a class of tranquilizing drugs called the **benzodiazepines.** These drugs include diazepam (Valium) and chlordiazepoxide (Librium), which are used to reduce anxiety, promote sleep, reduce seizure activity, and produce muscle relaxation. The third site binds with barbiturates. The fourth site binds with various steroids, including some steroids used to produce general anesthesia. The fifth site binds with picrotoxin, a poison found in an East Indian shrub. In addition, alcohol binds with one of these sites—probably the benzodiazepine binding site. (See ***Figure 4.12.***)

Figure 4.12

A schematic illustration of a $GABA_A$ receptor, with its binding sites.

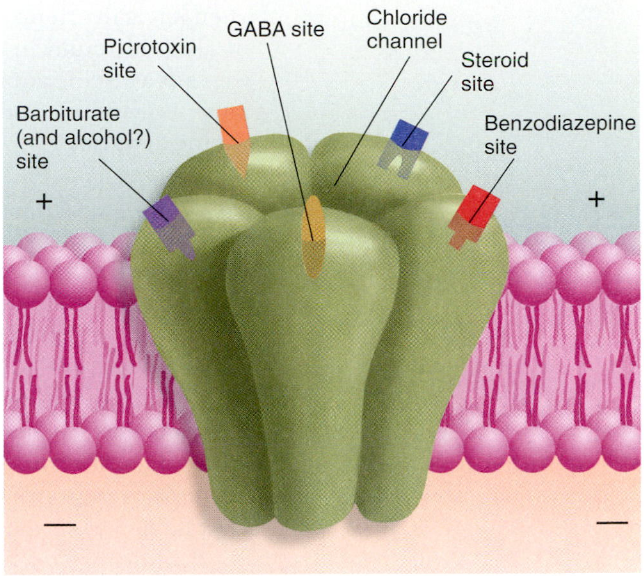

Barbiturates, drugs that bind to the steroid site, and benzodiazepines all promote the activity of the $GABA_A$ receptor; thus, all these drugs serve as indirect agonists. The benzodiazepines are very effective **anxiolytics,** or "anxiety-dissolving" drugs. They are often used to treat people with anxiety disorders. In addition, some benzodiazepines serve as effective sleep medications, and others are used to treat some types of seizure disorder.

In low doses barbiturates have a calming effect. In progressively higher doses they produce difficulty in walking and talking, unconsciousness, coma, and death. Although veterinarians sometimes use barbiturates to produce anesthesia for surgery, the therapeutic index—the ratio between a dose that produces anesthesia and one that causes fatal depression of the respiratory centers of the brain—is small. As a consequence, these drugs are rarely used by themselves to produce surgical anesthesia in humans.

Picrotoxin has effects opposite to those of benzodiazepines and barbiturates: It *inhibits* the activity of the $GABA_A$ receptor, thus serving as an indirect antagonist. In high enough doses this drug causes convulsions.

Various steroid hormones are normally produced in the body, and some hormones related to progesterone (the principal pregnancy hormone) act on the steroid binding site of the $GABA_A$ receptor, producing a sedative effect. However, the brain does not produce Valium, barbiturates, or picrotoxin. What are the natural ligands for these binding sites? So far, most research has concentrated on the benzodiazepine binding site. These binding sites are more complex than the others. They can be activated by drugs such as the benzodiazepines, which promote the activity of the receptor and thus serve as indirect agonists. They can also be activated by other drugs that have the opposite effect—that inhibit the activity of the receptor, thus serving as indirect antagonists. Presumably, the brain produces natural ligands that act as indirect agonists or antagonists at the benzodiazepine binding site, but so far, such a chemical has not been identified.

What about the $GABA_B$ receptor? This metabotropic receptor, coupled to a G protein, serves as both a postsynaptic receptor and a presynaptic autoreceptor. A $GABA_B$ agonist, baclofen, serves as a muscle relaxant. Another drug, CGP 335348, serves as an antagonist. The activation of $GABA_B$ receptors opens potassium channels, producing hyperpolarizing inhibitory postsynaptic potentials.

Glycine

The amino acid **glycine** appears to be the inhibitory neurotransmitter in the spinal cord and lower portions of the brain. Little is known about its biosynthetic pathway; there are several possible routes, but not enough is known to decide how neurons produce glycine. The bacteria that cause tetanus (lockjaw) release a

benzodiazepine (*ben zoe dy* ***azz*** *a peen*) A category of anxiolytic drugs; an indirect agonist for the $GABA_A$ receptor.

anxiolytic (*angz ee oh* ***lit*** *ik*) An anxiety-reducing effect.

glycine (***gly*** *seen*) An amino acid; an important inhibitory neurotransmitter in the lower brain stem and spinal cord.

chemical that prevents the release of glycine (and GABA as well); the removal of the inhibitory effect of these synapses causes muscles to contract continuously.

The glycine receptor is ionotropic, and it controls a chloride channel. Thus, when it is active, it produces inhibitory postsynaptic potentials. The drug **strychnine,** an alkaloid found in the seeds of the *Strychnos nux vomica,* a tree found in India, serves as a glycine antagonist. Strychnine is very toxic, and even relatively small doses cause convulsions and death. No drugs have yet been found that serve as specific glycine agonists.

Peptides

Recent studies have discovered that the neurons of the central nervous system release a large variety of peptides. Peptides consist of two or more amino acids linked together by peptide bonds. All the peptides that have been studied so far are produced from precursor molecules. These precursors are large polypeptides that are broken into pieces by special enzymes. A neuron manufactures both the polypeptides and the enzymes that it needs to break them apart in the right places. The appropriate sections are retained, and the other ones are destroyed. Because the synthesis of peptides takes place in the soma, vesicles containing these chemicals must be delivered to the terminal buttons by axoplasmic transport.

Peptides are released from all parts of the terminal button, not just from the active zone; thus, only a portion of the molecules are released into the synaptic cleft. The rest presumably act on receptors belonging to other cells in the vicinity. Once released, peptides are destroyed by enzymes. There is no mechanism for reuptake and recycling of peptides.

Several different peptides are released by neurons. Although most peptides appear to serve as neuromodulators, some act as neurotransmitters. One of the best known families of peptides is the **endogenous opioids.** (*Endogenous* means "produced from within"; *opioid* means "like opium.") Several years ago it became clear that opiates (drugs such as opium, morphine, and heroin) reduce pain because they have direct effects on the brain. (Please note that the term *opioid* refers to endogenous chemicals, and *opiate* refers to drugs.) Pert, Snowman, and Snyder (1974) discovered that neurons in a localized region of the brain contain specialized receptors that respond to opiates. Then, soon after the discovery of the opiate receptor, other neuroscientists discovered the natural ligands for these receptors (Terenius and Wahlström, 1975; Hughes et al., 1975), which they called **enkephalins** (from the Greek word *enkephalos,* "in the head"). We now know that the enkephalins are only two members of a family of endogenous opioids, all of which are synthesized from one of three large peptides that serve as precursors. In addition, we know that there are at least three different types of opiate receptors: μ (mu), δ (delta), and κ (kappa).

Several different neural systems are activated when opiate receptors are stimulated. One type produces analgesia, another inhibits species-typical defensive responses such as fleeing and hiding, and another stimulates a system of neurons involved in reinforcement ("reward"). The last effect explains why opiates are often abused. The situations that cause neurons to secrete endogenous opioids are discussed in Chapter 7, and the brain mechanisms of opiate addiction are discussed in Chapter 16.

So far, pharmacologists have developed only two types of drugs that affect neural communication by means of opioids: direct agonists and antagonists. Many synthetic opiates, including heroin (dihydromorphine) and Percodan (levorphanol), have been developed and are used clinically as analgesics (step 6 of Figure 4.4). Several opiate receptors blockers have also been developed (step 7 of Figure 4.4). One of them, **naloxone,** is used clinically to reverse opiate intoxication. This drug has saved the lives of many drug abusers who would otherwise have died of an overdose of heroin.

Several peptide hormones are also found in the brain, where they serve as neuromodulators. In some cases the peripheral and central peptides perform related functions. For example, outside the nervous system the hormone angiotensin acts

strychnine (***strik*** *neen*) A direct antagonist for the glycine receptor.

endogenous opioid (*en* ***dodge*** *en us* ***oh*** *pee oyd*) A class of peptides secreted by the brain that act as opiates.

enkephalin (*en* ***keff*** *a lin*) One of the endogenous opioids.

naloxone (*na* ***lox*** *own*) A drug that blocks opiate receptors.

directly on the kidneys and blood vessels to produce effects that help the body cope with the loss of fluid, and inside the nervous system circuits of neurons that use angiotensin as a neurotransmitter perform similar functions, including the activation of neural circuits that produce thirst.

Many peptides produced in the brain have interesting behavioral effects, which will be discussed in subsequent chapters.

Lipids

Various substances derived from lipids can serve to transmit messages within or between cells. At least two of them appear to be **cannabinoids**—natural ligands for the receptors that are responsible for the physiological effects of the active ingredient in marijuana. Matsuda et al. (1990) discovered that THC (tetrahydrocannibinal, the active ingredient of marijuana) stimulates cannabinoid receptors located in specific regions of the brain. (See ***Figure 4.13.***)

Figure 4.13

An autoradiogram of a sagittal section of a rat brain that has been incubated in a solution containing a radioactive ligand for THC receptors. The receptors are indicated by dark areas. (Autoradiography is described in Chapter 5.) (Br St = brain stem, Cer = cerebellum, CP = caudate nucleus/putamen, Cx = cortex, EP = entopeduncular nucleus, GP = globus pallidus, Hipp = hippocampus, SNr = substantia nigra.)

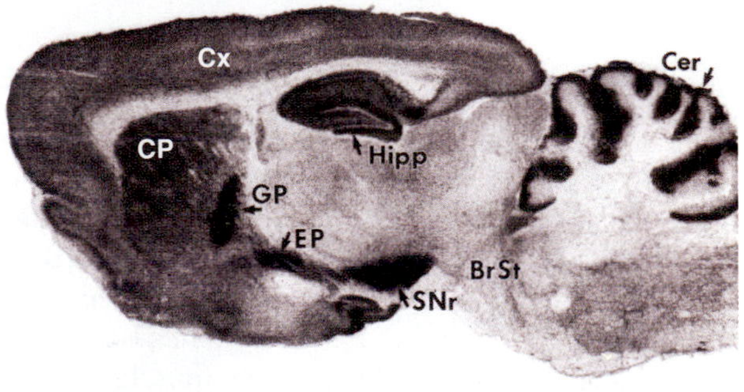

Courtesy of Miles Herkenham, National Institute of Mental Health, Bethesda, MD.

THC produces analgesia and sedation, stimulates appetite, reduces nausea caused by drugs used to treat cancer, relieves asthma attacks, decreases pressure within the eyes in patients with glaucoma, and reduces the symptoms of certain motor disorders. On the other hand, THC interferes with concentration and memory, alters visual and auditory perception, and distorts perceptions of the passage of time (Kunos and Batkai, 2001). Devane et al. (1992) discovered the first natural ligand for the THC receptor: a lipidlike substance that they named **anandamide,** from the Sanskrit word *ananda,* or "bliss." Anandamide seems to be synthesized on demand; that is, it is produced and released as it is needed and is not stored in synaptic vesicles.

Another of the effects of THC is interference with the functioning of 5-HT_3 receptors. As we saw earlier, these receptors are involved in vomiting; thus, THC serves as an antiemetic (antivomiting) drug. Fride and Mechoulam (1996) discovered that the behavioral effects of THC were not seen in young mice, which suggested that the immature brain lacked at least some of the neural mechanisms responsible for these effects. On the basis of this observation, they tried using THC to control the nausea and vomiting caused by chemotherapy for cancer in young children (Abrahamov et al., 1995). The drug successfully blocked the side effects of the chemotherapy without producing the psychotropic effects that THC produces in adults. In fact, the investigators were able to administer very high doses of THC that adults would not have been able to tolerate.

Nucleosides

A nucleoside is a compound that consists of a sugar molecule bound with a purine or pyrimidine base. One of these compounds, **adenosine** (a combination of ribose and adenine), serves as a neuromodulator in the brain.

Adenosine is known to be released, apparently by glial cells as well as neurons, when cells are short of fuel or oxygen. The release of adenosine activates receptors on nearby blood vessels and causes them to dilate, increasing the flow of blood and helping bring more of the needed substances to the region. Adenosine also acts as a neuromodulator, through its action on at least three different types of adenosine receptors. Adenosine receptors are coupled to G proteins, and their effect is to open potassium channels, producing inhibitory postsynaptic potentials. Because adenosine is present in all cells, investigators have not yet succeeded in distinguishing neurons that release this chemical as a neuromodulator. Thus, circuits of adenosinergic neurons have not yet been identified.

cannabinoid (*can **ob** in oid*) A lipid; an endogenous ligand for receptors that bind with THC, the active ingredient of marijuana.

anandamide (*a **nan** da mide*) The first cannabinoid to be discovered and probably the most important one.

adenosine (*a **den** oh seen*) A nucleoside; a combination of ribose and adenine; serves as a neuromodulator in the brain.

Because adenosine receptors suppress neural activity, adenosine and other adenosine receptor agonists have generally inhibitory effects on behavior. In fact, as we will see in Chapter 8, some investigators believe that adenosine receptors may be involved in the control of sleep. A very common drug, **caffeine,** blocks adenosine receptors (step 7 of Figure 4.4) and hence produces excitatory effects. Caffeine is a bitter-tasting alkaloid found in coffee, tea, cocoa beans, and other plants. In much of the world a majority of the adult population ingests caffeine every day—fortunately, without apparent harm.

Soluble Gases

Recently, investigators have discovered that neurons use at least two simple, soluble gases—nitric oxide and carbon monoxide—to communicate with one another. One of these, **nitric oxide (NO),** has received the most attention. Nitric oxide (not to be confused with nitrous oxide, or laughing gas) is a soluble gas that is produced by the activity of an enzyme found in certain neurons. Researchers have found that NO is used as a messenger in many parts of the body; for example, it is involved in the control of the muscles in the wall of the intestines, it dilates blood vessels in regions of the brain that become metabolically active, and it stimulates the changes in blood vessels that produce penile erections (Culotta and Koshland, 1992). As we will see in Chapter 12, it may also play a role in the establishment of neural changes that are produced by learning.

All of the neurotransmitters and neuromodulators discussed so far (with the exception of anandamide and perhaps adenosine) are stored in synaptic vesicles and released by terminal buttons. Nitric oxide is produced in several regions of a nerve cell—including dendrites—and is released as soon as it is produced. More accurately, it diffuses out of the cell as soon as it is produced. It does not activate membrane-bound receptors but enters neighboring cells, where it activates an enzyme responsible for the production of a second messenger, cyclic GMP. Within a few seconds of being produced, nitric oxide is converted into biologically inactive compounds.

Nitric oxide is produced from arginine, an amino acid, by the activation of an enzyme known as **nitric oxide synthase.** This enzyme can be inactivated (step 2 of Figure 4.4) by a drug called L-NAME (nitro-L-arginine methyl ester).

INTERIM SUMMARY

Neurotransmitters and Neuromodulators

The nervous system contains a variety of neurotransmitters, each of which interacts with a specialized receptor. Those that have received the most study are acetylcholine and the monoamines: dopamine, norepinephrine, and 5-hydroxytryptamine (serotonin). The synthesis of these neurotransmitters is controlled by a series of enzymes. Several amino acids also serve as neurotransmitters, the most important of which are glutamate (glutamic acid), GABA, and glycine. Glutamate serves as an excitatory neurotransmitter; the others serve as inhibitory neurotransmitters.

Peptide neurotransmitters consist of chains of amino acids. Like proteins, peptides are synthesized at the ribosomes according to sequences coded for by the chromosomes. The best-known class of peptides in the nervous system includes the endogenous opioids, whose effects are mimicked by drugs such as opium and heroin. One lipid appears to serve as a chemical messenger: anandamide, the endogenous ligand for the THC (marijuana) receptor. Adenosine, a nucleoside that has inhibitory effects on synaptic transmission, is released by neurons and glial cells in the brain. In addition, two soluble gases—nitric oxide and carbon monoxide—can diffuse out of the cell in which they are produced and trigger the production of a second messenger in adjacent cells.

This chapter has mentioned many drugs and their effects. They are summarized for your convenience in ***Table 4.3.***

caffeine A drug that blocks adenosine receptors.

nitric oxide (NO) A gas produced by cells in the nervous system; used as a means of communication between cells.

nitric oxide synthase The enzyme responsible for the production of nitric oxide.

Table 4.3

Drugs Mentioned in This Chapter

Neurotransmitter	Name of Drug	Effect of Drug	Effect on Synaptic Transmission
Acetylcholine (ACh)	Botulinum toxin	Block release of ACh	Antagonist
	Black widow spider venom	Stimulate release of ACh	Agonist
	Nicotine	Stimulate nicotinic receptors	Agonist
	Curare	Block nicotinic receptors	Antagonist
	Muscarine	Stimulate muscarinic receptors	Agonist
	Atropine	Block muscarinic receptors	Antagonist
	Neostigmine	Inhibit acetylcholinesterase	Agonist
Dopamine (DA)	L-DOPA	Facilitate synthesis of DA	Agonist
	AMPT	Inhibit synthesis of DA	Antagonist
	Reserpine	Inhibit storage of DA in synaptic vesicles	Antagonist
	Chlorpromazine	Block D_2 receptors	Antagonist
	Clozapine	Block D_4 receptors	Antagonist
	Cocaine, methylphenidate	Block DA reuptake	Agonist
	Amphetamine	Stimulate release of DA	Agonist
	Deprenyl	Block MAO-B	Agonist
Norepinephrine (NE)	Fusaric acid	Inhibit synthesis of NE	Antagonist
	Reserpine	Inhibit storage of NE in synaptic vesicles	Antagonist
	Idazoxan	Block α_2 autoreceptors	Agonist
	Desipramine	Inhibit reuptake of NE	Agonist
	MDMA, amphetamine	Stimulate release of NE	Agonist
Serotonin (5-HT)	PCPA	Inhibit synthesis of 5-HT	Antagonist
	Reserpine	Inhibit storage of 5-HT in synaptic vesicles	Antagonist
	Fenfluramine	Stimulate release of 5-HT	Agonist
	Fluoxetine	Inhibit reuptake of 5-HT	Agonist
	LSD	Stimulate 5-HT_{2A} receptors	Agonist
	MDMA	Stimulate release of 5-HT	Agonist
Glutamate	AMPA	Stimulate AMPA receptor	Agonist
	Kainic acid	Stimulate kainate receptor	Agonist
	NMDA	Stimulate NMDA receptor	Agonist
	AP5	Block NMDA receptor	Antagonist
GABA	Allylglycine	Inhibit synthesis of GABA	Antagonist
	Muscimol	Stimulate $GABA_A$ receptors	Agonist
	Bicuculline	Block $GABA_A$ receptors	Antagonist
	Benzodiazepines	Serve as indirect $GABA_A$ agonist	Agonist
Glycine	Strychnine	Block glycine receptors	Antagonist
Opioids	Opiates (morphine, heroin, etc.)	Stimulate opiate receptors	Agonist
	Naloxone	Block opiate receptors	Antagonist
Adenosine	Caffeine	Block adenosine receptors	Antagonist
Nitric oxide (NO)	L-NAME	Inhibit synthesis of NO	Antagonist

EPILOGUE

Helpful Hints from a Tragedy

The discovery that MPTP damages the brain and causes the symptoms of Parkinson's disease galvanized researchers interested in the disease. (I recently checked PubMed, a web site maintained by the U.S. National Institutes of Health, and found that 3,067 scientific publications referred to MPTP.) The first step was to find out whether the drug would have the same effect in laboratory animals so that the details of the process could be studied. It did; Langston et al. (1984) found that injections of MPTP produced parkinsonian symptoms in squirrel monkeys and that these symptoms could be reduced by L-DOPA therapy. And just as the investigators had hoped, examination of the animals' brains showed a selective loss of dopamine-secreting neurons in the substantia nigra.

It turns out that MPTP itself does not cause neural damage; instead, the drug is converted by an enzyme present in glial cells into another substance, MPP+. *That* chemical is taken up by dopamine-secreting neurons, by means of the reuptake mechanism that normally retrieves dopamine that is released by terminal buttons. MPP+ accumulates in mitochondria in these cells and blocks their ability to metabolize nutrients, thus killing the cells (Maret et al., 1990). The enzyme that converts MPTP into MPP+ is none other than monoamine oxidase (MAO), which, as you now know, is responsible for deactivating excess amounts of monoamines present in terminal buttons. Because pharmacologists had already developed MAO inhibitors, Langston and his colleagues decided to see whether one of these drugs (pargyline) would protect squirrel monkeys from the toxic effects of MPTP by preventing its conversion into MPP+ (Langston et al., 1984). It worked; when MAO was inhibited by pargyline, MPTP injections had no effects.

These results made researchers wonder whether MAO inhibitors might possibly protect against the degeneration of dopamine-secreting neurons in patients with Parkinson's disease. No one thought that Parkinson's disease was caused by MPP+, but perhaps some other toxins were involved. Epidemiologists have found that Parkinson's disease is more common in highly industrialized countries, which suggests that environmental toxins produced in these societies may be responsible for the brain damage (Tanner, 1989; Veldman et al., 1998). Fortunately, several MAO inhibitors have been tested and approved for use in humans. One of them, deprenyl, was tested and appeared to slow down the progression of neurological symptoms (Tetrud and Langston, 1989).

As a result of this study, many neurologists are now treating their Parkinson's patients with deprenyl, especially during the early stages of the disease. More recent studies found that deprenyl does not protect dopaminergic neurons indefinitely (Shoulson et al., 2002), but researchers are trying to develop other drugs with more sustained neuroprotective effects.

KEY CONCEPTS

PRINCIPLES OF PSYCHOPHARMACOLOGY

1. Pharmacokinetics is the process by which drugs are absorbed, distributed within the body, metabolized, and excreted.
2. Drugs can act at several different sites and have several different effects. The effectiveness of a drug is the magnitude of the effects of a given quantity of the drug.
3. A drug's therapeutic index is its margin of safety: the difference between an effective dose and a dose that produces toxic side effects.
4. When a drug is administered repeatedly, it often produces tolerance, and withdrawal effects often occur when the drug is discontinued. Sometimes, repeated administration of a drug causes sensitization.
5. Researchers must control for placebo effects in both humans and laboratory animals.

PHARMACOLOGY OF SYNAPSES

6. Each of the steps involved in synaptic transmission can be interfered with by drugs, and some can be facilitated. These steps include synthesis of the neurotransmitter, storage in synaptic vesicles, release, activation of postsynaptic and presynaptic receptors, and termination of postsynaptic potentials through reuptake or enzymatic deactivation.

NEUROTRANSMITTERS AND NEUROMODULATORS

7. Neurons use a variety of chemicals as neurotransmitters, including acetylcholine, the monoamines (dopamine, norepinephrine, and 5-HT), the amino acids (glutamic acid, GABA, and glycine), various peptides, lipids, nucleosides, and soluble gases.

SUGGESTED READINGS

Cooper, J. R., Bloom, F. E., and Roth, R. H. *The Biochemical Basis of Neuropharmacology*, 8th ed. New York: Oxford University Press, 2002.

Feldman, R. S., Meyer, J. S., and Quenzer, L. F. *Principles of Neuropsychopharmacology*. Sunderland, MA: Sinauer Associates, 1997.

Grilly, D. M. *Drugs and Human Behavior*, 4th ed. Boston: Allyn and Bacon, 2002.

SUGGESTED WEB SITES

Animations: How Drugs Work
www.pbs.org/wnet/closetohome/science/html/animations.html

This site provides a series of color animations that illustrate the action of drugs such as alcohol, opiates, and cocaine on synaptic function.

Internet Mental Health
www.mentalhealth.com

This site is a general resource that provides links to sites dealing with common mental disorders and the drugs that are used to treat mental disorders.

Drugs That Alter Anxiety
http://salmon.psy.plym.ac.uk/year2/anxiety.htm

This site provides student access to a comprehensive set of materials relating to the study of anxiety and the drugs that are used to treat anxiety.

The Search for Novel Antipsychotic Drugs
http://salmon.psy.plym.ac.uk/year2/schizo1.htm

This site provides student access to a comprehensive set of materials relating to the pharmacology of schizophrenia.

Pharmacology Information Network
http://pharminfo.com/

This site is a general resource site providing access to a database on common drugs.

Psychopharmocology Resources
www.psychwatch.com/psychopharm_page.htm

Links to sites dealing with the topic of psychopharmacology are provided by this site.

Classroom Psychopharmacology
www.unl.edu/tcweb/pharm/cpp.start.html

This site focuses on the topic of drugs that are used to treat children for problems within the classroom. The site provides an overview of synaptic function, of conditions that are treated by drugs, and of the drugs that are most commonly used for children.

Methods and Strategies of Research

chapter 5

CHAPTER OUTLINE

LEARNING OBJECTIVES

1. Discuss the research method of experimental ablation: the rationale, the evaluation of behavioral effects resulting from brain damage, and the production of brain lesions.
2. Describe stereotaxic surgery.
3. Describe research methods for preserving, sectioning, and staining the brain and for studying its parts and interconnections.
4. Describe research methods for tracing efferent and afferent axons and for studying the living human brain.
5. Describe how the neural activity of the brain is measured and recorded, both electrically and chemically.
6. Describe how neural activity in the brain is stimulated, both electrically and chemically.
7. Describe research methods for locating particular neurochemicals, the neurons that produce them, and the receptors that respond to them.
8. Discuss research techniques to identify genetic factors that may affect the development of the nervous system and influence behavior.

PROLOGUE

Heart Repaired, Brain Damaged

All her life, Mrs. H. had been active. She had never been particularly athletic, but she and her husband often went hiking and camping with their children when they were young, and they continued to hike and go for bicycle rides after their children left home. Her husband died when she was 60, and even though she no longer rode her bicycle, she enjoyed gardening and walking around the neighborhood with her friends.

A few years later, Mrs. H. was digging in her garden when a sudden pain gripped her chest. She felt as if a hand were squeezing her heart. She gasped and dropped her spade. The pain crept toward her left shoulder and then traveled down her left arm. The sensation was terrifying; she was sure that she was having a heart attack and was going to die. But after a few minutes the pain melted away, and she walked slowly back to her house.

Her physician examined her and performed some tests and later told her that she had not had a heart attack. Her pain was that of angina pectoris, caused by insufficient flow of blood to the heart. Some of her coronary arteries had become partially obstructed with atherosclerotic plaque—cholesterol-containing deposits on the walls of the blood vessels. Her efforts in her garden had increased her heart rate, and as a consequence, the metabolic activity of her heart muscle had also increased. Her clogged coronary arteries simply could not keep up with the demand, and the accumulation of metabolic by-products caused intense pain. Her physician cautioned her to avoid unnecessary exertion and prescribed nitroglycerine tablets to place under her tongue if another attack occurred.

Mrs. H. stopped working in her garden but continued to walk around the neighborhood with her friends. Then one evening, while climbing the stairs to get ready for bed, she felt another attack grip her heart. With difficulty, she made her way to her bathroom cabinet, where she found her nitroglycerine tablets. Fumbling with the childproof cap, she extracted a tablet and placed it under her tongue. As the tablet dissolved and the nitroglycerine entered her bloodstream, she felt the tightness in her chest loosen, and she stumbled to her bed.

Over the next year the frequency and intensity of Mrs. H.'s attacks increased. Finally, the specialist to whom the physician had referred her, recommended that she consider having a coronary artery bypass performed. She readily agreed. The surgeon, Dr. G., replaced two of her coronary arteries with sections of vein that he had removed from her leg. During the procedure, an artificial heart took over the pumping of her blood so that the surgeon could cut out the diseased section of the arteries and delicately sew in the replacements.

Several days later, Dr. G. visited Mrs. H. in her hospital room. "How are you feeling, Mrs. H?"

"I'm feeling fine," she said, "but I'm having trouble with my vision. Everything looks so confusing, and I feel disoriented. I can't. . . ."

"Don't worry," he cut in. "It's normal to feel confused after such serious surgery. Your tests look fine, and we don't expect a recurrence of your angina. You should be good for many years!" He flashed a broad smile at her and left the room.

But Mrs. H.'s visual problems and her confusion did not get better. Although the surgeon's notes indicated a successful outcome, her family physician saw that something was wrong and asked Dr. J., a neuropsychologist, to evaluate her. Dr. J.'s report confirmed the physician's fears: Mrs. H. had Balint's syndrome. She could still see, but she could not control her eye movements. The world confused her because she saw only fleeting, fragmentary images. She could no longer read, and she could no longer locate and grasp objects in front of her. In short, her vision was almost useless. Her heart was fine, but she would henceforth have to live in a nursing home, where others could care for her.

Study of the physiology of behavior involves the efforts of scientists in many disciplines, including physiology, neuroanatomy, biochemistry, psychology, endocrinology, and histology. Pursuing a research project in behavioral neuroscience requires competence in many experimental techniques. Because different procedures often produce contradictory results, investigators must be familiar with the advantages and limitations of the methods they employ. Scientific investigation entails a process of asking questions of nature. The method that is used frames the question. Often we receive a puzzling answer, only to realize later that we were not asking the question we thought we were. As we will see, the best conclusions about the physiology of behavior are made not by any single experiment, but by a program of research that enables us to compare the results of studies that approach the problem with different methods.

An enormous—and bewildering—array of research methods is available to the investigator. If I merely presented a catalog of them, it would not be surprising if you got lost—or simply lost interest. Instead, I will present only the most important and commonly used procedures, organized around a few problems that researchers have studied. This way, it should be easier to see the types of information provided by various research methods and to understand their advantages and disadvantages. It will also permit me to describe the strategies that researchers employ as they follow up the results of one experiment by designing and executing another one.

Experimental Ablation

One of the most important research methods used to investigate brain functions involves destroying part of the brain and evaluating the animal's subsequent behavior. This method is called **experimental ablation** (from the Latin word *ablatus,* a "carrying away"). In most cases experimental ablation does not involve the removal of brain tissue; instead, the researcher destroys some tissue and leaves it in place. Experimental ablation is the oldest method used in neuroscience, and it remains one of the most important ones today.

Evaluating the Behavioral Effects of Brain Damage

A *lesion* is a wound or injury, and a researcher who destroys part of the brain usually refers to the damage as a *brain lesion.* Experiments in which part of the brain is damaged and the animal's behavior is subsequently observed are called **lesion studies.** The rationale for lesion studies is that the function of an area of the brain can be inferred from the behaviors that the animal can no longer perform after the area is damaged. For example, if, after part of the brain is destroyed, an animal can no longer perform tasks that require vision, we can conclude that the animal is blind—and that the damaged area plays some role in vision.

We must be very careful in interpreting the effects of brain lesions. For example, how do we ascertain that the lesioned animal is blind? Does it bump into objects, or fail to run through a maze toward a light that signals the location of food, or no longer constrict its pupils to light? An animal could bump into objects because of deficits in motor coordination, it could have lost its appetite for food (and thus its motivation to run through the maze), or it could see quite well but could have lost its visual reflexes. Researchers can often be fooled. Years ago they thought that the albino rat was blind. (It isn't.) Think about it: How would you test whether a rat can see? Remember that rats have vibrissae (whiskers) that can be used to detect a wall before bumping into it or the edge of a table before walking off it. They can also find their way around a room by following odor trails.

Just what can we learn from lesion studies? Our goal is to discover what functions are performed by different regions of the brain and then to understand how these functions are combined to accomplish particular behaviors. The distinction between *brain function* and *behavior* is an important one. Circuits within the brain perform functions, not behaviors. No one brain region or neural circuit is solely responsible for a behavior; each region performs a function (or set of functions) that contributes to performance of the behavior. For example, the act of reading involves functions required for controlling eye movements, focusing the lens of the eye, perceiving and recognizing words and letters, comprehending the meaning of the words, and so on. Some of these functions also participate in other behaviors; for example, controlling eye movement and focusing are required for any task that involves looking, and brain mechanisms used for comprehending the meanings of words also participate in comprehending speech. The researcher's task is to understand the functions that are required for performing a particular behavior and to determine what circuits of neurons in the brain are responsible for each of these functions.

experimental ablation The removal or destruction of a portion of the brain of a laboratory animal; presumably, the functions that can no longer be performed are the ones the region previously controlled.

lesion study A synonym for experimental ablation.

excitotoxic lesion (*ek sigh tow* ***tok*** *sik*) A brain lesion produced by intracerebral injection of an excitatory amino acid, such as kainic acid.

Producing Brain Lesions

How do we produce brain lesions? It is easy to destroy parts of the brain immediately beneath the skull; we anesthetize the animal, cut open its scalp, remove part of its skull, and cut through the dura mater, bringing the cortex into view. Then we can use a suction device to aspirate the brain tissue. To accomplish this tissue removal, we place a glass pipette on the surface of the brain and suck away brain tissue with a vacuum pump attached to the pipette.

More often, we want to destroy regions that are hidden away in the depths of the brain. Brain lesions of subcortical regions (regions located beneath the cortex) are usually produced by passing electrical current through a stainless steel wire that is coated with an insulating varnish except for the very tip. We guide the wire stereotaxically so that its end reaches the appropriate location. (Stereotaxic surgery is described in the next subsection.) Then we turn on a lesion-making device, which produces radio frequency (RF) current—alternating current of a very high frequency. The passage of the current through the brain tissue produces heat that kills cells in the region surrounding the tip of the electrode. (See ***Figure 5.1.***)

Lesions produced by these means destroy everything in the vicinity of the electrode tip, including neural cell bodies and the axons of neurons that pass through the region. A more selective method of producing brain lesions employs an excitatory amino acid such as *kainic acid,* which kills neurons by stimulating them to death. (As we saw in Chapter 4, kainic acid stimulates glutamate receptors.) Lesions produced this way are referred to as **excitotoxic lesions.** When an excitatory amino acid is injected through a cannula into a region of the brain, the chemical destroys neural cell bodies in the vicinity but spares axons that belong to different neurons that happen to pass nearby. (See ***Figure 5.2.***) This selectivity permits the investigator to determine whether the behavioral effects of destroying a particular brain structure are caused by the death of neurons located there or by the destruction of axons that pass nearby.

Figure 5.1

Radio frequency lesion. The arrows point to very small lesions produced by passing radio frequency current through the tips of stainless steel electrodes placed in the medial preoptic nucleus of a rat brain. The oblong hole in the middle of the photograph is the third ventricle. (Frontal section, cell-body stain.)

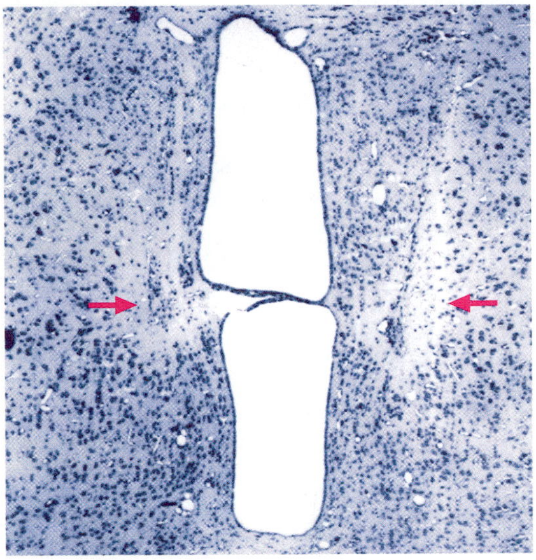

From Turkenburg, J. L., Swaab, D. F., Endert, E., Louwerse, A. L., and van de Poll, N. E. *Brain Research Bulletin,* 1988, *21,* 215–224.

Figure 5.2

Excitotoxic lesion. (a) Section through a normal hippocampus of a rat brain. (b) A lesion produced by infusion of an excitatory amino acid in a region of the hippocampus. Arrowheads mark the ends of the region in which neurons have been destroyed.

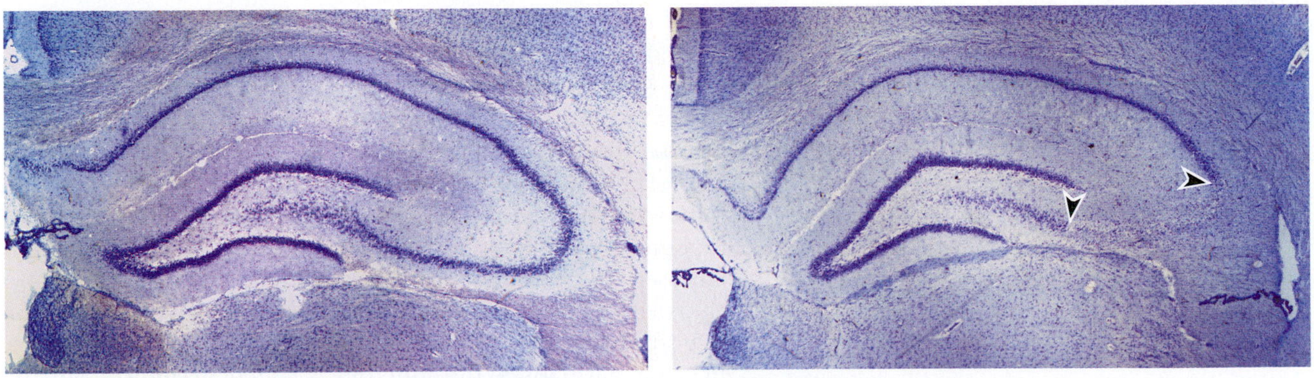

(a) (b)

Courtesy of Benno Roozendaal, University of California, Irvine.

sham lesion A "placebo" procedure that duplicates all the steps of producing a brain lesion except for the one that actually causes the brain damage.

stereotaxic surgery (*stair ee oh **tak** sik*) Brain surgery using a stereotaxic apparatus to position an electrode or cannula in a specified position of the brain.

bregma The junction of the sagittal and coronal sutures of the skull; often used as a reference point for stereotaxic brain surgery.

Note that when we produce subcortical lesions by passing RF current through an electrode or infusing a chemical through a cannula, we always cause additional damage to the brain. When we pass an electrode or a cannula through the brain to get to our target, we inevitably cause a small amount of damage even before turning on the lesion maker or starting the infusion. Therefore, we cannot simply compare the behavior of brain-lesioned animals with that of unoperated control animals; the incidental damage to the brain regions above the lesion may actually be responsible for some of the behavioral deficits we see. What we do is operate on a group of animals and produce **sham lesions.** To do so, we anesthetize each animal, put it in the stereotaxic apparatus (described below), cut open the scalp, drill the holes, insert the electrode or cannula, and lower it to the proper depth. In other words, we do everything we would do to produce the lesion except turn on the lesion maker or start the infusion. This group of animals serves as a control group; if the behavior of the animals with brain lesions is different from that of the sham-operated control animals, we can conclude that the lesions caused the behavioral deficits. (As you can see, a sham lesion serves the same purpose as a placebo does in a pharmacology study.)

Most of the time, investigators produce permanent brain lesions, but sometimes it is advantageous to disrupt the activity of a particular region of the brain temporarily. The easiest way to do so is to inject a local anesthetic or a drug called *muscimol* into the appropriate part of the brain. The anesthetic blocks action potentials in axons from entering or leaving that region, thus effectively producing a temporary lesion (usually called a *reversible* brain lesion). Muscimol, a drug that stimulates GABA receptors, inactivates a region of the brain by inhibiting the neurons located there. (You will recall that GABA is the most important inhibitory neurotransmitter in the brain.)

Figure 5.3

Relation of the skull sutures to a rat's brain, and the location of a target for an electrode placement. *Top:* Dorsal view. *Bottom:* Midsagittal view.

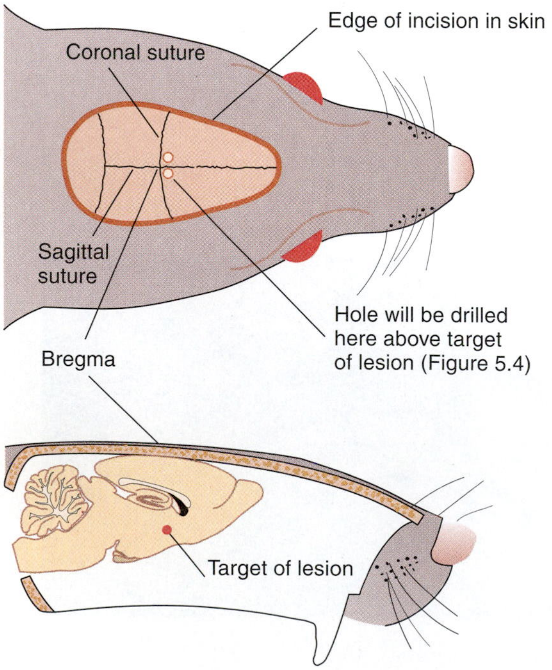

Stereotaxic Surgery

So how do we get the tip of an electrode or cannula to a precise location in the depths of an animal's brain? The answer is **stereotaxic surgery.** *Stereotaxis* literally means "solid arrangement"; more specifically, it refers to the ability to locate objects in space. A *stereotaxic apparatus* contains a holder that fixes the animal's head in a standard position and a carrier that moves an electrode or a cannula through measured distances in all three axes of space. However, to perform stereotaxic surgery, one must first study a *stereotaxic atlas.*

The Stereotaxic Atlas

No two brains of animals of a given species are completely identical, but there is enough similarity among individuals to predict the location of particular brain structures relative to external features of the head. For instance, a subcortical nucleus of a rat might be so many millimeters ventral, anterior, and lateral to a point formed by the junction of several bones of the skull. Figure 5.3 shows two views of a rat skull: a drawing of the dorsal surface and, beneath it, a midsagittal view. (See ***Figure 5.3.***) The skull is composed of several bones that grow together and form *sutures* (seams). The heads of newborn babies contain a soft spot at the junction of the coronal and sagittal sutures called the *fontanelle.* Once this gap closes, the junction is called **bregma,** from the Greek word meaning "front of head." We can find bregma on a rat's skull, too, and it serves as a convenient reference point. If the animal's skull is oriented as shown in the illustration, a particular region of the brain is found in a fairly constant position, relative to bregma.

A **stereotaxic atlas** contains photographs or drawings that correspond to frontal sections taken at various distances rostral and caudal to bregma. For example, the page shown in Figure 5.4 is a drawing of a slice of the brain that contains a brain structure (shown in red) that we are interested in. If we wanted to place the tip of a wire in this structure (the fornix), we would have to drill a hole through the skull immediately above it. (See ***Figure 5.4.***) Each page of the stereotaxic atlas is labeled according to the distance of the section anterior or posterior to bregma. The grid on each page indicates distances of brain structures ventral to the top of the skull and lateral to the midline. To place the tip of a wire in the fornix, we would drill a hole above the target and then lower the electrode through the hole until the tip was at the correct depth, relative to the skull height at bregma. (See ***Figures 5.3*** and ***5.4.***) Thus, by finding a neural structure (which we cannot see in our animal) on one of the pages of a stereotaxic atlas, we can determine the structure's location relative to bregma (which we can see). Note that because of variations in different strains and ages of animals, the atlas gives only an approximate location. We always have to try out a new set of coordinates, slice and stain the animal's brain, see the actual location of the lesion, correct the numbers, and try again. (Slicing and staining of brains are described later.)

stereotaxic atlas A collection of drawings of sections of the brain of a particular animal with measurements that provide coordinates for stereotaxic surgery.

stereotaxic apparatus A device that permits a surgeon to position an electrode or cannula into a specific part of the brain.

The Stereotaxic Apparatus

A **stereotaxic apparatus** operates on simple principles. The device includes a head holder, which maintains the animal's skull in the proper orientation, a holder for the electrode, and a calibrated mechanism that moves the electrode holder in measured distances along the three axes: anterior–posterior, dorsal–ventral, and lateral–medial. Figure 5.5 illustrates a stereotaxic apparatus designed for small animals; various head holders can be used to outfit this device for such diverse species as rats, mice, hamsters, pigeons, and turtles. (See ***Figure 5.5.***)

Figure 5.4

A sample page from a stereotaxic atlas of the rat brain. The target (the fornix) is indicated in red. Labels have been removed for the sake of clarity.

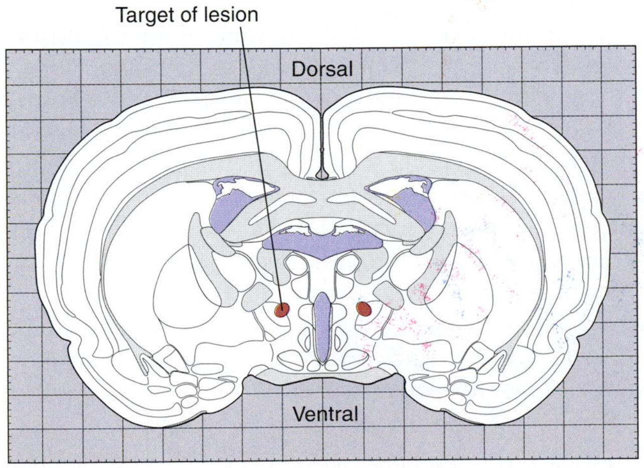

Adapted from Swanson, L. W. *Brain Maps: Structure of the Rat Brain.* New York: Elsevier, 1992.

Figure 5.5

A stereotaxic apparatus for performing brain surgery on rats.

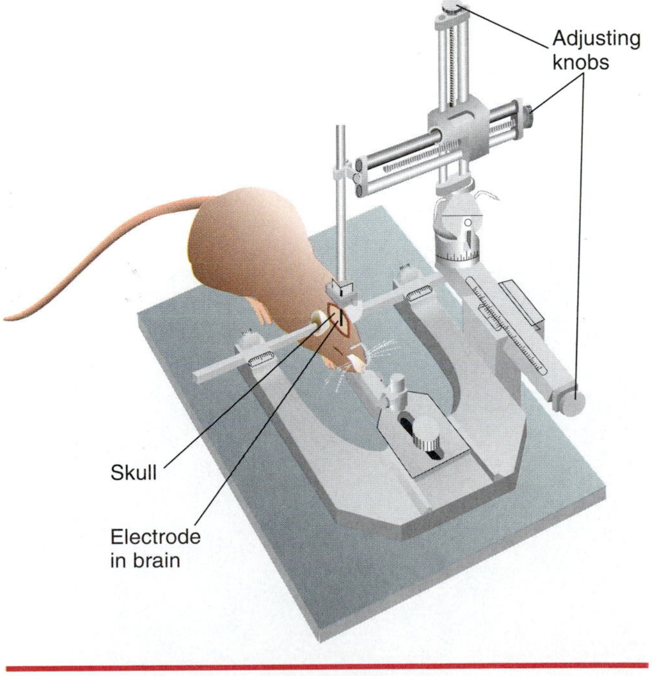

Figure 5.6

Stereotaxic surgery being performed on a human patient.

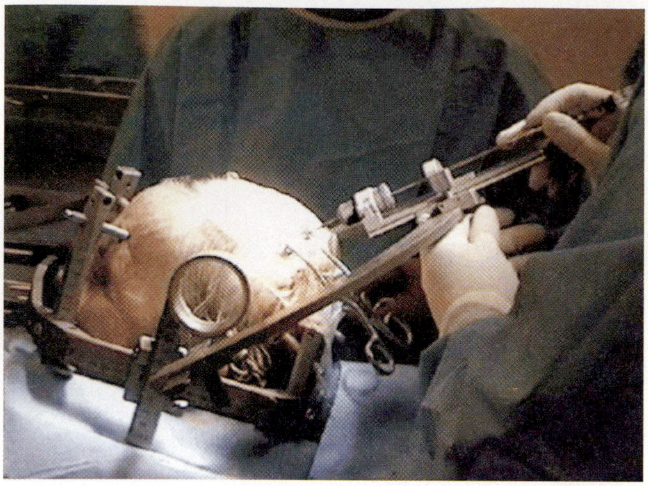

Photograph courtesy of John W. Snell, University of Virginia Health System.

Once we obtain the coordinates from a stereotaxic atlas, we anesthetize the animal, place it in the apparatus, and cut the scalp open. We locate bregma, dial in the appropriate numbers on the stereotaxic apparatus, drill a hole through the skull, and lower the device into the brain by the correct amount. Now the tip of the cannula or electrode is where we want it to be, and we are ready to produce the lesion.

Of course, stereotaxic surgery may be used for purposes other than lesion production. Wires placed in the brain may be used to stimulate neurons as well as destroy them, and drugs can be injected that stimulate neurons or block specific receptors. We can attach cannulas or wires permanently by following a procedure that will be described later in this chapter. In all cases, once surgery is complete, the wound is sewn together, and the animal is taken out of the stereotaxic apparatus and allowed to recover from the anesthetic.

Stereotaxic apparatuses are also made for humans, by the way. Sometimes a neurosurgeon produces subcortical lesions—for example, to reduce the symptoms of Parkinson's disease. Usually, the surgeon uses multiple landmarks and verifies the location of the wire (or other device) inserted into the brain by taking MRI scans before producing a brain lesion. (See ***Figure 5.6.***)

Histological Methods

After producing a brain lesion and observing its effects on an animal's behavior, we must slice and stain the brain so that we can observe it under the microscope and see the location of the lesion. Brain lesions often miss the mark, so we have to verify the precise location of the brain damage after testing the animal behaviorally. To do so, we must fix, slice, stain, and examine the brain. Together, these procedures are referred to as *histological methods.* (The prefix *histo-* refers to body tissue.)

Fixation and Sectioning

If we hope to study the tissue in the form it had at the time of the organism's death, we must destroy the autolytic enzymes (*autolytic* means "self-dissolving"), which will otherwise turn the tissue into mush. The tissue must also be preserved to prevent its decomposition by bacteria or molds. To achieve both of these objectives, we place the neural tissue in a **fixative.** The most commonly used fixative is **formalin,** an aqueous solution of formaldehyde, a gas. Formalin halts autolysis, hardens the very soft and fragile brain, and kills any microorganisms that might destroy it.

Figure 5.7

A microtome.

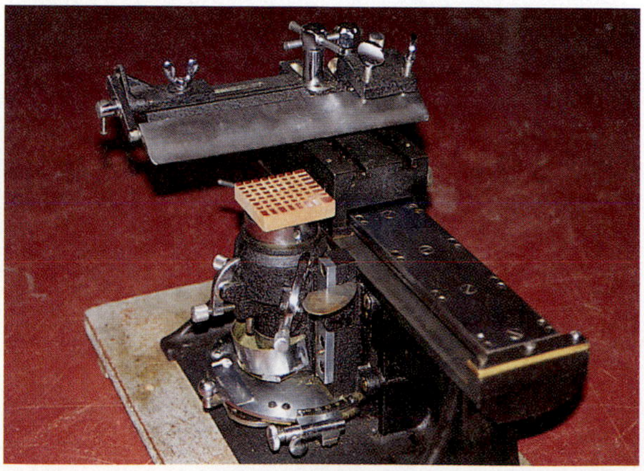

Once the brain has been fixed, we must slice it into thin sections and stain various cellular structures to see anatomical details. Slicing is done with a **microtome** (literally, "that which slices small"). (See ***Figure 5.7.***) Slices prepared for examination under a light microscope are typically 10 to 80 μm in thickness; those prepared for the electron microscope are generally cut at less than 1 μm. (A μm, or *micrometer,* is one-millionth of a meter, or one-thousandth of a millimeter.) For some reason, slices of brain tissue are usually referred to as *sections.*

After the tissue is cut, we attach the slices to glass microscope slides. We can then stain the tissue by putting the entire slide into various chemical solutions. Finally, we cover the stained sections with a small amount of a transparent liquid known as a *mounting medium* and place a very thin glass coverslip over the sections. The mounting medium keeps the coverslip in position. ***Animation 5.1, Histological Methods,*** shows these procedures.

Animation 5.1, Histological Methods, contains a video demonstrating the preparation of brain tissue for examination under a microscope.

Staining

If you looked at an unstained section of brain tissue under a microscope, you would be able to see the outlines of some large cellular masses and the more prominent fiber bundles. However, no fine details would be revealed. For this reason the study of microscopic neuroanatomy requires special histological stains. Researchers have developed many different stains to identify specific substances within and outside of cells. For verifying the location of a brain lesion, we will use one of the simplest: a cell-body stain.

In the late nineteenth century Franz Nissl, a German neurologist, discovered that a dye known as methylene blue would stain the cell bodies of brain tissue. The material that takes up the dye, known as the *Nissl substance,* consists of RNA, DNA, and associated proteins located in the nucleus and scattered, in the form of granules, in the cytoplasm. Many dyes besides methylene blue can be used to stain cell bodies found in slices of the brain, but the most frequently used is cresyl violet. Incidentally, the dyes were not developed specifically for histological purposes but were originally formulated for use in dyeing cloth.

The discovery of cell-body stains made it possible to identify nuclear masses in the brain. Figure 5.8 shows a frontal section of a cat brain stained with cresyl violet. Note that you can observe fiber bundles by their lighter appearance; they do not take up the stain. (See ***Figure 5.8.***) The stain is not selective for *neural* cell bodies; all cells are stained, neurons and glia alike. It is up to the investigator to determine which is which—by size, shape, and location.

fixative A chemical such as formalin; used to prepare and preserve body tissue.

formalin (***for*** *ma lin*) The aqueous solution of formaldehyde gas; the most commonly used tissue fixative.

microtome (***my*** *krow tome*) An instrument that produces very thin slices of body tissues.

Electron Microscopy

The light microscope is limited in its ability to resolve extremely small details. Because of the nature of light itself, magnification of more than approximately 1500 times does not add any detail. To see such small anatomical structures as synaptic

Figure 5.8

A frontal section of a cat brain, stained with cresyl violet, a cell-body stain. The arrowheads point to *nuclei,* or groups of cell bodies.

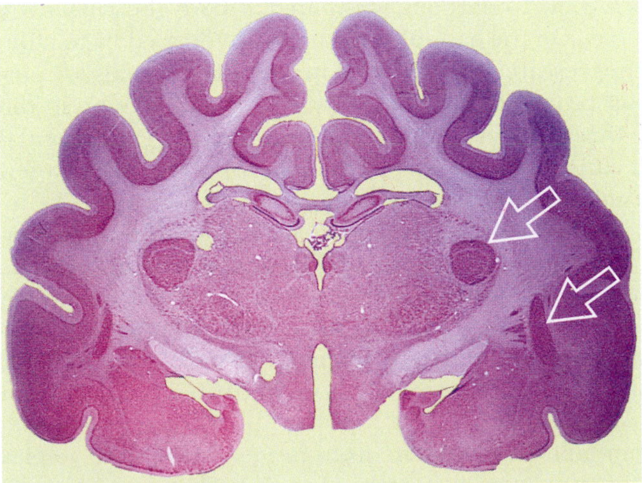

Histological material courtesy of Mary Carlson.

Figure 5.9

An electron photomicrograph of a section through an axodendritic synapse. Two synaptic regions are indicated by arrows, and a circle points out a region of pinocytosis in an adjacent terminal button, presumably representing recycling of vesicular membrane. T = terminal button; f = microfilaments; M = mitochondrion.

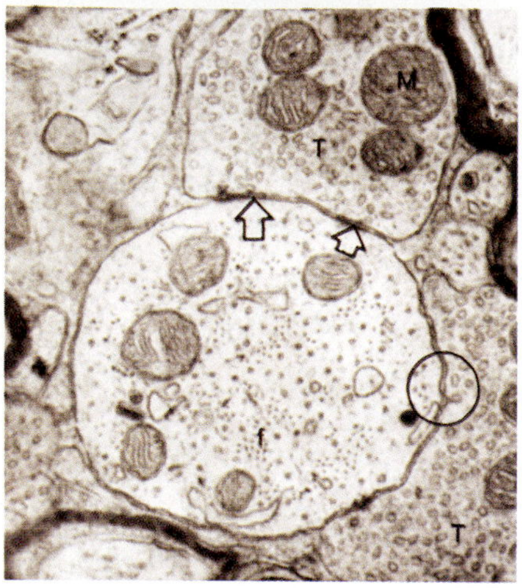

From Rockel, A. J., and Jones, E. G. *Journal of Comparative Neurology,* 1973, *147,* 61–92. Copyright © 1973. Reprinted by permission of Wiley-Liss, Inc., a subsidiary of John Wiley & Sons, Inc.

Figure 5.10

A scanning electron micrograph of neurons and glia.

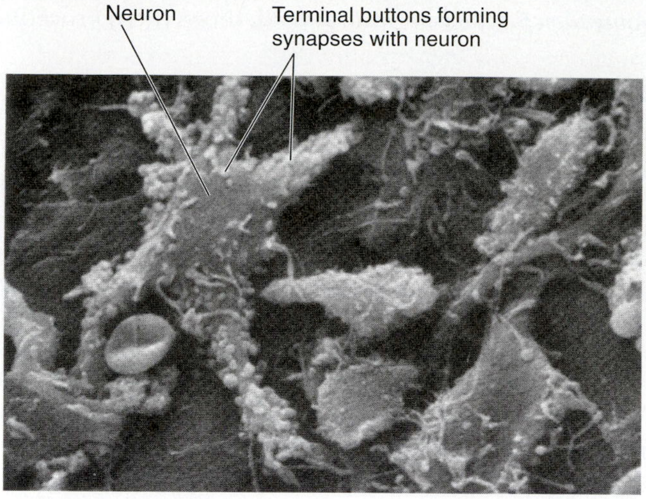

From Kessel, R. G., and Kardon, R. H. *Tissues and Organs: A Text-Atlas of Scanning Electron Microscopy.* San Francisco: W. H. Freeman, 1979. By permission.

vesicles and details of cell organelles, investigators must use an electron microscope. A beam of electrons is passed through the tissue to be examined. A shadow of the tissue is then cast onto a sheet of photographic film, which is exposed by the electrons. Electron photomicrographs produced in this way can provide information about structural details on the order of a few tens of nanometers. (See ***Figure 5.9.***)

A **scanning electron microscope** provides less magnification than a standard transmission electron microscope, which transmits the electron beam through the tissue. However, it shows objects in three dimensions. The microscope scans the tissue with a moving beam of electrons. The information received from the reflection of the beam is used to produce a remarkably detailed three-dimensional view. (See ***Figure 5.10.***)

Tracing Neural Connections

Let's suppose that we were interested in discovering the neural mechanisms responsible for reproductive behavior. To start out, we wanted to study the physiology of sexual behavior of female rats. On the basis of some hints we received by reading reports of experiments by other researchers published in scientific journals, we performed stereotaxic surgery on two groups of female rats. We made a lesion in the ventromedial nucleus of the hypothalamus (VMH) of the rats in the experimental group and performed sham surgery on the rats in the control group. After a few days' recovery we placed the animals (individually, of course) with male rats. The females in the control group responded positively to the males' attention; they engaged in courting behavior followed by copulation. However, the females with the VMH lesions rejected the males' attention and refused to copulate with them. We confirmed with histology that the VMH was indeed destroyed in the brains of the experimental animals. (One experimental rat did copulate, but we discovered later that the lesion had missed the VMH in that animal, so we discarded the data from that subject.)

The results of our experiment indicate that neurons in the VMH appear to play a role in functions required for copulatory behavior in females. (By the way, it turns

scanning electron microscope A microscope that provides three-dimensional information about the shape of the surface of a small object.

out that these lesions do not affect copulatory behavior in males.) So where do we go from here? What is the next step? In fact, there are many questions that we could pursue. One question concerns the system of brain structures that participate in female copulatory behavior. Certainly, the VMH does not stand alone; it receives inputs from other structures and sends outputs to still others. Copulation requires integration of visual, tactile, and olfactory perceptions and organization of patterns of movements in response to those of the partner. In addition, the entire network requires activation by the appropriate sex hormones. What is the precise role of the VMH in this complicated system?

Before we can hope to answer this question, we must know more about the connections of the VMH with the rest of the brain. What structures send their axons to the VMH, and to what structures does the VMH, in turn, send its axons? Once we know what the connections are, we can investigate the role of these structures and the nature of their interactions. (See ***Figure 5.11.***)

Figure 5.11

Once we know that a particular brain region is involved in a particular function, we may ask what structures provide inputs to the region and what structures receive outputs from it.

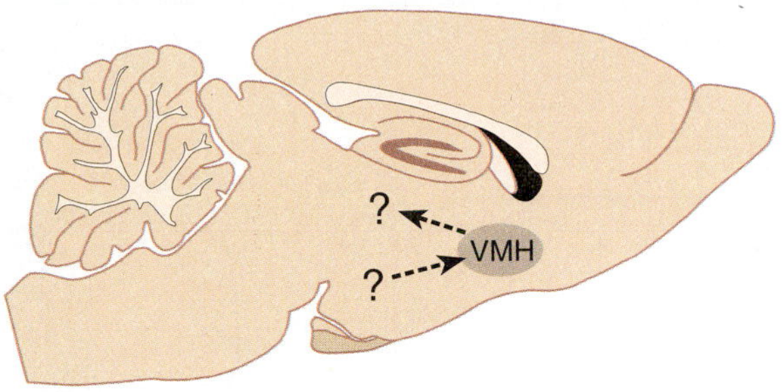

How do we investigate the connections of the VMH? The question cannot be answered by means of histological procedures that stain all neurons, such as cell-body stains. If we look closely at a brain that has been prepared by these means, we see only a tangled mass of neurons. But in recent years researchers have developed very precise methods that make specific neurons stand out from all of the others.

Tracing Efferent Axons

Because neurons in the VMH are not directly connected to muscles, they cannot affect behavior directly. Neurons in the VMH must send axons to parts of the brain that contain neurons that are responsible for muscular movements. The pathway is probably not direct; more likely, neurons in the VMH affect neurons in other structures, which influence those in yet other structures until, eventually, the appropriate motor neurons are stimulated. To discover this system, we want to be able to identify the paths followed by axons leaving the VMH. In other words, we want to trace the *efferent axons* of this structure.

We will use an **anterograde labeling method** to trace these axons. (*Anterograde* means "moving forward.") Anterograde labeling methods employ chemicals that are taken up by dendrites or cell bodies and are then transported through the axons toward the terminal buttons.

Over the years neuroscientists have developed several different methods for tracing the pathways followed by efferent axons. A recently developed method is replacing earlier ones, so this is what we will use. Cell biologists have discovered that a family of proteins produced by plants bind with specific complex molecules present in cells of the immune system. These proteins, called *lectins,* have also found a use in tracing neural pathways. A particular lectin produced by the kidney bean, **PHA-L** (*phaseolus vulgaris leukoagglutinin,* if you really want to know), is used to identify efferent axons.

To discover the destination of the efferent axons of neurons located within the VMH, we inject a minute quantity of PHA-L into that nucleus. (We use a stereotaxic apparatus to do so, of course.) The molecules of PHA-L are taken up by dendrites and are transported through the soma to the axon, where they travel by means of fast axoplasmic transport to the terminal buttons. Within a few days the cells are filled in their entirety with molecules of PHA-L: dendrites, soma, axons and all their branches, and terminal buttons. Then we kill the animal, slice the brain, and mount the sections on microscope slides. A special *immunocytochemical* method is used to

anterograde labeling method (***ann*** *ter oh grade*) A histological method that labels the axons and terminal buttons of neurons whose cell bodies are located in a particular region.

PHA-L Phaseolus vulgaris leukoagglutinin; a protein derived from kidney beans and used as an anterograde tracer; taken up by dendrites and cell bodies and carried to the ends of the axons.

Figure 5.12

The rationale for the use of PHA-L to trace efferent axons.

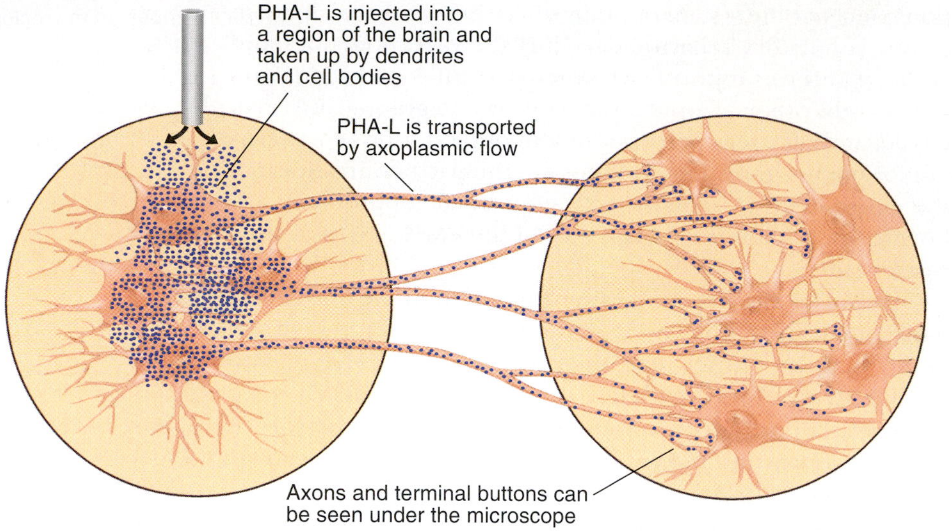
PHA-L is injected into a region of the brain and taken up by dendrites and cell bodies
PHA-L is transported by axoplasmic flow
Axons and terminal buttons can be seen under the microscope

immunocytochemical method A histological method that uses radioactive antibodies or antibodies bound with a dye molecule to indicate the presence of particular proteins of peptides.

make the molecules of PHA-L visible, and the slides are examined under a microscope. (See ***Figure 5.12.***)

Immunocytochemical methods take advantage of the immune reaction. The body's immune system has the ability to produce antibodies in response to antigens. *Antigens* are proteins (or peptides), such as those found on the surface of bacteria or viruses. *Antibodies,* which are also proteins, are produced by white blood cells to destroy invading microorganisms. Antibodies either are secreted by white blood cells or are located on their surface, in the way neurotransmitter receptors are located on the surface of neurons. When the antigens that are present on the surface of an invading microorganism come into contact with the antibodies that recognize them, the antibodies trigger an attack on the invader by the white blood cells.

Cell biologists have developed methods for producing antibodies to any peptide or protein. The antibody molecules are attached to various types of dye molecules. Some of these dyes react with other chemicals and stain the tissue a brown color. Others are fluorescent; they glow when they are exposed to light of a particular wavelength. To determine where the peptide or protein (the antigen) is located in the brain, the investigator places fresh slices of brain tissue in a solution that contains the antibody/dye molecules. The antibodies attach themselves to their antigen. When the investigator examines the slices with a microscope (under light of a particular wavelength in the case of fluorescent dyes), he or she can see which parts of the brain—even which individual neurons—contain the antigen.

Figure 5.13 shows how PHA-L can be used to identify the efferents of a particular region of the brain. Molecules of this chemical were injected into the VMH. Two days later, after the PHA-L had been taken up by the neurons in this region and transported to the ends of their axons, the animal was killed. Slices of the brain were treated

Figure 5.13

An anterograde labeling method. PHA-L was injected into the ventromedial nucleus of the hypothalamus (VMH), where it was taken up by dendrites and carried through the cells' axons to their terminal buttons. Labeled axons and terminal buttons are seen in the periaqueductal gray matter (PAG).

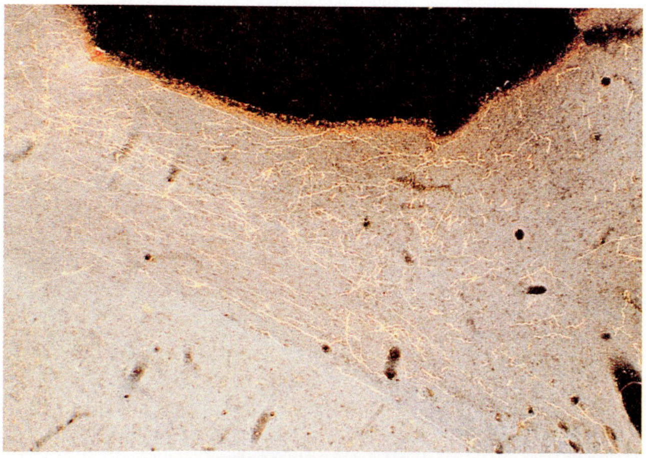

Courtesy of Kirsten Nielsen Ricciardi and Jeffrey Blaustein, University of Massachusetts.

with a chemical procedure that stains the tissue containing molecules of PHA-L a brown color. Figure 5.13 shows a photomicrograph of the periaqueductal gray matter (PAG). As you can see, this region contains some axons and terminal buttons labeled by the PHA-L, which proves that some of the efferent axons of the VMH terminate in the PAG. (See ***Figure 5.13.***)

To continue our study of the role of the VMH in female sexual behavior, we would find the structures that receive information from neurons in the VMH (such as the PAG) and see what happens when each of them is destroyed. Let's suppose that damage to some of these structures also impairs female sexual behavior. We will inject these structures with PHA-L and see where *their* axons go. Eventually, we will discover the relevant pathways from the VMH to the motor neurons whose activity is necessary for copulatory behavior. (In fact, researchers have done so, and some of their results are presented in Chapter 9.)

retrograde labeling method A histological method that labels cell bodies that give rise to the terminal buttons that form synapses with cells in a particular region.

fluorogold (***flew*** *roh gold*) A dye that serves as a retrograde label; taken up by terminal buttons and carried back to the cell bodies.

pseudorabies virus A weakened form of a pig herpes virus; used for transneuronal tracing, which labels a series of neurons that are interconnected synaptically.

Tracing Afferent Axons

Tracing efferent axons from the VMH will tell us only part of the story about the neural circuitry involved in female sexual behavior: the part between the VMH and the motor neurons. What about the circuits *before* the VMH? Is the VMH somehow involved in the analysis of sensory information (such as the sight, odor, or touch of the male)? Or perhaps the activating effect of a female's sex hormones on her behavior act through the VMH or through neurons whose axons form synapses there. To discover the parts of the brain that are involved in the "upstream" components of the neural circuitry, we need to find the inputs of the VMH—its afferent connections. To do so, we will employ a **retrograde labeling method.**

Retrograde means "moving backward." Retrograde labeling methods employ chemicals that are taken up by terminal buttons and carried back through the axons toward the cell bodies. The method for identifying the afferent inputs to a particular region of the brain is similar to the method used for identifying its efferents. First, we inject a small quantity of a chemical called **fluorogold** into the VMH. The chemical is taken up by terminal buttons and is transported back by means of retrograde axoplasmic transport to the cell bodies. A few days later we kill the animal, slice its brain, and examine the tissue under light of the appropriate wavelength. The molecules of fluorogold fluoresce under this light. We discover that the medial amygdala is one of the regions that provides input to the VMH. (See ***Figure 5.14.***)

The anterograde and retrograde labeling methods that I have described identify a single link in a chain of neurons—neurons whose axons enter or leave a particular brain region. *Transneuronal* tracing methods identify a series of two, three, or more neurons that form serial synaptic connections with each other. The most effective transneuronal tracing method uses a **pseudorabies virus**—a weakened form of a pig herpes virus that was originally developed as a vaccine. The virus is injected directly into a brain region, is taken up by neurons there, and infects them. The virus spreads throughout the infected neurons and is eventually released, passing on the infection to neurons with which they form synaptic connections. Some neurons are killed by the virus; others survive the infection. This method can be used to trace circuits in either the anterograde or the retrograde direction.

The longer the experimenter waits after injecting the virus, the larger the number of neurons that become

Figure 5.14

A retrograde tracing method. Fluorogold was injected in the VMH, where it was taken up by terminal buttons and transported back through the axons to their cell bodies. The photograph shows these cell bodies, located in the medial amygdala.

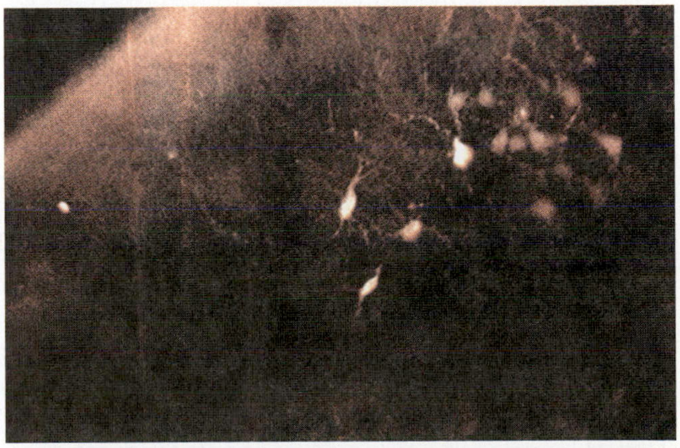

Courtesy of Yvon Delville, University of Massachusetts Medical School.

Figure 5.15

One of the inputs to the VMH and one of the outputs, as revealed by anterograde and retrograde labeling methods.

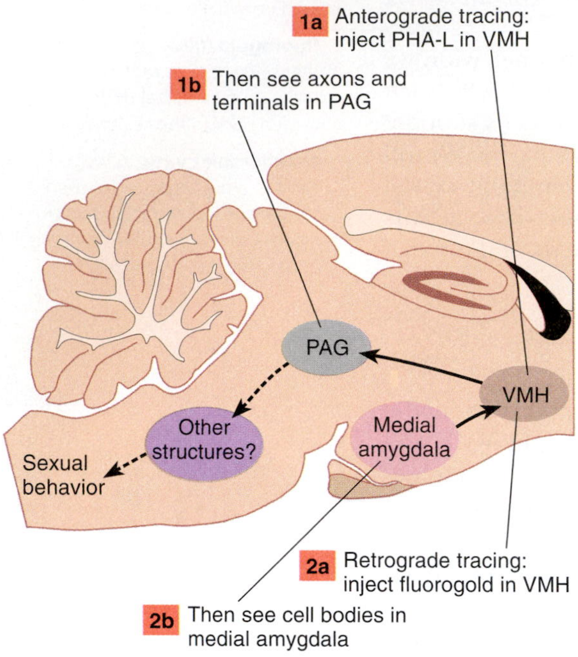

infected. After the animal is killed and the brain is sliced, immunocytochemical methods are used to localize a protein produced by the virus. For example, Daniels, Miselis, and Flanagan-Cato (1999) injected pseudorabies virus in the muscles responsible for female rats' mating posture. After a few days the rats were killed, and their brains were examined for evidence of viral infection. The study indicated that the virus found its way up the motor nerves to the motor neurons in the spinal cord, then to the reticular formation of the medulla, then to the periaqueductal gray matter, and finally to the VMH. These results confirm the results of the anterograde and retrograde labeling methods I just described. (Infected neurons were found in other structures as well, but they are not relevant to this discussion.)

Together, anterograde and retrograde labeling methods—including transneuronal methods—enable us to discover circuits of interconnected neurons. Thus, these methods help to provide us with a "wiring diagram" of the brain. (See ***Figure 5.15.***) Armed with other research methods (including some to be described later in this chapter), we can try to discover the functions of each component of this circuit.

Study of the Living Human Brain

There are many good reasons to investigate the functions of brains of animals other than humans. For one thing, we can compare the results of studies made with different species in order to make some inferences about the evolution of various neural systems. Even if our primary interest is in the functions of the human brain, we certainly cannot ask people to submit to brain surgery for the purposes of research. But diseases and accidents do occasionally damage the human brain, and if we know where the damage occurs, we can study the people's behavior and try to make the same sorts of inferences we make with deliberately produced brain lesions in laboratory animals. The problem is, where is the lesion?

In past years a researcher might study the behavior of a person with brain damage and never find out exactly where the lesion was located. The only way to be sure was to obtain the patient's brain when he or she died and examine slices of it under a microscope. But it was often impossible to do so. Sometimes the patient outlived the researcher. Sometimes the patient moved out of town. Sometimes (often, perhaps) the family refused permission for an autopsy. Because of these practical problems, study of the behavioral effects of damage to specific parts of the human brain made rather slow progress.

Recent advances in X-ray techniques and computers have led to the development of several methods for studying the anatomy of the living brain. These advances permit researchers to study the location and extent of brain damage while the patient is still living. The first method that was developed is called **computerized tomography (CT)** (from the Greek for *tomos,* "cut," and *graphein,* "to write"). This procedure, usually referred to as a *CT scan,* works as follows: The patient's head is placed in a large doughnut-shaped ring. The ring contains an X-ray tube and, directly opposite it (on the other side of the patient's head), an X-ray detector. The X-ray beam passes through the patient's head, and the detector measures the amount of radioactivity that gets through it. The beam scans the head from all angles, and a computer translates the numbers it receives from the detector into pictures of the skull and its contents. (See ***Figure 5.16.***)

computerized tomography (CT) The use of a device that employs a computer to analyze data obtained by a scanning beam of X-rays to produce a two-dimensional picture of a "slice" through the body.

magnetic resonance imaging (MRI) A technique whereby the interior of the body can be accurately imaged; involves the interaction between radio waves and a strong magnetic field.

Figure 5.17 shows a series of these CT scans taken through the head of a patient who sustained a stroke. The stroke damaged a part of the brain involved in bodily awareness and perception of space. The patient lost her awareness of the left side of her body and of items located on her left. You can see the damage as a white spot in the lower left corner of scan 5. (See ***Figure 5.17.***)

An even more detailed picture of what is inside a person's head is provided by a process called **magnetic resonance imaging (MRI)**. The MRI scanner resembles a CT scanner, but it does not use X-rays. Instead, it passes an extremely strong magnetic field through the patient's head. When a person's body is placed in a strong magnetic field, the nuclei of some atoms in molecules in the body spin with a particular orientation. If a radio frequency wave is then passed through the body, these nuclei emit radio waves of their own. Different molecules emit energy at different frequencies. The MRI scanner is tuned to detect the radiation from hydrogen atoms. Because these atoms are present in different concentrations in different tissues, the scanner can use the information to prepare pictures of slices of the brain. Unlike CT scans, which are generally limited to the horizontal plane, MRI scans can be taken in the sagittal or frontal planes as well. (See ***Figure 5.18.***)

Figure 5.16

A computerized tomography (CT) scanner.

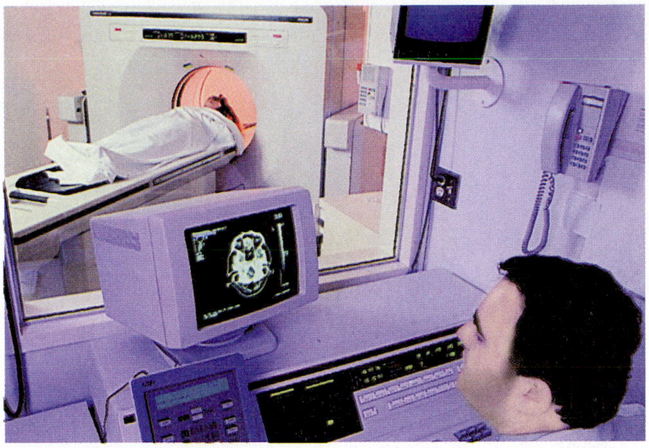

Larry Mulvihill/Rainbow.

Figure 5.17

A series of CT scans from a patient with a lesion in the right occipital-parietal area (scan 5). The lesion appears white because it was accompanied by bleeding; blood absorbs more radiation than does the surrounding brain tissue. Rostral is up, caudal is down; left and right are reversed. Scan 1 shows a section through the eyes and the base of the brain.

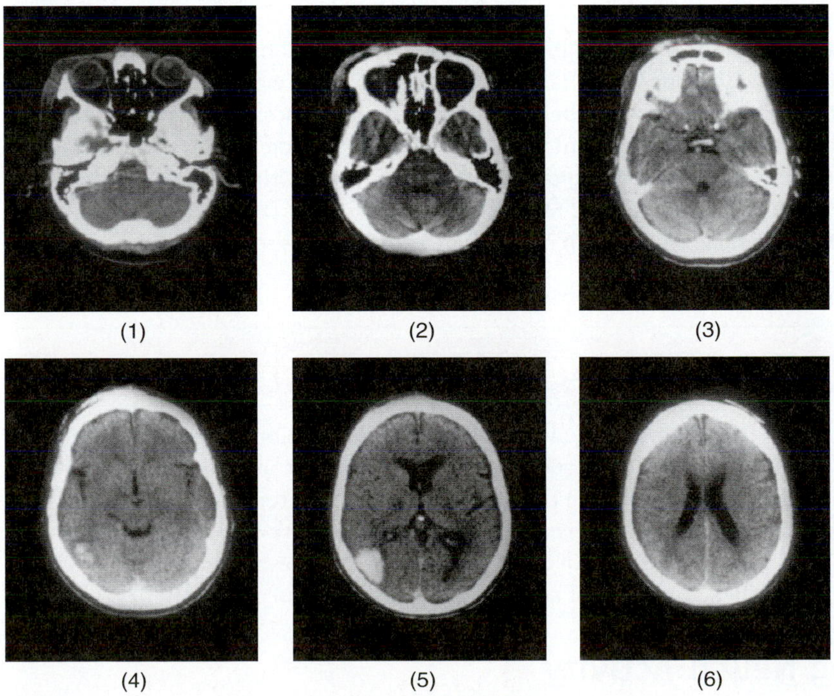

Courtesy of J. McA. Jones, Good Samaritan Hospital, Portland, Oregon.

Figure 5.18

A midsagittal MRI scan of a human brain.

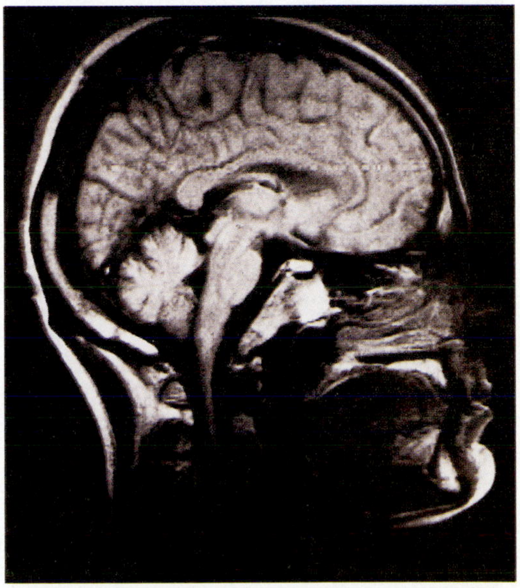

Photo courtesy of Philips Medical Systems.

INTERIM SUMMARY

Experimental Ablation

The goal of research in behavioral neuroscience is to understand the brain functions required for the performance of a particular behavior and then to learn the location of the neural circuits that perform these functions. The lesion method is the oldest one employed in such research, and it remains one of the most useful. A subcortical lesion is made under the guidance of a stereotaxic apparatus. The coordinates are obtained from a stereotaxic atlas, and the tip of an electrode or cannula is placed at the target. A lesion is made by passing radio frequency current through the electrode or infusing an excitatory amino acid through the cannula, producing an excitotoxic lesion. The advantage of excitotoxic lesions is that they destroy only neural cell bodies; axons passing through the region are not damaged.

The location of a lesion must be determined after the animal's behavior is observed. The animal is killed by humane means, and the brain is removed and placed in a fixative such as formalin. A microtome is used to slice the brain, which is usually frozen to make it hard enough to cut into thin sections. These sections are mounted on glass slides, stained with a cell-body stain, and examined under a microscope.

Light microscopes enable us to see cells and their larger organelles, but an electron microscope is needed to see small details, such as individual mitochondria and synaptic vesicles. Scanning electron microscopes provide a three-dimensional view of tissue, but at a lower magnification than transmission electron microscopes.

The next step in a research program often requires the investigator to discover the afferent and efferent connections of the region of interest with the rest of the brain. Efferent connections (those that carry information from the region in question to other parts of the brain) are revealed with anterograde tracing methods, such as the one that uses PHA-L. Afferent connections (those that bring information to the region in question from other parts of the brain) are revealed with retrograde tracing methods, such as the one that uses fluorogold. Chains of neurons that form synaptic connections are revealed by the transneuronal tracing method, which uses the pseudorabies virus.

Although brain lesions are not deliberately made in the human brain for the purposes of research, diseases and accidents can cause brain damage, and if we know where the damage is located, we can study people's behavior and make inferences about the location of the neural circuits that perform relevant functions. If the patient dies and the brain is available for examination, ordinary histological methods can be used. Otherwise, the living brain can be examined with CT scanners and MRI scanners.

Table 5.1 summarizes the research methods presented in this section.

Recording and Stimulating Neural Activity

The first section of this chapter dealt with the anatomy of the brain and the effects of damage to particular regions. This section considers a different approach: studying the brain by recording or stimulating the activity of particular regions. Brain functions involve activity of circuits of neurons; thus, different perceptions and behavioral responses involve different patterns of activity in the brain. Researchers have devised methods to record these patterns of activity or to artificially produce them.

Recording Neural Activity

Axons produce action potentials, and terminal buttons elicit postsynaptic potentials in the membrane of the cells with which they form synapses. These electrical events can be recorded (as we saw in Chapter 2), and changes in the electrical activity of a

Table 5.1

Research Methods: Part I

Goal of Method	Method	Remarks
Destroy or inactivate specific brain region	Radio frequency lesion	Destroys all brain tissue near tip of electrode
	Excitotoxic lesion; uses excitatory amino acid such as kainic acid	Destroys only cell bodies near tip of cannula; spares axons passing through region
	Infusion of local anesthetic or muscimol (drug that stimulates GABA receptors)	Temporarily inactivates specific brain region; animal can serve as its own control
Place electrode or cannula in specific region within brain	Stereotaxic surgery	Consult stereotaxic atlas for coordinates
Find location of lesion	Fix brain; slice brain; stain sections	
Identify axons leaving a particular region and the terminal buttons of these axons	Anterograde tracing method, such as PHA-L	
Identify location of neurons whose axons terminate in a particular region	Retrograde tracing method, such as fluorogold	
Identify chain of neurons that are interconnected synaptically	Transneuronal tracing method; uses pseudorabies virus	Can be used for both anterograde and retrograde tracing
Find location of lesion in living human brain	Computerized tomography (CT scanner)	Slows "slice" of brain; uses X-rays
	Magnetic resonance imaging (MRI scanner)	Shows "slice" of brain; better detail than CT scan; uses a magnetic field and radio waves

particular region can be used to determine whether that region plays a role in various behaviors. For example, recordings can be made during stimulus presentations, decision making, or motor activities.

Recordings can be made *chronically,* over an extended period of time after the animal recovers from surgery, or *acutely,* for a relatively short period of time during which the animal is kept anesthetized. Acute recordings, made while the animal is anesthetized, are usually restricted to studies of sensory pathways. Acute recordings seldom involve behavioral observations, since the behavioral capacity of an anesthetized animal is limited, to say the least.

Recordings with Microelectrodes

Drugs that affect serotonergic and noradrenergic neurons also affect REM sleep. Suppose that, knowing this fact, we wondered whether the activity of serotonergic and noradrenergic neurons would vary during different stages of sleep. To find out, we would record the activity of these neurons with microelectrodes. **Microelectrodes** have a very fine tip, small enough to record the electrical activity of individual neurons. This technique is usually called **single-unit recording** (a unit refers to an individual neuron).

Because we want to record the activity of single neurons over a long period of time in unanesthetized animals, we want more durable electrodes. We can purchase arrays of very fine wires, gathered together in a bundle. The wires are insulated with

microelectrode A very fine electrode, generally used to record activity of individual neurons.

single-unit recording Recording of the electrical activity of a single neuron.

Figure 5.19

A permanently attached set of electrodes, with a connecting socket cemented to the skull.

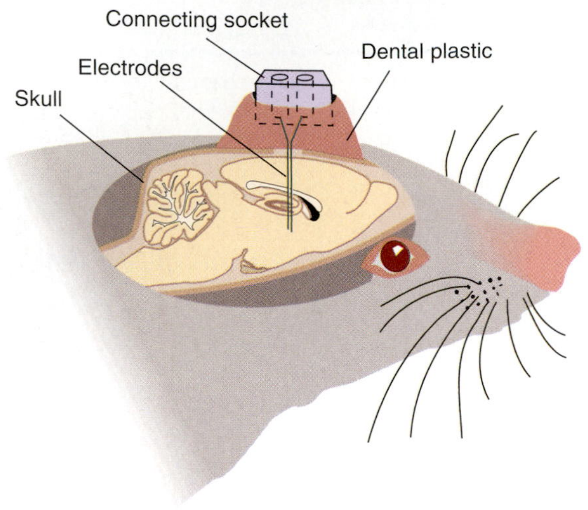

a special varnish so that only their tips are bare. The wires are flexible enough that they can follow movements of the brain tissue caused by movements of the animal's head. As a result, they are less likely to damage the neurons whose signals they are receiving. In addition, we can record the activity of several individual neurons in a particular region of the brain.

We implant the electrodes in the brains of animals through stereotaxic surgery. We attach them to miniaturized electrical sockets and bond the sockets to the animals' skull, using plastics that were originally developed for the dental profession. Then, after recovery from surgery, the animal can be "plugged in" to the recording system. Laboratory animals pay no heed to the electrical sockets on their skulls and behave quite normally. (See ***Figure 5.19.***)

Researchers often attach rather complex devices to the animals' skulls when they implant microelectrodes. These devices include screw mechanisms that permit the experimenter to move the electrode—or array of electrodes—deeper into the brain so that they can record from several different parts of the brain during the course of their observations.

The electrical signals detected by microelectrodes are quite small and must be amplified. Amplifiers used for this purpose work just like the amplifiers in a stereo system, converting the weak signals recorded at the brain into stronger ones. These signals can be displayed on an oscilloscope and stored in the memory of a computer for analysis at a later time.

What about the results of our recordings from serotonergic and noradrenergic neurons? As you will learn in Chapter 9, if we record the activity of these neurons during various stages of sleep, we will find that their firing rates fall almost to zero during REM sleep. This observation suggests that these neurons have an *inhibitory* effect on REM sleep. That is, REM sleep cannot occur until these neurons stop firing.

macroelectrode An electrode used to record the electrical activity of large numbers of neurons in a particular region of the brain; much larger than a microelectrode.

electroencephalogram (EEG) An electrical brain potential recorded by placing electrodes on in the scalp.

magnetoencephalography A procedure that detects groups of synchronously activated neurons by means of the magnetic field induced by their electrical activity; uses an array of superconducting quantum interference devices (SQUIDs).

2-deoxyglucose (2-DG) (*dee ox ee* ***gloo*** *kohss*) A sugar that enters cells along with glucose but is not metabolized.

autoradiography A procedure that locates radioactive substances in a slice of tissue; the radiation exposes a photographic emulsion or a piece of film that covers the tissue.

Recordings with Macroelectrodes

Sometimes, we want to record the activity of a region of the brain as a whole, not the activity of individual neurons located there. To do this, we would use macroelectrodes. **Macroelectrodes** do not detect the activity of individual neurons; rather, the records that are obtained with these devices represent the postsynaptic potentials of many thousands—or millions—of cells in the area of the electrode. These electrodes can consist of unsharpened wires inserted into the brain, screws attached to the skull, or even metal disks attached to the human scalp with a special paste that conducts electricity. Recordings taken from the scalp, especially, represent the activity of an enormous number of neurons, whose electrical signals pass through the meninges, skull, and scalp before reaching the electrodes.

Occasionally, neurosurgeons implant macroelectrodes directly into the human brain. The reason for doing so is to detect the source of abnormal electrical activity that is giving rise to frequent seizures. Once the source is determined, the surgeon can open the skull and remove the source of the seizures—usually scar tissue caused by brain damage that occurred earlier in life. Most often, the electrical activity of a human brain is recorded through electrodes attached to the scalp and displayed on an *ink-writing oscillograph,* commonly called a *polygraph.*

A polygraph contains a mechanism that moves a very long strip of paper past a series of pens. These pens are essentially the pointers of large voltmeters, moving up and down in response to the electrical signal sent to them by the biological amplifiers. Figure 5.20 illustrates a record of electrical activity recorded from macroelectrodes attached to various locations on a person's scalp. (See ***Figure 5.20.***) Such records are called **electroencephalograms (EEGs),** or "writings of electricity from the head." They can be used to diagnose epilepsy or brain tumors or to study the stages of sleep and wakefulness, which are associated with characteristic patterns of electrical activity.

Another use of the EEG is to monitor the condition of the brain during procedures that could potentially damage it. I witnessed just such a procedure several years ago.

Magnetoencephalography

As you undoubtedly know, when electrical current flows through a conductor, it induces a magnetic field. This means that as action potentials pass down axons or as postsynaptic potentials pass down dendrites or sweep across the somatic membrane of a neuron, magnetic fields are also produced. These fields are exceedingly small, but engineers have developed superconducting detectors (called superconducting quantum interference devices, or SQUIDs), that can detect magnetic fields that are approximately one-billionth of the size of the earth's magnetic field. **Magnetoencephalography** is performed with *neuromagnetometers,* devices that contain an array of several SQUIDs, oriented so that a computer can examine their output and calculate the source of particular signals in the brain. The neuromagnetometer shown in Figure 5.21 contains 275 SQUIDs. These devices can be used clinically—for example, to find the sources of seizures so that they can be removed surgically. They can also be used in experiments to measure regional brain activity that accompanies the perception of various stimuli or the performance of various behaviors or cognitive tasks. (See ***Figure 5.21.***)

Figure 5.20

A record from an ink-writing oscillograph.

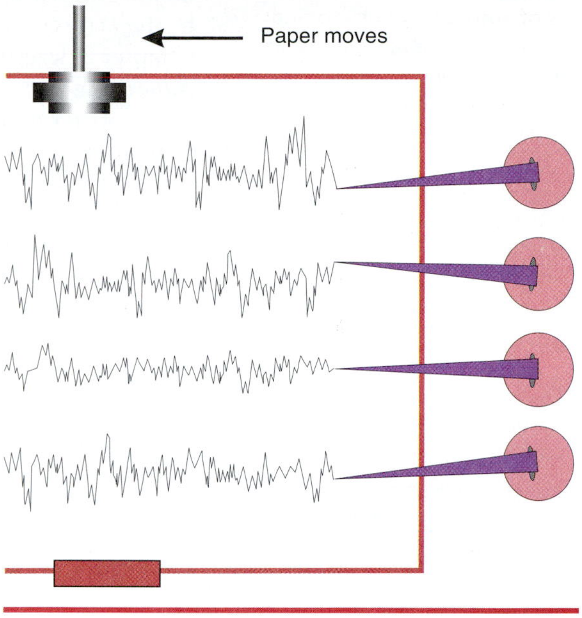

Recording the Brain's Metabolic and Synaptic Activity

Electrical signals are not the only signs of neural activity. If the neural activity of a particular region of the brain increases, the metabolic rate of this region increases, too, largely as a result of increased operation of ion pumps in the membrane of the cells. This increased metabolic rate can be measured. The experimenter injects radioactive **2-deoxyglucose (2-DG)** into the animal's bloodstream. Because this chemical resembles glucose (the principal food for the brain), it is taken into cells. Thus, the most active cells, which use glucose at the highest rate, will take up the highest concentrations of radioactive 2-DG. But unlike normal glucose, 2-DG cannot be metabolized, so it stays in the cell. The experimenter then kills the animal, removes the brain, slices it, and prepares it for *autoradiography.*

Autoradiography can be translated roughly as "writing with one's own radiation." Sections of the brain are mounted on microscope slides. The slides are then taken into a darkroom, where they are coated with a photographic emulsion (the substance found on photographic film). Several weeks later, the slides, with their coatings of emulsion, are developed, just like photographic film. The molecules of radioactive 2-DG show themselves as spots of silver grains in the developed emulsion because the radioactivity exposes the emulsion, just as X-rays or light will do.

Figure 5.21

Magnetoencephalography. The neuromagnetometer is shown on the monitor to the left. The regions of increased electrical activity are shown on the monitor to the right, superimposed on an image of the brain derived from an MRI scan.

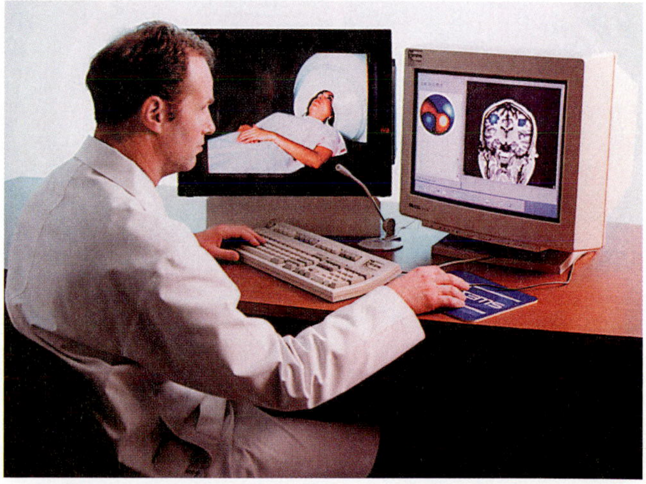

Courtesy of CTF Systems Inc.

Animation 5.2, Autoradiography, contains a video demonstrating the use of autoradiography to find the location of a neurotransmitter in the brain.

The most active regions of the brain contain the most radioactivity, showing this radioactivity in the form of dark spots in the developed emulsion. Figure 5.22 shows an autoradiograph of a slice of a rat brain; the dark spots at the bottom (indicated by the arrow) are nuclei of the hypothalamus with an especially high metabolic rate. Chapter 9 describes these nuclei and their function. (See ***Figure 5.22.***) ***Animation 5.2, Autoradiography,*** shows this procedure.

Another method of identifying active regions of the brain capitalizes on the fact that when neurons are activated (for example, by the terminal buttons that form synapses with them), particular genes in the nucleus called *immediate early genes* are turned on and particular proteins are produced. These proteins then bind with the chromosomes in the nucleus. The presence of these nuclear proteins indicates that the neuron has just been activated.

One of the nuclear proteins produced during neural activation is called **Fos.** You will remember that we already did some research on the neural circuitry involved in the sexual behavior of female rats. Suppose we want to use the Fos method in this research project to see what neurons are activated during a female rat's sexual activity. We place female rats with males and permit the animals to copulate. Then we remove the rats' brains, slice them, and follow a procedure that stains Fos protein. Figure 5.23 shows the results: Neurons in the medial amygdala of a female rat that has just mated show the presence of dark spots, indicating the presence of Fos protein. Thus, these neurons appear to be activated by copulatory activity—perhaps by the physical stimulation of the genitals that occurs then. As you will recall, when we injected a retrograde tracer (fluorogold) into the VMH, we found that this region receives input from the medial amygdala. (See ***Figure 5.23.***)

The metabolic activity of specific brain regions can be measured in human brains, too, using a method known as **positron emission tomography (PET).** First, the patient receives an injection of radioactive 2-DG. (Eventually, the chemical is broken down and leaves the cells. The dose given to humans is harmless.) The person's head is placed in a machine similar to a CT scanner. When the radioactive molecules of 2-DG decay, they emit subatomic particles called positrons, which are

Fos (*fahs*) A protein produced in the nucleus of a neuron in response to synaptic stimulation.

positron emission tomography (PET) The use of a device that reveals the localization of a radioactive tracer in a living brain.

functional MRI (fMRI) A modification of the MRI procedure that permits the measurement of regional metabolism in the brain.

microdialysis A procedure for analyzing chemicals present in the interstitial fluid through a small piece of tubing made of a semipermeable membrane that is implanted in the brain.

Figure 5.22

A 2-DG autoradiogram of a rat brain (frontal section, dorsal is at top), showing especially high regions of activity in the pair of nuclei in the hypothalamus, at the base of the brain.

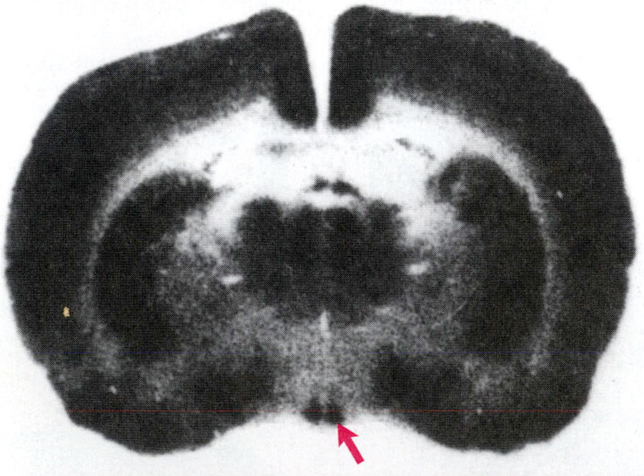

From Schwartz, W. J., and Gainer, H. *Science,* 1977, *197,* 1089–1091. Copyright 1977 American Association for the Advancement of Science. Reprinted with permission.

Figure 5.23

Localization of Fos protein. The photomicrograph shows a frontal section of the brain of a female rat, taken through the medial amygdala. The dark spots indicate the presence of Fos protein, localized by means of immunocytochemistry. The synthesis of Fos protein was stimulated by permitting the animal to engage in copulatory behavior.

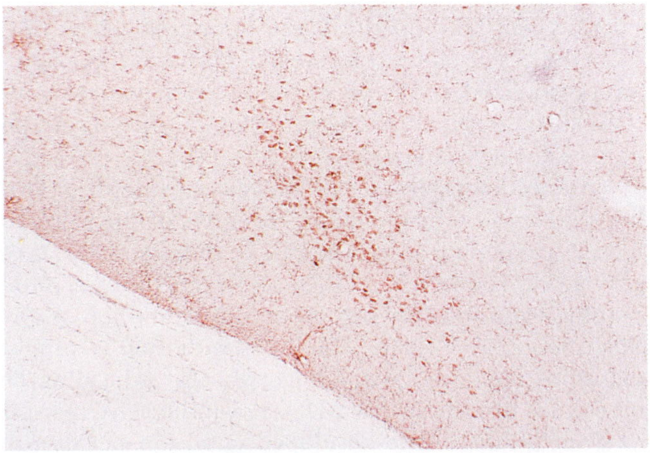

Courtesy of Marc Tetel, Skidmore College.

detected by the scanner. The computer determines which regions of the brain have taken up the radioactive substance, and it produces a picture of a slice of the brain, showing the activity level of various regions in that slice. (See ***Figure 5.24.***)

One of the disadvantages of PET scanners is their operating cost. For reasons of safety the radioactive chemicals that are administered have very short half-lives; that is, they decay and lose their radioactivity very quickly. For example, the half-life of radioactive 2-DG is 110 minutes; the half-life of radioactive water (also used for PET scans) is only 2 minutes. Because these chemicals decay so quickly, they must be produced on site, in an atomic particle accelerator called a *cyclotron.* Therefore, to the cost of the PET scanner must be added the cost of the cyclotron and the salaries of the personnel who operate it.

The most recent development in brain imaging is **functional MRI (fMRI).** Engineers have devised modifications to existing MRI scanners that acquire images very rapidly and permit the measurement of regional metabolism by detecting levels of oxygen in the brain's blood vessels. Functional MRI scans have a higher resolution than PET scans do, and they can be acquired much faster. Thus, they reveal more detailed information about the activity of particular brain regions. (See ***Figure 5.25.***)

Measuring the Brain's Secretions

Sometimes we are interested not in the general metabolic activity of particular regions of the brain, but in the secretion of specific neurotransmitters or neuromodulators in these regions. For example, suppose we know that acetylcholinergic neurons in the brain stem participate in the control of REM sleep. (The experiments that provided this knowledge are described in the next section of this chapter.) One of the characteristics of REM sleep is muscular paralysis, which prevents us from getting out of bed and acting out our dreams. We decide to measure the secretion of acetylcholine in a region of the medulla known to contain glycine-secreting neurons that inhibit motor neurons in the spinal cord. To do so, we use a procedure called **microdialysis.**

Dialysis is a process in which substances are separated by means of an artificial membrane that is permeable to some molecules but not others. A microdialysis probe consists of a small metal tube that introduces a solution into a section of dialysis tubing—a piece of artificial membrane shaped in the form of a cylinder, sealed at the bottom. Another small metal tube leads the solution away after it has circulated through the pouch. A drawing of such a probe is shown in ***Figure 5.26.***

We use stereotaxic surgery to place a microdialysis probe in a rat's brain so that the tip of the probe is located in the region we are interested in. We pump a small amount of a solution similar to extracellular fluid

Figure 5.24

PET scans of a human brain (horizontal sections). The top row shows three scans from a person at rest. The bottom row shows three scans from the same person while he was clenching and unclenching his right fist. The scans show increased uptake of radioactive 2-deoxyglucose in regions of the brain that are devoted to the control of movement, which indicates increased metabolic rate in these areas. Different computer-generated colors indicate different rates of uptake of 2-DG, as shown in the scale at the bottom.

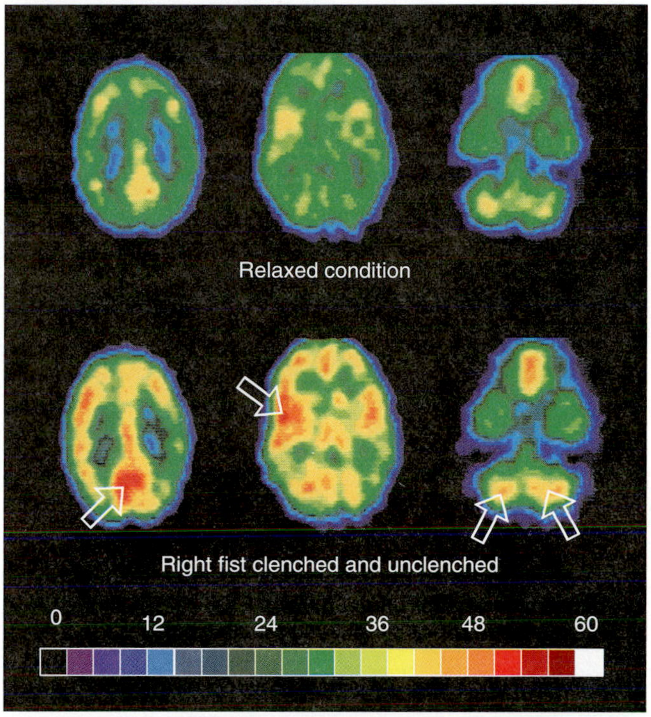

Courtesy of the Brookhaven National Laboratory and the State University of New York, Stony Brook.

Figure 5.25

A functional MRI scan of a human brain. Localized increases in neural activity of males (left) and females (right) while they were judging whether pairs of written words rhymed.

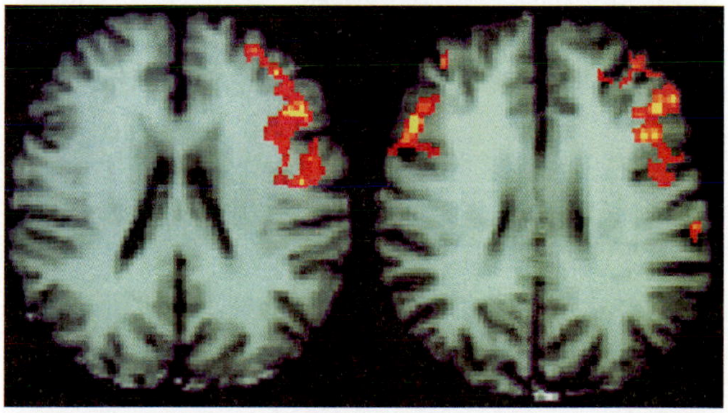

From Shaywitz, B. A., et al., *Nature,* 1995, *373,* 607–609. Copyright 1995 Macmillan Magazines Limited. Reprinted with permission.

Figure 5.26

Microdialysis. A dilute salt solution is slowly infused into the microdialysis tube, where it picks up molecules that diffuse in from the extracellular fluid. The contents of the fluid are then analyzed.

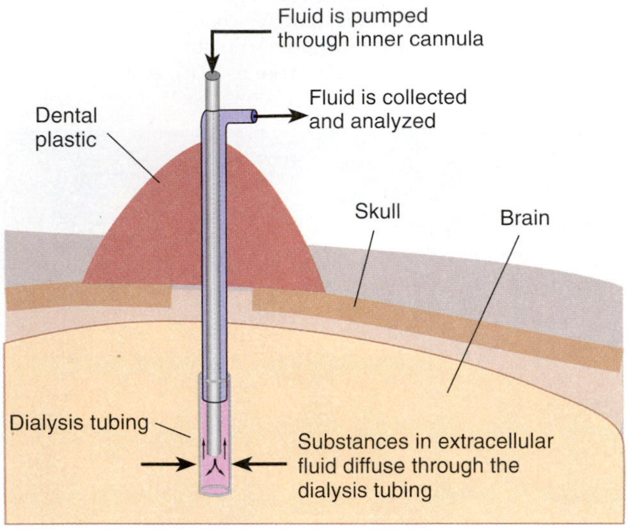

Adapted from Hernandez, L., Stanley, B. G., and Hoebel, B. G. *Life Sciences,* 1986, *39,* 2629–2637.

Figure 5.27

PET scans showing uptake of radioactive L-DOPA in the basal ganglia of a patient with parkinsonian symptoms induced by a toxic chemical before and after receiving a transplant of fetal dopaminergic neurons. (a) Preoperative scan. (b) Scan taken 13 months postoperatively. The increased uptake of L-DOPA indicates that the fetal transplant was secreting dopamine.

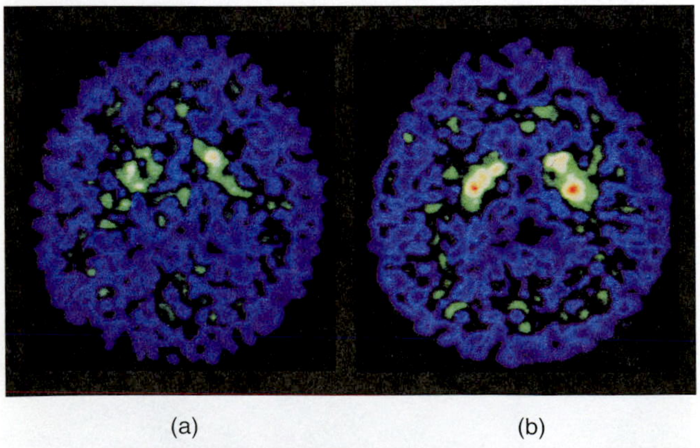

Adapted from Widner, H., Tetrud, J., Rehncrona, S., Snow, B., Brundin, P., Gustavii, B., Björklund, A., Lindvall, O., and Langston, J. W. *New England Journal of Medicine,* 1992, *327,* 1556–1563. Scans reprinted with permission.

through one of the small metal tubes into the dialysis tubing. The fluid circulates through the dialysis tubing and passes through the second metal tube, from which it is taken for analysis. As the fluid passes through the dialysis tubing, it collects molecules from the extracellular fluid of the brain, which are pushed across the membrane by the force of diffusion.

We analyze the contents of the fluid that has passed through the dialysis tubing by an extremely sensitive analytical method. This method is so sensitive that it can detect neurotransmitters (and their breakdown products) that have been released by the terminal buttons and have escaped from the synaptic cleft into the rest of the extracellular fluid. In fact, we find that the amount of acetylcholine present in the extracellular fluid of the nucleus in the medulla *does* increase during REM sleep.

In a few special cases (for example, in monitoring brain chemicals of people with intracranial hemorrhages or head trauma), the microdialysis procedure has been applied to study of the human brain, but ethical reasons prevent us from doing so for research purposes. Fortunately, there is a noninvasive way to measure neurochemicals in the human brain. Although PET scanners are expensive machines, they are also versatile. They can be used to localize *any* radioactive substance that emits positrons.

As we saw in the prologue to Chapter 4, several years ago, several people injected themselves with an illicit drug that was contaminated with a chemical that destroyed their dopaminergic neurons. As a result, they suffered from severe parkinsonism. Recently, neurosurgeons used stereotaxic procedures to transplant fetal dopaminergic neurons into the basal ganglia of some of these patients. Figure 5.27 shows PET scans of the brain of one of them. The patient was given an injection of radioactive L-DOPA one hour before each scan was made. As you learned in Chapter 4, L-DOPA is taken up by the terminals of dopaminergic neurons, where it is converted to dopamine; thus, the radioactivity shown in the scans indicates the presence of dopamine-secreting terminals in the basal ganglia. The scans show the amount of radioactivity before (part a) and after (part b) the patient received the transplant, which greatly diminished his symptoms. (See ***Figure 5.27.***)

Stimulating Neural Activity

So far, this section has been concerned with research methods that measure the activity of specific regions of the brain. But sometimes we may want to artificially change the activity of these regions to see what effects these changes have on the animal's behavior. For example, female rats will copulate with males only if certain female sex hormones are present. If we remove the rats' ovaries, the loss of these hormones will abolish their sexual behavior. We found in our earlier studies that VMH lesions disrupt this behavior. Perhaps if we *activate* the VMH, we will make up for the lack of female sex hormones and the rats will copulate again.

How do we activate neurons? We can do so by electrical or chemical stimulation. Electrical stimulation simply involves passing an electrical current through a wire inserted into the brain, as you saw in Figure 5.19. Chemical stimulation is usually accomplished by injecting a small amount of an excitatory amino acid, such as kainic acid or glutamic acid, into the brain. As you learned in Chapter 3, the principal excitatory neurotransmitter in the brain is glutamic acid (glutamate), and both of these chemicals stimulate glutamate receptors, thus activating the neurons on which these receptors are located.

Injections of chemicals into the brain can be done through an apparatus that is permanently attached to the skull so that the animal's behavior can be observed several times. We place a metal cannula (a guide cannula) in an animal's brain and cement its top to the skull. At a later date we place a smaller cannula of measured length inside the guide cannula and then inject a chemical into the brain. Because the animal is free to move about, we can observe the effects of the injection on its behavior. (See ***Figure 5.28.***) ***Animation 5.3, Cannula Implantation,*** shows this surgical procedure.

Animation 5.3, Cannula Implantation, contains a video demonstrating the use of a stereotaxic apparatus to implant a cannula in the brain.

The principal disadvantage of chemical stimulation is that it is slightly more complicated than electrical stimulation; chemical stimulation requires cannulas, tubes, special pumps or syringes, and sterile solutions of excitatory amino acids. However, it has a distinct advantage over electrical stimulation: It activates cell bodies but not axons. Because only cell bodies (and their dendrites, of course) contain glutamate receptors, we can be assured that an injection of an excitatory amino acid into a particular region of the brain excites the cells there, but not the axons of

Figure 5.28

An intracranial cannula. A guide cannula is permanently attached to the skull, and at a later time a thinner cannula can be inserted through the guide cannula into the brain. Chemicals can be infused into the brain through this device.

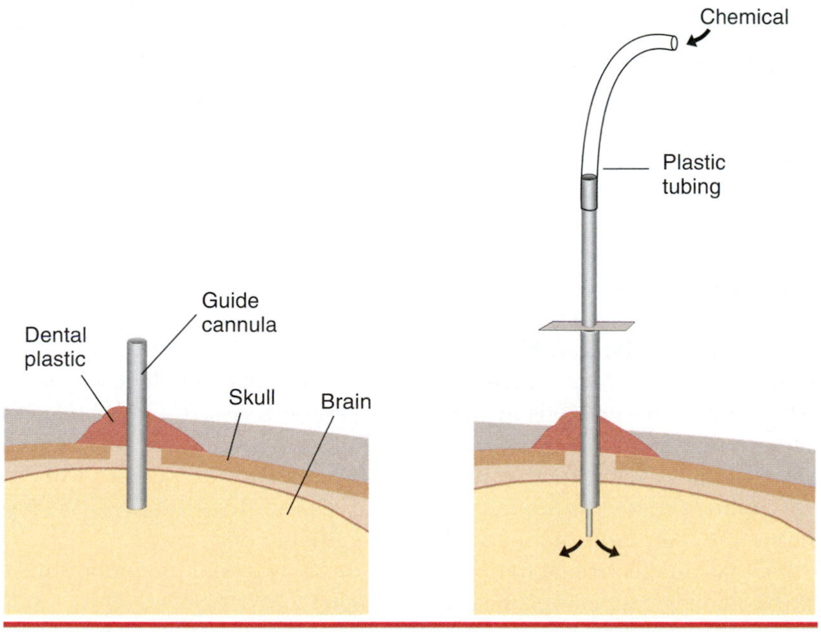

other neurons that happen to pass through the region. Thus, the effects of chemical stimulation are more localized than the effects of electrical stimulation.

You might have noticed that I just said that kainic acid, which I described earlier as a neurotoxin, can be used to stimulate neurons. These two uses are not really contradictory. Kainic acid produces excitotoxic lesions by stimulating neurons to death. Whereas large doses of a concentrated solution kill neurons, small doses of a dilute solution simply stimulate them.

What about the results of our experiment? In fact (as we shall see in Chapter 9), VMH stimulation *does* substitute for female sex hormones. Perhaps, then, the female sex hormones exert their effects in this nucleus. We will see how to test this hypothesis in the final section of this chapter.

Behavioral Effects of Electrical Brain Stimulation

Stimulation of the brain of a freely moving animal often produces behavioral changes. For example, hypothalamic stimulation can elicit behaviors such as feeding, drinking, grooming, attack, or escape, a finding that suggests that the hypothalamus is involved in their control. Stimulation of part of the caudate nucleus often halts ongoing behavior, which suggests that this structure is involved in motor inhibition. Brain stimulation can serve as a signal for a learned task or can even serve as a rewarding or punishing event, as we will see in Chapter 12.

There are problems in interpreting the significance of the effects of brain stimulation, especially when it is produced with electricity. An electrical stimulus (usually a series of pulses) can never duplicate the natural neural processes that go on in the brain. The normal interplay of spatial and temporal patterns of excitation and inhibition is destroyed by the artificial stimulation of an area. Electrical brain stimulation is probably as natural as attaching ropes to the arms of the members of an orchestra and then shaking all the ropes simultaneously to see what they can play. In fact, local stimulation is sometimes used to produce a "temporary lesion," by which the region is put out of commission by the meaningless artificial stimulation.

The surprising finding is that stimulation sometimes *does* produce orderly changes in behavior. This occurs when the stimulation takes place in regions of the brain that exert modulatory functions on neural circuits located in other parts of the brain. For example, the axons of acetylcholinergic neurons in the basal forebrain innervate much of the cerebral cortex. If these neurons are artificially stimulated, the widespread release of acetylcholine activates the cerebral cortex and facilitates information processing taking place there.

As we saw earlier in this chapter, neural activity induces magnetic fields that can be detected by means of magnetoencephalography. Similarly, magnetic fields can be used to stimulate neurons by inducing electrical currents in brain tissue. **Transcranial magnetic stimulation (TMS)** uses a coil of wires, usually arranged in the shape of the numeral 8, to stimulate neurons in the human cerebral cortex. The stimulating coil is placed on top of the skull so that the crossing point in the middle of the 8 is located immediately above the region to be stimulated. Pulses of electricity send magnetic fields that activate neurons in the cortex. The effects are very similar to those of direct stimulation of the exposed brain. For example, as we shall see in Chapter 6, stimulation of a particular region of the visual association cortex will disrupt a person's ability to detect movements in visual stimuli. In addition, TMS has been used to treat the symptoms of mental disorders such as depression.

transcranial magnetic stimulation (TMS) Stimulation of the cerebral cortex by means of magnetic fields produced by passing pulses of electricity through a coil of wire placed next to the skull; interferes with the functions of the brain region that is stimulated.

Figure 5.29 shows an electromagnetic coil used in transcranial magnetic stimulation and its placement on a person's head. (See ***Figure 5.29.***)

Figure 5.29

Transcranial magnetic stimulation. (a) The coil used to apply the stimulation. (b) An illustration of the use of the coil. The wires on the man's face supply electrical current to light-emitting diodes, which provide reference points to keep track of head movements.

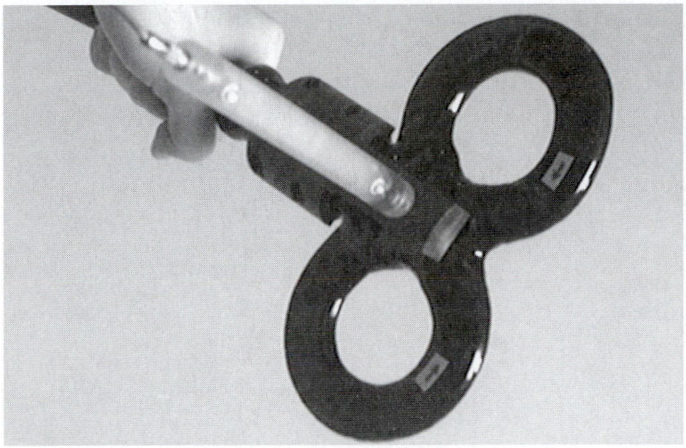

(a)

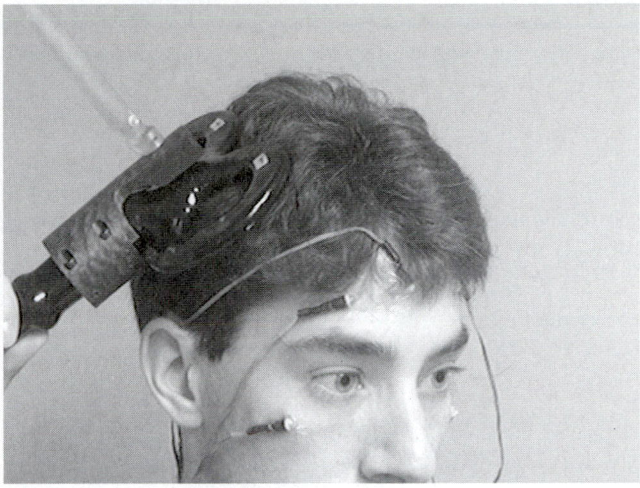

(b)

Photographs courtesy of Michael Leventon and the MIT AI Laboratory.

INTERIM SUMMARY

Recording and Stimulating Neural Activity

When circuits of neurons participate in their normal functions, their electrical activity, metabolic activity, and chemical secretions increase. Thus, by observing these processes as an animal perceives various stimuli or engages in various behaviors, we can make some inferences about the functions performed by various regions of the brain. Microelectrodes can be used to record the electrical activity of individual neurons. Chronic recordings require that the electrode be attached to an electrical socket, which is fastened to the skull with a plastic adhesive. Macroelectrodes record the activity of large groups of neurons. In rare cases macroelectrodes are placed in the depths of the human brain, but most often they are placed on the scalp and their activity is recorded on a polygraph.

Metabolic activity can be measured by giving an animal an injection of radioactive 2-DG, which accumulates in metabolically active neurons. The presence of the radioactivity is revealed through autoradiography: Slices of the brain are placed on microscope slides, covered with a photographic emulsion, left to sit a while, and then developed like photographic negatives. When neurons are stimulated, they synthesize the nuclear protein Fos. The presence of Fos, revealed by a special staining method, provides another way to discover active regions of the brain. The metabolic activity of various regions of the living human brain can be revealed by the 2-DG method, but a PET scanner is used to detect the active regions. Another noninvasive method of measuring regional brain activity is provided by functional MRI, which detects localized changes in oxygen level.

The secretions of neurotransmitters and neuromodulators can be measured by implanting the tip of a microdialysis probe in a particular region of the brain. A PET scanner can be used to perform similar observations of the human brain.

Researchers can stimulate various regions of the brain by implanting a macroelectrode and applying mild electrical stimulation. Alternatively, they can implant a guide cannula in

Table 5.2

Research Methods: Part II

Goal of Method	Method	Remarks
Record electrical activity of single neurons	Glass or metal microelectrodes	Metal microelectrodes can be implanted permanently to record neural activity as animal moves
Record electrical activity of regions of brain	Metal macroelectrodes	In humans, usually attached to the scalp with a special paste
Record magnetic fields induced by neural activity	Magnetoencephalography; uses a neuromagnetometer, which contains an array of SQUIDs	Can determine the location of a group of neurons firing synchronously
Record metabolic activity of regions of brain	2-DG autoradiography	Measures local glucose utilization
	Measurement of Fos protein	Identifies neurons that have recently been stimulated
	2-DG PET scan Functional MRI	Measures regional metabolic activity of human brain
Measure neurotransmitters and neuromodulators released by neurons	Microdialysis	A wide variety of substances can be analyzed
Measure neurochemicals in the living human brain	PET scan	Can localize any radioactive substance in the human brain
Stimulate neural activity	Electrical stimulation	Stimulates neurons near the tip of the electrode and axons passing through region
	Chemical stimulation with excitatory amino acid	Stimulates only neurons near the tip of the cannula, not axons passing through region
	Transcranial magnetic stimulation	Stimulate neurons in the human cerebral cortex with an electromagnet placed on the head

the brain; after the animal has recovered from the surgery, they insert a smaller cannula and inject a weak solution of an excitatory amino acid into the brain. The advantage of this procedure is that only neurons whose cell bodies are located nearby will be stimulated; axons passing through the region will not be affected. Transcranial magnetic stimulation induces electrical activity in the human cerebral cortex, which temporarily disrupts the functioning of neural circuits located there.

Table 5.2 summarizes the research methods presented in this section.

Neurochemical Methods

I have already described some neurochemical methods in the context of damaging or stimulating the brain or measuring neural activity. This section describes several other neurochemical methods that are useful in studying the physiology of behavior.

Physicians discovered that exposure to insecticides that contained acetylcholinesterase inhibitors could cause intense, bizarre dreams and waking hallucinations.

Finding Neurons That Produce Particular Neurochemicals

Suppose we learn that a particular drug affects behavior. How would we go about discovering the neural circuits that are responsible for the drug's effects? To answer this question, let's take a specific example. Physicians discovered several years ago that farm workers who had been exposed to certain types of insecticides (the organophosphates) had particularly intense and bizarre dreams and even reported having hallucinations while awake. A plausible explanation for these symptoms is that the drug stimulates the neural circuits responsible for dreaming. (After all, dreams are hallucinations that we have while sleeping.) Alternatively, the drug could disrupt inhibitory mechanisms that *prevent* dreaming while we are awake. Other evidence (which will not be described here) indicates that the former hypothesis is true: Organophosphate insecticides directly activate the neural circuits responsible for dreaming.

The first question to ask relates to how the organophosphate insecticides work. Pharmacologists have the answer: These drugs are acetylcholinesterase inhibitors. As you learned in Chapter 4, acetylcholinesterase inhibitors are potent acetylcholine agonists. By inhibiting AChE, the drugs prevent the rapid destruction of ACh after it is released by terminal buttons and thus prolong the postsynaptic potentials at acetylcholinergic synapses.

Now that we understand the action of the insecticides, we know that these drugs act at acetylcholinergic synapses. What neurochemical methods should we use to discover the sites of action of the drugs in the brain? There are three possibilities: We could look for neurons that contain acetylcholine, we could look for the enzyme acetylcholinesterase (which must be present in the postsynaptic membranes of cells that receive synaptic input from acetylcholinergic neurons), or we could look for acetylcholine receptors. Let's see how these three methods work.

First, let's consider methods by which we can localize particular neurochemicals, such as neurotransmitters and neuromodulators. (In our case we are interested in acetylcholine.) There are two basic ways of localizing neurochemicals in the brain: localizing the chemicals themselves or the enzymes that produce them.

Peptides (or proteins) can be localized directly by means of immunocytochemical methods, which were described in the first section of this chapter. Slices of brain tissue are exposed to an antibody for the peptide, linked to a dye (usually, a fluorescent dye). The slices are then examined under a microscope using light of a particular wavelength. For example, Figure 5.30 shows the location of axons in the forebrain that contain vasopressin, a peptide neurotransmitter. Two sets of axons are shown. One set, which forms a cluster around the third ventricle at the base of the brain, shows up as a rusty color. The other set, scattered through the lateral septum, looks like strands of gold fibers. (As you can see, a properly stained brain section can be beautiful. See ***Figure 5.30.***)

But we are interested in acetylcholine, which is not a peptide. Therefore, we cannot use immunocytochemical methods to find this neurotransmitter. However, we can use these methods to localize the enzyme that produces it. The synthesis of acetylcholine is made possible by the enzyme choline acetyltransferase (ChAT). Thus, neurons that contain this enzyme almost certainly secrete ACh. Figure 5.31 shows acetylcholinergic neurons in the pons that have been identified by means of immunocytochemistry; the brain tissue was exposed to an antibody to ChAT attached to a fluorescent dye. (See ***Figure 5.31.***)

Localizing Particular Receptors

As we saw in Chapters 3 and 4, neurotransmitters, neuromodulators, and hormones convey their messages to their target cells by binding with receptors. The location of these receptors can be determined by two different procedures.

The first procedure uses autoradiography. We expose slices of brain tissue to a solution containing a radioactive ligand for a particular receptor. Next, we rinse the slices so that the only radioactivity remaining in them is that of the molecules of the ligand bound to their receptors. Finally, we use autoradiographic methods to localize the radioactive ligand—and thus the re-

Figure 5.30

Localization of a peptide by means of immunocytochemistry. The photomicrograph shows a portion of a frontal section through the rat forebrain. The gold- and rust-colored fibers are axons and terminal buttons that contain vasopressin, a peptide neurotransmitter.

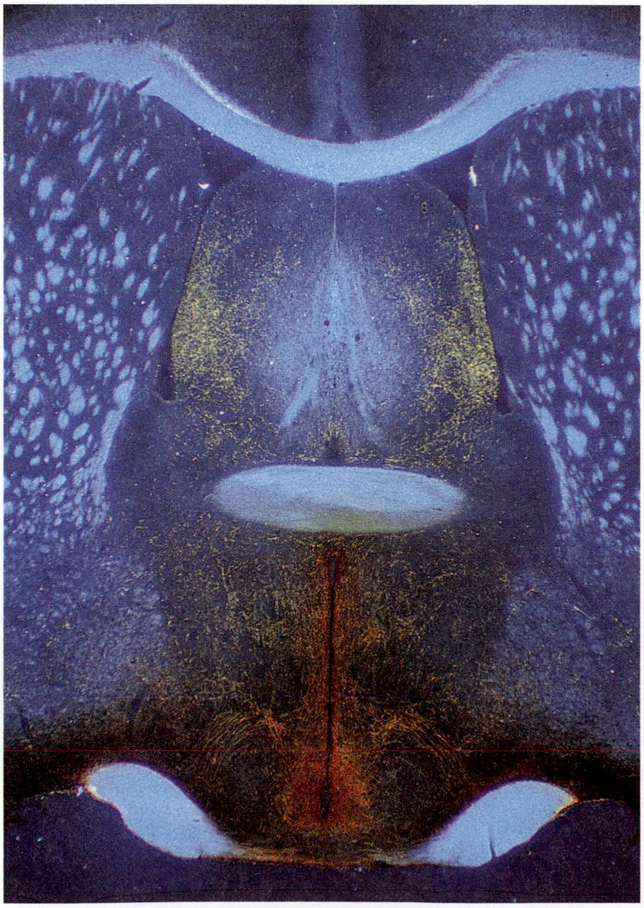

Courtesy of Geert DeVries, University of Massachusetts.

Figure 5.31

Localization of an enzyme responsible for the synthesis of a neurotransmitter, revealed by immunocytochemistry. The photomicrograph shows a section through the pons. The orange neurons contain choline acetyltransferase, which implies that they produce (and thus secrete) acetylcholine.

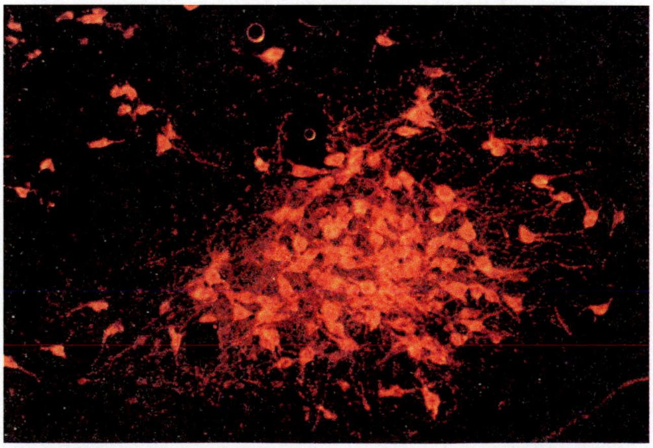

Courtesy of David A. Morilak and Roland Ciaranello, Nancy Pritzker Laboratory of Developmental and Molecular Neurobiology, Department of Psychiatry and Behavioral Sciences, Stanford University School of Medicine.

ceptors. Figure 5.32 shows an example of the results of this procedure. We see an autoradiogram of a slice of a rat's brain that was soaked in a solution that contained radioactive morphine, which bound with the brain's opiate receptors. (See ***Figure 5.32.***)

The second procedure uses immunocytochemistry. Receptors are proteins; therefore, we can produce antibodies against them. We expose slices of brain tissue to the appropriate antibody (labeled with a fluorescent dye) and look at the slices with a microscope under light of a particular wavelength.

Let's apply the method for localizing receptors to the first line of investigation we considered in this chapter: the role of the ventromedial hypothalamus (VMH) in the sexual behavior of female rats. As we saw, lesions of the VMH abolish this behavior. We also saw that the behavior does not occur if the rat's ovaries are removed but that it can be activated by stimulation of the VMH with electricity or an excitatory amino acid. These results suggest that the sex hormones produced by the ovaries act on neurons in the VMH.

This hypothesis suggests two experiments. First, we could use the procedure shown in Figure 5.28 to place a small amount of the appropriate sex hormone directly into the VMH of female rats whose ovaries we had previously removed. As we shall see in Chapter 9, this procedure works; the hormone *does* reactivate the animals' sexual behavior. The second experiment would use autoradiography to look for the receptors for the sex hormone. We would expose slices of rat brain to the radioactive hormone, rinse them, and perform autoradiography. If we did so, we would indeed find radioactivity in the VMH. (And if we compared slices from the brains of female and male rats, we would find evidence of more hormone receptors in the females' brains.) We could also use immunocytochemistry to localize the hormone receptors, and we would obtain the same results.

Figure 5.32

An autoradiogram of a rat brain (horizontal section, rostral is at top) that was incubated in a solution containing radioactive morphine, a ligand for opiate receptors. The receptors are indicated by white areas.

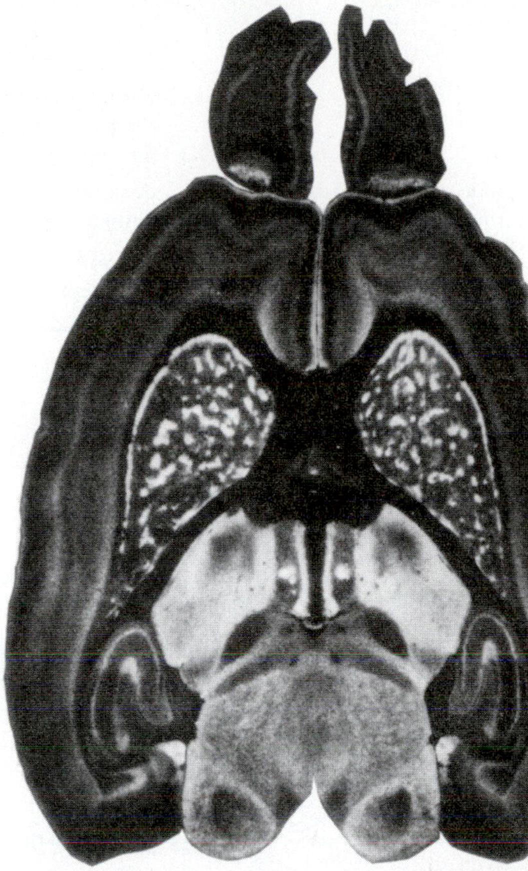

From Herkenham, M. A., and Pert, C. B. *Journal of Neuroscience,* 1982, *2,* 1129–1149. Copyright 1982 by the Society for Neuroscience.

INTERIM SUMMARY

Neurochemical Methods

Neurochemical methods can be used to determine the location of an enormous variety of substances in the brain. They can identify neurons that secrete a particular neurotransmitter or neuromodulator and those that possess receptors that respond to the presence of these substances. Peptides and proteins can be directly localized, through immunocytochemical methods; the tissue is exposed to an antibody that is linked to a molecule that fluoresces under light of a particular wavelength. Other substances can be detected by immunocytochemical localization of an enzyme that is required for their synthesis.

Receptors for neurochemicals can be localized by two means. The first method uses autoradiography to reveal the distribution of a radioactive ligand to which the tissue has been exposed. The second method uses immunocytochemistry to detect the presence of the receptors themselves, which are proteins.

Table 5.3 summarizes the research methods presented in this section.

Table 5.3

Research Methods: Part III

Goal of method	Method	Remarks
Identify neurons producing a particular neurotransmitter or neuromodulator	Immunocytochemical localization of peptide or protein	Requires a specific antibody
	Immunocytochemical localization of enzyme responsible for synthesis of substance	Useful if substance is not a peptide or protein
Identify neurons that contain a particular type of receptor	Autoradiographic localization of radioactive ligand	
	Immunocytochemical localization of receptor	Requires a specific antibody

Genetic Methods

All behavior is determined by interactions between an individual's brain and his or her environment. Many behavioral characteristics—such as talents, personality variables and mental disorders—seem to run in families. This fact suggests that genetic factors may play a role in the development of physiological differences that are ultimately responsible for these characteristics. In some cases the genetic link is very clear: A defective gene interferes with brain development, and a neurological abnormality causes behavioral deficits. In other cases the links between heredity and behavior are much more subtle, and special genetic methods must be used to reveal them.

Twin Studies

A powerful method for estimating the influence of heredity on a particular trait is to compare the *concordance rate* for this trait in pairs of monozygotic and dizygotic twins. Monozygotic twins (identical twins) have identical genotypes—that is, their chromosomes, and the genes they contain, are identical. In contrast, the genetic similarity between dizygotic twins (fraternal twins) is, on the average, 50 percent. Investigators study records to identify pairs of twins in which at least one member has the trait—for example, a diagnosis of a particular mental disorder. If both twins have been diagnosed with this disorder, they are said to be *concordant*. If only one has received this diagnosis, the twins are said to be *discordant*. Thus, if a disorder has a genetic basis, the percentage of monozygotic twins who are concordant for the diagnosis will be higher than the percentage of dizygotic twins. For example, as we will see in Chapter 15, the concordance rate for schizophrenia in twins is at least four times higher for monozygotic twins than for dizygotic twins, a finding that provides strong evidence that schizophrenia is a heritable trait. Twin studies have found that many individual characteristics, including personality traits, prevalence of obesity, incidence of alcoholism, and a wide variety of mental disorders, are influenced by genetic factors.

Twin studies provide a powerful method for estimating the relative roles of heredity and environment in the development of particular behavioral traits.

Adoption Studies

Another method for estimating the heritability of a particular behavioral trait is to compare people who were adopted early in life with their biological and adoptive parents. All behavioral traits are affected to some degree by hereditary factors, environmental factors, and an interaction between hereditary and environmental factors. Environmental factors are both social and biological in nature. For example, the mother's health, nutrition, and drug-taking behavior during pregnancy are prenatal environmental factors, and the child's diet, medical care, and social environment (both inside and outside the home) are postnatal environmental factors. If a child is adopted soon after birth, most of the postnatal environmental factors will be associated with the adoptive parents, the genetic factors will be associated with the biological parents, and the prenatal environmental factors will be associated with the biological mother.

Adoption studies require that the investigator know the identity of the parents of the people being studied and be able to measure the behavioral trait in the biological and adoptive parents. If the people being studied strongly resemble their biological parents, we conclude that the trait is probably influenced by genetic factors. To be certain, we will have to rule out possible differences in the prenatal environment of the adopted children. If, instead, the people resemble their adoptive parents, we conclude that the trait is influenced by environmental factors. (It would take further study to determine just what these environmental factors might be.) Of course, it is possible that both hereditary and environmental factors play a role, in which case the people being studied will resemble both their biological and adoptive parents.

Targeted Mutations

A recently developed method has put a powerful tool in the hands of neuroscientists. **Targeted mutations** are mutated genes produced in the laboratory and inserted into the chromosomes of mice. These mutated genes (also called knockout genes) are defective—They fail to produce a functional protein. In many cases the target of the mutation is an enzyme that controls a particular chemical reaction. For example, we will see in Chapter 12 that lack of a particular enzyme interferes with learning. This result suggests that the enzyme is partly responsible for changes in the structure of synapses required for learning to occur. In other cases the target of the mutation is a protein that itself serves useful functions in the cell. For example, we will see in Chapter 16 that a particular type of opiate receptor is involved in the reinforcing and analgesic effects of opiates.

INTERIM SUMMARY

Genetic Methods

Because genes direct an organism's development, genetic methods are very useful in studies of the physiology of behavior. Twin studies compare the concordance rates of monozygotic (identical) and dizygotic (fraternal) twins for a particular trait. A higher concordance rate for monozygotic twins provides evidence that the trait is influenced by heredity. Adoption studies compare people who were adopted during infancy with their biological and adoptive parents. If the people resemble their biological parents, evidence is seen for genetic factors. If the people resemble their adoptive parents, evidence is seen for a role of factors in the family environment.

Targeted mutations permit neuroscientists to study the effects of a lack of a particular protein—for example, an enzyme, structural protein, or receptor—on an animal's physiological and behavioral characteristics.

targeted mutation A mutated gene (also called a "knockout gene") produced in the laboratory and inserted into the chromosomes of mice; fails to produce a functional protein.

THOUGHT QUESTIONS

1. You have probably read news reports about studies of the genetics of human behavioral traits or seen them on television. What does it really mean when a laboratory reports the discovery of, say, a "gene for shyness"?
2. Most rats do not appear to like the taste of alcohol, but researchers have bred some rats that will drink alcohol in large quantities. Can you think of ways to use these animals to investigate the possible role of genetic factors in alcoholism in humans?

EPILOGUE

Watch the Brain Waves

What went wrong? Why did Mrs. H.'s "successful" surgery cause a neurological problem? And can anything be done for her?

First, let's consider the cause of the problem. As you will recall, a machine—an artificial heart—circulated Mrs. H.'s blood while the surgeon was removing two of her coronary arteries and replacing them with veins taken from her leg. The output of the machine is adjustable; that is, the person operating it can control the patient's blood pressure. The surgeon tries to keep the blood pressure just high enough to sustain the patient but not so high as to interfere with the delicate surgery on the coronary arteries. Unfortunately, Mrs. H.'s coronary arteries were not the only blood vessels to be partially blocked; the arteries in her brain, too, contained atherosclerotic plaque. When the machine took over the circulation of her blood, some parts of her brain received an inadequate blood flow, and the cells in these regions were damaged.

If Mrs. H.'s blood pressure had been maintained at a slightly higher level during the surgery, her brain damage might have been prevented. For most patients, the blood pressure would have been sufficient, but in her case it was not. Mrs. H.'s brain damage is irreversible, but are there steps that can be taken to prevent others from sharing her fate?

The answer is yes. The solution is to use a method described in this chapter: electroencephalography. What we need is a warning system to tell the surgeon that the brain is not receiving a sufficient blood flow so that he or she can adjust the machine and increase the patient's blood pressure. That warning can be provided by an EEG. For many years, clinical electroencephalographers (specialists who perform EEGs to diagnose neurological disorders) have known that diffuse, widespread brain damage caused by various poisons, anoxia, or extremely low levels of blood glucose produces slowing of the regular rhythmic pattern of the EEG. Fortunately, this pattern begins right away, as soon as the damage commences. Thus, if EEG leads are attached to a patient undergoing cardiac surgery, an electroencephalographer can watch the record coming off the polygraph and warn the surgeon if the record shows slowing. If it does, the patient's blood flow can be increased until the EEG reverts to normal, and brain damage can be averted.

Mrs. H. was operated on over 15 years ago, at a time when only a few cardiac surgeons had their patient's brain waves monitored. Today, the practice is common, and it is used during other surgical procedures that may reduce blood flow to the brain. For example, when the carotid arteries (the vessels that provide most of the brain's blood supply) become obstructed by atherosclerotic plaque, a surgeon can cut open the arteries and remove the plaque. During this procedure, called *carotid endarterectomy,* clamps must be placed on the carotid artery, completely stopping the blood flow. Some patients can tolerate the temporary clamping of one carotid artery without damage; others cannot. If the EEG record shows no slowing while the artery is clamped, the surgeon can proceed. If it does, the surgeon must place the ends of a plastic tube into the artery above and below the clamped region to maintain a constant blood flow. This procedure introduces a certain amount of additional risk to the patient, so most surgeons would prefer to do it only if necessary. The EEG provides the essential information.

KEY CONCEPTS

EXPERIMENTAL ABLATION

1. Neuroscientists produce brain lesions to try to infer the functions of the damaged region from changes in the animals' behavior.
2. Brain lesions may be produced in the depths of the brain by passing electrical current through an electrode placed there or by infusing an excitatory amino

acid; the latter method kills cells but spares axons that pass through the region.

3. The behavior of animals with brain lesions must be compared with that of a control group consisting of animals with sham lesions.
4. A stereotaxic apparatus is used to place electrodes or cannulas in particular locations in the brain. The coordinates are obtained from a stereotaxic atlas.
5. The location of a lesion is verified by means of histological methods, which include fixation, slicing, staining, and examination of the tissue under a microscope.
6. Special histological methods have been devised to trace the afferent and efferent connections of a particular brain region.
7. The structure of the living human brain can be revealed through CT scans or MRI scans.

RECORDING AND STIMULATING NEURAL ACTIVITY

8. The electrical activity of single neurons can be recorded with microelectrodes, and that of entire regions of the brain can be recorded with macroelectrodes. EEGs are recorded on polygraphs and recorded from macroelectrodes pasted on a person's scalp.
9. Metabolic activity of particular parts of animals' brains can be assessed by means of 2-DG autoradiography or by measurement of the production of Fos protein. The metabolic activity of specific regions of the human brain can be revealed through PET scans or functional MRI scans.
10. Microdialysis permits a researcher to measure the secretion of particular chemicals in specific regions of the brain.
11. Neurons can be stimulated electrically, through electrodes, or chemically, by infusing dilute solutions of excitatory amino acids through cannulas.

NEUROCHEMICAL METHODS

12. Immunocytochemical methods can be used to localize peptides in the brain or localize the enzymes that produce substances other than peptides.
13. Receptors can be localized by exposing the brain tissue to radioactive ligands and assessing the results with autoradiography or immunocytochemistry.

GENETIC METHODS

14. Twin studies and adoption studies enable investigators to estimate the role of hereditary factors in a particular physiological characteristic or behavior.
15. Targeted mutations are artificially produced mutations that interfere with the action of one or more genes, which enables investigators to study the effects of the lack of a particular gene product.

SUGGESTED READINGS

STEREOTAXIC ATLASES

Paxinos, G., and Watson, C. *The Rat Brain in Stereotaxic Coordinates,* 4th ed. San Diego, CA: Academic Press, 1998.

Slotnick, B. M., and Leonard, C. M. *A Stereotaxic Atlas of the Albino Mouse Forebrain.* Rockville, MD: Public Health Service, 1975. (U.S. Government Printing Office Stock Number 017-024-00491-0)

Snider, R. S., and Niemer, W. T. *A Stereotaxic Atlas of the Cat Brain.* Chicago: University of Chicago Press, 1961.

Swanson, L. W. *Brain Maps: Structure of the Rat Brain.* Amsterdam: Elsevier, 1992.

HISTOLOGICAL METHODS

Heimer, L., and Záborsky, L. *Neuroanatomical Tract-Tracing Methods 2: Recent Progress.* New York: Plenum Press, 1989.

SUGGESTED WEB SITES

Online Mendelian Inheritance

www3.ncbi.nlm.nih.gov/Omim/

This site contains an online catalog of human genes and genetic disorders and links to other genetic inheritance sites.

Bioscience Research: Methods

http://biochemie.net/links/Methods/

Protocols for various techniques in molecular biology are the focus of this site.

Tutorial of Functional MRI

www.mhri.edu.au/~nab/gregg.html

This site provides an advanced overview of the functional MRI technique and provides comprehensive references for the technique.

Vision

chapter 6

CHAPTER OUTLINE

LEARNING OBJECTIVES

1. Describe the characteristics of light and color, outline the anatomy of the eye and its connections with the brain, and describe the process of transduction of visual information.
2. Describe the coding of visual information by photoreceptors and ganglion cells in the retina.
3. Describe the striate cortex and discuss how its neurons respond to orientation, movement, and spatial frequency.
4. Discuss how neurons in the striate cortex respond to retinal disparity and color, and explain the modular organization of striate cortex.
5. Describe the anatomy of the visual association cortex and discuss the location and functions of the two streams of visual analysis that take place there.
6. Discuss the perception of color and the analysis of form by neurons in the ventral stream.
7. Describe the two basic forms of visual agnosia: apperceptive visual agnosia and associative visual agnosia.
8. Describe how neurons in the visual association cortex respond to movement and location and discuss the effects of brain damage on perception of these features.

PROLOGUE

Seeing with His Hands

One Sunday morning, a colleague called me and asked whether I would like to meet him at a nearby hospital to interview a patient with an interesting disorder. I joined him there and met a pleasant man in his mid-thirties. Mr. M. had sustained brain damage from an inflammatory disease that affected the blood vessels in his brain. His speech appeared to be normal, but he had great difficulty recognizing objects or pictures of them. We went through a book of pictures that is ordinarily used to test children's vocabularies, and we found that he was unable to say what many of them were. However, he sometimes made unintentional gestures when he was studying a picture that gave him enough of a clue to identify it. For example, on one occasion while he was puzzling over a picture of a cow, he held his fists together and started making alternating up-and-down movements with them. Unmistakably, he was acting as if he were milking a cow. He looked at his hands and said, "Oh, a cow!" He laughed. "I live on a farm, you know."

We later learned that his tendency to make movements that helped him "see" things was first discovered by a speech therapist. The brain damage had destroyed his ability to read as well as to recognize objects, and she was trying to help him regain this ability. She wanted to capitalize on the potential of his visual perceptions to trigger automatic hand movements, even though he could not describe those perceptions in words. Therefore, she decided to try to teach him the manual alphabet used by deaf people, in which letters are represented by particular hand and finger movements. (This system is commonly called finger spelling.) She showed Mr. M. a letter and asked him to say what it was. He was unable to do so. Then she held his fingers and moved them into the position that "spelled" the letter. Over several sessions she was able to teach him to make the proper movements, which he could do even though he was unable to say what each letter was. Once his fingers moved, he could feel their position and say what the letter must be. He was able to use this ability to read whole words; he looked at individual letters of a word, made the appropriate movements, observed the sequence of letters that he spelled, and recognized the word. The process was slow, but it worked.

As we saw in Chapter 3, the brain performs two major functions: It controls the movements of the muscles, producing useful behaviors, and it regulates the body's internal environment. To perform both these tasks, the brain must be informed about what is happening both in the external environment and within the body. Such information is received by the sensory systems. This chapter and the next are devoted to a discussion of the ways in which sensory organs detect changes in the environment and the ways in which the brain interprets neural signals from these organs.

We receive information about the environment from **sensory receptors**—specialized neurons that detect a variety of physical events. (Do not confuse *sensory receptors* with receptors for neurotransmitters, neuromodulators, and hormones. Sensory receptors are specialized neurons, and the other types of receptors are specialized proteins that bind with certain molecules.) Stimuli impinge on the receptors and, through various processes, alter their membrane potentials. This process is known as **sensory transduction** because sensory events are *transduced* ("transferred") into changes in the cells' membrane potential. These electrical changes are called **receptor potentials.** Most receptors lack axons; a portion of their somatic membrane forms synapses with the dendrites of other neurons. Receptor potentials affect the release of neurotransmitters and hence modify the pattern of firing in neurons with which these cells form synapses. Ultimately, the information reaches the brain.

This chapter considers vision, the sensory modality that receives the most attention from psychologists, anatomists, and physiologists. One reason for this attention derives from the fascinating complexity of the sensory organs of vision and the relatively large proportion of the brain that is devoted to the analysis of visual information. Another reason, I am sure, is that vision is so important to us as individuals. A natural fascination with such a rich source of information about the world leads to curiosity about how this sensory modality works. Chapter 7 deals with the other sensory modalities: audition, the vestibular senses, the somatosenses, gustation, and olfaction.

sensory receptor A specialized neuron that detects a particular category of physical events.

sensory transduction The process by which sensory stimuli are transduced into slow, graded receptor potentials.

receptor potential A slow, graded electrical potential produced by a receptor cell in response to a physical stimulus.

Figure 6.1

The electromagnetic spectrum.

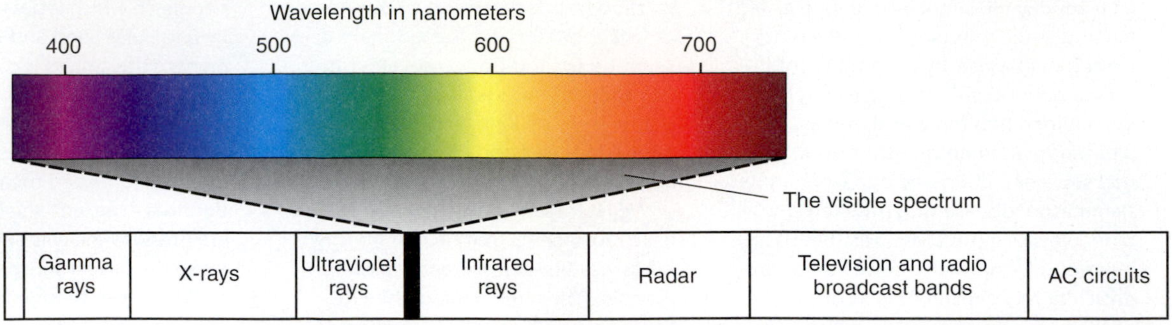

The Stimulus

As we all know, our eyes detect the presence of light. For humans light is a narrow band of the spectrum of electromagnetic radiation. Electromagnetic radiation with a wavelength between 380 and 760 nm (a nanometer, nm, is one-billionth of a meter) is visible to us. (See ***Figure 6.1.***) Other animals can detect different ranges of electromagnetic radiation. For example, honeybees can detect differences in ultraviolet radiation reflected by flowers that appear white to us. The range of wavelengths we call *light* is not qualitatively different from the rest of the electromagnetic spectrum; it is simply the part of the continuum that we humans can see.

The perceived color of light is determined by three dimensions: *hue, saturation,* and *brightness.* Light travels at a constant speed of approximately 300,000 kilometers (186,000 miles) per second. Thus, if the frequency of oscillation of the wave varies, the distance between the peaks of the waves will similarly vary, but in inverse fashion. Slower oscillations lead to longer wavelengths, and faster ones lead to shorter wavelengths. Wavelength determines the first of the three perceptual dimensions of light: **hue.** The visible spectrum displays the range of hues that our eyes can detect.

Light can also vary in intensity, which corresponds to the second perceptual dimension of light: **brightness.** If the intensity of the electromagnetic radiation is increased, the apparent brightness increases, too. The third dimension, **saturation,** refers to the relative purity of the light that is being perceived. If all the radiation is of one wavelength, the perceived color is pure, or fully saturated. Conversely, if the radiation contains all wavelengths, it produces no sensation of hue—it appears white. Colors with intermediate amounts of saturation consist of different mixtures of wavelengths. Figure 6.2 shows some color samples, all with the same hue but with different levels of brightness and saturation. (See ***Figure 6.2.***)

hue One of the perceptual dimensions of color; the dominant wavelength.

brightness One of the perceptual dimensions of color; intensity.

saturation One of the perceptual dimensions of color; purity.

accommodation Changes in the thickness of the lens of the eye, accomplished by the ciliary muscles, that focus images of near or distant objects on the retina.

retina The neural tissue and photoreceptive cells located on the inner surface of the posterior portion of the eye.

rod One of the receptor cells of the retina; sensitive to light of low intensity.

cone One of the receptor cells of the retina; maximally sensitive to one of three different wavelengths of light and hence encodes color vision.

photoreceptor One of the receptor cells of the retina; transduces photic energy into electrical potentials.

fovea (*foe vee a*) The region of the retina that mediates the most acute vision of birds and higher mammals. Color-sensitive cones constitute the only type of photoreceptor found in the fovea.

Anatomy of the Visual System

For an individual to see, an image must be focused on the retina, the inner lining of the eye. This image causes changes in the electrical activity of millions of neurons in the retina, which results in messages being sent through the optic nerves to the rest of the brain. (I said "the rest" because the retina is actually part of the brain; it and the optic nerve are in the central—not peripheral—nervous system.) This section describes the anatomy of the eyes, the photoreceptors in the retina that detect the presence of light, and the connections between the retina and the brain.

Some animals, such as this honeybee, can detect wavelengths of electromagnetic radiation that are invisible to us.

The Eyes

The eyes are suspended in the *orbits,* bony pockets in the front of the skull. They are held in place and moved by six extraocular muscles attached to the tough, white outer coat of the eye called the *sclera.* Normally, we cannot look behind our eyeballs and see these muscles, because their attachments to the eyes are hidden by the *conjunctiva.* These mucous membranes line the eyelid and fold back to attach to the eye (thus preventing a contact lens that has slipped off the cornea from "falling behind the eye"). Figure 6.3 illustrates the anatomy of the eye. (See ***Figure 6.3.***)

The outer layer of most of the eye, the sclera, is opaque and does not permit entry of light. However, the cornea, the outer layer at the front of the eye, is transparent and admits light. The amount of light that enters is regulated by the size of the pupil, which is an opening in the iris, the pigmented ring of muscles situated behind the cornea. The lens, situated immediately behind the iris, consists of a series of transparent, onionlike layers. Its shape can be altered by contraction of the ciliary muscles. These changes in shape permit the eye to focus images of near or distant objects on the retina—a process called **accommodation.**

After passing through the lens, light traverses the main part of the eye, which is filled with *vitreous humor* ("glassy liquid"), a clear, gelatinous substance. After passing through the vitreous humor, light falls on the **retina,** the interior lining of the back of the eye. In the retina are located the receptor cells, the **rods** and **cones** (named for their shapes), collectively known as **photoreceptors.**

The human retina contains approximately 120 million rods and 6 million cones. Although they are greatly outnumbered by rods, cones provide us with most of the information about our environment. In particular, they are responsible for our daytime vision. They provide us with information about small features in the environment and thus are the source of vision of the highest sharpness, or *acuity* (from *acus,* "needle"). The **fovea,** or central region of the retina, which mediates our most acute vision, contains only cones. Cones are also responsible for color vision—our ability to discriminate light of different wavelengths. Although rods do not

Figure 6.2

Examples of colors with the same dominant wavelength (hue) but different levels of saturations or brightness.

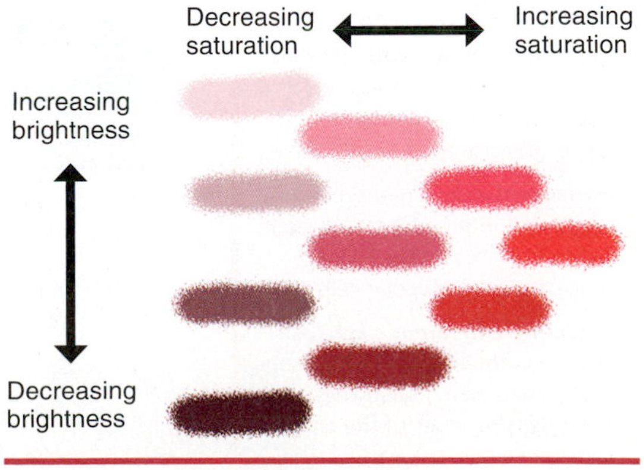

Figure 6.3

The human eye.

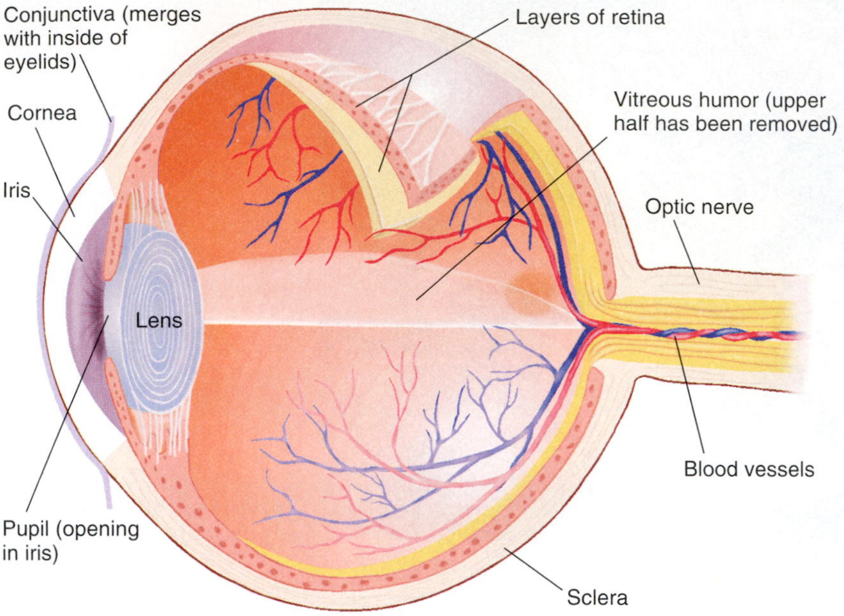

detect different colors and provide vision of poor acuity, they are more sensitive to light. In a very dimly lighted environment we use our rod vision; therefore, in dim light we are color-blind and lack foveal vision. You may have noticed, while out on a dark night, that looking directly at a dim, distant light (that is, placing the image of the light on the fovea) causes it to disappear. (See ***Table 6.1.***)

Another feature of the retina is the **optic disk,** where the axons conveying visual information gather together and leave the eye through the optic nerve. The optic disk produces a *blind spot* because no receptors are located there. We do not normally perceive our blind spots, but their presence can be demonstrated. If you have not found yours, you may want to try the exercise described in ***Figure 6.4.***

Close examination of the retina shows that it consists of several layers of neuron cell bodies, their axons and dendrites, and the photoreceptors. Figure 6.5 illustrates a cross section through the primate retina, which is divided into three main layers: the photoreceptive layer, the bipolar cell layer, and the ganglion cell layer. Note that the photoreceptors are at the *back* of the retina; light must pass through the overlying layers to get to them. Fortunately, these layers are transparent. (See ***Figure 6.5.***)

optic disk The location of the exit point from the retina of the fibers of the ganglion cells that form the optic nerve; responsible for the blind spot.

bipolar cell A bipolar neuron located in the middle layer of the retina, conveying information from the photoreceptors to the ganglion cells.

ganglion cell A neuron located in the retina that receives visual information from bipolar cells; its axons give rise to the optic nerve.

horizontal cell A neuron in the retina that interconnects adjacent photoreceptors and the outer processes of the bipolar cells.

amacrine cell (***amm*** *a krin*) A neuron in the retina that interconnects adjacent ganglion cells and the inner processes of the bipolar cells.

Table 6.1

Locations and Response Characteristics of Photoreceptors

Cones	Rods
Most prevalent in the central retina; found in the fovea	Most prevalent in the peripheral retina; not found in the fovea
Sensitive to moderate-to-high levels of light	Sensitive to low levels of light
Provide information about hue	Provide only monochromatic information
Provide excellent acuity	Provide poor acuity

Figure 6.4

A test for the blind spot. With your left eye closed, look at the + with your right eye and move the page nearer to and farther from you. When the page is about 20 cm from your face, the green circle disappears because its image falls on the blind spot of your right eye.

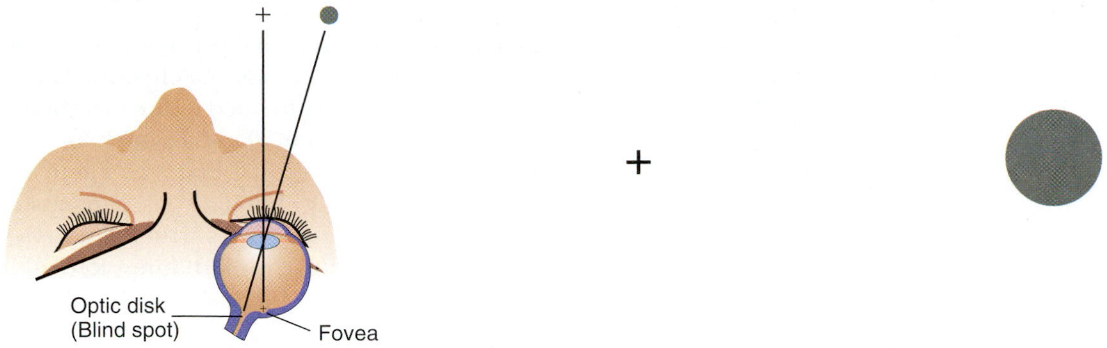

The photoreceptors form synapses with **bipolar cells,** neurons whose two arms connect the shallowest and deepest layers of the retina. In turn, these neurons form synapses with the **ganglion cells,** neurons whose axons travel through the optic nerves (the second cranial nerves) and carry visual information into the brain. In addition, the retina contains **horizontal cells** and **amacrine cells,** both of which transmit information in a direction parallel to the surface of the retina and thus combine messages from adjacent photoreceptors. (See ***Figure 6.5.***)

The primate retina contains approximately fifty-five different types of neurons: one type of rod, three types of cones, two types of horizontal cells, ten types of bipolar cells, twenty-four to twenty-nine types of amacrine cells, and ten to fifteen types of ganglion cells (Masland, 2001).

Figure 6.5

Details of retinal circuitry.

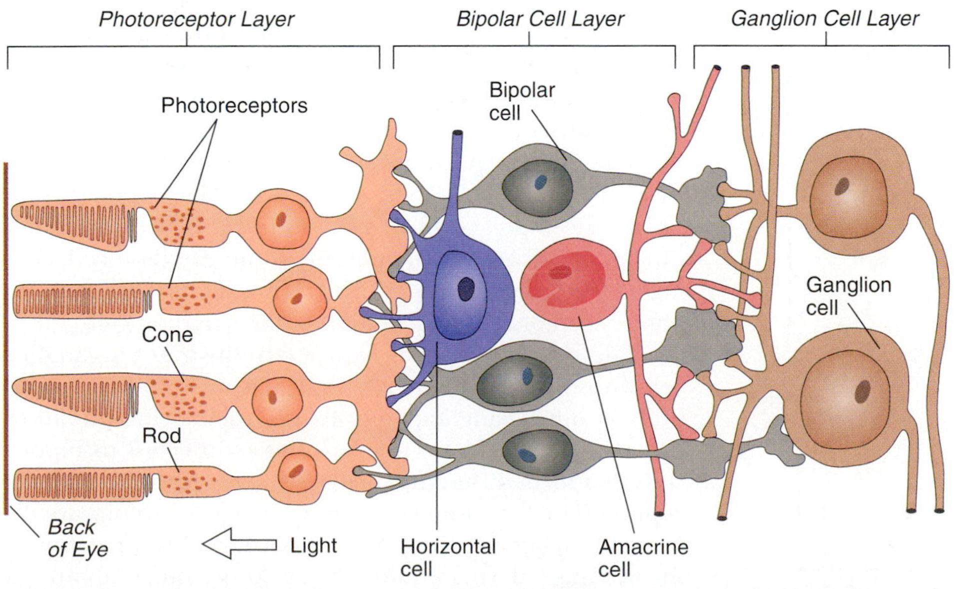

Adapted from Dowling, J. E., and Boycott, B. B. *Proceedings of the Royal Society of London, B,* 1966, *166,* 80–111.

lamella A layer of membrane containing photopigments; found in rods and cones of the retina.

photopigment A protein dye bonded to retinal, a substance derived from vitamin A; responsible for transduction of visual information.

opsin (*opp sin*) A class of protein that, together with retinal, constitutes the photopigments.

retinal (*rett i nahl*) A chemical synthesized from vitamin A; joins with an opsin to form a photopigment.

rhodopsin (*roh dopp sin*) A particular opsin found in rods.

Photoreceptors

Rods and cones consist of an outer segment connected by a cilium to an inner segment, which contains the nucleus. (See ***Figure 6.5.***) The outer segment contains several hundred **lamellae,** or thin plates of membrane. (*Lamella* is the diminutive form of *lamina,* "thin layer.")

Let's consider the nature of transduction of visual information. The first step in the chain of events that leads to visual perception involves a special chemical called a photopigment. **Photopigments** are special molecules embedded in the membrane of the lamellae; a single human rod contains approximately 10 million of them. The molecules consist of two parts: an **opsin** (a protein) and **retinal** (a lipid). There are several forms of opsin; for example, the photopigment of human rods, **rhodopsin,** consists of *rod opsin* plus retinal. (*Rhod-* refers to the Greek *rhodon,* "rose," not to *rod.* Before it is bleached by the action of light, rhodopsin has a pinkish hue.) Retinal is synthesized from vitamin A, which explains why carrots, which are rich in this vitamin, are said to be good for your eyesight.

When a molecule of rhodopsin is exposed to light, it breaks into its two constituents: rod opsin and retinal. When that happens, the rod opsin changes from its rosy color to a pale yellow; hence, we say that the light *bleaches* the photopigment. The splitting of the photopigment causes a change in the membrane potential of the photoreceptor (the receptor potential), which changes the rate at which the photoreceptor releases its neurotransmitter, glutamate.

In the vertebrate retina, photoreceptors provide input to both bipolar cells and horizontal cells. Figure 6.6 shows the neural circuitry from a photoreceptor to a ganglion cell. The circuitry is much simplified and omits the horizontal cells and amacrine cells. The first two types of cells in the circuit—photoreceptors and bipolar cells—do not produce action potentials. Instead, their release of neurotransmitter is regulated by the value of their membrane potential; depolarizations increase the release, and hyperpolarizations decrease it. The circles indicate what would be seen on an oscilloscope screen recording changes in the cells' membrane potentials in response to a spot of light shining on the photoreceptor.

The hyperpolarizing effect of light on the membranes of photoreceptors is shown in the left graph. The hyperpolarization *reduces* the release of neurotransmitter by the photoreceptor. Because the neurotransmitter normally hyperpolarizes the dendrites of the bipolar cell, a *reduction* in its release causes the membrane of the bipolar cell to *depolarize.* Thus, light hyperpolarizes the photoreceptor and depolarizes the bipolar cell. (See ***Figure 6.6.***) The depolarization causes the bipolar cell to release more neurotransmitter, which depolarizes the membrane of the ganglion cell, causing it to increase its rate of firing. Thus, light shining on the photoreceptor causes excitation of the ganglion cell.

The circuit shown in Figure 6.6 illustrates a ganglion cell whose firing rate increases in response to light. As we will see, other ganglion cells *decrease* their firing rate in response to light. These neurons are connected to bipolar cells that form different types of synapses with the photoreceptors. The functions of these two types of circuits are discussed in a later section, "Coding of Visual Information in the Retina." If you would like to know more about the neural circuitry of the retina, you should consult the book by Rodieck (1998).

Figure 6.6

Neural circuitry in the retina. Light striking a photoreceptor produces a hyperpolarization, so the photoreceptor releases *less* neurotransmitter. Because the neurotransmitter normally hyperpolarizes the membrane of the bipolar cell, the reduction causes a *depolarization.* This depolarization causes the bipolar cell to release *more* neurotransmitter, which excites the ganglion cell.

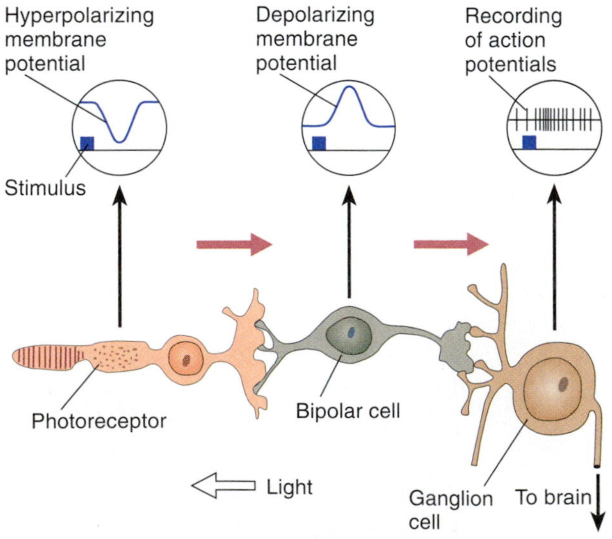

Adapted from Dowling, J. E., in *The Neurosciences: Fourth Study Program,* edited by F. O. Schmitt and F. G. Worden. Cambridge, Mass.: MIT Press, 1979.

Connections Between Eye and Brain

The axons of the retinal ganglion cells bring information to the rest of the brain. They ascend through the optic nerves and reach the **dorsal lateral geniculate nucleus** of the thalamus. This nucleus receives its name from its resemblance to a bent knee (*genu* is Latin for "knee"). It contains six layers of neurons, each of which receives input from only one eye. The neurons in the two inner layers contain cell bodies that are larger than those in the outer four layers. For this reason, the inner two layers are called the **magnocellular layers,** and the outer four layers are called the **parvocellular layers** (*parvo-* refers to the small size of the cells). A third set of neurons in the **koniocellular sublayers** are found ventral to each of the magnocellular and parvocellular layers. (*Konis* is the Greek word for "dust.") As we will see later, these three sets of layers belong to different systems, which are responsible for the analysis of different types of visual information. They receive input from different types of retinal ganglion cells. (See ***Figure 6.7.***)

The neurons in the dorsal lateral geniculate nucleus send their axons through a pathway known as the *optic radiations* to the primary visual cortex—the region surrounding the **calcarine fissure** (*calcarine* means "spur-shaped"), a horizontal fissure located in the medial and posterior occipital lobe. The primary visual cortex is often called the **striate cortex** because it contains a dark-staining layer (*striation*) of cells.

Figure 6.8 shows a diagrammatical view of a horizontal section of the human brain. The optic nerves join together at the base of the brain to form the X-shaped

dorsal lateral geniculate nucleus A group of cell bodies within the lateral geniculate body of the thalamus; receives inputs from the retina and projects to the primary visual cortex.

magnocellular layer One of the inner two layers of neurons in the dorsal lateral geniculate nucleus; transmits information necessary for the perception of form, movement, depth, and small differences in brightness to the primary visual cortex.

parvocellular layer One of the four outer layers of neurons in the dorsal lateral geniculate nucleus; transmits information necessary for perception of color and fine details to the primary visual cortex.

koniocellular sublayer (*koh nee oh* ***sell*** *yew lur*) One of the sublayers of neurons in the dorsal lateral geniculate nucleus found ventral to each of the magnocellular and parvocellular layers; transmits information from short-wavelength ("blue") cones to the primary visual cortex.

calcarine fissure (***kal*** *ka rine*) A horizontal fissure on the inner surface of the posterior cerebral cortex; the location of the primary visual cortex.

striate cortex (***stry*** *ate*) The primary visual cortex.

Figure 6.7

A photomicrograph of a section through the right lateral geniculate nucleus of a rhesus monkey (cresyl violet stain). Layers 1, 4, and 6 receive input from the contralateral (left) eye, and layers 2, 3, and 5 receive input from the ipsilateral (right) eye. Layers 1 and 2 are the magnocellular layers; layers 3 to 6 are the parvocellular layers. The koniocellular sublayers are found ventral to each of the parvocellular and magnocellular other layers. The receptive fields of all six principal layers are in almost perfect registration; cells located along the line of the unlabeled arrow have receptive fields centered on the same point.

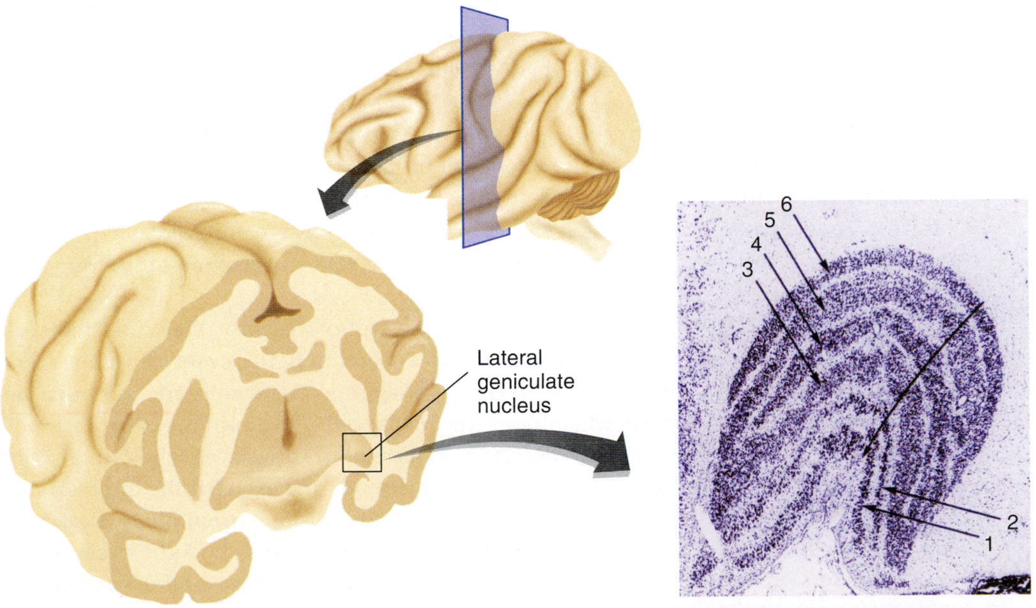

From Hubel, D. H., Wiesel, T. N., and Le Vay, S. *Philosophical Transactions of the Royal Society of London, B,* 1977, *278,* 131–163.

Figure 6.8

The primary visual pathway.

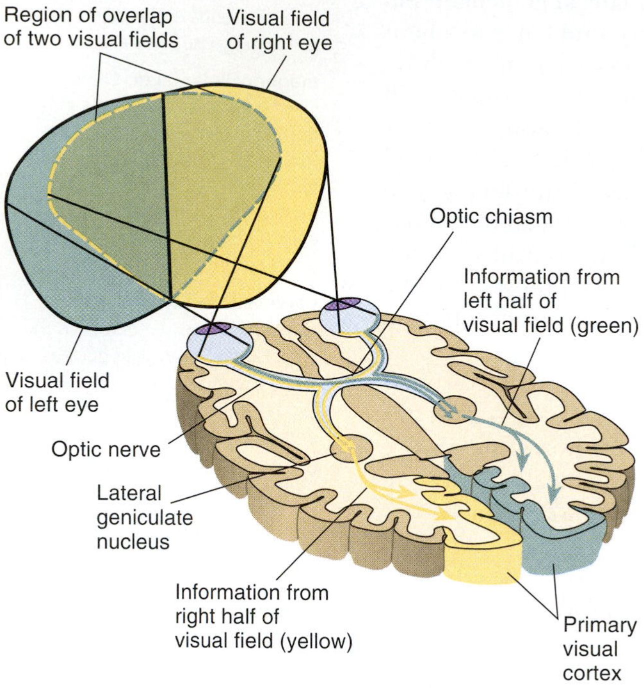

optic chiasm (*khiasma* means "cross"). There, axons from ganglion cells serving the inner halves of the retina (the nasal sides) cross through the chiasm and ascend to the dorsal lateral geniculate nucleus of the opposite side of the brain. The axons from the outer halves of the retina (the temporal sides) remain on the same side of the brain. (See ***Figure 6.8.***) The lens inverts the image of the world projected on the retina (and similarly reverses left and right). Therefore, because the axons from the nasal halves of the retinas cross to the other side of the brain, each hemisphere receives information from the contralateral half (opposite side) of the visual scene. That is, if a person looks straight ahead, the right hemisphere receives information from the left half of the visual field, and the left hemisphere receives information from the right. (See ***Figure 6.8.***)

Besides the primary retino-geniculo-cortical pathway, several other pathways are taken by fibers from the retina. For example, one pathway to the hypothalamus synchronizes an animal's activity cycles to the 24-hour rhythms of day and night. (We will study this system in Chapter 8.) Other pathways, especially those that travel to the optic tectum and the pretectal nuclei, coordinate eye movements, control the muscles of the iris (and thus the size of the pupil) and the ciliary muscles (which control the lens), and help to direct our attention to sudden movements in the periphery of our visual field.

INTERIM SUMMARY

The Stimulus and Anatomy of the Visual System

Light consists of electromagnetic radiation, similar to radio waves but of a different frequency and wavelength. Color can vary in three perceptual dimensions: hue, brightness, and saturation, which correspond to the physical dimensions of wavelength, intensity, and purity, respectively.

The photoreceptors in the retina—the rods and the cones—detect light. Muscles move the eyes so that images of the environment fall on the retina. Accommodation is accomplished by the ciliary muscles, which change the shape of the lens. Photoreceptors communicate through synapses with bipolar cells, which communicate through synapses with ganglion cells. In addition, horizontal cells and amacrine cells combine messages from adjacent photoreceptors.

When light strikes a molecule of photopigment in a photoreceptor, the retinal molecule detaches from the opsin molecule, a process known as bleaching. This event causes the membrane potential to become more polarized. This change in the membrane potential decreases the release of glutamate and informs the bipolar cell with which the photoreceptors communicate that light has just been detected. As a result of this process, the rate of firing of the ganglion cell changes, and a message is sent through the axons of the optic nerves.

Visual information from the retina reaches the striate cortex surrounding the calcarine fissure after being relayed through the magnocellular, parvocellular, and koniocellular layers of the dorsal lateral geniculate nuclei. Several other regions of the brain, including the hypothalamus and the tectum, also receive visual information. These regions help to regulate activity during the day–night cycle, coordinate eye and head movements, control attention to visual stimuli, and regulate the size of the pupils.

optic chiasm (***ky*** *az'm*) A cross-shaped connection between the optic nerves, located below the base of the brain, just anterior to the pituitary gland.

THOUGHT QUESTION

People who try to see faint, distant lights at night are often advised to look just to the side of the location where they expect to see the lights. Can you explain the reason for this advice?

Coding of Visual Information in the Retina

This section describes the way in which cells of the retina encode information they receive from the photoreceptors.

Coding of Light and Dark

One of the most important methods for studying the physiology of the visual system is the use of microelectrodes to record the electrical activity of single neurons. As we saw in the previous section, some ganglion cells become excited when light falls on the photoreceptors with which they communicate. The **receptive field** of a neuron in the visual system is the part of the visual field that an individual neuron "sees"—that is, the part in which light must fall for the neuron to be stimulated. Obviously, the location of the receptive field of a particular neuron depends on the location of the photoreceptors that provide it with visual information. If a neuron receives information from photoreceptors located in the fovea, its receptive field will be at the fixation point—the point at which the eye is looking. If the neuron receives information from photoreceptors located in the periphery of the retina, its receptive field will be located off to one side.

receptive field That portion of the visual field in which the presentation of visual stimuli will produce an alteration in the firing rate of a particular neuron.

At the periphery of the retina many individual receptors converge on a single ganglion cell, bringing information from a relatively large area of the retina—and hence a relatively large area of the visual field. However, foveal vision is more direct, with approximately equal numbers of ganglion cells and cones. These receptor-to-axon relationships explain the fact that our foveal (central) vision is very acute but our peripheral vision is much less precise. (See ***Figure 6.9.***)

Over sixty years ago, Hartline (1938) discovered that the frog retina contained three types of ganglion cells. ON cells responded with an excitatory burst when the retina was illuminated, OFF cells responded when the light was turned off, and ON/OFF cells responded briefly when the light went on and again when it went off. Kuffler (1952, 1953), recording from ganglion cells in the retina of the cat, discovered that their receptive field consists of a roughly circular center, surrounded by a ring. Stimulation of the center or surrounding fields had contrary effects: ON cells were excited by light falling in the central field (*center*) and were inhibited by light falling in the surrounding field (*surround*), whereas OFF cells responded in the opposite manner. ON/OFF ganglion cells were briefly excited when light was turned on or off. In primates these ON/OFF cells project primarily to the superior colliculus, which is primarily involved in visual reflexes (Schiller and Malpeli, 1977); thus, they do not appear to play a direct role in form perception. (See ***Figure 6.10.***)

Figure 6.9

Central versus peripheral acuity. Ganglion cells in the fovea receive input from a smaller number of photoreceptors than in the periphery and hence provide more acute visual information.

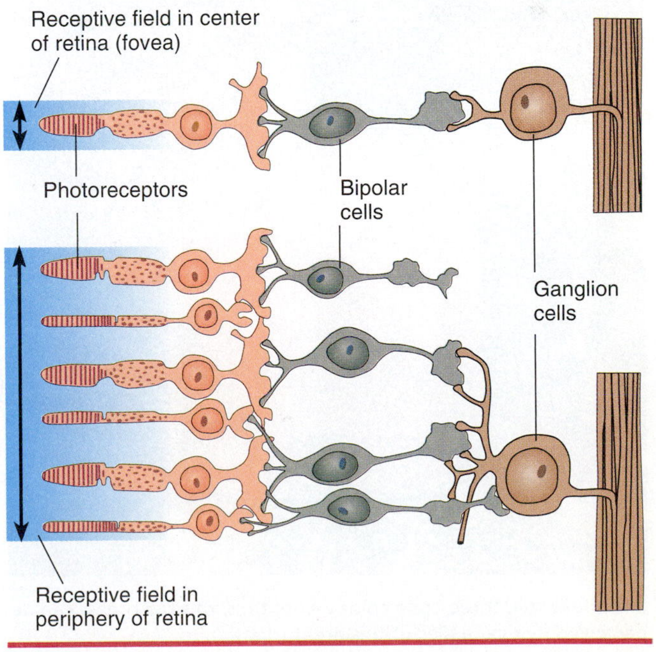

Figure 6.10

Responses of ON and OFF ganglion cells to stimuli presented in the center or the surround of the receptive field.

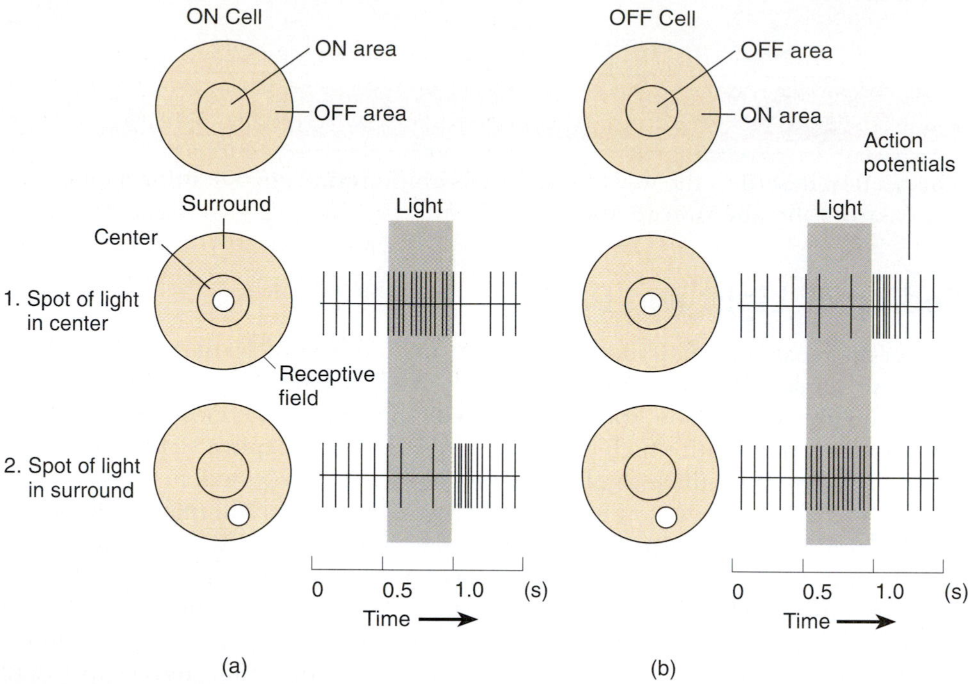

Adapted from Kuffler, S. W. *Cold Spring Harbor Symposium for Quantitative Biology,* 1952, *17,* 281–292.

Birds have full, three-cone color vision; thus, this red breast can be perceived by rival males of this great frigate bird.

Several studies have shown that ON cells and OFF cells signal different kinds of information. Schiller, Sandell, and Maunsell (1986) injected monkeys with APB (2-amino-4-phosphonobutyrate), a drug that selectively blocks synaptic transmission in ON bipolar cells. They found that the animals had difficulty detecting light spots on a dark background but had no difficulty detecting dark spots on a light background.

Coding of Color

So far, we have been examining the monochromatic properties of ganglion cells—that is, their responses to light and dark. But, of course, objects in our environment selectively absorb some wavelengths of light and reflect others, which, to our eyes, gives them different colors. The retinas of humans, Old World monkeys, one species of New World monkey, and apes contain three different types of cones, which provides them (and us) with the most elaborate form of color vision (Jacobs, 1996; Hunt et al., 1998). Although monochromatic (black-and-white) vision is perfectly adequate for most purposes, color vision gave our primate ancestors the ability to distinguish ripe fruit from unripe fruit and made it more difficult for other animals to hide themselves by means of camouflage

(Mollon, 1989). In fact, the photopigments of primates with three types of cones seem well suited for distinguishing red and yellow fruits against a background of green foliage (Regan et al., 2001).

Photoreceptors: Trichromatic Coding

Various theories of color vision have been proposed for many years—long before it was possible to disprove or validate them by physiological means. In 1802 Thomas Young, a British physicist and physician, proposed that the eye detected different colors because it contained three types of receptors, each sensitive to a single hue. His theory was referred to as the *trichromatic* (three-color) *theory*. It was suggested by the fact that for a human observer any color can be reproduced by mixing various quantities of three colors judiciously selected from different points along the spectrum.

I must emphasize that *color mixing* is different from *pigment mixing*. If we combine yellow and blue pigments (as when we mix paints), the resulting mixture is green. Color mixing refers to the addition of two or more light sources. If we shine a beam of red light and a beam of bluish green light together on a white screen, we will see yellow light. If we mix yellow and blue light, we get white light. When white appears on a color television screen or computer monitor, it actually consists of tiny dots of red, blue, and green light. (See ***Figure 6.11.***)

Physiological investigations of retinal photoreceptors in higher primates have found that Young was right: Three different types of photoreceptors (three different types of cones) are responsible for color vision. Investigators have studied the absorption characteristics of individual photoreceptors, determining the amount of light of different wavelengths that is absorbed by the photopigments. These characteristics are controlled by the particular opsin a photoreceptor contains; different opsins absorb particular wavelengths more readily. Figure 6.12 shows the absorption characteristics of the four types of photoreceptors in the human retina: rods and the three types of cones. (See ***Figure 6.12.***)

Figure 6.11

Additive color mixing and paint mixing. When blue, red, and green light of the proper intensity are all shone together, the result is white light. When red, blue, and yellow paints are mixed together, the result is a dark gray.

Figure 6.12

Relative absorbance of light of various wavelengths by rods and the three types of cones in the human retina.

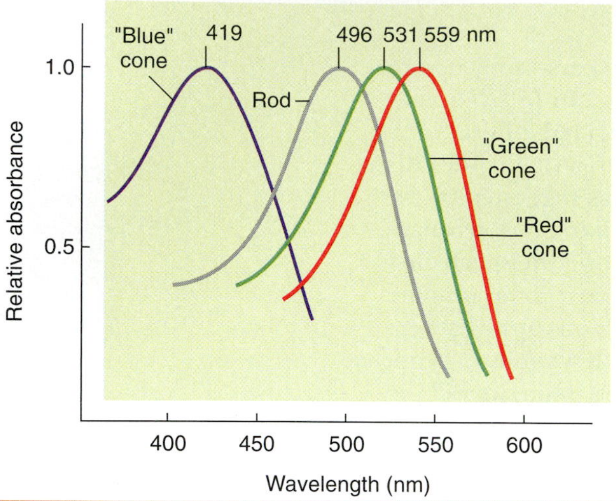

From Dartnall, H. J. A., Bowmaker, J. K., and Mollon, J. D. Human visual pigments: Microspectrophotometric results from the eyes of seven persons. *Proceedings of the Royal Society of London, B,* 1983, *220,* 115–130.

The peak sensitivities of the three types of cones are approximately 420 nm (blue-violet), 530 nm (green), and 560 nm (yellow-green). The peak sensitivity of the short-wavelength cone is actually 440 nm in the intact eye because the lens absorbs some short-wavelength light. For convenience the short-, medium-, and long-wavelength cones are traditionally called "blue," "green," and "red" cones, respectively. The retina contains approximately equal numbers of "red" and "green" cones but a much smaller number of "blue" cones (approximately 8 percent of the total).

Genetic defects in color vision appear to result from anomalies in one or more of the three types of cones (Boynton, 1979; Nathans et al., 1986; Wissinger and Sharpe, 1998). The first two kinds of defective color vision described here involve genes on the X chromosome; thus, because males have only one X chromosome, they are much more likely to have this disorder. (Females are likely to have a normal gene on one of their X chromosomes, which compensates for the defective one.) People with **protanopia** ("first-color defect") confuse red and green. They see the world in shades of yellow and blue; both red and green look yellowish to them. Their visual acuity is normal, which suggests that their retinas do not lack "red" or "green" cones. This fact, and their sensitivity to lights of different wavelengths, suggests that their "red" cones are filled with "green" cone opsin. People with **deuteranopia** ("second-color defect") also confuse red and green and also have normal visual acuity. Their "green" cones appear to be filled with "red" cone opsin.

Tritanopia ("third-color defect") is rare, affecting fewer than 1 in 10,000 people. This disorder involves a faulty gene that is not located on an X chromosome; therefore, it is equally prevalent in males and females. People with tritanopia have difficulty with hues of short wavelengths and see the world in greens and reds. To them a clear blue sky is a bright green, and yellow looks pink. Their retinas lack "blue" cones. Because the retina contains so few of these cones, their absence does not noticeably affect visual acuity.

Retinal Ganglion Cells: Opponent-Process Coding

At the level of the retinal ganglion cell the three-color code gets translated into an *opponent-color* system. Daw (1968) and Gouras (1968) found that these neurons respond specifically to pairs of primary colors, with red opposing green and blue opposing yellow. Thus, the retina contains two kinds of color-sensitive ganglion cells: *red-green* and *yellow-blue*. Some color-sensitive ganglion cells respond in a center-surround fashion. For example, a cell might be excited by red and inhibited by green in the center of their receptive field while showing the opposite response in the surrounding ring. (See ***Figure 6.13.***) Other ganglion cells that receive input from cones do not respond differentially to different wavelengths but simply encode relative brightness in the center and surround. These cells serve as "black-and-white detectors."

The response characteristics of retinal ganglion cells to light of different wavelengths are obviously determined by the particular circuits that connect the three types of cones with the two types of ganglion cells. These circuits involve different types of bipolar cells, amacrine cells, and horizontal cells.

Figure 6.13

Receptive fields of color-sensitive ganglion cells. When a portion of the receptive field is illuminated with the color shown, the cell's rate of firing increases. When a portion is illuminated with the complementary color, the cell's rate of firing decreases.

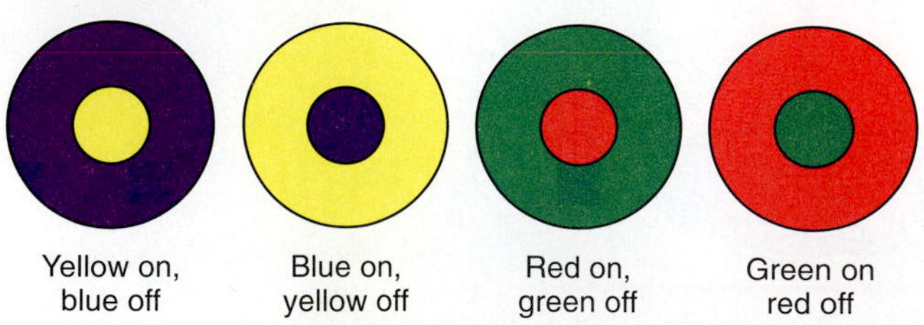

Figure 6.14

Color coding in the retina. (a) Red light stimulating a "red" cone, which causes excitation of a red-green ganglion cell. (b) Green light stimulating a "green" cone, which causes inhibition of a red-green ganglion cell. (c) Yellow light stimulating "red" and "green" cones equally but not affecting "blue" cones. The stimulation of "red" and "green" cones causes excitation of a yellow-blue ganglion cell. (d) Blue light stimulating a "blue" cone, which causes inhibition of a yellow-blue ganglion cell. The arrows labeled E and I represent neural circuitry within the retina that translates excitation of a cone into excitation or inhibition of a ganglion cell. For clarity only some of the circuits are shown.

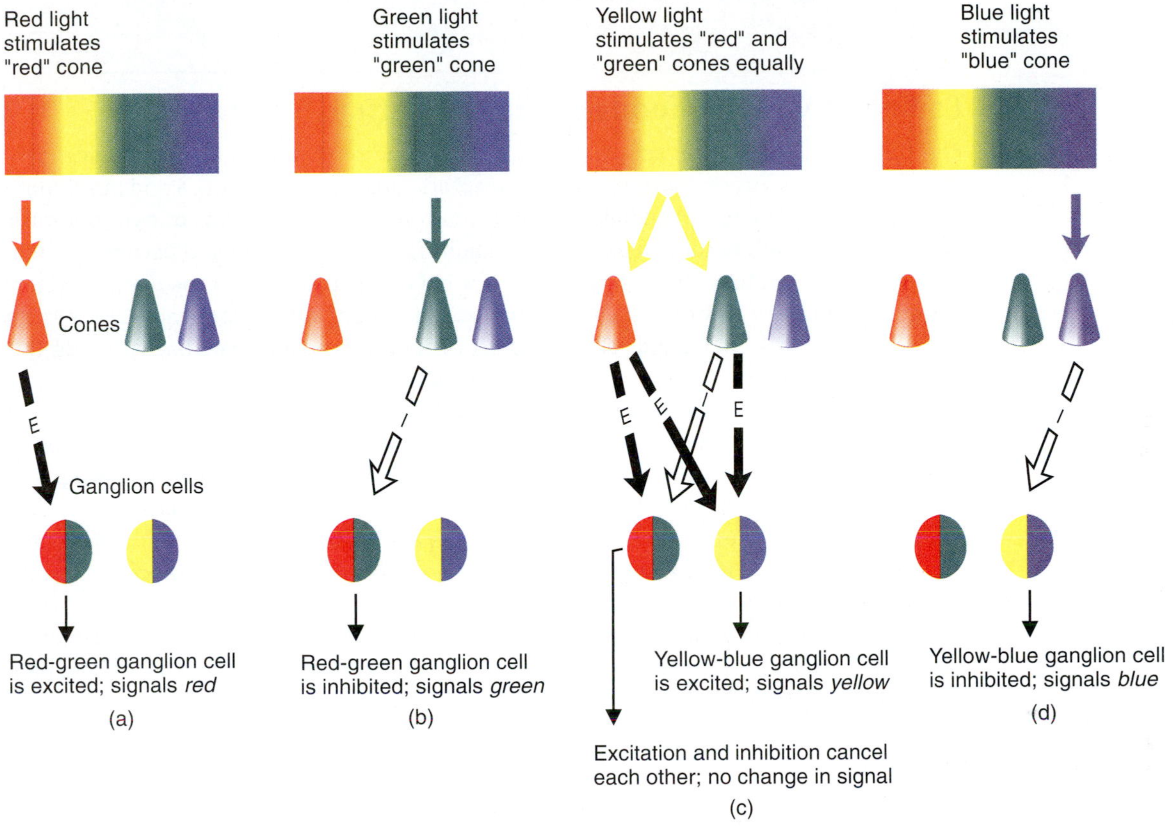

Figure 6.14 helps to explain how particular hues are detected by the "red," "green," and "blue" cones and translated into excitation or inhibition of the red-green and yellow-blue ganglion cells. The diagram does not show the actual neural circuitry, which includes the retinal neurons that connect the cones with the ganglion cells. The arrows in Figure 6.14 refer merely to the *effects* of the light falling on the retina. The book by Rodieck (1998) describes the actual neural circuitry in considerable detail.

Detection and coding of pure red, green, or blue light is the easiest to understand. For example, red light excites "red" cones, which causes the excitation of red-green ganglion cells. (See ***Figure 6.14a.***) Green light excites "green" cones, which causes the *inhibition* of red-green cells. (See ***Figure 6.14b.***) But consider the effect of yellow light. Because the wavelength that produces the sensation of yellow is intermediate between red and green, it will stimulate both "red" and "green" cones about equally. Yellow-blue ganglion cells are excited by both "red" and "green" cones, so their rate of firing increases. However, red-green ganglion cells are excited by red and inhibited by green, so their firing rate does not change. The brain detects an increased firing rate from the axons of yellow-blue ganglion cells, which it interprets as yellow. (See ***Figure 6.14c.***) Blue light simply inhibits the activity of yellow-blue ganglion cells. (See ***Figure 6.14d.***)

protanopia (*pro tan **owe** pee a*) An inherited form of defective color vision in which red and green hues are confused; "red" cones are filled with "green" cone opsin.

deuteranopia (*dew ter an **owe** pee a*) An inherited form of defective color vision in which red and green hues are confused; "green" cones are filled with "red" cone opsin.

tritanopia (*try tan **owe** pee a*) An inherited form of defective color vision in which hues with short wavelengths are confused; "blue" cones are either lacking or faulty.

The opponent-color system employed by the ganglion cells explains why we cannot perceive a reddish green or a bluish yellow: An axon that signals red or green (or yellow or blue) can either increase or decrease its rate of firing; it cannot do both at the same time. A reddish green would have to be signaled by a ganglion cell firing slowly and rapidly at the same time, which is obviously impossible.

See Animation 6.1, Complementary Colors, for a demonstration of negative afterimages.

Animation 6.1, Complementary Colors, demonstrates an interesting phenomenon that emerges from opponent-process coding.

INTERIM SUMMARY

Coding of Visual Information in the Retina

Recordings of the electrical activity of single neurons in the retina indicate that each ganglion cell receives information from photoreceptors—just one in the fovea and many more in the periphery. The receptive field of most retinal ganglion cells consists of two concentric circles, with the cells becoming excited when light falls in one region and becoming inhibited when it falls in the other. This arrangement enhances the ability of the nervous system to detect contrasts in brightness. ON cells are excited by light in the center, and OFF cells are excited by light in the surround. ON cells detect light objects against dark backgrounds; OFF cells detect dark objects against light backgrounds.

Color vision occurs as a result of information provided by three types of cones, each of which is sensitive to light of a certain wavelength: long, medium, or short. The absorption characteristics of the cones are determined by the particular opsin that their photopigment contains. Most forms of defective color vision appear to be caused by alterations in cone opsins. The "red" cones of people with protanopia are filled with "green" cone opsin, and the "green" cones of people with deuteranopia are filled with "red" cone opsin. The retinas of people with tritanopia appear to lack "blue" cones.

Most color-sensitive ganglion cells respond in an opposing center-surround fashion to the pairs of primary colors: red and green, and blue and yellow. The responses of these neurons is determined by the retinal circuitry that connects them with the photoreceptors.

THOUGHT QUESTION

Why is color vision useful? Birds, some fish, and some primates have full, three-cone color vision. Considering our own species, what other benefits (besides the ability to recognize ripe fruit, which I mentioned in the previous section) might come from the evolution of color vision?

Analysis of Visual Information: Role of the Striate Cortex

The retinal ganglion cells encode information about the relative amounts of light falling on the center and surround regions of their receptive field and, in many cases, about the wavelength of that light. The striate cortex performs additional processing of this information, which it then transmits to the visual association cortex.

Anatomy of the Striate Cortex

The striate cortex consists of six principal layers (and several sublayers), arranged in bands parallel to the surface. These layers contain the nuclei of cell bodies and dendritic trees that show up as bands of light or dark in sections of tissue that have been dyed with a cell-body stain. (See ***Figure 6.15.***)

simple cell An orientation-sensitive neuron in the striate cortex whose receptive field is organized in an opponent fashion.

complex cell A neuron in the visual cortex that responds to the presence of a line segment with a particular orientation located within its receptive field, especially when the line moves perpendicularly to its orientation.

hypercomplex cell A neuron in the visual cortex that responds to the presence of a line segment with a particular orientation that ends at a particular point within the cell's receptive field.

In primates, information from the parvocellular and magnocellular layers of the dorsal lateral geniculate nucleus enters the middle layer (layer 4C) of the striate cortex. From there it is relayed to the upper layers, where it is analyzed by circuits of neurons. Axons bringing information from the koniocellular layers form synapses with neurons in layer 3.

If we consider the striate cortex of one hemisphere as a whole—if we imagine that we remove it and spread it out on a flat surface—we find that it contains a map of the contralateral half of the visual field. (Remember that each side of the brain sees the opposite side of the visual field.) The map is distorted; approximately 25 percent of the striate cortex is devoted to the analysis of information from the fovea, which represents a small part of the visual field. (The area of the visual field seen by the fovea is approximately the size of a large grape held at arm's length.)

The pioneering studies of David Hubel and Torsten Wiesel at Harvard University during the 1960s began a revolution in the study of the physiology of visual perception (see Hubel and Wiesel, 1977, 1979). Hubel and Wiesel discovered that neurons in the visual cortex did not simply respond to spots of light; they selectively responded to specific *features* of the visual world. That is, the neural circuitry within the visual cortex combines information from several sources (for example, from axons carrying information received from several different ganglion cells) in such a way as to detect features that are larger than the receptive field of a single ganglion cell. The following subsections describe the visual characteristics that researchers have studied so far: orientation and movement, spatial frequency, retinal disparity, and color.

Figure 6.15

A photomicrograph of a small section of striate cortex, showing the six principal layers. The letter W refers to the white matter that underlies the visual cortex; beneath the white matter is layer VI of the striate cortex on the opposite side of the gyrus.

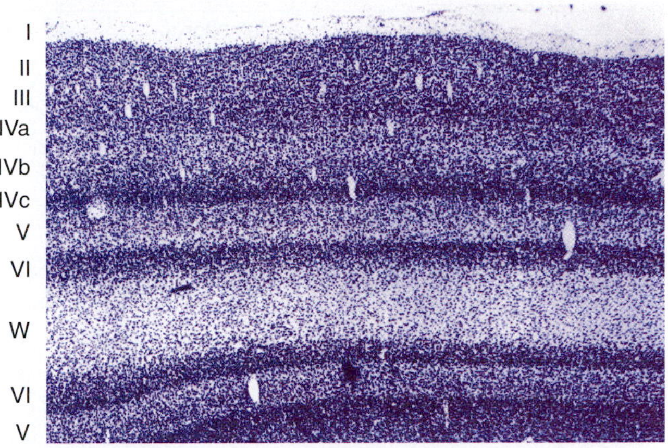

From Hubel, D. H., and Wiesel, T. N. *Proceedings of the Royal Society of London, B*, 1977, *198*, 1–59. Reprinted with permission.

Figure 6.16

Orientation sensitivity. An orientation-sensitive neuron in the striate cortex will become active only when a line of a particular orientation appears within its receptive field. For example, the neuron depicted in this figure responds best to a bar that is vertically oriented.

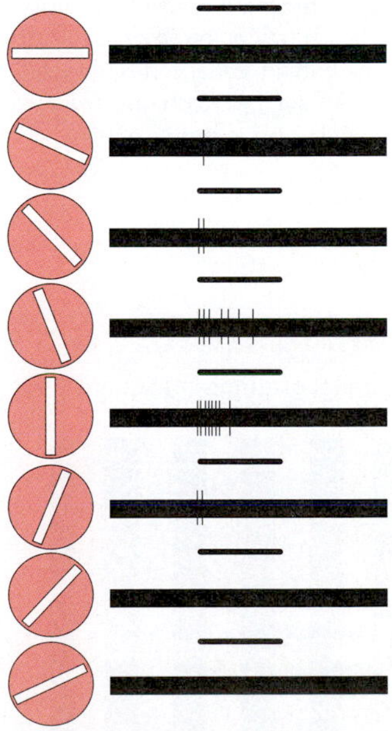

Adapted from Hubel, D. H., and Wiesel, T. N. *Journal of Physiology (London)*, 1959, *148*, 574–591.

Orientation and Movement

Most neurons in the striate cortex are sensitive to *orientation*. That is, if a line is positioned in the cell's receptive field and rotated around its center, the cell will respond only when the line is in a particular position—a particular orientation. Some neurons respond best to a vertical line, some to a horizontal line, and some to a line oriented somewhere in between. Figure 6.16 shows the responses of a neuron in the striate cortex when lines were presented at various orientations. As you can see, this neuron responded best when a vertical line was presented in its receptive field. (See ***Figure 6.16.***)

Some orientation-sensitive neurons have receptive fields organized in an opponent fashion. Hubel and Wiesel referred to them as **simple cells.** For example, a line of a particular orientation (say, a dark 45° line against a white background) might excite a cell if placed in the center of the receptive field but inhibit it if moved away from the center. (See ***Figure 6.17a.***) Another type of neuron, which the researchers referred to as a **complex cell,** also responded best to a line of a particular orientation but did not show an inhibitory surround; that is, it continued to respond while the line was moved within the receptive field. In fact, many complex cells increased their rate of firing when the line was moved perpendicular to its angle of orientation—often only in one direction. Thus, these neurons also served as movement detectors. In addition, complex cells responded equally well to white lines against black backgrounds and black lines against white backgrounds. (See ***Figure 6.17b.***) Finally, **hypercomplex cells** responded to lines of a particular orientation but had an inhibitory region at the end (or ends) of the lines, which meant that the cells detected the location of *ends* of lines of a particular orientation. (See ***Figure 6.17c.***)

Figure 6.17

Response characteristics of neurons to orientation in the primary visual cortex. (a) Simple cell. (b) Complex cell. (c) Hypercomplex cell.

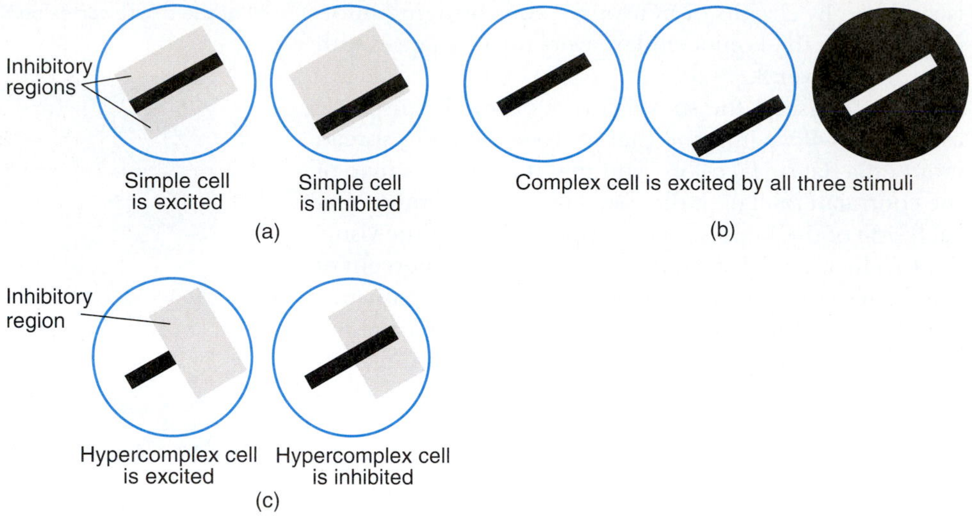

sine-wave grating A series of straight parallel bands varying continuously in brightness according to a sine-wave function, along a line perpendicular to their lengths.

spatial frequency The relative width of the bands in a sine-wave grating, measured in cycles per degree of visual angle.

retinal disparity The fact that points on objects located at different distances from the observer will fall on slightly different locations on the two retinas; provides the basis for stereopsis.

cytochrome oxidase (CO) blob The central region of a module of the primary visual cortex, revealed by a stain for cytochrome oxidase; contains wavelength-sensitive neurons; part of the parvocellular system.

Spatial Frequency

Although the early studies by Hubel and Wiesel suggested that neurons in the primary visual cortex detected lines and edges, subsequent research found that they actually responded best to sine-wave gratings (De Valois, Albrecht, and Thorell, 1978). Figure 6.18 compares a sine-wave grating with a more familiar square-wave grating. A square-wave grating consists of a simple set of rectangular bars that vary in brightness; the brightness along the length of a line perpendicular to them would vary in a stepwise (square-wave) fashion. (See ***Figure 6.18a.***) A **sine-wave grating** looks like a series of fuzzy, unfocused parallel bars. Along any line perpendicular to the long axis of the grating, the brightness varies according to a sine-wave function. (See ***Figure 6.18b.***)

A sine-wave grating is designated by its spatial frequency. We are accustomed to the expression of frequencies (for example, of sound waves or radio waves) in terms of time or distance (such as cycles per second or cycles per meter). But because the image of a stimulus on the retina varies in size according to how close it is to the eye, the visual angle is generally used instead of the physical distance between adjacent cycles. Thus, the **spatial frequency** of a sine-wave grating is its variation in brightness measured in cycles per degree of visual angle. (See ***Figure 6.19.***)

Figure 6.18

Parallel gratings. (a) Square-wave grating. (b) Sine-wave grating.

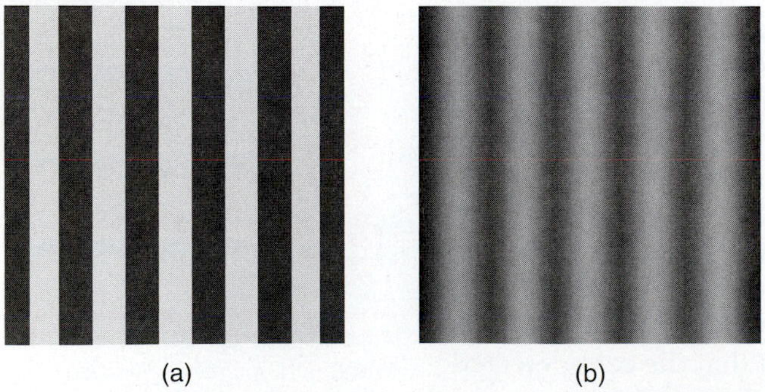

Most neurons in the striate cortex respond best when a sine-wave grating of a particular spatial frequency is placed in the appropriate part of the visual field. But what is the point of having neural circuits that analyze spatial frequency? A complete answer requires some rather complicated mathematics, so I will give a simplified one here. (If you are interested, you can consult De Valois and De Valois, 1988.) Consider the types of information provided by high and low spatial frequencies. Small objects, details within a large object, and large objects with sharp edges provide a signal rich in high frequencies, whereas large areas of light and dark are represented by low frequencies. An image that is deficient in high-frequency information looks fuzzy and out of focus, like the image seen by a nearsighted person who is not wearing corrective lenses. This image still provides much information about forms and objects in the environment; thus, the most important visual information is that contained in *low spatial frequencies.* When low-frequency information is removed, the shapes of images are very difficult to perceive. (As we will see, the more primitive magnocellular system provides low-frequency information.)

Figure 6.19

The concepts of visual angle and spatial frequency. Angles are drawn between the sine waves, with the apex at the viewer's eye. The *visual angle* between adjacent sine waves is smaller when the waves are closer together.

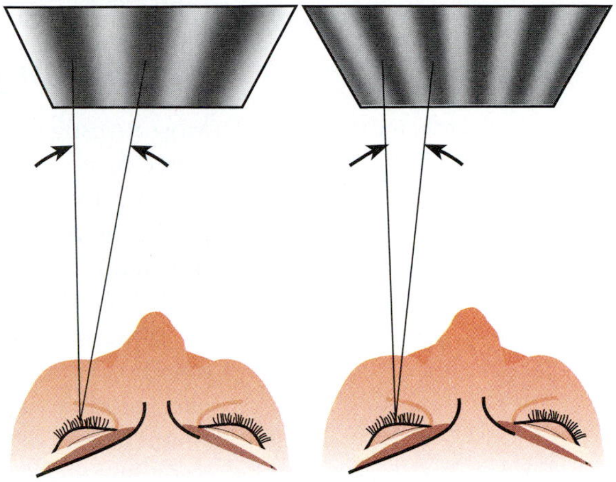

Retinal Disparity

We perceive depth by many means, most of which involve cues that can be detected monocularly, by one eye alone. For example, perspective, relative retinal size, loss of detail through the effects of atmospheric haze, and relative apparent movement of retinal images as we move our heads all contribute to depth perception and do not require binocular vision. However, binocular vision provides a vivid perception of depth through the process of stereoscopic vision, or *stereopsis.* If you have used a stereoscope (such as a View-Master) or have seen a three-dimensional movie, you know what I mean. Stereopsis is particularly important in the visual guidance of fine movements of the hands and fingers, such as we use when we thread a needle.

Most neurons in the striate cortex are *binocular*—that is, they respond to visual stimulation of either eye. Many of these binocular cells, especially those found in a layer that receives information from the magnocellular system, have response patterns that appear to contribute to the perception of depth (Poggio and Poggio, 1984). In most cases the cells respond most vigorously when each eye sees a stimulus in a slightly *different* location. That is, the neurons respond to **retinal disparity,** a stimulus that produces images on slightly different parts of the retina of each eye. This is exactly the information that is needed for stereopsis; each eye sees a three-dimensional scene slightly differently, and the presence of retinal disparity indicates differences in the distance of objects from the observer.

Color

In the striate cortex, information from color-sensitive ganglion cells is transmitted, through the parvocellular and koniocellular layers of the dorsal lateral geniculate nucleus, to special cells grouped together in **cytochrome oxidase (CO) blobs.** CO blobs were discovered by Wong-Riley (1978), who found that a stain for cytochrome oxidase, an enzyme that is present in mitochondria, showed a patchy distribution. Subsequent research with the stain (Horton and Hubel, 1980; Humphrey and Hendrickson, 1980) revealed the presence of a polka-dot pattern of dark columns extending through layers 2 and 3 and (more faintly) layers 5 and 6. The columns are oval in cross section, approximately 150 × 200 μm in diameter, and spaced at 0.5-mm intervals (Fitzpatrick, Itoh, and Diamond, 1983; Livingstone and Hubel, 1987).

Figure 6.20 shows a photomicrograph of a slice through a macaque monkey visual cortex that has been flattened out and stained for the mitochondrial enzyme. You can clearly see the CO blobs within the striate cortex. Because the curvature of the cortex prevents it from being perfectly flattened, some of the tissue is missing in the center of the slice. (See ***Figure 6.20.***)

Until recently, researchers believed that the parvocellular system transmitted all information pertaining to color to the striate cortex. However, it now appears that the parvocellular system receives information only from "red" and "green" cones;

Figure 6.20

A photomicrograph of a slice through the primary visual cortex of a macaque monkey, parallel to the surface. The dark spots are the blobs, colored by a stain for cytochrome oxidase.

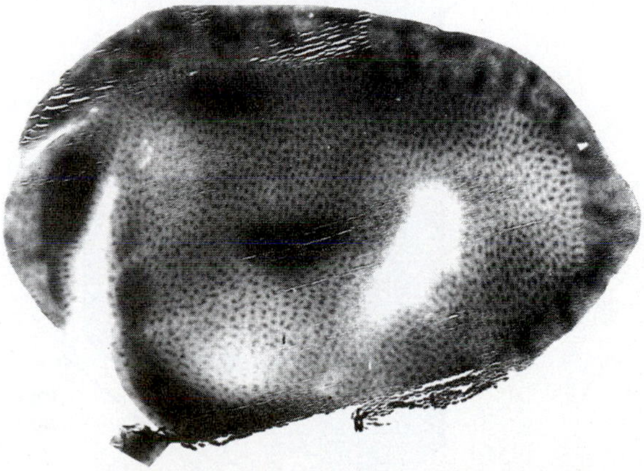

From Hubel, D. H., and Livingstone, M. S. *Journal of Neuroscience,* 1989, *7,* 3378–3415. Copyright 1989 by the Society for Neuroscience.

additional information from "blue" cones is transmitted through the koniocellular system (Hendry and Yoshioka, 1994; Martin et al., 1997; Komatsu, 1998).

To summarize, neurons in the striate cortex respond to several different features of a visual stimulus, including orientation, movement, spatial frequency, retinal disparity, and color. Now let us turn our attention to the way this information is organized within the striate cortex.

Modular Organization of the Striate Cortex

ocular dominance The extent to which a particular neuron receives more input from one eye than from the other.

Most investigators believe that the brain is organized in modules, which probably range in size from a hundred thousand to a few million neurons. Each module receives information from other modules, performs some calculations, and then passes the results to other modules. In recent years investigators have been learning the characteristics of the modules that are found in the visual cortex (De Valois and De Valois, 1988; Livingstone and Hubel, 1988).

The striate cortex is divided into approximately 2500 modules, each approximately 0.5 × 0.7 mm and containing approximately 150,000 neurons. The neurons in each module are devoted to the analysis of various features contained in one very small portion of the visual field. Collectively, these modules receive information from the entire visual field, the individual modules serving like the tiles in a mosaic mural. Input from the parvocellular, koniocellular, and magnocellular layers of the dorsal lateral geniculate nucleus is received by different sublayers of the striate cortex: The parvocellular input is received by layer 4Cβ, the magnocellular input is received by layer 4Cα, and the koniocellular input is received by layer 3.

The modules actually consist of two segments, each surrounding a CO blob. Neurons located within the blobs have a special function: They are sensitive to color and to low spatial frequencies but are relatively insensitive to other visual features. Outside the CO blob, neurons show sensitivity to orientation, movement, spatial frequency, texture, and binocular disparity—but most do not respond to color (Livingstone and Hubel, 1984; Born and Tootell, 1991; Edwards, Purpura, and Kaplan, 1995). Each half of the module receives input from only one eye, but the circuitry within the module combines the information from both eyes, which means that most of the neurons are binocular. Depending on their locations within the module, neurons receive varying percentages of input from each of the eyes.

If we record from neurons anywhere within a single module, we will find that all of their receptive fields overlap. Thus, all the neurons in a module analyze information from the same region of the visual field. Furthermore, if we insert a microelectrode straight down into an interblob region of the striate cortex (that is, in a location in a module outside one of the CO blobs), we will find both simple and complex cells, but all of the orientation-sensitive cells will respond to lines of the same orientation. In addition, they will all share the same **ocular dominance**—that is, the same percentage of input from each of the eyes. If we move our electrode around the module, we will find that these two characteristics—orientation sensitivity and ocular dominance—vary systematically and are arranged at right angles to each other. (See ***Figure 6.21.***)

How does spatial frequency fit into this organization? Edwards, Purpura, and Kaplan (1995) found that neu-

Figure 6.21

One of the modules of the primary visual cortex.

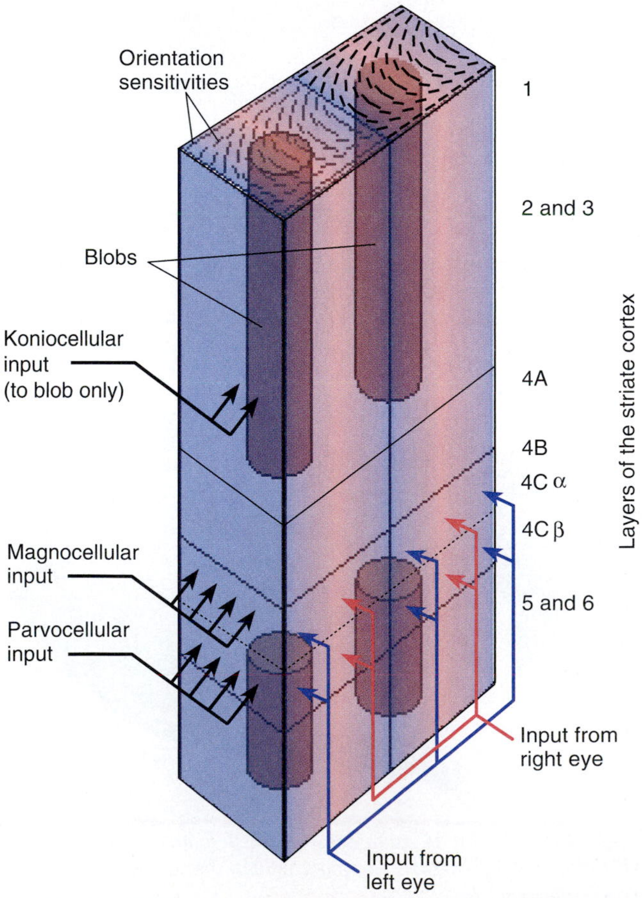

rons within the CO blobs responded to low spatial frequencies but were sensitive to small differences in brightness. Outside the blobs, sensitivity to spatial frequency varied with the distance from the center of the nearest blob. Higher frequencies were associated with greater distances. (See ***Figure 6.22.***) However, neurons outside the blobs were less sensitive to contrast; the difference between the bright and dark areas of the sine-wave grating had to be greater for these neurons than for neurons within the blobs.

Figure 6.22

Optimal spatial frequency of neurons in striate cortex as a function of the distance of the neuron from the center of the nearest cytochrome oxidase blob.

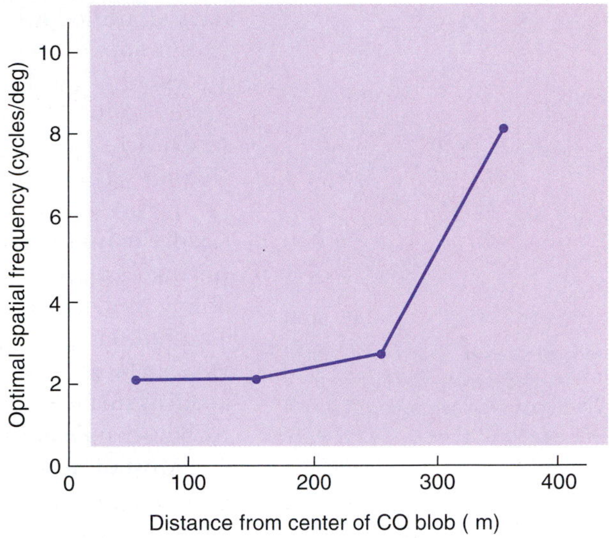

Adapted from Edwards, D. P., Purpura, K. P., and Kaplan, E. *Vision Research,* 1995, *35,* 1501–1523. Copyright 1995, with permission from Elsevier.

INTERIM SUMMARY

Analysis of Visual Information: Role of the Striate Cortex

The striate cortex consists of six layers and several sublayers. Visual information is received from the magnocellular, parvocellular, and koniocellular layers of the dorsal lateral geniculate nucleus. The magnocellular system is more primitive, color-blind, and sensitive to movement, depth, and small differences in brightness. The parvocellular system is more recent, color-sensitive (receiving information from "red" and "green" cones), and able to discriminate finer details. The koniocellular system provides additional information about color, received from "blue" cones.

The striate cortex is organized into modules, each surrounding a pair of CO blobs, which are revealed by a stain for cytochrome oxidase, an enzyme found in mitochondria. Each half of a module receives information from one eye; but because information is shared, most of the neurons respond to input to both eyes. The neurons in the CO blobs are sensitive to color and to low-frequency sine-wave gratings, whereas those between the blobs are sensitive to sine-wave gratings of higher spatial frequencies, orientation, retinal disparity, and movement.

THOUGHT QUESTION

Look at the scene in front of you and try to imagine how its features are encoded by neurons in your striate cortex. Try to picture how the objects you see can be specified by an analysis of orientation, spatial frequency, texture, and color.

Analysis of Visual Information: Role of the Visual Association Cortex

Although the striate cortex is necessary for visual perception, perception of objects and of the totality of the visual scene does not take place there. Each module of the striate cortex sees only what is happening in one tiny part of the visual field. Thus, for us to perceive objects and entire visual scenes, the information from these individual modules must be combined. That combination takes place in the visual association cortex.

Two Streams of Visual Analysis

Visual information received from the striate cortex is analyzed in the visual association cortex. Neurons in the striate cortex send axons to the **extrastriate cortex,** the region of the visual association cortex that surrounds the striate cortex (Zeki and

extrastriate cortex A region of visual association cortex; receives fibers from the striate cortex and from the superior colliculi and projects to the inferior temporal cortex.

Shipp, 1988). The primate extrastriate cortex (sometimes called the prestriate cortex or circumstriate cortex) consists of several regions, each of which contains one or more independent maps of the visual field. Each region is specialized, containing neurons that respond to a particular feature of visual information, such as orientation, movement, spatial frequency, retinal disparity, or color. So far, investigators have identified twenty-five distinct regions and subregions of the visual cortex of the rhesus monkey. These regions are arranged hierarchically, beginning with the striate cortex (Van Essen, Anderson, and Felleman, 1992). Most of the information passes up the hierarchy; each region receives information from regions located beneath it in the hierarchy, analyzes the information, and passes the results on to "higher" regions for further analysis.

Figure 6.23 shows the most important regions of the striate and extrastriate cortex of the human brain. The views of the brain in Figures 6.23a and 6.23b are nearly normal in appearance. Figures 6.23c and 6.23d show "inflated" cortical surfaces, enabling us to see regions that are normally hidden in the depths of sulci and fissures. The hidden regions are shown in dark gray, and regions that are normally visible (the surfaces of gyri) are shown in light gray. Figure 6.23e shows an unrolling of the cortical surface caudal to the dotted red line and green lines in Figure 6.23c and 6.23d. (See ***Figure 6.23.***)

dorsal stream A system of interconnected regions of visual cortex involved in the perception of spatial location, beginning with the striate cortex and ending with the posterior parietal cortex.

ventral stream A system of interconnected regions of visual cortex involved in the perception of form, beginning with the striate cortex and ending with the inferior temporal cortex.

Most of the outputs of the striate cortex—often called V1, because it is the first region of visual cortex—are sent to area V2, a region of the extrastriate cortex just adjacent to V1. At this point, the pathways diverge. On the basis of their own research and a review of the literature, Ungerleider and Mishkin (1982) concluded that the visual association cortex contains two streams of analysis: the **dorsal stream** and the **ventral stream.** Subsequent anatomical studies have confirmed this conclusion (Baizer, Ungerleider, and Desimone, 1991). Some of the outputs of area V2 con-

Figure 6.23

Striate cortex and regions of extrastriate cortex of the human brain. (a) A nearly normal lateral view. (b) A nearly normal midsagittal view. (c) An "inflated" lateral view. (d) An "inflated" midsagittal view. (e) An unrolling of the cortical surface caudal to the dotted red line and green lines shown in (c) and (d).

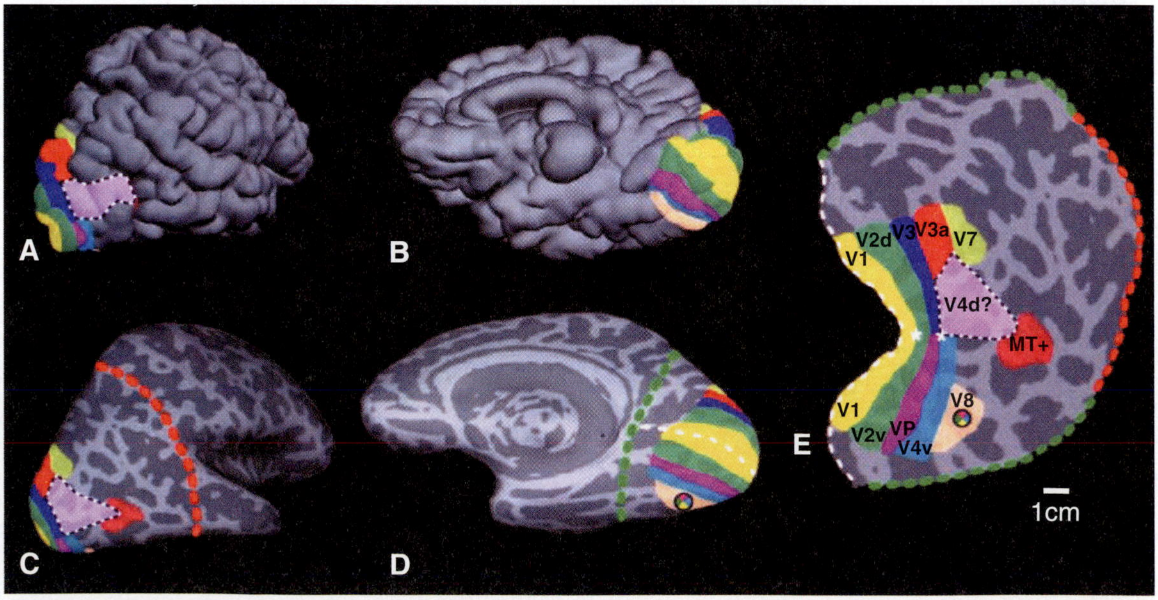

From Tootell, B. H., and Hadjikhani, N. *Cerebral Cortex,* 2001,*11,* 298–311.

tinue forward toward a series of regions that constitute the ventral stream; others ascend into regions of the dorsal stream. The ventral stream recognizes *what* an object is, and the dorsal stream recognizes *where* the object is located. (See ***Figure 6.24.***)

As we saw, the parvocellular, koniocellular, and magnocellular systems provide different kinds of information. The magnocellular system is found in all mammals, whereas the parvocellular and koniocellular systems are found only in primates. These systems receive information from different types of ganglion cells, which are connected to different types of bipolar cells and photoreceptors. Only the cells in the parvocellular and koniocellular system receive information about wavelength from cones; thus, these systems analyze information concerning color. Cells in the parvocellular system also show high spatial resolution and low temporal resolution; that is, they are able to detect very fine details, but their response is slow and prolonged. The koniocellular system, which receives information only from "blue" cones, which are much less numerous than "red" and "green" cones, does not provide information about fine details. In contrast, neurons in the magnocellular system are color-blind. They are not able to detect fine details, but they can detect smaller contrasts between light and dark. They are also especially sensitive to movement. (See ***Table 6.2.***)

Figure 6.24

The human visual system, from the eye to the two streams of visual association cortex.

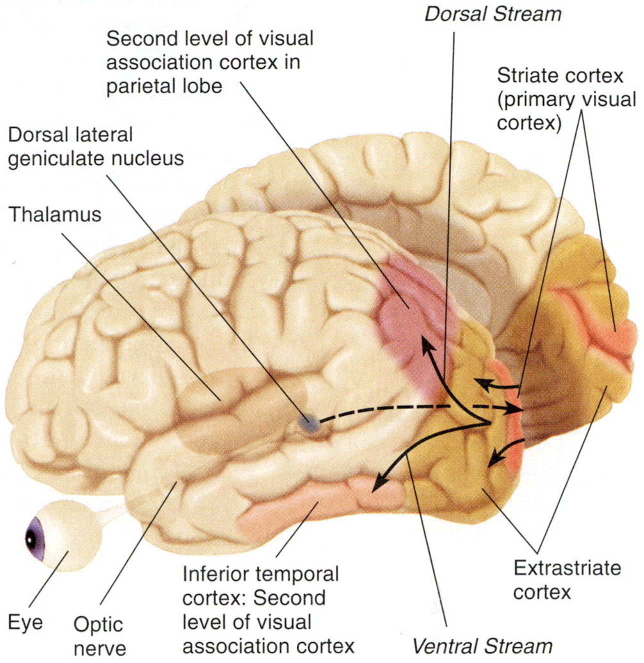

Perception of Color

As we saw earlier, neurons within the CO blobs in the striate cortex respond to colors. Like the ganglion cells in the retina (and the parvocellular and koniocellular neurons in the dorsal lateral geniculate nucleus), these neurons respond in opponent fashion. This information is analyzed by the regions of the visual association cortex that constitute the ventral stream.

Table 6.2

Properties of the Magnocellular, Parvocellular, and Koniocellular Divisions of the Visual System

Property	Magnocellular Division	Parvocellular Division	Koniocellular Division
Color	No	Yes (from "red" and "green" cones)	Yes (from "blue" cones)
Sensitivity to contrast	High	Low	?
Spatial resolution (ability to detect fine details)	Low	High	Low
Temporal resolution	Fast (transient response)	Slow (sustained response)	?

Studies with Laboratory Animals

In the monkey brain, neurons in the CO blobs send information about color to a specific subarea of the extrastriate cortex. Zeki (1980) found that neurons in this subarea (called *V4*) also respond selectively to colors, but their response characteristics are much more complex. Unlike the neurons we have encountered so far, these neurons respond to a variety of wavelengths, not just those that correspond to red, green, yellow, and blue.

The appearance of the colors of objects remains much the same whether we observe them under artificial light, under an overcast sky, or at noon on a cloudless day. This phenomenon is known as **color constancy.** Our visual system does not simply respond according to the wavelength of the light reflected by objects in each part of the visual field; instead, it compensates for the source of the light. Walsh et al. (1993) found that damage to area V4 disrupts color constancy. The investigators found that although monkeys could still discriminate between different colors after area V4 had been damaged, their performance was impaired when the color of the overall illumination was changed. But the fact that the monkeys could still perform a color discrimination task under constant illumination means that some region besides area V4 must be involved in color vision. ***Animation 6.2, Color Constancy,*** illustrates the effects of the color of overall illumunation on color perception.

Animation 6.2, Color Constancy, demonstrates the effects of apparent illumination on our perception of color.

A study by Heywood, Gaffan, and Cowey (1995) appears to have found the region responsible for color vision in the monkey brain: area TEO, a portion of the inferior temporal cortex just anterior to area V4. The investigators destroyed area TEO, leaving area V4 intact, and observed severe impairment in color discrimination. The monkeys had no difficulty discriminating shades of gray, so the deficit on this task appeared to be restricted to color perception. (As we will see later, lesions of the inferior temporal cortex also disrupt the ability to perceive and recognize objects.)

Studies with Humans

Lesions of a restricted region of the human extrastriate cortex in the medial occipital lobe can cause loss of color vision without disruption of visual acuity. The patients describe their vision as resembling a black-and-white film. (Damasio et al., 1980; Kennard et al., 1995). The condition is known as **achromatopsia** ("vision without color"). If the brain damage is unilateral, people will lose color vision in only half of the visual field. In addition, they cannot even imagine colors or remember the colors of objects they saw before their brain damage occurred.

A functional MRI study by Hadjikhani et al. (1998) found a color-sensitive region in the inferior temporal cortex, in a position corresponding to TEO in the monkey's cortex, which they called area V8. Indeed, lesions that cause achromatopsia damage V8 or other brain regions that provide input to V8. (Refer to ***Figure 6.23.***)

Of course, perception of colors is useless in itself. The function of our ability to perceive different colors is to help us perceive different objects in our environment. Therefore, to perceive and understand what is in front of us, we must have information about color combined with other forms of information. Some people with brain damage lose the ability to perceive shapes but can still perceive colors. For example, Zeki et al. (1999) described a patient who could identify colors but was otherwise blind. Patient P. B. received an electrical shock that caused both cardiac and respiratory arrest. He was revived, but the period of anoxia caused extensive damage to his extrastriate cortex. As a result, he lost all form perception. However, he could identify the colors of objects presented on a video monitor.

color constancy The relatively constant appearance of the colors of objects viewed under varying lighting conditions.

achromatopsia (*ay krohm a* ***top*** *see a*) Inability to discriminate among different hues; caused by damage to the visual association cortex.

Analysis of Form

The analysis of form by the visual cortex begins with neurons in the striate cortex that are sensitive to orientation and spatial frequency. These neurons send information to the extrastriate cortex, which consists of several subregions. These subregions analyze the information and send it along the ventral stream toward the temporal neocortex.

Studies with Laboratory Animals

In primates, the recognition of visual patterns and identification of particular objects take place in the **inferior temporal cortex,** located on the ventral part of the temporal lobe. This region of visual association cortex is located at the end of the ventral stream. It is here that analyses of form and color are put together and perceptions of three-dimensional objects and backgrounds are achieved. Damage to the inferior temporal cortex causes severe deficits in visual discrimination (Mishkin, 1966; Gross, 1973; Dean, 1976). (See ***Figure 6.25.***)

Figure 6.25

Areas of visual cortex in the rhesus monkey brain.

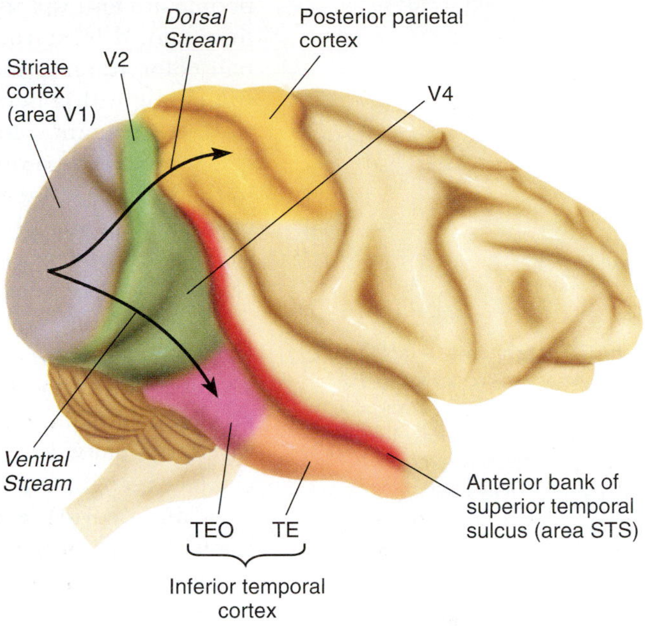

Adapted from Zeki, S. M. *Journal of Physiology,* 1978, *277,* 227–244.

Neurons in the inferior temporal cortex respond best to three-dimensional objects (or photographs of them). They respond poorly to simple stimuli such as spots, lines, or sine-wave gratings. Most of them continue to respond even when these stimuli are moved to a different location, are changed in size, are placed against a different background, or are partially occluded by another object (Rolls and Baylis, 1986; Kovács, Vogels, and Orban, 1995). Thus, they appear to participate in the recognition of objects rather than the analysis of specific features.

Like other regions of the visual cortex, the inferior temporal cortex is arranged in columns. Neurons in adjacent regions usually respond to slightly different versions of the same stimuli. For example, several studies (for example, Desimone et al., 1984) have found neurons in the temporal lobe of the rhesus monkey that are specifically excited by the sight of another face—either that of another monkey or that of a human. Some of these neurons respond to full-face views, and others respond to profiles. Most of these face-sensitive cells are located in area TE and in the cortex that lines the anterior bank of the superior temporal sulcus (area STS). (See ***Figure 6.25.***)

Studies with Humans

Damage to the human visual association cortex can cause a category of deficits known as **visual agnosia.** *Agnosia* ("failure to know") refers to an inability to perceive or identify a stimulus by means of a particular sensory modality, even though its details can be detected by means of that modality and the person retains relatively normal intellectual capacity. *Apperceptive* visual agnosias are failures in high-level perception, whereas *associative* visual agnosias are disconnections between these perceptions and verbal systems. The distinction will be described in more detail later in this section.

Apperceptive Visual Agnosia. People with **apperceptive visual agnosia** cannot identify common objects by sight, even though they may have relatively normal visual acuity. However, they normally can still read—even small print. When they are permitted to hold an object that they cannot recognize visually, they can normally recognize it right away by touch and say what it is. This ability demonstrates that they have not lost their memory for the object or have simply forgotten how to say its name.

Are Faces Special? A common symptom of apperceptive visual agnosia is **prosopagnosia,** inability to recognize particular faces (*prosopon* is Greek for "face"). That is, patients with this disorder can recognize that they are looking at a face, but

inferior temporal cortex In primates the highest level of the ventral stream of the visual association cortex; located on the inferior portion of the temporal lobe.

visual agnosia (*ag* ***no*** *zha*) Deficits in visual perception in the absence of blindness; caused by brain damage.

apperceptive visual agnosia Failure to perceive objects, even though visual acuity is relatively normal.

prosopagnosia (*prah soh pag* ***no*** *zha*) Failure to recognize particular people by the sight of their faces.

they cannot say whose face it is—even if it belongs to a relative or close friend. They see eyes, ears, a nose, a mouth—but cannot recognize the particular configuration of these features that identifies an individual face. They still remember who these people are and will usually recognize them when they hear their voice. As one patient said, "I have trouble recognizing people from just faces alone. I look at their hair color, listen to their voices . . . I use clothing, voice, and hair. I try to associate something with a person one way or another . . . what they wear, how their hair is worn" (Buxbaum, Glosser, and Coslett, 1999, p. 43).

Some investigators believe that facial recognition is mediated by special circuits in the brain that are devoted to the specific analysis of facial features. The most recent evidence suggests that faces are indeed recognized by special circuits in the visual association cortex, but that these circuits are not genetically programmed as a "face-recognizing device." Instead, they develop through experience, and can be used for learning to recognize other types of visual stimuli.

fusiform face area A region of the extrastriate cortex located at the base of the brain; involved in perception of faces and other complex objects that require expertise to recognize.

To recognize a particular person's face, we must have neural circuits that can analyze subtle differences in the configuration of eyes, eyebrows, nose, cheekbones, lips, chin, and all the other features that distinguish one face from another. Studies with brain-damaged people and functional imaging studies suggest that these special face-recognizing circuits are found in the **fusiform face area,** a region of visual association cortex located in the extrastriate cortex at the base of the brain. (See Kanwisher, McDermott, and Chun, 1997, for a review.) Most studies indicate that the right hemisphere is more important than the left. (See ***Figure 6.26.***)

Perhaps the strangest piece of evidence for a special face-recognition region comes from a report by Moscovitch, Winocur, and Behrmann (1997), who studied a man with a visual agnosia for objects but not for faces. For example, he recognized the face shown in Figure 6.27 but not the flowers and vegetables that compose it. (See ***Figure 6.27.***) Presumably, his general-purpose object-recognition circuits were damaged, but the fusiform face region was not.

Figure 6.26

The fusiform face area, located in the extrastriate cortex of the occipital lobe on the base of the brain.

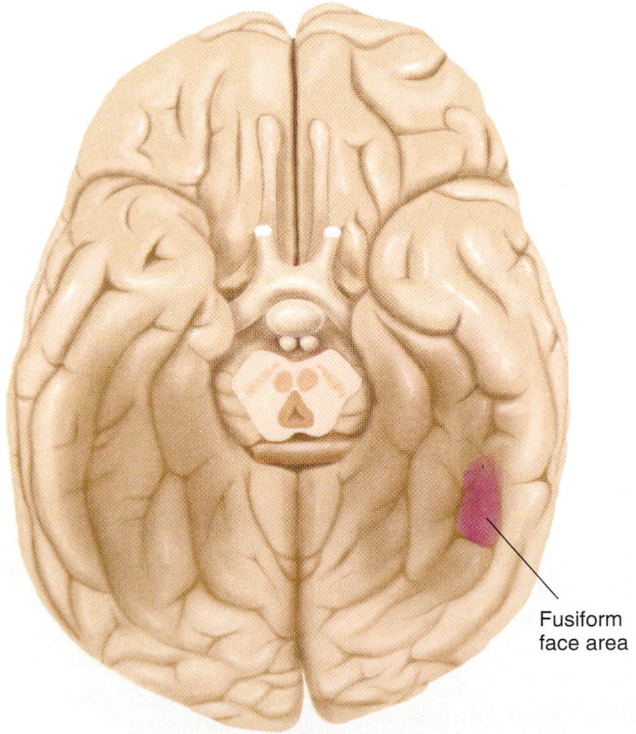

So there seems to be a special region devoted to recognition of faces. But must we conclude that the development of this region is a result of natural selection? Several kinds of evidence suggest that the answer is no—that the face-recognition circuits develop as a result of the extensive experience we have seeing people's faces. Because of this experience, we are all experts at recognizing faces. What about people who have become experts at recognizing other types of objects? It appears that recognition of specific complex stimuli by experts, too, is disrupted by lesions that cause prosopagnosia: inability of a farmer to recognize his cows, inability of a bird expert to recognize different species of birds, and inability of a driver to recognize his own car except by reading its license plate (Bornstein, Stroka, and Munitz, 1969; Damasio, Damasio, and Van Hoesen, 1982).

In a functional imaging study, Gauthier et al. (2000) found that when bird or car experts (but not nonexperts) viewed pictures of birds or cars, the fusiform face area was activated. Another study (Gauthier et al., 1999) found that when people had spent a long time becoming familiar with computer-generated objects they called "greebles," viewing the greebles activated the fusiform face area. (See ***Figure 6.28.***)

As we will see in Chapter 15, people with autistic disorder fail to develop normal social relationships with

Figure 6.27

Visual object agnosia without prosopagnosia. A patient could recognize the face in this painting but not the flowers and vegetables that compose it.

Giuseppe Arcimboldo. 1527–1593. *Vertumnus.* Erich Lessing/Art Resource, New York.

Figure 6.28

Some "greebles," computer-created objects from the study by Gauthier and Tarr (1997). Greebles were categorized by family and gender, and different individuals each had their own particular shapes. Two greebles of the same gender and family would resemble each other more closely than any other two greebles.

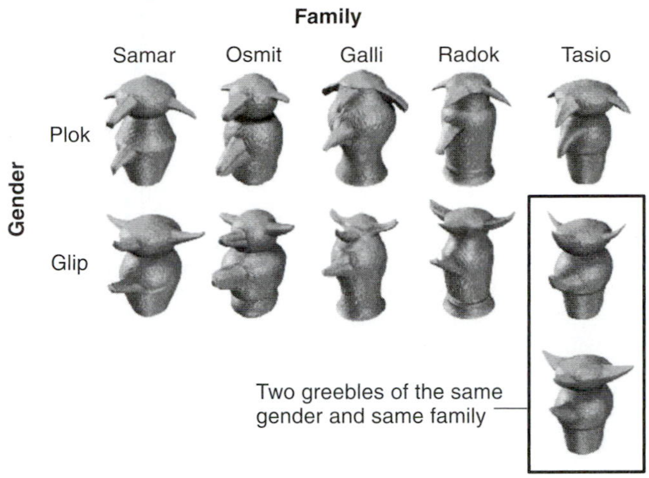

From Gauthier, I., and Tarr, M. J. *Vision Research,* 1997, *37,* 1673–1682. Copyright 1995 with permission from Elsevier.

other people. Indeed, in severe cases they give no signs that they recognize that other people exist. Grelotti, Gauthier, and Schultz (2002) found that people with autistic disorder showed a deficit in the ability to recognize faces and that looking at faces failed to activate the fusiform gyrus. The authors speculate that the lack of interest in other people, caused by the brain abnormalities responsible for autism, resulted in a lack of motivation that normally promotes the acquisition of expertise in recognizing faces as a child grows up.

In summary, a face-recognition region does appear to exist in the right fusiform gyrus, but the circuits there are specialized for acquiring expertise in recognizing a variety of closely related complex visual stimuli. The neural circuitry that is responsible for our ability to recognize faces does not seem to be genetically programmed for only one type of expertise.

Associative Visual Agnosia. A person with apperceptive agnosia who cannot recognize common objects also cannot draw them or copy other people's drawings; therefore, we properly speak of a deficit in perception. However, the brains of people with an **associative visual agnosia** appear to contain the neural circuits necessary for object recognition but the people seem to be unaware of these perceptions. For example, a patient studied by Ratcliff and Newcombe (1982) could copy a drawing of an anchor (better than I could have done). Therefore, he must have been able to

associative visual agnosia Inability to identify objects that are perceived visually, even though the form of the perceived object can be drawn or matched with similar objects.

Figure 6.29

Associative visual agnosia. (a) Model. (b) Patient's successful attempt to copy model. (c) and (d) Patient's unsuccessful attempts to comply with a request to "draw an anchor."

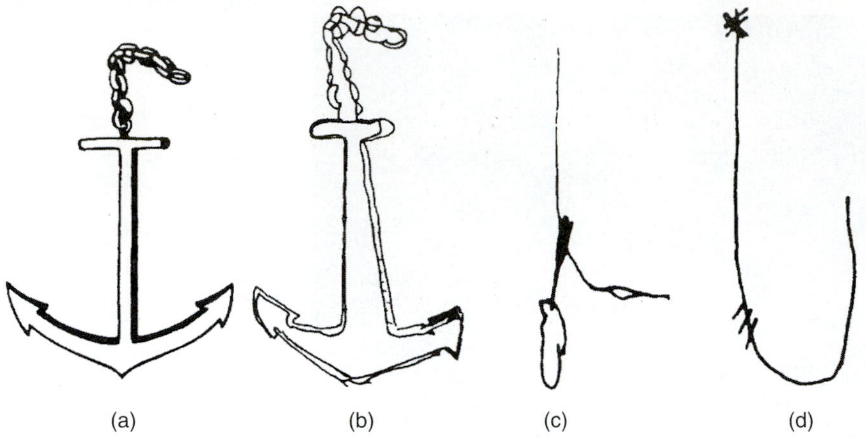

From Ratcliff, G., and Newcombe, F., in *Normality and Pathology in Cognitive Functions,* edited by A. W. Ellis. London: Academic Press, 1982.

perceive the shape of the anchor. However, he did not *recognize* either the sample or the copy that he had just drawn as being an anchor. When asked on another occasion to draw a picture of an anchor from memory (not from a picture), he could not do so. Even though he could copy a real image of an anchor, the word *anchor* failed to produce a mental image of one. (See ***Figure 6.29.***) When asked on yet another occasion to define *anchor,* he said, "a brake for ships," so we can conclude that he knew what the word meant.

Associative visual agnosia appears to involve a deficit in the ability to transfer information between the visual association cortex and brain mechanisms involved in language. That is, the person perceives the object well enough to draw it, but his or her verbal mechanisms do not receive the necessary information to produce the appropriate word or to think about what the object is. In the prologue to this chapter I described Mr. M., a man who was unable to recognize a picture of a cow until he observed himself making milking movements with his hands. We might speculate that his perceptual mechanisms in the visual association cortex were relatively normal but that connections between these mechanisms and the speech mechanisms of the left hemisphere were disrupted. However, the connections between the perceptual mechanisms and the motor mechanisms of the frontal lobe were spared, permitting him to make appropriate movements when looking at some pictures.

Perception of Movement

We need to know not only what things are, but also where they are and where they are going. Without the ability to perceive the direction and velocity of movement of objects, we would have no way to predict where they will be. We would be unable to catch them (or avoid letting them catch us). This section examines the perception of movement; the final section examines the perception of location.

Studies with Laboratory Animals

One of the regions of the extrastriate cortex—area V5, also known as area MT, for medial temporal—contains neurons that respond to movement. Damage to this region severely disrupts a monkey's ability to perceive moving stimuli (Siegel and Andersen, 1986). Area V5 receives input directly from the magnocellular system via

A tennis player must be able to perceive the direction and velocity of a tennis ball to predict its trajectory and intercept it with his racket. Perception of motion is disrupted by damage to a particular region of the extrastriate cortex.

the striate cortex and from several regions of the extrastriate cortex. It also receives input from the superior colliculus.

A region adjacent to area V5 (sometimes called V5a but more often referred to as MST, for *medial superior temporal*) receives information about movement from V5 and performs a further analysis. MST neurons respond to complex patterns of movement, including radial, circular, and spiral motion (see Vaina, 1998, for a review). One important function of this region—in particular, the dorsolateral MST, or MSTd—appears to be analysis of **optic flow.** As we move around in our environment or as objects in our environment move in relation to us, the sizes, shapes, and locations of environmental features on our retinas change. Imagine the image seen by a video camera as you walk along a street, pointing the lens of the camera straight in front of you. Suppose your path will pass just to the right of a mailbox. The image of the mailbox will slowly get larger. Finally, as you pass it, it will veer to the left and disappear. Points on the sidewalk will move downward, and branches of trees that you pass under will move upward. Analysis of the relative movement of the visual elements of your environment—the optic flow—will tell you where you are heading, how fast you are approaching different items in front of you, and whether you will pass to the left or right (or under or over) these items. The point toward which you are moving does not move, but all other points in the visual scene move away from it. Therefore, this point is called the *center of expansion.* If you keep moving in the same direction, you will eventually bump into an object that lies at the center of expansion. We can also use optic flow to determine whether an object approaching us will hit us or pass us by. Neurons in MSTd of monkeys respond selectively to optic flow, and disruption of the activity of MSTd neurons disrupts monkeys' ability to perceive direction of heading (Bradley et al., 1996; Britten and van Wezel, 1998).

Studies with Humans

Bilateral damage to parts of the visual association cortex of the human brain can produce an inability to perceive movement—**akinetopsia.** For example, Zihl et al. (1991) reported the case of a woman with bilateral lesions of the lateral occipital cortex and area V5.

Patient L. M. had an almost total loss of movement perception. She was unable to cross a street without traffic lights because she could not judge the speed at which

optic flow The complex motion of points in the visual field caused by relative movement between the observer and environment; provides information about the relative distance of objects from the observer and of the relative direction of movement.

akinetopsia Inability to perceive movement, caused by damage to area V5 (also called MST) of the visual association cortex.

cars were moving. Although she could perceive movements, she found moving objects very unpleasant to look at. For example, while talking with another person, she avoided looking at the person's mouth because she found its movements very disturbing. When the investigators asked her to try to detect movements of a visual target in the laboratory, she said, "First the target is completely at rest. Then it suddenly jumps upwards and downwards" (p. 2244). She was able to see that the target was constantly changing its position, but she was unaware of any sensation of movement.

Animation 6.3, Motion Aftereffects, demonstrates variations on the "waterfall effect."

As we saw in the previous subsection, neurons in area MSTd of the monkey brain respond to optic flow, an important source of information about the direction in which the animal is heading. A functional imaging study by Peuskens et al. (2001) found that the same region became active when subjects judged their heading while viewing a display showing optic flow. In addition, Vaina and her colleagues (Jornales et al., 1997; Vaina, 1998) found that people with lesions that included this region were able to perceive motion but could not perceive heading from optic flow. (***Animation 6.3, Motion Aftereffects,*** illustrates movement-related phenomena.)

Perception of movement can even help us perceive three-dimensional forms—a phenomenon known as *form from motion*. Johansson (1973) demonstrated just how much information we can derive from movement. He dressed actors in black and attached small lights to several points on their bodies, such as their wrists, elbows, shoulders, hips, knees, and feet. He made movies of the actors in a darkened room while they were performing various behaviors, such as walking, running, jumping, limping, doing push-ups, and dancing with a partner who was also equipped with lights. Even though observers who watched the films could see only a pattern of moving lights against a dark background, they could readily perceive the pattern as belonging to a moving human and could identify the behavior the actor was performing. Subsequent studies (Kozlowski and Cutting, 1977; Barclay, Cutting, and Kozlowski, 1978) showed that people could even tell, with reasonable accuracy, the sex of the actor wearing the lights. The cues appeared to be supplied by the relative amounts of movement of the shoulders and hips as the person walked.

Animation 6.4, Form from Motion, shows how familiar movements of people can be recognized from the coordinated movement of a few points of light.

A functional imaging study by Grossman et al. (2000) found that when people viewed a video that showed form from motion, a small region on the ventral bank of the posterior end of the superior temporal sulcus became active. More activity was seen in the right hemisphere, whether the images were presented to the left or right visual field. (For a demonstration of this phenomenon, see ***Animation 6.4, Form from Motion.***) Grossman and Blake (2001) found that this region became active even when people *imagined* that they were watching points of light representing form from motion. (See ***Figure 6.30.***)

Figure 6.30

Responses to viewing form from motion. Horizontal and lateral views of neural activity while the subject was viewing videos of biological motion such as those shown in Animation 6.3. Maximum activity is seen in a small region on the ventral bank of the posterior end of the superior temporal sulcus, primarily in the right hemisphere.

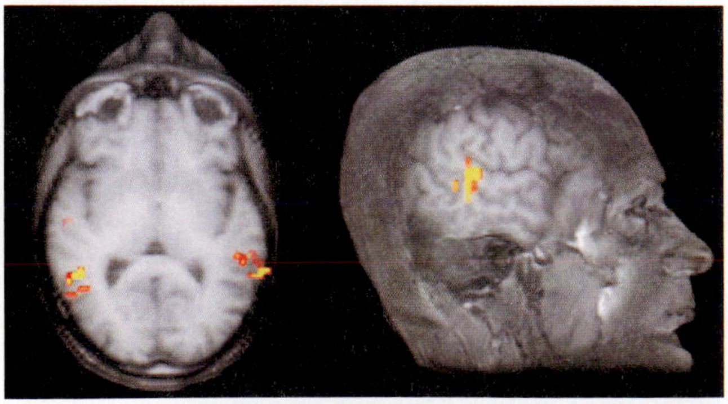

From Grossman, E. D., and Blake, R. *Vision Research*, 2001, *41*, 1475–1482. Copyright 2001, with permission from Elsevier.

Perception of Spatial Location

As we just saw, all subareas of the extrastriate cortex send information to the inferior temporal cortex, the region in which object perception appears to take place. In addition, three subareas of the extrastriate cortex—those involved with color, orientation, and movement—send information through area V5 to the parietal cortex. (Refer to ***Figure 6.25.***) The parietal lobe is involved in spatial perception, and it is through these connections that it receives its visual input. Damage to the parietal lobes disrupts performance on a variety of tasks that require perceiving and remembering the locations of objects (Ungerleider and Mishkin, 1982), and functional imaging studies have revealed increased activation of the dor-

Figure 6.31

Construction of a mental image. Subjects imagined the construction of an assembly of cubes as the experimenter indicated the location of each new block. (a) An assembly produced by the following directions: right, down, down, back, back, back, up, up, back, back, right. (b) Neural activity during the imaginary construction task, as measured by functional MRI.

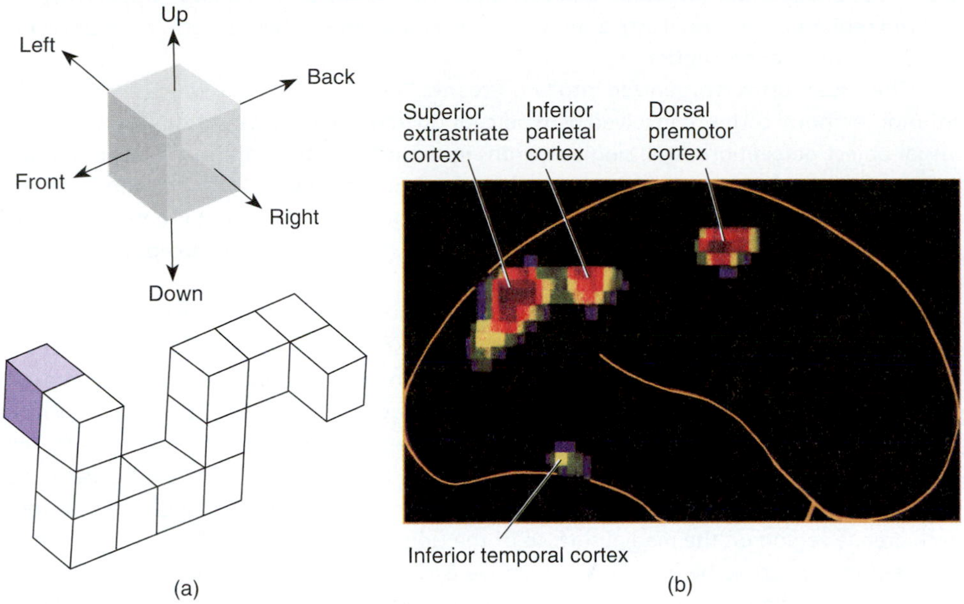

From Mellett, E., Tzourio, N., Crivello, F., Joliot, M., Denis, M., and Mazoyer, B. *Journal of Neuroscience,* 1996, *16,* 6504–6512. Copyright 1996 by the Society for Neuroscience.

sal stream when people perform tasks that require them to remember the spatial location of visual stimuli (Haxby et al., 1994).

A functional imaging study by Mellet et al. (1996) showed that the dorsal stream is involved in the construction of mental images of three-dimensional objects according to verbal instructions. The investigators asked people to imagine an assembly of cube-shaped blocks, put together one by one. For example, the assembly in Figure 6.31 begins with the block shown in blue. The second block goes to the right of the first, the third goes below the second, the fourth goes below the third, and so on. (See ***Figure 6.31a.***) Functional MRI images that were taken while the subjects were constructing the mental images of these objects found increased activity in a bilateral occipitoparietal-frontal network that included the superior extrastriate cortex of the occipital lobe, inferior parietal cortex, and dorsal premotor cortex of the frontal lobe. Activity was also seen in the right inferior temporal cortex. (See ***Figure 6.31b.***) Thus, imagining the construction of a three-dimensional assembly involves the dorsal stream (where spatial perception takes place) and the frontal lobes (where planning of movements takes place). The involvement of the ventral stream of the right hemisphere may reflect the people's recognition of the imaginary shape they had constructed.

INTERIM SUMMARY

Analysis of Visual Information: Role of the Visual Association Cortex

The visual cortex consists of the striate cortex, the extrastriate cortex, and the visual association cortex of the inferior temporal lobe and the posterior parietal lobe. There are at least twenty-five different subregions of the visual cortex, arranged in a hierarchical fashion. The color-sensitive cells in the CO blobs in the striate cortex send information to areas V4 and V8 of the extrastriate cortex. Damage to the area V4 abolishes color constancy (accurate perception of color under different lighting conditions), and damage to area V8 causes achromatopsia, a loss of color vision but not of form perception. A condition opposite to achromatopsia can also be seen: A patient with extensive damage to the extrastriate cortex was functionally blind but could still recognize colors. His brain damage apparently destroyed regions of the visual association cortex that are responsible for form perception but not those for color perception.

The visual cortex is organized into two streams. The ventral stream, which ends with the inferior temporal cortex, is involved with perception of objects. Lesions of this region disrupt visual object perception. Also, single neurons in the inferior temporal cortex respond best to complex stimuli and continue to do so even if the object is moved to a different location, changed in size, placed against a different background, or partially hidden. The dorsal stream, which ends with the posterior parietal cortex, is involved with perception of spatial location and movement.

Functional imaging studies indicate that specific regions of the cortex are involved in perception of form, movement, and color, and these studies are enabling us to discover the correspondences between the anatomy of the human visual system and that of laboratory animals. Studies of humans who have sustained damage to the visual association cortex have discovered two basic forms of visual agnosia. Apperceptive visual agnosia involves difficulty in perceiving the shapes of objects, even though fine details can often be detected. Prosopagnosia—failure to recognize faces—appears to be caused by damage to the fusiform face area, a region on the medial surface of the right occipital cortex. The development of this region appears to be a result of extensive experience looking at faces; expertise with other complex stimuli such as cows, birds, cars, or even artificial creatures (greebles) causes the development of circuits devoted to the perception of these stimuli as well. The fusiform face region fails to develop in people with autism, presumably because of insufficient motivation to become expert in recognizing other people's faces.

The second basic form of visual agnosia, associative visual agnosia, is characterized by relatively good object perception (shown by the fact that the patients can copy drawings of objects) but the inability to recognize what is perceived. This disorder is probably caused by damage to axons that connect the visual association cortex with regions of the brain that are important for verbalization and thinking in words. Some patients with this disorder can describe or mime actions appropriate to the objects they see but cannot recognize.

Damage to area V5 (also called area MT) disrupts an animal's ability to perceive movement, and damage to the posterior parietal cortex disrupts perception of the spatial location of objects. Damage to the human visual association cortex corresponding to area V5 disrupts perception of movement, producing a disorder known as akinetopsia. In addition, functional imaging studies show that perception of moving stimuli activate this region. In both monkeys and humans, area MSTd, a region of extrastriate cortex that receives information from area V5, appears to be specialized for perceiving optic flow, one of the cues we use to perceive the direction in which we are heading. The ability to perceive form from motion—recognition of complex movements of people indicated by lights attached to parts of their body—is probably related to the ability to recognize people by the way they walk. This ability apparently depends on a region of cerebral cortex on the ventral bank of the posterior end of the superior temporal sulcus.

THOUGHT QUESTIONS

1. Some psychologists are interested in "top-down" processes in visual perception—that is, the effects of context on perceiving ambiguous stimuli. For example, if you are in a dimly lighted kitchen and see a shape that could be either a loaf of bread or a country mailbox, you will be more likely to perceive the object as a loaf of bread. Where in the brain might contextual information affect perception?
2. A neurologist friend once told me about a patient he saw who had such severe prosopagnosia that he could not even recognize his wife by sight. One day, while

my friend was examining the patient, the patient's wife entered the hospital room. "Can you tell me who that is?" he asked, wanting to determine whether the patient's symptoms had improved. "I don't know," he said, "but it certainly can't be my dear Lucie." But it was. What type of prosopagnosia did the man have, apperceptive or associative? How might we explain his behavior?

EPILOGUE

Case Studies

The discussion of Mr. M. in the prologue raises an issue about research that I would like to address: the issue of making generalizations from the study of an individual patient. Some researchers have argued that because no two people are alike, we cannot make generalizations from a single individual like Mr. M. They say that valid inferences can be made only from studies that involve *groups* of people, so that individual differences can be accounted for statistically. Is this criticism valid?

The careful, detailed investigation of the abilities and disabilities of a single person is called a *case study.* In my opinion, case studies of people with brain damage can provide very useful information. In the first place, even if we were not able to make firm conclusions from the study of one person, a careful analysis of the pattern of deficits shown by an individual patient might give us some useful ideas for further research, and sources of good ideas for research should not be neglected. But under some circumstances we *can* draw conclusions from a single case.

Before describing what kinds of inferences we can and cannot make from case studies, let me review what we hope to accomplish by studying the behavior of people with brain damage. The brain seems to be organized in modules. A given module receives information from other modules, performs some kinds of analysis, and sends the results on to other modules with which it communicates. In some cases, the wiring of the module may change. That is, synaptic connections may be modified so that in the future the module will respond differently to its inputs. (As you will see in Chapter 12, the ability of modules to modify their synaptic connections serves as the basis for the ability to learn and remember.)

If we want to understand how the brain works, we have to know what the individual modules do. A particular module is not *responsible* for a behavior; instead, it performs one of the many functions that are necessary for a set of behaviors. For example, as I sit here typing this epilogue, I am using modules that perform functions related to posture and balance, to the control of eye movements, to memories related to the topic I am writing about, to memories of English words and their spellings, to control of finger movements . . . well, you get the idea. We would rarely try to analyze such a complex task as sitting and writing an epilogue; but we might try to analyze how we spell a familiar English word. Possibly, we use modules that perform functions normally related to hearing: We use these modules to "hear" the word in our head and then use other modules to convert the sounds into the appropriate patterns of letters. Alternatively, we may picture the word we want to spell, which would use modules that perform functions related to vision. I do not want to go into the details of spelling and writing here (they will be covered in Chapter 13), but I do want you to see why it is important to try to understand the functions performed by groups of modules located in particular parts of the brain. In practice, this means studying and analyzing the pattern of deficits shown by people with brain damage.

What kinds of conclusions can we make by studying a single individual? We *cannot* conclude that because two behaviors are impaired, the deficit is caused by damage to a set of common modules needed for both behaviors. Instead, it could be that behavior X is impaired by damage to module A and behavior Y is impaired by damage to module B and it just happens that modules A and B were both damaged by the brain lesion. However, we *can* conclude that if a brain lesion causes a loss of behavior X but not of behavior Y, then the functions performed by the damaged modules are not required to perform behavior Y. The study of a single patient permits us to make this conclusion.

The conclusion might seem rather modest, but it can advance our understanding of the types of brain functions involved in particular behaviors. For example, Mr. M. could not tell us that a picture he was looking at showed a cow, but he could make hand movements that a person would make only with respect to a cow. Therefore, we can conclude with certainty that brain damage that prevents a person from verbally identifying a particular visual image will not necessarily prevent the person from making hand movements appropriate to that image. Perhaps the brain has two perceptual systems, each with an independent set of modules devoted to analyzing visual images: one perceptual system connected to verbal mechanisms and the other connected to mechanisms involved with hand movements. Although we cannot rule out this possibility, it seems unlikely that the organization of the brain is so wasteful of resources. Instead, it seems more likely that a single set of modules is devoted to analyzing visual images, and the information analyzed there is sent to several different parts of the brain. Possibly, then, Mr. M.'s brain lesion disrupted the pathway bringing visual information to modules involved in verbal mechanisms but did not disrupt the pathway bringing it to modules involved in control of hand movements. (If this conclusion were true, we would say that associative visual agnosia is a *disconnection syndrome*—a syndrome caused by a disconnection between particular sets of modules.) Of course, to confirm this hypothesis, we need to make further observations on other patients.

You can see that although case studies do not permit us to make sweeping conclusions, under the right circumstances we can properly draw firm if modest conclusions that help us to understand the organization of the brain and suggest hypotheses to test with further research.

KEY CONCEPTS

THE STIMULUS

1. Light, a form of electromagnetic radiation, can vary in wavelength, intensity, and purity; it can thus give rise to differences in perceptions of hue, brightness, and saturation.

ANATOMY OF THE VISUAL SYSTEM

2. The eyes are complex sensory organs that focus an image of the environment on the retina. The retina consists of three layers: the photoreceptor layer (rods and cones), the bipolar cell layer, and the ganglion cell layer.
3. Information from the eye is sent to the parvocellular and magnocellular layers of the dorsal lateral geniculate nucleus and then to the primary visual cortex (striate cortex).

CODING OF VISUAL INFORMATION IN THE RETINA

4. When light strikes a molecule of photopigment in a photoreceptor, the molecule splits and initiates a receptor potential.
5. Ganglion cells of the retina respond in an opposing center/surround fashion.
6. Colors are detected by three types of cones, and the code is changed into an opponent-process system by the time it reaches the retinal ganglion cells.

ANALYSIS OF VISUAL INFORMATION: ROLE OF THE STRIATE CORTEX

7. Neurons in the striate cortex are organized in modules, each containing two blobs. Neurons within the blobs respond to color; those outside the blobs respond to orientation, spatial frequency, movement, and retinal disparity.
8. Visual information is processed by two parallel systems, the magnocellular system and the parvocellular system.

ANALYSIS OF VISUAL INFORMATION: ROLE OF THE VISUAL ASSOCIATION CORTEX

9. Specific regions of the prestriate cortex receive information about specific features of the visual scene from the striate cortex, analyze it, and send their information on to higher levels of association cortex.
10. The association cortex of the inferior temporal gyrus (ventral stream) recognizes the shape of objects, whereas the parietal cortex (dorsal stream) recognizes their location.
11. Damage to the visual association cortex can produce apperceptive or associative visual agnosia in humans. The fusiform gyrus on the base of the occipital lobe is involved in perception of faces and other particularly complex stimuli. A region located in the extrastriate cortex (V8) is involved in color vision. The region corresponding to area V5 is involved in perception of movement, and a nearby region (MSTd) is involved in perception of optic flow.

SUGGESTED READINGS

Gregory, R. L. *Eye and Brain: The Psychology of Seeing,* 5th ed. Princeton, NJ: Princeton University Press, 1997.

Oyster, C. W. *The Human Eye: Structure and Function.* Sunderland, MA: Sinauer Associates, 1999.

Rodieck, R. W. *The First Steps in Seeing.* Sunderland, MA: Sinauer Associates, 1998.

Tanaka, K. Inferotemporal cortex and object vision. *Annual Review of Neuroscience,* 1996, *19,* 100–139.

Wandell, B. A. *Foundations of Vision.* Sunderland, MA: Sinauer Associates, 1995.

Zeki, S. *A Vision of the Brain.* Oxford: Blackwell Scientific Publications, 1992.

SUGGESTED WEB SITES

Retina Reference

http://retina.anatomy.upenn.edu/~lance/retina/retina.html

The anatomy of the retina is the focus of this site. The site contains some marvelous images and diagrams of the retina and visual system.

***Perception: An Introduction to the Gestalt-Theorie* by Kurt Koffka (1992)**

www.yorku.ca/dept/psych/classics/Koffka/Perception/perception.htm

This site contains a translation of portions of a book by Kurt Koffka (1992) which outlines the general Gestalt view of perception.

Tutorials in Sensation and Perception

http://psych.hanover.edu/Krantz/sen_tut.html

This perception site contains tutorials and demonstrations on visual perception including visual aftereffects, motion illusions, and receptive fields.

Blindsight Demonstration

http://serendip.brynmawr.edu/bb/blindsight.html

This site provides an online demonstration of the phenomenon known as blindsight.

Audition, the Body Senses, and the Chemical Senses

chapter 7

CHAPTER OUTLINE

LEARNING OBJECTIVES

1. Describe the parts of the ear and the auditory pathway.
2. Describe the detection of pitch, timbre, and the location of the source of a sound.
3. Describe the structures and functions of the vestibular system.
4. Describe the cutaneous senses and their response to touch, temperature, and pain.
5. Describe the somatosensory pathways and the perception of pain.
6. Describe the four taste qualities, the anatomy of the taste buds and how they detect taste, and the gustatory pathway and neural coding of taste.
7. Describe the major structures of the olfactory system, explain how odors are detected, and describe the patterns of neural activity produced by these stimuli

PROLOGUE

All in Her Head?

Melissa, a junior at the state university, had volunteered to be a subject in an experiment at the dental school. She had been told that she might feel a little pain but that everything was under medical supervision and no harm would come to her. She didn't particularly like the idea of pain, but she would be well paid; and she saw in the experience an opportunity to live up to her own self-image as being as brave as anyone.

She entered the reception room, where she signed consent forms saying that she agreed to participate in the experiment and knew that a physician would be giving her a drug and that her reaction to pain would be measured. The experimenter greeted her, led her to a room, and asked her to be seated in a dental chair. He inserted a needle attached to a plastic tube into a vein in her right arm so that he could inject drugs.

"First," he said, "we want to find out how sensitive you are to pain." He showed her a device that looked something like an electric toothbrush with a metal probe on the end. "This device will stimulate nerves in the pulp of your tooth. Do you have some fillings?" She nodded. "Have you ever bitten on some aluminum foil?" She winced and nodded again. "Good, then you will know what to expect." He adjusted a dial on the stimulator, touched the tip of it to a tooth, and pressed the button. No response. He turned the dial and stimulated the tooth again. Still no response. He turned the dial again, and this time, the stimulation made her gasp and wince. He recorded the voltage setting in his notebook.

"Okay, now we know how sensitive this tooth is to pain. Now I'm going to give you a drug we are testing. It should decrease the pain quite a bit." He injected the drug and after a short while said, "Let's try the tooth again." The drug apparently worked; he had to increase the voltage considerably before she felt any pain.

"Now," he said, "I want to give you some more of the drug to see if we can make you feel even less pain." He gave another injection and, after a little wait, tested her again. But the drug had not further decreased her pain sensitivity; instead, it had *increased* it; she was now as sensitive as she had been before the first injection.

After the experiment was over, the experimenter walked with Melissa into a lounge. "I want to tell you about the experiment you were in, but I'd like to ask you not to talk about it with other people who might also serve as subjects." She nodded her head in agreement.

"Actually, you did not receive a painkiller. The first injection was pure salt water."

"It was? But I thought it made me less sensitive to pain."

"It did. When an innocuous substance such as an injection of salt water or a sugar pill has an effect like that, we call it a placebo effect."

"You mean that it was all in my mind? That I only *thought* that the shock hurt less?"

"No. Well, that is, it was necessary for you to think that you had received a painkiller. But the effect was a physiological one. We know that, because the second injection contained a drug that counteracts the effects of opiates."

"Opiates? You mean like morphine or heroin?"

"Yes." He saw her start to protest, shook his head, and said, "No, I'm sure you don't take drugs. But your brain makes them. For reasons we still do not understand, your believing that you had received a painkiller caused some cells in your brain to release a chemical that acts the way opiates do. The chemical acts on other neurons in your brain and decreases your sensitivity to pain. When I gave you the second injection—the drug that counteracts opiates—your sensitivity to pain came back."

"But then, did my mind or my brain make the placebo effect happen?"

"Well, think about it. Your mind and your brain are not really separate. Experiences can change the way your brain functions, and these changes can alter your experiences. Mind and brain have to be studied together, not separately."

One chapter was devoted to vision, but the rest of the sensory modalities must share a chapter. This unequal allocation of space reflects the relative importance of vision to our species and the relative amount of research that has been devoted to it. This chapter is divided into five major sections, which discuss audition, the vestibular system, the somatosenses, gustation, and olfaction.

Audition

For most people audition is the second most important sense. The value of verbal communication makes it even more important than vision in some respects; for example, a blind person can join others in conversation far more easily than a deaf person can. (Of course, deaf people can use sign language to converse.) Acoustic stimuli

pitch A perceptual dimension of sound; corresponds to the fundamental frequency.

hertz (Hz) Cycles per second.

loudness A perceptual dimension of sound; corresponds to intensity.

timbre (***tim*** *ber* or ***tamm*** *ber*) A perceptual dimension of sound; corresponds to complexity.

tympanic membrane The eardrum.

ossicle (***ahss*** *i kul*) One of the three bones of the middle ear.

malleus The "hammer"; the first of the three ossicles.

incus The "anvil"; the second of the three ossicles.

stapes (***stay*** *peez*) The "stirrup"; the last of the three ossicles.

cochlea (***cock lee uh***) The snail-shaped structure of the inner ear that contains the auditory transducing mechanisms.

also provide information about things that are hidden from view, and our ears work just as well in the dark. This section describes the nature of the stimulus, the sensory receptors, the brain mechanisms devoted to audition, and some of the details of the physiology of auditory perception.

The Stimulus

We hear sounds, which are produced by objects that vibrate and set molecules of air into motion. When an object vibrates, its movements cause molecules of air surrounding it alternately to condense and rarefy (pull apart), producing waves that travel away from the object at approximately 700 miles per hour. If the vibration ranges between approximately 30 and 20,000 times per second, these waves will stimulate receptor cells in our ears and will be perceived as sounds. (See ***Figure 7.1.***)

In Chapter 6 we saw that light has three perceptual dimensions—hue, brightness, and saturation—that correspond to three physical dimensions. Similarly, sounds vary in their pitch, loudness, and timbre. The perceived **pitch** of an auditory stimulus is determined by the frequency of vibration, which is measured in **hertz (Hz),** or cycles per second. (The term honors Heinrich Hertz, a nineteenth-century German physicist.) **Loudness** is a function of intensity—the degree to which the condensations and rarefactions of air differ from each other. More vigorous vibrations of an object produce more intense sound waves and hence louder ones. **Timbre** provides information about the nature of the particular sound—for example, the sound of an oboe or a train whistle. Most natural acoustic stimuli are complex, consisting of several different frequencies of vibration. The particular mixture determines the sound's timbre. (See ***Figure 7.2.***)

Anatomy of the Ear

Figure 7.3 shows a section through the ear and auditory canal and illustrates the apparatus of the middle and inner ear. (See ***Figure 7.3.***) Sound is funneled via the *pinna* (external ear) through the ear canal to the **tympanic membrane** (eardrum), which vibrates with the sound.

The *middle ear* consists of a hollow region behind the tympanic membrane, approximately 2 ml in volume. It contains the bones of the middle ear, called the **ossicles,** which are set into vibration by the tympanic membrane. (As we saw in Chapter 1, two of these bones evolved from part of the reptilian jaw.) The **malleus** (hammer) connects with the tympanic membrane and transmits vibrations via the **incus** (anvil) and **stapes** (stirrup) to the **cochlea,** the structure that contains the receptors. The

Figure 7.1

Sound waves. Changes in air pressure from sound waves move the eardrum in and out. Air molecules are closer together in regions of higher pressure and farther apart in regions of lower pressure.

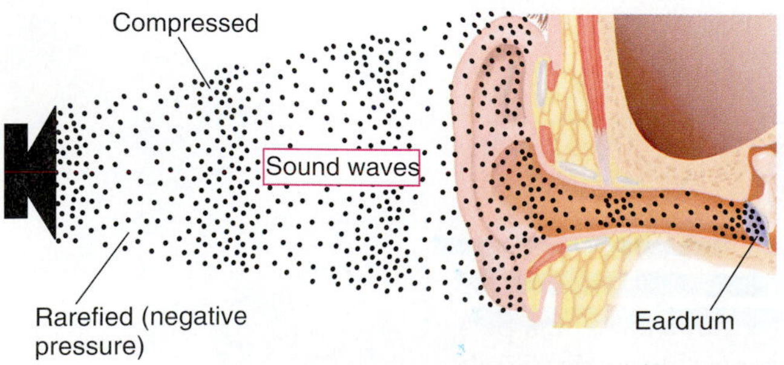

Figure 7.2

The physical and perceptual dimensions of sound waves.

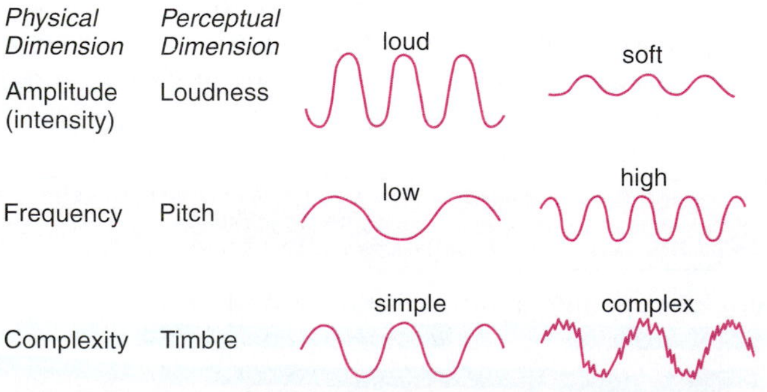

Figure 7.3

The auditory apparatus.

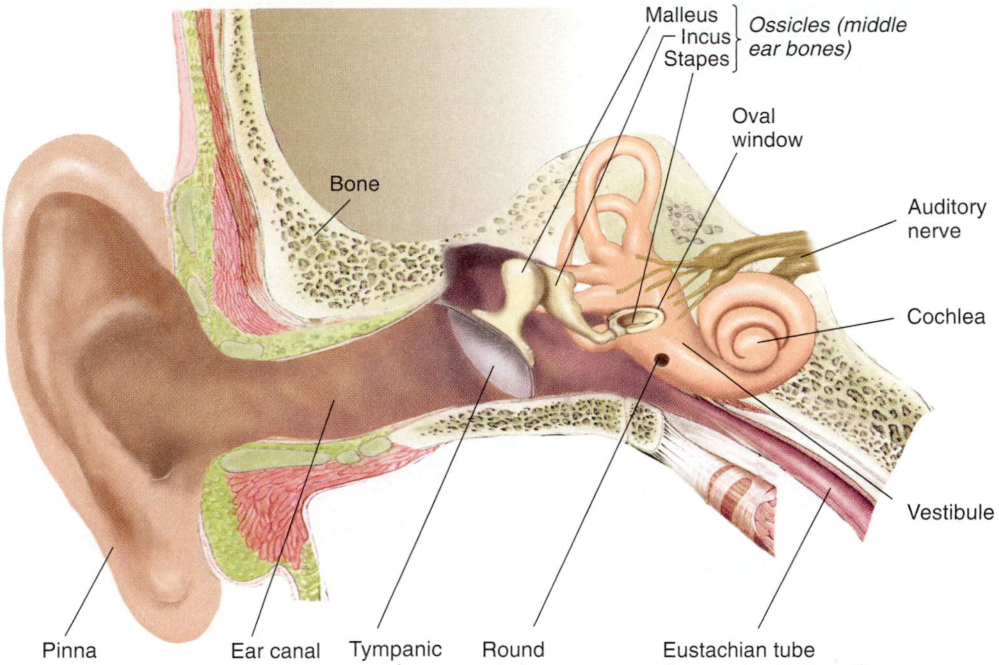

baseplate of the stapes presses against the membrane behind the **oval window,** the opening in the bony process surrounding the cochlea. (See ***Figure 7.3.***)

The cochlea is part of the *inner ear.* It is filled with fluid; therefore, sounds transmitted through the air must be transferred into a liquid medium. This process normally is very inefficient—99.9 percent of the energy of airborne sound would be reflected away if the air impinged directly against the oval window of the cochlea. The chain of ossicles serves as an extremely efficient means of energy transmission. The bones provide a mechanical advantage, with the baseplate of the stapes making smaller but more forceful excursions against the oval window than the tympanic membrane makes against the malleus.

The name *cochlea* comes from the Greek word *kokhlos,* or "land snail." It is indeed snail-shaped, consisting of two and three-quarters turns of a gradually tapering cylinder, 35 mm (1.37 in.) long. The cochlea is divided longitudinally into three sections, the *scala vestibuli* ("vestibular stairway"), the *scala media* ("middle stairway"), and the *scala tympani* ("tympanic stairway"), as shown in ***Figure 7.4.*** The receptive organ, known as the **organ of Corti,** consists of the *basilar membrane,* the *hair cells,* and the *tectorial membrane.* The auditory receptor cells are called **hair cells,** and they are anchored, via rodlike **Deiters's cells,** to the **basilar membrane.** The cilia of the hair cells pass through the *reticular membrane,* and the ends of some of them attach to the fairly rigid **tectorial membrane,** which projects overhead like a shelf. (See ***Figure 7.4.***) Sound waves cause the basilar membrane to move relative to the tectorial membrane, which bends the cilia of the hair cells. This bending produces receptor potentials.

Georg von Békésy—in a lifetime of brilliant studies on the cochleas of various animals, from human cadavers to elephants—found that the vibratory energy exerted on the oval window causes the basilar membrane to bend (von Békésy, 1960). Because of the physical characteristics of the basilar membrane, the portion that bends the most is determined by the frequency of the sound: High-frequency sounds cause the end nearest the oval window to bend.

oval window An opening in the bone surrounding the cochlea that reveals a membrane, against which the baseplate of the stapes presses, transmitting sound vibrations into the fluid within the cochlea.

organ of Corti The sensory organ on the basilar membrane that contains the auditory hair cells.

hair cell The receptive cell of the auditory apparatus.

Deiters's cell (***dye*** *terz*) A supporting cell found in the organ of Corti; sustains the auditory hair cells.

basilar membrane (***bazz*** *i ler*) A membrane in the cochlea of the inner ear; contains the organ of Corti.

tectorial membrane (*tek* ***torr*** *ee ul*) A membrane located above the basilar membrane; serves as a shelf against which the cilia of the auditory hair cells move.

Figure 7.4

A cross section through the cochlea, showing the organ of Corti.

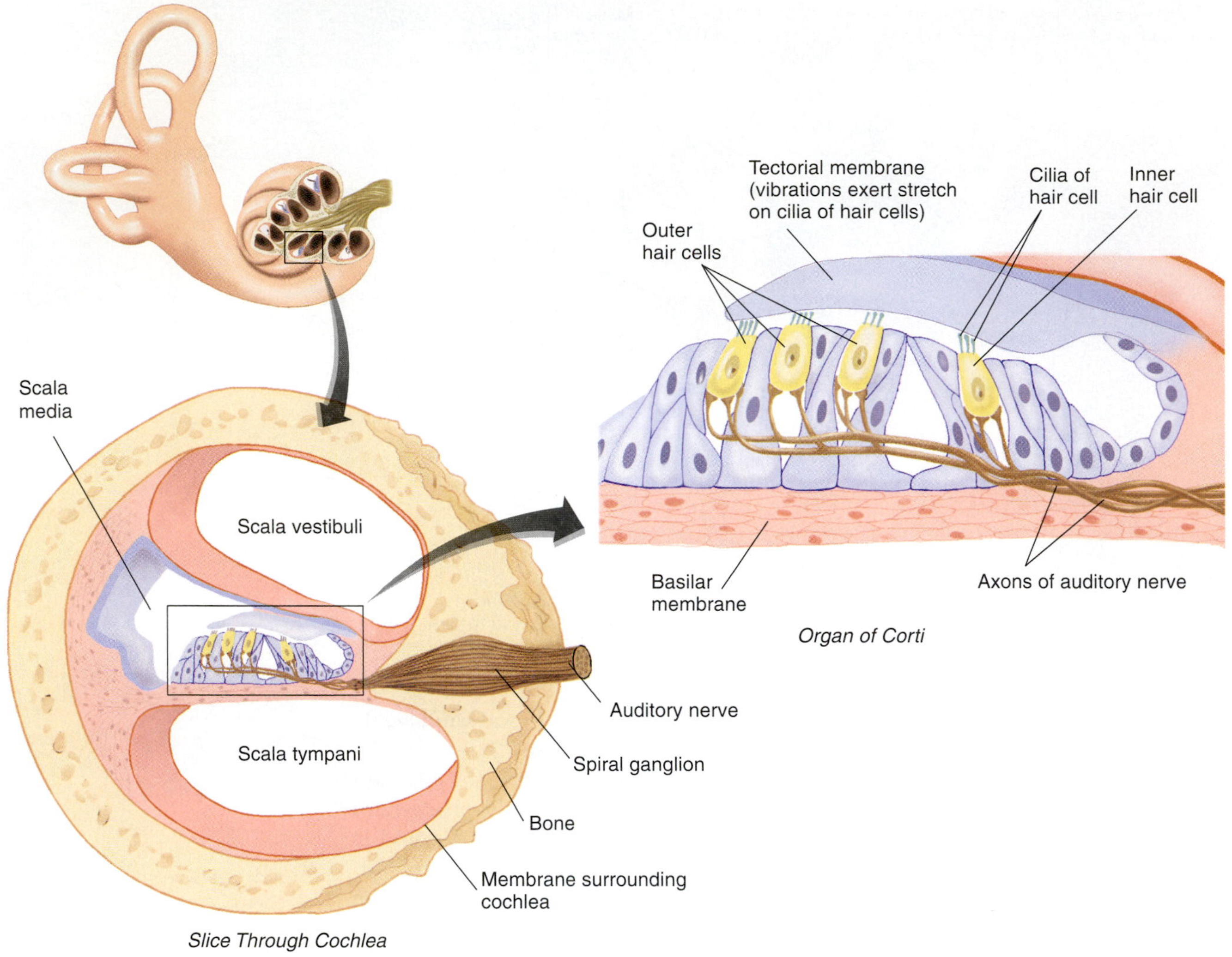

Figure 7.5 shows this process in a cochlea that has been partially straightened. If the cochlea were a closed system, no vibration would be transmitted through the oval window, because liquids are essentially incompressible. However, there is a membrane-covered opening, the **round window,** that allows the fluid inside the cochlea to move back and forth. The baseplate of the stapes vibrates against the membrane behind the oval window and introduces sound waves of high or low frequency into the cochlea. The vibrations cause part of the basilar membrane to flex back and forth. Pressure changes in the fluid underneath the basilar membrane are transmitted to the membrane of the round window, which moves in and out in a manner opposite to the movements of the oval window. That is, when the baseplate of the stapes pushes in, the membrane behind the round window bulges out. As we will see in a later subsection, different frequencies of sound vibrations cause different portions of the basilar membrane to flex. (See ***Figure 7.5.***)

round window An opening in the bone surrounding the cochlea of the inner ear that permits vibrations to be transmitted, via the oval window, into the fluid in the cochlea.

Some people suffer from a middle ear disease that causes bone to grow over the round window. Because their basilar membrane cannot easily flex back and forth, these people have a severe hearing loss. However, their hearing can be restored by a surgical procedure called *fenestration* ("window making"), in which a tiny hole is drilled in the bone where the round window should be.

Figure 7.5

Responses to sound waves. When the stapes pushes against the membrane behind the oval window, the membrane behind the round window bulges outward. Different high-frequency and medium-frequency sound vibrations cause flexing of different portions of the basilar membrane. In contrast, low-frequency sound vibrations cause the tip of the basilar membrane to flex in synchrony with the vibrations.

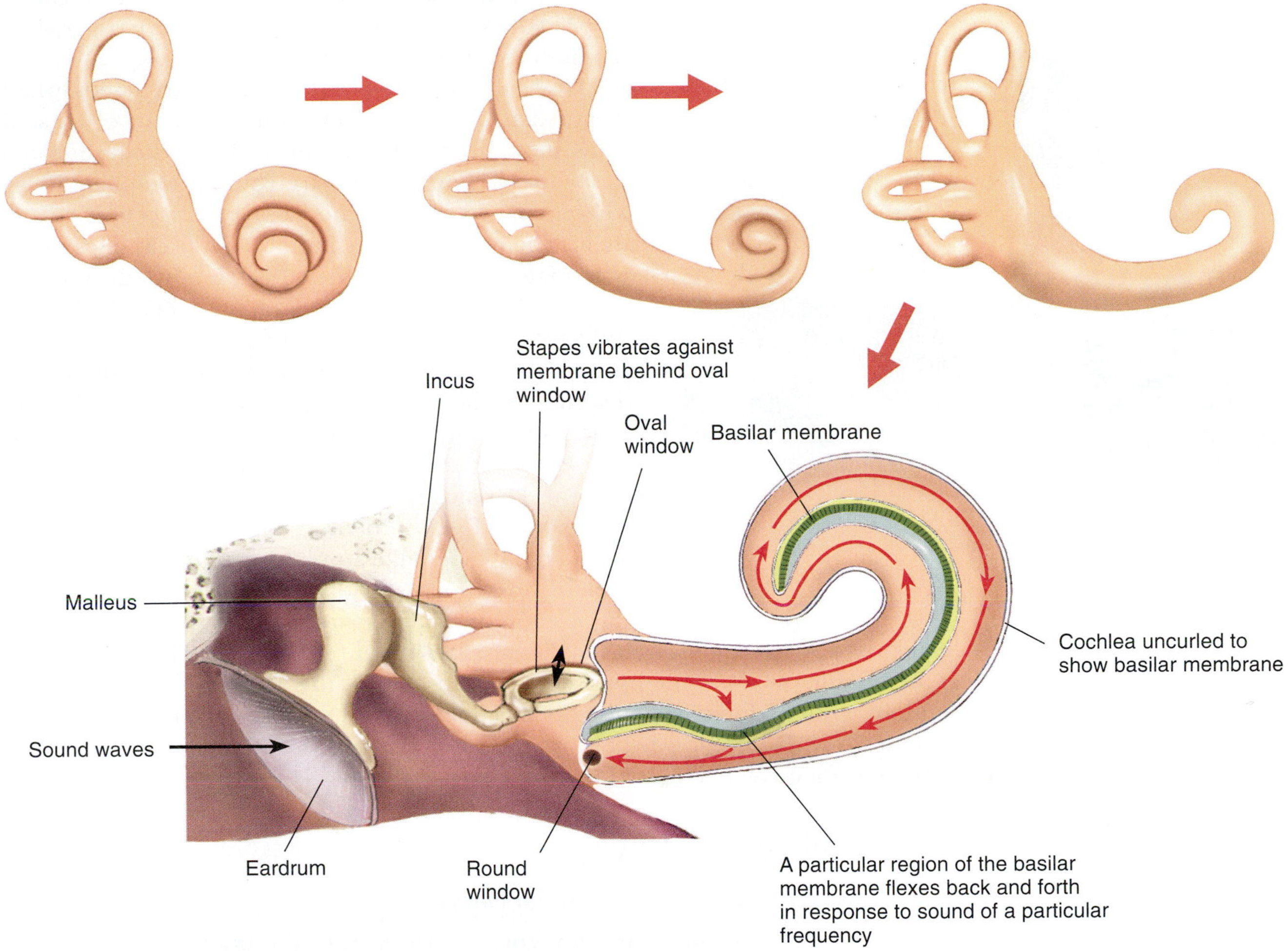

Stapes vibrates against membrane behind oval window
Incus
Oval window
Basilar membrane
Malleus
Cochlea uncurled to show basilar membrane
Sound waves
Eardrum
Round window
A particular region of the basilar membrane flexes back and forth in response to sound of a particular frequency

Auditory Hair Cells and the Transduction of Auditory Information

Two types of auditory receptors, *inner* and *outer* auditory hair cells, lie on the inside and outside of the cochlear coils, respectively. Hair cells contain **cilia** ("eyelashes"), fine hairlike appendages, arranged in rows according to height. The human cochlea contains approximately 3500 inner hair cells, arranged in a single row, and 12,000 outer hair cells, arranged in three rows. The hair cells form synapses with dendrites of bipolar neurons whose axons bring auditory information to the brain. (Refer to *Figure 7.4*.)

Sound waves cause both the basilar membrane and the tectorial membrane to flex up and down. These movements bend the cilia of the hair cells in one direction or the other. The tips of the cilia of outer hair cells are attached directly to the tectorial membrane. The cilia of the inner hair cells do not touch the overlying tectorial membrane, but the relative movement of the two membranes causes the fluid within the cochlea to flow past them, making them bend back and forth too.

cilium A hairlike appendage of a cell involved in movement or in transducing sensory information; found on the receptors in the auditory and vestibular system.

Figure 7.6

Electron micrographs of the transduction apparatus in hair cells. (a) Longitudinal section through three adjacent cilia. Tip links, elastic filaments attached to insertional plaques, link adjacent cilia. (b) A cross section through several cilia, showing an insertional plaque.

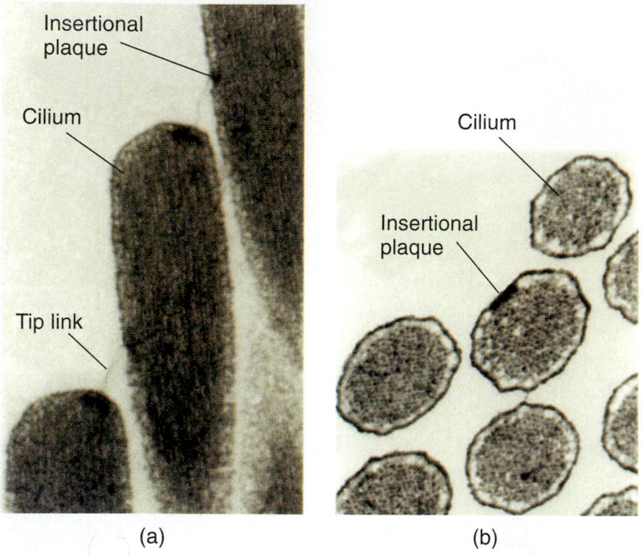

From Hudspeth, A. J., and Gillespie, P. G. *Neuron*, 1994, *12*, 1–9.

Cilia contain a core of actin filaments surrounded by myosin filaments, and these proteins make the cilia stiff and rigid (Flock, 1977). Adjacent cilia are linked to each other by elastic filaments known as **tip links.** Each tip link is attached to the end of one cilium and to the side of an adjacent cilium. The points of attachment, known as **insertional plaques,** look dark under an electron microscope. As we will see, receptor potentials are triggered at the insertional plaques. (See ***Figure 7.6.***)

Normally, tip links are slightly stretched, which means that they are under a small amount of tension. Thus, movement of the bundle of cilia in the direction of the tallest of them further stretches these linking fibers, whereas movement in the opposite direction relaxes them. The bending of the bundle of cilia causes receptor potentials (Pickles and Corey, 1992; Hudspeth and Gillespie, 1994; Gillespie, 1995; Jaramillo, 1995). Unlike the fluid that surrounds most neurons, the fluid that surrounds the auditory hair cells is rich in potassium. Each insertional plaque contains a single cation channel. When the bundle of cilia is straight, the probability of an individual ion channel being open is approximately 10 percent. This means that a small amount of the cations K^+ and Ca^{2+} diffuses into the cilium. When the bundle moves toward the tallest one, the increased tension on the tip links opens all the ion channels, the flow of cations into the cilium increases, and the membrane depolarizes. As a result, the release of neurotransmitter by the hair cell increases. When the bundle moves in the opposite direction, toward the shortest cilium, the relaxation of the tip links allows the opened ion channels to close. The influx of cations ceases, the membrane hyperpolarizes, and the release of neurotransmitter decreases. (See ***Figure 7.7.***)

The Auditory Pathway

Connections with the Cochlear Nerve

The organ of Corti sends auditory information to the brain by means of the **cochlear nerve,** a branch of the auditory nerve (eighth cranial nerve). The neurons that give rise to the afferent axons that travel through this nerve are of the bipolar type. Their cell bodies reside in the *cochlear nerve ganglion.* (This ganglion is also called the *spiral ganglion* because it consists of clumps of cell bodies arranged in a spiral caused by the curling of the cochlea.) These neurons have axonal processes, capable of sustaining action potentials, that protrude from both ends of the soma. The end of one process acts like a dendrite, responding with excitatory postsynaptic potentials when the neurotransmitter is released by the auditory hair cells. The excitatory postsynaptic potentials trigger action potentials in the auditory nerve axons, which form synapses with neurons in the medulla. (Refer to ***Figure 7.4.***)

Each cochlear nerve contains approximately 50,000 afferent axons. The dendrites of approximately 95 percent of these axons form synapses with the inner hair cells. Most afferent fibers make contact with only one inner hair cell, but each inner hair cell forms synapses with approximately twenty fibers (Dallos, 1992). The axons that receive information from the inner hair cells are thick and myelinated. The other 5 percent of the sensory fibers in the cochlear nerve form synapses with the much more numerous outer hair cells, at a ratio of approximately one fiber per thirty outer hair cells. In addition, these axons are thin and unmyelinated. Thus, al-

tip link An elastic filament that attaches the tip of one cilium to the side of the adjacent cilium.

insertional plaque The point of attachment of a tip link to a cilium.

cochlear nerve The branch of the auditory nerve that transmits auditory information from the cochlea to the brain.

Figure 7.7

Transduction in hair cells of the inner ear. (a) Appearance of the cilia of an auditory hair cell. (b) Movement of the bundle of cilia toward the tallest one increases the firing rate of the cochlear nerve axon attached to the hair cell, while movement away from the tallest one decreases it. (c) Movement toward the tallest cilium increases tension on the tip links, which opens the ion channels and increases the influx of K^+ and Ca^{2+} ions. Movement toward the shortest cilium removes tension from the tip links, which permits the ion channels to close, stopping the influx of cations.

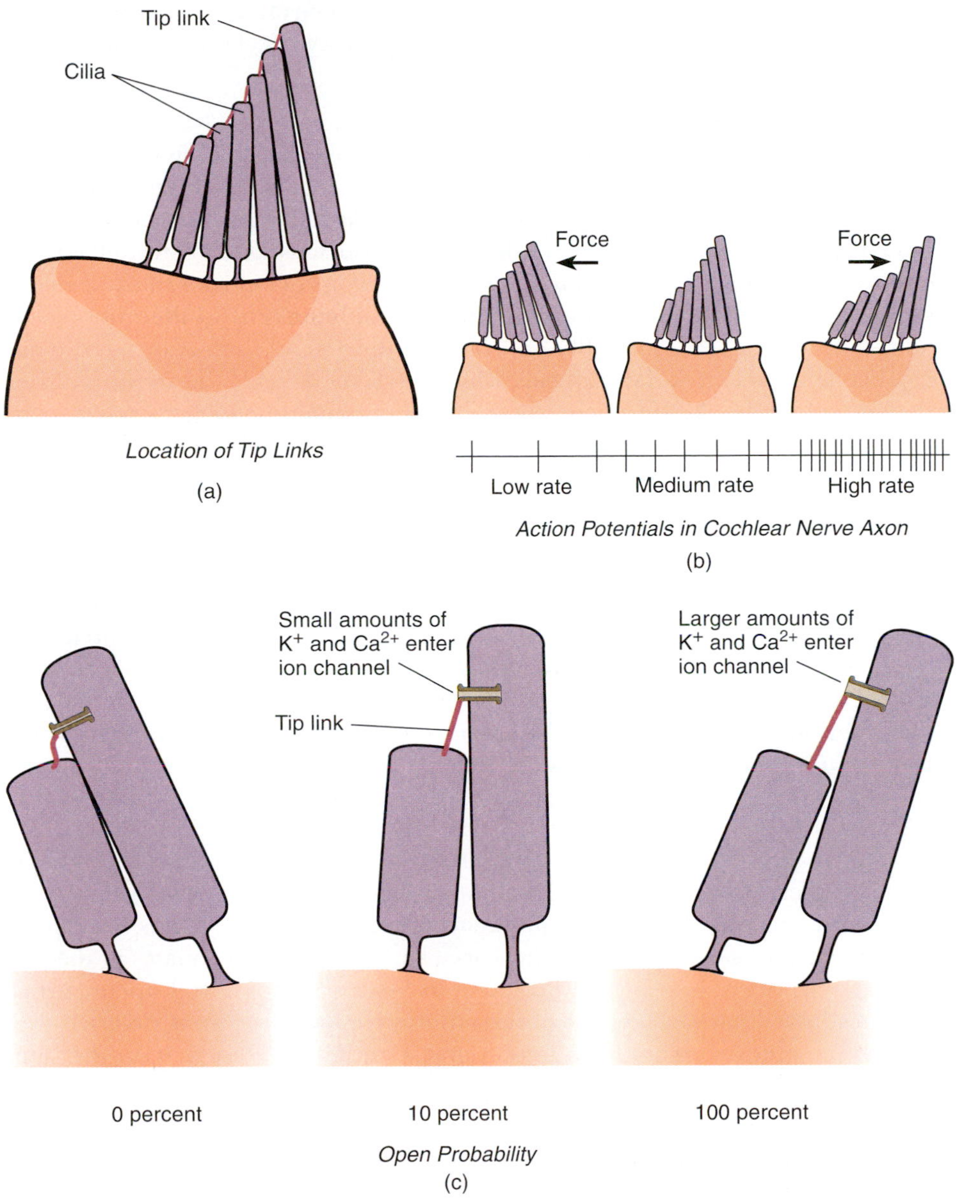

though the inner hair cells represent only 29 percent of the total number of receptor cells, their connections with auditory nerves suggest that they are of primary importance in the transmission of auditory information to the central nervous system.

Physiological and behavioral studies confirm the inferences made from the synaptic connections of the two types of hair cells: The inner hair cells are necessary for normal hearing. In fact, Deol and Gluecksohn-Waelsch (1979) found that a mutant strain of mice whose cochleas contain *only* outer hair cells apparently cannot hear at all. Subsequent research indicates that the outer hair cells are *effector* cells, involved in altering the mechanical characteristics of the basilar membrane and thus influencing the effects of sound vibrations on the inner hair cells. I will discuss the role of outer hair cells in the section on place coding of pitch.

The cochlear nerve contains efferent axons as well as afferent ones. The source of the efferent axons is the superior olivary complex, a group of nuclei in the medulla; thus, the efferent fibers constitute the **olivocochlear bundle.** The fibers form synapses directly on outer hair cells and on the dendrites that serve the inner hair cells. The neurotransmitter at the afferent synapses is glutamate. The efferent terminal buttons secrete acetylcholine, which appears to have an inhibitory effect on the hair cells.

The Central Auditory System

The anatomy of the auditory system is more complicated than that of the visual system. Rather than giving a detailed verbal description of the pathways, I will refer you to ***Figure 7.8.*** Note that axons enter the **cochlear nucleus** of the medulla and synapse there. Most of the neurons in the cochlear nucleus send axons to the **superior olivary complex,** also located in the medulla. Axons of neurons in these nuclei pass through a large fiber bundle called the **lateral lemniscus** to the inferior colliculus, located in the dorsal midbrain. Neurons there send their axons to the medial geniculate nucleus of the thalamus, which sends its axons to the auditory cortex of the temporal lobe. As you can see, there are many synapses along the way to complicate the story. Each hemisphere receives information from both ears but primarily from the contralateral one. Auditory information is relayed to the cerebellum and reticular formation as well.

If we unrolled the basilar membrane into a flat strip and followed afferent axons serving successive points along its length, we would reach successive points in the nuclei of the auditory system and ultimately successive points along the surface of the primary auditory cortex. The *basal* end of the basilar membrane (the end toward the oval window) is represented most medially in the auditory cortex, and the *apical* end is represented most laterally there. Because, as we will see, different parts of the basilar membrane respond best to different frequencies of sound, this relationship between cortex and basilar membrane is referred to as **tonotopic representation** (*tonos* means "tone," and *topos* means "place").

Neurons in the primary auditory cortex send axons to the auditory association cortex. In Chapter 3 we saw that the primary auditory cortex lies hidden on the inside of the lateral fissure and that the auditory association cortex lies on the superior part of the temporal lobe. Like the visual cortex, the auditory cortex is arranged in two streams, dorsal and ventral. The dorsal stream, which terminates in the posterior parietal cortex, is involved with sound localization; the ventral stream, which terminates in the parabelt region of the anterior temporal lobe, is involved with analysis of complex sounds (Rauschecker and Tian, 2000). Research on the functions of these streams is described later.

olivocochlear bundle A bundle of efferent axons that travel from the olivary complex of the medulla to the auditory hair cells on the cochlea.

cochlear nucleus One of a group of nuclei in the medulla that receive auditory information from the cochlea.

superior olivary complex A group of nuclei in the medulla; involved with auditory functions, including localization of the source of sounds.

lateral lemniscus A band of fibers running rostrally through the medulla and pons; carries fibers of the auditory system.

tonotopic representation (*tonn oh* ***top*** *ik*) A topographically organized mapping of different frequencies of sound that are represented in a particular region of the brain.

Perception of Pitch

As we have seen, the perceptual dimension of pitch corresponds to the physical dimension of frequency. The cochlea detects frequency by two means: moderate to high frequencies by place coding and low frequencies by rate coding. These two types of coding are described next.

Place Coding

The work of von Békésy has shown us that because of the mechanical construction of the cochlea and basilar membrane, acoustic stimuli of different frequencies cause different parts of the basilar membrane to flex back and forth. Figure 7.9 il-

Figure 7.8

The pathway of the auditory system. The major pathways are indicated by heavy arrows.

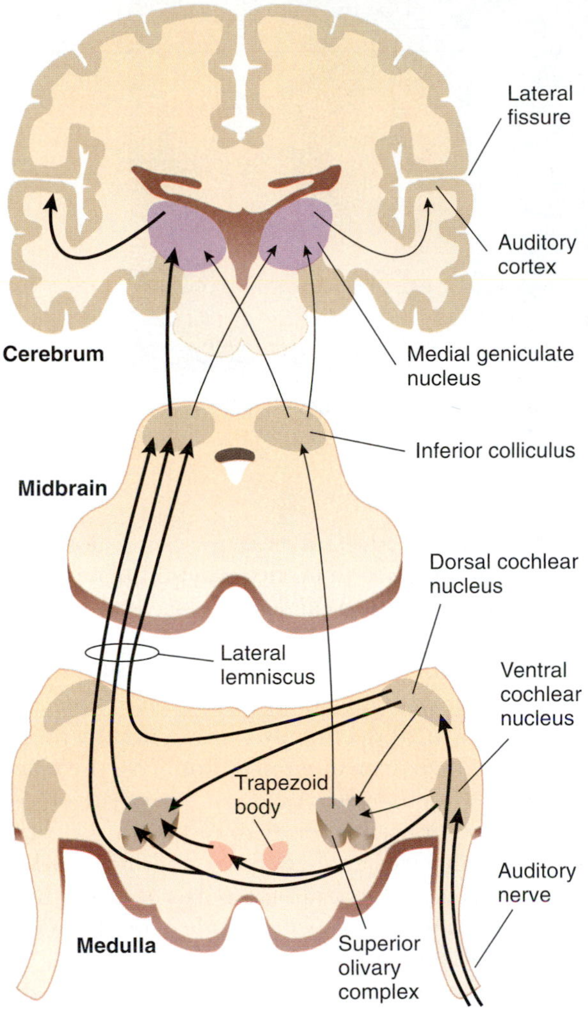

Figure 7.9

Anatomical coding of pitch. Stimuli of different frequencies maximally deform different regions of the basilar membrane.

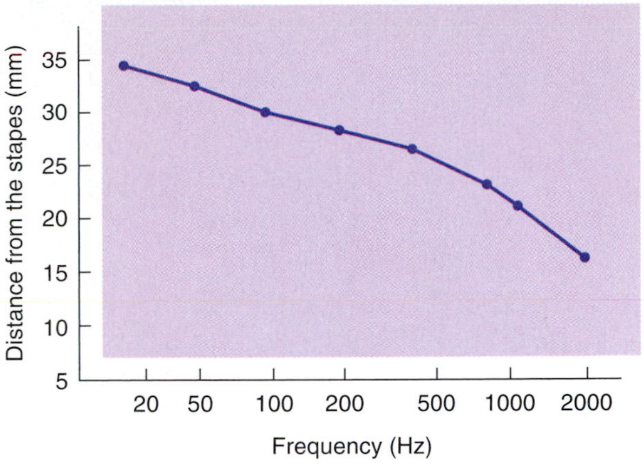

From von Békésy, G. *Journal of the Acoustical Society of America*, 1949, *21*, 233–245.

lustrates the amount of deformation along the length of the basilar membrane produced by stimulation with tones of various frequencies. Note that higher frequencies produce more displacement at the basal end of the membrane (the end closest to the stapes). (See ***Figure 7.9.***)

These results suggest that at least some frequencies of sound waves are detected by means of a **place code.** In this context a code represents a means by which neurons can represent information. Thus, if neurons at one end of the basilar membrane are excited by higher frequencies and those at the other end by lower frequencies, we can say that the frequency of the sound is *coded* by the particular neurons that are active. In turn, the firing of particular axons in the cochlear nerve tells the brain about the presence of particular frequencies of sound.

Evidence for place coding of pitch comes from several sources. Perhaps the best evidence (at least in humans) comes from the effectiveness of cochlear implants. **Cochlear implants** are devices used to restore hearing in people with deafness caused by damage to the hair cells. The external part of a cochlear implant consists of a microphone and a miniaturized electronic signal processor. The internal part contains a very thin, flexible array of electrodes, which the surgeon carefully inserts into the

place code The system by which information about different frequencies is coded by different locations on the basilar membrane.

cochlear implant An electronic device surgically implanted in the inner ear that can enable a deaf person to hear.

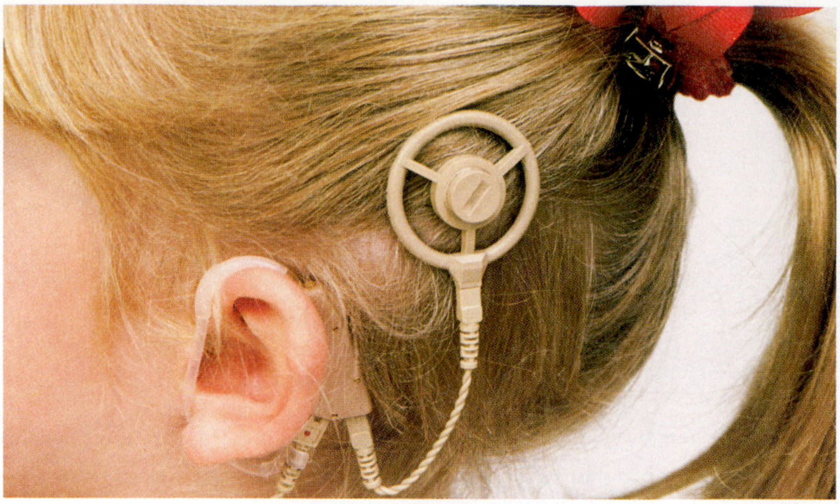

Cochiear implants are devices used to restore hearing in deaf people. They show that electrical stimulation of different regions of the basilar membrane produce perceptions of sounds of different pitches.

cochlea in such a way that it follows the snail-like curl and ends up resting along the entire length of the basilar membrane. Each electrode in the array stimulates a different part of the basilar membrane. Information from the signal processor is passed to the electrodes by means of flat coils of wire implanted under the skin.

The primary purpose of a cochlear implant is to restore a person's ability to understand speech. Because most of the important acoustical information in speech is contained in frequencies that are too high to be accurately represented by a rate code, the multichannel electrode was developed in an attempt to duplicate the place coding of pitch on the basilar membrane (Loeb, 1990). When different regions of the basilar membrane are stimulated, the person perceives sounds with different pitches. The signal processor in the external device analyzes the sounds detected by the microphone and sends separate signals to the appropriate portions of the basilar membrane. This device can work well; some people with cochlear implants can understand speech well enough to use a telephone.

As I mentioned earlier, the brain receives auditory information solely from the axons of inner hair cells. What role, then, do outer hair cells play? These cells contain contractile proteins, just as muscle fibers do. When they are exposed to an electrical current, outer hair cells contract by up to 10 percent of their length (Brownell et al., 1985; Zenner, Zimmermann, and Schmitt, 1985).

When the basilar membrane vibrates, movement of the cilia of the outer hair cells opens and closes ion channels, causing changes in the membrane potential. These changes cause movements of the contractile proteins, thus lengthening and shortening the cells. These changes in length amplify the vibrations of the basilar membrane. As a consequence, the signal that is received by inner hair cells is enhanced, which greatly increases the sensitivity of the inner ear to sound waves.

rate code The system by which information about different frequencies is coded by the rate of firing of neurons in the auditory system.

fundamental frequency The lowest, and usually most intense, frequency of a complex sound; most often perceived as the sound's basic pitch.

overtone The frequency of complex tones that occurs at multiples of the fundamental frequency.

Rate Coding

We have seen that the frequency of a sound can be detected by place coding. However, the lowest frequencies do not appear to be accounted for in this manner. Kiang (1965) was unable to find any cells that responded best to frequencies of less than 200 Hz. How, then, can animals distinguish low frequencies? It appears that lower frequencies are detected by neurons that fire in synchrony with the movements of the apical end of the basilar membrane. Thus, lower frequencies are detected by means of **rate coding.**

The most convincing evidence of rate coding of pitch comes from studies of people with cochlear implants. Pijl and Schwartz (1995a, 1995b) found that stimulation of a single electrode with pulses of electricity produced sensations of pitch that were proportional to the frequency of the stimulation. In fact, the subjects could even recognize familiar tunes produced by modulating the pulse frequency. (The subjects had become deaf later in life, after they had already learned to recognize the tunes.) As we would expect, the subjects' perceptions were best when the tip of the basilar membrane was stimulated, and only low frequencies could be distinguished by this method. (See ***Animation 7.1, Perception of Pitch.***)

Animation 7.1, Perception of Pitch, illustrates the coding of pitch by the basilar membrane.

Perception of Timbre

Although laboratory investigations of the auditory system often employ pure sine waves as stimuli, these waves are seldom encountered outside the laboratory. Instead, we hear sounds with a rich mixture of frequencies—sounds of complex timbre. For example, consider the sound of a clarinet playing a particular note. If we hear it, we can easily say that it is a clarinet and not a flute or a violin. The reason we can do so is that these three instruments produce sounds of different timbre, which our auditory system can distinguish.

Figure 7.10 shows the waveform from a clarinet playing a steady note (*top*). The shape of the waveform repeats itself regularly at the **fundamental frequency,** which corresponds to the perceived pitch of the note. A Fourier analysis of the waveform shows that it actually consists of a series of sine waves that includes the fundamental frequency and many **overtones,** multiples of the fundamental frequency. Different instruments produce overtones with different intensities. (See ***Figure 7.10.***) Electronic synthesizers simulate the sounds of real instruments by producing a series of overtones of the proper intensities, mixing them, and passing them through a loudspeaker.

When the basilar membrane is stimulated by the sound of a clarinet, different portions respond to each of the overtones. This response produces a unique anatomically coded pattern of activity in the cochlear nerve, which is subsequently identified by circuits in the auditory association cortex.

Actually, the recognition of complex sounds is not quite that simple. Figure 7.10 shows the analysis of a *sustained* sound of a clarinet. But most sounds (including those produced by a clarinet) are dynamic; that is, their beginning, middle, and end are different from each other. The beginning of a note played on a clarinet (the *attack*) contains frequencies that appear and disappear in a few milliseconds. And at the end of the note (the *decay*), some harmonics disappear before others. If we are to recognize different sounds, the auditory cortex must analyze a complex sequence of multiple frequencies that appear, change in amplitude, and disappear. And when you consider the fact that we can listen to an orchestra and identify several instruments that are playing simultaneously, you can appreciate the complexity of the analysis performed by the auditory system. We will revisit this process later in this chapter.

Figure 7.10

The shape of a sound wave from a clarinet (*top*) and the individual frequencies into which it can be analyzed.

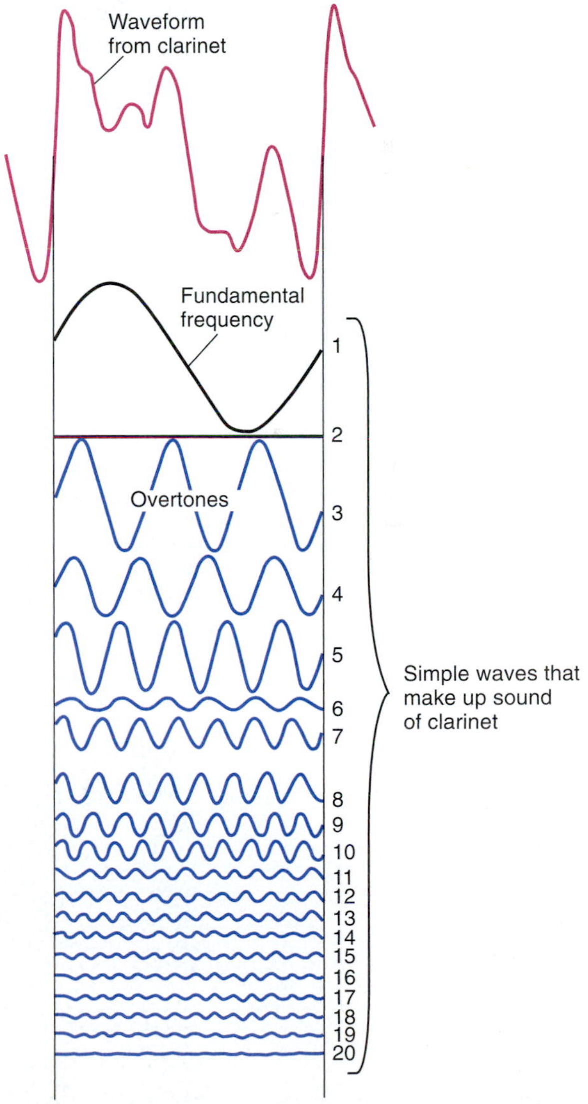

Reprinted from *Stereo Review,* copyright © 1977 by Diamandis Communications Inc.

Perception of Spatial Location

So far, I have discussed coding of pitch and timbre (the latter of which is actually a complex frequency analysis). The auditory system also responds to other qualities of acoustic stimuli. For example, our ears are very good at determining whether the source of a sound is to the right or left of us. Two separate physiological mechanisms detect the location of sound sources: We use phase differences for low frequencies (less than approximately 3000 Hz) and intensity differences for high frequencies. In addition, we use another mechanism—analysis of timbre—to determine whether the source of a sound is in front of us or behind us.

If we are blindfolded, we can still determine with rather good accuracy the location of a stimulus that emits a click. We do so because neurons respond selectively to different *arrival times* of the sound waves at the left and right ears. If the source of the click is to the right or left of the midline, the sound pressure wave will reach one ear sooner and initiate action potentials there first. Only if the stimulus is straight ahead will the ears be stimulated simultaneously. Neurons in the superior olivary complex of the medulla detect differences in arrival times of sound waves produced by clicks.

phase difference The difference in arrival times of sound waves at each of the eardrums.

Of course, we can hear continuous sounds as well as clicks, and we can also perceive the location of their source. We detect the source of continuous low-pitched sounds by means of phase differences. **Phase differences** refer to the simultaneous arrival, at each ear, of different portions (phases) of the oscillating sound wave. For example, if we assume that sound travels at 700 miles per hour through the air, adjacent cycles of a 1000-Hz tone are 12.3 inches apart. Thus, if the source of the sound is located to one side of the head, one eardrum is pulled out while the other is pushed in. The movement of the eardrums will reverse, or be 180° *out of phase.* If the source were located directly in front of the head, the movements would be perfectly in phase (0° out of phase). (See ***Figure 7.11.***) Because some auditory neurons respond only when the eardrums (and thus the bending of the basilar membrane) are at least somewhat out of phase, neurons in the superior olivary complex in the brain are able to use the information they provide to detect the source of a continuous sound. (See ***Animation 7.2, Sound Localization.***)

Animation 7.2, Sound Localization, shows how neurons in the superior olivary complex use phase differences to detect the source of a sound.

Figure 7.11

Localizing the source of low-frequency and medium-frequency sounds through phase differences. (a) Source of a 1000-Hz tone to the right. The pressure waves on each eardrum are out of phase; one eardrum is pushed in while the other is pushed out. (b) Source of a sound directly in front. The vibrations of the eardrums are synchronized (in phase).

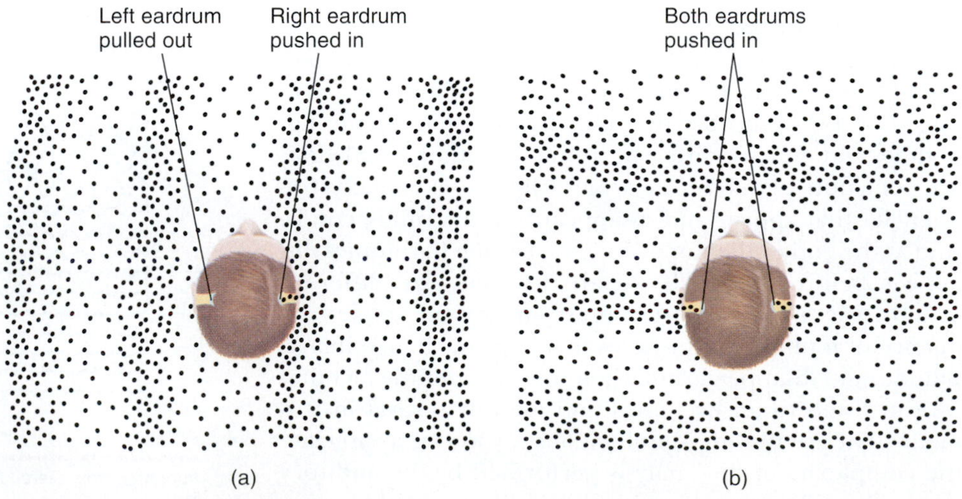

The auditory system cannot readily detect binaural phase differences of high-frequency stimuli; the differences in phases of such rapid sine waves are just too short to be measured by the neurons. However, high-frequency stimuli that occur to the right or left of the midline stimulate the ears unequally. The head absorbs high frequencies, producing a "sonic shadow," so the ear closest to the source of the sound receives the most intense stimulation. Some neurons in the superior olivary complex respond differentially to binaural stimuli of different intensity in each ear, which means that they provide information that can be used to detect the source of tones of high frequency.

How can we determine whether the source of a sound is in front of us or behind us? One answer is that we can turn our heads, thus transforming the discrimination into a left–right decision. But we have another means by which we can distinguish front from back: analysis of timbre. This method involves a part of the auditory system that I have not said much about: the external ear (pinna). If you look at someone's external ear, you will see that it contains several folds and ridges. Most of the sound waves that we hear bounce off the folds and ridges of the pinna before they enter the ear canal. This process changes the nature of the sounds that we hear. Depending on the angle at which the sound waves strike these folds and ridges, different frequencies will be enhanced or attenuated. In other words, the pattern of reflections will change with the location of the source of the sound, which will alter the timbre of the sound that is perceived. Sounds coming from behind the head will sound different from those coming from above the head or in front of it.

Behavioral Functions of the Auditory System

Hearing has three primary functions: to detect sounds, to determine the location of their sources, and to recognize the identity of these sources—and thus their meaning and relevance to us (Heffner and Heffner, 1990; Yost, 1991). Let us consider the third function: recognizing the identity of a sound source. Unless you are in a completely silent location, pay attention to what you can hear. Right now, I am sitting in an office and can hear the sound of a fan in a computer, the tapping of the keys as I write this, the footsteps of someone passing outside the door, and the voices of some people talking in the hallway. How can I recognize these sources? The axons in my cochlear nerve contain a constantly changing pattern of activity corresponding to the constantly changing mixtures of frequencies that strike my eardrums. Somehow, the auditory system of my brain recognizes particular patterns that belong to particular sources, and I perceive each of them as an independent entity.

The task of the auditory system in identifying sound sources, then, is one of *pattern recognition.* The auditory system must recognize that particular patterns of constantly changing activity belong to different sound sources. And as we saw, few patterns are simple mixtures of fixed frequencies. For example, the notes played on a clarinet have a characteristic attack and decay. And notes of different pitches produce different patterns of activity in our cochlear nerve, yet we recognize each of the notes as belonging to a clarinet. Needless to say, we are far from understanding how this pattern recognition works.

As we saw earlier, the auditory cortex, like the visual cortex, is organized into two streams: a dorsal stream, involved in perception of location, and a ventral stream, involved in perception of form. Anatomical studies have shown that the auditory cortex is similarly organized in two streams, with a similar dichotomy of functions (Romanski et al., 1999). In a single-unit recording study, Rauschecker and Tian (2000) found that neurons in the "what" system discriminated between different monkey calls, while neurons in the "where" system discriminated between different locations of loudspeakers presenting these calls.

Alain et al. (2001) found that the human auditory cortex shows a similar arrangement. In a functional-imaging study, they presented subjects with discrimination tasks

Figure 7.12

Evidence for the existence of dorsal and ventral streams of analysis in the cerebral cortex. Regions of the brain that became activated when subjects made judgments about pitch of sounds (yellow and orange) or about their locations (blue).

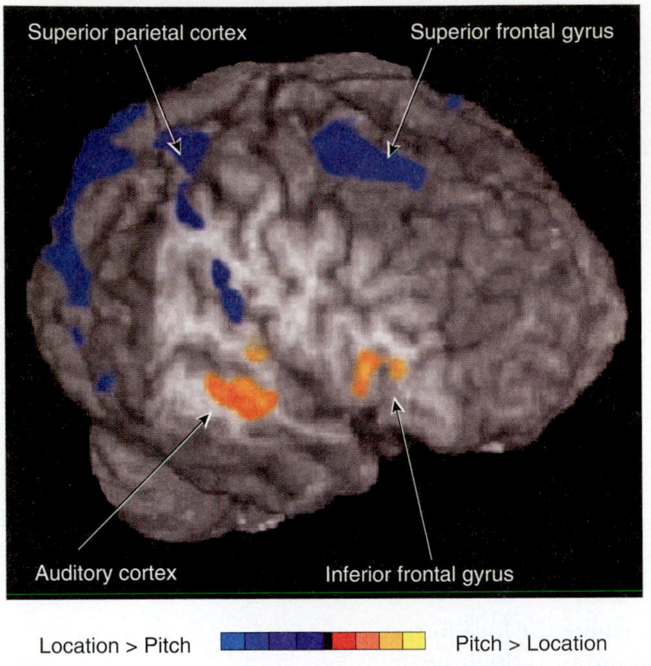

From Alain, C., Arnott, S. R., Hevenor, S., Graham, S., and Grady, C. L. *Proceedings of the National Academy of Science, USA*, 2001, *98*, 12301–12306. Copyright 2001 National Academy of Science, U.S.A.

that required them to determine the pitch of a sound or the location of its source. As Figure 7.12 shows, judgments of pitch activated ventral regions ("what"), and judgments of location activated dorsal regions ("where"). (See ***Figure 7.12.***)

As we saw in Chapter 6, lesions of the visual association cortex in humans can produce visual agnosias—the inability to recognize objects even though the visual acuity may be good. Similarly, lesions of the auditory association cortex can produce auditory agnosias, the inability to comprehend the meaning of sounds even though the individuals are not deaf. If the lesion occurs in the left hemisphere, the person will sustain a particular form of language disorder. If it occurs in the right hemisphere, the person will be unable to recognize the nature or location of nonspeech sounds. Because of the importance of audition to language, these topics are discussed in much more detail in Chapter 13.

INTERIM SUMMARY

Audition

The receptive organ for audition is the organ of Corti, located on the basilar membrane. When sound strikes the tympanic membrane, it sets the ossicles into motion, and the baseplate of the stapes pushes against the membrane behind the oval window. Pressure changes thus applied to the fluid within the cochlea cause a portion of the basilar membrane to flex, causing the basilar membrane to move laterally with respect to the tectorial membrane that overhangs it. This movement pulls directly on the cilia of the outer hair cells and changes their membrane potential. This change causes contractions or relaxations of contractile proteins within the cell, which amplify movements of the basilar membrane and sharpen their focus. These events cause movements in the fluid within the cochlea, which, in turn, causes the cilia of the inner hair cells to wave back and forth. These mechanical forces open potassium channels in the tips of the hair cells and thus produce receptor potentials.

The inner hair cells form synapses with the dendrites of the bipolar neurons whose axons give rise to the cochlear branch of the eighth cranial nerve. The central auditory system involves several brain stem nuclei, including the cochlear nuclei, superior olivary complexes, and inferior colliculi. The medial geniculate nucleus relays auditory information to the primary auditory cortex on the medial surface of the temporal lobe. Further analysis is performed by the auditory association cortex.

Pitch is encoded by two means. High-frequency sounds cause the base of the basilar membrane (near the oval window) to flex; low-frequency sounds cause the apex (opposite end) to flex. Because high and low frequencies thus stimulate different groups of auditory hair cells, frequency is encoded anatomically. The lowest frequencies cause the apex of the basilar membrane to flex back and forth in time with the acoustic vibrations. The outer hair cells act as motive elements rather than as sensory transducers, contracting in response to activity of the efferent axons and modifying the mechanical properties of the basilar membrane.

The auditory system discriminates between sounds with different timbres by detecting the individual overtones that constitute the sounds and producing unique patterns of neural firing in the auditory system.

Left–right localization is performed by analyzing binaural differences in arrival time, in phase relations, and in intensity. The location of the azimuth of the sources of brief sounds (such as clicks) and sounds of frequencies below approximately 3000 Hz is detected by neurons in the superior olivary complex, which respond most vigorously when one ear receives the click first or when the phase of a sine wave received by one ear leads that received by the other. The location of the azimuth of the sources of high-frequency sounds is also detected by neurons in the superior olivary complex, which respond most vigorously when one organ of Corti is stimulated more intensely than the other. Localization of the elevation of the sources of sounds can be accomplished by turning the head or by perception of subtle differences in the timbre of sounds coming from different directions. The folds and ridges in the external ear (pinna) reflect different frequencies into the ear canal, changing the timbre of the sound according to the location of its source.

To recognize the source of sounds, the auditory system must recognize the constantly changing patterns of activity received from the axons in the cochlear nerve. Like the visual cortex, the auditory cortex is organized into two streams. The ventral stream is involved in the analysis of the sound, and the dorsal stream is involved in perception of its location. In humans, left-hemisphere damage to the auditory cortex impairs recognition of language, and right-hemisphere damage impairs the analysis of nonspeech sounds.

THOUGHT QUESTION

A naturalist once noted that when a male bird stakes out his territory, he sings with a very sharp, staccato song that says, in effect, "Here I am, and stay away!" In contrast, if a predator appears in the vicinity, many birds will emit alarm calls that consist of steady whistles that start and end slowly. Knowing what you do about the two means of localizing sounds, what do these two types of calls have different characteristics?

Vestibular System

The vestibular system has two components: the vestibular sacs and the semicircular canals. They represent the second and third components of the *labyrinths* of the inner ear. (We just studied the first component, the cochlea.) The **vestibular sacs** respond to the force of gravity and inform the brain about the head's orientation. The **semicircular canals** respond to angular acceleration—changes in the rotation of the head—but not to steady rotation. They also respond (but rather weakly) to changes in position or to linear acceleration.

The functions of the vestibular system include balance, maintenance of the head in an upright position, and adjustment of eye movement to compensate for head movements. Vestibular stimulation does not produce any readily definable sensation; certain low-frequency stimulation of the vestibular sacs can produce nausea, and stimulation of the semicircular canals can produce dizziness and rhythmic eye movements (*nystagmus*). However, we are not directly aware of the information received from these organs. This section describes the vestibular system: the vestibular apparatus, the receptor cells, and the vestibular pathway in the brain.

Anatomy of the Vestibular Apparatus

Figure 7.13 shows the labyrinths of the inner ear, which include the cochlea, the semicircular canals, and the two vestibular sacs: the **utricle** ("little pouch") and the **saccule** ("little sack"). (See ***Figure 7.13.***) The semicircular canals approximate the three major planes of the head: sagittal, transverse, and horizontal. Receptors in each canal respond maximally to angular acceleration in one plane. The semicircular canal consists of a membranous canal floating within a bony one; the membranous canal contains a fluid called *endolymph*. An enlargement called the **ampulla** contains the organ in which the sensory receptors reside. The sensory receptors are hair cells similar to those found in the cochlea. Their cilia are embedded in a gelatinous mass called the **cupula,** which blocks part of the ampulla. (See ***Figure 7.13.***)

vestibular sac One of a set of two receptor organs in each inner ear that detect changes in the tilt of the head.

semicircular canal One of the three ringlike structures of the vestibular apparatus that detect changes in head rotation.

utricle (***you*** *trih kul*) One of the vestibular sacs.

saccule (***sak*** *yule*) One of the vestibular sacs.

ampulla (*am* ***pull*** *uh*) An enlargement in a semicircular canal; contains the cupula and the crista.

cupula (***kew*** *pew luh*) A gelatinous mass found in the ampulla of the semicircular canals; moves in response to the flow of the fluid in the canals.

Figure 7.13

The receptive organ of the semicircular canals.

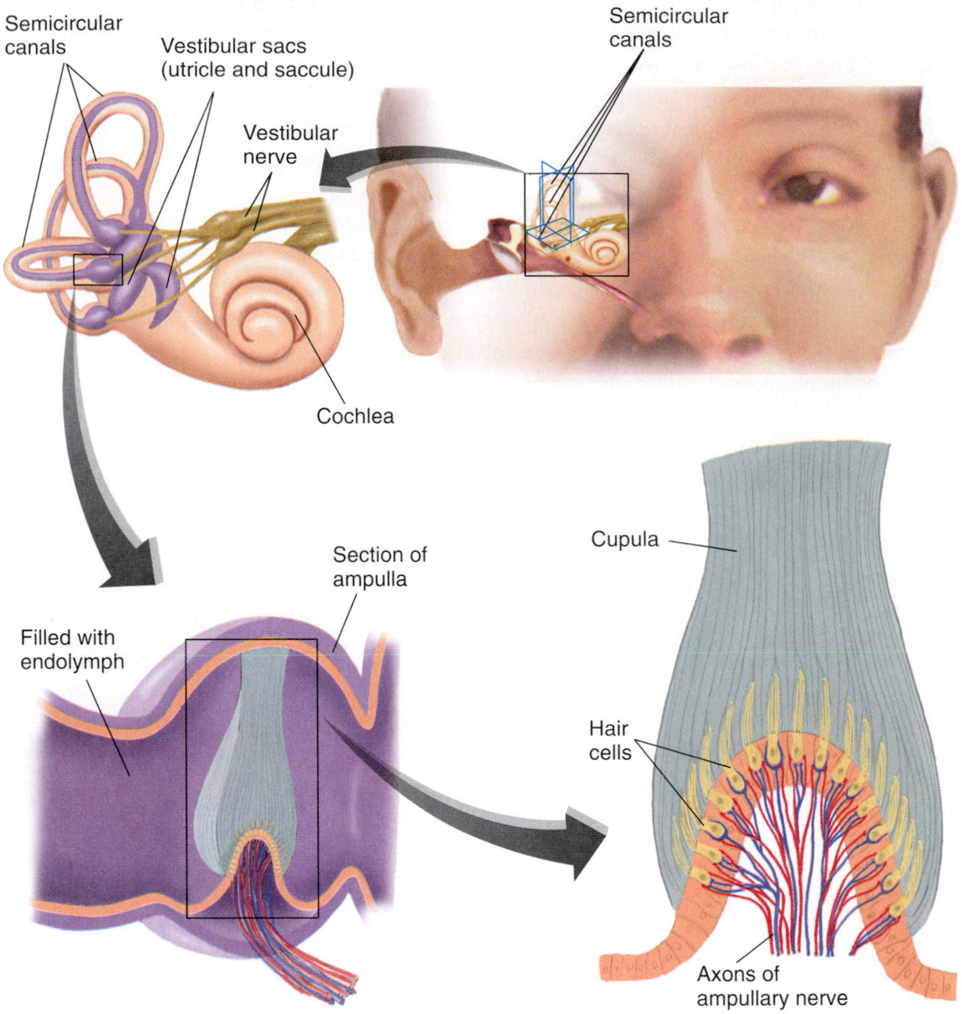

The vestibular sacs (the utricle and saccule) work very differently. These organs are roughly circular, and each contains a patch of receptive tissue. The receptive tissue is located on the "floor" of the utricle and on the "wall" of the saccule when the head is in an upright position. The receptive tissue, like that of the semicircular canals and cochlea, contains hair cells. The cilia of these receptors are embedded in an overlying gelatinous mass, which contains something rather unusual: *otoconia*, which are small crystals of calcium carbonate. (See ***Figure 7.14***.) The weight of the crystals causes the gelatinous mass to shift in position as the orientation of the head changes. Thus, movement produces a shearing force on the cilia of the receptive hair cells.

The Receptor Cells

vestibular ganglion A nodule on the vestibular nerve that contains the cell bodies of the bipolar neurons that convey vestibular information to the brain.

The hair cells of the semicircular canal and vestibular sacs are similar in appearance. Each hair cell contains several cilia, graduated in length from short to long. These hair cells resemble the auditory hair cells found in the cochlea, and their transduction mechanism is also similar: A shearing force of the cilia opens ion channels, and the entry of potassium ions depolarizes the ciliary membrane. Figure 7.15 shows two

Figure 7.14

The receptive tissue of the vestibular sacs: the utricle and the saccule.

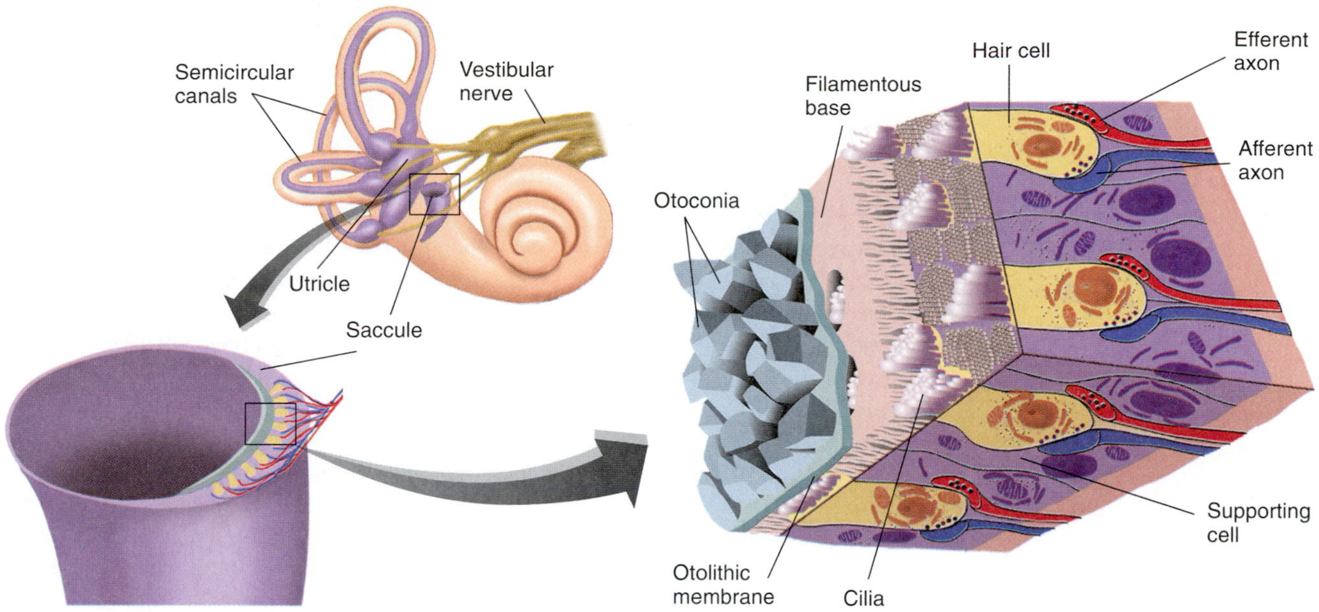

views of a hair cell of a bullfrog saccule made by a scanning electron microscope. (See ***Figure 7.15.***)

The Vestibular Pathway

The vestibular and cochlear nerves constitute the two branches of the eighth cranial nerve (auditory nerve). The bipolar cell bodies that give rise to the afferent axons of the vestibular nerve (a branch of the eighth cranial nerve) are located in the **vestibular ganglion,** which appears as a nodule on the vestibular nerve.

Most of the axons of the vestibular nerve synapse within the vestibular nuclei in the medulla, but some axons travel directly to the cerebellum. Neurons of the vestibular nuclei send their axons to the cerebellum, spinal cord, medulla, and pons. There also appear to be vestibular projections to the temporal cortex, but the precise pathways have not been determined. Most investigators believe that the cortical projections are responsible for feelings of dizziness; the activity of projections to the lower brain stem can produce the nausea and vomiting that accompany motion sickness. Projections to brain stem nuclei controlling neck muscles are clearly involved in maintaining an upright position of the head.

Perhaps the most interesting connections are those to the cranial nerve nuclei (third, fourth, and sixth) that control the eye muscles. As we walk or (especially) run, the head is jarred quite a bit. The vestibular system exerts direct control on eye movement, to compensate for the sudden head movements. This process, called the

Figure 7.15

(a) Oblique view of a normal bundle of vestibular hair cells. (b) Top view of a bundle of hair cells from which the longest has been detached.

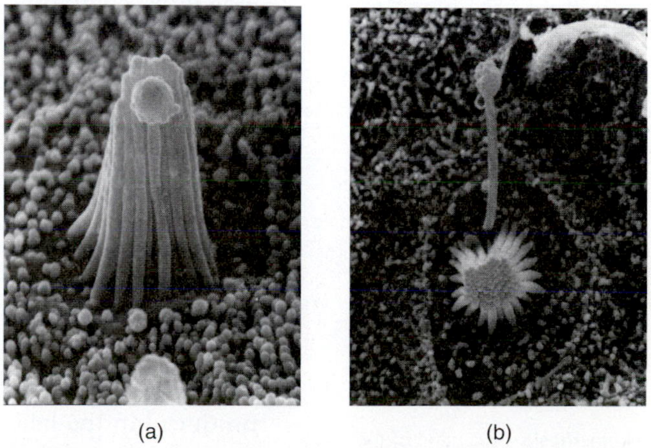

From Hudspeth, A. J., and Jacobs, R. *Proceedings of the National Academy of Sciences, USA,* 1979, *76,* 1506–1509. Copyright 1979 National Academy of Sciences, U.S.A.

vestibulo-ocular reflex, maintains a fairly steady retinal image. Test this reflex yourself: Look at a distant object and hit yourself (gently) on the side of the head. Note that your image of the world jumps a bit, but not too much. People who have suffered vestibular damage and who lack the vestibulo-ocular reflex have difficulty seeing anything while walking or running. Everything becomes a blur of movement.

INTERIM SUMMARY

Vestibular System

The semicircular canals are filled with fluid. When the head begins rotating or comes to rest after rotation, inertia causes the fluid to push the cupula to one side or the other. This movement exerts a shearing force on the cupula, the organ containing the vestibular hair cells. The vestibular sacs contain a patch of receptive tissue that contains hair cells whose cilia are embedded in a gelatinous mass. The weight of the otoconia in the gelatinous mass shifts when the head tilts, causing a shearing force on some of the cilia of the hair cells.

Each hair cell contains one long cilium and several shorter ones. These cells form synapses with dendrites of bipolar neurons whose axons travel through the vestibular nerve. The receptors also receive efferent terminal buttons from neurons located in the cerebellum and medulla, but the function of these connections is not known. Vestibular information is received by the vestibular nuclei in the medulla, which relay it on to the cerebellum, spinal cord, medulla, pons, and temporal cortex. These pathways are responsible for control of posture, head movements, and eye movements and the puzzling phenomenon of motion sickness.

THOUGHT QUESTIONS

Why can slow, repetitive vestibular stimulation cause nausea and vomiting? Obviously, there are connections between the vestibular system and the area postrema, which (as you learned in Chapter 2) controls vomiting. Can you think of any useful functions that might be served by these connections?

Somatosenses

The somatosenses provide information about what is happening on the surface of our body and inside it. The **cutaneous senses** (skin senses) include several submodalities commonly referred to as *touch.* **Kinesthesia** provides information about body position and movement and arises from receptors in joints, tendons, and muscles. The **organic senses** arise from receptors in and around the internal organs, providing us with unpleasant sensations, such as stomachaches or gallbladder attacks, or pleasurable ones, such as those provided by a warm drink on a cold winter day. Because the cutaneous senses are the most studied of the somatosenses, both perceptually and physiologically, I will devote most of my discussion to them.

The Stimuli

The cutaneous senses respond to several different types of stimuli: pressure, vibration, heating, cooling, and events that cause tissue damage (and hence pain). Feelings of pressure are caused by mechanical deformation of the skin. Vibration is produced in the laboratory or clinic by tuning forks or mechanical devices, but it more commonly occurs when we move our fingers across a rough surface. Thus, we use vibration sensitivity to judge an object's roughness. Obviously, sensations of warmth and coolness are produced by objects that change skin temperature from normal. Sensations of pain can be caused by many different types of stimuli, but it appears that most cause at least some tissue damage.

cutaneous sense (*kew **tane** ee us*) One of the somatosenses; includes sensitivity to stimuli that involve the skin.

kinesthesia Perception of the body's own movements.

organic sense A sense modality that arises from receptors located within the inner organs of the body.

Kinesthesia is provided by stretch receptors in skeletal muscles that report changes in muscle length to the central nervous system and by stretch receptors in tendons that measure the force being exerted by the muscles. Receptors within joints between adjacent bones respond to the magnitude and direction of limb movement. Muscle length detectors, located within the muscles, do not give rise to conscious sensations; their information is used to control movement.

Additional information about the internal organs is provided by receptors in the linings of muscles, outer layers of the gastrointestinal system and other internal organs, and linings of the abdominal and thoracic cavities. Many of these tissues are sensitive only to stretch and do not report sensations when cut, burned, or crushed. In addition, the stomach and esophagus are responsive to heat and cold and to some chemicals.

Anatomy of the Skin and Its Receptive Organs

The skin is a complex and vital organ of the body—one that we tend to take for granted. We cannot survive without it; extensive skin burns are fatal. Our cells, which must be bathed by a warm fluid, are protected from the hostile environment by the skin's outer layers. The skin participates in thermoregulation by producing sweat, thus cooling the body, or by restricting its circulation of blood, thus conserving heat. Its appearance varies widely across the body, from mucous membrane to hairy skin to the smooth, hairless skin of the palms and the soles of the feet.

Skin consists of subcutaneous tissue, dermis, and epidermis and contains various receptors scattered throughout these layers. Figure 7.16 shows cross sections through hairy and **glabrous skin** (hairless skin, found on our fingertips and palms and on the bottoms of our toes and feet). Hairy skin contains unencapsulated (free) nerve endings; **Ruffini corpuscles,** which respond to indentation of the skin; and

Figure 7.16

Cutaneous receptors.

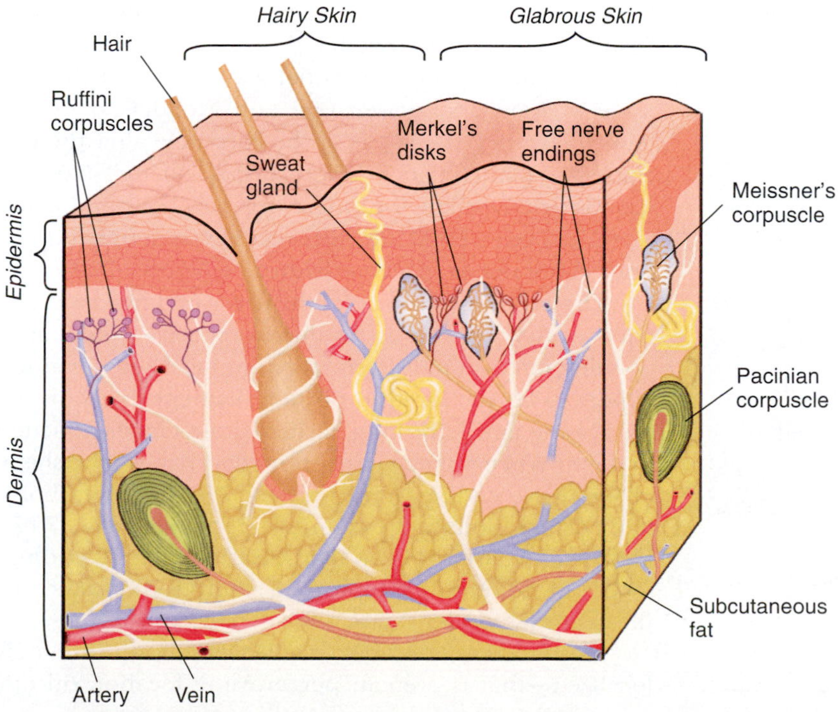

glabrous skin (*glab* russ) Skin that does not contain hair; found on the palms and the soles of the feet.

Ruffini corpuscle A vibration-sensitive organ located in hairy skin.

Pacinian corpuscle (*pa chin ee un*) A specialized, encapsulated somatosensory nerve ending that detects mechanical stimuli, especially vibrations.

Meissner's corpuscle The touch-sensitive end organs located in the papillae, small elevations of the dermis that project up into the epidermis.

Merkel's disk The touch-sensitive end organs found at the base of the epidermis, adjacent to sweat ducts.

Pacinian corpuscles, which respond to rapid vibrations. Pacinian corpuscles are the largest sensory end organs in the body. Their size, approximately 0.5 × 1.0 mm, makes them visible to the naked eye. They consist of up to seventy onionlike layers wrapped around the dendrite of a single myelinated axon. Free nerve endings, which detect painful stimuli and changes in temperature, are found just below the surface of the skin. Other free nerve endings are found in a basketwork around the base of hair follicles and around the emergence of hair shafts from the skin. These fibers detect movement of hairs. (See ***Figure 7.16.***)

Glabrous skin contains a more complex mixture of free nerve endings and axons that terminate within specialized end organs (Iggo and Andres, 1982). The increased complexity reflects the fact that we use the palms of our hands and the inside surfaces of our fingers to explore the environment actively: We use them to hold and touch objects. In contrast, the rest of our body most often contacts the environment passively; that is, other things come into contact with it.

Glabrous skin, like hairy skin, contains free nerve endings, Ruffini corpuscles and Pacinian corpuscles. (Pacinian corpuscles are also found in the joints and in various internal organs.) Glabrous skin also contains **Meissner's corpuscles,** which are found in *papillae* ("nipples"), small elevations of the dermis that project up into the epidermis. These end organs are innervated by between two and six axons. They respond to low-frequency vibration or to brief taps on the skin. **Merkel's disks,** which respond to indentation of the skin, are found at the base of the epidermis, in the same general locations as Meissner's corpuscles, adjacent to sweat ducts. (See ***Figure 7.16.***)

Perception of Cutaneous Stimulation

The three most important qualities of cutaneous stimulation are touch, temperature, and pain. These qualities are described in the sections that follow.

Touch

Sensitivity to pressure and vibration is caused by movement of the skin. The best-studied receptor is the Pacinian corpuscle, which primarily detects vibration. When the corpuscle is bent relative to the axon, the membrane becomes depolarized. If the threshold of excitation is exceeded, an action potential is produced at the first node of Ranvier. Loewenstein and Mendelson (1965) have shown that the layers of the corpuscle alter the mechanical characteristics of the organ, so the axon responds briefly when the intact organ is bent and again when it is released. Thus, this receptor is sensitive to vibration but not to steady pressure.

The bending of the tip of the nerve ending in a Pacinian corpuscle appears to produce a receptor potential by opening ion channels in the membrane. These channels appear to be anchored to protein filaments beneath the membrane and have long carbohydrate chains attached to them. When a mechanical stimulus changes the shape of the nerve ending, tension is exerted on the carbohydrate chains, pulling the channel open. (See ***Figure 7.17.***) Most investigators believe that the encapsulated endings serve only to modify the physical stimulus transduced by the axons that enter them.

Most information about tactile sensation is precisely localized—that is, we can perceive the location on our

Figure 7.17

A hypothetical explanation of transduction of somatosensory information. Mechanical force on carbohydrate chains linked to ion channels opens the channels, permitting the entry of cations, which depolarizes the membrane potential.

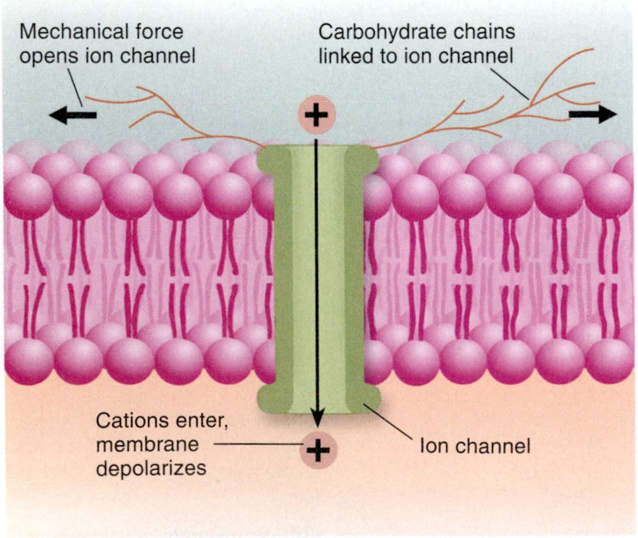

skin where we are being touched. Until very recently, neuroscientists believed that in humans this information was transmitted to the central nervous system only by fast-conducting myelinated axons. However, a recent study discovered a new category of tactile sensation that is transmitted by small-diameter unmyelinated axons. Olausson et al. (2002) reported the case of patient G. L., a woman whose large-diameter myelinated somatosensory axons were damaged by a disease. As a result, she could no longer feel when the skin below her nose was touched. She could still detect the stimuli that are conveyed by small-diameter unmyelinated axons—temperature, pain, and itch. But when the hairy skin on her forearm or the back of her hand was stroked with a soft brush, she reported a faint, pleasant sensation, although she could not determine the direction of the stroking or its precise location. Functional MRI (fMRI) analysis showed that this stimulation activated the insular cortex, a region that is known to be associated with emotional responses. The somatosensory cortex was not activated.

The investigators conclude that besides conveying information about noxious and thermal stimuli, small-diameter unmyelinated axons constitute a "system for limbic touch that may underlie emotional, hormonal and affiliative responses to caress-like, skin-to-skin contact between individuals" (Olausson et al., 2002, p. 900) The investigators reported that G. L. could no longer perceive tickle, which indicates that this sensation is apparently transmitted by the large-diameter myelinated axons that had been destroyed.

Investigators have known for a long time that a moderate, constant stimulus applied to the skin fails to produce any sensation after it has been present for a while. For example, not only do we ignore the pressure of a wristwatch, but we cannot feel it at all if we keep our arm still (assuming that the band is not painfully tight). Physiological studies have shown that the reason for the lack of sensation is the absence of receptor firing; the receptors adapt to a constant stimulus.

This adaptation is not caused by "fatigue" of physical or chemical processes within the receptor. Instead, adaptation occurs because of the physical construction of the skin and the cutaneous sensory organs. Nafe and Wagoner (1941) recorded the sensations reported by human subjects as a stimulus weight gradually moved downward, deforming the skin. Pressure was reported until the weight finally stopped moving. When the weight was increased, pressure was reported until downward movement stopped again. Pressure sensations were also briefly recorded when the weight was removed, while the surface of the skin regained its normal shape. (You might have noticed that when you first take your hat off, it feels for a few moments as if you were still wearing it.)

After wearing a wristwatch for several minutes, this man can no longer feel it unless it moves on his wrist.

Temperature

Feelings of warmth and coolness are relative, not absolute (except at the extremes). There is a temperature level that, for a particular region of skin, will produce a sensation of temperature neutrality—neither warmth nor coolness. This neutral point is not an absolute value but depends on the prior history of thermal stimulation of that area. If the temperature of a region of skin is raised by a few degrees, the initial feeling of warmth is replaced by one of neutrality. If the skin temperature is lowered to its initial value, it now feels cool. Thus, increases in temperature lower the sensitivity of warmth receptors and raise the sensitivity of cold receptors. The converse holds for decreases in skin temperature. This adaptation to ambient temperature can be demonstrated easily by placing one hand in a bucket of warm water and the other in a bucket of cool water until some adaptation has taken place. If you then simultaneously immerse both hands in water at room temperature, it will feel warm to one hand and cool to the other.

There are two types of thermal receptors: one that responds to warmth and one that responds to coolness. (As we will see in the next section, another category of cutaneous receptor responds to intense heat and gives rise to a sensation of pain.) The transduction of temperature changes into the rate of axonal firing is not yet understood. Spray (1986) suggested that the sodium-potassium pump may be responsible for sensory transduction in coolness receptors. A drop in temperature would slow the action of the pump, which would permit sodium to accumulate in the free nerve ending and depolarize its membrane. In support of this suggestion he found that *ouabain,* a toxin that inactivates the sodium-potassium pump, produced a brief burst of activity in cold-receptive fibers in the skin of a frog. After that burst, the fibers became unresponsive to temperature changes. Obviously, detectors of warmth must operate by a different mechanism.

Pain

Pain reception, like thermosensation, is accomplished by the networks of free nerve endings in the skin. There appears to be at least three types of pain receptors (usually referred to as *nociceptors,* or "detectors of noxious stimuli"). High-threshold mechanoreceptors are free-nerve endings that respond to intense pressure, which might be caused by something striking, stretching, or pinching the skin. A second type of free nerve ending appears to respond to extremes of heat, to acids, and to the presence of *capsaicin,* the active ingredient in chile peppers. (Note that we say that chile peppers make food taste "hot.") This type of fiber contains VR1 receptors—ionotropic receptors that contain a cation channel (Kress and Zeilhofer, 1999). Caterina et al. (2000) found that mice with a targeted mutation against the VR1 receptor showed less sensitivity to painful high temperature stimuli and would drink water to which capsaicin had been added. They responded normally to noxious mechanical stimuli. Presumably, this receptor is responsible for pain produced by burning of the skin and for pain caused by inflammation, which is reduced by applying a cold compress.

Another type of nociceptive fiber contains receptors that are sensitive to ATP (Burnstock and Wood, 1996). These receptors are ionotropic and control channels that admit sodium and calcium ions. You will recall that ATP is produced by mitochondria and serves as an energy source for the cell's metabolic processes. ATP is also released when the blood supply to a region of the body is disrupted (a condition called *ischemia,* which occurs during the spasms of blood vessels that cause angina or migraine) or when a muscle is damaged. It is also released by rapidly growing tumors. Thus, these nociceptors may be at least partly responsible for the pain caused by angina, migraine, damage to muscles, and cancer.

The Somatosensory Pathways

Somatosensory axons from the skin, muscles, or internal organs enter the central nervous system via spinal nerves. Those located in the face and head primarily enter through the trigeminal nerve (fifth cranial nerve). The cell bodies of the unipolar neurons are located in the dorsal root ganglia and cranial nerve ganglia. Axons that convey precisely localized information, such as fine touch, ascend through the *dorsal columns* in the white matter of the spinal cord to nuclei in the lower medulla. From there axons cross the brain and ascend through the *medial lemniscus* to the *ventral posterior nuclei of the thalamus,* the relay nuclei for somatosensation. Axons from the thalamus project to the primary somatosensory cortex, which in turn sends axons to the secondary somatosensory cortex. In contrast, axons that convey poorly localized information, such as pain or temperature, form synapses with other neurons as soon as they enter the spinal cord. The axons of these neurons cross to the other side of the spinal cord and ascend through the *spinothalamic tract* to the ventral posterior nuclei of the thalamus. (See ***Figure 7.18.***)

As we saw in Chapter 6, damage to the visual association cortex can cause visual agnosia, and as we saw earlier in this chapter, damage to the auditory association cortex can cause auditory agnosia. You will not be surprised to learn that damage to the somatosensory association cortex can cause of tactile agnosia. For example, Reed, Caselli, and Farah (1996) described patient E. C., a woman with left parietal lobe damage who was unable to recognize common objects by touch. For example, the patient identified a pine cone as a brush, a ribbon as a rubber band, and a snail shell as a bottle cap. The deficit was not due to a simple loss of tactile sensitivity; the patient was still sensitive to light touch and to warm and cold objects, and she could easily discriminate objects by their size, weight, and roughness.

Recognition of objects by touch requires cooperation between the somatosensory and motor systems. When we attempt to identify objects by touch alone, we explore them with moving fingers. Valenza et al. (2001) reported the case of a patient with brain damage to the right hemisphere that produced a disorder they called *tactile apraxia.* (*Apraxia* refers to a difficulty in carrying out purposeful movements without the loss of muscle strength or coordination.) When the experimenters gave the patient objects to identify by touch with her left hand, the patient explored the object with her fingers in a disorganized fashion. (Exploration and identification using her right hand were normal.) If the experimenters guided the patient's fingers and explored the object the way people normally do, she was able to recognize the object's shape. Thus, her deficit was caused by a movement disorder and not by damage to brain mechanisms involved in tactile perception.

Figure 7.18

The somatosensory pathways from the spinal cord to the somatosensory cortex. Note that precisely localized information (such as fine touch) and imprecisely localized information (such as pain and temperature) are transmitted by different pathways.

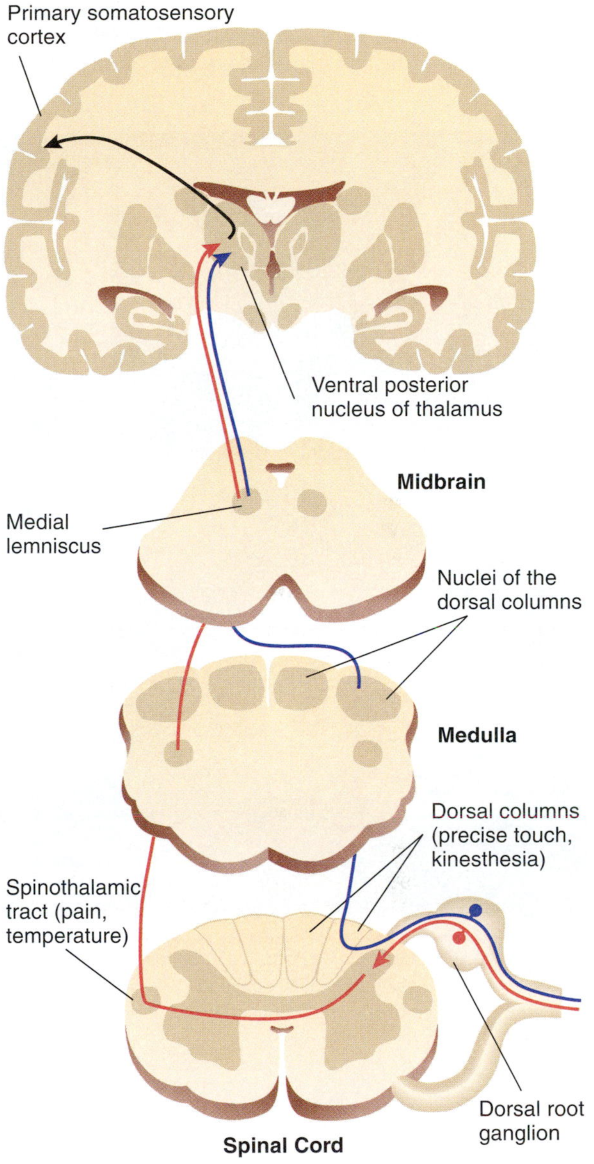

Perception of Pain

Pain is a curious phenomenon. It is more than a mere sensation; it can be defined only by some sort of withdrawal reaction or, in humans, by verbal report. Pain can be modified by the circumstances under which it occurs. For example, a person who is concentrating intently on an important task is less likely to be bothered by a painful stimulus than is someone who is sitting quietly. Pain can also be modified by opiates, by hypnosis, by the administration of pharmacologically inert sugar pills, by emotions, and even by other forms of stimulation, such as acupuncture. Recent research efforts have made remarkable progress in discovering the physiological bases of these phenomena.

Pain appears to have three different perceptual and behavioral effects (Price, 2000). First is the sensory component—the pure perception of the intensity of a painful stimulus. The second component is the immediate emotional consequences of pain—the unpleasantness or degree to which the individual is bothered by the painful stimulus. The third component is the long-term emotional implications of chronic pain—the threat that such pain represents to one's future comfort and well-being.

Figure 7.19

PET scans showing brain regions that respond to sensory and emotional components of pain. *Top:* Dorsal views of the brain. Activation of the primary somatosensory cortex (circled in red) by a painful stimulus was not affected by a hypnotically suggested reduction in unpleasantness of a painful stimulus, indicating that this region responded to the sensory component of pain. *Bottom:* Midsagittal views of the brain. The anterior cingulate cortex (circled in red) showed much less activation when the unpleasantness of the painful stimulus was reduced by hypnotic suggestion.

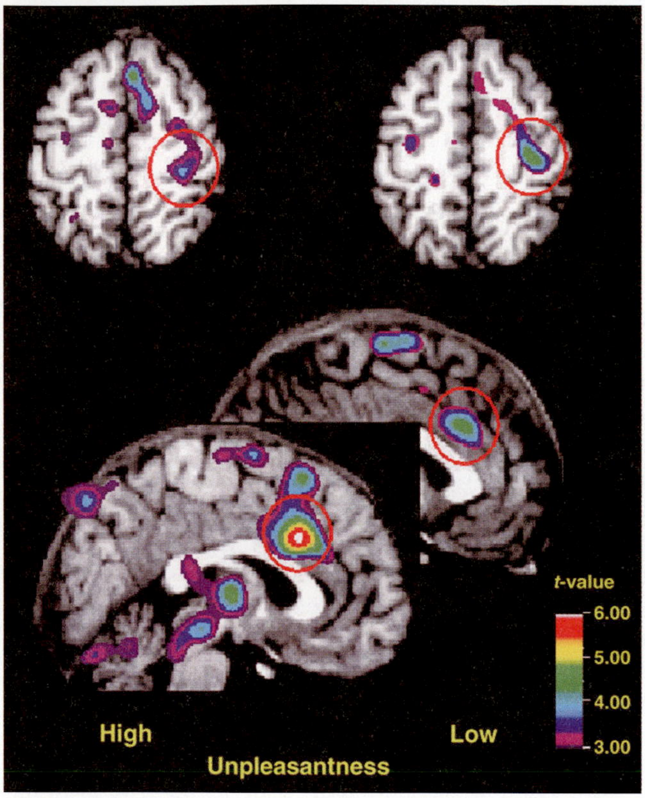

From Rainville, P., Duncan, G. H., Price, D. D., Carrier, Benoit, and Bushnell, M. C. *Science,* 1997, *277,* 968–971. Copyright 1997 American Association for the Advancement of Science. Reprinted with permission.

These three components of pain appear to involve different brain mechanisms. The purely sensory component of pain is mediated by a pathway from the spinal cord to the ventral posterolateral thalamus to the primary and secondary somatosensory cortex and the unpleasantness of pain appears to be mediated by pathways that reach the anterior cingulate cortex and insular cortex.

Rainville et al. (1997) produced pain sensations in human subjects by having them put their arms in ice water. Under one condition the researchers used hypnosis to diminish the unpleasantness of the pain. The hypnosis worked; the subjects said the pain was less unpleasant, even though it was still as intense. Meanwhile, the investigators used a PET scanner to measure regional activation of the brain. They found that the painful stimulus activated both the primary somatosensory cortex and the anterior cingulate cortex. When the subjects were hypnotized and found the pain less unpleasant, the activity of the anterior cingulate cortex decreased—but the activity of the primary somatosensory cortex remained high. Thus, the primary somatosensory cortex is involved in the perception of pain, and the anterior cingulate cortex is involved in its immediate emotional effects—its unpleasantness. (See ***Figure 7.19.***)

The third component of pain—the emotional consequences of chronic pain—appears to involve the prefrontal cortex. As we will see in Chapter 10, damage to the prefrontal cortex impairs people's ability to make plans for the future and to recognize the personal significance of situations in which they are involved. Along with the general lack of insight, people with prefrontal damage tend not to be concerned with the implications of chronic conditions—including chronic pain—for their future.

A particularly interesting form of pain sensation occurs after a limb has been amputated. After the limb is gone, up to 70 percent of amputees report that they feel as though the missing limb still existed and that it often hurts. This phenomenon is referred to as the **phantom limb** (Melzak, 1992). People with phantom limbs report that the limb feels very real, and they often say that if they try to reach out with it, it feels as though it were responding. Sometimes, they perceive it as sticking out, and they may feel compelled to avoid knocking it against the side of a doorframe or sleeping in a position that would make it come between them and the mattress. People have reported all sorts of sensations in phantom limbs, including pain, pressure, warmth, cold, wetness, itching, sweatiness, and prickliness.

The classic explanation for phantom limbs has been activity of the sensory axons belonging to the amputated limb. Presumably, the nervous system interprets this activity as coming from the missing limb. When nerves are cut and connections cannot be reestablished between the proximal and distal portions, the cut ends of the proximal portions form nodules known as *neuromas.* The treatment for phantom pain has been to cut the nerves above these neuromas, to cut the dorsal roots that bring the afferent information from these nerves into the spinal cord, or to make lesions in somatosensory pathways in the spinal cord, thalamus, or cerebral cortex. Sometimes these procedures work for a while, but often the pain returns.

phantom limb Sensations that appear to originate in a limb that has been amputated.

Melzak suggested that the phantom limb sensation is inherent in the organization of the parietal cortex. As we saw in Chapter 3, the parietal cortex is involved in our awareness of our own bodies. Indeed, people with lesions of the parietal lobe (especially in the right hemisphere) have been known to push their own leg out of bed, believing that it actually belongs to someone else. Melzak reports that some people who were born with missing limbs nevertheless experience phantom limb sensations, which would suggest that our brains are genetically programmed to provide sensations for all four limbs.

INTERIM SUMMARY

Somatosenses

Cutaneous sensory information is provided by specialized receptors in the skin. Pacinian corpuscles provide information about vibration. Ruffini corpuscles, similar to Pacinian corpuscles but considerably smaller, respond to indentation of the skin. Meissner's corpuscles, found in papillae and innervated by several axons, respond to low-frequency vibration or to brief taps on the skin. Merkel's disks, also found in papillae, consist of single, flattened dendritic endings next to specialized epithelial cells. These receptors respond to pressure. Painful stimuli and changes in temperature are detected by free nerve endings.

Our somatosensory system is most sensitive to changes in mechanical stimuli. Unless the skin is moving, we do not detect nonpainful stimuli, because the receptors adapt to constant mechanical pressure. Temperature receptors also adapt; moderate changes in skin temperature are soon perceived as neutral, and deviations above or below this temperature are perceived as warmth or coolness. Transduction in temperature receptors might be accomplished by changes in the rate of the sodium-potassium pump. There are at least three different types of pain receptors: high-threshold mechanoreceptors: fibers with capsaicin receptors, which detect extremes of heat, acids, and the presence of capsaicin (and, undoubtedly, a yet-undiscovered natural ligand); and fibers with receptors sensitive to ATP, which is released during ischemia, after muscle damage, and by rapidly growing tumors.

Precise, well-localized somatosensory information is conveyed by a pathway through the dorsal columns and their nuclei and the medial lemniscus, connecting the dorsal column nuclei with the ventral posterior nuclei of the thalamus. Information about pain and temperature ascends the spinal cord through the spinothalamic system. Organic sensibility reaches the central nervous system by means of axons that travel through nerves of the autonomic nervous systems.

Pain perception is not a simple function of stimulation of pain receptors; it is a complex phenomenon with sensory and emotional components that can be modified by experience and the immediate environment. The sensory component is mediated by the primary and secondary somatosensory cortex, the immediate emotional component appears to be mediated by the anterior cingulate cortex and the insular cortex, and the long-term emotional component appears to be mediated by the prefrontal cortex. Functional imaging studies using hypnotic suggestion found that a decrease in the unpleasantness of pain reduced the activation of the anterior cingulate cortex without affecting the activity of the somatosensory cortex. The phantom limb phenomenon, which often is accompanied by phantom pain, appears to be inherent in the organization of the parietal lobe.

THOUGHT QUESTIONS

Our fingertips and our lips are the most sensitive parts of our bodies; relatively large amounts of the primary somatosensory cortex are devoted to analyzing information from these parts of the body. It is easy to understand why our fingertips are so sensitive: We use them to explore object by touch. But why are our lips so sensitive? Does it have something to do with eating?

Gustation

The stimuli we have encountered so far produce receptor potentials by imparting physical energy: thermal, photic (involving light), or kinetic. However, the stimuli received by the last two senses to be studied—gustation and olfaction—interact with their receptors chemically. This section discusses the first of them: gustation.

The Stimuli

Gustation is clearly related to eating; this sense modality helps us to determine the nature of things we put in our mouths. For a substance to be tasted, molecules of it must dissolve in the saliva and stimulate the taste receptors on the tongue. Tastes of different substances vary, but much less than we generally realize. There are only five qualities of taste: *bitterness, sourness, sweetness, saltiness,* and *umami.* You are familiar with the first four qualities, and I will explain the fifth one later. Flavor, as opposed to taste, is a composite of olfaction and gustation. Much of the flavor of a steak depends on its odor; to an *anosmic* person (one who lacks the sense of smell) or to a person whose nostrils are stopped up, an onion tastes like an apple, and a steak tastes like salty cardboard.

Most vertebrates possess gustatory systems that respond to all five taste qualities. (An exception is the cat family; lions, tigers, leopards, and house cats do not detect sweetness—but then, none of the food they normally eat is sweet.) Clearly, sweetness receptors are food detectors. Most sweet-tasting foods, such as fruits and some vegetables, are safe to eat (Ramirez, 1990). Saltiness receptors detect the presence of sodium chloride. In some environments inadequate amounts of this mineral are obtained from the usual source of food, so sodium chloride detectors help the animal to detect its presence. Injuries that cause bleeding deplete an organism of its supply of sodium rapidly, so the ability to find it quickly can be critical.

Most species of animals will readily ingest substances that taste sweet or somewhat salty. However, they will tend to avoid substances that taste sour or bitter. Because of bacterial activity, many foods become acidic when they spoil. The acidity tastes sour and causes an avoidance reaction. (Of course, we have learned to make highly preferred mixtures of sweet and sour, such as lemonade.) Bitterness is almost universally avoided and cannot easily be improved by adding some sweetness. Many plants produce poisonous alkaloids, which protect them from being eaten by animals. Alkaloids taste bitter; thus, the bitterness receptor undoubtedly serves to warn animals away from these chemicals.

Anatomy of the Taste Buds and Gustatory Cells

The tongue, palate, pharynx, and larynx contain approximately 10,000 taste buds. Most of these receptive organs are arranged around *papillae,* small protuberances of the tongue. *Fungiform papillae,* located on the anterior two-thirds of the tongue, contain up to eight taste buds, along with receptors for pressure, touch, and temperature. *Foliate papillae* consist of up to eight parallel folds along each edge of the back of the tongue. Approximately 1300 taste buds are located in these folds. *Circumvallate papillae,* arranged in an inverted V on the posterior third of the tongue, contain approximately 250 taste buds. They are shaped like little plateaus surrounded by moatlike trenches. Taste buds consist of groups of twenty to fifty receptor cells, specialized neurons arranged somewhat like the segments of an orange. Cilia are located at the end of each cell and project through the opening of the taste bud (the pore) into the saliva that coats the tongue. Tight junctions between adjacent taste cells prevent substances in the saliva from diffusing freely into the taste bud itself. Figure 7.20 shows the appearance of a circumvallate papilla; a cross section through the surrounding trench contains a taste bud. (See ***Figure 7.20.***)

Figure 7.20

The tongue. (a) Papillae on the surface of the tongue. (b) Taste buds.

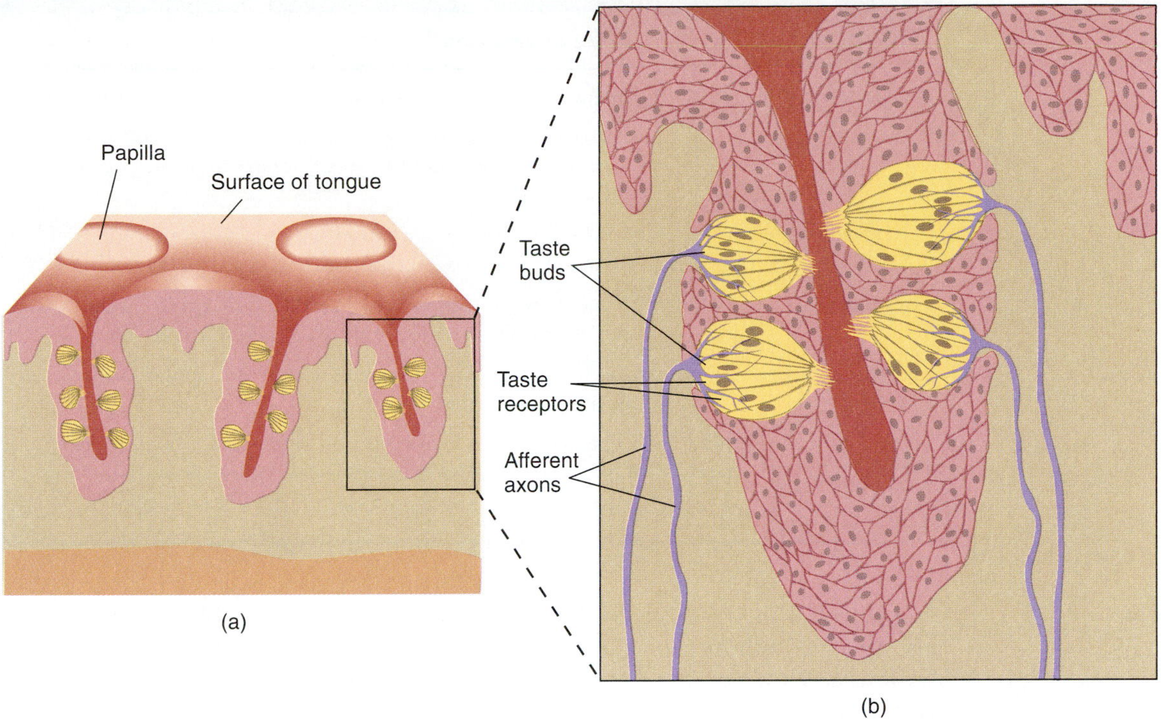

Taste receptor cells form synapses with dendrites of bipolar neurons whose axons convey gustatory information to the brain through the seventh, ninth, and tenth cranial nerves. The receptor cells have a life span of only ten days. They quickly wear out, being directly exposed to a rather hostile environment. As they degenerate, they are replaced by newly developed cells; the dendrite of the bipolar neuron is passed on to the new cell (Beidler, 1970).

Perception of Gustatory Information

Transduction of taste is similar to the chemical transmission that takes place at synapses: The tasted molecule binds with the receptor and produces changes in membrane permeability that cause receptor potentials. Different substances bind with different types of receptors, producing different taste sensations. In this section I will describe what we know about the nature of the molecules with particular tastes and the receptors that detect their presence. I should note that in some cases researchers have found that more than one type of receptor detects a particular taste and that different types of receptors may be found in different species. Thus, the following description, and the information in Table 7.1, should be seen as representative rather than definitive. (See ***Table 7.1.***)

To taste salty, a substance must ionize. Although the best stimulus for saltiness receptors is sodium chloride (NaCl), a variety of salts containing metallic cations (such as Na^+, K^+, and Li^+) with a small anion (such as Cl^-, Br^-, SO_4^{2-}, or NO_3^-) taste salty. The receptor for saltiness seems to be a simple sodium channel. When present in the saliva, sodium enters the taste cell and depolarizes it, triggering action potentials that cause the cell to release neurotransmitter (Avenet and Lindemann, 1989; Kinnamon and Cummings, 1992). The best evidence that sodium channels

Table 7.1

Detection of Gustatory Information

Taste Quality	Nature of Detection
Saltiness	Sodium ions enter sodium channels, depolarize taste cell
Sourness	Hydrogen ions bind with sites on potassium channels and close them, blocking outflow of potassium ions; depolarizes membrane
Sweetness	Molecule with hydrogen ion 0.3 nm away from a site that will accept a hydrogen ion binds with unknown receptor
Bitterness	Molecule with hydrophobic residue (and often a region with a positive charge) binds with unknown receptor
Umami (glutamate)	Glutamate ion binds with a metabotropic glutamate receptor (mGluR4)
Fatty acids (possible)	Triglycerides are broken down to fatty acids, which enter the receptor cells and close potassium channels, blocking outflow of potassium ions; depolarizes membrane

are involved is the fact that amiloride, a drug that is known to block sodium channels, prevents sodium chloride from activating taste cells and decreases sensations of saltiness. However, the drug does not completely block these sensations in humans, so most investigators believe that more than one type of receptor is involved (Schiffman, Lockhead, and Maes, 1983; Ossebaard, Polet, and Smith, 1997).

Sourness receptors appear to respond to the hydrogen ions present in acidic solutions. However, because the sourness of a particular acid is not simply a function of the concentration of hydrogen ions, the anions must have an effect as well. The reason for this anion effect is not yet known. Kinnamon, Dionne, and Beam (1988) suggest that sourness is detected by sites on potassium channels in the membrane of taste cell cilia. These channels are normally open, permitting K^+ to flow out of the cell. Hydrogen ions bind with these sites and close the channels. Their closure prevents this outward current and depolarizes the membrane, producing action potentials.

Bitter and sweet substances are more difficult to characterize. The typical stimulus for bitterness is a plant alkaloid such as quinine; for sweetness it is a sugar such as glucose or fructose. The fact that some molecules elicit both sensations suggests that bitterness and sweetness receptors may be similar. For example, the Seville orange rind contains a glycoside (complex sugar) that tastes extremely bitter; the addition of a hydrogen ion to the molecule makes it taste intensely sweet (Horowitz and Gentili, 1974). Some amino acids taste sweet. Indeed, the commercial sweetener aspartame consists simply of two amino acids: aspartate and phenylalanine.

The structure of molecules that taste bitter appears to include a hydrophobic residue—that is, a region that is repelled by the presence of water. Especially bitter substances also have a region with a positive charge (Kurihara et al., 1994). The bitterness receptors are coupled with a G protein called **gustducin,** which is very similar in structure to *transducin,* the G protein involved in transduction of photic information in the retina (McLaughlin et al., 1993). When a bitter molecule binds with the receptor, gustducin activates phosphodiesterase, an enzyme that destroys cyclic AMP. Thus, detection of a bitter-tasting molecule by the receptor causes a decrease in intracellular cyclic AMP. In taste receptor cells, as in photoreceptors, it appears that potassium channels in the body of the taste receptor cell are normally held open by the action of cyclic AMP, which permits a constant efflux of K^+ cations.

gustducin (*gust* ***doo*** *sin*) A G protein that plays a vital role in the transduction of sweetness and bitterness.

A fall in the level of cyclic AMP causes potassium channels to close, and the membrane depolarizes.

Most molecules that taste sweet have a hydrogen ion situated 0.3 nm from a site that will accept a hydrogen ion. Presumably, the sweetness receptor has sites that match these. Sweetness receptors, like bitterness receptors, appear to be coupled to gustducin. Wong, Gannon, and Margolskee (1996) produced a mutation in mice using genetic engineering techniques that permit investigators to "knock out" a particular gene—in this case the gene responsible for the production of gustducin. As expected, the mice did not respond to bitter substances. But in addition, they failed to respond to sweet substances. (They did respond to sour and salty substances.) The binding of sweet-tasting molecules with their receptors causes an increase in the level of cyclic AMP in the cell. This second messenger causes calcium channels to open, and the subsequent influx of calcium causes the cell to release its neurotransmitter (Lindemann, 1996).

In recent years, researchers have recognized the existence of a fifth taste quality: *umami.* **Umami,** a Japanese word that means "good taste," refers to the taste of monosodium glutamate (MSG), a substance that is often used as a flavor enhancer in Asian cuisine (Kurihara, 1987; Scott and Plata-Salaman, 1991). MSG is present naturally in meats, cheeses, and some vegetables. Chaudhari et al. (1996) suggest that a specialized metabotropic glutamate receptor (mGluR4) may be responsible for detecting the taste of glutamate. The investigators found this receptor in taste buds but not in other parts of the tongue. They also reported that rats did not distinguish the taste of MSG from that of a ligand for this receptor, L-AP4. Activation of the mGluR4 receptor appears to close a cation channel, thus depolarizing the membrane (Bigiani et al., 1997).

A sixth taste quality has been proposed. Fats (triglycerides) consist of three fatty acids molecules joined to a molecule of glycerol, a carbohydrate. Because a gram of fat contains almost twice as many calories as a gram of protein or carbohydrate, it seems reasonable that there could be a natural selection for receptors that identify fat. The fact that people show such strong preference for foods that are rich in fat suggests that we can detect the presence of this compound.

Actually, these receptors, if they exist, appear to detect fatty acids. The tongue contains *lingual lipase,* an enzyme that breaks down fat molecules into their constituents (Lohse et al., 1997). Furthermore, the apical membranes of taste buds contain fatty-acid transporters, molecules that permit the entry of fatty acids into the cell (Fukuwatari et al., 1997). Gilbertson et al. (1997) found that the presence of fatty acids closes a potassium channel that is normally open, depolarizing the membrane. Only essential fatty acids—those that must be obtained from an animal's diet—had this effect, suggesting that the receptors identify the fats that are nutritionally the most important.

The Gustatory Pathway

Gustatory information is transmitted through cranial nerves 7, 9, and 10. Information from the anterior part of the tongue travels through the **chorda tympani,** a branch of the seventh cranial nerve (facial nerve). Taste receptors in the posterior part of the tongue send information through the lingual (tongue) branch of the ninth cranial nerve (glossopharyngeal nerve); the tenth cranial nerve (vagus nerve) carries information from receptors of the palate and epiglottis. The chorda tympani gets its name because it passes through the middle ear just beneath the tympanic membrane. Because of its convenient location, it is accessible to a recording or stimulating electrode. Investigators have even recorded from this nerve during the course of human ear operations.

The first relay station for taste is the **nucleus of the solitary tract,** located in the medulla. In primates the taste-sensitive neurons of this nucleus send their axons to

umami (*oo mah mee*) The taste sensation produced by glutamate.

chorda tympani A branch of the facial nerve that passes beneath the eardrum; conveys taste information from the anterior part of the tongue and controls the secretion of some salivary glands.

nucleus of the solitary tract A nucleus of the medulla that receives information from visceral organs and from the gustatory system.

Figure 7.21

Neural pathways of the gustatory system.

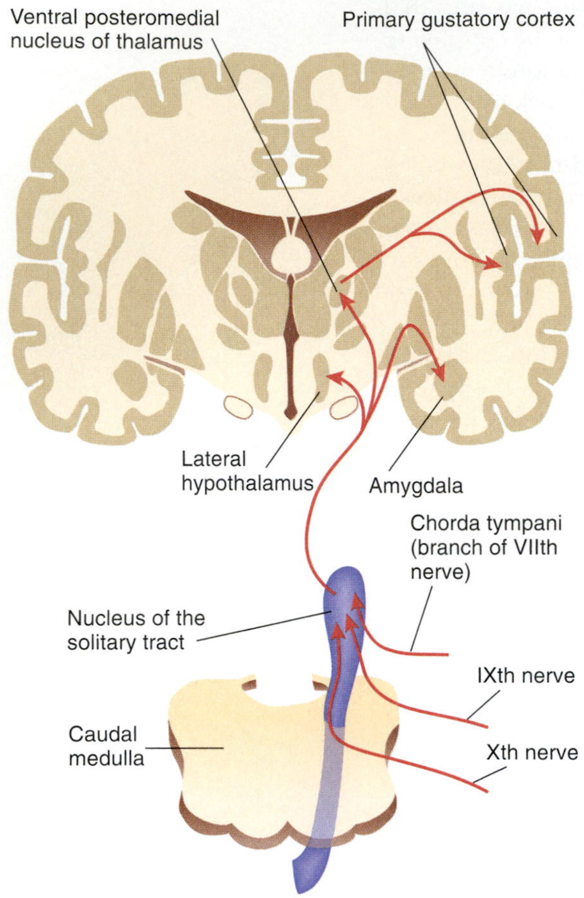

the ventral posteromedial thalamic nucleus, a nucleus that also receives somatosensory information received from the trigeminal nerve (Beckstead, Morse, and Norgren, 1980). Thalamic taste-sensitive neurons send their axons to the primary gustatory cortex, which is located in the base of the frontal cortex and in the insular cortex (Pritchard et al., 1986). Neurons in this region project to the secondary gustatory cortex, located in the caudolateral orbitofrontal cortex (Rolls, Yaxley, and Sienkiewicz, 1990). Unlike most other sense modalities, taste is ipsilaterally represented in the brain—that is, the right side of the tongue projects to the right side of the brain, and the left projects to the left. (See ***Figure 7.21.***)

Gustatory information also reaches the amygdala and the hypothalamus and adjacent basal forebrain (Nauta, 1964; Russchen, Amaral, and Price, 1986). Many investigators believe that the hypothalamic pathway plays a role in mediating the reinforcing effects of sweet and salty tastes. In fact, some neurons in the hypothalamus respond to sweet stimuli only when the animal is hungry (Rolls et al., 1986).

INTERIM SUMMARY

Gustation

Taste receptors detect only five sensory qualities: bitterness, sourness, sweetness, saltiness, and umami (umaminess?). Bitter foods often contain plant alkaloids, many of which are poisonous. Sour foods have usually undergone bacterial fermentation, which can produce toxins. On the other hand, sweet foods (such as fruits) are usually nutritious and safe to eat, and salty foods contain an essential cation: sodium. The fact that people in affluent cultures today tend to ingest excessive amounts of sweet and salty foods suggests that these taste qualities are naturally reinforcing. Umami, the taste of glutamate, identifies proteins.

Saltiness receptors appear to be simple sodium channels. Sourness receptors appear to detect the presence of hydrogen ions, which closes potassium channels located on the cilia and depolarizes the membrane of the cell. Both bitter and sweet tastes are detected by receptors bound to gustducin, a G protein. The structure of molecules that taste bitter appears to include a hydrophobic residue, and some also have a region with a positive charge. Bitter molecules activate phosphodiesterase, which destroys cyclic AMP and closes potassium channels, thus depolarizing the membrane of the cell. Most molecules that taste sweet have a hydrogen ion situated 0.3 nm from a site that will accept a hydrogen ion. Sweet molecules *increase* cyclic AMP levels, which opens calcium channels and thus causes the release of the neurotransmitter. The taste of glutamate (umami) is detected by a particular metabotropic glutamate receptor (mGluR4). Fats, an important component of the diet, may also be tasted, at least indirectly. The tongue contains an enzyme that converts some of the fat in the mouth to fatty acids, which appear to be transported into taste cells, where they stimulate specialized receptors.

Gustatory information from the anterior part of the tongue travels through the chorda tympani, a branch of the facial nerve that passes beneath the eardrum on its way to the brain. The posterior part of the tongue sends gustatory information through the glossopharyngeal nerve, and the palate and epiglottis send gustatory information through the vagus nerve. Gustatory information is received by the nucleus of the solitary tract (located in the medulla) and is relayed by the ventral posteromedial thalamus to the primary gustatory cortex in the opercular and insular areas. The caudolateral orbitofrontal cortex contains the secondary gustatory cortex. Gustatory information is also sent to the amygdala, hypothalamus, and basal forebrain.

THOUGHT QUESTIONS

Bees and birds can taste sweet substances, but cats and alligators cannot. Obviously, the ability to taste particular substances is related to the range of foods a species eats. If, through the process of evolution, a species develops a greater range of foods, what do you think comes first: the food or the receptor? Would a species start eating something with a new taste (say, something sweet) and later develop the appropriate taste receptors, or would the taste receptors evolve first and then lead the animal to a new taste?

Olfaction

Olfaction, the second chemical sense, helps us to identify food and avoid food that has spoiled and is unfit to eat. It helps the members of many species to track prey or detect predators and to identify friends, foes, and receptive mates. For humans olfaction is the most enigmatic of all sensory modalities. Odors have a peculiar ability to evoke memories, often vague ones that seem to have occurred in the distant past—a phenomenon that Marcel Proust vividly described in his book *Remembrance of Things Past.* Although people can discriminate among many thousands of different odors, we lack a good vocabulary to describe them. It is relatively easy to describe sights we have seen or sounds we have heard, but the description of an odor is difficult. At best, we can say that it smells like something else. Thus, the olfactory system appears to be specialized for *identifying things,* not for analyzing particular qualities.

The Stimulus

The stimulus for odor (known formally as *odorants*) consists of volatile substances having a molecular weight in the range of approximately 15 to 300. Almost all odorous compounds are lipid soluble and of organic origin. However, many substances that meet these criteria have no odor at all, so we still have much to learn about the nature of odorants.

Anatomy of the Olfactory Apparatus

Our six million olfactory receptor cells reside within two patches of mucous membrane (the **olfactory epithelium**), each having an area of about 1 square inch. The olfactory epithelium is located at the top of the nasal cavity, as shown in ***Figure 7.22.*** Less than 10 percent of the air that enters the nostrils reaches the olfactory epithelium; a sniff is needed to sweep air upward into the nasal cavity so that it reaches the olfactory receptors.

The inset in Figure 7.22 illustrates a group of olfactory receptor cells, along with their supporting cells. (See ***inset, Figure 7.22.***) Olfactory receptor cells are bipolar neurons whose cell bodies lie within the olfactory mucosa that lines the *cribriform plate,* a bone at the base of the rostral part of the brain. There is a constant production of new olfactory receptor cells, but their life is considerably longer than those of gustatory receptor cells. Supporting cells contain enzymes that destroy odorant molecules and thus help to prevent them from damaging the olfactory receptor cells.

Olfactory receptor cells send a process toward the surface of the mucosa, which divides into 10 to 20 cilia that penetrate the layer of mucus. Odorous molecules must dissolve in the mucus and stimulate receptor molecules on the olfactory cilia. Approximately 35 bundles of axons, ensheathed by glial cells, enter the skull through

olfactory epithelium The epithelial tissue of the nasal sinus that covers the cribriform plate; contains the cilia of the olfactory receptors.

Figure 7.22

The olfactory system.

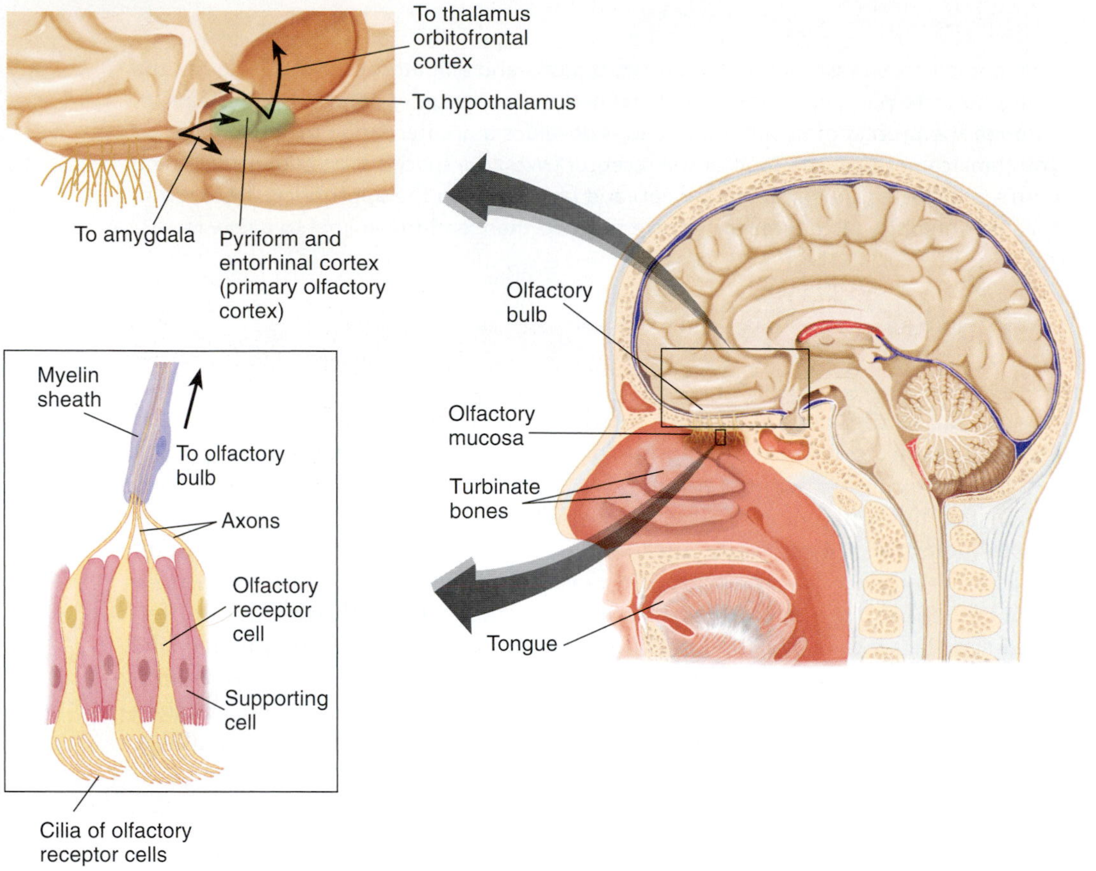

small holes in the cribriform ("perforated") plate. The olfactory mucosa also contains free nerve endings of trigeminal nerve axons; these nerve endings presumably mediate sensations of pain that can be produced by sniffing some irritating chemicals, such as ammonia.

The **olfactory bulbs** lie at the base of the brain on the ends of the stalklike olfactory tracts. Each olfactory receptor cell sends a single axon into the olfactory bulb, where it forms synapses with dendrites of **mitral cells** (named for their resemblance to a bishop's miter). These synapses take place in the complex axonal and dendritic arborizations called **olfactory glomeruli** (from *glomus,* "ball"). There are approximately 10,000 glomeruli, each of which receives input from a bundle of approximately 2000 axons. The axons of the mitral cells travel to the rest of the brain through the olfactory tracts. Some of these axons terminate in other regions of the ipsilateral forebrain; others cross the brain and terminate in the contralateral olfactory bulb.

Olfactory tract axons project directly to the amygdala and to two regions of the limbic cortex: the pyriform cortex and the entorhinal cortex. (See ***Figure 7.22.***) The amygdala sends olfactory information to the hypothalamus, the entorhinal cortex sends it to the hippocampus, and the pyriform cortex sends it to the hypothalamus and to the orbitofrontal cortex, via the dorsomedial nucleus of the thalamus (Buck, 1996; Shipley and Ennis, 1996). As you may recall, the orbitofrontal cortex also receives gustatory information; thus, it may be involved in the combining of taste and olfaction into flavor. The hypothalamus also receives a considerable amount of olfactory information, which is probably important for the acceptance or rejection of

olfactory bulb The protrusion at the end of the olfactory tract; receives input from the olfactory receptors.

mitral cell A neuron located in the olfactory bulb that receives information from olfactory receptors; axons of mitral cells bring information to the rest of the brain.

olfactory glomerulus (*glow* ***mare*** *you luss*) A bundle of dendrites of mitral cells and the associated terminal buttons of the axons of olfactory receptors.

food and for the olfactory control of reproductive processes seen in many species of mammals.

Most mammals have another organ that responds to chemicals in the environment: the *vomeronasal organ.* Because it plays an important role in animals' responses to pheromones, chemicals produced by other animals that affect reproductive physiology and behavior, its structure and function are described in Chapter 9.

Efferent fibers from several locations in the brain enter the olfactory bulbs. These include acetylcholinergic, noradrenergic, dopaminergic, and serotonergic inputs (Shipley and Ennis, 1996). As we shall see in Chapter 9, the noradrenergic input appears to be involved in olfactory memories, particularly those involved in reproduction.

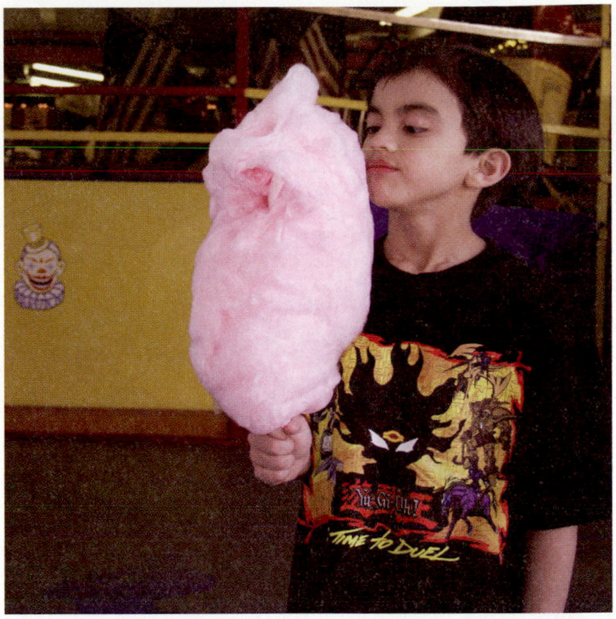

Particular odors that we experience when we are young often have the ability to evoke poignant memories later in life.

Transduction of Olfactory Information

For many years researchers have recognized that olfactory cilia contain receptors that are stimulated by molecules of odorants, but the nature of the receptors was unknown. Jones and Reed (1989) identified a particular G protein, which they called G_{olf}. This protein is able to activate an enzyme that catalyzes the synthesis of cyclic AMP, which, in turn, can open sodium channels and depolarize the membrane of the olfactory cell (Nakamura and Gold, 1987; Firestein, Zufall, and Shepherd, 1991; Menco et al., 1992).

As we saw in Chapter 2, G proteins serve as the link between metabotropic receptors and ion channels: When a ligand binds with a metabotropic receptor, the G protein either opens ion channels directly or does so indirectly, by triggering the production of a second messenger. The discovery of G_{olf} suggested that olfactory cilia contained odorant receptors linked to this G protein. Indeed, Buck and Axel (1991) used molecular genetics techniques and discovered a family of genes that code for a family of olfactory receptor proteins. So far, olfactory receptor genes have been isolated in more than twelve species of vertebrates, including mammals, birds, and amphibians (Mombaerts, 1999). In humans there appear to be between five hundred and one thousand different receptors, each sensitive to different odorants (Ressler, Sullivan, and Buck, 1994a). Thus, molecules of odorant bind with receptors, and the G proteins coupled to these receptors open sodium channels and produce depolarizing receptor potentials.

Perception of Specific Odors

For many years recognition of specific odors has been an enigma. Humans can recognize up to ten thousand different odorants, and other animals can probably recognize even more of them (Shepherd, 1994). Even if we have several hundred (or even one thousand) different types of olfactory receptors, that leaves many odors unaccounted for. And every year, chemists synthesize new chemicals, many with odors unlike those that anyone has previously detected. How can we use a relatively small number of receptors to detect so many different odorants?

Before I answer this question, we should look more closely at the relationship between receptors, olfactory neurons, and the glomeruli to which the axons of these neurons project. First, the cilia of each olfactory neuron contain only one type of receptor (Nef et al., 1992; Vassar, Ngai, and Axel, 1993). As we saw, each glomerulus receives information from approximately two thousand different olfactory receptor cells. Using special histochemical methods to identify particular receptor proteins in individual cells, Ressler, Sullivan, and Buck (1994b) discovered that although a given

Figure 7.23

Details of the connections of olfactory receptor cells with the glomeruli of the olfactory bulb. Each glomerulus receives information from only one type of receptor cell. Olfactory receptor cells of different colors contain different types of receptor molecules.

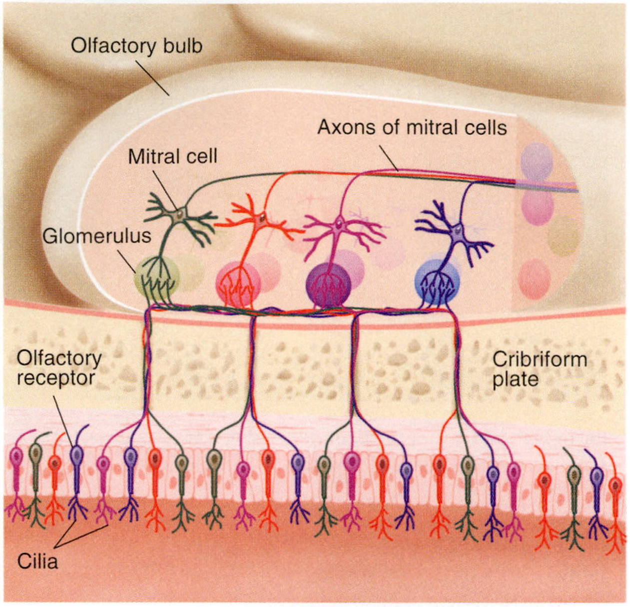

glomerulus receives information from approximately two thousand different olfactory receptor cells, each of these cells contains the same type of receptor molecule. Thus, there are as many types of glomeruli as there are types of receptor molecules. Furthermore, the location of particular types of glomeruli (defined by the type of receptor that sends information to them) appears to be the same in each of the olfactory bulbs in a given animal and may even be the same from one animal to another (Zou et al., 2001). (See ***Figure 7.23.***)

Now let's get back to the question I just posed: How can we use a relatively small number of receptors to detect so many different odorants? The answer is that a particular odorant binds to more than one receptor. Thus, because a given glomerulus receives information from only one type of receptor, different odorants produce different *patterns* of activity in different glomeruli. Recognizing a particular odor, then, is a matter of recognizing a particular pattern of activity in the glomeruli. The task of chemical recognition is transformed into a task of spatial recognition.

Figure 7.24 illustrates this process (Malnic et al., 1999). The left side of the figure shows the shapes of eight hypothetical odorants. The right side shows four hypothetical odorant receptor molecules. If a portion of the odorant molecule fits the binding site of the receptor molecule, it will activate it and stimulate the olfactory neuron. As you can see, each odorant molecule fits the binding site of at least one of the receptors and in most cases fits more than one of them. Notice also that the *pattern* of receptors activated by each of the eight odorants is different, which means that if we know which pattern of receptors is activated, we know which odorant is present. Of course, even though a particular odorant might bind with several different types of receptor molecules, it might not bind equally well with each of them. For example, it might bind very well with one receptor molecule, moderately well with another, weakly with another, and so on. (See ***Figure 7.24.***) As we just saw, the spatial pattern of "olfactotopic" information is maintained in the olfactory cortex. Presumably, the brain recognizes particular odors by recognizing different patterns of activation there.

Just how the brain recognizes these patterns is not yet known. The task is obviously complex. Cain (1988) noted that although most odors are produced by mixtures of many different chemicals, we identify odors as belonging to particular objects. For example, the smells of coffee, fried bacon, and cigarette smoke are each made of up to several hundred different types of molecules. Although each of these odors is a mixture, we recognize them as being unique—We do not detect the individual components. However, if the smells of coffee, fried bacon, and cigarette smoke are mixed together (as they might be at a breakfast counter that permits smoking), we still recognize all three odors, even though each one of them is itself a mixture!

INTERIM SUMMARY

Olfaction

The olfactory receptors consist of bipolar neurons located in the olfactory epithelium that lines the roof of the nasal sinuses, on the bone that underlies the frontal lobes. The receptors send processes toward the surface of the mucosa, which divide into cilia. The membranes of these cilia contain receptors that detect aromatic molecules dissolved in the air that sweeps past the olfactory mucosa. The axons of the olfactory receptors pass through the perforations of the cribriform plate into the olfactory bulbs, where they form synapses in the glomeruli with the dendrites of the mitral cells. These neurons send axons through the olfactory tracts to the brain, principally to the amygdala, the pyriform cortex, and the entorhinal cortex. The hippocampus, hypothalamus, and orbitofrontal cortex receive olfactory information indirectly,

Aromatic molecules produce membrane potentials by interacting with a newly discovered family of receptor molecules, which may number up to one thousand. These receptor molecules are coupled to a special G protein, G_{olf}. When an odorant molecule bind with and stimulates one of these receptors, G_{olf} catalyzes the synthesis of cyclic AMP, which opens sodium channels and depolarizes the membrane. Each glomerulus receives information from only one type of olfactory receptor, and "olfactotopic" coding is maintained all the way to the olfactory cortex. This means that the task of detecting different odors is a spatial one; the brain recognizes odors by means of the patterns of activity created in the olfactory cortex.

THOUGHT QUESTIONS

As I mentioned in the preceding section, odors have a peculiar ability to evoke memories, a phenomenon that Marcel Proust vividly described in his book *Remembrance of Things Past.* Have you ever encountered an odor that you knew was somehow familiar, but you couldn't say exactly why? Can you think of any explanations? Might this phenomenon have something to do with the fact that the sense of olfaction developed very early in our evolutionary history?

Figure 7.24

A hypothetical explanation of coding of olfactory information. Different odorant molecules attach to different combinations of receptor molecules. (Activated receptor molecules are shown in blue.) Unique patterns of activation represent particular odorants.

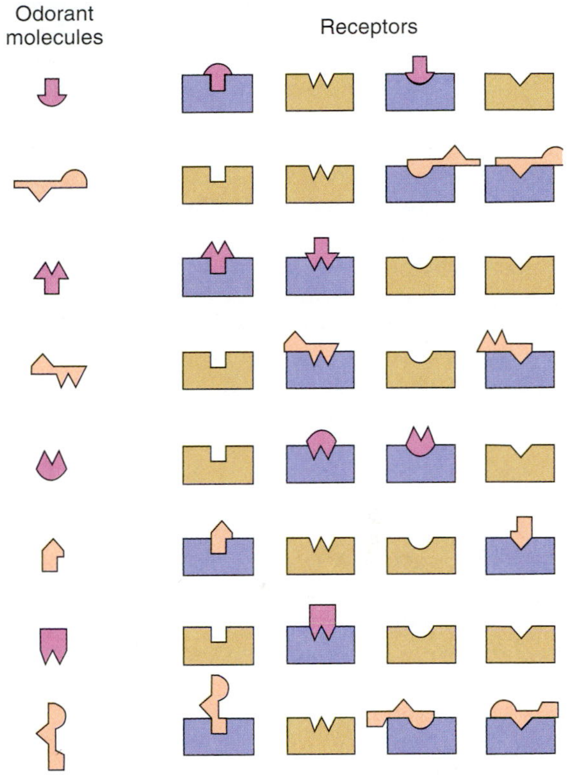

Adapted from Malnic, B., Hirono, J, Sato, T., and Buck, L. B. *Cell,* 1999, *96,* 713–723.

EPILOGUE

Natural Analgesia

As we have seen, the brain contains an elaborate system through which certain types of stimuli can produce analgesia primarily through the release of the endogenous opiates. What functions does this system perform? Most researchers believe that it prevents pain from disrupting animals' behavior in situations in which pain is unavoidable and in which the damaging effect of the painful stimuli are less important than the goals of the animals' behavior. This explanation accounts for several types of situations that produce analgesia, but not all of them; some mysteries still remain.

When an animal encounters a noxious stimulus, it usually stops what it is doing and engages in withdrawal or escape behaviors. Obviously, these responses are quite appropriate. However, they are sometimes counterproductive. For example, if an animal sustains a wound that causes chronic pain, a tendency to engage in withdrawal responses will interfere with its performance of everyday activities, such as obtaining food. Thus, the inhibitory effects of chronic, unavoidable pain would best be diminished.

Another useful function of analgesia is the suppression of pain during important behaviors such as fighting or mating. For example, males fighting for access to females during mating season will fail to pass on their genes if pain elicits withdrawal responses that interfere with fighting. As you will see, these conditions (fighting or mating) *do* diminish pain.

Let us consider the effects of unavoidable pain. Several experiments have shown that analgesia can be produced by the application of painful stimuli or even by the presence of nonpainful stimuli that have been paired with painful ones. For example, Maier, Drugan, and Grau (1982) administered inescapable shocks to rats' tails or administered shocks that the animals could learn to escape by making a response. Although both groups of animals received the same amount of shock, only those that received *inescapable* shocks showed analgesia. That is, when their pain sensitivity was tested, it was found to be lower than that of control subjects. The analgesia was abolished by administration of naloxone, which indicates that it was mediated by the release of endogenous opiates. (Naloxone is a drug that blocks opiate receptors. The experimenter in the chapter prologue used this drug when he blocked the analgesic effect of Melissa's own endogenous opiates.) The results make good sense, biologically. If pain is escapable, it serves to motivate the animal to make appropriate responses. If it occurs no matter what the animal does, then a reduction in pain sensitivity is in the animal's best interest.

There is evidence that engaging in behaviors that are important to survival also reduces sensitivity to pain. For example, Komisaruk and Larsson (1971) found that genital stimulation produced analgesia. They gently probed the cervix of female rats with a glass rod and found that the procedure diminished the animals' sensitivity to pain. It also increased the activity of neurons in the periaqueductal gray matter and decreased the pain response in the thalamus (Komisaruk and Steinman, 1987). The phenomenon also occurs in humans; Whipple and Komisaruk (1988) found that self-administered vaginal stimulation reduces women's sensitivity to painful stimuli but not to neutral tactile stimuli. Presumably, copulation also triggers analgesic mechanisms. The adaptive significance of this phenomenon is clear: Painful stimuli that are encountered during the course of copulation are less likely to cause the behavior to be interrupted; thus, the chances of pregnancy are increased. (As you will recall, passing on one's genes is the ultimate criterion of the adaptive significance of a trait.)

As we saw in the chapter prologue, pain can also be reduced at least in some people by administering a *placebo,* a pharmacologically inert substance. (The term *placebo* comes from the Latin *placere,* which means "to please." The physician pleases an anxious patient by giving him or her an innocuous substance.) The pain reduction seems to be mediated by the release of endogenous opiates, because it is blocked by naloxone (Levine, Gordon, and Fields, 1979). Thus, *believing* that pain is going to diminish is a self-fulfilling prophecy. *Why* this particular phenomenon occurs is still a mystery.

Pain can be also reduced by stimulating regions other than those that hurt. For example, people often rub or scratch the area around a wound in an apparent attempt to diminish the severity of the pain. And as you know, acupuncturists insert needles into various parts of the body to reduce pain. The needle is usually then rotated, thus stimulating axons and nerve endings in the vicinity. Often, the region that is stimulated is far removed from the region that becomes less sensitive to pain.

Several experimental studies have shown that acupuncture can produce analgesia. Mayer, Price, Rafii, and Barber (1976) reported that the analgesic effects of acupuncture could be blocked by naloxone. However, when pain was reduced by hypnotic suggestion, naloxone had no effect. Thus, acupuncture, but not hypnosis, appears to cause analgesia through the release of endogenous opiates.

The endogenous opiates were first discovered by scientists who were investigating the perception of pain; thus, many of the studies using these peptides have examined their role in mechanisms of analgesia. However, their role in other functions may be even more important. As you will see in subsequent chapters, the endogenous opiates may even be involved in learning, especially in mechanisms of reinforcement. This connection should not come as a surprise; as you know, many people have found injections of opiates like morphine or heroin to be extremely pleasurable.

KEY CONCEPTS

AUDITION

1. The bones of the middle ear transmit sound vibrations from the eardrum to the cochlea, which contains the auditory receptors the hair cells.
2. The hair cells send information through the eighth cranial nerve to nuclei in the brain stem; it is then relayed to the medial geniculate nucleus and finally to the primary auditory cortex.
3. The ear is analytical; it detects individual frequencies by means of place coding and rate coding. Left–right localization is also accomplished by two means: arrival time (phase differences) and binaural differences in intensity.

VESTIBULAR SYSTEM

4. The vestibular system helps us to maintain our balance and makes compensatory eye movements to help us maintain fixation when our head moves. The semicircular canals detect head rotations and the vestibular sacs detect changes in the tilt of the head.

SOMATOSENSES

5. Cutaneous receptors in the skin provide information about touch, pressure, vibration, changes in temperature, and stimuli that cause tissue damage.

6. Pain perception helps protect us from harmful stimuli. Sensitivity to pain is modulated by the release of the endogenous opiates by cells in the brain.

GUSTATION

7. Taste receptors on the tongue respond to bitterness, sourness, sweetness, saltiness, and perhaps umami and fatty acids. Together with olfactory information, gustation provides us with information about complex flavors.

OLFACTION

8. The olfactory system detects the presence of aromatic molecules. The discovery of a family of receptors coupled to a special G protein (G_{olf}) suggests that several hundred different receptors may be involved in olfactory discrimination. Patterns of activation of these receptors lead to perception of different odorants.

SUGGESTED READINGS

AUDITION

Ehret, G., and Romand, R. *The Central Auditory System.* New York: Oxford University Press, 1997.

Moore, B. C. J. *Hearing: Handbook of Perception and Cognition,* 2nd ed. San Diego: Academic Press, 1995.

Yost, W. A. *Fundamentals of Hearing: An Introduction,* 3rd ed. San Diego: Academic Press, 1994.

VESTIBULAR SYSTEM

Cohen, B., Tomko, D. L., and Guedry, F. E. *Sensing and Controlling Motion: Vestibular and Sensorimotor Function.* New York: New York Academy of Sciences, 1992.

SOMATOSENSES

Bromm, B., and Desmedt, J. E. *Pain and the Brain: From Nociception to Cognition.* New York: Raven Press, 1995.

García-Añoveros, J., and Corey, D. P. The molecules of mechanosensation. *Annual Review of Neuroscience,* 1997, *20,* 567–594.

Kruger, L. *Pain and Touch: Handbook of Perception and Cognition,* 2nd ed. San Diego: Academic Press, 1996.

Melzak, R. Phantom limbs. *Scientific American,* 1992, *266(4),* 120–126.

OLFACTION AND GUSTATION

Doty, R. L. Olfaction. *Annual Review of Psychology,* 2001, *52,* 423–452.

Herness, M. S., and Gilbertson, T. A. Cellular mechanisms of taste transduction. *Annual Review of Physiology,* 1999, *61,* 873–900.

Hildebrand, J. G., and Shepherd, G. M. Mechanisms of olfactory discrimination: Converging evidence for common principles across phyla. *Annual Review of Neuroscience,* 1997, *20,* 595–632.

SUGGESTED WEB SITES

Somatosensory Pathways

http://thalamus.wustl.edu/course/body.html

This site contains a tutorial on somatosensory pathways and a variety of related images.

Relief of Pain and Suffering

www.library.ucla.edu/libraries/biomed/his/PainExhibit/

The measurement and treatment of pain is the focus of this site. Topics covered on the site include pain measurement, analgesia and anesthesia, and the phantom limb phenomenon.

The Nature of Pain

http://msnews.org/mchenryone.htm

The focus of this site is a general tutorial on pain.

Auditory System Function

http://penguin.d.umn.edu/undergrad/audsyfunctweb/sld001.htm

This site provides faculty with access to a PowerPoint slide set dealing with auditory system structure and function (30 slides).

Somatosensory Mapping

http://alpha.nmrlab.hscsyr.edu/mnr_lab/jake_home.html

This site contains an fMRI image showing the mapping of somatosensory cortex.

Sleep and Biological Rhythms

chapter 8

LEARNING OBJECTIVES

1. Describe the course of a night's sleep: its stages and their characteristics.
2. Discuss insomnia, sleeping medications, and sleep apnea.
3. Discuss sleep disorders associated with REM sleep and slow-wave sleep.
4. Review the hypothesis that sleep serves as a period of restoration by discussing the effects of sleep deprivation, exercise, and mental activity.
5. Discuss the functions of REM sleep.
6. Evaluate evidence that the onset and amount of sleep is chemically controlled, and describe the neural control of arousal.
7. Discuss the neural control of slow-wave sleep, including the sleep–waking "flip-flop" and the role of hypocretinergic neurons.
8. Discuss the neural control of REM sleep.
9. Describe circadian rhythms and discuss research on the neural and physiological bases of biological clocks.

CHAPTER OUTLINE

PROLOGUE

Waking Nightmares

Lately, Michael felt almost afraid of going to bed because of the unpleasant experiences he had been having. His dreams seemed to have become more intense, in a rather disturbing way. Several times in the past few months, he felt as if he were paralyzed as he lay in bed, waiting for sleep to come. It was a strange feeling; was he *really* paralyzed, or was he just not trying hard enough to move? He always fell asleep before he was able to decide. A couple of times he woke up just before it was time for his alarm to go off and felt unable to move. Then the alarm would ring, and he would quickly shut it off. That meant that he really wasn't paralyzed, didn't it? Was he going crazy?

Last night brought the worst experience of all. As he was falling asleep, he felt again as if he were paralyzed. Then he saw his old roommate enter his bedroom. But that wasn't possible! Since the time he graduated from college, he had lived alone, and he always locked the door. He tried to say something, but he couldn't. His roommate was holding a hammer. He walked up to the bed, stood over Michael, and suddenly raised the hammer, as if to smash in Michael's forehead. When Michael awoke in the morning, he shuddered at the remembrance. It had seemed so real! It must have been a dream, but he didn't think he was asleep. He was in bed. Can a person really dream that he is lying in bed, not yet asleep?

That day at the office he had trouble concentrating on his work. He forced himself to review his notes, because he had to present the details of the new project to the board of directors. This was his big chance; if the project were accepted, he would certainly be chosen to lead it, and that would mean a promotion and a substantial raise. Naturally, with so much at stake, he felt nervous when he entered the boardroom. His boss introduced Michael and asked him to begin. Michael glanced at his notes and opened his mouth to speak. Suddenly, he felt his knees buckle. All his strength seemed to slip away. He fell heavily to the floor. He could hear people running over and asking what had happened. He couldn't move anything except his eyes. His boss got down on his knees, looked into his face, and asked, "Michael, are you all right?" Michael looked at his boss and tried to answer, but he couldn't say a thing. A few seconds later, he felt his strength coming back. He opened his mouth and said, "I'm okay." He struggled to his knees and then sat in a chair, feeling weak and frightened.

"You undoubtedly have a condition known as narcolepsy," said the doctor whom Michael visited. "It's a problem that concerns the way your brain controls sleep. I'll have you spend a night in the sleep clinic and get some recordings done to confirm my diagnosis, but I'm sure that I'll be proved correct. You told me that lately you've been taking short naps during the day. What were these naps like? Were you suddenly struck by an urge to sleep?" Michael nodded. "I just had to put my head on the desk, even though I was afraid that my boss might see me. But I don't think I slept more than five minutes or so." "Did you still feel sleepy when you woke?" "No," he replied, "I felt fine again." The doctor nodded. "All the symptoms you have reported—the sleep attacks, the paralysis you experienced before sleeping and after waking up, the spell you had today—they all fit together. Fortunately, we can usually control narcolepsy with medication. In fact, we have a new one that does an excellent job. I'm sure we'll have you back to normal, and there is no reason why you can't continue with your job. If you'd like, I can talk with your boss and reassure him, too."

Why do we sleep? Why do we spend at least one-third of our lives doing something that provides most of us with only a few fleeting memories? I will attempt to answer this question in several ways. In the first two parts of this chapter I will describe what is known about the phenomenon of sleep and its disorders: How much do we sleep? What do we do while asleep? Are sleeping medications effective? What do we know about narcolepsy, sleepwalking, and other sleep-related disorders? In the third part I will discuss research on the causes of sleep: What happens if we do not get enough sleep? Does sleep perform a restorative function? In the fourth part of the chapter I will describe the search for the chemicals and the neural circuits that control sleep and wakefulness. In the final part of the chapter I will discuss the brain's biological clock—the mechanism that controls daily rhythms of sleep and activity.

A Physiological and Behavioral Description of Sleep

Sleep is a behavior. That statement might seem peculiar, because we usually think of behaviors as activities that involve movements, such as walking or talking. Except for

Figure 8.1

A subject prepared for a night's sleep in a sleep laboratory.

Philippe Platilly/Science Photo Library/Photo Researchers Inc.

the rapid eye movements that accompany a particular stage, sleep is not distinguished by movement. What characterizes sleep is that the insistent urge of sleepiness forces us to seek out a quiet, comfortable place; lie down; and remain there for several hours. Because we remember very little about what happens while we sleep, we tend to think of sleep more as a state of consciousness than as a behavior. The change in consciousness is undeniable, but it should not prevent us from noticing the behavioral changes.

The best research on human sleep is conducted in a sleep laboratory. A sleep laboratory, usually located at a university or medical center, consists of one or several small bedrooms adjacent to an observation room, where the experimenter spends the night (trying to stay awake). The experimenter prepares the sleeper for electrophysiological measurements by attaching electrodes to the scalp to monitor the electroencephalogram (EEG) and to the chin to monitor muscle activity, recorded as the **electromyogram (EMG)**. Electrodes attached around the eyes monitor eye movements, recorded as the **electro-oculogram (EOG)**. In addition, other electrodes and transducing devices can be used to monitor autonomic measures such as heart rate, respiration, and skin conductance. (See ***Figure 8.1.***)

During wakefulness the EEG of a normal person shows two basic patterns of activity: *alpha activity* and *beta activity.* **Alpha activity** consists of regular, medium-frequency waves of 8–12 Hz. The brain produces this activity when a person is resting quietly, not particularly aroused or excited and not engaged in strenuous mental activity (such as problem solving). Although alpha waves sometimes occur when a person's eyes are open, they are much more prevalent when the eyes are closed. The other type of waking EEG pattern, **beta activity,** consists of irregular, mostly low-amplitude waves of 13–30 Hz. This activity occurs when a person is alert and attentive to events in the environment or is thinking actively. (See ***Figure 8.2.***)

Let us look at a typical night's sleep of a female college student on her third night in the laboratory. (Of course, we would obtain similar results from a male, with one exception, which is noted later.) The experimenter attaches the electrodes, turns the lights off, and closes the door. Our subject becomes drowsy and soon enters stage 1 sleep, marked by the presence of some **theta activity** (3.5–7.5 Hz). This stage is actually a transition between sleep and wakefulness; if we watch our volunteer's eyelids, we will see that from time to time they slowly open and close and that her eyes roll upward and downward. (See ***Figure 8.2.***) About 10 minutes later she enters stage 2 sleep. The EEG during this stage is generally irregular but contains periods of theta activity, *sleep spindles,* and *K complexes.* Sleep spindles are short bursts of waves of 12–14 Hz that occur between two and five times a minute during stages 1–4 of sleep. Some investigators believe that sleep spindles represent the activity of a mechanism that is involved in keeping a person asleep (Bowersox, Kaitin, and Dement, 1985; Steriade, 1992; Nicolas et al., 2001). K complexes are sudden, sharp waveforms, which, unlike sleep spindles, are usually found only during stage 2 sleep. They spontaneously occur at the rate of approximately one per minute but often can be triggered by noises—especially unexpected noises. According to De Gennaro, Ferrara, and Bertini (2000), they appear to be the forerunner of delta waves, which appear in deeper levels of sleep. (See ***Figure 8.2.***)

electromyogram (EMG) (*my oh gram*) An electrical potential recorded from an electrode placed on or in a muscle.

electro-oculogram (EOG) (*ah kew loh gram*) An electrical potential from the eyes, recorded by means of electrodes placed on the skin around them; detects eye movements.

alpha activity Smooth electrical activity of 8–12 Hz recorded from the brain; generally associated with a state of relaxation.

beta activity Irregular electrical activity of 13–30 Hz recorded from the brain; generally associated with a state of arousal.

theta activity EEG activity of 3.5–7.5 Hz that occurs intermittently during early stages of slow-wave sleep and REM sleep.

The subject is sleeping soundly now; but if awakened, she might report that she has not been asleep. This phenomenon often is reported by nurses who awaken loudly snoring patients early in the night (probably to give them a sleeping pill) and find that the patients insist they were lying there awake all the time. About 15 minutes later the subject enters stage 3 sleep, signaled by the occurrence of high-amplitude **delta activity** (slower than 3.5 Hz). (See ***Figure 8.2.***) The distinction between stage 3 and stage 4 is not clear-cut; stage 3 contains 20–50 percent delta activity, and stage 4 contains more than 50 percent. (See ***Figure 8.2.***)

About 90 minutes after the beginning of sleep (and about 45 minutes after the onset of stage 4 sleep), we notice an abrupt change in a number of physiological measures recorded from our subject. The EEG suddenly becomes mostly desynchronized, with a sprinkling of theta waves, very similar to the record obtained during stage 1 sleep. (See ***Figure 8.2.***) We also note that her eyes are rapidly darting back and forth beneath her closed eyelids. We can see this activity in the EOG, recorded from electrodes attached to the skin around her eyes, or we can observe the eye movements directly—the cornea produces a bulge in the closed eyelids that can be seen to move about. We also see that the EMG becomes silent; there is a profound loss of muscle tonus. In fact, physiological studies have shown that, aside from occasional twitching, a person actually becomes paralyzed during REM sleep. This peculiar stage of sleep is quite distinct from the quiet sleep we saw earlier. It is usually referred to as **REM sleep** (for the **r**apid **e**ye **m**ovements that characterize it).

At this point I should introduce some terminology. Stages 1–4 are usually referred to as **non-REM sleep.** Stages 3 and 4 are referred to as **slow-wave sleep,** because of the presence of delta activity. As we will see, research has focused on the role of REM sleep and of slow-wave sleep; most investigators believe that the other stages of non-REM sleep, stages 1 and 2, are less important. (As we shall see, when people are sleep deprived, they make up most of their slow-wave sleep and REM sleep but not their stage 1 and stage 2 sleep.) Stage 4 is the deepest stage of sleep; only loud noises will cause a person to awaken, and when awakened, the person acts groggy and confused. During REM sleep a person might not react to noises, but he or she is easily aroused by meaningful stimuli, such as the sound of his or her name. Also, when awakened from REM sleep, a person appears alert and attentive.

If we arouse our volunteer during REM sleep and ask her what was going on, she will almost certainly report that she had been dreaming. The dreams of REM sleep tend to be narrative in form; there is a storylike progression of events. If we wake her during slow-wave sleep and ask, "Were you dreaming?" she will most likely say, "No." However, if we question her more carefully, she might report the presence of a thought, an image, or some emotion.

During the rest of the night our subject's sleep alternates between periods of REM and non-REM sleep. Each cycle is approximately 90 minutes long, containing a 20- to 30-minute bout of REM sleep. Thus, an 8-hour sleep will contain four or five periods of REM sleep. Figure 8.3 shows a graph of a typical night's sleep. The vertical axis indicates the EEG activity that is being recorded; thus REM sleep and stage 1 sleep are placed on the same line because similar patterns of EEG activity occur at these times. Note that most slow-wave sleep (stages 3 and 4) occurs during the first half of night. Subsequent bouts of non-REM sleep contain more and more stage 2

Figure 8.2

An EEG recording of the stages of sleep.

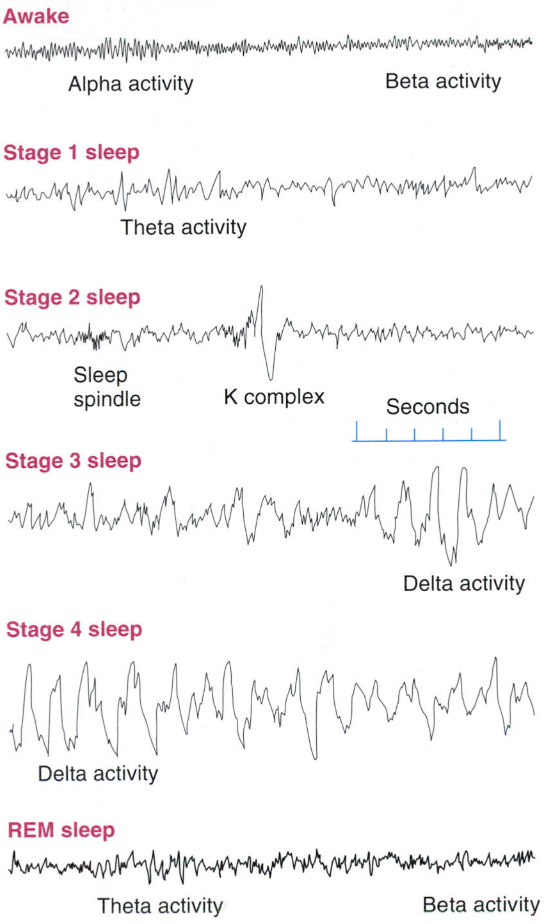

From Horne, J. A. *Why We Sleep: The Functions of Sleep in Humans and Other Mammals.* Oxford, England: Oxford University Press, 1988.

delta activity Regular, synchronous electrical activity of less than 4 Hz recorded from the brain; occurs during the deepest stages of slow-wave sleep.

REM sleep A period of desynchronized EEG activity during sleep, at which time dreaming, rapid eye movements, and muscular paralysis occur; also called *paradoxical sleep.*

non-REM sleep All stages of sleep except REM sleep.

slow-wave sleep Non-REM sleep, characterized by synchronized EEG activity during its deeper stages.

Figure 8.3

A typical pattern of the stages of sleep during a single night. The dark blue shading indicates REM sleep.

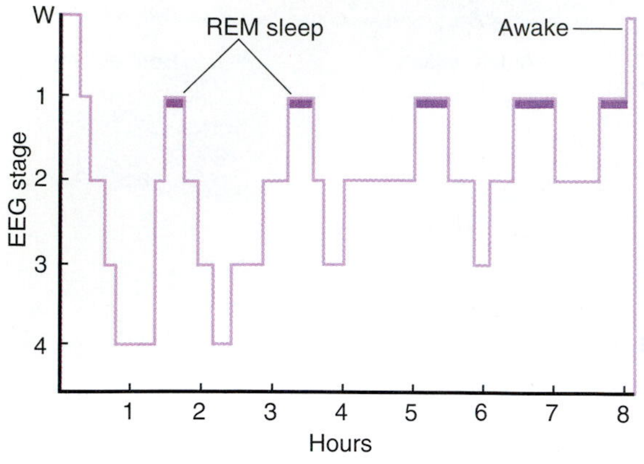

sleep, and bouts of REM sleep (indicated by the horizontal bars) become more prolonged. (See ***Figure 8.3.***)

The fact that REM sleep occurs at regular 90-minute intervals suggests that a brain mechanism alternately causes REM and slow-wave sleep. Normally, a period of slow-wave sleep must precede REM sleep. In addition, there seems to be a refractory period after each occurrence of REM sleep, during which time REM sleep cannot take place again. In fact, the cyclical nature of REM sleep appears to be controlled by a "clock" in the brain that also controls an activity cycle that continues through waking. The first suggestion that a 90-minute activity cycle occurs throughout the day came from the observation that infants who are fed on demand show regular feeding patterns (Kleitman, 1961). Later studies found 90-minute cycles of rest and activity, including such activities as eating, drinking, smoking, heart rate, oxygen consumption, stomach motility, urine production, and performance on various tasks that make demands on a person's ability to pay attention. Kleitman termed this phenomenon the **basic rest–activity cycle** (Kleitman, 1982.) An internal "clock," as yet undiscovered, appears to cause regular changes in activity and alertness during the day and control periods of slow-wave and REM sleep at night.

As we saw, during REM sleep we become paralyzed; most of our spinal and cranial motor neurons are strongly inhibited. (Obviously, the ones that control respiration and eye movements are spared.) At the same time the brain is very active. Cerebral blood flow and oxygen consumption are accelerated. In addition, a male's penis will become at least partially erect, and a female's vaginal secretions will increase. However, Fisher, Gross, and Zuch (1965) found that in males, genital changes do not signify that the person is experiencing a dream with sexual content. (Of course, people can have dreams with frank sexual content. In males some dreams culminate in ejaculation—the so-called nocturnal emissions, or "wet dreams." Females, too, sometimes experience orgasm during sleep.)

The fact that penile erections occur during REM sleep, independent of sexual arousal, has been used clinically to assess the causes of impotence (Karacan, Salis, and Williams, 1978; Singer and Weiner, 1996). A subject sleeps in the laboratory with a device attached to his penis that measures its circumference. If penile enlargement occurs during REM sleep, then his failure to obtain an erection during attempts at intercourse is not caused by physiological problems such as nerve damage or a circulatory disorder. (A neurologist told me that there is a less expensive way to gather the same data. The patient obtains a strip of postage stamps, moistens them, and applies them around his penis before going to bed. In the morning he checks to see whether the perforations are broken.)

The important differences between REM and slow-wave sleep are listed in ***Table 8.1.***

Table 8.1

Principal Characteristics of REM and Slow-Wave Sleep

REM Sleep	Slow-Wave Sleep
EEG desynchrony (rapid, irregular waves)	EEG synchrony (slow waves)
Lack of muscle tonus	Moderate muscle tonus
Rapid eye movements	Slow or absent eye movements
Penile erection or vaginal secretion	Lack of genital activity
Dreams	

basic rest–activity cycle A 90-minute cycle (in humans) of waxing and waning alertness, controlled by a biological clock in the caudal brain stem; controls cycles of REM sleep and slow-wave sleep.

INTERIM SUMMARY

A Physiological and Behavioral Description of Sleep

Sleep is generally regarded as a state, but it is nevertheless a behavior. The stages of non-REM sleep, stages 1–4, are defined by EEG activity. Slow-wave sleep (stages 3 and 4) includes the two deepest stages. Alertness consists of desynchronized beta activity (13–30 Hz); relaxation and drowsiness consist of alpha activity (8–12 Hz); stage 1 sleep consists of alternating periods of alpha activity, irregular fast activity, and theta activity (3.5–7.5 Hz); the EEG of stage 2 sleep lacks alpha activity but contains sleep spindles (short periods of 12–14 Hz activity) and occasional K complexes; stage 3 sleep consists of 20–50 percent delta activity (less than 3.5 Hz); and stage 4 sleep consists of more than 50 percent delta activity. About 90 minutes after the beginning of sleep, people enter REM sleep. Cycles of REM and slow-wave sleep alternate in periods of approximately 90 minutes.

REM sleep consists of rapid eye movements, a desynchronized EEG, sensitivity to external stimulation, muscular paralysis, genital activity, and dreaming.

THOUGHT QUESTIONS

1. Have you ever been resting quietly and suddenly heard someone tell you that you had obviously been sleeping because you were snoring? Did you believe them, or were you certain that you were really awake? Do you think it was likely that you had actually entered stage 1 sleep?
2. What is accomplished by dreaming? Some researchers believe that the subject matter of a dream does not matter; it is the REM sleep itself that is important. Others believe that the subject matter *does* count. Some researchers believe that if we remember a dream, then the dream failed to accomplish all of its functions; others say that remembering dreams is useful, because it can give us some insights into our problems. What do you think of these controversies?
3. Some people report that they are "in control" of some of their dreams, that they feel as if they determine what comes next and are not simply swept along passively. Have you ever had this experience? And have you ever had a "lucid dream," in which you aware of the fact that you were dreaming?

Disorders of Sleep

Because we spend about one-third of our lives sleeping, sleep disorders can have a significant impact on our quality of life. They can also affect the way we feel while we are awake.

Insomnia

Insomnia is a problem that is said to affect approximately 25 percent of the population occasionally and 9 percent regularly (Ancoli-Israel and Roth, 1999). But we need to define *insomnia* carefully. First, there is no single definition of insomnia that can apply to all people. The amount of sleep that individuals require is quite variable. A short sleeper may feel fine with five hours; a long sleeper may still feel unrefreshed after ten hours of sleep. Insomnia must be defined in relation to a person's particular sleep needs. Some short sleepers have sought medical assistance because they thought that they were supposed to get more sleep, even though they felt fine. These people should be reassured that whatever amount of sleep seems to be enough *is* enough.

Ironically, one of the most important causes of insomnia seems to be sleeping medication. Insomnia is not a disease that can be corrected with a medicine in the way that diabetes can be treated with insulin. Insomnia is a symptom. If it is caused by pain or discomfort, the physical ailment that leads to the sleeplessness should be treated. If it is secondary to personal problems or psychological disorders, these problems should be dealt with directly. Patients who receive a sleeping medication develop a tolerance to the drug and suffer rebound symptoms if it is withdrawn (Weitzman, 1981). That is, the drug loses its effectiveness, so the patient requests larger doses from the physician. If the patient attempts to sleep without the accustomed medication or even takes a smaller dose one night, he or she is likely to experience a withdrawal effect: a severe disturbance of sleep. The patient becomes convinced that the insomnia is even worse than before and turns to more medication for relief. This common syndrome is called **drug dependency insomnia.** Kales et al. (1979) found that withdrawal of some sleeping medications produced a rebound insomnia after the drugs were used for as few as three nights.

The second consideration in defining insomnia is the unreliability of self reports. Very few patients are observed during a night's sleep in a sleep laboratory; thus, insomnia is one of the few medical problems that physicians treat without having direct clinical evidence for its existence. But studies on the sleep of people who complain of insomnia show that most of them grossly underestimate the amount of time they actually sleep.

For many years the goal of sleeping medication was to help people fall asleep, and when drug companies evaluated potential medications, they concentrated on that property. However, if we think about the ultimate goal of sleeping medication, it is to make the person feel more refreshed the next day. If a medication puts people to sleep right away but produces a hangover of grogginess and difficulty concentrating the next day, it is worse than useless. In fact, many drugs that are traditionally used to treat insomnia had just this effect. More recently, researchers have recognized that the true evaluation of a sleeping medication must be made during wakefulness the following day, and "hangover-free" drugs are finally being developed (Hajak et al., 1995).

A particular form of insomnia is caused by an inability to sleep and breathe at the same time. Patients with this disorder, called **sleep apnea,** fall asleep and then cease to breathe. (Nearly all people, especially people who snore, have occasional episodes of sleep apnea, but not to the extent that it interferes with sleep.) During a period of sleep apnea the level of carbon dioxide in the blood stimulates chemoreceptors (neurons that detect the presence of certain chemicals), and the person wakes up, gasping for air. The oxygen level of the blood returns to normal, the person falls asleep, and the whole cycle begins again. Fortunately, many cases of sleep apnea are caused by an obstruction of the airway that can be corrected surgically or relieved by a device that attaches to the sleeper's face and provides pressurized air that keeps the airway open (Sher, 1990; Piccirillo, Duntley, and Schotland, 2000).

Narcolepsy

Narcolepsy (*narke* means "numbness," and *lepsis* means "seizure") is a neurological disorder characterized by sleep (or some of its components) at inappropriate times. The symptoms can be described in terms of what we know about the phenomena of sleep. The primary symptom of narcolepsy is the **sleep attack.** The narcoleptic sleep attack is an overwhelming urge to sleep that can happen at any time but occurs most often under monotonous, boring conditions. Sleep (which appears to be entirely normal) generally lasts for 2–5 minutes. The person usually wakes up feeling refreshed.

Another symptom of narcolepsy—in fact, the most striking one—is **cataplexy** (from *kata,* "down," and *plexis,* "stroke"). During a cataplectic attack a person will suddenly wilt and fall like a sack of flour. The person will lie there, *fully conscious,* for a few seconds to several minutes. What apparently happens is that one of the phe-

drug dependency insomnia An insomnia caused by the side effects of ever-increasing doses of sleeping medications.

sleep apnea (***app*** *nee a*) Cessation of breathing while sleeping.

narcolepsy (***nahr*** *ko lep see*) A sleep disorder characterized by periods of irresistible sleep, attacks of cataplexy, sleep paralysis, and hypnagogic hallucinations.

sleep attack A symptom of narcolepsy; an irresistible urge to sleep during the day, after which the person awakes feeling refreshed.

cataplexy (***kat*** *a plex ee*) A symptom of narcolepsy; complete paralysis that occurs during waking.

nomena of REM sleep—muscular paralysis—occurs at an inappropriate time. As we saw, this loss of tonus is caused by massive inhibition of motor neurons in the spinal cord. When this happens during waking, the victim of a cataplectic attack falls as suddenly as if a switch had been thrown.

Cataplexy is quite different from a narcoleptic sleep attack; cataplexy is usually precipitated by strong emotion or by sudden physical effort, especially if the patient is caught unawares. Laughter, anger, or an effort to catch a suddenly thrown object can trigger a cataplectic attack. In fact, as Guilleminault, Wilson, and Dement (1974) noted, even people who do not have cataplexy sometimes lose muscle strength after a bout of intense laughter. (Perhaps that is why we say a person can become "weak from laughter.") Common situations that bring on cataplexy are attempting to discipline one's children and making love (an awkward time to become paralyzed!). Michael, the man described in the chapter prologue, had his first cataplectic attack when he was addressing the board of directors of the company he worked for.

REM sleep paralysis sometimes intrudes into waking but at a time that does not present any physical danger—just before or just after normal sleep, when a person is already lying down. This symptom of narcolepsy is referred to as **sleep paralysis,** an inability to move just before the onset of sleep or upon waking in the morning. A person can be snapped out of sleep paralysis by being touched or by hearing someone call his or her name. Sometimes, the mental components of REM sleep intrude into sleep paralysis; that is, the person dreams while lying awake, paralyzed. These episodes, called **hypnagogic hallucinations,** are often alarming or even terrifying. (The term *hypnagogic* comes from the Greek words *hupnos,* "sleep," and *agogos,* "leading.")

As we will see later in this chapter, narcolepsy is produced by a brain abnormality that disrupts the neural mechanisms that control various aspects of sleep and arousal. Narcoleptic patients have difficulty staying awake, and aspects of REM sleep intrude into the waking state. In addition, they generally skip the slow-wave sleep that normally begins a night's sleep; instead, they go directly into REM sleep from waking. Finally, their sleep is often disrupted by periods of wakefulness.

Human narcolepsy is a genetic disorder that is influenced by unknown environmental factors (Mignot, 1998). Years ago, researchers began a program to maintain breeds of dogs that are afflicted with narcolepsy, in the hope that discovery of the causes of canine narcolepsy would further our understanding of the causes of human narcolepsy. (See ***Figure 8.4.***) This research has finally paid off. Lin et al. (1999) discovered that a mutation of a specific gene is responsible for canine narcolepsy.

sleep paralysis A symptom of narcolepsy; paralysis occurring just before a person falls asleep.

hypnagogic hallucination (*hip na* ***gah*** *jik*) A symptom of narcolepsy; vivid dreams that occur just before a person falls asleep; accompanied by sleep paralysis.

Figure 8.4

A dog undergoing a cataplectic attack triggered by its excitement at finding some food on the floor. (a) Sniffing the food. (b) Muscles beginning to relax. (c) The dog is temporarily paralyzed, as it would be during REM sleep.

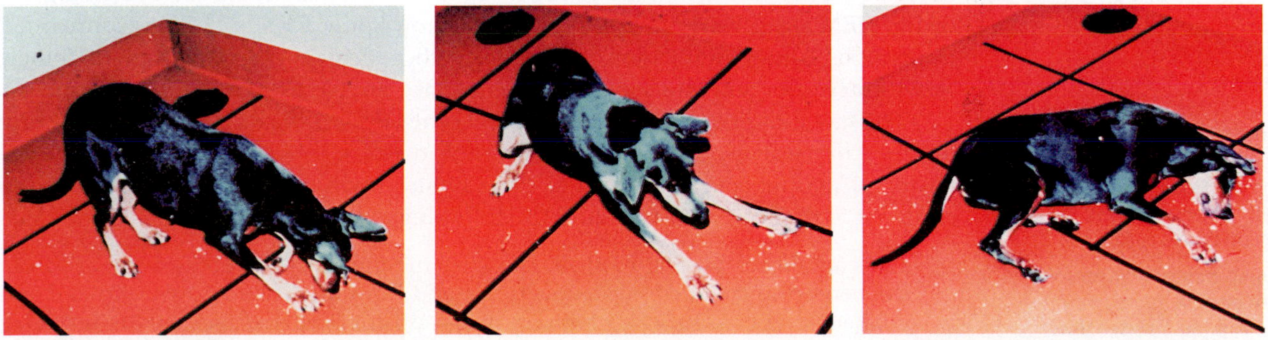

(a) (b) (c)

Photos courtesy of the Sleep Disorders Foundation, Stanford University.

The product of this gene is a receptor for a recently discovered peptide neurotransmitter called **hypocretin** (also known by some researchers as *orexin*). The name "hypocretin" comes from the fact that the lateral *hypo*thalamus contains the cell bodies of all of the neurons that se*crete* this peptide. The name "orexin" comes from the role this peptide plays in the control of eating and metabolism, which are discussed in Chapter 11. (*Orexis* means "appetite" in Greek.)

Chemelli et al. (1999) prepared a targeted mutation in mice against the hypocretin gene and found that the animals showed symptoms of narcolepsy. Like human patients with narcolepsy, they went directly into REM sleep from waking and showed periods of cataplexy while they were awake. (Videos of narcoleptic dogs, mice, and people are shown in ***Animation 8.1, Narcolepsy.***) Hara et al. (2001) created a strain of mice with a genetic mutation that caused the eventual death of hypocretinergic neurons. The mice were born with these neurons, but the neurons degenerated later in life, at which time the mice showed the symptoms of narcolepsy: behavioral arrests (cataplexy), early-onset REM sleep, and fragmented sleep.

Animation 8.1, Narcolepsy, contains videos of dogs, mice, and people undergoing attacks of cataplexy.

Abnormalities in the hypocretin system appear to be the cause of narcolepsy in humans as well (Nishino et al., 2000). The cause of narcolepsy appears to be a hereditary disorder that stimulates the immune system to attack and destroy hypocretin-secreting neurons. Most patients with narcolepsy are born with hypocretinergic neurons, but during adolescence the immune system attacks these neurons, and the symptoms of narcolepsy begin.

The symptoms of narcolepsy can be successfully treated with drugs. Sleep attacks can be diminished by stimulants such a methylphenidate (Ritalin), a catecholamine agonist (Vgontzas and Kales, 1999). The REM sleep phenomena (cataplexy, sleep paralysis, and hypnagogic hallucinations) can be alleviated by antidepressant drugs, which facilitate both serotonergic and noradrenergic activity (Mitler, 1994; Hublin, 1996). As we will see in Chapter 15, abnormalities in patterns of REM sleep are seen in people suffering from depression. The fact that drugs that reduce depression also suppress the phenomena of REM sleep is probably not coincidental.

More recently, modafinil, a stimulant drug whose precise site of action is still unknown, has been used to treat narcolepsy (Fry, 1998). (Michael, the man discussed in the chapter prologue, is now taking this drug.) A study by Scammell et al. (2000) suggests that modafinil acts, directly or indirectly, on hypocretinergic neurons. The investigators found that administration of modafinil increased the expression of Fos protein in hypocretinergic neurons, which indicates that the neurons had been activated.

The connections of hypocretinergic neurons with other regions of the brain is discussed later in this chapter.

REM Sleep Behavior Disorder

Several years ago, Schenck et al. (1986) reported the existence of an interesting disorder: **REM sleep behavior disorder.** As you now know, REM sleep is accompanied by paralysis. Although the motor cortex and subcortical motor systems are extremely active (McCarley and Hobson, 1979), people are unable to move at this time.

The fact that people are paralyzed while they dream suggests the possibility that but for the paralysis, they would act out their dreams. Indeed, they would. The behavior of people who exhibit REM sleep behavior disorder corresponds with the contents of their dreams. Consider the following case:

> I was a halfback playing football, and after the quarterback received the ball from the center he lateraled it sideways to me and I'm supposed to go around end and cut back over tackle and—this is very vivid—as I cut back over tackle there is this big 280-pound tackle waiting, so I, according to football rules, was to give him my shoulder and bounce him out of the way . . . when I came to I was standing in front of our dresser and I had [gotten up out of bed and run and] knocked lamps, mirrors and

hypocretin A peptide, also known as *orexin,* produced by neurons whose cell bodies are located in the hypothalamus; their destruction causes narcolepsy.

REM sleep behavior disorder (*ay **tone** ee a*) A neurological disorder in which the person does not become paralyzed during REM sleep and thus acts out dreams.

everything off the dresser, hit my head against the wall and my knee against the dresser. (Schenck et al., 1986, p. 294)

Like narcolepsy, REM sleep behavior disorder appears to be a neurodegenerative disorder with at least some genetic component (Schenck et al., 1996). It is often associated with better-known neurodegenerative disorders such as Parkinson's disease and multiple system atrophy (Boeve et al., 2001). The symptoms of REM sleep behavior disorder are the opposite of those of cataplexy; that is, rather than exhibiting paralysis outside REM sleep, patients with REM sleep behavior disorder *fail* to exhibit paralysis *during* REM sleep. As you might expect, the drugs that are used to treat the symptoms of cataplexy will aggravate the symptoms of REM sleep behavior disorder (Schenck and Mahowald, 1992). REM sleep behavior disorder is usually treated by clonazepam, a benzodiazepine (Schenck, Hurwitz, and Mahowald, 1993).

Problems Associated with Slow-Wave Sleep

Some maladaptive behaviors occur during slow-wave sleep, especially during its deepest phase, stage 4. These behaviors include bed-wetting (*nocturnal enuresis*), sleepwalking (*somnambulism*), and night terrors (*pavor nocturnus*). All three events occur most frequently in children. Often bed-wetting can be cured by training methods, such as having a special electronic circuit ring a bell when the first few drops of urine are detected in the bed sheet (a few drops usually precede the ensuing flood). Night terrors consist of anguished screams, trembling, a rapid pulse, and usually no memory of what caused the terror. Night terrors and somnambulism usually cure themselves as the child gets older. Neither of these phenomena is related to REM sleep; a sleepwalking person is *not* acting out a dream. Most authorities firmly advise that the best treatment for these two disorders is no treatment at all. There is no evidence that they are associated (at least in childhood) with mental disorders or personality variables.

INTERIM SUMMARY

Disorders of Sleep

Although many people believe that they have insomnia—that they do not obtain as much sleep as they would like—insomnia is not a disease. Insomnia can be caused by depression, pain, illness, or even excited anticipation of a pleasurable event. Far too many people receive sleeping medications, which often lead to a condition called drug dependency insomnia. Sometimes, insomnia is caused by sleep apnea, which can often be corrected surgically or treated by wearing a mask that delivers pressurized air.

Narcolepsy is characterized by four symptoms. *Sleep attacks* consist of overwhelming urges to sleep for a few minutes. *Cataplexy* is sudden paralysis, during which the person remains conscious. *Sleep paralysis* is similar to cataplexy, but it occurs just before sleep or on waking. *Hypnagogic hallucinations* are dreams that occur during periods of sleep paralysis, just before a night's sleep. Sleep attacks are treated with stimulants such as amphetamine, and the other symptoms are treated with serotonin agonists. Studies with narcoleptic dogs and humans indicate that this disorder is caused by pathologies in a system of neurons that secrete a neuropeptide known as hypocretin (also known as orexin). Another disorder associated with REM sleep, REM sleep behavior disorder, is a neurodegenerative disease that damages brain mechanisms that produce paralysis during REM sleep.

During slow-wave sleep, especially during stage 4, some people are afflicted by bed-wetting (nocturnal enuresis), sleepwalking (somnambulism), or night terrors (pavor nocturnus). These problems are most common in children, who usually outgrow them. Only if they occur in adults do they suggest the existence of a physical or psychological disorder.

THOUGHT QUESTION

Suppose you spent the night at a friend's house and, hearing a strange noise during the night, got out of bed and found your friend walking around, still asleep. How would you tell whether your friend was sleepwalking or had REM sleep behavior disorder?

Why Do We Sleep?

We all know how insistent the urge to sleep can be and how uncomfortable we feel when we have to resist it and stay awake. With the exception of the effects of severe pain and the need to breathe, sleepiness is probably the most insistent drive. People can commit suicide by refusing to eat or drink, but even the most stoical person cannot indefinitely defy the urge to sleep. Sleep will come, sooner or later, no matter how hard a person tries to stay awake. Although the issue is not yet settled, most researchers believe that the primary function of slow-wave sleep is to permit the brain to rest. REM sleep appears to promote brain development and learning, but how it might do so is not yet understood.

Functions of Slow-Wave Sleep

Sleep is a universal phenomenon among vertebrates. As far as we know, all mammals and birds sleep (Durie, 1981). Reptiles also sleep, and fish and amphibians enter periods of quiescence that probably can be called sleep. However, only warm-blooded vertebrates (mammals and birds) exhibit unequivocal REM sleep, with muscular paralysis, EEG signs of desynchrony, and rapid eye movements.

Sleep appears to be essential to survival. Evidence for this assertion comes from the fact that sleep is found in some species of mammals that would seem to be better off without it. For example, the Indus dolphin (*Platanista indi*) lives in the muddy waters of the Indus estuary in Pakistan (Pilleri, 1979). Over evolutionary time, it has become blind, presumably because vision is not useful in the animal's environment. (It has an excellent sonar system, which it uses to navigate and find prey.) However, despite the dangers caused by sleeping, sleep has not disappeared in this species. The Indus dolphin never stops swimming; doing so would result in injury, because of the dangerous currents and the vast quantities of debris carried by the river during the monsoon season. Pilleri captured two of the dolphins and studied their habits. He found that they slept a total of 7 hours a day, in brief naps of 4–60 seconds each. If sleep were simply an adaptive response, why was it not eliminated (as vision was) through the process of natural selection?

The two cerebral hemispheres of some species of porpoises take turns sleeping—although probably not when the animals are as active as the one shown here.

Some other species of marine mammals have developed an extraordinary pattern of sleep: The cerebral hemispheres take turns sleeping, presumably because that strategy always permits at least one hemisphere to be alert. The bottlenose dolphin (*Tursiops truncatus*) and the porpoise (*Phocoena phocoena*) both sleep this way (Mukhametov, 1984). Figure 8.5 shows the EEG recordings from the two hemispheres; note that slow-wave sleep occurs independently in the left and right hemispheres. (See ***Figure 8.5.***)

Effects of Sleep Deprivation

When we are forced to miss a night's sleep, we become very sleepy. The fact that sleepiness is so motivating suggests that sleep is a necessity of life. If so, it should be possible to deprive people of sleep and see what functions are disrupted. We should then be able to infer the role that sleep plays. The results of sleep deprivation studies suggest that the restorative effects sleep are more important for the brain than for the rest of the body.

Sleep deprivation studies with human subjects have provided little evidence that sleep is needed to keep the body functioning normally. Horne (1978) reviewed over fifty experiments in which people had been deprived of sleep. He reported that most of them found that sleep deprivation did not interfere with people's ability to perform physical exercise. In addition, the studies found no evidence of a physiological stress response to sleep deprivation. Thus, the primary role of sleep does not seem to be rest and recuperation of the body. However, people's cognitive abilities were affected; some people reported perceptual distortions or even hallucinations and had trouble concentrating on mental tasks. Perhaps sleep provides the opportunity for the brain to rest.

Figure 8.5

Sleep in a dolphin. The two hemispheres sleep independently, presumably so that the animal remains behaviorally alert.

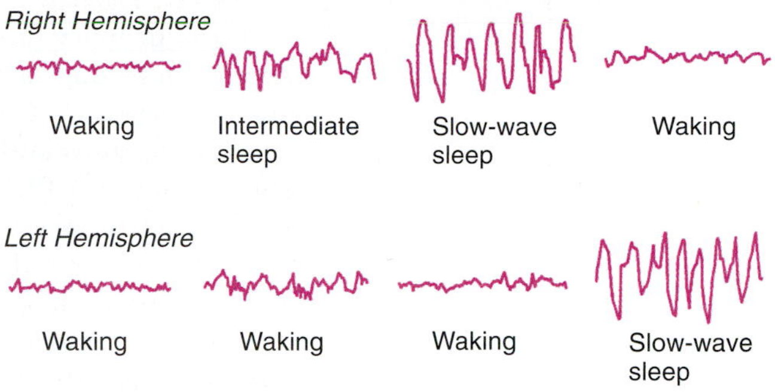

Adapted from Mukhametov, L. M., in *Sleep Mechanisms,* edited by A. A. Borbély and J. L. Valatx. Munich: Springer-Verlag, 1984.

During slow-wave sleep, both cerebral metabolic rate and cerebral blood flow decline, falling to about 75 percent of the waking level during stage 4 sleep (Sakai et al., 1979; Buchsbaum et al., 1989; Maquet, 1995). In particular, the regions that have the highest levels of activity during waking show the highest levels of delta waves—and the lowest levels of activity—during slow-wave sleep. Thus, the presence of delta activity in a particular region of the brain appears to indicate that that region is resting. As we know from behavioral observation, people are unreactive to all but intense stimuli during slow-wave sleep and, if awakened, act groggy and confused, as if their cerebral cortex has been shut down and has not yet resumed its functioning. These observations suggest that during stage 4 sleep the brain is indeed resting.

An inherited neurological disorder called **fatal familial insomnia** results in damage to portions of the thalamus (Sforza et al., 1995; Gallassi et al., 1996). The symptoms of this disease include deficits in attention and memory, followed by a dreamlike, confused state; loss of control of the autonomic nervous system and the endocrine system; and insomnia. The first signs of sleep disturbances are reductions in sleep spindles and K complexes. As the disease progresses, slow-wave sleep completely disappears, and only brief episodes of REM sleep (without the accompanying paralysis) remain. As the name indicates, the disease is fatal. Whether the insomnia, caused by the brain damage, contributes to the other symptoms and to the patient's death is not known.

Effects of Exercise on Sleep

Sleep deprivation studies with humans suggest that the brain may need slow-wave sleep to recover from the day's activities but that the rest of the body does not. Another way to determine whether sleep is needed for restoration of physiological functioning is to look at the effects of daytime activity on nighttime sleep. If the function of sleep is to repair the effects of activity during waking hours, then we should expect that sleep and exercise are related. That is, we should sleep more after a day of vigorous exercise than after a day spent quietly at an office desk.

However, the relationship between sleep and exercise is not very compelling. For example, Ryback and Lewis (1971) found no changes in slow-wave or REM sleep of healthy subjects who spent six weeks resting in bed. If sleep repairs wear and tear, we would expect these people to sleep less. Adey, Bors, and Porter (1968) studied the sleep of *completely* immobile quadriplegics and paraplegics and found only a small decrease in slow-wave sleep as compared with uninjured people. Thus, although

fatal familial insomnia A fatal inherited disorder characterized by progressive insomnia.

sleep certainly provides the body with rest, its primary function appears to be something else.

Effects of Mental Activity on Sleep

If the primary function of slow-wave sleep is to permit the brain to rest and recover from its daily activity, then we might expect that a person would spend more time in slow-wave sleep after a day of intense cerebral activity. First of all, tasks that demand alertness and mental activity *do* increase glucose metabolism in the brain, as measured by a PET scanner (Roland, 1984). The most significant increases are seen in the frontal lobes, where delta activity is most intense during slow-wave sleep. In an experiment that supports this interpretation, Kattler, Dijk, and Borbély (1994) stimulated a person's hand with a vibrator, which activated the contralateral somatosensory cortex. The next night, a recording of the subject's EEG showed more delta activity in that region of the brain. Presumably, the increased activity of the cortical neurons called for more rest during the following night's sleep.

In an ingenious study Horne and Minard (1985) found a way to increase mental activity without affecting physical activity and without causing stress. The investigators told subjects to show up for an experiment in which they were supposed to take some tests designed to measure reading skills. When the subjects turned up, however, they were told that the plans had been changed. They were invited for a day out, at the expense of the experimenters. (Not surprisingly, the subjects willingly accepted.) They spent the day visiting an art exhibition, a shopping center, a museum, an amusement park, a zoo, and an interesting mansion. After a scenic drive through the countryside they watched a movie in a local theater. They were driven from place to place and certainly did not become overheated by exercise. After the movie they returned to the sleep laboratory. They said they were tired, and they readily fell asleep. Their sleep duration was normal, and they awoke feeling refreshed. However, their slow-wave sleep—particularly stage 4 sleep—was increased. After all that mental exercise, the brain appears to have needed more rest than usual.

Functions of REM Sleep

Clearly, REM sleep is a time of intense physiological activity. The eyes dart about rapidly, the heart rate shows sudden accelerations and decelerations, breathing becomes irregular, and the brain becomes more active. It would be unreasonable to expect that REM sleep has the same functions as slow-wave sleep. An early report on the effects of REM sleep deprivation (Dement, 1960) observed that as the deprivation progressed, subjects had to be awakened from REM sleep more frequently; the "pressure" to enter REM sleep built up. Furthermore, after several days of REM sleep deprivation, subjects would show a **rebound phenomenon** when permitted to sleep normally; they spent a much greater-than-normal percentage of the recovery night in REM sleep. This rebound suggests that there is a need for a certain amount of REM sleep—that REM sleep is controlled by a regulatory mechanism. If selective deprivation causes a deficiency in REM sleep, the deficiency is made up later, when uninterrupted sleep is permitted.

Researchers have long been struck by the fact that the highest proportion of REM sleep is seen during the most active phase of brain development. Perhaps, then, REM sleep plays a role in this process (Roffwarg, Muzio, and Dement, 1966). The association could go either way; brain development could cause REM sleep (perhaps to tidy up after spurts of neural growth), or REM sleep could be setting the stage for brain growth to occur. The developmental hypothesis is supported by the fact that infant animals born with well-developed brains (such as guinea pigs) spend proportionally less time in REM sleep than do infant animals born with less-developed

rebound phenomenon The increased frequency or intensity of a phenomenon after it has been temporarily suppressed; for example, the increase in REM sleep seen after a period of REM sleep deprivation.

brains (such as rats, cats, or humans). Studies of human fetuses and infants born prematurely indicate that REM sleep begins to appear 30 weeks after conception and peaks at around 40 weeks (Roffwarg, Muzio, and Dement, 1966; Petre-Quadens and De Lee, 1974; Inoue et al., 1986). Approximately 70 percent of a newborn infant's sleep is REM sleep. By six months of age this proportion has declined to approximately 30 percent. By eight years of age it has fallen to approximately 22 percent, and by late adulthood it is less than 15 percent.

But if the function of REM sleep is to promote brain development, why do adults have REM sleep? One possibility is that REM sleep facilitates the massive changes in the brain that occur during development but also the more modest changes responsible for learning that occur later in life. Some investigators have suggested that memories of events of the previous day—especially those dealing with emotionally related information—are consolidated and integrated with existing memories (Greenberg and Pearlman, 1974); others have suggested that this time is utilized to accomplish the opposite function: to flush useless information from memory, to prevent the storage of useless clutter (Crick and Mitchison, 1983, 1995).

Studies with laboratory animals suggest that REM sleep does indeed perform functions that facilitate learning. Investigators have carried out two types of experiments. In the first they train animals in a learning task and then deprive them of REM sleep for a period of time. If REM sleep facilitates learning—perhaps by promoting changes in the brain that store the information just acquired—then animals that are deprived of the opportunity to engage in REM sleep after the training session should not learn as well as control subjects. In the second type of experiment, investigators train animals in a learning task and then monitor their sleep for several hours. An increase in REM sleep suggests that learning increases the need for this stage of sleep.

Experiments of both types have obtained positive results. For example, when animals are deprived of REM sleep after participating in a training session, they learn the task more slowly; thus, REM sleep deprivation retards memory formation (Smith, 1996). In an example of the second type of experiment, Bloch, Hennevin, and Leconte (1977) gave rats daily training trials in a complex maze. They found that the experience enhanced subsequent REM sleep. Moreover, daily performance was related to subsequent REM sleep. The lower curve in Figure 8.6 shows REM sleep as a percentage of total sleep. The upper curve illustrates the animals' performance in the maze. You can see that the largest increase in running speed (possibly representing the largest increase in learning) was accompanied by the largest amount of REM sleep. Also note that once the task was well learned (after day 6), REM sleep declined to baseline levels. (See ***Figure 8.6.***)

Studies with human subjects have found that REM sleep deprivation has only a small effect on a person's ability to learn or to remember what was previously learned. But several studies have found that learning can affect the amount of REM sleep a person obtains. For example, several studies found that retarded children engaged in less REM sleep than normal children and that intellectually gifted children engaged in more (Dujardin, Guerrien, and Leconte, 1990). In addition, Smith and Lapp (1991) found that REM sleep of college students increased during exam time, when they presumably were spending more time learning new information.

Figure 8.6

Percentage of sleep time spent in REM sleep (*lower curve*) as a function of maze-learning performance (*upper curve*).

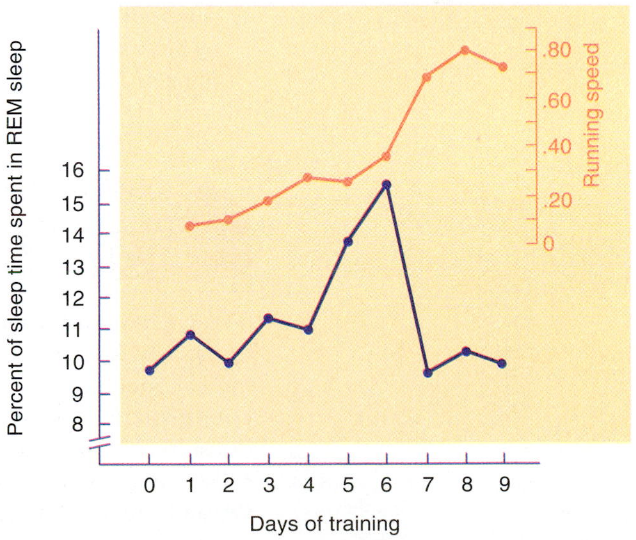

From Bloch, V., Hennevin, E., and Leconte, P., in *Neurobiology of Sleep and Memory,* edited by R. R. Drucker-Colín and J. L. McGaugh. New York: Academic Press, 1978.

INTERIM SUMMARY

Why Do We Sleep?

Sleep appears to provide a period of rest for the brain. The fact that all vertebrates sleep, including some that would seem to be better off without it, suggests that sleep is an essential phenomenon. In humans the effects of several days of sleep deprivation include perceptual distortions and (sometimes) mild hallucinations and difficulty performing tasks that require prolonged concentration. These effects suggest that sleep deprivation impairs cerebral functioning. Deep slow-wave sleep appears to be the most important stage, and perhaps its function is to permit the brain to recuperate. Fatal familial insomnia is an inherited disease that results in degeneration of parts of the thalamus, deficits in attention and memory, a dreamlike state, loss of control of the autonomic nervous system and the endocrine system, insomnia, and death.

The primary function of sleep does not seem to be to provide an opportunity for the body to repair the wear and tear that occurs during waking hours. Changes in a person's level of exercise do not significantly alter the amount of sleep the person needs the following night. Instead, the most important function of slow-wave sleep seem to be to lower the brain's metabolism and permit it to rest. In support of this hypothesis, research has shown that slow-wave sleep does indeed reduce the brain's metabolic rate and that increased mental activity (the surprise treat experiment) can cause an increase in slow-wave sleep the next night.

The functions of REM sleep are less understood than those of slow-wave sleep. REM sleep may promote brain development and learning. So far, the evidence is inconclusive, although several studies have shown a moderate relationship between REM sleep and learning.

THOUGHT QUESTIONS

The evidence presented in this section suggests that the primary function of sleep is to permit the brain to rest. But could sleep also have some other functions? For example, could sleep serve as an adaptive response, keeping animals out of harm's way *as well as* provide some cerebral repose? Sleep researcher William Dement pointed out that one of the functions of the lungs is communication. Obviously, the *primary* function of our lungs is to provide oxygen and rid the body of carbon dioxide, and this function explains the evolution of the respiratory system. But we can also use our lungs to vibrate our vocal cords and provide sounds used to talk, so they play a role in communication, too. Other functions of our lungs are to warm our cold hands (by breathing on them), to kindle fires by blowing on hot coals, or to blow out candles. With this perspective in mind, can you think of some other useful functions of sleep?

Physiological Mechanisms of Sleep and Waking

So far, I have discussed the nature of sleep, problems associated with it, and its functions. Now it is time to examine what researchers have discovered about the physiological mechanisms that are responsible for the behavior of sleep and for its counterpart, alert wakefulness. But before doing so, I must emphasize that sleep does not occur simply because neurons get tired and begin to fire more slowly. Like other behaviors, sleep occurs when a particular neural circuit becomes *active.* Activation of this circuit puts us to sleep.

Chemical Control of Sleep

As we have seen, sleep is *regulated;* that is, if an organism is deprived of slow-wave sleep or REM sleep, the organism will make up at least part of the missed sleep when permitted to do so. In addition, the amount of slow-wave sleep that a person obtains during a daytime nap is deducted from the amount of slow-wave sleep he or she obtains the next night (Karacan et al., 1970). These facts suggest that some physiological mechanism monitors the amount of sleep that an organism receives. What might this mechanism be? Perhaps prolonged wakefulness produces a *sleep-promoting substances* or sleep produces a *wakefulness-promoting* substances.

Where might these substances be located? They do not appear to be found in the general circulation of the body. As we saw earlier, the cerebral hemispheres of the bottlenose dolphin sleep at different times (Mukhametov, 1984). If sleep were controlled by chemicals carried in the blood, the hemispheres should sleep at the same time. This observation suggests that if sleep is controlled by chemicals, these chemicals are produced within the brain and act there. In support of this suggestion, Oleksenko et al. (1992) obtained evidence that indicates that each hemisphere of the brain incurs its own sleep debt. The researchers deprived a bottlenose dolphin of sleep in only one hemisphere. When they allowed the animal to sleep normally, they saw a rebound of slow-wave sleep only in the deprived hemisphere.

Benington, Kodali, and Heller (1995) suggested that a nucleoside neurotransmitter, *adenosine,* might play a primary role in the control of sleep. The primary nutrient of the brain is glucose, carried to the brain by the blood. The blood supply usually delivers an adequate amount of glucose, but if some regions of the brain become especially active, the cells located there consume the glucose faster than it can be supplied. In such cases extra nutrients are supplied by astrocytes (Swanson, 1992; Swanson and Choi, 1993). Astrocytes maintain a small stock of nutrients in the form of glycogen, an insoluble carbohydrate that is also stocked by the liver and the muscles. The metabolism of glycogen causes an increase in the levels of **adenosine,** a neuromodulator that has inhibitory effects. Benington and his colleagues suggested that this accumulation of adenosine increases the amount of delta activity during the next night's sleep. The cells in that region rest, and the astrocytes renew their stock of glycogen. In support of this hypothesis, the investigators found that when they administered a drug that stimulates adenosine receptors, they saw increases in delta activity during the animals' slow-wave sleep. And as we saw in Chapter 4, caffeine blocks adenosine receptors. (I don't have to tell you the effect that caffeine has on sleepiness.)

More recent evidence supports the hypothesis that adenosine plays a role in regulating sleep and suggests that it acts on particular neural mechanisms involved in sleep and waking. The adenosine hypothesis is discussed later in this chapter, in a section on the neural control of sleep.

Neural Control of Arousal

As we have seen, sleep is not a uniform condition but consists of several different stages with very different characteristics. The waking state, too, is nonuniform; sometimes we are alert and attentive, and sometimes we fail to notice much about what is happening around us. Of course, sleepiness has an effect on wakefulness; if we are fighting to stay awake, the struggle might impair our ability to concentrate on other things. But everyday observations suggest that even when we are not sleepy, our alertness can vary. For example, when we observe something very interesting (or frightening or simply surprising), we feel ourselves become more alert and aware of our surroundings.

Circuits of neurons that secrete at least five different neurotransmitters play a role in some aspect of an animal's level of alertness and wakefulness—what is commonly called arousal: acetylcholine, norepinephrine, serotonin, histamine, and hypocretin (Wada et al., 1991; McCormick, 1992; Marrocco, Witte, and Davidson, 1994; Hungs and Mignot, 2001).

Acetylcholine

One of the most important neurotransmitters involved in arousal—especially of the cerebral cortex—is acetylcholine. Two groups of acetylcholinergic neurons, one

adenosine A chemical produced when increased neural activity requires the breakdown of glycogen stored in astrocytes; may increase delta activity during the next night's sleep and thus enable the region to recover from its energy expenditure.

locus coeruleus (*sa* ***roo*** *lee us*) A dark-colored group of noradrenergic cell bodies located in the pons near the rostral end of the floor of the fourth ventricle; involved in arousal and vigilance.

raphe nuclei (*ruh* ***fay***) A group of nuclei located in the reticular formation of the medulla, pons, and midbrain, situated along the midline; contain serotonergic neurons.

in the pons and one located in the basal forebrain, produce activation and cortical desynchrony when they are stimulated (Jones, 1990; Steriade, 1996).

Researchers have long known that acetylcholinergic antagonists decrease EEG signs of cortical arousal and that acetylcholinergic agonists increase them (Vanderwolf, 1992). Day, Damsma, and Fibiger (1991) used microdialysis probes to measure the release of acetylcholine in the striatum, hippocampus, and frontal cortex—three regions whose activity is closely related to an animal's alertness and behavioral arousal. They found that levels of ACh in these regions were highest when the animals were active and lowest when they were inactive. In addition, Rasmusson, Clow, and Szerb (1994) found that electrical stimulation of a region of the dorsal pons activated the cerebral cortex and increased the release of acetylcholine there by 350 percent. A group of acetylcholinergic neurons located in the basal forebrain forms an essential part of the pathway that is responsible for this effect. The investigators found that if these neurons were deactivated by infusing a local anesthetic or drugs that blocked synaptic transmission, the activating effects of the pontine stimulation were abolished.

Norepinephrine

Investigators have long known that catecholamine agonists such as amphetamine produce arousal and sleeplessness. These effects appear to be mediated primarily by the noradrenergic system of the **locus coeruleus,** located in the dorsal pons. Neurons of the locus coeruleus give rise to axons that branch widely, releasing norepinephrine (from axonal varicosities) throughout the neocortex, hippocampus, thalamus, cerebellar cortex, pons, and medulla; thus, they potentially affect widespread and important regions of the brain. (See ***Figure 8.7.***)

Figure 8.7

A section through the pons of a rat, showing the location of the locus coeruleus, which contains the cell bodies of most of the brain's noradrenergic neurons. Also shown are some structures that play a role in REM sleep, which is discussed later.

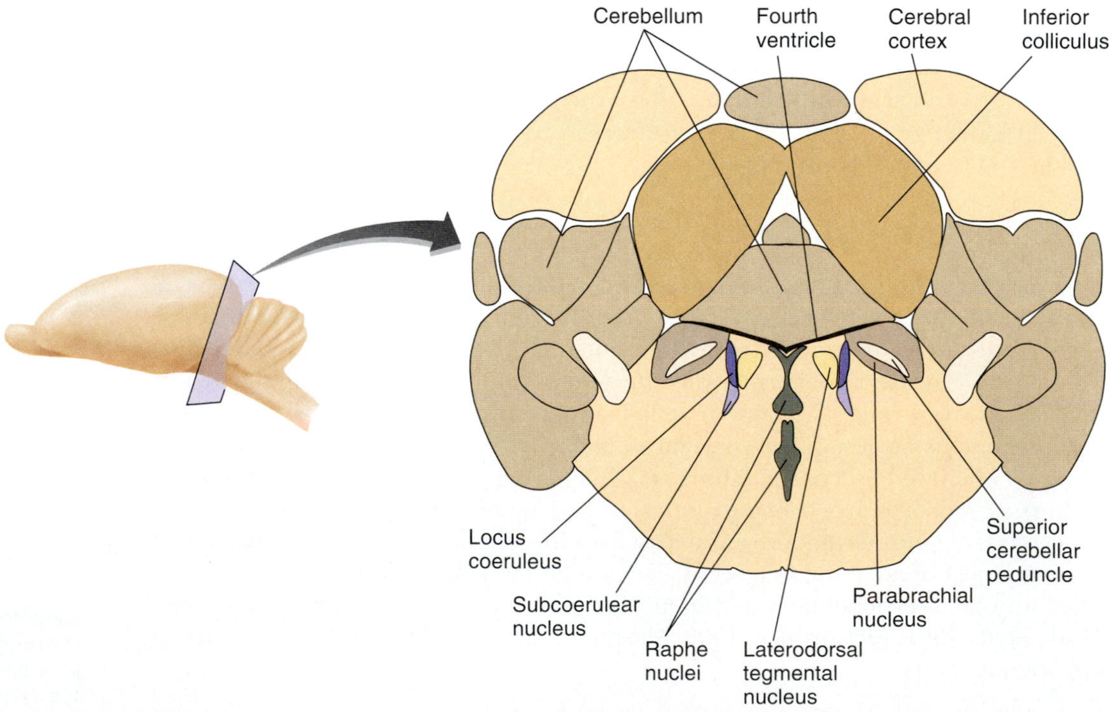

Adapted from Paxinos, G., and Watson, C. *The Rat Brain in Stereotaxic Coordinates.* Sydney: Academic Press, 1982. Redrawn with permission.

Figure 8.8

Activity of noradrenergic neurons in the locus coeruleus of freely moving rats during various stages of sleep and waking.

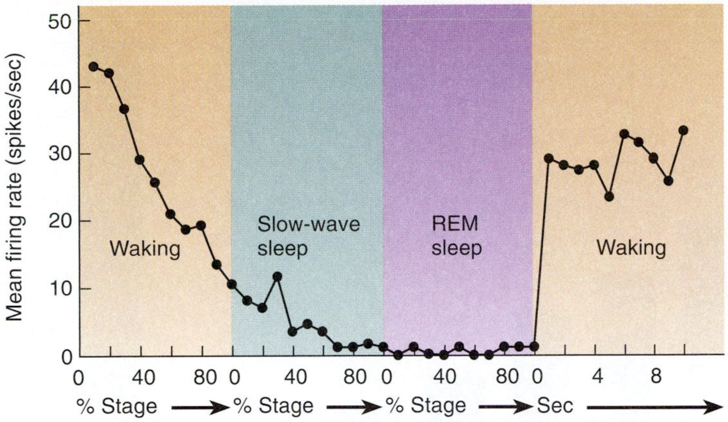

From Aston-Jones, G., and Bloom, F. E. *The Journal of Neuroscience,* 1981, *1,* 876–886. Copyright 1981 by The Society for Neuroscience.

Aston-Jones and Bloom (1981a) recorded from noradrenergic neurons of the locus coeruleus (LC) across the sleep-waking cycle in unrestrained rats. As Figure 8.8 shows, these neurons exhibited a close relationship to behavioral arousal. Note the decline in firing rate before and during sleep and the abrupt increase when the animal wakes. The rate of firing of neurons in the locus coeruleus falls almost to zero during REM sleep and increases dramatically when the animal wakes. As we shall see later in this chapter, these facts suggest that these neurons (along with serotonergic neurons) play a role in controlling REM sleep. (See ***Figure 8.8.***) Most investigators believe that activity of noradrenergic LC neurons increases an animal's vigilance—its ability to pay attention to stimuli in the environment. In fact, a study by Aston-Jones et al. (1994) found that the moment-to-moment activity of noradrenergic LC neurons was directly related to the animals' current performance on a task that required vigilance.

Serotonin

A third neurotransmitter, serotonin (5-HT), also appears to play a role in activating behavior. Almost all of the brain's serotonergic neurons are found in the **raphe nuclei,** which are located in the medullary and pontine regions of the reticular formation. (See ***Figure 8.9.***) The axons of these neurons project to many parts of the brain, including the thalamus, hypothalamus, basal ganglia, hippocampus, and neocortex. Stimulation of the raphe nuclei causes locomotion and cortical arousal (as measured by the EEG), whereas PCPA, a drug that prevents the synthesis of serotonin, reduces cortical arousal (Peck and Vanderwolf, 1991).

Figure 8.10 shows the activity of serotonergic neurons, recorded by Trulson and Jacobs (1979). As you can see, these neurons, like the noradrenergic neurons studied by Aston-Jones and Bloom (1981a), were most active during waking. Their firing rate declined during slow-wave sleep

Figure 8.9

The raphe nuclei, the location of the cell bodies of most of the brain's serotonergic neurons.

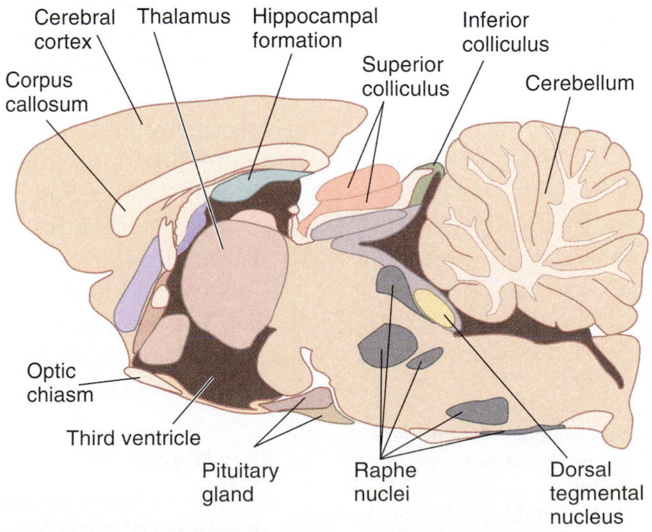

Adapted from Paxinos, G., and Watson, C. *The Rat Brain in Stereotaxic Coordinates.* Sydney: Academic Press, 1982. Redrawn with permission.

Figure 8.10

Activity of serotonergic (5-HT-secreting) neurons in the dorsal raphe nuclei of freely moving cats during various stages of sleep and waking.

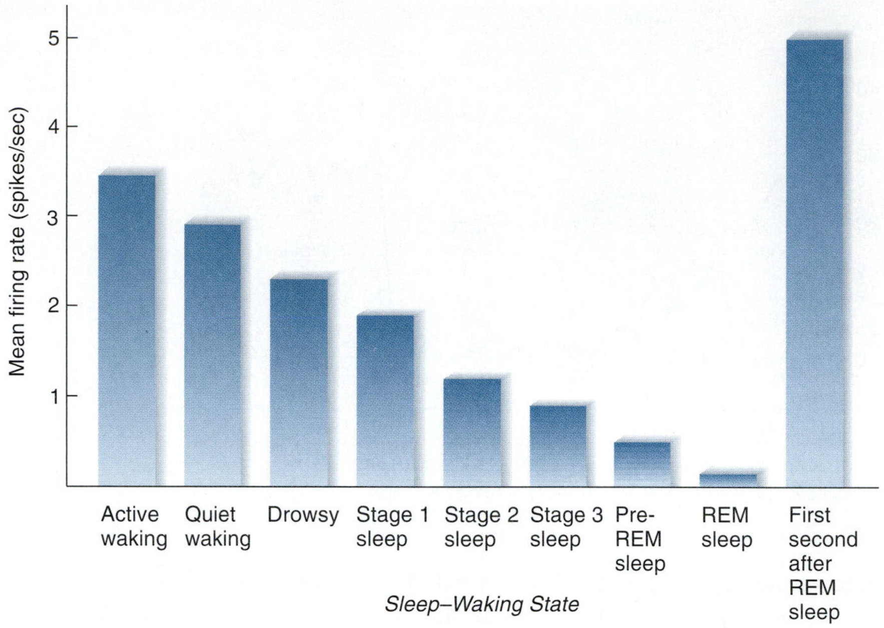

Adapted from Trulson, M. E., and Jacobs, B. L. *Brain Research,* 1979, *163,* 135–150. Redrawn with permission.

and became virtually zero during REM sleep. However, once the period of REM sleep ended, the activity of the neurons immediately increased. (See ***Figure 8.10.***)

Histamine

The fourth neurotransmitter implicated in the control of wakefulness and arousal is histamine, a compound synthesized from histidine, an amino acid. The cell bodies of histaminergic neurons are located in the **tuberomammillary nucleus** of the hypothalamus, located at the base of the brain just rostral to the mammillary bodies. The axons of these neurons project primarily to the cerebral cortex, thalamus, basal ganglia, basal forebrain, and hypothalamus. The projections to the cerebral cortex directly increase cortical activation and arousal, and projections to acetylcholinergic neurons of the basal forebrain and dorsal pons do so indirectly, by increasing the release of acetylcholine in the cerebral cortex (Khateb et al., 1995; Brown, Stevens, and Haas, 2001). Injections of drugs that prevent the synthesis of histamine or block histamine H_1 receptors decrease waking and increase sleep (Lin, Sakai, and Jouvet, 1988). Also, the activity of histaminergic neurons is high during waking but low during slow-wave sleep and REM sleep (Steininger et al., 1996).

You are undoubtedly aware that some antihistamines, used to treat allergies, can cause drowsiness. They do so by blocking histamine H_1 receptors. More modern antihistamines cannot cross the blood–brain barrier, so they do not cause drowsiness.

tuberomammillary nucleus A nucleus in the ventral posterior hypothalamus, just rostral to the mammillary bodies; contains histaminergic neurons involved in cortical activation and behavioral arousal.

Hypocretin

As we saw in the section on sleep disorders, recent investigations discovered that the cause of narcolepsy is degeneration of hypocretinergic neurons in humans and a hereditary absence of hypocretin-2 receptors in dogs. The cell bodies of neurons that secrete hypocretin (as we saw, also called orexin) are located in the lateral hypothalamus. The axons of these neurons terminate in several regions involved in arousal, including the locus coeruleus, raphe nuclei, tuberomammillary nucleus, acetylcholinergic neurons in the dorsal pons and basal forebrain, and cerebral cortex (Saper, Chou, and Scammell, 2001). Hypocretin has an excitatory, wakefulness-promoting effect in all of these regions.

Estabrooke et al. (2001) found that hypocretinergic neurons are active (as measured by production of Fos protein) during wakefulness and inactive during sleep. High levels of hypocretinergic activity were seen during spontaneous wakefulness or through wakefulness caused by tapping on the rats' cages while they were asleep.

Neural Control of Slow-Wave Sleep

Although sleep is a behavior that involves most of the brain, one region seems to play a particularly important role in putting us to sleep: the **ventrolateral preoptic area (VLPA)**. The preoptic area is located just rostral to the hypothalamus. Studies with rats (Nauta, 1946) and cats (McGinty and Sterman, 1968) found that destruction of the preoptic area caused insomnia, followed by coma and death. Sterman and Clemente (1962a, 1962b) found that electrical stimulation of this region produced opposite effects: drowsiness, EEG desynchrony, and, in many cases, sleep.

Several recording studies confirm these findings. For example, Sherin et al. (1996) found increased levels of Fos protein during sleep in a cluster of neurons in the ventrolateral preoptic area. Lu et al. (2000) found that excitotoxic lesions of this cluster of neurons suppressed sleep. Szymusiak et al. (1998) found that the activity of single neurons in the VLPA increased during sleep. When the animals were kept awake for 12–14 hours and were then allowed to sleep, neurons in the VLPA showed an especially high rate of firing, as if the drive to sleep were particularly intense.

Anatomical and histochemical studies indicate that the VLPA contains inhibitory GABA-secreting neurons and that these neurons send their axons to the tuberomammillary nucleus, dorsal pons, raphe nuclei, and locus coeruleus (Sherin et al., 1998). As we saw in the previous section, activity of neurons in these brain regions causes cortical activation and behavioral arousal. The fact that stimulation of the VLPA inhibits these regions is consistent with other evidence indicating that activation of the VLPA induces sleep.

The VLPA receives inhibitory inputs from many of the same regions it inhibits, including the tuberomammillary nucleus, raphe nuclei, and locus coeruleus (Chou et al., 2002). As Saper et al. (2001) suggest, this mutual inhibition may provide the basis for establishing periods of sleep and waking. They note that reciprocal inhibition also characterizes an electronic circuit known as a *flip-flop*. A flip-flop can assume one of two states, usually referred to as on or off—or 0 or 1 in computer applications. Thus, either the VLPA is active and inhibits the wakefulness-promoting regions or the wakefulness-promoting regions are active and inhibit the VLPA. Because these regions are mutually inhibitory, it is impossible for neurons in both sets of regions to be active at the same time. (See ***Figure 8.11.***)

A flip-flop has an important advantage: When it switches from one state to another, it does so quickly. Clearly, it is most advantageous to be either asleep or awake; a state that has some of the characteristics of both sleep and wakefulness would be maladaptive. However, there is one problem with flip-flops: They can be unstable, switching on and off spontaneously. In fact, people with narcolepsy and animals with damage to the hypocretinergic system of neurons exhibit just this characteristic. They have great difficulty remaining awake when nothing interesting is happening, and they have trouble remaining asleep for an extended amount of time.

Saper et al. (2001) suggest that an important function of hypocretinergic neurons is to help stabilize the "flip-flop." Activity of this system of neurons promotes wakefulness and inhibits sleep. As far as we know, hypocretinergic neurons do not receive inhibitory input from either side of the "flip-flop," so activation of either side

ventrolateral preoptic area (VLPA) A group of GABAergic neurons in the preoptic area whose activity suppresses alertness and behavioral arousal and promotes sleep.

Figure 8.11

A schematic diagram of the sleep/waking flip-flop proposed by Saper et al. (2001). The major sleep-promoting region (the VLPA) and the major wakefulness-promoting regions (the basal forebrain and peribrachial regions, which contain acetylcholinergic neurons; the locus coeruleus, which contains noradrenergic neurons; the raphe nuclei, which contain serotonergic neurons; and the tuberomammillary nucleus of the hypothalamus, which contains histaminergic neurons) are reciprocally connected by inhibitory GABAergic neurons. When the flip-flop is "on," the arousal systems are active and the VLPA is inhibited, and the animal is awake. When the flip-flop is "off," the VLPA is active and the arousal systems are inhibited, and the animal is asleep.

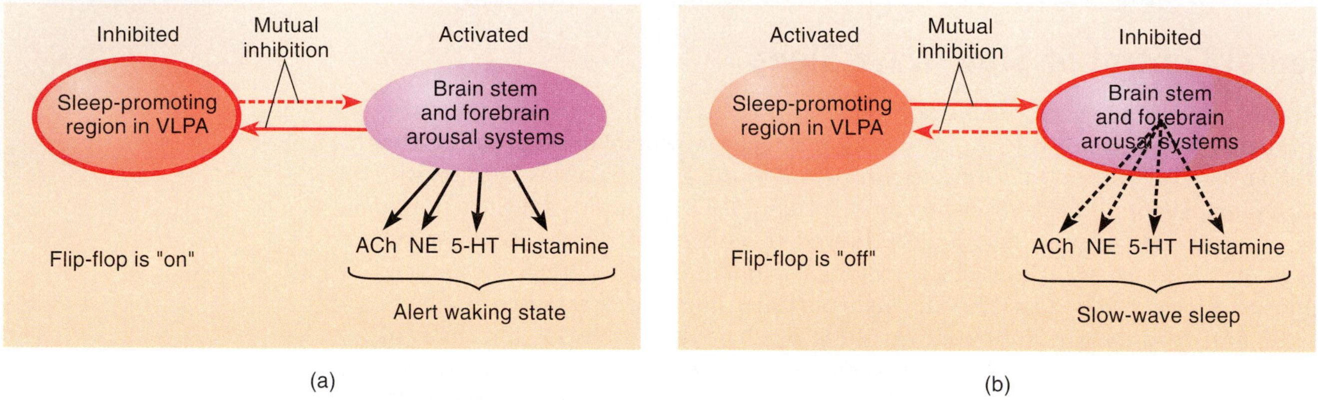

does not affect them. As we saw in the previous subsection, Estabrooke et al. (2001) found that enforced wakefulness increased the activity of hypocretinergic neurons. Perhaps, then, events that keep an animal awake do so by activating these neurons. Perhaps your success at staying awake during a boring lecture depends on maintaining a high rate of firing of your hypocretinergic neurons. This event would keep the flip-flop in the on (waking) state. Because we know very little about the inputs to hypocretinergic neurons, we cannot yet say how we manage to control the firing of these neurons. (See ***Figure 8.12.***)

PGO wave Bursts of phasic electrical activity originating in the pons, followed by activity in the lateral geniculate nucleus and visual cortex; a characteristic of REM sleep.

As we saw earlier in this chapter, adenosine is produced when neurons become especially active, and accumulated adenosine may be at least one of the chemicals that stimulates drowsiness and sleep. Porkka-Heiskanen, Strecker, and McCarley (2000) found that levels of adenosine in the brain increased during wakefulness and slowly decreased during sleep, especially in the region of the basal forebrain that contains acetylcholinergic neurons.

As we just saw, the VLPA appears to be a critical brain region in the production of sleep. Thus, if the accumulation of adenosine is one of the factors that makes us sleepy, we would expect this chemical to activate the VLPA. As far as we know, the activation of adenosine receptors has an inhibitory effect, which means that any excitatory action this chemical has on the VLPA must be indirect. Scammell et al. (2001) found that an infusion of an adenosine agonist in the subarachnoid space adjacent to the VLPA activated neurons there (as measured by levels of Fos protein), decreased the activity of histaminergic neurons of the tuberomammillary nucleus, and increased slow-wave sleep. The investigators suggested that adenosine might increase sleep by inhibiting neurons that normally inhibit VLPA neurons. The release from inhibition would activate these neurons. (See ***Figure 8.13.***)

Figure 8.12

A schematic diagram of the effect of activation of the hypocretinergic system of neurons of the lateral hypothalamus on the sleep/waking flip-flop. Motivation to remain awake or events that disturb sleep activate the hypocretinergic neurons.

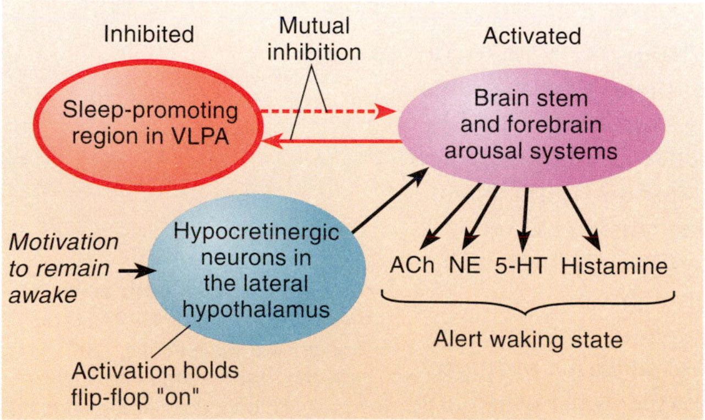

A study by Thakkar, Winston, and McCarley (2002) suggests another possibility. These investigators found that hypocretinergic neurons in the lateral hypothalamus contain adenosine A1 receptors. They suggest that the inhibition of these neurons caused by the accumulation of adenosine during wakefulness may also be one of the signals that promotes sleep.

Figure 8.13

Possible role of adenosine in sleep and waking. Prolonged neural activity causes adenosine to accumulate, which disinhibits the sleep-promoting neurons of the VLPA.

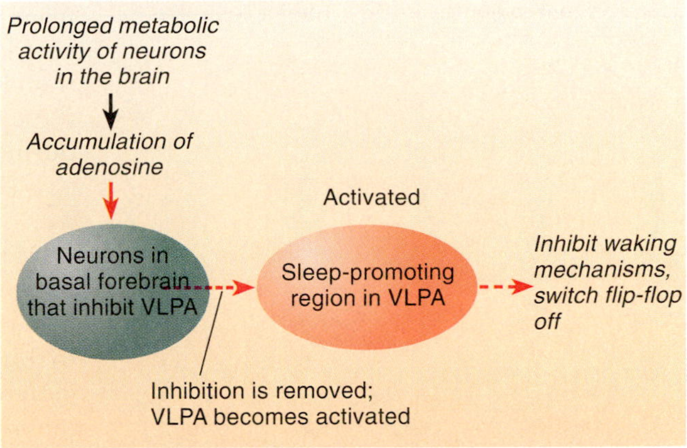

Neural Control of REM Sleep

As we saw earlier in this chapter, REM sleep consists of desynchronized EEG activity, muscular paralysis, rapid eye movements, and (in humans, at least) increased genital activity. The rate of cerebral metabolism is as high as it is during waking (Maquet et al., 1990), and were it not for the state of paralysis, the level of *physical* activity would also be high. In laboratory animals REM sleep also includes *PGO waves.* **PGO waves** (for **p**ons, **g**eniculate, and **o**ccipital) are the first manifestation of REM sleep. They consist of brief, phasic bursts of electrical activity that originate in the pons and are propagated to the lateral geniculate nuclei and then to the primary visual (occipital) cortex. They can be seen only when electrodes are placed directly into the brain, so they have not been recorded in humans. It seems likely, however, that they occur in our species, too.

Figure 8.14 shows the typical onset of REM sleep, recorded in a cat. The first sign of an impending bout of REM sleep is the presence of PGO waves—in this case recorded from electrodes implanted in the lateral geniculate nucleus. Next, the EEG becomes desynchronized, and then muscular activity ceases and rapid eye movements commence. (See ***Figure 8.14.***)

As we shall see, REM sleep is controlled by mechanisms located within the pons. The executive mechanism (that is, the one whose activity turns on the various components of REM sleep) consists of a group of neurons in the dorsal pons that secrete acetylcholine. During waking and slow-wave sleep, REM sleep is inhibited by the serotonergic neurons of the raphe nuclei and the noradrenergic neurons of the locus coeruleus.

The Executive Mechanism

Researchers have long known that acetylcholinergic agonists facilitate REM sleep. Stoyva and Metcalf (1968) found that people who have been exposed to organophosphate insecticides, which act as acetylcholine agonists, spend an increased time in REM sleep. In a controlled experiment with human subjects, Sitaram, Moore, and Gillin (1978) found that an ACh agonist (arecoline) shortened the interval between periods of REM sleep and that an acetylcholinergic antagonist (scopolamine) lengthened it.

Jasper and Tessier (1969) analyzed the levels of acetylcholine that had been released by terminal buttons in the

Figure 8.14

Onset of REM sleep in a cat. The arrows indicate the onset of PGO waves, EEG desynchrony, loss of muscular activity, and rapid eye movements. LG = lateral geniculate nucleus; EOG = electro-oculogram (eye movements).

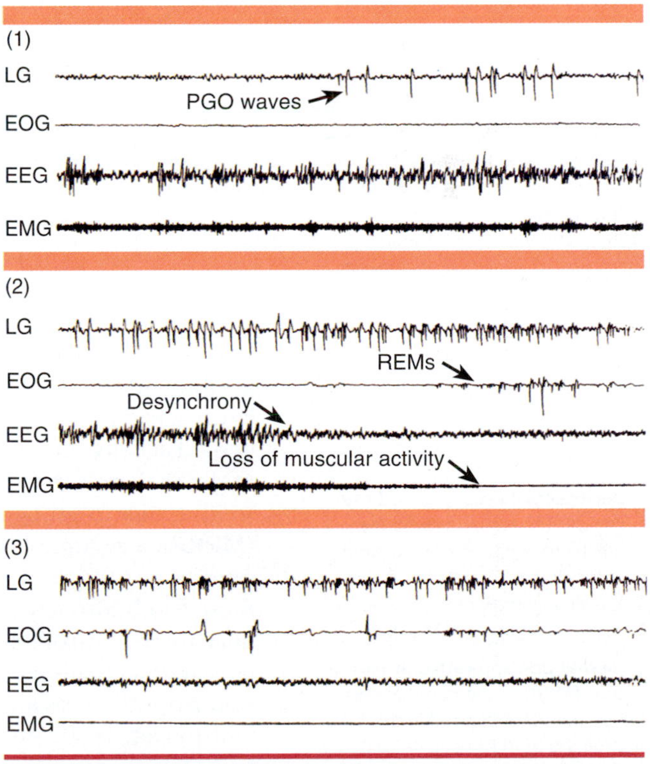

Adapted from Steriade, M., Paré, D., Bouhassira, D., Deschênes, M., and Oakson, G. *Journal of Neuroscience*, 1989, *9*, 2215–2229. Reprinted with permission.

Figure 8.15

Acetylcholinergic neurons (colored circles) in the peribrachial area of the cat, as revealed by a stain for choline acetyltransferase. LDT = lateral tegmental nucleus; PPT = pedunculopontine tegmental nucleus; bc = brachium conjunctivum; IC = inferior colliculus.

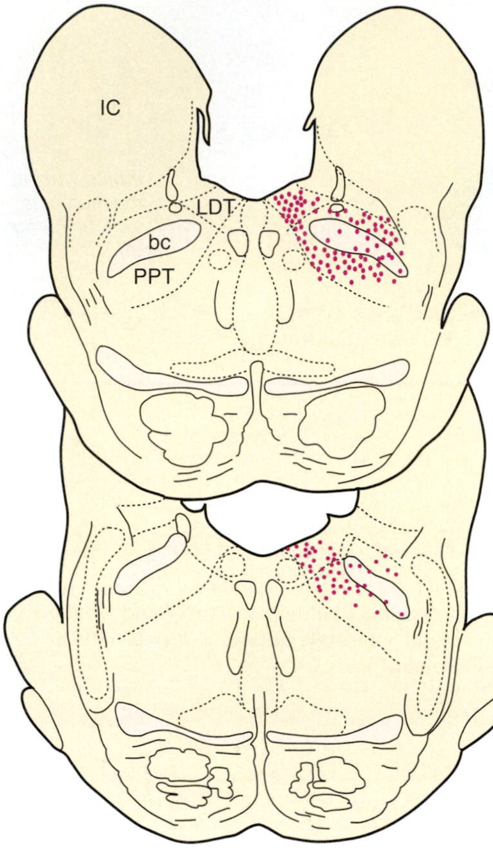

Adapted from Jones, B. E., and Beaudet, A. *Journal of Comparative Neurology,* 1987, *261,* 15–32. Copyright © 1987. Reprinted by permission of Wiley-Liss, Inc., a subsidiary of John Wiley & Sons, Inc.

cat cerebral cortex. They found that the levels of ACh were highest during waking and REM sleep and were lowest during slow-wave sleep. Using 2-DG autoradiography in cats, Lydic et al. (1991) found that the rate of glucose metabolism was elevated in the regions of the brain that contain ACh-secreting neurons or that receive input from the axons of these neurons. As we saw earlier in this chapter, acetylcholinergic neurons play an important role in cerebral activation during alert wakefulness. The findings I just cited suggest that these neurons are also responsible for the cerebral activation seen during REM sleep.

The brain contains several groups of acetylcholinergic neurons. The ones that play the most central role in triggering the onset of REM sleep are found in the dorsolateral pons, primarily in the *pedunculopontine tegmental nucleus* (PPT) and *laterodorsal tegmental nucleus* (LDT) (Jones and Beaudet, 1987). Many investigators now refer to this region as the **peribrachial area,** because it is located in the region of the brachium conjunctivum. Figure 8.15 contains two drawings through the brain stem of a cat, prepared by Jones and Beaudet (1987). The locations of acetylcholinergic cell bodies (identified by a stain for choline acetyltransferase) are shown by colored circles. As you can see, these neurons surround the brachium conjunctivum (bc). (See ***Figure 8.15.***)

Several studies (for example, El Mansari, Sakai, and Jouvet, 1989; Steriade et al., 1990; Kayama, Ohta, and Jodo, 1992) have shown that the activity of single neurons in the peribrachial area is related to the sleep cycle. Most of these neurons fire at a high rate during REM sleep or during both REM sleep and active wakefulness. Figure 8.16 shows the activity of a so-called *REM-ON* cell, which fires at a high rate only during REM sleep. As you can see, this neuron increased its activity approximately 80 sec before the onset of REM sleep. The increase in the activity of these acetylcholinergic cells may be the event that initiates a bout of REM sleep. (See ***Figure 8.16.***)

Webster and Jones (1988) made excitotoxic lesions of the peribrachial area. They found that REM sleep was drastically reduced. The amount of REM sleep that remained was directly related to the number of cholinergic neurons that were spared.

Figure 8.17 shows the connections of the acetylcholinergic neurons of the peribrachial area with the regions of the brain that are responsible for the phenomena of REM sleep. (See ***Figure 8.17.***) Let's consider each of these phenomena. If the acetylcholinergic neurons in the peribrachial area of the pons are responsible for the onset of REM sleep, how do they control each of its components: cortical arousal, PGO waves, rapid eye movements, genital activity, and muscular paralysis? These neurons send axons directly to regions of the thalamus that are involved in the control of cortical arousal. In addition, they send axons to glutamatergic neurons in the **medial pontine reticular formation (MPRF),** a region of the pons ventral to the locus coeruleus. Neurons in the MPRF send axons to the acetylcholinergic neurons of the basal forebrain. Activation of these forebrain neurons produces arousal and cortical desynchrony. PGO waves appear to be controlled by direct connections between the peribrachial area and the lateral geniculate nucleus, the region of the thalamus that receives visual information from the eyes and passes it on to the primary visual cortex and tectum. (Sakai and Jouvet, 1980; Steriade, Paré, Datta, Oakson, and Curró Dossi, 1990). The control of rapid eye movements appears to be achieved by projections from the peribrachial area to the tectum (Webster and Jones, 1988).

peribrachial area (*pair ee* ***bray*** *kee ul*) The region around the brachium conjunctivum, located in the dorsolateral pons; contains acetylcholinergic neurons involved in the initiation of REM sleep.

medial pontine reticular formation (MPRF) A region that contains neurons involved in the initiation of REM sleep; activated by acetylcholinergic neurons of the peribrachial area.

Figure 8.16

Firing pattern of an acetylcholinergic REM-ON cell in the peribrachial area of the pons. (a) Action potentials during 60-minute intervals during waking, slow-wave sleep, and REM sleep. (b) Rate of firing just before and after the transition from slow-wave sleep to REM sleep. The increase in activity begins approximately 80 seconds before the onset of REM sleep.

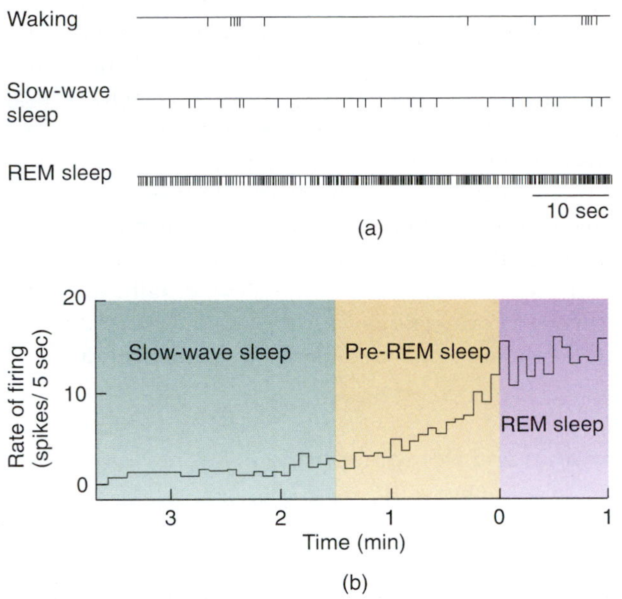

Adapted from El Mansari, M., Sakai, K., and Jouvet, M. *Experimental Brain Research,* 1989, *76,* 519–529.

Figure 8.17

A summary of the neural circuitry that is thought to be responsible for the components of REM sleep.

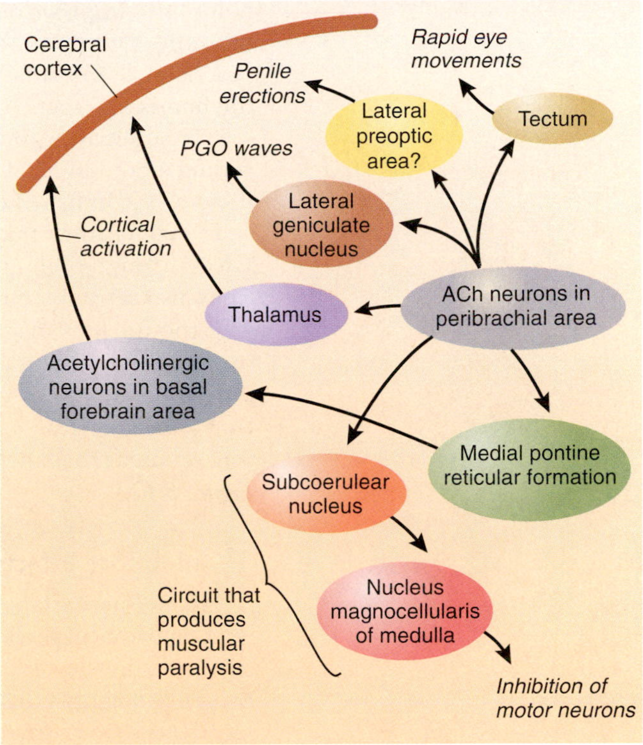

Little is known about the function of genital activity that occurs during REM sleep or about the neural mechanisms responsible for them. A study by Schmidt et al. (2000) found that excitotoxic lesions of the lateral preoptic area in rats suppressed penile erections during REM sleep but had no effect on erections during waking. Further research will be needed to investigate possible connections between the brain stem regions responsible for REM sleep and the lateral preoptic area.

The last of the REM-related phenomena, muscular paralysis, is particularly interesting. As we saw earlier, patients with REM sleep behavior disorder fail to become paralyzed during REM sleep and thus act out their dreams. The same thing happens—that is, assuming that cats dream—when a lesion is placed just caudal to the peribrachial area of the pons. Jouvet (1972) described this phenomenon:

> To a naive observer, the cat, which is standing, looks awake since it may attack unknown enemies, play with an absent mouse, or display flight behavior. There are orienting movements of the head or eyes toward imaginary stimuli, although the animal does not respond to visual or auditory stimuli. These extraordinary episodes . . . are a good argument that "dreaming" occurs during [REM sleep] in the cat. (Jouvet, 1972, pp. 236–237)

Jouvet's lesions destroyed a set of neurons that are responsible for the muscular paralysis that occurs during REM sleep. These neurons are located just ventral to the locus coeruleus—in the subcoerulear region. Their axons travel caudally to the **magnocellular nucleus,** located in the medial medulla (Sakai, 1980). Neurons in the magnocellular nucleus send axons to the spinal cord, where they form inhibitory synapses with motor neurons (Morales, Boxer, and Chase, 1987).

magnocellular nucleus A nucleus in the medulla; involved in the muscular paralysis that accompanies REM sleep.

The fact that our brains contain an elaborate mechanism whose sole function is to keep us paralyzed while we dream—that is, to prevent us from acting out our dreams—suggests that the motor components of dreams are as important as the sensory components. Perhaps the practice our motor system gets during REM sleep helps us to improve our performance of behaviors we have learned that day. The inhibition of the motor neurons in the spinal cord prevents the movements being practiced from actually occurring, with the exception of a few harmless twitches of the hands and feet.

To summarize the information presented in this subsection: The first event preceding a bout of REM sleep appears to be activation of acetylcholinergic neurons in the peribrachial area of the dorsolateral pons. These neurons directly activate brain stem mechanisms that are responsible for rapid eye movements and trigger PGO waves through their connections with the lateral geniculate nucleus of the thalamus. They also activate neurons in the subcoerulear area that, through their connections with the nucleus magnocellularis of the medulla, produce muscular paralysis. Presumably, they also activate neurons in the lateral preoptic area that are responsible for penile erections (and perhaps vaginal secretions in females). Finally, these neurons cause cortical activation through connections with the thalamus, medial pontine reticular formation, and acetylcholinergic neurons of the basal forebrain. (See ***Figure 8.17.***)

Inhibitory Effects of Serotonin and Norepinephrine

As we saw earlier (in Figures 8.8 and 8.10), the rate of activity in the noradrenergic neurons of the locus coeruleus and the serotonergic neurons of the raphe nuclei are at low levels during sleep and at their very lowest levels during REM sleep. Evidence suggests that the activity of neurons in the locus coeruleus and the dorsal raphe nucleus normally inhibits REM sleep and that a reduction in the rate of firing of these neurons may be the event that triggers a bout of REM sleep. Acetylcholinergic neurons in the peribrachial area receive both serotonergic and noradrenergic inputs (Honda and Semba, 1994; Leonard et al., 1995), and infusion of inhibitors of norepinephrine or serotonin into the pons causes an increase in REM sleep (Bier and McCarley, 1994; Portas et al., 1996).

Several unanswered questions await further research. As we saw in an earlier section, neurons in the sleep-promoting region of the VLPA inhibit the wakefulness-promoting regions of the forebrain and pons, which explains why the activity of noradrenergic and serotonergic neurons decreases during sleep. But what is responsible for the further inhibition of these neurons during REM sleep? Is there an excitatory input to the peribrachial area as well as the inhibitory ones whose activity *increases* at the beginning of REM sleep? Where is the pacemaker that controls the regular cycles of REM and slow-wave sleep, and how is this pacemaker connected to the REM sleep mechanisms in the pons? (See ***Figure 8.18.***)

Figure 8.18

Interactions between serotonergic, noradrenergic, and acetylcholinergic neurons in the control of REM sleep.

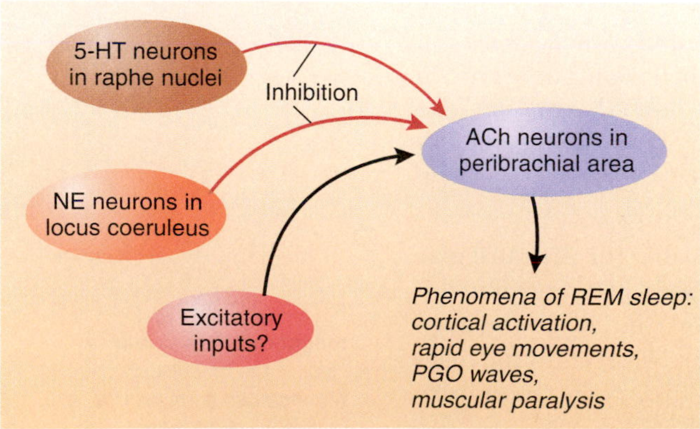

INTERIM SUMMARY

Physiological Mechanisms of Sleep and Waking

The fact that the amount of sleep is regulated suggests that sleep-promoting substances (produced during wakefulness) or wakefulness-promoting substances (produced during sleep) may exist. The sleeping pattern of the dolphin brain suggests that such substances do not accumulate in the blood. Evidence suggests that adenosine, released when neurons are obliged to utilize the supply of glycogen stored in astrocytes, serves as the link between increased brain metabolism and the necessity of sleep.

Five systems of neurons appear to be important for alert, active wakefulness: the acetylcholinergic system of the peribrachial area of the pons and the basal forebrain, the noradrenergic system of the locus coeruleus, the serotonergic system of the raphe nuclei, the histaminergic neurons of the tuberomammillary nucleus, and the hypocretinergic system of the lateral hypothalamus.

Slow-wave sleep occurs when neurons in the ventrolateral preoptic area (VLPA) become active. These neurons inhibit the histaminergic neurons of the tuberomammillary nucleus, the noradrenergic neurons of the locus coeruleus, and the serotonergic neurons of the raphe nuclei. In turn, the VLPA is inhibited by the wakefulness-promoting regions of the brain, forming a kind of flip-flop that keeps us either awake or asleep. The accumulation of adenosine may also promote sleep by inhibiting the acetylcholinergic neurons in the basal forebrain and activating the neurons of the VLPA. Activity of the hypocretinergic neurons of the lateral hypothalamus may keep the flip-flop that controls sleep and waking in the "on" state, thus maintaining wakefulness. Evidence suggests that adenosine also has an inhibitory effect on hypocretinergic neurons.

REM sleep occurs when the activity of acetylcholinergic neurons in the peribrachial area increases. These neurons initiate PGO waves and cortical arousal through their connections with the thalamus, and they activate neurons in the MPRF that in turn activate the acetylcholinergic neurons of the basal forebrain. The peribrachial neurons also produce rapid eye movements through their connections with motor neurons in the tectum. Penile erections during REM sleep (but not during waking) are abolished by lesions of the lateral preoptic area. The muscular paralysis that prevents our acting out our dreams is produced by a group of acetylcholinergic neurons located in the subcoerulear nucleus that activate other neurons located in the magnocellular nucleus of the medulla, which in turn produce inhibition of motor neurons in the spinal cord.

The noradrenergic neurons of the locus coeruleus and the serotonergic neurons of the raphe nuclei have inhibitory effects on pontine neurons responsible for REM sleep. Bouts of REM sleep begin only after the activity of the noradrenergic and serotonergic neurons ceases; whether this event is the only one to trigger REM sleep or whether direct excitation of acetylcholinergic neurons also occurs is not yet known.

THOUGHT QUESTION

Have you ever been lying in bed, almost asleep, when you suddenly thought of something important you had forgotten to do? Did you then suddenly become fully awake and alert? If so, neurons in your reticular formation undoubtedly became active, which aroused your cerebral cortex. What do you think the source of this activation was? What activated your reticular formation? How would you go about answering this question? What research methods described in Chapter 5 would be helpful?

Biological Clocks

Much of our behavior follows regular rhythms. For example, we saw that the stages of sleep are organized around a 90-minute cycle of REM and slow-wave sleep. The same rhythm continues during the day as the basic rest–activity cycle. And, of course, our daily pattern of sleep and waking follows a 24-hour cycle. Finally, many animals display seasonal breeding rhythms in which reproductive behaviors and hormone levels show yearly fluctuations. In recent years investigators have learned much about the neural mechanisms that are responsible for these rhythms.

Circadian Rhythms and Zeitgebers

Daily rhythms in behavior and physiological processes are found throughout the plant and animal world. These cycles are generally called **circadian rhythms.** (*Circa* means "about," and *dies* means "day"; therefore, a circadian rhythm is one that varies on a cycle of approximately 24 hours.) Some of these rhythms are passive responses to changes in illumination. However, other rhythms are controlled by mechanisms within the organism—by "internal clocks." For example, if a rat is housed in a room where lights are on for 12 hours each day, its circadian rhythm will follow the cycle of illumination: The animal will sleep when the light is on and become active when the room is dark. If the lights are now turned on (or off) all day, the animal will continue to show rhythms of sleep and wakefulness. In the absence of external stimuli, the rhythm must be provided by some sort of internal clock. In fact, the internal clock tends to run a little slow. The cycle of the internal clock of most mammals tends to be approximately 25 hours.

In the natural environment, where day and night are defined by the rising and setting of the sun, the internal clock is reset each day so that the cycles take 24 hours. Light serves as a **zeitgeber** (German for "time giver"); it synchronizes the endogenous rhythm. Studies with many species of animals have shown that if they are maintained in constant darkness (or constant dim light), a brief period of bright light will reset their internal clock, advancing or retarding it, depending upon when the light flash occurs (Aschoff, 1979). For example, if an animal is exposed to bright light soon after dusk, the biological clock is set back to an earlier time—as if dusk had not yet arrived. On the other hand, if the light occurs late at night, the biological clock is set ahead to a later time—as if dawn had already come.

People, too, have circadian rhythms, but without the benefits of modern civilization we would probably go to sleep earlier and get up earlier than we do; we use artificial lights to delay our bedtime and window shades to extend our time for sleep. Under constant illumination our biological clocks will run free, gaining or losing time like a watch that runs too slow or too fast. Different people have different cycle lengths, but most people in that situation will begin to live a "day" that is approximately 25 hours long. This works out quite well, because the morning light, acting as a zeitgeber, simply resets the clock.

The Suprachiasmatic Nucleus

Researchers working independently in two laboratories (Moore and Eichler, 1972; Stephan and Zucker, 1972) discovered that the primary biological clock of the rat is located in the **suprachiasmatic nucleus (SCN)** of the hypothalamus; they found that lesions disrupted circadian rhythms of wheel running, drinking, and hormonal secretion. The SCN also provides the primary control over the timing of sleep cycles. Rats are nocturnal animals; they sleep during the day and forage and feed at night. Lesions of the SCN abolish this pattern; sleep occurs in bouts randomly dispersed throughout both day and night (Ibuka and Kawamura, 1975; Stephan and Nuñez, 1977). However, rats with SCN lesions still obtain the same amount of sleep that normal animals do. The lesions disrupt the circadian pattern but do not affect the total amount of sleep.

circadian rhythm (*sur* ***kay*** *dee un* or *sur ka* ***dee*** *un*) A daily rhythmical change in behavior or physiological process.

zeitgeber (***tsite*** *gay ber*) A stimulus (usually the light of dawn) that resets the biological clock that is responsible for circadian rhythms.

suprachiasmatic nucleus (SCN) (*soo pra ky az* ***mat*** *ik*) A nucleus situated atop the optic chiasm. It contains a biological clock that is responsible for organizing many of the body's circadian rhythms.

melanopsin (*mell a* ***nop*** *sin*) A photopigment present in ganglion cells in the retina whose axons transmit information to the SCN, the thalamus, and the olivary pretectal nuclei.

Anatomy and Connections

Figure 8.19 shows the suprachiasmatic nuclei in a cross section through the hypothalamus of a rat; they appear as two clusters of dark-staining neurons at the base of the brain, just above the optic chiasm. (See ***Figure 8.19.***) The suprachiasmatic nuclei of the rat consist of approximately 10,000 small neurons, tightly packed into a volume of between 0.1 and 0.3 mm^3 (Meijer and Rietveld, 1989). The dendrites of these neurons form synapses with one another—a phenomenon that is found only in this part of the hypothalamus and that probably relates to the special function of these nuclei. A group of neurons is found clustered around the capillaries that serve the SCN, which suggests that they may be neurosecretory cells (Card, Riley, and Moore, 1980; Moore, Card, and Riley, 1980). Thus, some of the control that the SCN exerts over other parts of the brain may be accomplished by the secretion of neuromodulators.

Because light is the primary zeitgeber for most mammals' activity cycles, we would expect that the SCN receives fibers from the visual system. Indeed, anatomical studies have revealed a direct projection of fibers from the retina to the SCN: the *retinohypothalamic pathway* (Hendrickson, Wagoner, and Cowan, 1972; Aronson et al., 1993). Pulses of light that reset an animal's circadian rhythm trigger the production of Fos protein in the SCN, which indicates that the light initiates a period of neural activity in this nucleus (Rusak et al., 1990, 1992). (The significance of the Fos protein as an indicator of neural activation was discussed in Chapter 5.) If you look carefully at Figure 8.19, you can see small dark spots within the optic chiasm, just ventral and medial to the base of the SCN; these are cell bodies of oligodendroglia that serve axons that enter the SCN and provide information from the retina. (See ***Figure 8.19.***)

Figure 8.19

A cross section through a rat brain, showing the location and appearance of the suprachiasmatic nuclei. Cresyl violet stain.

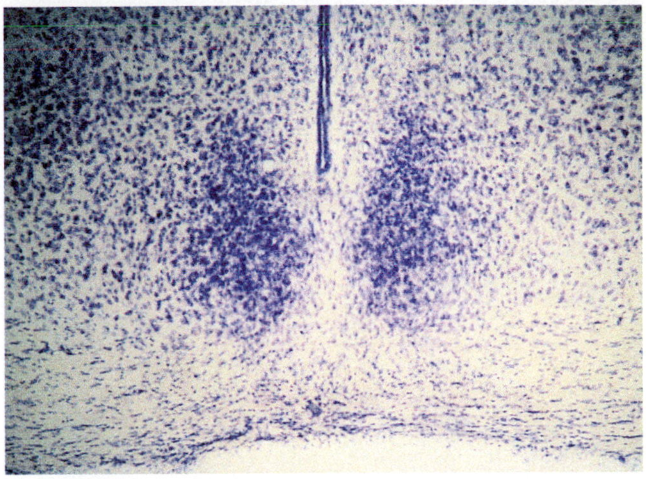

Courtesy of Geert DeVries, University of Massachusetts.

The photoreceptors in the retina that provide photic information to the SCN are neither rods nor cones—the cells that provide us with the information used for visual perception. Indeed, Freedman et al. (1999) found that targeted mutations against genes necessary for production of both rods and cones did not disrupt the synchronizing effects of light. However, when they removed the mice's eyes, these effects *were* disrupted. These results suggest that there is a special photoreceptor that is responsible for synchronization of diurnal rhythms. Provencio et al. (2000) found the photochemical responsible for these effects, which they named **melanopsin.**

Unlike the other retinal photopigments, which are found in rods and cones, melanopsin is present in ganglion cells—the neurons whose axons transmit information from the eyes to the rest of the brain. Melanopsin-containing ganglion cells are sensitive to light, and their axons terminate in the SCN and in a region of the tectum involved in the response of the pupils to light (Berson, Dunn, and Takao, 2002; Hattar et al., 2002). (See ***Figure 8.20.***)

Figure 8.20

Melanopsin-containing ganglion cells in the retina whose axons form the retinohypothalamic tract. These neurons detect the light of dawn that resets the biological clock in the SCN.

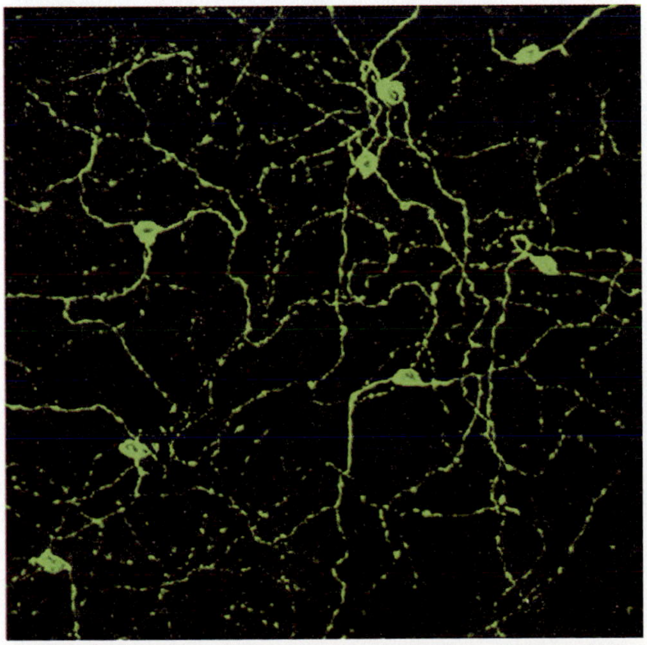

From Hattar, S., Liao, H.-W., Takao, M., Berson, D. M., and Yau, K.-W. *Science,* 2002, *295,* 1065–1070. Copyright 2002 American Association for the Advancement of Science. Reprinted with permission.

How does the SCN control drinking, eating, sleep cycles, and hormone secretion? Although neurons of the SCN project to several parts of the brain, transplantation studies suggest that the SCN controls some functions by releasing chemical signals. Lehman et al. (1987) destroyed the SCN and then transplanted in their place a new set of suprachiasmatic nuclei obtained from donor animals. The grafts succeeded in reestablishing circadian rhythms, even though very few efferent connections were observed between the graft and the recipient's brain. Even more convincing evidence comes from a transplantation study by Silver et al. (1996). Silver and her colleagues first destroyed the SCN in a group of hamsters,

Figure 8.21

Autoradiographs of cross sections through the brains of rats that had been injected with carbon 14-labeled 2-deoxyglucose during the day (*left*) and the night (*right*). The dark region at the base of the brain (*arrows*) indicates increased metabolic activity of the suprachiasmatic nuclei.

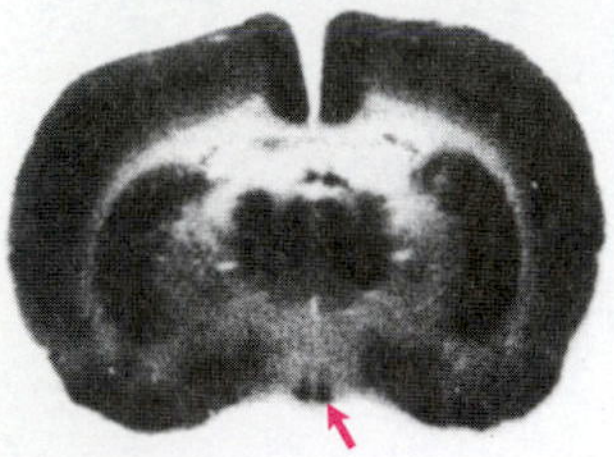

From Schwartz, W. J., and Gainer, H. *Science*, 1977, *197*, 1089–1091. Copyright 1977 American Association for the Advancement of Science. Reprinted with permission.

Figure 8.22

Firing rate of individual SCN neurons in a tissue culture. Color bars have been added to emphasize the daily peaks. Note that although each neuron has a period of approximately 1 day, the neurons' activity cycles are not synchronized.

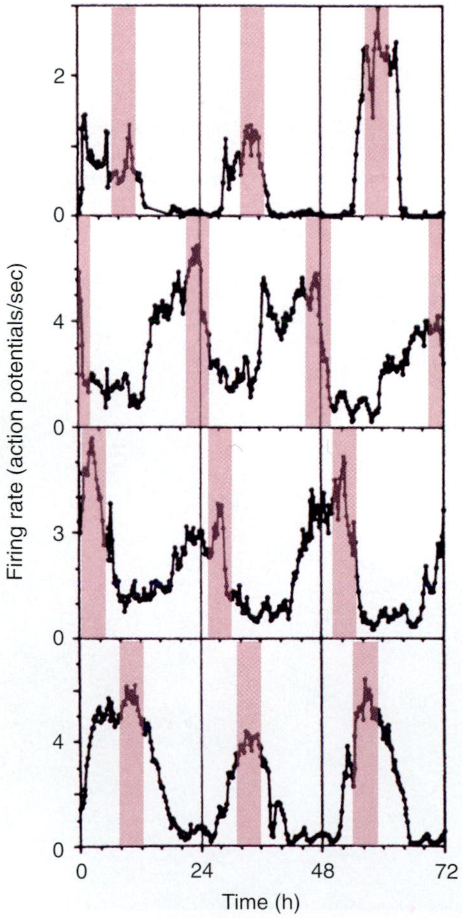

From Welsh, D. K., Logothetis, D. E., Meister, M., and Reppert, S. M. *Neuron,* 1995, *14,* 697–706.

abolishing their circadian rhythms. Then, a few weeks later, they removed SCN tissue from donor animals and placed it in very small semipermeable capsules, which they then implanted in the animals' third ventricles. Nutrients and other chemicals could pass through the walls of the capsules, keeping the SCN tissue alive, but the neurons inside the capsules were not able to establish synaptic connections with the surrounding tissue. Nevertheless, the transplants reestablished circadian rhythms in the recipient animals.

The Nature of the Clock

All clocks must have a time base. Mechanical clocks use flywheels or pendulums; electronic clocks use quartz crystals. The SCN, too, must contain a physiological mechanism that parses time into units. After years of research, investigators are finally beginning to discover the nature of the biological clock in the SCN.

Several studies have demonstrated daily activity rhythms in the SCN, which indicates that the circadian clock is located there. A study by Schwartz and Gainer (1977) nicely demonstrated day–night fluctuations in the activity of the SCN. These investigators injected rats with radioactive 2-deoxyglucose (2-DG).

Schwartz and Gainer injected some rats with radioactive 2-DG during the day and injected others at night. The animals were then killed, and autoradiographs of cross sections through the brain were prepared. Figure 8.21 shows photographs of two of these cross sections. Note the evidence of radioactivity (and hence a high metabolic rate) in the SCN of the brain that was injected during the day (*left*). (See ***Figure 8.21.***)

The "ticking" of the biological clock within the SCN could involve interactions of circuits of neurons, or it could be intrinsic to individual neurons themselves. Evidence suggests the latter—that each neuron contains a clock. Several studies have succeeded in keeping individual SCN neurons alive in a culture medium. For example, Welsh et al. (1995) removed tissue from the rat SCN and dissolved the connections between the cells with papain, an enzyme sometimes used as a meat tenderizer. The cells were placed on top of an array of microelectrodes so that their electrical activity could be measured. Although these neurons did re-establish synaptic connections with each other, they displayed individual, independent, circadian rhythms in activity. Figure 8.22 shows the activity cycles of four neurons. As you can see, all showed circadian rhythms, but their periods of peak activity occurred at different times of day. (See ***Figure 8.22.***)

What causes SCN neurons to "tick"? For many years investigators have believed that circadian rhythms were produced by the production of a protein that, when it reached a certain level in the cell, inhibited its own production. As a result, the levels of the protein would begin to decline, which would remove the inhibition, starting the production cycle again. (See ***Figure 8.23.***)

Just such a mechanism was discovered in *Drosophila melanogaster,* the common fruit fly. Subsequent research with mammals discovered a similar system (Shearman et al., 2000; Reppert and Weaver, 2001). The system involves at least seven genes and their proteins and two interlocking feedback loops. When one of the proteins produced by the first loop reaches a sufficient level, it starts the second loop, which eventually inhibits the production of proteins in the first loop, and the cycle begins again. Thus, the intracellular ticking is regulated by the time it takes to produce and degrade a set of proteins.

Control of Seasonal Rhythms: The Pineal Gland and Melatonin

Although the SCN has an intrinsic rhythm of approximately 24 hours, it plays a role in much longer rhythms. (We could say that it is involved in a biological calendar as well as a biological clock.) Male hamsters show annual rhythms of testosterone secretion, which appear to be based on the amount of light that occurs each day. Their breeding season begins as the day length increases and ends when it decreases. Lesions of the SCN abolish these annual breeding cycles; the animals' testes then secrete testosterone all year (Rusak and Morin, 1976). Possibly, the lesions disrupt these annual cycles because they destroy the 24-hour clock against which the daily light period is measured to determine the season. That is, if the light period is considerably shorter than 12 hours, the season is winter; if it is considerably longer than 12 hours, the season is summer.

The control of seasonal rhythms involves another part of the brain: the **pineal gland** (Bartness et al., 1993; Moore, 1995). This structure sits on top of the midbrain, just in front of the cerebellum. (See ***Figure 8.24.***) The pineal gland secretes a hormone called **melatonin,** so named because it has the ability in certain animals (primarily fish, reptiles, and amphibians) to turn the skin temporarily dark. (The dark

pineal gland (*py* ***nee*** *ul*) A gland attached to the dorsal tectum; produces melatonin and plays a role in circadian and seasonal rhythms.

melatonin (*mell a* ***tone*** *in*) A hormone secreted during the night by the pineal body; plays a role in circadian and seasonal rhythms.

Figure 8.23

A schematic, simplified explanation of the molecular control of the "ticking" of neurons of the SCN.

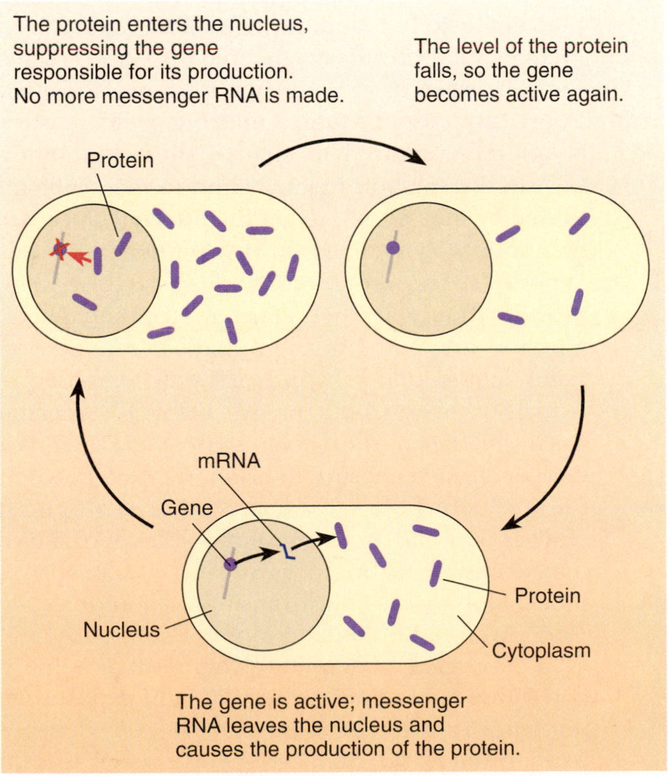

The protein enters the nucleus, suppressing the gene responsible for its production. No more messenger RNA is made.
The level of the protein falls, so the gene becomes active again.
Protein
mRNA
Gene
Protein
Nucleus
Cytoplasm
The gene is active; messenger RNA leaves the nucleus and causes the production of the protein.

Figure 8.24

The pineal gland, located on the dorsal surface of the midbrain.

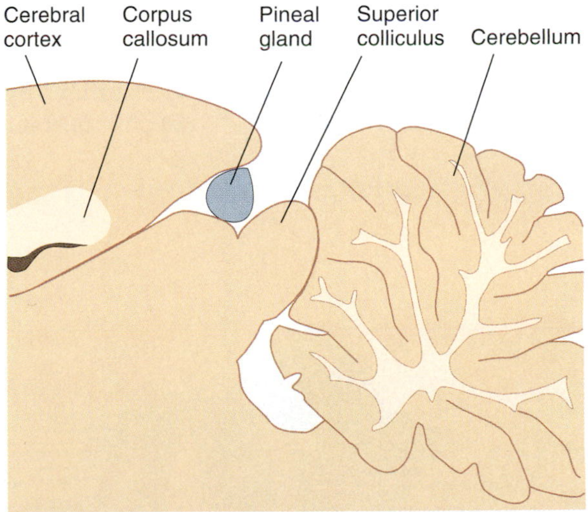

Cerebral cortex
Corpus callosum
Pineal gland
Superior colliculus
Cerebellum

Adapted from Paxinos, G., and Watson, C. *The Rat Brain in Stereotaxic Coordinates.* Sydney: Academic Press, 1982. Redrawn with permission.

color is produced by a chemical known as *melanin.*) In mammals melatonin controls seasonal rhythms. Neurons in the SCN make synaptic connections with neurons in the *paraventricular nucleus of the hypothalamus* (the PVN). The axons of these neurons travel all the way to the spinal cord, where they form synapses with preganglionic neurons of the sympathetic nervous system. The postganglionic neurons innervate the pineal gland and control the secretion of melatonin.

In response to input from the SCN, the pineal gland secretes melatonin during the night. This melatonin acts back on various structures in the brain (including the SCN, whose cells contain melatonin receptors) and controls hormones, physiological processes, and behaviors that show seasonal variations. During long nights a large amount of melatonin is secreted, and the animals go into the winter phase of their cycle. Lesions of the SCN, the paraventricular nucleus (PVN), or the pineal gland disrupt seasonal rhythms that are controlled by day length—and so do knife cuts that interrupt the neural connection between the SCN and the PVN, which indicates that this is one function of the SCN that is mediated through its neural connections with another structure. Furthermore, although transplants of fetal suprachiasmatic nuclei will restore circadian rhythms, they will not restore seasonal rhythms, because the transplanted tissue does not establish neural connections with the PVN (Ralph and Lehman, 1991).

Changes in Circadian Rhythms: Shift Work and Jet Lag

When people abruptly change their daily rhythms of activity, their internal circadian rhythms, controlled by the SCN, become desynchronized with those in the external environment. For example, if a person who normally works on the day shift begins working on a night shift or if someone travels east or west across several time zones, his or her SCN will signal the rest of the brain that it is time to sleep during the work shift (or the middle of the day, in the case of jet travel). This disparity between internal rhythms and the external environment results in sleep disturbances and mood changes and interferes with people's ability to function during waking hours.

Jet lag is a temporary phenomenon; after several days, people who have crossed several time zones find it easier to fall asleep at the appropriate time, and their daytime alertness improves. Shift work can present a more enduring problem when people are required to change shifts frequently. Clearly, the solution to jet lag and to the problems caused by shift work is to get the internal clock synchronized with the external environment as quickly as possible. The most obvious way to start is to try to provide strong zeitgebers at the appropriate time. If a person is exposed to bright light before the low point in the daily rhythm of body temperature (which occurs an hour or two before the person usually awakens), the person's circadian rhythm is delayed. If the exposure to bright light occurs after the low point, the circadian rhythm is advanced (Dijk et al., 1995). In fact, several studies have shown that exposure to bright lights at the appropriate time helps to ease the transition (Boulos et al., 1995). Houpt, Boulos, and Moore-Ede (1996) have even developed a computer program that helps to determine the optimal pattern of light exposure to minimize the effects of jet travel between various parts of the world. Similarly, people adapt to shift

Researchers are beginning to understand the role of the suprachiasmatic nucleus and the pineal gland in phenomena such as jet lag.

work more rapidly if artificial light is kept at a brighter level and if their bedroom is kept as dark as possible (Eastman et al., 1995).

As we saw in the previous subsection, the role of melatonin in seasonal rhythms is well established. Studies in recent years suggest that melatonin may also be involved in circadian rhythms. As we saw, melatonin is secreted during the night, which, for diurnal mammals such as ourselves, is the period during which we sleep. But although our species lacks strong seasonal rhythms, the daily rhythm of melatonin secretion persists. Thus, melatonin must have some functions besides regulation of seasonal rhythms.

Recent studies have found that melatonin, acting on receptors in the SCN, can affect the sensitivity of SCN neurons to zeitgebers and can itself alter circadian rhythms (Gillette and McArthur, 1995; Starkey et al., 1995). Researchers do not yet understand exactly what role melatonin plays in the control of circadian rhythms, but they have already discovered practical applications. Melatonin secretion normally reaches its highest levels early in the night, at around bedtime. Investigators have found that the administration of melatonin at the appropriate time (in most cases, just before going to bed) significantly reduces the adverse effects of both jet lag and shifts in work schedules (Arendt et al., 1995; Deacon and Arendt, 1996). Bedtime melatonin has even helped to synchronize circadian rhythms and improve the sleep of blind people for whom light cannot serve as a zeitgeber (Skene, Lockley, and Arendt, 1999).

INTERIM SUMMARY

Biological Clocks

Our daily lives are characterized by cycles in physical activity, sleep, body temperature, secretion of hormones, and many other physiological changes. Circadian rhythms—those with a period of approximately one day—are controlled by biological clocks in the brain. The principal biological clock appears to be located in the suprachiasmatic nuclei of the hypothalamus; lesions of these nuclei disrupt most circadian rhythms, and the activity of neurons located there correlates with the day–night cycle. Light, detected by special cells in the retina that are not involved in visual perception, serves as a zeitgeber for most circadian rhythms. That is, the biological clocks tend to run a bit slow, with a period of approximately 25 hours. The presence of sunlight in the morning is detected by melanopsin-containing photoreceptors in the retina and conveyed to the SCN. The effect of the light is to reset the clock to the start of a new cycle.

Individual neurons, rather than circuits of neurons, are responsible for the "ticking." Studies with tissue cultures suggest that synchronization of the firing patterns of individual neurons is accomplished by means of chemical communication between cells. "Ticking" is accomplished by cycles of production and destruction of proteins. At least seven genes and their proteins and two interlocking feedback loops are involved in this process. A human genetic disorder, familial advanced sleep phase syndrome, is caused by a mutation of one of the genes responsible for circadian rhythms.

The SCN and the pineal gland control seasonal rhythms. During the night the SCN signals the pineal gland to secrete melatonin. Prolonged melatonin secretion, which occurs during winter, causes the animals to enter the winter phase of their annual cycle. Melatonin also appears to be involved in synchronizing circadian rhythms: The hormone can help people to adjust to the effects of shift work or jet lag and even synchronize the daily rhythms of blind people for whom light cannot serve as a zeitgeber.

THOUGHT QUESTION

Until recently (in terms of the evolution of our species), our ancestors tended to go to sleep when the sun set and wake up when it rose. Once our ancestors learned how to control fire, they undoubtedly stayed up somewhat later, sitting in front of a fire. But it was only with the development of cheap, effective lighting that many members of our species adopted the habit of staying up late and waking several hours after sunrise. Considering that our biological clock and the neural mechanisms it controls evolved long ago, do you think the changes in our daily rhythms impair any of our physical and intellectual abilities?

EPILOGUE

Functions of Dreams

Even though we are still not sure why REM sleep occurs, the elaborate neural circuitry involved with its control indicates that it must be important. Nature would probably not invent this circuitry if it did not do something useful. Michael's attacks of sleep paralysis, hypnagogic hallucinations, and cataplexy, described in the chapter prologue, occurred when two of the aspects of REM sleep (paralysis and dreaming) occurred at inappropriate times. Normally, the brain mechanisms responsible for these phenomena are inhibited during waking; perhaps this inhibition is too weak in Michael's case.

As we saw, researchers have proposed four categories of hypothetical explanations for REM sleep: vigilance, learning, species-typical reprogramming, and brain development. Each of these explanations has some support, and REM sleep possibly performs more than one function. But what about the subjective aspect of REM sleep dreaming? Is there some special purpose served by those vivid, storylike hallucinations we have while we sleep, or are dreams just irrelevant side effects of more important things going on in the brain?

Since ancient times, people have regarded dreams as important, using them to prophesy the future, decide whether to go to war, or determine the guilt or innocence of a person accused of a crime. In the twentieth century Sigmund Freud proposed a very influential theory about dreaming. He said that dreams arise out of inner conflicts between unconscious desires (primarily sexual ones) and prohibitions against acting out these desires, which we learn from society. According to Freud, although all dreams represent unfulfilled wishes, their contents are disguised. The *latent content* of the dream (from the Latin word for "hidden") is transformed into the *manifest content* (the actual story line or plot). Taken at face value, the manifest content is innocuous, but a knowledgeable psychoanalyst can recognize unconscious desires disguised as symbols in the dream. For example, climbing a set of stairs might represent sexual intercourse. The problem with Freud's theory is that it is not disprovable; even if it is wrong, a psychoanalyst can always provide a plausible interpretation of a dream that reveals hidden conflicts, disguised in obscure symbols.

Many sleep researchers—especially those who are interested in the biological aspects of dreaming—disagree with Freud and suggest alternative explanations. For example, Hobson (1988) suggests that the brain activation that occurs during REM sleep leads to hallucinations that we try to make sense of by creating a more or less plausible story. As you learned in this chapter, REM sleep occurs when a circuit of acetylcholinergic neurons in the peribrachial region becomes active, stimulating rapid eye movements and cortical arousal. The visual system is especially active. So is the motor system—in fact, we have a mechanism that paralyzes and prevents the activity of the motor system from causing us to get out of bed and doing something that might harm us. (As we saw, people who suffer from REM without atonia actually *do* act out their dreams and sometimes injure themselves. On occasion they have even attacked their spouses while dreaming that they were fighting with someone.)

Research indicates that the two systems of the brain that are most active, the visual system and the motor system, account for most of the sensations that occur during dreams. Many dreams are silent, but almost all are full of visual images. In addition, many dreams contains sensations of movements, which are probably caused by feedback from the activity of the motor system. Very few dreamers report tactile sensations, smells, or tastes. Hobson, a wine lover, reported that although he has drunk wine in his dreams, he has never experienced any taste or smell. (He reported this fact rather wistfully; I suspect that he would have appreciated the opportunity to taste a fine wine without having to open one of his own bottles.) Why are these sensations absent? Is it because our "hidden desires" involve only sight and movement, or is it because the neural activation that occurs during REM sleep simply does not involve other systems to a very great extent? Hobson suggests the latter, and I agree with him.

KEY CONCEPTS

A PHYSIOLOGICAL AND BEHAVIORAL DESCRIPTION OF SLEEP

1. Sleep consists of slow-wave sleep, divided into four stages, and REM sleep. Dreaming occurs during REM sleep.

DISORDERS OF SLEEP

2. People sometimes suffer from such sleep disorders as insomnia, sleep apnea, narcolepsy, REM without atonia, bed-wetting, sleepwalking, or night terrors. Three symptoms of narcolepsy (cataplexy, sleep

paralysis, and hypnagogic hallucinations) can be understood as components of REM sleep occurring at inappropriate times. Narcolepsy is caused by a hereditary disorder that causes the degeneration of hypocretin-secreting neurons during adolescence.

WHY DO WE SLEEP?

3. Slow-wave sleep appears to permit the cerebral cortex to rest. REM sleep may be important in brain development, and it appears to be somehow involved in learning.

PHYSIOLOGICAL MECHANISMS OF SLEEP AND WAKING

4. Adenosine, a neuromodulator that is produced as a by-product of cerebral metabolism, may play a role in initiating sleep.
5. The brain stem contains an arousal mechanism with five major components: the acetylcholinergic system of the dorsolateral pons and basal forebrain, the noradrenergic system originating in the locus coeruleus, the serotonergic system originating in the raphe nuclei, the histaminergic system originating in the tuberomammillary nucleus of the hypothalamus, and the hypocretinergic system originating in the lateral hypothalamus. The ventrolateral preoptic area (VLPA) appears to be necessary for sleep; its neurons inhibit the brain regions responsible for arousal.
6. Hypocretinergic neurons help stabilize the sleep/waking "flip-flop," which consists of reciprocal inhibitory connections between the VLPA and the regions involved in arousal.
7. REM sleep is produced by the activity of acetylcholinergic neurons in the dorsolateral pons, which are normally inhibited by both noradrenergic and serotonergic synapses. The circuit responsible for the muscular paralysis that accompanies REM sleep has been located, and damage to it is responsible for REM without atonia.

BIOLOGICAL CLOCKS

8. Circadian rhythms are largely under the control of a mechanism located in the suprachiasmatic nucleus. They are synchronized by the day–night light cycle, which is detected by newly discovered photoreceptors in the retina. The ticking of the internal clock responsible for these rhythms appears to involve the production and degradation of a protein.

SUGGESTED READINGS

Hastings, J. W., Rusak, B., and Boulos, Z. Circadian rhythms: The physiology of biological timing. In *Neural and Integrative Animal Physiology*, edited by C. L. Prosser. New York: Wiley-Liss, 1991.

Horne, J. *Why We Sleep: The Functions of Sleep in Humans and Other Mammals.* Oxford, England: Oxford University Press, 1988.

Kryger, M. H., Roth, T., and Dement, W. C. *Principles and Practice of Sleep Medicine.* Philadelphia: Saunders, 1994.

Mancia, M., and Marini, G. *The Diencephalon and Sleep.* New York: Raven Press, 1990.

Moorcroft, W. H. *Sleep, Dreaming, and Sleep Disorders: An Introduction.* Lanham, MD: University Press of America, 1993.

Schwartz, W. J. *Sleep Science: Integrating Basic Research and Clinical Practice.* Basel: Karger, 1997.

Webb, W. *Sleep: The Gentle Tyrant,* 2nd ed. Bolton, MA: Anker, 1992.

SUGGESTED WEB SITES

The Sleep Well

www.stanford.edu/~dement/alphaindex.html

The topic of sleep is the focus of this site. The Sleep Well site provides a number of links to basic research on sleep and to sites that cover sleep disorders.

SleepNet

www.sleepnet.com/

SleepNet contains a forum on sleep issues, a set of links to sleep lab sites and to sleep disorders. In addition, the site contains a column written by the sleep scientist Dr. William Dement.

Basic of Sleep Behavior

http://bisleep.medsch.ucla.edu/sleepsyllabus/

This site provides coverage on a number of sleep lecture topics including NREM and REM sleep, chemical and neuronal control of sleep, and sleep functions.

National Centers on Sleep Disorders Research

www.nhlbi.nih.gov/about/ncsdr/

This NIH site provides an interactive quiz on sleep, and contains a series of fact sheets and education materials on sleep and sleep disorders.

Reproductive Behavior

chapter 9

CHAPTER OUTLINE

LEARNING OBJECTIVES

1. Describe mammalian sexual development and explain the factors that control it.
2. Describe the hormonal control of the female reproductive cycle and of male and female sexual behavior.
3. Describe the role of pheromones in reproductive physiology and sexual behavior.
4. Discuss the activational effects of gonadal hormones on the sexual behavior of women and men.
5. Discuss sexual orientation, the prenatal androgenization of genetic females, and the failure of androgenization of genetic males.
6. Discuss the neural control of male sexual behavior.
7. Discuss the neural control of female sexual behavior.
8. Describe the maternal behavior of rodents and explain its significance.
9. Explain the hormonal and neural mechanisms that control maternal behavior and the neural control of paternal behavior.

PROLOGUE

From Boy to Girl

The aftermath of a tragic surgical accident suggested that people's sexual identity and sexual orientation were not under the strong control of biological factors and that these characteristics could be shaped by the way a child was raised (Money and Ehrhardt, 1972). Identical twin boys were raised normally until seven months of age, at which time one of the boys' penis was accidentally destroyed during circumcision. The cautery (a device that cuts tissue by means of electric current) was adjusted too high, and instead of removing the foreskin, the current burned off the entire penis. After a period of agonized indecision, the parents decided, on the advice of an expert in human sexuality, to raise the child as a girl. Bruce became Brenda.

Bruce's parents started dressing her in girl's clothing and treating her like a little girl. Surgeons removed the child's testes. Reports of this case stated that Brenda was a normal, happy girl, and many experts concluded that children's sexual identities were determined by the way that they were raised, and not by their chromosomes or sex hormones. After all, Brenda's identical twin brother provided the perfect control. Many writers saw this case as a triumph of socialization over biology.

As you will see in the chapter epilogue, this conclusion was premature.

Reproductive behaviors constitute the most important category of social behaviors, because without them, most species would not survive. These behaviors—which include courting, mating, parental behavior, and most forms of aggressive behaviors—are the most striking categories of **sexually dimorphic behaviors,** that is, behaviors that differ in males and females (*di* + *morphous,* "two forms"). As you will see, hormones that are present both before and after birth play a very special role in the development and control of sexually dimorphic behaviors.

This chapter describes male and female sexual development and then discusses the neural and hormonal control of two sexually dimorphic behaviors that are most important to reproduction: sexual behavior and parental behavior.

Sexual Development

A person's chromosomal sex is determined at the time of fertilization. However, this event is merely the first in a series of steps that culminate in the development of a male or female. This section considers the major features of sexual development.

Production of Gametes and Fertilization

All cells of the human body (other than sperms or ova) contain twenty-three pairs of chromosomes. The genetic information that programs the development of a human is contained in the DNA that constitutes these chromosomes. We pride ourselves on our ability to miniaturize computer circuits on silicon chips, but that accomplishment looks primitive when we consider that the blueprint for a human being is too small to be seen by the naked eye.

The production of **gametes** (ova and sperms; *gamein* means "to marry") entails a special form of cell division. This process produces cells that contain one member of each of the twenty-three pairs of chromosomes. The development of a human begins at the time of fertilization, when a single sperm and ovum join, sharing their twenty-three single chromosomes to reconstitute the twenty-three pairs.

A person's genetic sex is determined at the time of fertilization by the father's sperm. Twenty-two of the twenty-three pairs of chromosomes determine the organism's physical development independent of its sex. The last pair consists of two **sex chromosomes,** which determine whether the offspring will be a boy or a girl.

sexually dimorphic behavior A behavior that has different forms or that occurs with different probabilities or under different circumstances in males and females.

gamete (***gamm*** *eet*) A mature reproductive cell; a sperm or ovum.

sex chromosome The X and Y chromosomes, which determine an organism's gender. Normally, XX individuals are female, and XY individuals are male.

Figure 9.1

Determination of gender. The gender of the offspring depends on whether the sperm cell that fertilizes the ovum carries an X or a Y chromosome.

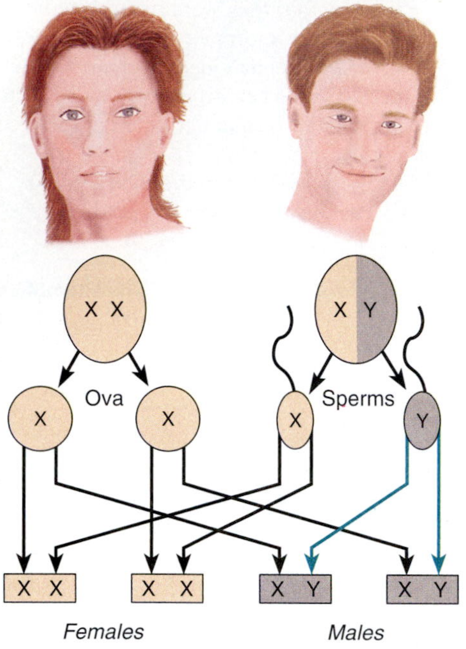

There are two types of sex chromosomes: X chromosomes and Y chromosomes. Females have two X chromosomes (XX); thus, all the ova that a woman produces will contain an X chromosome. Males have an X and a Y chromosome (XY). When a man's sex chromosomes divide, half the sperms contain an X chromosome and the other half contain a Y chromosome. A Y-bearing sperm produces an XY-fertilized ovum and therefore a male. An X-bearing sperm produces an XX-fertilized ovum and therefore a female. (See ***Figure 9.1.***)

Development of the Sex Organs

Men and women differ in many ways: Their bodies are different, parts of their brains are different, and their reproductive behaviors are different. Are all these differences encoded on the tiny Y chromosome, the sole piece of genetic material that distinguishes males from females? The answer is no. The X chromosome and the twenty-two nonsex chromosomes found in the cells of both males and females contain all the information needed to develop the bodies of either sex. Exposure to sex hormones, both before and after birth, is responsible for our sexual dimorphism. What the Y chromosome does control is the development of the glands that produce the male sex hormones.

Gonads

There are three general categories of sex organs: the gonads, the internal sex organs, and the external genitalia. The **gonads—**testes or ovaries—are the first to develop. Gonads (from the Greek *gonos,* "procreation") have a dual function: They produce ova or sperms, and they secrete hormones. Through the sixth week of prenatal development, male and female fetuses are identical. Both sexes have a pair of identical undifferentiated gonads, which have the potential of developing into either testes or ovaries. The factor that controls their development appears to be a single gene on the Y chromosome called *Sry.* This gene produces a protein called *testis-determining factor,* which binds to the DNA of cells in the undifferentiated gonads and causes them to become testes. (Testes are also known as *testicles,* Latin for "little testes." Believe it or not, the words "testis" and "testify" have the same root, meaning "witness." Legend has it that ancient Roman men placed their right hand over their testes while swearing that they would tell the truth in court.) If the *Sry* gene is not present, they become ovaries (Sinclair et al., 1990; Smith, 1994; Koopman, 2001). In fact, a few cases of XX males have been reported. This anomaly can occur when the *Sry* gene becomes translocated from the Y chromosome to the X chromosome during production of sperms (Warne and Zajac, 1998).

Once the gonads have developed, a series of events is set into action that determines the individual's gender. These events are directed by hormones, which affect sexual development in two ways. During prenatal development these hormones have **organizational effects,** which influence the development of a person's sex organs and brain. These effects are permanent; once a particular path is followed in the course of development, there is no going back. The second role of sex hormones is their **activational effect.** These effects occur later in life, after the sex organs have developed. For example, hormones activate the production of sperms, make erection and ejaculation possible, and induce ovulation. Because the bodies of adult males and females have been organized differently, sex hormones will have different activational effects in the two sexes.

gonad (rhymes with ***moan*** *ad*) An ovary or testis.

organizational effect (of hormone) The effect of a hormone on tissue differentiation and development.

activational effect (of hormone) The effect of a hormone that occurs in the fully developed organism; may depend on the organism's prior exposure to the organizational effects of hormones.

Müllerian system The embryonic precursors of the female internal sex organs.

Wolffian system The embryonic precursors of the male internal sex organs.

anti-Müllerian hormone A peptide secreted by the fetal testes that inhibits the development of the Müllerian system, which would otherwise become the female internal sex organs.

Internal Sex Organs

Early in embryonic development, the internal sex organs are *bisexual;* that is, all embryos contain the precursors for both female and male sex organs. However, during the third month of gestation, only one of these precursors develops; the other withers away. The precursor of the internal female sex organs, which develops into the *fimbriae* and *Fallopian tubes,* the *uterus,* and the *inner two-thirds of the vagina,* is called the **Müllerian system.** The precursor of the internal male sex organs, which develops into the *epididymis, vas deferens,* and *seminal vesicles,* is called the **Wolffian system.** (These systems were named after their discoverers, Müller and Wolff. See ***Figure 9.2.***)

The gender of the internal sex organs of a fetus is determined by the presence or absence of hormones secreted by the testes. If these hormones are present, the Wolffian system develops. If they are not, the Müllerian system develops. The Müllerian (female) system needs no hormonal stimulus from the gonads to develop; it just normally does so. In contrast, the cells of the Wolffian (male) system do not develop unless they are stimulated to do so by a hormone. Thus, testes secrete two types of hormones. The first, a peptide hormone called **anti-Müllerian hormone,** does exactly what its name says: It prevents the Müllerian (female) system from developing. It therefore has a **defeminizing effect.** The second, a set of steroid hormones called **androgens,** stimulates the development of the Wolffian system. (This class of hormone is also aptly named: *Andros* means "man," and *gennan* means "to produce.") Androgens have a **masculinizing effect.**

Two different androgens are responsible for masculinization. The first, **testosterone,** is secreted by the testes and gets its name from these glands. An enzyme converts some of the testosterone into another androgen, known as **dihydrotestosterone.**

defeminizing effect An effect of a hormone present early in development that reduces or prevents the later development of anatomical or behavioral characteristics typical of females.

androgen (***an*** *dro jen*) A male sex steroid hormone. Testosterone is the principal mammalian androgen.

masculinizing effect An effect of a hormone present early in development that promotes the later development of anatomical or behavioral characteristics typical of males.

testosterone (*tess* ***tahss*** *ter own*) The principal androgen found in males.

dihydrotestosterone (*dy hy dro tess* ***tahss*** *ter own*) An androgen, produced from testosterone through the action of the enzyme 5α reductase.

Figure 9.2

Development of the internal sex organs.

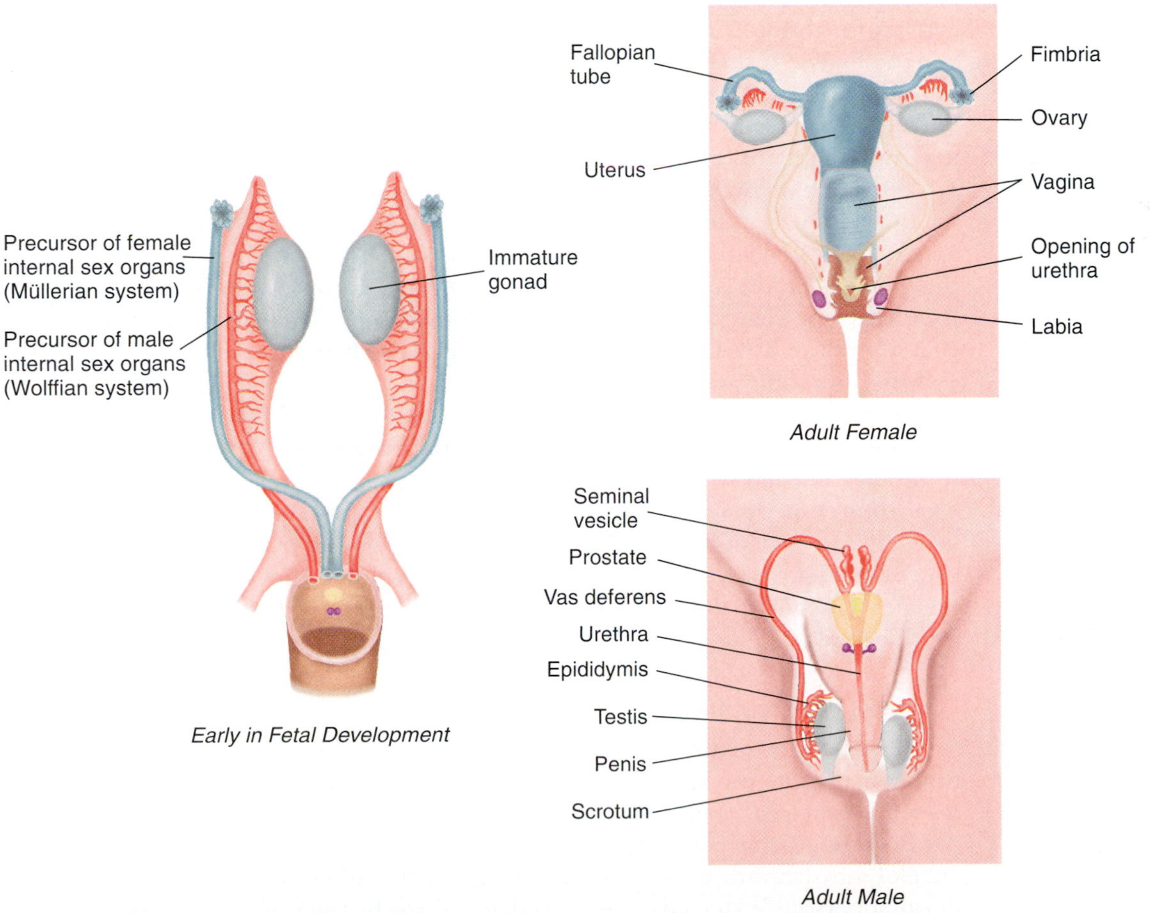

As you will recall from Chapter 2, hormones exert their effects on target cells by stimulating the appropriate hormone receptor. Thus, the precursor of the male internal sex organs—the Wolffian system—contains androgen receptors that are coupled to cellular mechanisms that promote growth and division. When molecules of androgens bind with these receptors, the epididymis, vas deferens, and seminal vesicles develop and grow. In contrast, the cells of the Müllerian system contain receptors for anti-Müllerian hormone that *prevent* growth and division. Thus, anti-Müllerian hormone prevents the development of the female internal sex organs.

The fact that the internal sex organs of the human embryo are bisexual and could potentially develop as either male or female is dramatically illustrated by two genetic disorders: *androgen insensitivity syndrome* and *persistent Müllerian duct syndrome.* Some people are insensitive to androgens; they have **androgen insensitivity syndrome,** one of the more aptly named disorders (Money and Ehrhardt, 1972; MacLean, Warne, and Zajac, 1995). The cause of androgen insensitivity syndrome is a genetic mutation that prevents the formation of functioning androgen receptors. (The gene for the androgen receptor is located on the X chromosome.) The primitive gonads of a genetic male fetus with androgen insensitivity syndrome become testes and secrete both anti-Müllerian hormone and androgens. The lack of androgen receptors prevents the androgens from having a masculinizing effect; thus, the epididymis, vas deferens, seminal vesicles, and prostate fail to develop. However, the anti-Müllerian hormone still has its defeminizing effect, preventing the female internal sex organs from developing. The uterus, fimbriae, and Fallopian tubes fail to develop, and the vagina is shallow. Their external genitalia are female, and at puberty they develop a woman's body. Of course, lacking a uterus and ovaries, these people cannot have children.

The second genetic disorder, **persistent Müllerian duct syndrome,** has two causes: either a failure to produce anti-Müllerian hormone or the absence of receptors for this hormone (Warne and Zajac, 1998). When this syndrome occurs in genetic males, androgens have their masculinizing effect but defeminization does not occur. Thus, the person is born with *both* sets of internal sex organs, male and female. The presence of the additional female sex organs usually interferes with normal functioning of the male sex organs.

So far, I have been discussing only male sex hormones. What about prenatal sexual development in females? A chromosomal anomaly indicates that female sex organs are not needed for development of the Müllerian system. This fact has led to the dictum "Nature's impulse is to create a female." People with **Turner's syndrome** have only one sex chromosome: an X chromosome. (Thus, instead of having XX cells, they have X0 cells—0 indicating a missing sex chromosome.) In most cases the existing X chromosome comes from the mother, which means that the cause of the disorder lies with a defective sperm (Knebelmann et al., 1991). Because a Y chromosome is not present, testes do not develop. In addition, because two X chromosomes are needed to produce ovaries, these glands are not produced either. But even though people with Turner's syndrome have no gonads at all, they develop into females, with normal female internal sex organs and external genitalia—which proves that fetuses do not need ovaries or the hormones they produce to develop as females. Of course, they cannot bear children, because without ovaries they cannot produce ova.

androgen insensitivity syndrome A condition caused by a congenital lack of functioning androgen receptors; in a person with XY sex chromosomes, causes the development of a female with testes but no internal sex organs.

persistent Müllerian duct syndrome A condition caused by a congenital lack of anti-Müllerian hormone or receptors for this hormone; in a male, causes development of both male and female internal sex organs.

Turner's syndrome The presence of only one sex chromosome (an X chromosome); characterized by lack of ovaries but otherwise normal female sex organs and genitalia.

gonadotropin-releasing hormone (*go nad oh* ***trow*** *pin*) A hypothalamic hormone that stimulates the anterior pituitary gland to secrete gonadotropic hormone.

gonadotropic hormone A hormone of the anterior pituitary gland that has a stimulating effect on cells of the gonads.

follicle-stimulating hormone (FSH) The hormone of the anterior pituitary gland that causes development of an ovarian follicle and the maturation of an ovum.

luteinizing hormone (LH) (***lew*** *tee a nize ing*) A hormone of the anterior pituitary gland that causes ovulation and development of the ovarian follicle into a corpus luteum.

External Genitalia

The external genitalia are the visible sex organs, including the penis and scrotum in males and the labia, clitoris, and outer part of the vagina in females. (See ***Figure 9.3.***) As we just saw, the external genitalia do not need to be stimulated by female sex hormones to become female; they just naturally develop that way. In the presence of dihydrotestosterone the external genitalia will become male. Thus, the gender of a person's external genitalia is determined by the presence or absence of an androgen, which explains why people with Turner's syndrome have female external genitalia even though they lack ovaries. People with androgen insensitivity syndrome have female external genitalia too, because without androgen receptors their cells cannot respond to the androgens produced by their testes.

Figure 9.4 summarizes the factors that control the development of the gonads, internal sex organs, and genitalia. (See ***Figure 9.4***.)

Sexual Maturation

The *primary* sex characteristics include the gonads, internal sex organs, and external genitalia. These organs are present at birth. The *secondary* sex characteristics, such as enlarged breasts and widened hips or a beard and deep voice, do not appear until puberty. Without seeing genitals, we must guess the sex of a prepubescent child from his or her haircut and clothing; the bodies of young boys and girls are rather similar. However, at puberty the gonads are stimulated to produce their hormones, and these hormones cause the person to mature sexually. The onset of puberty occurs when cells in the hypothalamus secrete **gonadotropin-releasing hormones** (GnRH), which stimulate the production and release of two **gonadotropic hormones** by the anterior pituitary gland. The gonadotropic ("gonad-turning") hormones stimulate the gonads to produce *their* hormones, which are ultimately responsible for sexual maturation. (See ***Figure 9.5***.)

The two gonadotropic hormones are **follicle-stimulating hormone (FSH)** and **luteinizing hormone (LH),** named for the effects they produce in the female (production of a *follicle* and its subsequent *luteinization,* to be described in the next section of this chapter). However, the same hormones are produced in the male, where they stimulate the testes to produce sperms and to secrete testosterone. If male and female pituitary glands are

Figure 9.3

Development of the external genitalia.

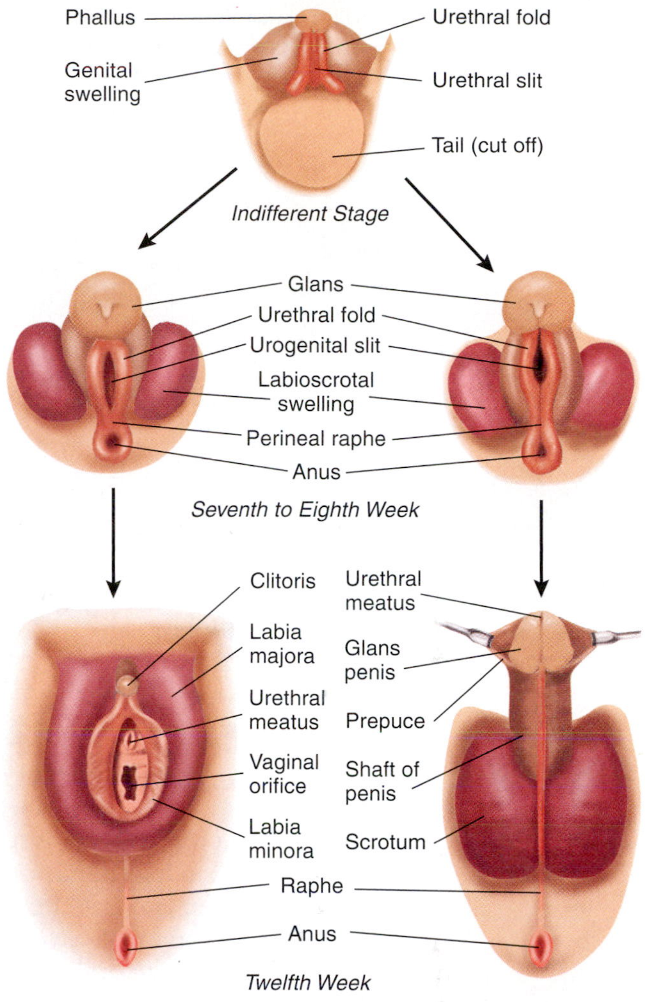

Adapted from Spaulding, M. H., in *Contributions to Embryology,* Vol. 13. Washington, DC: Carnegie Institute of Washington, 1921.

Figure 9.4

Hormonal control of development of the internal sex organs.

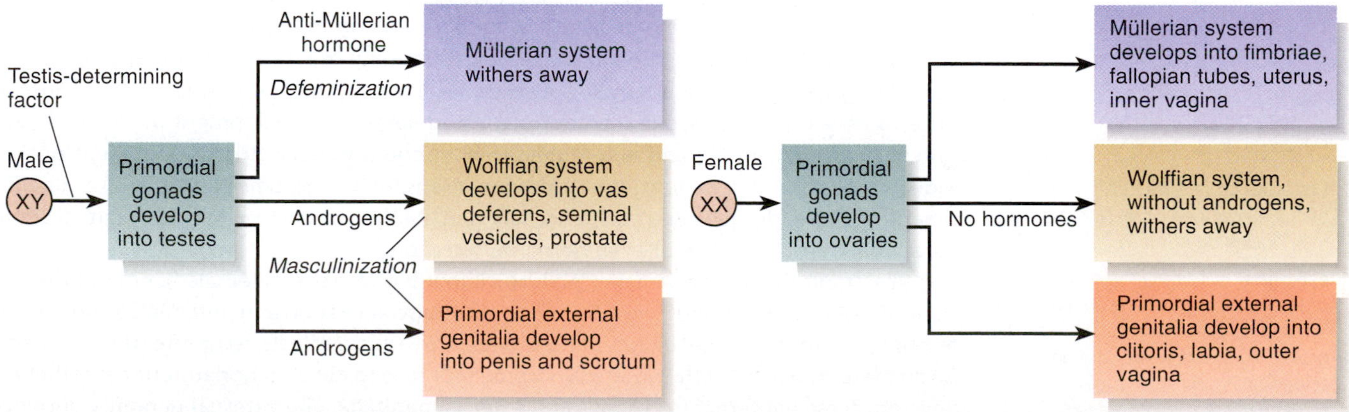

Figure 9.5

Sexual maturation. Puberty is initiated when the hypothalamus secretes gonadotropin-releasing hormones, which stimulate the anterior pituitary gland to secrete gonadotropic hormones.

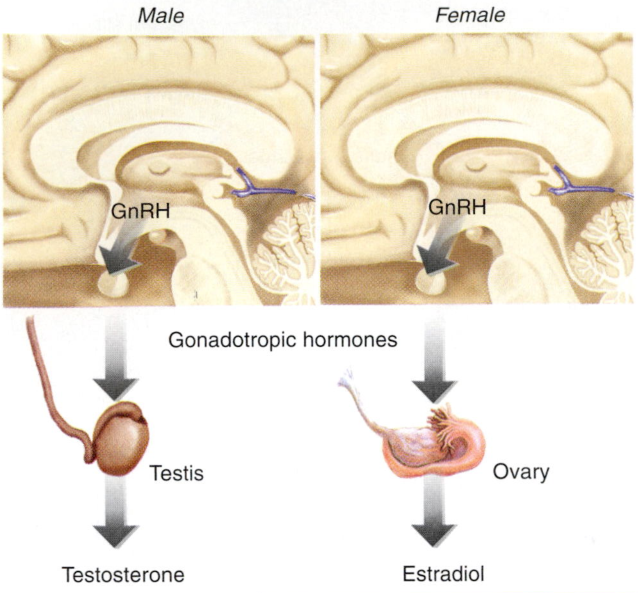

exchanged in rats, the ovaries and testes respond perfectly to the hormones secreted by the new glands (Harris and Jacobsohn, 1951–1952).

In response to the gonadotropic hormones (usually called *gonadotropins*) the gonads secrete steroid sex hormones. The ovaries produce **estradiol,** one of a class of hormones known as **estrogens.** As we saw, the testes produce testosterone, an androgen. Both types of glands also produce a small amount of the hormones of the other sex. The gonadal steroids affect many parts of the body. Both estradiol and androgens initiate closure of the growing portions of the bones and thus halt skeletal growth. Estradiol also causes breast development, growth of the lining of the uterus, changes in the deposition of body fat, and maturation of the female genitalia. Androgens stimulate growth of facial, axillary (underarm), and pubic hair; lower the voice; alter the hairline on the head (often causing baldness later in life); stimulate muscular development; and cause genital growth. This description leaves out two of the female secondary characteristics: axillary and pubic hair. These characteristics are produced not by estradiol but rather by androgens secreted by the cortex of the adrenal glands. Even a male who is castrated before puberty (whose testes are removed) will grow axillary and pubic hair, stimulated by his own adrenal androgens.

A list of the principal sex hormones and examples of their effects are presented in Table 9.1. Note that some of these effects are discussed later in this chapter. (See ***Table 9.1.***)

The bipotentiality of some of the secondary sex characteristics remains throughout life. If a man is treated with an estrogen (for example, to control an androgen-dependent tumor), he will grow breasts, and his facial hair will become finer and softer. However, his voice will remain low, because the enlargement of the larynx is permanent. Conversely, a woman who receives high levels of an androgen (usually from a tumor that secretes androgens) will grow a beard, and her voice will become lower.

INTERIM SUMMARY

Sexual Development

Gender is determined by the sex chromosomes: XX produces a female, and XY produces a male. Males are produced by the action of the *Sry* gene on the Y chromosome, which contains the code for the production of the testis-determining protein, which in turn causes the primitive gonads to become testes. The testes secrete two kinds of hormones that cause a male to develop. Testosterone (an androgen) stimulates the development of the Wolffian system (masculinization), and anti-Müllerian hormone suppresses the development of the Müllerian system (defeminization). Androgen insensitivity syndrome results from a hereditary defect in androgen receptors, and persistent Müllerian duct syndrome results from a hereditary defect in anti-Müllerian hormone receptors.

By default the body is female ("Nature's impulse is to create a female"); only by the actions of testicular hormones will it become male. Masculinization and defeminization are referred to as *organizational* effects of hormones; *activational* effects occur after development is complete. A person with Turner's syndrome (X0) fails to develop gonads but nevertheless develops female internal sex organs and external genitalia. The external genitalia develop

estradiol (*ess tra* ***dye*** *ahl*) The principal estrogen of many mammals, including humans.

estrogen (***ess*** *trow jen*) A class of sex hormones that cause maturation of the female genitalia, growth of breast tissue, and development of other physical features characteristic of females.

Table 9.1

Classification of Sex Hormones

Class	Principal Hormone in Humans (Where Produced)	Examples of Effects
Androgens	Testosterone (testes)	Development of Wolffian system; production of sperms; growth of facial, pubic, and axillary hair; muscular development; enlargement of larynx; inhibition of bone growth; sex drive in men (and women?)
	Dihydrotestosterone (produced from testosterone by action of 5α reductase)	Maturation of male external genitalia
	Androstenedione (adrenal glands)	In women, growth of pubic and axillary hair; less important than testosterone and dihydrotestosterone in men
Estrogens	Estradiol (ovaries)	Maturation of female genitalia; growth of breasts; alterations in fat deposits; growth of uterine lining; inhibition of bone growth; sex drive in women (?)
Gestagens	Progesterone (ovaries)	Maintenance of uterine lining
Hypothalamic hormones	Gonadotropin-releasing hormone (hypothalamus)	Secretion of gonadotropins
Gonadotropins	Follicle-stimulating hormone (anterior pituitary)	Development of ovarian follicle
	Luteinizing hormone (anterior pituitary)	Ovulation; development of corpus luteum
Other hormones	Prolactin (anterior pituitary)	Milk production; male refractory period (?)
	Oxytocin (posterior pituitary)	Milk ejection; orgasm

from common precursors. In the absence of gonadal hormones the precursors develop the female form; in the presence of androgens (primarily dihydrotestosterone, which derives from testosterone through the action of an enzyme), they develop the male form (masculinization).

Sexual maturity occurs when the hypothalamus begins secreting gonadotropin-releasing hormone, which stimulates the secretion of follicle-stimulating hormone and luteinizing hormone by the anterior pituitary gland. These hormones stimulate the gonads to secrete their hormones, thus causing the genitals to mature and the body to develop the secondary sex characteristics (activational effects).

THOUGHT QUESTIONS

1. Suppose that people could determine the sex of their child, say, by having one of the would-be parents take a drug before conceiving the baby. What would the consequences be?
2. With appropriate hormonal treatment, the uterus of a postmenopausal woman can be made ready for the implantation of another woman's ovum, fertilized in vitro, and she can become a mother. In fact, several women in their fifties and sixties have done so. What do you think about this procedure? Should decisions about using it be left to couples and their physicians, or does the rest of society (represented by their legislators) have an interest?

Hormonal Control of Sexual Behavior

We have seen that hormones are responsible for sexual dimorphism in the structure of the body and its organs. Hormones have organizational and activational effects on the internal sex organs, genitals, and secondary sex characteristics. Naturally, all of these effects influence a person's behavior. Simply having the physique and genitals of a man or a woman exerts a powerful effect. But hormones do more than give us masculine or feminine bodies; they also affect behavior by interacting directly with the nervous system. Androgens that are present during prenatal development affect the development of the nervous system. In addition, both male and female sex hormones have activational effects on the adult nervous system that influence both physiological processes and behavior. This section considers some of these hormonal effects.

Hormonal Control of Female Reproductive Cycles

The reproductive cycle of female primates is called a **menstrual cycle** (from *mensis,* meaning "month"). Females of other species of mammals also have reproductive cycles, called **estrous cycles.** *Estrus* means "gadfly"; when a female rat is in estrus, her hormonal condition goads her to act differently than she does at other times. (For that matter, it goads male rats to act differently, too.) The primary feature that distinguishes menstrual cycles from estrous cycles is the monthly growth and loss of the lining of the uterus. The other features are approximately the same—except that the estrous cycle of rats takes four days. Also, the sexual behavior of female mammals with estrous cycles is linked with ovulation, whereas most female primates can mate at any time during their menstrual cycle.

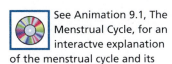

See Animation 9.1, The Menstrual Cycle, for an interactve explanation of the menstrual cycle and its control.

Menstrual cycles and estrous cycles consist of a sequence of events that are controlled by hormonal secretions of the pituitary gland and ovaries. These glands interact, the secretions of one affecting those of the other. A cycle begins with the secretion of gonadotropins by the anterior pituitary gland. These hormones (especially FSH) stimulate the growth of **ovarian follicles,** small spheres of epithelial cells surrounding each ovum. Women normally produce one ovarian follicle each month; if two are produced and fertilized, dizygotic (fraternal) twins will develop. As ovarian follicles mature, they secrete estradiol, which causes the growth of the lining of the uterus in preparation for implantation of the ovum, should it be fertilized by a sperm. Feedback from the increasing level of estradiol eventually triggers the release of a surge of LH by the anterior pituitary gland. (See ***Figure 9.6*** and ***Animation 9.1, The Menstrual Cycle.***)

Figure 9.6

Neuroendocrine control of the menstrual cycle.

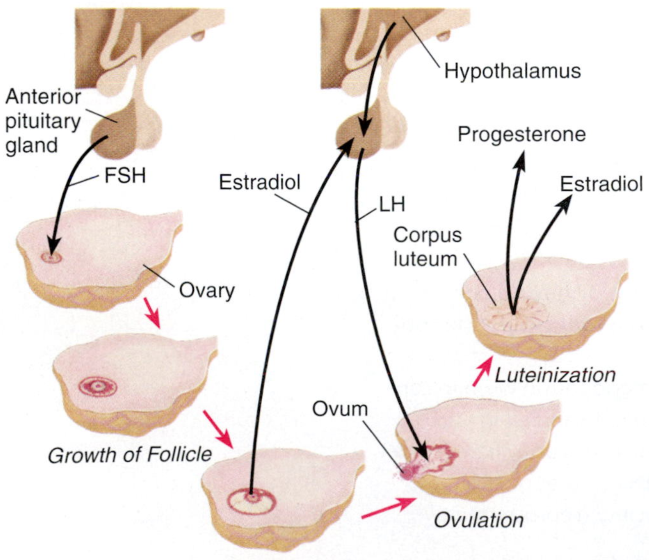

The LH surge causes *ovulation*: The ovarian follicle ruptures, releasing the ovum. Under the continued influence of LH, the ruptured ovarian follicle becomes a **corpus luteum** ("yellow body"), which produces estradiol and **progesterone.** (See ***Figure 9.6.***) The latter hormone promotes pregnancy (*gestation*). It maintains the lining of the uterus, and it inhibits the ovaries from producing another follicle. Meanwhile, the ovum enters one of the Fallopian tubes and begins its progress toward the uterus. If it meets sperm cells during its travel down the Fallopian tube and becomes fertilized, it begins to divide, and several days later it attaches itself to the uterine wall.

If the ovum is not fertilized or if it is fertilized too late to develop sufficiently by the time it gets to the uterus, the corpus luteum will stop producing estradiol and progesterone, and then the lining of the walls of the uterus will slough off. At this point menstruation will commence.

Hormonal Control of Sexual Behavior of Laboratory Animals

The interactions between sex hormones and the human brain are difficult to study. We must turn to two sources of information: experiments with animals and various developmental disorders in humans, which serve as nature's own "experiments." Let us first consider the evidence gathered from research with laboratory animals.

Males

Male sexual behavior is quite varied, although the essential features of *intromission* (entry of the penis into the female's vagina), *pelvic thrusting* (rhythmic movement of the hindquarters, causing genital friction), and *ejaculation* (discharge of semen) are characteristic of all male mammals. Humans, of course, have invented all kinds of copulatory and noncopulatory sexual behavior. For example, the pelvic movements leading to ejaculation may be performed by the woman, and sex play can lead to orgasm without intromission.

The sexual behavior of rats has been studied more than that of any other laboratory animal. When a male rat encounters a receptive female, he will spend some time nuzzling her and sniffing and licking her genitals, mount her, and engage in pelvic thrusting. He will mount her several times, achieving intromission on most of the mountings. After eight to fifteen intromissions approximately 1 minute apart (each lasting only about one-quarter of a second), the male will ejaculate.

After ejaculating, the male refrains from sexual activity for a period of time (minutes, in the rat). Most mammals will return to copulate again and again, showing a longer pause, called a **refractory period,** after each ejaculation. (The term comes from the Latin *refringere,* "to break off.") An interesting phenomenon occurs in some mammals. If a male, after finally becoming "exhausted" by repeated copulation with the same female, is presented with a new female, he begins to respond quickly—often as fast as he did in his initial contact with the first female. Successive introductions of new females can keep up his performance for prolonged periods of time. This phenomenon is undoubtedly important in species in which a single male inseminates all the females in his harem. Species with approximately equal numbers of reproductively active males and females are less likely to act this way.

The rejuvenating effect of a new female, also seen in roosters, is usually called the **Coolidge effect.** The following story is reputed to be true, but I cannot vouch for that fact. (If it is not true, it ought to be.) The late former U.S. president Calvin Coolidge and his wife were touring a farm, when Mrs. Coolidge asked the farmer whether the continuous and vigorous sexual activity among the flock of hens was the work of just one rooster. The reply was yes. She smiled and said, "You might point that out to Mr. Coolidge." The president looked thoughtfully at the birds and then asked the farmer whether a different hen was involved each time. The answer, again, was yes. "You might point *that* out to Mrs. Coolidge," he said.

Sexual behavior of male rodents depends on testosterone, a fact that has long been recognized (Bermant and Davidson, 1974). If a male rat is castrated (that is, if his testes are removed), his sexual activity eventually ceases. However, the behavior can be reinstated by injections of testosterone. I will describe the neural basis of this activational effect later in this chapter.

Females

The mammalian female has been described as the passive participant in copulation. It is true that in some species the female's role during the act of copulation

menstrual cycle (***men*** *strew al*) The female reproductive cycle of most primates, including humans; characterized by growth of the lining of the uterus, ovulation, development of a corpus luteum, and (if pregnancy does not occur), menstruation.

estrous cycle The female reproductive cycle of mammals other than primates.

ovarian follicle A cluster of epithelial cells surrounding an *oocyte,* which develops into an ovum.

corpus luteum (***lew*** *tee um*) A cluster of cells that develops from the ovarian follicle after ovulation; secretes estradiol and progesterone.

progesterone (*pro* ***jess*** *ter own*) A steroid hormone produced by the ovary that maintains the endometrial lining of the uterus during the later part of the menstrual cycle and during pregnancy; along with estradiol it promotes receptivity in female mammals with estrous cycles.

refractory period (*ree* ***frak*** *to ree*) A period of time after a particular action (for example, an ejaculation by a male) during which that action cannot occur again.

Coolidge effect The restorative effect of introducing a new female sex partner to a male that has apparently become "exhausted" by sexual activity.

is merely to assume a posture that exposes her genitals to the male. This behavior is called the **lordosis** response (from the Greek *lordos,* meaning "bent backward"). The female will also move her tail away (if she has one) and stand rigidly enough to support the weight of the male. However, the behavior of a female rodent in *initiating* copulation is often very active. Certainly, if a male attempts to copulate with a nonestrous rodent, the female will either actively flee or rebuff him. But when the female is in a receptive state, she will often approach the male, nuzzle him, sniff his genitals, and show behaviors characteristic of her species. For example, a female rat will exhibit quick, short, hopping movements and rapid ear wiggling, which most male rats find irresistible (McClintock and Adler, 1978).

Sexual behavior of female rodents depends on the gonadal hormones present during estrus: estradiol and progesterone. In rats estradiol increases about 40 hours before the female becomes receptive; just before receptivity occurs, the corpus luteum begins secreting large quantities of progesterone (Feder, 1981). Ovariectomized rats (rats whose ovaries have been removed) are not sexually receptive. Although sexual receptivity can be produced in ovariectomized rodents by administering large doses of estradiol alone, the most effective treatment duplicates the normal sequence of hormones: a small amount of estradiol, followed by progesterone. Progesterone alone is ineffective; thus, the estradiol "primes" its effectiveness. Priming with estradiol takes about 16–24 hours, after which an injection of progesterone produces receptive behaviors within an hour (Takahashi, 1990). The neural mechanisms that are responsible for these effects will be described later in this chapter.

The sequence of estradiol followed by progesterone has three effects on female rats: It increases their receptivity, their proceptivity, and their attractiveness. *Receptivity* refers to their ability and willingness to copulate—to accept the advances of a male by holding still and displaying lordosis when he attempts to mount her. *Proceptivity* refers to a female's eagerness to copulate, as shown by the fact that she seeks out a male and engages in behaviors that tend to arouse his sexual interest. *Attractiveness* refers to physiological and behavioral changes that affect the male. The male rat (along with many other male mammals) is most responsive to females who are in estrus ("in heat"). Males will ignore a female whose ovaries have been removed, but injections of estradiol and progesterone will restore her attractiveness (and also change her behavior toward the male). The stimuli that arouse a male rat's sexual interest include her odor and her behavior. In some species visible changes, such as the swollen sex skin in the genital region of a female monkey, also affect sex appeal.

lordosis A spinal sexual reflex seen in many four-legged female mammals; arching of the back in response to approach of a male or to touching the flanks, which elevates the hindquarters.

pheromone (***fair*** *oh moan*) A chemical released by one animal that affects the behavior or physiology of another animal; usually smelled or tasted.

Lee-Boot effect The slowing and eventual cessation of estrous cycles in groups of female animals that are housed together; caused by a pheromone in the animals' urine; first observed in mice.

Whitten effect The synchronization of the menstrual or estrous cycles of a group of females, which occurs only in the presence of a pheromone in a male's urine.

Vandenbergh effect The earlier onset of puberty seen in female animals that are housed with males; caused by a pheromone in the male's urine; first observed in mice.

Bruce effect Termination of pregnancy caused by the odor of a pheromone in the urine of a male other than the one that impregnated the female; first identified in mice.

vomeronasal organ (VNO) (*voah mer oh* ***nay*** *zul*) A sensory organ that detects the presence of certain chemicals, especially when a liquid is actively sniffed; mediates the effects of some pheromones.

Organizational Effects of Androgens on Behavior: Masculinization and Defeminization

The dictum "Nature's impulse is to create a female" applies to sexual behavior as well as to sex organs. That is, if a rodent's brain is *not* exposed to androgens during a critical period of development, the animal will engage in female sexual behavior as an adult (if then given estradiol and progesterone). Fortunately for experimenters this critical time comes shortly after birth for rats and for several other species of rodents that are born in a rather immature condition. Thus, if a male rat is castrated immediately after birth, permitted to grow to adulthood, and then given injections of estradiol and progesterone, it will respond to the presence of another male by arching its back and presenting its hindquarters. In other words, it will act as if it were a female (Blaustein and Olster, 1989).

In contrast, if a rodent brain is exposed to androgens during development, two phenomena occur: behavioral defeminization and behavioral masculinization. *Behavioral defeminization* refers to the organizational effect of androgens that prevents the animal from displaying female sexual behavior in adulthood. As we shall see later, this effect is accomplished by suppressing the development of neural circuits controlling female sexual behavior. For example, if a female rodent is ovariectomized and given an injection of testosterone immediately after birth, she will *not* respond to a male rat when, as an adult, she is given injections of estradiol and progesterone. *Behavioral masculinization* refers to the organizational effect of androgens that enables animals to engage in male sexual behavior in adulthood. This effect is accomplished by stimulating the development of neural circuits controlling male sexual behavior. For example, if the female rodent in my previous example is given testosterone in adulthood rather than estradiol and progesterone, she will mount and attempt to copulate with a receptive female. (See Breedlove, 1992, and Carter, 1992, for references to specific studies.) (See ***Figure 9.7.***)

Figure 9.7

Organizational effects of testosterone. Around the time of birth, testosterone masculinizes and defeminizes rodents' sexual behavior.

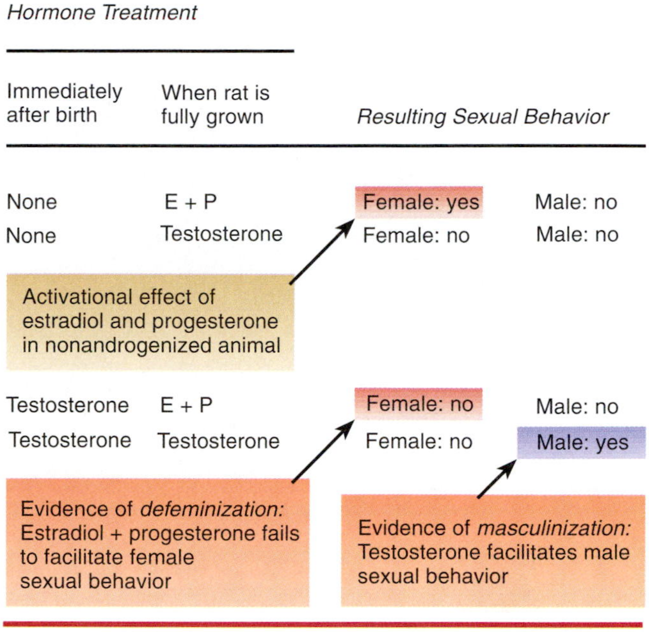

Hormone Treatment
Immediately after birth
When rat is fully grown
Resulting Sexual Behavior
None
E + P
Female: yes
Male: no
None
Testosterone
Female: no
Male: no
Activational effect of estradiol and progesterone in nonandrogenized animal
Testosterone
E + P
Female: no
Male: no
Testosterone
Testosterone
Female: no
Male: yes
Evidence of defeminization: Estradiol + progesterone fails to facilitate female sexual behavior
Evidence of masculinization: Testosterone facilitates male sexual behavior

Effects of Pheromones

Hormones transmit messages from one part of the body (the secreting gland) to another (the target tissue). Another class of chemicals, called **pheromones,** carries messages from one animal to another. Some of these chemicals, like hormones, affect reproductive behavior. Karlson and Luscher (1959) coined the term, from the Greek *pherein,* "to carry," and *horman,* "to excite." Pheromones are released by one animal and directly affect the physiology or behavior of another. In mammalian species most pheromones are detected by means of olfaction.

Pheromones can affect reproductive physiology or behavior. First, let us consider the effects on reproductive physiology. When groups of female mice are housed together, their estrous cycles slow down and eventually stop. This phenomenon is known as the **Lee-Boot effect** (van der Lee and Boot, 1955). If groups of females are exposed to the odor of a male (or of his urine), they begin cycling again, and their cycles tend to be synchronized. This phenomenon is known as the **Whitten effect** (Whitten, 1959). The **Vandenbergh effect** (Vandenbergh, Whitsett, and Lombardi, 1975) is the acceleration of the onset of puberty in a female rodent caused by the odor of a male. Both the Whitten effect and the Vandenbergh effect are caused by a group of compounds that are present only in the urine of intact adult males (Ma, Miao, and Novotny, 1999; Novotny et al., 1999); the urine of a juvenile or castrated male has no effect. Thus, the production of the pheromone requires the presence of testosterone.

The **Bruce effect** (Bruce, 1960a, 1960b) is a particularly interesting phenomenon: When a recently impregnated female mouse encounters a normal male mouse other than the one with which she mated, the pregnancy is very likely to fail. This effect, too, is caused by a substance secreted in the urine of intact males—but not of males that have been castrated. Thus, a male mouse that encounters a pregnant female is able to prevent the birth of infants carrying another male's genes and subsequently impregnate the female himself. This phenomenon is advantageous even from the female's point of view. The fact that the new male has managed to take over the old male's territory indicates that he is probably healthier and more vigorous, and therefore his genes will contribute to the formation of offspring that are more likely to survive.

As you learned in Chapter 7, detection of odors is accomplished by the olfactory bulbs, which constitute the primary olfactory system. However, the four effects that pheromones have on reproductive cycles appear to be mediated by another organ—the **vomeronasal organ**—which consists of a small group of sensory receptors arranged around a pouch connected by a duct to the nasal passage. The vomeronasal

Figure 9.8

The rodent accessory olfactory system.

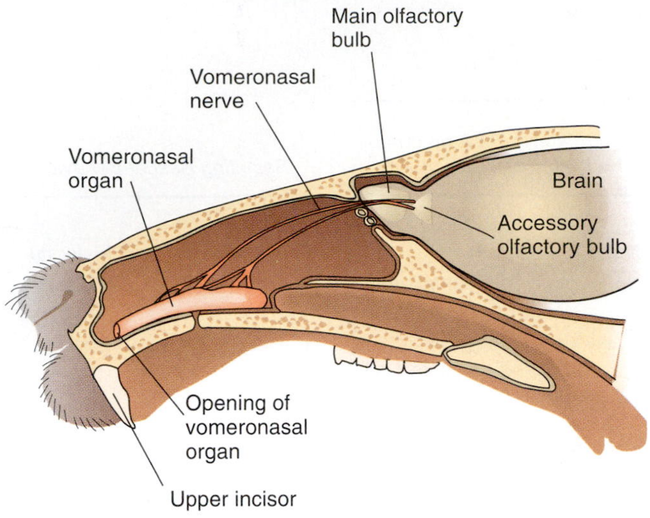

Adapted from Wysocki, C. J. *Neuroscience & Biobehavioral Reviews,* 1979, *3,* 301–341.

Figure 9.9

A cross section through the rat brain showing the location of the amygdala.

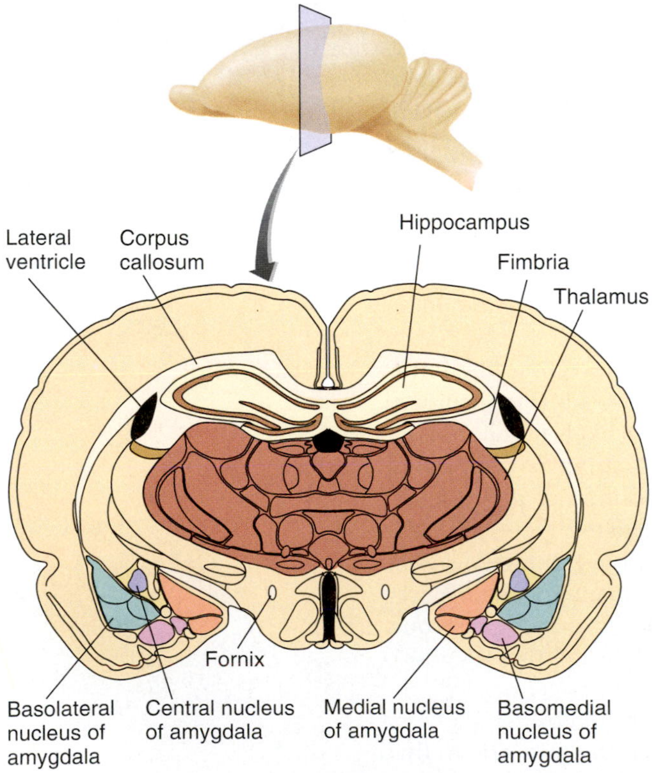

Adapted from Swanson, L. W. *Brain Maps: Structure of the Rat Brain.* New York: Elsevier, 1992.

organ, which is present in all orders of mammals except for cetaceans (whales and dolphins), projects to the **accessory olfactory bulb,** located immediately behind the olfactory bulb (Wysocki, 1979). (See ***Figure 9.8.***) The vomeronasal organ probably does not detect airborne molecules, as the olfactory bulbs do, but instead is sensitive to nonvolatile compounds found in urine or other substances. In fact, stimulation of a nerve that serves the nasal region of the hamster causes fluid to be pumped into the vomeronasal organ, which exposes the receptors to any substances that may be present (Meredith and O'Connell, 1979). This pump is activated whenever the animal encounters a novel stimulus (Meredith, 1994).

Removal of the accessory olfactory bulb disrupts the Lee-Boot effect, the Whitten effect, the Vandenbergh effect, and the Bruce effect; thus, the vomeronasal system is essential for these phenomena (Halpern, 1987). The accessory olfactory bulb sends axons to the **medial nucleus of the amygdala,** which in turn projects to the preoptic area and anterior hypothalamus and to the ventromedial nucleus of the hypothalamus. (As you learned in Chapter 7, so does the main olfactory bulb.) Thus, the neural circuit responsible for the effects of these pheromones appears to involve these regions. As we shall see, the preoptic area, the medial amygdala, and the ventromedial nucleus of the hypothalamus all play important roles in reproductive behavior. (See ***Figure 9.9.***)

Besides having effects on reproductive physiology, some pheromones directly affect behavior. For example, pheromones present in the vaginal secretions of female hamsters stimulate sexual behavior in males. Males are attracted to the secretions of females, and they sniff and lick the female's genitals before copulating. In fact, there may be two categories of pheromones: one detected by the vomeronasal organ and another detected by the olfactory epithelium; mating behavior of male hamsters is disrupted only if *both* systems are interrupted (Powers and Winans, 1975; Winans and Powers, 1977). As we saw, both the primary and accessory olfactory systems send fibers to the medial nucleus of the amygdala. Lehman and Winans (1982) found that lesions of the medial amygdala abolished the sexual behavior of male hamsters. Thus, the amygdala is part of the system that mediates the effects of pheromones on the sexual behavior of male hamsters.

Stowers et al. (2002) found that a targeted mutation against a protein that is essential for the detection of pheromones by the vomeronasal organ abolishes a male mouse's ability to discriminate between males and females. As a result, male mice with this mutation attempted to copulate with both males and females. (The behavior of these mice is shown in Animation 10.1.)

It appears that at least some pheromone-related phenomena occur in humans. McClintock (1971) studied the menstrual cycles of women attending an all-female college. She found that women who spent a large amount of

The presence of pheromone-related phenomena in humans was confirmed by the discovery that women who regularly spend time together tend to have synchronized menstrual cycles.

time together tended to have synchronized cycles—Their menstrual periods began within a day or two of one another. In addition, women who regularly spent some time in the presence of men tended to have shorter cycles than those who rarely spent time with (smelled?) men.

Russell, Switz, and Thompson (1980) obtained direct evidence that olfactory stimuli can synchronize women's menstrual cycles. The investigators collected daily samples of a woman's underarm sweat. They dissolved the samples in alcohol and swabbed them on the upper lips of a group of women three times each week, in the order in which they were originally taken. The cycles of the women who received the extract (but not those of control subjects whose lips were swabbed with pure alcohol) began to synchronize with the cycle of the odor donor. These results were confirmed by a similar study by Stern and McClintock (1998), who found that compounds from the armpits of women taken around the time of ovulation lengthened other women's menstrual cycles, and compounds taken late in the cycle shortened them. Shinohara et al. (2001) found that these effects were caused by pheromone-induced changes in the rate of LH secretion.

Several studies have found that two compounds present in human sweat have different effects in men and women. Jacob and McClintock (2000) found that the androgenic chemical *androstadienone* increases alertness and positive mood in women but decreased positive mood in men. A functional imaging study by Savic et al. (2001) found that the androstadienone activated the preoptic area and ventromedial hypothalamus in women, whereas the estrogenic chemical *estratetraene* activated the paraventricular nucleus and dorsomedial hypothalamus in men.

Whether or not pheromones play a role in sexual attraction in humans, the familiar odor of a sex partner probably has a positive effect on sexual arousal—just like the sight of a sex partner or the sound of his or her voice. We are not generally conscious of the fact, but we can identify other people on the basis of olfactory cues. For example, a study by Russell (1976) found that people were able to distinguish by odor between T-shirts that they had worn and those previously worn by other people. They could also tell whether the unknown owner of a T-shirt was male or female. Thus, it is likely that men and women can *learn* to be attracted by their partners' characteristic odors, just as they can learn to be attracted by the sound of their voice. In an instance like this, the odors are serving simply as sensory cues, not as pheromones.

Although the human nose contains a vomeronasal organ (Garcia-Velasco and Mondragon, 1991), not all investigators agree that this organ detects pheromones.

accessory olfactory bulb A neural structure located in the main olfactory bulb that receives information from the vomeronasal organ.

medial nucleus of the amygdala (*a **mig** da la*) A nucleus that receives olfactory information from the olfactory bulb and accessory olfactory bulb; involved in the effects of odors and pheromones on reproductive behavior.

The density of neurons in the VNO is very sparse, and investigators have not yet succeeded in tracing neural connections from this organ to the brain (Doty, 2001), which has led some researchers to conclude that the human VNO is a vestigial organ like the human appendix. Evidence clearly shows that human reproductive physiology is affected by pheromones, but it seems likely that these chemical signals are detected by the "standard" olfactory system—the receptor cells in the olfactory epithelium—and not by cells in the VNO.

Human Sexual Behavior

Human sexual behavior, like that of other mammals, is influenced by activational effects of gonadal hormones and, almost certainly, organizational effects as well. But as we will see in the following subsections, the effects of these hormones are different in our species—especially in women.

If hormones have organizational effects on human sexual behavior, they must exert these effects by altering the development of the brain. Although there is good evidence that prenatal exposure to androgens affects development of the human brain, we cannot yet be certain that this exposure has long-lasting behavioral effects. The evidence pertaining to these issues is discussed later, in a section on sexual orientation.

Activational Effects of Sex Hormones in Women

As we saw, the sexual behavior of most female mammals other than higher primates is controlled by the ovarian hormones estradiol and progesterone. (In some species, such as cats and rabbits, only estradiol is necessary.) As Wallen (1990) pointed out, the ovarian hormones control not only the *willingness* (or even eagerness) of an estrous female to mate but also her *ability* to mate. That is, a male rat cannot copulate with a female rat that is not in estrus. Even if he would overpower her and mount her, her lordosis response would not occur, and he would be unable to achieve intromission. Thus, the evolutionary process seems to have selected animals that mate only at a time when the female is able to become pregnant. (The neural control of the lordosis response and the effects of ovarian hormones on it are described later in this chapter.)

In higher primates (including our own species) the ability to mate is not controlled by ovarian hormones. There are no physical barriers to sexual intercourse during any part of the menstrual cycle. If a woman or other female primate consents to sexual activity at any time (or is forced to submit by a male), intercourse can certainly take place.

Although ovarian hormones do not *control* women's sexual activity, they may still have an influence on their sexual interest. Early studies reported that fluctuations in the level of the ovarian hormones had only a minor effect on women's sexual interest (Adams, Gold, and Burt, 1978; Morris et al., 1987). However, as Wallen (1990) pointed out, these studies have almost all involved married women who live with their husbands. In stable, monogamous relationships in which the partners are together on a daily basis, sexual activity can be instigated by either of them. Normally, a husband does not force his wife to have intercourse with him, but even if she is not interested in engaging in sexual activity at that moment, she may find that she wants to do so because of her affection for him. Thus, changes in sexual interest and arousability might not always be reflected in changes in sexual behavior. In fact, a study of lesbian couples (whose menstrual cycles are likely to be synchronized) found a significant increase in sexual interest and activity during the middle portions of the women's cycles (Matteo and Rissman, 1984), which suggests that ovarian hormones *do* influence women's sexual interest.

These results pose an interesting question. If all of a woman's sexual encounters were initiated by her, without regard to her partner's desires, would we find an effect of ovarian hormones on the women's sexual activity? Van Goozen et al. (1997) found that the sexual activity initiated by men and women showed very different relationships to the woman's menstrual cycle (and hence to her level of ovarian hormones). Men initiated sexual activity at about the same rate throughout the woman's cycle, whereas sexual activity initiated by women showed a distinct peak around the time of ovulation, when estradiol levels are highest. (See ***Figure 9.10.***)

Wallen (2001) points out that although ovarian hormones may affect a woman's sexual interest, her behavior can be influenced by other factors as well. For example, if a woman does not want to become pregnant and does not have absolute confidence in her method of birth control, she may avoid sexual intercourse at mid-cycle, around the time of ovulation—even if her potential sexual interest is at a peak. In fact, Harvey (1987) found that women were more likely to engage in autosexual activity at this time. On the other hand, women who *want* to become pregnant are more likely to initiate sexual intercourse during the time when they are most likely to conceive.

Figure 9.10

The distribution of sexual activity of heterosexual couples initiated by the man and by the woman.

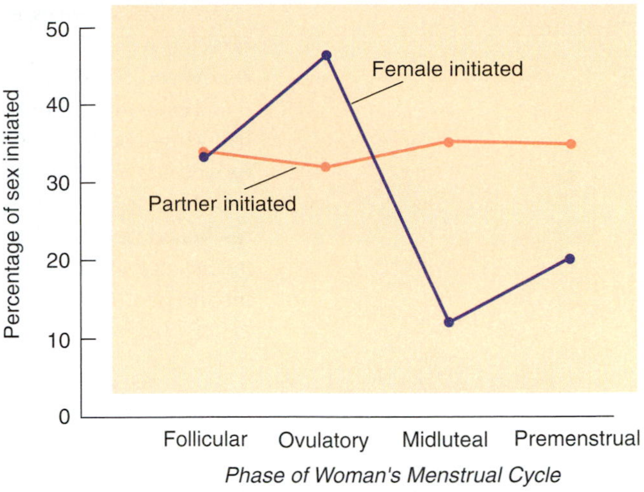

Adapted from Wallen, K. *Hormones and Behavior,* 2001, *40,* 339–357. After data from Van Goozen et al., 1997.

Several investigators have suggested that women's sexual interest can be stimulated by androgens. However, at the present time, the most likely conclusion seems to be that although androgens by themselves (in the absence of estradiol) do not stimulate women's sexual interest, they appear to amplify the effects of estradiol (Wallen, 2001). For example, Shifren et al. (2000) studied ovariectomized women aged 31–56 years who were receiving estrogen-replacement therapy. The women were given, in addition to the estrogen, either a placebo or one of two different doses of testosterone, delivered through transdermal patches. Although the placebo produced a positive effect, the testosterone further increased sexual activity and rate of orgasm. At the higher dose, the percentage of women who had sex fantasies, masturbated, and had intercourse increased two to three times over baseline levels and reported higher levels of well-being.

Activational Effects of Sex Hormones in Men

Although women and mammals with estrous cycles differ in their behavioral responsiveness to sex hormones, men resemble other mammals in their behavioral responsiveness to testosterone. With normal levels they can be potent and fertile; without testosterone sperm production ceases, and sooner or later, so does sexual potency. In a double-blind study, Bagatell et al. (1994) gave a placebo or a gonadotropin-releasing hormone (GnRH) antagonist to young male volunteers to suppress secretion of testicular androgens. Within two weeks the subjects who received the GnRH antagonist reported a decrease in sexual interest, sexual fantasy, and intercourse. Men who received replacement doses of testosterone along with the antagonist did not show these changes.

The decline of sexual activity after castration is quite variable. As reported by Money and Ehrhardt (1972), some men lose potency immediately, whereas others show a slow, gradual decline over several years. Perhaps at least some of the variability is a function of prior experience; practice not only may "make perfect," but may also forestall a decline in function. Although there is no direct evidence with respect to this possibility in humans, Wallen and his colleagues (Wallen et al., 1991; Wallen, 2001) injected a GnRH antagonist in seven adult male rhesus monkeys that were part of a larger group. The injection suppressed testosterone secretion, and sexual behavior declined after one week. However, the decline was related to the animal's social rank and sexual experience: More sexually experienced, high-ranking males continued to copulate. In fact, the highest-ranking male continued to copulate and ejaculate at the same rate as before, even though his testosterone secretion was suppressed for almost eight weeks. The mounting behavior of the lowest-ranking monkey completely ceased and did not resume until testosterone secretion recovered from the anti-GnRH treatment.

Testosterone not only affects sexual activity but also is affected by it—or even by thinking about it. A scientist stationed on a remote island (Anonymous, 1970) removed his beard with an electrical shaver each day and weighed the clippings. Just before he left for visits to the mainland (and to the company of a female companion), his beard began growing faster. Because rate of beard growth is related to androgen levels, the effect indicates that his anticipation of sexual activity stimulated testosterone production. Confirming these results, Hellhammer, Hubert, and Schurmeyer (1985) found that watching an erotic film increased men's testosterone level.

Sexual Orientation

After puberty most people develop a sexual and romantic attraction to members of the opposite sex. However, some people find themselves attracted to members of their own sex. What controls a person's sexual orientation—the gender of people to whom a person is sexually and romantically attracted? Some investigators believe that homosexuality is a result of childhood experiences, especially interactions between the child and parents. A large-scale study of several hundred male and female homosexuals reported by Bell, Weinberg, and Hammersmith (1981) attempted to assess the effects of these factors. The researchers found no evidence that homosexuals had been raised by domineering mothers or submissive fathers, as some clinicians had suggested. The best predictor of adult homosexuality was a self-report of homosexual feelings, which usually preceded homosexual activity by three years. The investigators concluded that their data did not support social explanations for homosexuality but were consistent with the possibility that homosexuality is at least partly biologically determined.

If homosexuality does have a physiological cause, it certainly is not variations in the levels of sex hormones during adulthood. Many studies have examined the levels of sex steroids in male homosexuals (Meyer-Bahlburg, 1984), and the vast majority of them found these levels to be similar to those of heterosexuals. A few studies suggest that about 30 percent of female homosexuals have elevated levels of testosterone (but still lower than those found in men). Whether these differences are related to a biological cause of lesbianism or whether differences in lifestyles may increase the secretion of testosterone is not yet known.

A more likely biological cause of homosexuality is a subtle difference in brain structure caused by differences in the amount of prenatal exposure to androgens. Perhaps, then, the brains of male homosexuals are neither masculinized nor defeminized, those of female homosexuals are masculinized and defeminized, and those of bisexuals are masculinized but not defeminized. Of course, these are *speculations* that so far cannot be supported by human data; they are not *conclusions*. They should be regarded as suggestions to guide future research.

Prenatal Androgenization of Genetic Females

Evidence suggests that prenatal androgens can affect human social behavior and sexual orientation, as well as anatomy. In a disorder known as **congenital adrenal hyperplasia (CAH),** the adrenal glands secrete abnormal amounts of androgens. (*Hyperplasia* means "excessive formation.") The secretion of androgens begins prenatally; thus, the syndrome causes prenatal masculinization. Boys born with

congenital adrenal hyperplasia (CAH) (*hy per* ***play*** *zha*) A condition characterized by hypersecretion of androgens by the adrenal cortex; in females, causes masculinization of the external genitalia.

CAH develop normally; the extra androgen does not seem to have significant effects. However, a girl with CAH will be born with an enlarged clitoris, and her labia may be partly fused together. (As Figure 9.3 shows, the scrotum and labia develop from the same tissue in the fetus.) If the masculinization of the genitals is pronounced, surgery will be performed to correct them. In any event, once the syndrome is identified, the person will be given a synthetic hormone that suppresses the abnormal secretion of androgens.

Money, Schwartz, and Lewis (1984) studied thirty young women with a history of CAH. They had all been born with enlarged clitorises and partly fused labia, which led to the diagnosis. (A few mild cases were not diagnosed for several years.) Once the diagnosis was made, they were treated with drugs that suppress the secretion of adrenal androgens, and, if necessary, genital surgery was performed. Money and his colleagues asked the young women to describe their sexual orientation. Thirty-seven percent of the women described themselves as bisexual or homosexual, 40 percent said they were exclusively heterosexual, and 23 percent refused to talk about their sex lives. If the noncommittal women are excluded from the sample, the percentage of homosexuality or bisexuality rises to 48 percent. These results suggest that the exposure of a female fetus to an abnormally high level of androgens does affect their subsequent sexual orientation.

A study by Iijima et al. (2001) found that prenatal androgenization may affect other sexually dimorphic behaviors besides sexual orientation. The investigators asked young children, including girls with CAH, to draw pictures. Typically, boys are more likely to make drawings that use dark or cold colors and to feature moving objects such as cars, trucks, trains, and airplanes, whereas girls are more likely to use light and warm colors and to include people, flowers, and butterflies. The investigators found that masculine motifs were much more likely to appear in the drawings of girls with CAH. (See ***Figure 9.11.***)

A plausible explanation for the high prevalence of masculine sexual orientation of women with CAH is that the androgens affect development of the brain. However, we must remember that the androgens also affect the genitals; possibly, the changes in the genitals played a role in shaping the development of the girls' sexual orientation. If the differences seen in sexual orientation *are* caused by effects of prenatal androgens on brain development, then we could reasonably conclude that prenatal androgens are responsible for establishing the sexual orientation of males, too. That is, these results support the hypothesis that male sexual orientation is at least partly determined by masculinizing (and defeminizing) effects of androgens on the human brain.

Failure of Androgenization of Genetic Males

As we saw, genetic males with androgen insensitivity syndrome develop as females, with female external genitalia—but also with testes and without uterus or Fallopian tubes. If an individual with this syndrome is raised as a girl, all is well. Normally, the testes are removed because they often become cancerous; but if they are not, the body will mature into that of a woman at the time of puberty through the effects of the small amounts of estradiol produced by the testes. (If the testes are removed, the person will be given estradiol to accomplish the same result.) At adulthood the individual will function sexually as a woman, although surgical lengthening of the vagina may be necessary. Women with this syndrome report average sex drives, including normal frequency of orgasm in intercourse. Most marry and have normal sex lives.

Studies of the social behavior of people with androgen insensitivity syndrome indicate that they tend to be very "feminine" (Money and Ehrhardt, 1972). There is no indication of sexual orientation toward women. Thus, the lack of androgen receptors appears to prevent both the masculinizing and defeminizing effects of androgens on

Figure 9.11

Prenatal androgens and children's drawings. (a) Drawing by a 5-year-old girl. (b) Drawing by a 5-year-old boy. (c) Drawing by a 5-year-old girl with congenital adrenal hyperplasia.

(a)

(b)

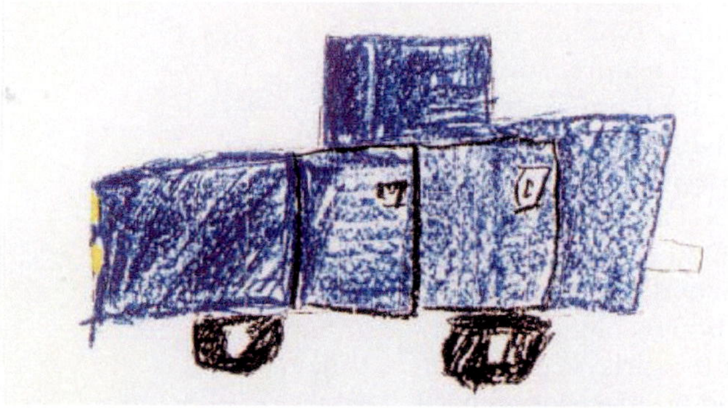

(c)

From Iijima, M., Arisaka, O., Minamoto, F., and Arai, Y. *Hormones and Behavior,* 2001, *20,* 99–104.

a person's sexual interest. If the lack of androgen receptors results in a person with a sexual orientation toward men, then perhaps events that interfere with prenatal androgenization in male fetuses could increase the likelihood of homosexuality. Of course, it is also possible that rearing an XY child with androgen insensitivity syndrome as a girl plays an important role in that person's sexual orientation.

Sexual Orientation and the Brain

The human brain is a sexually dimorphic organ. This fact has long been suspected, even before confirmation was received from anatomical studies and studies of regional cerebral metabolism using PET and functional MRI. For example, neurologists discovered that the two hemispheres of a woman's brain appear to share functions more than those of a man's brain do. If a man sustains a stroke that damages the left side of the brain, he is more likely to show impairments in language than is a woman with similar damage. Presumably, the woman's right hemisphere shares language functions with the left, so that damage to one hemisphere is less devastating than it is in men. In addition, the sizes of some specific regions of the telencephalon and diencephalon are different in males and females, and the shape of the corpus callosum may also be sexually dimorphic. (See Breedlove, 1994, and Swaab, Gooren, and Hofman, 1995, for specific references.)

Most investigators believe that the sexual dimorphism of the human brain is a result of differential exposure to androgens prenatally and during early postnatal life. Of course, additional changes could occur at the time of puberty, when another surge in androgens occurs. The differences could even be a result of differences in the social environments of males and females. We cannot manipulate the hormone levels of humans before and after birth as we can with laboratory animals, so it might be a long time before enough evidence is gathered to permit us to make definite conclusions.

Several studies have examined the brains of deceased heterosexual and homosexual men and heterosexual women. So far, these studies have found differences in the size of three different subregions of the brain: the suprachiasmatic nucleus, a sexually dimorphic nucleus of the hypothalamus, and the anterior commissure (Swaab and Hofman, 1990; LeVay, 1991; Allen and Gorski, 1992). You are already familiar with the suprachiasmatic nucleus from Chapter 8; the anterior commissure is a fiber bundle that interconnects parts of the left and right temporal lobes. The suprachiasmatic nucleus was found to be larger in homosexual men and smaller in heterosexual men and women; a sexually dimorphic nucleus of the hypothalamus (the *third interstitial nucleus of the anterior hypothalamus,* or *INAH-3*) was found to be larger in heterosexual men and smaller in homosexual men and heterosexual women; and the anterior commissure was found to be larger in homosexual men and heterosexual women and smaller in heterosexual men. However, a follow-up study failed to replicate this effect. Byne et al. (2002) found that the INAH-3 was larger in heterosexual men than in women but failed to find a relationship between size and sexual orientation in men.

We cannot necessarily conclude that any of the brain regions I mentioned in this section are directly involved in people's sexual orientation (or sexual identity), but the results do suggest the following: The brains of heterosexual women, heterosexual men, and homosexual men may have been exposed to different patterns of hormones prenatally. The *real* differences—if indeed sexual orientation is determined by prenatal exposure to androgens—may lie elsewhere in the brain, but at least we have an indication that differences do exist and that exposure to prenatal hormones has a profound effect on the nature of a person's sexuality.

Heredity and Sexual Orientation

Another factor that may play a role in sexual orientation is heredity. Twin studies take advantage of the fact that identical twins have identical genes, whereas the genetic similarity between fraternal twins is, on the average, 50 percent. Bailey and Pillard (1991) studied pairs of male twins in which at least one member identified himself as homosexual. If both twins are homosexual, they are said to be *concordant* for this trait. If only one is homosexual, the twins are said to be *discordant.* Thus, if homosexuality has a genetic basis, the percentage of monozygotic twins who are concordant for homosexuality should be higher than that for dizygotic twins. This is exactly what Bailey and Pillard found: The concordance rate was 52 percent for identical twins and only 22 percent for fraternal twins.

Genetic factors also appear to affect female homosexuality. Bailey et al. (1993) found that the concordance of female monozygotic twins for homosexuality was 48 percent, while that of dizygotic twins was 16 percent. Another study, by Pattatucci and Hamer (1995), found an increased incidence of homosexuality and bisexuality in sisters, daughters, nieces, and female cousins (through a paternal uncle) of homosexual women.

To summarize, evidence suggests that two biological factors—prenatal hormonal exposure and heredity—may affect a person's sexual orientation. These research findings certainly contradict the suggestion that a person's sexual orientation is a moral issue. It appears that homosexuals are no more responsible for their sexual orientation than heterosexuals are. Ernulf, Innala, and Whitam (1989) found that people who believed that homosexuals were "born that way" expressed more positive attitudes toward them than did people who believed that they "chose to be" or "learned to be" that way. Thus, we can hope that research on the origins of homosexuality will reduce prejudice based on a person's sexual orientation. The question "Why does someone become homosexual?" will probably be answered when we find out why someone becomes *heterosexual.*

INTERIM SUMMARY

Hormonal Control of Sexual Behavior

Sexual behaviors are controlled by the organizational and activational effects of hormones. The female reproductive cycle (menstrual cycle or estrous cycle) begins with the maturation of one or more ovarian follicles, which occurs in response to the secretion of FSH by the anterior pituitary gland. As the ovarian follicle matures, it secretes estradiol, which causes the lining of the uterus to develop. When estradiol reaches a critical level, it causes the pituitary gland to secrete a surge of LH, triggering ovulation. The empty ovarian follicle becomes a corpus luteum, under the continued influence of LH, and secretes estradiol and progesterone. If pregnancy does not occur, the corpus luteum dies and stops producing hormones, and menstruation begins.

The sexual behavior of males of all mammalian species appears to depend on the presence of androgens. The proceptivity, receptivity, and attractiveness of female mammals other than primates depend primarily on estradiol and progesterone. In particular, estradiol has a priming effect on the subsequent appearance of progesterone.

In most mammals female sexual behavior is the norm, just as the female body and female sex organs are the norm. That is, unless prenatal androgens masculinize and defeminize the animal's brain, its sexual behavior will be feminine. Behavioral masculinization refers to the androgen-stimulated development of neural circuits that respond to testosterone in adulthood, producing male sexual behavior. Behavioral defeminization refers to the inhibitory effects of androgens on the development of neural circuits that respond to estradiol and progesterone in adulthood, producing female sexual behavior.

Pheromones can affect sexual physiology and behavior. Odorants present in the urine of female mice affect their estrous cycles, lengthening and eventually stopping them (the Lee-Boot effect). Odorants present in the urine of male mice abolish these effects and cause the females' cycles to become synchronized (the Whitten effect). (Phenomena similar to the Lee-Boot effect and the Whitten effect also occur in women.) Odorants can also accelerate the onset of puberty in females (the Vandenbergh effect). In addition, the odor of the urine from a male other than the one that impregnated a female mouse will cause her to abort (Bruce effect).

In the hamster the attractiveness of an estrous female to the male derives in part from chemicals present in her vaginal secretions, detected by the olfactory epithelium and vomeronasal organ. Connections between the olfactory system and the amygdala appear to be important in stimulating male sexual behavior.

The search for sex attractant pheromones in humans has so far been fruitless, although we might well recognize our sex partners by their odors. Some studies have found that compounds present in human sweat have different effects on the mood states of men and women.

The behavioral effects of prenatal exposure to androgens in humans, if any, are not well understood. Studies of prenatally androgenized girls suggest that organizational effects might well influence the development of sexual orientation; androgenization appears to increase the incidence of homosexuality. If androgens cannot act (as they cannot in cases of androgen insensitivity syndrome), then the person's anatomy and behavior are feminine. Testosterone has an activational effect on the sexual behavior of men, just as it does on the behavior of other male mammals. Women do not require estradiol or progesterone to experience sexual interest or to engage in sexual behavior. These hormones may affect the quality and intensity of their sex drive. Studies suggest that variations in levels of ovarian hormones across the menstrual cycle do affect a woman's sexual interest but that other factors (such as initiation of sexual activity by partners or a desire to avoid or attain pregnancy) can affect behavior. In addition, the presence of androgens may have a facilitating effect in women's sexual interest.

Sexual orientation (that is, heterosexuality or homosexuality) may be influenced by prenatal exposure to androgens. So far, researchers have obtained evidence that suggests that the sizes of three brain regions are related to a man's sexual orientation. In addition, twin studies suggest that heredity may play a role in sexual orientation in both men and women.

THOUGHT QUESTION

Whatever the relative roles played by biological and environmental factors may be, most investigators believe that a person's sexual orientation is not a matter of choice. Why do you think so many people consider sexual orientation to be a moral issue?

Neural Control of Sexual Behavior

The control of sexual behavior—at least in laboratory animals—involves different brain mechanisms in males and females. This section describes these mechanisms.

Males

Erection and ejaculation are controlled by circuits of neurons that reside in the spinal cord. However, brain mechanisms have both excitatory and inhibitory control of these circuits. The **medial preoptic area (MPA),** located just rostral to the hypothalamus, is the forebrain region most critical for male sexual behavior. (As we will see later in this chapter, it is also critical for other sexually dimorphic behavior, including maternal behavior.) Electrical stimulation of this region elicits male copulatory behavior (Malsbury, 1971), and sexual activity increases the firing rate of single neurons in the MPA (Shimura, Yamamoto, and Shimokochi, 1994; Mas, 1995). In addition, the act of copulation increases the metabolic activity of the MPA and induces the production of Fos protein (Oaknin et al., 1989; Robertson et al., 1991; Wood and Newman, 1993). (The significance of the Fos protein as an indicator of neural activation was discussed in Chapter 5.) Finally, destruction of the MPA abolishes male sexual behavior (Heimer and Larsson, 1966/1967).

The organizational effects of androgens are responsible for sexual dimorphisms in brain structure. Gorski et al. (1978) discovered a nucleus within the MPA of the rat that is three to seven times larger in males than in females. This area is called (appropriately enough) the **sexually dimorphic nucleus (SDN)** of the preoptic area. The size of this nucleus is controlled by the amount of androgens present during fetal development. According to Rhees, Shryne, and Gorski (1990a, 1990b), the critical period for masculinization of the SDN appears to start on the eighteenth day of gestation and end once the animals are five days old. (Normally, rats are born on the twenty-second day of gestation.)

Of course, the MPA does not stand alone. It receives chemosensory input from the vomeronasal organ through connections with the medial amygdala and the bed nucleus of the stria terminalis (BNST). The MPA also receives somatosensory information from the genitals through connections with the central tegmental field of the midbrain and the medial amygdala. (See ***Figure 9.12.***)

The medial amygdala, like the medial preoptic area, is sexually dimorphic: One region within this structure (which contains an especially high concentration of androgen receptors) is 85 percent larger in male rats than in female rats (Hines, Allen, and Gorski, 1992). In addition, destruction of the medial amygdala disrupts the

medial preoptic area (MPA) An area of cell bodies just rostral to the hypothalamus; plays an essential role in male sexual behavior.

sexually dimorphic nucleus A nucleus in the preoptic area that is much larger in males than in females; first observed in rats; plays a role in male sexual behavior.

Figure 9.12

Cross sections through the rat brain showing the location of the medial preoptic area, the medial amygdala, the bed nucleus of the stria terminalis, and the central tegmental field of the midbrain.

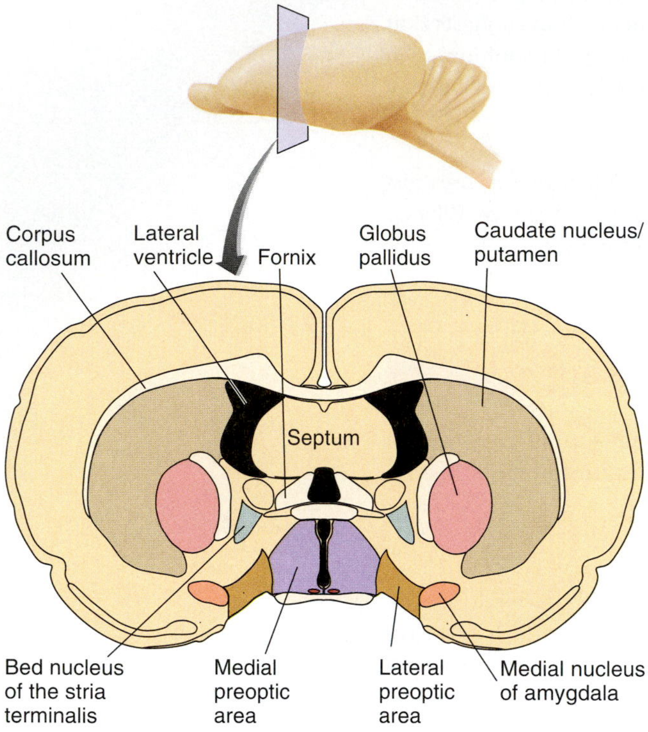

Adapted from Swanson, L. W. *Brain Maps: Structure of the Rat Brain.* New York: Elsevier, 1992.

sexual behavior of male rats. De Jonge et al. (1992) found that the rats with these lesions took longer to mount receptive females and to ejaculate. Wood and Newman (1993) observed that mating increased the production of Fos protein in the medial amygdala.

Androgens exert their activational effects on neurons in the MPA and associated brain regions. If a male rodent is castrated in adulthood, its sexual behavior will cease. However, the behavior can be reinstated by implanting a small amount of testosterone directly into the MPA or in two regions whose axons project to the MPA: the central tegmental field and the medial amygdala (Sipos and Nyby, 1996; Coolen and Wood, 1999). Both of these regions contain a high concentration of androgen receptors in the male rat brain (Cottingham and Pfaff, 1986).

The motor neurons that innervate the pelvic organs involved in copulation are located in the dorsomedial and dorsolateral nuclei of the lumbar and sacral regions of the spinal cord. Anatomical tracing studies suggest that the most important connections between the MPA and the motor neurons of the spinal cord are accomplished through the **periaqueductal gray matter (PAG)** of the midbrain and the **nucleus paragigantocellularis (PGi)** of the medulla. (See Murphy and Hoffman, 2001, for particular references.) The PGi has inhibitory effects on spinal cord sexual reflexes, so one of the tasks of the pathway originating in the MPA is to suppress this inhibition (Marson and McKenna, 1996). Excitatory input to the spinal mechanisms from the MPA appear to be conveyed via the PAG.

Figure 9.13 summarizes the evidence I have presented in this section. (See ***Figure 9.13.***)

Figure 9.13

A possible explanation of the interacting excitatory effects of pheromones, genital stimulation, and testosterone on male sexual behavior.

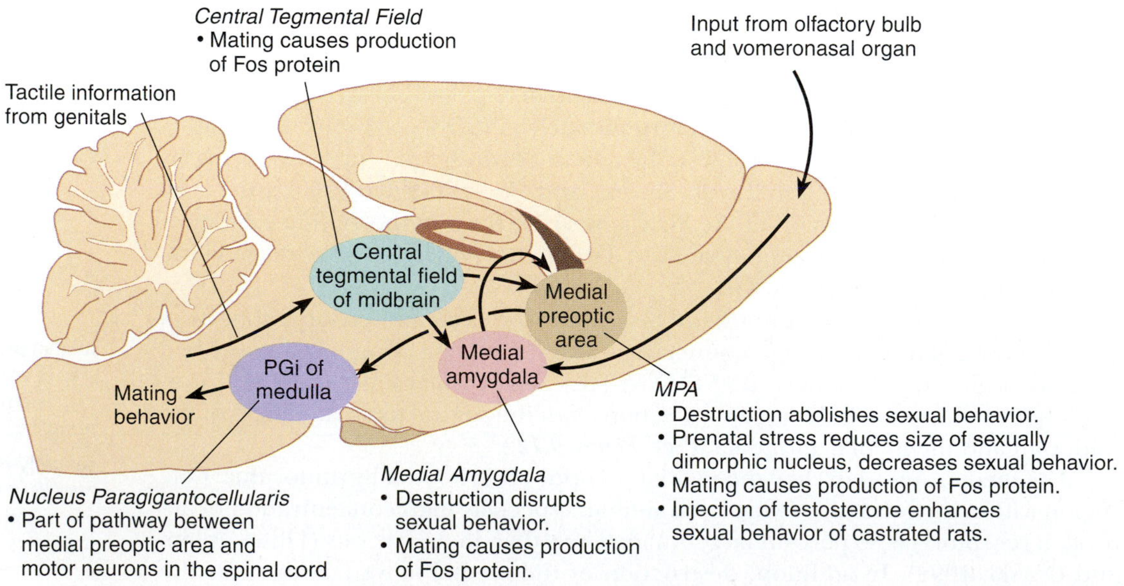

Females

Just as the MPA plays an essential role in male sex behavior, another region in the ventral forebrain plays a similar role in female sexual behavior: the **ventromedial nucleus of the hypothalamus (VMH)**. A female rat with bilateral lesions of the ventromedial nuclei will not display lordosis, even if she is treated with estradiol and progesterone. Conversely, electrical stimulation of the ventromedial nucleus facilitates female sexual behavior (Pfaff and Sakuma, 1979). (See ***Figure 9.14***.)

As we saw in the previous section, the medial amygdala of males receives chemosensory information from the vomeronasal system and somatosensory information from the genitals, and it sends efferent axons to the medial preoptic area. These connections are found in females as well. In addition, neurons in the medial amygdala also send efferent axons to the VMH. In fact, copulation or mechanical stimulation of the genitals or flanks increases the production of Fos protein in both the medial amygdala and the VMH (Pfaus et al., 1993; Tetel, Getzinger, and Blaustein, 1993).

As we saw earlier, sexual behavior of female rats is activated by a priming dose of estradiol, followed by progesterone. The estrogen sets the stage, so to speak, and the progesterone stimulates the sexual behavior. Injections of these hormones directly into the VMH will stimulate sexual behavior even in females whose ovaries have been removed (Rubin and Barfield, 1980; Pleim and Barfield, 1988). And if a chemical that blocks the production of progesterone receptors is injected into the VMH, the animal's sexual behavior is disrupted (Ogawa et al., 1994). Thus, estradiol and progesterone exert their effects on female sexual behavior by activating neurons in this nucleus.

Figure 9.14

A cross section through the rat brain showing the location of the ventromedial nucleus of the hypothalamus.

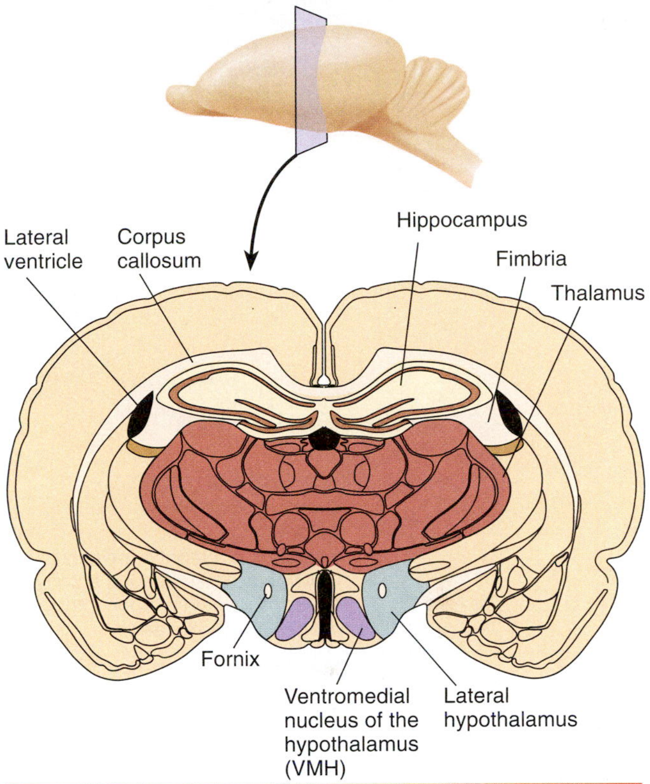

Adapted from Swanson, L. W. *Brain Maps: Structure of the Rat Brain.* New York: Elsevier, 1992.

Rose (1990) recorded from single neurons in the ventromedial hypothalamus of freely moving female hamsters and found that injections of progesterone (following estradiol pretreatment) increased the activity level of these neurons, particularly when the animals were displaying lordosis. Tetel, Celentano, and Blaustein (1994) found that neurons in both the VMH and the medial amygdala that showed increased Fos production when the animal's genitals were stimulated also contained estrogen receptors. Thus, the stimulating effects of estradiol and genital stimulation converge on the same neurons.

The neurons of the ventromedial nucleus send axons to the periaqueductal gray matter (PAG) of the midbrain, which surrounds the cerebral aqueduct. This region, too, has been implicated in female sexual behavior; Sakuma and Pfaff (1979a, 1979b) found that electrical stimulation of the PAG facilitates lordosis in female rats and that lesions there disrupt it. In addition, Hennessey et al. (1990) found that lesions that disconnect the VMH from the PAG abolish female sexual behavior. Finally, Sakuma and Pfaff (1980a, 1980b) found that estradiol treatment or electrical stimulation of the ventromedial nuclei increased the firing rate of neurons in the PAG. (The PAG contains both estrogen and progesterone receptors.)

Daniels, Miselis, and Flanagan-Cato (1999) injected a transneuronal retrograde tracer, pseudorabies virus, in the muscles responsible for the lordosis response in female rats. They found that the pathway innervating these muscles was as previous studies predicted: VMH → PAG → medullary reticular formation → motor neurons in the ventral horn of the lumbar region of the spinal cord.

periaqueductal gray matter (PAG) The region of the midbrain that surrounds the cerebral aqueduct; plays an essential role in various species-typical behaviors, including female sexual behavior.

nucleus paragigantocellularis (PGi) A nucleus of the medulla that receives input from the medial preoptic area and contains neurons whose axons form synapses with motor neurons in the spinal cord that participate in sexual reflexes in males.

ventromedial nucleus of the hypothalamus (VMH) A large nucleus of the hypothalamus located near the walls of the third ventricle; plays an essential role in female sexual behavior.

Figure 9.15

A possible explanation of the interacting excitatory effects of pheromones, genital stimulation, and estradiol and progesterone on female sexual behavior.

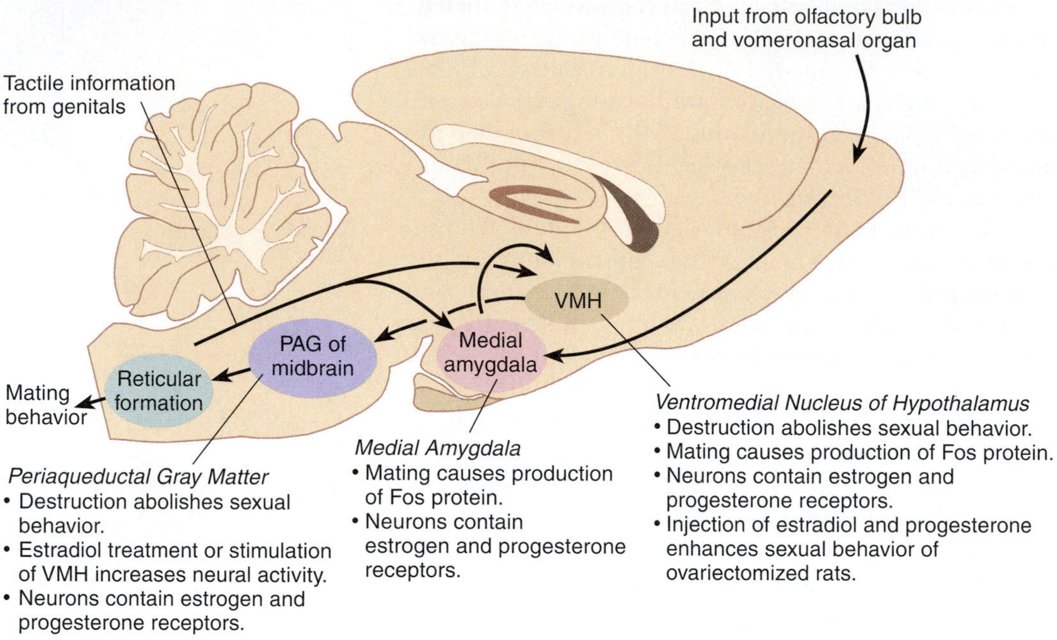
Input from olfactory bulb and vomeronasal organ
Tactile information from genitals
VMH
PAG of midbrain
Medial amygdala
Reticular formation
Mating behavior
Ventromedial Nucleus of Hypothalamus
• Destruction abolishes sexual behavior.
• Mating causes production of Fos protein.
• Neurons contain estrogen and progesterone receptors.
• Injection of estradiol and progesterone enhances sexual behavior of ovariectomized rats.
Medial Amygdala
• Mating causes production of Fos protein.
• Neurons contain estrogen and progesterone receptors.
Periaqueductal Gray Matter
• Destruction abolishes sexual behavior.
• Estradiol treatment or stimulation of VMH increases neural activity.
• Neurons contain estrogen and progesterone receptors.

As we saw in the previous subsection, the brain regions that control male genital reflexes include the MPA, PAG, and PGi. Marson (1995) injected pseudorabies virus into the clitorises of female rats and found retrograde labeling in these three brain structures (and some others, as well). Thus, it seems likely that erections of the penis and clitoris are controlled by similar brain mechanisms. This finding is not surprising, because these organs derive from the same embryonic tissue.

Figure 9.15 summarizes the evidence I have presented in this section. (See ***Figure 9.15.***)

INTERIM SUMMARY

Neural Control of Sexual Behavior

In laboratory animals different brain mechanisms control male and female sexual behavior. The medial preoptic area is the forebrain region that is most critical for male sexual behavior. Stimulating this area produces copulatory behavior; destroying it permanently abolishes the behavior. The sexually dimorphic nucleus, located in the medial preoptic area, develops only if an animal is exposed to androgens early in life. Its destruction impairs male sexual behavior. This nucleus is found in humans as well.

Neurons in the MPA contain testosterone receptors. Copulatory activity causes an increase in the activity of neurons in this region. Implantation of testosterone directly into the MPA reinstates copulatory behavior that was previously abolished by castration in adulthood. Neurons in the MPA are part of a circuit that includes the periaqueductal gray matter, the nucleus paragigantocellularis of the medulla, and motor neurons controlling genital reflexes in the spinal cord. Connections of the PGi with the spinal cord are inhibitory.

The most important forebrain region for female sexual behavior is the ventromedial nucleus of the hypothalamus (VMH). Its destruction abolishes copulatory behavior, and its stimulation facilitates this behavior. Both estradiol and progesterone exert their facilitating effects on female sexual behavior in this region, and studies have confirmed the existence of progesterone and estrogen receptors there. The steroid-sensitive neurons of the VMH send axons to the periaqueductal gray matter (PAG) of the midbrain; these neurons, through their connections with the medullary reticular formation, control the particular responses that constitute female sexual behavior.

Parental Behavior

In most mammalian species reproductive behavior takes place after the offspring are born as well as at the time they are conceived. This section examines the role of hormones in the initiation and maintenance of maternal behavior and the role of the neural circuits that are responsible for their expression. Most of the research has involved rodents; less is known about the neural and endocrine bases of maternal behavior in primates.

Although most research on the physiology of parental behavior has focused on maternal behavior, some researchers are now studying paternal behavior shown by the males of some species of rodents. It goes without saying that human paternal behavior is very important for the offspring of our species, but the physiological basis of this behavior has not yet been studied.

Maternal Behavior of Rodents

The final test of the fitness of an animal's genes is the number of offspring that survive to a reproductive age. Just as the process of natural selection favors reproductively competent animals, it favors those that care adequately for their young, if their young in fact require care. Rat and mouse pups certainly do; they cannot survive without a mother to attend to their needs.

At birth rats and mice resemble fetuses. The infants are blind (their eyes are still shut), and they can only wriggle helplessly. They are poikilothermous ("cold-blooded"); their brain is not yet developed enough to regulate body temperature. They even lack the ability to release their own urine and feces spontaneously and must be helped to do so by their mother. As we will see shortly, this phenomenon actually serves a useful function.

During gestation female rats and mice build nests. The form this structure takes depends on the material available for its construction. In the laboratory the animals are usually given strips of paper or lengths of rope or twine. A good *brood nest,* as it is called, is shown in Figure 9.16(a). This nest is made of hemp rope; a piece of the rope is shown below the nest. The mouse laboriously shredded the rope and then wove an enclosed nest, with a small hole for access to the interior. (See ***Figure 9.16a.***)

At the time of **parturition** (delivery of offspring) the female begins to groom and lick the area around her vagina. As a pup begins to emerge, she assists the uterine contractions by pulling the pup out with her teeth. She then eats the placenta and umbilical cord and cleans off the fetal membranes—a quite delicate operation. (A newborn pup looks as though it is sealed in very thin plastic wrap.) After all the pups are born and cleaned up, the mother will probably nurse them. Milk is usually present in the mammary glands very near the time of birth.

Periodically, the mother licks the pups' anogenital region, stimulating reflexive urination and defecation. Friedman and Bruno (1976) have shown the utility of this mechanism. They noted that a lactating female rat produces approximately 48 grams (g) of milk on the tenth day of lactation. This milk contains approximately 35 milliliters (ml) of water. The experimenters injected some of the pups with tritiated (radioactive) water and later found radioactivity in the mother and in the littermates.

parturition (*par tew **ri** shun*) The act of giving birth.

Figure 9.16

(a) A mouse's brood nest. Beside it is a length of the kind of rope the mouse used to construct it. (b) A female mouse carrying one of her pups.

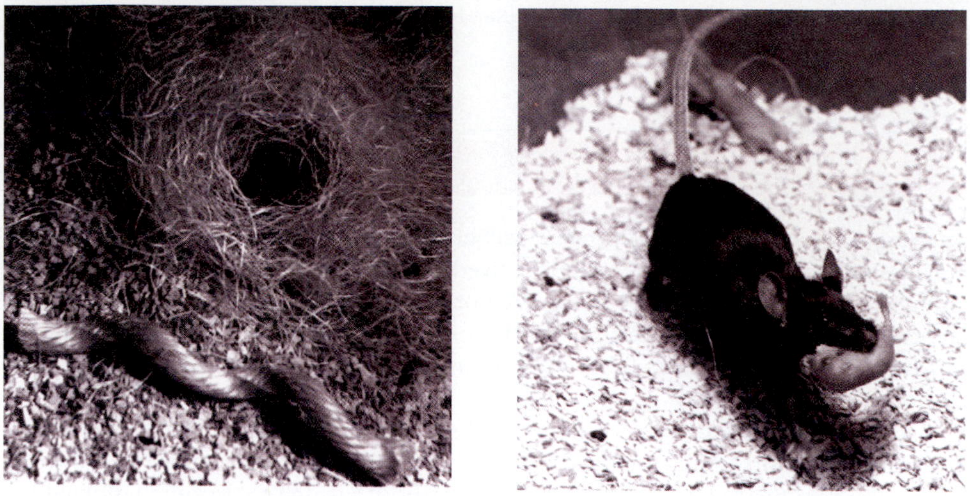

(a) (b)

They calculated that a lactating rat normally consumes 21 ml of water in the urine of her young, thus recycling approximately two-thirds of the water she gives to the pups in the form of milk. The water, traded back and forth between mother and young, serves as a vehicle for the nutrients—fats, protein, and sugar—contained in milk. Because each day the milk production of a lactating rat is approximately 14 percent of her body weight (for a human weighing 120 pounds, that would be around 2 gallons), the recycling is extremely useful, especially when the availability of water is a problem.

Besides cleaning, nursing, and purging her offspring, a female rodent will retrieve pups if they leave or are removed from the nest. The mother will even construct another nest in a new location and move her litter there, should the conditions at the old site become unfavorable (for example, when an inconsiderate experimenter puts a heat lamp over it). The way a female rodent picks up her pup is quite consistent: She gingerly grasps the animal by the back, managing not to injure it with her very sharp teeth. (I can personally attest to the ease with which these teeth can penetrate skin.) She then carries the pup with a characteristic prancing walk, her head held high. (See ***Figure 9.16b***.) The pup is brought back to the nest and is left there. The female then leaves the nest again to search for another pup. She continues to retrieve pups until she finds no more; she does not count her pups and stop retrieving when they are all back. A mouse or rat will usually accept all the pups she is offered, if they are young enough. I once observed two lactating female mice with nests in corners of the same cage, diagonally opposite each other. I disturbed their nests, which triggered a long bout of retrieving, during which each mother stole youngsters from the other's nest. The mothers kept up their exchange for a long time, passing each other in the middle of the cage.

Hormonal Control of Maternal Behavior

As we saw earlier in this chapter, most sexually dimorphic behaviors are controlled by the organizational and activational effects of sex hormones. Maternal behavior is somewhat different in this respect. First, there is no evidence that organizational effects of hormones play a role; as we will see, under the proper conditions even males will take care of infants. (Obviously, they cannot provide them with milk.) Second, although maternal behavior is affected by hormones, it is not *controlled* by them. Most virgin female rats will begin to retrieve and care for young pups after having infants placed with them for several days (Wiesner and Sheard, 1933). And once the rats are sensitized, they will thereafter take care of pups as soon as they encounter them; sensitization lasts for a lifetime.

Although hormones are not essential for the activation of maternal behavior, many aspects of maternal behavior are facilitated by hormones. Nest-building behavior is facilitated by progesterone, the principal hormone of pregnancy (Lisk, Pretlow, and Friedman, 1969). After parturition, mothers continue to maintain their nests, and they construct new nests if necessary, even though their blood level of progesterone is very low then. Voci and Carlson (1973) found that hypothalamic implants of prolactin as well as progesterone facilitated nest building in virgin female mice. Presumably, nest building can be facilitated by either hormone: progesterone during pregnancy and prolactin after parturition. Prolactin, produced by the anterior pituitary gland, is responsible for milk production. Unlike many other peptides, special mechanisms transport this hormone from the blood into the brain (Grattan et al., 2001).

Although pregnant female rats will not immediately care for foster pups that are given to them during pregnancy, they will do so as soon as their pups are born. The hormones that influence a female rodent's responsiveness to her offspring are the ones that are present shortly before parturition. Figure 9.17 shows the levels of the three hormones that have been implicated in maternal behavior: progesterone, estradiol, and prolactin. Note that just before parturition the level of estradiol begins rising, then the level of progesterone falls dramatically, followed by a sharp increase in prolactin. (See ***Figure 9.17.***) If ovariectomized virgin female rats are given estradiol and progesterone in a pattern that duplicates this sequence, the time it takes to sensitize their maternal behavior is drastically reduced (Moltz, Lubin, Leon, and Numan, 1970; Bridges, 1984). Prolactin is not necessary.

Figure 9.17

Blood levels of progesterone, estradiol, and prolactin in pregnant rats.

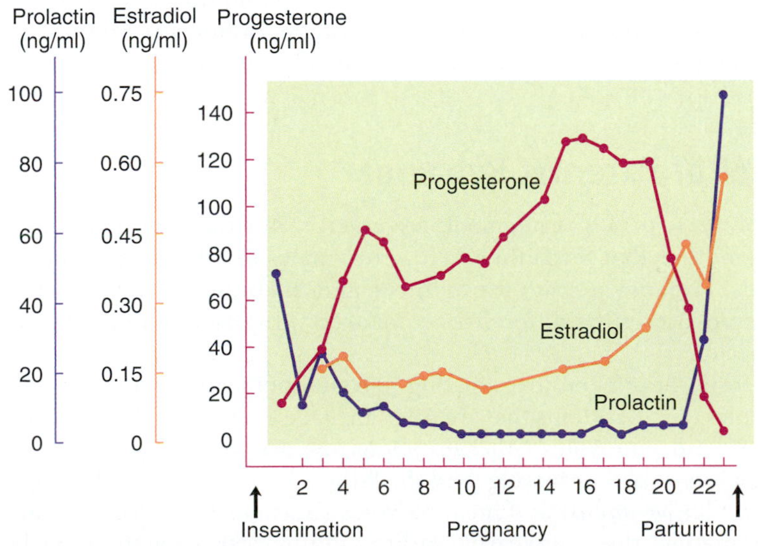

From Rosenblatt, J. S., Siegel, H. I., and Mayer, A. D. *Advances in the Study of Behavior,* 1979, *10,* 225–310.

Another hormone that is present during lactation—prolactin—may also have stimulating effects on maternal behavior; and its effects, like those of estradiol, may be exerted in the medial preoptic area. Bridges et al. (1990) infused minute quantities of prolactin into the lateral ventricles or directly into the MPA of virgin female rats. They found that the animals quickly began taking care of pups. The effect occurred only if the animals were first given a series of injections of progesterone and estradiol; thus, the maternal behavior of normal females may depend on an interaction between several hormones. Lucas et al. (1998) found that mice with a targeted mutation against the gene for the prolactin receptor showed deficient maternal behavior, which supports the importance of prolactin in this behavior.

Neural Control of Maternal Behavior

The medial preoptic area, the region of the forebrain that plays the most critical role in male sexual behavior, appears to play a similar role in maternal behavior. Numan (1974) found that lesions of the MPA disrupted both nest building and pup care. The mothers simply ignored their offspring. However, female sexual behavior was unaffected by these lesions.

As you learned earlier, in the discussion of the neural basis of male sexual behavior, the MPA sends axons to the midbrain and lower brain stem. Numan and Numan (1977) found that neurons of the MPA that were activated by the performance of maternal behavior (as indicated by the production of Fos protein) sent their axons to two regions of the midbrain: the ventral tegmental area (VTA) and retrorubral field. The retrorubral field of the midbrain sends axons to regions of the brain stem reticular formation that may be involved in the expression of maternal behavior. Cutting the connections of the MPA with the brain stem abolishes maternal behavior (Numan and Smith, 1984).

The medial preoptic area appears to be the place where estradiol affects maternal behavior. The MPA contains estrogen receptors (Pfaff and Keiner, 1973). Giordano et al. (1989) found that the concentration of estrogen receptors in the MPA increases during pregnancy and appears to reflect the priming effect produced by the sequence of hormones that occurs during pregnancy. In addition, direct implants of estradiol in the MPA facilitate maternal behavior (Numan, Rosenblatt, and Komisaruk, 1977), and injections of an antiestrogen into the MPA block it (Adieh, Mayer, and Rosenblatt, 1987).

Prolactin also appears to affect maternal behavior by acting on neurons in the MPA. Bridges et al. (1990) found that an infusion of prolactin into the MPA of virgin female rats that had been primed with estradiol and progesterone stimulated maternal behavior.

Neural Control of Paternal Behavior

Newborn infants of most species of mammals are cared for by their mother, and it is, of course, their mother that feeds them. However, males of a few species of rodents share the task of infant care with the mothers, and the brains of these nurturing fathers show some interesting differences compared with those of nonpaternal fathers of other species.

Several laboratories have been investigating parental behavior in some closely related species of voles (small rodents that are often mistaken for mice). Prairie voles (*Microtus ochrogaster*) and pine voles (*Microtus pinetorum*) are monogamous; males and females form pair bonds after mating, and the fathers help to care for the pups. Montane voles (*Microtus montanus*) and meadow voles (*Microtus pennsylvanicus*) are promiscuous; after mating, the male leaves, and the mother cares for the pups by herself. The size of the MPA, which plays an essential role in maternal behavior, shows less sexual dimorphism in monogamous prairie voles than in promiscuous montane voles (Shapiro et al., 1991).

Kirkpatrick, Kim, and Insel (1994) found that when male prairie voles were exposed to a pup, Fos production increased in the MPA (and also several other regions of the forebrain). In addition, electrolytic or excitotoxic lesions of the MPA produce severe deficits in paternal behavior of male rats (Rosenblatt, Hazelwood, and Poole, 1996; Sturgis and Bridges, 1997). Finally, implants of estradiol in the MPA of male rats shortened the time it took to stimulate paternal behavior by exposure to pups. Thus, the MPA appears to play a similar roles in parental behavior of both males and females.

INTERIM SUMMARY

Parental Behavior

Many species must care for their offspring. Among most rodents this duty falls to the mother, which must build a nest, deliver her own pups, clean them, keep them warm, nurse them, and retrieve them if they are moved out of the nest. They must even induce their pups' urination and defecation, and the mother's ingestion of the urine recycles water, which is often a scarce commodity.

Exposure of virgin females to young pups stimulates maternal behavior within a few days. The stimuli that normally induce maternal behavior are those produced by the act of parturition and the hormones present around the end of pregnancy. Nest building appears to be facilitated by progesterone during pregnancy and by prolactin during the lactation period. Injections of progesterone and estradiol that duplicate the sequence that occurs during pregnancy facilitate of maternal behavior, as does injection of prolactin directly into the brain.

The medial preoptic area is the most important forebrain structure for maternal behavior, and the ventral tegmental area and retrorubal field of the midbrain are the most important brain stem structures. Neurons in the medial preoptic area send axons caudally to the ventral tegmental area and the retrorubral reticular formation of the pons and medulla. If the connections of the MPA with the brain stem are interrupted, rats cease to provide maternal care.

Paternal behavior is relatively rare in mammalian species, but research indicates that sexual dimorphism of the MPA is less pronounced in male voles of monogamous, but not promiscuous, species. Lesions of the MPA abolish paternal behavior of male rats, and implants of estradiol in this region facilitate it.

THOUGHT QUESTION

As you saw, both male sexual behavior and maternal behavior are disrupted by lesions of the medial preoptic area; thus, the MPA performs some functions necessary for both behaviors. Do you think that the functions are common to both categories of behavior, or do you think that different functions are involved? If you think the former possibility is true, what might these functions be? Can you think of any common features of male sexual behavior and maternal behavior?

EPILOGUE

From Boy to Girl and Back Again

Unfortunately, the case of Bruce/Brenda was not what it seemed to be (Diamond and Sigmundson, 1997). It turned out that although Brenda did not know she had been born as a boy, she was unhappy as a girl. As her twin brother said, "I recognized Brenda as my sister, [b]ut she never, ever acted the part. . . . When I say there was nothing feminine about Brenda, . . . I mean there was *nothing* feminine. She walked like a guy. Sat with her legs apart. She talked about guy things, didn't give a crap about cleaning house, getting married, wearing makeup. . . . She played with *my* toys: Tinkertoys, dump trucks. This toy sewing machine she got just sat" (Colapinto, 2000, p. 57).

Brenda's childhood was lonely and miserable. She had no real friends. She was teased by her classmates, who recognized that there was something different about her. Brenda tried, unsuccessfully, to convince the girls in her class to play games like boys played. One of her classmates asked the teacher, "How come Brenda stands *up* when she goes to the bathroom?" (Colapinto, 2000, p. 61). When Brenda was seven years old, she daydreamed of herself as a man with a mustache, driving a sports car. Yet reports of her case described "the identical twin boy whose penis was cauterized at birth and who, now that his parents have opted for surgical reconstruction to make him appear female, has been sailing contentedly through childhood as a genuine girl" (Wolfe, 1975, quoted by Colapinto, 2000, p. 107).

In the summer of 1977 Brenda began taking estrogen pills to stimulate the changes that normally occur at puberty. The hormone caused her breasts to grow, which mortified her. She began to overeat so that her breasts would be hidden by fat; in fact, her waist grew to forty inches. She started throwing the estrogen tablets down the toilet, but when her parents discovered that she was doing so, they insisted on watching her swallow them.

At age fourteen, Brenda stopped wearing girls' clothing. She began wearing a worn denim jacket, corduroy pants, and heavy workman's boots. Her classmates continued to taunt her. As one said, "You're a f—ing *gorilla*" (Colapinto, 2000, p. 165).

By this time the family was in turmoil. Finally, Brenda's father explained what had happened. "He told me that I was born a boy, and about the accident when they were trying to circumcise me, and how they saw all kinds of specialists, and they took the best advice they had at the time, which was to try to change me over. My dad got very upset" (Colapinto, 2000, p. 180).

Brenda received this revelation with great relief. She (now I should say "he") stopped taking estrogen pills, had a mastectomy, and began taking testosterone pills. Later, he underwent several operations that included construction of a penis and implantation of plastic testicular prostheses, designed to provide an appearance as normal as possible. He changed his name to David. He is now happily married and has adopted his wife's children. After several years of anonymity David decided to reveal his identity. A book has told his story (Colapinto, 2000), and a 2002 television documentary (Nova's "Sex: Unknown") presented interviews with David, his mother, and others involved in this unfortunate case.

This case suggests that people's sexual identity and sexual orientation are strongly influenced by biological factors and cannot easily be changed by the way a child is raised. Presumably, the exposure of Bruce's brain to testosterone prenatally and during the first few months of life affected neural development, favoring the emergence of male sexual identity and an orientation toward women as romantic and sexual partners. Fortunately, cases like this one are rare. Another case of penile ablation in infancy followed by a sex reassignment was reported by Bradley et al. (1998). As a child, the girl was described as a "tomboy" but appears to have accepted her identity as a female. However, she described herself as primarily attracted to women and was currently living with a woman.

KEY CONCEPTS

SEXUAL DEVELOPMENT

1. Gender is determined by the sex chromosomes, which control development of the gonads. Two hormones secreted by the testes, testosterone and anti-Müllerian hormone, cause masculinization and defeminization, respectively; otherwise, the organism will be female.
2. Sexual maturation occurs when the anterior pituitary gland secretes gonadotropic hormones, which instruct the gonads to secrete sex steroid hormones.

HORMONAL CONTROL OF SEXUAL BEHAVIOR

3. Female reproductive cycles are caused by interactions between the ovaries and the anterior pituitary gland.
4. Androgens cause behavioral masculinization and defeminization by affecting brain development.
5. In mammals other than primates, estradiol and progesterone activate female sexual behavior. Testosterone activates male sexual behavior in all mammalian species.
6. Pheromones, detected by the vomeronasal organ or by the olfactory receptors, permit animals to affect the reproductive status or sexual interest of other members of their species by their mere presence.
7. In humans organizational effects of androgens may manifest themselves in sexual preference. Androgens appear to have the most important activational effects for both men and women.

NEURAL CONTROL OF SEXUAL BEHAVIOR

8. In laboratory animals the sexually dimorphic nucleus of the medial preoptic area is critical for male sexual behavior, and the ventromedial nucleus of the hypothalamus is critical for female sexual behavior. In addition, sex hormones exert their behavioral effects on neurons in these brain regions, and on those in

the medial amygdala, which receive pheromone-related information.

PARENTAL BEHAVIOR

9. Maternal behavior is influenced by hormones—primarily estradiol and prolactin—but depends also on the stimuli provided by the female's offspring. Some of the neural circuitry that controls the behaviors involves a pathway from the medial preoptic area to the ventral tegmental area. The medial preoptic area also appears to be involved in paternal behavior.

SUGGESTED READINGS

Becker, J. B., Breedlove, S. M., and Crews, D. *Behavioral Endocrinology,* 2nd ed. Cambridge, MA: MIT Press, 2002.

Bornstein, M. H. *Handbook of Parenting. Vol. 2: Biology and Ecology of Parenting.* Mahwah, NJ: Lawrence Erlbaum Associates, 1995.

Gerall, A. A., Moltz, H., and Ward, I. I. *Handbook of Behavioral Neurobiology. Vol. 11: Sexual Differentiation.* New York: Plenum Press, 1992.

Kandeel, F. R., Koussa, V. K. T., and Swerdloff, R. S. Male sexual function and its disorders: Physiology, pathophysiology, clinical investigation, and treatment. *Endocrine Reviews,* 2001, *22,* 342–388.

Krasnegor, N. A., and Bridges, R. S. *Mammalian Parenting: Biochemical, Neurobiological, and Behavioral Determinants.* New York: Oxford University Press, 1990.

Numan, M., and Insel, T. R. *The Neurobiology of Parental Behavior.* New York: Springer-Verlag, 2003.

SUGGESTED WEB SITES

Archive for Sexology

www.rki.de/GESUND/ARCHIV/FIRST.HTM

This German Web site contains a series of links on the history of sexology, various WHO reports on sexology, and links to scientific sites dealing with sexology.

Neurobiology of Sexual Behavior

http://salmon.psy.plym.ac.uk/year2/sexbehav.htm

The focus of this site is an online course in the neurobiology of sexual behavior. Topics include gender identity, the genetics of homosexuality, and the impact of hormones on sexual behavior.

Scientific Study of Human Sexuality: Academia

www.byz.org/~sexuality/html/body_academia.html

The focus of this site is advisory material on the academic study of human sexuality.

Hormones and Sexual Behavior

http://salmon.psy.plym.ac.uk/year1/sexbehav.htm

The impact of hormones on sexual behavior and function is the focus of this online course.

Emotion

chapter 10

CHAPTER OUTLINE

LEARNING OBJECTIVES

1. Discuss the behavioral, autonomic, and hormonal components of an emotional response and the role of the amygdala in controlling them.
2. Discuss the nature, functions, and neural control of aggressive behavior.
3. Discuss the role of the orbitofrontal cortex in the analysis of social situations and the effects of damage to this region.
4. Discuss the hormonal control of intermale aggression and interfemale aggression.
5. Discuss the effects of androgens on human aggressive behavior.
6. Discuss cross-cultural studies on the expression and comprehension of emotions.
7. Discuss the neural control of the recognition of emotional expression in normal people and people with brain damage.
8. Discuss the neural control of emotional expression in normal people and people with brain damage.
9. Discuss the James-Lange theory of feelings of emotion and evaluate relevant research.

PROLOGUE

Intellect and Emotion

Several years ago, while I was on a sabbatical leave, a colleague stopped by my office and asked whether I would like to see an interesting patient. The patient, a 72-year-old man, had suffered a massive stroke in his right hemisphere that had paralyzed the left side of his body. Three of us went to see him: Dr. W.; Lisa, an undergraduate psychology student who was on a summer internship; and I.

Mr. V. was seated in a wheelchair equipped with a large tray on which his right arm was resting; his left arm was immobilized in a sling, to keep it out of the way. He greeted us politely, almost formally, articulating his words carefully with a slight European accent.

Mr. V. seemed intelligent, and this impression was confirmed when we gave him some of the subtests of the Wechsler Adult Intelligence Test. He could define rather obscure words, provide the meanings of proverbs, supply information, and do mental arithmetic. In fact, his verbal intelligence appeared to be in the upper 5 percent of the population. The fact that English was not his native language made his performance even more remarkable. But as we expected, he did poorly on simple tasks that required him to deal with shapes and geometry. He failed to solve even the sample problem for the block design subtest, in which colored blocks must be put together to duplicate a pattern shown in a drawing.

The most interesting aspect of Mr. V.'s behavior after his stroke was his lack of reaction to his symptoms. After we had finished with the testing, we asked him to tell us a little about himself and his lifestyle. What, for example, was his favorite pastime?

"I like to walk," he said. "I walk at least two hours each day around the city, but mostly I like to walk in the woods. I have maps of most of the national forests in the state on the walls of my study, and I mark all of the trails I've taken. I figure that in about six months I will have walked all of the trails that are short enough to do in a day. I'm too old to camp out in the woods."

"You're going to finish up those trails in the next six months?" asked Dr. W.

"Yes, and then I'll start over again!" he replied.

"Mr. V., are you having any trouble?" asked Dr. W.

"Trouble? What do you mean?"

"I mean physical difficulty."

"No." Mr. V. gave him a slightly puzzled look.

"Well, what are you sitting in?"

Mr. V. gave him a look that indicated he thought that the question was rather stupid—or perhaps insulting. "A wheelchair, of course," he answered.

"Why are you in a wheelchair?"

Now Mr. V. looked frankly exasperated; he obviously did not like to answer foolish questions. "Because my left leg is paralyzed!" he snapped.

The word *emotion* can mean several things. Most of the time, it refers to positive or negative feelings that are produced by particular situations. For example, being treated unfairly makes us angry, seeing someone suffer makes us sad, and being close to a loved one makes us feel happy. Emotions consist of patterns of physiological responses and species-typical behaviors. In humans these responses are accompanied by feelings. In fact, most of us use the word *emotion* to refer to the feelings, not to the behaviors. But it is behavior, and not private experience, that has consequences for survival and reproduction. Thus, the useful purposes served by emotional behaviors are what guided the evolution of our brain. The feelings that accompany these behaviors came rather late in the game.

This chapter is divided into three major sections. The first considers the patterns of behavioral and physiological responses that constitute the negative emotions of fear and anger. It describes the nature of these response patterns and their neural and hormonal control. The second section describes the communication of emotions—their expression and recognition. The third section examines the nature of the feelings that accompany emotions.

Emotions as Response Patterns

An emotional response consists of three types of components: behavioral, autonomic, and hormonal. The *behavioral* component consists of muscular movements that are appropriate to the situation that elicits them. For example, a dog defending its territory against an intruder first adopts an aggressive posture, growls, and shows its teeth. If the intruder does not leave, the defender runs toward it and attacks. *Autonomic* responses facilitate the behaviors and provide quick mobilization of energy for vigorous movement. In this example the activity of the sympathetic branch increases while that of the parasympathetic branch decreases. As a consequence, the dog's heart rate increases, and changes in the size of blood vessels shunt the circulation of blood away from the digestive organs toward the muscles. *Hormonal* responses reinforce the autonomic responses. The hormones secreted by the adrenal medulla—epinephrine and norepinephrine—further increase blood flow to the muscles and cause nutrients stored in the muscles to be converted into glucose. In addition, the adrenal cortex secretes steroid hormones, which also help to make glucose available to the muscles.

This section discusses research on the control of overt emotional behaviors and the autonomic and hormonal responses that accompany them. Special behaviors that serve to communicate emotional states to other animals, such as the threat gestures that precede an actual attack and the smiles and frowns used by humans, are discussed in the second section of the chapter. As you will see, negative emotions receive much more attention than positive ones. Most of the research on the physiology of emotions has been confined to fear and anger—emotions associated with situations in which we must defend ourselves or our loved ones. The physiology of behaviors associated with positive emotions—such as those associated with lovemaking, caring for one's offspring, or enjoying a good meal or a cool drink of water (or an alcoholic beverage)—is described in other chapters but not in the specific context of emotions. And Chapter 16 discusses the consequences of situations that evoke negative emotions: stress.

Fear

As we saw, emotional responses involve behavioral, autonomic, and hormonal components. These components are controlled by separate neural systems. The *integration* of the components of fear appears to be controlled by the amygdala.

medial nucleus A group of subnuclei of the amygdala that receives sensory input, including information about the presence of odors and pheromones, and relays it to the medial basal forebrain and hypothalamus.

lateral nucleus (LA) A nucleus of the amygdala that receives sensory information from the neocortex, thalamus, and hippocampus and send projections to the basal, accessory basal, and central nucleus of the amygdala.

central nucleus (CE) The region of the amygdala that receives information from the basal, lateral, and accessory basal nuclei and sends projections to a wide variety of regions in the brain; involved in emotional responses.

conditioned emotional response A classically conditioned response that occurs when a neutral stimulus is followed by an aversive stimulus; usually includes autonomic, behavioral, and endocrine components such as changes in heart rate, freezing, and secretion of stress-related hormones.

Research with Laboratory Animals

The amygdala plays a special role in physiological and behavioral reactions to objects and situations that have special biological significance, such as those that warn of pain or other unpleasant consequences or signify the presence of food, water, salt, potential mates or rivals, or infants in need of care. Researchers in several different laboratories have shown that single neurons in various nuclei of the amygdala become active when emotionally relevant stimuli are presented. For example, these neurons are excited by such stimuli as the sight of a device that has been used to squirt either a bad-tasting solution or a sweet solution into the animal's mouth, the sound of another animal's vocalization, the sound of the opening of the laboratory door, the smell of smoke, or the sight of another animal's face (O'Keefe and Bouma, 1969; Jacobs and McGinty, 1972; Rolls, 1982; Leonard et al., 1985). And as we have already seen in Chapter 9, the amygdala is involved in the effects of pheromones on reproductive physiology and behavior (including maternal behavior). This section describes research on the role of the amygdala in organizing emotional responses produced by aversive stimuli.

The amygdala (or, more precisely, the *amygdaloid complex*) is located within the temporal lobes. It consists of several groups of nuclei, each with different inputs and outputs—and with different functions (Amaral et al., 1992; Pitkänen et al., 1997). The amygdala has been subdivided into approximately twelve regions, each containing several subregions. However, we need concern ourselves with just five major regions: the *medial nucleus*, the *lateral nucleus*, the *basal nucleus*, the *accessory basal nucleus*, and the *central nucleus*.

The **medial nucleus** consists of several subnuclei that receive sensory input (including information about the presence of odors and pheromones) and relay the information to the medial basal forebrain and to the hypothalamus. Reproductive functions of the medial nucleus were discussed in Chapter 9. The **lateral nucleus (LA)** receives sensory information from the primary sensory cortex, association cortex, thalamus, and hippocampal formation. The lateral nucleus sends information to other parts of the brain, including the ventral striatum (a region involved in the effects of reinforcing stimuli on learning) and the dorsomedial nucleus of the thalamus, whose projection region is the prefrontal cortex. The lateral nucleus also sends information to the basal (B) and accessory basal (AB) nuclei. The LA, B, and AB nuclei all send information to the **central nucleus (CE),** which is the part of the amygdala that will most concern us in this chapter. The central nucleus projects to regions of the hypothalamus, midbrain, pons, and medulla that are responsible for the expression of the various components of emotional responses. As we will see, activation of the central nucleus elicits a variety of emotional responses: behavioral, autonomic, and hormonal. (See ***Figure 10.1.***)

Figure 10.1

A much-simplified diagram of the major divisions and connections of the amygdala that play a role in emotions.

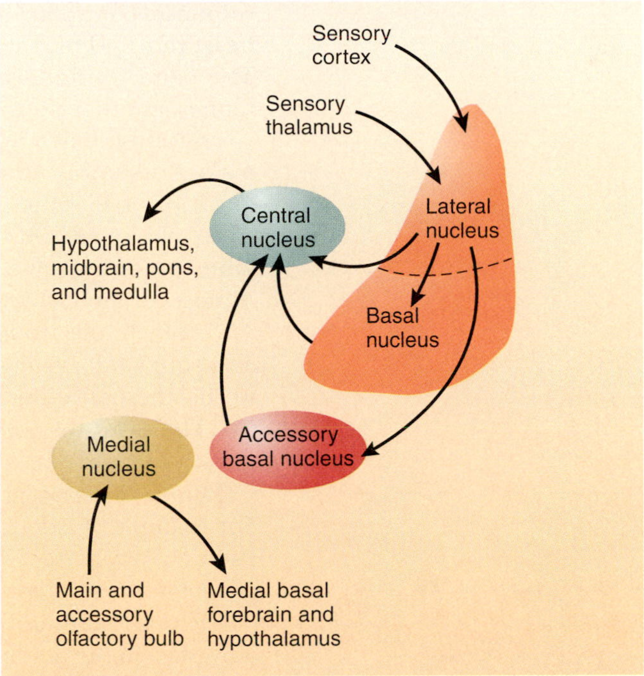

The central nucleus of the amygdala is the single most important part of the brain for the expression of emotional responses provoked by aversive stimuli. When threatening stimuli are presented, both the neural activity of the central nucleus and the production of Fos protein increase (Pascoe and Kapp, 1985; Campeau et al., 1991). Damage to the central nucleus (or to the nuclei that provide it with sensory information) reduces or abolishes a wide range of emotional behaviors and physiological responses. After the central nucleus has been destroyed, animals no longer show signs of fear when confronted with stimuli that have been paired with aversive events. They also act more tamely when handled by humans, their blood levels of stress hormones are lower, and they are less likely to develop ulcers or other forms of stress-induced illnesses (Coover, Murison, and Jellestad, 1992; Davis, 1992b; LeDoux, 1992). In contrast, when the central amygdala is stimulated by means of electricity or by an injection of an excitatory amino acid, the animal shows physiological and behavioral signs of fear and agitation (Davis, 1992b), and long-term stimulation of the central nucleus produces stress-induced illnesses such as gastric ulcers (Henke, 1982). These observations suggest that the autonomic and endocrine responses controlled by the central nucleus are among those responsible for the harmful effects of long-term stress, which are discussed in Chapter 16.

The central nucleus of the amygdala is particularly important for aversive emotional learning. A few stimuli automatically produce fear reactions—for example, loud unexpected noises, the approach of large animals, heights, or (for some species) specific sounds or odors. Even more important, however, is the fact that we can *learn* that a particular situation is dangerous or threatening. Once the learning has taken place, we will become frightened when we encounter that situation. Our heart rate and blood pressure will increase, our muscles will become more tense, our adrenal glands will secrete epinephrine, and we will proceed cautiously, alert and ready to respond.

Let's examine a specific (if somewhat contrived) example. A **conditioned emotional response** is produced by a neutral stimulus that has been paired with an emotion-producing stimulus. For example, suppose you are helping a friend prepare a meal. You pick up an electric mixer to mix some batter for a cake. Before you can turn the mixer on, the device makes a sputtering noise and then gives you a painful electrical shock. Your first response would be a defensive reflex: You would let go of the mixer, which would end the shock. This response is *specific;* it is aimed at terminating the painful stimulus. In addition, the painful stimulus would elicit *nonspecific* responses controlled by your autonomic nervous system: Your eyes would dilate, your heart rate and blood pressure would increase, you would breathe faster, and so on. The painful stimulus would also trigger the secretion of some stress-related hormones, another nonspecific response.

Suppose that a while later you visit your friend again and once more agree to make a cake. Your friend tells you that the electric mixer is perfectly safe. It has been fixed. Just seeing the mixer and thinking of holding it again makes you a little nervous, but you accept your friend's assurance and pick it up. Just then, it makes the same sputtering noise that it did when it shocked you. What would your response be? Almost certainly, you would drop the mixer again, even if it did not give you a shock. And your pupils would dilate, your heart rate and blood pressure would increase, and your endocrine glands would secrete some stress-related hormones. In other words, the sputtering sound would trigger a conditioned emotional response.

The word *conditioned* refers to the process of *classical conditioning,* which is described in more detail in Chapter 12. Briefly, classical conditioning occurs when a neutral stimulus is regularly followed by a stimulus that automatically evokes a response. For example, if a dog regularly hears a bell ring just before it receives some food that makes it salivate, it will begin salivating as soon as it hears the sound of the bell. (You probably already know that this phenomenon was discovered by Ivan Pavlov.)

Several laboratories have investigated the role of the central nucleus of the amygdala in the development of classically conditioned emotional responses. For example, LeDoux and his colleagues have studied these responses in rats by pairing an auditory stimulus with a brief electrical shock delivered to the feet (reviewed by LeDoux, 1995). In their studies they presented an 800-Hz tone for 10 sec, and then they delivered a brief (0.5-sec) shock to the floor on which the animals were standing. (See ***Figure 10.2.***) By itself the shock produces an *unconditional* emotional response: The animal jumps into the air, its heart rate and blood pressure increase, its breathing becomes more rapid, and its adrenal glands secrete catecholamines and steroid stress hormones. The experimenters presented several pairings of the two stimuli, which established classical conditioning.

The investigators tested conditioned emotional responses the next day by presenting the 800-Hz tone several times and measuring the animals' blood pressure and heart rate and observing their behavior. (This time, they did not present the shock.) Upon hearing the tone, the rats showed the same type of physiological responses as they had when they were shocked the previous day. In addition, they showed behavioral arrest—a species-typical defensive response called *freezing.* That is, the animals acted as if they were expecting to receive a shock.

LeDoux and his colleagues have shown that the central nucleus is necessary for the development of a conditioned emotional response (LeDoux, 1995). If this nucleus is destroyed, conditioning does not take place. In addition, LeDoux et al. (1988) destroyed two regions that receive projections from the central nucleus: the lateral hypothalamus and the caudal periaqueductal gray matter. They found that lesions of the lateral hypothalamus interfered with the change in blood pressure, whereas lesions of the periaqueductal gray matter interfered with the freezing response. Thus, two different mechanisms, both under the control of the central nucleus of the amygdala, are responsible for the autonomic and behavioral components of conditioned emotional responses.

Research on the details of the physical changes responsible for classical conditioning—including the role of the cen-

Figure 10.2

The procedure used to produce conditioned emotional responses.

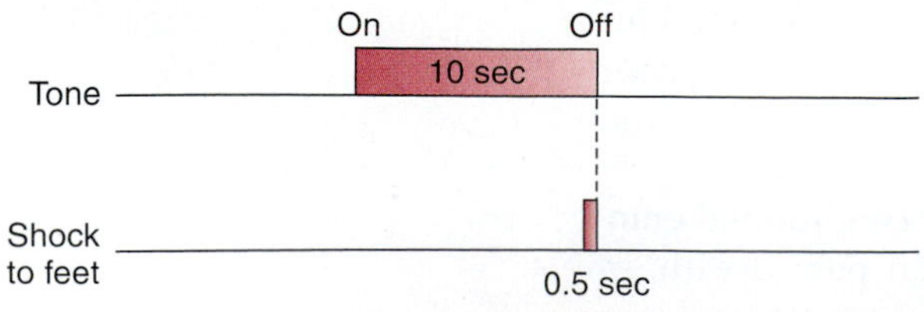

tral nucleus of the amygdala—has provided some interesting information about the physiology of learning and memory. This research will be discussed in more detail in Chapter 12.

Some of the effects of anxiolytic (anxiety-reducing) drugs appear to be produced through the central nucleus. The amygdala contains a high concentration of benzodiazepine receptors, especially the regions that project to the central nucleus, and the central nucleus itself contains a high concentration of opiate receptors. The infusion of either opiates or benzodiazepine tranquilizers into the amygdala decreases both the learning and the expression of conditioned emotional responses (Kapp et al., 1982; Davis, 1992a). In addition, Sanders and Shekhar (1995) found that an injection of a benzodiazepine antagonist into the amygdala blocked the anxiolytic effects of an intraperitoneal injection of chlordiazepoxide (*Librium*). Thus, tranquilizers and opiates appear to exert their anxiolytic effect in the amygdala. It is possible that some other regions of the brain are also involved in the effects of these drugs; Yadin et al. (1991) found that even after the amygdala is destroyed, benzodiazepines still have some anxiolytic effect.

As we will see in Chapter 15, some evidence suggests that increased activity of the neural mechanisms described in this section is associated with a fairly common category of psychological disorders: the *anxiety disorders.* Some investigators have suggested that anxiety disorders are caused by hyperactivity of the central nucleus of the amygdala. Whether the primary cause of the increased anxiety lies within these circuits or elsewhere in the brain has yet to be determined.

Research with Humans

A considerable amount of evidence indicates that the amygdala is involved in emotional responses in humans. One of the earliest studies observed the reactions of people who were being evaluated for surgical removal of parts of the brain to treat severe seizure disorders. These studies found that stimulation of parts of the brain (for example, the hypothalamus) produced autonomic responses that are often associated with fear and anxiety but that only when the amygdala was stimulated did people also report that they actually *felt* afraid (White, 1940; Halgren et al., 1978; Gloor et al., 1982).

Lesions of the amygdala decrease people's emotional responses. Two studies (LaBar et al., 1995; Bechara et al., 1995) found that people with lesions of the amygdala showed impaired acquisition of a conditioned emotional response, just as rats do. Damage to the amygdala also interferes with the effects of emotions on memory. Mori et al. (1999) questioned patients with Alzheimer's disease who had witnessed the devastating earthquake that struck Kobe, Japan, in 1955. They found that memory of this frightening event was inversely correlated with amygdala damage: The more a patient's amygdala was degenerated, the less likely it was that the patient remembered the earthquake.

Several imaging studies have shown that the human amygdala participates in emotional responses. For example, Cahill et al. (1996) had people watch both neutral and emotionally arousing films (such as scenes of violent crimes). Later, the experimenters placed the subjects in a PET scanner and asked them to recall the films. The activity of the right amygdala increased while the subjects recalled the emotionally arousing films but not when they recalled the neutral ones. In addition, the subjects were most likely to recall the emotionally arousing films that produced the highest level of activity in the right amygdala when they were originally viewed.

In another PET study, Isenberg et al. (1999) found that seeing words that denote threatening situations increases the activity of the amygdala. The investigators had people look at words presented in various colors on a computer screen. Some of the words were neutral (e. g., list, dial, wheel, label, bookcase, spin, cups, repeat), and

Figure 10.3

An averaged PET scan from a group of people while looking at threatening words. The scan shows increased activity in the amygdala.

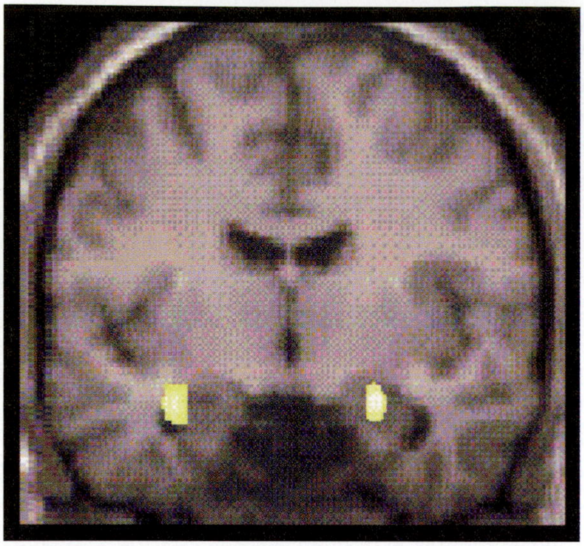

From Isenberg, N., Silbersweig, D., Engelien, A., Emmerich, S., Malavade, K., Beattie, B., Leon, A. C., and Stern, E. *Proceedings of the National Academy of Sciences, USA,* 1999, *96,* 10456–10459. Copyright 1999 National Academy of Sciences, U.S.A.

Figure 10.4

Results of the studies by Shaikh, Siegel, and their colleagues. The diagram shows interconnections of parts of the amygdala, hypothalamus, and periaqueductal gray matter and their effects on defensive rage and predation in cats. Black arrows indicate excitation; red arrows indicate inhibition.

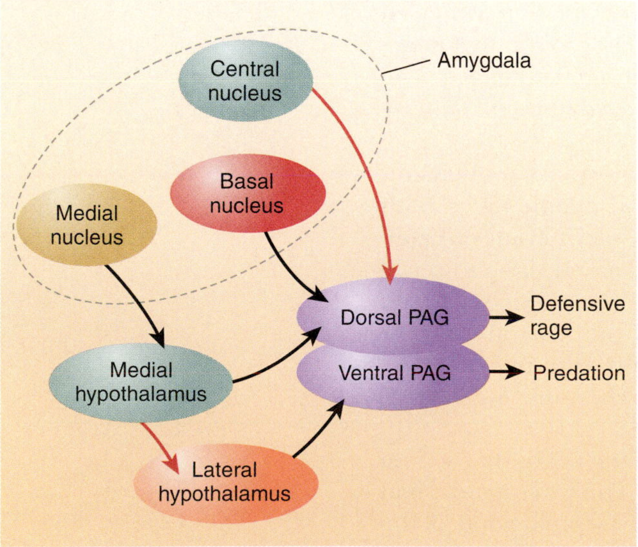

some were threatening (e. g., slaughter, prisoner, evil, rape, knife, suffer, mutilate, danger). The subjects were not asked to read the words, but simply asked to name the color of the letters. Seeing the threatening words (but not the neutral ones) caused a bilateral increase in the activity of the amygdala. (See ***Figure 10.3.***)

Anger and Aggression

Almost all species of animals engage in aggressive behaviors, which involve threatening gestures or actual attack directed toward another animal. Aggressive behaviors are species-typical; that is, the patterns of movements (for example, posturing, biting, striking, and hissing) are organized by neural circuits whose development is largely programmed by an animal's genes. Many aggressive behaviors are related to reproduction. For example, aggressive behaviors that gain access to mates, defend territory needed to attract mates or to provide a site for building a nest, or defend offspring against intruders can all be regarded as reproductive behaviors. Other aggressive behaviors are related to self-defense, such as that of an animal threatened by a rival or a predator.

Research with Laboratory Animals

Neural Control of Aggressive Behavior. The neural control of aggressive behavior is hierarchical. That is, the particular muscular movements an animal makes in attacking or defending itself are programmed by neural circuits in the brain stem. Whether an animal attacks depends on many factors, including the nature of the eliciting stimuli in the environment and the animal's previous experience. The activity of the brain stem circuits appears to be controlled by the hypothalamus and the amygdala, which also influence many other species-typical behaviors. And, of course, the activity of the limbic system is controlled by perceptual systems that detect the status of the environment, including the presence of other animals.

A series of studies by Shaikh, Siegel, and their colleagues (reviewed by Siegel et al., 1999) investigated the neural circuitry involved in defensive behavior and predation in cats. The investigators placed electrodes in various regions of the brain and observed the effects of electrical stimulation of these regions on the animals' behavior. In some cases the electrode was actually a stainless-steel cannula, coated with an insulating material except for the tip. These devices (called *cannula electrodes*) could be used to infuse chemicals into the brain as well as to stimulate it. The investigators found that defensive behavior and predation can be elicited by stimulation of different parts of the periaqueductal gray matter of the midbrain (PAG) and that the hypothalamus and the amygdala influence these behaviors through excitatory and inhibitory connections with the PAG. They found that the three principal regions of the amygdala and two regions of the hypothalamus affect defensive rage and predation, both of which appear to be organized by the PAG. (They assessed predation by presenting the cats with an anesthetized rat, so no pain was inflicted.) A possible connection between the lateral hypothalamus and the ventral PAG has not yet been verified. Rather than list the connections and their effects, I will direct you to ***Figure 10.4.***

Studies of groups of vervet monkeys confirm the role of serotonin in control of aggression.

Role of Serotonin. An overwhelming amount of evidence suggests that the activity of serotonergic synapses inhibits aggression. In contrast, destruction of serotonergic axons in the forebrain facilitates aggressive attack, presumably by removing an inhibitory effect (Vergnes et al., 1988).

A group of researchers has studied the relationship between serotonergic activity and aggressiveness in a free-ranging colony of rhesus monkeys (Mehlman et al., 1995; Higley et al., 1996a, 1996b). They assessed serotonergic activity by capturing the monkeys, removing a sample of cerebrospinal fluid, and analyzing it for 5-HIAA, a metabolite of serotonin (5-HT). When 5-HT is released, most of the neurotransmitter is taken back into the terminal buttons by means of reuptake, but some escapes and is broken down to 5-HIAA, which finds its way into the cerebrospinal fluid. Thus, high levels of 5-HIAA in the CSF indicates an elevated level of serotonergic activity. The investigators found that young male monkeys with the lowest levels of 5-HIAA showed a pattern of risk-taking behavior, including high levels of aggression directed toward animals that were older and much larger than themselves. They were much more likely to take dangerous unprovoked long leaps from tree to tree at a height of more than 7 m (27.6 ft). They were also more likely to pick fights that they could not possibly win. Of 49 preadolescent male monkeys that the investigators followed for four years, 46 percent of those with the lowest 5-HIAA levels died, while all of the monkeys with the highest levels survived. (See ***Figure 10.5.***) Most of the monkeys were killed by other monkeys. In fact, the first monkey to be killed had the lowest level of 5-HIAA and was seen attacking two mature males the night before his death.

It is clear that serotonin does not merely inhibit aggression; rather, it exerts a controlling influence on risky behavior, which includes aggression. A study by Raleigh et al. (1991) removed the dominant male from each of several groups of vervet monkeys and treated the top two remaining males with serotonergic drugs: One received an agonist, and the other received an antagonist. The monkeys that received the serotonin agonist became dominant, while the status of those that received the antagonist declined. You might think that removing some inhibitory control over aggressiveness would increase a monkey's dominance. However, dominance and aggression are not synonymous. Certainly, a dominant animal will use aggression if it is overtly challenged by a rival. However, becoming the dominant animal in a group of monkeys requires good social skills. As Mehlman et al. (1995)

Figure 10.5

Percentage of young male monkeys alive or dead as a function of 5-HIAA level in the CSF, measured four years previously.

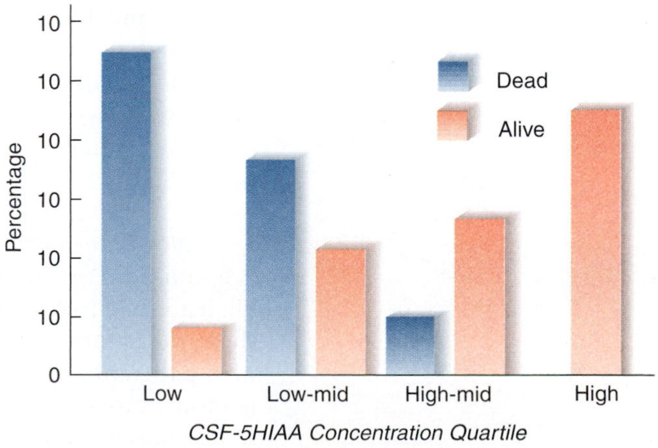

Adapted from Higley, J. D., Mehlman, P. T., Higley, S. B., Fernald, B., Vickers, J., Lindell, S. G., Taub, D. M., Suomi, S. J., and Linnoila, M., *Archives of General Psychiatry,* 1996, *53,* 537–543.

noted in their naturalistic study, the monkeys with low levels of serotonergic activity showed the lowest levels of social competency.

Several studies with targeted mutations in mice confirm the conclusion that serotonin has an inhibitory role in aggression. For example, Saudou et al. (1994) and Bouwknecht et al. (2001) found that mice lacking 5-HT_{1B} receptors attacked an intruder more quickly and intensely than normal mice did, but otherwise, their behavior appeared normal.

Research with Humans

Human violence and aggression are serious social problems. Consider the following case histories:

> Born to an alcoholic teen mother who raised him with an abusive alcoholic stepfather, Steve was hyperactive, irritable, and disobedient as a toddler. . . . After dropping out of school at age 14, Steve spent his teen years fighting, stealing, taking drugs, and beating up girlfriends. . . . School counseling, a probation officer, and meetings with child protective service failed to forestall disaster: At 19, several weeks after his last interview with researchers, Steve visited a girlfriend who had recently dumped him, found her with another man, and shot him to death. The same day he tried to kill himself. Now he's serving a life sentence without parole. (Holden, 2000, p. 580)

> By the time Joshua had reached the age of 2, . . . he would bolt out of the house and into traffic. He kicked and head-butted relatives and friends. He poked the family hamster with a pencil and tried to strangle it. He threw regular temper tantrums and would stage toy-throwing frenzies. At one point he was hurting himself—banging his head against a wall, pinching himself, not to mention leaping off the refrigerator. . . . Showering Joshua with love . . . made little difference: By age 3, his behavior got him kicked out of his preschool. (Holden, 2000, p. 581)

Role of Serotonin. Several studies have found that serotonergic neurons play an inhibitory role in human aggression. For example, a depressed rate of serotonin release (indicated by low levels of 5-HIAA in the CSF) are associated with aggression and other forms of antisocial behavior, including assault, arson, murder, and child beating (Lidberg et al., 1984, 1985; Virkkunen et al., 1989). Coccaro et al. (1994) studied a group of men with personality disorders (including a history of impulsive aggression). They found that the men with the lowest serotonergic activity were most likely to have close relatives with a history of similar behavior problems.

If low levels of serotonin release contribute to aggression, perhaps drugs that act as serotonin agonists might help to reduce antisocial behavior. In fact, a study by Coccaro and Kavoussi (1997) found that fluoxetine (Prozac), a serotonin agonist, decreased irritability and aggressiveness, as measured by a psychological test. Joshua, the little boy described in the introduction to this subsection, came under the care of a psychiatrist who prescribed monoaminergic agonists and began a course of behavior therapy that managed to stem Joshua's violent outbursts and risk-taking behaviors.

Role of the Prefrontal Cortex. Many investigators believe that impulsive violence is a consequence of faulty emotional regulation. For most of us, frustrations may elicit an urge to respond emotionally, but we manage to calm ourselves and suppress these urges. As we shall see, the prefrontal cortex plays an important role in recognizing the emotional significance of complex social situations and in regulating our responses to such situations. The analysis of social situations involves much more than sensory analysis; it involves experiences and memories, inferences and judgments. In fact, the skills involved include some of the most complex ones we possess. These skills are not localized in any one part of the cerebral cortex, although research does suggest that the right hemisphere is more important than the left. But one region of the prefrontal cortex—the orbitofrontal cortex—plays a special role.

The **orbitofrontal cortex** is located at the base of the frontal lobes. It covers the part of the brain just above the *orbits*—the bones that form the eye sockets—hence the term *orbitofrontal.* (See ***Figure 10.6.***) The orbitofrontal cortex receives direct inputs from the dorsomedial thalamus, temporal cortex, ventral tegmental area, olfactory system, and amygdala. Its outputs go to several brain regions, including the cingulate cortex, hippocampal formation, temporal cortex, lateral hypothalamus, and amygdala. Finally, it communicates with other regions of the frontal cortex. Thus, its inputs provide it with information about what is happening in the environment and what plans are being made by the rest of the frontal lobes, and its outputs permit it to affect a variety of behaviors and physiological responses, including emotional responses organized by the amygdala.

Figure 10.6

The orbitofrontal cortex.

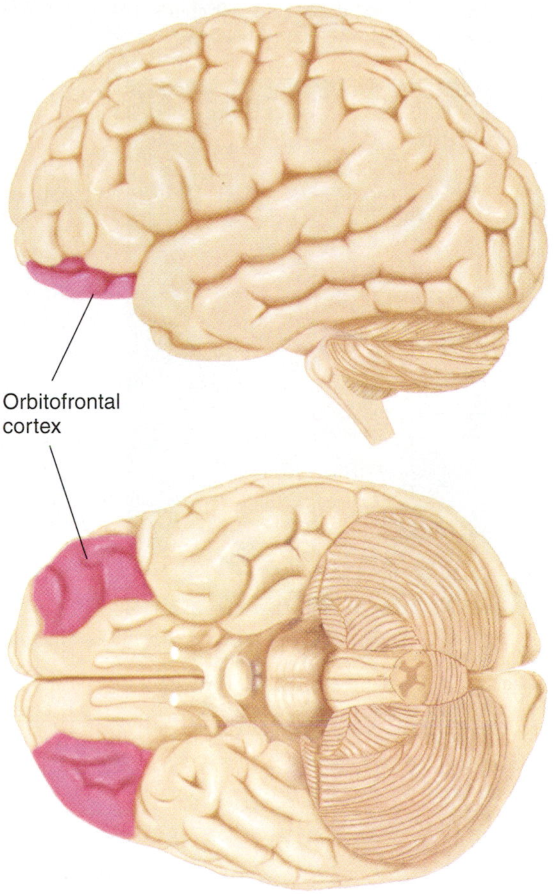

The fact that the orbitofrontal cortex plays an important role in control of emotional behavior is shown by the effects of damage to this region. The first—and most famous—case comes from the mid-1800s. Phineas Gage, the foreman of a railway construction crew, was using a steel rod to ram a charge of blasting powder into a hole drilled in solid rock. Suddenly, the charge exploded and sent the rod into his cheek, through his brain, and out the top of his head. (See ***Figure 10.7.***) He survived, but he was a different man. Before his injury he was serious, industrious, and energetic. Afterward, he became childish, irresponsible, and thoughtless of others. His outbursts of temper led some people to remark that it looked as if Dr. Jekyll had become Mr. Hyde. He was unable to make or carry out plans, and his actions appeared to be capricious and whimsical. His accident largely destroyed the orbitofrontal cortex (Damasio et al., 1994).

What, exactly, does the orbitofrontal cortex do? Evidence suggests that it serves as in interface between brain mechanisms involved in automatic emotional responses (both learned and unlearned) and those involved in the control of complex behaviors. This role includes using our emotional reactions to guide our behavior and controlling the occurrence of emotional reactions in various social situations.

People whose orbitofrontal cortex has been damaged by disease or accident are still able to accurately assess the significance of particular situations, but only in a *theoretical* sense. For example, Eslinger and Damasio (1985) found that a patient with bilateral damage of the orbitofrontal cortex (produced by a benign tumor, which was successfully removed) displayed excellent social judgment. When he was given hypothetical situations that required him to make decisions about what the people involved should do—situations involving moral, ethical, or practical dilemmas—he always gave sensible answers and justified them with carefully reasoned logic. However, his own life was a different matter. He frittered away his life's savings on investments that his family and friends pointed out were bound to fail. He lost one job after another because of his irresponsibility. He became unable to distinguish between trivial decisions and important ones, spending hours trying to decide where to have dinner but failing to use good judgment in situations that concerned his occupation and family life. (His wife finally left him and sued for divorce.) As the authors noted, "He had learned and used normal patterns of social behavior

orbitofrontal cortex The region of the prefrontal cortex at the base of the anterior frontal lobes.

Figure 10.7

A reconstruction of the skull of Phineas Gage and the rod that passed through his head. The steel rod entered his left cheek and exited through the top of his head.

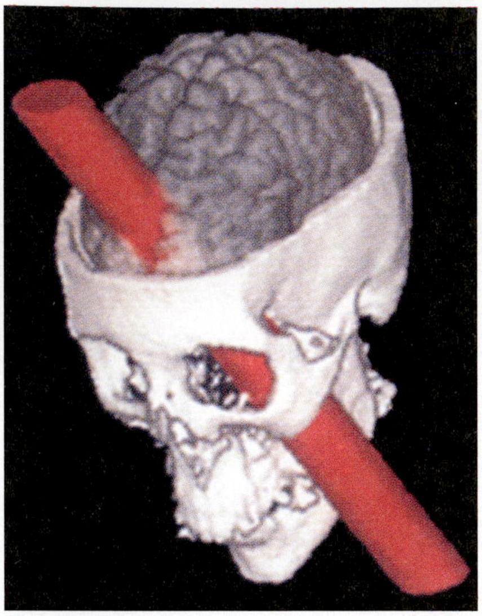

From Damasio, H., Grabowski, T., Frank, R., Galaburda, A. M., and Damasio, A. R. *Science*, 1994, *264*, 1102–1105. Copyright 1994 American Association for the Advancement of Science. Reprinted with permission.

before his brain lesion, and although he could recall such patterns when he was questioned about their applicability, *real-life situations failed to evoke them*" (p. 1737). Thus, it appears that the orbitofrontal cortex is not directly involved in making judgments and conclusions about events (these occur elsewhere in the brain); rather, it is involved in translating these judgments into appropriate feelings and behaviors.

Mr. V., described in the chapter prologue, had brain damage that impaired his judgment without affecting traditional measures of verbal intelligence. This damage included both the right frontal and parietal lobes, so we cannot attribute his symptoms to any single region.

Evidence suggests that emotional reactions guide moral judgments as well as other kinds of decisions and that the prefrontal cortex plays a role in these judgments. Consider the following moral dilemma: You see a runaway trolley with five people aboard hurtling down a track leading to a cliff. Without your intervention these people will soon die. However, you are standing near a switch that will shunt the trolley off to another track, where the vehicle will stop safely. But a worker is standing on that track, and he will be killed if you throw the switch to save the five helpless passengers. Should you stand by and watch the trolley go off the cliff, or should you save them—and kill the man on the track?

Most people conclude that the better choice would be to throw the switch; saving five people justifies the sacrifice of one man. But consider a variation of this dilemma. As before, the trolley is hurtling toward doom, but there is no switch at hand to shunt it to another track. Instead, you are standing on a bridge over the track. An obese man is standing there too, and if you give him a push, his body will fall on the track and stop the trolley. (You are too small to stop the trolley, so you cannot save the five people by sacrificing yourself.) What should you do?

Most people balk at pushing the man off the bridge, even though the result would be the same as the first dilemma: one person lost, five people saved. Whether we kill someone by sending a trolley his way or by pushing him off a bridge into the path of an oncoming trolley, he dies when the trolley strikes him. But somehow pushing a person's body and causing his death seems more emotionally wrenching than throwing a switch that changes the course of a runaway trolley. Thus, moral judgments appear to be guided by emotional reactions and are not simply the products of rational, logical decision making processes.

In a functional imaging study, Greene et al. (2001) presented people with the moral dilemmas such as the one I just described and found that thinking about them activated several brain regions involved in emotional reactions, including the medial prefrontal cortex. (Making innocuous decisions, such as whether to take a bus or train to some destination, did not activate these regions.) Perhaps, then, our reluctance to push someone to his death is guided by the emotional reaction we feel when we contemplate this action.

It might seem that I have been getting away from the topic of this section: anger and aggression. However, recall that many investigators believe that impulsive violence is a consequence of faulty emotional regulation. The amygdala plays an important role in provoking anger and violent emotional reactions, and the prefrontal cortex plays an important role in suppressing such behavior by making us see its negative consequences. Let's look at some evidence. A functional imaging study by Dougherty et al. (1999) found that when subjects read and thought about stories from their own lives that had made them angry, they became angry again, and their orbitofrontal cortex and medial prefrontal cortex became activated. The activation of the prefrontal cortex may reflect its role in inhibiting aggressive behavior.

Raine et al. (1998) found evidence of decreased prefrontal activity and increased subcortical activity (including the amygdala) in the brains of convicted murderers. These changes were primarily seen in impulsive, emotional murderers. Cold-blooded, calculating, predatory murderers—whose crimes were not accompanied by anger and rage—showed more normal prefrontal activity. Presumably, increased activation of the amygdala reflected an increased tendency for display of negative emotions, and the decreased activation of the prefrontal cortex reflected a decreased ability to control one's emotions. In fact, Raine et al. (2002) found that people with antisocial personality disorder showed an 11 percent reduction in volume of the gray matter of the prefrontal cortex.

In an earlier section of this chapter we saw that decreased activity of serotonergic neurons is associated with aggression, violence, and risk taking. As we saw in this subsection, decreased activity of the prefrontal cortex is also associated with antisocial behavior. These two fact appear to be linked. The prefrontal cortex receives a major projection of serotonergic axons. Research indicates that serotonergic input to the prefrontal cortex activates this region; thus, an abnormally low level of serotonin release can result in decreased activity of the prefrontal cortex.

A functional imaging study by Mann et al. (1996) showed that fenfluramine, a drug that stimulates the release of 5-HT, increases the activity of the prefrontal cortex. A study by New et al. (2002) found that a serotonin-releasing drug increased the activity of the orbitofrontal cortex in normal, nonviolent subjects but failed to do so in subjects with a history of impulsive aggression.

In summary, the prefrontal cortex appears to provide information about our ongoing emotional states to regions of the brain involved in rational, logical cognitive processes. This information plays a critical role our ability to regulate and control our emotional responses, including those that would result in anger and violence. The inhibitory role that serotonin plays in aggression and risk-taking behavior may reflect the fact that serotonin activates the prefrontal cortex and hence enhances the ability of this brain region to control these behaviors.

Hormonal Control of Aggressive Behavior

As we saw, many instances of aggressive behavior are in some way related to reproduction. For example, males of some species establish territories that attract females during the breeding season. To do so, they must defend the territories against the intrusion of other males. Even in species in which breeding does not depend on the establishment of a territory, males may compete for access to females, which also involves aggressive behavior. Females, too, often compete with other females for space in which to build nests or dens in which to rear their offspring, and they will defend their offspring against the intrusion of other animals. As you learned in Chapter 9, most reproductive behaviors are controlled by the organizational and activational effects of hormones; thus, we should not be surprised that many forms of aggressive behavior are, like mating, affected by hormones.

Aggression in Males

Adult males of many species fight for territory or access to females. In laboratory rodents androgen secretion occurs prenatally, decreases, and then increases again at the time of puberty. Intermale aggressiveness also begins around the time of puberty, which suggests that the behavior is controlled by neural circuits that are stimulated by androgens. Indeed, many years ago Beeman (1947) found that castration reduced aggressiveness and that injections of testosterone reinstated it.

In Chapter 9 we saw that early androgenization has an *organizational effect*. The secretion of androgens early in development modifies the developing brain, making

Figure 10.8

Organizational and activational effects of testosterone on social aggression.

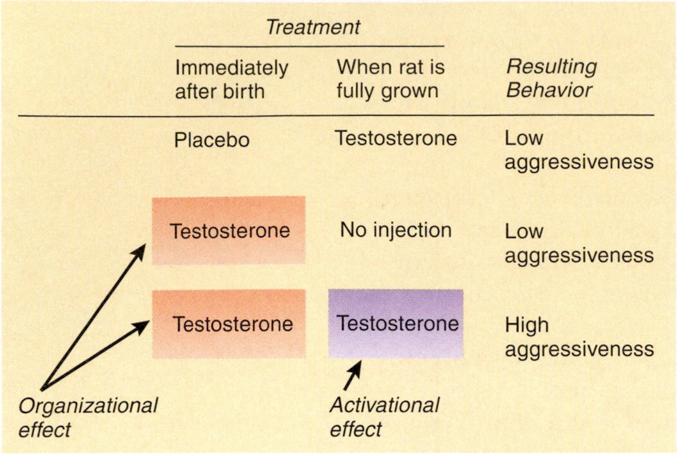

neural circuits that control male sexual behavior become more responsive to testosterone. Similarly, early androgenization has an organizational effect that stimulates the development of testosterone-sensitive neural circuits that facilitate intermale aggression. (See ***Figure 10.8.***)

Treatment
Immediately after birth
When rat is fully grown
Resulting Behavior
Placebo
Testosterone
Low aggressiveness
Testosterone
No injection
Low aggressiveness
Testosterone
Testosterone
High aggressiveness
Organizational effect
Activational effect

The organizational effect of androgens on intermale aggression (aggressive displays or actual fights between two males of the same species) is important, but it is not an all-or-none phenomenon. Prolonged administration of testosterone will eventually induce intermale aggression even in rodents that were castrated immediately after birth. Data reviewed by vom Saal (1983) show that exposure to androgens early in life decreases the amount of exposure that is necessary to activate aggressive behavior later in life. Thus, early androgenization *sensitizes* the neural circuits—The earlier the androgenization, the more effective the sensitization.

We also saw in Chapter 9 that androgens stimulate male sexual behavior by interacting with androgen receptors in neurons located in the medial preoptic area (MPA). This region also appears to be important in mediating the effects of androgens on intermale aggression. Bean and Conner (1978) found that implanting testosterone in the MPA reinstated intermale aggression in castrated male rats. Presumably, the testosterone directly activated the behavior by stimulating the androgen-sensitive neurons located there. The medial preoptic area, then, appears to be involved in several behaviors related to reproduction: male sexual behavior, maternal behavior, and intermale aggression.

Males readily attack other males but usually do not attack females. Their ability to discriminate the sex of the intruder appears to be based on the presence of particular pheromones. Bean (1982) found that intermale aggression was abolished in mice by cutting the vomeronasal nerve, which deprives the brain of input from the vomeronasal organ. And if the urine of female mice is painted on a male mouse, that

Aggressive behavior can be seen at all ages and in both sexes, but its frequency generally increases in males after puberty.

mouse will not be attacked if it is introduced into another male's cage (Dixon and Mackintosh, 1971; Dixon, 1973). In fact, a targeted mutation against a protein that is essential for the detection of pheromones by the vomeronasal organ abolishes a male mouse's ability to discriminate between males and females. The authors of this study (Stowers et al., 2002) also found that the mutation abolished intermale aggression. Because male intruders were not recognized as rival males, they were not attacked. (See ***Animation 10.1, Role of Pheromones in Intermale Aggression.***)

Animation 10.1, Role of Pheromones in Intermale Aggression, contains videos showing the effects of genetically engineered interference with detection of pheromones on aggressive behavior of male mice.

Aggression in Females

Two adult female rodents that meet in a neutral territory are less likely than males to fight. But aggression between females, like aggression between males, appears to be facilitated by testosterone. Van de Poll et al. (1988) ovariectomized female rats and then give them daily injections of testosterone, estradiol, or a placebo for 14 days. The animals were then placed in a test cage, and an unfamiliar female was introduced. As Figure 10.9 shows, testosterone increased aggressiveness, whereas estradiol had no effect. (See ***Figure 10.9.***)

Androgens have an organizational effect on the aggressiveness of females, and a certain amount of prenatal androgenization appears to occur naturally. Most rodent fetuses share their mother's uterus with brothers and sisters, arranged in a row like peas in a pod. A female mouse may have zero, one, or two brothers adjacent to her. Researchers refer to these females as 0M, 1M, or 2M, respectively. (See ***Figure 10.10.***) Being next to a male fetus has an effect on a female's blood levels of androgens prenatally. Vom Saal and Bronson (1980) found that females located between two males had significantly higher levels of testosterone in their blood than females located between two females (or between a female and the end of the uterus). When they are tested as adults, 2M females are more likely to exhibit interfemale aggressiveness.

Figure 10.9

Effects of estradiol and testosterone on interfemale aggression in rats.

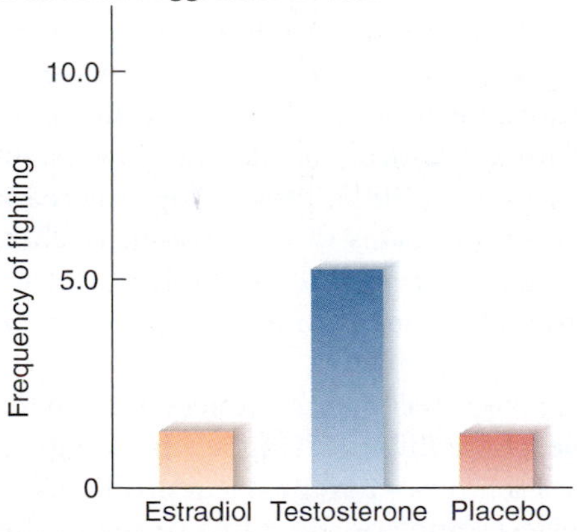

Adapted from van de Poll, N. E., Taminiau, M. S., Endert, E., and Louwerse, A. L., *International Journal of Neuroscience,* 1988, *41,* 271–286.

Figure 10.10

0M, 1M, and 2M female mouse fetuses.

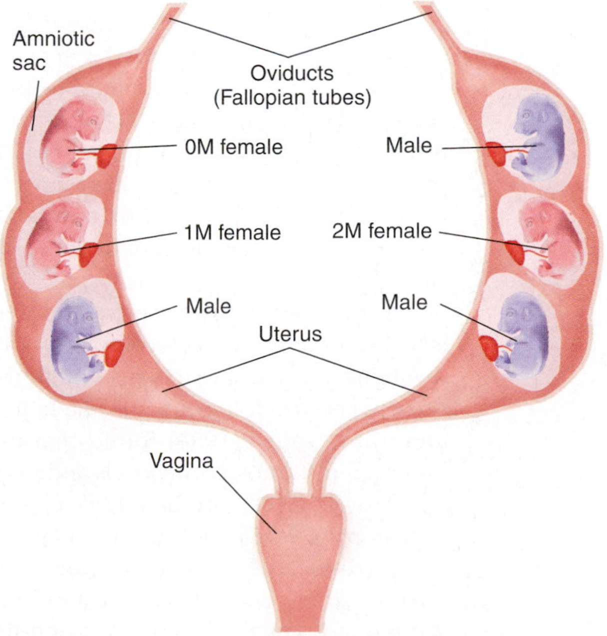

Adapted from vom Saal, F. S., in *Hormones and Aggressive Behavior,* edited by B. B. Svare. New York: Plenum Press, 1983.

Females of some primate species (for example, rhesus monkeys and baboons) are more likely to engage in fights around the time of ovulation (Carpenter, 1942; Saayman, 1971). This phenomenon is probably caused by their increased sexual interest and consequent proximity to males. As Carpenter noted, "She actively approaches males and must overcome their usual resistance to close association, hence she becomes an object of attacks by them" (p. 136). Another period of fighting occurs just before menstruation (Sassenrath, Powell, and Hendrickx, 1973; Mallow, 1979). During this time females tend to attack other females.

Effects of Androgens on Human Aggressive Behavior

Boys are generally more aggressive than girls. Clearly, Western society tolerates assertiveness and aggressive behavior from boys more than from girls. Without doubt the way we treat boys and girls and the models to which we expose them play important roles in sex differences in aggressiveness in our species. The question is not whether socialization has an effect (certainly, it does) but whether biological influences, such as exposure to androgens, have an effect too.

Prenatal androgenization increases aggressive behavior in all species that have been studied, including primates. Therefore, if androgens did not affect aggressive behavior in humans, our species would be exceptional. After puberty androgens also begin to have activational effects. Boys' testosterone levels begin to increase during the early teens, at which time aggressive behavior and intermale fighting also increase (Mazur, 1983). Of course, boys' social status changes during puberty, and their testosterone affects their muscles as well as their brains, so we cannot be sure that the effect is hormonally produced or, if it is, that it is mediated by the brain.

Scientifically rigorous evidence that androgens increase aggression in humans is difficult to obtain. Obviously, we cannot randomly castrate some men to find out whether their aggressiveness declines. In the past authorities attempted to suppress sex-related aggression by castrating convicted male sex offenders. Investigators have reported that both heterosexual and homosexual aggressive attacks disappear, along with the offender's sex drive (Hawke, 1951; Sturup, 1961; Laschet, 1973). However, the studies typically lack appropriate control groups and usually do not measure aggressive behavior directly.

Some cases of aggressiveness, especially sexual assault, have been treated with synthetic steroids that inhibit the production of androgens by the testes. Clearly, treatment with drugs is preferable to castration, because the effects are not irreversible. However, the efficacy of treatment with antiandrogens has yet to be established conclusively. According to Walker and Meyer (1981), these drugs decrease sex-related aggression but have no effect on other forms of aggression. In fact, Zumpe et al. (1991) found that one of these drugs decreased sexual activity and aggression toward females when administered to male monkeys but that it actually *increased* intermale aggression.

Another way to determine whether androgens affect aggressiveness in humans is to examine the testosterone levels of people who exhibit varying levels of aggressive behavior. However, even though this approach poses fewer ethical problems, it presents methodological ones. First, let me review some evidence. In a review of the literature Archer (1994) found that most studies found a positive relationship between men's testosterone levels and their level of aggressiveness. For example, Dabbs and Morris (1990) studied 4462 U.S. military veterans. The men with the highest testosterone levels had records of more antisocial activities, including assaults of other adults and histories of more trouble with parents, teachers, and classmates during adolescence. The largest effects were seen in men of lower socioeconomic status. Dabbs et al. (1987) measured the testosterone levels of male prison inmates and found a significant correlation with several measures of violence, including the nature of the crime for which they were convicted, infractions of prison rules, and ratings of "toughness" by their peers. These relationships are also seen in female prison inmates; Dabbs et al. (1988) found that women prisoners who showed unprovoked violence and had several prior convictions also showed higher levels of testosterone than the other female inmates. (As we saw earlier, testosterone increases interfemale aggression in laboratory animals as well.)

In any event we must remember that *correlation* does not necessarily indicate *causation.* A person's environment can affect his or her testosterone level. For example, losing a tennis match or a wrestling competition causes a fall in blood levels of testosterone (Mazur and Lamb, 1980; Elias, 1981). Even winning or losing a simple game of chance carried out in a psychology laboratory can affect participants' testosterone levels: Winners feel better afterward and have a higher level of testosterone (McCaul, Gladue, and Joppa, 1992). Bernhardt et al. (1998) found that basketball and soccer fans showed an increase in testosterone levels if their team won and a decrease if it lost. Thus, we cannot be sure in any correlational study that high testosterone levels *cause* people to become dominant or aggressive; perhaps their success in establishing a position of dominance increases their testosterone levels relative to those of the people they dominate.

A few studies have looked at the behavioral effects of administering androgens. Because of ethical concerns, people cannot be given androgen supplements for any length of time merely to find out whether they become more aggressive; excessive amounts of androgens have deleterious effects on a person's health. Thus, the only evidence we have of the effects of long-term administration comes from case studies in which people with abnormally low levels of testosterone (the *hypogonadal syndrome*) are given an androgen to replace what would normally be present. In general, such people feel happier and their sexual activity increases, but they do not usually show more aggressiveness (Skakkebaek et al., 1981; O'Carroll, Shapiro, and Bancroft, 1985). One double-blind study (Su et al., 1993) did administer testosterone for several days to a group of normal volunteers, men aged 18 to 42 years. Those receiving the highest doses reported more euphoria and sexual arousal but also more irritability and feelings of hostility. However, the effects were small, and the investigators did not observe behaviors, only self-reports of feelings.

As everyone knows, some athletes take anabolic steroids to increase their muscle mass and strength and, supposedly, to increase their competitiveness. Anabolic steroids include natural androgens and synthetic hormones with androgenic effects. Thus, we might expect that these hormones would increase aggressiveness. Indeed, several studies have found exactly that. For example, Yates, Perry, and Murray (1992) found male weight lifters who were taking anabolic steroids to be more aggressive and hostile than those who were not. But as the authors note, we cannot be certain that the steroid is responsible for the increased aggressiveness; it could simply be that the men who were already more competitive and aggressive were the ones who chose to take the steroids.

INTERIM SUMMARY

Emotions as Response Patterns

The word *emotion* refers to behaviors, physiological responses, and feelings. This section has discussed emotional response patterns, which consist of behaviors that deal with particular situations and physiological responses (both autonomic and hormonal) that support the behaviors. The amygdala organizes behavioral, autonomic, and hormonal responses to a variety of situations, including those that produce fear, or anger. In addition, it is involved in the effects of odors and pheromones on sexual and maternal behavior. It receives inputs from the olfactory system, the association cortex of the temporal lobe, the frontal cortex, and the rest of the limbic system. Its outputs go to the frontal cortex, hypothalamus, hippocampal formation, and brain stem nuclei that control autonomic functions and some species-typical behaviors. Damage to specific brain regions that receive these outputs will abolish particular components of emotional response patterns. Electrical recordings of single neurons in the amygdala indicate that some of them respond when the animal perceives particular stimuli with emotional significance. Stimulation of the amygdala leads to emotional responses, and its destruction disrupts them. Receptors in the amygdala are largely responsible for the anxiolytic effects of the benzodiazepine tranquilizers and the opiates. Studies of people with amygdala lesions and PET and functional MRI studies with humans indicate that the amygdala is involved in emotional reactions in our species, too.

Aggressive behaviors are species-typical and serve useful functions most of the time. In addition, animals may exhibit threat or submissive behaviors, which may avoid an actual fight. The periaqueductal gray matter appears to be involved in defensive behavior and predation. These mechanisms are modulated by the hypothalamus and amygdala.

The activity of serotonergic neurons appears to inhibit risk-taking behaviors, including aggression. Destruction of serotonergic axons in the forebrain enhances aggression, and administration of drugs that facilitate serotonergic transmission reduces it. Low CSF levels of 5-HIAA (a metabolite of serotonin) are correlated with increased risk-taking and aggressive behavior in monkeys and humans.

The ventromedial prefrontal cortex (which includes the orbitofrontal cortex) plays an important role in emotional reactions. This region communicates with other regions of the frontal lobes, the temporal pole, and the amygdala and other parts of the limbic system. People with orbitofrontal lesions show impulsive behavior and often display outbursts of inappropriate anger. They are able to explain the implications of complex situations but are often unable to respond appropriately when these situations concern *them.* Their lack of an emotional response in a situation that has important consequences for them often leads to poor decision making. Evidence suggests that the prefrontal cortex is involved in making moral judgments.

The prefrontal cortex plays an important role in regulation of emotional expression, including anger and aggression. In a laboratory setting, anger activates this region, perhaps reflecting inhibitory control on behavior. Violent criminals generally show a low level of activity of this region, and the volume of gray matter in this region was lower than normal in a group of people with antisocial personality disorder. The release of serotonin in the prefrontal cortex activates this region, and some investigators believe that the serotonergic input to this region is responsible for the ability of serotonin to inhibit aggression and risky behavior.

Because many aggressive behaviors are related to reproduction, they are influenced by hormones, especially sex steroid hormones. In males androgens have organizational and activational effects on offensive attack, just as they have on male sexual behavior. The effects of androgens on intermale aggression appear to be mediated by the medial preoptic area.

Females rodents will fight when they meet in neutral territory but less often than males. Female rodents that have been slightly androgenized (2M females) are more likely to attack other females. Female primates are most likely to fight around the time of ovulation, perhaps because their increased sexual interest brings them closer to males.

Androgens apparently promote aggressive behavior in humans, but this topic is more difficult to study in our species than in laboratory animals. Differences in testosterone levels have been observed in criminals with a history of violence. Research suggests that the primary effect of androgens may be to increase motivation to achieve dominance and that increased aggression may be secondary to this effect. In any case we cannot be sure whether higher androgen levels promote dominance or whether successful dominance increases androgen levels.

THOUGHT QUESTIONS

1. Phobias can be seen as dramatic examples of conditioned emotional responses. These responses can even be contagious; we can acquire them without direct experience with an aversive stimulus. For example, a child who sees a parent show signs of fright in the presence of a dog may also develop a fear reaction to the dog. Do you think that some prejudices might be learned in this way, too?

2. From the point of view of evolution, aggressive behavior and a tendency to establish dominance have useful functions. In particular, they increase the likelihood that only the most healthy and vigorous animals will reproduce. Can you think of examples of good and bad effects of these tendencies among members of our own species?

Communication of Emotions

The previous section described emotions as organized responses (behavioral, autonomic, and hormonal) that prepare an animal to deal with existing situations in the environment, such as events that pose a threat to the organism. For our earliest premammalian ancestors that is undoubtedly all there was to emotions. But over time other responses, with new functions, evolved. Many species of animals (including our own) communicate their emotions to others by means of postural changes, facial expressions, and nonverbal sounds (such as sighs, moans, and growls). These expressions serve useful social functions; they tell other individuals how we feel and—more to the point—what we are likely to do. For example, they warn a rival that we are angry or tell friends that we are sad and would like some comfort and reassurance. In many species they indicate that a danger might be present or that something interesting seems to be happening. This section examines such expression and communication of emotions.

Facial Expression of Emotions: Innate Responses

Charles Darwin (1872/1965) suggested that human expressions of emotion have evolved from similar expressions in other animals. He said that emotional expressions are innate, unlearned responses consisting of a complex set of movements, principally of the facial muscles. Thus, a man's sneer and a wolf's snarl are biologically determined response patterns, both controlled by innate brain mechanisms, just as coughing and sneezing are. (Of course, men can sneer and wolves can snarl for quite different reasons.) Some of these movements resemble the behaviors themselves and may have evolved from them. For example, a snarl shows one's teeth and can be seen as an anticipation of biting.

Darwin obtained evidence for his conclusion that emotional expressions were innate by observing his own children and by corresponding with people living in various isolated cultures around the world. He reasoned that if people all over the world, no matter how isolated, show the same facial expressions of emotion, then these expressions must be inherited instead of learned. The logical argument goes like this: When groups of people are isolated for many years, they develop different languages. Thus, we can say that the words people use are arbitrary; there is no biological basis for using particular words to represent particular concepts. However, if facial expressions are inherited, then they should take approximately the same form in people from all cultures, despite their isolation from one another. And Darwin did, indeed, find that people in different cultures used the same patterns of movement of facial muscles to express a particular emotional state.

Research by Ekman and his colleagues (Ekman and Friesen, 1971; Ekman, 1980) tends to confirm Darwin's hypothesis that facial expression of emotion uses an innate, species-typical repertoire of movements of facial muscles (Darwin, 1872/1965). For example, Ekman and Friesen (1971) studied the ability of members of an isolated tribe in New Guinea to recognize facial expressions of emotion produced by Westerners. They had no trouble doing so and themselves produced facial expressions that Westerners readily recognized. Figure 10.11 shows four photographs taken from videotapes of a man from this tribe reacting to stories designed

Figure 10.11

A member of an isolated New Guinea tribe, studied by Ekman and Friesen, making faces when told stories. (a) "Your friend has come and you are happy." (b) "Your child had died." (c) "You are angry and about to fight." (d) "You see a dead pig that has been lying there a long time."

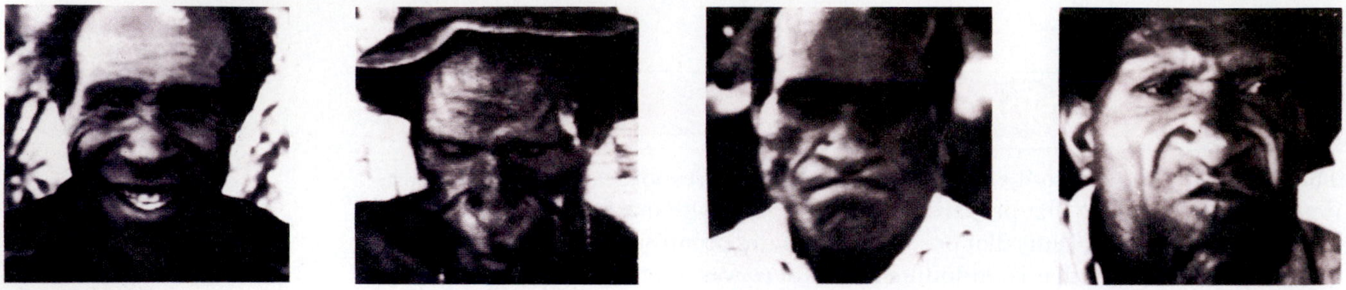

From Ekman, P., *The Face of Man: Expressions of Universal Emotions in a New Guinea Village*. New York: Garland STPM Press, 1980. Reprinted with permission.

to evoke facial expressions of happiness, sadness, anger, and disgust. I am sure that you will have no trouble recognizing which is which. (See ***Figure 10.11.***)

Because the same facial expressions were used by people who had not previously been exposed to each other, Ekman and Friesen concluded that the expressions were unlearned behavior patterns. In contrast, different cultures use different words to express particular concepts; production of these words does not involve innate responses but must be learned.

Other researchers have compared the facial expressions of blind and normally sighted children. They reasoned that if the facial expressions of the two groups are similar, then the expressions are natural for our species and do not require learning by imitation. (Studies of blind adults would not be conclusive, because adults would probably have heard enough descriptions of facial expressions to be able to pose them.) In fact, the facial expressions of young blind and sighted children are very similar (Woodworth and Schlosberg, 1954; Izard, 1971). Thus, both the cross-cultural studies and the investigations with blind children confirm the naturalness of these expressions.

Researchers have not yet determined whether other means of communicating emotions, such as tone of voice or changes in body posture, are learned or are at least partly innate. However, as we will see, some progress has been made in studying the neuroanatomical basis of expressing and recognizing emotions.

Neural Basis of the Communication of Emotions: Recognition

Effective communication is a two-way process. That is, the ability to display one's emotional state by changes in expression is useful only if other people are able to recognize them. In fact, Kraut and Johnston (1979) unobtrusively observed people in circumstances that would be likely to make them happy. They found that happy situations (such as making a strike while bowling, seeing the home team score, or experiencing a beautiful day) produced only small signs of happiness when the people were alone. However, when the people were interacting socially with other people, they were much more likely to smile. For example, bowlers who made a strike usually did not smile when the ball hit the pins, but when they turned around to face their companions, they often smiled. Jones et al. (1991) found that even 10-month-old children showed this tendency.

We recognize other people's feelings by means of vision and audition—seeing their facial expressions and hearing their tone of voice and choice of words. Many studies have found that the right hemisphere plays a more important role than the left hemisphere in comprehension of emotion. For example, many investigators have found a left-ear and a left-visual field advantage in recognition of emotionally related stimuli. The rationale for these studies is that each hemisphere directly receives information from the contralateral part of the environment. When a person looks directly ahead, visual stimuli to the left of the fixation point (seen with *both* eyes) are transmitted to the right hemisphere, and stimuli to the right are transmitted to the left hemisphere. Of course, the hemispheres exchange information by means of the corpus callosum, but it appears that this transcommissural information is not as precise and detailed as information that is directly received. Similarly, although each hemisphere receives auditory information from both ears, the contralateral projections are richer than the ipsilateral ones. Thus, when stimuli are presented to the left visual field or left ear, the right hemisphere receives more specific information than the left hemisphere does.

Although a skilled actor or model can learn to produce realistic facial expressions, genuine smiles are controlled by neural circuits that we cannot voluntarily activate.

In studies of hemispherical differences in visual recognition, stimuli are usually presented to the left or right visual field so rapidly that the subject does not have time to move his or her eyes. Many studies (reviewed by Bryden and Ley, 1983) have shown that the left hemisphere is better than the right at recognizing words or letter strings but that the right hemisphere is better at detecting differences in facial expressions of emotion. Similarly, subjects can more easily understand the verbal content of a message that is presented to the left hemisphere but can more accurately detect the emotional tone of the voice presented to the right hemisphere. These results suggest that when a message is heard, the right hemisphere assesses the emotional expression of the voice while the left hemisphere assesses the meaning of the words.

Blonder, Bowers, and Heilman (1991) found that patients with right hemisphere lesions had no difficulty making emotional judgments about particular situations but were severely impaired in judging the emotions conveyed by facial expressions or hand gestures. For example, they had no difficulty deciding what emotion would be evoked by the situations described in sentences such as *After you drink the water, you see the sign* (fear) or *Your house seems empty without her* (sadness). However, these patients had difficulty recognizing the emotions depicted by sentences such as *He scowled, Tears fell from her eyes,* or *He shook his fist.*

Several PET studies have confirmed these results. For example, George et al. (1996) measured subjects' regional cerebral blood flow with a PET scanner while the subjects listened to some sentences and identified their emotional content. In one condition the subjects listened to the meaning of the words and said whether they described a situation in which someone would be happy, sad, angry, or neutral. In another condition they judged the emotional state from the tone of the voice. In a control condition they simply repeated the second word they heard from each sentence. The investigators found that comprehension of emotion from word meaning increased the activity of both frontal lobes, the left more than the right. Comprehension of emotion from tone of voice increased the activity of only the right prefrontal cortex. (See ***Figure 10.12.***)

Heilman, Watson, and Bowers (1983) recorded a particularly interesting case of a man with a disorder called *pure word deafness* (described in Chapter 13). The man was not deaf, but he could not comprehend the meaning of speech. Nevertheless, he had no difficulty identifying the emotion being expressed by its intonation. This case, like the study by George et al. (1996), indicates that comprehension of words and recognition of tone of voice are independent functions.

Adolphs et al. (2000) compiled computerized information about the locations of brain damage in 108 patients with localized brain lesions. They correlated this information with the patients' ability to recognize and identify facial expressions of

Figure 10.12

PET scans indicating brain regions activated by listening to emotions expressed by tone of voice (green) or meanings of words (red).

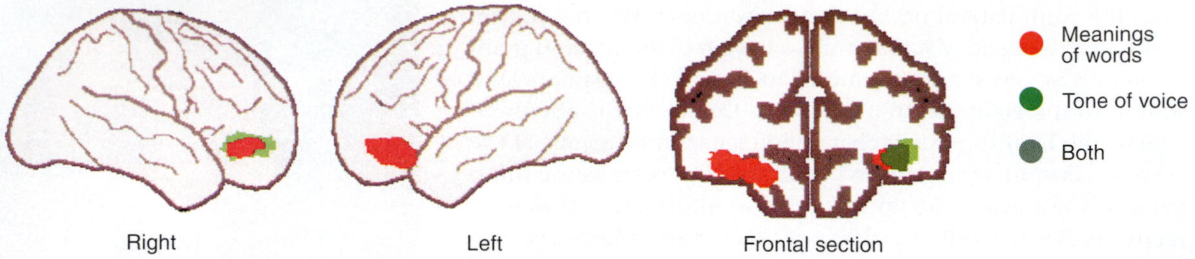

From George, M. S., Parekh, P. I., Rosinsky, N., Ketter, T. A., Kimbrell, T. A., Heilman, K. M., Herscovitch, P., and Post, R. M., *Archives of Neurology,* 1996, *53,* 665–670.

emotions. They found that the most severe damage to this ability was caused by damage to the somatosensory cortex of the right hemisphere. (See ***Figure 10.13.***)

Adolphs and his colleagues propose a possible explanation for the apparent relationship between somatosensation and emotional recognition. They suggest that when we see a facial expression of an emotion, we unconsciously imagine ourselves making that expression. (In fact, as we will see in the final section of this chapter, we often do more than imagine—we often actually imitate other people's expressions.) The somatosensory representation of what it feels like to make the perceived expression provide the cues we use to recognize the emotion being expressed in the face we are viewing. In support of this hypothesis, Adolphs and his colleagues report that the ability of patients with right hemisphere lesions to recognize facial expressions of emotions is correlated with their ability to perceive somatosensory stimuli. That is, patients with somatosensory impairments (caused by right-hemisphere lesions) also had impairments in recognition of emotions.

As we saw in Chapter 6, damage to a region of the visual association cortex can cause *prosopagnosia*—inability to recognize particular faces. However, if the lesions do not involve other parts of the brain, they do not impair recognition of facial expressions of emotions. Some patients can recognize faces but not the emotions they express, and others can recognize the emotions but not the faces (Bowers and Heilman, 1981; Humphreys, Donnelly, and Riddoch, 1993). This finding means that just as recognition of the meaning of words and the emotion expressed by tone of voice are accomplished by different brain functions, so are recognition of particular faces and facial expressions of emotions.

As we saw in the previous section, the amygdala plays a special role in emotional responses. It might play a role in emotional recognition as well. For example, several studies have found that lesions of the amygdala (the result of degenerative diseases or surgery for severe seizure disorders) impair people's ability to recognize facial expressions of emotion, especially expressions of fear (Adolphs et al., 1994, 1995; Young et al., 1995; Calder et al., 1996; Adolphs et al., 1999). In addition, functional imaging studies (Morris et al., 1996; Whalen et al., 1998) have found large increases in the activity of the amygdala when people view photographs of faces expressing fear but only small increases (or even decreases) when they look at photographs of happy faces.

Damage to a particular part of the brain—the basal ganglia—disrupts a person's ability to recognize a particular emotion: disgust. Disgust (literally, "bad taste") is an

Figure 10.13

A computer-generated representation of performance of subjects with localized brain damage on recognition of facial expressions of emotion. The colored areas outline the site of the lesions. Good performance is shown in shades of blue; poor performance is shown in red and yellow. A green line shows the central sulcus.

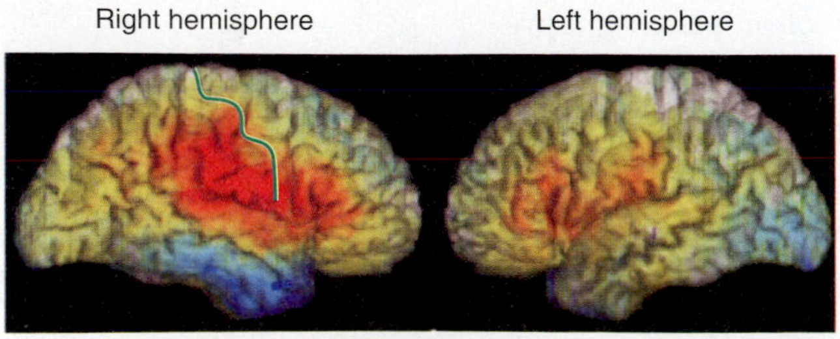

From Adolphs, R., Damasio, H., Tranel, D., Cooper, G., and Damasio, A. R. *The Journal of Neuroscience,* 2000, 20, 2683–2690. Copyright 2000 by the Society for Neuroscience.

emotion provoked by something that tastes or smells bad—or by an action that we consider to be in bad taste (figuratively, not literally). Disgust has a very characteristic facial expression. (If you want to see a good example, refer to Figure 10.11d or Figure 10.16.) Several studies have found that people with Huntington's disease or obsessive-compulsive disorder have lost the ability to recognize facial expressions of disgust (Sprengelmeyer et al., 1996, 1997). Huntington's disease (described in Chapter 14) is a progressive, fatal, genetic disorder that involves the degeneration of the putamen and caudate nucleus, two components of the basal ganglia. Obsessive-compulsive disorder (described in Chapter 15) is a mental disorder that appears to be caused by abnormalities in the basal ganglia. Results of functional imaging studies by Sprengelmeyer et al. (1998) and Phillips et al. (1998) support these findings. These investigators found that subjects who viewed pictures of faces showing expressions of disgust showed increased activity in the basal ganglia and also in the anterior insular region (a portion of the frontal lobe that is normally hidden behind the temporal lobe). As we saw in Chapter 7, the insular region contains the primary gustatory cortex, so perhaps it is not a coincidence that this region is also involved in recognition of "bad taste."

volitional facial paresis Difficulty in moving the facial muscles voluntarily; caused by damage to the face region of the primary motor cortex or its subcortical connections.

emotional facial paresis Lack of movement of facial muscles in response to emotions in people who have no difficulty moving these muscles voluntarily; caused by damage to the insular prefrontal cortex, subcortical white matter of the frontal lobe, or parts of the thalamus.

Neural Basis of the Communication of Emotions: Expression

Facial expressions of emotion are automatic and involuntary. It is not easy to produce a realistic facial expression of emotion when we do not really feel that way. In fact, Ekman and Davidson have confirmed an early observation by a nineteenth-century neurologist, Guillaume-Benjamin Duchenne de Boulogne, that genuinely happy smiles, as opposed to false smiles or social smiles people make when they greet someone else, involve contraction of a muscle near the eyes, the lateral part of the orbicularis oculi—now sometimes referred to as Duchenne's muscle (Ekman, 1992; Ekman and Davidson, 1993). As Duchenne put it, "The first [zygomatic major muscle] obeys the will but the second [orbicularis oculi] is only put in play by the sweet emotions of the soul; the . . . fake joy, the deceitful laugh, cannot provoke the contraction of this latter muscle" (Duchenne, 1862/1990, p. 72). (See ***Figure 10.14.***) The difficulty actors have in voluntarily producing a convincing facial expression of emotion is one of the reasons that led Konstantin Stanislavsky to develop his system of *method acting,* in which actors attempt to imagine themselves in a situation that would lead to the desired emotion. Once the emotion is evoked, the facial expressions follow naturally.

This observation is confirmed by two neurological disorders with complementary symptoms (Hopf et al., 1992; Topper et al., 1995; Urban et al., 1998). The first, **volitional facial paresis,** is caused by damage to the face region of the primary motor cortex or to the fibers connecting this region with the motor nucleus of the facial nerve, which controls the muscles responsible for movement of the facial muscles. (*Paresis,* from the Greek "to let go," refers to a partial paralysis.) The interesting thing about volitional facial paresis is that the patient cannot voluntarily move the facial muscles but will involuntarily express a genuine emotion with those muscles. For example, Figure 10.15(a) shows a woman trying to pull her lips apart and show her teeth. Because of the lesion in the face region of her right primary motor cortex, she could not move the left side of her face. However, when she laughed (Figure 10.15b), both sides of her face moved normally. (See ***Figures 10.15a*** and ***10.15b.***)

In contrast, **emotional facial paresis** is caused by damage to the insular region of the prefrontal cortex, to the white matter of the frontal

Figure 10.14

A photograph of Dr. Duchenne electrically stimulating muscles in the face of a volunteer, causing contraction of muscles around the mouth that become active during a smile. As Duchenne discovered, however, a true smile also involves muscles around the eyes.

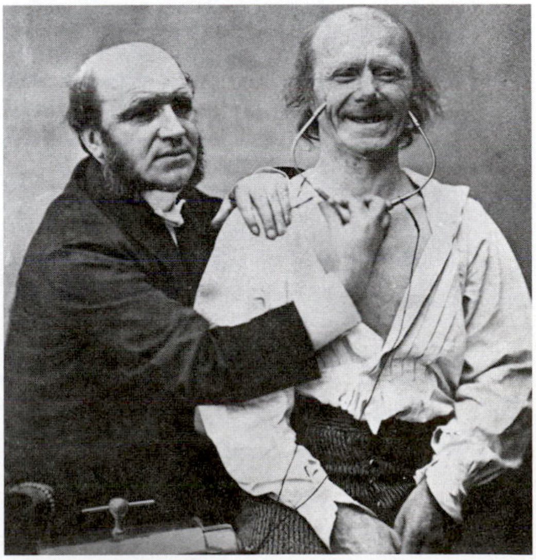

Figure 10.15

Emotional and volitional paresis. (a) A woman with volitional facial paresis caused by a right hemisphere lesion trying to pull her lips apart and show her teeth. Only the right side of her face responds. (b) The same woman showing a genuine smile. (c) A man with emotional facial paresis caused by a left-hemisphere lesion showing his teeth. (d) The same man smiling. Only the left side of his face responds.

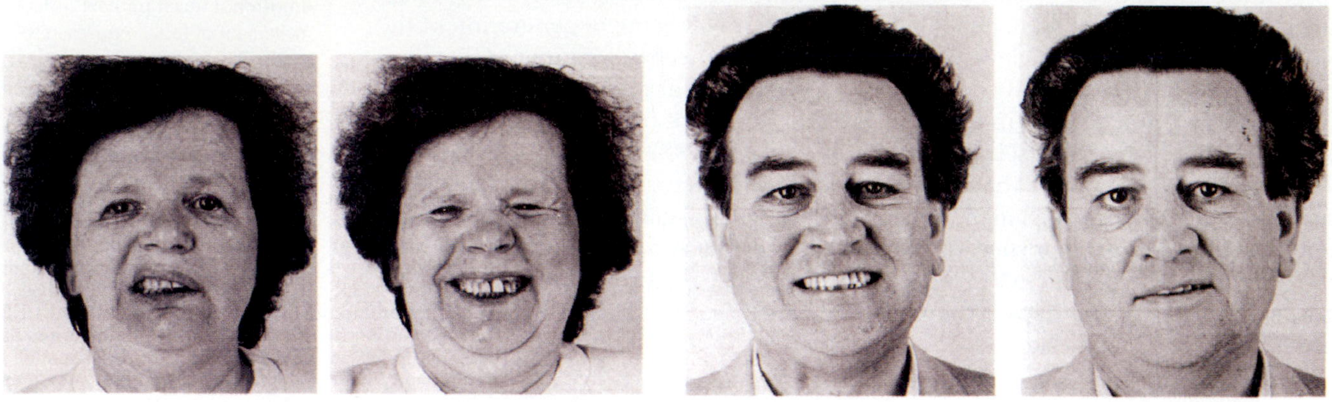

(a) (b) (c) (d)

From Hopf, H. C., Mueller-Forell, W., and Hopf, N. J., *Neurology,* 1992, *42,* 1918–1923.

lobe, or to parts of the thalamus. This system joins the system responsible for voluntary movements of the facial muscles in the medulla or caudal pons. People with this disorder can move their face muscles voluntarily but do not express emotions on the affected side of the face. Figure 10.15(c) shows a man pulling his lips apart to show his teeth, which he had no trouble doing. Figure 10.15(d) shows him smiling; as you can see, only the left side of his mouth is raised. He had a stroke that damaged the white matter of the left frontal lobe. (See ***Figures 10.15c*** and ***10.15d.***) These two syndromes clearly indicate that different brain mechanisms are responsible for voluntary movements of the facial muscles and automatic, involuntary expression of emotions involving the same muscles.

As we saw in the previous subsection, the right hemisphere plays a more significant role in recognizing emotions in the voice or facial expressions of other people—especially negative emotions. The same hemispheric specialization appears to be true for expressing emotions. When people show emotions with their facial muscles, the left side of the face usually makes a more intense expression. For example, Sackeim and Gur (1978) cut photographs of people who were expressing emotions into right and left halves, prepared mirror images of each of them, and pasted them together, producing so-called *chimerical faces* (from the mythical Chimera, a fire-breathing monster, part goat, part lion, and part serpent). They found that the left halves were more expressive than the right ones. (See ***Figure 10.16.***) Because motor control is contralateral, the results suggest that the right hemisphere is more expressive than the left.

Moscovitch and Olds (1982) made more natural observations of people in restaurants and parks and found that the left side of their faces appeared to make stronger expressions of emotions. They confirmed these results in the laboratory by analyzing videotapes of people telling sad or humorous stories. A review of the literature by Borod et al. (1998) found 48 other studies that obtained similar results.

Left hemisphere lesions do not usually impair vocal expressions of emotion. For example, people with Wernicke's aphasia (described in Chapter 13) usually modulate their voice according to mood, even though the words they say make no sense. In contrast, right-hemisphere lesions do impair expression of emotion, both facially and by tone of voice.

We saw in the previous subsection that the amygdala is involved in the recognition of facial expression of emotions. Research indicates that it is not involved in

Figure 10.16

An example of a stimulus used by Sackeim and Gur (1978). (a) Original photo. (b) Composite of the right side of the man's face. (c) Composite of the left side of the man's face.

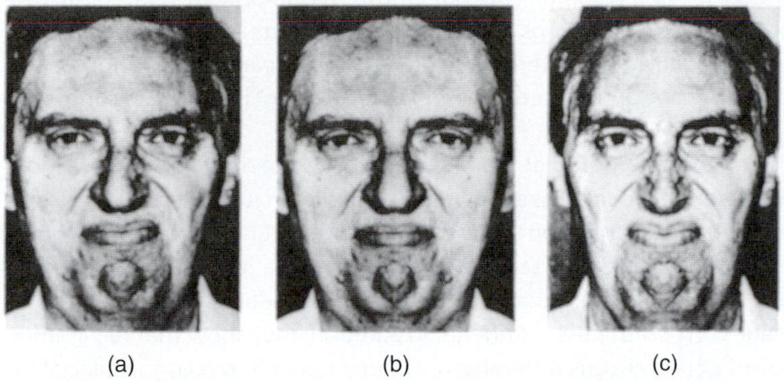

Reprinted with permission from *Neuropsychologia, 16,* H. A. Sackeim and R. C. Gur, Lateral asymmetry in intensity of emotional expression. Copyright 1978, Pergamon Press.

emotional *expression*. Anderson and Phelps (2000) reported the case of S. P., a 54-year-old woman whose right amygdala was removed to treat a serious seizure disorder. Because of a preexisting lesion of the left amygdala, the surgery resulted in a bilateral amygdalectomy. After the surgery, S. P. lost the ability to recognize facial expressions of emotion, but she had no difficulty recognizing individual faces, and she could easily identify male and female faces and accurately judge their ages. What is particularly interesting is that the amygdala lesions did not impair S. P.'s ability to produce her own facial expressions of emotions. Figure 10.17 shows S. P. displaying a neutral expression (1) and six emotional expressions: fear, anger, happiness, sadness, disgust, and surprise. By the way, when she saw these pictures of herself, she could not tell what emotions her face had been expressing. (See ***Figure 10.17.***)

Figure 10.17

Photographs of posed facial expressions of emotions (from a videotape) by Patient S. P., a woman with bilateral amygdala lesions who was unable to recognize such expressions—even her own. (1) Neutral expression, (2) fear, (3) anger, (4) happiness, (5) sadness, (6) disgust, (7) surprise.

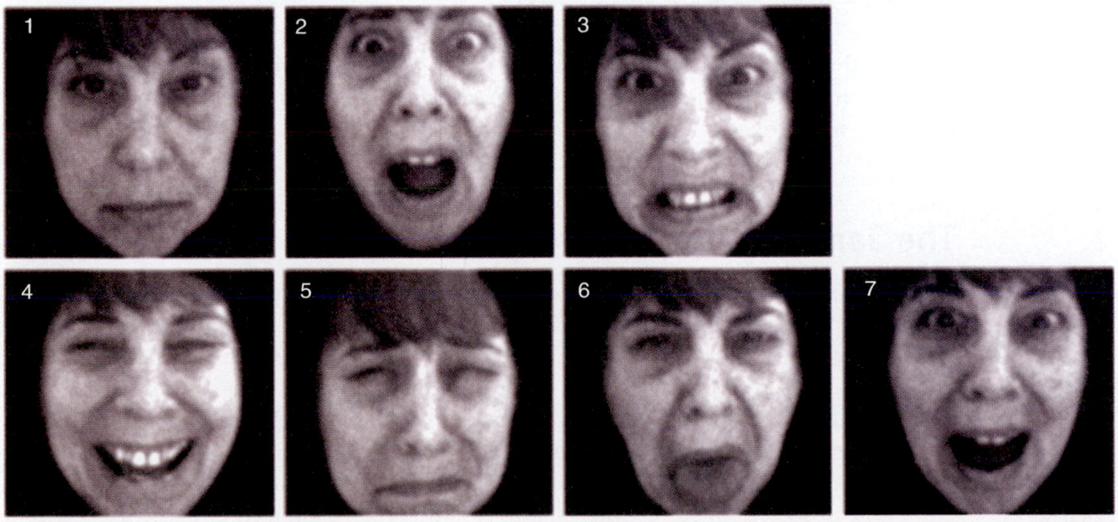

From Anderson, A. K., and Phelps, E. A. *Psychological Science,* 2000, *11,* 106–111.

INTERIM SUMMARY

Communication of Emotions

We (and members of other species) communicate our emotions primarily through facial gestures. Darwin believed that such expressions of emotion were innate—that these muscular movements were inherited behavioral patterns. Ekman and his colleagues performed cross-cultural studies with members of an isolated tribe in New Guinea. Their results supported Darwin's hypothesis.

Recognition of other people's emotional expressions involves the right hemisphere more than the left. Studies with normal people have shown that people can judge facial expressions or tone of voice better when the information is presented to the right hemisphere than when it is presented to the left hemisphere. PET scans made while people judge the emotions of voices activate the right hemisphere more than the left. Studies of people with left- or right-hemisphere brain damage corroborate these findings. In addition, they show that recognition of particular faces involves neural circuits different from those needed to recognize facial expressions of emotions. Finally, the amygdala plays a role in recognition of facial expressions of emotions; lesions of the amygdala disrupt this ability, and PET scans show increased activity of the amygdala while the subject is engaging in this task. Damage to the caudate nucleus and putamen (components of the basal ganglia) disrupts recognition of facial expressions of disgust, and functional imaging studies suggest that both the basal ganglia and the insular cortex (which contains the primary gustatory cortex) are involved in this emotion.

Facial expression of emotions (and other stereotypical behaviors such as laughing and crying) are difficult to simulate. For example, only a genuine smile of pleasure causes the contraction of the lateral part of the orbicularis oculi (Duchenne's muscle). Genuine expressions of emotion are controlled by special neural circuits. The best evidence for this assertion comes from the complementary syndromes of emotional and volitional facial paresis. People with emotional facial paresis can move their facial muscles voluntarily but not in response to an emotion, whereas people with volitional facial paresis show the opposite symptoms. In addition, the left halves of people's faces tend to be more expressive than the right halves. Although damage to the amygdala disrupts people's ability to recognize emotional expressions in other people, the patients can still produce emotional expressions of their own.

Feelings of Emotions

So far, we have examined two aspects of emotions: the organization of patterns of responses that deal with the situation that provokes the emotion and the communication of emotional states with other members of the species. The final aspect of emotion to be examined in this chapter is the subjective component: feelings of emotion.

The James-Lange Theory

William James (1842–1910), an American psychologist, and Carl Lange (1834–1900), a Danish physiologist, independently suggested similar explanations for emotion, which most people refer to collectively as the **James-Lange theory** (James, 1884; Lange, 1887). Basically, the theory states that emotion-producing situations elicit an appropriate set of physiological responses, such as trembling, sweating, and increased heart rate. The situations also elicit behaviors, such as clenching of the fists or fighting. The brain receives sensory feedback from the muscles and from the organs that produce these responses, and it is this feedback that constitutes our feeling of emotion.

James-Lange theory A theory of emotion that suggests that behaviors and physiological responses are directly elicited by situations and that feelings of emotions are produced by feedback from these behaviors and responses.

James says that our own emotional feelings are based on what we find ourselves doing and on the sensory feedback we receive from the activity of our muscles and internal organs. Thus, when we find ourselves trembling and feel queasy, we experience fear. Where feelings of emotions are concerned, we are self-observers. Thus, the two aspects of emotions reported in the first two sections of this chapter (patterns of emotional responses and expressions of emotions) give rise to the third: feelings. (See ***Figure 10.18.***)

Figure 10.18

A diagrammatic representation of the James-Lange theory of emotion. An event in the environment triggers behavioral, autonomic, and endocrine responses. Feedback from these responses produces feelings of emotions.

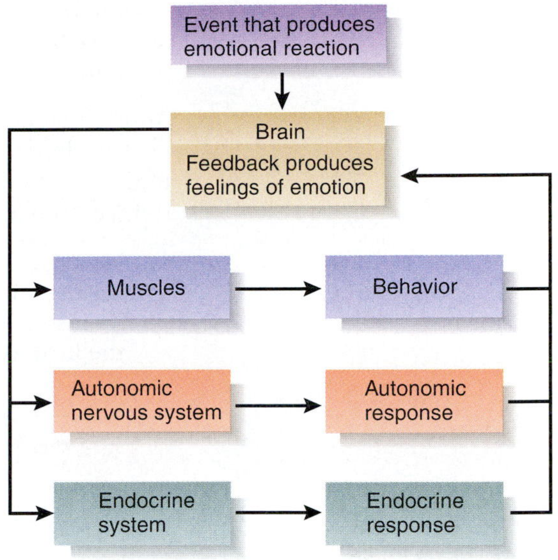

James's description of the process of emotion might strike you as being at odds with your own experience. Many people think that they experience emotions directly, internally. They consider the outward manifestations of emotions to be secondary events. But have you ever found yourself in an unpleasant confrontation with someone else and discovered that you were trembling, even though you did not think that you were so bothered by the encounter? Or did you ever find yourself blushing in response to some public remark that was made about you? Or did you ever find tears coming to your eyes while you watched a film that you did not think was affecting you? What would you conclude about your emotional states in situations like these? Would you ignore the evidence from your own physiological reactions?

A well-known physiologist, Walter Cannon, criticized James's theory. He said that the internal organs were relatively insensitive and that they could not respond very quickly, so feedback from them could not account for our feelings of emotions. In addition, he observed that cutting the nerves that provide feedback from the internal organs to the brain did not alter emotional behavior (Cannon, 1927). However, subsequent research indicated that Cannon's criticisms are not relevant. For example, although the viscera are not sensitive to some kinds of stimuli, such as cutting and burning, they provide much better feedback than Cannon suspected. Moreover, many changes in the viscera can occur rapidly enough that they could be the causes of feelings of emotion.

Cannon cited the fact that cutting the sensory nerves between the internal organs and the central nervous system does not abolish emotional behavior in laboratory animals. However, this observation misses the point. It does not prove that feelings of emotion survive this surgical disruption—only that emotional *behaviors* do. We do not know how the animals feel; we know only that they will snarl and attempt to bite if threatened. In any case James did not attribute all feelings of emotion to the internal organs; he also said that feedback from muscles was important. The threat might make the animal snarl and bite, and the feedback from the facial and neck muscles might constitute a "feeling" of anger, even if feedback from the internal organs was cut off. But we have no way to determine how the animal felt.

James's theory is difficult to verify experimentally, because it attempts to explain *feelings* of emotion, not the causes of emotional responses, and feelings are private events. Some anecdotal evidence supports the theory. For example, Sweet (1966) reported the case of a man in whom some sympathetic nerves were severed on one side of the body to treat a cardiovascular disorder. The man—a music lover—reported that the shivering sensation he felt while listening to music now occurred only on the unoperated side of his body. He still enjoyed listening to music, but the surgery altered his emotional reaction.

In one of the few tests of James's theory, Hohman (1966) collected data from people with spinal cord damage. He asked these people about the intensity of their emotional feelings. If feedback is important, one would expect that emotional feelings would be less intense if the injury were high (that is, close to the brain) than if it were low, because a high spinal cord injury would make the person become insensitive to a larger part of the body. In fact, this result is precisely what Hohman found: The higher the injury, the less intense the feeling was. As one of Hohman's subjects said:

> I sit around and build things up in my mind, and I worry a lot, but it's not much but the power of thought. I was at home alone in bed one day and dropped a cigarette where I couldn't reach it. I finally managed to scrounge around and put it out. I could have burned up right there, but the funny thing is, I didn't get all shook up about it. I just didn't feel afraid at all, like you would suppose. (Hohman, 1966, p. 150)

Another subject showed that angry behavior (an emotional response) does not appear to depend on *feelings* of emotion. Instead, the behavior is evoked by the situation (and by the person's evaluation of it) even if the spinal cord damage has reduced the intensity of the person's emotional feelings.

> Now, I don't get a feeling of physical animation, it's sort of cold anger. Sometimes I act angry when I see some injustice. I yell and cuss and raise hell, because if you don't do it sometimes, I've learned people will take advantage of you, but it doesn't have the heat to it that it used to. It's a mental kind of anger. (Hohman, 1966, p. 151)

INTERIM SUMMARY

Feelings of Emotions

From the earliest times people recognized that emotions were accompanied by feelings that seemed to come from inside the body, which probably provided the impetus for developing physiological theories of emotion. James and Lange suggested that emotions were primarily responses to situations. Feedback from the physiological and behavioral reactions to emotion-producing situations gave rise to the feelings of emotion; thus, feelings are the *results,* not the *causes,* of emotional reactions. Hohman's study of people with spinal cord damage supported the James-Lange theory; people who could no longer feel the reactions from most of their body reported that they no longer experienced intense emotional states.

EPILOGUE

Mr. V. Revisited

After our visit to Mr. V. (described in the chapter prologue), we were discussing the case. Lisa, the student, asked why Mr. V. talked about continuing his walking schedule when he obviously knew that he couldn't walk. Did he think that he would recover soon?

"No, that's not it," said Dr. W. "He *knows* what his problem is, but he doesn't really *understand* it. The people at the rehab center are having trouble with him because he keeps trying to go outside for a walk. The first time, he managed to wheel his chair to the top of the stairs, but someone caught him just in time. Now they have a chain across the door frame of his room so that he can't get into the hall without an attendant.

"Mr. V.'s problem is not that he can't verbally recognize what's going on; it's that he just can't grasp its significance. The right hemisphere is specialized in seeing many things at once: in seeing all the parts of a geometric shape and grasping its form or in seeing all the elements of a situation and understanding what they mean. That's what's wrong. He can tell you about his paralyzed leg, about the fact that he is in a wheelchair, and so on, but he can't put these facts together and realize that his days of walking are over.

"As you could see, Mr. V. can still express emotions." We all smiled at the thought of the contemptuous look on Mr. V.'s face. "But the right hemisphere is especially important in assessing the significance of a situation and making conclusions that lead to our being happy or sad or whatever. People with certain right-hemisphere lesions are not bothered at all by their conditions. They can *tell* you about their problems, so I guess they verbally understand it, but their problems just don't affect them emotionally."

He turned to me. "Neil, do you remember Mr. P.?" I nodded. "Mr. P. had a left-hemisphere lesion. He had a severe aphasia and could hardly say a word. We showed him a picture of some objects and asked him to try to name them. He looked at them and started crying. Although he couldn't talk, he knew that he had a serious problem and that things would never be the same for him. His right hemisphere was still working. It could assess the situation and give rise to feelings of sadness and despair."

Dr. W. suggested that the right hemisphere's special role in emotional processes is related to its ability to deal with perception and evaluation of patterns of stimuli that occur simultaneously. His suggestion is plausible, but we still do not know enough about hemispheric differences to be sure that it is correct. In any event, many studies have shown that the right hemisphere does play a special role in evaluating the emotional significance of a situation. I described some of these studies in the chapter, but let's look at a few more examples. Bear and Fedio (1977) reported that people with seizures that primarily involve the left hemisphere tend to have thought disorders, whereas those with right-hemisphere seizures tend to have emotional disorders. Mesulam (1985) reported that people with damage to the right temporal lobe (but not the left temporal lobe) are likely to lose their sensitivity to social cues. Obviously, this observation is meaningful only for patients who were sensitive to social cues before the brain damage; if someone is socially insensitive *before* having a stroke, we can hardly blame the behavior on brain damage. In particular, people with right temporal lobe lesions tend to show bad manners. They talk when they feel like it and do not yield the floor to someone else who has something to say; they simply ignore the social cues that polite people observe and follow. They also adopt a familiar conversational style with people to whom they would normally be deferential (usually, the physician who is treating them and writes up a report of their behavior).

Perhaps my favorite example of possible hemispheric specialization is hypnosis. Sackeim (1982) reported that when people are hypnotized, the left side of their body is more responsive to hypnotic suggestion than the right side. Because the left side of the body is controlled by the right hemisphere, this observation indicates that the right hemisphere may be more susceptible to hypnotic suggestion. In addition, Sackeim, Paulus, and Weiman (1979) found that students who are easily hypnotized tend to sit on the right side of the classroom. In this position they see most of the front of the room (including the teacher) with their right hemispheres, so perhaps their choice represents a preference for right-hemisphere involvement in watching another person.

One of the reasons I enjoy writing these epilogues is that I can permit myself to be more speculative than I am in the text of the chapter itself. Why might the right hemisphere be more involved in hypnosis? One explanation of hypnosis that I find appealing is that it derives from our ability to get emotionally involved in a story—to get wrapped up in what is happening to the characters in a film or a novel (Barber, 1975). When we become involved in a story, we experience genuine feelings of emotion: happiness, sadness, fear, or anger. We laugh, cry, and show the same sorts of physiological changes that we would if the story were really happening to us. Similarly, according to Barber, we become involved in the "story" that the hypnotist is creating for us, and we suspend our disbelief and act it out. According to this explanation, hypnosis is related to our susceptibility to social situations and to our ability to empathize with others. In fact, people with the ability to produce vivid mental images, a high capacity for becoming involved in imaginative activities, and a rich, vivid imagination are those who are most likely to be susceptible to hypnosis (Kihlstrom, 1985).

As we saw in this chapter, the right hemisphere appears to play a special role in assessing social situations and appreciating their emotional significance. If Barber's explanation of hypnosis is correct, then we can see why the right hemisphere might play a special role in hypnosis, too. Perhaps researchers interested in hypnosis will begin studying patients with right- or left-hemisphere damage, and neuropsychologists already studying these people will start investigating hypnosis and its possible relation to social and emotional variables and either confirm or disprove these speculations.

KEY CONCEPTS

EMOTIONS AS RESPONSE PATTERNS

1. Emotional responses consist of three components: behavioral, autonomic, and hormonal.
2. The amygdala plays a central role in coordinating all three components in response to threatening or aversive stimuli. In particular, the central nucleus is involved in conditioned emotional responses.
3. The orbitofrontal cortex plays a special role in regulation of emotional responses, especially in response to social situations.
4. Species-typical aggressive behaviors are controlled by neural circuits in the periaqueductal gray matter and the ventral tegmental area, which are modulated by the circuits in the hypothalamus and the amygdala.
5. Androgens have both organizational and activational effects on aggression in males and females.
6. Androgens may be at least partly responsible for the increased level of aggression seen in males of our species, but ethical considerations make it difficult to

be certain. Antiandrogens have been used in an attempt to control sex-related violence.

COMMUNICATION OF EMOTIONS

7. Facial expressions of emotions appear to be species-typical responses, even in humans.
8. Recognition of facial expressions of emotions may involve the somatosensory cortex, which is responsible for perception of the sensations that accompany emotional responses.
9. Expression and recognition of emotions is largely accomplished by neural mechanisms located in the right hemisphere.
10. The amygdala is involved in recognition of facial expressions of emotion but not in their production.

FEELINGS OF EMOTION

11. The James-Lange theory suggests that we experience our own emotions through feedback from the expression of the physiological and behavioral components. Evidence from people with spinal cord injuries supports this theory.

SUGGESTED READINGS

Damasio, A. R. *Descartes' Error: Emotion, Reason, and the Human Brain.* New York: G. P. Putnam, 1994.

Damasio, A. R. *The Feeling of What Happens: Body and Emotion in the Making of Consciousness.* New York: Harcourt Brace, 1999.

Ekman, P. *Emotions Revealed.* New York: Times Books, 2003.

LeDoux, J. E. *The Emotional Brain: The Mysterious Underpinnings of the Emotional Life.* New York: Simon and Schuster, 1996.

Stoff, D. M., and Cairns, R. B. (eds.) *Aggression and Violence: Genetic, Neurobiological, and Biosocial Perspectives.* Mahwah, NJ: Lawrence Erlbaum Associates, 1996.

SUGGESTED WEB SITES

The Emotion Home Page
http://emotion.salk.edu/Emotion/History/Hgeneral.html

The Emotion Page provides a series of lecture outlines on the history of emotion theories, ranging from Plato through the 20th century.

***What is an Emotion?* by William James**
www.yorku.ca/dept/psych/classics/James/emotion.htm

The Classics in the History of Psychology site provides the original text of an article on emotions published by William James in 1884.

Dr. Ivan's Depression Central
www.psycom.net/depression.central.html

Depression is the focus of this site by Dr. Ivan Goldberg. The site provides fact sheets on the genetics of depression, treatments for depression, and a host of links to other depression Web sites.

Research on Human Emotion
http://www-white.media.mit.edu/vismod/demos/affect/AC_research/emotions.html

This site contains an overview of three theories of emotion and provides links to various research projects on the topic of emotion.

Emotions and Emotional Intelligence
http://trochim.human.cornell.edu/gallery/young/emotion.htm

The focus of this site is on theories of emotion and of emotional intelligence.

Ingestive Behavior

chapter 11

CHAPTER OUTLINE

LEARNING OBJECTIVES

1. Explain the characteristics of a regulatory mechanism.
2. Describe the fluid compartments of the body.
3. Explain the control of osmometric thirst and volumetric thirst and the role of angiotensin.
4. Describe the neural control of thirst.
5. Describe characteristics of the two nutrient reservoirs and the absorptive and fasting phases of metabolism.
6. Discuss social and environmental factors that begin a meal.
7. Discuss the long-term and short-term factors responsible for stopping a meal.
8. Describe research on the role of the brain stem and hypothalamus in hunger and satiety.
9. Discuss the physiological factors that may contribute to obesity.
10. Discuss the physiological factors that may contribute to anorexia nervosa and bulimia nervosa.

PROLOGUE

Not Her Fault?

Emily and her younger brother, Jonathan, prided themselves on their lack of racial and religious prejudice. Jonathan was a self-proclaimed feminist and enjoyed telling his friends how well his sister was doing in her engineering courses at a prestigious university. He and his sister shared a contempt for intolerance and chauvinism and believed that if other people were more like themselves, the world would be a better place in which to live. The few times that acquaintances had told jokes in their presence that stereotyped other cultures or racial groups, Emily and Jonathan immediately pounced on them and chided them for their bigotry.

Just before the end of Emily's first year of college, she saw a notice asking for students to provide living accommodations for foreign students who could not afford to return home during summer vacation. She called her parents, who readily agreed to put someone up at their house. The whole family felt that they would enjoy getting to know a foreign student really well and looked forward to showing how nice a North American family could be.

When Emily met her guest at a party that was held to introduce the students to their hosts, she was dismayed. The girl, Norella, was fat! Well, not grossly obese, but certainly far heavier than she should be. Her face was pretty, and she was intelligent and witty; why didn't she pay attention to her diet?

Emily and her brother exchanged a significant glance when she introduced Norella to her family. However, within a few days Norella had fit right into the family routine, and they almost forgot that she was fat. She helped to prepare the meals and do the dishes afterward; she charmed the whole family with her stories of her own country and delighted them with her astute observations of life in their country.

Three weeks after Norella had come to live with them, Emily and Jonathan began talking about a topic they previously had studiously ignored. "You know," Jonathan said, "I just realized this evening that Norella eats less than you do."

Emily looked startled, then said, "You're right! I hadn't thought about that! How can that be?"

"I don't know," he said. "Does she eat between meals?"

"No," answered Emily, "I don't think I've ever seen her do that." She paused, looking pensive, then shook her head. "No. I'm positive that I've never seen her eat between meals. When we've gone out shopping together, I always buy something to eat, but Norella never does. I've offered her some of mine, but she's always said, 'No.' "

Emily and Jonathan sat together in silence. "You know," Jonathan said, "I've never really liked fat people, because it seems like they don't have enough self-respect to keep from overeating. I've always thought that they ate like pigs. But Norella doesn't even eat as much as you do, and she's fat! Maybe it's not her fault."

As the French physiologist Claude Bernard (1813–1878) said, "The constancy of the internal milieu is a necessary condition for a free life." This famous quotation says succinctly what organisms must do to be able to exist in environments that are hostile to the living cells that compose them (that is, to live a "free life"): They must provide a barrier between their cells and the external environment—in the case of mammals this barrier consists of skin and mucous membrane. Within the barrier they must regulate the nature of the internal fluid that bathes the cells.

The physiological characteristics of the cells that constitute our bodies evolved long ago, when these cells floated freely in the ocean. In essence, what the evolutionary process has accomplished is the ability to make our own seawater for bathing our cells, to add to this seawater the oxygen and nutrients that our cells need, and to remove from it waste products that would otherwise poison them. To perform these functions, we have digestive, respiratory, circulatory, and excretory systems. We also have the behaviors necessary for finding and ingesting food and water.

Regulation of the fluid that bathes our cells is part of a process called **homeostasis** ("similar standing"). This chapter discusses the means by which we mammals achieve homeostatic control of the vital characteristics of our extracellular fluid through our **ingestive behavior:** intake of food, water, and minerals such as sodium. First, we will examine the general nature of regulatory mechanisms; then we will consider drinking and eating and the neural mechanisms that are responsible for these behaviors. Finally, we will look at some research on the eating disorders.

homeostasis (*home ee oh **stay** sis*) The process by which the body's substances and characteristics (such as temperature and glucose level) are maintained at their optimal level.

ingestive behavior (*in **jess** tiv*) Eating or drinking.

Physiological Regulatory Mechanisms

A physiological regulatory mechanism is one that maintains the constancy of some internal characteristic of the organism in the face of external variability—for example, keeping body temperature constant despite changes in the ambient temperature. A regulatory mechanism contains four essential features: the **system variable** (the characteristic to be regulated), a **set point** (the optimal value of the system variable), a **detector** that monitors the value of the system variable, and a **correctional mechanism** that restores the system variable to the set point.

An example of a regulatory system is a room whose temperature is regulated by a thermostatically controlled heater. The system variable is the air temperature of the room, and the detector for this variable is a thermostat. This device can be adjusted so that contacts of a switch will be closed when the temperature falls below a preset value (the set point). Closure of the contacts turns on the correctional mechanism—the coils of the heater. (See ***Figure 11.1.***) If the room cools below the set point of the thermostat, the thermostat turns the heater on, and the heater warms the room. The rise in room temperature causes the thermostat to turn the heater off. Because the activity of the correctional mechanism (heat production) feeds back to the thermostat and causes it to turn the heater off, this process is called **negative feedback.** Negative feedback is an essential characteristic of all regulatory systems.

This chapter considers regulatory systems that involve ingestive behaviors: drinking and eating. These behaviors are correctional mechanisms that replenish the body's depleted stores of water or nutrients. Because of the delay between ingestion and replenishment of the depleted stores, ingestive behaviors are controlled by **satiety mechanisms** as well as by detectors that monitor the system variables. Satiety mechanisms are required because of the physiology of our digestive system. For example, suppose you spend some time in a hot, dry environment and lose body water. The loss of water causes internal detectors to initiate the correctional mechanism—drinking. You quickly drink a glass or two of water and then stop. What stops your ingestive behavior? The water is still in your digestive system, not yet in the fluid surrounding your cells, where it is needed. Therefore, although drinking was initiated by detectors that measure your body's need for water, *it was stopped by other means.* There must be a satiety mechanism that says, in effect, "Stop—this water, when absorbed by the digestive system into the blood, will eventually replenish the body's need." Satiety mechanisms monitor the activity of the correctional mechanism (in this case, drinking), not the system variables themselves. When a sufficient amount of drinking occurs, the satiety mechanisms stop further drinking *in anticipation* of the replenishment that will occur later. (See ***Figure 11.2.***)

system variable A variable that is controlled by a regulatory mechanism—for example, temperature in a heating system.

set point The optimal value of the system variable in a regulatory mechanism.

detector In a regulatory process, a mechanism that signals when the system variable deviates from its set point.

correctional mechanism In a regulatory process, the mechanism that is capable of changing the value of the system variable.

negative feedback A process whereby the effect produced by an action serves to diminish or terminate that action; a characteristic of regulatory systems.

satiety mechanism A brain mechanism that causes cessation of hunger or thirst, produced by adequate and available supplies of nutrients or water.

Figure 11.1

An example of a regulatory system.

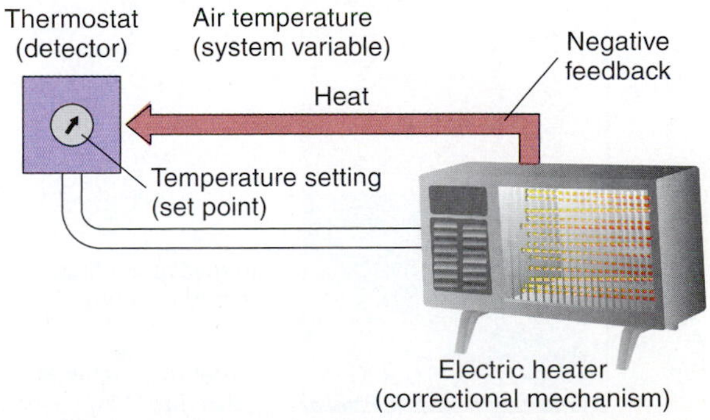

Drinking

To maintain our internal milieu at its optimal state, we have to drink some water from time to time. This section describes the control of this form of ingestive behavior.

Some Facts About Fluid Balance

Before you can understand the physiological control of drinking, you must know something about the fluid compartments of the body and their relationships with each other. The body contains four major fluid compartments: one compartment of

Figure 11.2

An outline of the system that controls drinking.

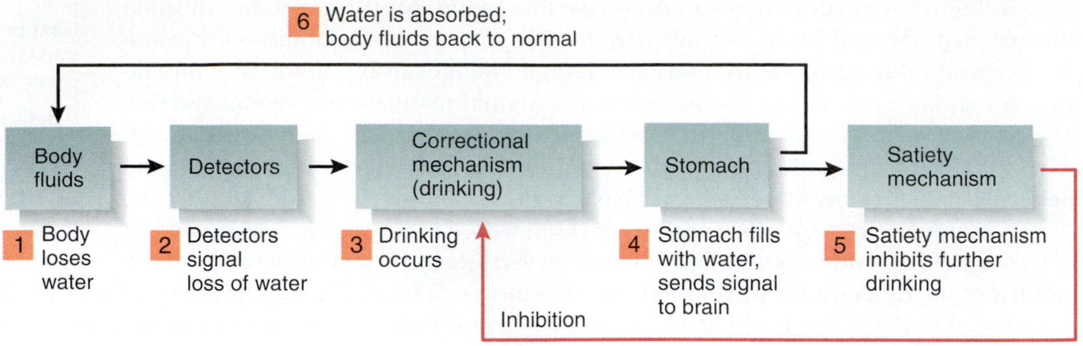

intracellular fluid and three compartments of extracellular fluid. Approximately two-thirds of the body's water is contained in the **intracellular fluid,** the fluid portion of the cytoplasm of cells. The rest is **extracellular fluid,** which includes the **intravascular fluid** (the blood plasma), the cerebrospinal fluid, and the **interstitial fluid.** *Interstitial* means "standing between"; indeed, the interstitial fluid stands between our cells—it is the "seawater" that bathes them. For the purposes of this chapter we will ignore the cerebrospinal fluid and concentrate on the other three compartments. (See ***Figure 11.3.***)

intracellular fluid The fluid contained within cells.

extracellular fluid All body fluids outside cells: interstitial fluid, blood plasma, and cerebrospinal fluid.

intravascular fluid The fluid found within the blood vessels.

interstitial fluid The fluid that bathes the cells, filling the space between the cells of the body (the "interstices").

isotonic Equal in osmotic pressure to the contents of a cell. A cell placed in an isotonic solution neither gains nor loses water.

Two of the fluid compartments of the body must be kept within precise limits: the intracellular fluid and the intravascular fluid. The intracellular fluid is controlled by the concentration of solutes in the interstitial fluid. (*Solutes* are the substances dissolved in a solution.) Normally, the interstitial fluid is **isotonic** (from *isos,* "equal," and *tonos,* "tension") with the intracellular fluid. That is, the concentration of solutes in the cells and in the interstitial fluid that bathes them is balanced, so that water does not tend to move into or out of the cells. If the interstitial fluid loses water (becomes more concentrated, or **hypertonic**), water will be pulled out of the cells. On the other hand, if the interstitial fluid gains water (becomes more dilute, or **hypotonic**), water will move into the cells. Either condition endangers cells; a loss of water deprives them of the ability to perform many chemical reactions, and a gain of water can cause their membranes to rupture. Therefore, the concentration of the interstitial fluid must be closely regulated. (See ***Figure 11.4.***)

The volume of the blood plasma must be closely regulated because of the mechanics of the operation of the heart. If the blood volume falls too low, the heart can no longer pump the blood effectively; if the volume is not restored, heart failure will result. This condition is called **hypovolemia,** literally "low volume of the blood" (*-emia* comes from the Greek *haima,* "blood"). The vascular system of the body can make some adjustments for loss of blood volume by contracting the muscles in smaller veins and arteries, thereby presenting a smaller space for the blood to fill, but this correctional mechanism has definite limits.

The two important characteristics of the body fluids—the solute concentration of the intracellular fluid and the volume of the blood—are monitored by two different sets of receptors. A single set of receptors would not work, because it is possible for one of these fluid compartments to be changed without affecting the other. For example, a loss of blood obviously reduces the vol-

Figure 11.3

The relative size of the body's fluid compartments.

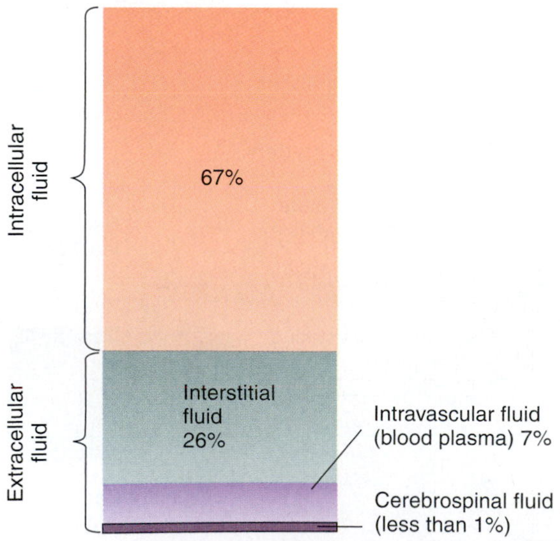

ume of the intravascular fluid, but it has no effect on the volume of the intracellular fluid. On the other hand, a salty meal will increase the solute concentration of the interstitial fluid, drawing water out of the cells, but it will not cause hypovolemia. Thus, the body needs two sets of receptors, one measuring blood volume and another measuring cell volume.

Figure 11.4

Effects of differences in solute concentration on the movement of water molecules.

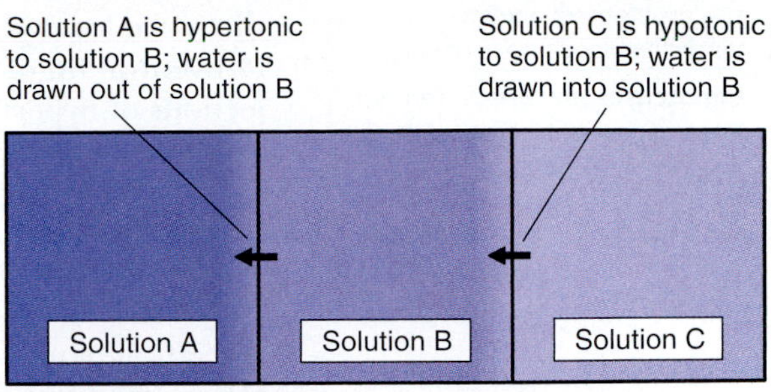
Solution A is hypertonic to solution B; water is drawn out of solution B
Solution C is hypotonic to solution B; water is drawn into solution B
Solution A
Solution B
Solution C

Two Types of Thirst

As we just saw, for our bodies to function properly, the volume of two fluid compartments—intracellular and intravascular—must be regulated. Most of the time, we ingest more water and sodium than we need and the kidneys excrete the excess. However, if the levels of water or sodium fall too low, correctional mechanisms—drinking water or ingesting sodium—are activated. Everyone is familiar with the sensation of thirst, which occurs when we need to ingest water. However, a salt appetite is much more rare, because it is difficult for people *not* to get enough sodium in their diet, even if they do not put extra salt on their food. Nevertheless, the mechanisms to increase sodium intake exist, even though they are seldom called upon in members of our species.

Because loss of water from either the intracellular or intravascular fluid compartment stimulates drinking, researchers have adopted the terms *osmometric thirst* and *volumetric thirst* to describe them. The term *volumetric* is clear; it refers to the metering (measuring) of the volume of the blood plasma. The term *osmometric* requires more explanation, which will be provided in the next section. The term *thirst* means different things in different circumstances. Its original definition referred to a sensation that people say they have when they are dehydrated. Here I use it in a descriptive sense. Because we do not know how other animals feel, *thirst* simply means a tendency to seek water and to ingest it.

hypertonic The characteristic of a solution that contains enough solute that it will draw water out of a cell placed in it, through the process of osmosis.

hypotonic The characteristic of a solution that contains so little solute that a cell placed in it will absorb water, through the process of osmosis.

hypovolemia (*hy poh voh* ***lee*** *mee a*) Reduction in the volume of the intravascular fluid.

osmometric thirst Thirst produced by an increase in the osmotic pressure of the interstitial fluid relative to the intracellular fluid, thus producing cellular dehydration.

osmoreceptor A neuron that detects changes in the solute concentration of the interstitial fluid that surrounds it.

Osmometric Thirst

Osmometric thirst occurs when the tonicity (solute concentration) of the interstitial fluid increases. This increase draws water out of the cells, and they shrink in volume. The term *osmometric* refers to the fact that the detectors are actually responding to (metering) changes in the concentration of the interstitial fluid that surrounds them. *Osmosis* is the movement of water through a semipermeable membrane from a region of low solute concentration to one of high solute concentration.

The existence of neurons that respond to changes in the solute concentration of the interstitial fluid was first hypothesized by Verney (1947). Verney suggested that these detectors, which he called **osmoreceptors,** were neurons whose firing rate was affected by their level of hydration. That is, if the interstitial fluid surrounding them became more concentrated, they would lose water through osmosis. The shrinkage would cause them to alter their firing rate, which would send signals to other parts of the brain. (See ***Figure 11.5***.)

When we eat a salty meal, we incur a pure osmometric thirst. The salt is absorbed from the digestive system into the blood plasma; hence, the blood plasma becomes hypertonic. This condition draws water from the interstitial fluid, which makes this compartment become hypertonic too and thus causes water to leave the cells. As the blood plasma increases in volume, the kidneys begin excreting large amounts of both sodium and water. Eventually, the

Figure 11.5

A hypothetical explanation of the workings of an osmoreceptor.

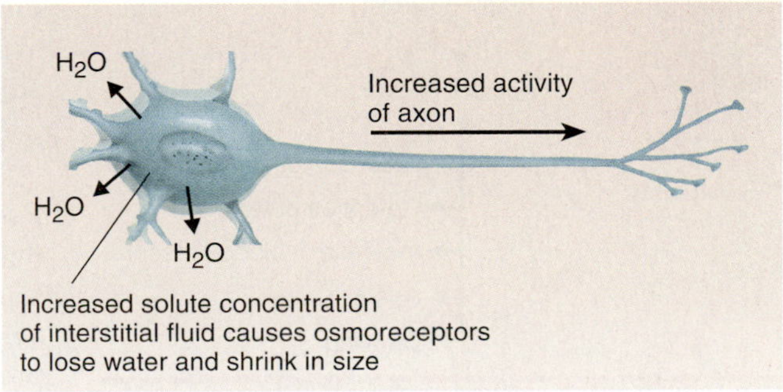
H2O
Increased activity of axon
H2O
H2O
Increased solute concentration of interstitial fluid causes osmoreceptors to lose water and shrink in size

volumetric thirst Thirst produced by hypovolemia.

renin (*ree* nin) A hormone secreted by the kidneys that causes the conversion of angiotensinogen in the blood into angiotensin.

angiotensin (*ann gee oh **ten** sin*) A peptide hormone that constricts blood vessels, causes the retention of sodium and water, and produces thirst and a salt appetite.

excess sodium is excreted, along with the water that was taken from the interstitial and intracellular fluid. The net result is a loss of water from the cells. *At no time does the volume of the blood plasma fall.*

Most researchers now believe that osmoreceptors responsible for osmometric thirst are located in the region of the anterior hypothalamus that borders the anteroventral tip of the third ventricle (the *AV3V*). Buggy et al. (1979) found that injections of hypertonic saline directly into the AV3V produced drinking.

Volumetric Thirst

Volumetric thirst occurs when the volume of the blood plasma—the intravascular volume—decreases. When we lose water through evaporation, we lose it from all three fluid compartments: intracellular, interstitial, and intravascular. Thus, evaporation produces both volumetric thirst and osmometric thirst. In addition, loss of blood, vomiting, and diarrhea all cause loss of blood volume (hypovolemia) without depleting the intracellular fluid.

Loss of blood causes pure volumetric thirst. From the earliest recorded history, reports of battles note that the wounded survivors called out for water. In addition, because hypovolemia involves a loss of sodium as well as water (that is, the sodium that was contained in the isotonic fluid that was lost), volumetric thirst leads to a salt appetite.

What detectors are responsible for initiating volumetric thirst and a salt appetite? There are two sets of receptors that accomplish this dual function: one set in the kidneys, which controls the production of angiotensin, and one set in the heart and large blood vessels (atrial baroreceptors).

The Role of Angiotensin. The kidneys contain cells that are able to detect decreases in the flow of blood to the kidneys. The usual cause of a reduced flow of blood is a loss of blood volume; thus, these cells detect the presence of hypovolemia. When the flow of blood to the kidneys decreases, these cells secrete an enzyme called **renin.** Renin enters the blood, where it catalyzes the conversion of a protein called *angiotensinogen* into a hormone called **angiotensin.** In fact, there are two forms of angiotensin. Angiotensinogen becomes angiotensin I, which is quickly converted by an enzyme to angiotensin II. The active form is angiotensin II, which I shall abbreviate as *AII.*

Angiotensin II has several physiological effects: It stimulates the secretion of hormones by the posterior pituitary gland and the adrenal cortex that cause the kidneys to conserve water and sodium, and it increases blood pressure by causing muscles in the small arteries to contract. In addition, AII has two behavioral effects: It initiates both drinking and a salt appetite. Therefore, a reduction in the flow of blood to the kidneys causes water and sodium to be retained by the body, helps to compensate for their loss by reducing the size of the blood vessels, and encourages the animal to find and ingest both water and salt. (See ***Figure 11.6.***)

Figure 11.6

Detection of hypovolemia by the kidney and the renin–angiotensin system.

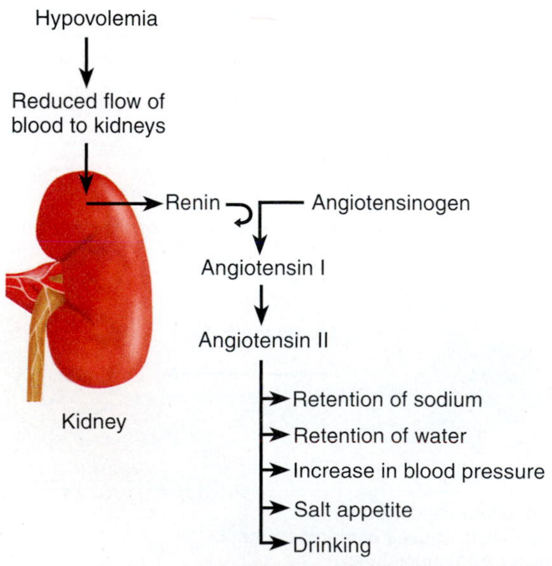

Atrial Baroreceptors. The second set of receptors for volumetric thirst lies within the heart. Physiologists had long known that the *atria* of the heart (the parts that receive blood from the veins) contain sensory neurons that detect stretch. (The term *baro-* comes from the Greek *baros,* "heavy," and refers to weight or pressure.) The atria are passively filled with blood being returned from the body by the veins. The more blood in the veins, the fuller the atria become just before each contraction of the heart. Thus, when the volume of the blood plasma falls, the atria become less full, and the stretch receptors within them will detect this change.

Fitzsimons and Moore-Gillon (1980) showed that information from these receptors can stimulate thirst. They operated on dogs and placed a small balloon in the inferior vena cava, the vein that brings blood from most of the body (excluding the head and arms) to the heart. When the balloon was inflated, it reduced the flow of blood to the heart and thus lowered the amount of blood that entered the right atrium. Within thirty minutes the dogs began to drink. Quillen, Keil, and Reid (1990) confirmed these results. They also found that when the nerves connecting the atrial baroreceptors with the brain were cut, animals drank much less water when the blood flow to their heart was temporarily reduced.

Figure 11.7

A sagittal section of the rat diencephalon, showing the location of the subfornical organ and its connection with the median preoptic nucleus.

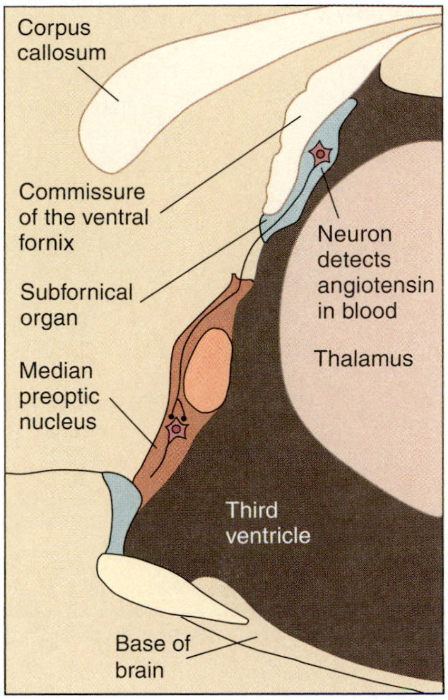

Neural Mechanisms of Thirst

As you have already learned, the osmoreceptors that initiate drinking are located in the brain tissue around the AV3V. The entire region around the anterior third ventricle—dorsal as well as ventral—seems to be the part of the brain where osmometric and volumetric signals are integrated to control drinking. The region around the AV3V also appears to receive information that can stimulate volumetric thirst. Sensory information from the baroreceptors located in the atria of the heart is sent to a nucleus in the medulla: the **nucleus of the solitary tract.** This nucleus sends efferent axons to many parts of the brain, including the region around the AV3V (see Johnson and Edwards, 1990).

The second signal for volumetric thirst is provided by angiotensin II. Because this peptide does not cross the blood–brain barrier, it cannot directly affect neurons in the brain except for those located in one of the circumventricular organs. In fact, research indicates that one of these organs, the **subfornical organ (SFO),** is the site at which blood angiotensin acts to produce thirst. This structure gets its name from its location, just below the commissure of the ventral fornix. (See ***Figure 11.7.***)

Simpson, Epstein, and Camardo (1978) found that very low doses of angiotensin injected directly into the SFO caused drinking and that destruction of the SFO or injection of a drug that blocks angiotensin receptors abolished the drinking that normally occurs when angiotensin is injected into the blood. In addition, Phillips and Felix (1976) found that injections of minute quantities of angiotensin into the SFO increased the firing rate of single neurons located there; evidently, these neurons contain angiotensin receptors.

Neurons in the subfornical organ send their axons to the **median preoptic nucleus** (not to be confused with the *medial* preoptic nucleus), a small nucleus wrapped around the front of the anterior commissure, a fiber bundle that connects the amygdala and anterior temporal lobe. (See ***Figure 11.7.***)

On the basis of these findings, Thrasher and his colleagues (see Thrasher, 1989) suggested that the region in front of the third ventricle acts as an integrating system for most or all of the stimuli for osmometric and volumetric thirst. As you just saw, the median preoptic nucleus receives information from angiotensin-sensitive neurons in the SFO. In addition, this nucleus receives information from the region around the AV3V (which contains osmoreceptors) and from the nucleus of the solitary tract (which receives information from the atrial baroreceptors). According to Thrasher and his colleagues, the median preoptic nucleus integrates the information it receives

nucleus of the solitary tract A nucleus of the medulla that receives information from visceral organs and from the gustatory system.

subfornical organ (SFO) A small organ located in the confluence of the lateral ventricles, attached to the underside of the fornix; contains neurons that detect the presence of angiotensin in the blood and excite neural circuits that initiate drinking.

median preoptic nucleus A small nucleus situated around the decussation of the anterior commissure; plays a role in thirst stimulated by angiotensin.

Figure 11.8

Neural circuitry concerned with the control of drinking. Not all connections are shown, and some connections may be indirect.

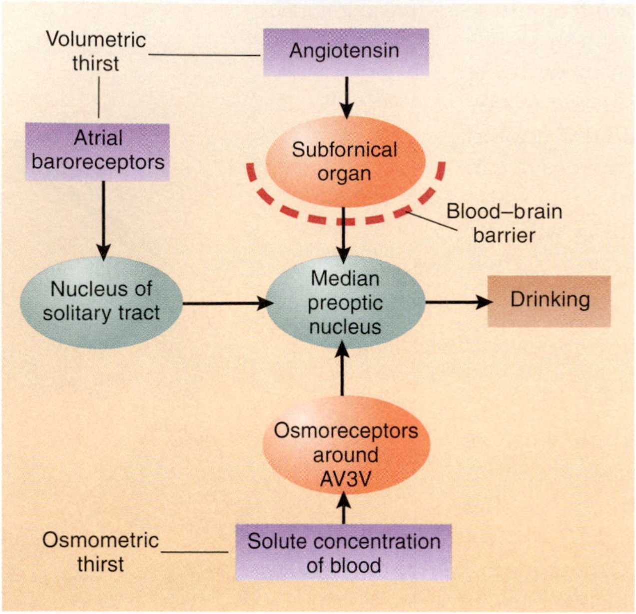

Adapted from Thrasher, T. N. *Acta Physiologica Scandanivica,* 1989, *136,* 141–150.

and, through its efferent connections with other parts of the brain, controls drinking. (See ***Figure 11.8.***)

The region of the AV3V seems to play a critical role in fluid regulation in humans as well. For example, McIver et al. (1991) report that brain damage that includes this region can cause *adipsia*—lack of drinking. The patients report no sensation of thirst even after they are given an injection of hypertonic saline. To survive, they must deliberately drink water at regular intervals each day, even though they feel no need to do so.

INTERIM SUMMARY

Physiological Regulatory Mechanisms and Drinking

A regulatory system contains four features: a system variable (the variable that is regulated), a set point (the optimal value of the system variable), a detector to measure the system variable, and a correctional mechanism to change it. Physiological regulatory systems, such as control of body fluids and nutrients, require a satiety mechanism to anticipate the effects of the correctional mechanism, because the changes brought about by eating and drinking occur only after a considerable period of time.

The body contains three major fluid compartments: intracellular, interstitial, and intravascular. Sodium and water can easily pass between the intravascular fluid and the interstitial fluid, but sodium cannot penetrate the cell membrane. The solute concentration of the interstitial fluid must be closely regulated. If it becomes hypertonic, cells lose water; if it becomes hypotonic, they gain water. The volume of the intravascular fluid (blood plasma) must also be kept within bounds.

Osmometric thirst occurs when the interstitial fluid becomes hypertonic, drawing water out of cells. This event, which can be caused by evaporation of water from the body or by ingestion of a salty meal, is detected by osmoreceptors in the region of the anteroventral third ventricle (the AV3V). Activation of the osmoreceptors stimulates drinking.

Volumetric thirst occurs along with osmometric thirst when the body loses fluid through evaporation. Pure volumetric thirst is caused by blood loss, vomiting, and diarrhea. One stimulus for volumetric thirst is provided by a fall in blood flow to the kidneys. This event triggers the secretion of renin, which converts plasma angiotensinogen to angiotensin I. Angiotensin I is subsequently converted to its active form, angiotensin II. Angiotensin II acts on neurons in the brain and stimulates thirst. The hormone also increases blood pressure and stimulates the secretion of pituitary and adrenal hormones that inhibit the secretion of water and sodium by the kidneys and induce a sodium appetite. (Sodium is needed to help restore the plasma volume.) Volumetric drinking can also be stimulated by a set of baroreceptors in the atria of the heart that detect decreased blood volume and send this information to the brain.

The region of the AV3V detects and integrates signals that produce both osmometric and volumetric thirst. Volumetric thirst stimulated by angiotensin involves another circumventricular organ: the subfornical organ. Volumetric thirst stimulated by the atrial stretch receptor system reaches the AV3V region via a relay in the nucleus of the solitary tract. Neurons in the SFO and the AV3V region (which, you will remember, contains osmoreceptors) send axons to the median preoptic nucleus. Neurons in this nucleus stimulate drinking through their connections with other parts of the brain.

THOUGHT QUESTION

How do we know that we are thirsty? What does thirst feel like? It cannot simply be a dry mouth or throat, because a real thirst is not quenched by taking a small sip of water, which moistens the mouth and throat as effectively as a big drink does.

Eating and Metabolism

Clearly, eating is one of the most important things we do, and it can also be one of the most pleasurable. Much of what an animal learns to do is motivated by the constant struggle to obtain food; thus, the need to ingest undoubtedly shaped the evolutionary development of our own species. After having read the first part of this chapter, in which you saw that the signals that cause thirst are well understood, you might be surprised to learn that researchers are only now discovering what the system variables for hunger are. Control of ingestive behavior is even more complicated than the control of drinking and sodium intake. We can achieve water balance by the intake of two ingredients: water and sodium chloride. When we eat, we must obtain adequate amounts of carbohydrates, fats, amino acids, vitamins, and minerals other than sodium. Thus, our food-ingestive behaviors are more complex, as are the physiological mechanisms that control them.

To stay alive, our cells must be supplied with fuel and oxygen. Obviously, fuel comes from the digestive tract, and its presence there is a result of eating. But the digestive tract is sometimes empty; in fact, most of us wake up in the morning in that condition. So there has to be a reservoir that stores nutrients to keep the cells of the body nourished when the gut is empty. Indeed, there are two reservoirs: one short-term and the other long-term. The short-term reservoir stores carbohydrates, and the long-term reservoir stores fats.

The short-term reservoir is located in the cells of the liver and the muscles, and it is filled with a complex, insoluble carbohydrate called **glycogen.** For simplicity I will consider only one of these locations: the liver. Cells in the liver convert glucose (a simple, soluble carbohydrate) into glycogen and store the glycogen. They are stimulated to do so by the presence of **insulin,** a peptide hormone produced by the pancreas. Thus, when glucose and insulin are present in the blood, some of the glucose is used as a fuel, and some of it is stored as glycogen. Later, when all of the food has been absorbed from the digestive tract, the level of glucose in the blood begins to fall.

The fall in glucose is detected by cells in the pancreas and in the brain. The pancreas responds by stopping its secretion of insulin and starting to secrete a different peptide hormone: **glucagon.** The effect of glucagon is opposite that of insulin: It stimulates the conversion of glycogen into glucose. (Unfortunately, the terms *glucose, glycogen,* and *glucagon* are similar enough that it is easy to confuse them. Even worse, you will soon encounter another one: *glycerol.*) (See ***Figure 11.9.***) Thus, the liver soaks up excess glucose and stores it as glycogen when plenty of glucose is available, and it releases glucose from its reservoir when the digestive tract becomes empty and the level of glucose in the blood begins to fall.

The carbohydrate reservoir in the liver is primarily reserved for the central nervous system. When you wake in the morning, your brain is being fed by your liver, which is in the process of converting glycogen to glucose and releasing it into the blood. The glucose reaches the CNS, where it is absorbed and metabolized by the neurons and the glia. This process can continue for a few hours, until all of the carbohydrate reservoir in the liver is used up. (The average liver holds approximately 300 calories of carbohydrate.) Usually, we eat

glycogen (*gly ko jen*) A polysaccharide often referred to as *animal starch;* stored in liver and muscle; constitutes the short-term store of nutrients.

insulin A pancreatic hormone that facilitates entry of glucose and amino acids into the cell, conversion of glucose into glycogen, and transport of fats into adipose tissue.

glucagon (*gloo ka gahn*) A pancreatic hormone that promotes the conversion of liver glycogen into glucose.

Figure 11.9

Effects of insulin and glucagon on glucose and glycogen.

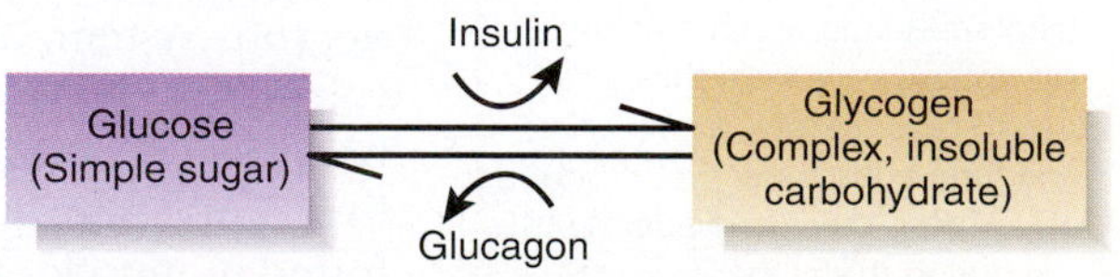

some food before this reservoir gets depleted, which permits us to refill it. But if we do not eat, the CNS has to start living on the products of the long-term reservoir.

Our long-term reservoir consists of adipose tissue (fat tissue). This reservoir is filled with fats, or, more precisely, with **triglycerides.** Triglycerides are complex molecules that contain **glycerol** (a soluble carbohydrate, also called *glycerine*) combined with three **fatty acids** (stearic acid, oleic acid, and palmitic acid). Adipose tissue is found just beneath the skin and in various locations in the abdominal cavity. It consists of cells that are capable of absorbing nutrients from the blood, converting them to triglycerides, and storing them. These cells can expand enormously in size; in fact, the primary physical difference between an obese person and a person of normal weight is the size of their fat cells, which is determined by the amount of triglycerides that these cells contain.

The long-term fat reservoir is obviously what keeps us alive when we are fasting. As we begin to use the contents of our short-term carbohydrate reservoir, fat cells start converting triglycerides into fuels that the cells can use and releasing these fuels into the bloodstream. As we just saw, when we awaken in the morning with an empty digestive tract, our brain (in fact, all of the central nervous system) is living on glucose released by the liver. But what about the other cells of the body? They are living on fatty acids, sparing the glucose for the brain. As you will recall from Chapter 3, the sympathetic nervous system is primarily involved in the breakdown and utilization of stored nutrients. When the digestive system is empty, there is an increase in the activity of the sympathetic axons that innervate adipose tissue, the pancreas, and the adrenal medulla. All three effects (direct neural stimulation, secretion of glucagon, and secretion of adrenal hormones) cause triglycerides in the long-term fat reservoir to be broken down into glycerol and fatty acids. The fatty acids can be directly metabolized by cells in all of the body *except the brain,* which needs glucose. That leaves glycerol. The liver takes up glycerol and converts it to glucose. That glucose, too, is available to the brain.

You may be asking why the cells of the rest of the body treat the brain so kindly, letting it consume almost all the glucose that the liver releases from its carbohydrate reservoir and constructs from glycerol. The answer is simple: Insulin has several other functions besides causing glucose to be converted to glycogen. One of these functions is controlling the entry of glucose into cells. To be taken into a cell, glucose must be transported there by *glucose transporters*—protein molecules that are situated in the membrane and are similar to those responsible for the reuptake of transmitter substances. Glucose transporters contain insulin receptors, which control their activity; only when insulin binds with these receptors can glucose be transported into the cell. But the cells of the nervous system are an exception to this rule. Their glucose transporters do not contain insulin receptors; thus, these cells can absorb glucose *even when insulin is not present.*

Figure 11.10 reviews what I have said so far about the metabolism that takes place while the digestive tract is empty, which physiologists refer to as the **fasting phase** of metabolism. A fall in the blood glucose level causes the pancreas to stop secreting insulin and to start secreting glucagon. The absence of insulin means that most of the cells of the body can no longer use glucose; thus, all the glucose present in the blood is reserved for the central nervous system. The presence of glucagon and the absence of insulin instructs the liver to start drawing on the short-term carbohydrate reservoir—to start converting its glycogen into glucose. The presence of glucagon and the absence of insulin, along with increased activity of the sympathetic nervous system, also instruct fat cells to start drawing on the long-term fat reservoir—to start breaking down triglycerides into fatty acids and glycerol. Most of the body lives on the fatty acids, and the glycerol, which is converted into glucose by the liver, gets used by the brain. If fasting is prolonged, proteins (especially protein found in muscle) will be broken down to amino acids, which can be metabolized by

triglyceride (*try **gliss** er ide*) The form of fat storage in adipose cells; consists of a molecule of glycerol joined with three fatty acids.

glycerol (***gliss** er all*) A substance (also called glycerine) derived from the breakdown of triglycerides, along with fatty acids; can be converted by the liver into glucose.

fatty acid A substance derived from the breakdown of triglycerides, along with glycerol; can be metabolized by most cells of the body except for the brain.

fasting phase The phase of metabolism during which nutrients are not available from the digestive system; glucose, amino acids, and fatty acids are derived from glycogen, protein, and adipose tissue during this phase.

Figure 11.10

Metabolic pathways during the fasting phase and absorptive phase of metabolism.

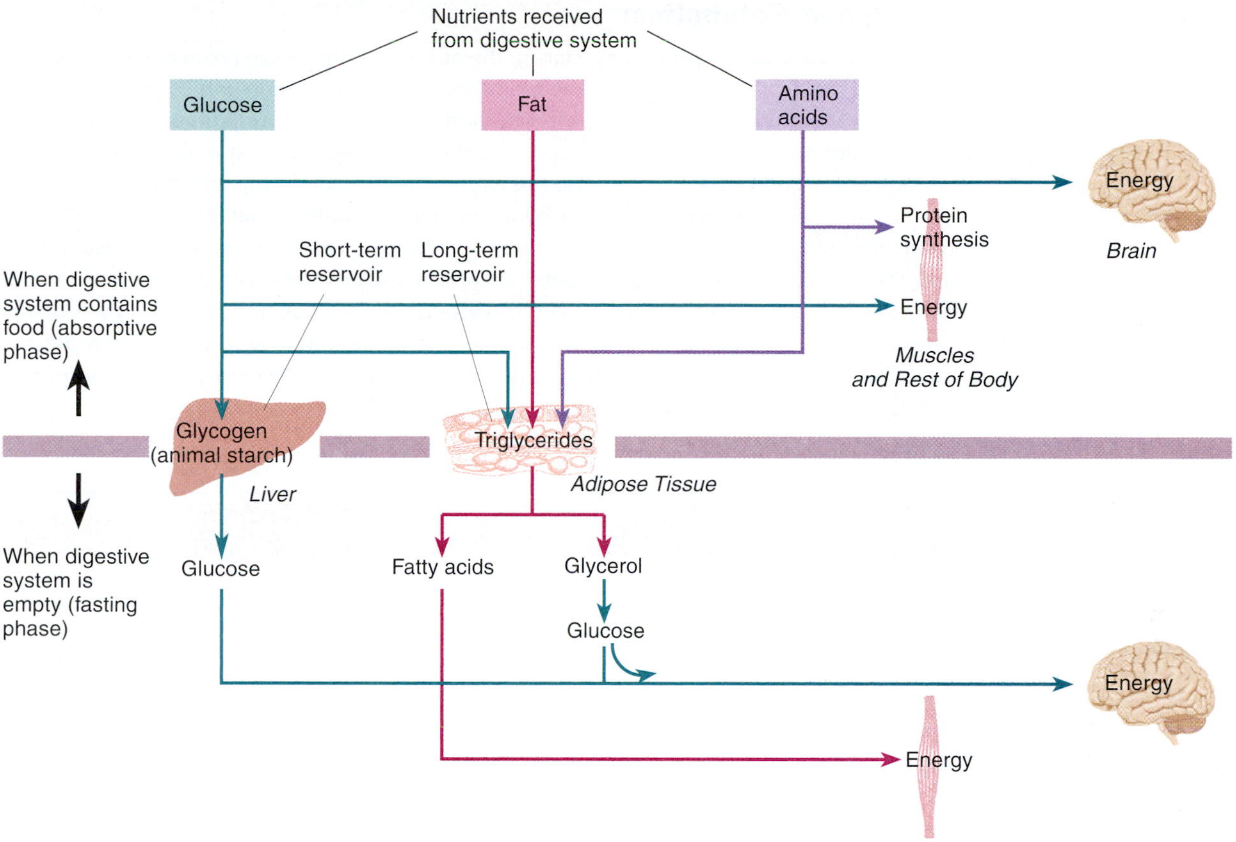

all of the body except the central nervous system. (See ***Figure 11.10*** and ***Animation 11.1, Metabolism.***)

The phase of metabolism that occurs when food is present in the digestive tract is called the **absorptive phase.** Now that you understand the fasting phase, this one is simple. Suppose that we eat a balanced meal of carbohydrates, proteins, and fats. The carbohydrates are broken down into glucose, and the proteins are broken down into amino acids. The fats basically remain as fats. Let us consider each of these three nutrients.

1. As we start absorbing the nutrients, the level of glucose in the blood rises. This rise is detected by cells in the brain, which causes the activity of the sympathetic nervous system to decrease and the activity of the parasympathetic nervous system to increase. This change tells the pancreas to stop secreting glucagon and to begin secreting insulin. The insulin permits all the cells of the body to use glucose as a fuel. Extra glucose is converted into glycogen, which fills the short-term carbohydrate reservoir. If some glucose is left over, it is converted into fat and absorbed by fat cells.
2. A small proportion of the amino acids received from the digestive tract are used as building blocks to construct proteins and peptides; the rest are converted to fats and stored in adipose tissue.
3. Fats are not used at this time; they are simply stored in adipose tissue. (See ***Figure 11.10.***)

Animation 11.1, Metabolism, reviews the storage and breakdown of nutrients during the fasting phase and absorptive phase of metabolism.

absorptive phase The phase of metabolism during which nutrients are absorbed from the digestive system; glucose and amino acids constitute the principal source of energy for cells during this phase, and excess nutrients are stored in adipose tissue in the form of triglycerides.

INTERIM SUMMARY

Eating and Metabolism

Metabolism consists of two phases. During the absorptive phase we receive glucose, amino acids, and fats from the intestines. The blood level of insulin is high, which permits all cells to metabolize glucose. In addition, the liver and the muscles convert glucose to glycogen, which replenishes the short-term reservoir. Excess carbohydrates and amino acids are converted to fats, and fats are placed into the long-term reservoir in the adipose tissue.

During the fasting phase the activity of the parasympathetic nervous system falls, and the activity of the sympathetic nervous system increases. In response the level of insulin falls, and the level of glucagon and the adrenal catecholamines rises. These events cause liver glycogen to be converted to glucose and triglycerides to be broken down into glycerol and fatty acids. In the absence of insulin only the central nervous system can use the glucose available in the blood; the rest of the body lives on fatty acids. Glycerol is converted to glucose by the liver, and the glucose is metabolized by the brain.

What Starts a Meal?

The heading to this section is a very simple question, but the answer is complex. The short answer, I suppose, is that we still are not sure, but that will not stop me from continuing to write. In fact, many factors start a meal, including the presence of appetizing food, the company of people who are eating, or the words "It's time to eat!" More fundamentally, there must be some sort of signal that tells the brain that the supply of nutrients has gotten low and that it is time to begin looking for, and ingesting, some food. This section considers all of these factors.

Before I begin, I will point out that the physiological signals that cause a meal to begin are different from the ones that cause it to end. As I said in the discussion of regulatory systems at the beginning of this chapter, there is a considerable delay between the act of eating (the correctional mechanism) and a change in the system variable. We may start eating because the supply of nutrients has fallen below a certain level, but we certainly do not stop eating because the level of those nutrients has been restored to normal. In fact, we stop eating long before that happens, because digestion takes several hours. Thus, the signals for hunger and satiety are sure to be different.

Social and Environmental Factors

Most people, if they were asked why they eat, would say that they do so because they get hungry. By that they probably mean that something happens inside their body that provides a sensation that makes them want to eat. In other words, we tend to think of eating as something provoked by physiological factors. But often we eat because of habit or because of some stimuli present in our environment. These stimuli may include a clock indicating that it is time to eat, the sight of a plate of food, the smell of food cooking in the kitchen, or the presence of other people sitting around the table.

One of the most important variables affecting appetite is the meal schedule. We tend to take our meals at fixed times: soon after waking, at midday, and in the evening. This custom makes it difficult for us to adjust the timing of our meals, as other animals can do. What we do instead is adjust the *size* of our meals. If we have eaten recently or if the previous meal was large, we tend to eat a smaller meal (Jiang and Hunt, 1983; de Castro et al., 1986). However, if someone else prepares and

Social factors, and not just physiological ones, affect when and how much we eat.

serves us our meal (for example, at a restaurant), we are more likely to ignore internal satiety signals and finish what is on our plate.

Physiological Hunger Signals

Most of the time, we begin a meal because it is time to eat. The amount of food we eat during that meal depends on several factors, including the amount and variety of food available to us and how good the food tastes to us. But the amount of food we eat also depends on metabolic factors. If we skip several meals, we get hungrier and hungrier, presumably because of physiological signals indicating that we have been withdrawing nutrients from our long-term reservoir.

A fall in blood glucose level (a condition known as *hypoglycemia*) is a potent stimulus for hunger. Hypoglycemia can be produced experimentally by giving an animal a large injection of insulin, which causes liver cells and fat cells to take up glucose and store it away. We can also deprive cells of glucose by injecting an animal with 2-deoxyglucose (2-DG). You are already familiar with this chemical, because I have described several experiments in previous chapters that used radioactive 2-DG in conjunction with PET scanners or autoradiography to study the metabolic rate of different parts of the brain. When (nonradioactive) 2-DG is given in large doses, it interferes with glucose metabolism by competing with glucose for access to the mechanism that transports glucose through the cell membrane and for access to the enzymes that metabolize glucose. (A similar chemical, *5-TG,* has the same effect.) Both hypoglycemia and 2-DG cause **glucoprivation;** that is, they deprive cells of glucose. And glucoprivation, whatever its cause, stimulates eating.

Hunger can also be produced by causing **lipoprivation**—depriving cells of lipids. More precisely, they are deprived of the ability to metabolize fatty acids through injection of one of two drugs, **methyl palmoxirate (MP)** or **mercaptoacetate (MA)**.

What is the nature of the detectors that monitor the level of metabolic fuels, and where are they located? The evidence that has been gathered so far indicates that there are two sets of detectors: one set located in the brain and the other set located in the liver.

Let's first review the evidence for the detectors in the liver. A study by Novin, VanderWeele, and Rezek (1973) suggested that receptors in the liver can stimulate glucoprivic hunger; when these neurons are deprived of nutrients, they cause eating.

glucoprivation A dramatic fall in the level of glucose available to cells; can be caused by a fall in the blood level of glucose or by drugs that inhibit glucose metabolism.

lipoprivation A dramatic fall in the level of fatty acids available to cells; usually caused by drugs that inhibit fatty acid metabolism.

methyl palmoxirate (MP) A drug that inhibits fatty acid metabolism and produces lipoprivic hunger.

mercaptoacetate (MA) A drug that inhibits fatty acid metabolism and produces lipoprivic hunger.

Figure 11.11

The hepatic portal blood supply. The liver receives water, minerals, and nutrients from the digestive system through this blood supply.

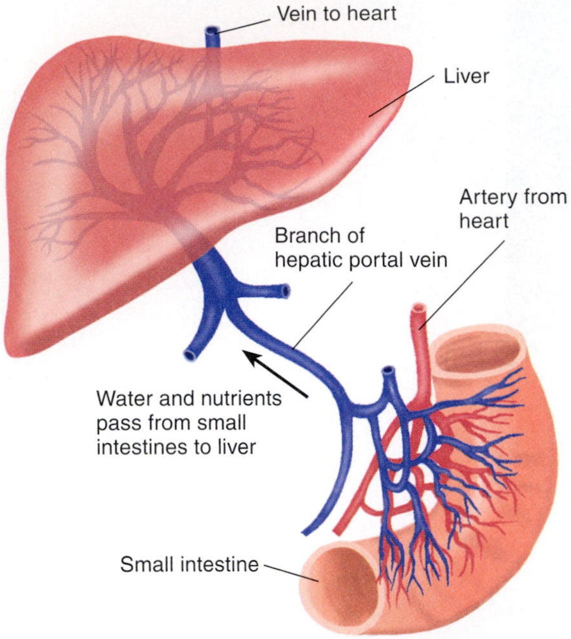
Vein to heart
Liver
Artery from heart
Branch of hepatic portal vein
Water and nutrients pass from small intestines to liver
Small intestine

Figure 11.12

Probable location of nutrient receptors responsible for hunger signals.

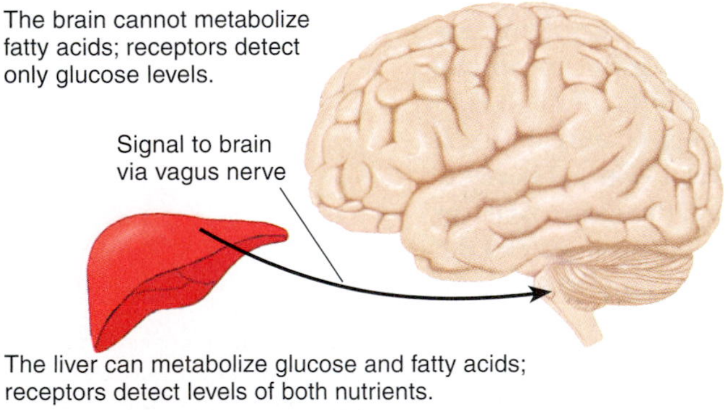
The brain cannot metabolize fatty acids; receptors detect only glucose levels.
Signal to brain via vagus nerve
The liver can metabolize glucose and fatty acids; receptors detect levels of both nutrients.

The investigators infused 2-DG into the **hepatic portal vein.** This vein brings blood from the intestines to the liver; thus, an injection of a drug into this vein delivers it directly to the liver. (See ***Figure 11.11.***) The investigators found that the intraportal infusions of 2-DG caused immediate eating. When they cut the vagus nerve, which connects the liver with the brain, the infusions no longer stimulated eating. Thus, the brain receives the hunger signal through this connection.

What about lipoprivic hunger? Ritter and Taylor (1990) induced lipoprivic hunger with an injection of MA and found that cutting the vagus nerve abolished this hunger. Furthermore, Lutz, Diener, and Scharrer (1997) found that infusion of MA into the hepatic portal vein increased the activity of afferent axons in the hepatic branch of the vagus nerve, Thus, the liver appears to contain receptors that detect low availability of glucose or fatty acids (glucoprivation or lipoprivation) and send this information to the brain through the vagus nerve.

Now let's look at some of the evidence that indicates that the brain has its own nutrient detectors. Because the brain can use only glucose, it would make sense that these detectors respond to glucoprivation—and, indeed, they do. Ritter, Slusser, and Stone (1981) injected 5-TG into either the third ventricle or the fourth ventricle. (5-TG, like 2-DG, produces glucoprivation.) Injections into the fourth ventricle stimulated eating, but injections into the third ventricle (located in the middle of the diencephalon) had no effect. Presumably, the 5-TG diffused out of the fourth ventricle into the surrounding brain tissue and inhibited glucose metabolism in neurons in the hindbrain.

The location of the hindbrain nutrient receptors is not yet known, but one possible location is the area postrema or the adjacent nucleus of the solitary tract, located in the medulla. Bird, Cardone, and Contreras (1983) found that after the area postrema had been destroyed, an injection of 5-TG into the ventricular system no longer stimulated food intake.

To summarize: The brain contains detectors that monitor the availability of glucose (its only fuel) inside the blood–brain barrier, and the liver contains detectors the monitor the availability of nutrients (glucose and fatty acids) outside the blood–brain barrier. (See ***Figure 11.12.***)

hepatic portal vein The vein that transports blood from the digestive system to the liver.

INTERIM SUMMARY

What Starts a Meal?

Many stimuli, environmental and physiological, can initiate a meal. Stimuli associated with eating—such as clocks pointing to lunchtime or dinnertime, the smell or sight of food, or (especially) the taste of food—increase appetite. The size of a meal taken by a rat (or a person living in isolation) determines the interval until the next one. In contrast, most people eat at relatively fixed times but vary their intake according to how much (or when) they ate the previous meal. The presence of other people tends to increase the size of our meal and removes the controlling effect of the previous meal.

Studies with inhibitors of the metabolism of glucose (2-DG or 5-TG) and fatty acids (MP or MA) indicate that low levels of both of these nutrients are involved in hunger; that is, animals will eat in response to both glucoprivation and lipoprivation. The signal for lipoprivic eating is detected by receptors in the liver and transmitted to the brain through sensory axons of the vagus nerve. Glucoprivic eating can also be stimulated by interfering with glucose metabolism in the region surrounding the fourth ventricle by injecting 5-TG into the fourth ventricle; thus, the brain stem contains its own glucose-sensitive detectors. Although the evidence is not yet conclusive, these detectors may lie in the area postrema/nucleus of the solitary tract.

THOUGHT QUESTION

Do you find hunger unpleasant? I find that when I'm looking forward to a meal I particularly like, I don't mind being hungry, knowing that I'll enjoy the meal that much more. But then, I've never gone without eating for several days.

What Stops a Meal?

As we saw, the signals that stop a meal are different from those that start it. However, these two types of signals interact. If a meal is started when there is not much physiological need for nutrients (that is, when the nutrient reservoirs are well stocked), the meal will be a small one. But if a meal is started after a long fast, when the nutrient reservoirs are somewhat depleted, the meal will be a large one. In other words, if the hunger signal is moderate, a moderate satiety signal will stop the meal. If the hunger signal is strong, only a strong satiety signal will stop it.

There are two primary sources of satiety signals—the signals that stop a meal. Short-term satiety signals come from the immediate consequence of eating a particular meal. To search for these signals, we follow the pathway traveled by ingested food: the stomach, the small intestine, and the liver. Each of these locations can potentially provide a signal to the brain that indicates that food has been ingested and is progressing on the way toward absorption. In addition, metabolic signals present in the blood inform the brain that the body is in the absorptive phase. Long-term satiety signals arise in the adipose tissue, which contains the long-term nutrient reservoir. These signals do not control the beginning and end of a particular meal, but they do, in the long run, control the intake of calories by modulating the sensitivity of brain mechanisms involved in hunger.

Gastric Factors

Although most people associate feelings of hunger with "hunger pangs" in the stomach and feelings of satiety with an impression of gastric fullness, the stomach is not necessary for feelings of hunger. Humans whose stomachs have been removed because of cancer or the presence of large ulcers still periodically get hungry (Ingelfinger, 1944). Of necessity these people eat frequent, small meals; in fact, a large meal causes nausea and discomfort, apparently because the duodenum quickly fills up. The **duodenum** is the part of the small intestine that attaches to the stomach. (The original Greek name for this part of the gut was *dodekadaktulon,* or "twelve fingers long." In fact, the duodenum is twelve finger *widths* long.) However, although the stomach might not be especially important in producing hunger, it does appear to play an important role in satiety.

The stomach apparently contains receptors that can detect the presence of nutrients. Davis and Campbell (1973) allowed rats to eat their fill, and shortly thereafter,

duodenum The first portion of the small intestine, attached directly to the stomach.

they removed food from the rats' stomachs through an implanted tube. When the rats were permitted to eat again, they ate almost exactly the same amount of food that had been taken out. This finding suggests that animals are able to monitor the amount of food in their stomachs.

Deutsch and Gonzalez (1980) confirmed and extended these findings. They found that when they removed food from the stomach of a rat that had just eaten all it wanted, the animal would immediately eat just enough food to replace what had been removed. The rats ate this amount even when the experimenters replaced the food with a nonnutritive saline solution. Obviously, the rats did not simply measure the volume of the food in their stomachs, because they were not fooled by the infusion of a saline solution. Of course, this study proves only that the stomach contains nutrient receptors; it does not prove that there are not detectors in the intestines as well.

Intestinal Factors

Indeed, the intestines do contain nutrient detectors. Studies have shown that afferent axons arising from the duodenum are sensitive to the presence of glucose, amino acids, and fatty acids (Ritter et al., 1992). These axons may transmit a satiety signal to the brain.

Feinle, Grundy, and Read (1997) placed an inflatable bag in people's stomachs. When the stomach and duodenum were empty, the subjects reported that they simply felt bloated when the bag was inflated, filling the stomach. However, when fats or carbohydrates were infused into the duodenum while the bag was being inflated, the people reported sensations of fullness like those experienced after eating a meal. Thus, stomach and intestinal satiety factors can interact. That's not surprising, given the fact that by the time we finish a normal meal, our stomachs are full and a small amount of nutrients have been received by the duodenum.

After food reaches the stomach, it is mixed with hydrochloric acid and pepsin, an enzyme that breaks proteins into their constituent amino acids. As digestion proceeds, food is gradually introduced into the duodenum. There, the food is mixed with bile and pancreatic enzymes, which continue the digestive process. The duodenum controls the rate of stomach emptying by secreting a peptide hormone called **cholecystokinin (CCK).** This hormone got its name from the fact that it causes the gallbladder (cholecyst) to contract, injecting bile into the duodenum. (Bile breaks fats down into small particles so that they can be absorbed from the intestines.) CCK is secreted in response to the presence of fats, which are detected by receptors in the walls of the duodenum. In addition to stimulating contraction of the gallbladder, CCK causes the pylorus to constrict and inhibits gastric contractions, thus keeping the stomach from giving it more food.

Obviously, the blood level of CCK must be related to the amount of nutrients (particularly fats) that the duodenum receives from the stomach. Thus, this hormone could potentially provide a satiety signal to the brain, telling it that the duodenum was receiving food from the stomach. Many studies have indeed found that injections of CCK suppress eating (Gibbs, Young, and Smith, 1973; Smith, Gibbs, and Kulkosky, 1982). In addition, a strain of rats with a genetic mutation that prevents the production of CCK receptors become obese, apparently because of a disruption in normal satiety (Moran et al., 1998). The suppressive effects are only temporary; if CCK is administered with each meal, the animal eats less but then compensates for the decreased food intake by taking more frequent meals (West, Fey, and Woods, 1984). Thus, CCK is involved in short-term satiety, not long-term satiety.

Recently, investigators have discovered a chemical produced by cells in the intestinal tract that may serve as a satiety signal. This chemical, **peptide $YY_{3\text{-}36}$** (let's just call it **PYY**) is released after a meal in amounts proportional to the calories that were just ingested (Pedersen-Bjergaard et al., 1996; Batterham et al., 2002; Batterham and Bloom, 2003). The secretion of PYY begins within 15 minutes and levels off 75 min-

cholecystokinin (CCK) (*coal i sis toe **ky** nin*) A hormone secreted by the duodenum that regulates gastric motility and causes the gallbladder (cholecyst) to contract; appears to provide a satiety signal transmitted to the brain through the vagus nerve.

peptide $YY_{3\text{-}36}$ (PYY) A peptide released by the gastrointestinal system after a meal in amounts proportional to the size of the meal.

utes later. Injections of PYY significantly decreased the amount of food that hungry rats or hungry humans would eat. (Yes, the peptide was tested in humans.) Because PYY interacts with peptide receptors in the hypothalamus that are involved with hunger and satiety, I will discuss the actions of this chemical later in this chapter, in a section dealing with brain mechanisms of ingestive behavior.

Liver Factors

Satiety produced by gastric factors or duodenal factors is anticipatory; that is, these factors predict that the food in the digestive system will, when absorbed, eventually restore the system variables that cause hunger. Food in the mouth or stomach does not restore the body's store of nutrients. Not until nutrients are absorbed from the intestines are the internal system variables that cause hunger returned to normal. The last stage of satiety appears to occur in the liver, which is the first organ to learn that food is finally being received by the intestines.

Evidence that nutrient detectors in the liver play a role in satiety comes from several sources. For example, Tordoff and Friedman (1988) infused small amounts of two nutrients, glucose and fructose, into the hepatic portal vein. The amounts they used were similar to those that are produced when a meal is being digested. The infusions "fooled" the liver; both nutrients reduced the amount of food that the rats ate. Fructose cannot cross the blood–brain barrier and is metabolized very poorly by cells in the rest of the body, but it can readily be metabolized by the liver. Therefore, the signal from this nutrient must have originated in the liver. These results strongly suggest that when the liver receives nutrients from the intestines, it sends a signal to the brain that produces satiety. (More accurately, the signal *continues* the satiety that was already started by signals arising from the stomach and intestines.)

Satiety During the Absorptive Phase: Role of Insulin

Satiety begins with the eating of a meal, which is detected by factors in the stomach, intestines, and liver. The liver absorbs some nutrients—particularly glucose, which it converts into glycogen and stores in the short-term reservoir. But soon, the level of nutrients in the blood begins to rise. When this happens, physiological changes occur, and the body enters the absorptive phase of metabolism. Perhaps some signals that arise from these changes provide a satiety signal to the brain.

As you will recall, the absorptive phase of metabolism is accompanied by an increased level of insulin in the blood. Insulin permits organs other than the brain to metabolize glucose, and it promotes the entry of nutrients into fat cells where they are converted into triglycerides. You will also recall that cells in the brain do not need insulin to metabolize glucose. Nevertheless, the brain contains insulin receptors (Unger et al., 1989). What purpose do these insulin receptors serve? The answer is that they appear to detect insulin present in the blood, which tells the brain that the body is probably in the absorptive phase of metabolism. Thus, insulin may serve as a satiety signal (Woods et al., 1979).

Brüning et al. (2000) prepared a mutation in mice that prevented the synthesis of insulin receptors in the brain without affecting their production elsewhere in the body. The mice became obese, especially when they were fed a tasty, high-fat diet, which would be expected if one of the factors that promotes satiety was absent.

Long-Term Satiety: Signals from Adipose Tissue

So far, I have discussed satiety factors arising from a meal. But as we saw in the first section of this chapter, total body fat appears to be regulated over a long-term basis.

Figure 11.13

Food intake and body weight of rats that received an excess of their normal food intake through force feeding. Their food intake fell during the period of force feeding and recovered only when their body weight returned to normal.

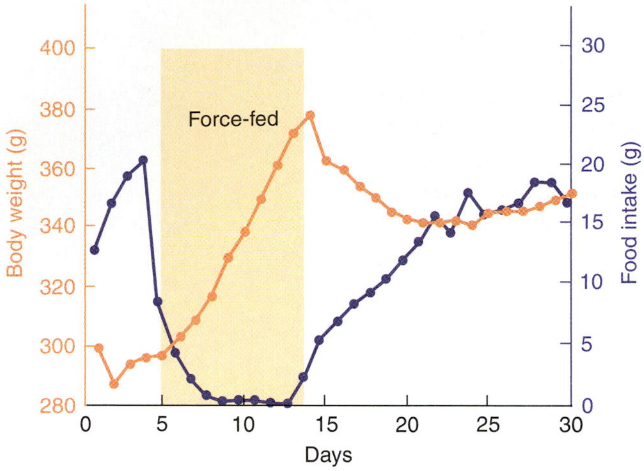

Adapted from Wilson, B. E., Meyer, G. E., Cleveland, J. C., and Weigle, D. S. *American Journal of Physiology,* 1990, *259,* R1148–R1155.

Figure 11.14

The effects of leptin on obesity in mice of the ob (obese) strain. The ob mouse on the left is untreated; the one on the right received daily injections of leptin.

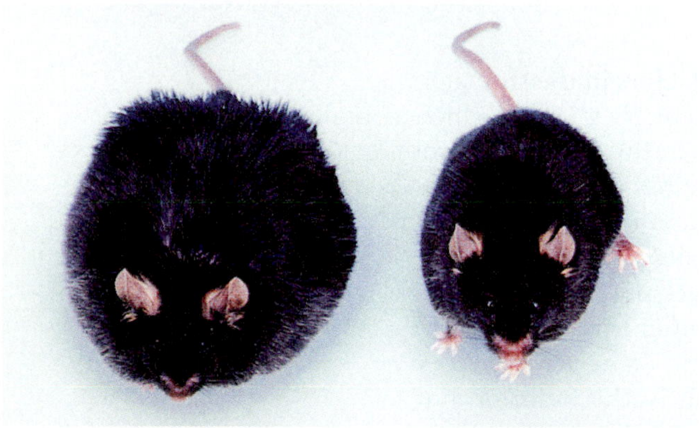

Photo courtesy of Dr. J. Sholtis, The Rockefeller University. Copyright © 1995 Amgen, Inc.

If an animal is force-fed so that it becomes fatter than normal, it will reduce its food intake once it is permitted to choose how much to eat (Wilson et al., 1990). (See ***Figure 11.13.***) Thus, signals arising from the long-term nutrient reservoir may either suppress hunger signals or augment short-term satiety signals.

What exactly is the system variable that permits the body weight of most organisms to remain relatively stable? The basic difference between obese and nonobese people is the amount of fat stored in their adipose tissue. Perhaps fat tissue provides a signal to the brain that indicates how much of it there is.

The discovery of such a signal came after years of study with a strain of genetically obese mice. The **ob mouse** (as this strain is called) has a low metabolism, overeats, and gets exceedingly fat. It also develops diabetes in adulthood, just as many obese people do. Researchers in several laboratories have discovered the cause of the obesity (Campfield et al., 1995; Halaas et al., 1995; Pelleymounter et al., 1995). A particular gene, called OB, normally produces a protein that has been given the name **leptin** (from the Greek word *leptos,* "thin"). Leptin is normally secreted by fat cells that contain a large amount of triglycerides. Because of a genetic mutation, the fat cells of ob mice are unable to produce leptin.

Leptin has profound effects on metabolism and eating, acting as an antiobesity hormone. If ob mice are given daily injections of leptin, their metabolic rate increases, their body temperature rises, they become more active, and they eat less. As a result, their weight returns to normal. Figure 11.14 shows a picture of an untreated ob mouse and an ob mouse that has received injections of leptin. (See ***Figure 11.14.***)

Leptin affects the metabolism and food intake of normal animals. If leptin is given to rats each day, the animals eat smaller meals and lose weight (Eckel et al., 1998; Kahler et al., 1998). The leptin affected only meal size; the animals ate the same number of meals each day. These results suggest that leptin sensitizes the brain to the satiety signals it receives from the stomach, liver, and intestines, causing meals to stop earlier than they otherwise would.

INTERIM SUMMARY

What Stops a Meal?

Because of the long delay between swallowing food and digesting it, the regulation of food intake requires a satiety mechanism; without it, we would overeat and damage our stomachs. The stomach contains nutrient detectors that tell the brain how much food has been received. If some food is removed from the stomach, the animal eats enough to replace it, and if the experimenter tries to fool the animal by injecting a saline solution into the stomach, food intake is not reduced.

Signals originating in the intestines may also produce satiety. Several investigators have suggested that cholecystokinin, released by the duodenum when it receives fat-rich food from the stomach, provides a short-term satiety signal. The duodenum also appears to contain nutrient detectors that send a satiety signal directly to the brain without the intermediate of a hormone. PYY, a peptide secreted after a meal by the intestines, also appears to act as a satiety signal.

Another satiety signal comes from the liver, which detects nutrients being received from the intestines. Infusion of glucose or fructose (which does not cross the blood–brain barrier) directly into the hepatic portal vein suppresses food intake of hungry animals. Insulin, which is present in high levels during the absorptive phase of metabolism, enters the brain and activates insulin receptors there, providing another satiety signal.

Signals arising from nutrient reservoirs affect food intake on a long-term basis. Studies of the ob mouse led to the discovery of leptin, a peptide hormone secreted by well-nourished adipose tissue that increases an animal's metabolic rate and decreases food intake. Leptin decreases meal size, apparently by increasing the brain's sensitivity to short-term satiety signals.

ob mouse A strain of mice whose obesity and low metabolic rate is caused by a mutation that prevents the production of leptin.

leptin A hormone secreted by adipose tissue; decreases food intake and increases metabolic rate, primarily by inhibiting NPY-secreting neurons in the arcuate nucleus.

decerebration A surgical procedure that severs the brain stem, disconnecting the hindbrain from the forebrain.

THOUGHT QUESTION

The drive-reduction hypothesis of motivation and reinforcement says that drives are aversive and satiety is pleasurable. Clearly, *satisfying* hunger is pleasurable, but what about *satiety?* Which do you prefer, eating a meal while you are hungry or feeling full afterward?

Brain Mechanisms

Although hunger and satiety signals originate in the digestive system and in the body's nutrient reservoirs, the target of these signals is the brain. This section looks at some of the research on brain mechanisms of food intake and metabolism.

Brain Stem

Ingestive behaviors are phylogenetically ancient; obviously, all our ancestors ate and drank or died. Therefore, we should expect that the basic ingestive behaviors of chewing and swallowing are programmed by phylogenetically ancient brain circuits. Indeed, studies have shown that these behaviors can be performed by decerebrate rats, whose brains were transected between the diencephalon and the midbrain (Norgren and Grill, 1982; Grill and Kaplan, 1990). **Decerebration** disconnects the motor neurons of the brain stem and spinal cord from the neural circuits of the cerebral hemispheres (such as the cerebral cortex and basal ganglia) that normally control them. The only behaviors that decerebrate animals can display are those that are directly controlled by neural circuits located within the brain stem. (See ***Figure 11.15.***)

Decerebrate rats cannot approach and eat food; the experimenters must place food, in liquid form, into their mouths. Decerebrate rats can distinguish between different tastes; they drink and swallow sweet or slightly salty liquids and spit out bitter ones. They even respond to hunger and satiety signals. They drink more sucrose after having been deprived of food for 24 hours, and they drink less of it if some sucrose is first injected directly into their

Figure 11.15

Decerebration. The operation disconnects the forebrain from the hindbrain so that the muscles involved in ingestive behavior are controlled solely by hindbrain mechanisms.

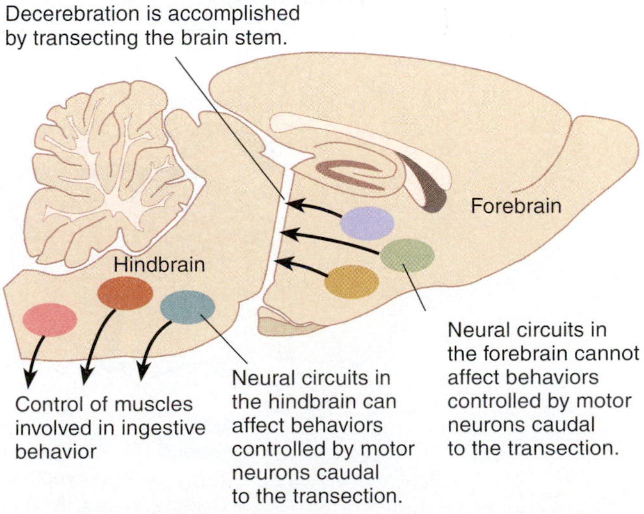
Decerebration is accomplished by transecting the brain stem.
Forebrain
Hindbrain
Control of muscles involved in ingestive behavior
Neural circuits in the hindbrain can affect behaviors controlled by motor neurons caudal to the transection.
Neural circuits in the forebrain cannot affect behaviors controlled by motor neurons caudal to the transection.

stomachs. These studies indicate that the brain stem contains neural circuits that can control at least some aspects of food intake.

melanin-concentrating hormone (MCH) A peptide neurotransmitter found in a system of lateral hypothalamic neurons that stimulate appetite and reduce metabolic rate.

orexin A peptide neurotransmitter found in a system of lateral hypothalamic neurons that stimulate appetite and reduce metabolic rate.

neuropeptide Y (NPY) A peptide neurotransmitter found in a system of neurons of the arcuate nucleus that stimulate feeding, insulin secretion, and glucocorticoid secretion; decrease the breakdown of triglycerides; and decrease body temperature.

Hypothalamus

Discoveries made in the 1940s and 1950s focused the attention of researchers interested in ingestive behavior on two regions of the hypothalamus: the lateral area and the ventromedial area. For many years investigators believed that these two regions controlled hunger and satiety, respectively; one was the accelerator, and the other was the brake. The basic findings were these: After the lateral hypothalamus was destroyed, animals stopped eating or drinking (Anand and Brobeck, 1951; Teitelbaum and Stellar, 1954). Electrical stimulation of the same region would produce eating, drinking, or both behaviors. Conversely, lesions of the ventromedial hypothalamus produced overeating that led to gross obesity, whereas electrical stimulation suppressed eating (Hetherington and Ranson, 1942). (See ***Figure 11.16.***)

Role in Hunger

Research in the latter half of the twentieth century has shown that the lateral hypothalamus does indeed play a role in eating. Neurotoxic lesions of the lateral hypothalamus made with ibotenic acid, which kills cells while sparing axons passing

Figure 11.16

Cross sections through the rat brain, showing the location of regions of the hypothalamus that play a role in the control of eating and metabolism.

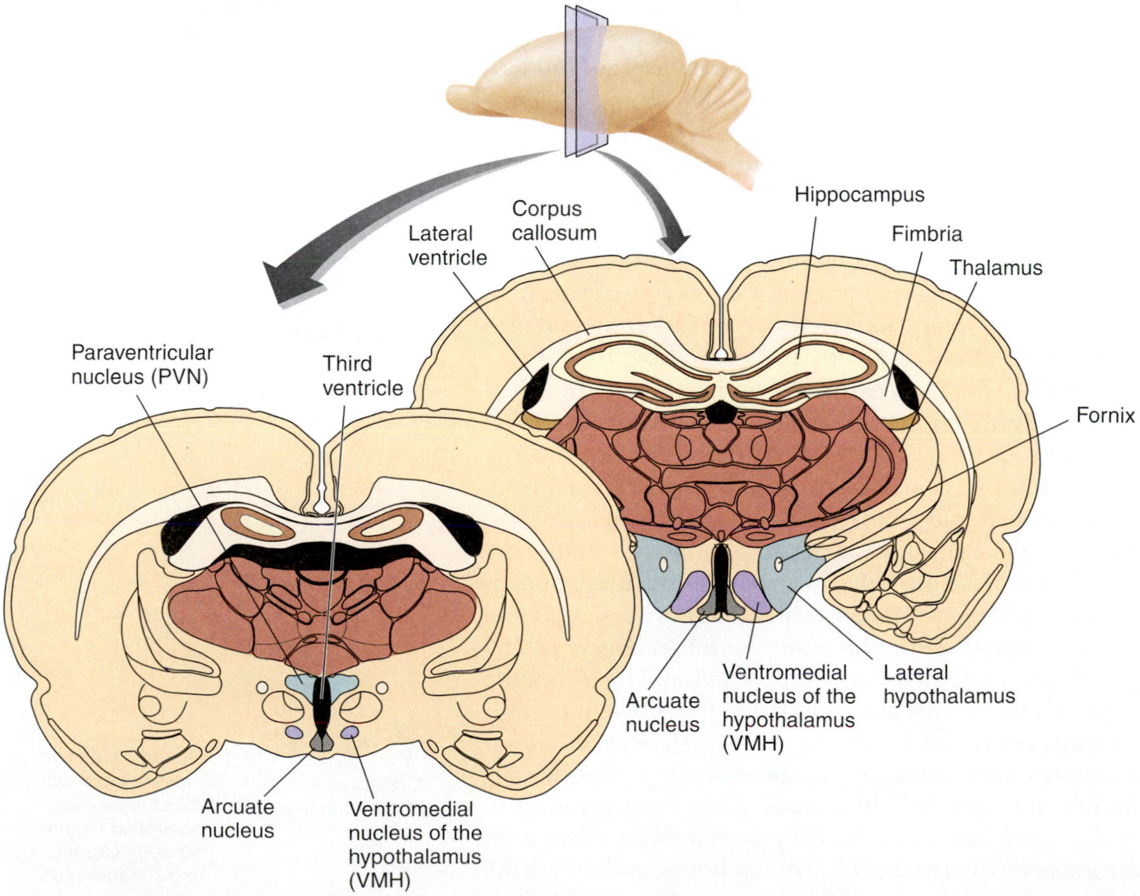

Adapted from Swanson, L. W. *Brain Maps: Structure of the Rat Brain.* New York: Elsevier, 1992.

through the region, produce a long-lasting decrease in food intake and body weight (Stricker, Swerdloff, and Zigmond, 1978; Dunnett, Lane, and Winn, 1985). In addition, stimulation of the lateral hypothalamus with direct injections of excitatory amino acids produces eating (Stanley et al., 1993a; Duva et al., 2001), and injections of a glutamate antagonist in this region decrease food intake (Stanley et al., 1996). (See ***Figure 11.17.***)

We now know that these injections activate two populations of neurons located in the lateral hypothalamus that stimulate hunger and decrease metabolic rate, thus preserving the body's energy stores. The neurons secrete two different peptide neurotransmitters: **melanin-concentrating hormone (MCH)** and **orexin.**

Melanin-concentrating hormone received its name from its role in regulating changes in skin pigmentation in fish and other nonmammalian vertebrates (Kawauchi et al., 1983). In mammals it serves as a neurotransmitter. Orexin (from the Greek word *orexis,* "appetite") was discovered by Sakurai et al. (1998). This peptide is also known as *hypocretin*—particularly by researchers studying sleep. As we saw in Chapter 8, degeneration of neurons that secrete hypocretin is responsible for narcolepsy. Of these two hypothalamic peptides, MCH appears to play the more important role.

Injections of either MCH or orexin into the lateral ventricles or various regions of the brain induce eating. If rats are deprived of food, messenger RNA levels for MCH and orexin in the lateral hypothalamus increase (Qu et al., 1996; Sakurai et al., 1998; Dube, Kalra, and Kalra, 1999). In addition, mice with a targeted mutation against the MCH gene eat less than normal mice and are consequently underweight (Shimada et al., 1998). Researchers refer to these peptides as *orexigens,* "appetite-inducing chemicals."

The axons of MCH and orexin neurons travel to a variety of brain structures that are known to be involved in motivation and movement, including the neocortex, periaqueductal gray matter, reticular formation, thalamus, and locus coeruleus. These neurons also have connections with neurons in the spinal cord that control the autonomic nervous system, which explains how they can affect the body's metabolic rate (Sawchenko, 1998; Nambu et al., 1999). These connections are shown in ***Figure 11.18.***

As we saw earlier, metabolic hunger signals caused by glucoprivation or lipoprivation arise from detectors in the liver and medulla. How do these signals activate the MCH and orexin neurons of the lateral hypothalamus? Part of the pathway involves a system of neurons that secrete a neurotransmitter called **neuropeptide Y (NPY)**, an extremely potent stimulator of food intake (Clark et al., 1984). Infusion of NPY into the hypothalamus produces ravenous, almost frantic eating. Rats who receive an infusion of this peptide will work very hard, pressing a lever many times for each morsel of food; they will eat food made bitter with quinine; and they will continue to drink

Figure 11.17

Body weight of rats that received twice-daily injections of a glutamate antagonist into the lateral hypothalamus.

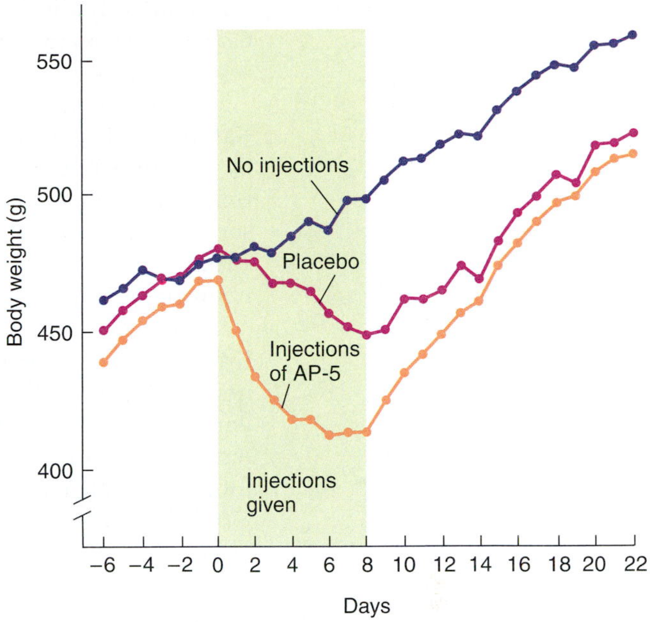

Adapted from Stanley, B. G., Willett, V. L., Donias, H. W., Dee, M. G., and Duva, M. A. *American Journal of Physiology: Regulatory, Integrative and Comparative Physiology,* 1996, *270,* R443–R449.

Figure 11.18

Connections of the MCH neurons and orexin neurons of the lateral hypothalamus.

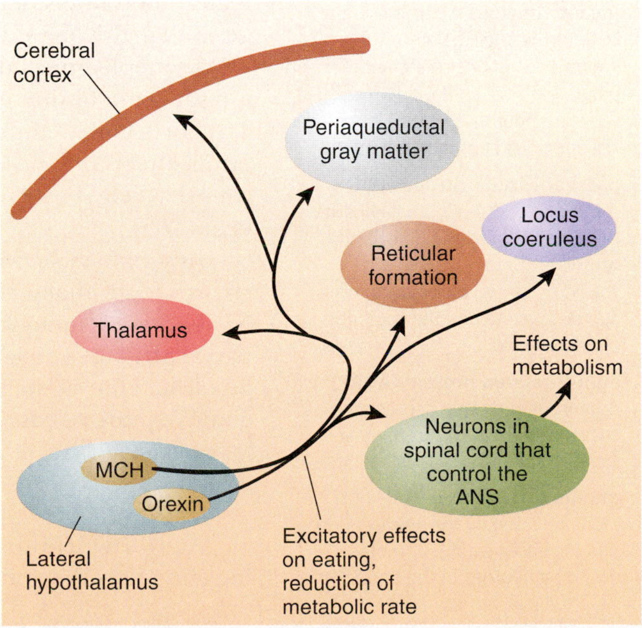

milk even when doing so means that they receive an electric shock to their tongue (Flood and Morley, 1991; Jewett et al., 1992).

Infusions of NPY also produce metabolic effects, including insulin and glucocorticoid secretion, decreased breakdown of triglycerides in adipose tissue, and a decrease in body temperature (Wahlestedt et al., 1987; Abe, Saito, and Shimazu, 1989; Currie and Coscina, 1996). These effects complement the increased appetite by preserving the body's energy supplies.

Levels of neuropeptide Y are affected by hunger and satiety signals; Sahu, Kalra, and Kalra (1988) found that hypothalamic levels of NPY are increased by food deprivation and lowered by eating. In addition, Myers et al. (1995) found that hypothalamic injections of a drug that blocks neuropeptide Y receptors suppress eating caused by food deprivation. This last finding, in particular, provides strong evidence that normal food intake is at least partially stimulated by neuropeptide Y.

The neurons that secrete NPY are found in the **arcuate nucleus,** located in the hypothalamus at the base of the third ventricle. The arcuate nucleus also contains neurosecretory cells whose hormones control the secretions of the anterior pituitary gland. (Refer to ***Figure 11.16.***) The NPY neurons send a dense projection of axons to the **paraventricular nucleus (PVN)**—a region of the hypothalamus where infusions of NPY affect metabolic functions (Bai et al., 1985). They also send a projection directly to MCH and orexin neurons in the lateral hypothalamus (Broberger et al., 1998; Elias et al., 1998a), which appears to be responsible for the feeding elicited by activation of NPY neurons.

The terminals of NPY neurons release another orexigenic peptide in addition to neuropeptide Y: **agouti-related peptide,** otherwise known as **AGRP** (Hahn et al., 1998). AGRP is a potent and extremely long-lasting orexigen. Infusion of a very small amount of this peptide into the third ventricle of rats produced an increase in food intake that lasted for six days (Lu et al., 2001).

Recently, researchers discovered that the gastrointestinal system (especially the stomach) releases a peptide hormone called **ghrelin** (Kojima et al., 1999). The name *ghrelin* is a contraction of *GH releasin,* which reflects the fact that this peptide is involved in controlling the release of growth hormone, usually abbreviated as *GH.* Although the physiological signal that triggers ghrelin release by the stomach is not yet known, researchers have discovered that blood levels of this peptide increase with fasting and are reduced after a meal. Cummings et al. (2001) discovered that in humans blood levels of ghrelin increase shortly before each meal, a finding that suggests that this peptide may be involved in the initiation of a meal. In addition, subcutaneous injections or infusions of ghrelin into the cerebral ventricles cause weight gain by increasing food intake and decreasing the metabolism of fats (Tschöp, Smiley, and Heiman, 2000; Nakazato et al., 2001). Ghrelin appears to exert its effects on appetite and metabolism by stimulating receptors located on neurons that release NPY and AGRP (Willesen, Kristensen, and Romer, 1999; Nakazato et al., 2001).

In summary, activity of MCH and orexin neurons of the lateral hypothalamus increases food intake and decreases metabolic rate. These neurons are activated by NPY-secreting neurons of the arcuate nucleus. The NPY neurons also project to the paraventricular nucleus, which plays a role in control of insulin secretion and metabolism. One of the signals that activates NPY/AGRP neurons is ghrelin, an orexigenic peptide released by the stomach. (See ***Figure 11.19.***)

arcuate nucleus A nucleus in the base of the hypothalamus that controls secretions of the anterior pituitary gland; contains NPY-secreting neurons involved in feeding and control of metabolism.

paraventricular nucleus (PVN) A nucleus of the hypothalamus located adjacent to the dorsal third ventricle; contains neurons involved in control of the autonomic nervous system and the posterior pituitary gland.

agouti-related protein (AGRP) A neuropeptide that acts as an antagonist at MC-4 receptors and increases eating.

ghrelin (***grell*** *in*) A peptide hormone released by the stomach that increases eating; also produced by neurons in the brain.

Role in Satiety

As we saw, leptin, a hormone secreted by well-fed adipose tissue, suppresses eating and raises the animal's metabolic rate. The interactions of this long-term satiety signal with neural circuits involved in hunger are now being discovered. Leptin produces its behavioral and metabolic effects by binding with receptors in the brain—in particular, on neurons that secrete the orexigenic peptides NPY and AGRP (Hakansson et al., 1996; Mercer et al., 1996).

Glaum et al. (1996) found that activation of leptin receptors on NPY-secreting neurons in the arcuate nucleus has an inhibitory effect on these neurons. As a consequence, leptin reduces the amount of the NPY and AGRP released in the hypothalamus (Wang et al., 1997; Li et al., 2000). Thus, leptin inhibits the release of the orexigens produced in the hypothalamus.

The arcuate nucleus contains two other systems of peptide-secreting neurons, both of which serve as *anorexigens* "appetite-suppressing chemicals." Douglass, McKinzie, and Couceyro (1995) discovered a peptide that is now called **CART** (for *cocaine- and amphetamine-regulated transcript*). When cocaine or amphetamine is administered to an animal, levels of this peptide increase, which might have something to do with the fact that these drugs suppress appetite. CART neurons appear to play an important role in satiety. If animals are deprived of food, levels of CART decrease. CART is almost totally absent in ob mice, which lack leptin, but injections of leptin in their cerebral ventricles will stimulate the production of CART. Injections of CART into their cerebral ventricles inhibit feeding, including the feeding stimulated by NPY. Finally, infusion of a CART antibody increases feeding (Kristensen et al., 1998).

CART neurons are located in the arcuate nucleus and send their axons to a variety of locations, including several other hypothalamic nuclei, the periaqueductal gray matter, and regions of the spinal cord that control the autonomic nervous system (Koylu et al., 1998). In the context of the present topic the most important connections are probably those with the paraventricular nucleus and those with the MCH and orexin neurons of the lateral hypothalamus. Activity of CART neurons increases metabolic rate through its connections with the paraventricular nucleus, and it appears to inhibit MCH and orexin neurons, thus suppressing eating. CART neurons contain leptin receptors that have an *excitatory* effect; thus, CART-secreting neurons appear to be responsible for at least part of the satiating effect of leptin (Elias et al., 1998b).

A second anorexigen, **α-melanocyte-stimulating hormone (α-MSH),** is also released by CART neurons. This peptide is an agonist of the **melanocortin-4 receptor (MC4-R)**; it binds with the receptor and inhibits feeding. You will recall that NPY neurons also release AGRP, which stimulates eating. Both α-MSH and AGRP bind with the MC4-R. However, whereas α-MSH binds with the MC4 receptor and inhibits eating, AGRP binds with the receptor and *causes* feeding (as we saw in the previous subsection). CART/α-MSH neurons are activated by leptin and NPY/AGRP neurons are inhibited by leptin. (See Elmquist, Elias, and Saper, 1999, for specific references.) So leptin stimulates the production of the anorexigens CART and α-MSH and inhibits the production of the orexigens NPY and AGRP.

Figure 11.19

Connections of the NPY neurons of the arcuate nucleus.

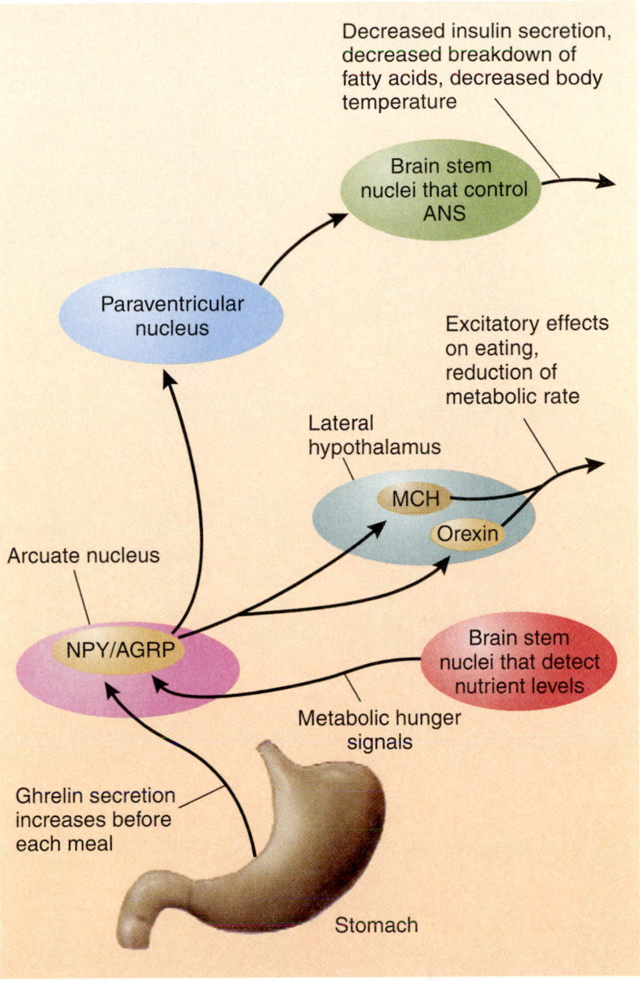

CART Cocaine- and amphetamine-regulated transcript; a peptide neurotransmitter found in a system of neurons of the arcuate nucleus that inhibit feeding.

α-melanocyte-stimulating hormone (α-MSH) A neuropeptide that acts as an agonist at MC-4 receptors and inhibits eating.

melanocortin-4 receptor (MC-4R) A receptor found in the brain that binds with α-MSH and agouti-related protein; plays a role in control of appetite.

Figure 11.20

Connections of CART neurons of the arcuate nucleus and effects of leptin on hypothalamic neurons involved in control of hunger, satiety, and metabolic rate.

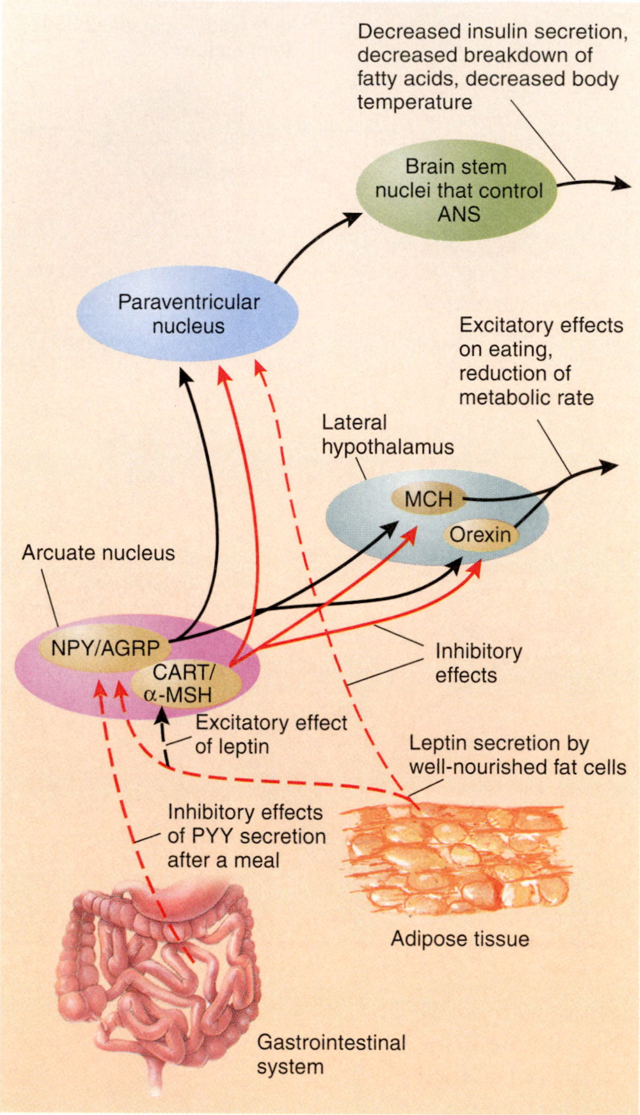

Earlier in this chapter, I mentioned an anorexigenic peptide, PYY, which is produced by cells in the gastrointestinal tract in amounts proportional to the calories that were just ingested. PYY binds with the Y2 receptor, an inhibitory autoreceptor found on NPY neurons in the arcuate nucleus of the hypothalamus. When PYY binds with the Y2 receptor, it suppresses the release of the orexigens NPY and AGRP. As we saw earlier, a single injection of PYY suppresses eating for up to 12 hours in both humans and rats (Batterham et al., 2002). In addition, mice with a targeted mutation against the Y2 receptor do not respond to injections of PYY. This evidence strongly suggests that PYY is a short-term (or perhaps medium-term) satiety signal. I am sure that several laboratories, including those supported by drug companies, are actively studying this peptide.

In summary, leptin appears to exert at least some of its satiating effects by stimulating receptors on neurons in the arcuate nucleus. Leptin inhibits NPY/AGRP neurons, which suppresses the feeding that these peptides stimulate and prevents the decrease in metabolic rate. Leptin activates CART/α-MSH neurons, which inhibit MCH and orexin neurons in the lateral hypothalamus and prevent their stimulatory effect on appetite. PYY, released by the gastrointestinal tract just after a meal, inhibits NPY/AGRP neurons. (See ***Figure 11.20.***)

Another neurotransmitter appears to play a role in satiety. Infusions of serotonin (5-HT) into various parts of the brain, including the PVN and ventromedial hypothalamus, suppress eating (Leibowitz, Weiss, and Suh, 1990). In addition, administration of serotonin agonists suppress eating (Blundell and Halford, 1998). In fact, such drugs have been used to treat people with obesity. In contrast, drugs that destroy serotonergic neurons, inhibit the synthesis of 5-HT, or block 5-HT receptors have an effect opposite that of 5-HT: They *increase* food intake, especially carbohydrates (Breisch, Zemlan, and Hoebel, 1976; Saller and Stricker, 1976; Stallone and Nicolaïdis, 1989). Dryden et al. (1995) found that an IP injection of methysergide, a 5-HT antagonist, increased the secretion of NPY in the hypothalamus and (as you might expect) increased food intake. This finding suggests that serotonergic neurons somehow inhibit the activity of NPY neurons. In addition, mice with a targeted mutation against the 5-HT_{2C} receptor eat more food and develop obesity in middle age (Nonogaki et al., 1998).

The neural circuits that are responsible for the suppressive effect of 5-HT on feeding are not yet understood. Although, as we saw, infusions of serotonin or serotonin agonists into the PVN suppress eating, Fletcher et al. (1993) found that IP injections of fenfluramine, a potent serotonin agonist, still decreased food intake after the PVN had been destroyed. Brain stem circuits may be involved in these effects; Li and Rowland (1995) found that injections of fenfluramine increased Fos production in neurons in the AP/NST and parabrachial nucleus, and Li, Spector, and Rowland (1994) found that the appetite-suppressing effect of the drug was reduced after destruction of the lateral parabrachial nucleus, which connects the AP/NST with the hypothalamus.

INTERIM SUMMARY

Brain Mechanisms

The brain stem contains neural circuits that are able to control acceptance or rejection of sweet or bitter foods and can even be modulated by satiation or physiological hunger signals, such as a decrease in glucose metabolism or the presence of food in the digestive system.

Stimulation of the lateral hypothalamus with electricity or excitatory amino acids produces eating, while lesions or infusion of glutamate antagonists decreases eating. The lateral hypothalamus contains two sets of neurons whose activity increases eating and decreases metabolic rate. These neurons secrete the peptides orexin and MCH (melanin-concentrating hormone). Food deprivation increases the level of these peptides, and mice with a targeted mutation against MCH undereat. The axons of these neurons project to regions of the brain involved in motivation, movement, and metabolism.

The release of neuropeptide Y in the lateral hypothalamus induces ravenous eating, an effect that appears to be produced by the connection of NPY-secreting neurons with the orexin and MCH neurons. When NPY is infused in the paraventricular nucleus, it decreases metabolic rate. Levels of NPY increase when an animal is deprived of food and fall again when the animal eats. A drug that blocks NPY receptors suppresses eating. NPY neurons also release a peptide called AGRP. This peptide serves as an antagonist at MC4 receptors and stimulates eating.

Leptin, the long-term satiety hormone secreted by well-stocked adipose tissue, desensitizes the brain to hunger signals. It binds with receptors in the arcuate nucleus of the hypothalamus, where it inhibits NPY/AGRP-secreting neurons, increasing metabolic rate and suppressing eating. The arcuate nucleus also contains neurons that secrete CART (cocaine- and amphetamine-regulated transcript), a peptide that suppresses eating. These neurons, which are *activated* by leptin, have inhibitory connections with MCH and orexin neurons in the lateral hypothalamus. CART neurons also secrete a peptide called α-MSH, which serves as an agonist at MC4 receptors and inhibits eating.

A monoaminergic transmitter substance, 5-HT, has an inhibitory effect on eating in the PVN. Serotonin agonists have been used to treat obesity in humans. The site of action of such drugs may be in the brain stem as well as in the hypothalamus.

Eating Disorders

Unfortunately, some people are susceptible to the development of eating disorders. Some people grow obese, even though our society regards this condition as unattractive and even though obese people generally have more health problems than people of normal weight and tend to die sooner. Other people (especially young women) can become obsessed with losing weight, eating little and increasing their activity level until their body weight becomes extremely low—sometimes fatally so. Others manage to keep from losing or gaining weight but often lose control of intake, eating enormous amounts of food and then taking strong laxatives or forcing themselves to vomit. Has what we have learned about the physiology of appetite helped us to understand these conditions?

Obesity

Obesity is a widespread problem that can have serious medical consequences. In the United States approximately 63 percent of men and 55 percent of women are overweight, defined as a body mass index (BMI) of over 25. The incidence of obesity, defined as a BMI of over 30, has increased by 50 percent in the past 20 years and stood at approximately 18 percent in 1998. In addition, the number of overweight children has doubled (Must et al., 1999; Yanovski and Yanovski, 1999; Hirsch, 2002). The known health hazards of obesity include cardiovascular disease, diabetes, strokes, arthritis, and some forms of cancer.

Obesity undoubtedly has many causes, including learning and innate or acquired differences in metabolism. The behavior of eating, like most other behaviors, is subject to modification through learning. Unfortunately, many aspects of modern, industrialized societies tend to weaken physiological controls over eating. For example, as children we learn to eat what is put on our plates; indeed, many children are praised for eating all they have been given and punished for failing to do so. As Birch et al. (1987) showed, the effect of this kind of training can be to make children less sensitive to the nutrient content of their diet. As we get older, our metabolic requirements decrease; and if we continue to eat as we did when we were younger, we tend to accumulate fat. The inhibitory signals associated with food consumption are certainly not absolute; they can be overridden by habit or by the simple pleasure of ingesting good-tasting food.

As we will see, genetic differences—and their effects on development of the brain and organs involved in metabolism—appear to be responsible for the overwhelming proportion of people with extreme obesity. But as we saw, the problem of obesity has been growing over recent years. Clearly, changes in the gene pool cannot account for this increase; instead, we must look to environmental causes that have produced changes in people's behavior.

Body weight is the result of the difference between two factors: calories consumed and energy expended. If we consume more calories than we expend as heat and work, we gain weight. If we expend more than we consume, we lose weight. In modern industrialized societies inexpensive, convenient, good-tasting, high-fat food is readily available, which promotes an increase in intake. Fast-food restaurants are close at hand, parking is convenient (or even unnecessary at restaurants with drive-up windows), and the size of the portions they serve has increased in recent years. People have begun to eat out more often, and most often they do so at inexpensive fast-food restaurants.

Of course, fast-food restaurants are not the only environmental factor responsible for the increased incidence of obesity. Snack foods are available in convenience stores and vending machines, and even school cafeterias make high-calorie, high-fat foods and sweetened beverages available to their young students. In fact, school administrators often welcome the installation of vending machines because of the income they provide. In addition, changes in the workplace affect people's expenditure of energy. The proportion of people employed in jobs that require a high level of physical activity has decreased considerably, which means that on the average we need less food than we did previously.

One reason that many people have so much difficulty losing weight is that metabolic factors appear to play an important role in obesity. In fact, most cases of extreme obesity are caused not by *eating disorders* (despite the title of this section) but rather by *metabolic disorders.*

Just as cars differ in their fuel efficiency, so do living organisms, and hereditary factors can affect the level of efficiency. For example, farmers have bred cattle, pigs, and chickens for their efficiency in converting feed into muscle tissue, and researchers have done the same with rats (Pomp and Nielsen, 1999). People differ in this form of efficiency too. Those with an efficient metabolism have calories left over to deposit in the long-term nutrient reservoir; thus, they have difficulty keeping this reservoir from growing. Researchers have referred to this condition as a "thrifty phenotype." In contrast, people with an inefficient metabolism (a "spendthrift phenotype") can eat large meals without getting fat. A fuel-efficient automobile is desirable, but a fuel-efficient body runs the risk of becoming obese—at least in an environment where food is cheap and plentiful.

Differences in body weight (perhaps reflecting physiological differences in metabolism or appetite) appear to have a hereditary basis. Twin studies suggest that between 40 percent and 85 percent of the variability in body fat is due to genetic differences (Price and Gottesman, 1991; Allison et al., 1996; Comuzzie and Allison, 1998). And the family environment in which people are raised apparently has no significant effect on their body weight as adults; Stunkard et al. (1986) found that the body weight of a sample of people who had been adopted as infants was highly correlated with their *biological* parents but not with their *adoptive* parents. Sørensen et al. (1989) came to similar conclusions in a study comparing adopted people with their full and half siblings with whom they had not been raised.

Why are there genetic differences in metabolic efficiency? Ravussin et al. (1994) studied two groups of Pima Indians, who live in the southwestern United States and northwestern Mexico. Members of the two groups appear to have the same genetic background; they speak the same language and have common historical traditions. The two groups separated 700–1000 years ago and now live under very different environmental conditions. The Pima Indians in the southwestern United States eat a high-fat American-style diet and weigh an average of 90 kg (198 lb), men and women combined. In contrast, the lifestyle of the Mexican Pimas is probably similar to that of their ancestors. They spend long hours working at subsistence farming and eat a low-fat diet—and weigh an average of 64 kg (141 lb). The cholesterol level of the American Pimas is much higher than that of the Mexican Pimas, and the American Pimas' rate of diabetes is more than five times higher. These findings show that genes that promote an efficient metabolism are of benefit to people who must work hard for their calories but that these same genes turn into a liability when people live in an environment where the physical demands are low and high-calorie food is cheap and plentiful. Genetic differences in people's metabolic rates may reflect the nature of the environment experienced by their ancestors.

As we saw earlier, study of the ob mouse led to the discovery of leptin, the hormone secreted by well-nourished adipose tissue. The explanation of obesity in the ob mouse was simple: The animals could not produce leptin. Following this discovery, researchers have been trying to determine whether understanding the role of leptin can help us understand at least some of the causes of obesity in humans.

So far, researchers have found several cases of familial obesity caused by the absence of leptin produced by the mutation of the gene responsible for its production (Montague et al., 1997; Strobel et al., 1998; Ozata, Ozdemir, and Licinio, 1999), and more will undoubtedly be discovered. Farooqi et al. (2001) found three unrelated families with mutations that caused slightly lower levels of leptin to be produced. These mutations, too, caused obesity. However, such mutations are rare, so they do not explain the vast majority of cases of obesity. Schwartz et al. (1996) found that plasma levels of leptin were related to total body fat in both lean and obese people. Therefore, most investigators believe that if leptin plays a role in human obesity, the likely mechanism is reduced *sensitivity* to the hormone and not decreased secretion.

How could people differ in sensitivity to leptin? One possible mechanism could be a mutation of the gene responsible for production of the leptin receptor. In fact, three strains of obese rodents—the *db mouse,* the *corpulent rat,* and the *Zucker rat*—all have mutations of the leptin receptor gene (Gura, 1997). But familial obesity in humans caused by a defective leptin receptor gene appears to be a very rare event (Clément et al., 1998).

Figure 11.21

Percent change in plasma leptin concentration in response to high-fat or low-fat meals of equal caloric value.

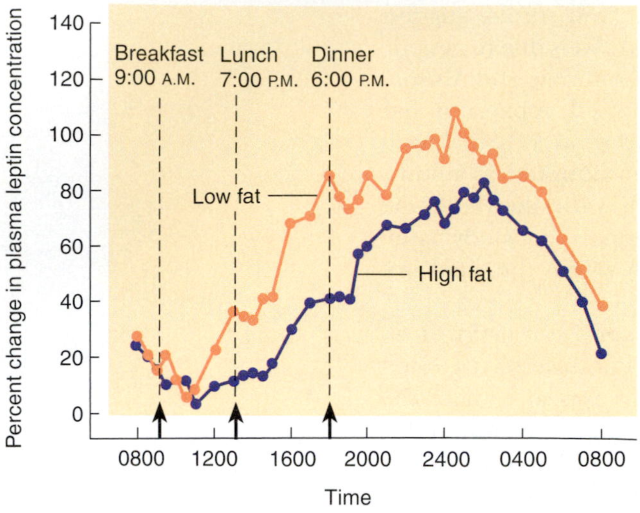

Adapted from Havel, P. J., Townsend, R., Chaump, L., and Teff, K. *Diabetes,* 1999, *48,* 334–341.

Leptin is a peptide, and peptides normally cannot cross the blood–brain barrier. However, an active mechanism transports molecules of leptin across this barrier so that it can exert its behavioral and metabolic effects (Banks et al., 1996; Golden, MacCagnan, and Pardridge, 1997). Caro et al. (1996) suggested that differences in the effectiveness of this transport system may be one cause of obesity. If not much leptin gets across the blood–brain barrier, the leptin signal in the brain will be weaker than it should be. Caro and his colleagues found that although the level of leptin in the blood was 318 percent higher in obese people, it was only 30 percent higher in the cerebrospinal fluid (which is presumably related to the concentration of the hormone in the brain). Thus, differences in sensitivity to leptin could be caused by differences in the transport of leptin molecules into the brain.

Evidence suggests that sensitivity to leptin can be affected by environmental factors. As you undoubtedly know, a high-fat diet encourages weight gain. This effect is partly caused by the fact that a gram of fat contains approximately nine calories, whereas a gram of carbohydrate or protein contain approximately five calories. But there appear to be other reasons as well. In a study with humans, Havel et al. (1999) found that high-fat meals produce less of an increase in plasma leptin levels than do low-fat meals equated for caloric content. This finding suggests that a high-fat diet decreases the strength of the primary long-term satiety factor. (See ***Figure 11.21.***)

As you have undoubtedly noticed, many people gain weight as they grow o lder. There are undoubtedly several causes for this tendency, including a decrease in levels of physical activity. But some evidence suggests that there can be age-related changes in sensitivity to leptin. Scarpace, Matheny, and Tümer (2001) found that hypothalamic neurons in aged obese rats showed a smaller response to leptin than did those in rats of normal weight. They also observed a 50 percent reduction in the number of leptin receptors, which may account for this difference.

The final physiological factor that I will mention in this section is a chemical known as **uncoupling protein (UCP)**. This protein is found in mitochondria and may be one of the factors that determine the rate at which an animal burns off its calories. In other words, it may be a factor in metabolic efficiency. Uncoupling protein affects the membranes of mitochondria, so instead of producing molecules of ATP that can be used as a source of energy in the cell, the energy derived from metabolizing fuels is "wasted" as heat (Nicholls and Wenner, 1972).

Using methods of molecular genetics, Clapham et al. (2000) prepared a strain of mice that produced an abnormally high level of UCP3 (a particular form of uncoupling protein) in their skeletal muscles. These animals ate more than normal mice but were lean and had a much lower level of body fat. In addition, Schrauwen et al. (1999) found that levels of UCP3 in Pima Indians were negatively correlated with body mass index and positively correlated with metabolic rate. In other words, Pima Indians with low levels of UCP3 became obese, whereas those with high levels of UCP3 had "spendthrift" phenotypes that helped to protect them from developing obesity. You will not be surprised to learn that pharmaceutical companies are studying the role the UCP3 plays in the hopes of finding a way to decrease the thriftiness of people who find it hard not to gain weight.

uncoupling protein (UCP) A mitochondrial protein that facilitates the conversion of nutrients into heat.

Anorexia Nervosa/Bulimia Nervosa

Most people, if they have an eating problem, tend to overeat. However, some people, especially adolescent women, have the opposite problem: They eat too little, even to the point of starvation. This disorder is called **anorexia nervosa.** Another eating disorder, **bulimia nervosa,** is characterized by a loss of control of food intake. (The term *bulimia* comes from the Greek *bous,* "ox," and *limos,* "hunger.") People with bulimia nervosa periodically gorge themselves with food, especially dessert or snack food and especially in the afternoon or evening. These binges are usually followed by self-induced vomiting or the use of laxatives, along with feelings of depression and guilt (Mawson, 1974; Halmi, 1978). With this combination of binging and purging, the net nutrient intake (and consequently, the body weight) of bulimics can vary; Weltzin et al. (1991) reported that 19 percent of bulimics undereat, 37 percent eat a normal amount, and 44 percent overeat. Episodes of bulimia are seen in some patients with anorexia nervosa. Bulimia nervosa is more common than anorexia nervosa, and its incidence seems to be increasing (Walsh and Devlin, 1998).

Figure 11.22

Effects of the sight and smell of a warm cinnamon roll on insulin secretion in anorexic women and thin, nonanorexic women.

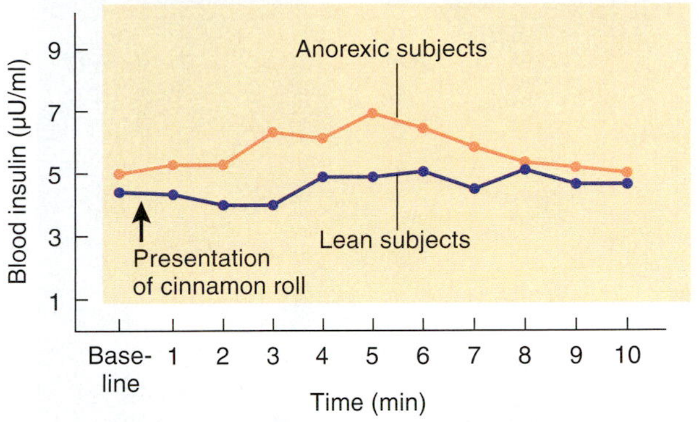

Adapted from Broberg, D. J., and Bernstein, I. L. *Physiology and Behavior,* 1989, *45,* 871–874.

The literal meaning of the word *anorexia* suggests a loss of appetite, but people with this disorder are usually interested in—even preoccupied with—food. They may enjoy preparing meals for others to consume, collect recipes, and even hoard food that they do not eat. Broberg and Bernstein (1989) presented anorexic and lean (but nonanorexic) young women with a warm, appetizing cinnamon roll. They cut the roll and said that the women could eat it if they wanted. For the next 10 minutes the experimenters withdrew blood samples and analyzed the insulin content. They found that both groups of subjects showed an increase in insulin level; surprisingly, the increase was even higher in the anorexic subjects. Thus, we cannot conclude that anorexics are simply unresponsive to food. (See ***Figure 11.22.***) Incidentally, as you might expect, the normal subjects ate the roll, but the anorexics did not, saying that they were not hungry.

Although anorexics might not be oblivious to the effects of food, they express an intense fear of becoming obese, which continues even if they become dangerously thin. Many exercise by cycling, running, or almost constant walking and pacing. Studies with animals suggest that the increased activity may be a result of the fasting. When rats are deprived of food, they will spend more and more time running in a wheel if one is available, even though doing so means that the animals will lose weight faster (Routtenberg, 1968). Some investigators believe that the exercise stimulates the breakdown of lipids into fatty acids and glycerol and thus actually reduces feelings of hunger. Wilckens, Schweiger, and Pirke (1992) found that deprivation-induced wheel running can be inhibited by drugs that stimulate 5-HT_{1C} receptors.

The fact that anorexia nervosa is seen primarily in young women has prompted both biological and social explanations. Most psychologists favor the latter, concluding that the emphasis our society places on slimness—especially in women—is responsible for this disorder. However, the success rate of therapy is not especially encouraging; Ratnasuriya et al. (1991) reported that twenty years later, only 29 percent of a group of patients treated for anorexia nervosa showed a good recovery. Almost 15 percent of the patients had died of suicide or complications of the disease. Many anorexics suffer from osteoporosis, and bone fractures are common.

anorexia nervosa A disorder that most frequently afflicts young women; exaggerated concern with overweight that leads to excessive dieting and often compulsive exercising; can lead to starvation.

bulimia nervosa Bouts of excessive hunger and eating, often followed by forced vomiting or purging with laxatives; sometimes seen in people with anorexia nervosa.

Anorexia nervosa most often occurs in young women. An especially high incidence of this eating disorder is seen in ballet dancers, who must be both athletic and thin.

When the weight loss becomes severe enough, the anorexics cease menstruating. Some disturbing reports (Artmann et al., 1985; Herholz, 1996; Kingston et al., 1996) indicate that CT scans revealed enlarged ventricles and widened sulci, which indicates shrinkage of brain tissue. The widened sulci, but not the enlarged ventricles, apparently return to normal after recovery.

There is good evidence, primarily from twin studies, that hereditary factors play an important role in the development of anorexia (Russell and Treasure, 1989; Walters and Kendler, 1995; Kortegaard et al., 2001). The existence of hereditary factors suggests that abnormalities in physiological mechanisms may be involved. As you might suspect, many investigators have suggested that anorexia and bulimia may be caused by biochemical or structural abnormalities in the brain mechanisms that control metabolism or eating. In a review of the literature Fava et al. (1989) reported that studies have found evidence for changes in NE, 5-HT, and opioids in people with anorexia nervosa and changes in NE and 5-HT in people with bulimia nervosa. Many studies have reported changes in endocrine levels of anorexic patients, but these changes are probably effects of the disorder, not causes. In most cases when a patient recovers, the endocrine system returns to normal.

Some investigators have suggested that neuropeptide Y may play a role in anorexia (Kaye et al., 1990; Kaye, 1996). Kaye and his colleagues found elevated levels of NPY in the cerebrospinal fluid of severely underweight anorexics. However, once the patients regained their normal weights, the levels of the peptide returned to normal. The investigators suggested that the increased level of NPY is a response to the loss of weight and at least partly accounts for the obsession with food that is typical in anorexia. In addition, the high level of NPY is probably responsible for the absence of menstruation in these patients. (You will recall that neuropeptide Y suppresses ovulation in laboratory animals.) CSF levels of leptin are, as one would expect, low in underweight anorexics. However, if the patients begin eating again, their leptin levels reach normal values even before their weight returns to normal, which may make it difficult for them to maintain their weight gain (Mantzoros et al., 1997).

We cannot rule out the possibility that some biochemical disturbance in brain functions related to metabolism or food intake underlie anorexia nervosa. Measurement of neurotransmitters, neuromodulators, and their metabolites in the cerebrospinal fluid is a crude and indirect indication of the release and activity of these substances in the brain. Unfortunately, we do not have a good animal model of anorexia to study in the laboratory.

Researchers have tried to treat anorexia nervosa with many drugs that increase appetite in nonanorexics or in laboratory animals—for example, antipsychotic medications, drugs that stimulate adrenergic α_2 receptors, L-DOPA, and THC (the active ingredient in marijuana). Unfortunately, none of these drugs have shown themselves to be helpful (Mitchell, 1989). One study (Halmi et al., 1986) found that cyproheptadine, an antihistaminergic drug that also has an antiserotonergic effect, may speed the recovery of anorexics. The drug aided only patients who did not exhibit bulimia; the drug actually interfered with the recovery of those who did exhibit bulimia. These results have not yet been confirmed by other investigators. In any event the fact that anorexics are usually obsessed with food (and show high levels of neuropeptide Y in their CSF) suggests that the disorder is not caused by the absence of hunger. Researchers have had better luck with bulimia nervosa; several studies suggest that serotonin agonists such as fluoxetine (an antidepressant drug that is best known as Prozac) may aid in the treatment of this disorder (Advokat and Kutlesic, 1995; Kaye et al., 2001). However, fluoxetine does not help anorexic patients (Attia et al., 1998).

Anorexia nervosa is a serious condition; understanding its causes is more than an academic matter. We can hope that research on the biological and social control of feeding and metabolism will help us to understand this puzzling and dangerous disorder.

INTERIM SUMMARY

Eating Disorders

Two sets of eating disorders—obesity and anorexia/bulimia nervosa—present serious health problems. Although the availability of cheap, tasty, high-calorie food in industrialized societies plays an important role in the increasing incidence of obesity, the most important cause of extreme obesity appears to be an efficient metabolism, which permits fat to accumulate easily. Metabolic rates are controlled by hereditary and environmental factors. Adoption studies find no evidence that a person's early family environment has a significant effect on his or her body weight in adulthood. But other environmental factors do play an important role in the development of obesity. A high percentage of Pima Indians who live in the United States and consume a high-fat diet become obese and, as a consequence, develop diabetes. In contrast, Mexican Pima Indians, who work hard at subsistence farming and eat a low-fat diet, remain thin and have a low incidence of obesity.

So far, there is little evidence that obesity in humans is related to a deficient secretion of leptin, as it is in ob mice; in general, obese people have very high levels of leptin in their blood. Nor is there good evidence that obese people have faulty leptin receptors, as do db mice, corpulent rats, and Zucker rats.

Anorexia nervosa is a serious—even life-threatening—disorder. Although anorexic patients avoid eating, they often remain preoccupied with food, and their insulin level rises when they are presented with an appetizing stimulus. Bulimia nervosa (sometimes associated with anorexia) consists of periodic binging and purging.

Researchers are beginning to study possible abnormalities in the regulation of transmitter substances and neuropeptides that seem to play a role in normal control of feeding to determine whether medical treatments for anorexia and bulimia can be discovered. So far, no useful drugs have been found to treat anorexia nervosa; but fluoxetine, a serotonin agonist used to treat depression, may help to suppress episodes of bulimia.

This section and the previous one introduced several neuropeptides and peripheral peptides that play a role in control of eating and metabolism. Table 11.1 summarizes information about these compounds. (See ***Table 11.1.***)

THOUGHT QUESTIONS

1. One of the last prejudices that people admit to publicly is a dislike of fat people. Is this fair, given that genetic differences in metabolism are such an important cause of obesity?
2. Undoubtedly, anorexia has both environmental and physiological causes. Do you think that sex differences in the incidence of this disorder (that is, the fact that almost all anorexics are female) is entirely caused by social factors (such as the emphasis on thinness in our society), or do you think that biological factors (such as hormonal differences) also play a role?

Table 11.1

Neuropeptides and Peripheral Peptides Involved in Control of Food Intake and Metabolism.

NEUROPEPTIDES

Name	Location of Cell Bodies	Location of Terminals	Interaction with Other Peptides	Physiological or Behavioral Effects
Melanin-concentrating hormone (MCH)	Lateral hypothalamus	Neocortex, periaqueductal gray matter, reticular formation, thalamus, locus coeruleus, neurons in spinal cord that control the sympathetic nervous system	Inhibited by leptin and CART/α-MSH; activated by NPY/AGRP	Eating, decreased metabolic rate
Orexin	Lateral hypothalamus	Similar to those of MCH neurons	Inhibited by leptin and CART/α-MSH; activated by NPY/AGRP	Eating, decreased metabolic rate
Neuropeptide Y (NPY)	Arcuate nucleus of hypothalamus	Paraventricular nucleus, MCH and orexin neurons of the perifornical region	Inhibited by leptin	Eating, decreased metabolic rate
Agouti-related peptide (AGRP)	Arcuate nucleus of hypothalamus (colocalized with NPY)	Same regions as NPY neurons	Inhibited by leptin	Eating, decreased metabolic rate; acts as antagonist at MC4 receptors
Cocaine- and amphetamine-regulated transcript (CART)	Arcuate nucleus of hypothalamus	Paraventricular nucleus, lateral hypothalamus, periaqueductal gray matter, neurons in spinal cord that control the sympathetic nervous system	Activated by leptin	Suppression of eating, increased metabolic rate
α-melanocyte stimulating hormone (α-MSH)	Arcuate nucleus of hypothalamus (colocalized with CART)	Same regions as CART neurons	Activated by leptin	Suppression of eating, increased metabolic rate; acts as agonist at MC4 receptors

PERIPHERAL PEPTIDES

Name	Where Produced	Site of Actions	Physiological or Behavioral Effects
Leptin	Fat tissue	Inhibits NPY/AGRP neurons; excites CART/α-MSH neurons	Suppression of eating, increased metabolic rate
Insulin	Pancreas	Similar to leptin	Similar to leptin
Ghrelin	Gastrointestinal system	Excites NPY/AGRP neurons	Eating
Cholecystokinin (CCK)	Duodenum	Neurons in pylorus	Suppression of eating
Peptide YY_{3-36} (PYY)	Gastrointestinal system	Inhibits NPY/AGRP neurons	Suppression of eating

EPILOGUE

Treatment of Obesity

As Emily and Jonathan, the students discussed in the chapter prologue, came to realize, some people become fat without eating enormous quantities of food. Heredity has given them efficient metabolisms that, in societies where food is plentiful, make weight gain easy and weight loss difficult. Of course, some fat people *do* eat enormous amounts of food; they may be addicted to eating the way some people are addicted to drugs.

Whatever the cause of obesity, the metabolic fact of life is this: If calories in exceed calories out, then body fat will increase. Because it is difficult to increase the "calories out" side of the equation enough to bring an obese person's weight back to normal, most treatments for obesity attempt to reduce the "calories in." The extraordinary difficulty that obese people have in reducing caloric intake for a sustained period of time (that is, for the rest of their lives) has led to the development of some extraordinary means. The rest of this discussion will describe mechanical and surgical methods that have been devised to make obese people eat less.

To eat, we must open our mouths. This obvious fact led to the development of jaw wiring, a procedure in which wires are attached to a person's teeth to keep the jaw from opening. The patient is not left to starve; he or she is given a liquid diet to sip through a straw. Of course, there is no guarantee that a person will ingest fewer calories each day simply because he or she is deprived of the opportunity to chew. In fact, Munro et al. (1987) reported that some of their patients managed to *gain* weight on a liquid diet. However, many patients do manage to lose weight. Unfortunately, almost all of them regain it once the wires are removed, and many become even more obese than they were when they started out.

To reduce the recidivism rate, some therapists have fastened a nylon cord around the waist of their patients after they had lost weight through a jaw-wiring procedure. The ends of the cord were fused together so that the cord could not be removed without cutting it. Unfortunately, about half of the patients did just that.

Surgeons have also become involved in trying to help obese people lose weight. The procedures they have developed either reduce the amount of food that can be eaten during a meal or interfere with absorption of calories from the intestines. Surgery has been aimed at the stomach, the small intestine, or both.

The most common surgical procedure for reducing food intake has been to make the person's stomach smaller. Early procedures actually removed some of the stomach, but more recent methods have stapled part of it shut or have put bands around it so that it can expand only a limited amount, a procedure known as *gastroplasty* (literally, "a reshaping of the stomach"). Ideally, gastroplasty should result in a feeling of satiety after the ingestion of a small amount of food. But in fact the surgery usually produces *nimiety,* or an aversive feeling of overfullness (from the Latin *nimius,* "excessive"). The meal stops not because the patients feel satisfied but because they feel so uncomfortable that they cannot go on.

Surgeons have developed several procedures that reduce the absorption of food from the intestines. All of these procedures rearrange the intestines so that food takes a shorter path to the large intestine, leaving less time for nutrients to be absorbed. The unabsorbed nutrients are evacuated from the body, of course, so it should come as no surprise that diarrhea and flatulence (excessive intestinal gas) are commonly associated with these procedure.

A less drastic form of therapy for obesity—exercise—has significant benefits. Exercise burns off calories, of course, but it also appears to have beneficial effects on metabolic rate. Bunyard et al. (1998) found that when middle-aged men participated in an aerobic exercise program for six months, their body fat decreased and their daily energy requirement increased.

King et al. (2001) studied the relationship between occupational and leisure-time activity and people's body weight. They found that both factors were important. People with jobs that required more physical activity weighed less than those with sedentary jobs, and people who reported that they regularly got moderate or vigorous exercise weighed less than people who were physically inactive during their leisure time. Of the two factors, leisure-time activity level was more important.

As we have seen, appetite can be stimulated by activation of NPY, MCH, orexin, and ghrelin receptors, and it can be suppressed by the activation of leptin, CCK, CART, and MC4 receptors. Appetite can also be suppressed by activation of inhibitory presynaptic Y2 autoreceptors by PYY. Most of these orexigenic and anorexigenic chemicals also affect metabolism: Orexigenic chemicals tend to decrease metabolic rate, and anorexigenic chemicals tend to increase it. In addition, uncoupling protein causes nutrients to be "burned"—converted into heat instead of adipose tissue. Do these discoveries hold any promise for the treatment of obesity? Is there any possibility that researchers will find drugs that will stimulate or block these receptors, thus decreasing people's appetite and increasing the rate at which they burn rather than store their calories? Drug companies certainly hope so, and they are working hard on developing medications that will do so, because they know that there will be a very large number of people willing to pay for them.

The variety of methods—surgical, mechanical, behavioral, and pharmacological—that therapists and surgeons have developed to treat obesity attests to the tenacity of the problem. The basic difficulty, beyond that caused by having an efficient metabolism, is that eating is pleasurable and satiety signals are easy to ignore or override. Despite the fact that relatively little success has been seen until now, I am personally optimistic about what the future may hold. I think that if we learn more about the physiology of hunger signals, satiety signals, and the reinforcement provided by eating, we will be able to develop drugs that attenuate the signals that encourage us to eat and strengthen those that encourage us to stop eating.

KEY CONCEPTS

PHYSIOLOGICAL REGULATORY SYSTEMS

1. Regulatory systems include four essential features: a system variable, a set point, a detector, and a correctional mechanism. Because of the time it takes for substances to be absorbed from the digestive system, eating and drinking behaviors are also controlled by satiety mechanisms.

DRINKING

2. The body's water is located in the intracellular and extracellular compartments; the latter consists of the interstitial fluid and the blood plasma.
3. Normal loss of water depletes both major compartments and produces both osmometric and volumetric thirst.
4. Osmometric thirst is detected by neurons in the OVLT and surrounding parts of the anterior hypothalamus; volumetric thirst is detected by the kidney, which secretes an enzyme that produces angiotensin, and by baroreceptors in the atria of the heart, which communicate directly with the brain.

EATING AND METABOLISM

5. The body has two nutrient reservoirs: a short-term reservoir containing glycogen (a carbohydrate) and a long-term reservoir containing fats.
6. Metabolism is divided into the absorptive and fasting phases, controlled primarily by the hormones insulin and glucagon.

WHAT STARTS A MEAL?

7. Hunger is affected by social and environmental factors, such as time of day and the presence of other people.
8. The most important physiological signal for hunger occurs when receptors located in the liver and the brain signal a low availability of nutrients.

WHAT STOPS A MEAL?

9. Satiety is controlled by receptors in several locations. Nutrient receptors in the stomach send signals to the brain. The release of CCK by the duodenum and PYY by other parts of the intestinal tract decrease food intake. Receptors in the small intestines and in the liver detect the presence of nutrients of a meal that is being digested and absorbed into the body.

NEURAL MECHANISMS

10. Neural mechanisms in the brain stem are able to control acceptance or rejection of food, even when they are isolated from the forebrain.
11. The hypothalamus is involved in the control of eating. Neurons in the lateral hypothalamus that secrete MCH or orexin increase appetite and decrease metabolic rate. These neurons are, in turn, activated by neurons that secrete neuropeptide Y and AGRP. Grehlin, secreted by the stomach, activates NPY/AGRP neurons and stimulates hunger.
12. Well-fed adipose tissue releases a hormone, leptin, that suppresses eating by binding with leptin receptors on neuropeptide-Y-secreting neurons in the paraventricular nucleus of the hypothalamus, inhibiting them. Leptin also inhibits lateral hypothalamic neurons that secrete MCH and orexin, and it stimulates CART- and α-MSH-secreting neurons, whose activity inhibits eating.

EATING DISORDERS

13. An important cause of obesity is an efficient metabolism, which may have a genetic basis. Uncoupling protein may be involved in determining the efficiency of a person's metabolism.
14. Drugs that interact with the MCH, orexin, NPY, CART, or MC-4 receptors or alter the activity of uncoupling protein may be helpful in treating obesity.
15. Some investigators believe that physiological mechanisms such as misregulation of the release of 5-HT or neuropeptide Y in the hypothalamus may play a role in anorexia nervosa, but so far, persuasive evidence is lacking.

SUGGESTED READINGS

Barsh, G. S., and Schwartz, M. W. Genetic approaches to studying energy balance: Perception and integration. *Nature Reviews: Genetics,* 2002, *3,* 589–600.

Bouchard, C., and Bray, G. A. *Regulation of Body Weight: Biological and Behavioral Mechanisms.* New York: John Wiley & Sons, 1996.

Brownell, K. D., and Fairburn, C. G. *Eating Disorders and Obesity: A Comprehensive Handbook.* New York: Guilford Press, 1995.

Chiesi, M., Huppertz, C., and Hofbauer, K. G. Pharmacotherapy of obesity: Targets and perspectives. *Trends in Pharmacological Sciences,* 2001, *22,* 247–254.

Havel, P. J. Peripheral signals conveying metabolic information to the brain: Short-term and long-term regulation of food intake and energy homeostasis. *Proceedings of the Society for Experimental Biology and Medicine,* 2001, *226,* 963–977.

Johnson, A. K., and Thunhorst, R. L. The neuroendocrinology of thirst and salt appetite: Visceral sensory signals and mechanisms of central integration. *Frontiers in Neuroendocrinology,* 1997, *18,* 292–353.

Kreipe, R. E., and Mou, S. M. Eating disorders in adolescents and young adults. *Obstetrics and Gynecology Clinics of North America,* 2000, *27,* 101–124.

SUGGESTED WEB SITES

The Society for the Study of Ingestive Behavior

http://lshome.utsa.edu/SSIB/

Eating and drinking are the research topics of scientists within this society. The site contains links to journals, a newsletter, and links relating to ingestive behavior.

Endocrine-Related Sites

http://www.endo-society.org/coolsite.htm

This site provides a comprehensive set of links to sites relating to the topic of endocrinology.

Eating Disorders

http://eatingdisorders.mentalhelp.net/

This site contains facts about eating disorders as well as links to sites dealing with treatments for eating disorders.

Nutrition and Obesity

http://www.niddk.nih.gov/health/nutrit/nutrit.htm

Nutrition and obesity issues and facts are contained within this site provided by the National Institutes of Health (NIH).

Obesity Links

http://www.dimensionsmagazine.com/links/scientific.html

This site provides a series of interesting and informative site related to obesity, weight loss, and surgical treatments for obesity.

North American Associations for the Study of Obesity (NAASO)

http://www.naaso.org/calendar/

This is the Web site of the North American Association for the Study of Obesity, a group dedicated to understanding and treating obesity. The site provides access to online abstracts of the journal *Obesity Research* and to an obesity discussion group.

Eating Disorders Tutorials

http://psy71.dur.ac.uk/Education/index.html

The site contains a comprehensive set of links to documents and tutorials on eating disorders.

Learning and Memory

chapter 12

CHAPTER OUTLINE

LEARNING OBJECTIVES

1. Describe each of four basic forms of learning: perceptual learning, stimulus-response learning, motor learning, and relational learning.
2. Describe the anatomy of the hippocampus, describe the establishment of long-term potentiation, and discuss the role of NMDA receptors in this phenomenon.
3. Discuss research on the physiological basis of synaptic plasticity during long-term potentiation and long-term depression.
4. Describe research on the role of the inferior temporal cortex in visual perceptual learning.
5. Discuss the physiology of the classically conditioned emotional response to aversive stimuli.
6. Describe the role of the basal ganglia in instrumental conditioning and motor learning.
7. Describe the role of dopamine in reinforcing brain stimulation and discuss the effects of administering dopamine antagonists and agonists.
8. Describe the nature of human anterograde amnesia and explain what it suggests about the organization of learning.
9. Describe the role of the hippocampus in relational learning, including spatial learning, and discuss the function of hippocampal place cells.

PROLOGUE

Every Day Is Alone

Patient H. M. has a relatively pure amnesia. His intellectual ability and his immediate verbal memory appear to be normal. He can repeat seven numbers forward and five numbers backward, and he can carry on conversations, rephrase sentences, and perform mental arithmetic. He is unable to remember events that occurred during several years preceding his brain surgery, but he can recall older memories very well. He showed no personality change after the operation, and he appears to be generally polite and good-natured.

However, since the operation, H. M. has been unable to learn anything new. He cannot identify by name people he has met since the operation (performed in 1953, when he was twenty-seven years old). His family moved to a new house after his operation, and he never learned how to get around in the new neighborhood. (He now lives in a nursing home, where he can be cared for.) He is aware of his disorder and often says something like this:

> Every day is alone in itself, whatever enjoyment I've had, and whatever sorrow I've had. . . . Right now, I'm wondering. Have I done or said anything amiss? You see, at this moment everything looks clear to me, but what happened just before? That's what worries me. It's like waking from a dream; I just don't remember. (Milner, 1970, p. 37)

H. M. is capable of remembering a small amount of verbal information as long as he is not distracted; constant rehearsal can keep information in his immediate memory for a long time. However, rehearsal does not appear to have any long-term effects; if he is distracted for a moment, he will completely forget whatever he had been rehearsing. He works very well at repetitive tasks. Indeed, because he so quickly forgets what previously happened, he does not easily become bored. He can endlessly reread the same magazine or laugh at the same jokes, finding them fresh and new each time. His time is typically spent solving crossword puzzles and watching television.

Experiences change us; encounters with our environment alter our behavior by modifying our nervous system. As many investigators have said, an understanding of the physiology of memory is the ultimate challenge to neuroscience research. The brain is complex, and so are learning and remembering. Although the individual changes that occur within the cells of the brain may be relatively simple, the brain consists of many billions of neurons. Therefore, isolating and identifying the particular changes that are responsible for a particular memory are exceedingly difficult. Similarly, although the elements of a particular learning task may be simple, its implications for an organism may be complex. The behavior that the investigator observes and measures may be only one of many that change as a result of an experience. However, despite the difficulties, the long years of work finally seem to be paying off. New approaches and new methods have evolved from old ones, and real progress has been made in understanding the anatomy and physiology of learning and remembering.

The Nature of Learning

Learning refers to the process by which experiences change our nervous system and hence our behavior. We refer to these changes as *memories*. Although it is convenient to describe memories as if they were notes placed in filing cabinets, this is certainly not the way experiences are reflected within the brain. Experiences are not "stored"; rather, they change the way we perceive, perform, think, and plan. They do so by physically changing the structure of the nervous system, altering neural circuits that participate in perceiving, performing, thinking, and planning. Learning can take at least four basic forms: perceptual learning, stimulus-response learning, motor learning, and relational learning. **Perceptual learning** is the ability to learn to recognize stimuli that have been perceived before. The primary function of this type of learning is the ability to identify and categorize objects (including other members of our

perceptual learning Learning to recognize a particular stimulus.

own species) and situations. Unless we have learned to recognize something, we cannot learn how we should behave with respect to it—We will not profit from our experiences with it, and profiting from experience is what learning is all about.

Each of our sensory systems is capable of perceptual learning. We can learn to recognize objects by their visual appearance, the sounds they make, how they feel, or how they smell. We can recognize people by the shape of their face, the movements they make when they walk, or the sound of their voice. When we hear people talk, we can recognize the words they are saying and perhaps their emotional state. As we shall see, perceptual learning appears to be accomplished primarily by changes in the sensory association cortex. That is, learning to recognize complex visual stimuli involves changes in the visual association cortex, learning to recognize complex auditory stimuli involves changes in the auditory association cortex, and so on.

Stimulus-response learning is the ability to learn to perform a particular behavior when a particular stimulus is present. Thus, it involves the establishment of connections between circuits involved in perception and those involved in movement. The behavior could be an automatic response such as a defensive reflex, or it could be a complicated sequence of movements that was learned previously. Stimulus-response learning includes two major categories of learning that psychologists have studied extensively: *classical conditioning* and *instrumental conditioning*.

Classical conditioning is a form of learning in which an unimportant stimulus acquires the properties of an important one. It involves an *association between two stimuli*. A stimulus that previously had little effect on behavior becomes able to evoke a reflexive, species-typical behavior. For example, a defensive eyeblink response can be conditioned to a tone. If we direct a brief puff of air toward a rabbit's eye, the eye will automatically blink. The response is called an **unconditional response (UR)** because it occurs unconditionally, without any special training. The stimulus that produces it (the puff of air) is called an **unconditional stimulus (US)**. Now we begin the training. We present a series of brief 1000-Hz tones, each followed 500 ms later by a puff of air. After several trials the rabbit's eye begins to close even before the puff of air occurs. Classical conditioning has occurred; the **conditional stimulus (CS**—the 1000-Hz tone) now elicits the **conditional response (CR**—the eye blink). (See ***Figure 12.1.***)

When classical conditioning takes place, what kinds of changes occur in the brain? Figure 12.1 shows a simplified neural circuit that could account for this type of learning. For the sake of simplicity we will assume that the US (the puff of air) is detected by a single neuron in the somatosensory system and that the CS (the 1000-Hz tone) is detected by a single neuron in the auditory system. We will also assume that the response—the eyeblink—is controlled by a single neuron in the motor system. (See ***Figure 12.1.***)

Now let us see how the circuits work. If we present a 1000-Hz tone, we find that the animal makes no reaction, because the synapse connecting the tone-sensitive neuron with the neuron in the motor system is weak. That is, when an action potential reaches the terminal button of synapse T (tone), the EPSP it produces in the dendrite of the motor neuron is too small to make that neuron fire. However, if we present a puff of air to the eye, the eye blinks. This reaction occurs because nature has provided the animal with a strong synapse between the somatosensory neuron and the motor neuron that causes a blink (synapse P, for "puff"). To establish classical conditioning, we first present the 1000-Hz tone and then almost immediately follow it with a puff of air. After we repeat these pairs of stimuli several times, we find that we can dispense with the air puff; the 1000-Hz tone produces the blink all by itself.

Figure 12.1

A simple neural model of classical conditioning. When the 1000-Hz tone is presented just before the puff of air to the eye, synapse T is strengthened.

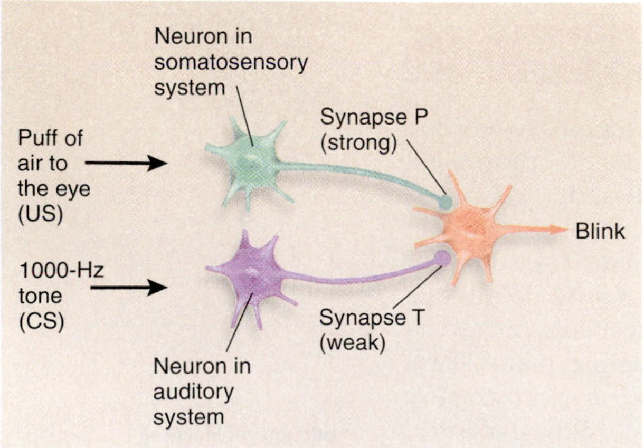

Over fifty years ago, Donald Hebb proposed a rule that might explain how neurons are changed by experience in a way that would cause changes in behavior (Hebb, 1949). The **Hebb rule** says that if a synapse repeatedly becomes active at about the same time that the postsynaptic neuron fires, changes will take place in the structure or chemistry of the synapse that will strengthen it. How would the Hebb rule apply to our circuit? If the 1000-Hz tone is presented first, then weak synapse T (for "tone") becomes active. If the puff is presented immediately afterward, then strong synapse P becomes active and makes the motor neuron fire. The act of firing then strengthens any synapse with the motor neuron *that has just been active.* Of course, this means synapse T. After several pairings of the two stimuli, and after several increments of strengthening, synapse T becomes strong enough to cause the motor neuron to fire by itself. Learning has occurred. (See ***Figure 12.1.***)

When Hebb formulated his rule, he was unable to determine whether it was true or false. Now, finally, enough progress has been made in laboratory techniques that the strength of individual synapses can be determined, and investigators are studying the physiological bases of learning. We will see the results of some of these approaches in the next section of this chapter.

The second major class of stimulus-response learning is **instrumental conditioning** (also called *operant conditioning*). Whereas classical conditioning involves automatic, species-typical responses, instrumental conditioning involves behaviors that have been learned. And whereas classical conditioning involves an association between two stimuli, instrumental conditioning involves an *association between a response and a stimulus.* Instrumental conditioning is a more flexible form of learning. It permits an organism to adjust its behavior according to the consequences of that behavior. That is, when a behavior is followed by favorable consequences, the behavior tends to occur more frequently; when it is followed by unfavorable consequences, it tends to occur less frequently. Collectively, "favorable consequences" are referred to as **reinforcing stimuli,** and "unfavorable consequences" are referred to as **punishing stimuli.** For example, a response that enables a hungry organism to find food will be reinforced, and a response that causes pain will be punished. (Psychologists often refer to these terms as *reinforcers* and *punishers.*)

Let's consider the process of reinforcement. Briefly stated, reinforcement causes changes in an animal's nervous system that increase the likelihood that a particular stimulus will elicit a particular response. For example, when a hungry rat is first put in an operant chamber (a "Skinner box"), it is not very likely to press the lever mounted on a wall. However, if it does press the lever and if it receives a piece of food immediately afterward, the likelihood of its making another response increases. Put another way, reinforcement causes the sight of the lever to serve as the stimulus that elicits the lever-pressing response. It is not accurate to say simply that a particular behavior becomes more frequent. If no lever is present, a rat that has learned to press one will not wave its paw around in the air. The *sight of a lever* is needed to produce the response. Thus, the process of reinforcement strengthens a connection between neural circuits involved in perception (the sight of the lever) and those involved in movement (the act of lever pressing). As we will see later in this chapter, the brain contains reinforcement mechanisms that control this process. (See ***Figure 12.2.***)

The third major category of learning, **motor learning**, is actually a component of stimulus-response learning. For simplicity's sake we can think of perceptual learning as the establishment of changes within the sensory systems of the brain, stimulus-response learning as the establishment of connections between sensory systems and motor systems, and motor learning as the establishment of changes within motor systems. But, in fact, motor learning cannot occur without sensory guidance from the environment. For example, most skilled movements involve interactions with objects: bicycles, pinball machines, tennis racquets, knitting needles, and so on. Even skilled movements that we make by ourselves, such as solitary dance steps, involve feedback from the joints, muscles, vestibular apparatus, eyes, and contact between

stimulus-response learning Learning to automatically make a particular response in the presence of a particular stimulus; includes classical and instrumental conditioning.

classical conditioning A learning procedure; when a stimulus that initially produces no particular response is followed several times by an **unconditional stimulus** that produces a defensive or appetitive response (the **unconditional response**), the first stimulus (now called a **conditional stimulus**) itself evokes the response (now called a **conditional response**).

Hebb rule The hypothesis proposed by Donald Hebb that the cellular basis of learning involves strengthening of a synapse that is repeatedly active when the postsynaptic neuron fires.

instrumental conditioning A learning procedure whereby the effects of a particular behavior in a particular situation increase (reinforce) or decrease (punish) the probability of the behavior; also called *operant conditioning*.

reinforcing stimulus An appetitive stimulus that follows a particular behavior and thus makes the behavior become more frequent.

punishing stimulus An aversive stimulus that follows a particular behavior and thus makes the behavior become less frequent.

motor learning Learning to make a new response.

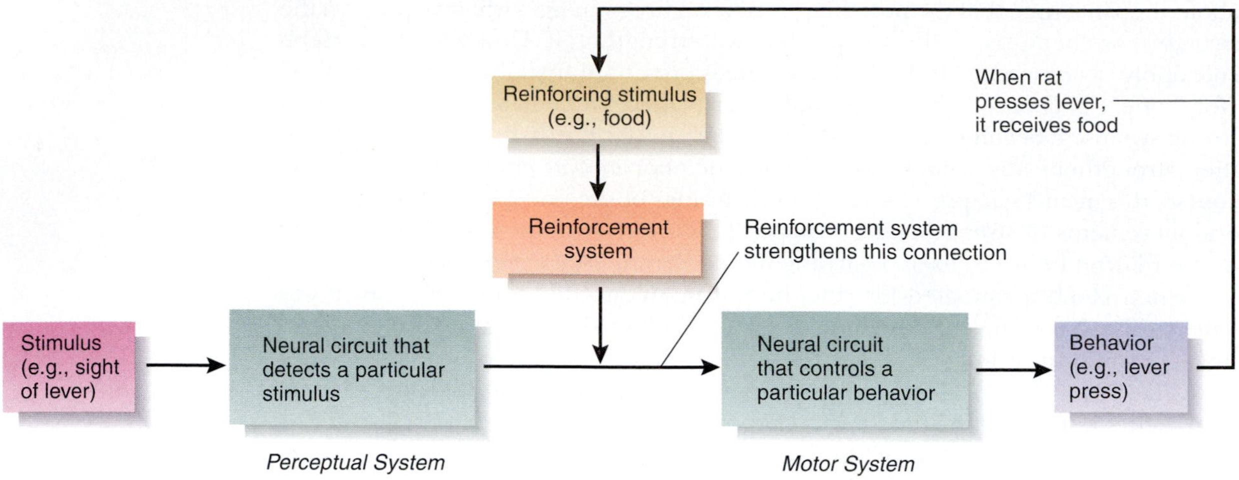

Figure 12.2
A simple neural model of instrumental conditioning.

the feet and the floor. Motor learning differs from other forms of learning primarily in the degree to which new forms of behavior are learned; the more novel the behavior, the more the neural circuits in the motor systems of the brain must be modified. (See ***Figure 12.3.***)

A particular learning situation can involve varying amounts of all three types of learning that I have described so far: perceptual, stimulus-response, and motor. For example, if we teach an animal to make a new response whenever we present a stimulus it has never seen before, it must learn to recognize the stimulus (perceptual learning) and make the response (motor learning), and a connection must be established between these two new memories (stimulus-response learning). If we teach it to make a response it has already learned whenever we present a new stimulus, only perceptual learning and stimulus-response learning will take place.

The three forms of learning I have described so far consist primarily of changes in one sensory system, between one sensory system and the motor system, or in the motor system. But obviously, learning is usually more complex than that. The fourth form of learning, **relational learning,** involves learning the relationships among individual stimuli. For example, consider what we must learn to become familiar with the contents of a room. First, we must learn to recognize each of the objects. In addition, we must learn the relative locations of the objects with respect to each other.

relational learning A complex form of learning that involves the relations among individual stimuli; includes spatial learning, episodic learning, and observational learning.

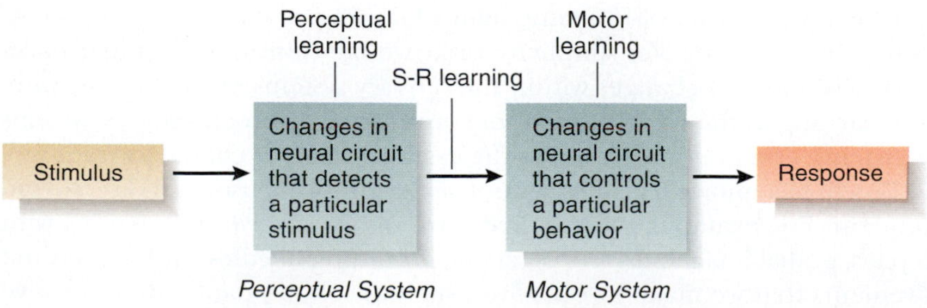

Figure 12.3
An overview of perceptual, stimulus-response (S-R), and motor learning.

As a result, when we find ourselves located in a particular place in the room, our perceptions of these objects and their locations relative to us tell us exactly where we are.

Other types of relational learning are even more complex. *Episodic learning*—remembering sequences of events (episodes) that we witness—requires us to keep track not only of individual stimuli but also of the order in which they occur. *Observational learning*—learning by watching and imitating other people—requires us to remember what someone else does, the situation in which the behavior is performed, and the relationship between the other person's movements and our own. As we will see in the last part of this chapter, a special system that involves the hippocampus and associated structures appears to perform coordinating functions that are necessary for many types of learning that go beyond simple perceptual, stimulus-response, or motor learning.

INTERIM SUMMARY

The Nature of Learning

Learning produces changes in the way we perceive, act, think, and feel. It does so by producing changes in the nervous system in the circuits responsible for perception, in those responsible for the control of movement, and in connections between the two.

Perceptual learning consists primarily of changes in perceptual systems that make it possible for us to recognize stimuli so that we can respond to them appropriately. Stimulus-response learning consists of connections between perceptual and motor systems. The most important forms are classical and instrumental conditioning. Classical conditioning occurs when a neutral stimulus is followed by an unconditional stimulus (US) that naturally elicits an unconditional response (UR). After this pairing, the neutral stimulus becomes a conditional stimulus (CS); it now elicits the response by itself, which we refer to as the conditional response (CR).

Instrumental conditioning occurs when a response is followed by a reinforcing stimulus, such as a drink of water for a thirsty animal. The reinforcing stimulus increases the likelihood that the other stimuli that were present when the response was made will evoke the response. Both forms of stimulus-response learning may occur as a result of strengthened synaptic connections, as described by the Hebb rule.

Motor learning, although it may primarily involve changes within neural circuits that control movement, is guided by sensory stimuli; thus, it is actually a form of stimulus-response learning. Relational learning, the most complex form of learning, is described later in this chapter. It includes the ability to recognize objects through more than one sensory modality, to recognize the relative location of objects in the environment, and to remember the sequence in which events occurred during particular episodes.

THOUGHT QUESTION

Can you think of specific examples of each of the categories of learning described in this section? Can you think of some examples that include more than one category?

Learning and Synaptic Plasticity

On theoretical considerations alone, it would appear that learning must involve synaptic plasticity: changes in the structure or biochemistry of synapses that alter their effects on postsynaptic neurons. Recent years have seen an explosion of research on this topic, largely stimulated by the development of methods that permit researchers to observe structural and biochemical changes in microscopically small structures: the presynaptic and postsynaptic components of synapses.

long-term potentiation A long-term increase in the excitability of a neuron to a particular synaptic input caused by repeated high-frequency activity of that input.

hippocampal formation A forebrain structure of the temporal lobe, constituting an important part of the limbic system; includes the hippocampus proper (Ammon's horn), dentate gyrus, and subiculum.

population EPSP An evoked potential that represents the EPSPs of a population of neurons.

associative long-term potentiation A long-term potentiation in which concurrent stimulation of weak and strong synapses to a given neuron strengthens the weak ones.

Induction of Long-Term Potentiation

Electrical stimulation of circuits within the hippocampal formation can lead to long-term synaptic changes that seem to be among those responsible for learning. Lømo (1966) discovered that intense electrical stimulation of axons leading from the entorhinal cortex to the dentate gyrus caused a long-term increase in the magnitude of excitatory postsynaptic potentials in the postsynaptic neurons; this increase has come to be called **long-term potentiation.** (The word *potentiate* means "to strengthen, to make more potent.")

First, let's review some anatomy. The **hippocampal formation** is a specialized region of the limbic cortex located in the temporal lobe. (Its location in a human brain is shown in Figure 3.11.) Because the hippocampal formation is folded in one dimension and then curved in another, it has a complex, three-dimensional shape. Therefore, it is difficult to show what it looks like with a diagram on a two-dimensional sheet of paper. Fortunately, the structure of the hippocampal formation is orderly; a slice taken anywhere perpendicular to its curving long axis contains the same set of circuits.

Figure 12.4 shows a slice of the hippocampal formation, illustrating a typical procedure for producing long-term potentiation. The primary input to the hippocampal formation comes from the *entorhinal cortex.* The axons of neurons in the entorhinal cortex pass through the *perforant path* and form synapses with the granule cells of the *dentate gyrus.* A stimulating electrode is placed in the perforant path, and a recording electrode is placed in the dentate gyrus, near the granule cells. (See ***Figure 12.4.***) First, a single pulse of electrical stimulation is delivered to the perforant

Figure 12.4

Connections of the components of the hippocampal formation.

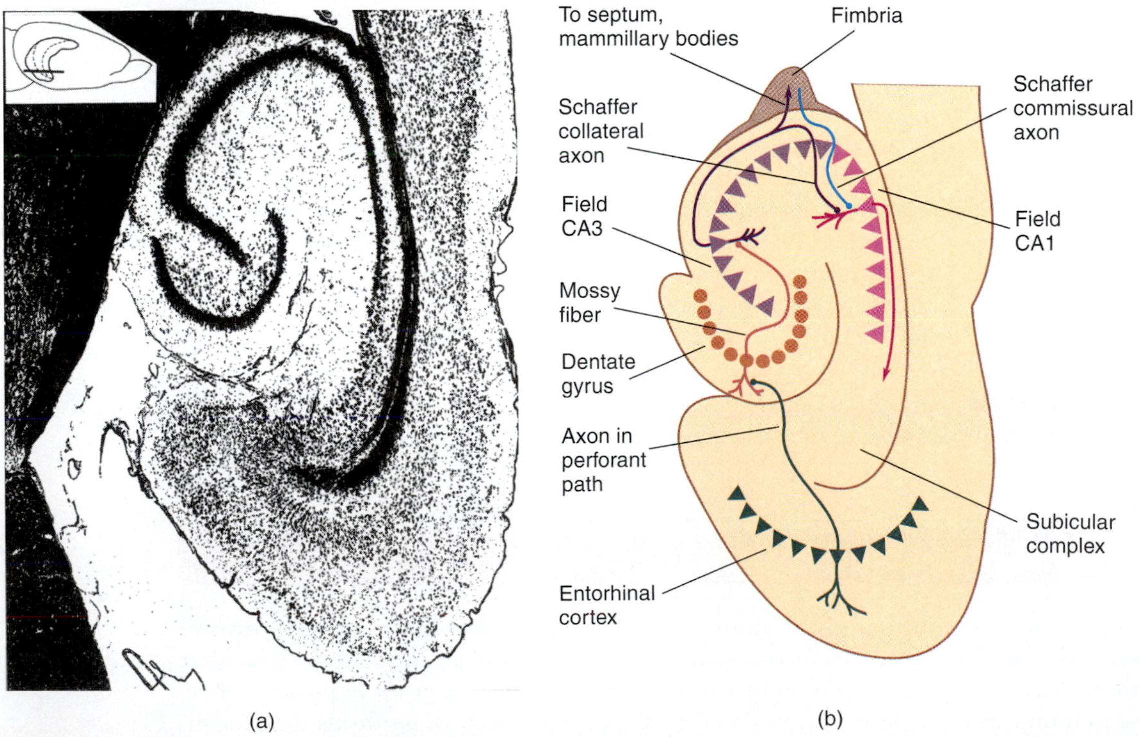

Photograph from Swanson, L. W., Köhler, C., and Björklund, A., in *Handbook of Chemical Neuroanatomy. Vol. 5: Integrated Systems of the CNS, Part I.* Amsterdam: Elsevier Science Publishers, 1987.

path, and then the resulting population EPSP is recorded in the dentate gyrus. The **population EPSP** is an extracellular measurement of the excitatory postsynaptic potentials (EPSP) produced by the synapses of the perforant path axons with the dentate granule cells. The size of the first population EPSP indicates the strength of the synaptic connections before long-term potentiation has taken place. Long-term potentiation can be induced by stimulating the axons in the perforant path with a burst of approximately one hundred pulses of electrical stimulation, delivered within a few seconds. Evidence that long-term potentiation has occurred is obtained by periodically delivering single pulses to the perforant path and recording the response in the dentate gyrus. If the response is greater than it was before the burst of pulses was delivered, long-term potentiation has occurred. (See ***Figure 12.5.***)

Figure 12.5

The procedure for producing long-term potentiation.

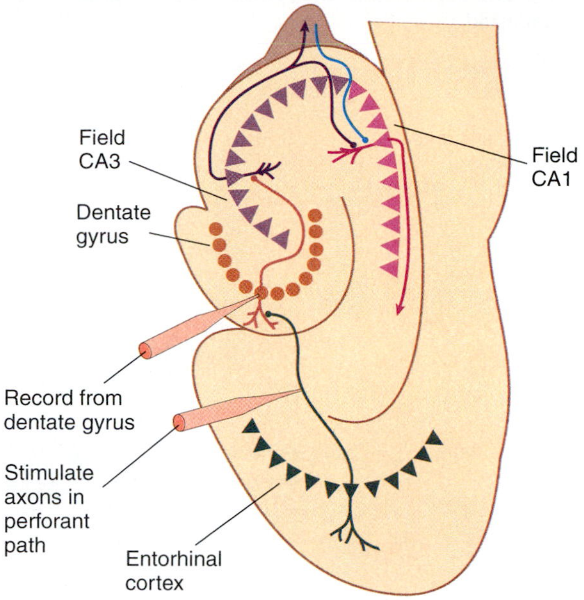

Long-term potentiation can be produced in other regions of the hippocampal formation and, as we shall see, in other places in the brain. It can last for several months (Bliss and Lømo, 1973). It can be produced in isolated slices of the hippocampal formation as well as in the brains of living animals, which allows researchers to stimulate and record from individual neurons and to analyze biochemical changes. The brain is removed from the skull, the hippocampal complex is dissected, and slices are placed in a temperature-controlled chamber filled with liquid that resembles interstitial fluid. Under optimal conditions a slice remains alive for up to forty hours.

Many experiments have demonstrated that long-term potentiation in hippocampal slices can follow the Hebb rule. That is, when weak and strong synapses to a single neuron are stimulated at approximately the same time, the weak synapse becomes strengthened. This phenomenon is called **associative long-term potentiation,** because it is produced by the association (in time) between the activity of the two sets of synapses. (See ***Figure 12.6.***)

Role of NMDA Receptors

Nonassociative long-term potentiation requires some sort of additive effect. That is, a series of pulses delivered at a high rate all in one burst will produce long-term potentiation, but the same number of pulses given at a slow rate will not. (In fact, as we shall see, low-frequency stimulation can lead to the opposite phenomenon: long-term *depression.*) The reason for this phenomenon is now clear. Several experiments have shown that synaptic strengthening occurs when molecules of the neurotransmitter bind with postsynaptic receptors located in a dendritic spine that is already depolarized. Kelso, Ganong, and Brown (1986) found that if they used a microelectrode to artificially depolarize CA1 neurons and then stimulated the axons that formed synapses with them, the synapses became stronger—that is, they produced a stronger postsynaptic potential in the dendritic spine. However, if the stimulation of the synapses and the depolarization of the neuron occurred at different times, no effect was seen; thus, the release of the neurotransmitter and depolarization of the

Figure 12.6

Population EPSPs recorded from the dentate gyrus before and after electrical stimulation that led to long-term potentiation.

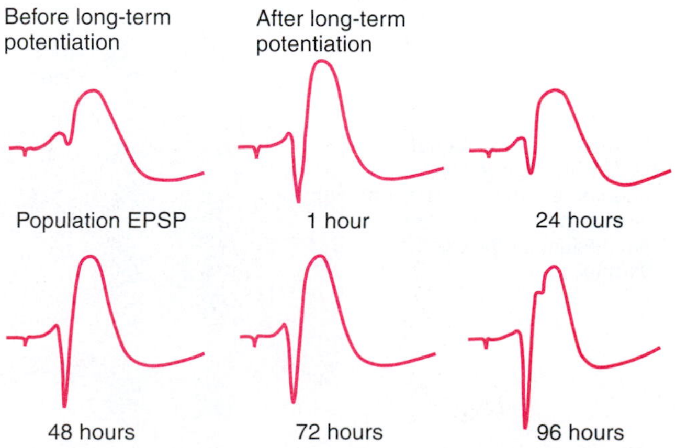

From Berger, T. W. *Science,* 1984, *224,* 627–630. Copyright 1984 by the American Association for the Advancement of Science. Reprinted with permission.

Figure 12.7

Long-term potentiation. Synaptic strengthening occurs when synapses are active while the membrane of the postsynaptic cell is depolarized.

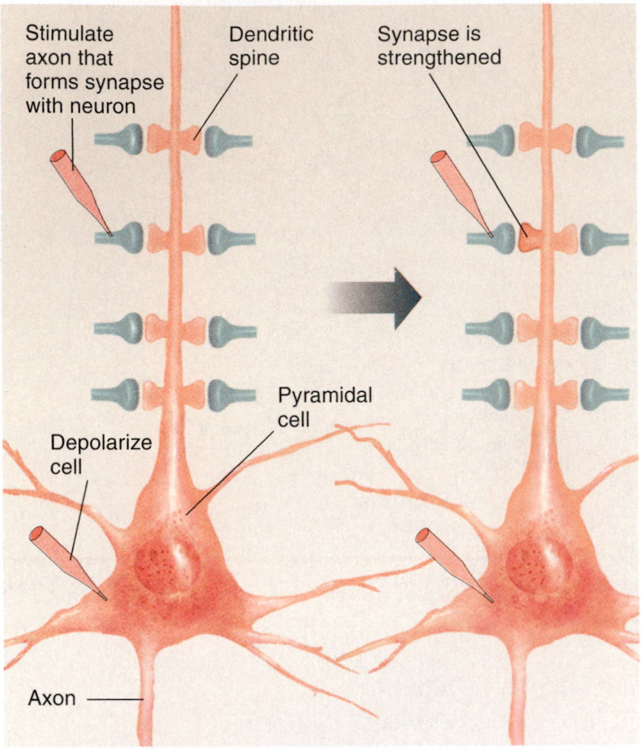

Stimulate axon that forms synapse with neuron
Dendritic spine
Synapse is strengthened
Pyramidal cell
Depolarize cell
Axon

postsynaptic membrane had to occur at the same time. (See ***Figure 12.7.***)

Experiments such as the ones I just described indicate that long-term potentiation requires two events: activation of synapses and depolarization of the postsynaptic neuron. The explanation for this phenomenon, at least in some parts of the brain, lies in the characteristics of a very special receptor. As we saw in Chapter 4, the most important excitatory neurotransmitter in the brain is glutamic acid (usually referred to as *glutamate*). We also saw that the postsynaptic effects of glutamate are mediated by several different types of receptors. One of them, the NMDA receptor, plays a critical role in long-term potentiation.

The **NMDA receptor** has some unusual properties. It is found in the hippocampal formation, especially in field CA1. It gets its name from the drug that specifically activates it: *N*-methyl-D-aspartate. The NMDA receptor controls a calcium ion channel. However, this channel is normally blocked by a magnesium ion (Mg^{2+}), which prevents calcium ions from entering the cell even when the receptor is stimulated by glutamate. But if the postsynaptic membrane is depolarized, the Mg^{2+} is ejected from the ion channel, and the channel is free to admit Ca^{2+} ions. Thus, calcium ions enter the cells through the channels controlled by NMDA receptors only when glutamate is present *and* when the postsynaptic membrane is depolarized. This means that the ion channel controlled by the NMDA receptor is a neurotransmitter *and* voltage-dependent ion channel. (See ***Figure 12.8*** and ***Animation 12.1, The NMDA receptor.***)

Figure 12.8

The NMDA receptor, a neurotransmitter- and voltage-dependent ion channel. (a) When the postsynaptic membrane is at the resting potential, Mg^{2+} blocks the ion channel, preventing Ca^{2+} from entering. (b) When the membrane is depolarized, the magnesium ion is evicted. Thus, the attachment of glutamate to the binding site causes the ion channel to open, allowing calcium ions to enter the dendritic spine.

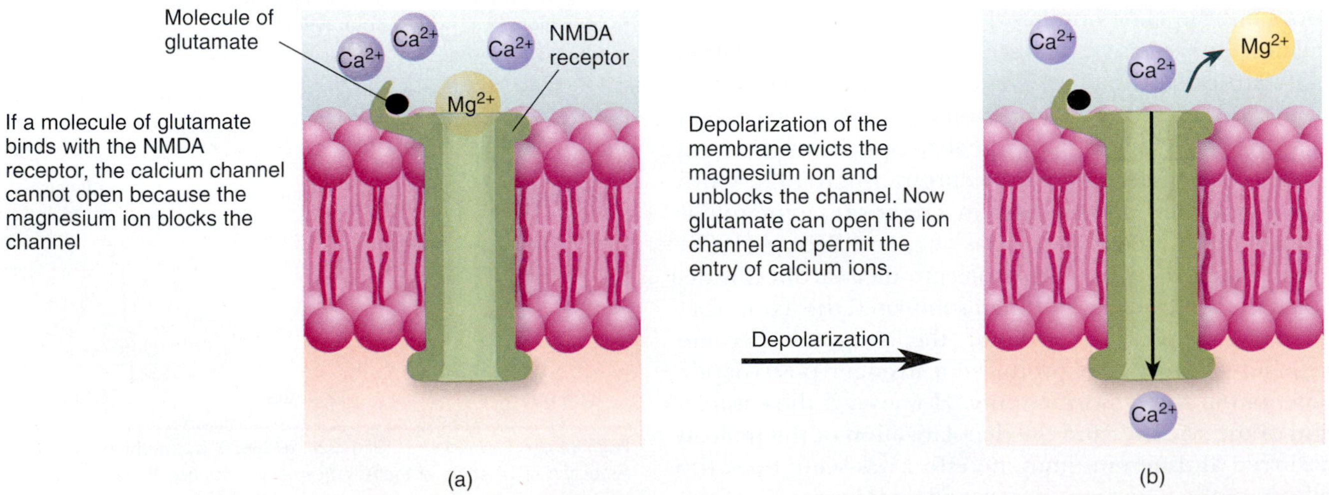

Molecule of glutamate
Ca2+
Ca2+
Ca2+
NMDA receptor
Mg2+
If a molecule of glutamate binds with the NMDA receptor, the calcium channel cannot open because the magnesium ion blocks the channel
(a)
Depolarization of the membrane evicts the magnesium ion and unblocks the channel. Now glutamate can open the ion channel and permit the entry of calcium ions.
Depolarization
Ca2+
Ca2+
Mg2+
Ca2+
(b)

The strongest evidence implicating NMDA receptors in long-term potentiation comes from research with drugs that block NMDA receptors, such as **AP5** (2-amino-5-phosphonopentanoate). AP5 prevents the establishment of long-term potentiation in field CA1 and the dentate gyrus.

Animation 12.1, The NMDA receptor, illustrates the role of the NMDA receptor as a neurotransmitter- and voltage-dependent ion channel.

Cell biologists have discovered that the calcium ion is used by many cells as a second messenger. The entry of calcium ions through the ion channels controlled by NMDA receptors is an essential step in long-term potentiation. Lynch et al. (1984) demonstrated this fact by injecting EGTA directly into hippocampal pyramidal cells. This chemical binds with calcium and makes it insoluble, destroying its biological activity. The EGTA blocked the establishment of long-term potentiation in the injected cells; their excitability was not increased by high-frequency stimulation of axons that formed synapses with them. However, neighboring cells, which were not injected with EGTA, showed long-term potentiation.

In Chapter 2 you learned that only axons are capable of producing action potentials. Actually, they can also occur in dendrites of some types of pyramidal cells, including those in field CA1 of the hippocampal formation. The threshold of excitation for **dendritic spikes** (as these action potentials are called) is rather high. As far as we know, they occur only when an action potential is triggered in the axon of the pyramidal cell. The backwash of depolarization across the cell body triggers a dendritic spike, which is propagated up the trunk of the dendrite. This means that whenever the axon of a pyramidal cell fires, all of its dendritic spines become depolarized for a brief time.

I think that considering what you already know about associative long-term potentiation, you can anticipate the role that NMDA receptors play in this phenomenon. If weak synapses are active by themselves, nothing happens, because the membrane of the dendritic spine does not depolarize sufficiently for the calcium channels controlled by the NMDA receptors to open. (Remember that for these channels to open, the postsynaptic membrane must depolarize and displace the Mg^{2+} ions that normally block them.) However, if the activity of strong synapses located elsewhere on the postsynaptic cell has caused the cell to fire, then a dendritic spike will depolarize the postsynaptic membrane enough for calcium to enter the ion channels controlled by the NMDA receptors. Thus, the special properties of NMDA receptors account not only for the existence of long-term potentiation but also for its associative nature. (See ***Figure 12.9*** and ***Animation 12.2, Associative LTP.***)

Animation 12.2, Associative LTP, illustrates the role of dendritic spikes in the strengthening of weak synapses by the coordinated activity of strong synapses.

Mechanisms of Synaptic Plasticity

What is responsible for the increases in synaptic strength that occur during long-term potentiation? Research indicates that at least two types of modifications occur when a synapse becomes strengthened: individual synapses are strengthened, and new synapses are produced. Strengthening of an individual synapse appears to be accomplished by an increase in the number of postsynaptic **AMPA receptors**—that is, *non*-NMDA glutamate receptors—present in that synapse.

Where do these new AMPA receptors come from? Shi et al. (1999) prepared a gene for a subunit of the AMPA receptor that had a fluorescent dye molecule attached to it. They used a harmless virus to insert this gene into neurons in hippocampal slices. This procedure permitted the investigators to use a two-photon laser scanning microscope to see the exact location of AMPA receptors in dendritic spines of CA1 neurons. The investigators induced long-term potentiation by stimulating axons that form synapses with these dendrites. Before long-term potentiation was induced, they saw AMPA receptors clustered at the base of the dendritic spines. Fifteen minutes after the induction of long-term potentiation, the AMPA receptors flooded into the spines and moved to their tips—the location of the postsynaptic membrane. This movement of AMPA receptors was prevented by AP5, the drug that blocks NMDA receptors. (See ***Figure 12.10.***)

NMDA receptor A specialized ionotropic glutamate receptor that controls a calcium channel that is normally blocked by Mg^{2+} ions; involved in long-term potentiation.

AP5 2-Amino-5-phosphonopentanoate, a drug that blocks NMDA receptors.

dendritic spike An action potential that occurs in the dendrite of some types of pyramidal cells.

AMPA receptor An ionotropic glutamate receptor that controls a sodium channel; when open, it produces EPSPs.

Figure 12.9

Associative long-term potentiation. If the activity of strong synapses is sufficient to trigger an action potential in the neuron, the dendritic spike will depolarize the membrane of dendritic spines, priming NMDA receptors so that any weak synapses active at that time will become strengthened.

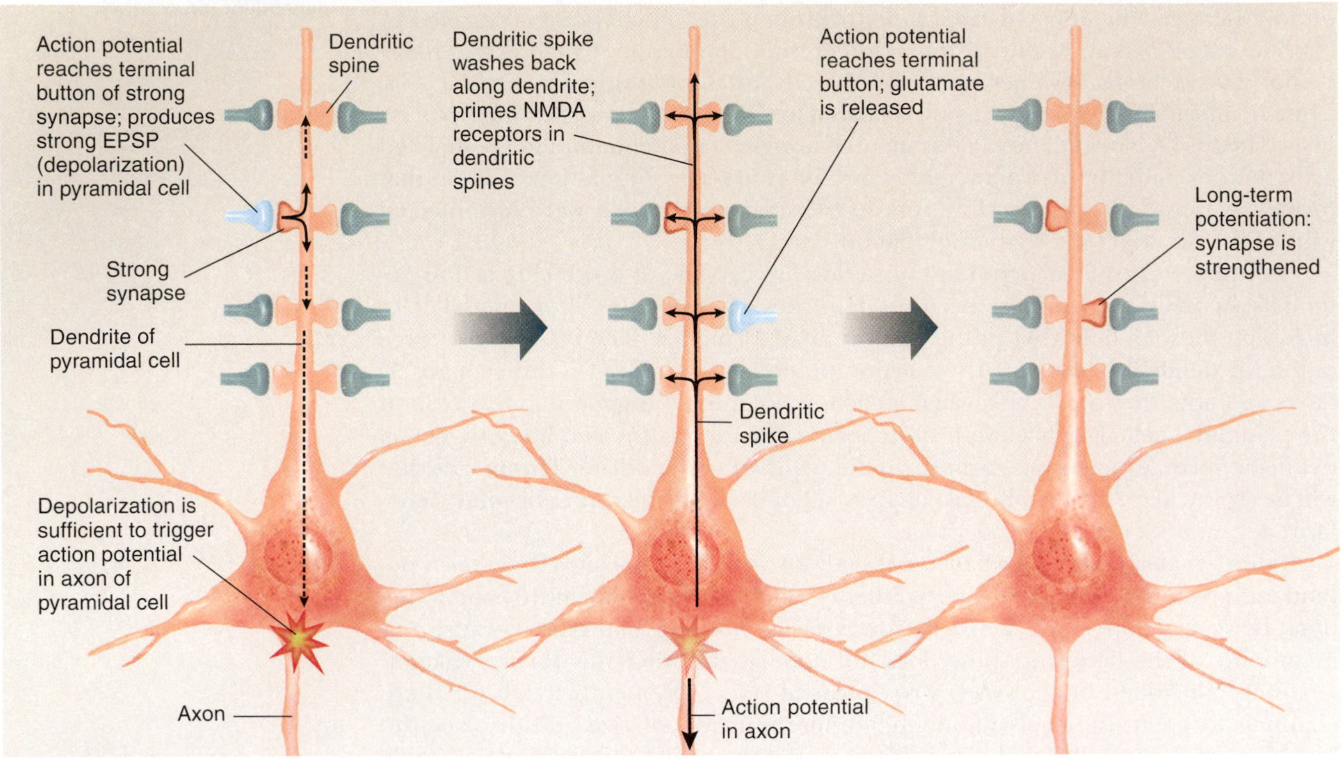

Figure 12.10

Two-photon laser scanning microscopy of the CA1 region of living hippocampal slices showing delivery of AMPA receptors into dendritic spines after long-term potentiation. The AMPA receptors were tagged with a fluorescent dye molecule. The two photographs at the bottom are higher magnifications of the ones above. The arrows labeled *a* and *b* point to dendritic spines that became filled with AMPA receptors after the induction of long-term potentiation.

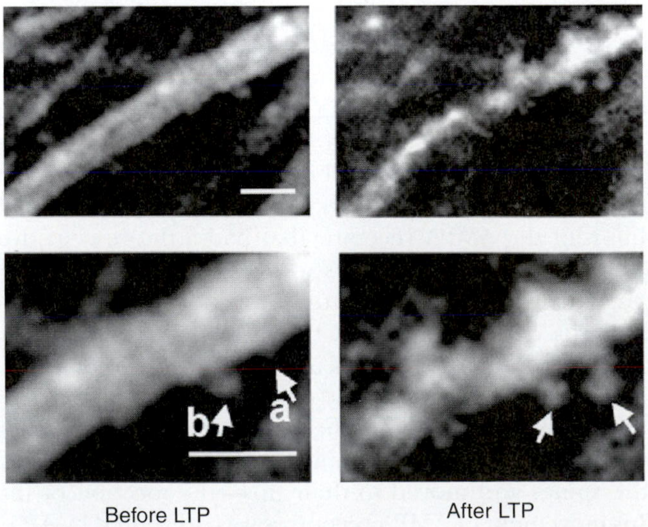

From Shi, S.-H., Hayashi, Y., Petralia, R. S., Zaman, S. H., Wenthold, R. J., Svoboda, K., and Malinow, R. *Science*, 1999, *284*, 1811–1816.

How does the entry of calcium ions into the dendritic spine cause AMPA receptors to move into the postsynaptic membrane? This process appears to involve **CaM-KII** (type II calcium-calmodulin kinase), an enzyme that is present in dendritic spines. CaM-KII is a *calcium-dependent* enzyme, which is inactive until a calcium ion binds with it and activates it. Many studies have shown that CaM-KII plays a critical role in long-term potentiation. For example, Silva et al. (1992a) produced a targeted mutation of the gene responsible for the production of CaM-KII in mice. The mice had no obvious neuroanatomical defects, and the responses of their NMDA receptors were normal. However, the investigators were unable to produce long-term potentiation in field CA1 of hippocampal slices taken from these animals. Lledo et al. (1995) found that injection of activated CaM-KII directly into CA1 pyramidal cells mimicked the effects of long-term potentiation: It strengthened synaptic transmission in those cells.

Lisman and Zhabotinsky (2001) present a hypothetical model to explain the role that activated CaM-KII plays in the insertion of new AMPA receptors into the postsynaptic membrane. NMDA receptors are normally anchored to a scaffolding protein known as PSD95, located inside the postsynaptic membrane. Research has shown that activated CaM-KII can bind with an intracellular component of the NMDA receptor—and also with a set of linking proteins that can attach to AMPA receptors. AMPA receptors are brought in vesicles to the postsynaptic membrane of dendritic spines. They attach to the NMDA receptors, linking proteins attach to them, and then AMPA receptors attach to the linking proteins. (See ***Figure 12.11.***)

CaM-KII Type II calcium-calmodulin kinase, an enzyme that must be activated by calcium; may play a role in the establishment of long-term potentiation.

Figure 12.11

A hypothetical model that describes the insertion of new AMPA receptors into the postsynaptic membrane of dendritic spines after long-term potentiation. The presence of glutamate and membrane depolarization open NMDA receptors. Calcium ions enter and activate molecules of CaM-KII by attaching phosphate groups (P), a process known as *phosphorylation.* Linking proteins attach to the activated CaM-KII, and AMPA receptors, brought to the postsynaptic membrane in vesicles, attach to the linking proteins. The addition of new AMPA receptors results in larger postsynaptic potentials when the terminal button releases glutamate.

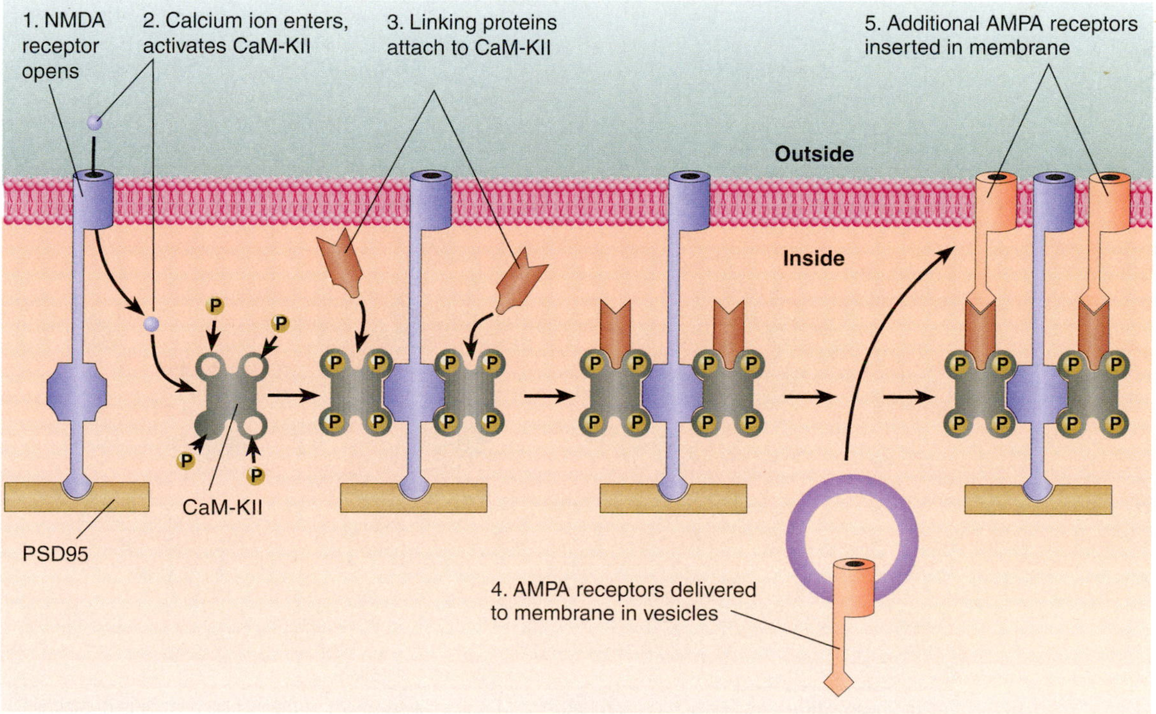

Adapted from Lisman, J., Schulman, H., and Cline, H. *Nature Reviews: Neuroscience,* 2002, *3,* 175–190.

A second change that appears to accompany long-term potentiation is alteration of synaptic structure. For example, Geinisman et al. (1991, 1996) have found that long-term potentiation increased the number of such features, which they referred to as "perforated synapses." Using a special stain that labeled calcium in dendritic spines, Buchs and Muller (1996) found that after long-term potentiation, most of the labeled spines formed perforated synapses with the presynaptic terminals. Thus, perforated synapses appear to be one of the characteristic features of strengthened synapses.

Toni et al. (1999) found evidence that supported the suggestion that perforated synapses are a waypoint on the path to production of new synapses. By examining different hippocampal slices at different times after the induction of long-term potentiation, they could follow the time course of structural changes. At first they saw perforated synapses, but these soon disappeared, to be replaced by a threefold increase in the number of terminal buttons forming synapses with two or more spines. They did not see multiple spine synapses when they pretreated the hippocampal slice with a chemical that prevents the formation of long-term potentiation. (See ***Figure 12.12*** and ***Animation 12.3, Long-Lasting LTP.***)

Animation 12.3, Long-Lasting LTP, shows structural changes that may be responsible for long-lasting long-term potentiation.

Researchers believe that long-term potentiation may also involve a third type of synaptic modifications: *presynaptic* changes, such as an increase in the amount of glutamate that is released by the terminal button. But how could a process that occurs postsynaptically, in the dendritic spines, cause presynaptic changes? A possible answer comes from the discovery that a simple molecule, nitric oxide, can communicate messages from one cell to another. As we saw in Chapter 4, nitric oxide is a soluble gas produced from the amino acid arginine by the activity of an enzyme known as **nitric oxide synthase.** Researchers have found that nitric oxide (NO) is used as a messen-

nitric oxide synthase An enzyme responsible for the production of nitric oxide.

Figure 12.12

A hypothetical series of changes that synapses undergo following long-term potentiation.

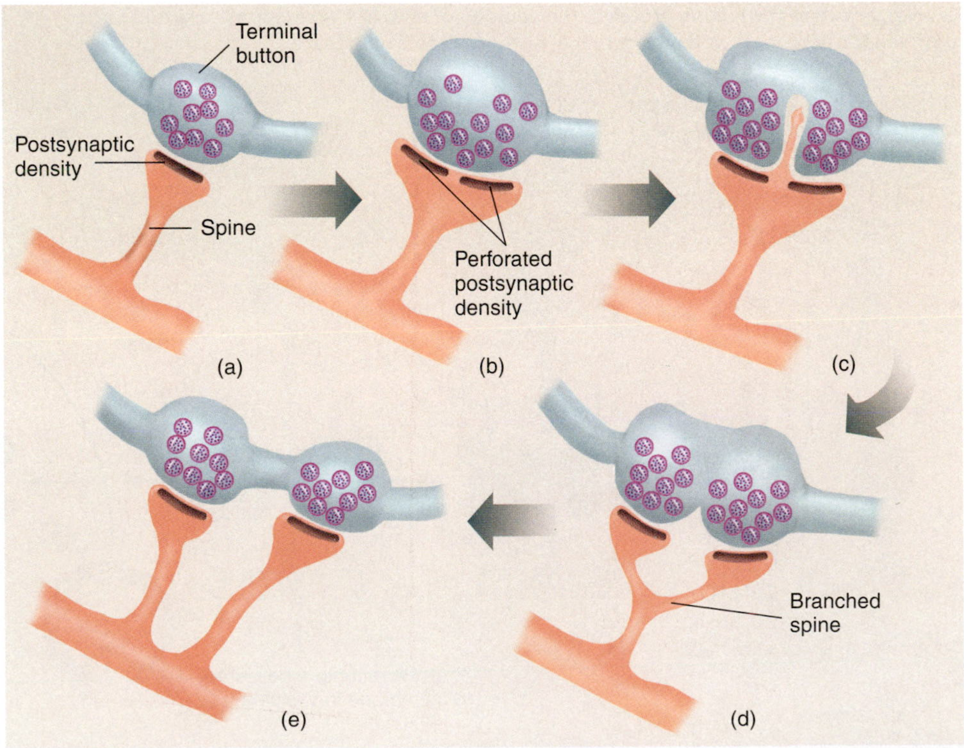

Adapted from Sorra, K. E., Fiala, J. C., and Harris, K. M. Critical assessment of the involvement of perforations, spinules, and spine branching in hippocampal synapse formation. *Journal of Comparative Neurology,* 1998, *398,* 225–240. Copyright © 1998. Reprinted with permission of Wiley-Liss, Inc., a subsidiary of John Wiley & Sons, Inc.

ger in many parts of the body; for example, it is involved in the control of the muscles in the wall of the intestines, it dilates blood vessels in regions of the brain that become metabolically active, and it stimulates the changes in blood vessels that produce penile erections (Culotta and Koshland, 1992). Once produced, NO lasts only a short time before it is destroyed. Thus, if it were produced in dendritic spines in the hippocampal formation, it could diffuse only as far as the nearby terminal buttons, where it might produce changes related to the induction of long-term potentiation.

Several experiments suggest that NO may indeed be a retrograde messenger involved in long-term potentiation. (*Retrograde* means "moving backward"; in this context it refers to messages sent from the dendritic spine back to the terminal button.) Almost simultaneously, four laboratories reported that drugs that block nitric oxide synthase prevented the establishment of long-term potentiation in hippocampal slices (O'Dell et al., 1991; Schuman and Madison, 1991; Bon et al., 1992; Haley, Wilcox, and Chapman, 1992). In addition, Endoh, Maiese, and Wagner (1994) found that a calcium-activated NO synthase is found in several regions of the brain, including the dentate gyrus and fields CA1 and CA3 of the hippocampus. Finally, Zhang and Wong-Riley (1996) found that most cells that contain NO synthase also contain NMDA receptors. Although there is good evidence that NO is one of the signals the dendritic spine uses to communicate with the terminal button, most investigators believe that there must be other signals as well. After all, alterations in synapses require coordinated changes in both presynaptic and postsynaptic elements.

For several years after its discovery, researchers believed that long-term potentiation involved a single process. Since then it has become clear that long-term potentiation consists of several stages. *Long-lasting* long-term potentiation—that is, long-term potentiation that lasts more than a few hours—requires protein synthesis. Frey and his colleagues (Frey et al., 1988; Frey and Morris, 1997) found that drugs that blocks protein synthesis could block the establishment of long-lasting long-term potentiation in field CA1. If the drug was administered before, during, or immediately after a prolonged burst of stimulation was delivered, long-term potentiation occurred, but it disappeared a few hours later. However, if the drug was administered one hour after the synapses had been stimulated, the long-term potentiation persisted. Apparently, the protein synthesis necessary for establishing the later phase of long-lasting, long-term potentiation is accomplished within an hour of stimulation.

Figure 12.13 summarizes the biochemistry discussed in this subsection. I suspect that you might feel overwhelmed by all the new terms I have introduced here, and I hope that the figure will help to clarify things. The evidence we have seen so far indicates that the entry of calcium ions through channels controlled by NMDA receptors activates CaM-KII, a calcium-dependent protein kinase. Activated CaM-KII travels to the postsynaptic density of dendritic spines, where it enables AMPA receptors, sent to the spines in vesicles, to bind with NMDA receptors, which themselves are anchored on strands of PSD95, the scaffolding protein that holds molecules in place in the postsynaptic density. In addition, long-term potentiation initiates rapid changes in synaptic structure such as development of perforated synaptic density. (See ***Figure 12.13.***) The entry of calcium also activates a calcium-dependent NO synthase, and the newly produced NO then presumably diffuses out of the dendritic spine, back to the terminal button. There, it may

Figure 12.13

Long-term potentiation. A summary of the chemical reactions that appear to be triggered by the entry of an adequate amount of calcium into the dendritic spine.

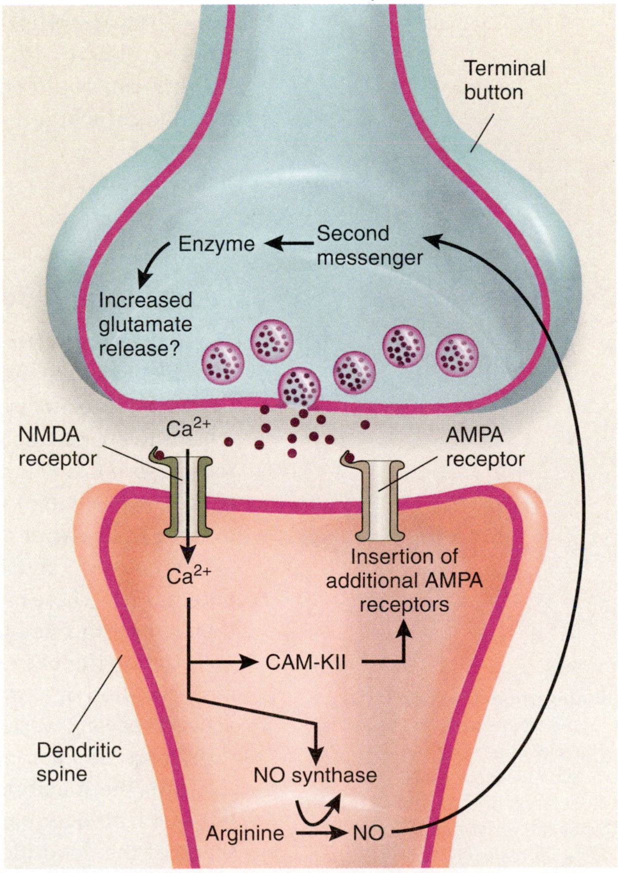

Animation 12.4, Chemistry of LTP, outlines the biochemical steps that appear to take place during long-term potentiation.

trigger unknown chemical reactions that increase the release of glutamate. (See ***Figure 12.13.***) Finally, long-lasting long-term potentiation requires the synthesis of new proteins, which may include components of the cytoskeleton, protein kinases, and receptors. (See ***Animation 12.4, Chemistry of LTP.***)

Long-Term Depression

I mentioned earlier that low-frequency stimulation of the synaptic inputs to a cell can *decrease* rather than increase their strength. This phenomenon, known as **long-term depression,** also plays a role in learning. After all, even though the number of synapses in the brain is very large, it is still finite, and animals can continue to learn throughout their lives. Thus, it seems unlikely that once a synapse is strengthened, it must remain that way forever.

Stanton and Sejnowski (1989) demonstrated associative long-term depression in field CA1. They found that when a weak input was paired with a strong input, long-term potentiation was produced. However, when the two inputs were stimulated at different times, long-term *depression* was produced. Other studies have shown that long-term depression is produced when synaptic inputs are activated at the same time that the postsynaptic membrane is either weakly depolarized or hyperpolarized (Debanne, Gähwiler, and Thompson, 1994; Thiels et al., 1996).

As we saw, long-term potentiation involves an increase in the number of AMPA receptors in the postsynaptic membrane of dendritic spines. Long-term depression appears to involve the opposite: a *decrease* in the number of AMPA receptors (Carroll et al., 1999). And just as AMPA receptors are brought into dendritic spines by vesicles during long-term potentiation, they are taken away from the spines in vesicles during long-term depression (Lüscher et al., 1999).

Thus, at least at some synapses the Hebb rule appears to work in both directions: Inputs that are correlated with strong inputs (or with activation of the postsynaptic neuron) are strengthened, whereas inputs that are *not* correlated with strong inputs (or correlated with *nonactivation* of the postsynaptic neuron) are weakened. This mechanism could conceivably allow for the reversal of previously established synaptic changes when the contingencies in the environment change.

INTERIM SUMMARY

Learning and Synaptic Plasticity

The study of long-term potentiation in the hippocampal formation has suggested a mechanism that might be responsible for at least some of the synaptic changes that occur during learning. High-frequency stimulation of axons in the hippocampal formation strengthens synapses; it leads to an increase in the size of the EPSPs in the dendritic spines of the postsynaptic neurons. Associative long-term potentiation can also occur, in which weak synapses are strengthened by the action of strong ones. In fact, the only requirement for long-term potentiation is that the postsynaptic membrane be depolarized at the same time that the synapses are active.

In field CA1 and in the dentate gyrus, NMDA receptors play a special role in long-term potentiation. These receptors, sensitive to glutamate, control calcium channels but can open them only if the membrane is already depolarized. Thus, the combination of membrane depolarization (for example, from a dendritic spike produced by the activity of strong synapses) and activation of a NMDA receptor causes the entry of calcium ions. The increase in calcium activates several calcium-dependent enzymes, including CaM-KII. Inhibition of CaM-KII disrupts long-term potentiation; presumably, this enzyme causes the insertion of AMPA receptors into the membrane of the dendritic spine, increasing their sensitivity to glutamate released by the terminal button. This change is accompanied by structural alterations in the shape of the dendritic spine, including the appearance of synapse perforated by "fingers" inserted into the terminal button, which may be the first step toward producing additional

long-term depression (LTD) A long-term decrease in the excitability of a neuron to a particular synaptic input caused by stimulation of the terminal button while the postsynaptic membrane is hyperpolarized or only slightly depolarized.

synapses. Long-term potentiation may also involve presynaptic changes, through the activation of NO synthase, an enzyme responsible for the production of nitric oxide. This soluble gas may diffuse into nearby terminal buttons where it facilitates the release of glutamate. Long-lasting, long-term potentiation requires protein synthesis, which appears to take place in the dendrite adjacent to the dendritic spines.

Long-term depression occurs when a synapse is activated at the time that the postsynaptic membrane is hyperpolarized or only slightly depolarized.

THOUGHT QUESTION

The brain is the most complex organ in the body, and it is also the most malleable. Every experience leaves at least a small trace, in the form of altered synapses. When we tell someone something or participate in an encounter that the other person will remember, we are (literally) changing connections in the person's brain. How many synapses change each day? What prevents individual memories from becoming confused?

Perceptual Learning

Learning enables us to adapt to our environment and to respond to changes in it. In particular, it provides us with the ability to perform an appropriate behavior in an appropriate situation. Situations can be as simple as the sound of a buzzer or as complex as the social interactions of a group of people. The first part of learning involves learning to perceive.

Perceptual learning involves learning *about* things, not *what to do* when they are present. (Learning what to do is discussed in the subsequent sections of this chapter.) Perceptual learning can involve learning to recognize entirely new stimuli, or it can involve learning to recognize changes or variations in familiar stimuli. For example, if a friend gets a new hairstyle or replaces glasses with contact lenses, our visual memory of that person changes. We also learn that particular stimuli are found in particular locations or contexts or in the presence of other stimuli. We can even learn and remember particular *episodes:* sequences of events taking place at a particular time and place. The more complex forms of perceptual learning will be discussed in the last section of this chapter, which is devoted to relational learning.

In mammals with large and complex brains, objects are recognized visually by circuits of neurons in the visual association cortex. As we saw in Chapter 6, the primary visual cortex receives information from the lateral geniculate nucleus of the thalamus. Within the primary visual cortex individual modules of neurons analyze information from restricted regions of the visual scene that pertain to movement, orientation, color, binocular disparity, and spatial frequency. Information about each of these attributes is collected in subregions of the extrastriate cortex, which surrounds the primary visual cortex (striate cortex). For example, specific regions are devoted to the analysis of form, color, and movement. After analyzing particular attributes of the visual scene, the subregions of the extrastriate cortex send the results of their analysis to the next level of the visual association cortex. As we saw in Chapter 6, the second level of the visual association cortex is divided into two "streams." The *ventral stream,* which is involved with object recognition, begins in the extrastriate cortex and continues ventrally into the inferior temporal cortex. The *dorsal stream,* which is involved with perception of the location of objects, also begins in the extrastriate cortex of the occipital lobe, but it continues dorsally into the posterior parietal cortex. As

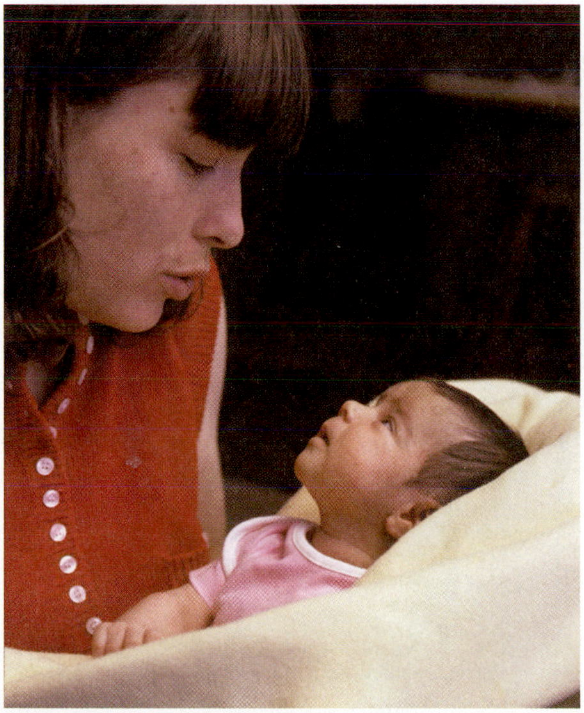

Learning to reorganize another person's face is an important form of perceptual learning.

Figure 12.14

The major divisions of the visual cortex of the rhesus monkey. The arrows indicate the primary direction of the flow of information in the dorsal and ventral streams.

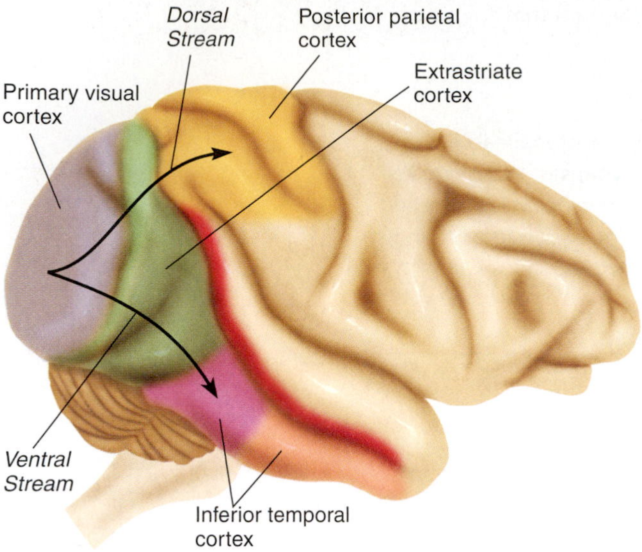

Figure 12.15

Evidence of retrieval of visual memories of movement. The bars represent the level of activation, measured by fMRI, of MT/MST, regions of the visual association cortex that respond to movement. Subjects looked at photographs of static scenes or scenes that implied motion similar to the ones shown here.

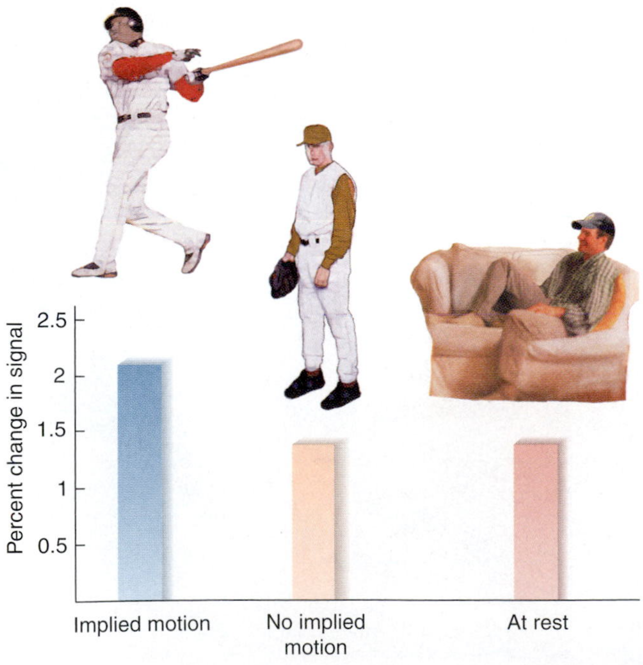

Adapted from Kourtzi, A., and Kanwisher, N. *Journal of Cognitive Neuroscience*, 2000, *12*, 48–55.

some investigators have said, the ventral stream is involved with the *what* of visual perception; the dorsal stream is involved with the *where.* (See ***Figure 12.14.***)

Damage to the visual association cortex impairs people's ability to perceive (and thus, to learn to recognize) particular kinds of visual information. As we saw in Chapter 6, people with damage to the inferior temporal cortex may have excellent vision but be unable to recognize familiar, everyday objects such as scissors, clothespins, or light bulbs—and faces of friends and relatives.

Presumably, learning to recognize a particular visual stimulus is accomplished by changes in synaptic connections in the inferior temporal cortex that establish new neural circuits—changes such as the ones described in the previous section of this chapter. At a later time, when the animal sees the same stimulus again and the same pattern of activity is transmitted to the inferior temporal cortex, these circuits become active again. This activity constitutes the recognition of the stimulus—the readout of the visual memory, so to speak.

As we saw in Chapter 6, some neurons in the inferior temporal cortex show remarkable specificity in their response characteristics, which suggests that they are part of circuits that detect the presence of specific stimuli. For example, neurons located near the superior temporal sulcus become active when an animal is shown pictures of faces. Baylis, Rolls, and Leonard (1985) found that most of these neurons are sensitive to *particular* faces.

Let's look at some evidence from studies with humans that supports the conclusion that activation of neural circuits in sensory association cortex constitutes the "readout" of a perceptual memory. Many years ago, Penfield and Perot (1963) discovered that when they stimulated the visual and auditory association cortex as patients were undergoing seizure surgery, the patients reported memories of images or sounds—for example, images of a familiar street or the sound of the patient's mother's voice. (Seizure surgery is usually performed under a local anesthetic so that the surgeons can talk with the patients and test the effects of brain stimulation on the patients' cognitive functions.)

Kourtzi and Kanwisher (2000) found that specific kinds of visual information can activate very specific regions of visual association cortex. As we saw in Chapter 6, two adjacent regions of the visual association cortex, MT and MST, play an essential role in perception of movement. Kourtzi and Kanwisher presented subjects with photographs that implied motion—for example, an athlete getting ready to throw a ball. They found that photographs like these, but not photographs of people remaining still, activated area MT/MST. Obviously, the photographs did not move, but presumably the subjects' memories contained information about movements they had previously seen. (See ***Figure 12.15.***)

Moscovitch et al. (1995) found that the recall of perceptual memories of the identities and locations of objects in the human brain involve activity in the ventral and

Figure 12.16

The results of PET scans taken while people were performing an object memory retrieval task or spatial memory retrieval task.

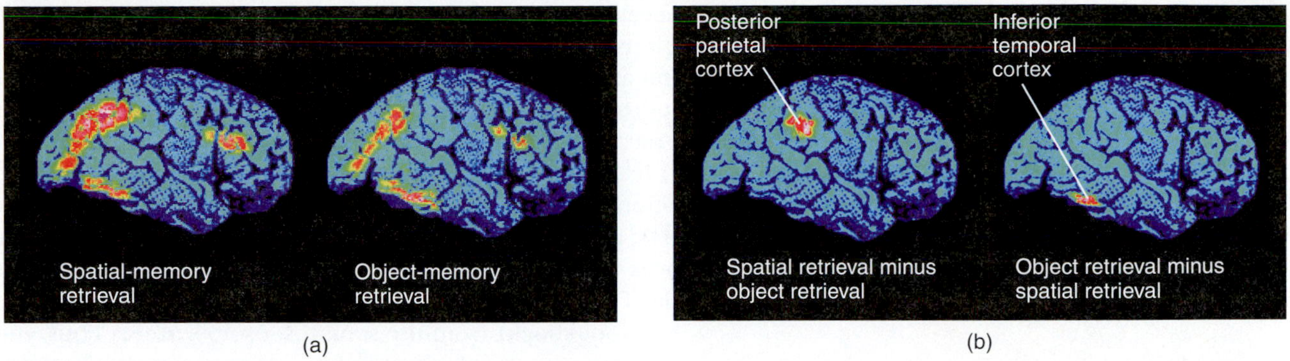

From Moscovitch, M., Kapur, S., Koehler, S., and Houle, S. *Proceedings of the National Academy of Sciences,* 1995, *92,* 3721–3725. Copyright 1995 National Academy of Sciences, U.S.A.

dorsal streams, respectively. These investigators measured the activity of the human brain during the recall of the identity and location of visual stimuli they had previously seen—in other words, the retrieval of perceptual memories of objects and their locations. Both tasks produced activity in the visual association cortex of the occipital, temporal, and parietal lobes, as well as a region of the frontal cortex. (See ***Figure 12.16a.***) The two scans on the right show the differences between the two scans on the left. As you can see, the object-memory retrieval task activated the ventral stream in the inferior temporal cortex, while the spatial-memory retrieval task activated the dorsal stream in the posterior parietal cortex. (See ***Figure 12.16b.***)

INTERIM SUMMARY

Perceptual Learning

Perceptual learning occurs as a result of changes in synaptic connections within the sensory association cortex. Information about the form of visual stimuli is analyzed in the ventral stream of the visual association cortex, and information about the location of visual stimuli is analyzed in the dorsal stream. Electrical recording studies have shown that some neurons in the monkey visual association cortex respond preferentially to particular complex stimuli, including faces. Functional imaging studies with humans have shown that retrieval of memories of pictures, movements, or spatial locations activate the appropriate regions of the visual association cortex.

THOUGHT QUESTION

How many perceptual memories does your brain hold? How many images, sounds, and odors can you recognize, and how many objects and surfaces can you recognize by touch? Is there any way we could estimate these quantities?

Classical Conditioning

Neuroscientists have studied the anatomy and physiology of classical conditioning using many models, such as the gill withdrawal reflex in *Aplysia* (a marine invertebrate) and the eyeblink reflex in the rabbit (Carew, 1989; Lavond, Kim, and Thompson, 1993). I have chosen to describe a simple mammalian model of classical conditioning—the conditioned emotional response—to illustrate the results of such investigations.

The amygdala plays an important role in organizing a pattern of emotional responses that are provoked by aversive stimuli, both learned and unlearned. As we saw in Chapter 10, when the central nucleus of the amygdala is activated, its efferent connections with other regions of the brain trigger several behavioral, autonomic, and endocrine responses that are elicited by aversive stimuli. Most stimuli that cause an aversive emotional response are not intrinsically aversive; we have to *learn* to fear them. The amygdala is part of an important system involved in a particular form of stimulus-response (S-R) learning: classically conditioned emotional responses.

A conditioned emotional response can occur in the absence of the auditory cortex (LeDoux et al., 1984); therefore, I will confine my discussion to the subcortical components of this process. Information about the CS (the tone) reaches the lateral nucleus of the amygdala. This nucleus also receives information about the US (the foot shock) from the somatosensory system. Thus, these two sources of information converge in the lateral nucleus, which means that synaptic changes responsible for learning could take place in this location.

A hypothetical neural circuit is shown in Figure 12.17. The lateral nucleus of the amygdala contains pyramidal cells whose axons project to the central nucleus. Terminal buttons from neurons that transmit auditory and somatosensory information to the lateral nucleus form synapses with dendritic spines on these pyramidal cells. When a rat encounters a painful stimulus, strong synapses in the lateral nucleus are activated; as a result, the pyramidal cells in this nucleus begin firing, which activates neurons in the central nucleus, evoking an unlearned (unconditional) emotional response. If a tone is paired with the painful stimulus, the weak synapses in the lateral amygdala are strengthened through the action of the Hebb rule. (See ***Figure 12.17.***)

This hypothesis has a considerable amount of support. Lesions of the lateral or central nucleus of the amygdala (but not other regions of the amygdala) disrupt conditioned emotional responses that involve a simple auditory stimulus as a CS and a shock to the feet as a US (Kapp et al., 1979; Nader et al., 2001). Thus, the synaptic changes responsible for this learning may take place within this circuit.

Wilensky, Schafe, and LeDoux (1999) temporarily inactivated the lateral amygdala by infusing muscimol, a drug that activates inhibitory GABA receptors, and hence suppresses neural firing. They found that if the lateral amygdala was inactivated during training, when the CS and US pairing were taking place, the animals did not acquire a conditioned emotional response.

Quirk, Repa, and LeDoux (1995) found evidence for synaptic changes in the lateral nucleus of the amygdala. They recorded the activity of neurons in this nucleus in freely moving rats before, during, and after pairing of a tone with a foot shock. Within a few trials the neurons became more responsive to the tone, and many neurons that had not previously responded to the tone began doing so. (See ***Figure 12.18.***) Maren (2000) confirmed these results and also found that the magnitude of the in-

Figure 12.17

The probable location of the changes in synaptic strength produced by the classically conditioned emotional response that results from pairing a tone with a foot shock.

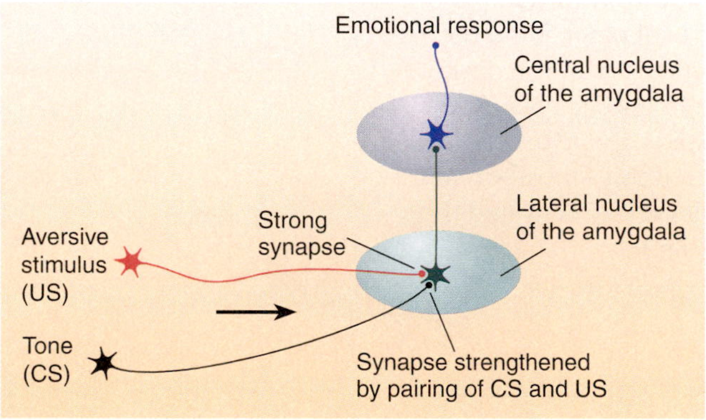

Figure 12.18

Change in rate of firing of neurons in the lateral amygdala in response to the tone, relative to baseline levels.

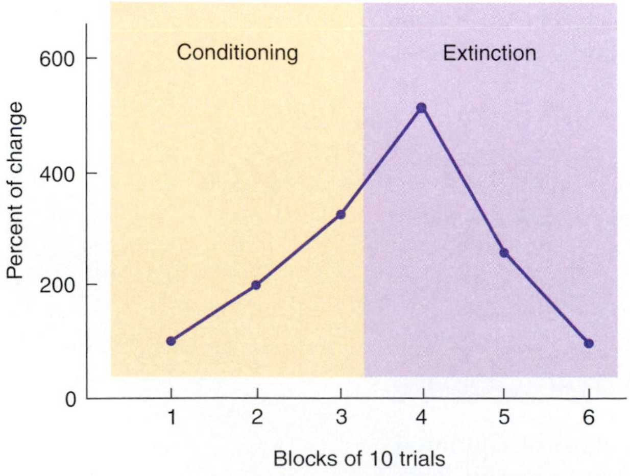

Adapted from Quirk, G. J., Repa, J. C., and LeDoux, J. E. *Neuron,* 1995, *15,* 1029–1039.

creased firing rate in neurons in the lateral nucleus correlated with the magnitude of the conditioned emotional response.

The evidence from several studies supports the hypothesis that the changes in the lateral amygdala responsible for acquisition of a conditioned emotional response involve long-term potentiation. Experiments have shown that long-term potentiation can take place in the synaptic connections in the lateral nucleus of the amygdala. In fact, Rogan and LeDoux (1995) found that when long-term potentiation was produced in the lateral nucleus of the amygdala, neurons there became more responsive to auditory stimuli.

As we saw, long-term potentiation in at least some parts of the brain is accomplished through the activation of NMDA receptors. Several experiments suggest that these receptors also participate in the synaptic plasticity that occurs in the amygdala. When AP5 is injected directly into the basolateral amygdala, rats no longer learned a conditioned emotional response. However, if the AP5 is injected *after* a classically conditioned emotional response has been established, the drug had no effect (Campeau, Miserendino, and Davis, 1992; Fanselow and Kim, 1994). Thus, it seems that AP5 can disrupt the establishment of learning by blocking synaptic plasticity in the basolateral amygdala, but the drug does not affect synaptic changes that have already taken place.

INTERIM SUMMARY

Classical Conditioning

You have already encountered the conditioned emotional response in Chapter 10. When an auditory stimulus (CS) is paired with a foot shock (US), the two types of information converge in the lateral nucleus of the amygdala. This nucleus is connected to the central nucleus, which is responsible for activating the various components of the emotional response. Lesions anywhere in this circuit disrupt the response.

Recordings of single neurons in the lateral nucleus of the amygdala indicate that classical conditioning changes the response of neurons to the CS. The mechanism of synaptic plasticity in this system appears to be NMDA-mediated long-term potentiation. Long-term potentiation can be established in the lateral amygdala, which increases the responses of neurons there to auditory stimuli. In addition, the infusion of an NMDA receptor blocker into the lateral amygdala prevents classical conditioning from taking place but has no effect on conditioning that was established earlier.

Instrumental Conditioning

Instrumental (operant) conditioning is the means by which we (and other animals) profit from experience. If, in a particular situation, we make a response that has favorable outcomes, we will tend to make the response again. Sometimes the response is one that we already know how to perform, which means that all that needs to occur is a strengthening of connections between neural circuits that detect the relevant stimuli and those that control the relevant response. However, if the response is one that we have not made before, our performance is likely to be slow and awkward. As we continue to practice the response, our behavior becomes faster, smoother, and more automatic. In other words, motor learning takes place as well. This section first describes the neural pathways involved in instrumental conditioning and then discusses the neural basis of reinforcement.

Role of the Basal Ganglia

As we saw earlier in this chapter, instrumental conditioning entails the strengthening of connections between neural circuits that detect a particular stimulus and neural circuits that produce a particular response. Clearly, the circuits responsible for instrumental conditioning begin in various regions of the sensory association cortex, where perception takes place, and end in the motor association cortex of the frontal lobe, which controls movements. But what pathways are responsible for these connections, and where do the synaptic changes responsible for the learning take place?

There are two major pathways between the sensory association cortex and the motor association cortex: direct transcortical connections and connections via the basal ganglia and thalamus. (A third pathway, involving the cerebellum and thalamus, also exists, but the role of this pathway in instrumental conditioning has until very recently received little attention from neuroscientists.) Both of these pathways appear to be involved in instrumental conditioning, but they play different roles.

The direct connections between the sensory association cortex and the motor association cortex are, as we saw earlier, involved in short-term memory. In conjunction with the hippocampal formation they are also involved in the acquisition of episodic memories—complex perceptual memories of sequences of events that we witness or are described to us. (The acquisition of these types of memories is discussed in the last section of this chapter.) The transcortical connections are also involved in the acquisition of complex behaviors that involve deliberation or instruction. For example, a person learning to drive a car with a manual transmission might say, "Let's see, push in the clutch, move the shift lever to the left and then away from me—there, it's in gear—now let the clutch come up—oh! It died—I should have given it more gas. Let's see, clutch down, turn the key . . . ." A memorized set of rules (or an instructor sitting next to us) provides a script for us to follow. Of course, this process does not have to be audible or even involve actual movements of the speech muscles; a person can think in words with neural activity that does not result in overt behavior. (Animals that cannot communicate by means of language can acquire complex responses by observing and imitating the behavior of other animals.)

At first, performing a behavior through observation or by following a set of rules is slow and awkward. And because so much of the brain's resources are involved with recalling the rules and applying them to our behavior, we cannot respond to other stimuli in the environment—we must ignore events that might distract us. But then, with practice, the behavior becomes much more fluid. Eventually, we perform it without thinking and can easily do other things at the same time, such as carrying on a conversation with passengers as we drive our car.

Evidence suggests that as learned behaviors become automatic and routine, they are "transferred" to the basal ganglia. The process seems to work like this. As we deliberately perform a complex behavior, the basal ganglia receive information about

When we are first learning a complex skill such as driving a car, we must give it our full attention. Eventually, we can drive without thinking much about it and can easily carry on a conversation with passengers at the same time.

the stimuli that are present and the responses we are making. At first the basal ganglia are passive "observers" of the situation, but as the behaviors are repeated again and again, the basal ganglia begin to learn what to do. Eventually, they take over most of the details of the process, leaving the transcortical circuits free to do something else. We need no longer think about what we are doing.

The basal ganglia receive sensory information from all regions of the cerebral cortex. They also receive information from the frontal lobes about movements that are planned or are actually in progress. (So as you can see, the basal ganglia have all the information they need to monitor the progress of someone learning to drive a car.) The outputs of the basal ganglia are sent to the frontal cortex—to the premotor and supplementary motor cortex, where plans for movements are made, and to the primary motor cortex, where they are executed.

Now let's review some evidence that supports the assertion that the basal ganglia are involved in learning. Studies with laboratory animals have found that lesions of the basal ganglia disrupt instrumental conditioning but do not affect other forms of learning. For example, Fernandez-Ruiz et al. (2001) destroyed the portions of the caudate nucleus and putamen that receive visual information from the ventral stream of the visual association cortex. They found that although the lesions did not disrupt visual perceptual learning, the monkeys' ability to learn to make a visually guided operant response was impaired.

As we saw in the previous section, long-term potentiation appears to play a critical role in classical conditioning. This form of neural plasticity appears to be involved in instrumental conditioning, as well. Packard and Teather (1997) found that blocking NMDA receptors in the basal ganglia with an injection of AP5 disrupted learning guided by a simple visual cue.

Studies with humans also indicate that the basal ganglia play an important role in automatic, nondeliberate learning. Investigators have studied people with Parkinson's disease, a neurological disorder that affects the basal ganglia. The symptoms of Parkinson's disease have been described as "motor deficits." However, some of them can be seen as failures of automated memories. For example, although people with Parkinson's disease usually have sufficient muscular strength, they have difficulty performing many everyday tasks, such as getting out of a chair. Also, if someone bumps into them while they are standing, they are likely to fall—and they will not put their hands out in front of them to catch themselves. These symptoms can, of course, be viewed as motor deficits. But we can also regard them as failure to remember how to do something. We do not think of rising from a chair as a learned behavior, but it surely must be. It involves leaning forward to bring our center of gravity over our feet before beginning to contract the extensor muscles of our legs. Unless the disease is well advanced, people with Parkinson's disease can eventually stand up from a chair, but it takes them some time, as if they have to think about how to do it. Similarly, we do not think of putting our hands out in front of us to break a fall as a learned response, but perhaps it is.

Several experiments have shown that people with diseases of the basal ganglia have deficits that can definitely be attributed to difficulty in learning automatic responses. For example, Owen et al. (1992) found that patients with Parkinson's disease were impaired on learning a visually cued instrumental conditioning task. The patients performed normally on a test of visual recognition, which indicates that their impairment was not caused by a perceptual deficit. Willingham and Koroshetz (1993) found that patients with Huntington's disease (a degenerative disease of the basal ganglia) failed to learn a sequence of button presses.

Reinforcement

Learning provides a means for us to profit from experience—to make responses that provide favorable outcomes. When good things happen (that is, when reinforcing stimuli occur), reinforcement mechanisms in the brain become active, and the establishment of synaptic changes is facilitated.

medial forebrain bundle (MFB) A fiber bundle that runs in a rostral–caudal direction through the basal forebrain and lateral hypothalamus; electrical stimulation of these axons is reinforcing.

ventral tegmental area (VTA) A group of dopaminergic neurons in the ventral midbrain whose axons form the mesolimbic and mesocortical systems; plays a critical role in reinforcement.

nucleus accumbens A nucleus of the basal forebrain near the septum; receives dopamine-secreting terminal buttons from neurons of the ventral tegmental area and is thought to be involved in reinforcement and attention.

Neural Circuits Involved in Reinforcement

Electrical stimulation of many parts of the brain is reinforcing (Olds and Fobes, 1981). The best and most reliable location is the **medial forebrain bundle (MFB),** a bundle of axons that travel in a rostral-caudal axis from the midbrain to the rostral basal forebrain. The MFB passes through the lateral hypothalamus, and it is in this region that most investigators place the tips of their electrodes.

Although there may well be more than one reinforcement mechanism, the activity of dopaminergic neurons plays a particularly important role in this phenomenon. As we saw in Chapter 4, there are three major systems of dopaminergic neurons: the *nigrostriatal system,* the *mesolimbic system,* and the *mesocortical system.* The mesolimbic system begins in the **ventral tegmental area (VTA)** of the midbrain and projects rostrally to several forebrain regions, including the amygdala, the hippocampus, and the **nucleus accumbens (NAC).** This nucleus is located in the basal forebrain rostral to the preoptic area and immediately adjacent to the septum. (In fact, the full name of this region is the *nucleus accumbens septi,* or "nucleus leaning against the septum.") (See ***Figure 12.19.***) The mesocortical system also plays a role in reinforcement. This system also begins in the ventral tegmental area but projects to the prefrontal cortex, the limbic cortex, and the hippocampus.

A large body of experimental evidence indicates that the projections of the mesolimbic pathway that terminate in the nucleus accumbens are at least partly responsible for the reinforcing effects of electrical brain stimulation. These neurons also play an important role in the reinforcing effects of amphetamine, cocaine, and other addictive drugs. (This role is discussed in more detail in Chapter 16.) Treatments that stimulate dopamine receptors in the nucleus accumbens will reinforce behaviors; thus, animals will press a lever that causes electrical stimulation of the ventral tegmental area, the medial forebrain bundle, or the nucleus accumbens itself (Routtenberg and Malsbury, 1969; Crow, 1972; Olds and Fobes, 1981). They will also press

Figure 12.19

Sections through a rat brain showing the location of the ventral tegmental area and the nucleus accumbens.

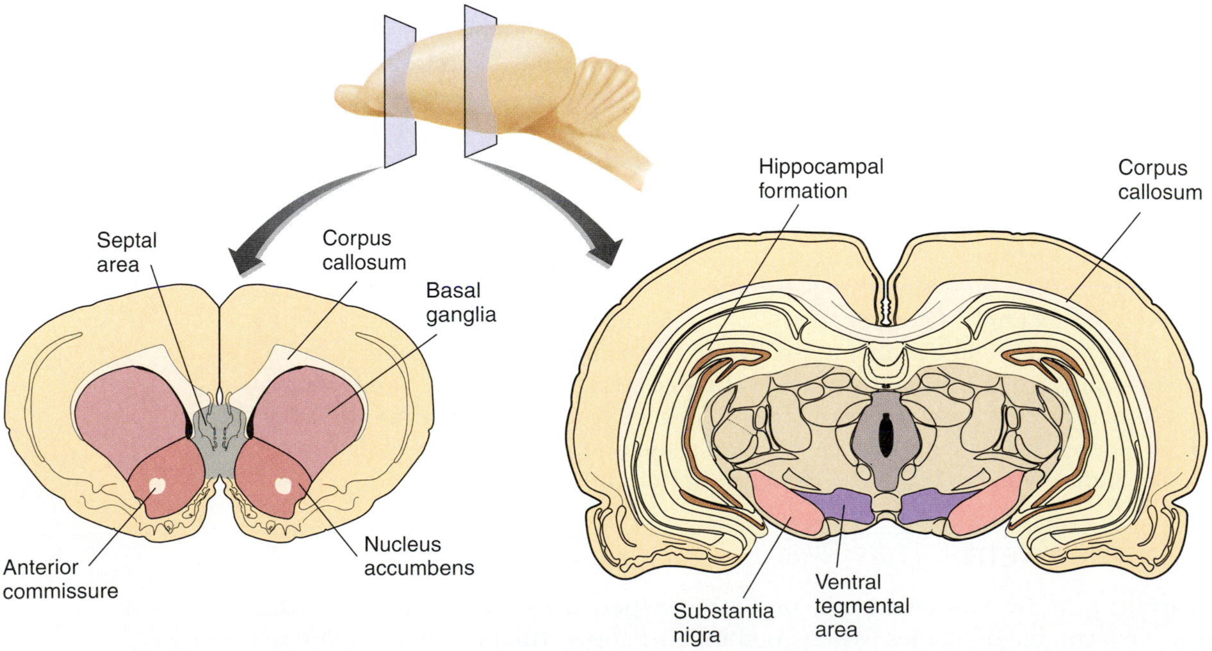

Adapted from Swanson, L. W. *Brain Maps: Structure of the Rat Brain.* New York: Elsevier, 1992.

Figure 12.20

The experiment by Stellar, Kelley, and Corbett (1983). Blocking dopamine receptors in the nucleus accumbens reduces the reinforcing effects of electrical stimulation of the medial forebrain bundle.

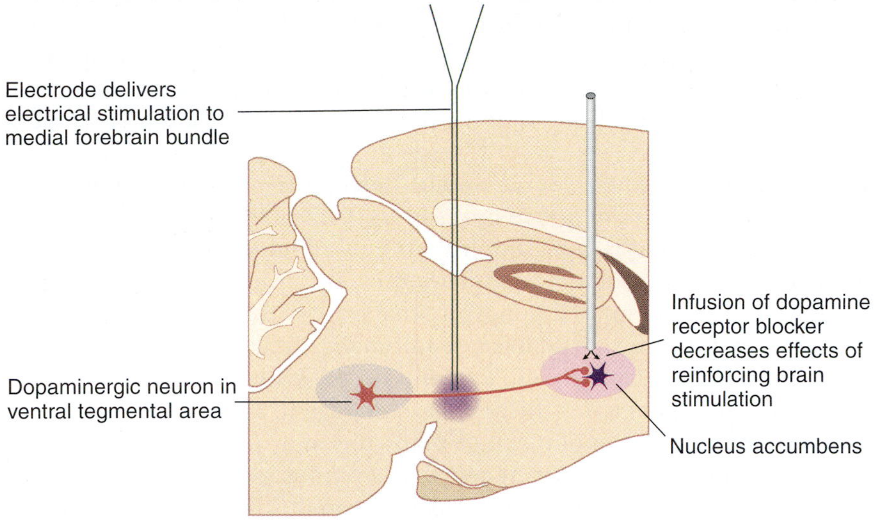

a lever that delivers injections of very small amounts of dopamine or amphetamine directly into the nucleus accumbens (Hoebel et al., 1983; Guerin et al., 1984). And if a drug that blocks dopamine receptors is injected directly into the nucleus accumbens, then electrical stimulation of the mesolimbic pathway becomes less reinforcing (Stellar, Kelley, and Corbett, 1983). (See ***Figure 12.20.***)

Chapter 5 described a research technique called *microdialysis,* which enables an investigator to analyze the contents of the interstitial fluid within a specific region of the brain. Researchers using this method have shown that reinforcing electrical stimulation of the medial forebrain bundle or the ventral tegmental area, or the administration of cocaine or amphetamine, causes the release of dopamine in the nucleus accumbens (Moghaddam and Bunney, 1989; Nakahara et al., 1989; Phillips et al., 1992). (See ***Figure 12.21.***) Microdialysis studies have also found that the presence of natural reinforcers, such as water, food, or a sex partner, stimulates the release of dopamine in the nucleus accumbens. Thus, the effects of reinforcing brain stimulation seem to be similar in many ways to those of natural reinforcers.

Although microdialysis probes are not placed in the brain of humans for experimental purposes, functional imaging studies have shown that reinforcing events activate the human nucleus accumbens. For example, Knutson et al. (2001) found that the nucleus accumbens became more active (and, presumably, dopamine was being released there) when people were presented with stimuli that indicated that they would be receiving money. Aharon et al. (2001) found that young heterosexual men would press a lever that presented pictures of beautiful women (but not handsome men) and that when they saw these pictures, the activity of the nucleus accumbens increased.

Figure 12.21

Release of dopamine in the nucleus accumbens, measured by microdialysis, produced when a rat pressed a lever that delivered electrical stimulation to the ventral tegmental area.

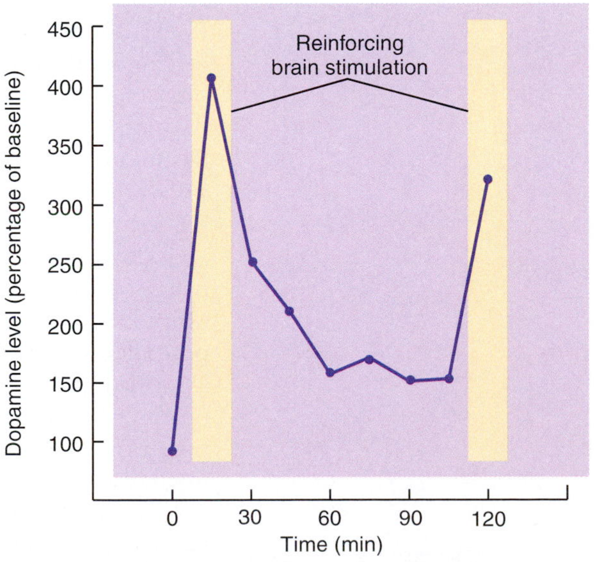

Adapted from Phillips, A. G., Coury, A., Fiorino, D., LePiane, F. G., Brown, E., and Fibiger, H. C. *Annals of the New York Academy of Sciences,* 1992, *654,* 199–206.

Functions of the Reinforcement System

What does reinforcing brain stimulation tell us about the brain mechanisms that are involved in instrumental conditioning? Almost all investigators believe that electrical stimulation of some parts of the brain is reinforcing because it activates the same systems that are activated by natural reinforcers, such as food, water, or sexual contact. A reinforcement system must perform two functions: detect the presence of a reinforcing stimulus (that is, recognize that something good has just happened) and strengthen the connections between the neurons that detect the discriminative stimulus (such as the sight of a lever) and the neurons that produce the instrumental response (a lever press).

Reinforcement occurs when neural circuits detect a reinforcing stimulus and cause the activation of dopaminergic neurons in the ventral tegmental area. Detection of a reinforcing stimulus is not a simple matter; a stimulus that serves as a reinforcer on one occasion may fail to do so on another. For example, the presence of food will reinforce the behavior of a hungry animal but not that of one that has just eaten. Thus, the reinforcement system is not automatically activated when particular stimuli are present; its activation also depends on the state of the animal.

In general, if a stimulus causes the animal to engage in an appetitive behavior (that is, if it approaches the stimulus rather than runs away from it), that stimulus can reinforce the animal's behavior. When that stimulus occurs, it activates the brain's reinforcement mechanism, and the link between the discriminative stimulus and the instrumental response is strengthened.

What neural circuits are responsible for detecting the presence of a reinforcing stimulus (primary or conditioned) and then activating dopaminergic neurons in this region? The ventral tegmental area receives inputs from many regions of the brain. Although we still know very little about how reinforcing stimuli are detected, the three inputs that probably play the most important role in reinforcement are the amygdala, the lateral hypothalamus, and the prefrontal cortex.

As we saw in Chapter 10 and again in this chapter, the amygdala is involved in classically conditioned emotional responses. Several studies suggest that it is also involved in reinforcement. For example, destruction of the amygdala or its disconnection from the visual system has no effect on monkeys' ability to recognize particular visual stimuli by sight, but it does disrupt their ability to remember which of them has been paired with food (Spiegler and Mishkin, 1981; Gaffan, Gaffan, and Harrison, 1988). In addition, Cador, Robbins, and Everitt (1989) and Everitt, Cador, and Robbins (1989) found that neurotoxic lesions of the basolateral amygdala reduced the reinforcing value of stimuli that had been paired with natural reinforcers: water (in thirsty rats) and sexual contact. The experimenters paired the reinforcing stimuli with a flashing light and found that later, the animals would press a lever that turned on the flashing light. Thus, the flashing light had become a conditioned reinforcer. The lesions of the amygdala severely depressed the animals' rate of responding for the flashing light without otherwise affecting their motor performance.

The inputs to the ventral tegmental area from the lateral hypothalamus may also play a role in the detection of reinforcing stimuli. For example, Burton, Rolls, and Mora (1976) studied the response characteristics of single neurons in the lateral hypothalamus and substantia innominata (a nearby region in the basal forebrain). They found that some neurons located there responded to either the sight or taste of food, but they did so *only if the animal was hungry.* Perhaps the connections between the neurons like these and neurons in the ventral tegmental area convey information about the presence of reinforcing stimuli.

The prefrontal cortex also provides an important input to the ventral tegmental area. The terminal buttons of the axons connecting these two areas secrete glutamate, an excitatory neurotransmitter, and the activity of these synapses makes dopaminergic neurons in the ventral tegmental area fire in a bursting pattern, which greatly increases the amount of dopamine they secrete in the nucleus accumbens

(Gariano and Groves, 1988). The prefrontal cortex is generally involved in devising strategies, making plans, evaluating progress made toward goals, judging the appropriateness of one's own behavior, and so on (Mesulam, 1986). Perhaps the prefrontal cortex turns on the reinforcement mechanism when it determines that the ongoing behavior is bringing the organism nearer to its goals—that the present strategy is working.

INTERIM SUMMARY

Instrumental Conditioning

Instrumental conditioning entails the strengthening of connections between neural circuits that detect stimuli and neural circuits that produce responses. One of the locations of these changes appears to be the basal ganglia, especially the changes responsible for learning of automated and routine behaviors. The basal ganglia receive sensory information and information about plans for movement from the neocortex. Damage to the basal ganglia disrupts instrumental conditioning in laboratory animals, and Parkinson's disease disrupts automatic motor responses (as opposed to deliberate ones) and even impairs learning of instrumental conditioning tasks.

Although several neurotransmitters may play a role in reinforcement, one is particularly important: dopamine. The cell bodies of the most important system of dopaminergic neurons are located in the ventral tegmental area, and their axons project to the nucleus accumbens, prefrontal cortex, and amygdala. Stimulation of the ventral tegmental area, nucleus accumbens, or the medial forebrain bundle, which unites these two structures, has reinforcing effects.

Infusions of dopamine agonists directly into the nucleus accumbens will reinforce an animal's behavior. Both laboratory animals and humans will self-administer dopamine agonists such as amphetamine or cocaine; laboratory animals will press a lever to have amphetamine injected directly into the nucleus accumbens. Microdialysis studies have also shown that natural and artificial reinforcers stimulate the release of dopamine in the nucleus accumbens. The system of neurons that detect reinforcing stimuli and activate the dopaminergic neurons in the mesolimbic and mesocortical systems probably involves the amygdala, lateral hypothalamus, and prefrontal cortex; these neurons fire in response to various categories of stimuli that are capable of reinforcing an animal's behavior. Damage to the amygdala disrupts conditioned reinforcement. The frontal cortex may play a role in reinforcement that occurs when our own behavior brings us nearer to a goal.

THOUGHT QUESTION

Have you ever been working hard on a problem and suddenly thought of a possible solution? Did the thought make you feel excited and happy? What would we find if we had a microdialysis probe in your nucleus accumbens?

Relational Learning

So far, I have discussed relatively simple forms of learning, which can be understood as changes in circuits of neurons that detect the presence of particular stimuli or as strengthened connections between neurons that analyze sensory information and those that produce responses. But most forms of learning are more complex; most memories of real objects and events are related to other memories. Seeing a photograph of an old friend may remind you of the sound of the person's name and of the movements you have to make to pronounce it. You may also be reminded of things you have done with your friend: places you have visited, conversations you have had, experiences you have shared. Each of these memories can contain a series of events, complete with sights and sounds, that you will be able to recall in the proper sequence. Obviously, the neural circuits in the visual association cortex that recognize your friend's face are connected to circuits in many other parts of the brain, and these circuits are connected to many others. This chapter discusses research on relational learning, which includes the establishment and retrieval of memories of events and episodes.

Human Anterograde Amnesia

One of the most dramatic and intriguing phenomena caused by brain damage is *anterograde amnesia,* which, at first glance, appears to be the inability to learn new information. However, when we examine the phenomenon more carefully, we find that the basic abilities of perceptual learning, stimulus-response learning, and motor learning are intact but that complex relational learning, of the type I just described, is gone. This section discusses the nature of anterograde amnesia in humans and its anatomical basis. The section that follows discusses related research with laboratory animals.

The term **anterograde amnesia** refers to difficulty in learning new information. A person with pure anterograde amnesia can remember events that occurred in the past, during the time before the brain damage occurred, but cannot retain information he or she encounters *after* the damage. In contrast, **retrograde amnesia** refers to the inability to remember events that happened *before* the brain damage occurred. (See ***Figure 12.22.***) Pure anterograde amnesia is rare; usually, there is also a retrograde amnesia for events that occurred for a period of time before the brain damage occurred.

In 1889 Sergei Korsakoff, a Russian physician, first described a severe memory impairment caused by brain damage, and the disorder was given his name. The most profound symptom of **Korsakoff's syndrome** is a severe anterograde amnesia: The patients appear to be unable to form new memories, although they can still remember old ones. They can converse normally and can remember events that happened long before their brain damage occurred, but they cannot remember events that happened afterward. Korsakoff's syndrome is usually (but not always) a result of chronic alcoholism.

Anterograde amnesia can also be caused by damage to the temporal lobes. Scoville and Milner (1957) reported that bilateral removal of the medial temporal lobe produced a memory impairment in humans that was apparently identical to that seen in Korsakoff's syndrome. Thirty operations had been performed on psychotic patients in an attempt to alleviate their mental disorder, but it was not until this operation was performed on patient H. M. that the anterograde amnesia was discovered. The psychotic patients' behavior was already so disturbed that their amnesia was not detected. However, patient H. M. was reasonably intelligent and was not psychotic; therefore, his postoperative deficit was discovered immediately. He had received the surgery in an attempt to treat his very severe epilepsy, which could not be controlled even by high doses of anticonvulsant medication. The epilepsy appears to have been caused by a head injury he received when he was struck by a bicycle at age nine (Corkin et al., 1997).

The surgery successfully treated H. M.'s seizure disorder, but it became apparent that the operation had produced a serious memory impairment. Subsequently, Scoville and Milner (1957) examined eight of the psychotic patients who were coherent enough to cooperate with them. Careful testing revealed that some of these patients also had anterograde amnesia; the

Figure 12.22

A schematic definition of retrograde amnesia and anterograde amnesia.

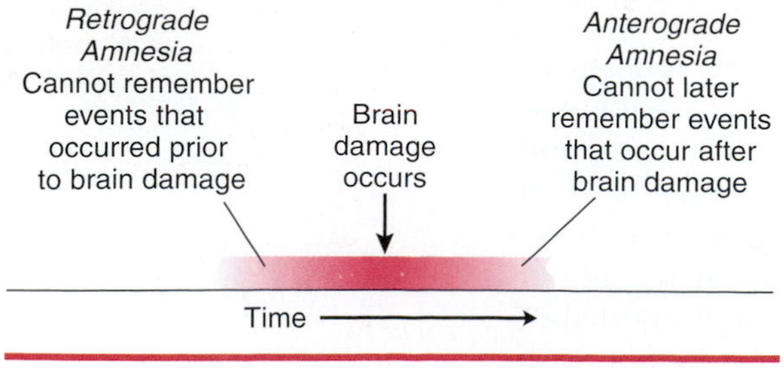
Retrograde Amnesia
Cannot remember events that occurred prior to brain damage
Brain damage occurs
Anterograde Amnesia
Cannot later remember events that occur after brain damage
Time

deficit appeared to occur only when the hippocampus was removed. They concluded that the hippocampus was the critical structure destroyed by the surgery. Once it was discovered that bilateral medial temporal lobectomy causes anterograde amnesia, neurosurgeons stopped performing them and are now careful to operate on only one temporal lobe. (Unilateral temporal lobectomy may cause minor memory problems, but nothing like what occurs after bilateral operations.)

Basic Description

H. M.'s history and memory deficits were described in the chapter prologue (Milner, Corkin, and Teuber, 1968; Milner, 1970; Corkin et al., 1981). Because of his relatively pure amnesia, he has been extensively studied. Milner and her colleagues based the following conclusions on his pattern of deficits:

1. *The hippocampus is not the location of long-term memories; nor is it necessary for the retrieval of long-term memories.* If it were, H. M. would not have been able to remember events from early in his life, he would not know how to talk, he would not know how to dress himself, and so on.
2. *The hippocampus is not the location of immediate (short-term) memories.* If it were, H. M. would not be able to carry on a conversation, because he would not remember what the other person said long enough to think of a reply.
3. *The hippocampus is involved in converting immediate (short-term) memories into long-term memories.* This conclusion is based on a particular hypothesis of memory function: that our immediate memory of an event is retained by neural activity and that long-term memories consist of relatively permanent biochemical or structural changes in neurons. The conclusion seems a reasonable explanation for the fact that when presented with new information, H. M. seems to understand it and remember it as long as he thinks about it but that a permanent record of the information is just never made.

As we will see, these three conclusions are too simple. Subsequent research on patients with anterograde amnesia indicates that the facts are more complicated—and more interesting—than they first appeared to be. But to appreciate the significance of the findings of more recent research, we must understand these three conclusions and remember the facts that led to them.

Many psychologists believe that learning consists of at least two stages: short-term memory and long-term memory. They conceive of short-term memory as a means of storing a limited amount of information temporarily and long-term memory as a means of storing an unlimited amount (or at least an enormously large amount) of information permanently. **Short-term memory** is an immediate memory for stimuli that have just been perceived. We can remember a new item of information (such as a telephone number) for as long as we want to by engaging in a particular behavior: rehearsal. However, once we stop rehearsing the information, we might or might not be able to remember it later; that is, the information might or might not get stored in **long-term memory.**

Short-term memory can hold only a limited amount of information. To demonstrate this fact, read the following numbers to yourself just once, and then close your eyes and recite them back.

1 4 9 2 3 0 7

You probably had no trouble remembering them. Now, try the following set of numbers, and go through them *only once* before you close your eyes.

7 2 5 2 3 9 1 6 5 8 4

Very few people can repeat eleven numbers; in fact, you might not have even bothered to try, once you saw how many numbers there were. Therefore, short-term

anterograde amnesia Amnesia for events that occur after some disturbance to the brain, such as head injury or certain degenerative brain diseases.

retrograde amnesia Amnesia for events that preceded some disturbance to the brain, such as a head injury or electroconvulsive shock.

Korsakoff's syndrome Permanent anterograde amnesia caused by brain damage resulting from chronic alcoholism or malnutrition.

short-term memory Immediate memory for events, which may or may not be consolidated into long-term memory.

long-term memory Relatively stable memory of events that occurred in the more distant past, as opposed to short-term memory.

memory has definite limits. But of course, if you wanted to, you could recite the numbers again and again until you had memorized them; that is, you could rehearse the information in short-term memory until it was eventually stored in long-term memory. Long-term memory has no known limits; and as its name suggests, it is relatively durable. Presumably, it is a result of changes in synaptic strength, such as the ones responsible for long-term potentiation. If we stop thinking about something we have just perceived (that is, something contained in short-term memory), we might or might not remember the information later. However, information in long-term memory need not be continuously rehearsed; once we have learned something, we can stop thinking about it until we need the information at a future time.

Figure 12.23

A simple model of the learning process.

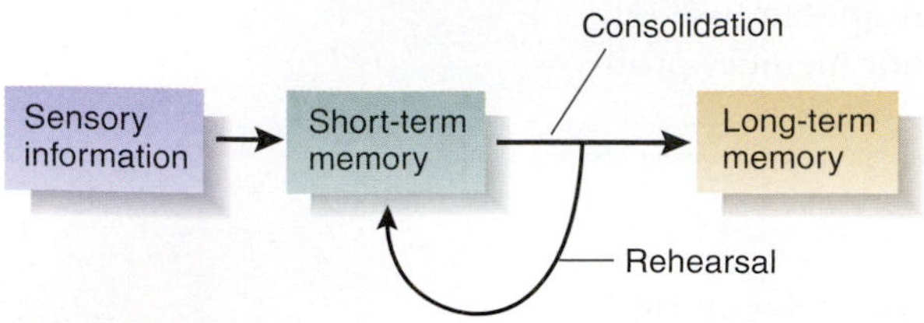

The simplest model of the memory process says that sensory information enters short-term memory, rehearsal keeps it there, and eventually, the information makes its way into long-term memory, where it is permanently stored. The conversion of short-term memories into long-term memories has been called **consolidation,** because the memories are "made solid," so to speak. (See ***Figure 12.23.***)

Now you can understand the original conclusions of Milner and her colleagues: If H. M.'s short-term memory is intact and if he can remember events from before his operation, then the problem must be that consolidation does not take place. Thus, the role of the hippocampal formation in memory is consolidation—converting short-term memories to long-term memories.

Spared Learning Abilities

H. M.'s memory deficit is striking and dramatic. However, when he and other patients with anterograde amnesia are studied more carefully, it becomes apparent that the amnesia does not represent a total failure in learning ability. When the patients are appropriately trained and tested, we find that they are capable of three of the four major types of learning described earlier in this chapter: perceptual learning, sensory-response learning, and motor learning. A review by Spiers, Maguire, and Burgess (2001) summarized 147 cases of anterograde amnesia that are consistent with the description that follow.

Figure 12.24

Examples of broken drawings.

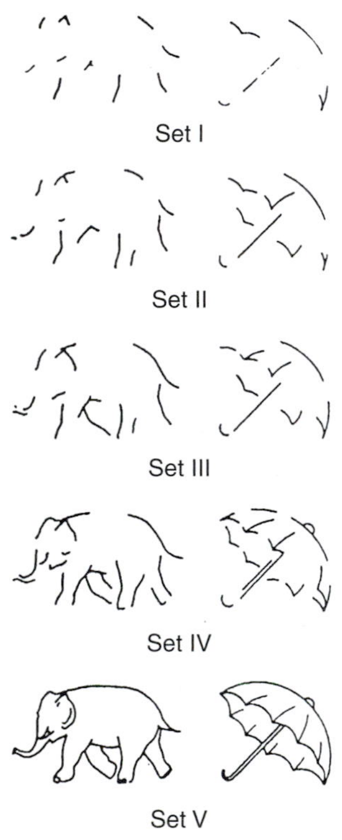

Reprinted with permission of author and publisher from Gollin, E. S. Developmental studies of visual recognition of incomplete objects. *Perceptual and Motor Skills,* 1960, *11,* 289–298.

First, let us consider perceptual learning. Figure 12.24 shows two sample items from a test of the ability to recognize broken drawings; note how the drawings are successively more complete. (See ***Figure 12.24.***) Subjects are first shown the least complete set (set I) of each of twenty different drawings. If they do not recognize a figure (and most people do not recognize set I), they are shown more complete sets until they identify it. One hour later, the subjects are tested again for retention, starting with set I. Patient H. M. was given this test and, when retested an hour later, showed considerable improvement (Milner, 1970). When he was retested four months later, he *still* showed this improvement. His performance was not as good as that of normal control subjects, but he showed unmistakable evidence of long-term retention. (You can try the broken drawing task yourself by running ***Animation 12.5, Implicit Memory Tasks.***)

Animation 12.5, Implicit Memory Tasks, includes interactive demonstrations of memory tasks that can successfully be performed by patients with anterograde amnesia.

Johnson, Kim, and Risse (1985) found that patients with anterograde amnesia could learn to recognize faces and melodies. They played unfamiliar melodies from Korean songs to amnesic patients and found that when they were tested later, the patients preferred these melodies to ones they had not heard before. The experimenters also presented photographs of two men along with stories of their lives: One man was said to be dishonest, mean, and vicious, and the other was described as nice enough to invite home to dinner. Twenty days later, the amnesic patients said they liked the picture of the "nice" man better than that of the "nasty" one.

consolidation The process by which short-term memories are converted into long-term memories.

Investigators have also succeeded in demonstrating stimulus-response learning by H. M. and other amnesic subjects. For example, Woodruff-Pak (1993) found that H. M. and another patient with anterograde amnesia could acquire a classically conditioned eyeblink response. H. M. even showed retention of the task two years later: He acquired the response again in one-tenth the number of trials that were needed previously. Sidman, Stoddard, and Mohr (1968) successfully trained patient H. M. on an instrumental conditioning task—a visual discrimination task in which pennies were given for correct responses.

Finally, several studies have demonstrated motor learning in patients with anterograde amnesia. For example, Reber and Squire (1998) found that subjects with anterograde amnesia could learn a sequence of button presses. They sat in front of a computer screen and watched an asterisk appear—apparently randomly—in one of four locations. Their task was to press the one of four buttons that corresponded to the location of the asterisk. As soon as they did so, the asterisk moved to a new location, and they pressed the corresponding button. (See ***Figure 12.25***.)

Figure 12.25

The procedure of the study by Reber and Squire (1998). Subjects pressed the button in a sequence indicated by movement of the asterisk on the computer screen.

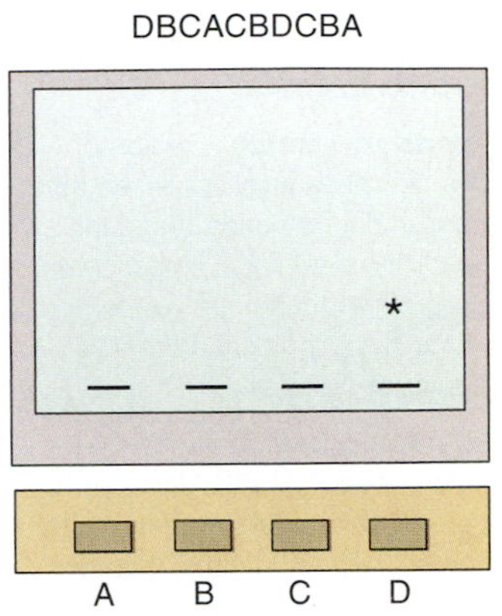

Although experimenters did not say so, the sequence of button presses specified by the moving asterisk was not random. For example, it might be DBCACBDCBA, a ten-item sequence that is repeated continuously. With practice subjects become faster and faster at this task. It is clear that their rate increases because they have learned the sequence, because if the sequence is changed, their performance decreases. The amnesic subjects learned this task just as well as normal subjects did.

As you can see, patients with anterograde amnesia are capable of a variety of forms of perceptual learning, stimulus-response learning, and motor learning.

Declarative and Nondeclarative Memories

If amnesic patients can learn tasks like these, you might ask, why do we call them *amnesic?* The answer is this: Although the patients can learn to perform these tasks, they do not remember anything about having learned them. They do not remember the experimenters, the room in which the training took place, the apparatus that was used, or any events that occurred during the training. Although H. M. learned to recognize the broken drawings, he denied that he had ever seen them before. Although the amnesic patients in the study by Johnson, Kim, and Risse learned to like some of the Korean melodies better, they did not recognize that they had heard them before; nor did they remember having seen the pictures of the two men. Although H. M. successfully acquired a classically conditioned eyeblink response, he did not remember the experimenter, the apparatus, or the headband he wore that held the device that delivered a puff of air to his eye.

In the experiment by Sidman, Stoddard, and Mohr, although H. M. learned to make the correct response (press a panel with a picture of a circle on it), he was unable to recall having done so. In fact, once H. M. had learned the task, the experimenters interrupted him, had him count his pennies (to distract him for a little while), and then asked him to say what he was supposed to do. He seemed puzzled by the question; he had absolutely no idea. But when they turned on the stimuli again, he immediately made the correct response. Finally, although the amnesic subjects in Reber and Squire's study obviously learned the sequence of finger movements, they were completely unaware that there was, in fact, a sequence; they thought that the movement of the asterisk was random.

Learning to ride a bicycle is a combination of stimulus-response learning and motor learning, both of which are nondeclarative in nature. Remembering when we learned to ride a bicycle is an episodic memory, a form of relational learning.

The distinction between what people with anterograde amnesia can and cannot learn is obviously important, because it reflects the basic organization of the learning process. Clearly,

declarative memory Memory that can be verbally expressed, such as memory for events in a person's past.

nondeclarative memory Memory whose formation does not depend on the hippocampal formation; a collective term for perceptual, stimulus-response, and motor memory.

perirhinal cortex A region of limbic cortex adjacent to the hippocampal formation that, along with the parahippocampal cortex, relays information between the entorhinal cortex and other regions of the brain.

parahippocampal cortex A region of limbic cortex adjacent to the hippocampal formation that, along with the perirhinal cortex, relays information between the entorhinal cortex and other regions of the brain.

there are at least two major categories of memories. Psychologists have given them several different names. For example, some investigators (Eichenbaum, Otto, and Cohen, 1992; Squire, 1992) suggest that patients with anterograde amnesia are unable to form **declarative memories,** which have been defined as those that are "explicitly available to conscious recollection as facts, events, or specific stimuli" (Squire, Shimamura, and Amaral, 1989, p. 218). The term *declarative* obviously comes from *declare,* which means "to proclaim; to announce." The term reflects the fact that patients with anterograde amnesia cannot talk about experiences that they have had since the time of their brain damage. Thus, according to Squire and his colleagues, declarative memory is memory of events and facts that we can think and talk about.

The other category of memories, often called **nondeclarative memories,** includes instances of perceptual, stimulus-response, and motor learning that we are not necessarily conscious of. (Some psychologists refer to these two categories as *explicit* and *implicit* memories, respectively.) Nondeclarative memories appear to operate automatically. They do not require deliberate attempts on the part of the learner to memorize something. They do not seem to include facts or experiences; instead, they control behaviors. For example, suppose we learn to ride a bicycle. We do so quite consciously and develop declarative memories about our attempts: who helped us learn, where we rode, how we felt, how many times we fell, and so on. But we also form nondeclarative stimulus-response and motor memories; *we learn to ride.* We learn to make automatic adjustments with our hands and bodies that keep our center of gravity above the wheels.

Graf, Squire, and Mandler (1984) demonstrated perceptual learning for verbal stimuli in subjects with anterograde amnesia. They showed lists of six-letter words to amnesic and nonamnesic subjects and asked them to study each one carefully and rate how much they liked them. The purpose of the rating was to make sure that the subjects spent some time thinking about each word. The investigators then administered two types of memory tests. In the *explicit memory* (declarative memory) condition they asked the subjects to recall the words they had seen. In the *implicit memory* (nondeclarative memory) condition they presented cards containing the first three letters of the words. For example, if one of the words had been DEFINE, they would have been shown a card on which DEF was printed. Several different six-letter words besides *define* begin with the letters DEF, such as *deface, defame, defeat, defect, defend, defied,* and *deform,* so there are several possible responses. The investigators asked the subjects simply to say the first word that started with those letters that came into their minds. As Figure 12.26 shows, the amnesic subjects explicitly remembered fewer than half as many words as the control subjects, but the two groups performed equally well on the implicit memory task. (See ***Figure 12.26.***)

Table 12.1 lists the declarative and nondeclarative memory tasks that I have described so far. (See ***Table 12.1.***)

Figure 12.26

Explicit and implicit memory of amnesic patients and control subjects. The performance of amnesic patients was impaired when they were instructed to try to recall the words they had previously seen but not when they were asked to say the first word that came into their minds.

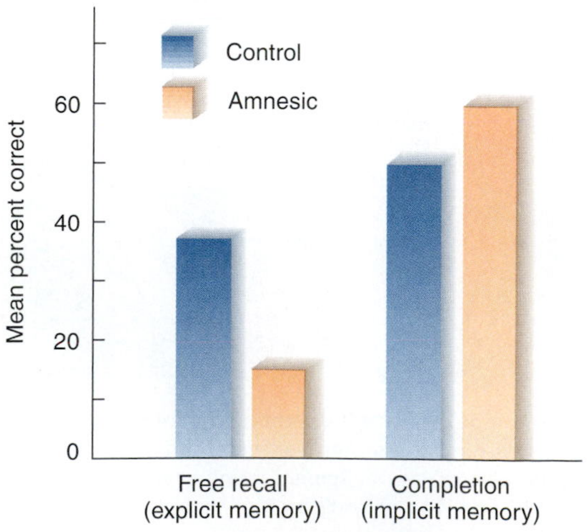

Based on data from Graf, Squire, and Mandler, 1984.

Anatomy of Anterograde Amnesia

The phenomenon of anterograde amnesia and its implications for the nature of relational learning have led investigators to study this phenomenon in laboratory animals. But before I review this research (which has provided some very interesting results), we should examine the brain damage that produces anterograde amnesia. One fact is clear: Damage to the hippocampus, or to regions that supply its inputs and receive its outputs, causes anterograde amnesia.

As we saw earlier in this chapter, the most important input to the hippocampal formation comes from the entorhinal cortex. The entorhinal cortex receives its inputs from the cingulate cortex and all regions of the association cortex, either directly or via two

Table 12.1

Examples of Declarative and Nondeclarative Memory Tasks.	
Declarative Memory Tasks	
Remembering past experiences	
Learning new words	
Recalling words (DEF___)	
Nondeclarative Memory Tasks	**Type of Learning**
Broken drawings	Perceptual
Recognizing faces	Perceptual (and stimulus-response?)
Recognizing melodies	Perceptual
Classical conditioning (eyeblink)	Stimulus-response
Instrumental conditioning (choose circle)	Stimulus-response
Sequence of button presses	Motor
Word completion (DEF___)	Stimulus-response

adjacent regions of limbic cortex: the **perirhinal cortex** and the **parahippocampal cortex.** (See ***Figure** 12.27.*) It also receives information from the amygdala, which may be responsible for the role that emotions play in memories. The outputs of the hippocampal system are relayed back through the entorhinal, perirhinal, and

Figure 12.27

Cortical connections of the hippocampal formation. (a) A view of the base of a monkey's brain. (b) Connections with the cerebral cortex.

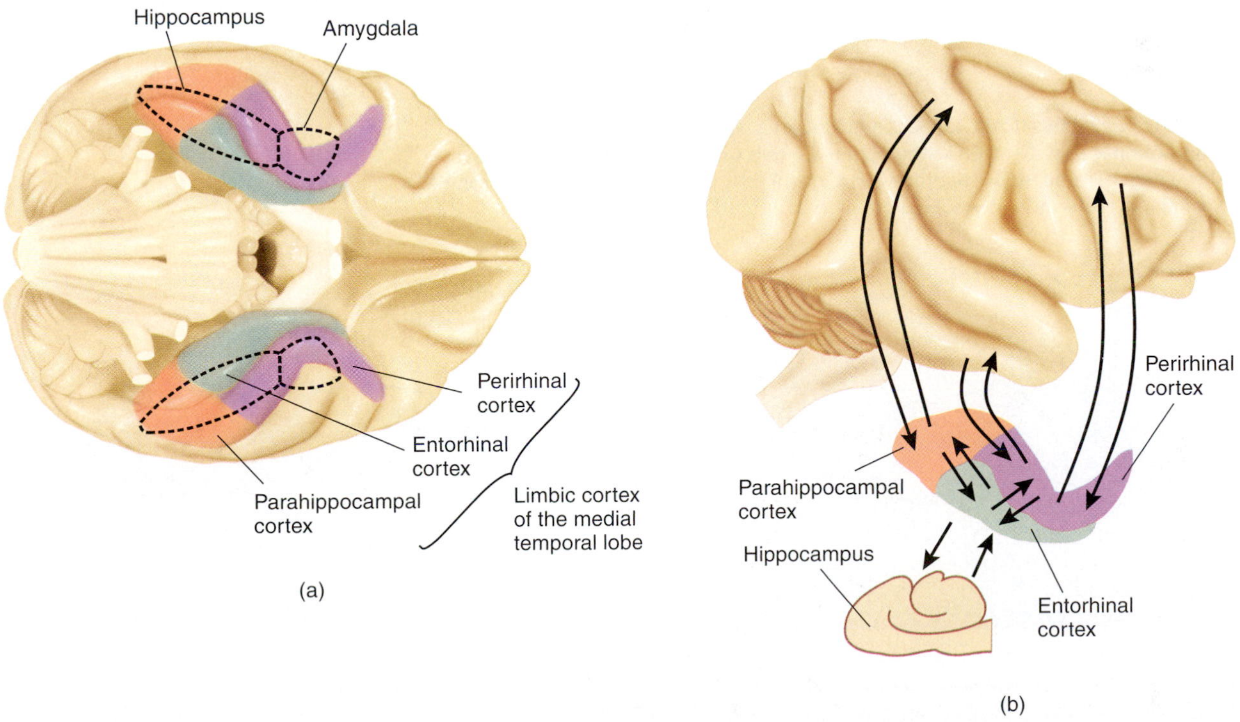

parahippocampal to the same regions that provide inputs: the cingulate cortex and all regions of the association cortex.

The hippocampal formation also receives input from subcortical regions via the fornix. As far as we know, these inputs select and modulate the functions of the hippocampal formation, but they do not supply it with specific information. (An analogy may make this distinction clearer. An antenna supplies a radio with information that is being broadcast, whereas the on–off switch, the volume control, and the station selector control the radio's functions.) The fornix carries dopaminergic axons from the ventral tegmental area, noradrenergic axons from the locus coeruleus, serotonergic axons from the raphe nuclei, and acetylcholinergic axons from the medial septum.

The clearest evidence that damage to the hippocampal formation produces anterograde amnesia came from a case studied by Zola-Morgan, Squire, and Amaral (1986). Patient R. B., a 52-year-old man with a history of heart trouble, sustained a cardiac arrest. Although his heart was successfully restarted, the period of anoxia caused by the temporary halt in blood flow resulted in brain damage. The primary symptom of this brain damage was a permanent anterograde amnesia, which Zola-Morgan and his colleagues carefully documented. Five years after the onset of the amnesia, R. B. died of heart failure. His family gave permission for histological examination of his brain.

The investigators discovered that field CA1 of the hippocampal formation was gone; its neurons had completely degenerated. Subsequent studies reported other patients with anterograde amnesia caused by CA1 damage (Victor and Agamanolis, 1990; Kartsounis, Rudge, and Stevens, 1995; Rempel-Clower et al., 1996). (See ***Figure 12.28.***) In addition, several studies have found that a period of anoxia causes damage to field CA1 in monkeys and in rats and that the damage causes anterograde amnesia in these species too (Auer, Jensen, and Whishaw, 1989; Zola-Morgan et al., 1992).

Why is field CA1 of the hippocampus so sensitive to anoxia? The answer appears to lie in the fact that this region is especially rich in NMDA receptors. For some reason metabolic disturbances of various kinds, including seizures, anoxia, or hypoglycemia, cause glutamatergic terminal buttons to release glutamate at abnormally high levels. The effect of this glutamate release is to stimulate NMDA receptors, which permit the entry of calcium. Within a few minutes excessive amounts of intracellular calcium begins to destroy the neurons. If animals are pretreated with

Figure 12.28

Damage to field CA1 caused by anoxia. (a) Section through a normal hippocampus. (b) Section through the hippocampus of patient G. D. The pyramidal cells of field CA1 (between the two arrowheads) have degenerated. (DG = dentate gyrus, gl, ml, pl = layers of the dentate gyrus, PaS = parasubiculum, PrS = presubiculum, S = subiculum.)

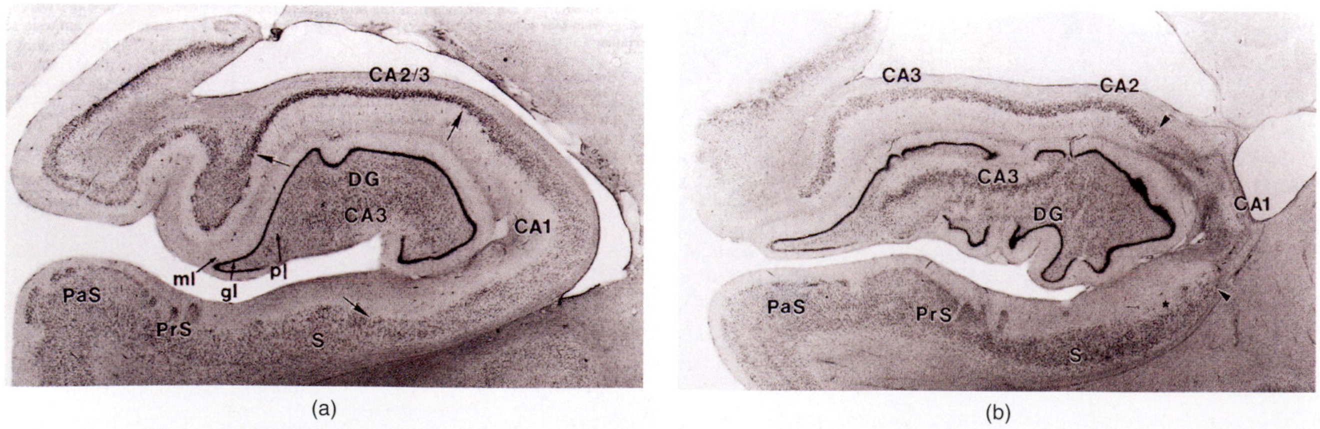

From Rempel-Clower, N. L., Zola, S. M., Squire, L. R., and Amaral, D. G. *Journal of Neuroscience,* 1996, *16,* 5233–5255. Copyright 1996 by the Society for Neuroscience.

drugs that block NMDA receptors, a period of anoxia is much less likely to produce brain damage (Rothman and Olney, 1987). CA1 neurons contain many NMDA receptors, so long-term potentiation can quickly become established there. This flexibility undoubtedly contributes to our ability to learn as quickly as we do. But it also renders these neurons particularly susceptible to damage by metabolic disturbances.

Anterograde Amnesia: Failure of Relational Learning

As we have seen, anterograde amnesia appears to be a loss of the ability to establish new declarative memories; the ability to establish new nondeclarative memories (perceptual, stimulus-response, or motor learning) is intact. What, exactly, are declarative memories? Are they *verbal* memories? Is it simply that people with anterograde amnesia cannot learn new verbal information?

The answer seems to be no. Declarative memories are not necessarily verbal memories; they are recollections of things or events we have previously experienced. Let's consider the most complex forms of declarative memories: memories of particular episodes. Episodic memories consist of collections of perceptions of events organized in time and identified by a particular context. For example, consider my memory of this morning's breakfast. I put on my robe and slippers, walked downstairs, made coffee, drank some orange juice, made waffle batter, baked a waffle, and ate it at the table next to the window. If I wanted to (and if I thought you were interested), I could give you many more details. The point is that the memory contains many events, organized in time. But would we say that my memory is a *verbal* memory? Clearly not; what I remember about my experience this morning is perceptions of a series of *events,* not a series of *words.* I remember not words but perceptions: the sight of the snow falling outside, the feel of the cold floor replaced by the comfortable warmth of my slippers, the smell of the coffee beans as I opened the container, the rasping sound made by the coffee grinder, and so on.

Obviously, memories must be organized. If you asked me about this morning's breakfast, your words would bring to mind a *set* of perceptual memories—memories of events that occurred at a particular time and place. What does the hippocampal formation have to do with that ability? The most likely explanation is that during the original experience, it somehow ties together a series of perceptions in such a way that their memories, too, are linked. The hippocampal formation enables us to learn the *relationship* between the stimuli that were present at the time—the *context* in which the episode occurred—and the events themselves. As we saw, people with anterograde amnesia can form perceptual memories. As studies have shown, once they see something, they are more likely to recognize it later. But their perceptual memories are isolated; the memories of individual objects and events are not tied together or to the context in which they occurred. Thus, seeing a particular person does not remind them of other times they have seen that person or of the things they have done together. Anterograde amnesia appears to be a loss of the ability to learn about the relationships among stimuli, including the time and place in which they occurred and the order of their occurrence.

Role of the Hippocampal Formation in Spatial Memory

I mentioned earlier in this chapter that patient H. M. has not been able to find his way around his present environment. Although spatial information need not be declared (we can demonstrate our topographical memories by successfully getting from place to place), people with anterograde amnesia are unable to consolidate information about the location of rooms, corridors, buildings, roads, and other important items in their environment.

Bilateral damage to the hippocampal formation produces the most profound impairment in spatial memory, but significant deficits can be produced by damage that is limited to the right hemisphere. For example, Luzzi et al. (2001) reported the case of a man with a lesion of the right parahippocampal cortex who lost his ability to find his way around a new environment. The only way he could find his room was by counting doorways from the end of the hall or by seeing a red napkin that was located on top of his bedside table.

Functional imaging studies have shown that the right hippocampal formation becomes active when a person is remembering or performing a navigational task. For example Maguire, Frackowiak, and Frith (1997) had London taxi drivers describe the routes they would take in driving from one location to another. A PET scan taken during their description of the route showed activation of the right hippocampal formation. Maguire et al. (1998) had subjects play a virtual reality computer game that permitted them to navigate around a town. The subjects played the game long enough that its streets, buildings, open spaces, and other features became familiar. The experimenters could close doors or put up barricades that required the subjects to follow alternative routes to get to a particular location. Then they arranged for the subjects to play the game while their heads were in a PET scanner that measured regional brain activation. The images they obtained indicated that the right hippocampal formation became active when the subjects were navigating. In fact, the amount of activity in this region was correlated with the subjects' accuracy in navigation. (See ***Figure 12.29.***)

Relational Learning in Laboratory Animals

The discovery that hippocampal lesions produced anterograde amnesia in humans stimulated interest in the exact role that this structure plays in the learning process. To pursue this interest, experimenters began making lesions of the hippocampal formation in animals and testing their learning ability. They quickly found that the animals remained capable of learning most tasks. At the time they were surprised; some even thought that the hippocampal formation had different functions in humans than it had in other animals. We now realize that most of the learning tasks that the animals were given tested simple stimulus-response learning, and as we saw in the

Figure 12.29

The experiment by Maguire et al. (1991). (a) A scene from the virtual reality game. (b) A PET scan showing activation of the right hippocampal formation from subjects navigating through the "town."

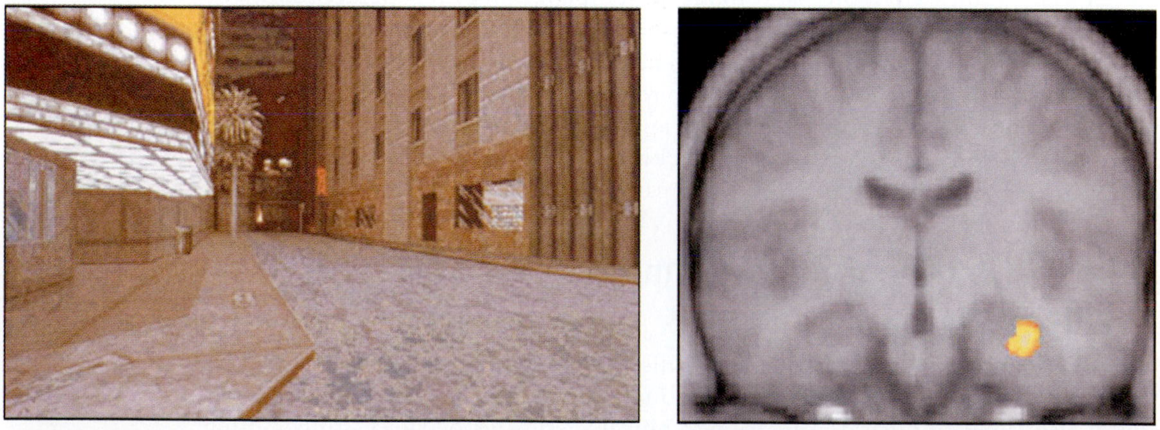

(a) (b)

From Maguire, E. A., Burgess, N., Donnett, J. G., Frackowiak, R. S. J., Frith, C. D., and O'Keefe, J. *Science,* 1998, *280,* 921–924.

previous section, even humans with anterograde amnesia can do well on such tasks. People's anterograde amnesia becomes apparent only when we talk with them, which is something we cannot do with other animals. However, researchers have developed other tasks that require relational learning, and on such tasks laboratory animals with hippocampal lesions show memory deficits, just as humans do.

Spatial Perception and Learning

As we saw, hippocampal lesions disrupt people's ability to keep track of and remember spatial locations. For example, H. M. never learned to find his way home when his parents moved after his surgery. Laboratory animals show similar problems in navigation. Morris et al. (1982) developed a task that has been adopted by other researchers as a standard test of rodents' spatial abilities. The task requires rats to find a particular location in space solely by means of visual cues external to the apparatus. The "maze" consists of a circular pool, 1.3 meters in diameter, filled with a mixture of water and something to increase the opacity of the water, such as powdered milk. The water hides the location of a small platform, situated just beneath the surface of the liquid. The experimenters put the rats into the water and let them swim until they encountered the hidden platform and climbed onto it. They released the rats from a new position on each trial. After a few trials normal rats learned to swim directly to the hidden platform from wherever they were released.

The Morris water maze requires relational learning; to navigate around the maze, the animals get their bearings from the relative locations of stimuli located outside the maze—furniture, windows, doors, and so on. But the maze can be used for nonrelational, stimulus-response learning too. If the animals are always released at the same place, they learn to head in a particular direction—say, toward a particular landmark they can see above the wall of the maze (Eichenbaum, Stewart, and Morris, 1990).

If rats with hippocampal lesions are always released from the same place, they learn this nonrelational, stimulus-response task about as well as normal rats do. However, if they are released from a new position on each trial, they swim in what appears to be an aimless fashion until they finally encounter the platform. (See ***Figure 12.30.***)

Many different types of studies have confirmed the importance of the hippocampus in spatial learning. For example, Gagliardo, Ioalé, and Bingman (1999) found that hippocampal lesions disrupted navigation in homing pigeons. The lesions did not disrupt the birds' ability to use the position of the sun at a particular time of day as a compass pointing toward their home roost. Instead, the lesions disrupted their ability to keep track of where they were when they got near the end of their flight—at a time when the birds begin to use familiar landmarks to determine where they are. In a review of the literature Sherry, Jacobs, and Gaulin (1992) reported that the hippocampal formation of species of birds and rodents that normally store seeds in hidden caches and later retrieve them (and that have excellent memories for spatial locations) is larger than that of animals without this ability.

You may recall from a discussion earlier in this chapter that the left hippocampal formation of London taxi drivers become activated when the drivers describe a complicated route they would take to get between two points in the city. London taxi drivers undergo extensive training to learn how to navigate efficiently in that city; in fact, this training takes about two years, and the drivers receive their license only after passing a rigorous set of tests. We would expect that this topographical learning would produce some changes in various parts of their brains, including their hippocampal formation. Using MRI scans, Maguire et al. (2000) found that the volume of the posterior hippocampus of London taxi drivers was larger than that of control subjects. On the other hand, the volume of the anterior hippocampus was smaller. Furthermore, the longer an individual taxi driver had spent in this occupation, the larger was the volume of the posterior hippocampus—and the smaller was the volume of the anterior hippocampus. As we will see later in this chapter, the dorsal hippocampus of rats (which corresponds to the posterior hippocampus of humans) contains *place cells*—neurons that are directly involved in navigation in space.

Figure 12.30

The Morris water maze. (a) Environmental cues present in the room provide information that permits the animals to orient themselves in space. (b) Variable and fixed starting positions. Normally, rats are released from a different position on each trial. If they are released from the same position every time, the rats can learn to find the hidden platform through stimulus-response learning. (c) Performance of normal rats and rats with hippocampal lesions using variable or fixed starting positions. Hippocampal lesions impair acquisition of the relational task. (d) Representative samples of the paths followed by normal rats and rats with hippocampal lesions on the relational task.

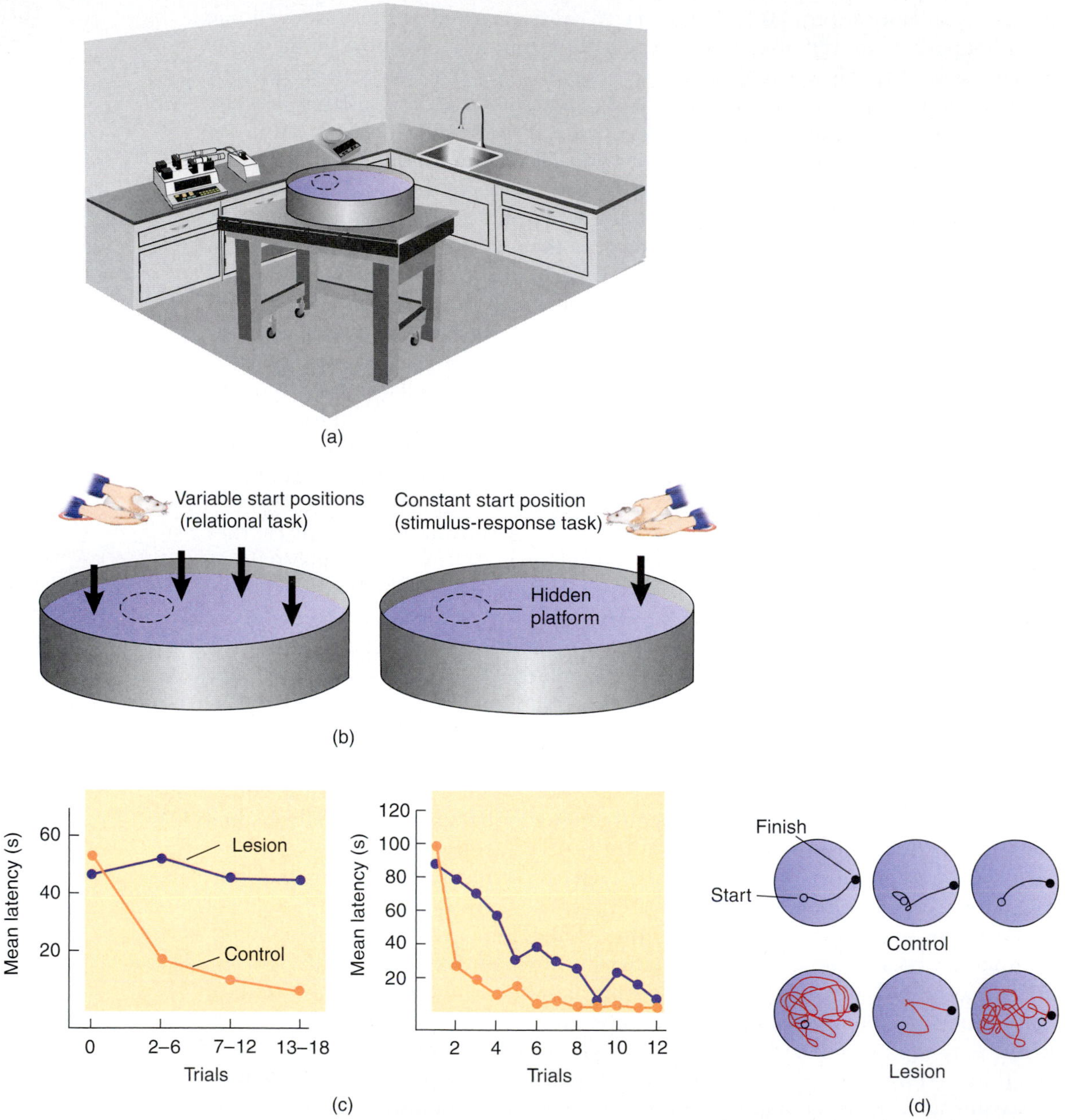

Adapted from Eichenbaum, H. *Nature Reviews: Neuroscience,* 2000, *1,* 41–50. Data from Eichenbaum et al., 1990.

Place Cells in the Hippocampal Formation

One of the most intriguing discoveries about the hippocampal formation was made by O'Keefe and Dostrovsky (1971), who recorded the activity of individual pyramidal cells in the hippocampus as an animal moved around the environment. The experimenters found that some neurons fired at a high rate only when the rat was in a particular location. Different neurons had different **spatial receptive fields;** that is, they responded when the animals were in different locations. A particular neuron might fire twenty times per second when the animal was in a particular location but only a few times per hour when it was located elsewhere. For obvious reasons these neurons were named **place cells.**

spatial receptive field The region of the environment into which the entry of an animal will produce an increase in the firing rate of a place cell in the animal's brain.

place cell A neuron that becomes active when the animal is in a particular location in the environment; most typically found in the hippocampal formation.

When a rat is placed in a symmetrical chamber, where there are few cues to distinguish one part of the apparatus from another, the animal must keep track of its location from objects it sees (or hears) in the environment outside the maze. Changes in these items affect the firing of the rats' place cells as well as their navigational ability. When experimenters move the stimuli as a group, maintaining their relative positions, the animals simply reorient their responses accordingly. However, when the experimenters interchange the stimuli so that they are arranged in a new order, the animals' performance (and the firing of their place cells) is disrupted. (Imagine how disoriented you might be if you entered a familiar room and found that the windows, doors, and furniture were in new positions.)

The fact that neurons in the hippocampal formation have spatial receptive fields does not mean that each neuron encodes a particular location. Instead, this information is undoubtedly represented by particular *patterns* of activity in circuits of neurons within the hippocampal formation. In rodents most hippocampal place cells are found in the dorsal hippocampus, which corresponds to the posterior hippocampus in humans (Best, White, and Minai, 2001).

Evidence indicates that firing of hippocampal place cells appears to reflect the location where an animal "thinks" it is. Skaggs and McNaughton (1998) constructed an apparatus that contained two nearly identical chambers connected by a corridor. Each day, rats were placed in one of the chambers, and a cluster of electrodes in the animals' brains recorded the activity of hippocampal place cells. Each rat was always placed in the same chamber each day. Some of the place cells showed similar patterns of activity in each of the chambers, and some showed different patterns, which suggests that the hippocampus "realized" that there were two different compartments but also "recognized" the similarities between them. Then, on the last day of the experiment, the investigators placed the rats in the other chamber of the apparatus. For example, if a rat was usually placed in the north chamber, on the last day it was placed in the south chamber. The firing pattern of the place cells in at least half of the rats indicated that the hippocampus "thought" it was in the usual chamber—the one to the north. However, once the rat left the chamber and entered the corridor, it saw that it had to turn to the left to get to the other chamber and not to the right. The animal apparently realized its mistake, because for the rest of that session the neurons fired appropriately. They displayed the "north" pattern in the north chamber and the "south" pattern in the south chamber. (See ***Figure 12.31.***)

Figure 12.31

The apparatus used in the study by Skaggs and McNaughton (1998). Place cells reflect the location where the animal "thinks" it is. Because the rat was normally placed in the north chamber, its hippocampal place cells responded as if it were there when it was placed in the south chamber one day. However, once it stuck its head into the corridor, it saw that the other chamber was located to its right, so it "realized" that it had just been in the south chamber. From then on, the pattern of firing of the hippocampal place cells accurately reflected the chamber in which the animal was located.

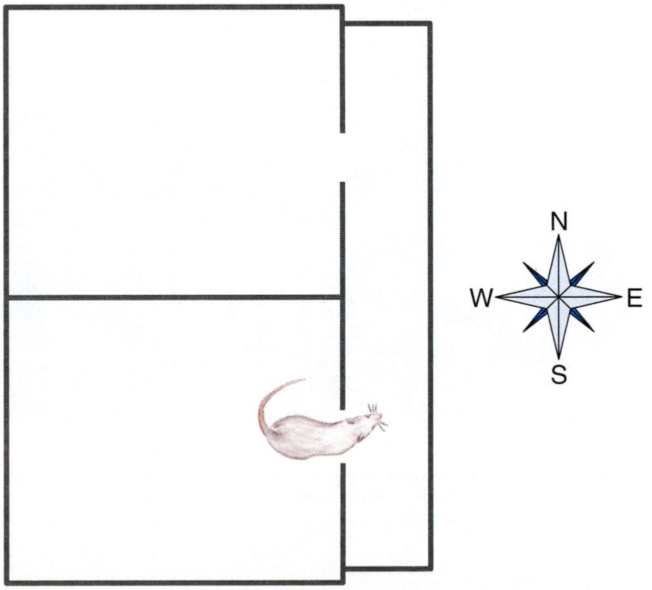

The hippocampal formations of monkeys, like those of rodents, also contain neurons that respond to location, but most of them encode information about what part of the environment the animal is *looking at* rather than where the animal is located. The firing of these cells is not affected by the position of the eye, the orientation of its head, or the position in which the monkey is located. Thus, the neurons seem to represent locations "out there" (Rolls, 1996; Georges-François, Rolls, and Robertson, 1999). Rolls and his colleagues refers to these neurons as *spatial view cells* and suggests that their presence in the hippocampus of the monkey reflects the fact that vision is such an important sense modality for primates. The hippocampus of the monkey also contains place cells that respond the way they do in the hippocampus of the rat, but there are many fewer of these cells (O'Mara et al., 1994). On the basis of these findings, I would predict that the posterior hippocampus of the human brain contains spatial view cells, which are probably also activated when a person *thinks about* a particular place.

Role of Long-Term Potentiation in Relational Learning

In the first part of this chapter we saw how synaptic connections could be quickly modified in the hippocampal formation, leading to long-term potentiation or long-term depression. Are these changes in synaptic strength related to the role the hippocampus plays in learning?

The answer appears to be yes. Recently, researchers have developed targeted mutations of the gene responsible for the production of NMDA receptors which are responsible for long-term potentiation in several parts of the hippocampal formation. Two studies from the same laboratory (McHugh et al., 1996; Tsien, Huerta, and Tonegawa, 1996) produced a targeted mutation of the NMDA receptor gene that affected only the CA1 pyramidal cells. NMDA receptors in these neurons failed to develop; in all other parts of the brain these receptors were normal. Figure 12.32 shows photomicrographs of slices through the hippocampus of a normal mouse and a knockout mouse that were stained for the messenger RNA for the NMDA receptor. As you can see, this chemical is missing in the CA1 field of the mouse with the targeted mutation. (See ***Figure 12.32.***)

As you might expect, the experimenters found that the lack of NMDA receptors prevented the establishment of long-term potentiation in field CA1 in the mice with the targeted mutation. In addition, although the pyramidal cells of CA1 did show spatial receptive fields, these fields were larger and less focused than those shown by cells in normal animals. Finally, the knockout mice learned a Morris water maze much more slowly than mice whose CA1 neurons contained NMDA receptors.

An extraordinary experiment from Tsien's laboratory (Tang et al., 1999) performed a genetic manipulation in mice that caused the increased production of a particular subunit of the NMDA receptor—NMDA-R2B—in the forebrain. The calcium channel of an NMDA receptor that contains this subunit produces a slightly larger excitatory postsynaptic potential than an NMDA receptor that contains the other subunit—NMDA-R2A. Thus, EPSPs produced by NMDA receptors in the hippocampus, amygdala, cortex, and basal ganglia were slightly longer in the genetically modified mice. As a consequence, long-term potentiation was enhanced in hippocampal slices taken from the genetically modified mice. The animals also learned to find the platform in a Morris water maze faster than animals with normal NMDA receptors, which strongly suggests that hippocampal long-term potentiation plays an important role in relational learning. Some commentators have suggested that this genetic manipulation might enable us to produce smarter animals—or even smarter people. However, if we would really be better off with more NMDA-R2B subunits in our brains, natural selection would probably have bequeathed them to us. Considering the fact that the large concentration of

Figure 12.32

Effects of a targeted mutation (knockout) of the NMDA receptor gene expressed only in field CA1 of the hippocampus. Photomicrographs of sections through the hippocampus stained for the messenger RNA responsible for the production of NMDA receptors. (a) Normal mouse. (b) Mouse with the targeted mutation (CA1 knockout). Ctx = neocortex, CA1 = hippocampal field CA1, DG = dentate gyrus.

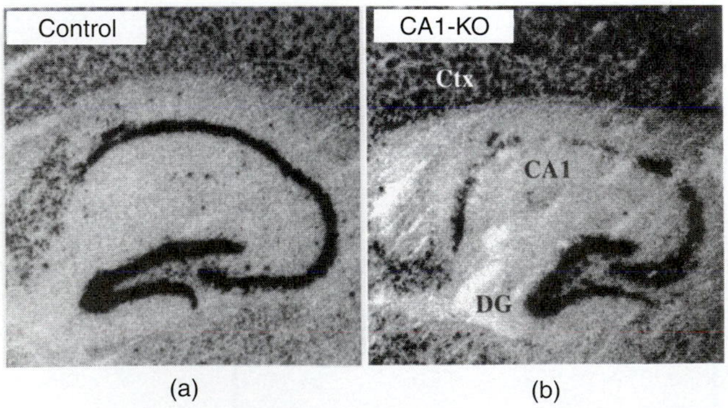

From Tsien, J. Z., Huerta, P. T., and Tonegawa, S. *Cell,* 1996, *87,* 1327–1338. Copyright 1996 Cell Press.

NMDA receptors already makes the hippocampus susceptible to seizure activity and to damage from anoxia, we are probably better off the way we are.

INTERIM SUMMARY

Relational Learning

Brain damage can produce anterograde amnesia, which consists of the inability to remember events that happen after the damage occurs, even though short-term memory (such as that needed to carry on a conversation) is largely intact. The patients also have a retrograde amnesia of several years' duration but can remember information from the distant past. Anterograde amnesia can be caused by the brain damage that sometimes accompanies chronic alcoholism (Korsakoff's syndrome), or it can be produced by bilateral removal of the medial temporal lobes.

The first explanation for anterograde amnesia was that the brain's ability to consolidate short-term memories into long-term memories was damaged. However, ordinary perceptual, stimulus-response, and motor learning do not appear to be impaired; people can learn to recognize new stimuli, they are capable of instrumental and classical conditioning, and they can acquire motor memories. But they are not capable of *declarative learning*—of describing events that happen to them. The amnesia has also been called a deficit in explicit memory. An even more descriptive term—one that applies to laboratory animals as well as to humans—is *relational learning.*

Although other structures may be involved, researchers are now confident that the primary cause of anterograde amnesia is damage to the hippocampal formation or to its inputs and outputs. Temporary anoxia damages field CA1 and produces anterograde amnesia. The entorhinal cortex receives information from all regions of the association cortex, directly and through its connections with the perirhinal and parahippocampal cortex that surrounds it. The outputs of the hippocampal formation are relayed through these same regions. Subcortical inputs and outputs to the hippocampal formation pass through the fornix and modulate hippocampal functions.

Studies with laboratory animals indicate that damage to the hippocampal formation disrupts the ability to learn spatial relations. For example, rats with hippocampal damage cannot learn the Morris water maze unless they can see the platform or they are always released from the same place in the maze. The basic deficit appears to be an inability to distinguish among different contexts, which includes locations in space and in time.

The hippocampal formation contains neurons that respond when the animal is in a particular location, which implies that the hippocampus contains neural networks that keep track of the relations among stimuli in the environment that define the animal's location. Place cells in primates tend to respond according to the particular location the animal is looking at.

Long-term potentiation appears to be related to learning. A unique targeted mutation against the NMDA receptor gene in field CA1 disrupts long-term potentiation and the ability to learn the Morris water maze. Conversely, both long-term potentiation and the ability to learn the Morris water maze were enhanced by a mutation that increased the amount of calcium ions admitted by NMDA receptors in the forebrain.

THOUGHT QUESTION

Although we can live only in the present, our memories are an important aspect of our identities. What do you think it would be like to have a memory deficit like H. M.'s? Imagine having no recollection of over thirty years of experiences. Imagine being surprised every time you see yourself in the mirror and discover someone who is more than thirty years older than you believe yourself to be.

EPILOGUE

What, Exactly, Does the Hippocampus Do?

As we saw earlier, people with anterograde amnesia can learn to recognize new stimuli, can learn new responses, and can learn to make a particular response when a particular stimulus is presented. What they cannot do is to talk about what they have learned. Anterograde amnesia appears to be a loss of the ability to learn about complex relations between many stimuli, including the order of their occurrence in time. How does research with laboratory animals help us to understand this process?

Many investigators have come to the conclusion that the deficit in spatial learning produced by hippocampal lesions is caused by a failure to learn complex relations among stimuli—patterns of stimuli rather than the individual stimuli themselves. I think it is likely that the original function of the hippocampus was to help the animal learn to navigate in the environment. Later, the process of evolution gave the hippocampus the ability to detect other types of contexts also.

Let's first consider the spatial functions of the hippocampal formation. Suppose you are standing in an environment similar to the circular water maze I described earlier: a large field covered with grass and surrounded by distinctive objects such as trees and buildings. You are familiar with the environment, having walked across it and played games on it many times. If someone blindfolds you and then picks you up and drops you somewhere on the field, you will recognize your location as soon as you remove the blindfold. Your location is defined by the *configuration* of objects you see—the *relationship* they have with respect to each other. You will get a different view of these objects from each position on the field. Of course, if there are distinctive objects present on the field itself (trees, garbage cans, drinking fountains), the task will be even easier because you can judge your position relative to nearby objects as well as distant ones.

How can we put all the information about the hippocampal complex together? As you will recall, the hippocampal complex receives information from all regions of the sensory association cortex and from the motor association cortex of the frontal lobe. It also receives information from the amygdala concerning odors and dangerous stimuli. Thus, the hippocampal complex knows what is going on in the environment, where we are located, and what responses we have just made. It also knows about our emotional state: whether we are hungry, frightened, and so on. Thus, when something happens, the hippocampal system has all the information necessary to put that event into the proper context.

What does context have to do with declarative memory deficits? Let's go back to a study involving someone with hippocampal damage and consider why that person can learn a nondeclarative task but cannot recall anything about the experience later. Consider a normal person learning to press a panel with a picture of a circle on it, as patient H. M. did in the experiment by Sidman, Stoddard, and Mohr (1968). While the person is seated in front of the apparatus, his or her hippocampal formation receives information about the context in which the learning is taking place: the room, the other people present, the person's mood, and so on. These pieces of information are collected and are somehow attached to the patterns of activity in the association cortex in several different regions of the brain. Later, when the person is asked about the task, the question reactivates the pattern of activity in the hippocampus, which causes the retrieval of the memory of the episode, pieces of which are stored all over the brain. Patient H. M., lacking a functioning hippocampal system, was unable to accomplish this act.

This analysis is certainly speculative, but I think it is consistent with the experimental data I have presented in this chapter. Of course, it is vague about many parts of the process. For example, just how does asking someone a question activate the pattern of activity in the hippocampus? And how, exactly, are memories "tied together"? How are pieces of information collected and attached to sets of neural circuits? Obviously, we need to think about these questions, design clever experiments to obtain useful information, think about the questions in light of the new information, design more clever experiments. . . .

KEY CONCEPTS

THE NATURE OF LEARNING

1. Learning takes many forms. The most important categories appear to be perceptual learning, stimulus-response learning, motor learning, and relational learning.
2. The Hebb rule describes the synaptic change that appears to be responsible for stimulus-response learning: If an initially weak synapse repeatedly fires at the same time that the postsynaptic neuron fires, the synapse will become strengthened.

LEARNING AND SYNAPTIC PLASTICITY

3. Long-term potentiation occurs when axons in the hippocampal formation are repeatedly stimulated.

4. Associative long-term potentiation appears to follow the Hebb rule and understanding it may help us understand the physiological basis of learning.
5. The special properties of NMDA receptors as both voltage- and neurotransmitter-dependent account for associative long-term potentiation.
6. The entry of calcium into dendritic spines activates enzymes that cause the insertion of AMPA receptors into the postsynaptic membrane and initiate structural changes in the synapse.

PERCEPTUAL LEARNING

7. Learning to recognize complex stimuli involves changes in the association cortex of the appropriate sensory modality.

CLASSICAL CONDITIONING

8. Study of the role of the amygdala and associated structures in learning conditioned emotional responses has furthered our understanding of the physiological basis of classical conditioning.

INSTRUMENTAL CONDITIONING

9. The basal ganglia appear to be involved in the retention of learned behaviors that have become automatic and routine.
10. Electrical stimulation of several parts of the brain—especially the medial forebrain bundle—can reinforce an animal's behavior.
11. Reinforcing brain stimulation and natural reinforcers are effective because they cause the activation of neurons in the mesolimbic system, which release dopamine in the nucleus accumbens.
12. Drugs that block dopaminergic transmission in the nucleus accumbens block the reinforcing effects of electrical stimulation of the brain.

RELATIONAL LEARNING

13. Damage to the hippocampal formation causes a syndrome of anterograde amnesia, in which people can still learn to perform perceptual, stimulus-response, or motor learning tasks but can no longer describe episodes from their lives that occur after the time of the brain damage.
14. Studies with laboratory animals suggest that the hippocampal formation, which may originally have developed as part of a mechanism for spatial learning, is now also responsible for other forms of relational learning, recognizing contexts, and coordinating learning that takes place in other parts of the brain.

SUGGESTED READINGS

Gazzaniga, M. S. *The Mind's Past.* Berkeley, CA: University of California Press, 1998.

Lisman, J., Schulman, H., and Cline, H. The molecular basis of CaMKII function in synaptic and behavioural memory. *Nature Reviews: Neuroscience,* 2002, *3,* 175–190.

McGaugh, J. L., Weinberger, N. M., and Lynch, G. *Brain and Memory: Modulation and Mediation of Neuroplasticity.* New York: Oxford University Press, 1995.

Squire, L. R., and Kandel, E. R. *Memory: From Mind to Molecules.* New York: Scientific American Library, 1999.

SUGGESTED WEB SITES

Neural Plasticity and LTP Page

http://hallux.medschool.hscbklyn.edu/~eric/#Plastica

The site contains tutorials relating to neural plasticity and to long-term potentiation.

Medial Temporal Lobe and Memory

http://thalamus.wustl.edu/course/limbic.html

The site contains an overview of the limbic system anatomy supplemented by several line-art diagrams illustrating the anatomy of the amygdala and hippocampus.

Learning and Memory

http://brembs.net/

This site provides a basic tutorial on mechanisms of learning and of memory.

Tutorials on Learning and Memory

http://psy71.dur.ac.uk/Education/memory/index.html

The site contains a link to a tutorial on learning and memory.

Human Communication

chapter 13

CHAPTER OUTLINE

LEARNING OBJECTIVES

1. Describe the use of subjects with brain damage in the study of language and explain the concept of lateralization.
2. Describe Broca's aphasia and the three major speech deficits that result from damage to Broca's area: agrammatism, anomia, and articulation difficulties.
3. Describe the symptoms of Wernicke's aphasia, pure word deafness, and transcortical sensory aphasia and explain how they are related.
4. Discuss the brain mechanisms that underlie our ability to understand the meanings of words and to express our own thoughts and perceptions in words.
5. Describe the symptoms of conduction aphasia and anomic aphasia and describe research on the neural basis of bilingualism.
6. Describe pure alexia and explain why this disorder is caused by damage to two specific parts of the brain.
7. Describe whole-word and phonetic reading and discuss three acquired dyslexias: surface dyslexia, phonological dyslexia, and direct dyslexia.
8. Explain the relationship between speaking and writing and describe the symptoms of phonological dysgraphia, orthographic dysgraphia, and semantic (direct) dysgraphia.
9. Describe research on the neurological basis of developmental dyslexias.

PROLOGUE

Can't Hear Words

Dr. D. presented the case. "Mr. S. had two strokes about ten years ago, which damaged both temporal lobes. His hearing, tested by an audiologist, is in the normal range. But as you will see, his speech comprehension is deficient."

Actually, as we soon saw, it was nonexistent. Mr. S. was ushered into the conference room and shown an empty chair at the head of the table, where we could all see and hear him. He looked calm and unworried; in fact, he seemed to be enjoying himself, and it occurred to me that this was probably not the first time he had been the center of attention. I had read about the syndrome I was about to see, and I knew that it was very rare.

"Mr. S., will you tell us how you are feeling?" asked Dr. D.

The patient turned his head at the sound of his voice and said, "Sorry, I can't understand you."

"*How are you feeling?*" he asked in a loud voice.

"Oh, I can hear you all right, I just can't understand you. Here," he said, handing Dr. D. a pencil and a small pad of paper.

Dr. D. took the pencil and paper and wrote something. He handed them back to Mr. S., who looked at it and said, "Fine. I'm just fine."

"Will you tell us about what you have been doing lately?" asked Dr. D. Mr. S. smiled, shook his head, and handed him the paper and pencil again.

"Oh sure," he said after reading the new question, and he proceeded to tell us about his garden and his other hobbies. "I don't get much from television unless there are a lot of close-ups, where I can read their lips. I like to listen to music on the radio, but, of course, the lyrics don't mean too much to me!" He laughed at his own joke, which had probably already seen some mileage.

"You mean that you can read lips?" someone asked.

Mr. S. immediately turned toward the sound of the voice and said, "What did you say? Say it slow, so I can try to read your lips." We all laughed, and Mr. S. joined us when the question was repeated slowly enough for him to decode. Another person tried to ask him a question, but apparently his Spanish accent made it impossible for Mr. S. to read his lips.

Suddenly, the phone rang. We all, including Mr. S., looked up at the wall where it was hanging. "Someone else had better get that," he said. "I'm not much good on the phone."

After Mr. S. had left the room, someone observed that although Mr. S.'s speech was easy to understand, it seemed a bit strange. "Yes," said a speech therapist, "he almost sounds like a deaf person who has learned to talk but doesn't get the pronunciation of the words just right."

Dr. D. nodded and played a tape for us. "This recording was made a few months after his strokes, ten years ago." We heard the same voice, but this time it sounded absolutely normal.

"Oh," said the speech therapist. "He has lost the ability to monitor his own speech, and over the years he has forgotten some of the details of how various words are pronounced."

"Exactly," said Dr. D. "The change has been a gradual one."

Verbal behaviors constitute one of the most important classes of human social behavior. Our cultural evolution has been possible because we can talk and listen, write and read. Language enables our discoveries to be cumulative; knowledge gained by one generation can be passed on to the next.

The basic function of verbal communication is seen in its effects on other people. When we talk to someone, we almost always expect our speech to induce the person to engage in some sort of behavior. Sometimes, the behavior is of obvious advantage to us, as when we ask for an object or for help in performing a task. At other times we are simply asking for a social exchange: some attention and perhaps some conversation. Even "idle" conversation is not idle, because it causes another person to look at us and say something in return.

This chapter discusses the neural basis of verbal behavior: talking, understanding speech, reading, and writing.

Speech Production and Comprehension: Brain Mechanisms

Our knowledge of the physiology of language has been obtained primarily by observing the effects of brain lesions on people's verbal behavior. Although investigators have studied people who have undergone brain surgery or who have sustained head injuries, brain tumors, or infections, most of the observations have been made on people who have suffered strokes, or **cerebrovascular accidents.** As we will see in Chapter 14, the most common type of cerebrovascular accident is caused by obstruction of a blood vessel. The interruption in blood flow deprives a region of the brain of its blood supply, which causes cells in that region to die.

A second source of information about the physiology of language comes from studies using functional imaging devices. In recent years, researchers have used PET functional MRI to gather information about language processes from normal subjects. In general, these studies have confirmed or complemented what we have learned by studying patients with brain damage.

The most important category of speech disorders is **aphasia,** a primary disturbance in the comprehension or production of speech, caused by brain damage. Not all speech disturbances are aphasias; a patient must have difficulty comprehending, repeating, or producing meaningful speech, and this difficulty must not be caused by simple sensory or motor deficits or by lack of motivation. For example, inability to speak caused by deafness or paralysis of the speech muscles is not considered to be aphasia.

Lateralization

Verbal behavior is a *lateralized* function; most language disturbances occur after damage to the left side of the brain, whether people are left-handed or right-handed. Using an ultrasonic procedure to measure changes in cerebral blood flow while people performed a verbal task, Knecht et al. (2000) assessed the relationship between handedness and lateralization of speech mechanisms in people without any known brain damage. They found that right-hemisphere speech dominance was seen in only 4 percent of right-handed people, in 15 percent of ambidextrous people, and in 27 percent of left-handed people. If the left hemisphere is malformed or damaged early in life, then language dominance is very likely to pass to the right hemisphere (Vikingstad et al., 2000). Because the left hemisphere of approximately 90 percent of the total population is dominant for speech, you can assume that the brain damage described in this chapter is located in the left (speech-dominant) hemisphere unless I say otherwise.

Why is one hemisphere specialized for speech? The perceptual functions of the left hemisphere are more specialized for the analysis of sequences of stimuli, occurring one after the other. The perceptual functions of the right hemisphere are more specialized for the analysis of space and geometrical shapes and forms, the elements of which are all present at the same time. Speech is certainly sequential; it consists of sequences of words, which are composed of sequences of sounds. Therefore, it makes sense for the left hemisphere to have become specialized at perceiving speech. In addition, the left hemisphere is involved in the control of sequences of voluntary movements. Perhaps this fact accounts for the localization of neural circuits involved in speech production, as well as speech perception, in the left hemisphere.

Although the circuits that are *primarily* involved in speech comprehension and production are located in one hemisphere (almost always the left hemisphere), it would be a mistake to conclude that the other hemisphere plays no role in speech. Speech is not simply a matter of talking; it is also having something to say. Similarly, listening is not simply hearing and recognizing words; it is understanding the meaning of what has been said. When we hear and understand words and when we talk about or think about our own perceptions or memories, we are using neural circuits besides those directly involved in speech. Thus, these circuits, too, play a role in verbal behavior. For example, damage to the right hemisphere makes it difficult for a person to read maps, perceive spatial relationships, and recognize complex geo-

cerebrovascular accident A "stroke"; brain damage caused by occlusion or rupture of a blood vessel in the brain.

aphasia Difficulty in producing or comprehending speech not produced by deafness or a simple motor deficit; caused by brain damage.

Broca's aphasia A form of aphasia characterized by agrammatism, anomia, and extreme difficulty in speech articulation.

function word A preposition, article, or other word that conveys little of the meaning of a sentence but is important in specifying its grammatical structure.

content word A noun, verb, adjective, or adverb that conveys meaning.

metrical forms. People with such damage also have trouble talking about things like maps and complex geometrical forms or understanding what other people say about them. The right hemisphere also appears to be involved in organizing a narrative—selecting and assembling the elements of what we want to say (Gardner et al., 1983). As we saw in Chapter 10, the right hemisphere is involved in the expression and recognition of emotion in the tone of voice. And as we shall see in this chapter, it is also involved in control of *prosody*—the normal rhythm and stress found in speech. Therefore, both hemispheres of the brain have a contribution to make to our language abilities.

Speech entails more than the production of words: Before we can communicate, we must have something to say.

Speech Production

Being able to talk—that is, to produce meaningful speech—requires several abilities. First, the person must have something to talk about. Let us consider what this means. We can talk about something that is currently happening or something that happened in the past. In the first case we are talking about our perceptions: things we are seeing, hearing, feeling, smelling, and so on. In the second case we are talking about our memories of what happened in the past. Both perceptions of current events and memories of events that occurred in the past involve brain mechanisms in the posterior part of the cerebral hemispheres (the occipital, temporal, and parietal lobes). Thus, this region is largely responsible for our having something to say.

Given that a person has something to say, actually saying it requires some additional brain functions. As we shall see in this section, the conversion of perceptions, memories, and thoughts into speech makes use of neural mechanisms located in the frontal lobes.

Damage to a region of the inferior left frontal lobe (Broca's area) disrupts the ability to speak: It causes **Broca's aphasia.** This disorder is characterized by slow, laborious, and nonfluent speech. When trying to talk with patients who have Broca's aphasia, most people find it hard to resist supplying the words the patients are obviously groping for. But although they often mispronounce words, the ones they manage to come out with are usually meaningful. The posterior part of the cerebral hemispheres has something to say, but the damage to the frontal lobe makes it difficult for the patients to express these thoughts.

People with Broca's aphasia find it easier to say some types of words than others. They have great difficulty saying the little words with grammatical meaning, such as *a, the, some, in,* or *about.* These words are called **function words,** because they have important grammatical functions. The words that they do manage to say are almost entirely **content words**—words that convey meaning, including nouns, verbs, adjectives, and adverbs, such as *apple, house, throw,* or *heavy.* Here is a sample of speech from a man with Broca's aphasia, who is trying to describe the scene shown in ***Figure 13.1.*** As you will see,

Figure 13.1

The drawing of the kitchen story, part of the Boston Diagnostic Aphasia Test.

From Goodglass, H., and Kaplan, E. *The Assessment of Aphasia and Related Disorders,* 2nd ed. Philadelphia: Lea & Febiger, 1983. Reprinted with permission.

Broca's area A region of frontal cortex, located just rostral to the base of the left primary motor cortex, that is necessary for normal speech production.

agrammatism One of the usual symptoms of Broca's aphasia; a difficulty in comprehending or properly employing grammatical devices, such as verb endings and word order.

anomia Difficulty in finding (remembering) the appropriate word to describe an object, action, or attribute; one of the symptoms of aphasia.

his words are meaningful, but what he says is certainly not grammatical. The dots indicate long pauses.

> kid . . . kk . . . can . . . candy . . . cookie . . . candy . . . well I don't know but it's writ . . . easy does it . . . slam . . . early . . . fall . . . men . . . many no . . . girl. Dishes . . . soap . . . soap . . . water . . . water . . . falling pah that's all . . . dish . . . that's all.
>
> Cookies . . . can . . . candy . . . cookies cookies . . . he . . . down . . . That's all. Girl . . . slipping water . . . water . . . and it hurts . . . much to do . . . Her . . . clean up . . . Dishes . . . up there . . . I think that's doing it. (Obler and Gjerlow, 1999, p. 41)

People with Broca's aphasia can comprehend speech much better than they can produce it. In fact, some observers have said that their comprehension is unimpaired, but as we will see, this is not quite true. Broca (1861) suggested that this form of aphasia is produced by a lesion of the frontal association cortex, just anterior to the face region of the primary motor cortex. Subsequent research proved him to be essentially correct, and we now call the region **Broca's area.** (See ***Figure 13.2.***)

Lesions that produce Broca's aphasia are certainly centered in the vicinity of Broca's area. However, damage that is restricted to the cortex of Broca's area does not appear to produce Broca's aphasia; the damage must extend to surrounding regions of the frontal lobe and to the underlying subcortical white matter (H. Damasio, 1989; Naeser et al., 1989). In addition, there is evidence that lesions of the basal ganglia—especially the head of the caudate nucleus—can also produce a Broca-like aphasia (Damasio, Eslinger, and Adams, 1984).

Watkins et al. (2002a, 2002b) studied three generations of the KE family, half of whose members are affected by a severe speech and language disorder caused by the mutation of a single gene found on chromosome 7. The primary deficit appears to involve the ability to perform the sequential movements necessary for speech, but the people also have difficulty repeating sounds they hear and forming the past tense of verbs. The mutation causes abnormal development of the caudate nucleus and the left inferior frontal cortex, including Broca's area.

What do the neural circuits in and around Broca's area do? Wernicke (1874) suggested that Broca's area contains motor memories—in particular, *memories of the sequences of muscular movements that are needed to articulate words.* Talking involves rapid movements of the tongue, lips, and jaw, and these movements must be coordinated with each other and with those of the vocal cords; thus talking requires some very sophisticated motor control mechanisms. Obviously, circuits of neurons somewhere in our brain will, when properly activated, cause these sequences of movements to be executed. Because damage to the inferior caudal left frontal lobe (including Broca's area) disrupts the ability to articulate words, this region is the most likely candidate for the location of these "programs." The fact that this region is directly connected to the part of the primary motor cortex that controls the muscles used for speech certainly supports this conclusion.

But the speech functions of the left frontal lobe include more than programming the movements used to speak. Broca's aphasia is much more than a deficit in pronouncing words. In general, three major speech deficits are produced by lesions in and around Broca's area: *agrammatism, anomia,* and *articulation difficulties.* Although most patients with Broca's aphasia will have all of these

Figure 13.2

The location of the primary speech areas of the brain. (Wernicke's area will be described later.)

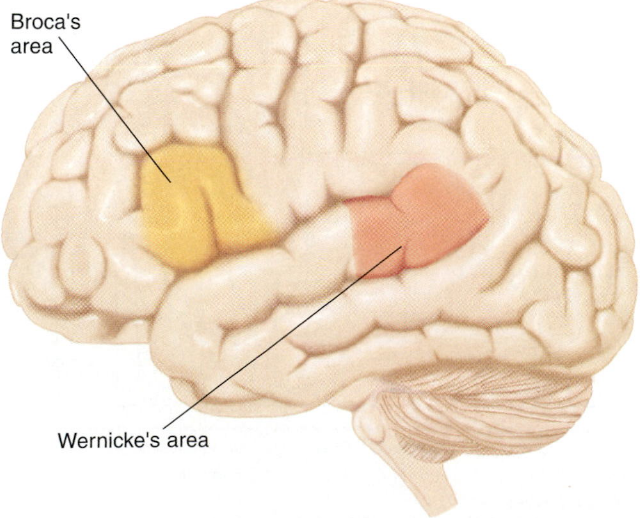

deficits to some degree, their severity can vary considerably from person to person—presumably, because their brain lesions differ. You can also hear the voice of an agrammatic patient and one with articulation difficulties in ***Animation 13.1, Voices of Aphasia: Broca's Aphasia.***

Animation 13.1, Voices of Aphasia: Broca's Aphasia, lets you hear the speech of patients with different forms of this disorder.

Agrammatism refers to a patient's difficulty in using grammatical constructions. This disorder can appear all by itself, without any difficulty in pronouncing words (Nadeau, 1988). As we saw, people with Broca's aphasia rarely use function words. In addition, they rarely use grammatical markers such as *-ed* or auxiliaries such as *have* (as in *I have gone*). For some reason, they *do* often use *-ing*, perhaps because this ending converts a verb into a noun. A study by Saffran, Schwartz, and Marin (1980) illustrates this difficulty. The following quotations are from agrammatic patients attempting to describe pictures:

> *Picture of a boy being hit in the head by a baseball*
>
> The boy is catch . . . the boy is hitch . . . the boy is hit the ball. (Saffran, Schwartz, and Marin, 1980, p. 229)
>
> *Picture of a girl giving flowers to her teacher*
>
> Girl . . . wants to . . . flowers . . . flowers and wants to. . . . The woman . . . wants to. . . . The girl wants to . . . the flowers and the woman. (Saffran, Schwartz, and Marin, 1980, p. 234)

So far, I have described Broca's aphasia as a disorder in speech *production.* The striking disparity between the speech and comprehension of people with Broca's aphasia often leads people to assume that their comprehension is normal. But it is not. Schwartz, Saffran, and Marin (1980) showed Broca's aphasics pairs of pictures in which agents and objects of the action were reversed: for example, a horse kicking a cow and a cow kicking a horse, a truck pulling a car and a car pulling a truck, and a dancer applauding a clown and a clown applauding a dancer. As they showed each pair of pictures, they read the subject a sentence, for example, *The horse kicks the cow.* The subjects' task was to point to the appropriate picture, indicating whether they understood the grammatical construction of the sentence. (See ***Figure 13.3.***) They performed very poorly.

Figure 13.3

An example of the stimuli used in the experiment by Schwartz, Saffran, and Marin (1980).

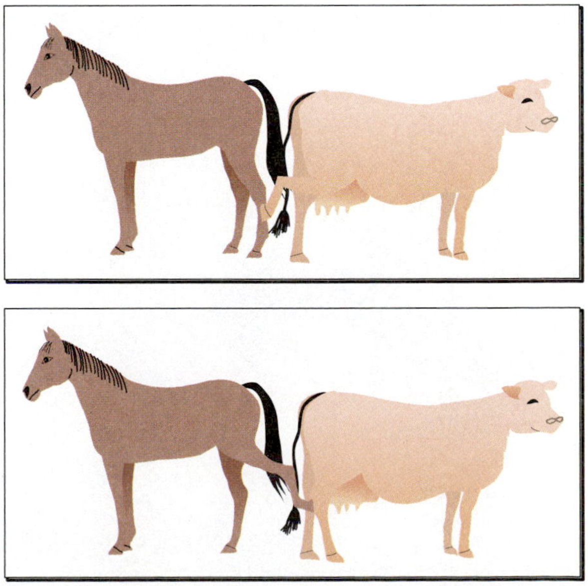

The correct picture in the study by Schwartz and her colleagues was specified by a particular aspect of grammar: word order. The agrammatism that accompanies Broca's aphasia appears to disrupt patients' ability to use grammatical information, including word order, to decode the meaning of a sentence. Thus, their deficit in comprehension parallels their deficit in production. If they heard a sentence such as *The man swats the mosquito,* they would understand that it concerns a man and a mosquito and the action of swatting. They would have no trouble figuring out who is doing what to whom. But a sentence such as *The horse kicks the cow* does not provide any extra cues; if the grammar is not understood, neither is the meaning of the sentence.

The second major speech deficit seen in Broca's aphasia is **anomia** ("without name"). Anomia refers to a word-finding difficulty; and because all aphasics omit words or use inappropriate ones, anomia is actually a primary symptom of *all* forms of aphasia. However, because the speech of Broca's aphasics lacks fluency, their anomia is especially apparent; their facial expression and frequent use of sounds like "uh" make it obvious that they are groping for the correct words.

The third major characteristic of Broca's aphasia is *difficulty with articulation.* Patients mispronounce words, often altering the sequence of sounds. For example, *lipstick* might be pronounced "likstip." People with Broca's aphasia recognize that their pronunciation is erroneous, and they usually try to correct it.

These three deficits are seen in various combinations in different patients, depending on the exact location of the lesion and, to a certain extent, on their stage of recovery. We can think of these deficits as constituting a hierarchy. On the lowest, most elementary level is control of the sequence of movements of the muscles of speech; damage to this ability leads to articulation difficulties. The next higher level is selection of the particular "programs" for individual words; damage to this ability leads to anomia. Finally, the highest level is selection of grammatical structure, including word order, use of function words, and word endings; damage to this ability leads to agrammatism.

We might expect that the direct control of articulation would involve the face area of the primary motor cortex and portions of the basal ganglia, while the selection of words, word order, and grammatical markers would involve Broca's area and adjacent regions of the frontal association cortex. Some recent studies indicate that different categories of symptoms of Broca's aphasia do, indeed, involve different brain regions. Dronkers (1996) appears to have found a critical location for control of speech articulation: the left precentral gyrus of the insula. The insular cortex is located on the lateral wall of the cerebral hemisphere behind the anterior temporal lobe. Normally, this region is hidden and can be seen only when the temporal lobe is dissected away. (See ***Figure 13.4.***) Dronkers discovered the apparent role of this region by plotting the lesions of patients with and without apraxia of speech who had strokes that damaged the same general area of the brain. (**Apraxia of speech** is an impairment in the ability to program movements of the tongue, lips, and throat that are required to produce the proper sequence of speech sounds.) Figure 13.5(a) shows the overlap of the lesions of twenty-five patients with apraxia of speech. As you can see, a region of 100 percent overlap, shown in yellow, falls on the left precentral gyrus of the insula. (See ***Figure 13.5a.***) In contrast, *none* of the lesions of nineteen patients who did not show apraxia of speech included damage to this region. (See ***Figure 13.5b.***)

Figure 13.4

The insular cortex, normally hidden behind the rostral temporal lobe.

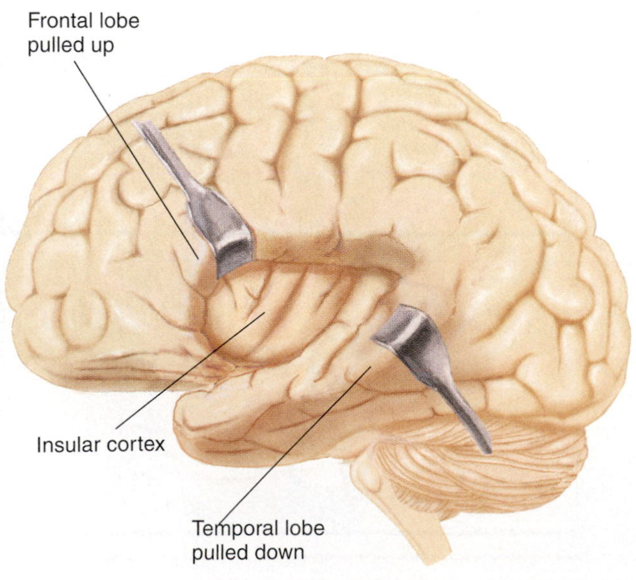

Figure 13.5

Evidence for involvement of the insular cortex in speech articulation. Percentage overlap in the lesions of twenty-five patients (a) with apraxia of speech and (b) without apraxia of speech. The only region common to all lesions that produced apraxia of speech was the precentral gyrus of the insular cortex.

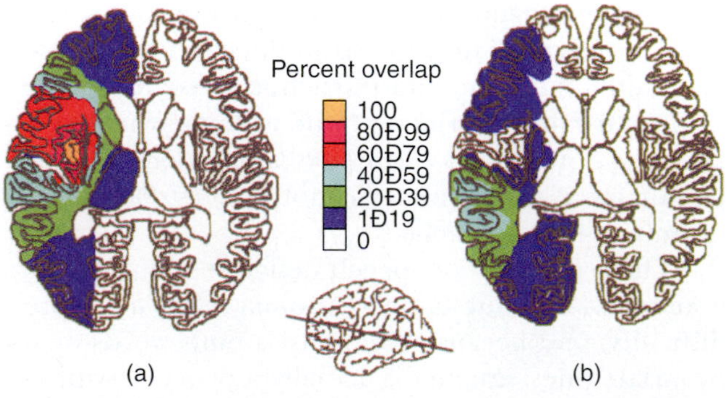

From Dronkers, N. F. *Nature,* 1996, *384,* 159–161. Copyright 1996 Macmillan Magazines Limited. Reprinted with permission.

At least two functional imaging studies support Dronkers's conclusion. Kuriki, Mori, and Hirata (1999) and Wise et al. (1999) found that pronunciation of words caused activation of the left anterior insula.

Speech Comprehension

Comprehension of speech obviously begins in the auditory system, which detects and analyzes sounds. But *recognizing* words is one thing; *comprehending* them—understanding their meaning—is another. For example, we can learn to recognize a foreign word we have heard several times even though we do not understand its meaning. Recognizing a spoken word is a complex perceptual task that relies on memories of sequences of sounds. This task appears to be accomplished by neural circuits in the middle and posterior portion of the superior temporal gyrus of the left hemisphere, a region that has come to be known as **Wernicke's area.** (Refer to ***Figure 13.2.***)

Wernicke's Aphasia: Description

The primary characteristics of **Wernicke's aphasia** are poor speech comprehension and production of meaningless speech. Unlike Broca's aphasia, Wernicke's aphasia is fluent and unlabored; the person does not strain to articulate words and does not appear to be searching for them. The patient maintains a melodic line, with the voice rising and falling normally. When you listen to the speech of a person with Wernicke's aphasia, it appears to be grammatical. That is, the person uses function words such as *the* and *but* and employs complex verb tenses and subordinate clauses. However, the person uses few content words, and the words that he or she strings together just do not make sense. In the extreme, speech deteriorates into a meaningless jumble, illustrated by the following quotation:

Examiner: What kind of work did you do before you came into the hospital?

Patient: Never, now mista oyge I wanna tell you this happened when happened when he rent. His—his kell come down here and is—he got ren something. It happened. In thesse ropiers were with him for hi—is friend—like was. And it just happened so I don't know, he did not bring around anything. And he did not pay it. And he roden all o these arranjen from the pedis on from iss pescid. In these floors now and so. He hadn't had em round here. (Kertesz, 1981, p. 73)

Because of the speech deficit of people with Wernicke's aphasia, when we try to assess their ability to comprehend speech, we must ask them to use nonverbal responses. That is, we cannot assume that they do not understand what other people say to them just because they do not give the proper answer. A commonly used test of comprehension assesses their ability to understand questions by pointing to objects on a table in front of them. For example, they are asked to "Point to the one with ink." If they point to an object other than the pen, they have not understood the request. When tested in this way, people with severe Wernicke's aphasia do indeed show poor comprehension.

A remarkable fact about people with Wernicke's aphasia is that they often seem unaware of their deficit. That is, they do not appear to recognize that their speech is faulty, nor do they recognize that they cannot understand the speech of others. They do not look puzzled when someone tells them something, even though they obviously cannot understand what they hear. Perhaps their comprehension deficit prevents them from realizing that what they say and hear makes no sense. They still follow social conventions, taking turns in conversation with the examiner, even though they do not understand what the examiner says and what they say in return makes little sense. They remain sensitive to the other person's facial expression and tone of voice and begin talking when he or she asks a question and pauses for an

apraxia of speech Impairment in the ability to program movements of the tongue, lips, and throat required to produce the proper sequence of speech sounds.

Wernicke's area A region of auditory association cortex on the left temporal lobe of humans, which is important in the comprehension of words and the production of meaningful speech.

Wernicke's aphasia A form of aphasia characterized by poor speech comprehension and fluent but meaningless speech.

answer. One patient with Wernicke's aphasia made the following responses when asked to name ten common objects.

toothbrush → "stoktery"

cigarette → "cigarette"

pen → "tankt"

knife → "nike"

fork → "fahk"

quarter → "minkt"

pen → "spentee"

matches → "senktr"

key → "seek"

comb → "sahk"

He acted sure of himself and gave no indication that he recognized that most of his responses were meaningless. The responses he made were not simply new words that he had invented; he was asked several times to name the objects and gave different responses each time (except for *cigarette,* which he always named correctly). You can hear the speech of people with Wernicke's aphasia in ***Animation 13.1, Voices of Aphasia: Wernicke's Aphasia.***

Animation 13.1, Voices of Aphasia: Wernicke's Aphasia, lets you hear the speech of patients with this disorder.

Animation 13.2, Speech Perception, lets you hear the transformed speech used in the experiment by Scott and her colleagues.

Wernicke's Aphasia: Analysis

Because the superior temporal gyrus is a region of auditory association cortex, and because a comprehension deficit is so prominent in Wernicke's aphasia, this disorder has been characterized as a *receptive* aphasia. Wernicke suggested that the region that now bears his name is the location of *memories of the sequences of sounds that constitute words.* This hypothesis is reasonable; it suggests that the auditory association cortex of the superior temporal gyrus recognizes the sounds of words, just as the visual association cortex of the inferior temporal gyrus recognizes the sight of objects.

But why should damage to an area that is responsible for the ability to recognize spoken words disrupt people's ability to speak? In fact, it does not; Wernicke's aphasia, like Broca's aphasia, actually appears to consist of several deficits. The abilities that are disrupted include *recognition of spoken words, comprehension of the meaning of words,* and the *ability to convert thoughts into words.* Let us consider each of these abilities in turn.

Recognition: Pure Word Deafness. As I said in the introduction to this section, *recognizing* a word is not the same as *comprehending* it. If you hear a foreign word several times, you will learn to recognize it; but unless someone tells you what it means, you will not comprehend it. Recognition is a perceptual task; comprehension involves retrieval of additional information from memory.

Damage to the left temporal lobe can produce a disorder of auditory word recognition, uncontaminated by other problems. This syndrome is called **pure word deafness.** (Mr. S., the patient described in the chapter prologue, had this disorder.) Although people with pure word deafness are not deaf, they cannot understand speech. As one patient put it, "I can hear you talking, I just can't understand what you're saying." Another said, "It's as if there were a bypass somewhere, and my ears were not connected to my voice" (Saffran, Marin, and Yeni-Komshian, 1976, p. 211). These patients can recognize nonspeech sounds such as the barking of a dog, the sound of a doorbell, and the chirping of a bird. Often, they can recognize the emotion expressed by the intonation of speech even though they cannot understand what is being said. More significantly, their own speech is excellent. They can often understand what other people are saying by reading their lips. They can also read and write, and they sometimes ask people to communicate with them in writing. Clearly, pure word deafness is not an inability to comprehend the meaning of words;

pure word deafness The ability to hear, to speak, and (usually) to read and write without being able to comprehend the meaning of speech; caused by damage to Wernicke's area or disruption of auditory input to this region.

if it were, people with this disorder would not be able to read people's lips or read words written on paper.

Functional imaging studies confirm that perception of speech sounds activates neurons in the auditory association cortex of the superior temporal gyrus. Belin et al. (2000) found that as they presented more and more distorted speech, they saw parallel decreases in the subjects' ability to recognize words and the level of activation of the superior temporal gyrus. They also found regions that were sensitive to nonspeech vocal sounds, such as laughs, coughs, and sighs.

Although several studies have found that speech sounds activate regions of the superior temporal cortex, Scott et al. (2000) prepared a computerized transformation of normal speech that preserved the complexity of the speech sounds but rendered it unintelligible. They also prepared a transformation that removed most of the complexity of speech but could nevertheless be understood. Scott and her colleagues found that two regions of the superior temporal lobe were activated by phonetic information—that is, speech sounds, regardless of intelligibility. Another region was activated only by intelligibility—speech that could be understood, regardless of complexity. Presumably, damage to this region (or to its inputs) is responsible for pure word deafness. (See ***Figure 13.6*** and listen to the transformations in ***Animation 13.2, Speech Perception.***)

Apparently, two types of brain injury can cause pure word deafness: disruption of auditory input to Wernicke's area or damage to Wernicke's area itself. Disruption of auditory input can be produced by bilateral damage to the primary auditory cortex, or it can be caused by damage to the white matter in the left temporal lobes that cuts axons bringing auditory information from the primary auditory cortex to Wernicke's area (Digiovanni et al., 1992; Takahashi et al., 1992). Either type of damage—disruption of auditory input or damage to Wernicke's area—disturbs the analysis of the sounds of words and hence prevents people from recognizing other people's speech. (See ***Figure 13.7.***)

Figure 13.6

Results of PET scans indicating regions of the superior temporal lobe that respond to speech sounds. *Red:* Regions that responded to phonetic information (normal speech sounds or a computerized transformation speech that preserved the complexity of the speech sounds but rendered it unintelligible). *Yellow:* Region that responded to intelligible speech (normal speech sounds or a computerized transformation that removed most normal frequencies but preserved intelligibility.

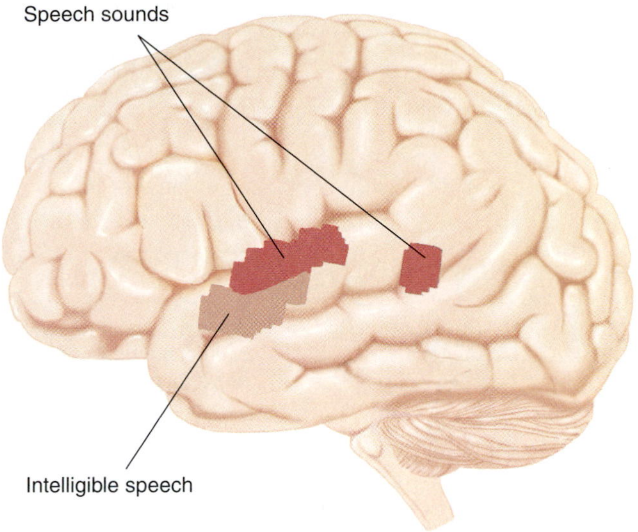
Speech sounds
Intelligible speech

Adapted from Scott, S. K., Blank, E. C., Rosen, S., and Wise, R. J. S. *Brain,* 2000, *123,* 2400–2406.

Figure 13.7

The brain damage that causes pure word deafness.

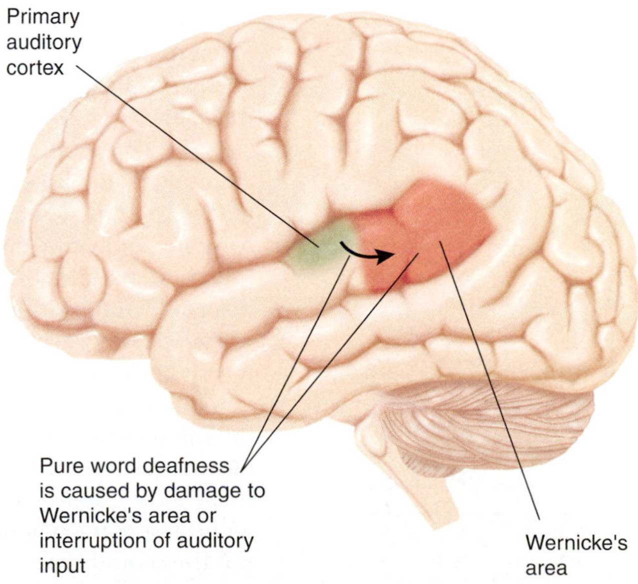
Primary auditory cortex
Pure word deafness is caused by damage to Wernicke's area or interruption of auditory input
Wernicke's area

Comprehension: Transcortical Sensory Aphasia. The other symptoms of Wernicke's aphasia—failure to comprehend the meaning of words and inability to express thoughts in meaningful speech—appear to be produced by damage that extends beyond Wernicke's area into the region that surrounds the posterior part of the lateral fissure, near the junction of the temporal, occipital, and parietal lobes. For want of a better term, I will refer to this region as the *posterior language area.* (See ***Figure 13.8.***) The posterior language area appears to serve as a place for interchanging information between the auditory representation of words and the meanings of these words, stored as memories in the rest of the sensory association cortex.

Damage to the posterior language area alone, which isolates Wernicke's area from the rest of the posterior

Figure 13.8

The location and interconnections of the posterior language area and an explanation of its role in transcortical sensory aphasia and Wernicke's aphasia.

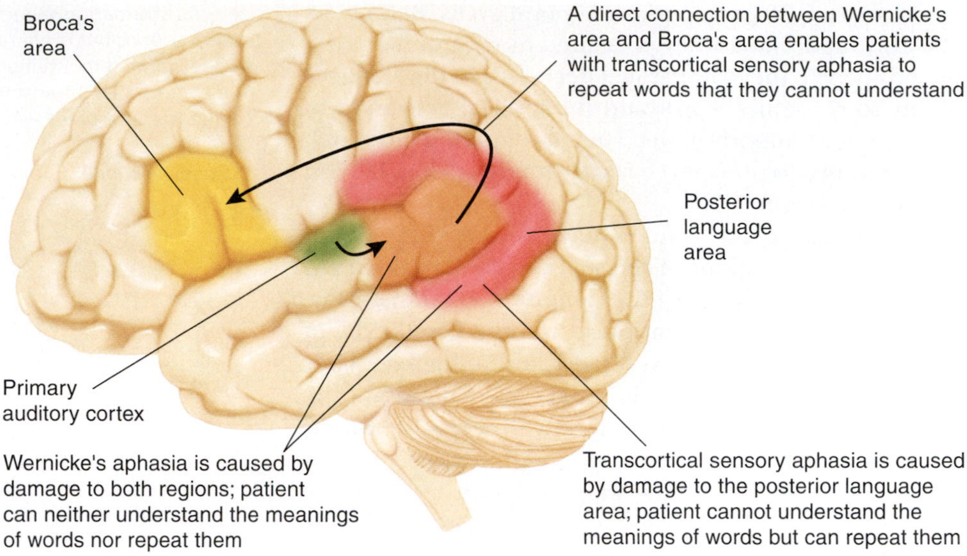
Broca's area
A direct connection between Wernicke's area and Broca's area enables patients with transcortical sensory aphasia to repeat words that they cannot understand
Posterior language area
Primary auditory cortex
Wernicke's aphasia is caused by damage to both regions; patient can neither understand the meanings of words nor repeat them
Transcortical sensory aphasia is caused by damage to the posterior language area; patient cannot understand the meanings of words but can repeat them

language area, produces a disorder known as **transcortical sensory aphasia.** (See ***Figure 13.8.***) The difference between transcortical sensory aphasia and Wernicke's aphasia is that patients with this disorder *can repeat what other people say to them;* therefore, they can recognize words. However, *they cannot comprehend the meaning of what they hear and repeat; nor can they produce meaningful speech of their own.* How can these people repeat what they hear? Because the posterior language area is damaged, repetition does not involve this part of the brain. Obviously, there must be a direct connection between Wernicke's area and Broca's area that bypasses the posterior language area. (See ***Figure 13.8.***)

Let me describe a case of transcortical sensory aphasia. A woman sustained extensive brain damage from breathing carbon monoxide produced by a faulty water heater. She spent several years in the hospital before she died, without ever saying anything meaningful on her own. She did not follow verbal commands or otherwise give signs of understanding them. However, she often repeated what was said to her. For example, if an examiner said "Please raise your right hand," she would reply "Please raise your right hand." The repetition was not parrotlike; she did not imitate accents different from her own, and if someone made a grammatical error while saying something to her, she sometimes repeated the sentence correctly, without the error. She could also recite poems if someone started them. For example, when an examiner said "Roses are red, violets are blue," she continued with "Sugar is sweet and so are you." She could sing and would do so when someone started singing a song she knew. She even learned new songs from the radio while in the hospital. Remember, though, that she gave *no signs of understanding anything she heard or said.* This disorder, along with pure word deafness, clearly confirms the conclusion that *recognizing* spoken words and *comprehending* them are different processes and involve different brain mechanisms (Geschwind, Quadfasel, and Segarra, 1968).

transcortical sensory aphasia A speech disorder in which a person has difficulty comprehending speech and producing meaningful spontaneous speech but can repeat speech; caused by damage to the region of the brain posterior to Wernicke's area.

Boatman et al. (2000) stimulated various language-related areas of the brains of people who were being evaluated for seizure surgery. They found that in most cases, electrical stimulation of the lateral temporal lobe, ventral or anteroventral to Wernicke's area, produced the symptoms of transcortical sensory aphasia: The patients could not comprehend what was said to them when the stimulation was turned on, but they could repeat what they heard. (See ***Figure 13.9.***) These findings suggest that perhaps my representation of the posterior language area should extend more rostrally than I have depicted it in Figure 13.8.

In conclusion, transcortical sensory aphasia can be seen as Wernicke's aphasia without a repetition deficit. To put it another way, the symptoms of Wernicke's aphasia (WA) consist of those of pure word deafness (PWD) plus those of transcortical sensory aphasia (TSA). As I tell my students, WA = TSA + PWD. By simple algebra, TSA = WA – PWD, and so on. (Refer to ***Figure 13.8.***)

Figure 13.9

Location of sites where electrical stimulation interfered with normal cortical activity and produced the symptoms of transcortical sensory aphasia: loss of speech comprehension but preservation of the ability to repeat speech.

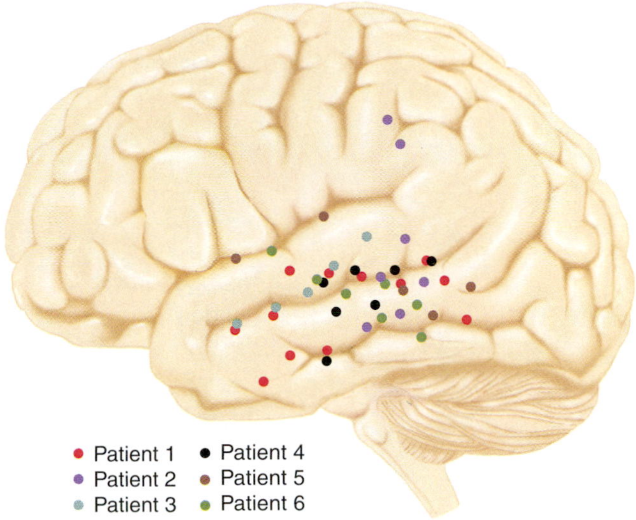

Adapted from Boatman, D., Gordon, B., Hart, J., Selnes, O., Miglioretti, D., and Lenz, F. *Brain,* 2000, *123,* 1634–1642.

What Is Meaning? As we have seen, Wernicke's area is involved in the analysis of speech sounds and thus in the recognition of words. Damage to the posterior language area does not disrupt people's ability to recognize words, but it does disrupt their ability to understand them or to produce meaningful speech of their own. But what, exactly, do we mean by the word *meaning*? And what types of brain mechanisms are involved?

Words refer to objects, actions, or relationships in the world. Thus, the meaning of a word is defined by particular memories associated with it. For example, knowing the meaning of the word *tree* means being able to imagine the physical characteristics of trees: what they look like, what the wind sounds like blowing through their leaves, what the bark feels like, and so on. It also means knowing facts about trees: about their roots, buds, flowers, nuts, and wood and the chlorophyll in their leaves. These memories are stored not in the primary speech areas but in other parts of the brain, especially regions of the association cortex. Different categories of memories may be stored in particular regions of the brain, but they are somehow tied together, so hearing the word *tree* activates all of them. (As we saw in Chapter 12, the hippocampal formation is involved in this process of tying related memories together.)

In thinking about the brain's verbal mechanisms involved in recognizing words and comprehending their meaning, I find that the concept of a dictionary serves as a useful analogy. Dictionaries contain entries (the words) and definitions (the meanings of the words). In the brain we have at least two types of entries: auditory and visual. That is, we can look up a word according to how it sounds or how it looks (in writing). Let us just consider just one type of entry: the sound of a word. (I will discuss reading and writing later in this chapter.) We hear a familiar word and understand its meaning. How do we do so?

First, we must recognize the sequence of sounds that constitute the word—We find the auditory entry for the word in our "dictionary." As we saw, this entry appears in Wernicke's area. Next, the memories that constitute the meaning of the word must be activated. Presumably, Wernicke's area is connected—through the posterior language area—with the neural circuits that contain these memories. (See ***Figure 13.10.***)

The Hebb rule, which we encountered in Chapter 12, can be invoked to explain the acquisition of words and their meanings. Recall that the Hebb rule says that when interconnected neurons are repeatedly active at the same time, the synaptic connections between them are strengthened. Thus, when we hear a word several times, a particular set of neurons in the superior temporal lobe become active, and their interconnections eventually become strengthened. (We could also hear the word once and repeat it to ourselves, thus activating these neurons enough to strengthen their interconnections.) As Hebb put it, the coactivated neurons became a *cell assembly*—an assembly of interconnected neurons.

Figure 13.10

The "dictionary" in the brain. Wernicke's area contains the auditory entries of words; the meanings are contained as memories in the sensory association areas. Black arrows represent comprehension of words—the activation of memories that correspond to a word's meaning. Red arrows represent translation of thoughts or perceptions into words.

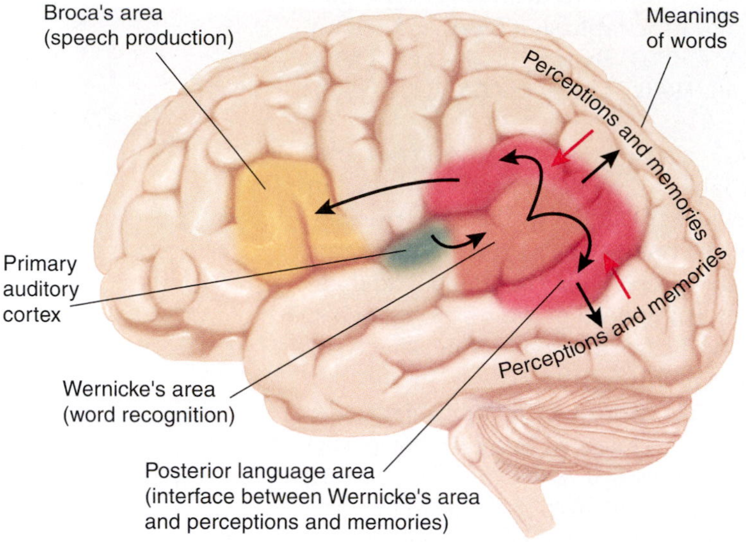

Suppose the word is "ball" and a child hears the word several times while she is playing with a ball or simply looking at one. Cell assemblies in Wernicke's area would constitute the memory of the sound of the word, while cell assemblies in the visual association cortex would constitute the memory of the child's ball. And because these two cell assemblies, which we can think of as the auditory entry of the word in the brain's dictionary and its definition, are active at the same time, they become linked through axons that interconnect these two regions. The Hebb rule predicts that other interconnections will also occur. For example, if the child successfully repeats the word "ball," a third cell assembly will develop in Broca's area that is responsible for the word's pronunciation. Eventually, interconnections will develop between all three areas, so the child will be able to say "ball" when she sees the ball or wants to play with it, and she will look for the ball when someone else says the word. In time, the child will learn that other round objects of different colors and sizes are also balls and so on. Pulvermüller (1999) develops this explanation of the "dictionary in the brain," (my words, not his) in more detail.

The process works in reverse when we describe our thoughts or perceptions in words. Suppose we want to tell someone about a tree that we just planted in our yard. Thoughts about the tree (for example, a visual image of it) occur in our association cortex—the visual association cortex, in this example. Information about the activity of these circuits first activates circuits of neurons in the posterior language area and then circuits of neurons in Broca's area, which cause the words to be set into a grammatical sentence and be pronounced. (See ***Figure 13.10.***)

What evidence do we have that meanings of words are represented by cell assemblies located in various regions of the association cortex? The best evidence comes from the fact that damage to particular regions of the sensory association cortex can damage particular kinds of information and thus abolish particular kinds of meanings.

Damage to part of the association cortex of the left parietal lobe can produce an inability to name the body parts. The disorder is called **autotopagnosia,** or "poor knowledge of one's own topography." (A better name would have been *autotopanomia,* "poor naming of one's own topography.") People who can otherwise converse normally cannot reliably point to their elbow, knee, or cheek when asked to do so and cannot name body parts when the examiner points to them. However, they have no difficulty understanding the meaning of other words.

autotopagnosia Inability to name body parts or to identify body parts that another person names.

Other investigators have reported verbal deficits that include disruption of particular categories of meaning. McCarthy and Warrington (1988) reported the case of a man with left temporal lobe damage (patient T. B.) who was unable to explain the meaning of words that denoted living things. For example, when he was asked to define the word *rhinoceros,* he said, "Animal, can't give you any functions." However, when he was shown a *picture* of a rhinoceros, he said, "Enormous, weighs over one ton, lives in Africa." Similarly, when asked what a *dolphin* was, he said, "a fish or a bird"; but he responded to a *picture* of a dolphin by saying, "Dolphin lives in water . . . they are trained to jump up and come out. . . . In America during the war years they started to get this particular animal to go through to look into ships." Clearly, patient T. B. has not lost his knowledge of specific animals but only the ability to name them. Presumably, the damage to his brain disconnected circuits involved in the recognition of words from those involved in his memories of animals. When T. B. was asked to define the meanings of words that denoted inanimate objects (such as *lighthouse* or *wheelbarrow*), he had no trouble at all.

Some patients have even more specific deficits; Semenza and Zettin (1989) described patient P. C., who had great difficulty with proper nouns (names of people and places). Damasio et al. (1991) studied several patients with similar deficits and concluded that anomia for proper nouns is caused by damage to the temporal pole (the rostral end of the temporal lobe), whereas anomia for common nouns is caused by damage to the inferior temporal cortex. An electrical recording study also found activation of different regions by common and proper nouns (Proverbio et al., 2001). Damasio and his colleagues suggest that the important distinction between the two types of words is that proper nouns are specific to particular individuals (people or places), whereas common nouns apply to *categories.* Presumably, the cortex of the temporal pole is specifically involved with recognition of individuals. This suggestion was supported by a functional imaging study from Damasio's laboratory (Grabowski et al., 2001). The investigators found that when people tried to name pictures of either famous landmarks or famous faces, their left temporal pole was activated.

Hamberger et al. (2001) asked patients who were being assessed for possible seizure surgery to try to name common objects. The items were presented visually or acoustically; the patients were shown drawings of objects or heard oral descriptions, such as "What a king wears on his head." While the patients were performing this task, the experimenters stimulated different regions of the temporal lobe and parietal lobe just dorsal to the lateral fissure. As you can see in Figure 13.11, stimulation of different regions disrupted naming elicited by visual and auditory cues. (See ***Figure 13.11.***)

Figure 13.11

Location of sites in and near the lateral temporal cortex where electrical stimulation interfered with visual naming (drawings of common objects) or auditory naming (spoken definitions of common items).

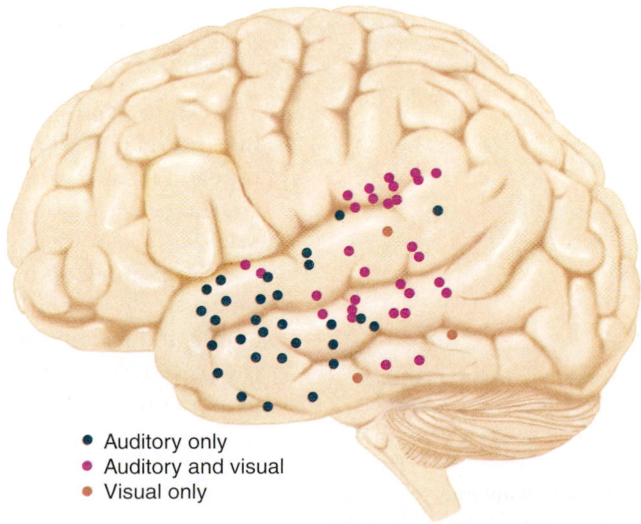

Adapted from Hamberger, M. J., Goodman, R. R., Perrine, K., and Tamny, T. *Neurology,* 2001, *56,* 56–61.

Repetition: Conduction Aphasia. As we saw earlier in this section, the fact that people with transcortical

Figure 13.12

MRI scans showing subcortical damage responsible for a case of conduction aphasia. This lesion damaged the arcuate fasciculus, a fiber bundle connecting Wernicke's area and Broca's area.

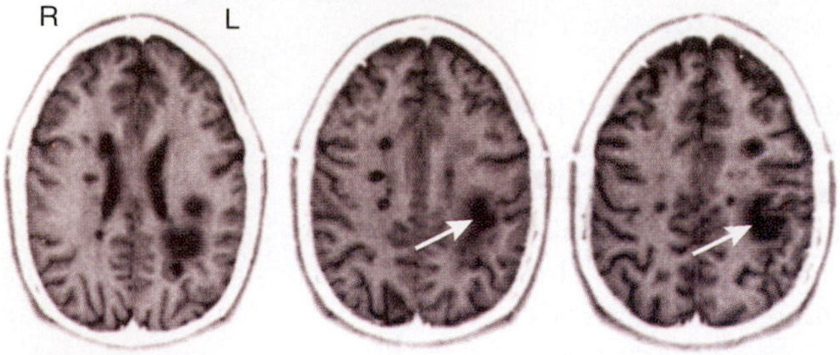

From Arnett, P. A., Rao, S. M., Hussain, M., Swanson, S. J., and Hammeke, T. A. *Neurology,* 1996, *47,* 576–578.

sensory aphasia can repeat what they hear suggests that there is a direct connection between Wernicke's area and Broca's area—and there is, the **arcuate fasciculus** ("arch-shaped bundle"). This bundle of axons appears to convey information about the *sounds* of words but not their *meanings.* The best evidence for this conclusion comes from a syndrome known as conduction aphasia, which is produced by damage to the inferior parietal lobe that extends into the subcortical white matter and damages the arcuate fasciculus (Damasio and Damasio, 1980). (See ***Figure 13.12.***)

Conduction aphasia is characterized by meaningful, fluent speech; relatively good comprehension; but very poor repetition. For example, the spontaneous speech of patient L. B. (observed by Margolin and Walker, 1981) was excellent; he made very few errors and had no difficulty naming objects. But let us see how patient L. B. performed when he was asked to repeat words. (You can hear this person's voice on ***Animation 13.1, Voices of Aphasia: Conduction Aphasia.***)

Animation 13.1, Voices of Aphasia: Conduction Aphasia, lets you hear the speech of a patient with this disorder.

Examiner: bicycle

Patient: bicycle

Examiner: hippopotamus

Patient: hippopotamus

Examiner: blaynge

Patient: I didn't get it.

Examiner: Okay, some of these won't be real words, they'll just be sounds. Blaynge.

Patient: I'm not . . .

Examiner: blanch

Patient: blanch

Examiner: north

Patient: north

Examiner: rilld

Patient: Nope, I can't say.

You will notice that the patient can repeat individual words (all nouns, in this case) but utterly fails to repeat nonwords. And as you can hear in the animation, he can repeat a meaningful three-word phrase but not three unrelated words. People with conduction aphasia can repeat speech sounds that they hear *only if these sounds have meaning.*

Sometimes, when a person with conduction aphasia is asked to repeat a word, he or she says a word with the same meaning—or at least one that is related. For example, if the examiner says *house,* the patient may say *home.* If the examiner says *chair,* the patient may say *sit.* One patient made the following response when asked to repeat an entire sentence:

Examiner: The auto's leaking gas tank soiled the roadway.

Patient: The car's tank leaked and made a mess on the street.

The symptoms that are seen in transcortical sensory aphasia and conduction aphasia lead to the conclusion that there are pathways connecting the speech mechanisms of the temporal lobe with those of the frontal lobe. The direct pathway

arcuate fasciculus A bundle of axons that connects Wernicke's area with Broca's area; damage causes conduction aphasia.

conduction aphasia An aphasia characterized by inability to repeat words that are heard but the ability to speak normally and comprehend the speech of others.

through the arcuate fasciculus simply conveys speech sounds from Wernicke's area to Broca's area. We use this pathway to repeat unfamiliar words—for example, when we are learning a foreign language or a new word in our own language or when we are trying to repeat a nonword such as *blaynge*. The second pathway, between the posterior language area and Broca's area, is indirect and is based on the *meaning* of words, not the sounds they make. When patients with conduction aphasia hear a word or a sentence, the meaning of what they hear evokes some sort of image related to that meaning. (The patient in the second example presumably imagined the sight of an automobile leaking fuel onto the pavement.) They are then able to describe that image, just as they would put their own thoughts into words. Of course, the words they choose might not be the same as the ones used by the person who spoke to them. (See ***Figure 13.13.***)

The symptoms of conduction aphasia indicate that the connection between Wernicke's area and Broca's area appears to play an important role in short-term memory of words and speech sounds that have just been heard. Presumably, rehearsal of such information can be accomplished by "talking to ourselves" inside our head without actually having to say anything aloud. Imagining ourselves saying the word activates the region of Broca's area, whereas imagining that we are hearing it activates the auditory association area of the temporal lobe. These two regions, connected by means of the arcuate fasciculus (which contains axons traveling in *both* directions) circulate information back and forth, keeping the short-term memory alive. Baddeley (1993) refers to this circuit as the *phonological loop*.

Memory of Words: Anomic Aphasia

As I have already noted, anomia, in one form or other, is a hallmark of aphasia. However, one category of aphasia consists of almost pure anomia, the other symptoms being inconsequential. Speech of patients with anomic aphasia is fluent and grammatical, and their comprehension is excellent, but they have difficulty finding the appropriate words. They often employ **circumlocutions** (literally, "speaking in a

circumlocution A strategy by which people with anomia find alternative ways to say something when they are unable to think of the most appropriate word.

Figure 13.13

A hypothetical explanation of conduction aphasia. A lesion that damages the arcuate fasciculus disrupts transmission of auditory information, but not of information related to meaning, to the frontal lobe.

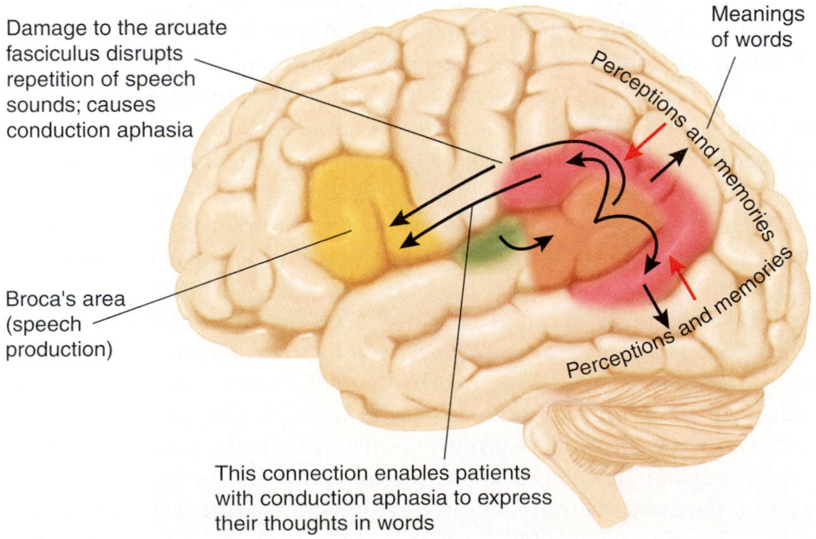
Damage to the arcuate fasciculus disrupts repetition of speech sounds; causes conduction aphasia
Meanings of words
Perceptions and memories
Perceptions and memories
Broca's area (speech production)
This connection enables patients with conduction aphasia to express their thoughts in words

roundabout way") to get around missing words. Anomic aphasia is different from Wernicke's aphasia. People with anomic aphasia can understand what other people say, and what they say makes perfect sense, even if they often choose roundabout ways to say it.

The following quotation is from a patient that some colleagues and I studied (Margolin, Marcel, and Carlson, 1985). We asked her to describe the kitchen picture shown in earlier, in ***Figure 13.1.*** Her pauses, which are marked with three dots, indicate word-finding difficulties. In some cases, when she could not find a word, she supplied a definition instead (a form of circumlocution) or went off on a new track. I have added the words in brackets that I think she intended to use. (You can hear this person's voice on ***Animation 13.1, Voices of Aphasia: Anomic Aphasia.***)

Animation 13.1, Voices of Aphasia: Anomic Aphasia, lets you hear the speech of a patient with this disorder.

Examiner: Tell us about that picture.

Patient: It's a woman who has two children, a son and a daughter, and her son is to get into the . . . cupboard in the kitchen to get out [*take*] some . . . cookies out of the [*cookie jar*] . . . that she possibly had made, and consequently he's slipping [*falling*] . . . the wrong direction [*backward*] . . . on the . . . what he's standing on [*stool*], heading to the . . . the cupboard [*floor*] and if he falls backwards he could have some problems [*get hurt*], because that [*the stool*] is off balance.

Anomia has been described as a partial amnesia for words. It can be produced by lesions in either the anterior or posterior regions of the brain, but only posterior lesions produce a *fluent* anomia. The most likely location of lesions that produce anomia without the other symptoms of aphasia, such as comprehension deficits, agrammatism, or difficulties in articulation, is the left temporal or parietal lobe, usually sparing Wernicke's area. In the case of the woman described above, the damage included the middle and inferior temporal gyri, which includes an important region of the visual association cortex. Wernicke's area was not damaged.

When my colleagues and I were studying this anomic patient, I was struck by the fact that she seemed to have more difficulty finding nouns than other types of words. I informally tested her ability to name actions by asking her what people shown in a series of pictures were doing. She made almost no errors in finding verbs. For example, although she could not say what a boy was holding in his hand, she had no trouble saying that he was *throwing* it. Similarly, she knew that a girl was *climbing* something but could not tell me the name of what she was climbing (a fence). In addition, she had no trouble finding nonvisual adjectives; for example, she could say that lemons tasted *sour,* that ice was *cold,* and that a cat's fur felt *soft.*

For several years I thought that our patient was unique. But other researchers have reported similar patterns of deficits. For example, Semenza and Zettin (1989) and Manning and Campbell (1992) described patients who had difficulty naming objects but not actions. Several studies have found that anomia for verbs (more correctly called *averbia*) is caused by damage to the frontal cortex, in and around Broca's area (Damasio and Tranel, 1993; Daniele et al., 1994; Bak et al., 2001). If you think about it, that makes sense. The frontal lobes are devoted to planning, organizing, and executing actions, so it should not surprise us that they are involved in the task of remembering the names of actions.

A study by Pulvermüller, Harle, and Hummel (2000) lends considerable support to this suggestion. These investigators recorded electrical activity evoked in the brain when people distinguished between verbs that referred to different actions. They found that verbs pertaining to the legs (for example, *to kick*) activated the region of the motor cortex controlling leg movements, while verbs pertaining to the face (for example, *to speak*) activated the face region of the motor cortex. Presumably, thinking about particular actions activated regions that control these actions.

A PET study by Martin et al. (1996) investigated the brain regions activated by naming pictures of animals and tools. They found that naming both categories acti-

Figure 13.14

PET scans showing the regions of activation when people named pictures of animals (left) or tools (right).

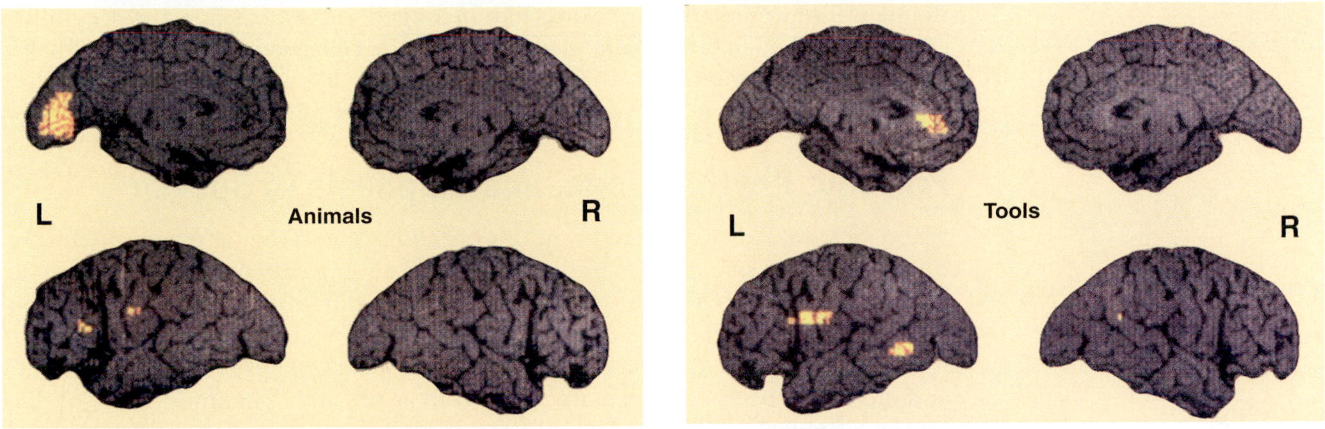

From Martin, A., Wiggs, C. L., Ungerleider, L. G., and Haxby, J. V. *Nature,* 1996, *379,* 649–652. Copyright 1996 Macmillan Magazines Limited. Reprinted with permission.

vated the inferior temporal cortex (the ventral stream of visual processing) and Broca's area. However, animal naming selectively activated the visual association cortex of the medial occipital lobe. Naming tools selectively activated the left middle temporal gyrus and the left premotor cortex—the same region that is activated when people imagine they are making hand movements. (See ***Figure 13.14.***)

The picture I have drawn so far suggests that comprehension of speech includes a flow of information from Wernicke's area to the posterior language area to various regions of sensory and motor association cortex, which contain memories that provide *meanings* to words. Production of spontaneous speech involves the flow of information concerning perceptions and memories from the sensory and motor association cortex to the posterior language area to Broca's area. This model is certainly an oversimplification, but it is a useful starting point in conceptualizing basic mental processes. For example, thinking in words probably involves two-way communication between the speech areas and surrounding association cortex (and subcortical regions such as the hippocampus, of course).

The Bilingual Brain

One question has long puzzled scientists who are interested in brain mechanisms of language: How does the brain handle two or more different languages? Obviously, we can learn new words in our native languages all our lives. (In fact, I hope you are doing so as you read this book.) Presumably, the cell assemblies that contain information about these words are intermingled with cell assemblies that contain information about words we already know. But when a second language is learned, are the cell assemblies that represent the newly learned words and grammatical conventions intermingled with the previously established ones, or are they stored in locations somewhat apart from those used for our native language?

Although the question cannot yet be answered with certainty, evidence suggests that first and second languages share the same brain regions. For example, Fabbro (2001a) studied the recovery of language functions in bilingual patients after they sustained a stroke that caused a severe aphasia. He found that 65 percent of the patients showed similar improvements in both languages, 20 percent showed a greater recovery in their second language, and 15 percent showed a greater recovery in their first language. In other words, there was no evidence that the brain damage was more likely to affect one language more than the other. In a review of the literature, Fabbro (2001b) reported that a variety of methods, including electrical brain stimulation, electrical recording of neural activity, and functional imaging, showed that the neural representations of words that belonged to people's first and second languages appeared to be intermingled. However, the cell assemblies required for storage of different grammatical rules appeared more likely to be separate, perhaps because languages can have different grammatical structures.

Prosody: Rhythm, Tone, and Emphasis in Speech

When we speak, we do not merely utter words. Our speech has a regular rhythm and cadence; we give some words stress (that is, we pronounce them louder), and we vary the pitch of our voice to indicate phrasing and to distinguish between assertions and questions. In addition, we can impart information about our emotional state through the rhythm, emphasis, and tone of our speech. These rhythmic, emphatic, and melodic aspects of speech are referred to as **prosody.** The importance of these aspects of speech is illustrated by our use of punctuation symbols to indicate some elements of prosody when we write. For example, a comma indicates a short pause; a period indicates a longer one with an accompanying fall in the pitch of the voice; a question mark indicates a pause and a rise in the pitch of the voice; an exclamation mark indicates that the words are articulated with special emphasis; and so on.

The prosody of people with fluent aphasias, caused by posterior lesions, sounds normal. Their speech is rhythmical, with pauses after phrases and sentences, and has a melodic line. Even when the speech of a person with severe Wernicke's aphasia makes no sense, the prosody sounds normal. As Goodglass and Kaplan (1972) note, a person with Wernicke's aphasia may "sound like a normal speaker at a distance, because of his fluency and normal melodic contour of his speech." (Up close, of course, we hear the speech clearly enough to realize that it is meaningless.)

prosody The use of changes in intonation and emphasis to convey meaning in speech besides that specified by the particular words; an important means of communication of emotion.

Evidence from studies of normal people and patients with brain lesions suggests that prosody is a special function of the right hemisphere. This function is undoubtedly related to the more general role of this hemisphere in musical skills and the expression and recognition of emotions: Production of prosody is rather like singing, and prosody often serves as a vehicle for conveying emotion.

When we speak we do not merely utter words. We can impart information about our emotional state through the rhythm, emphasis, and tone of our speech.

Weintraub, Mesulam, and Kramer (1981) tested the ability of patients with right-hemisphere damage to recognize and express prosodic elements of speech. In one experiment they showed their subjects two pictures, named one of them, and asked the subjects to point to the appropriate one. For example, they showed them a picture of a greenhouse and a house that was painted green. In speech we distinguish between *greenhouse* and *green house* by stress: *GREEN house* means the former, and *GREEN HOUSE* (syllables equally stressed) means the latter. In a second experiment Weintraub and her colleagues tested the subjects' ability simply to detect differences in prosody. They presented pairs of sentences and asked the subjects whether they were the same or different. The pairs of sentences either were identical or differed in terms of intonation (for example, *Margo plays the piano?* and *Margo plays the piano*) or location of stress (for example, *STEVE drives the car* and *Steve drives the CAR*). The patients with right-hemisphere lesions (but not control subjects) performed poorly on both of these tasks. Thus, they showed a deficit in prosodic comprehension.

To test production, the investigators presented two written sentences and asked a question about them. For example, they presented the following pair:

The man walked to the grocery store.

The woman rode to the shoe store.

The subjects were instructed to answer questions by reading one of the sentences. Try this one yourself. Read the question below and then read aloud the sentence (above) that answers it.

Who walked to the grocery store, the man or the woman?

The question asserts that someone walked to the grocery store but asks who that person was. When answering a question like this, people normally stress the requested item of information; in this case they say, "The *man* walked to the grocery store." However, Weintraub and her colleagues found that although patients with right-hemisphere brain damage chose the correct sentence, they either failed to stress a word or stressed the wrong one. Thus, the right hemisphere plays a role in production as well as perception of prosody.

INTERIM SUMMARY

Speech Production and Comprehension: Brain Mechanisms

Two regions of the brain are especially important in understanding and producing speech. Broca's area, in the left frontal lobe just rostral to the region of the primary motor cortex that controls the muscles of speech, is involved with speech production. This region contains memories of the sequences of muscular movements that produce words, each of which is connected with its auditory counterpart in the posterior part of the brain. Broca's aphasia—which is caused by damage to Broca's area, adjacent regions of the frontal cortex, and underlying white matter—consists of varying degrees of agrammatism, anomia, and articulation difficulties.

Wernicke's area, in the posterior superior temporal lobe, is involved with speech perception. The region just adjacent to Wernicke's area, which I have called the posterior language area, is necessary for speech comprehension and the translation of thoughts into words. Presumably, Wernicke's area contains memories of the sounds of words, each of which is connected through the posterior language area with circuits that contain memories about the properties of the things the words denote and with circuits that are responsible for pronouncing the words. Damage restricted to Wernicke's area causes pure word deafness—loss of the ability to understand speech but intact speech production, reading, and writing. Wernicke's aphasia, caused by damage to Wernicke's area and the posterior language area, consists of poor speech comprehension, poor repetition, and production of fluent, meaningless speech. Transcortical sensory aphasia, caused by damage to the posterior speech area, consists of poor speech comprehension and production, but the patients can repeat what they hear. Thus, the symptoms of Wernicke's aphasia consist of those of transcortical sensory aphasia plus those of pure word deafness (WA = TSA + PWD). The fact that people with transcortical sensory aphasia can repeat words they cannot understand suggests that there is a direct connection between Wernicke's area and Broca's area. Indeed, there is: the arcuate fasciculus. Damage to this bundle of axons produces conduction aphasia: disruption of the ability to repeat exactly what was heard without disruption of the ability to comprehend or produce meaningful speech.

The meanings of words are our memories of objects, actions, and other concepts associated with them. These meanings are memories and are stored in the association cortex, not in the speech areas themselves. Pure anomia, caused by damage to the temporal or parietal lobes, consists of difficulty in word finding, particularly in naming objects. Some patients have a specific difficulty with proper nouns, while others have difficulty with common nouns; most patients have little difficulty with verbs. Damage to Broca's area and surrounding regions disrupts the ability to name actions—to think of appropriate verbs. Brain damage can also disrupt the "definitions" as well as the "entries" in the mental dictionary; damage to specific regions of the association cortex effectively erases some categories of the meanings of words.

The location of cell assemblies that encode words in different languages in the brains of bilingual people appear to be located in approximately the same places. The separation of cell assemblies that represent the grammatical rules of different languages can be more substantial.

Prosody includes changes in intonation, rhythm, and stress that add meaning, especially emotional meaning, to the sentences that we speak. The neural mechanisms that control the prosodic elements of speech appear to be in the right hemisphere.

Because so many terms and symptoms were described in this section, I have provided a table that summarizes them. (See ***Table 13.1.***)

Table 13.1

Aphasic Syndromes Produced by Brain Damage

Disorder	Areas of Lesion	Spontaneous Speech	Comprehension	Repetition	Naming
Wernicke's aphasia	Posterior portion of superior temporal gyrus (Wernicke's area) and posterior language area	Fluent	Poor	Poor	Poor
Pure word deafness	Wernicke's area or its connection with primary auditory cortex	Fluent	Poor	Poor	Good
Broca's aphasia	Frontal cortex rostral to base of primary motor cortex (Broca's area)	Nonfluent	Good	Poor[a]	Poor
Conduction aphasia	White matter beneath parietal lobe superior to lateral fissure (arcuate fasciculus)	Fluent	Good	Poor	Good
Anomic aphasia	Various parts of parietal and temporal lobes	Fluent	Good	Good	Poor
Transcortical sensory aphasia	Posterior language area	Fluent	Poor	Good	Poor

[a]May be better than spontaneous speech.

THOUGHT QUESTION

Suppose you were asked to determine the abilities and deficits of people with aphasia. What tasks would you include in your examination to test for the presence of particular deficits?

Disorders of Reading and Writing

Reading and writing are closely related to listening and talking; thus, oral and written language abilities have many brain mechanisms in common. This section discusses the neural basis of reading and writing disorders. As you will see, the study of these disorders has provided us with some useful and interesting information.

pure alexia Loss of the ability to read without loss of the ability to write; produced by brain damage.

Relationship to Aphasia

The reading and writing skills of people with aphasia almost always resemble their speaking and comprehending abilities. For example, patients with Wernicke's aphasia have as much difficulty reading and writing as they do speaking and understanding speech. Patients with Broca's aphasia comprehend what they read about as well as they can understand speech, but their reading aloud is poor, of course. If their speech is agrammatical, so is their writing; and to the extent that they fail to comprehend grammar when listening to speech, they fail to do so when reading. Patients with conduction aphasia generally have some difficulty reading; and when they read aloud, they often make semantic paraphasias (saying synonyms for some of the words they read), just as they do when attempting to repeat what they hear. Depending on the location of the lesion, some patients with transcortical sensory aphasia can read aloud accurately but fail to comprehend what they read.

Figure 13.15

A letter written to Dr. Elizabeth Warrington by a patient with pure alexia. The letter reads as follows: "Dear Dr. Warrington, Thank you for your letter of September 16th. I shall be pleased to be at your office between 10–10:30 am on Friday 17th october. I still find it very odd to be able to write this letter but not to be able to read it back a few minutes later. I much appreciate the opportunity to see you. Yours sincerely, Harry X.

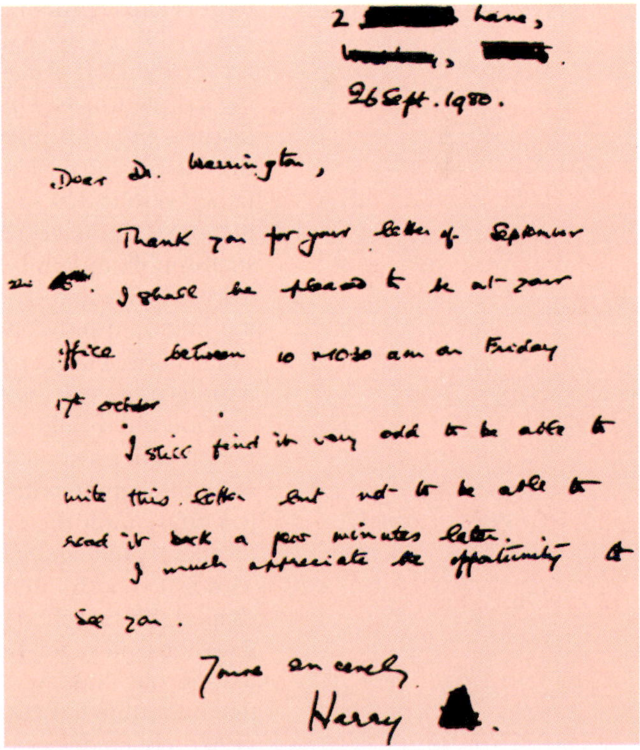
2 [redacted] Lane,
[redacted], [redacted].
26 Sept. 1980.

Dear Dr. Warrington,

Thank you for your letter of September 16th. I shall be pleased to be at your office between 10–10.30 am on Friday 17th october.

I still find it very odd to be able to write this letter but not to be able to read it back a few minutes later.

I much appreciate the opportunity to see you.

Yours sincerely,
Harry [redacted].

From McCarthy, R. A., and Warrington, E. K. *Cognitive Neuropsychology: A Clinical Introduction.* San Diego: Academic Press, 1990. Reprinted with permission.

Pure Alexia

Dejerine (1892) described a remarkable syndrome, which we now call **pure alexia,** or sometimes *pure word blindness* or *alexia without agraphia.* His patient had a lesion in the visual cortex of the left occipital lobe and the posterior end of the corpus callosum. The patient could still write, although he had lost the ability to read. In fact, if he was shown some of his own writing, he could not read it.

Several years ago, some colleagues and I studied a man with pure alexia who discovered his ability to write in an interesting way. A few months after he sustained a head injury that caused his brain damage, he and his wife were watching a service person repair their washing machine. The patient wanted to say something privately to his wife, so he picked up a pad of paper and jotted a note. As he was handing it to her, they suddenly realized with amazement that although he could not read, he was able to write! His wife brought the note to their neurologist, who asked the patient to read it. Although he remembered the gist of the message, he could not read the words. Unfortunately, I do not have that note, but Figure 13.15 shows the writing of another person with pure alexia. (See ***Figure 13.15.***)

Although patients with pure alexia cannot read, they can recognize words that are spelled aloud to them;

Animation 13.3, Pure Alexia, explains the role of lesions of the left primary visual cortex and posterior corpus callosum in this disorder.

therefore, they have not lost their memories of the spellings of words. Pure alexia is obviously a perceptual disorder; it is similar to pure word deafness, except that the patient has difficulty with visual input, not auditory input. The disorder is caused by lesions that prevent visual information from reaching the extrastriate cortex of the left hemisphere (Damasio and Damasio, 1983, 1986). Figure 13.16 explains why Dejerine's original patient could not read. (***Animation 13.3, Pure Alexia,*** also illustrates the brain damage responsible for this disorder.) The first diagram shows the pathway that visual information would take if a person had damage *only to the left primary visual cortex.* In this case the person's right visual field would be blind; he or she would see nothing to the right of the fixation point. But people with this disorder can read. Their only problem is that they must look to the right of each word so that they can see all of it, which means that they read somewhat more slowly than someone with full vision.

Let us trace the flow of visual information for a person with this brain damage. Information from the left side of the visual field is transmitted to the right striate cortex (primary visual cortex) and then to the lingual and fusiform gyri—a region of extrastriate cortex involved in the recognition of written text. From there, the information crosses the posterior corpus callosum and is transmitted to the left extrastriate cortex and then to speech mechanisms located in the left frontal lobe. Thus, the person can read the words aloud. (See ***Figure 13.16a.***)

The second diagram shows Dejerine's patient. Notice how the additional lesion of the corpus callosum prevents visual information concerning written text from reaching the posterior left hemisphere. Without this information, the patient cannot read. (See ***Figure 13.16b.***)

I must note that the diagrams shown in Figure 13.16 are as simple and schematic as possible. They illustrate only the pathway involved in seeing a word and pronouncing it, and they ignore neural structures that would be involved in understanding its meaning. As we will see later in this chapter, evidence from patients with brain lesions indicates that seeing and pronouncing words can take place independently of understanding them. Thus, although the diagrams are simplified, they are not unreasonable, given what we know about the neural components of the reading process.

Presumably, some parts of the visual association cortex are involved in perceiving written words. The fact that damage to the posterior end of the corpus callosum disrupts the exchange of information concerning the shape of words suggests that the extrastriate cortex may be responsible for this analysis. Petersen et al. (1990) obtained results that support this suggestion. The investigators used a PET scanner to measure regional cerebral blood flow while presenting subjects with four types of visual stimuli: unfamiliar letterlike forms, strings of consonants, pronounceable nonwords, and real words. They found that one region of the medial extrastriate cortex was activated only when a person viewed pronounceable nonwords or real words. Their finding suggests that this region plays a role in recognition of familiar combinations of letters. (See ***Figure 13.17.***)

You will recall from Chapter 6 that visual agnosia is a perceptual deficit in which people with bilateral damage to the visual association cortex cannot recognize objects by sight. Patients with pure alexia do *not* have visual agnosia; they can recognize objects and supply their names. Similarly, people with visual agnosia can still read. Thus, the perceptual analysis of objects and words requires different brain mechanisms. This fact is both interesting and puzzling. Certainly, the ability to read cannot have shaped the evolution of the human brain, because the invention of writing is only a few thousand years old, and until very recently, the vast majority of the world's population was illiterate. Thus, reading and object recognition use brain mechanisms that undoubtedly existed long before the invention of writing. As Patterson and Ralph (1999) conclude, natural selection has provided us with brain mechanisms for visual perception, speaking, and comprehending spoken language. Our ability to recognize words and understand them undoubtedly utilizes these mechanisms. Although

Figure 13.16

Pure alexia. Red arrows indicate the flow of information that has been interrupted by brain damage. (a) The route followed by information as a person with damage to the left primary visual cortex reads aloud. (b) Additional damage to the posterior corpus callosum interrupts the flow of information and produces pure alexia.

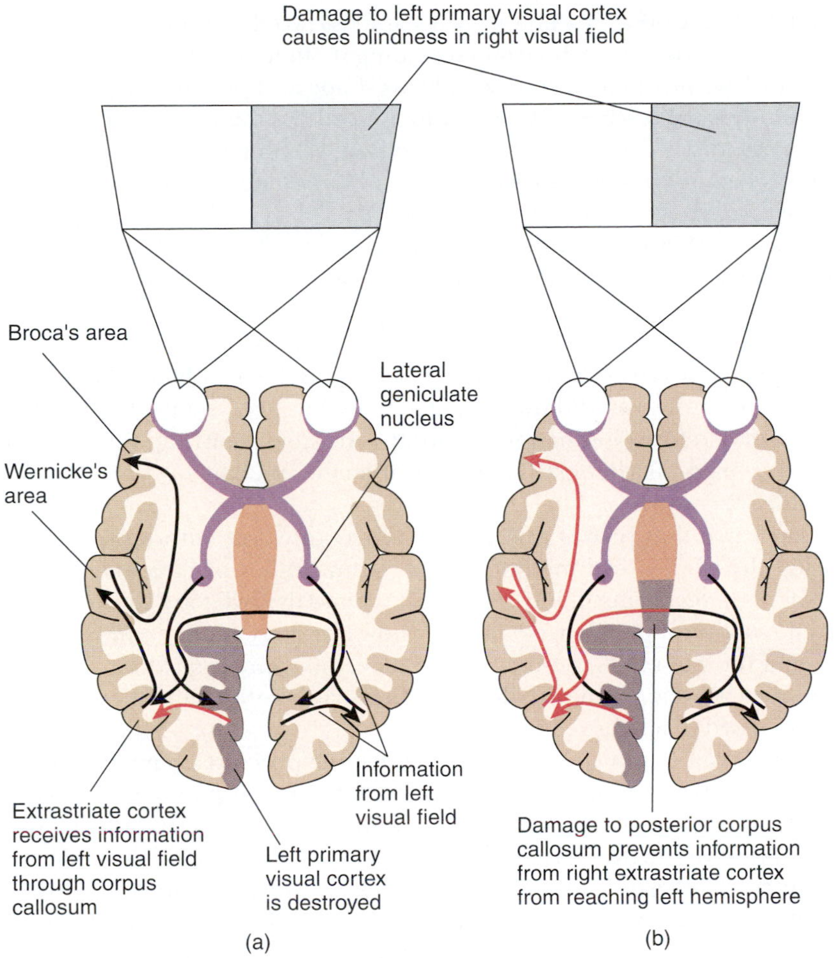
Damage to left primary visual cortex causes blindness in right visual field
Broca's area
Lateral geniculate nucleus
Wernicke's area
Extrastriate cortex receives information from left visual field through corpus callosum
Left primary visual cortex is destroyed
Information from left visual field
Damage to posterior corpus callosum prevents information from right extrastriate cortex from reaching left hemisphere
(a)
(b)

Figure 13.17

PET scans of the medial surface of the brains of subjects who read (a) letterlike forms, (b) strings of consonants, (c) pronounceable nonwords, or (d) real words

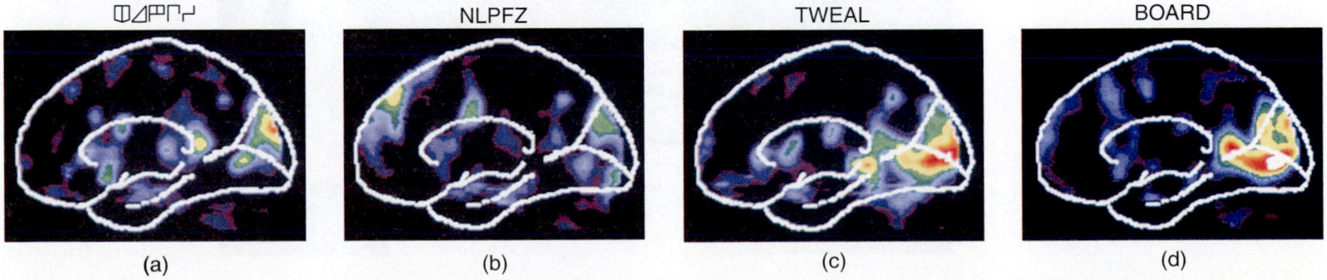
NLPFZ
TWEAL
BOARD
(a)
(b)
(c)
(d)

From Petersen, S. E., Fox, P. T., Snyder, A. Z., and Raichle, M. E. *Science,* 1990, *249,* 1041–1044. Reprinted with permission.

the argument can be made that we have inherited brain mechanisms that play a special role in *language,* the same cannot be said for the brain mechanisms we use to read and write.

Toward an Understanding of Reading

Most investigators believe that reading involves at least two different processes: direct recognition of the word as a whole and sounding it out letter by letter. When we see a familiar word, we normally recognize it by its shape and pronounce it—a process known as **whole-word reading.** (With very long words we might instead perceive segments of several letters each.) The second method, which we use for unfamiliar words, requires recognition of individual letters and knowledge of the sounds they make. This process is known as **phonetic reading.**

Evidence for our ability to sound out words is easy to obtain. In fact, you can prove to yourself that phonetic reading exists by trying to read the following words:

glab trisk chint

Well, as you can see, they are not really words, but I doubt that you had trouble pronouncing them. Obviously, you did not *recognize* them, because you probably never saw them before. Therefore, you had to use what you know about the sounds that are represented by particular letters (or groups of letters, such as *ch*) to figure out how to pronounce the words.

The best evidence that proves that people can read words without sounding them out, using the whole-word method, comes from studies of patients with acquired dyslexias. *Dyslexia* means "faulty reading." *Acquired* dyslexias are those caused by damage to the brains of people who already know how to read. In contrast, *developmental* dyslexias refer to reading difficulties that become apparent when children are learning to read. Developmental dyslexias, which may involve anomalies in brain circuitry, are discussed in a later section.

Figure 13.18 illustrates some elements of the reading processes. The diagram is an oversimplification of a very complex process, but it helps to organize some of the facts that investigators have obtained. It considers only reading and pronouncing single words, not understanding the meaning of text. When we see a familiar word, we normally recognize it as a whole and pronounce it. If we see an unfamiliar word or a pronounceable nonword, we must try to read it phonetically. (See ***Figure 13.18.***)

whole-word reading Reading by recognizing a word as a whole; "sight reading."

phonetic reading Reading by decoding the phonetic significance of letter strings; "sound reading."

surface dyslexia A reading disorder in which a person can read words phonetically but has difficulty reading irregularly spelled words by the whole-word method.

phonological dyslexia A reading disorder in which a person can read familiar words but has difficulty reading unfamiliar words or pronounceable nonwords.

Japanese writing uses two forms of characters, which encode information phonetically or nonphonetically.

Although investigators have reported several types of acquired dyslexias, I will mention three of them here. **Surface dyslexia** is a deficit in whole-word reading, usually caused by a lesion of the left lateral temporal lobe (Marshall and Newcombe, 1973; McCarthy and Warrington, 1990; Patterson and Ralph, 1999). The term *surface* reflects the fact that people with this disorder make errors related to the visual appearance of the words and to pronunciation rules, not to the meaning of the words, which is metaphorically "deeper" than the appearance.

Because patients with surface dyslexia have difficulty recognizing words as a whole, they are obliged to sound them out. Thus, they can easily read words with regular spelling, such as *hand, table,* or *chin.* However, they have difficulty reading words with irregular spelling, such as *sew, pint,* and *yacht.* In fact, they may read these words as *sue, pinnt,* and *yatchet.* They have no difficulty reading pronounceable nonwords, such as *glab, trisk,* and *chint.* Because people with surface dyslexia cannot recognize whole words by their appearance, they must, in effect, listen to their own pronunciation to understand what they are reading. If they read the word *pint* and pronounce it *pinnt,* they will say that it is not an English word (which it is not, pronounced that way). If the word is one member of a homophone, it will be impossible to understand it unless it is read in the context of a sentence. For example, if you hear the single word "pair" without additional information, you cannot know whether the speaker is referring to *pair, pear,* or *pare.* Thus, a patient with surface dyslexia who reads the word *pair* might say, ". . . it could be two of a kind, apples and . . . or what you do with your fingernails" (Gurd and Marshall, 1993, p. 594). (See ***Figure 13.19.***)

Patients with **phonological dyslexia** have the opposite problem; they can read by the whole-word method but cannot sound words out. Thus, they can read words that they are already familiar with but have great difficulty figuring out how to read unfamiliar words or pronounceable nonwords (Beauvois and Dérouesné, 1979; Dérouesné and Beauvois, 1979). (In this context, *phonology*—loosely translated as "laws of sound"—refers to the relation between letters and the sounds they represent.) People with phonological dyslexia may be excellent readers if they had already acquired a good reading vocabulary before their brain damage occurred.

Phonological dyslexia provides further evidence that whole-word reading and phonological reading involve different brain mechanisms. Phonological reading, which is the only way we can read nonwords or words we have not yet learned, entails some sort of letter-to-sound decoding. Obviously, phonological reading of English requires more than decoding of the sounds produced by single letters, because, for example, some sounds are transcribed as two-letter sequences (such as *th* or *sh*) and the addition of the letter *e* to the end of a word lengthens an internal vowel (*can* becomes *cane*). (See ***Figure 13.20.***)

Phonological dyslexia is usually caused by damage to the left frontal lobe (Price, 1998; Fiez and Petersen, 1998). A PET

Figure 13.18

A simplified model of the reading process, showing whole-word and phonetic reading. Whole-word reading is used for most familiar words; phonetic reading is used for unfamiliar words and for nonwords such as *glab, trisk,* or *chint.*

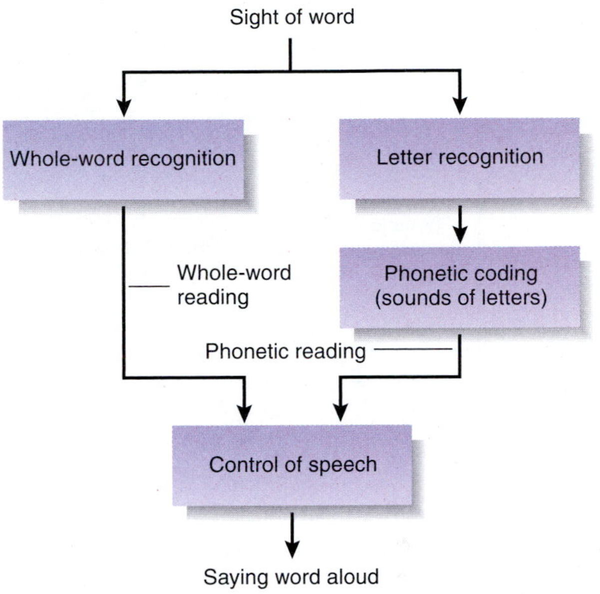

Figure 13.19

A hypothetical explanation of surface dyslexia. Whole-word reading is damaged; only phonetic reading remains.

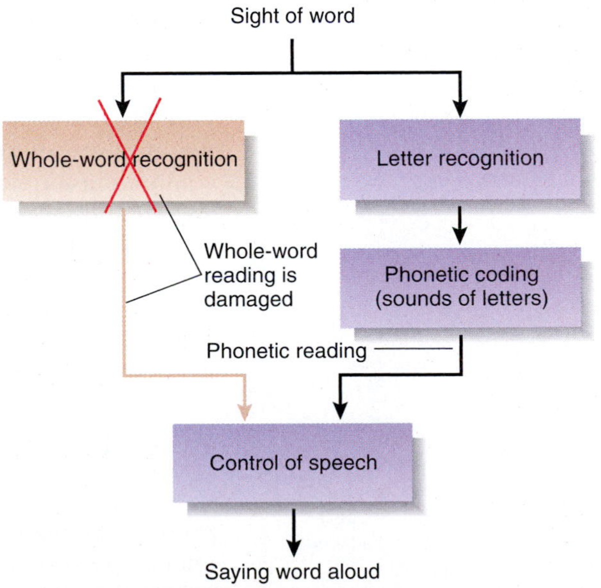

Figure 13.20

A hypothetical explanation of phonological dyslexia. Phonetic reading is damaged; only whole-word reading remains.

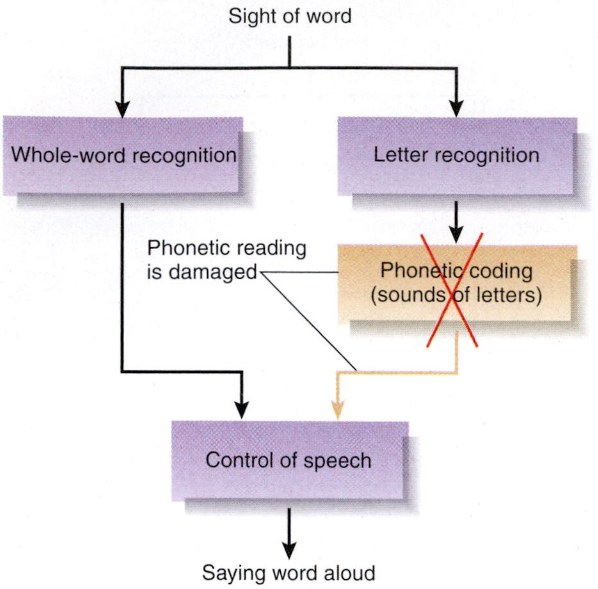

study by Fiez et al. (1999) found that phonological reading activated Broca's area and the left insular region. They suggest that "phonological" reading may actually involve articulation—that we sound out words not so much by "hearing" them in our heads as by feeling ourselves pronounce them silently to ourselves. Of course, the two processes could be taking place simultaneously.

The Japanese language provides a particularly interesting distinction between phonetic and whole-word reading. The Japanese language makes use of two kinds of written symbols. *Kanji* symbols are pictographs, adopted from the Chinese language (although they are pronounced as Japanese words). Thus, they represent concepts by means of visual symbols but do not provide a guide to their pronunciation. Reading words expressed in kanji symbols is analogous, then, to whole-word reading. *Kana* symbols are phonetic representations of syllables; thus, they encode acoustical information. These symbols are used primarily to represent foreign words or Japanese words that the average reader would be unlikely to recognize if they were represented by their kanji symbols. Reading words expressed in kana symbols is obviously phonetic.

Studies of Japanese people with localized brain damage have shown that the reading of kana and kanji symbols involves different brain mechanisms (Iwata, 1984; Sakurai et al., 1994; Sakurai, Ichikawa, and Mannen, 2001). Difficulty reading kanji symbols is analogous to surface dyslexia, whereas difficulty reading kana symbols is analogous to phonological dyslexia. A functional imaging study suggests that two different brain regions are involved in reading of kanji and kana symbols (Sakurai et al., 2000).

As we saw earlier in this chapter, recognizing a spoken word is different from understanding it. For example, patients with transcortical sensory aphasia can repeat what is said to them even though they show no signs of understanding what they hear or say. The same is true for reading. **Direct dyslexia** resembles transcortical sensory aphasia, except that the words in question are written, not spoken (Schwartz, Marin, and Saffran, 1979; Lytton and Brust, 1989; Gerhand, 2001). Patients with direct dyslexia are able to read aloud *even though they cannot understand the words they are saying.* After sustaining a stroke that damaged his left frontal and temporal lobes, Lytton and Brust's patient lost the ability to communicate verbally; his speech was meaningless, and he was unable to comprehend what other people said to him. However, he could read words with which he was already familiar. He could *not* read pronounceable nonwords; therefore, he had lost the ability to read phonetically. His comprehension deficit seemed complete; when the investigators presented him with a word and several pictures, one of which corresponded to the word, he read the word correctly but had no idea what picture went with it. Gerhand's patient showed a similar pattern of deficits, except that she was able to read phonetically: She could sound out pronounceable nonwords. These findings indicate that the brain regions responsible for phonetic reading and whole-word reading are each directly connected with brain regions responsible for speech.

Toward an Understanding of Writing

direct dyslexia A language disorder caused by brain damage in which the person can read words aloud without understanding them.

Writing depends on knowledge of the words that are to be used, along with the proper grammatical structure of the sentences they are to form. Thus, if a patient is unable to express himself or herself by speech, we should not be surprised to see a writing disturbance as well.

One type of writing disorder involves difficulties in motor control—in directing the movements of a pen or pencil to form letters and words. Investigators have reported surprisingly specific types of writing disorders that fall under this category. For example, some patients can write numbers but not letters, some can write uppercase letters but not lowercase letters, some can write consonants but not vowels, some can write cursively but not print uppercase letters, and others can write letters normally but have difficulty placing them in an orderly fashion on the page (Cubelli, 1991; Alexander et al., 1992; Margolin and Goodman-Schulman, 1992; Silveri, 1996).

Writing normally involves holding a pen or pencil and moving its point across a piece of paper. But we can create visual records with the keyboard of a typewriter or a computer. However, the movements we make with our hands and fingers are different when we write or type. Skilled typists learn automatic sequences of movements that produce frequently used words, but these are different from the movements we would make when we write these words. Otsuki et al. (2002) reported the case of a man who lost the ability to type after a stroke that damaged the ventral left frontal lobe. His ability to speak and understand speech, his ability to read, and his ability to write were not affected, and he showed no other obvious motor impairments besides his *dystypia,* as the investigators named it.

A more basic type of writing disorder involves problems in the ability to spell words, as opposed to problems with making accurate movements of the fingers. I will devote the rest of this section to this type of disorder. Like reading, writing (or more specifically, spelling) involves more than one method. The first is related to audition. When children acquire language skills, they first learn the sounds of words, then learn to say them, then learn to read, and then learn to write. Undoubtedly, reading and writing depend heavily on the skills that are learned earlier. For example, to write most words, we must be able to "sound them out in our heads," that is, to hear them and to articulate them subvocally. If you want to demonstrate this to yourself, try to write a long word such as *antidisestablishmentarianism* from memory and see whether you can do it without saying the word to yourself. If you recite a poem or sing a song to yourself under your breath at the same time, you will see that the writing comes to a halt.

A second way of writing involves transcribing an image of what a particular word looks like—copying a visual mental image. Have you ever looked off into the distance to picture a word so that you can remember how to spell it? Some people are not very good at phonological spelling and have to write some words down to see whether they look correct. This method obviously involves *visual* memories, not acoustical ones.

Neurological evidence supports these speculations. Brain damage can impair either phonetic or visually based writing. Impaired phonetic writing is called **phonological dysgraphia** (Shallice, 1981). (*Dysgraphia* refers to a writing deficit just as *dyslexia* refers to a reading deficit.) People with this disorder are unable to sound out words and write them phonetically. Thus, they cannot write unfamiliar words or pronounceable nonwords, such as the ones I presented in the section on reading. They can, however, visually imagine familiar words and then write them. **Orthographic dysgraphia** is just the opposite—a disorder of visually based writing. People with orthographic dysgraphia can *only* sound words out; thus, they can spell regular words such as *care* or *tree,* and they can write pronounceable nonwords. However, they have difficulty spelling irregular words such as *half* or *busy* (Beauvois and Dérouesné, 1981); they may write *haff* or *bizzy.*

Japanese patients show writing deficits similar to those of patients whose languages use the Roman alphabet; some patients have difficulty writing kana symbols, whereas others have difficulty with kanji symbols (Iwata, 1984; Yokota et al., 1990). Kawamura, Hirayama, and Yamamoto (1989) reported a particularly interesting case of a man with damage to the middle part of the corpus callosum who could write kana symbols with both hands and could write kanji symbols with the right hand but

phonological dysgraphia A writing disorder in which the person cannot sound out words and write them phonetically.

orthographic dysgraphia A writing disorder in which the person can spell regularly spelled words but not irregularly spelled ones.

Figure 13.21

The writing of a Japanese patient with damage to the middle part of the corpus callosum. He could write both kanji and kana characters with his right hand, but he could not write kanji characters with his left hand (color). He could, however, *copy* kanji characters with his left hand if he was given a model to look at.

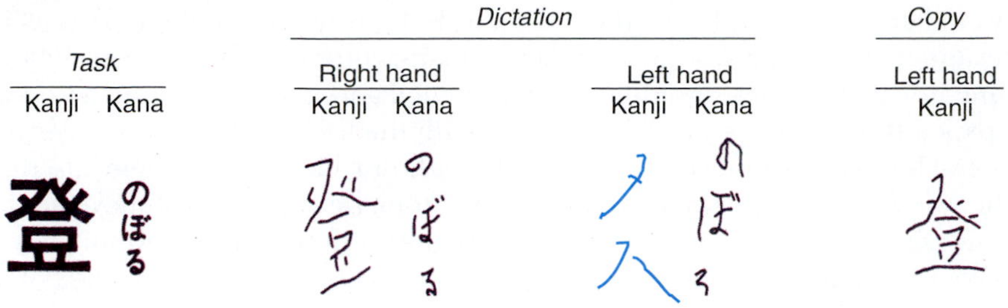

From Kawamura, M., Hirayama, K., and Yamamoto, H. *Brain,* 1989, *112,* 1011–1018. Reprinted by permission of Oxford University Press.

developmental dyslexia A reading difficulty in a person of normal intelligence and perceptual ability; of genetic origin or caused by prenatal or perinatal factors.

not the left. He could *copy* kanji symbols with his left hand; he just could not write them down when the investigators dictated them to him. (See ***Figure 13.21.***) Another patient, reported by Tei, Soma, and Maruyama (1994), had the opposite symptoms: very bad kana writing with the nondominant hand but better kanji writing.

These results have interesting implications. Writing appears to be organized in the speech-dominant hemisphere (normally, the left hemisphere). That is, the information needed to specify the shape of the symbols is provided by circuits in this hemisphere. When a person uses his or her left hand to write these symbols, the information must be sent across the corpus callosum to the motor cortex of the right hemisphere, which controls the left hand. Apparently, information about the two forms of Japanese symbols is transmitted through different parts of the corpus callosum; the brain damage of the patient studied by Kawamura and his colleagues disrupted one of these pathways but not the other. (See ***Figure 13.22.***)

As we saw in the section on reading, some patients (those with direct dyslexia) can read aloud without being able to understand what they are reading. Similarly, some patients can write words that are dictated to them even though they cannot understand these words (Roeltgen, Rothi, and Heilman, 1986; Lesser, 1989). Of course, they cannot communicate by means of writing, because they cannot translate their thoughts into words. (In fact, because most of these patients have sustained extensive brain damage, their thought processes themselves are severely disturbed.) Some of these patients can even spell pronounceable nonwords, which indicates that their ability to spell phonetically is intact. Roeltgen et al. (1986) referred to this disorder as *semantic agraphia,* but perhaps the term *direct dysgraphia* would be more appropriate, because of the parallel with direct dyslexia.

Figure 13.22

The role of the corpus callosum in Japanese writing. Information about kana and kanji characters apparently crosses different parts of the corpus callosum.

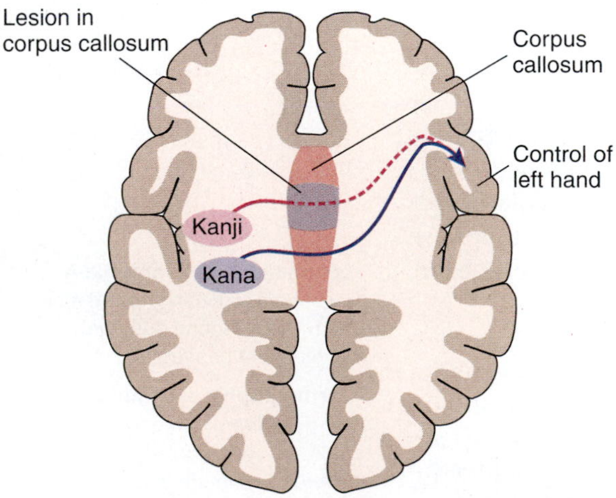

Developmental Dyslexias

Some children have great difficulty learning to read and never become fluent readers, even though they are otherwise intelligent. Specific language learning disorders, called **developmental dyslexias,** tend to occur in families, a finding that suggests a genetic (and hence biological) component (Pennington et al., 1991; Wolff and Melngailis, 1994). Linkage studies suggest that the chromosomes 6 and 15 may contain genes responsible for different components of this disorder (Grigorenko et al., 1997; Fisher et al., 1999; Gayán et al., 1999; Petryshen et al., 2001). Taipale et al. (2003) found that alterations in a gene on chromosome 15 that produces a nuclear protein appear to be associated with developmental dyslexia. The function of this protein has not yet been identified.

A study of fifty-six dyslexic boys in Sydney, Australia, found that two-thirds of them showed impairments in both phonological and word-form reading. Among the other third, 64 percent had difficulty only with phonological reading, and 46 percent had difficulty only with word-form reading (Castles and Coltheart, 1993). (You will recall that phonological difficulty is the primary symptom of phonological dyslexia, while word-form difficulty is the primary symptom of surface dyslexia.)

As we saw earlier, the fact that written language is a recent invention means that natural selection could not have given us brain mechanisms whose only role is to interpret written language. Thus, we should not expect that developmental dyslexia involves only deficits in reading. Indeed, researchers have found a variety of language deficits that do *not* involve reading. One common deficit is deficient phonological awareness. That is, people with developmental dyslexia have difficulty blending or rearranging the sounds of words that they hear (Eden and Zeffiro, 1998). For example, they have difficulty recognizing that if we remove the first sound from "cat," we are left with the word "at." They also have difficulty distinguishing the order of sequences of sounds (Helenius, Uutela, and Hari, 1999). Problems such as these might be expected to impair the ability to read phonetically. Dyslexic children also tend to have great difficulty in writing: They make spelling errors, they show poor spatial arrangements of letters, they omit letters, and their writing tends to have weak grammatical development (Habib, 2000).

Some evidence has been obtained from functional imaging that suggests that the brains of dyslexics process written information differently than do proficient readers. For example, Shaywitz et al. (2002) had seventy dyslexic and seventy-four nondyslexic children read words and pronounceable nonwords. They found significantly different patterns of brain activation in the two groups. The proficient readers showed activation of the left occipitotemporal and parietotemporal regions and of the left and right inferior frontal cortex (which included Broca's area). A child's reading skill was positively correlated with activation of the left occipitotemporal cortex. (See ***Figure 13.23.***)

Most languages—including English—contain many irregular words. For example, consider *cough, rough, bough,* and *through.* Because there is no phonetic rule that describes how these words are to be pronounced, readers of English are obliged to memorize them. In fact, the forty sounds that distinguish English words can be spelled in up to 1120 different ways. In contrast, Italian is much more regular; it contains twenty-five different sounds that can be spelled in only thirty-three combinations of letters (Helmuth, 2001). Paulesu et al. (2001) found that developmental dyslexia is rare among people who speak Italian and is much more common among speakers of English and French (another language with many irregular words). Paulesu and his colleagues identified college students with a history of dyslexia from Italy, France, and Great Britain. Italian dyslexics were much harder to find, and their disorders were much less severe than those of their English-speaking and French-speaking counterparts. However, when all three groups were asked to read

Figure 13.23

Three regions of the brain activated in the brains of children as they read words and pronounceable nonwords. Proficient readers showed activation of all three areas: the left occipitotemporal and parietotemporal regions, and the left and right inferior frontal cortex. Reading ability was positively correlated the level of activation of the occipitotemporal region; activation of this area was lower in dyslexic children.

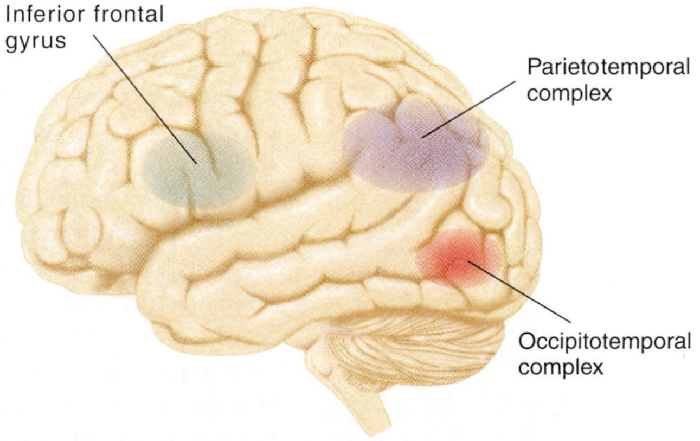

Adapted from Shaywitz, B. A., Shaywitz, S. E., Pugh, K. R., Mencl, W. E., Fulbright, R. K., Skudlarski P., Constable, R. T., Marchione, K. E., Fletcher, J. M., Lyon, G. R., and Gore, J. C. *Biological Psychiatry,* 2002, *52,* 101–110.

while their heads were in a PET scanner, their scans all showed the same pattern: a decrease in the activity of the left occipitotemporal region—the same general region that Shaywitz et al. (2002) identified. (See the green region of ***Figure 13.23.***)

Paulesu and his colleagues concluded that the brain anomalies that cause dyslexia are similar in the three countries they studied but that the regularity of Italian spelling made it much easier for potential dyslexics in Italy to learn to read. By the way, other "dyslexia-friendly" languages include Spanish, Finnish, Czech, and Japanese. One of the authors of this study, Chris D. Frith, cites the case of an Australian boy who lived in Japan. He learned to read Japanese normally but was dyslexic in English (Recer, 2001).

INTERIM SUMMARY

Disorders of Reading and Writing

Brain damage can produce reading and writing disorders. With few exceptions, aphasias are accompanied by writing deficits that parallel the speech production deficits and by reading deficits that parallel the speech comprehension deficits. Pure alexia is a perceptual deficit caused by lesions that produce blindness in the right visual field and destruction of fibers of the posterior corpus callosum.

Research in the past few decades has discovered that acquired reading disorders (dyslexias) can fall into one of several categories, and the study of these disorders has provided neuropsychologists and cognitive psychologists with thought-provoking information that has helped them understand the brain mechanisms involved in reading. Surface dyslexia, usually caused by damage to the left lateral temporal lobe, is a loss of whole-word reading ability. Phonological dyslexia, usually caused by damage to the left frontal lobe, is loss of the ability to read phonetically. Reading of kana (phonetic) and kanji (pictographic) symbols by Japanese people are equivalent to phonetic and whole-word reading, and damage to different parts of the brain interfere with these two forms of reading. Direct dyslexia is analogous to transcortical sensory aphasia; the patients can read words aloud but cannot understand what they are reading. Some can read both real words and pronounceable nonwords, so both phonetic and whole-word reading can be preserved.

Brain damage can disrupt writing ability by impairing people's ability to form letters—or even specific types of letters, such as uppercase or lowercase letters or vowels. One case of dystypia—a specific deficit in the ability to type without other reading or writing disorders—has been reported. Other deficits involve the ability to spell words. We normally use at least two different strategies to spell words: phonetic (sounding the word out), and visual (remembering how it looks on paper). Two types of dysgraphia—phonological and orthographic—represent difficulties implementing phonetic and visual strategies, respectively. The existence of these two disorders indicates that several different brain mechanisms are involved in the process of writing. In addition, some patients have a deficit parallel to direct dyslexia; they can write words they cannot understand.

Developmental dyslexia is a hereditary condition that may involve abnormal development of parts of the brain that play a role in language. Most developmental dyslexics have difficulty with phonological processing—of spoken words as well as written ones. Functional imaging studies report decreased activation of a region of the left occipitotemporal cortex may be involved in reading deficits. Children who learn to read languages that have writing with regular correspondence between spelling and pronunciation (such as Italian) are much less likely to become dyslexic than those who learn to read languages with irregular spelling (such as English or French). A better understanding of the components of reading and writing may help us to develop effective teaching methods that will permit people with dyslexia to take advantage of the abilities that they do have.

Table 13.2 summarizes the disorders that were described in this section.

Table 13.2

Reading and Writing Disorder Produced by Brain Damage

Reading Disorder	Whole-Word Reading	Phonetic Reading	Remarks
Pure alexia	Poor	Poor	Can write
Surface dyslexia	Poor	Good	
Phonological dyslexia	Good	Poor	
Direct dyslexia	Good	Good	Cannot comprehend words
Writing Disorder	**Whole-Word Writing**	**Phonetic Writing**	**Remarks**
Phonological dysgraphia	Good	Poor	
Orthographic dysgraphia	Poor	Good	
Semantic agraphia (direct dysgraphia)	Good	Good	Cannot comprehend words

THOUGHT QUESTION

Suppose someone close to you received a head injury that caused phonological dyslexia. What would you do to try to help this person read better? (It would probably be best to build on the person's remaining abilities.) Suppose this person needed to learn to read some words she or he had never seen before. How would you help the person to do so?

EPILOGUE

Analysis of Speech Sounds

Mr. S., the man described in the chapter prologue, had pure word deafness. As you learned in this chapter, pure word deafness is a perceptual deficit that does not affect people's general language abilities, nor does it affect their ability to recognize nonspeech sounds.

As you saw in this chapter, pure word deafness is caused by lesions that damage Wernicke's area or prevent it from receiving auditory input. Thus, Wernicke's area appears to contain the neural network responsible for analyzing speech sounds. The auditory association cortex of the right hemisphere is apparently involved in perception of nonspeech sounds and of the rhythmic elements of speech (such as those we use for emphasis or to express emotions). Many patients with pure word deafness can recognize the emotion expressed by the intonation of speech even though they cannot understand what is being said. In addition, perception of the melodic and harmonic structure of music is accomplished by the right hemisphere; damage to this hemisphere can result in *amusia,* or loss of musical ability.

Hemispheric specialization in auditory function is not limited to the human brain. Heffner and Heffner (1990) reviewed a series of experiments from their laboratory indicating that the auditory system of the left hemisphere in monkeys plays a special role in recognizing vocal communications. Although Japanese macaques obviously cannot talk, they do have a repertoire of vocal calls that they use to communicate with each other. Heffner and Heffner found that lesions of the left auditory cortex produce a much more severe impairment than right-hemisphere lesions.

Exactly what do we mean when we say that the auditory system of the left hemisphere is specialized for the analysis of speech sounds? First, the specialization is only for the discrimination of the sounds that distinguish one word from another, not the sounds related to the rhythmic aspects of speech. In general, the sounds that distinguish between words are very brief, whereas those that convey emphasis or emotion are of longer duration. Perhaps the auditory system of the left hemisphere is simply specialized for the recognition of acoustical events of short duration.

In a review of the literature, Phillips and Farmer (1990) suggest precisely this hypothesis. They note that careful studies of patients with pure word deafness have shown that the patients can distinguish between different vowels but not between different consonants—especially between different stop consonants, such as /t/, /d/, /k/, or /p/. (Linguists represent speech sounds by putting letters or special phonetic symbols between slashes.) Patients with pure word deafness *can* generally recognize consonants with a long duration, such as /s/, /z/, or /f/. (Say these consonants to yourself, and you will see how different they sound.)

Phillips and Farmer note that the important acoustical events in speech sounds fall within a time range of a few milliseconds to a few tens of milliseconds. Speech sounds are made by rapidly moving the lips, tongue, and soft palate, which can produce acoustical events that can be distinguished only by a fine-grained analysis. In contrast, most environmental sounds do not contain such a fine temporal structure. The authors also note that "pure" word deafness is not absolutely pure. That is, when people with this disorder are tested carefully with recordings of a variety of environmental sounds, they have difficulty recognizing at least some of them. Although *most* environmental sounds do not contain a fine temporal structure, some do, and patients have difficulty recognizing these.

Several studies have found deficits in auditory perception that support Phillips and Farmer's "temporal grain" hypothesis of pure word deafness. For example, normal subjects can perceive a series of clicks as being separate events when they are separated by only 1–3 msec; in contrast, patients with pure word deafness require a separation of 15–30 msec. In addition, although normal subjects can count clicks that are presented at a rate of up to 9–11 per second, patients with pure word deafness cannot count clicks presented faster than 2 per second. This perceptual difficulty shows up in recognition of nonspeech sounds in which the timing of brief events is important; one study reported that a patient with pure word deafness could no longer understand messages in Morse code, although he could still *send* messages that way. Thus, his deficit was perceptual, not motor.

Although more research needs to be done on hemispheric differences in the functions of the auditory system, the temporal grain hypothesis appears to be quite reasonable and has considerable support. Most investigators have focused on the linguistic aspects of language deficits produced by brain damage; it is clear that study of the brain mechanisms involved in the perceptual aspects of speech deserves attention, too.

KEY CONCEPTS

SPEECH PRODUCTION AND COMPREHENSION: BRAIN MECHANISMS

1. Broca's area, located in the left frontal lobe, is important in articulating words and producing and understanding grammatical constructions.
2. Wernicke's area, located in the auditory association cortex of the left hemisphere, is important in recognizing the sounds of words.
3. Comprehension of speech involves connections between Wernicke's area and memories that define words. These memories are located in the sensory association cortex, and the connections are made via the posterior language area.
4. Conduction aphasia occurs when Wernicke's area and Broca's area can no longer communicate directly.

DISORDERS OF READING AND WRITING

5. Brain damage can produce a variety of reading and writing disorders. Study of these disorders is helping investigators discover the brain functions necessary for these behaviors.
6. Reading takes two forms: whole-word and phonetic. Writing can be based on memories of the sounds the words make or their visual shape.
7. Developmental dyslexia may be a genetic disorder that results in abnormal development of the brain regions involved in language abilities.

SUGGESTED READINGS

Davis, G. A. *Aphasiology: Disorders and Clinical Practice.* Boston: Allyn and Bacon, 2000.

Obler, L. K., and Gjerlow, K. *Language and the Brain.* Cambridge, England: Cambridge University Press, 1999.

Parkin, A. J. *Explorations in Cognitive Neuropsychology.* Oxford, England: Blackwell Publishers, 1996.

Posner, M. I., and Raichle, M. E. *Images of Mind.* New York: Scientific American Library, 1994.

Sarno, M. T. *Acquired Aphasia* (3rd ed.). New York: Academic Press, 1998.

SUGGESTED WEB SITES

Sleep and Language
http://thalamus.wustl.edu/course/sleep.html

This Web site provides an overview of sleep phenomena and of language.

Dyslexia Web Resources
http://www.krgraphics.co.uk/texthelp/d_web.htm

The focus of the collection of Web links is on the topic of dyslexia

Aphasia: Treatment, Prevention, and Cure
http://www.healthlinkusa/A.html

This page contains a series of links that will take you to a page devoted to the topic of aphasia.

Neurological Disorders

chapter 14

CHAPTER OUTLINE

LEARNING OBJECTIVES

1. Discuss the causes, symptoms, and treatment of brain tumors, seizure disorders, and cerebrovascular accidents.
2. Discuss developmental disorders resulting from toxic chemicals, inherited metabolic disorders, and Down syndrome.
3. Discuss research on the role of misfolded prion proteins in the transmissible spongiform encephalopathies.
4. Discuss the causes, symptoms, and available treatments for the degeneration of the basal ganglia that occurs in Parkinson's disease and Huntington's disease.
5. Discuss the causes, symptoms, and potential treatments for the brain degeneration caused by Alzheimer's disease and multiple sclerosis.
6. Discuss the causes, symptoms, and available treatments for encephalitis, dementia caused by the AIDS virus, and meningitis.

PROLOGUE

It Started with Her Foot

Mrs. R., a divorced, fifty-year-old elementary school teacher, was sitting in her car, waiting for the traffic light to change. Suddenly, her right foot began to shake. Afraid that she would inadvertently press the accelerator and lurch forward into the intersection, she quickly grabbed the shift lever and switched the transmission into neutral. Now her lower leg was shaking; then her upper leg, as well. With horrified fascination she felt her body, then her arm, begin to shake in rhythm with her leg. The shaking slowed and finally stopped. By this time the light had changed to green, and the cars behind her began honking at her. She missed that green light, but by the time the light changed again, she had recovered enough to put the car in gear and drive home.

Mrs. R. was frightened by her experience and tried in vain to think what she might have done to cause it. The next evening, some close friends visited her apartment for dinner. She found it hard to concentrate on their conversation and thought of telling them about her spell, but she finally decided not to bring up the matter. After dinner, while she was clearing the dishes off the table, her right foot began shaking again. This time she was standing up, and the contractions—much more violent than before—caused her to fall. Her friends, seated in the living room, heard the noise and came running to see what had happened. They saw Mrs. R. lying on the floor, her legs and arms held out stiffly before her, vibrating uncontrollably. Her head was thrown back and she seemed not to hear their anxious questions. The convulsion soon ceased; less than a minute later, Mrs. R. regained consciousness but seemed dazed and confused.

Mrs. R. was brought by ambulance to a hospital. After learning about her first spell and hearing her friends describe the convulsion, the emergency room physician immediately called a neurologist, who ordered a CT scan. The scan showed a small, circular white spot right where the neurologist expected it, between the frontal lobes, above the corpus callosum. Two days later, a neurosurgeon removed a small benign tumor, and Mrs. R. made an uneventful recovery.

When my colleagues and I met Mrs. R., we saw a pleasant, intelligent woman, much relieved to know that her type of brain tumor rarely produces brain damage if it is removed in time. Indeed, although we tested her carefully, we found no signs of intellectual impairment.

Although the brain is the most protected organ, many pathological processes can damage it or disrupt its functioning. Because much of what we have learned about the functions of the human brain has been gained by studying people with brain damage, you have already encountered many neurological disorders in this book: movement disorders, such as Parkinson's disease; perceptual disorders, such as visual agnosia and blindness caused by damage to the visual system; language disorders such as aphasia, alexia, and agraphia; and memory disorders, such as Korsakoff's syndrome. This chapter describes the major categories of the neuropathological conditions that the brain can sustain—tumors, seizure disorders, cerebrovascular accidents, disorders of development, degenerative disorders, and disorders caused by infectious diseases—and discusses the behavioral effects of these conditions and their treatments.

Tumors

A tumor is a mass of cells whose growth is uncontrolled and that serves no useful function. Some are **malignant,** or cancerous, and others are **benign** ("harmless"). The major distinction between malignancy and benignancy is whether the tumor is *encapsulated:* whether there is a distinct border between the mass of tumor cells and the surrounding tissue. If there is such a border, the tumor is benign; the surgeon can cut it out, and it will not regrow. However, if the tumor grows by *infiltrating* the surrounding tissue, there will be no clear-cut border between the tumor and normal tissue. If the surgeon removes the tumor, some cells may be missed, and these cells will produce a new tumor. In addition, malignant tumors often give rise to **metastases.** A metastasizing tumor will shed cells, which then travel through the bloodstream, lodge

malignant tumor A cancerous (literally, "harm-producing") tumor; lacks a distinct border and may metastasize.

benign tumor (*bee* ***nine***) A noncancerous (literally, "harmless") tumor; has a distinct border and cannot metastasize.

metastasis (*meh* ***tass*** *ta sis*) The process by which cells break off of a tumor, travel through the vascular system, and grow elsewhere in the body.

Figure 14.1

A slice of a human brain, showing how a large nonmalignant tumor (a meningioma) has displaced the right side of the brain toward the left. (The dashed line indicates the location of the midline.) The right lateral ventricle is almost completely occluded.

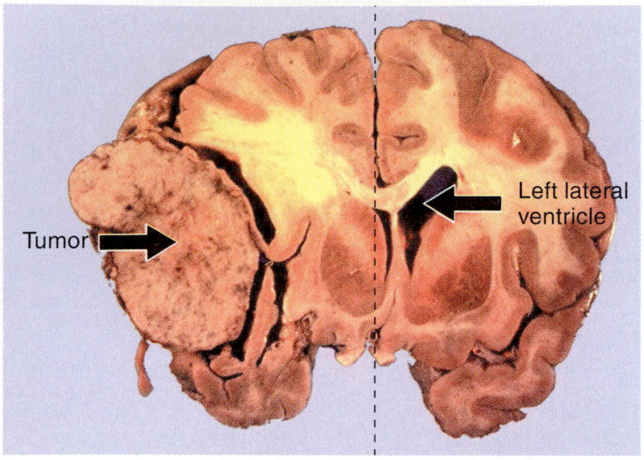

Courtesy of A. D'Agostino, Good Samaritan Hospital, Portland, Oregon.

Table 14.1

Types of Brain Tumors
Gliomas
Glioblastoma multiformae (poorly-differentiated glial cells)
Astrocytoma (astrocytes)
Ependymoma (ependymal cells that line ventricles)
Medulloblastoma (cells in roof of fourth ventricle)
Oligodendrocytoma (oligodendrocytes)
Meningioma (cells of the meninges)
Pituitary adenoma (hormone-secreting cells of the pituitary gland)
Neurinoma (Schwann cells or cells of connective tissue covering cranial nerves)
Metastatic carcinoma (depends on nature of primary tumor)
Angioma (cells of blood vessels)
Pinealoma (cells of pineal gland)

in capillaries, and serve as seeds for the growth of new tumors in different locations in the body.

Tumors damage brain tissue by two means: compression and infiltration. Obviously, *any* tumor growing in the brain, malignant or benign, can produce neurological symptoms and threaten the patient's life. Even a benign tumor occupies space and thus pushes against the brain. The compression can directly destroy brain tissue, or it can do so indirectly by blocking the flow of cerebrospinal fluid and causing hydrocephalus. Even worse are malignant tumors, which cause both compression and infiltration. As a malignant tumor grows, it invades the surrounding region and destroys cells in its path. Figure 14.1 illustrates the compressive effect of a large nonmalignant tumor. As you can see, the tumor has displaced the lateral and third ventricles. (See ***Figure 14.1.***)

Tumors do not arise from nerve cells, which are not capable of dividing. Instead, they arise from other cells found in the brain or from metastases originating elsewhere in the body. The most common types are listed in Table 14.1. (See ***Table 14.1.***) The most serious types of tumors are metastases and the **gliomas** (derived from various types of glial cells), which are usually very malignant and fast growing. Figures 14.2 and 14.3 show gliomas located in the basal ganglia and the pons, respectively. (See ***Figures 14.2*** and ***14.3.***) Figure 14.4 shows an ependymoma in the lateral ventricles. (See ***Figure 14.4.***) Some tumors are sensitive to radiation and can be destroyed by a beam of radiation focused on them. Usually, a neurosurgeon first removes as much of the tumor as possible, and then the remaining cells are targeted by the radiation.

The chapter prologue described a woman whose sudden onset of seizures suggested the presence of a tumor near the top of the primary motor cortex. Indeed, she had a **meningioma,** an encapsulated, benign tumor consisting of cells that constitute the dura mater or arachnoid membrane. Such tumors tend to originate in the part of the dura mater that is found between the two cerebral hemispheres, or along the tentorium, the sheet of dura mater that lies between the occipital lobes and the cerebellum. (See ***Figure 14.5.***)

glioma (*glee* ***oh*** *mah*) A cancerous brain tumor composed of one of several types of glial cells.

meningioma (*men in jee* ***oh*** *ma*) A benign brain tumor composed of the cells that constitute the meninges.

Figure 14.2

A slice of a human brain, showing a large glioma located in the basal ganglia, which has invaded both the left and right lateral ventricles.

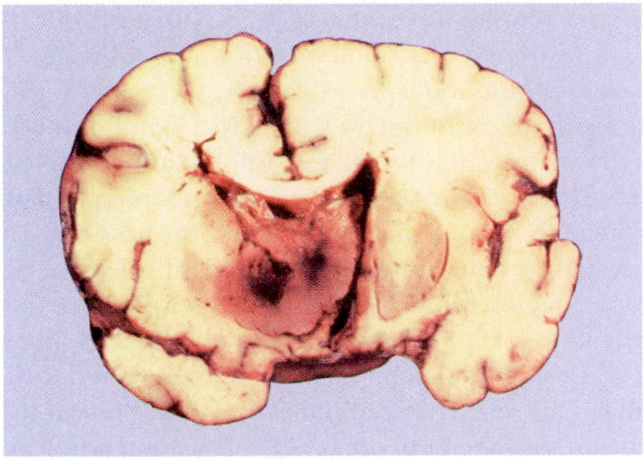

Courtesy of A. D'Agostino, Good Samaritan Hospital, Portland, Oregon.

Figure 14.3

A midsagittal view of a human brain, showing a glioma located in the dorsal pons (*arrowhead*).

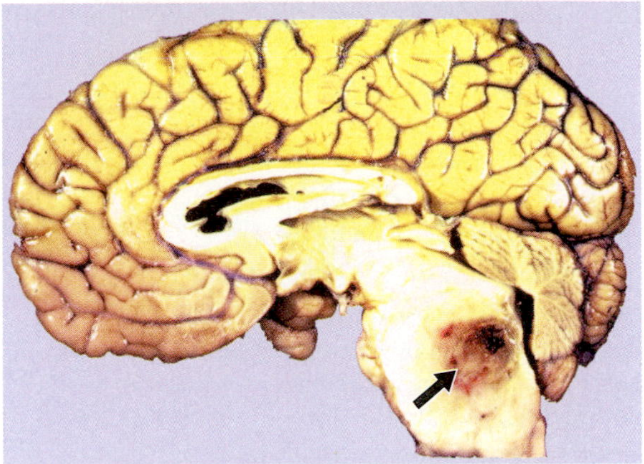

Courtesy of A. D'Agostino, Good Samaritan Hospital, Portland, Oregon.

Figure 14.4

A slice of a human brain, showing an ependymoma of the left lateral ventricle (*arrowhead*).

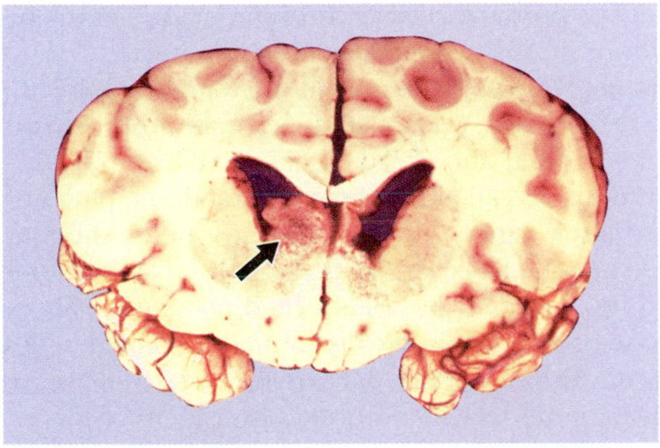

Courtesy of A. D'Agostino, Good Samaritan Hospital, Portland, Oregon.

Figure 14.5

A CT scan of a brain, showing the presence of a meningioma (round white spot indicated by the arrow).

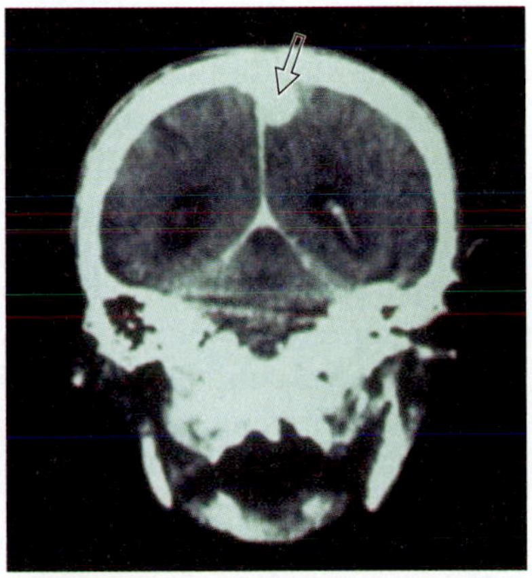

Courtesy of J. McA. Jones, Good Samaritan Hospital, Portland, Oregon.

Seizure Disorders

Because of negative connotations that were acquired in the past, many physicians prefer not to use the term *epilepsy*. Instead, they use the phrase **seizure disorder** to refer to a condition that has many causes. Seizure disorders constitute the second most important category of neurological disorders, following stroke. A *seizure* is a period of sudden, excessive activity of cerebral neurons. Sometimes, if neurons that make up the motor system are involved, a seizure can cause a **convulsion,** which is wild, uncontrollable activity of the muscles. But not all seizures cause convulsions; in fact, most do not.

seizure disorder The preferred term for epilepsy.

convulsion A violent sequence of uncontrollable muscular movements caused by a seizure.

Table 14.2

The Classification of Seizure Disorders

I. Generalized seizures (with no apparent local onset)
   A. Tonic-clonic (grand mal)
   B. Absence (petit mal)
   C. Atonic (loss of muscle tone; temporary paralysis)

II. Partial seizures (starting from a focus)
   A. Simple (no major change in consciousness)
      1. Localized motor seizure
      2. Motor seizure, with progression of movements as seizure spreads along the primary motor cortex
      3. Sensory (somatosensory, visual, auditory, olfactory, vestibular)
      4. Psychic (forced thinking, fear, anger, etc.)
      5. Autonomic (e.g., sweating, salivating, etc.)
   B. Complex (with altered consciousness)
      Includes 1–5, as above

III. Partial seizures (simple or complex) evolving to generalized cortical seizure: Starts as IIA or IIB, then becomes a grand mal seizure

Table 14.2 presents a summary of the most important categories of seizure disorders. Two distinctions are important: *partial* versus *generalized* seizures and *simple* versus *complex* ones. **Partial seizures** have a definite *focus,* or source of irritation: typically, a scarred region caused by an old injury. The neurons that become involved in the seizure are restricted to a small part of the brain. **Generalized seizures** are widespread, involving most of the brain. In many cases they grow from a focus, but in some cases their origin is not discovered. Simple and complex seizures are two categories of partial seizures. **Simple partial seizures** often cause *changes* in consciousness but do not cause *loss* of consciousness. In contrast, because of their particular location and severity, **complex partial seizures** lead to loss of consciousness. (See *Table 14.2.*)

The most severe form of seizure is often referred to as **grand mal.** This seizure is generalized, and because it includes the motor systems of the brain, it is accompanied by convulsions. Often, before having a grand mal seizure, a person has warning symptoms, such as changes in mood or perhaps a few sudden jerks of muscular activity on awakening. (Almost everyone sometimes experiences these jolts while falling asleep.) A few seconds before the seizure occurs, the person often experiences an **aura,** which is presumably caused by excitation of neurons surrounding a seizure focus. This excitation has effects similar to those that would be produced by electrical stimulation of the region. Obviously, the nature of an aura varies according to the location of the focus. For example, because structures in the temporal lobe are involved in the control of emotional behaviors, seizures that originate from a focus located there often begin with feelings of fear and dread or, occasionally, euphoria.

The beginning of a grand mal seizure is called the **tonic phase.** All the patient's muscles contract forcefully. The arms are rigidly outstretched, and he or she may make an involuntary cry as the tense muscles force air out of the lungs. (At this point the patient is completely unconscious.) The patient holds a rigid posture for about 15 seconds, and then the **clonic phase** begins. (*Clonic* means "agitated.") The muscles begin trembling, then start jerking convulsively—quickly at first, then more and more slowly. Meanwhile, the eyes roll, the patient's face is contorted with violent grimaces, and the tongue may be bitten. Intense activity of the autonomic nervous system manifests itself in sweating and salivation. After about 30 seconds, the patient's muscles relax; only then does breathing begin again. The patient falls into a stuporous, unresponsive sleep, which lasts for about 15 minutes. After that the patient may awaken briefly but usually falls back into an exhausted sleep that may last for a few hours.

Recordings made during grand mal seizures from electrodes implanted into patients' brains show that neural firing first begins in the focus at the time of the aura; it then spreads to other regions of the brain (Adams and Victor, 1981). The activity spreads to regions surrounding the focus and then to the contralateral cortex (through the corpus callosum), the basal ganglia, the thalamus, and various nuclei of the brain stem reticular formation. At this point the symptoms begin. The excited subcortical regions feed back more excitation to the cortex, amplifying the activity there. Neurons in the motor cortex begin firing continuously, producing the tonic phase. Next, diencephalic structures begin quenching the seizure by sending inhibitory messages to the cortex. At first the inhibition comes in brief bursts; this causes the jerking movements of the clonic phase, as the muscles repeatedly relax and then contract again. Then the bursts of inhibition become more and more pro-

partial seizure A seizure that begins at a focus and remains localized, not generalizing to the rest of the brain.

generalized seizure A seizure that involves most of the brain, as contrasted with a partial seizure, which remains localized.

simple partial seizure A partial seizure, starting from a focus and remaining localized, that does not produce loss of consciousness.

complex partial seizure A partial seizure, starting from a focus and remaining localized, that produces loss of consciousness.

grand mal seizure A generalized, tonic-clonic seizure, which results in a convulsion.

longed, and the jerks occur more and more slowly. Finally, the inhibition wins, and the patient's muscles relax.

Other types of seizures are far less dramatic. Partial seizures involve relatively small portions of the brain. The symptoms can include sensory changes, motor activity, or both. For example, a simple partial seizure that begins in or near the motor cortex can involve jerking movements that begin in one place and spread throughout the body as the excitation spreads along the precentral gyrus. In the chapter prologue I described such a progression, caused by a seizure triggered by a meningioma. The tumor was pressing against the "foot" region of the left primary motor cortex. When the seizure began, it involved the foot; as it spread, it began involving the other parts of the body. (See ***Figure 14.6.***) Mrs. R.'s first spell was a simple partial seizure, but her second one—much more severe—would be classed as a complex partial seizure, because she lost consciousness. A seizure beginning in the occipital lobe may produce visual symptoms such as spots of color, flashes of light, or temporary blindness; one originating in the parietal lobe can evoke somatosensations, such as feelings of pins and needles or heat and cold. Seizures in the temporal lobes may cause hallucinations that include old memories; presumably, neural circuits involved in these memories are activated by the spreading excitation. Depending on the location and extent of the seizure, the patient may or may not lose consciousness.

Figure 14.6

Primary motor cortex and seizures. Mrs. R.'s seizure began in the foot region of the primary motor cortex, and as the seizure spread, more and more parts of her body became involved.

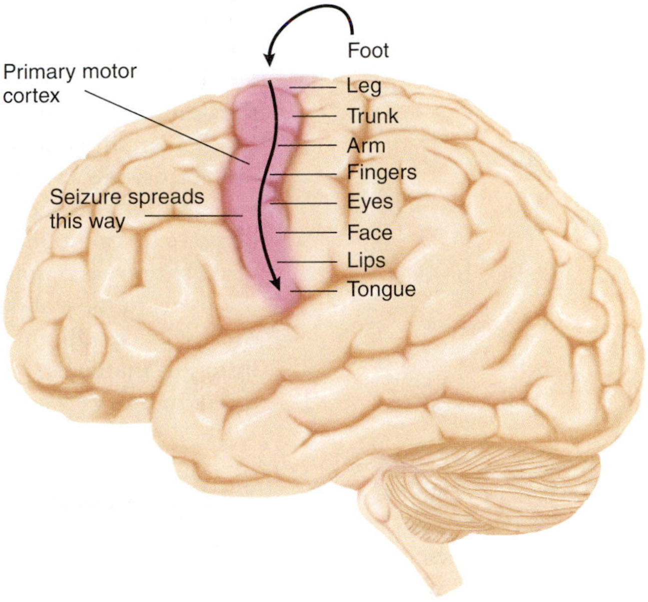

Children are especially susceptible to seizure disorders. Many of them do not have grand mal episodes but, instead, have very brief seizures that are referred to as spells of **absence.** During an absence seizure, which is a *generalized* seizure disorder, they stop what they are doing and stare off into the distance for a few seconds, often blinking their eyes repeatedly. (These spells are also sometimes referred to as *petit mal* seizures.) During this time they are unresponsive, and they usually do not notice their attacks. Because absence seizures can occur up to several hundred times each day, they can disrupt a child's performance in school. Unfortunately, many of these children are considered to be inattentive and unmotivated unless the disorder is diagnosed.

Seizures can have serious consequences: They can cause brain damage. Approximately 50 percent of patients with seizure disorders show evidence of damage to the hippocampus. The amount of damage is correlated with the number and severity of seizures the patient has had. Significant hippocampal damage can be caused by a single episode of **status epilepticus,** a condition in which the patient undergoes a series of seizures without regaining consciousness. The damage appears to be caused by an excessive release of glutamate during the seizure (Thompson et al., 1996).

Seizures have many causes. The most common cause is scarring, which may be produced by an injury, a stroke, or the irritating effect of a growing tumor. For injuries the development of seizures may take a considerable amount of time. Often, a person who receives a head injury from an automobile accident will not start having seizures until several months later.

Various drugs and infections that cause a high fever can also produce seizures. In addition, seizures are commonly seen in alcohol or barbiturate addicts who suddenly stop taking the drug; the sudden release from the inhibiting effects of the alcohol or barbiturate leaves the brain in a hyperexcitable condition. In fact, this condition is a medical emergency, because it can be fatal.

Evidence suggests that NMDA receptors may be involved in the seizures caused by alcohol withdrawal. As you saw in Chapter 12, NMDA receptors are specialized

aura A sensation that precedes a seizure; its exact nature depends on the location of the seizure focus.

tonic phase The first phase of a grand mal seizure, in which all of the patient's skeletal muscles are contracted.

clonic phase The phase of a grand mal seizure in which the patient shows rhythmic jerking movements.

absence A type of seizure disorder often seen in children; characterized by periods of inattention, which are not subsequently remembered; also called *petit mal* seizure.

status epilepticus A condition in which a patient undergoes a series of seizures without regaining consciousness.

glutamate receptors that control calcium channels. These channels open only when glutamate binds with the receptor *and* the membrane is depolarized. This double contingency is what seems to be responsible for at least one kind of synaptic modification involved in learning. Several studies have shown that alcohol blocks NMDA receptors (Gonzales, 1990). Perhaps, then, long-term suppression of NMDA receptors caused by chronic alcohol intake results in supersensitivity or "up-regulation," a compensatory mechanism produced by long-term inhibition of the receptors. When an alcoholic suddenly stops drinking, the NMDA receptors, which have been suppressed for so long, suddenly rebound. The increased activity causes seizures.

Seizure disorders are treated with anticonvulsant drugs, many of which work by increasing the effectiveness of inhibitory synapses. Most disorders respond well enough that the patient can lead a normal life. In a few instances drugs provide little or no help. Sometimes, seizure foci remain so irritable that despite drug treatment, brain surgery is required. The surgeon removes the region of the brain surrounding the focus (almost always, the medial temporal lobe). Most patients recover well, with their seizures eliminated or greatly reduced in frequency. Mrs. R.'s treatment was a different matter; in her case the removal of a meningioma eliminated the source of the irritation and ended her seizures. No healthy brain tissue was removed.

Cerebrovascular Accidents

You have already learned about the *effects* of cerebrovascular accidents, or *strokes*, in earlier chapters. For example, we saw that strokes can produce impairments in perception, emotional recognition and expression, memory, and language. This section will describe only their causes and treatments.

The incidence of strokes in the United States is approximately 550,000 per year. The likelihood of having a stroke is related to age; the probability doubles each decade after 45 years of age and reaches 1–2 percent per year by age 75 (Wolfe et al., 1992). The two major types of strokes are *hemorrhagic* and *obstructive*. **Hemorrhagic strokes** are caused by bleeding within the brain, usually from a malformed blood vessel or from one weakened by high blood pressure. The blood that seeps out of the defective blood vessel accumulates within the brain, putting pressure on the surrounding brain tissue and damaging it. **Obstructive strokes**—those that plug up a blood vessel and prevent the flow of blood—can be caused by thrombi or emboli. (Loss of blood flow to a region is called **ischemia,** from the Greek *ischein,* "to hold back," and *haima,* "blood.") A **thrombus** is a blood clot that forms in blood vessels, especially in places where their walls are already damaged. Sometimes, thrombi become so large that blood cannot flow through the vessel, causing a stroke. People who are susceptible to the formation of thrombi are often advised to take a drug such as aspirin, which helps to prevent clot formation. An **embolus** is a piece of material that forms in one part of the vascular system, breaks off, and is carried through the bloodstream until it reaches an artery too small to pass through. It lodges there, damming the flow of blood through the rest of the vascular tree (the "branches" and "twigs" arising from the artery). Emboli can consist of a variety of materials, including bacterial debris from an infection in the lining of the heart or pieces broken off from a blood clot. As we will see in a later section, emboli can introduce a bacterial infection into the brain. (See ***Figure 14.7.***)

Research with both animals and humans has shown that exercise and sensory stimulation facilitate recovery of functions lost as a result of brain damage.

Figure 14.7

Strokes. (a) Formation of thrombi and emboli. (b) An intracerebral hemorrhage.

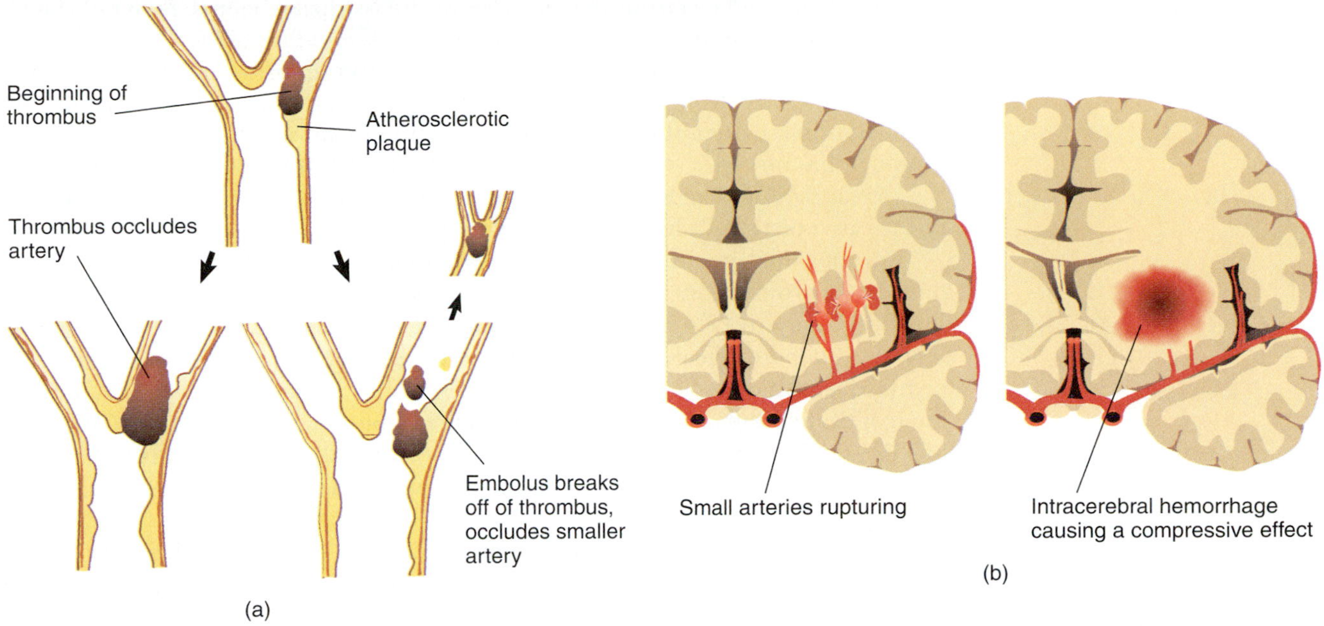

Strokes produce permanent brain damage, but depending on the size of the affected blood vessel, the amount of damage can vary from negligible to massive. If a hemorrhagic stroke is caused by high blood pressure, medication is given to reduce it. If one is caused by weak and malformed blood vessels, brain surgery may be used to seal off the faulty vessels to prevent another hemorrhage. If a thrombus was responsible for the stroke, anticoagulant drugs will be given to make the blood less likely to clot, reducing the likelihood of another stroke. If an embolus broke away from a bacterial infection, antibiotics will be given to suppress the infection.

What, exactly, causes the death of neurons when the blood supply to a region of the brain is interrupted? We might expect that the neurons simply starve to death because they lose their supply of glucose and oxygen to metabolize it. However, research indicates that the immediate cause of neuron death is the presence of excessive amounts of glutamate. In other words, the damage produced by loss of blood flow to a region of the brain is actually an excitotoxic lesion, just like one produced in a laboratory animal by the injection of a chemical such as kainic acid. (See Koroshetz and Moskowitz, 1996, for a review.)

When the blood supply to a region of the brain is interrupted, the oxygen and glucose in that region are quickly depleted. As a consequence, the sodium-potassium transporters, which regulate the balance of ions inside and outside the cell, stop functioning. Neural membranes become depolarized, which causes the release of glutamate. The activation of glutamate receptors further increases the inflow of sodium ions and causes cells to absorb excessive amounts of calcium. (As we saw in Chapter 4, different types of glutamate receptors control different ion channels: NMDA receptors control calcium channels, and kainate and AMPA receptors control sodium channels.) The presence of excessive amounts of sodium and calcium within cells is toxic. The intracellular sodium causes the cells to absorb water and swell. The inflammation attracts microglia and activates them, causing them to become phagocytic. The phagocytic microglia begin destroying injured cells. Inflammation also attracts white blood cells, which can adhere to the walls of capillaries near the ischemic region and obstruct

hemorrhagic stroke A cerebrovascular accident caused by the rupture of a cerebral blood vessel.

obstructive stroke A cerebrovascular accident caused by occlusion of a blood vessel.

ischemia (*is **kee** mee uh*) The interruption of the blood supply to a region of the body.

thrombus A blood clot that forms within a blood vessel, which may occlude it.

embolus (***emm** bo lus*) A piece of matter (such as a blood clot, fat, or bacterial debris) that dislodges from its site of origin and occludes an artery; in the brain an embolus can lead to a stroke.

free radical A molecule with unpaired electrons; acts as a powerful oxidizing agent; toxic to cells.

them. The presence of excessive amounts of calcium in the cells activates a variety of calcium-dependent enzymes, many of which destroy molecules that are vital for normal cell functioning. Finally, damaged mitochondria produce **free radicals**—molecules with unpaired electrons that act as powerful oxidizing agents. Free radicals are extremely toxic; they destroy nucleic acids, proteins, and fatty acids.

In recent years, researchers have sought ways to minimize the amount of brain damage caused by strokes. One approach has been to administer drugs that dissolve blood clots in an attempt to reestablish circulation to an ischemic brain region. This approach has met with some success. Marler et al. (2000) found that administration of a clot-dissolving drug called *rt-PA* (recombinant tissue plasminogen activator) after the onset of a stroke had clear benefits, especially if it was given within 90 minutes.

Another therapeutic approach has been to prevent the death of cells in the region that surrounds the ischemic region. Cells in this region live as long as several days but are eventually killed by inflammation, free radicals, and the effects of excessive glutamate release. Researchers are experimenting with anti-inflammatory agents, drugs that block glutamate receptors, chemicals that bind with free radicals and inactivate them, and drugs that stimulate inhibitory GABA receptors (Koroshetz and Moskowitz, 1996). Research with laboratory animals and preliminary clinical trials provide hope that such treatments may minimize the damage to the human brain caused by strokes.

Depending on the location of the brain damage, people who have strokes will receive physical therapy, and perhaps speech therapy, to help them recover from their disability. Several studies have shown that exercise and sensory stimulation can facilitate recovery from the effects of brain damage. For example, Taub et al. (1993) studied patients with strokes that impaired their ability to use one arm and hand. They forced the patients to use the impaired limb by putting the *unaffected* arm in a sling for fourteen days. This procedure produced long-term improvement in the patients' ability to use the affected arm. And in a laboratory study with rats, Hamm et al. (1996) found that environmental stimulation facilitated recovery from traumatic brain injury similar to a concussion that might be caused by an automobile accident. After producing the brain injury, the investigators placed one group of rats in a complex environment that contained objects to explore. The other rats were placed in empty cages that contained only food and water. Ten days later, both groups were trained on the Morris milk maze. (As we saw in Chapter 12, learning this task involves relational memory, a relatively complex cognitive ability.) The environmental stimulation provided to the first group clearly facilitated the animals' recovery from the effects of the brain damage. (See ***Figure 14.8.***)

Figure 14.8

Effects of environmental stimulation (exposure to a complex environment) on recovery from traumatic brain injury. Latency to reach the platform of a Morris milk maze as a function of days of training.

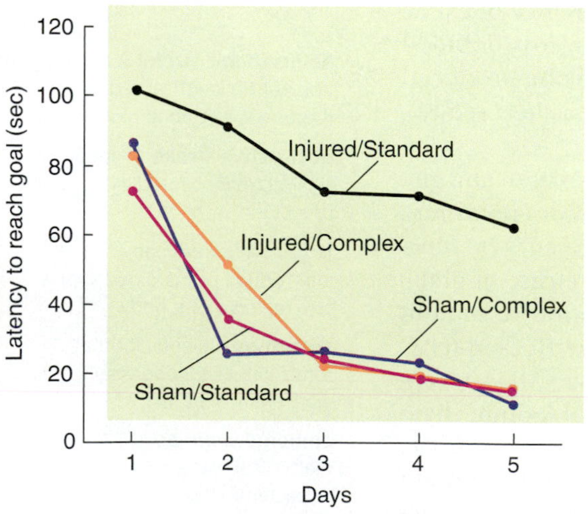

Adapted from Hamm, R. J., Temple, M. D., O'Dell, D. M., Pike, B. R., and Lyeth, B. G. *Journal of Neurotrauma*, 1996, *13*, 41–47.

INTERIM SUMMARY

Tumors, Seizure Disorders, and Cerebrovascular Accidents

Neurological disorders have many causes. Because we have learned much about the functions of the human brain from studying the behavior of people with various neurological disorders, you have already learned about many of them in previous chapters of this book. Brain tumors are caused by the uncontrolled growth of various types of cells *other than neurons.* They can be benign or malignant. Benign tumors are encapsulated and thus have a distinct border; when one is surgically removed, the surgeon has a good chance of getting all of it. Tumors produce brain damage by compression and, in the case of malignant tumors, infiltration.

Seizures are periodic episodes of abnormal electrical activity of the brain. Partial seizures are localized, beginning with a focus—usually, some scar tissue caused by previous damage or a tumor. When they begin, they often produce an aura, consisting of particular sensations or changes in mood. Simple partial seizures do not produce profound changes in consciousness; complex partial seizures do. Generalized seizures may or may not originate at a single focus, but they involve most of the brain. Some seizures involve motor activity; the most serious are the grand mal convulsions that accompany generalized seizures. The convulsions are caused by involvement of the brain's motor systems; the patient first shows a tonic phase, consisting of a few seconds of rigidity, and then a clonic phase, consisting of rhythmic jerking. Absence seizures, also called petit mal seizures, are common in children. These generalized seizures are characterized by periods of inattention and temporary loss of awareness. Seizures produced by abstinence after prolonged heavy intake of alcohol appear to be produced by supersensitivity (up-regulation) of NMDA receptors.

Cerebrovascular accidents damage parts of the brain through rupture of a blood vessel or occlusion (obstruction) of a blood vessel by a thrombus or embolus. A thrombus is a blood clot that forms within a blood vessel. An embolus is a piece of debris that is carried through the bloodstream and lodges in an artery. Emboli can arise from infections within the chambers of the heart or can consist of pieces of thrombi. The lack of blood flow appears to damage neurons primarily by stimulating a massive release of glutamate, which causes inflammation, phagocytosis by activated microglia, the production of free radicals, and activation of calcium-dependent enzymes. Potential treatments for stroke include administration of drugs that dissolve clots, reduce inflammation, block glutamate receptors, inactivate free radicals, or stimulate inhibitory GABA receptors. After a stroke has occurred, physical therapy can facilitate recovery and minimize a patient's deficits.

Disorders of Development

As you will see in this section, brain development can be affected adversely by the presence of toxic chemicals during pregnancy and by genetic abnormalities, both hereditary and nonhereditary. In some instances the result is mental retardation.

Toxic Chemicals

A common cause of mental retardation is the presence of toxins that impair fetal development during pregnancy. For example, if a woman contracts rubella (German measles) early in pregnancy, the toxic chemicals released by the virus interfere with the chemical signals that control normal development of the brain. Most women who receive good health care will be immunized for rubella to prevent them from contracting it during pregnancy.

In addition to the toxins produced by viruses, various drugs can adversely affect fetal development. For example, mental retardation can be caused by the ingestion of alcohol during pregnancy. Babies born to alcoholic women are typically smaller than average and develop more slowly. Many of them exhibit **fetal alcohol syndrome,** which is characterized by abnormal facial development and deficient brain development. Figure 14.9 shows photographs of the face of a child with fetal alcohol syndrome, of a rat fetus whose mother was fed alcohol during pregnancy, and of a normal rat fetus. As you can see, alcohol produces similar abnormalities in the offspring of both species. The facial abnormalities are relatively unimportant, of course. Much more serious are the abnormalities in the development of the brain. (See ***Figure 14.9.***)

Recent research suggests that alcohol disrupts normal brain development by interfering with a **neural adhesion protein**—a protein that helps to guide the growth of neurons in the developing brain (Braun, 1996). Prenatal exposure to alcohol even appears to have direct effects on neural plasticity. Sutherland, McDonald, and

fetal alcohol syndrome A birth defect caused by ingestion of alcohol by a pregnant woman; includes characteristic facial anomalies and faulty brain development.

neural adhesion protein A protein that plays a role in brain development; helps to guide the growth of neurons.

Figure 14.9

A child with fetal alcohol syndrome, along with magnified views of a rat fetus. (a) Fetus whose mother received alcohol during pregnancy. (b) Normal rat fetus.

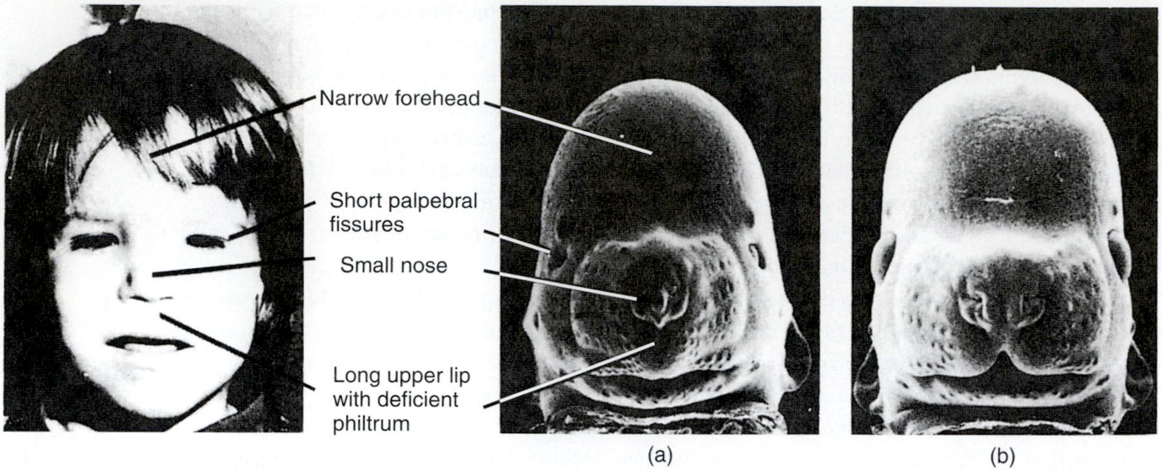

Photographs courtesy of Katherine K. Sulik.

Savage (1997) found that the offspring of female rats that are given moderate amounts of alcohol during pregnancy showed smaller amounts of long-term potentiation (described in Chapter 12).

A woman need not be an alcoholic to impair the development of her offspring; some investigators believe that fetal alcohol syndrome can be caused by a single alcoholic binge during a critical period of fetal development. Now that we recognize the dangers of this syndrome, pregnant women are advised to abstain from alcohol (and from other drugs not specifically prescribed by their physician) while their bodies are engaged in the task of sustaining the development of another human being.

Inherited Metabolic Disorders

Several inherited "errors of metabolism" can cause brain damage or impair brain development. Normal functioning of cells requires intricate interactions among countless biochemical systems. As you know, these systems depend on enzymes, which are responsible for constructing or breaking down particular chemical compounds. Enzymes are proteins and therefore are produced by mechanisms involving the chromosomes, which contain the recipes for their synthesis. "Errors of metabolism" refer to genetic abnormalities in which the recipe for a particular enzyme is in error, so the enzyme cannot be synthesized. If the enzyme is a critical one, the results can be very serious.

There are at least a hundred different inherited metabolic disorders that can affect the development of the brain. The most common and best-known is called **phenylketonuria (PKU).** This disease is caused by an inherited lack of an enzyme that converts phenylalanine (an amino acid) into tyrosine (another amino acid). Excessive amounts of phenylalanine in the blood interfere with the myelinization of neurons in the central nervous system. Much of the myelinization of the cerebral hemispheres takes place after birth. Thus, when an infant born with PKU receives foods containing phenylalanine, the amino acid accumulates, and the brain fails to develop normally. The result is severe mental retardation, with an average IQ of approximately 20 by six years of age.

Fortunately, PKU can be treated by putting the infant on a low-phenylalanine diet. The diet keeps the blood level of phenylalanine low, and myelinization of the

phenylketonuria (PKU) (*fee nul kee ta* ***new*** *ree uh*) A hereditary disorder caused by the absence of an enzyme that converts the amino acid phenylalanine to tyrosine; the accumulation of phenylalanine causes brain damage unless a special diet is implemented soon after birth.

central nervous system takes place normally. Once myelinization is complete, the dietary restraints can be relaxed somewhat, because a high level of phenylalanine no longer threatens brain development. During prenatal development a fetus is protected by its mother's normal metabolism, which removes the phenylalanine from its circulation. However, if the *mother* has PKU, she must follow a strict diet during pregnancy or her infant will be born with brain damage. If she eats a normal diet, rich in phenylalanine, the high blood level of this compound will not damage her brain, but it will damage that of her fetus.

Diagnosing PKU immediately after birth is imperative so that the infant's brain is never exposed to high levels of phenylalanine. Consequently, many governments have passed laws that mandate a PKU test for all newborn babies. The test is inexpensive and accurate, and it has prevented many cases of mental retardation.

Other genetic errors of metabolism can be treated in similar fashion. For example, untreated **pyridoxine dependency** results in damage to cerebral white matter, to the thalamus, and to the cerebellum. It is treated by large doses of vitamin B_6. Another error of metabolism, **galactosemia,** is an inability to metabolize galactose, a sugar found in milk. If it is not treated, it, too, causes damage to cerebral white matter and to the cerebellum. The treatment is use of a milk substitute that does not contain galactose. (Galactosemia should not be confused with *lactose intolerance,* which is caused by an insufficient production of lactase, the digestive enzyme that breaks down lactose. Lactose intolerance leads to digestive disturbance, not brain damage.)

Some other inherited metabolic disorders cannot yet be treated successfully. For example, **Tay-Sachs disease,** which occurs mainly in children of Eastern European Jewish descent, causes the brain to swell and damage itself against the inside of the skull and against the folds of the dura mater than encase it. The neurological symptoms begin by four months of age and include an exaggerated startle response to sounds, listlessness, irritability, spasticity, seizures, dementia, and, finally, death.

Tay-Sachs disease is one of several metabolic "storage" disorders. All cells contain sacs of material encased in membrane, called lysosomes ("dissolving bodies"). These sacs constitute the cell's rubbish-removal system; they contain enzymes that break down waste substances that cells produce in the course of their normal activities. The broken-down waste products are then recycled (used by the cells again) or excreted. Metabolic storage disorders are genetic errors of metabolism in which one or more vital enzymes are missing. Particular kinds of waste products cannot be destroyed by the lysosomes, so they accumulate. The lysosomes get larger and larger, the cells get larger and larger, and eventually the brain begins to swell and become damaged.

Researchers investigating hereditary errors of metabolism hope to prevent or treat these disorders in several ways. Some will be treated like PKU or galactosemia, by avoiding a constituent of the diet that cannot be tolerated. Others, such as pyridoxine dependency, will be treated by administering a substance that the body requires. Still others may be cured some day by the techniques of genetic engineering. Viruses infect cells by inserting their own genetic material into them and thus taking over the cells' genetic machinery, using it to reproduce themselves. Perhaps one day, researchers will develop special viruses that will "infect" an infant's cells with genetic information that is needed to produce the enzymes that the cells lack, leaving the rest of the cells' functions intact. Such viruses have already yielded useful results, such as the development of bacteria that produce human insulin. Some day they might cure human genetic disorders as well.

Down Syndrome

Down syndrome is a congenital disorder that results in abnormal development of the brain, producing mental retardation in varying degrees. *Congenital* does not necessarily mean *hereditary;* it simply refers to a disorder that one is born with. Down syndrome is caused not by the inheritance of a faulty gene but by the possession of an

pyridoxine dependency (*peer i* ***dox*** *een*) A metabolic disorder in which an infant requires larger-than-normal amounts of pyridoxine (vitamin B_6) to avoid neurological symptoms.

galactosemia (*ga lak tow* ***see*** *mee uh*) An inherited metabolic disorder in which galactose (milk sugar) cannot easily be metabolized.

Tay-Sachs disease A heritable, fatal, metabolic storage disorder; lack of enzymes in lysosomes causes accumulation of waste produces and swelling of cells of the brain.

Down syndrome A disorder caused by the presence of an extra twenty-first chromosome, characterized by moderate to severe mental retardation and often by physical abnormalities.

People with Down syndrome, caused by the presence of an extra twenty-first chromosome, are often only mildly retarded, and many of them can function well with only minimal supervision.

extra twenty-first chromosome. The syndrome is closely associated with the mother's age; in most cases something goes wrong with some of her ova, resulting in the presence of two (rather than one) twenty-first chromosomes. When fertilization occurs, the addition of the father's twenty-first chromosome makes three, rather than two. The extra chromosome presumably causes biochemical changes that impair normal brain development. The development of *amniocentesis,* a procedure whereby some fluid is withdrawn from a pregnant woman's uterus through a hypodermic syringe, has allowed physicians to identify fetal cells with chromosomal abnormalities and thus determine whether the fetus carries Down syndrome.

Down syndrome, described in 1866 by John Langdon Down, occurs in approximately 1 out of 700 births. An experienced observer can recognize people with this disorder; they have round heads, thick, protruding tongues that tend to keep the mouth open much of the time, stubby hands, short stature, low-set ears, and somewhat slanting eyelids. They are slow to learn to talk, but most do talk by age 5. The brain of a person with Down syndrome is approximately 10 percent lighter than that of a normal person, the convolutions (gyri and sulci) are simpler and smaller, the frontal lobes are small, and the superior temporal gyrus (the location of Wernicke's area) is thin. After age 30 the brain develops abnormal microscopic structures and begins to degenerate. Because this degeneration resembles that of Alzheimer's disease, it will be discussed in the next section.

Although the occurrence of any form of mental retardation is a tragedy, people with Down syndrome are often only moderately retarded. Given proper training, many of them can function well with only minimal supervision.

INTERIM SUMMARY

Disorders of Development

Developmental disorders can result in brain damage serious enough to cause mental retardation. During pregnancy the fetus is especially sensitive to toxins, such as alcohol or chemicals produced by some viruses. Several inherited metabolic disorders can also impair brain development. For example, phenylketonuria is caused by the lack of an enzyme that converts phenylalanine into tyrosine. Brain damage can be averted by feeding the infant a diet low in phenylalanine, so early diagnosis is essential. Other inherited metabolic disorders include pyridoxine dependency, which can be treated by vitamin B_6, and galactosemia, which can be treated with a diet that does not contain milk sugar. Storage disorders, such as Tay-Sachs disease, are caused by the inability of cells to destroy waste products within the lysosomes, which causes the cells to swell and eventually die. So far, these disorders cannot be treated. Down syndrome is produced by the presence of an extra twenty-first chromosome. The brain development of people with Down syndrome is abnormal, and after age 30 their brains develop features similar to those of people with Alzheimer's disease.

Degenerative Disorders

Many disease processes cause degeneration of the cells of the brain. Some of these conditions injure particular kinds of cells, a fact that provides the hope that research will uncover the causes of the damage and find a way to halt it and prevent it from occurring in other people.

Transmissible Spongiform Encephalopathies

The outbreak of bovine spongiform encephalopathy (BSE, or "mad cow disease") in Great Britain in the late 1980s and early 1990s brought a peculiar form of brain disease to public attention. BSE is a **transmissible spongiform encephalopathy (TSE)**—a contagious brain disease ("encephalopathy") whose degenerative process gives the brain a sponge-like (or Swiss cheese-like) appearance. Besides BSE, these diseases include Creutzfeldt-Jakob disease, fatal familial insomnia, and kuru, which affect humans, and scrapie, which primarily affects sheep. Although scrapie cannot be transmitted to humans, BSE can, and produces a variant of Creutzfeldt-Jakob disease. Although they can have a long incubation period, TSEs are ultimately fatal.

Unlike other transmissible diseases, TSEs are not caused by microorganisms, but by simple proteins, which have been called **prions,** or "protein infectious agents" (Prusiner, 1982). Prion proteins are primarily found in the membrane of neurons, where they are believed to play a role in synaptic function. The sequence of amino acids of normal prion protein (PrPc) and infectious prion (PrPSc) are identical. How, then, can two proteins with the same amino acid sequences have such different effects? The answer is that the functions of proteins are largely determined by their three-dimensional shapes. The only difference between PrPc and PrPSc is the way the protein is folded. And once misfolded PrPSc is introduced into a cell, it causes normal PrPc to become misfolded too, so abnormal proteins accumulate within neurons, ultimately killing them. (See Hetz et al., 2003, for a review.)

Whatever role normal PrPc plays, it does not seem essential for the life of a cell. Bueler et al. (1993) found that mice with a targeted mutation of the prion protein gene showed normal development and behavior, despite the fact that they contained absolutely no prion protein. Moreover, they did not develop mouse scrapie when they were inoculated with the misfolded prions that cause this disease. Normal mice inoculated with these prions died within six months.

Mallucci et al. (2003) prepared a genetically modified mouse strain whose neurons produced an enzyme at 12 weeks of age that destroyed normal prion protein. At a few weeks of age the experimenters infected the animals with misfolded mouse scrapie prions. Soon thereafter, the animals began developing spongy holes in their brains, indicating that they were infected with mouse scrapie. Then, at 12 weeks, the enzyme became active and started destroying normal PrPc. Although analysis showed that glial cells in the brain still contained misfolded PrPSc, the disease process stopped. Neurons stopped making normal PrPc, which could no longer be converted into PrPSc, so the mice went on to live normal lives. The disease process continued to progress in mice without the special enzyme, and these animals soon died. The authors concluded that the process of conversion of PrPc to PrPSc is what kills cells. The mere presence of PrPSc in the brain (found in nonneuronal cells) does not cause the disease. Figure 14.10 shows the development of spongiform degeneration and its disappearance after the PrPc-destroying enzyme became active at 12 weeks of age. (See ***Figure 14.10.***)

How might misfolded prion protein kill neurons? As we will see later in this chapter, the brains of people with several other degenerative diseases, including Parkinson's disease, Alzheimer's disease, and Huntington's disease contain aggregations of misfolded proteins (Soto, 2003). As we saw in Chapter 3, cells contain the means by which they can commit suicide—a process known as *apoptosis.* Apoptosis can be triggered either externally, by a chemical signal telling the cell it is no longer needed (for example, during development), and internally, by evidence that biochemical processes in the cell have become disrupted so that the cell is no longer functioning properly. Perhaps the accumulation of misfolded, abnormal proteins provides such a signal. Apoptosis involves production of "killer enzymes" called **caspases.** Mallucci et al. (2003) suggest that inactivation of caspase-12, the enzyme that appears to be responsible for the death of neurons infected with PrPSc, may provide a treatment that could arrest the progress of transmissible spongiform encephalopathies. Let's hope they are right.

transmissible spongiform encephalopathy A contagious brain disease whose degenerative process gives the brain a sponge-like appearance; caused by accumulation of misfolded prion protein.

prion (***pree*** *on*) A protein that can exist in two forms that differ only in their three-dimensional shape; accumulation of misfolded prion protein is responsible for transmissible spongiform encephalopathies.

caspase A "killer enzyme" that plays a role in apoptosis, or programmed cell death.

Figure 14.10

Prevention of neural death and reversal of early spongiosis in scrapie-infected mice after a genetically engineered enzyme began to destroy PrPc at 12 weeks of age. Arrows point to degenerating neurons in mice without the prion-destroying enzyme. Spongiosis is seen as holes in the brain tissue (*arrowheads*).

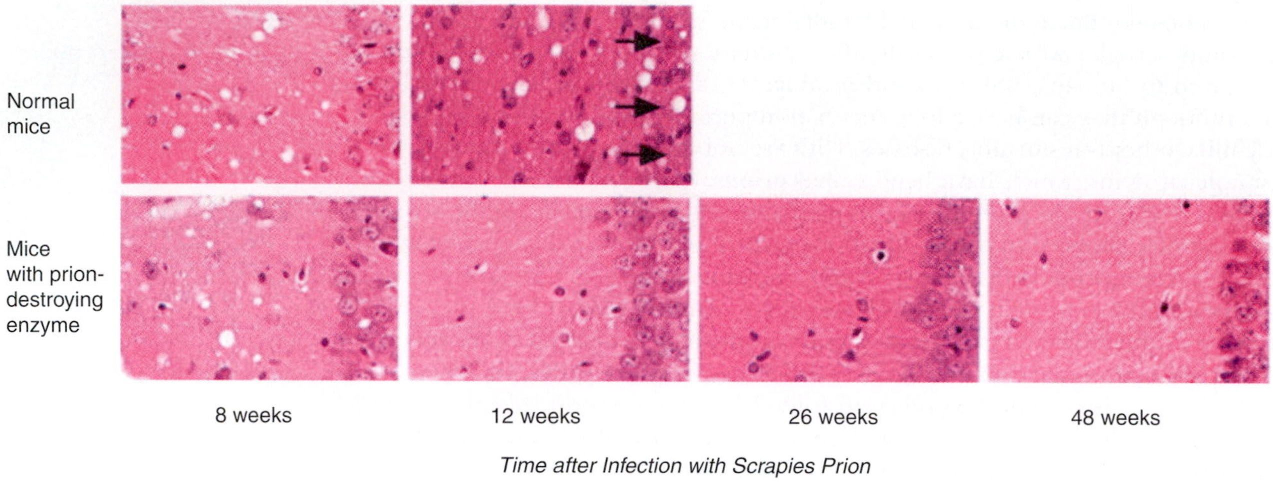

From Mallucci, G., Dickinson, A., Linehan, J., Klöhn, P. C., Brandner, S., and Collinge, J. *Science,* 2003, *302,* 871–874.

Parkinson's Disease

One of the most common degenerative neurological disorders, Parkinson's disease, is caused by degeneration of the nigrostriatal system—the dopamine-secreting neurons of the substantia nigra that send axons to the basal ganglia. The primary symptoms of Parkinson's disease are muscular rigidity, slowness of movement, a resting tremor, and postural instability. For example, once a person with Parkinson's disease is seated, he or she finds it difficult to arise. Once the person begins walking, he or she has difficulty stopping. Thus, a person with Parkinson's disease cannot easily pace back and forth across a room. Reaching for an object can be accurate, but the movement usually begins only after a considerable delay. Writing is slow and labored, and as it progresses, the letters get smaller and smaller. Postural movements are impaired. A normal person who is bumped while standing will quickly move to restore balance—for example, by taking a step in the direction of the impending fall or by reaching out with the arms to grasp onto a piece of furniture. However, a person with Parkinson's disease fails to do so and simply falls. A person with this disorder is even unlikely to put out his or her arms to break the fall.

Parkinson's disease also produces a resting tremor—vibratory movements of the arms and hands that diminish somewhat when the individual makes purposeful movements. The tremor is accompanied by rigidity; the joints appear stiff. However, the tremor and rigidity are not the cause of the slow movements. In fact, some patients with Parkinson's disease show extreme slowness of movements but little or no tremor.

Examination of the brains of patients who had Parkinson's disease shows, of course, the near-disappearance of nigrostriatal dopaminergic neurons. Many surviving dopaminergic neurons show **Lewy bodies,** abnormal circular structures found within the cytoplasm. Lewy bodies have a dense protein core, surrounded by a halo of radiating fibers (Forno, 1996). (See ***Figure 14.11.***) Although most cases of Parkinson's disease do not appear to have genetic origins, researchers have discovered a particular mutation of a gene located on chromosome 4 that will produce this disorder (Polymeropoulos et al., 1996). This gene produces a protein known as **α-synuclein,** which is normally found in the presynaptic membrane and is thought to be involved

Lewy body Abnormal circular structures with a dense core consisting of α-synuclein protein; found in the cytoplasm of nigrostriatal neurons in people with Parkinson's disease.

α-synuclein (*sin **oo** klee in*) A protein normally found in the presynaptic membrane, where it is apparently involved in synaptic plasticity. Abnormal accumulations are apparently the cause of neural degeneration in Parkinson's disease.

in synaptic plasticity. The mutation causes the formation of aggregations of misfolded α-synuclein, especially in dopaminergic neurons (Goedert, 2001). The dense core of Lewy bodies consists primarily of these aggregations. Another hereditary form of Parkinson's disease is caused by mutation of a gene that has been named *parkin* (Kitada et al., 1998). The protein it produces appears to play a role in ferrying defective or degraded proteins to the **proteosomes**—organelles responsible for destroying these proteins (Fishman and Oyler, 2002). This mutation, too, permits toxic levels of α-synuclein to accumulate in dopaminergic neurons.

Although there are several forms of hereditary parkinsonism, including the mutation I just described, the overwhelming majority of the cases of this disease are *sporadic*. That is, they occur in people without a family history of Parkinson's disease. What, then, triggers the accumulation of α-synuclein and the destruction of dopaminergic neurons? Research suggests that Parkinson's disease may be caused by toxins present in the environment, by faulty metabolism, or by unrecognized infectious disorders. As you saw in the prologue and epilogue of Chapter 4, several young people who took a drug contaminated with MPTP developed Parkinsonism. Besides MPTP, the insecticides rotenone and paraquat can also cause Parkinson's disease—and, presumably, so can some other unidentified toxins. All of these chemicals inhibit some mitochondrial functions, which leads to the aggregation of misfolded α-synuclein, especially in dopaminergic neurons. These accumulated proteins eventually kill the cells (Dawson and Dawson, 2003).

Figure 14.11

A photomicrograph of the substantia nigra of a patient with Parkinson's disease. A Lewy body is indicated by the arrow.

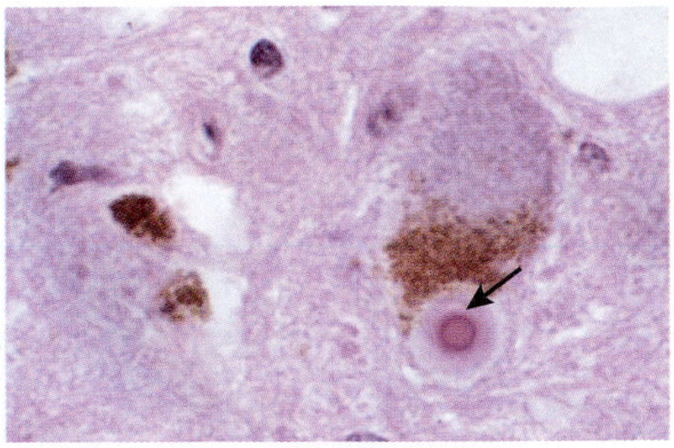

Photograph courtesy of Dr. Don Born, University of Washington.

As we saw in Chapter 4, the standard treatment for Parkinson's disease is L-DOPA, the precursor of dopamine. An increased level of L-DOPA in the brain causes a patient's remaining dopaminergic neurons to produce and secrete more dopamine and, for a time, alleviates the symptoms of the disease. But this compensation does not work indefinitely; eventually, the number of nigrostriatal dopaminergic neurons declines to such a low level that the symptoms become worse. In addition, high levels of L-DOPA produce side effects by acting on dopaminergic systems other than the nigrostriatal system. Some patients—especially those whose symptoms began when they were relatively young—become bedridden, scarcely able to move.

Neurosurgeons have been developing three stereotaxic procedures designed to alleviate the symptoms of Parkinson's disease that no longer respond to treatment with L-DOPA. The first one, transplantation of fetal tissue, attempts to reestablish the secretion of dopamine in the neostriatum. The tissue is obtained from the substantia nigra of aborted human fetuses and implanted into the caudate nucleus and putamen by means of stereotaxically guided needles. Although the procedure is still experimental, some good results have been obtained. As we saw in Chapter 5, PET scans have shown that dopaminergic fetal cells are able to grow in their new host and secrete dopamine, reducing the patient's symptoms. In a study of 32 patients with fetal tissue transplants, Freed et al. (2002) found that those whose symptoms had previously responded to L-DOPA were most likely to benefit from the surgery. Presumably, these patients had a sufficient number of basal ganglia neurons with receptors that could be stimulated by the dopamine secreted by either the medication or the transplanted tissue.

Because of ethical and practical issues, investigators have continued to search for other sources of dopamine-secreting neurons. Fetal dopaminergic cells are difficult to obtain, and about 90 percent of them die through apoptosis once they are transplanted into the human brain. One potential source of neurons could come from cultures of fetal stem cells—undifferentiated cells that have the ability, if appropriately stimulated, to develop into a variety of types of cells, including dopaminergic neurons (Freed, 2002). A significant advantage of human stem cells is that large numbers of cells could be transplanted, thus increasing the numbers of surviving cells in the patients' brains.

proteosome An organelle responsible for destroying defective or degraded proteins within the cell.

Another procedure has a long history, but only recently have technological developments in imaging methods and electrophysiological techniques led to an increase in its popularity. The principal output of the basal ganglia comes from the **internal division of the globus pallidus (GP_i).** (The caudate nucleus, putamen, and globus pallidus are the three major components of the basal ganglia.) This output, which is directed through the thalamus to the motor cortex, is inhibitory. Furthermore, a decrease in the activity of the dopaminergic input to the caudate nucleus and putamen causes an *increase* in the activity of the GP_i. Thus, damage to the GP_i might be expected to relieve the symptoms of Parkinson's disease. (See ***Figure 14.12.***)

In the 1950s, Leksell and his colleagues performed pallidotomies (surgical destruction of the internal division of the globus pallidus) in patients with severe Parkinson's disease (Svennilson et al., 1960; Laitinen, Bergenheim, and Hariz, 1992). The surgery often reduced the rigidity and enhanced the patient's ability to move. Unfortunately, the surgery occasionally made the patient's symptoms worse and sometimes resulted in partial blindness. (The optic tract is located next to the GP_i.)

With the development of L-DOPA therapy in the late 1960s, pallidotomies were abandoned. However, it eventually became evident that L-DOPA worked for a limited time and that the symptoms of Parkinson's disease would eventually return. For that

internal division of the globus pallidus (GP_i) A division of the globus pallidus that provides inhibitory input to the motor cortex via the thalamus; sometimes stereotaxically lesioned to treat the symptoms of Parkinson's disease.

Figure 14.12

The major connections of the basal ganglia and associated structures. Excitatory connections are shown as black lines; inhibitory connections are shown as red lines. Many connections, such as the inputs to the substantia nigra, are omitted for clarity. Two regions that have been targets of stereotaxic surgery for Parkinson's disease—the internal division of the globus pallidus and the subthalamus—are outlined in gray. Damage to these regions reduces inhibitory input to the thalamus and facilitates movement.

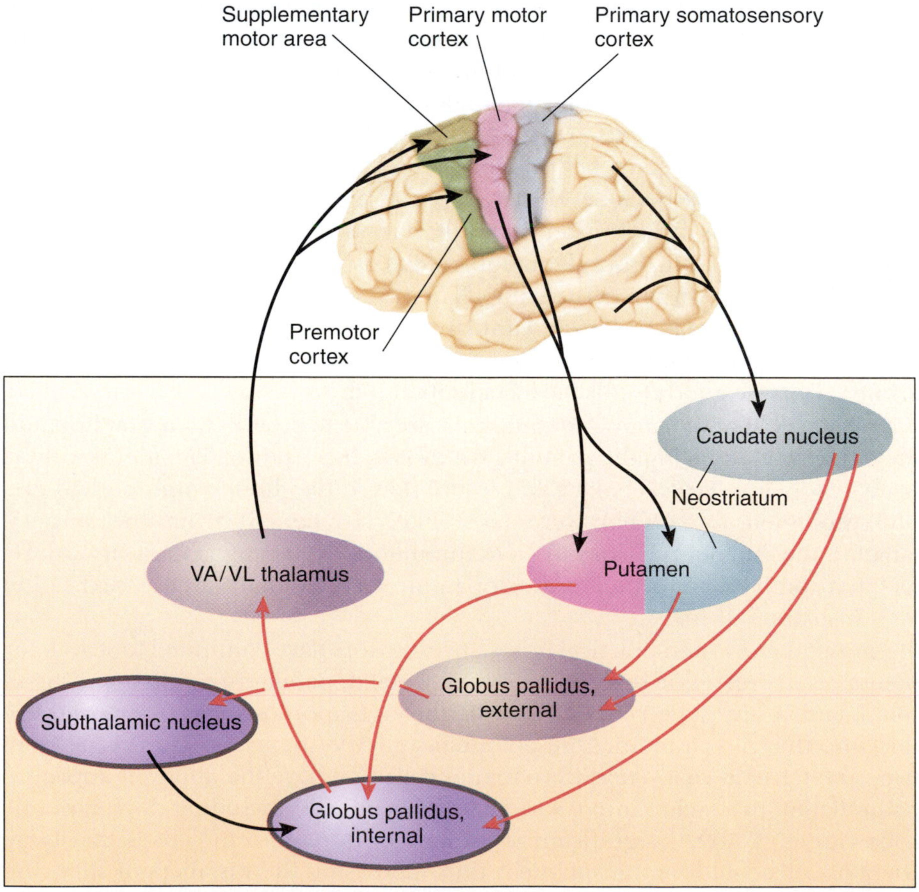

reason, in the 1990s neurosurgeons again began experimenting with pallidotomies, first with laboratory animals and then with humans (Graybiel, 1996; Lai et al., 2000). This time, they used MRI scans to find the location of the GP_i and then inserted an electrode into the target region. They could then pass low-intensity, high-frequency stimulation through the electrode, thus temporarily disabling the region around its tip. If the patient's rigidity disappeared (obviously, the patient is awake during the surgery), then the electrode was in the right place. To make the lesion, the surgeon passes radiofrequency current of sufficient strength to heat and destroy the brain tissue. The results of this procedure have been so promising that several neurological teams have begun promoting its use in the treatment of relatively young patients whose symptoms no longer respond to L-DOPA. PET studies have found that after pallidotomy, the metabolic activity in the premotor and supplementary motor areas of the frontal lobes, normally depressed in patients with Parkinson's disease, returns to normal levels (Grafton et al., 1995), a result indicating that lesions of the GP_i do indeed release the motor cortex from inhibition.

Neurosurgeons have also targeted the subthalamus in patients with advanced Parkinson's disease. As Figure 14.12 shows, the subthalamus has an excitatory effect on the GP_i; thus, damage to the subthalamus decreases the activity of this region and removes some of the inhibition on motor output. (See ***Figure 14.12.***) Normally, damage to the subthalamus causes involuntary jerking and twitching movements. However, in people with Parkinson's disease, damage to this region brings motor activity, which is normally depressed, back to normal (Guridi and Obeso, 2001).

Huntington's disease An inherited disorder that causes degeneration of the basal ganglia; characterized by progressively more severe uncontrollable jerking movements, writhing movements, dementia, and finally death.

The third stereotaxic procedure aimed at relieving the symptoms of Parkinson's disease involves implanting electrodes in the subthalamic nucleus and attaching a device that permits the patient to electrically stimulate the brain through the electrodes. (See ***Figure 14.13.***) According to some studies, deep brain stimulation is as effective as brain lesions in suppressing tremors and has fewer adverse side effects (Simuni et al., 2002; Speelman et al., 2002). The fact that either lesions or stimulation alleviates tremors suggests that the stimulation has an inhibitory effect on subthalamic neurons, but this hypothesis has not yet been confirmed.

Figure 14.13

Deep brain stimulation. Electrodes are implanted in the patient's brain, and wires are run under the skin to stimulation devices implanted near the collarbone.

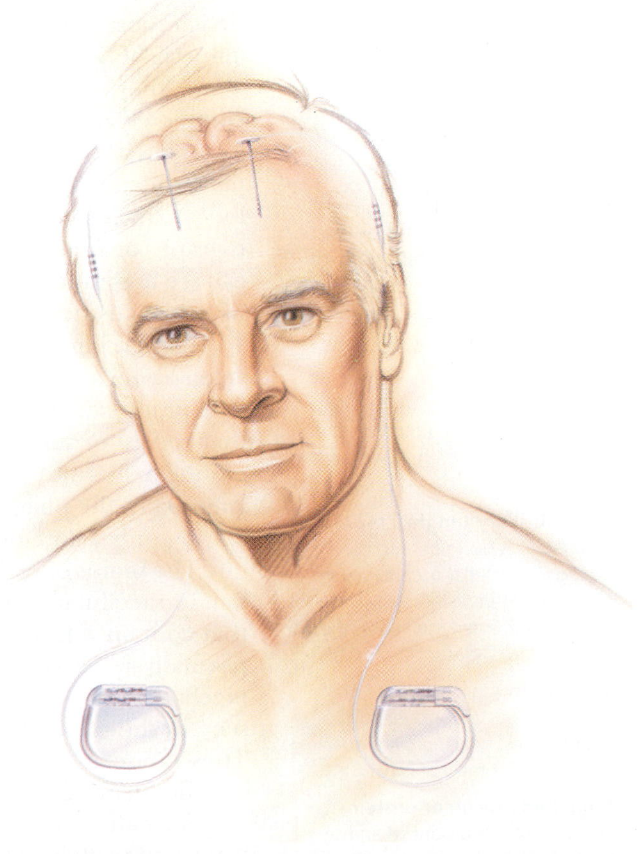

Illustration used with permission by Medtronic, Inc.

Huntington's Disease

Another basal ganglia disease, **Huntington's disease,** is caused by degeneration of the caudate nucleus and putamen, especially of GABAergic and acetylcholinergic neurons. Whereas Parkinson's disease causes a poverty of movements, Huntington's disease causes uncontrollable ones, especially jerky limb movements. The movements of Huntington's disease look like fragments of purposeful movements but occur involuntarily. This disease is progressive and eventually causes death.

The symptoms of Huntington's disease usually begin in the thirties and forties but can sometimes begin in the early twenties. The first signs of neural degeneration occur in the putamen, in a specific group of inhibitory neurons. Damage to these neurons removes some inhibitory control exerted on the premotor and supplementary motor areas of the frontal cortex. Loss of this control leads to involuntary movements.

Huntington's disease is a hereditary disorder, caused by a dominant gene on chromosome 4. In fact, the gene has been located, and its defect has been identified as a repeated sequence of bases that code for the amino acid glutamine (Collaborative Research Group, 1993). This repeated sequence causes the gene product—a protein called *huntingtin*—to contain an elongated stretch of glutamine. Longer stretches of glutamine are associated with patients whose symptoms began at a younger age, a finding that strongly suggests that this abnormal portion of the huntingtin molecule is responsible for the disease.

Normal huntingtin is found in the cytoplasm, where it apparently plays a role in production of certain cell organelles (Hilditch-Maguire et al., 2000). In cells of genetically altered HD mice that express long huntingtin and develop a disorder that closely resembles Huntington's disease, fragments of huntingtin begin to accumulate in the nucleus, which apparently triggers the production of caspase. (As we saw in the section on transmissible spongiform encephalopathies, caspase is a "killer enzyme" that plays a role in apoptosis, or programmed cell death. Li et al. (2000) found that HD mice lived longer if they were given a caspase inhibitor, which suppresses apoptosis. Further research will undoubtedly clarify the role of faulty huntingtin protein in the neuropathology of Huntington's disease. Unfortunately, there is at present no treatment for the disorder.

Alzheimer's Disease

Several neurological disorders result in **dementia,** a deterioration of intellectual abilities resulting from an organic brain disorder. A common form of dementia is called **Alzheimer's disease,** which occurs in approximately 7 percent of the population above the age of sixty-five and up to 40 percent of people older than eighty years. It is characterized by progressive loss of memory and other mental functions. At first, people may have difficulty remembering appointments and sometimes fail to think of words or other people's names. As time passes, they show increasing confusion, and increasing difficulty with tasks such as balancing a checkbook. The memory deficit most critically involves recent events, and thus it resembles the anterograde amnesia of Korsakoff's syndrome. If people with Alzheimer's disease venture outside alone, they are likely to get lost. They eventually become bedridden, then become completely helpless, and finally succumb (Terry and Davies, 1980).

Alzheimer's disease produces severe degeneration of the hippocampus, entorhinal cortex, neocortex (especially the association cortex of the frontal and temporal lobes), nucleus basalis, locus coeruleus, and raphe nuclei. Figure 14.14 shows photographs of the brain of a patient with Alzheimer's disease and of a normal brain. You can see how much wider the sulci are in the patient's brain, indicating substantial loss of cortical tissue. (See ***Figure 14.14.***)

Earlier, I mentioned that the brains of patients with Down syndrome usually develop abnormal structures that are also seen in patients with Alzheimer's disease: *neuritic plaques* and *neurofibrillary tangles.* **Neuritic plaques** are extracellular deposits that consist of a dense core of a protein known as **β-amyloid,** surrounded by degenerating axons and dendrites, along with activated microglia and reactive astrocytes. Eventually, the phagocytic glial cells destroy the degenerating axons and dendrites, leaving only a core of β-amyloid.

The brains of Alzheimer's patients (and patients with Down syndrome) also contain intracellular abnormalities: **neurofibrillary tangles,** consisting of dying neurons that contain intracellular accumulations of twisted filaments of **tau protein,** which normally serve as a component of microtubules, which provide the cells' transport mechanism. During the progression of Alzheimer's disease, abnormal filaments are seen in the soma and proximal dendrites of pyramidal cells in the cerebral cortex. These abnormal filaments disrupt transport of substances within the cell, and the cell dies, leaving behind a tangle of protein filaments. (See ***Figure 14.15.***)

Formation of neuritic plaques is caused by the production of a defective form of β-amyloid protein. The production of β-amyloid takes several steps. First, a gene encodes the production of the **β-amyloid precursor protein (APP),** a chain of approxi-

dementia (*da* ***men*** *sha*) A loss of cognitive abilities such as memory, perception, verbal ability, and judgment; common causes are multiple strokes and Alzheimer's disease.

Alzheimer's disease A degenerative brain disorder of unknown origin; causes progressive memory loss, motor deficits, and eventual death.

neuritic plaque An extracellular deposit containing a dense core of β-amyloid protein surrounded by degenerating axons and dendrites and activated microglia and reactive astrocytes.

β-amyloid (***amm*** *i loyd*) A protein found in excessive amounts in the brains of patients with Alzheimer's disease.

neurofibrillary tangle (*new row* ***fib*** *ri lair y*) A dying neuron containing intracellular accumulations β-amyloid and twisted protein filaments that formerly served as the cell's internal skeleton.

tau protein A protein that normally serves as a component of microtubules, which provide the cell's transport mechanism.

β-amyloid precursor protein (APP) A protein produced and secreted by cells that serves as the precursor for β-amyloid protein.

Figure 14.14

Alzheimer's disease. (a) A lateral view of the right side of the brain of a person with Alzheimer's disease. (Rostral is to the right; dorsal is up.) Note that the sulci of the temporal lobe and parietal lobe are especially wide, indicating degeneration of the neocortex (*arrowheads*). (b) A lateral view of the right side of a normal brain.

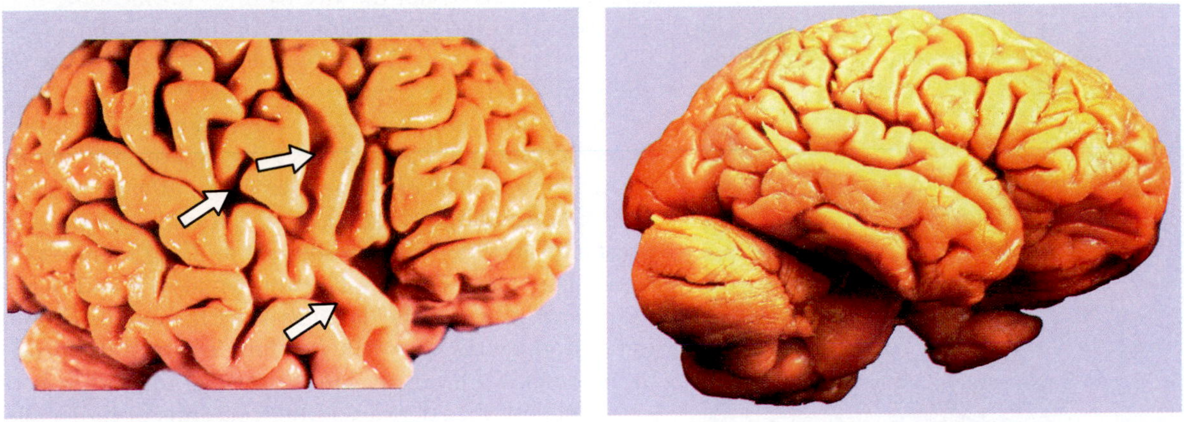

(a) (b)

Photo of diseased brain courtesy of A. D'Agostino, Good Samaritan Hospital, Portland, Oregon; photo of normal brain © Dan McCoy/Rainbow.

mately 700 amino acids. APP is then cut apart in two places by enzymes known as **secretases** to produce β-amyloid. The first, β-secretase, cuts the "tail" off of an APP molecule. The second, γ-secretase (gamma-secretase), cuts the "head off." The result is a molecule of β-amyloid that contains either 40 or 42 amino acids. The location of the second cut of the APP molecule by γ-secretase determines which form is produced. In normal brains, 90–95 percent of the β-amyloid molecules are of the short form; the other 5–10 percent are of the long form. In patients with Alzheimer's disease, the proportion of long β-amyloid rises to as much as 40 percent of the total. High concentrations of the long form have a tendency to fold themselves improperly and form aggregations, which have toxic effects on the cell. (As we saw, abnormally folded prions form aggregations that cause brain degeneration.) Small amounts of long β-amyloid can easily be cleared from the cell. The molecules are given a tag that marks them for destruction, and they are transported to the proteosomes, where they are rendered harmless. However, this system cannot keep up with abnormally high levels of production of long β-amyloid.

secretase (***see*** *cre tayss*) A class of enzymes that cut the β-amyloid precursor protein into smaller fragments, including β-amyloid.

Figure 14.16 shows the abnormal accumulation of β-amyloid protein in the brain of a person with Alzheimer's disease. Klunk et al. (2003) developed a drug that binds with β-amyloid protein and readily crosses the blood–brain barrier. They gave the patient and a healthy control subject an injection of a radioactive form of this drug and examined their brains with a PET scanner. You can see the accumulation of the protein in the patient's cerebral cortex. (See ***Figure 14.16.***) The ability to measure the levels of β-amyloid in the brains of Alzheimer's patients will enable researchers to evaluate the effectiveness of potential treatments for the disease. And if such a treatment is devised, the ability to identify the accumulation of β-amyloid early in the development of the disease will make it possible to begin a patient's treatment before significant degeneration—and the accompanying decline in cognitive abilities—has occurred.

Figure 14.15

A neuritic plaque (center) and neurofibrillary tangles (arrows). The dark mass in the center of the neuritic plaque is β-amyloid protein.

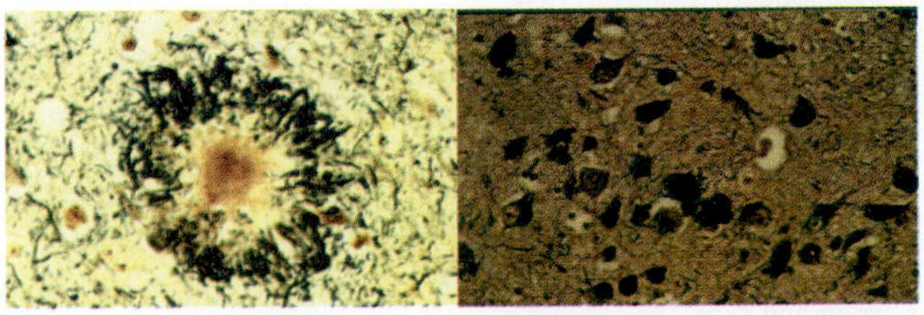

(a) (b)

Photo courtesy of D. J. Selkoe, Brigham and Women's Hospital, Boston.

Figure 14.16

Accumulation of β-amyloid protein in the brains of a patient with Alzheimer's disease. AD = Alzheimer's disease, MR = structural magnetic resonance image, [C-11]PIB PET = PET scan of brains after an injection of a radioactive ligand for β-amyloid protein.

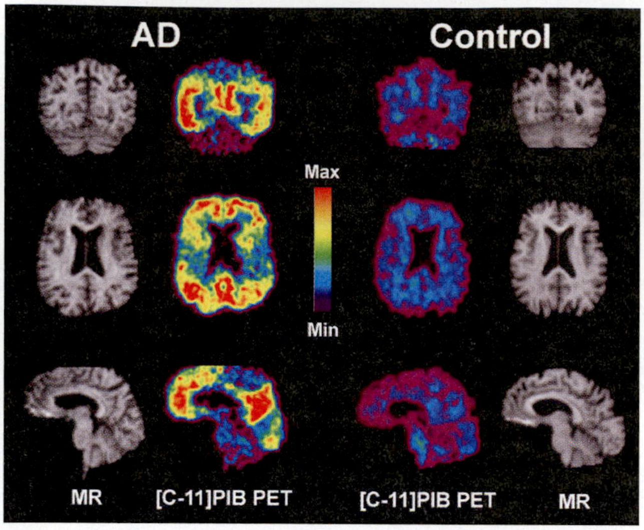

Courtesy of William Klunk, Western Psychiatric Institute and Clinic, Pittsburgh, PA.

Research has shown that at least some forms of Alzheimer's disease appear to run in families and thus appear to be hereditary. Because the brains of people with Down syndrome (caused by an extra twenty-first chromosome) also contain deposits of β-amyloid, some investigators hypothesized that the twenty-first chromosome may be involved in the production of this protein. In fact, St. George-Hyslop et al. (1987) found that chromosome 21 *does* contains the gene that produces APP.

Since the discovery of the APP gene, several studies found specific mutations of this gene that produce familial Alzheimer's disease (Martinez et al., 1993; Farlow et al., 1994). In addition, other studies found mutations of **presenilin** genes on chromosomes 1 and 14 that also produce Alzheimer's disease. The abnormal APP and presenilin genes all cause the defective long form of β-amyloid to be produced (Hardy, 1997). The identity of the presenilin proteins are not yet known for certain, but investigators believe that they are either secretins or molecules that interact with secretins.

Yet another genetic cause of Alzheimer's disease is a mutation in the gene for **apolipoprotein E (apoE),** a glycoprotein that transports cholesterol in the blood and also plays a role in cellular repair. One allele of the apoE gene, known as E4, increases the risk of late-onset Alzheimer's disease, apparently by interfering with the removal of the long form of β-amyloid from the extracellular space in the brain (Roses, 1997; Price and Sisodia, 1998; Mahley and Rall, 2000).

As we saw earlier, the brains of Alzheimer's patients contain abnormal forms of two types of proteins: β-amyloid protein and tau protein. It appears that excessive amounts of abnormal β-amyloid protein, and not tau protein, are responsible for the disease. Mutations in the β-amyloid precursor, APP, produce both forms of abnormal proteins and cause the development of both neuritic plaques and neurofibrillary tangles. However, mutations in the gene for tau protein produce only neurofibrillary tangles. The result of these mutations is a disorder known as *frontotemporal dementia,* which causes degeneration of the frontal and temporal cortex along with the symptoms of Parkinson's disease (Goate, 1998; Goedert and Spillantini, 2000).

Although the studies I have cited indicate that the production of abnormal β-amyloid plays an important role in the development of Alzheimer's disease, the fact is that most forms of Alzheimer's disease are *not* hereditary. What causes the accumulation of β-amyloid in these cases? The answer is that we do not know, although some investigators have proposed that head injury, infections, excessive use of alcohol or other drugs, and exposure to toxic substances can trigger the formation of amyloid plaques. For example, examination of the brains of people who have sustained closed head injuries (including those that occur during prize fights) often reveals a widespread distribution of amyloid plaques. The finding that estrogen replacement therapy substantially reduces the risk of Alzheimer's disease in postmenopausal women indicates yet another link between physiological factors and the development of this disease (Henderson, 1997).

Acting on observations that people who had been treated with anti-inflammatory drugs (for diseases such as rheumatoid arthritis or leprosy) seemed to have a particularly low rate of Alzheimer's disease, Rogers et al. (1993) administered indomethacin, a nonsteroid anti-inflammatory drug (NSAID) or a placebo to 44 patients with mild to moderate symptoms of Alzheimer's disease. They found that the cognitive performance of the drug-treated patients improved by 1.3 percent over the six-month period, while that of the placebo patients declined by 8.4 percent. As

presenilin (*pree sen **ill** in*) A protein produced by a faulty gene that causes β-amyloid precursor protein to be converted to the abnormal short form; may be a cause of Alzheimer's disease.

apolipoprotein E (apoE) (*ay po lye po **proh** teen*) A glycoprotein that transports cholesterol in the blood and plays a role in cellular repair; presence of the E4 allele of the apoE gene increases the risk of late-onset Alzheimer's disease.

Rogers noted, "We lost about 20 percent of our placebo patients because they went down hill behaviorally, so much that they wouldn't take medicine or sit for the test anymore. . . . This didn't happen with the indomethacin patients" (Schnabel, 1993, p. 1719). As you might expect, these findings have stimulated further research, and drug companies are trying to develop even more effective anti-inflammatory drugs. Recent studies (Sastre, et al., 2003; Weggen et al., 2003) suggest that NSAIDs reduce the production of β-amyloid by modulating the activity of secretases.

Perhaps the most promising approaches to the prevention of Alzheimer's disease come from recent research with *AD mice*—a strain of genetically modified mice that contain a human gene that leads to the development of Alzheimer's disease. Schenck et al. (1999) and Bard et al. (2000) attempted to sensitize the immune system against β-amyloid. They injected AD mice with a vaccine that, they hoped, would stimulate the immune system to destroy β-amyloid. The treatment worked: The vaccine suppressed the development of amyloid plaques in the brains of mice that received the vaccine from an early age and halted or even reversed the development of plaques in mice that received the vaccine later in life. Another approach also reduced levels of β-amyloid in AD mice. Dovey et al. (2001) developed a drug that inhibits γ-secretase and found that this drug did indeed reduce the levels of β-amyloid in the brains of AD mice.

A recent clinical trial with Alzheimer's patients attempted to destroy β-amyloid by sensitizing the patient's immune systems to the protein (Monsonego and Weiner, 2003). In a double-blind study, thirty patients with mild-to-moderate Alzheimer's disease were given injections of a portion of the β-amyloid protein. Twenty of these patients generated antibodies against β-amyloid, which slowed the course of the disease, presumably because their immune systems began destroying β-amyloid in their brain and reducing the neural destruction caused by the accumulation of this protein. Hock et al. (2003) compared the cognitive abilities of the patients who generated β-amyloid antibodies to those who did not. As Figure 14.17 shows, antibody production significantly reduced cognitive decline. (See ***Figure 14.17***.)

One of the patients whose immune system generated antibodies against β-amyloid died of a pulmonary embolism (a blood clot in a blood vessel serving the lungs).

Figure 14.17

Effect of immunization against β-amyloid protein on the cognitive decline of patients who generated β-amyloid antibodies (Successfully immunized patients) and those who did not (Controls).

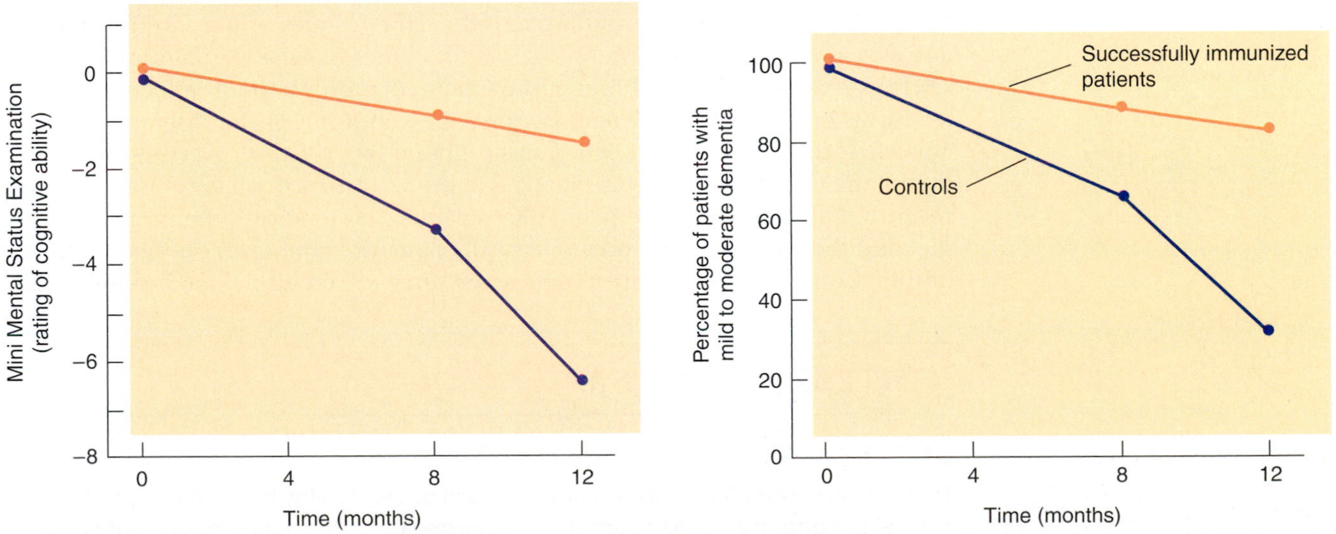

Adapted from Hock, C., Konietzko, U., Streffer, J. R., Tracy, J., Signorell, A., Müller-Tillmans, B., Lemke, U., Henke, K., Moritz, E., Garcia, E., Wollmer, M. A., Umbricht, D., de Quervain, D. J. F., Hofmann, M., Maddalena, A., Papassotiropoulos, A., and Nitsch, R. M. *Neuron,* 2003, *38,* 547–554.

Figure 14.18

A slice of a human brain of a person who had multiple sclerosis. The arrowheads point to sclerotic plaques in the white matter.

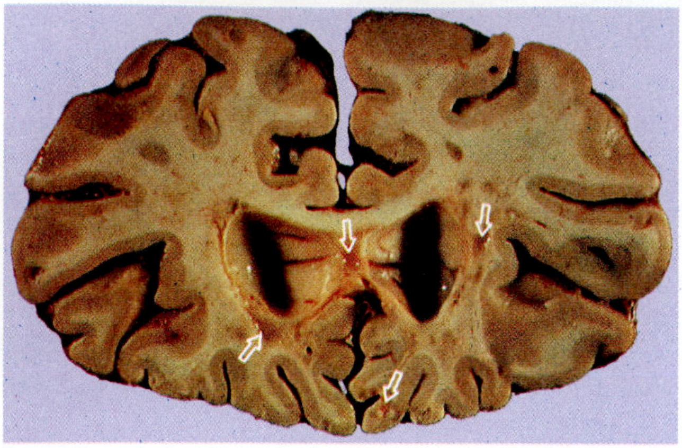

Courtesy of A. D'Agostino, Good Samaritan Hospital, Portland, Oregon.

Nicoll et al. (2003) examined this patient's brain and found evidence that the immune system had removed β-amyloid from many regions of the cerebral cortex. Unfortunately, the injections of the β-amyloid antigen caused an inflammatory reaction in the brains of 5 percent of the patients, so the clinical trial was terminated. However, Monsonego and Weiner (2003) suggest some possible solutions to this problem: preparation of a vaccine using a different portion of the β-amyloid protein or attempting to establish a passive immunity by administering antibodies developed in tissue cultures. All of us who look forward to growing old and retaining our cognitive abilities should hope that one of these approaches is successful.

Multiple Sclerosis

Multiple sclerosis is an autoimmune demyelinating disease. At scattered locations within the central nervous system, myelin sheaths are attacked by the person's immune system, leaving behind hard patches of debris called *sclerotic plaques.* (See ***Figure 14.18.***) The normal transmission of neural messages through the demyelinated axons is interrupted. Because the damage occurs in white matter located throughout the brain and spinal cord, a wide variety of neurological disorders are seen.

Multiple sclerosis afflicts women somewhat more frequently than men, and the disorder usually occurs in people in their late twenties or thirties. People who spend their childhood in places far from the equator are more likely to come down with the disease than are those who live close to it. In addition, people born during the late winter and early spring are at higher risk. Hence, it is likely that some disease contracted during a childhood spent in a region in which the virus is prevalent causes the person's immune system to attack his or her own myelin. Perhaps a virus weakens the blood–brain barrier, allowing myelin protein into the general circulation and sensitizing the immune system to it, or perhaps the virus attaches itself to myelin. In any event, the process is a long-lived one, lasting for many decades.

The only treatment for multiple sclerosis that has shown any promise is *interferon β,* a protein that modulates the responsiveness of the immune system. Administration of interferon β has been shown to reduce the frequency and severity of attacks and slow the progression of neurological disabilities in some patients with multiple sclerosis (Arnason, 1999). However, the treatment is only partially effective, and better forms of therapy are needed. Because the symptoms of the disease are usually episodic—new or worsening symptoms followed by partial recovery—patients and their families often attribute the changes in the symptoms to whatever has happened recently. For example, if the patient has taken a new medication or gone on a new diet and the symptoms get worse, they will blame the symptoms on the medication or diet. Conversely, if the patient gets better, they will credit the medication or diet.

INTERIM SUMMARY

Degenerative Disorders

Transmissible spongiform encephalopathies such as Creutzfeldt-Jakob disease, scrapie, and bovine spongiform encephalopathy ("mad cow disease") are unique among contagious diseases: They are produced by a simple protein molecule, not by a virus or microbe. The sequence of amino acids of normal prion protein (PrPc) and infectious prion protein (PrPSc) are identical, but their three-dimensional shapes differ in the way that they are folded. Somehow, the presence of a misfolded prion protein in a neuron causes normal prion proteins to become misfolded, and a chain reaction ensues. PrPSc accumulates and kills the cell, apparently by triggering apoptosis.

Parkinson's disease is caused by degeneration of dopamine-secreting neurons of the substantia nigra that send axons to the basal ganglia. Study of rare hereditary forms of Parkinson's disease reveal that death of these neurons is caused by the aggregation of misfolded protein, α-synuclein. The accumulation of this protein can be triggered by some toxins, which suggests that nonhereditary forms of the disease may be caused by toxic substances present in the environment. Treatment of Parkinson's disease includes administration of L-DOPA, implantation of fetal dopaminergic neurons in the basal ganglia, stereotaxic destruction of a portion of the globus pallidus or subthalamus, and implantation of electrodes that enable the patient to electrically stimulate the subthalamus.

Alzheimer's disease, another degenerative disorder, involves much more of the brain; the disease process eventually destroys most of the hippocampus and cortical gray matter. The brains of affected individuals contain many amyloid plaques, which contain a core of misfolded long-form β-amyloid protein surrounded by degenerating axons and dendrites, and neurofibrillary tangles, composed of dying neurons that contain intracellular accumulations of twisted filaments of tau protein. Hereditary forms of Alzheimer's disease involve defective genes for the amyloid precursor protein (APP), for the secretases that cut APP into smaller pieces, or for apolipoprotein E (apoE), a glycoprotein involved in transport of cholesterol and the repair of cell membranes. Anti-inflammatory drugs may be useful in fighting this disorder. Other promising treatments include vaccination against β-amyloid and drugs that inactivate γ-secretase. Multiple sclerosis, a demyelinating disease, is characterized by periodic attacks of neurological symptoms, usually with partial remission between attacks. The damage appears to be caused by the body's immune system, which attacks the protein contained in myelin.

Disorders Caused by Infectious Diseases

Several neurological disorders can be caused by infectious diseases, transmitted by bacteria, fungi or other parasites, or viruses. The most common are encephalitis and meningitis. **Encephalitis** is an infection that invades the entire brain. The most common cause of encephalitis is a virus that is transmitted by mosquitoes, which pick up the infectious agent from horses, birds, or rodents. The symptoms of acute encephalitis include fever, irritability, and nausea, often followed by convulsions, delirium, and signs of brain damage, such as aphasia or paralysis. Unfortunately, there is no specific treatment besides supportive care, and between 5 and 20 percent of cases are fatal; 20 percent of the survivors show some residual neurological symptoms.

Encephalitis can also be caused by the **herpes simplex virus,** which is the cause of cold sores (or "fever blisters") that most people develop in and around their mouth from time to time. Normally, the viruses live quietly in the *trigeminal nerve ganglia* nodules on the fifth cranial nerve that contain the cell bodies of somatosensory neurons that serve the face. The viruses proliferate periodically, traveling down to the ends of nerve fibers, where they cause sores to develop in mucous membrane. Unfortunately, they occasionally (but rarely) go the other way into the brain. Herpes encephalitis is a serious disease; the virus attacks the frontal and temporal lobes in particular and can severely damage them.

Two other forms of viral encephalitis are probably already familiar to you: polio and rabies. **Acute anterior poliomyelitis** ("polio") is fortunately very rare in developed countries since the development of vaccines that immunize people against the disease. The virus causes specific damage to motor neurons of the brain and spinal cord: neurons in the primary motor cortex; in the motor nuclei of the thalamus,

encephalitis (*en seff a* ***lye*** *tis*) An inflammation of the brain; caused by bacteria, viruses, or toxic chemicals.

herpes simplex virus A virus that normally causes cold sores near the lips but that can also cause brain damage.

acute anterior poliomyelitis A viral disease that destroys motor neurons of the brain and spinal cord.

hypothalamus, and brain stem; in the cerebellum; and in the ventral horns of the gray matter of the spinal cord. Undoubtedly, these motor neurons contain some chemical substance that either attracts the virus or in some way makes the virus become lethal to them.

Rabies is caused by a virus that is passed from the saliva of an infected mammal directly into a person's flesh by means of a bite wound. The virus travels through peripheral nerves to the central nervous system and there causes severe damage. The symptoms include a short period of fever and headache, followed by anxiety, excessive movement and talking, difficulty in swallowing, movement disorders, difficulty in speaking, seizures, confusion, and, finally, death within two to seven days of the onset of the symptoms. The virus has a special affinity for cells in the cerebellum and hippocampus, and damage to the hippocampus probably accounts for the emotional changes that are seen in the early symptoms.

Fortunately, the incubation period for rabies lasts up to several months while the virus climbs through the peripheral nerves. (If the bite is received in the face or neck, the incubation time will be much shorter, because the virus has a smaller distance to travel before it reaches the brain.) During the incubation period a person can receive a vaccine that will confer an immunity to the disease; the person's own immune system will destroy the virus before it reaches the brain.

Several infectious diseases cause brain damage even though they are not primarily diseases of the central nervous system. One such disease is acquired immune deficiency syndrome (AIDS). Records of autopsies have revealed that at least 75 percent of people who died of AIDS show evidence of brain damage (Levy and Bredesen, 1989). The brain damage often results in a syndrome called *AIDS dementia,* which is characterized by a loss of cognitive and motor functions. At first the patients may become forgetful, they may think and reason more slowly, and they may have word-finding difficulties (anomia). Eventually, they may become almost mute. Motor deficits may begin with tremor and difficulty in making complex movement but then may progress so much that the patient becomes bedridden (Maj, 1990).

Evidence suggests that the cause of AIDS dementia may be the entry of excessive amounts of calcium into neurons. For several years, researchers have been puzzled by the fact that although AIDS certainly causes neural damage, neurons are not themselves infected by the HIV virus (the organism responsible for the disease). Lipton et al. (1990) found that the cause of neural death appears to be the entry of excessive amounts of calcium. (As we saw earlier, the death of neurons caused by seizures and by anoxia also involves the entry of excessive amounts of Ca^{2+}.) Lipton and his colleagues (Lipton, 1996, 1997) suggest that virus-infected astrocytes and white blood cells may be the cause of the calcium inflow. The infection causes these cells to secrete excitotoxic substances (including glutamate) that activate NMDA receptors. The investigators suggest that the drugs being developed to reduce the damage caused by strokes may also be useful in treating AIDS dementia. In fact, a clinical trial of nimodipine, a drug that blocks calcium channels, found no signs of toxicity, and further studies will investigate the effectiveness of this drug in preventing the development of neurological symptoms (Navia et al., 1998).

Another category of infectious diseases of the brain actually involves inflammation of the meninges, the layers of connective tissue that surround the central nervous system. **Meningitis** can be caused by viruses or bacteria. The symptoms of all forms include headache, a stiff neck, and, depending on the severity of the disorder, convulsions, confusion or loss of consciousness, and sometimes death. The stiff neck is one of the most important symptoms. Neck movements cause the meninges to stretch; because they are inflamed, the stretch causes severe pain. Thus, the patient resists having his or her neck moved.

The most common form of viral meningitis usually does not cause significant brain damage. However, various forms of bacterial meningitis do. The usual cause is spread of a middle-ear infection into the brain, introduction of an infection into the

rabies A fatal viral disease that causes brain damage; usually transmitted through the bite of an infected animal.

meningitis (*men in **jy** tis*) An inflammation of the meninges; can be caused by viruses or bacteria.

brain from a head injury, or the presence of emboli that have dislodged from a bacterial infection present in the chambers of the heart. Such an infection is often caused by unclean hypodermic needles; therefore, drug addicts are at particular risk for meningitis (as well as many other diseases). The inflammation of the meninges can damage the brain by interfering with circulation of blood or by blocking the flow of cerebrospinal fluid through the subarachnoid space, causing hydrocephalus. In addition, the cranial nerves are susceptible to damage. Fortunately, bacterial meningitis can usually be treated effectively with antibiotics. Of course, early diagnosis and prompt treatment are essential, because neither antibiotics nor any other known treatment can repair a damaged brain.

INTERIM SUMMARY

Disorders Caused by Infectious Diseases

Infectious diseases can damage the brain. Encephalitis, usually caused by a virus, affects the entire brain. One form is caused by the herpes simplex virus, which infects the trigeminal nerve ganglia of most of the population. This virus tends to attack the frontal and temporal lobes. The polio virus attacks motor neurons in the brain and spinal cord, resulting in motor deficits or even paralysis. The rabies virus, acquired by an animal bite, travels through peripheral nerves and attacks the brain, particularly the cerebellum and hippocampus. An AIDS infection also produces brain damage, perhaps because infected white blood cells and astrocytes release excitotoxic chemicals that open calcium channels that permit a lethal dose of the ion to enter the cells of the brain. Meningitis is an infection of the meninges, caused by viruses or bacteria. The bacterial form, which is usually more serious, is generally caused by an ear infection, a head injury, or an embolus from a heart infection.

EPILOGUE

Seizure Surgery

Mrs. R.'s surgery was performed to remove a noncancerous brain tumor that, incidentally, produced seizures. As I mentioned in this chapter, neurosurgeons occasionally perform surgery specifically to remove brain tissue that contains a seizure focus. Such an operation, called *seizure surgery,* is performed only when drug therapy is unsuccessful.

Because seizure surgery often involves the removal of a substantial amount of brain tissue (usually from one of the temporal lobes), we might expect it to cause behavioral deficits. But in most cases the reverse is true; people's performance on tests of neuropsychological functioning usually *improves.* How can the removal of brain tissue improve a person's performance?

The answer is provided by looking at what happens in the brain not *during* seizures but *between* them. The seizure focus, usually a region of scar tissue, irritates the brain tissue surrounding it, causing increased neural activity that tends to spread to adjacent regions. Between seizures this increased excitatory activity is held in check by a compensatory increase in inhibitory activity. That is, inhibitory neurons in the region surrounding the seizure focus become more active. (This phenomenon is known as *interictal inhibition; ictus* means "stroke" in Latin.) A seizure occurs when the excitation overcomes the inhibition.

The problem is that the compensatory inhibition does more than hold the excitation in check; it also suppresses the normal functions of a rather large region of brain tissue surrounding the seizure focus. Thus, even though the focus may be small, its effects are felt over a much larger area even between seizures. Removing the seizure focus and some surrounding brain tissue eliminates the source of the irritation and makes the compensatory inhibition unnecessary. Freed from interictal inhibition, the brain tissue located near the site of the former seizure focus can now function normally, and the patient's neuropsychological abilities will show an improvement.

As I mentioned in this chapter, seizures often occur after a head injury, but only after a delay of several months. The cause of the delay is related to some properties of neurons that make learning possible. Goddard (1967) implanted electrodes in the brains of rats and administered a brief, weak electrical stimulus once a day. At first the stimulation produced no effects, but after several days the stimulation began to trigger small, short seizures. As days went by, the seizures became larger and longer until the animal was finally having full-blown clonic-tonic convulsions. Goddard called the phenomenon *kindling,* because it resembled the way a small fire can be kindled to start a larger one.

Kindling appears to be analogous to learning, and it presumably involves changes in synaptic strength like those seen in long-term potentiation. It can most easily be induced in the temporal lobe, which is the place where seizure foci are most likely to occur. The probable reason for the delayed occurrence of seizures after a head injury is that it takes time for kindling to occur. The irritation produced by the brain injury eventually causes increased synaptic strength in excitatory synapses located nearby.

Kindling has become an animal model of focal-seizure disorders, and it has proved useful in research on the causes and treatment of these disorders. For example, Silver, Shin, and McNamara (1991) produced seizure foci in rats through kindling and compared the effects of some commonly used medications on both seizures (the electrical events within the brain) and convulsions (the motor manifestations of the seizures). They found that one of the drugs they tested prevented the convulsions but left seizures intact, whereas another prevented both seizures and convulsions. Because each seizure is capable of producing some brain damage through overstimulation of neurons (especially those in the hippocampal formation, which become especially active during a seizure), the goal of medical treatment should be the elimination of seizures, not simply the convulsions that accompany them. Research with the animal model of kindling will undoubtedly contribute to the effective treatment of focal-seizure disorders.

KEY CONCEPTS

TUMORS

1. Brain tumors are uncontrolled growths of cells other than neurons within the skull that damage normal tissue by compression or infiltration.

SEIZURE DISORDERS

2. Seizures are periodic episodes of abnormal neural firing, which can produce a variety of symptoms. They usually originate from a focus, but some have no apparent source of localized irritation.

CEREBROVASCULAR ACCIDENTS

3. Cerebrovascular accidents, hemorrhagic or obstructive in nature, produce localized brain damage. The two most common sources of obstructive strokes are emboli and thrombi.

DISORDERS OF DEVELOPMENT

4. Developmental disorders can be caused by drugs or disease-produced toxins, or by chromosomal or genetic abnormalities.

DEGENERATIVE DISORDERS

5. Several degenerative disorders of the nervous system, including transmissible spongiform encephalopathies, Parkinson's disease, Huntington's disease, Alzheimer's disease, and multiple sclerosis, have received much attention from scientists in recent years. All of these diseases except multiple sclerosis appear to involve accumulations of abnormal proteins.

DISORDERS CAUSED BY INFECTIOUS DISEASES

6. Infectious diseases, either viral bacterial, can damage the brain. The two most important infections of the central nervous system are encephalitis and meningitis, but with the rise of the AIDS epidemic, AIDS dementia complex has become more common.

SUGGESTED READINGS

Adams, R. D., Victor, M., and Ropper, A. H. *Principles of Neurology,* 6th ed. New York: McGraw-Hill, 1997.

Feldman, R. S., Meyer, J. S., and Quenzer, L. F. *Principles of Neuropsychopharmacology.* Sunderland, MA: Sinauer Associates, 1997.

Terry, R. D., Katzman, R., Sisodia, S. S., and Bick, K. L. *Alzheimer Disease,* 2nd ed. Baltimore, MD: Lippincott Williams & Wilkins, 1999.

SUGGESTED WEB SITES

Neuropathology on the Internet

www.neuropat.dote.hu/

An excellent compilation of links to neuroanatomy and neuropathology sites on the internet, prepared by the Department of Neurology, University of Debrecen, Hungary.

Neurophysiology Figures

http://w3.uokhsc.edu/human_physiology/neurofigs.html

Links to several sites prepared by the Oklahoma University College of Medicine. Includes an excellent atlas of neuroanatomy.

Databases of Neuropathology Images

http://www-medlib.med.utah.edu/WebPath/CNSHTML/CNSIDX.html

Neuropathology images prepared by the University of Utah Medical School.

Washington University Alzheimer's Disease Research Center

www.biostat.wustl.edu/alzheimer/

Links to resources and information about Alzheimer's disease.

Parkinson's Disease Web Ring

www.pdring.com/

Links to resources and information about Parkinson's Disease.

Schizophrenia, Affective Disorders, and Anxiety Disorders

chapter 15

CHAPTER OUTLINE

LEARNING OBJECTIVES

1. Describe the symptoms of schizophrenia and discuss evidence concerning its heritability.
2. Discuss drugs that alleviate or produce the positive symptoms of schizophrenia and discuss research on the dopamine hypothesis of schizophrenia.
3. Describe evidence that schizophrenia may result from abnormal brain development.
4. Describe evidence linking both the positive and negative symptoms to decreased activity of the prefrontal cortex.
5. Describe the two major affective disorders, their heritability, and their physiological treatments.
6. Summarize the monoamine hypothesis of depression and review evidence for brain abnormalities in people with affective disorders.
7. Explain the role of circadian rhythms in affective disorders: the effects of REM sleep deprivation and total sleep deprivation and the symptoms and treatment of seasonal affective disorder.
8. Describe the symptoms and possible causes of panic disorder.
9. Describe the symptoms and possible causes of obsessive-compulsive disorder.

PROLOGUE

Side Effects

Larry had become a permanent resident of the state hospital. His parents had originally hoped that treatment would help him enough that he could live in a halfway house with a small group of other young men, but his condition was so serious that he required constant supervision. Larry had severe schizophrenia. The medication he was taking helped, but he still exhibited severe psychotic symptoms. In addition, he had begun showing signs of a neurological disorder that seemed to be getting worse.

Larry had always been a difficult child, shy and socially awkward. He had no real friends. During adolescence he became even more withdrawn and insisted that his parents and older sister keep out of his room. He stopped taking meals with the family, and he even bought a small refrigerator of his own for his room so that he could keep his own food, which he said he preferred to that "pesticide-contaminated" food his parents ate. His grades in school, which were never outstanding, got progressively worse, and when he was seventeen years old, he dropped out of high school.

Larry's parents recognized that something was seriously wrong with him. Their family physician suggested that he see a psychiatrist and gave them the name of a colleague that he respected, but Larry flatly refused to go. Within a year after he quit high school, he became frankly psychotic. He heard voices talking to him, and sometimes his parents could hear him shouting for the voices to go away. He was convinced that his parents were trying to poison him, and he would eat only factory-sealed food that he had opened himself. Although he kept his body clean—sometimes he would stand in the shower for an hour "purifying" himself—his room became frightfully messy. He insisted on keeping old cans and food packages because, he said, he needed to compare them with items his parents brought from the store to be sure they were not counterfeit.

One day, while Larry was in the shower purifying himself, his mother cleaned his room. She filled several large plastic garbage bags with the cans and packages and put them out for the trash collector. As she re-entered the house, she heard a howling noise from upstairs. Larry had emerged from the shower and discovered that his room had been cleaned. When he saw his mother coming up the stairs, he screamed at her, cursed her savagely, and rushed down the stairs toward her. He hit her so hard that she flew through the air, landing heavily on the floor below. He wheeled around, ran up the stairs, and went into his room, slamming the door behind him.

An hour later, Larry's father discovered his wife unconscious at the foot of the stairs. She soon recovered from the mild concussion she had sustained, but Larry's parents realized that it was time for him to be put in custody. Because he had attacked his mother, a judge ordered that he be temporarily detained and, as a result of a psychiatric evaluation, had him committed to the state hospital. The diagnosis was "schizophrenia, paranoid type."

In the state hospital, Larry was given Thorazine (chlorpromazine), which helped considerably. For the first few weeks, he showed some symptoms commonly seen in Parkinson's disease—tremors, rigidity, a shuffling gait, and lack of facial expression—but these symptoms cleared up spontaneously, as his physician had predicted. The voices still talked to him occasionally, but less often than before, and even then he could ignore them most of the time. His suspiciousness decreased, and he was willing to eat with the residents in the dining room. But he still obviously had paranoid delusions, and the psychiatric staff was unwilling to let him leave the hospital. For one thing, he refused to take his medication voluntarily. Once, after he had suffered a serious relapse, the staff discovered that he had only been pretending to swallow his pills and was later throwing them away. After that, they made sure that he swallowed them.

After several years, Larry began developing more serious neurological symptoms. He began pursing his lips and making puffing sounds, and later, he started grimacing, sticking his tongue out, and turning his head sharply to the left. The symptoms became so severe that they interfered with his ability to eat. His physician prescribed an additional drug, which reduced the symptoms considerably but did not eliminate them. As he explained to Larry's parents, "His neurological problems are caused by the medication that we are using to help with his psychiatric symptoms. These problems usually do not develop until a patient has taken the medication for many years, but Larry appears to be one of the unfortunate exceptions. If we take him off the medication, the neurological symptoms will get even worse. We could reduce the symptoms by giving him a higher dose of the medication, but then the problem would come back later, and it would be even worse. All we can do is try to treat the symptoms with another drug, as we have been doing. We really need a medication that helps treat schizophrenia without producing these tragic side effects."

Most of the discussion in this book has concentrated on the physiology of normal, adaptive behavior. The last two chapters summarize research on the nature and physiology of syndromes characterized by maladaptive behavior: mental disorders, attention-deficit/hyperactivity disorder, autism, stress disorders, and drug abuse. The symptoms of mental disorders include deficient or inappropriate social behaviors; illogical, incoherent, or obsessional thoughts; inappropriate emotional responses, including depression, mania, or anxiety; and delusions and hallucinations. Research in recent years indicates that many of these symptoms are caused by abnormalities in the brain, both structural and biochemical.

Schizophrenia

Description

Schizophrenia is a serious mental disorder that afflicts approximately 1 percent of the world's population. Its monetary cost to society is enormous; in the United States this figure exceeds that of the cost of all cancers (Thaker and Carpenter, 2001). Descriptions of symptoms in ancient writings indicate that the disorder has been around for thousands of years (Jeste et al., 1985). The major symptoms of schizophrenia are universal, and clinicians have developed criteria for reliably diagnosing the disorder in people of a wide variety of cultures (Flaum and Andreasen, 1990). *Schizophrenia* is probably the most misused psychological term in existence. The word literally means "split mind," but it does *not* imply a split or multiple personality. People often say that they "feel schizophrenic" about an issue when they really mean that they have mixed feelings about it. A person who sometimes wants to build a cabin in Alaska and live off the land and at other times wants to take over the family insurance agency might be undecided, but he or she is not schizophrenic. The man who invented the term, Eugen Bleuler (1911/1950), intended it to refer to a break with reality caused by disorganization of the various functions of the mind, such that thoughts and feelings no longer worked together normally.

Schizophrenia is characterized by two categories of symptoms: positive and negative (Crow, 1980; Andreasen, 1995). **Positive symptoms** make themselves known by their presence. They include thought disorders, hallucinations, and delusions. A **thought disorder**—disorganized, irrational thinking—is probably the most important symptom of schizophrenia. Schizophrenics have great difficulty arranging their thoughts logically and sorting out plausible conclusions from absurd ones. In conversation they jump from one topic to another as new associations come up. Sometimes, they utter meaningless words or choose words for rhyme rather than for meaning. **Delusions** are beliefs that are obviously contrary to fact. Delusions of *persecution* are false beliefs that others are plotting and conspiring against oneself. Delusions of *grandeur* are false beliefs in one's power and importance, such as a conviction that one has godlike powers or has special knowledge that no one else possesses. Delusions of *control* are related to delusions of persecution; the person believes (for example) that he or she is being controlled by others through such means as radar or tiny radio receivers implanted in his or her brain.

The third positive symptom of schizophrenia is **hallucinations,** perceptions of stimuli that are not actually present. The most common schizophrenic hallucinations are auditory, but they can also involve any of the other senses. The typical schizophrenic hallucination consists of voices talking to the person. Sometimes, the voices order the person to do something; sometimes, they scold the person for his or her unworthiness; sometimes, they just utter meaningless phrases. Olfactory hallucinations are also fairly common; often they contribute to the delusion that others are trying to kill the person with poison gas. (See ***Table 15.1.***)

Table 15.1

Positive and Negative Symptoms of Schizophrenia

Positive Symptom	Negative Symptom
Hallucinations	Flattened emotional response
Thought disorders	Poverty of speech
Delusions	Lack of initiative and persistence
Persecution	Anhedonia (inability to experience pleasure)
Grandeur	Social withdrawal
Control	

In contrast to the positive symptoms, the **negative symptoms** of schizophrenia are known by the absence of normal behaviors: flattened emotional response, poverty of speech, lack of initiative and persistence, inability to experience pleasure, and social withdrawal. Negative symptoms are not specific to schizophrenia; they are seen in many neurological disorders that involve brain damage, especially to the frontal lobes. As we will see later in this chapter, research suggests that these two sets of symptoms are caused by different abnormalities in the brain: Positive symptoms appear to involve excessive activity in some neural circuits that include dopamine as a neurotransmitter, and negative symptoms appear to be caused by developmental or degenerative processes that impair the normal functions of some regions of the brain. Recent evidence suggests that these two sets of symptoms may involve a common set of underlying causes. (See ***Table 15.1.***)

Heritability

One of the strongest pieces of evidence that schizophrenia is a biological disorder is that it appears to be heritable. Both adoption studies (Kety et al., 1968, 1994) and twin studies (Gottesman and Shields, 1982; Tsuang, Gilbertson, and Faraone, 1991) indicate that schizophrenia is a heritable trait.

If schizophrenia were a simple trait produced by a single gene, we would expect to see this disorder in at least 75 percent of the children of two schizophrenic parents if the gene were dominant. If it were recessive, *all* children of two schizophrenic parents should become schizophrenic. However, the actual incidence is less than 50 percent, which means either that several genes are involved or that having a "schizophrenia gene" imparts a *susceptibility* to develop schizophrenia, the disease itself being triggered by other factors.

So far, researchers have not yet located a "schizophrenia gene," although many candidates have been found. A review by Shastry (2002) notes that evidence for linkage to susceptibility for schizophrenia has been reported for chromosomes 1, 2, 4, 5, 6, 7, 8, 9, 10, 11, 13, 15, 18, 22, and X. (That includes all but 3, 12, 14, 16, 17, 19, 20, 21, and Y—at least, so far.) If susceptibility to schizophrenia is caused by a small number of genes, geneticists will undoubtedly succeed in finding them some day. Once they are found, other researchers will try to determine what role these genes play, which should provide useful information about the causes of schizophrenia.

Pharmacology of Schizophrenia: The Dopamine Hypothesis

Pharmacological evidence suggests that the positive symptoms of schizophrenia are caused by a biochemical disorder. The explanation that has received the most attention from researchers is the *dopamine hypothesis,* which suggests that schizophrenia is caused by overactivity of dopaminergic synapses, probably those in the mesolimbic pathway, which projects from the ventral tegmental area to the nucleus accumbens and amygdala.

Effects of Dopamine Agonists and Antagonists

Almost fifty years ago, a French surgeon named Henri Laborit discovered that a drug used to prevent surgical shock seemed also to reduce anxiety (Snyder, 1974). A French drug company developed a related compound called **chlorpromazine,** which seemed to be even more effective. The discovery of the antipsychotic effects of chlorpromazine profoundly altered the way in which physicians treated schizophrenic patients and made prolonged hospital stays unnecessary for many of them (the patients, that is).

Since the discovery of chlorpromazine, many other drugs have been developed that relieve the positive symptoms of schizophrenia. These drugs were found to

schizophrenia A serious mental disorder characterized by disordered thoughts, delusions, hallucinations, and often bizarre behaviors.

positive symptom A symptom of schizophrenia evident by its presence: delusions, hallucinations, or thought disorders.

thought disorder Disorganized, irrational thinking.

delusion A belief that is clearly in contradiction to reality.

hallucination Perception of a nonexistent object or event.

negative symptom A symptom of schizophrenia characterized by the absence of behaviors that are normally present: social withdrawal, lack of affect, and reduced motivation.

chlorpromazine A dopamine receptor blocker; a commonly prescribed antischizophrenic drug.

have one property in common: They block dopamine receptors (Creese, Burt, and Snyder, 1976). Other drugs that interfere with dopaminergic transmission, such as reserpine (which prevents the storage of monoamines in synaptic vesicles) or α-methyl *p*-tyrosine (which blocks the synthesis of dopamine), either facilitate the antipsychotic action of drugs such as chlorpromazine or themselves exert antipsychotic effects (Tamminga et al., 1988). Thus, the positive symptoms of schizophrenia are reduced by a variety of drugs with one common effect: antagonism of dopaminergic transmission.

Another category of drugs has the opposite effect, namely, *production* of the positive symptoms of schizophrenia. The drugs that can produce these symptoms have one known pharmacological effect in common: They act as dopamine agonists. These drugs include amphetamine, cocaine, and methylphenidate (which block the reuptake of dopamine) and L-DOPA (which stimulates the synthesis of dopamine). The symptoms that these drugs produce can be alleviated with antipsychotic drugs, a result that further strengthens the argument that the antipsychotic drugs exert their therapeutic effects by blocking dopamine receptors.

How might we explain the apparent link between overactivity of dopaminergic synapses and the positive symptoms of schizophrenia? Most researchers believe that the mesolimbic pathway, which begins in the ventral tegmental area and ends in the nucleus accumbens and amygdala, is more likely to be involved in the symptoms of schizophrenia. As we saw in Chapter 12, the activity of dopaminergic synapses in the nucleus accumbens appears to be a vital link in the process of reinforcement. Snyder (1974) notes that schizophrenics often report feelings of elation and euphoria at the beginning of a schizophrenic episode, when their symptoms flare up. Presumably, this euphoria is caused by hyperactivity of dopaminergic neurons involved in reinforcement.

The positive symptoms of schizophrenia also include disordered thinking and unpleasant, often terrifying delusions. The disordered thinking may be caused by disorganized attentional processes; the indiscriminate activity of the dopaminergic synapses in the nucleus accumbens makes it difficult for the patients to follow an orderly, rational thought sequence. Fibiger (1991) suggests that paranoid delusions may be caused by increased activity of the dopaminergic input to the amygdala. As we saw in Chapter 10, the central nucleus of the amygdala is involved with conditioned emotional responses elicited by aversive stimuli. The central nucleus receives a strong projection from the mesolimbic dopaminergic system, so Fibiger's suggestion is certainly plausible.

The Search for Abnormalities in Dopamine Transmission in the Brains of Schizophrenic Patients

Is there any evidence that dopaminergic activity in the brains of schizophrenic patients is indeed abnormal? Before I discuss the search for abnormalities, let's consider the possibilities. (These possibilities are based on what you learned about the pharmacology of neurons in Chapter 4.) Too much dopamine might be released, neurons that receive dopaminergic input could be excessively sensitive to this input, or a slow reuptake process in dopaminergic terminals could keep molecules of dopamine in the synaptic cleft for an unusually long time, resulting in prolonged activation of the postsynaptic dopamine receptors. (See ***Table 15.2.***)

Table 15.2

Possible Causes of Increased Dopaminergic Transmission in the Brains of Schizophrenic Patients
Increased dopamine release:
More excitatory input to dopaminergic neurons
Less inhibitory input to dopaminergic neurons
Fewer or defective autoreceptors on dopaminergic neurons
Increased postsynaptic response to dopamine release:
More postsynaptic dopamine receptors
More response in postsynaptic neuron to activation of dopamine receptors
Prolonged activation of postsynaptic receptors:
Decreased reuptake of dopamine by dopaminergic terminal button

Let's look at some of the evidence. Studies have found evidence that dopaminergic neurons in the brain of schizophrenic patients may indeed release more dopamine (Laruelle et al., 1996; Breier et al., 1997). Laruelle and colleagues used a device similar to a PET scanner to estimate the release of dopamine caused by an intravenous injection of amphetamine. As we saw in Chapter 4, amphetamine stimulates the release of dopamine, apparently by causing the dopamine transporters that are present in the terminal buttons to run backward, pumping dopamine out rather than retrieving it after it has been released. Of course, this effect inhibits the reuptake of dopamine as well. Laruelle and his colleagues found that the amphetamine caused the release of more dopamine in the striatum of schizophrenic patients. They also found that subjects with greater amounts of dopamine release showed greater increases in positive symptoms. (See ***Figure 15.1.***)

Another possibility—that the brains of schizophrenic patients contain a greater number of dopamine receptors—received much attention for several years. However, although some studies have found evidence for increased numbers of dopamine receptors, others have not; and some researchers suggest that the positive results may be caused by antipsychotic medication that the patients received. A review by Kestler, Walker, and Vega (2001) concludes that there might be moderate increases in the numbers of D_2 receptors in the brains of schizophrenics.

The older antipsychotic drugs certainly act as D_2 receptor antagonists, and they have a strong effect in the neostriatum. But the affinity for D_2 receptors does not necessarily account for the ability of these drugs to relieve the symptoms of schizophrenia. **Clozapine,** a more recently developed drug, is a very effective antipsychotic medication whose site of action is primarily in the nucleus accumbens (Kinon and Lieberman, 1996). This drug has little effect on D_2 receptors (Pickar, 1995), a feature that has earned it the label of *atypical* antischizophrenic medication. Clozapine serves as a potent blocker of D_4 dopamine receptor; in fact, it has ten times more affinity for

clozapine An atypical antipsychotic drug; blocks D_4 receptors in the nucleus accumbens.

Figure 15.1

Results of the study by Laruelle et al. (1996). (a) Relative amount of dopamine released in response to amphetamine. (b) Relationship between dopamine release and changes in positive symptoms of schizophrenic patients.

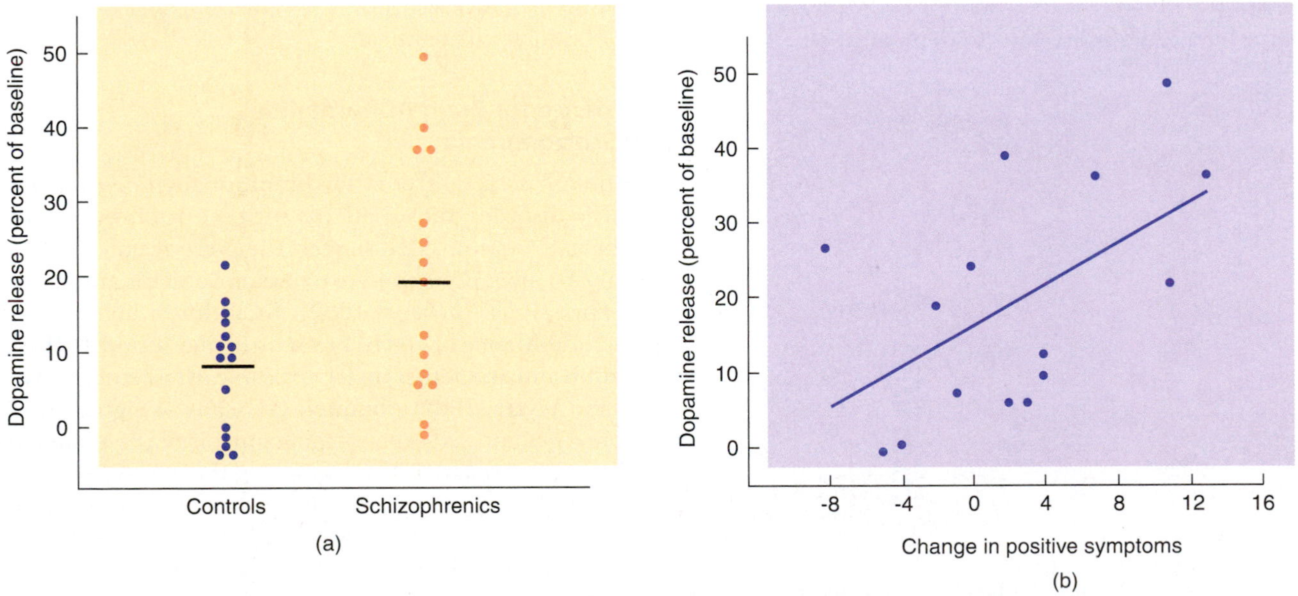

Adapted from Laruelle, M., Abi-Dargham, A., Van Dyck, C. H., Gil, R., D'Souza, C. D., Erdos, J., McCance, E., Rosenblatt, W., Fingado, C., Zoghbi, S. S., Baldwin, R. M., Seibyl, J. P., Krystal, J. H., Charney, D. S., and Innis, R. B. *Proceedings of the National Academy of Sciences, USA,* 1996, *93,* 9235–9240. Copyright 1996 National Academy of Sciences, USA.

Figure 15.2

Pseudocolor images of concentrations of D_3-receptor binding in the human striatum. (a) Control subject. (b) Unmedicated schizophrenic patient. (c) Schizophrenic patient receiving antipsychotic medication. Cd = caudate nucleus, Pt = putamen, NA = nucleus accumbens.

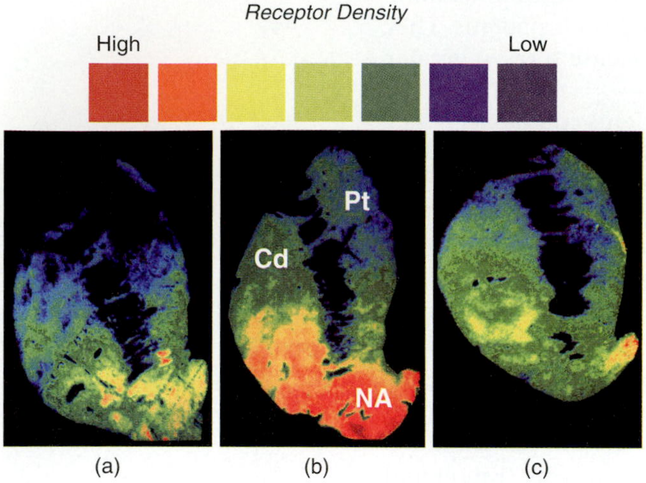

From Gurevich, E. V., Bordelon, Y., Shapiro, R. M., Arnold, S. E., Gur, R. E., and Joyce, J. N. *Archives of General Psychiatry,* 1997, *54,* 225–232.

D_4 receptors than for D_2 receptors (Van Tol et al., 1991). Consequently, researchers are beginning to turn their attention to these receptors. They are also beginning to examine the possible role of another dopamine receptor: the D_3 receptor, which is found in especially high concentrations in the human nucleus accumbens (Murray et al., 1994).

Two studies have found evidence for increased amounts of D_3 and D_4 dopamine receptors in the brains of deceased schizophrenics. Murray et al. (1995) found a twofold increase in the concentration of D_4 receptors in the nucleus accumbens. Gurevich et al. (1997) found a twofold increase in D_3 receptors in both the neostriatum and the nucleus accumbens of schizophrenic patients. The patients had been drug free for at least one month before their deaths, so the increased concentration of D_3 receptors is unlikely to have been caused by medication. (See ***Figure 15.2.***)

Schizophrenia as a Neurological Disorder

So far, I have been discussing the physiology of the positive symptoms of schizophrenia—principally, hallucinations, delusions, and thought disorders. These symptoms could very well be related to one of the known functions of dopaminergic neurons: reinforcement. But the negative symptoms of schizophrenia—flattened emotional response, poverty of speech, lack of initiative and persistence, inability to experience pleasure, and social withdrawal—are very different. Whereas the positive symptoms are unique to schizophrenia (and to amphetamine or cocaine psychosis), the negative symptoms are similar to those produced by brain damage caused by several different means. Many pieces of evidence suggest that the negative symptoms of schizophrenia are indeed a result of brain abnormalities.

Figure 15.3

Relative ventricular size in chronic schizophrenics and controls.

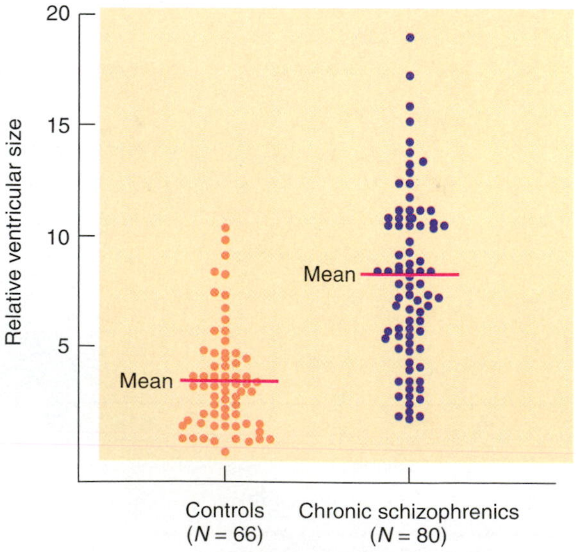

From Weinberger, D. R., and Wyatt, R. J., in *Schizophrenia as a Brain Disease,* edited by F. A. Henn and H. A. Nasrallah. New York: Oxford University Press, 1982. Reprinted with permission.

Evidence for Brain Abnormalities in Schizophrenia

Although schizophrenia has traditionally been labeled a psychiatric disorder, most patients with schizophrenia exhibit neurological symptoms that suggest the presence of brain damage—in particular, poor control of eye movements and unusual facial expressions (Stevens, 1982). In addition, many studies have found evidence of loss of brain tissue in CT and MRI scans of schizophrenic patients. In one of the earliest studies, Weinberger and Wyatt (1982) obtained CT scans of eighty chronic schizophrenics and sixty-six normal controls of the same mean age (twenty-nine years). They found that the relative size of the lateral ventricles of the schizophrenic patients was more than twice as great as that of the normal control subjects. (See ***Figure 15.3.***) The most likely cause of the enlarged ventricles is loss of brain tissue; thus, the CT scans provide evidence that chronic schizophrenia is associated with brain abnormalities. In fact, Hulshoff-Pol et al. (2002) found that although everyone loses some cerebral gray matter as they age, the rate of tissue loss is greater in schizophrenic patients. (See ***Figure 15.4.***)

Possible Causes of the Brain Abnormalities

As we saw earlier, schizophrenia is a heritable disease, but its heritability is less than perfect. Why do fewer than half the children of parents with chronic schizophrenia become schizophrenic? Perhaps what is inherited is a defect that renders people susceptible to some environmental factors that adversely affect brain development or cause brain damage later in life. Let's look at the evidence concerning environmental factors that increase the risk of schizophrenia.

Epidemiological Studies. **Epidemiology** is the study of the distribution and causes of diseases in populations. Thus, epidemiological studies examine the relative frequency of diseases in groups of people in different environments and try to correlate the disease frequencies with factors that are present in these environments. Evidence from these studies indicates that the incidence of schizophrenia is related to several environmental factors, including season of birth, viral epidemics, population density, Rh incompatibility, and maternal stress. Let's examine each of these factors in turn.

Many studies have shown that people born during the late winter and early spring are more likely to develop schizophrenia—a phenomenon known as the **seasonality effect.** For example, Kendell and Adams (1991) studied the month of birth of over 13,000 schizophrenic patients born in Scotland between 1914 and 1960. They found that disproportionately more patients were born in February, March, April, and May. (See ***Figure 15.5.***)

What factors might be responsible for the seasonality effect? One possibility is that pregnant women may be more likely to contract a viral illness during a critical phase of their infants' development. The brain development of their fetuses may be adversely affected either by a toxin produced by the virus or by the mother's antibodies against the virus. As Pallast et al. (1994) note, the winter flu season coincides with the second trimester of pregnancy of babies born in late winter and early spring. (As we shall see later, evidence suggests that critical aspects of brain development occur during the second trimester.) In fact, Kendell and Adams (1991) found that the

epidemiology The study of the distribution and causes of diseases in populations.

seasonality effect The increased incidence of schizophrenia in people born during late winter and early spring.

Figure 15.4

Changes in volume of cerebral gray matter with age in normal subjects and people with schizophrenia.

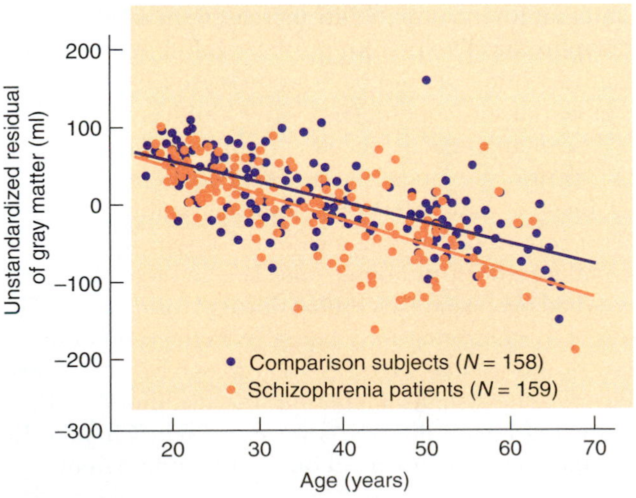

Adapted from Hulshoff-Pol, H. E., Schnack, H. G., Bertens, M. G. B. C., van Haren, N. E. M., Staal, W. G., Baaré, W. F. C., and Kahn, R. S. *American Journal of Psychiatry,* 2002, *159,* 244–250.

Figure 15.5

The seasonality effect. The graph shows the number of schizophrenic births per 10,000 live births.

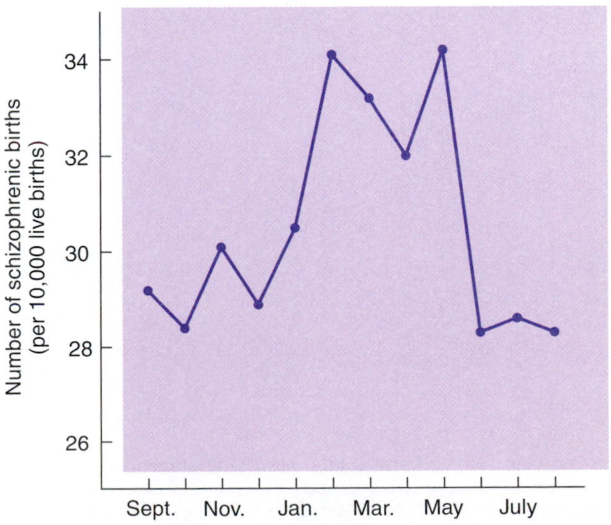

Based on data from Kendell, R. E., and Adams, W. *British Journal of Psychiatry,* 1991, *158,* 758–763.

Epidemiological studies have provided important information about the possible causes of schizophrenia. For example, the fact that schizophrenia is more prevalent in crowded urban areas with cold winter climates suggests that viral infections may play a role.

relative number of schizophrenic births in late winter and early spring was especially high if the temperature was lower than normal during the previous autumn—a condition that keeps people indoors and favors the transmission of viral illnesses.

Several studies have found that the seasonality effect occurs primarily in cities but is rarely found in the countryside. In fact, the likelihood of developing schizophrenia is approximately three times higher in people who live in the middle of large cities than in those who live in rural areas (Eaton, Mortensen, and Frydenberg, 2000). Because viruses are more readily transmitted in regions with high population densities, this finding is consistent with the hypothesis that at least one of the causes of the seasonality effect is exposure of pregnant women to viral illnesses during the second trimester.

If the viral hypothesis is true, then an increased incidence of schizophrenia should be seen in babies born a few months after an influenza epidemic, whatever the season. Several studies have observed just that. For example, Sham et al. (1992) studied the medical histories of infants born to mothers who were pregnant during several influenza epidemics in England and Wales between 1939 and 1960. As Figure 15.6 shows, the number of schizophrenic births peaked five months after the start of the epidemic, which means that the greatest susceptibility appears to occur during the second trimester of pregnancy. (See ***Figure 15.6.***)

Figure 15.6

Average number of schizophrenic births in each of the ten months following an influenza epidemic in England and Wales between 1939 and 1960.

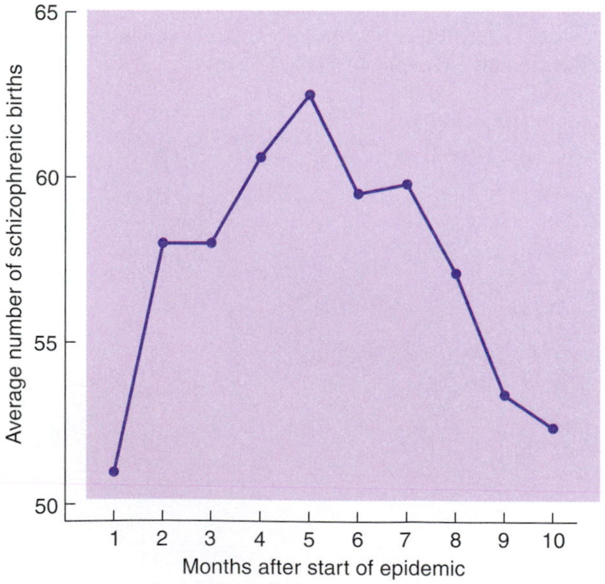

Adapted from Sham, P. C., O'Callaghan, E., Takei, N., Murray, G. K., Hare, E. H., and Murray, R. M. *British Journal of Psychiatry,* 1992, *160,* 461–466. Reprinted with permission.

Rh incompatibility may be another prenatal condition that increases the risk of schizophrenia. The red blood cells of an Rh-positive person contain a protein—the Rh factor—while those of an Rh-negative person do not. If an RH-negative woman is pregnant with an Rh-positive fetus, her immune system will begin to produce antibodies against the protein. If the woman carries another Rh-positive fetus during a subsequent pregnancy, her Rh antibodies will attach the fetus's red blood cells, causing anemia. Hollister, Laing, and Mednick (1996) found that Rh incompatibility increased the likelihood of schizophrenia. The first Rh-positive child born to an Rh-negative mother did not have an increased risk of schizophrenia, but subsequent Rh-positive children did.

The final prenatal effect that I will mention may be independent of the ones I have described so far, or it may also involve viral infections. Huttunen and Niskanen (1978) reported a higher incidence of schizophrenia in the children born to women who learned that their husbands had been killed in combat during World War II. The stress of this news may have had direct effects on development of the women's fetuses, or it may have suppressed their immune systems, increasing the likelihood of their contracting a viral illness. As we will see in Chapter 16, stress has an inhibitory effect on the immune system.

Evidence for Abnormal Brain Development. Is there any direct evidence that abnormal prenatal development is associated with schizophrenia? The answer is yes; studies have reported evidence for developmental abnormalities. Walker and her colleagues (Walker, Savoie, and Davis, 1994; Walker, Lewine, and Neumann, 1996) obtained home movies from families with a schizophrenic child. They had independent observers examine the behavior of the children. In comparison with their normal siblings the children who subsequently became schizophrenic displayed more negative affect in their facial expressions and were more likely to show abnormal movements. (The ratings were done blind; the observers did not know which children subsequently became schizophrenic.) In addition, a study by Cannon et al. (1997) found that children who later became schizophrenic had poorer social adjustment and did more poorly in school. These studies suggest that the prenatal brain development of the children who became schizophrenic was not entirely normal.

Table 15.3

Examples of Minor Physical Abnormalities Associated with Schizophrenia

Location	Description
Head	Two or more hair whorls
	Head circumference outside normal range
Eyes	Skin fold at inner corner of eye
	Wide-set eyes
Ears	Low-seated ears
	Asymmetrical ears
Mouth	High-steepled palate
	Furrowed tongue
Hands	Curved fifth finger
	Single transverse crease in palm
Feet	Third toe longer than second toe
	Partial webbing of two middle toes

Source: Adapted from Schiffman, J., Ekstrom, M., LaBrie, J., Schulsinger, F., Sorensen, H., and Mednick, S. *American Journal of Psychiatry,* 2002, *159,* 238–243.

Minor physical anomalies, such as a high-steepled palate or especially wide-set or narrow-set eyes, have also been shown to be associated with the incidence of schizophrenia (Schiffman et al., 2002). (See ***Table 15.3.***) These differences were first reported in the late nineteenth century by Kraepelin, one of the pioneers in schizophrenia research. As Schiffman and his colleagues note, these anomalies provide evidence of factors that have adverse effects on development. They found that people with schizophrenic relatives normally have an 11.9 percent likelihood of developing schizophrenia. This likelihood increases to 30.8 percent in people who also have minor physical anomalies; thus, the factors that produce minor physical anomalies are independent of the genetic factors associated with schizophrenia.

Some monozygotic twins are discordant for schizophrenia; that is, one of them develops schizophrenia, and the other does not. In the past most researchers assumed that discordance for schizophrenia in monozygotic twins must be caused by differential exposure to some environmental factors after birth. Not only are monozygotic twins genetically identical, but they also share the same intrauterine environment. However, some investigators have pointed out that the prenatal environment of monozygotic twins is *not* identical. In fact, there are two types of monozygotic twins: monochorionic and dichorionic. The formation of monozygotic twins occurs when the blastocyst (the developing organism) splits in two—when it clones itself. If twinning occurs before day 4, the two organisms develop independently, each forming its own placenta. (That is, the twins are *dichorionic.* The *chorion* is the outer layer of the blastocyst, which gives rise to the placenta.) If twinning occurs after day 4, the two organisms become *monochorionic,* sharing a single placenta. (See ***Figure 15.7.***)

The placenta transports nutrients to the developing organism from the mother's circulation and transports waste products to her, which she metabolizes in her liver or excretes in her urine. It also constitutes the barrier through which toxins or infectious agents must pass if they are to affect fetal development. The prenatal environments of monochorionic twins, who share a single placenta, are obviously more similar than those of dichorionic twins. Thus, we might expect that the concordance rates for schizophrenia of *monochorionic* monozygotic twins should be higher than those of *dichorionic* monozygotic twins. In fact, they are. Davis, Phelps, and Bracha (1995) found that the concordance rate for schizophrenia was 10.7 percent in the dichorionic twins and 60 percent in the monochorionic twins. These results provide

Figure 15.7

Monozygotic twins. (a) Monochorionic twins, sharing a single placenta. (b) Dichorionic twins, each with its own placenta.

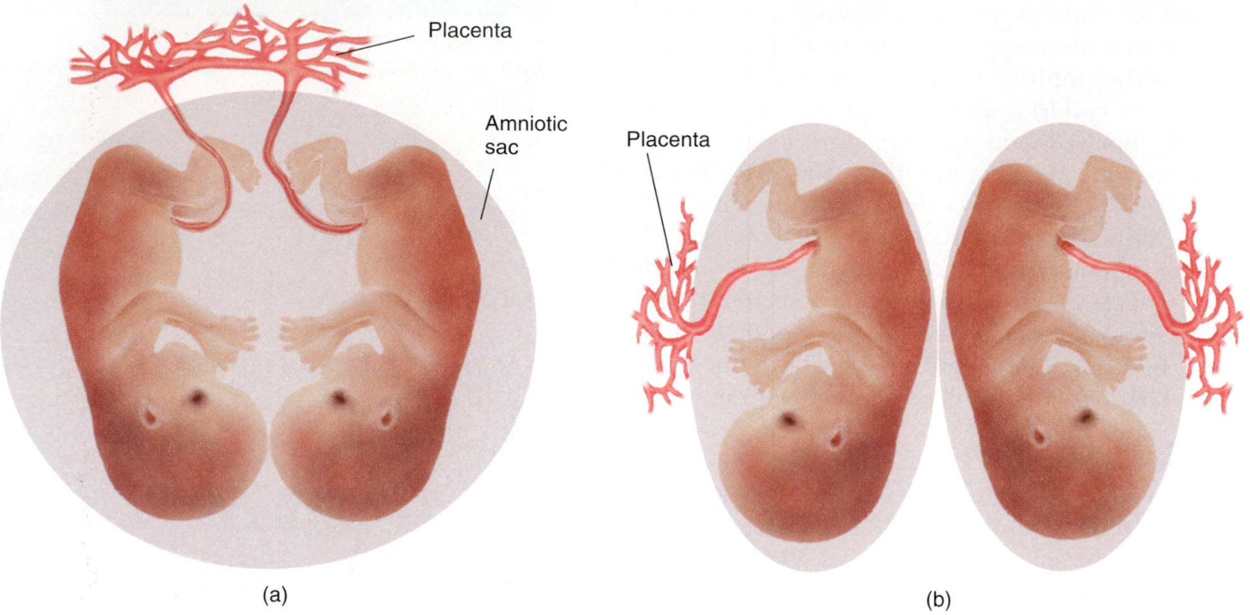

strong evidence for an interaction between heredity and environment during prenatal development.

Although studies have found that people who develop schizophrenia show some abnormalities even during childhood, the symptoms of schizophrenia itself rarely occur before late adolescence or early adulthood. (They also rarely first occur later in life.) Figure 15.8 shows a graph of the ages of first signs of mental disorder in males and females diagnosed with schizophrenia. (See ***Figure 15.8.***) Even if most cases of schizophrenia involve abnormalities in prenatal brain development, something else must happen later in life to cause the onset of schizophrenic symptoms.

Figure 15.8

Age at first sign of psychotic symptoms in schizophrenic patients.

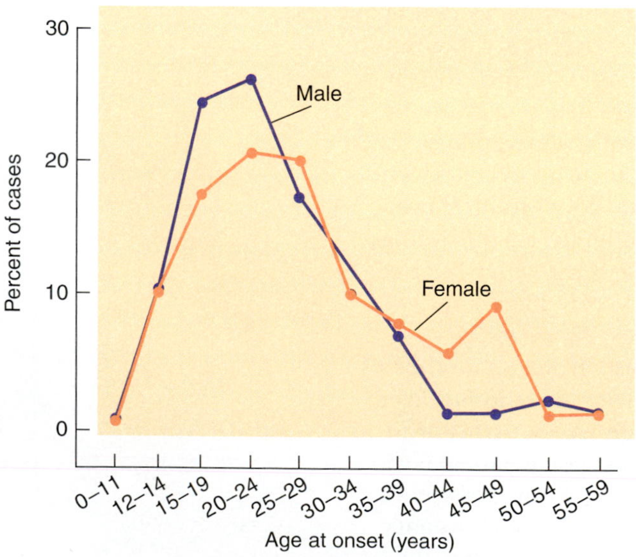

Adapted from Häfner H., Riecher-Rössler A., an der Heiden W., Maurer K., Fätkenheuer B., and Löffler W. *Psychological Medicine,* 1993, *23,* 925–940.

In a review of the literature, Woods (1998) notes that MRI studies suggest that schizophrenia is not caused by a degenerative process, as are Parkinson's disease, Huntington's disease, or Alzheimer's disease, in which neurons continue to die over a period of years. Instead, a sudden, rapid loss of brain volume occurs during young adulthood, with little evidence for continuing degeneration. Woods suggests that the disease process of schizophrenia begins prenatally and then lies dormant until puberty, when some unknown mechanism triggers degeneration of some population of neurons. The brain abnormalities that develop prenatally account for the deficits in social behavior and poor academic performance seen in people who later become schizophrenic. Then, sometime after puberty, when many developmental changes occur in the brain, more serious degeneration occurs, and the symptoms of schizophrenia begin to appear.

A study by Thompson et al. (2001) found dramatic evidence for loss of cortical gray matter during adolescence in patients with early-onset schizophrenia. The investigators used MRI procedures to measure the volume of the gray matter of the cerebral cortex at two-year intervals in schizophrenic patients and control subjects. Adolescence is a time when some synaptic "pruning" takes place in the brain, and the MRI scans showed an expected loss of cortical gray matter in nonschizophrenic subjects of about 0.5–1.0 percent. However, the loss of tissue was approximately twice as large in schizophrenic subjects. The degeneration started in the parietal lobes, and the wave of destruction continued rostrally, including the temporal lobes, somatosensory and motor cortex, and dorsolateral prefrontal cortex. The symptoms shown by the patients were associated with the cortical regions that were undergoing tissue loss. For example, auditory hallucinations occurred with changes in the temporal lobes, and their severity was correlated with the amount of tissue that was lost. Figure 15.9 shows the regions of the brain that underwent the greatest amount of tissue loss. (See ***Figure 15.9.***)

Figure 15.9

Average annual rate of loss of cortical gray matter in normal and schizophrenic adolescents.

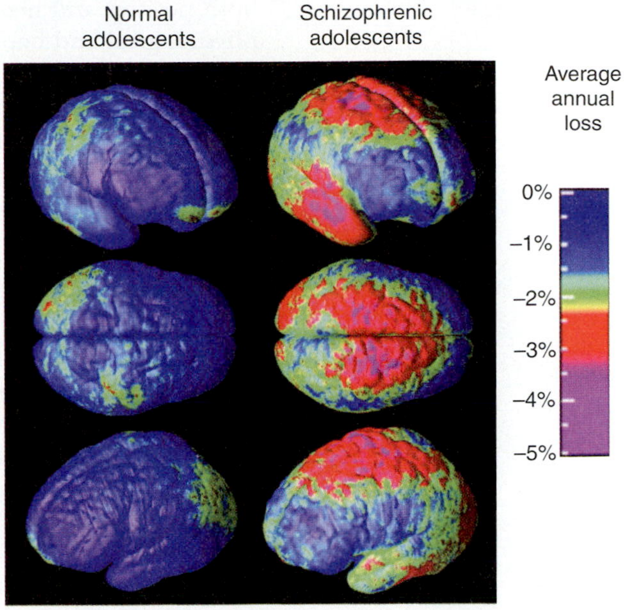

From Thompson, P. M., Vidal, C., Giedd, J. N., Gochman, P., Blumenthal, J., Nicolson, R., Toga, A. W., and Rapoport, J. L. *Proceedings of the National Academy of Science, USA,* 2001, *98,* 11650–11655. Copyright 2001 National Academy of Sciences, USA.

The evidence I have cited so far suggests that the most important cause of schizophrenia is disturbance of normal prenatal brain development. Presumably, genetic factors make some fetuses more sensitive to events that can disturb development. There is good evidence that obstetric complications can also cause schizophrenia. In fact, several studies have found that if a schizophrenic person does *not* have relatives with a schizophrenic disorder, that person is more likely to have had a history of complications at or around the time of childbirth, and the person is more likely to develop the schizophrenic symptoms at an earlier age (Schwarzkopf et al., 1989; O'Callaghan et al., 1992; Cannon, Jones, and Murray, 2002.) In other words, if the schizophrenia is not a result of genetic factors, then nongenetic factors such as obstetric complications are the most likely cause. Thus, brain damage that is *not related to heredity* may also be a cause of schizophrenia.

Relationship Between Positive and Negative Symptoms: Role of the Prefrontal Cortex

As we saw, schizophrenia has both positive and negative symptoms. The positive symptoms may be caused by hyperactivity of dopaminergic synapses, and the negative symptoms may be caused by brain abnormalities. Is there a relationship between the two categories of schizophrenic symptoms? An accumulating amount of evidence suggests that the causes of positive and negative symptoms may indeed be related.

Weinberger (1988) suggested that the negative symptoms of schizophrenia are caused primarily by **hypofrontality,** decreased activity of the frontal lobes—in particular, of the dorsolateral prefrontal cortex. Many studies have shown that schizophrenic patients do poorly on neuropsychological tests that are sensitive to prefrontal damage. In a review of the literature, Taylor (1996) found that most functional imaging studies of the prefrontal cortex of schizophrenic patients found evidence for decreased activity, particularly when the patients were being challenged by tasks that require the use of the prefrontal cortex.

hypofrontality Decreased activity of the prefrontal cortex; believed to be responsible for the negative symptoms of schizophrenia.

As we saw, dopamine agonists such as cocaine and amphetamine can cause positive symptoms of schizophrenia. Two other drugs, PCP (phencyclidine, also known as "angel dust") and ketamine ("Special K"), can cause both positive and negative symptoms of schizophrenia (Adler et al., 1999; Lahti et al., 2001; Avila et al., 2002). Chronic abuse of PCP impairs a person's working memory; causes deficits in attention; decreases drive; interferes with planning; and causes thought disorders, hallucinations, and delusions (Javitt and Zukin, 1991). Because PCP and ketamine elicit both positive and negative symptoms, many researchers believe that studying the physiological and behavioral effects of these drugs will help to solve the puzzle of schizophrenia.

The negative symptoms caused by chronic abuse of PCP are apparently a result of decreased metabolic activity of the frontal lobes (Hertzmann, Reba, and Kotlyarov, 1990; Wu, Buchsbaum, and Bunney, 1991). Jentsch et al. (1997) found that chronic administration of PCP (twice a day for two weeks) impaired the performance of monkeys on an object-retrieval task that is sensitive to prefrontal damage. They also found that the atypical antipsychotic drug clozapine, which reduces both the positive and negative symptoms of schizophrenia, improved the performance of the treated monkeys on this task.

What is the relationship between hypoactivity of the prefrontal cortex and the positive symptoms of schizophrenia, which appear to be produced by hyperactivity of dopaminergic synapses in the nucleus accumbens? Several investigators have suggested that the events are linked—that decreased prefrontal activity causes mesolimbic dopamine hyperactivity (Weinberger, 1988; Grace, 1991; Deutch, 1992). The primary effects of PCP appear to take place in the prefrontal cortex; Jentsch et al. (1998) found that infusing PCP directly into the prefrontal cortex increased the level of dopamine utilization in the nucleus accumbens. Neurons of the prefrontal cortex send axons to the ventral tegmental area, where they form synapses with GABA-secreting neurons that project to the nucleus accumbens (Carr and Sesack, 2000). Jackson, Frost, and Moghaddam (2001) found that electrical stimulation of the prefrontal cortex inhibited the release of dopamine in the nucleus accumbens, as measured by microdialysis. It makes sense, then, that decreased activity of the prefrontal cortex causes an increase in the release of dopamine in the nucleus accumbens. (See ***Figure 15.10.***)

The studies I have cited suggest that schizophrenia may begin with brain abnormalities that cause hypofrontality—perhaps by reducing the volume of the gray matter in the dorsolateral prefrontal cortex. The hypofrontality produces the negative symptoms of schizophrenia. It also causes an increase in the activity of the dopaminergic neurons in the mesolimbic system, which produces positive symptoms. (See ***Figure 15.11.***) If this hypothesis is true, then we might expect to see structural or biochemical abnormalities in the prefrontal cortex of schizophrenic patients. Indeed, as we saw earlier, the volume of gray matter in several regions of the cerebral cortex of schizophrenic patients significantly declines during adolescence.

The PCP model of schizophrenia has stimulated research that could lead to the development of more drugs that can be used to treat this disorder. First, let's look at the site of action of PCP. PCP acts as an indirect (noncompetitive) antagonist for NMDA receptors. It binds with a site on the NMDA receptor and prevents the ion channel from opening, even if glutamate—the neurotransmitter that binds with this receptor—is present. (As we saw in Chapter 12, NMDA receptors are involved in synaptic plasticity. Whether this special property of the NMDA receptor is relevant in this context is not known.)

If disrupting the activity of NMDA receptors causes the symptoms of schizophrenia, then we might expect drugs that act as NMDA agonists to reduce these symptoms. Unfortunately, direct NMDA agonists (such as NMDA itself) cannot be used, because they increase the risk of seizures and might even

Figure 15.10

Effects of electrical stimulation of the prefrontal cortex on the release of dopamine in the nucleus accumbens (NAC), as measured by microdialysis.

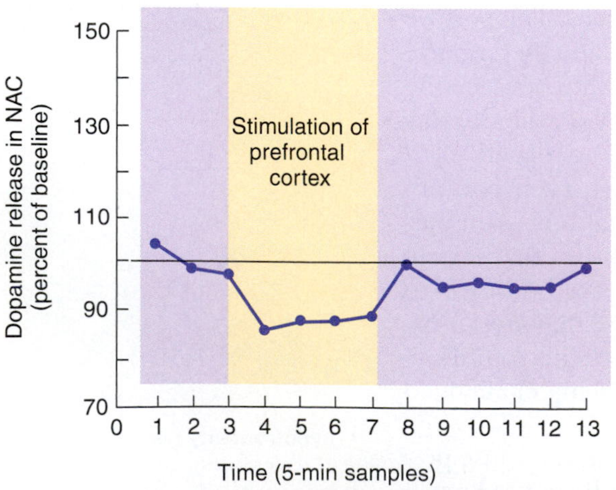

Adapted from Jackson, M. E., Frost, A. D., and Moghaddam, B. *Journal of Neurochemistry,* 2001, *78,* 920–923.

cause brain abnormalities. But you might remember from Chapter 4 that NMDA receptors have several other sites to which ligands can bind, besides the glutamate site and the PCP site. Glycine binds to one of these sites, where it acts as an indirect agonist. Normally, adequate amounts of glycine are present, but it is possible that increasing the level of glycine or administering a glycine agonist might facilitate NMDA activity and reduce schizophrenic symptoms. Several studies have found exactly that. (See Tsai and Coyle, 2002, for a review.) In a double-blind, randomized clinical trial, Goff et al. (1999) found that D-cycloserine, a glycine agonist, improved negative symptoms of schizophrenic patients. In another double-blind study, Heresco-Levy et al. (1999) found that very large doses of oral glycine reduced patients' negative (but not positive) symptoms. The large doses were necessary because only a small percentage of the glycine crossed the blood–brain barrier. (See ***Figure 15.12.***)

Before I conclude this section, I want to mention an interesting sidelight that might have some relevance to the causes of schizophrenia. As we saw, ketamine and PCP have similar effects. Ketamine is used as an anesthetic for children and animals. It is not often used as an anesthetic in adult humans because it produces episodes of psychosis when the person awakens after the surgery. Ketamine does not have this effect in prepubertal children (Marshall and Longnecker, 1990). (You might recall that THC, the active ingredient of marijuana, does not have a psychotropic effect in children either.) No one knows why ketamine (and probably PCP) produces psychotic behavior only in adults; perhaps the explanation is related to the fact that the symptoms of schizophrenia also emerge after puberty. Whatever developmental changes occur after puberty that make the brain susceptible to the psychotic effects of NMDA antagonists may also be related to the emergence of symptoms of schizophrenia at this time.

Farber et al. (1995) found that large doses of another noncompetitive NMDA antagonist, MK-801, produced brain abnormalities when given to adult rats but not to prepubertal rats. Between the age of puberty and full adulthood, the animals' brains became more and more sensitive to the effects of the drug. These findings support the hypothesis that developmental changes that begin around the time of puberty may play a role in the development of schizophrenia.

Figure 15.11

A hypothetical explanation for the role of the dorsolateral prefrontal cortex in positive and negative symptoms of schizophrenia.

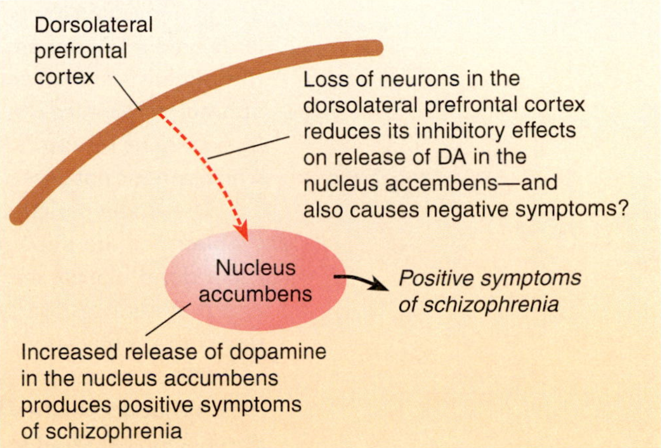

Figure 15.12

Effects of large doses of oral glycine on the negative symptoms of schizophrenia. Individual curves represent individual patients.

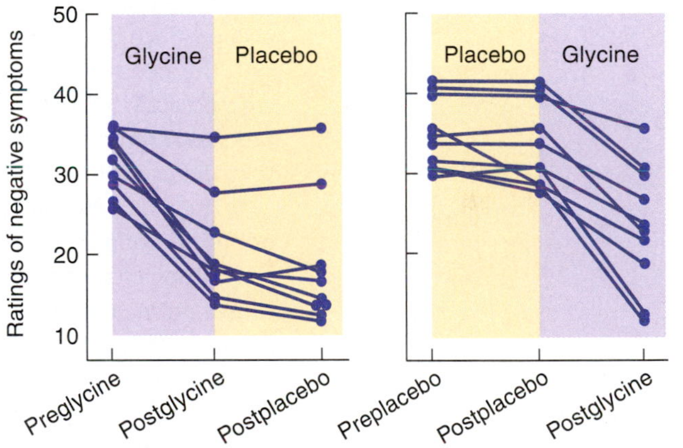

Adapted from Heresco-Levy, U., Javitt, D. C., Ermilov, M., Mordel, C., Silipo, G., and Lichtenstein, M. *Archives of General Psychiatry,* 1999, *56,* 29–36.

INTERIM SUMMARY

Schizophrenia

Researchers have made considerable progress in the past few years in their study of the physiology of mental disorders, but many puzzles still remain. Schizophrenia consists of positive and negative symptoms, the former involving the presence of unusual behavior and the latter involving the absence of normal behavior. Because schizophrenia is at least somewhat heritable, it appears to have a biological basis.

The dopamine hypothesis—inspired by the findings that dopamine antagonists alleviate the positive symptoms of schizophrenia and that dopamine agonists increase or even produce them—has received much attention from researchers. This hypothesis states that the positive symptoms of schizophrenia are caused by hyperactivity of dopaminergic synapses. Paranoid thoughts may be caused by dopaminergic activation of the central nucleus of the amygdala, a region involved in negative emotional responses. There is no evidence that an abnormally large amount of dopamine is released under resting conditions, but PET studies indicate that the administration of amphetamine causes a larger release of dopamine in the brains of schizophrenics. Evidence that the brains of schizophrenic patients contain increased numbers of D_2 dopamine receptors is mixed. Studies suggest that the nucleus accumbens in the brains of schizophrenic patients may contain increased numbers of D_3 or D_4 dopamine receptors.

That some patients are not helped by "classic" antipsychotic drugs poses an unsolved problem for the dopamine hypothesis. Atypical antipsychotic drugs, including clozapine, risperidone, olanzapine, and amisulpride, reduce both positive symptoms and negative ones, and they reduces the symptoms of some patients who are not helped by traditional antipsychotic medication.

MRI scans and the presence of signs of neurological impairments indicate the presence of brain abnormalities in schizophrenic patients. Studies of the epidemiology of schizophrenia indicate that season of birth, viral epidemics during pregnancy, population density, Rh incompatibility, and prenatal stress all contribute to the occurrence of schizophrenia. In addition, home movies of children who later became schizophrenic indicate the early presence of abnormalities in movements and facial expressions. All these factors provide evidence for problems with prenatal development. The higher concordance rate of monochorionic monozygotic twins provides further evidence that hereditary and prenatal environmental factors may interact.

The symptoms of schizophrenia usually emerge soon after puberty, when the brain is undergoing important maturational changes. Some investigators believe that the disease process of schizophrenia begins prenatally, lies dormant until puberty, and then causes a period of neural degeneration that causes the symptoms to appear. Obstetric complications can also produce the symptoms of schizophrenia.

The negative symptoms of schizophrenia appear to be a result of hypofrontality (decreased activity of the dorsolateral prefrontal cortex). Schizophrenic patients do poorly on tasks that require activity of the prefrontal cortex, and functional imaging studies indicate that the prefrontal cortex is hypoactive when the patients attempt to perform these tasks.

The drugs PCP and ketamine mimics both the positive and negative symptoms of schizophrenia. Long-term administration of PCP to monkeys disrupts their performance of an object-retrieval task that requires the prefrontal cortex. Evidence suggests that hypofrontality causes an increase in the activity of dopaminergic neurons in the mesolimbic system, thus producing the positive symptoms of schizophrenia. Connections between the prefrontal cortex and the ventral tegmental area appear to be responsible for this phenomenon. Clozapine reduces hypofrontality, increases the performance of monkeys on the object retrieval task, and decreases the release of dopamine in the ventral tegmental area—and decreases both the positive and negative symptoms of schizophrenia.

PCP and ketamine act as indirect antagonists for NMDA receptors. Glycine and D-cycloserine, which serve as NMDA receptor agonists, produce modest reductions in negative symptoms of schizophrenia, providing further support for the PCP model of this disorder. Ketamine causes psychotic reactions in adults but not children. Another indirect NMDA antagonist causes brain abnormalities in adult, but not juvenile, rats. These disparities may be related to the apparent changes in the brain that are responsible for the emergence of the symptoms of schizophrenia after puberty.

THOUGHT QUESTION

Suppose that a young schizophrenic woman insists on living in the streets and refuses to take antipsychotic medication. She is severely disturbed; she is undernourished and often takes intravenous drugs, which expose her to the risk of AIDS. Her parents have tried to get her to seek help, but she believes that they are plotting against her. Suppose further that we can predict with 90 percent accuracy that she will die within a few years. She is not violent, and she has never talked about committing suicide, so we cannot prove that her behavior constitutes an immediate threat to herself or to others. Should her parents be able to force her to receive treatment, or does she have an absolute right to be left alone, even if she is mentally ill?

Major Affective Disorders

Affect, as a noun, refers to feelings or emotions. Just as the primary symptom of schizophrenia is disordered thoughts, the **major affective disorders** (also called *mood disorders*) are characterized by disordered feelings.

Description

Feelings and emotions are essential parts of human existence; they represent our evaluation of the events in our lives. In a very real sense, feelings and emotions are what human life is all about. The emotional state of most of us reflects what is happening to us: Our feelings are tied to events in the real world, and they are usually the result of reasonable assessments of the importance these events have for our lives. But for some people, affect becomes divorced from reality. These people have feelings of extreme elation (*mania*) or despair (*depression*) that are not justified by events in their lives. For example, depression that accompanies the loss of a loved one is normal, but depression that becomes a way of life—and will not respond to the sympathetic effort of friends and relatives or even to psychotherapy—is pathological.

There are two principal types of major affective disorders. The first type is characterized by alternating periods of mania and depression—a condition called **bipolar disorder.** This disorder afflicts men and women in approximately equal numbers. Episodes of mania can last a few days or several months, but they usually take a few weeks to run their course. The episodes of depression that follow generally last three times as long as the mania. The second type is **unipolar depression,** or depression without mania. This depression may be continuous and unremitting or, more typically,

major affective disorder A serious mood disorder; includes unipolar depression and bipolar disorder.

bipolar disorder A serious mood disorder characterized by cyclical periods of mania and depression.

unipolar depression A serious mood disorder that consists of unremitting depression or periods of depression that do not alternate with periods of mania.

Normally, our feelings and emotions are tied to events that affect us. People with depression feel sad, unworthy, and guilty independent of events in their daily lives.

may come in episodes. Unipolar depression strikes women two to three times more often than men. Mania without periods of depression sometimes occurs, but it is rare.

Severely depressed people usually feel extremely unworthy and have strong feelings of guilt. The affective disorders are dangerous; a person who suffers from a major affective disorder runs a considerable risk of death by suicide. According to Chen and Dilsaver (1996), 15.9 percent of people with unipolar depression and 29.2 percent of people with bipolar disorder attempt to commit suicide. Schneider, Muller, and Philipp (2001) found that the rate of death by unnatural causes (not all suicides are diagnosed as such) for people with affective disorders was 28.8 times higher than expected for people of the same age in the general population. Depressed people have very little energy, and they move and talk slowly, sometimes becoming almost torpid. At other times they may pace around restlessly and aimlessly. They may cry a lot. They are unable to experience pleasure; they lose their appetite for food and sex. Their sleep is disturbed; they usually have difficulty falling asleep and awaken early and find it difficult to get to sleep again. Even their body functions become depressed; they often become constipated, and secretion of saliva decreases.

> [A psychiatrist] asked me if I was suicidal, and I reluctantly told him yes. I did not particularize—since there seemed no need to—did not tell him that in truth many of the artifacts of my house had become potential devices for my own destruction: the attic rafters (and an outside maple or two) a means to hang myself, the garage a place to inhale carbon monoxide, the bathtub a vessel to receive the flow from my opened arteries. The kitchen knives in their drawers had but one purpose for me. Death by heart attack seemed particularly inviting, absolving me as it would of active responsibility, and I had toyed with the idea of self-induced pneumonia—a long frigid, shirt-sleeved hike through the rainy woods. Nor had I overlooked an ostensible accident . . . by walking in front of a truck on the highway nearby. . . . Such hideous fantasies, which cause well people to shudder, are to the deeply depressed mind what lascivious daydreams are to persons of robust sexuality. (Styron, 1990, pp. 52–53)

Episodes of mania are characterized by a sense of euphoria that does not seem to be justified by circumstances. The diagnosis of mania is partly a matter of degree; one would not call exuberance and a zest for life pathological. People with mania usually exhibit nonstop speech and motor activity. They flit from topic to topic and often have delusions, but they lack the severe disorganization that is seen in schizophrenia. They are usually full of their own importance and often become angry or defensive if they are contradicted. Frequently, they go for long periods without sleep, working furiously on projects that are often unrealistic. (Sometimes, their work is fruitful; George Frideric Handel wrote *Messiah,* one of the masterpieces of choral music, during one of his periods of mania.)

Heritability

The tendency to develop an affective disorder appears to be heritable. (See Moldin, Reich, and Rice, 1991, for a review.) For example, Rosenthal (1971) found that close relatives of people who suffer from affective psychoses are ten times more likely to develop these disorders than are people without afflicted relatives. Gershon et al. (1976) found that if one member of a set of monozygotic twins was afflicted with an affective disorder, the likelihood that the other twin was similarly afflicted was 69 percent. In contrast, the concordance rate for dizygotic twins was only 13 percent. Furthermore, the concordance rate for monozygotic twins appears to be the same whether the twins were raised together or apart (Price, 1968). The heritability of the affective disorders implies that they have a physiological basis.

Physiological Treatments

There are four effective biological treatments for unipolar depression: monoamine oxidase (MAO) inhibitors, drugs that inhibit the reuptake of norepinephrine or serotonin, electroconvulsive therapy (ECT), and sleep deprivation. (Sleep deprivation is discussed in a later section.) Bipolar disorder can be effectively treated by lithium and some anticonvulsant drugs. The fact that these disorders respond to medical treatment provides additional evidence that they have a physiological basis. Furthermore, the fact that lithium is very effective in treating bipolar affective disorders but not unipolar depression suggests that there is a fundamental difference between these two illnesses (Soares and Gershon, 1998).

Before the 1950s there was no effective drug treatment for depression. In the late 1940s clinicians noticed that some drugs used for treating tuberculosis seemed to elevate the patient's mood. Researchers subsequently found that a derivative of these drugs, iproniazid, reduced symptoms of psychotic depression (Crane, 1957). Iproniazid inhibits the activity of MAO, which destroys excess monoamine transmitter substances within terminal buttons. Thus, the drug increases the release of dopamine, norepinephrine, and serotonin. Other MAO inhibitors were soon discovered. Unfortunately, MAO inhibitors can have harmful side effects, so they must be used with caution.

Fortunately, another class of antidepressant drugs was soon discovered that did not produce harmful side effects: the **tricyclic antidepressants.** These drugs were found to inhibit the reuptake of 5-HT and norepinephrine by terminal buttons. By retarding reuptake, the drugs keep the neurotransmitter in contact with the postsynaptic receptors, thus prolonging the postsynaptic potentials. Thus, both the MAO inhibitors and the tricyclic antidepressant drugs are monoaminergic agonists.

Since the discovery of the tricyclic antidepressants, other drugs have been discovered that have similar effects. The most important of these are the **specific serotonin reuptake inhibitors,** whose action is described by their name. They are widely prescribed for their antidepressant properties and for their ability to reduce the symptoms of obsessive-compulsive disorder and social phobia.

The third biological treatment for depression has an interesting history. Earlier in this century, a physician named von Meduna noted that psychotic patients who were also subject to epileptic seizures showed improvement immediately after each attack. He reasoned that the violent storm of neural activity in the brain that constitutes an epileptic seizure somehow improved the patients' mental condition. He developed a way to produce seizures by administering a drug, but the procedure was dangerous to the patient. In 1937 Ugo Cerletti, an Italian psychiatrist, developed a less dangerous method for producing seizures. He had previously learned that the local slaughterhouse applied a jolt of electricity to animals' heads to stun them before killing them. The electricity appeared to produce a seizure that resembled an epileptic attack. He decided to attempt to use electricity to induce a seizure more safely.

Cerletti tried the procedure on dogs and found that an electrical shock to the skull did produce a seizure and that the animals recovered with no apparent ill effects. He then used the procedure on humans and found it to be safer than the chemical treatment that had previously been used. As a result, **electroconvulsive therapy (ECT)** became a common treatment for mental illness. Before a person receives ECT, he or she is anesthetized and is given a drug similar to curare, which paralyzes the muscles, preventing injuries that might be produced by a convulsion. (Of course, the patient is attached to a respirator until the effects of this drug wear off.) Electrodes are placed on the patient's scalp (most often to the non-speech-dominant hemisphere, to avoid damaging verbal memories), and a jolt of electricity triggers a seizure. Usually, a patient receives three treatments per week until maximum improvement is seen, which usually involves six to twelve treatments. The effectiveness of ECT has been established by placebo studies, in which some patients are anesthetized but not given shocks (Weiner and Krystal, 1994). Although ECT was originally used for a variety of disorders, including schizophrenia, we now know that its usefulness is limited to treatment of mania and depression. (See ***Figure 15.13.***)

A depressed patient does not respond immediately to treatment with antidepressant drugs; improvement in symptoms is not usually seen before two to three

tricyclic antidepressant A class of drugs used to treat depression; inhibits the reuptake of norepinephrine and serotonin; named for the molecular structure.

specific serotonin reuptake inhibitor A drug that inhibits the reuptake of serotonin without affecting the reuptake of other neurotransmitters.

electroconvulsive therapy (ECT) A brief electrical shock, applied to the head, that results in an electrical seizure; used therapeutically to alleviate severe depression.

Figure 15.13

A patient being prepared for electroconvulsive therapy.

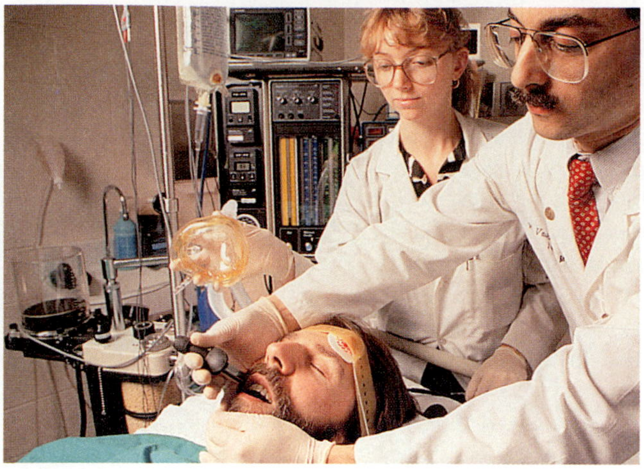

Photo Researchers, Inc.

weeks of drug treatment. In contrast, the effects of ECT are more rapid. A few seizures induced by ECT can often snap a person out of a deep depression within a few days. Although prolonged and excessive use of ECT causes brain damage, resulting in long-lasting impairments in memory (Squire, 1974), the judicious use of ECT during the interim period before antidepressant drugs become effective has undoubtedly saved the lives of some suicidal patients (Baldessarini, 1977). A study by Ende et al. (2000) found no evidence of hippocampal damage after a typical course of ECT. In addition, some severely depressed people are not helped by drug therapy; for them occasional ECT is the only effective treatment.

Another procedure may provide at least some of the benefits of ECT without introducing the risk of cognitive impairments or memory loss. As we saw in Chapter 5, transcranial magnetic stimulation (TMS) is accomplished by applying a strong localized magnetic field into the brain by passing an electrical current through a coil of wire placed on the scalp. The magnetic field induces a weak electrical current in the brain. Several studies have found that TMS applied to the prefrontal cortex reduces the symptoms of depression without producing any apparent negative side effects (George et al., 1995; Klein et al., 1999; Szuba et al., 2001). Further investigations will have to determine whether this procedure produces long-term beneficial effects.

The therapeutic effect of **lithium,** the drug used to treat bipolar affective disorders, is very rapid. This drug, which is administered in the form of lithium carbonate, is most effective in treating the manic phase of a bipolar affective disorder; once the mania is eliminated, depression usually does not follow (Gerbino, Oleshansky, and Gershon, 1978; Soares and Gershon, 1998). Many clinicians and investigators have referred to lithium as psychiatry's wonder drug: It does not suppress normal feelings of emotions, but it leaves patients able to feel and express joy and sadness in response to events in their lives. Similarly, it does not impair intellectual processes; many patients have received the drug continuously for years without any apparent ill effects (Fieve, 1979). Between 70 and 80 percent of patients with bipolar disorder show a positive response to lithium within a week or two (Price and Heninger, 1994).

Researchers have found that lithium has many physiological effects, but they have not yet discovered the pharmacological effects of lithium that are responsible for its ability to eliminate mania (Phiel and Klein, 2001). Some suggest that the drug stabilizes the population of certain classes of neurotransmitter receptors in the brain (especially serotonin receptors), thus preventing wide shifts in neural sensitivity. This effect may involve interference with the production of a class of second messengers, the *phosphoinositide system* (Atack, Broughton, and Pollack, 1995; Jope et al., 1996; Manji and Lenox, 1999). Others have shown that lithium may increase the production of neuroprotective proteins—proteins that help to prevent cell death (Manji, Moore, and Chen, 2001). In fact, Moore et al. (2000) found that four weeks of lithium treatment for bipolar disorder increased the volume of cerebral gray matter in the patients' brains, a finding that suggests that lithium facilitates neural or glial growth. As we will see later in this chapter, many studies have found decreased cerebral gray matter in patients suffering from depression.

Because some patients cannot tolerate the side effects of lithium, and because of the potential danger of overdose, researchers have been searching for alternative medications for bipolar disorder. One medication that has shown considerable promise is **carbamazepine** (Tegretol), a drug used to treat seizures that originate in the medial temporal lobes. Although carbamazepine is effective in treating the de-

lithium A chemical element; lithium carbonate is used to treat bipolar disorder.

carbamazepine A drug (trade name: Tegretol) that is used to treat seizures originating from a focus, generally in the medial temporal lobe.

pressed phase of bipolar disorder, its effects on mania are more impressive (Post et al., 1984). (See *Figure 15.14.*)

Role of Monoamines

The fact that depression can be treated effectively with MAO inhibitors and drugs that inhibit the reuptake of serotonin and norepinephrine suggested the **monoamine hypothesis:** Depression is caused by insufficient activity of monoaminergic neurons. Because the symptoms of depression do not respond to potent dopamine agonists such as amphetamine or cocaine, most investigators have focused their research efforts on the other two monoamines: norepinephrine and serotonin.

As we saw earlier in this chapter, the dopamine hypothesis of schizophrenia receives support from the fact that dopamine agonists can produce the symptoms of schizophrenia. Similarly, the monoamine hypothesis of depression receives support from the fact that depression can be caused by monoamine antagonists. Many hundreds of years ago, an alkaloid extract from *Rauwolfia serpentina,* a shrub of Southeast Asia, was found to be useful for treating snakebite, circulatory disorders, and insanity.

Reserpine, formerly used to treat high blood pressure, has a serious side effect: It can cause depression. Reserpine interferes with the storage of monoamines in synaptic vesicles, reducing the amount of neurotransmitter released by the terminal buttons. Thus, a monoamine antagonist produces depression, whereas monoamine agonists alleviate it.

Figure 15.14

The effects of lithium carbonate and carbamazepine on symptoms of mania in patients with bipolar disorder.

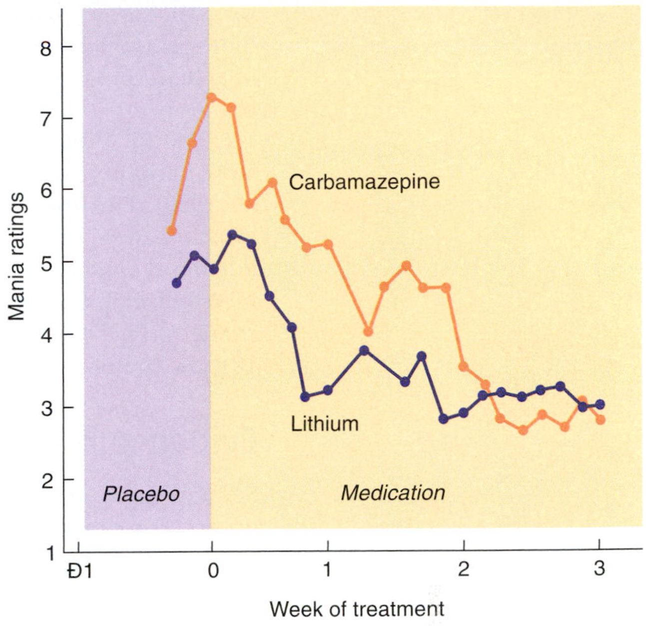

Adapted from Feldman, R. S., Meyer, J. S., and Quenzer, L. F. *Principles of Neuropsychopharmacology.* Sunderland, MA: Sinauer Associates, 1997. After Post et al., 1984.

Several studies have found that suicidal depression is related to decreased CSF levels of **5-HIAA** (5-hydroxyindoleacetic acid), a metabolite of serotonin that is produced when serotonin is destroyed by MAO. A decreased level of 5-HIAA implies that less 5-HT (serotonin) is being produced and released in the brain. Träskmann et al. (1981) found that CSF levels of 5-HIAA in people who had attempted suicide were significantly lower than those in controls. In a follow-up study of depressed and potentially suicidal patients, 20 percent of those with levels of 5-HIAA below the median subsequently killed themselves, whereas none of those with levels above the median committed suicide. More recent studies have confirmed these results (Roy, De Jong, and Linnoila, 1989).

Sedvall et al. (1980) analyzed the CSF of healthy, nondepressed volunteers. The families of subjects with unusually low levels of 5-HIAA were more likely to include people with depression. The results suggest that serotonin metabolism or release is genetically controlled and is linked to depression. Yatham et al. (2000) found a lower level of 5-HT_2 receptors in the neocortex of depressed patients. These findings clearly support the monoamine hypothesis.

Delgado et al. (1990) used a different approach to study of the role of serotonin in depression—the **tryptophan depletion procedure.** They studied depressed patients who were receiving antidepressant medication and were currently feeling well. For one day they had the patients follow a low-tryptophan diet (for example, salad, corn, cream cheese, and a gelatin dessert). Then the next day, the patients drank an amino acid "cocktail" that contained no tryptophan. The uptake of amino acids through the blood–brain barrier is accomplished by amino acid transporters. Because the patients' blood level of tryptophan was very low and that of the other amino acids was high, very little tryptophan found its way into the brain, and the

monoamine hypothesis A hypothesis that depression is caused by a low level of activity of one or more monoaminergic synapses.

5-HIAA A breakdown product of the neurotransmitter serotonin (5-HT).

tryptophan depletion procedure A procedure involving a low-tryptophan diet and a tryptophan-free amino acid "cocktail" that lowers brain tryptophan and consequently decreases the synthesis of 5-HT.

level of tryptophan in the brain fell drastically. As you will recall, tryptophan is the precursor of 5-HT, or serotonin. Thus, the treatment lowered the level of serotonin in the brain.

Delgado and his colleagues found that the tryptophan depletion caused most of the patients to relapse back into depression. Then when they began eating a normal diet again, they recovered. These results strongly suggest that the therapeutic effect of at least some antidepressant drugs depends on the availability of serotonin in the brain.

Two PET studies attempted to determine the brain regions involved in the relapse of depression caused by tryptophan depletion (Bremner et al., 1997; Smith et al., 1999). The investigators measured patients' regional cerebral metabolic rate before and after the patients drank a placebo or the amino acid "cocktail." Both studies found that patients whose depression returned showed a decrease in brain metabolism in the prefrontal cortex. Patients who did not relapse did not show these changes. These results are consistent with the general finding (discussed in Chapter 10) that the prefrontal cortex is involved in emotions.

Evidence for Brain Abnormalities

Several studies have found abnormalities in the brains of patients with affective disorders. For example, Elkis et al. (1996) found evidence for a decreased amount of tissue in the prefrontal cortex of young patients with unipolar depression, which suggests the presence of a developmental abnormality or a degenerative process that occurs early in life. A structural MRI study by Strakowski et al. (2002) found evidence that repeated episodes of depression and mania caused an increase in the size of the lateral ventricles, which implies a loss of brain tissue.

In a review of the relevant literature, Drevets (2001) suggests that the amygdala and several regions of the prefrontal cortex play special roles in the development of depression. As we saw in Chapter 10, the amygdala is critically involved in the expression of negative emotions. Functional imaging studies indicate an increase in blood flow and metabolism of 50–75 percent (Drevets et al., 1992; Links et al., 1996). A study by Abercrombie et al. (1998) found that the activity of the amygdala of depressed patients was correlated with the severity of their depression. In addition, the metabolic activity of the amygdala increases in normal subjects when they look at pictures of faces with expressions of sadness, and it also increases when depressed subjects remember episodes in their lives that made them sad (Drevets, 2000b; Liotti et al., 2002).

Figure 15.15

Composite fMRI image showing increased metabolic rate in the amygdala and medial orbitofrontal cortex of patients with unipolar depression.

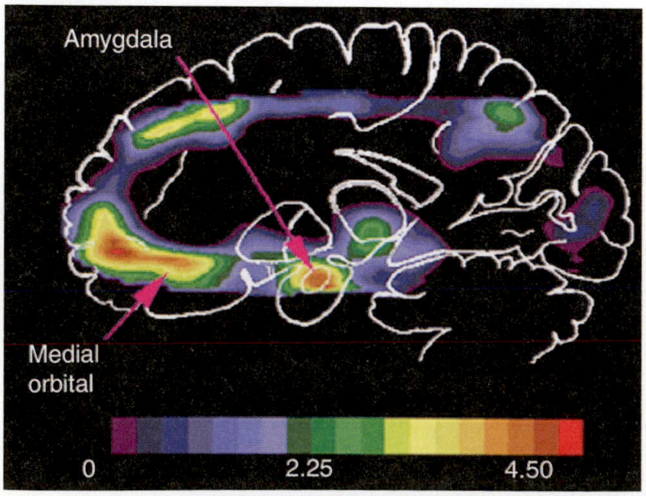

From Drevets, W. C., *Current Opinion in Neurobiology,* 2001, *11,* 240–249.

Several areas of the prefrontal cortex are involved in modulating emotional behavior. Like the amygdala, the orbitofrontal cortex is generally more activated in depressed patients than in healthy subjects (Drevets, 2000a). Damage to the orbitofrontal cortex disrupts the ability to abandon previously reinforced behaviors that are no longer fruitful (Bechara et al., 1998). Drevets (2001) suggests that the activation of this region in depressed patients may reflect their attempt to suppress unreinforced, unpleasant thoughts and emotions. Figure 15.15 illustrates the increased activity of the amygdala and orbitofrontal cortex in depressed patients. (See ***Figure 15.15.***)

Another region of the medial prefrontal cortex—the *subgenual prefrontal cortex*—shows a *lower* level of activation in depressed patients (Drevets et al., 1997). If you look at a sagittal view of the corpus callosum, you will notice that the front of this structure looks like a bent knee—*genu,* in Latin. The subgenual prefrontal cortex is located below

Figure 15.16

Metabolic rate of the subgenual prefrontal cortex in mania and depression. (a) Composite fMRI image showing decreased metabolic activity of this region in depressed patients. (b) Mean relative metabolic rate of the subgenual prefrontal cortex in normal controls and depressed and manic patients.

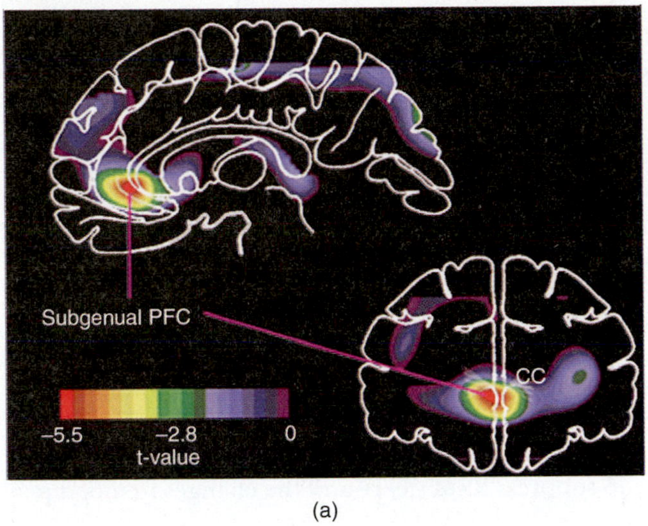

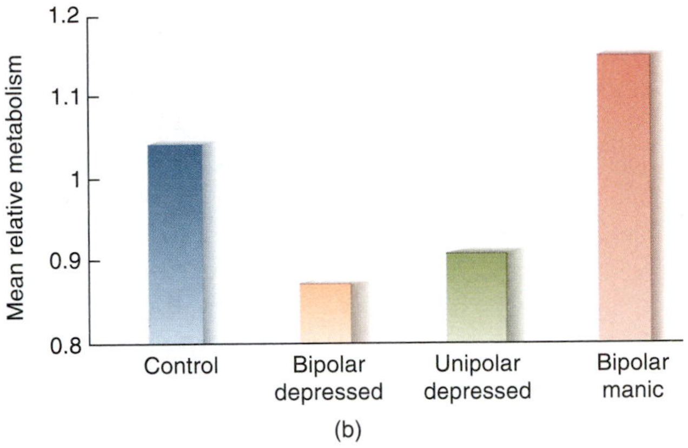

From Drevets, W. C., *Current Opinion in Neurobiology,* 2001, *11,* 240–249.

the "knee" at the front of the corpus callosum. Studies with laboratory animals indicate that this region plays an inhibitory role in emotions and emotional memories. Figure 15.16 shows the decreased activity of the subgenual prefrontal cortex in depressed patients. As the bar graph shows, the activity of this region is *increased* during a manic episode in patients with bipolar disorder (Drevets et al., 1997). Thus, the activity of this region decreases during times of negative mood and increased during times of positive mood. (See ***Figure 15.16.***)

As we saw earlier in this chapter, evidence indicates that schizophrenia can be produced by brain damage resulting from obstetric complications. Kinney et al. (1993) found that patients with bipolar disorder were more likely than their normal siblings to have a record of obstetric complications. The complications were mostly minor, so the authors suggest that they probably served as a contributing factor to the development of the disorder rather than the sole cause. A subsequent study with a larger sample of subjects confirmed these results (Kinney et al., 1998).

Role of Circadian Rhythms

One of the most prominent symptoms of depression is disordered sleep. The sleep of people with depression tends to be shallow; slow-wave delta sleep (stages 3 and 4) is reduced, and stage 1 is increased. Sleep is fragmented; people tend to waken frequently, especially toward the morning. In addition, REM sleep occurs earlier, the first half of the night contains a higher proportion of REM periods, and REM sleep contains an increased number of rapid eye movements (Kupfer, 1976; Vogel et al., 1980). (See ***Figure 15.17.***)

Figure 15.17

Patterns of the stages of sleep of a normal subject and of a patient with major depression. Note the reduced sleep latency, reduced REM latency, reduction in slow-wave sleep (stages 3 and 4), and general fragmentation of sleep (arrows) in the depressed patient.

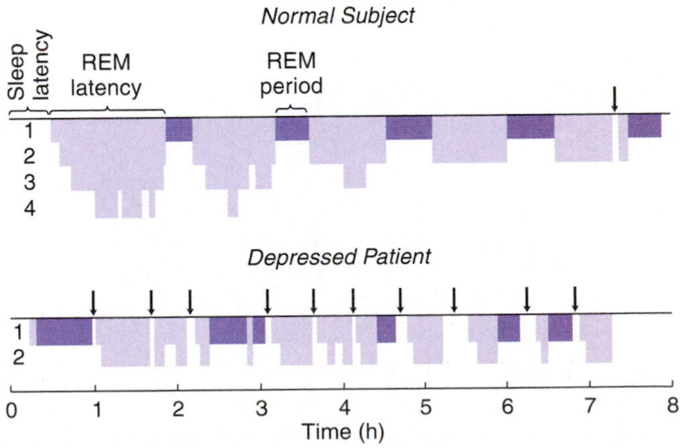

From Gillin, J. C., and Borbély, A. A. *Trends in Neurosciences,* 1985, *8,* 537–542. Reprinted with permission.

REM Sleep Deprivation

One of the most effective antidepressant treatments is sleep deprivation, either total or selective. Selective deprivation of REM sleep, accomplished by monitoring people's EEG and awakening them whenever they show signs of REM sleep, alleviates depression (Vogel et al., 1975; Vogel et al., 1990). The therapeutic effect, like that of the antidepressant medications, occurs slowly, over the course of several weeks. Some patients show long-term improvement even after the deprivation is discontinued; thus, it is a practical as well as an effective treatment. In addition, regardless of their specific pharmacological effects, other treatments for depression suppress REM sleep, delaying its onset and decreasing its duration. These facts suggest that some common mechanism may affect both REM sleep and mood.

Scherschlicht et al. (1982) examined the effects of twenty antidepressant drugs on the sleep cycles of cats and found that all of them profoundly reduced REM sleep and most of them increased slow-wave sleep. In an extensive review of the literature, Vogel et al. (1990) found that all drugs that suppressed REM sleep (and produced a rebound effect when their administration was discontinued) acted as antidepressants. As a consequence, an increased amount of delta sleep occurs during the first pre-REM period. Kupfer et al. (1994) found that the effects of antidepressant drugs on sleep persisted throughout long-term treatment. (They observed patients for as long as three years.) These results suggest that the primary effect of successful antidepressant treatment may be to suppress REM sleep, and the changes in mood may be a result of this suppression.

Studies of families with a history of major depression also suggest a link between this disorder and abnormalities in REM sleep. For example, Giles, Roffwarg, and Rush (1987) found that first-degree relatives of people with depression are likely to show a short REM sleep latency, even if they have not yet had an episode of depression. Giles et al. (1988) found that the members of these families who had the lowest REM latency had the highest risk of subsequently becoming depressed. Abnormalities in REM sleep are seen early in life; Coble et al. (1988) found that newborn infants of mothers with a history of major depression showed patterns of REM sleep that were different from those of the infants of mothers without such a history.

Total Sleep Deprivation

Total sleep deprivation also has an antidepressant effect. Unlike specific deprivation of REM sleep, which takes several weeks to reduce depression, total sleep deprivation produces immediate effects (Wu and Bunney, 1990). Figure 15.18 shows the mood rating of a patient who stayed awake one night; as you can see, the depression was lifted by the sleep deprivation but returned the next day, after a normal night's sleep. (See ***Figure 15.18.***)

Figure 15.18

Changes in the depression rating of a depressed patient produced by a single night's total sleep deprivation.

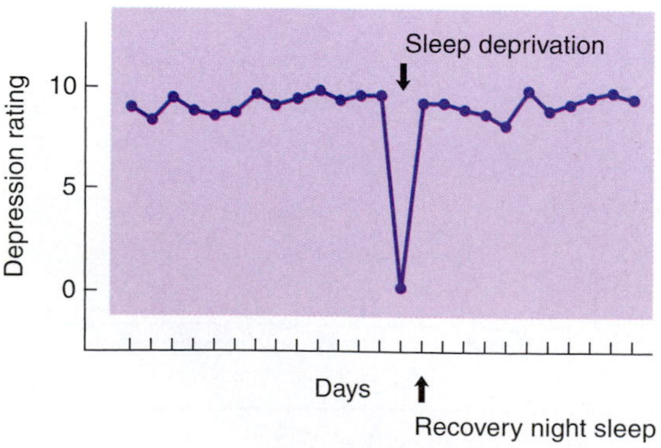

From Wu, J. C., and Bunney, W. E. *American Journal of Psychiatry,* Vol. 147, pp. 14–21, 1990. Copyright 1990, the American Psychiatric Association. Reprinted by permission.

Wu and Bunney suggest that during sleep a substance is produced that has a *depressogenic* effect. That is, the substance produces depression in a susceptible person. Presumably, this substance is produced in the brain and acts as a neuromodulator. During waking, this substance is gradually metabolized and hence inactivated. Some of the evidence for this hypothesis is presented in Figure 15.19. The data are taken from eight different studies (cited by Wu and Bunney, 1990) and show self-ratings of depression of people who did and did not respond to sleep deprivation. (Total sleep deprivation improves the mood of patients with major depression approximately two-thirds of the time.) (See ***Figure 15.19.***)

Why do only some people profit from sleep deprivation? In general, depressed patients whose mood remains stable will probably not benefit from sleep depression, whereas those whose mood fluctuates probably will. The patients who are most likely to respond are those who feel depressed in the morning but then gradually feel better as the day progresses (Riemann, Wiegand, and Berger, 1991; Haug, 1992; Wirz-Justice and Van den Hoofdakker, 1999). In these people sleep deprivation appears to prevent the depressogenic effects of sleep from taking place and simply permits the trend to continue. If you examine Figure 15.19, you can see that the responders were already feeling better by the end of the day. This improvement continued through the sleepless night and during the following day. The next night they were permitted to sleep normally, and their depression was back the following morning. As Wu and Bunney note, these data are consistent with the hypothesis that sleep produces a substance with a depressogenic effect. (See ***Figure 15.19.***)

Figure 15.19

Mean mood rating of responding and nonresponding patients deprived of one night's sleep as a function of the time of day.

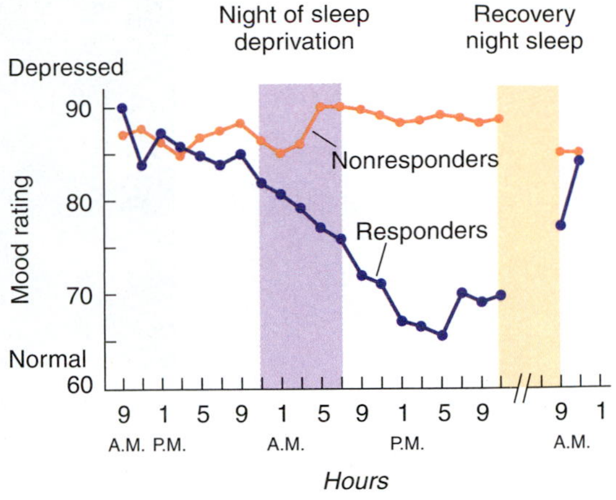

From Wu, J. C., and Bunney, W. E. *American Journal of Psychiatry,* Vol. 147, pp. 14–21, 1990. Copyright 1990, the American Psychiatric Association. Reprinted by permission.

The antidepressant effect of REM sleep deprivation and that of total sleep deprivation appear to be different; one is slow and long-lasting, whereas the other is fast and short-lived. In addition, total sleep deprivation can even trigger an episode of mania in patients with bipolar disorder (Wehr, 1992). (Even nondepressed people often report feeling "high" after spending a night without sleep.) The fact that a person's mood can be altered so quickly suggests that it would be worthwhile to look for physiological changes before and after sleep deprivation to try to identify those that may play a role in the control of mood.

Although total sleep deprivation is not a practical method for treating depression (it is impossible to keep people awake indefinitely), several studies suggest that *partial* sleep deprivation can hasten the beneficial effects of antidepressant drugs (Szuba, Baxter, and Fairbanks, 1991; Leibenluft and Wehr, 1992). Some investigators have found that *intermittent* total sleep deprivation (say, twice a week for four weeks) can have beneficial results (Papadimitriou et al., 1993).

Riemann et al. (1999) found that advancing the time of day that depressed patients sleep can prolong the beneficial effects of total sleep deprivation. They deprived patients of sleep for one night and continued to study those who showed a good response to the deprivation. The next night, the experimenters had some of the patients go to bed six hours earlier than usual, while the others went to bed three hours *later* than normal. Gradually, over several days, the subjects' bedtimes were returned to normal. Seventy-five percent of the early sleepers showed a continued remission of their depression, compared with only 40 percent of the late sleepers. As Riemann, Berger, and Voderholzer (2001) note, only sleep in the morning seems to be able to produce depression; thus, the best advice to depressed patients may be to get out of bed early in the morning and go to bed early at night.

Role of Zeitgebers

Yet another phenomenon relates depression to sleep and waking—or, more specifically, to the mechanisms that are responsible for circadian rhythms. Some people become depressed during the winter season, when days are short and nights are long (Rosenthal et al., 1984). The symptoms of this form of depression, called **seasonal affective disorder,** are somewhat different from those of major depression; both forms include lethargy and sleep disturbances, but seasonal depression includes a craving for carbohydrate and an accompanying weight gain. (As you will recall, people with major depression tend to lose their appetite.) A much smaller percentage of the population becomes depressed during the summer (Wehr, Sack, and Rosenthal, 1987). People with **summer depression** are more likely to sleep less, lose their appetite, and lose weight (Wehr et al., 1991).

Seasonal affective disorder, like unipolar depression and bipolar disorder, appears to have a genetic basis. In a study of 6439 adult twins, Madden et al. (1996) found that seasonal affective disorder ran in families, and they estimated that at least

seasonal affective disorder A mood disorder characterized by depression, lethargy, sleep disturbances, and craving for carbohydrates during the winter season when days are short.

summer depression A mood disorder characterized by depression, sleep disturbances, and loss of appetite.

Seasonal affective disorder, which is provoked by the long nights and short days of winter, can be treated by daily exposure to bright lights.

29 percent of the variance in seasonal mood disorders could be attributed to genetic factors. Molecular genetic studies suggest that seasonal affective disorder may be linked to genes involved in production of the 5-HT transporter and the 5-HT_{2A} receptor (Sher et al., 1999).

Seasonal affective disorder can be treated by **phototherapy:** exposing people to bright light for several hours a day (Rosenthal et al., 1985; Stinson and Thompson, 1990). As you will recall, circadian rhythms of sleep and wakefulness are controlled by the activity of the suprachiasmatic nucleus of the hypothalamus. Light serves as a *zeitgeber;* that is, it synchronizes the activity of the biological clock to the day–night cycle. One possibility is that people with seasonal affective disorder require a stronger-than-normal zeitgeber to reset their biological clock. The evidence on this issue is mixed: Two studies found that light therapy had an antidepressant effect no matter what time of day it occurred (Wirz-Justice et al., 1993; Meesters et al., 1995), and two studies found that morning light exposure was effective but evening exposure was not (Lewy et al., 1998; Terman, Terman, and Ross, 1998). If the light serves as a zeitgeber, we would expect different effects depending on the time of day the phototherapy occurred, so it is important to resolve the conflicting evidence.

Phototherapy appears to be a treatment without any adverse side effects besides a higher electric bill. According to a study by Wirz-Justice et al. (1996), even this side effect can be avoided. They found that a one-hour walk outside each morning reduced the symptoms of seasonal affective disorder. The investigators note that even on an overcast winter day, the early morning sky provides considerably more illumination than normal indoor artificial lighting, so a walk outside increases a person's exposure to light. The exercise probably doesn't hurt, either.

In fact, exercise appears to have a beneficial effect on depression. Singh, Clements, and Fiatarone (1997) enrolled depressed patients (aged 60–84 years) in a supervised weight-training program. The exercise program improved both their depression and their sleep.

INTERIM SUMMARY

Major Affective Disorders

The major affective disorders include bipolar affective disorder, with its cyclical episodes of mania and depression, and unipolar depression. Heritability studies suggest that genetic anomalies are at least partly responsible for these disorders. Unipolar depression can be successfully treated by for biological treatments: MAO inhibitors, drugs that block the reuptake of norep-

phototherapy Treatment of seasonal affective disorder by daily exposure to bright light.

inephrine and serotonin, electroconvulsive therapy, and sleep deprivation. Bipolar disorder can be successfully treated by lithium salts. Lithium appears to stabilize neural transmission, especially in serotonin-secreting neurons. It may do so by interfering with the phosphoinositide system, which is responsible for the production of several categories of second messengers. It also appears to protect neurons from damage and perhaps facilitate their repair.

The therapeutic effect of noradrenergic and serotonergic agonists and the depressant effect of reserpine, a monoaminergic antagonist, suggested the monoamine hypothesis of depression. Several other lines of evidence support this hypothesis. Low levels of 5-HIAA (a serotonin metabolite) in the cerebrospinal fluid correlate with attempts at suicide. It is possible that these results are related to the effects of serotonin on (self-directed) aggression. Depletion of tryptophan (the precursor of 5-HT) in the brain reverses the therapeutic effects of antidepressant medication in depressed patients, which lends further support to the conclusion that 5-HT plays a role in mood. Some evidence also suggests that drugs that block NK_1 receptors, which normally respond to a peptide known as substance P, reduce the symptoms of depression.

Several studies have looked for abnormalities in the brains of depressed patients. In general, patients with unipolar depression show abnormalities in the prefrontal cortex, basal ganglia, and cerebellum, while patients with bipolar disorder show abnormalities in the cerebellum and (perhaps) temporal lobe. One hypothesis suggests that depression results from hyperactivity activity of the amygdala and orbitofrontal cortex and hypoactivity of the subgenual prefrontal cortex.

Sleep disturbances are characteristic of affective disorders. In fact, total sleep deprivation rapidly (but temporarily) reduces depression in many people, and selective deprivation of REM sleep does so slowly (but more lastingly). In addition, almost all effective antidepressant treatments suppress REM sleep. Finally, a specific form of depression, seasonal affective disorder, can be treated by exposure to bright light. Spending time outdoors—especially when exposure to natual lighting is accompanied by exercise—is an effective (and inexpensive) form of therapy for depression. Clearly, the mood disorders are somehow linked to biological rhythms.

THOUGHT QUESTION

A television commentator, talking in particular about the suicide of a young pop star and in general about unhappy youth, asked with exasperation, "What would all these young people be doing if they had real problems like a Depression, World War II, or Vietnam?" People with severe depression often try to hide their pain because they fear others will scoff at them and say that they have nothing to feel unhappy about. If depression is caused by abnormal brain functioning, are these remarks justified? How would you feel if you were severely depressed and people close to you berated you for feeling so sad and told you to snap out of it and quit feeling sorry for yourself?

Anxiety Disorders

As we saw earlier, the affective disorders are characterized by unrealistic extremes of emotion: depression or elation (mania). The **anxiety disorders** are characterized by unrealistic, unfounded fear and anxiety. This section describes two of the anxiety disorders that appear to have biological causes: panic disorder and obsessive-compulsive disorder. The causes of other anxiety disorders, such as generalized anxiety disorder and phobic disorders, seem to be similar to those of panic disorder, so they will not be discussed separately here.

anxiety disorder A psychological disorder characterized by tension, overactivity of the autonomic nervous system, expectation of an impending disaster, and continuous vigilance for danger.

panic disorder A disorder characterized by episodic periods of symptoms such as shortness of breath, irregularities in heartbeat, and other autonomic symptoms, accompanied by intense fear.

Panic Disorder

Description

People with **panic disorder** suffer from episodic attacks of acute anxiety—periods of acute and unremitting terror that grip them for variable lengths of time, from a

Figure 15.20

Percentage of men and women who receive a diagnosis of panic disorder earlier and later in life.

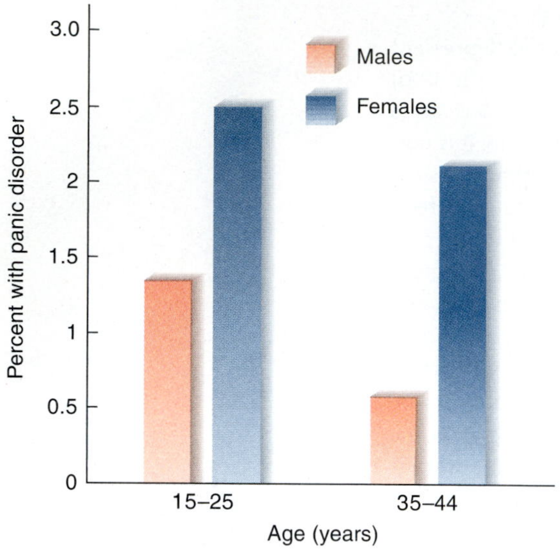

Based on data from Eaton, W. W., Kessler, R. C., Wittchen, H. U., and Magee, W. J. *American Journal of Psychiatry,* 1994, *151,* 413–420.

few seconds to a few hours. The disorder usually has its onset in young adulthood. Women appear to be about 2.5 times more likely than men to suffer from panic disorder (Eaton et al., 1994. See ***Figure 15.20***).

The basic symptoms of panic attack appear to be universal. For example, these symptoms are similar in residents of the United States, Puerto Rico, Germany, Lebanon, Korea, and New Zealand (Weissman et al., 1995). Panic attacks include many physical symptoms, such as shortness of breath, clammy sweat, irregularities in heartbeat, dizziness, faintness, and feelings of unreality. The victim of a panic attack often feels that he or she is going to die. Anxiety is a normal reaction to many stresses of life, and none of us is completely free from it. In fact, anxiety is undoubtedly useful in causing us to be more alert and to take important things seriously. However, the anxiety that we all feel from time to time is obviously different from the intense fear and terror experienced by a person gripped by a panic attack.

Between panic attacks many people with panic disorder suffer from **anticipatory anxiety**—the fear that another panic attack will strike them. This anticipatory anxiety often leads to the development of a serious phobic disorder: **agoraphobia** (*agora* means "open space"). According to the American Psychiatric Association's official *Diagnostic and Statistical Manual IV (DSM-IV),* agoraphobia associated with panic attacks is a fear of "being in places or situations from which escape might be difficult (or embarrassing) or in which help might not be available in the event of . . . a Panic Attack" (American Psychiatric Association, 1994, p. 200). Agoraphobia can be severely disabling; some people with this disorder have stayed inside their houses or apartments for years, afraid to venture outside.

Possible Causes

Because the physical symptoms of panic attacks are so overwhelming, many patients reject the suggestion that they have a mental disorder, insisting that their problem is medical. In fact, a considerable amount of evidence suggests that panic disorder may have biological origins. First, the disorder appears to be hereditary. In a review of the literature, Hettema, Neale, and Kendler (2001) found five family studies and three twin studies that indicate a significant genetic factor in panic disorder.

Several studies have shown a peculiar and puzzling genetic association between loose joints (*joint hypermobility syndrome,* or "double-jointedness") and panic disorder. Martin-Santos et al. (1998) reported that joint hypermobility syndrome was seen in 68 percent of patients with panic disorder but only 12.5 percent of control subjects. Gratacos et al. (2001) found that both joint hypermobility syndrome and panic and phobic disorders appear to be associated with a duplicated region of chromosome 15.

Anxiety disorders were previously treated by a combination of behavior therapy and a benzodiazepine. As we saw in Chapter 4, benzodiazepines have strong anxiolytic ("anxiety-dissolving") effects. The brain possesses benzodiazepine receptors, which are part of the $GABA_A$ receptor complex. When a benzodiazepine agonist binds with its receptor, it increases the sensitivity of the GABA-binding site and produces an anxiolytic effect. On the other hand, when a benzodiazepine antagonist occupies the receptor site, it *reduces* the sensitivity of the GABA-binding site and *increases* anxiety. Anxiety disorders, then, might be caused by a diminished number of benzodiazepine receptors or by the secretion of a neuromodulator that blocks the benzodiazepine-binding site at the $GABA_A$ receptor. Nutt et al. (1990) found that administration of flumazenil, a benzodiazepine antagonist (having an action opposite that of the benzodiazepine tranquilizers), produced panic in patients with panic

anticipatory anxiety A fear of having a panic attack; may lead to the development of agoraphobia.

agoraphobia A fear of being away from home or other protected places.

disorder but not in control subjects. In addition, a functional imaging study by Malizia et al. (1998) found evidence for a reduction in $GABA_A$ receptors in the brains of patients with panic disorder.

As we saw earlier, serotonin appears to play a role in depression. Much evidence suggests that serotonin may play a role in anxiety disorders too. Even though the symptoms of panic disorder and obsessive-compulsive disorder (described in the next section) are very different, specific serotonin reuptake inhibitors, which serve as potent serotonin agonists have become the first-line medications for treating both of these disorders (American Psychiatric Association, 1998; Asnis et al., 2001). Figure 15.21 shows the effect of fluvoxamine, a serotonin reuptake inhibitor, on the number of panic attacks in patients with panic disorder. (See ***Figure 15.21***.)

Figure 15.21

Effects of fluvoxamine (a specific serotonin reuptake inhibitor) on the severity of panic disorder.

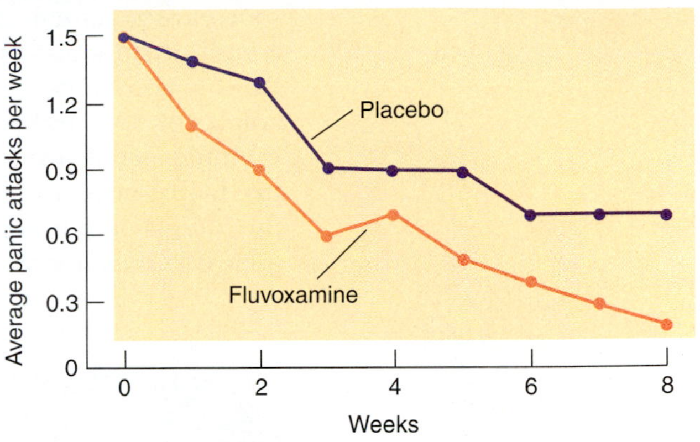

Adapted from Asnis, G. M., Hameedi, F. A., Goddard, A. W., Potkin, S. G., Black, D., Jameel, M., Desagani, K., and Woods, S. W. *Psychiatry Research*, 2001, *103*, 1–14.

Functional imaging studies suggest that the cingulate, prefrontal, and anterior temporal cortices are involved in panic attack. For example, Johanson et al. (1998) measured regional cerebral blood flow in women with severe spider phobias. He showed the women videos of spiders, which provoked panic attacks in half of the subjects. Those who panicked showed a decrease in the frontal cortex. Those who did not panic showed an *increase* in the frontal cortex. Johanson and his colleagues suggest that the increased frontal activity in those who managed to suppress their panic reflected brain mechanisms involved in control of fear. (All the subjects reported intense fear when they viewed the spider videos.)

Obsessive-Compulsive Disorder

Description

As the name implies, people with an **obsessive-compulsive disorder (OCD)** suffer from **obsessions**—thoughts that will not leave them—and **compulsions**—behaviors that they cannot keep from performing. Obsessions are seen in a variety of mental disorders, including schizophrenia. However, unlike schizophrenics, people with obsessive-compulsive disorder recognize that their thoughts and behaviors are senseless and desperately wish that they would go away. Compulsions often become more and more demanding until they interfere with people's careers and daily lives.

The incidence of obsessive-compulsive disorder is 1–2 percent. Females are slightly more likely than males to have this diagnosis. Like panic disorder, OCD most commonly begins in young adulthood (Robbins et al., 1984). Cross-cultural studies find that the symptoms of this disorder are similar in various racial and ethnic groups (Akhtar et al., 1975; Khanna and Channabasavanna, 1987; Hinjo et al., 1989). People with this disorder are unlikely to marry, perhaps because of the common obsessional fear of dirt and contamination or because of the shame associated with the rituals they are compelled to perform, which causes them to avoid social contacts (Turner, Beidel, and Nathan, 1985).

Most compulsions fall into one of four categories: *counting, checking, cleaning,* and *avoidance.* For example, people might repeatedly check burners on the stove to see that they are off and windows and locks to be sure that they are locked. Davison and Neale (1974) reported the case of a woman who washed her hands more than five hundred times a day because she feared being contaminated by germs. The hand washing persisted even when her hands became covered with painful sores. Other people meticulously clean their apartment or endlessly wash, dry, and fold their clothes. Some become afraid to leave home because they fear contamination,

obsessive-compulsive disorder (OCD) A mental disorder characterized by obsessions and compulsions.

obsession An unwanted thought or idea with which a person is preoccupied.

compulsion The feeling that one is obliged to perform a behavior, even if one prefers not to do so.

and they refuse to touch other members of their family. If they do accidentally become "contaminated," they usually have lengthy purification rituals. (See ***Table 15.4.***)

Some investigators believe that the compulsive behaviors seen in OCD are forms of species-typical behaviors—for example, grooming, cleaning, and attention to sources of potential danger—that are released from normal control mechanisms by a brain dysfunction (Wise and Rapoport, 1988). Fiske and Haslam (1997) suggest that the behaviors seen in obsessive-compulsive disorder are simply pathological examples of a natural behavioral tendency to develop and practice social rituals. For example, people perform cultural rituals to mark transitions or changes in social status, to diagnose or treat illnesses, to restore relationships with deities, or to ensure the success of hunting or planting. These rituals define the status of individuals and their relationships with other members of the society, and they provide comfort in

Table 15.4

Reported Obsessions and Compulsions of Child and Adolescent Patients

Major Presenting Symptoms	Percent Reporting Symptom at Initial Interview
OBSESSION	
Concern or disgust with bodily wastes or secretions (urine, stool, saliva), dirt, germs, environmental toxins, etc.	43
Fear something terrible might happen (fire, death/illness of loved one, self, or others)	24
Concern or need for symmetry, order, or exactness	17
Scrupulosity (excessive praying or religious concerns out of keeping with patient's background)	13
Lucky/unlucky numbers	18
Forbidden or perverse sexual thoughts, images, or impulses	14
Intrusive nonsense sounds, words, or music	11
COMPULSION	
Excessive or ritualized hand washing, showering, bathing, toothbrushing, or grooming	85
Repeating rituals (going in/out of door, up/down from chair, etc.)	51
Checking doors, locks, stove, appliances, car brakes, etc.	46
Cleaning and other rituals to remove contact with contaminants	23
Touching	20
Ordering/arranging	17
Measures to prevent harm to self or others (e.g., hanging clothes a certain way)	16
Counting	18
Hoarding/collecting	11
Miscellaneous rituals (e.g., licking, spitting, special dress pattern)	26

Source: From Rapoport, J. L. *Journal of the American Medical Association,* 1988, *260,* 2888–2890.

knowing that the structure of the society approves the transition or change in status or is doing all it can to avert misfortune. Consider the following scenario (from Fiske and Haslam, 1997):

> Imagine that you are traveling in an unfamiliar country. Going out for a walk, you observe a man dressed in red, standing on a red mat in a red-painted gateway. . . . He utters the same prayer six times. He brings out six basins of water and meticulously arranges them in a symmetrical configuration in front of the gateway. Then he washes his hands six times in each of the six basins, using precisely the same motions each time. As he does this, he repeats the same phrase, occasionally tapping his right finger on his earlobe. Through your interpreter, you ask him what he is doing. He replies that there are dangerous polluting substances in the ground, . . . [and that] he must purify himself or something terrible will happen. He seems eager to tell you about his concerns. (p. 211)

Why is the man acting this way? Is he a priest following a sacred ritual or does he have obsessive-compulsive disorder? Without knowing more about the spiritual rituals followed by the man's culture, we cannot say. Fiske and Haslam compared the features of OCD and other psychological disorders in descriptions of rituals, work, or other activities in fifty-two cultures. They found that the features of OCD (for example, observing lucky or unlucky numbers or colors with special significance, repeating activities, ordering or arranging things in specific configurations, or paying special attention to thresholds or entrances) were found in rituals in these cultures. The features of other psychological disorders were much less common. On the whole, the evidence suggests that the symptoms of obsessive-compulsive disorder represent an exaggeration of natural human tendencies.

Possible Causes

Evidence is beginning to accumulate suggesting that obsessive-compulsive disorder might have a genetic origin. So far, no properly controlled twin studies have studied people with a diagnosis of OCD, but several studies have found a greater concordance for obsessions and compulsions in monozygotic twins than in dizygotic twins (Hettema, Neale, and Kendler, 2001).

Family studies have found that OCD is associated with a neurological disorder that appears during childhood (Pauls and Leckman, 1986; Pauls et al., 1986). This disorder, **Tourette's syndrome,** is characterized by muscular and vocal tics: facial grimaces, squatting, pacing, twirling, barking, sniffing, coughing, grunting, or repeating specific words (especially vulgarities). Treatment for Tourette's syndrome includes antischizophrenic medications that block dopamine D_2 receptors, such as haloperidol or pimozide; risperidone (an atypical antipsychotic medication); or clonidine, an α_2 adrenoreceptor agonist (Swerdlow, 2001).

As with schizophrenia, not all cases of OCD have a genetic origin; the disorder sometimes occurs after brain damage caused by various means, such as birth trauma, encephalitis, and head trauma (Berthier et al., 1996; Hollander et al., 1990). In particular, the symptoms appear to be associated with damage to or dysfunction of the basal ganglia, cingulate gyrus, and prefrontal cortex (Giedd et al., 1995; Robinson et al., 1995).

Tic disorders (including OCD) can be caused by a group A β-hemolytic streptococcal infection. This infection can trigger several autoimmune diseases, in which the patient's immune system attacks and damages certain tissues of the body, including the valves of the heart, the kidneys, and—in this case—parts of the brain. Figure 15.22 shows the parallel course of a young girl's symptoms and the level of antistreptococcal DNA-B in her blood, indicating the presence of an active infection (Perlmutter et al., 1998). (See ***Figure 15.22.***) The symptoms of OCD appear to be produced by damage to the basal ganglia. Bodner, Morshed, and Peterson (2001) report the case of a 25-year-old man whose untreated sore throat (he lived in a religious

Tourette's syndrome A neurological disorder characterized by tics and involuntary vocalizations and sometimes by compulsive uttering of obscenities and repetition of the utterances of others.

Figure 15.22

The parallel course of a young girl's symptoms and the level of antistreptococcal DNA-B in her blood, which indicates the presence of an active infection. This relation provides evidence that a group A β-hemolytic streptococcal infection can produce tics and the symptoms of OCD, presumably by affecting the basal ganglia.

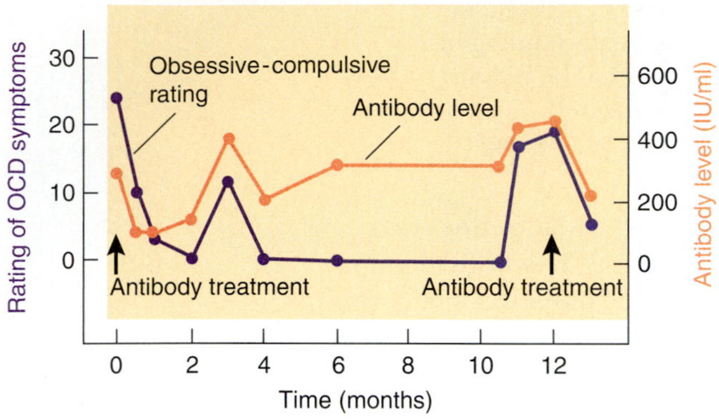

Adapted from Perlmutter, S. J., Garvey, M. A., Castellanos, X., Mittleman, B. B., Giedd, J., Rapoport, J. L., and Swedo, S. E. *American Journal of Psychiatry*, 1998, *155*, 1592–1598.

group that prohibited antibiotics) developed into an autoimmune disease that produced obsessions and compulsions. The investigators found antibodies to type A β-hemolytic streptococcus, and MRI scans indicated abnormalities in the basal ganglia.

Several studies using PET scans have found evidence of increased activity in the frontal lobes and caudate nucleus in patients with OCD. A review by Saxena et al. (1998) reported on six PET studies. Five studies found increased activity in the orbitofrontal cortex, two studies found increased activity in the cingulate cortex, and two studies found increased activity in the caudate nucleus. Saxena and his colleagues also reported on several studies that measured regional brain activity of OCD patients before and after successful treatment with drugs or behavior therapy. In general, the improvement in a patient's symptoms was correlated with a reduction in the activity of the caudate nucleus and orbitofrontal cortex. The fact that behavior therapy and drug therapy produced similar results is especially remarkable: It indicates that very different procedures may be bringing about physiological changes that alleviate a serious mental disorder.

As we saw in Chapter 10, the prefrontal cortex (particularly the orbitofrontal cortex) and the cingulate cortex are involved in emotional reactions, so it is not surprising to learn that they might be implicated in OCD. In fact, some patients with severe OCD have been successfully treated with **cingulotomy**—surgical destruction of specific fiber bundles in the subcortical frontal lobe, including the cingulum bundle (which connects the prefrontal and cingulate cortex with the limbic cortex of the temporal lobe) and a region that contains fibers that connect the basal ganglia with the prefrontal cortex (Ballantine et al., 1987; Mindus, Rasmussen, and Lindquist, 1994). These operations, which are performed only when a patient has serious obsessive and compulsive symptoms that do not respond to behavior therapy or drugs, have a reasonably good success rate. Dougherty et al. (2002) reported that 32 percent of patients showed definite improvement after cingulotomy, 14 percent showed partial improvement, and 54 percent were unchanged. Of course, neurosurgery cannot be undone, so such procedures must be considered only as a last resort.

In one extraordinary case a patient performed his own psychosurgery. Solyom, Turnbull, and Wilensky (1987) reported the case of a young man with a serious obsessive-compulsive disorder whose ritual hand washing and other behaviors made it impossible for him to continue his schooling or lead a normal life. Finding that his life was no longer worthwhile, he decided to end it. He placed the muzzle of a .22-caliber rifle in his mouth and pulled the trigger. The bullet entered the base of the brain and damaged the frontal lobes. He survived, and he was amazed to find that his compulsions were gone. Fortunately, the damage did not disrupt his ability to make or execute plans; he went back to school and completed his education and now has a job. His IQ was unchanged. Ordinary surgery would have been less hazardous and messy, but it could hardly have been more successful.

cingulotomy The surgical destruction of the cingulum bundle, which connects the prefrontal cortex with the limbic system; helps to reduce intense anxiety and the symptoms of obsessive-compulsive disorder.

The symptoms of OCD can be treated by specific serotonin reuptake inhibitors such as clomipramine, fluoxetine, and fluvoxamine. Although these drugs are also effective antidepressants, their antidepressant action does not seem to be related to their ability to relieve the symptoms of OCD. For example, Leonard et al. (1989) compared the effects of clomipramine and desipramine (an antidepressant drug that inhibits the reuptake of norepinephrine but not serotonin) on the symptoms of children and adolescents with severe obsessive-compulsive disorder. For three weeks, all patients received a placebo. Then for five weeks half of them received clomipramine (CMI), and the other half received desipramine (DMI), on a double-blind basis. At the end of that time the drugs were switched. As Figure 15.23 shows, CMI was a much more effective drug; in fact, when the patients were switched from CMI to DMI, their symptoms got worse. (See ***Figure 15.23.***)

The importance of serotonergic activity in inhibiting compulsive behaviors is underscored by three interesting compulsions: trichotillomania, onychophagia, and acral lick dermatitis. *Trichotillomania* is compulsive hair pulling. People with this disorder (almost always females) often spend hours each night pulling hairs out one by one, sometimes eating them (Rapoport, 1991). *Onychophagia* is compulsive nail biting, which in its extreme can cause severe damage to the ends of the fingers. (For those who are sufficiently agile, toenail biting is not uncommon.) Double-blind studies have shown that both of these disorders can be treated successfully by clomipramine, the drug of choice for obsessive-compulsive disorder (Leonard et al., 1992a).

Acral lick dermatitis is a disease of dogs, not humans. Some dogs will continuously lick at a part of their body, especially their wrist or ankle (called the *carpus* and the *hock*). The licking removes the hair and often erodes away the skin as well. The disorder seems to be genetic; it is seen almost exclusively in large breeds such as Great Danes, Labrador retrievers, and German shepherds, and it runs in families. A double-blind study found that clomipramine reduces this compulsive behavior (Rapoport, Ryland, and Kriete, 1992). At first, when I read the term "double-blind" in the report by Rapoport and her colleagues, I was amused to think that the investigators were careful not to let the dogs learn whether they were receiving clomipramine or a placebo. Then I realized that, of course, it was the dogs' owners who had to be kept in the dark.

Figure 15.23

Mean rating of symptom severity of patients with obsessive-compulsive disorder treated with desipramine (DMI) or clomipramine (CMI).

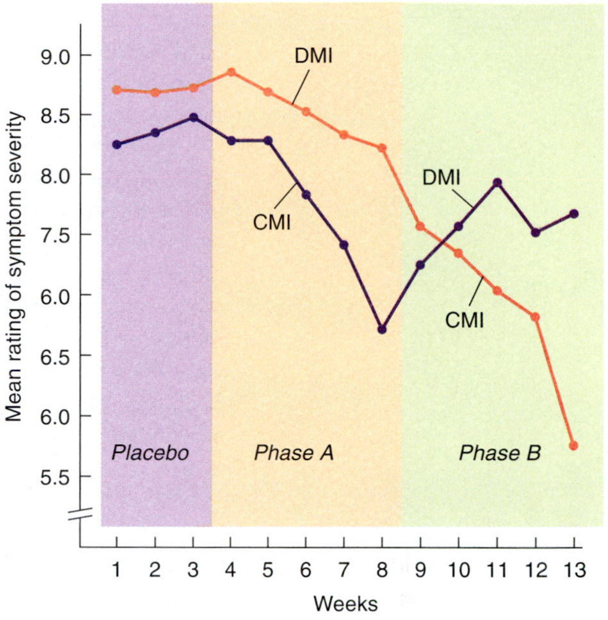

From Leonard, H. L., Swedo, S. E., Rapoport, J. L., Koby, E. V., Lenane, M. C., Cheslow, D. L., and Hamburger, S. D. *Archives of General Psychiatry,* 1989, *46,* 1088–1092. Copyright 1989, American Medical Association.

INTERIM SUMMARY

Anxiety Disorders

The anxiety disorders severely disrupt some people's lives. Panic disorder is approximately 2.5 times more frequent in females than in males. People with panic disorder periodically have panic attacks, during which they experience intense symptoms of autonomic activity and often feel as if they are going to die. Frequently, panic attacks lead to the development of agoraphobia, an avoidance of being away from a safe place, such as home. Family and twin studies have shown that panic disorder is at least partly heritable, which suggests that it has biological causes. An association between joint hypermobility syndrome ("double-jointedness") and panic disorder and panic disorder may involve a region of chromosome 15.

Panic attacks can be alleviated by the administration of a benzodiazepine, a finding that suggests that the disorder may involve decreased numbers of benzodiazepine receptors or an inadequate secretion of an endogenous benzodiazepine agonist. A benzodiazepine antagonist can trigger a panic attack, and a study found evidence for a reduction of $GABA_A$ receptors in the brains of people with panic disorder. Nowadays, the first choice of medical treatment for panic attacks is specific serotonin reuptake inhibitors. Functional imaging studies suggest that the prefrontal, cingulate, and anterior temporal cortices are involved in panic attacks.

Obsessive-compulsive disorder (OCD) is characterized by obsessions—unwanted thoughts—and compulsions—uncontrollable behaviors, especially those involving cleanliness and attention to danger. Some investigators believe that these behaviors represent overactivity of species-typical behavioral tendencies.

OCD has a heritable basis and is related to Tourette's syndrome, a neurological disorder characterized by tics and strange verbalizations. It can also be caused by brain damage at birth, encephalitis, and head injuries, especially when the basal ganglia are involved. A type A β-hemolytic streptococcus infection can stimulate an autoimmune attack—presumably on the basal ganglia—that produces the symptoms of OCD.

PET scans indicate that people with obsessive-compulsive disorder tend to show increased activity in the orbitofrontal cortex, cingulate cortex, and caudate nucleus. Drug treatment or behavior therapy that successfully reduces the symptoms of OCD generally reduces the activity of the orbitofrontal cortex and caudate nucleus. Cingulotomy, the destruction of the cingulum bundle, which links the prefrontal cortex and cingulate cortex with the limbic cortex of the temporal lobe, reduces the symptoms of OCD, as do drugs that specifically block the reuptake of serotonin. Some investigators believe that clomipramine and related drugs alleviate the symptoms of OCD by increasing the activity of serotonergic pathways that play an inhibitory role on species-typical behaviors. Three other compulsions, hair pulling, nail biting, and (in dogs) acral lick syndrome, are also suppressed by clomipramine.

THOUGHT QUESTION

Most reasonable people would agree that a person with mental disorders cannot be blamed for his or her thoughts and behaviors. Most of us would sympathize with someone whose life is disrupted by panic attacks or obsessions and compulsions, and we would not see their plight as a failure of will power. After all, whether these disorders are caused by traumatic experiences or brain abnormalities (or both), the afflicted person has not chosen to be the way he or she is. But what about less dramatic examples: Should we blame people for their shyness or hostility or other maladaptive personality traits? If, as many psychologists believe, people's personality characteristics are largely determined by their heredity (and thus by the structure and chemistry of their brains), what are the implications for our concepts of "blame" and "personal responsibility"?

EPILOGUE

Tardive Dyskinesia

As a result of taking an antipsychotic medication, Larry, the schizophrenic man described in the chapter prologue, developed a neurological disorder called *tardive dyskinesia. Tardus* means "slow," and *dyskinesia* means "faulty movement"; thus, tardive dyskinesia is a late-developing movement disorder. (In Larry's case it actually came rather early.)

Tardive dyskinesia appears to be the opposite of Parkinson's disease. Whereas patients with Parkinson's disease have difficulty moving, patients with tardive dyskinesia are unable to stop moving. Indeed, dyskinesia commonly occurs when patients with Parkinson's disease receive too much L-DOPA. In schizophrenic patients, tardive dyskinesia is made *worse* by discontinuing the antipsychotic drug and is improved by increasing the dose. The symptoms are also intensified by dopamine agonists such as L-DOPA or amphetamine. Therefore, the disorder appears to be produced by an overstimulation of dopamine receptors. But if it is, why should it be originally caused by antipsychotic drugs, which are dopamine *antagonists?*

The answer seems to be provided by a phenomenon known as *supersensitivity.* Supersensitivity is a compensatory mechanism in which some types of receptors become more sensitive if they are inhibited for a period of time by a drug that blocks them. For tardive dyskinesia the relevant receptors are D_2 receptors found in the caudate nucleus, an important component of the motor system. (You will recall that Parkinson's disease is caused by degeneration of dopamine-secreting neurons that connect the substantia nigra with the caudate nucleus.) When these receptors are chronically blocked by an antipsychotic drug, they become supersensitive. In some cases the supersensitivity becomes so great that it overcompensates for the effects of the drug, causing the neurological symptoms to occur (Adler et al., 2002; Tarsy, Baldessarini, and Tarazi, 2002).

Fortunately, the wish expressed by Larry's physician has come true. Researchers *have* discovered medications that treat the symptoms of schizophrenia without producing neurological side effects, and early indications suggest that tardive dyskinesia may become a thing of the past. The incidence of tardive dyskinesia is absent or much reduced in patients who are treated with the atypical medications, apparently because they do not block D_2 receptors (Llorca et al., 2002). Even patients who are treated with the "classic" antipsychotic medications are unlikely to develop tardive schizophrenia if they are treated with low doses (Lohr et al., 2002; Turrone, Remington, and Nobrega, 2002). Clozapine, the first of the atypical antipsychotic medications, has been joined by several others, including risperidone, olanzapine, and amisulpride. As we saw in the previous section, these drugs, unlike the "classic" antipsychotic medication, reduce the negative symptoms of schizophrenia as well as the positive ones.

KEY CONCEPTS

SCHIZOPHRENIA

1. Because a tendency to develop schizophrenia is heritable, biological factors appear to be important in the development of this disorder.
2. The effects of dopamine agonists and antagonists on the positive symptoms of schizophrenia give support to the dopamine hypothesis.
3. Because evidence of brain damage is found in people who display the negative symptoms of schizophrenia, some researchers believe that a pathological process, perhaps triggered by a virus, is responsible for schizophrenia.
4. Evidence suggests that the negative symptoms of schizophrenia are primarily caused by decreased activity of the prefrontal cortex, which may increase the release of dopamine in the nucleus accumbens and provoke the positive symptoms.

MAJOR AFFECTIVE DISORDERS

5. The major affective disorders include major depression and bipolar disorder. Evidence suggests that both types are heritable.
6. The monoamine hypothesis was suggested by the findings that dopamine agonists and antagonists affect the symptoms of the affective disorders, and that depressed people tend to have a low level of a serotonin metabolite in their CSF.
7. The affective disorders are related to sleep disturbances and can be relieved by REM sleep deprivation or total sleep deprivation. In addition, some people suffer from seasonal affective disorders. Thus, affective disorders may be caused by malfunctions of the neural systems that regulate circadian rhythms.

ANXIETY DISORDERS

8. The two most serious anxiety disorders are panic disorder and obsessive-compulsive disorder. Both disorders appear to have a strong hereditary component.
9. Panic disorder is treated with benzodiazepines and may involve abnormalities in these receptors. It is also treated with serotonin agonists such as fluoxetine.
10. Obsessive-compulsive disorder may be related to the species-typical behaviors of grooming, cleaning, and attention to danger. It is treated with specific serotonin reuptake inhibitors such as clomipramine, which inhibit these behaviors in laboratory animals.

SUGGESTED READINGS

Breier, A. *The New Pharmacotherapy of Schizophrenia.* Washington, DC: American Psychiatric Press, 1996.

Coleman, M., and Gillberg, C. *The Schizophrenias: A Biological Approach to the Schizophrenia Spectrum Disorders.* New York: Springer, 1996.

Goodwin, D. W., and Guze, S. B. *Psychiatric Diagnosis,* 6th ed. New York: Oxford University Press, 1996.

Hollander, E. *Obsessive-Compulsive Related Disorders.* Washington, DC: American Psychiatric Press, 1993.

Mann, J. J., and Kupfer, D. J. *Biology of Depressive Disorders.* New York: Plenum Press, 1993.

Strange, P. G. *Brain Biochemistry and Brain Disorders.* Oxford, England: Oxford University Press, 1992.

Tsai, G., and Coyle, J. T. Glutamatergic mechanisms in schizophrenia. *Annual Review of Pharmacology and Toxicology,* 2002, *42,* 165–179.

Waddington, J. L., and Buckley, P. F. *The Neurodevelopmental Basis of Schizophrenia.* New York: Chapman & Hall, 1996.

SUGGESTED WEB SITES

Schizophrenia
www.schizophrenia.com/

This comprehensive site contains discussion areas devoted to schizophrenia as well as fact sheets about schizophrenia.

Dana Brain Web
www.dana.org/brainweb/

The focus of the Dana Brain Web is on sites relating to brain diseases and disorders.

All About Depression
http://depression.mentalhelp.net/

This site from the Mental Health Network contains links on depression diagnosis, therapy, and organizations.

The Search for Novel Antipsychotic Drugs
http://salmon.psy.plym.ac.uk/year2/schizo1.htm

This site provides student access to a comprehensive set of materials relating to the pharmacology of schizophrenia.

Autistic, Attention-Deficit/Hyperactivity, Stress, and Substance Abuse Disorders

chapter 16

CHAPTER OUTLINE

LEARNING OBJECTIVES

1. Describe the symptoms and possible causes of autism.
2. Describe the symptoms and possible causes of attention-deficit/hyperactivity disorder.
3. Describe the physiological responses to stress and their effects on health.
4. Discuss some of the long-term effects of stress, including posttraumatic stress disorder, and describe the role of the coping response.
5. Discuss the interactions between stress, the immune system, and infectious diseases.
6. Review the general characteristics and definitions of addiction.
7. Describe two common features of addictive drugs: positive and negative reinforcement.
8. Review the neural basis of the reinforcing effects and withdrawal effects of opiates.
9. Describe the behavioral and pharmacological effects of cocaine,amphetamine, and nicotine.
10. Describe the behavioral and pharmacological effects of alcohol and cannabis.
11. Describe research on the role that heredity plays in addiction in humans.
12. Discuss methods of therapy for drug abuse.

PROLOGUE

A Sudden Craving

John was beginning to feel that perhaps he would be able to get his life back together. It looked like his drug habit was going to be licked. He had started taking drugs several years ago. At first he had used them only on special occasions—mostly on weekends with his friends—but heroin proved to be his undoing. One of his acquaintances had introduced him to the needle, and he had found the rush so blissful that he couldn't wait a whole week for his next fix. Soon he was shooting up daily. Shortly after that, he lost his job and, to support his habit, began earning money through car theft and small-time drug dealing. As time went on, he needed more and more heroin at shorter and shorter intervals, which necessitated even more money. Eventually, he was arrested and convicted of selling heroin to an undercover agent.

The judge gave John the choice of prison or a drug rehabilitation program, and he chose the latter. Soon after starting the program, he realized that he was relieved to have been caught. Now that he was clean and could reflect on his life, he realized what would have become of him had he continued to take drugs. Withdrawal from heroin was not an experience he would want to live through again, but it turned out not to be as bad as he had feared. The counselors in his program told him to avoid his old neighborhood and to break contact with his old acquaintances, and he followed their advice. He had been clean for eight weeks, he had a job, and he had met a woman who really seemed sympathetic. He knew that he hadn't completely kicked his habit, because every now and then, despite his best intentions, he found himself thinking about the wonderful glow that heroin provided him. But things were definitely looking up.

Then one day, while walking home from work, he turned a corner and saw a new poster plastered on the wall of a building. The poster, produced by an antidrug agency, showed all sorts of drug paraphernalia in full color: glassine envelopes with white powder spilling out of them, syringes, needles, a spoon and candle used to heat and dissolve the drug. He was seized with a sudden, intense compulsion to take some heroin. He closed his eyes, trying to will the feeling away, but all he could feel was his churning stomach and his trembling limbs, and all he could think about was getting a fix. He hopped on a bus and went back to his old neighborhood.

Chapter 15 discussed mental disorders characterized by maladaptive emotions and thought processes. This chapter considers four more disorders with a physiological basis: autistic disorder, attention-deficit/hyperactivity disorder, stress disorders, and drug abuse. Autistic disorder appears to be a hereditary disorder that affects development of the brain. Most autistic children show mental retardation, but some do not. However, all of them exhibit severe deficiencies in social behavior; some do not even seem to recognize the existence of people other than themselves. Attention-deficit/hyperactivity disorder can cause severe impairments in children's social and academic adjustments.

Although we tend to think of stress disorders and drug abuse as the consequences of modern civilization, stress and drugs have probably been familiar to our species from its very beginnings. Modern research has shown that communal living in groups of nonhuman primates generates much stress—so much that some members die of stress-related illness. And our ancestors long ago discovered that eating or smoking certain plants (or drinking fermented fruit juice) had interesting effects on one's perception, mood, and behavior. Of course, the development of modern chemistry has enabled us to refine drugs found in plant tissue or produce chemicals that are not normally found in nature, and some of these drugs are much more potent (and potentially addictive) than those our ancestors encountered.

Autistic Disorder

Description

autistic disorder A chronic disorder whose symptoms include failure to develop normal social relations with other people, impaired development of communicative ability, lack of imaginative ability, and repetitive, stereotyped movements.

When a baby is born, the parents normally expect to love and cherish the child and to be loved and cherished in return. Unfortunately, approximately 4 in every 10,000 infants are born with a disorder that impairs their ability to return their parents' affection. The symptoms of **autistic disorder** include a failure to develop normal social

When a baby is born, the parents normally expect to love and cherish the child and to be loved and cherished in return.

relationships with other people, impaired development of communicative ability, and lack of imaginative ability. The syndrome was named and characterized by Kanner (1943), who chose the term (*auto,* "self," *-ism,* "condition") to refer to the child's apparent self-absorption. The disorder afflicts boys three times more often than girls.

Infants with autistic disorder do not seem to care whether they are held, or they may arch their backs when picked up, as if they do not want to be held. They do not look or smile at their caregivers. If they are ill, hurt, or tired, they will not look to someone else for comfort. As they get older, they do not enter into social relationships with other children and avoid eye contact with them. Their language development is abnormal or even nonexistent. They often echo what is said to them, and they may refer to themselves as others do—in the second or third person. For example, they may say, "You want some milk?" to mean "I want some milk." They may learn words and phrases by rote, but they fail to use them productively and creatively. Those who do acquire reasonably good language skills talk about their own preoccupations without regard for other people's interests. They usually interpret other people's speech literally. For example, when an autistic person is asked, "Can you pass the salt?," he might simply say "Yes"—and not because he is trying to be funny or sarcastic.

Autistic people generally show abnormal interests and behaviors. For example, they may show stereotyped movements, such as flapping their hand back and forth or rocking back and forth. They may become obsessed with investigating objects, sniffing them, feeling their texture, or moving them back and forth. They may become attached to a particular object and insist on carrying it around with them. They may become preoccupied in lining up objects or in forming patterns with them, oblivious to everything else that is going on around them. They often insist on following precise routines and may become violently upset when they are hindered from doing so. They show no make-believe play and are uninterested in stories that involve fantasy. Although most autistic people are mentally retarded, not all are; and unlike most retarded people, they may be physically adept and graceful. Some have isolated skills, such as the ability to multiply two four-digit numbers very quickly, without apparent effort.

Autistic disorder is one of several pervasive developmental disorders that have similar symptoms (Rapin, 1999). *Asperger's disorder* is generally less severe, and its symptoms do not include a delay in language development or the presence of important cognitive deficits. The primary symptoms are deficient or absent social interactions and repetitive and stereotyped behaviors and obsessional interest in narrow subjects.

Figure 16.1

Responses of the fusiform face area in normal and autistic adults looking at pictures of human faces. This region received very little activation in the autistic subjects, but in every normal subject this region was the most active one in the brain. FG = fusiform gyrus, STS = superior temporal sulcus, Amy = amygdala.

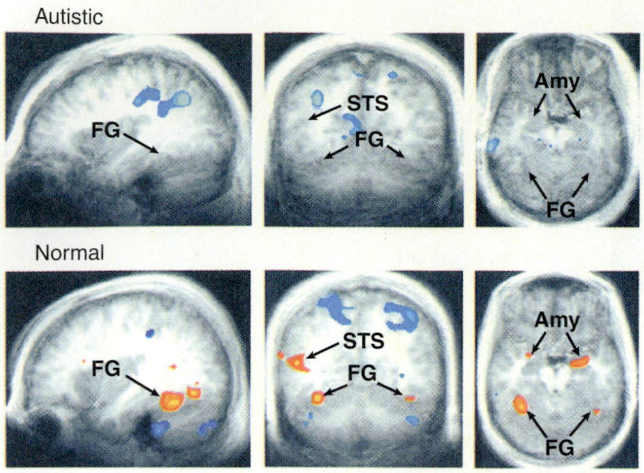

From Pierce, K., Müller, R.-A., Ambrose, J., Allen, G., and Courchesne, E. *Brain,* 2001, *124,* 2059–2073.

Rett's disorder is a genetic neurological syndrome seen in girls that accompanies an arrest of normal brain development that occurs during infancy. Children with *childhood disintegrative disorder* show normal intellectual and social development and then, sometime between the ages of 2 and 10 years, show a severe regression into autism. When autistic children with mental retardation reach puberty, many of them develop epileptic seizures, an occurrence that suggests that abnormal changes take place in the brain at this stage of development (Rapin, 1995). The prevalence of all forms of pervasive developmental disorders is 18.7 in 10,000 (Fombonne, 1999).

As you can see, autistic disorder includes affective, cognitive, and behavioral abnormalities. The lack of interest in or understanding of other people is reflected in the response of the autistic brain to the sight of the human face. As we saw in Chapter 6, the *fusiform face area,* located on the fusiform gyrus, a region of visual association cortex on the base of the brain, is involved in the recognition of individual faces. A functional imaging study by Pierce et al. (2001) found little or no activity in the fusiform face area of autistic adults looking at pictures of human faces. In contrast, this region showed the greatest increase of all brain regions of control subjects performing the same task. (See ***Figure 16.1.***) As Pierce and her colleagues note, autistics are poor at recognizing facial expressions of emotion or the direction of another person's gaze and have low rates of eye contact with other people. It seems likely that the fusiform face area of autistics fails to respond to the sight of the human face because these people spend very little time studying other people's faces and hence do not develop the expertise the rest of us acquire through normal interpersonal interactions.

Possible Causes

When Kanner first described autism, he suggested that it was of biological origin; but not long afterward, influential clinicians argued that autism was learned. More precisely, it was taught—by cold, insensitive, distant, demanding, introverted parents. Bettelheim (1967) believed that autism was similar to the apathetic, withdrawn, and hopeless behavior seen in some of the survivors of the German concentration camps of World War II. You can imagine the guilt felt by parents who were told by a mental health professional that they were to blame for their child's pitiful condition. Some professionals saw the existence of autism as evidence for child abuse and advocated that autistic children be removed from their families and placed with foster parents.

Nowadays, researchers and mental health professionals are convinced that autism is caused by biological factors and that parents should be given help and sympathy, not blame. Careful studies have shown that the parents of autistic children are just as warm, sociable, and responsive as other parents (Cox et al., 1975). In addition, parents with one autistic child often raise one or more normal children. If the parents were at fault, we should expect *all* of their offspring to be autistic.

Heritability

Like all the mental disorders I have described so far, at least some forms of autism appear to be heritable. As we shall see, there appear to be *several* hereditary causes, as well as some nonhereditary ones. Between 2 and 3 percent of the siblings of people with autism are themselves autistic (Folstein and Piven, 1991; Bailey, 1993). That figure might seem low, but it is between 50 and 100 times the expected frequency of autism in the general population (4 cases per 10,000 people). As Jones and Szatmari (1988) note, many parents stop having children after an autistic child is born for fear of having another one with the same disorder; if they did not, the percentage of autistic siblings would be even larger.

The best evidence for genetic factors in autism comes from twin studies. These studies indicate that the concordance rate for monozygotic twins is approximately 70 percent, while the rate for dizygotic twins studied so far is 0 percent (Folstein and Rosen-Sheidley, 2001). In addition, most of the nonautistic members of discordant monozygotic twins exhibited deficient language development and showed signs of social withdrawal (Bailey et al., 1995). These results indicate that autism is highly heritable. Genetic investigations have suggested that genes involved in autistic disorder may be located on chromosomes 2, 7, 15, and X (Folstein and Rosen-Sheidley, 2001). Evidence obtained by Wassink et al. (2001) suggests that the *WNT2* gene, located on chromosome 7 and involved in development, may play a role in autism.

Brain Pathology

The fact that autism is highly heritable is presumptive evidence that the disorder is a result of structural or biochemical abnormalities in the brain. In addition, a variety of nongenetic pathological conditions—especially those that occur during prenatal development—can produce the symptoms of autism. Evidence suggests that approximately 20 percent of all cases of autism have definable biological causes, such as rubella (German measles) during pregnancy; prenatal thalidomide; encephalitis caused by the herpes virus; and tuberous sclerosis, a genetic disorder that causes the formation of benign tumors in many organs, including the brain (De Long, 1999; Rapin, 1999). Hollander et al. (1999) found evidence for an autoimmune process in some cases of autism. As we saw in Chapter 15, tic disorders and obsessive-compulsive disorder can be produced by an autoimmune reaction provoked by a group A β-hemolytic streptococcal infection. Hollander and his colleagues found streptococcal antibodies in blood samples from 78 percent of the autistic patients but only 21 percent of the normal subjects. All these findings suggest that autistic disorder can result from a wide variety of factors that damage the brain or impair its development.

Studies by Miller and Strömland (1993) and Strömland et al. (1994) identified a drug that can increase the likelihood of autism. Thalidomide, a drug that was given to pregnant women in some countries during the 1960s to treat the symptoms of morning sickness, was later found to cause serious birth defects. Miller, Strömland, and their colleagues studied eighty-six people whose mothers had taken thalidomide during pregnancy and found that five of them were autistic. (This rate is 145 times higher than the rate of autism in the population as a whole.) All of the autistic people had been exposed to thalidomide between prenatal days 20 and 24. As Rodier et al. (1996) note, the only part of the central nervous system that forms at this time is the brain stem. They suggest that either genetic abnormalities or exposure of a developing embryo to toxic chemicals just after closure of the neural tube may be responsible for anomalies in brain development that are responsible for autism. By the way, studies have failed to find evidence that autism is linked to childhood immunization (Farrington, Miller, and Taylor, 2001; Andrews et al., 2002; Taylor et al., 2002).

Researchers have found evidence for structural abnormalities in the brains of autistics, but so far we cannot point to any single abnormality as the cause of the disorder. Courchesne et al. (2001) use structural MRI to study the brain development of autistic and normal boys. They found that although the average head size (and presumably the brain size) of the two groups was identical at birth, by ages 2–4 years the brains of children who became autistic were larger than normal. MRI scans showed increased growth of white matter in the cerebellum and gray and white matter in the cerebral hemispheres. The cerebellar gray matter grew more slowly than normal. One region of the cerebellum—the vermis, a structure located on the midline—was much smaller than normal. Bailey et al. (1998) studied the brains of six deceased autistics and found enlarged brain size in most cases, along with developmental abnormalities in the cortex, brain stem, and cerebellum. They found a 31 percent decrease in the number of Purkinje cells, the largest neurons found in the cerebellar cortex. The relationship between these abnormalities and the symptoms of autism is not yet understood.

INTERIM SUMMARY

Autistic Disorder

Autistic disorder occurs in approximately 4 of 10,000 infants. It is characterized by poor or absent social relations, communicative abilities, and imaginative abilities and the presence of repetitive, purposeless movements. Although autistics are usually, but not always, retarded, they may have a particular, isolated talent. Autistic people tend not to pay attention to other people's faces, which is reflected in the lack of activation of the fusiform face area when they do so.

In the past, clinicians blamed parents for autism, but now it is generally accepted as a disorder with biological roots. Twin studies have shown that autism is highly heritable but that several genes are responsible for its development. Autism can also be caused by events that interfere with prenatal development, such as prenatal thalidomide or maternal infection with rubella. Evidence suggests that the most critical period occurs between the 20th and 24th days of gestation. Autism does not appear to be associated with childhood vaccinations. MRI studies indicate that although the brain size of babies who become autistic is normal at birth, their brains are larger than normal by ages 2–4 years. Parts of the brain, such as the vermis of the cerebellum, are much smaller than normal. Studies of the brains of deceased autistics have found abnormalities in the cortex, brain stem, and cerebellum.

Attention-Deficit/Hyperactivity Disorder

Description

Some children have difficulty concentrating, remaining still, and working on a task. At one time or other, *most* children exhibit these characteristics. But children with **attention-deficit/hyperactivity disorder (ADHD)** display these symptoms so often that they interfere with the children's ability to learn. ADHD is the most common behavior disorder that shows itself in childhood. It is usually first discovered in the classroom, where children are expected to sit quietly and pay attention to the teacher or work steadily on a project. Some children's inability to meet these expectations then becomes evident. They have difficulty withholding a response, act without reflecting, often show reckless and impetuous behavior, and let interfering activities intrude into ongoing tasks.

According to the DSM-IV, the diagnosis of ADHD requires the presence of six or more of nine symptoms of inattention and six or more of nine symptoms of hyperactivity and impulsivity that have persisted for at least six months. Symptoms of inattention include such things as "often had difficulty sustaining attention in tasks of play activities" or "is often easily distracted by extraneous stimuli"; and symptoms of hyperactivity and impulsivity include such things as "often runs about or climbs excessively in situations in which it is inappropriate" or "often interrupts or intrudes on others (e. g., butts into conversations or games)" (American Psychiatric Association, 1994, pp. 64–65).

attention-deficit/hyperactivity disorder (ADHD) A disorder characterized by uninhibited responses, lack of sustained attention, and hyperactivity; first shows itself in childhood.

ADHD can be very disruptive of a child's education and that of other children in the same classroom. (See Wilens, Biederman, and Spencer, 2002, for a review.) It is seen in 4–5 percent of grade school children. Boys are about ten times more likely than girls to receive a diagnosis of ADHD, but in adulthood the ratio is approximately 2 to 1, which suggests that many girls with this disorder fail to be diagnosed. Because the symptoms can vary—some children's symptoms are primarily those of inattention, some are those of hyperactivity, and some show mixed symptoms—most investigators believe that this disorder has more than one cause. Diagnosis is often difficult, because the symptoms are not well defined. ADHD is often associated with aggression, conduct disorder, learning disabilities, depression, anxiety, and low self-esteem. Approximately 60 percent of children with ADHD continue to display symptoms of this disorder into adulthood, at which time a disproportionate number develop antisocial personality disorder and substance abuse disorder (Ernst et al., 1998). Adults with ADHD are also more likely to show cognitive impairments and lower occupational attainment than would be predicted by their education (Seidman et al., 1998). The most common treatment for ADHD is administration of methylphenidate (Ritalin), a drug that inhibits the reuptake of dopamine. Amphetamine, another dopamine agonist, also reduces the symptoms of ADHD, but this drug is used much less often.

Possible Causes

There is strong evidence from both family studies and twin studies for hereditary factors in a person's likelihood of developing ADHD (Faraone and Biederman, 1994; Levy et al., 1997). In their twin study, Levy and her colleagues conclude that "ADHD is best viewed as the extreme of a behavior that varies genetically throughout the entire population rather than as a disorder with discrete determinants" (p. 737).

According to Sagvolden and Sergeant (1998), the impulsive and hyperactive behavior that are seen in children with ADHD are the result of a *delay of reinforcement gradient* that is steeper than normal. As we saw in Chapter 12, the occurrence of an appetitive stimulus can reinforce the behavior that just preceded it. For example, a piece of food can reinforce the lever press that a rat just made, and a smile can reinforce a person's attempts at conversation. Reinforcing stimuli are most effective if they immediately follow a behavior: The longer the delay, the less effective the reinforcement. Sagvolden and Sergeant suggest that some physiological differences in the brains of children with ADHD increase the steepness of their delay of reinforcement gradient, which means that immediate reinforcement is even more effective in these children, but even slightly delayed reinforcement loses its potency. (See ***Figure 16.2.***)

Why would a steeper delay of reinforcement gradient produce the symptoms of ADHD? According to Sagvolden and Sergeant, for people with a steep gradient, reinforcement with a short delay will be even more effective, thus producing overactivity. On the other hand, these people will be less likely to engage in behaviors that are followed by delayed reinforcement, as many of our behaviors (especially classroom activities) are. In support of this hypothesis, Sagvolden et al. (1998) trained normal boys and boys with ADHD on an instrumental conditioning task. When a signal was present, responses would be reinforced every 30 seconds with coins or trinkets. When the signal was not present, responses were never reinforced. The normal boys learned to respond only when

Figure 16.2

Different delay of reinforcement gradients, hypothesized by Sagvolden and Sergeant (1998) to be responsible for the impulsive behavior of children with ADHD.

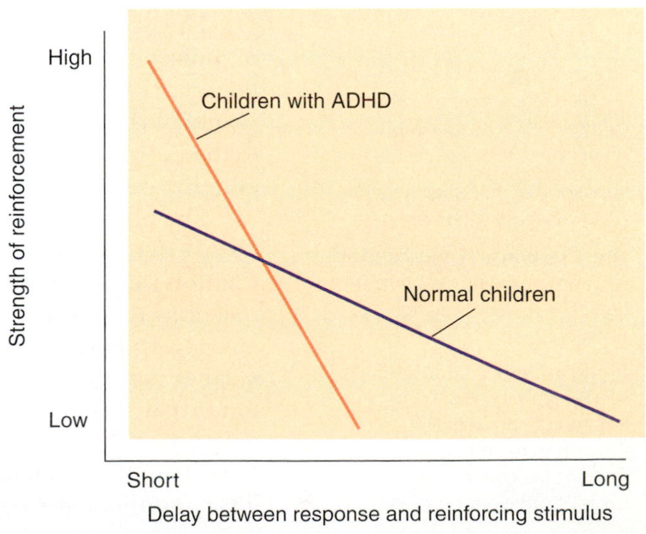

the signal was present. When the signal was off, they waited patiently until it came on again. In contrast, the boys with ADHD showed impulsive behavior—intermittent bursts of rapid responses whether the signal was present or not. According to the investigators, this pattern of responding was what would be expected by a steep delay of reinforcement gradient.

Studies of brain structure of people with ADHD do not reveal any localized abnormalities, though the total volume of their brains is approximately 4 percent smaller than normal (Castellanos et al., 2002). However, a special functional imaging method that estimates the blood volume in various regions of the brain revealed decreased blood volumes in the basal ganglia and cerebellar vermis of boys with ADHD (Teicher et al., 2000; Anderson et al., 2002).

INTERIM SUMMARY

Attention-Deficit/Hyperactivity Disorder

Attention-deficit/hyperactivity disorder is the most common behavior disorder that first appears in childhood. Children with ADHD show symptoms of inattention, hyperactivity, and impulsivity. This disorder is seen in 4–5 percent of grade school children and is more frequent in boys. The symptoms of about 60 percent of children with ADHD continue into adulthood, and the disorder is associated with antisocial personality disorder and substance abuse disorder. The most common medical treatment is methylphenidate, a dopamine agonist.

Family and twin studies indicate a heritable component in this disorder. Evidence suggests that a steeper delay of reinforcement gradient may account for impulsiveness and hyperactivity. The brains of people with ADHD are approximately 4 percent smaller than normal, and functional imaging indicates a decreased blood volume in the basal ganglia and cerebellar vermis.

Stress Disorders

Aversive stimuli can harm people's health. Many of these harmful effects are produced not by the stimuli themselves but by our reactions to them. Walter Cannon, the physiologist who criticized the James-Lange theory described in Chapter 10, introduced the term **stress** to refer to the physiological reaction caused by the perception of aversive or threatening situations.

The word *stress* was borrowed from engineering, in which it refers to the action of physical forces of mechanical structures. The word can be a noun or a verb; and the noun can refer to situations or the individual's response to them. Because of this potential confusion, I will refer to "stressful" stimuli and situations as **stressors** and to the individual's reaction as a **stress response.** The word *stress* will refer to the general process (as in the title to this section).

The physiological responses that accompany the negative emotions prepare us to threaten rivals or fight them or to run away from dangerous situations. Walter Cannon introduced the phrase **fight-or-flight response** to refer to the physiological reactions that prepare us for the strenuous efforts required by fighting or running away. Normally, once we have bluffed or fought with an adversary or run away from a dangerous situation, the threat is over and our physiological condition can return to normal. The fact that the physiological responses may have adverse long-term effects on our health is unimportant as long as the responses are brief. But sometimes, the threatening situations are continuous rather than episodic, producing a more or less continuous stress response.

stress A general, imprecise term that can refer either to a stress response or to a stressor (stressful situation).

stressor A stimulus (or situation) that produces a stress response.

stress response A physiological reaction caused by the perception of aversive or threatening situations.

fight-or-flight response A species-typical response preparatory to fighting or fleeing; thought to be responsible for some of the deleterious effects of stressful situations on health.

Physiology of the Stress Response

As we saw in Chapter 10, emotions consist of behavioral, autonomic, and endocrine responses. The latter two components, the autonomic and endocrine responses, are the ones that can have adverse effects on health. (Well, I guess the behavioral components can too, if a person rashly gets into a fight with someone who is much bigger and stronger.) Because threatening situations generally call for vigorous activity, the autonomic and endocrine responses that accompany them are catabolic; that is, they help to mobilize the body's energy resources. The sympathetic branch of the autonomic nervous system is active, and the adrenal glands secrete epinephrine, norepinephrine, and steroid stress hormones. Because the effects of sympathetic activity are similar to those of the adrenal hormones, I will limit my discussion to the hormonal responses.

Epinephrine affects glucose metabolism, causing the nutrients stored in muscles to become available to provide energy for strenuous exercise. Along with norepinephrine, the hormone also increases blood flow to the muscles by increasing the output of the heart. In doing so, it also increases blood pressure, which, over the long term, contributes to cardiovascular disease.

Besides serving as a stress hormone, norepinephrine is (as you know) secreted in the brain as a neurotransmitter. Some of the behavioral and physiological responses produced by aversive stimuli appear to be mediated by noradrenergic neurons. For example, microdialysis studies have found that stressful situations increase the release of norepinephrine in the hypothalamus, frontal cortex, and lateral basal forebrain (Yokoo et al. 1990; Cenci et al., 1992). Presumably, the release of norepinephrine in the brain is produced by a pathway from the central nucleus of the amygdala to the norepinephrine-secreting regions of the brain stem (Van Bockstaele et al., 2001).

The other stress-related hormone is *cortisol,* a steroid secreted by the adrenal cortex. Cortisol is called a **glucocorticoid** because it has profound effects on glucose metabolism. In addition, glucocorticoids help to break down protein and convert it to glucose, help to make fats available for energy, increase blood flow, and stimulate behavioral responsiveness, presumably by affecting the brain. They decrease the sensitivity of the gonads to luteinizing hormone, which suppresses the secretion of the sex steroid hormones. In fact, Singer and Zumoff (1992) found that the blood level of testosterone in male hospital residents (doctors, not patients) was severely depressed, presumably because of the stressful work schedule they were obliged to follow. Glucocorticoids have other physiological effects, too, some of which are only poorly understood. Almost every cell in the body contains glucocorticoid receptors, which means that few of them are unaffected by these hormones.

The secretion of glucocorticoids is controlled by neurons in the paraventricular nucleus of the hypothalamus (PVN). The neurons of the PVN secrete a peptide called **corticotropin-releasing hormone (CRH),** which stimulates the anterior pituitary gland to secrete **adrenocorticotropic hormone (ACTH).** ACTH enters the general circulation and stimulates the adrenal cortex to secrete glucocorticoids. (See ***Figure 16.3.***)

CRH is also secreted within the brain, where it serves as a neuromodulator/neurotransmitter, especially in regions of the limbic system that are involved in emotional responses, such as the periaqueductal gray matter, the locus coeruleus, and the central nucleus of the amygdala. The

glucocorticoid One of a group of hormones of the adrenal cortex that are important in protein and carbohydrate metabolism, secreted especially in times of stress.

corticotropin-releasing hormone (CRH) A hypothalamic hormone that stimulates the anterior pituitary gland to secrete ACTH (adrenocorticotropic hormone).

adrenocorticotropic hormone (ACTH) A hormone released by the anterior pituitary gland in response to CRH; stimulates the adrenal cortex to produce glucocorticoids.

Figure 16.3

Control of the secretion of glucocorticoids by the adrenal cortex and of catecholamines by the adrenal medulla.

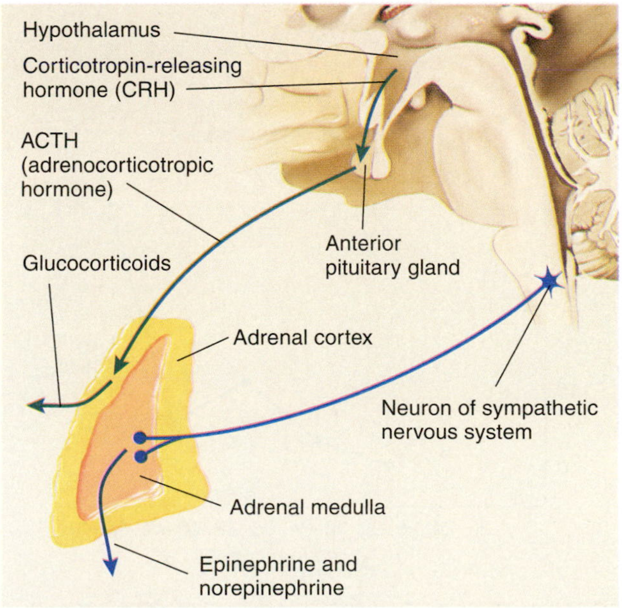

behavioral effects produced by an injection of CRH into the brain are similar to those produced by aversive situations; thus, some elements of the stress response appear to be produced by the release of CRH by neurons in the brain. For example, intracerebroventricular injection of CRH decreases the amount of time a rat spends in the center of a large open chamber (Britton et al., 1982), enhances the acquisition of a classically conditioned fear response (Cole and Koob, 1988), and increases the startle response elicited by a sudden loud noise (Swerdlow et al., 1986). On the other hand, intracerebroventricular injection of a CRH antagonist *reduces* the anxiety caused by a variety of stressful situations (Kalin, Sherman, and Takahashi, 1988; Heinrichs et al., 1994; Skutella et al., 1994).

The secretion of glucocorticoids does more than help an animal react to a stressful situation: It helps the animal to survive. If a rat's adrenal glands are removed, the rat becomes much more susceptible to the effects of stress. In fact, a stressful situation that a normal rat would take in its stride might kill one whose adrenal glands have been removed. And physicians know that if an adrenalectomized human is subjected to stressors, he or she must be given additional amounts of glucocorticoid (Tyrell and Baxter, 1981).

Health Effects of Long-Term Stress

Many studies of humans who have been subjected to stressful situations have found evidence of ill health. For example, survivors of concentration camps, who were obviously subjected to long-term stress, have generally poorer health later in life than other people of the same age (Cohen, 1953). Drivers of subway trains that injure or kill people are more likely to suffer from illnesses several months later (Theorell et al., 1992). Air traffic controllers, especially those who work at busy airports where the danger of collisions is greatest, show a greater incidence of high blood pressure, which gets worse as they grow older (Cobb and Rose, 1973). (See ***Figure 16.4.***) They also are more likely to suffer from ulcers or diabetes.

Figure 16.4

Incidence of hypertension in various age groups of air traffic controllers at high-stress and low-stress airports.

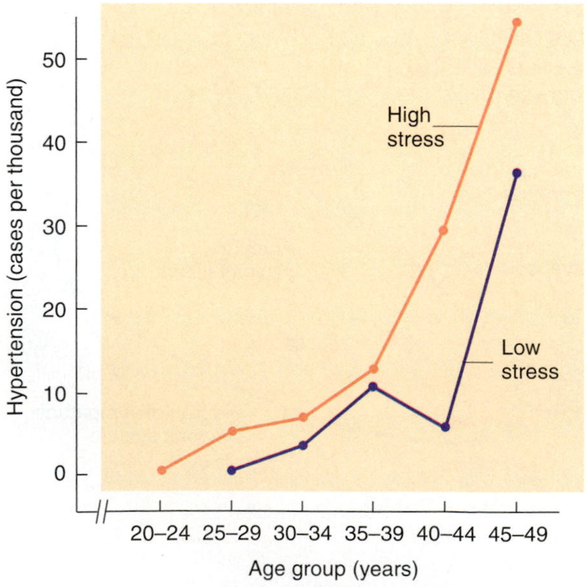

Based on data from Cobb and Rose, 1973.

A pioneer in the study of stress, Hans Selye, suggested that most of the harmful effects of stress were produced by the prolonged secretion of glucocorticoids (Selye, 1976). Although the short-term effects of glucocorticoids are essential, the long-term effects are damaging. These effects include increased blood pressure, damage to muscle tissue, steroid diabetes, infertility, inhibition of growth, inhibition of the inflammatory responses, and suppression of the immune system. High blood pressure can lead to heart attacks and stroke. Inhibition of growth in children who are subjected to prolonged stress prevents them from attaining their full height. Inhibition of the inflammatory response makes it more difficult for the body to heal itself after an injury, and suppression of the immune system makes an individual vulnerable to infections. Long-term administration of steroids to treat inflammatory diseases often produces cognitive deficits and can even lead to *steroid psychosis,* whose symptoms include profound distractibility, anxiety, insomnia, depression, hallucinations, and delusions (Lewis and Smith, 1983).

The adverse effects of stress on healing were demonstrated in a study by Kiecolt-Glaser et al. (1995), who performed punch biopsy wounds in the subjects' forearms, a harmless procedure that is used often in medical research. The subjects were people who were providing long-term care for relatives with Alzheimer's disease—a situation that is known to cause stress—and control subjects of the same approximate age and family income. The investigators found that healing of the wounds took significantly longer in the caregivers (48.7 days versus 39.3 days). (See ***Figure 16.5.***)

Sapolsky and his colleagues have investigated one rather serious long-term effect of stress: brain damage. As you learned in Chapter 12, the hippocampal formation plays a crucial role in learning and memory, and evidence suggests that one of the causes of memory loss that occurs with aging is degeneration of this brain structure. Research with animals has shown that long-term exposure to glucocorticoids destroys neurons located in field CA1 of the hippocampal formation. The hormone appears to destroy the neurons by decreasing the entry of glucose and decreasing the reuptake of glutamate (Sapolsky, 1992, 1995; McEwen and Sapolsky, 1995). Both of these effects make neurons more susceptible to potentially harmful events, such as decreased blood flow, which often occurs as a result of the aging process. The increased amounts of extracellular glutamate permit calcium to enter through NMDA receptors. (You will recall that the entry of excessive amounts of calcium can kill neurons.) Perhaps, then, the stressors to which people are subjected throughout their lives increase the likelihood of memory problems as they grow older. In fact, Lupien et al. (1996) found that elderly people with elevated blood levels of glucocorticoids learned a maze more slowly than did those with normal levels.

Even acute exposure to stress can have adverse effects on normal brain functioning. Diamond and his colleagues (Diamond et al., 1999; Mesches et al., 1999) placed rats individually in a Plexiglas box and then placed the box in a cage with a cat for 75 minutes. Although the cat could not harm the rats, the cat's presence (and odor) clearly alarmed the rats and elicited a stress response; the stressed rats' blood glucocorticoid increased to approximately five times its normal level. The investigators found that this short-term stress affected the functioning of the animals' hippocampus. The stressed rats' ability to learn a spatial task (which requires the hippocampus) was impaired, and primed-burst potentiation (a form of long-term potentiation) was impaired in hippocampal slices taken from stressed rats. (See ***Figure 16.6.***)

Uno et al. (1989) found that if long-term stress is intense enough, it can even cause brain damage in young primates. The investigators studied a colony of vervet monkeys housed in a primate center in Kenya. They found that some monkeys died, apparently from stress. Vervet monkeys have a hierarchical society, and monkeys near the bottom of the hierarchy are picked on by the others; thus, they are almost continuously subjected to stress. (Ours is not the only species with social structures that cause a stress reaction in some of its members.) The deceased monkeys had gastric ulcers and enlarged adrenal glands, which are signs of chronic stress. And as Figure 16.7 shows, neurons in the CA1 field of the hippocampal formation were completely destroyed. (See ***Figure 16.7.***) Severe stress appears to cause brain damage in

Figure 16.5

Percentage of caregivers and control subjects whose wounds had healed as a function of time after the biopsy was performed.

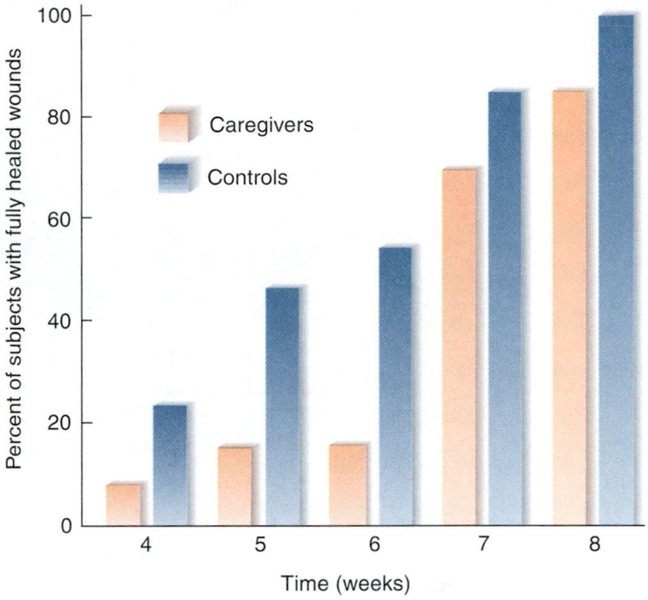

Adapted from Kiecolt-Glaser, J. K., Marucha, P. T., Malarkey, W. B., Mercado, A. M., and Glaser, R. *Lancet,* 1995, *346,* 1194–1196.

Figure 16.6

Effects of acute stress caused by exposing a rat to the sight and smell of a cat. The stress raised the glucocorticoid level (corticosterone, in the case of a rat), impaired the development of primed-burst potentiation (a form of long-term potentiation) in slices taken from these animals, and interfered with learning of a spatial task that requires the hippocampus.

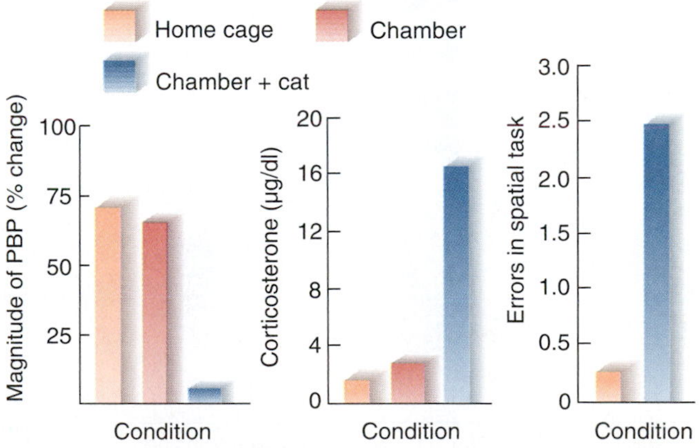

Adapted from Diamond, D. M., Park, C. R., Heman, K. L., and Rose, G. M. *Hippocampus,* 1999, *9,* 542–552, and Mesches, M. H., Fleshner, M., Heman, K. L., Rose, G. M., and Diamond, D. M. *Journal of Neuroscience,* 1999, *19,* RC18(1–5). Copyright 1989 by the Society for Neuroscience.

Figure 16.7

Photomicrographs showing brain damage caused by stress. (a) Section through the hippocampus of a normal monkey. (b) Section through the hippocampus of a monkey of low social status subjected to stress. Compare the regions between the arrowheads, which are normally filled with large pyramidal cells.

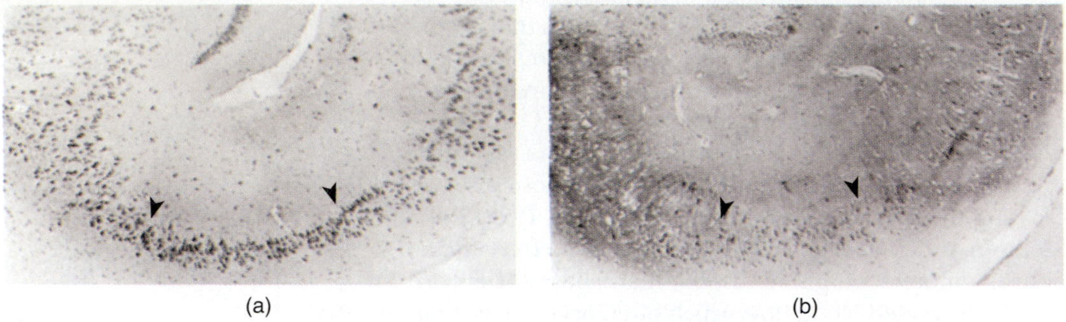

From Uno, H., Tarara, R., Else, J. G., Suleman, M. A., and Sapolsky, R. M. *Journal of Neuroscience,* 1989, *9,* 1706–1711. Reprinted by permission of the *Journal of Neuroscience.* Copyright 1989 by the Society for Neuroscience.

humans as well; Jensen, Genefke, and Hyldebrandt (1982) found evidence of brain degeneration in CT scans of people who had been subjected to torture.

As we saw in Chapter 10, prenatal stress tends to inhibit androgenization of the fetuses. That is, when a pregnant female is exposed to stressors, the behavior and brain structure of her male offspring appear less masculinized and defeminized than those of control animals. Prenatal stress also appears to produce long-term effects on animals' stress reactions. At least some of the effects of prenatal stress on the fetus appear to be mediated by the secretion of glucocorticoids. Barbazanges et al. (1996) subjected pregnant female rats to stress and later observed the effects of this treatment on their offspring once they grew up. They found that the prenatally stressed rats showed a prolonged secretion of glucocorticoids when they were subjected to restraint stress. However, if the mothers' adrenal glands had been removed so that glucocorticoid levels could not increase during the stressful situation, their offspring reacted normally in adulthood. (The experimenters gave the adrenalectomized mothers controlled amounts of glucocorticoids to maintain them in good health.) (See ***Figure 16.8.***)

Figure 16.8

Effects of prenatal stress and glucocorticoid level on the stress response of adult rats. Adrenalectomy of the mother before she was subjected to stress prevented the development of an elevated stress response in the offspring during adulthood.

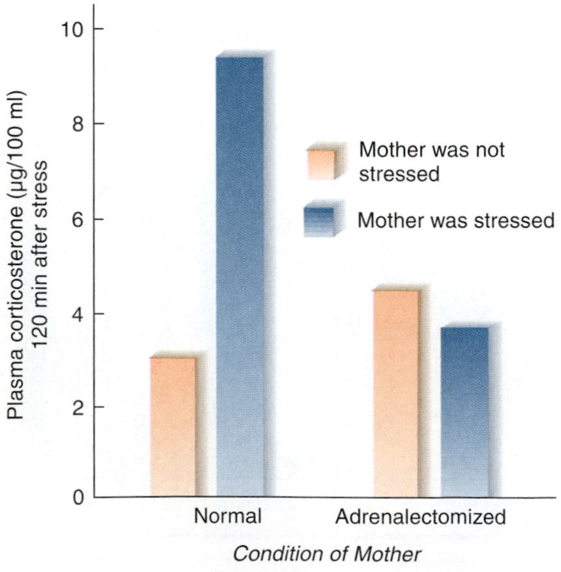

Adapted from Barbazanges, A., Piazza, P. V., Le Moal, M., and Maccari, S. *Journal of Neuroscience,* 1996, *16,* 3943–3949.

Posttraumatic Stress Disorder

The aftermath of tragic and traumatic events such as those that accompany wars and natural disasters often includes psychological symptoms that persist long after the stressful events are over. According to the DSM IV, **posttraumatic stress disorder (PTSD)** is caused by a situation in which a person "experienced, witnessed, or was confronted with an event or events that involved actual or threatened death or serious injury, or a threat to the physical integrity of self or others" that provoked a response that "involved intense fear, helplessness, or horror." The symptoms produced by such exposure include recurrent dreams or recollections of the event, feelings that the traumatic event is recurring ("flashback" episodes), and intense psychological distress.

These dreams, recollections, or flashback episodes can lead the person to avoid thinking about the traumatic event, which often results in diminished interest in social activities, feelings of detachment from others, suppressed emotional feelings, and a sense that the future is bleak and empty. Particular psychological symptoms include difficulty falling or staying asleep, irritability, outbursts of anger, difficulty in concentrating, and heightened reactions to sudden noises or movements. As this description indicates, people with PTSD have impaired mental health functioning. They also tend to have generally poor physical health (Zayfert et al., 2002). Although men are exposed to traumatic events more often than women are, women are approximately four times more likely to develop PTSD after being exposed to such events (Fullerton et al., 2001).

posttraumatic stress disorder (PTSD) A psychological disorder caused by exposure to a situation of extreme danger and stress; symptoms include recurrent dreams or recollections; can interfere with social activities and cause a feeling of hopelessness.

Posttraumatic stress disorder can strike people at any age. Children may show particular symptoms that are not usually seen in adulthood, such as loss of recently acquired language skills or toilet training, and somatic complaints such as stomachaches and headaches. Usually, the symptoms begin immediately after the traumatic event, but they are sometimes delayed for several months or years.

Evidence from twin studies suggest that genetic factors play a role in a person's susceptibility to develop PTSD. In fact, genetic factors influence not only the likelihood of developing PTSD after being exposed to traumatic events, but also the likelihood that the person will be involved in such an event (Stein et al., 2002). For example, people with a genetic predisposition toward irritability and anger are more likely to be assaulted, and those with a predisposition toward risky behavior are more likely to be involved in accidents. In a review of the Vietnam Era Twin Registry, Koenen et al. (2002) reported that the following demographic and personality factors predict an increased risk for being exposed to traumatic events: military service in Southeast Asia during the Vietnam war, a preexisting conduct disorder or substance dependence, and a family history of mood disorders. The following factors predict the risk of developing PTSD after exposure: earlier age at the time of the traumatic event, exposure to more than one traumatic event, a father with a depressive disorder, a low educational level, and a preexisting conduct disorder, panic disorder, generalized anxiety disorder, or depressive disorder.

As we saw earlier in this chapter, prolonged exposure to stress can cause brain damage, particularly in the hippocampus. At least two MRI studies have found evidence of hippocampal damage in veterans with combat-related posttraumatic stress disorder (Bremner et al., 1995; Gurvits et al., 1996). In the study by Gurvits et al. the volume of the hippocampal formation was reduced by over 20 percent, and the loss was proportional to the amount of combat exposure the veteran had experienced. Other studies have found similar effects in adult patients with posttraumatic stress disorder who had been subjected to severe childhood abuse (Bremner, 1999).

Although many investigators have assumed that the reduction in hippocampal volume in posttraumatic stress disorder is caused by hypersecretion of cortisol, evidence indicates that people with PTSD actually have *lower* levels of cortisol, and evidence suggests that trauma victims who develop PTSD show smaller increases in cortisol secretion at the time of the trauma. Resnick et al. (1995) analyzed blood samples from female rape victims that were obtained in the emergency room soon after the rape. They found that women who had been previously assaulted had the highest likelihood of developing PTSD—and the

For many American veterans of the Vietnam war, this memorial symbolizes the grief they feel from the loss of their comrades and the horrors experienced during conflict. The experience of wars and other disasters can produce posttraumatic stress disorder in some participants.

Figure 16.9

Concentrations of CRH in the cerebrospinal fluid of normal subjects and subjects with PTSD.

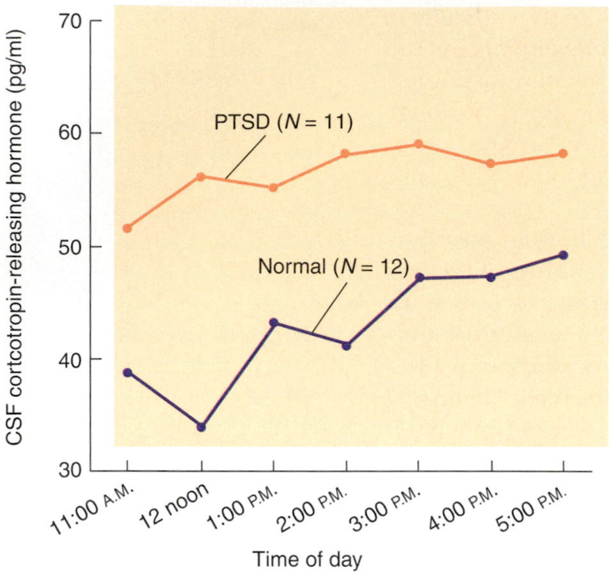

Adapted from Baker, D. G., West, S. A., Nicholson, W. E., Ekhator, N. N., Kasckow, J. W., Hill, K. K., Bruce, A. B., Orth, D. N., and Geracioti, T. D. *American Journal of Psychiatry,* 1999, *156,* 585–588.

Figure 16.10

A hypothetical explanation by Yehuda (2001) of the pattern of cortisol secretion in response to stress seen in patients with PTSD.

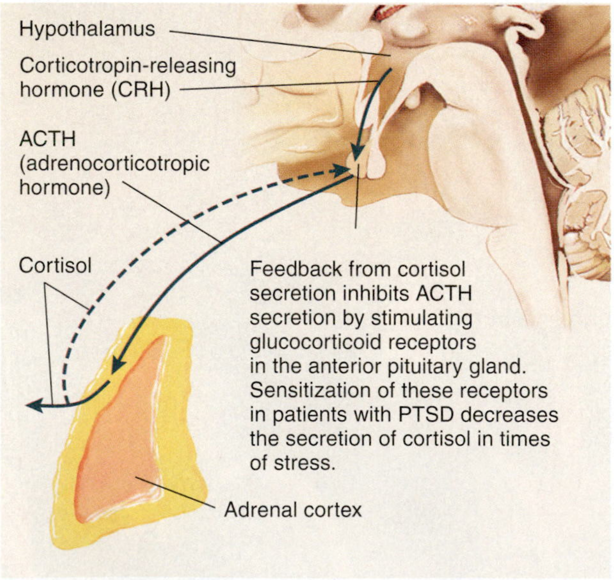

lowest levels of cortisol. McFarlane, Atchison, and Yehuda (1997) found similar effects in people involved in motor vehicle accidents.

Why should people who have been exposed to traumatic events show *decreased* cortisol secretion when they are exposed to stressful situations? Yehuda (2001) suggests that exposure to severe stress increases the number and sensitivity of glucocorticoid receptors in the hypothalamus and anterior pituitary gland. These receptors regulate cortisol secretion: If cortisol levels rise, stimulation of these receptors inhibits the secretion of ACTH. However, other factors (perhaps including the amygdala) continue to stimulate the release of CRH. Baker et al. (1999) placed a catheter in the subarachnoid space of the lumbar spine of combat veterans with PTSD and normal volunteers and withdrew samples of cerebrospinal fluid over a six-hour period. They found significantly elevated CRH levels in the men with PTSD. However, the levels of cortisol were not elevated; in fact, the patients with the lowest cortisol levels had the highest levels of PTSD symptoms. As we saw earlier in this chapter, CRH has anxiety-producing effects on the brain. Thus, high levels of CRH, rather than high levels of cortisol, may play a role in the development of the symptoms of PTSD. (See ***Figures 16.9 and 16.10.***)

The Coping Response

As we have seen, many of the harmful effects of long-term stress are caused by our own reactions—primarily the secretion of stress hormones. Some events that cause stress responses, such as prolonged exertion or extreme cold, cause damage directly. These stressors will affect everyone; their severity will depend on each person's physical capacity. The effects of other stressors, such as situations that cause fear or anxiety, depend on people's perceptions and emotional reactivity. That is, because of individual differences in temperament or experience with a particular situation, some people may find a situation stressful and others may not. In these cases it is the perception that counts.

One of the most important variables that determines whether an aversive stimulus will cause a stress reaction is the degree to which the situation can be controlled. When an animal can learn a **coping response**—a response that avoids contact with an aversive stimulus or decreases its severity, the animal's emotional response will decrease or even disappear. Weiss (1968) found that rats who learned to minimize (but not completely avoid) shocks by making a response whenever they heard a warning tone developed fewer stomach ulcers than did rats who had no control over the shocks. The effect was not caused by the pain itself, because both groups of animals received exactly the same number of shocks. Thus, being able to exert some control over an aversive situation reduces an animal's stress response. Humans react similarly. Situations that permit some control are less likely to produce signs of stress than are those in which other people (or machines) control the situation (Gatchel, Baum, and Krantz, 1989). Perhaps this phenomenon explains why some people like to have a magic charm or other "security blanket" with them in stressful situations. Perhaps even the *illusion* of control can be reassuring.

Foy et al. (1987) found that restraint stress or tail shock impaired the establishment of long-term potentiation in hippocampal slices taken from the stressed animals. A subsequent study from the same laboratory (Shors et al., 1989) found that this effect did not occur if the rats were given a chance to escape from the shock. (The study used a yoked control group so that rats that could escape the shock received just as many as those that could not.) Thus, the opportunity to make a coping response decreases the negative impact of stress on the hippocampus. The neural or hormonal mechanisms that are responsible for the beneficial effects of coping responses are not yet understood.

Stress and Infectious Diseases

As we have seen, long-term stress can be harmful to one's health and can even result in brain damage. The most important cause of these effects is elevated levels of glucocorticoids, but the high blood pressure caused by epinephrine and norepinephrine also plays a contributing role. In addition, the stress response can impair the functions of the immune system, which protects us from assault from viruses, microbes, fungi, and other types of parasites.

The immune system is one of the most complex systems of the body. Its function is to protect us from infection; and because infectious organisms have developed devious tricks through the process of evolution, our immune system has evolved devious tricks of its own. The immune system derives from white blood cells that develop in the bone marrow and in the thymus gland. Some of the cells roam through the blood or lymphatic system; others reside permanently in one place. Infectious microorganisms have unique proteins on their surfaces, called **antigens.** These proteins serve as the invaders' calling cards, identifying them to the immune system. Through exposure to the microorganisms, the immune system learns to recognize these proteins. (I will not try to explain the mechanism by which this learning takes place.) The result of this learning is the development of special lines of cells that produce specific **antibodies**—proteins that recognize antigens and help to kill the invading microorganism.

Often when a married person dies, his or her spouse dies soon afterward, frequently of an infection. In fact, a wide variety of stress-producing events in a person's life can increase the susceptibility to illness. For example, Glaser et al. (1987) found that medical students were more likely to contract acute infections and to show evidence of suppression of the immune system during the time that final examinations were given. In addition, autoimmune diseases often get worse when a person is subjected to stress, as Feigenbaum, Masi, and Kaplan (1979) found for rheumatoid arthritis.

Stone, Reed, and Neale (1987) attempted to determine whether stressful events in people's daily lives might predispose them to upper respiratory infection. If a person is exposed to a microorganism that might cause such a disease, the symptoms do not occur for several days; that is, there is an incubation period between exposure and signs of the actual illness. Thus, the authors reasoned that if stressful events suppressed the immune system, one might expect to see a higher likelihood of respiratory infections several days after such stress. To test their hypothesis, they asked volunteers to keep a daily record of desirable and undesirable events in their lives over a twelve-week period. The volunteers also kept a daily record of any discomfort or symptoms of illness.

The results were as predicted: During the three-to-five-day period just before showing symptoms of an upper respiratory infection, people experienced an increased number of undesirable events and a decreased number of desirable events in their lives. (See ***Figure 16.11.***) Stone et al. (1987) suggest that the effect is caused by decreased production of a particular type of antibody that is present in the secretions

coping response A response through which an organism can avoid, escape from, or minimize an aversive stimulus; reduces the stressful effects of an aversive stimulus.

antigen A protein present on a microorganism that permits the immune system to recognize the microorganism as an invader.

antibody A protein produced by a cell of the immune system that recognizes antigens present on invading microorganisms.

Figure 16.11

Mean percentage change in frequency of undesirable and desirable events during the ten-day period preceding the onset of symptoms of upper respiratory infections.

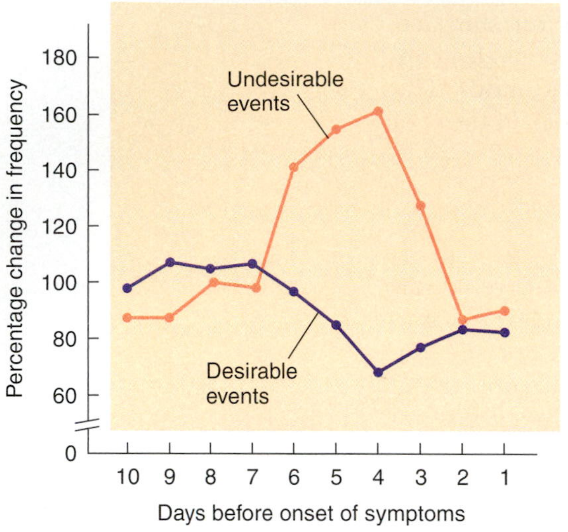

Based on data from Stone, A. A., Reed, B. R., and Neale, J. M. *Journal of Human Stress,* 1987, *13,* 70–74.

Figure 16.12

Percent of subjects with colds as a function of an index of psychological stress.

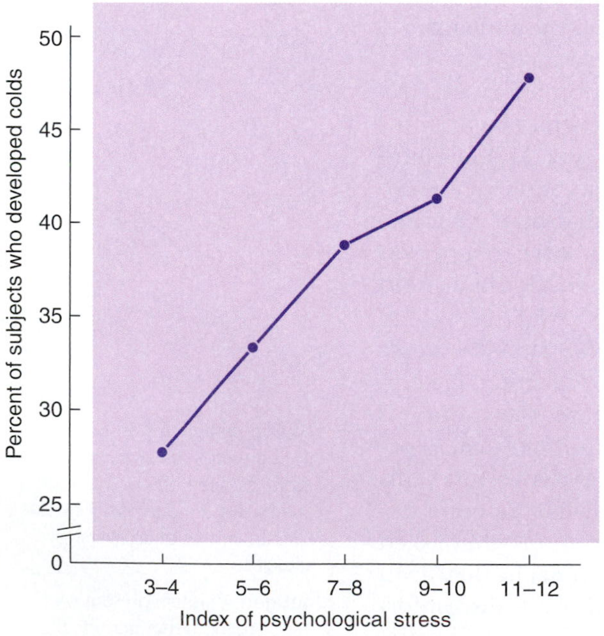

Adapted from Cohen, S., Tyrrell, D. A. J., and Smith, A. P. *New England Journal of Medicine,* 1991, *325,* 606–612.

of mucous membranes, including those in the nose, mouth, throat, and lungs. This antibody, *IgA,* serves as the first defense against infectious microorganisms that enter the nose or mouth. They found that IgA is associated with mood; when a subject is unhappy or depressed, IgA levels are lower than normal. The results suggest that the stress caused by undesirable events may, by suppressing the production of IgA, lead to a rise in the likelihood of upper respiratory infections.

The results of the study by Stone and his colleagues were confirmed by an experiment by Cohen, Tyrrell, and Smith (1991). The investigators found that subjects who were given nasal drops containing cold viruses were much more likely to develop colds if they reported stressful experiences during the past year and if they said they felt threatened, out of control, or overwhelmed by events. (See ***Figure 16.12.***)

What is the physiological explanation for the effects of stress on people's susceptibility to infectious diseases? Probably the most important cause is that stress increases the secretion of glucocorticoids, and as we saw, these hormones directly suppress the activity of the immune system (Keller et al., 1983). Because the secretion of glucocorticoids is controlled by the brain (through its secretion of CRH), the brain is obviously responsible for the suppressing effect of these hormones on the immune system. Neurons in the central nucleus of the amygdala send axons to CRH-secreting neurons in the paraventricular nucleus of the hypothalamus; thus, we can reasonably expect that the mechanism that is responsible for negative emotional responses is also responsible for the stress response and the immunosuppression that accompanies it. Several studies have shown that stress increases the activity of neurons in brain regions that have been shown to play a role in emotional responses, including the central nucleus of the amygdala and the paraventricular nucleus (Sharp et al., 1991; Imaki et al., 1992).

INTERIM SUMMARY

Stress Disorders

People's emotional reactions to aversive stimuli can harm their health. The stress response, which Cannon called the fight-or-flight response, is useful as a short-term response to threatening stimuli but is harmful in the long term. This response includes increased activity of the sympathetic branch of the autonomic nervous system and increased secretion of hormones by the adrenal gland: epinephrine, norepinephrine, and glucocorticoids. Corticotropin-releasing hormone, which stimulates the secretion of ACTH by the anterior pituitary gland, is also secreted in the brain, where it elicits some of the emotional responses to stressful situations.

Although increased levels of epinephrine and norepinephrine can raise blood pressure, most of the harm to health comes from glucocorticoids. Prolonged exposure to high levels of these hormones can increase blood pressure, damage muscle tissue, lead to infertility, inhibit growth, inhibit the inflammatory response, and suppress the immune system. It can also damage the hippocampus. Acute stress can also impair hippocampal functioning. At least some of these effects involve the amygdala; lesions of this structure reduce the effects of short-term stress. Prenatal exposure to excessive levels of glucocorticoids (caused by maternal stress) causes developmental changes that appear to predispose animals to react more to stressful situations.

Exposure to extreme stress can also have long-lasting effects; it can lead to the development of posttraumatic stress disorder. This disorder, to which women appear to be more susceptible than men, is associated with memory deficits, poorer health, and a decrease in the size of the hippocampus. Twin studies indicate a hereditary component to susceptibility to PTSD. Functional imaging studies have found an increase in the activity of the prefrontal cortex and amygdala when patients think about the situations that led to their disorder. People with PTSD generally show a smaller cortisol response to a traumatic experience; however, they secrete large amounts of CRH. This pattern of secretion suggests that glucocorticoid receptors in the hypothalamus and anterior pituitary that inhibit ACTH secretion have become hypersensitive.

Because the harm of most forms of stress comes from our own response to it, individual differences in personality variables can alter the effects of stressful situations. Another important variable is the ability to perform a coping response; being able to do so considerably reduces the aversive effects of stressful situations.

The immune system consists of white blood cells that develop in the bone marrow or the thymus gland. They produce antibodies that recognize antigens—unique proteins present on the surface of infectious microorganisms. Recognition of these antigens triggers an attack against the invaders.

A wide variety of stressful situations have been shown to increase people's susceptibility to infectious diseases. The most important mechanism by which stress impairs immune function is the increased blood levels of glucocorticoids. In addition, the neural input to the bone marrow, lymph nodes, and thymus gland may also play a role.

THOUGHT QUESTION

Researchers are puzzled by the fact that glucocorticoids suppress the immune system. Can you think of any potential benefits that come from the fact that our immune system is suppressed during times of danger and stress?

Substance Abuse Disorders

Drug addiction poses a serious problem to our species. Consider the disastrous effects caused by the abuse of one of our oldest drugs, alcohol: automobile accidents, fetal alcohol syndrome, cirrhosis of the liver, Korsakoff's syndrome, increased rate of heart disease, and increased rate of intracerebral hemorrhage. Smoking (addiction to nicotine) greatly increases the chances of dying of lung cancer, heart attack, and stroke; and women who smoke give birth to smaller, less healthy babies. Cocaine addiction can cause psychotic behavior, brain damage, and death from overdose; use of cocaine by pregnant women can result in the birth of babies with brain damage and consequent psychological problems; and competition for lucrative markets terrorizes neighborhoods, subverts political and judicial systems, and causes many deaths. The use of "designer drugs" exposes users to unknown dangers of untested and often contaminated products, as several people discovered when they acquired Parkinson's disease after taking a synthetic opiate tainted with a neurotoxin. Addicts who take their drugs intravenously run a serious risk of contracting AIDS. What makes these drugs so attractive to so many people?

The answer is that all of these substances stimulate brain mechanisms that are responsible for positive reinforcement. In addition, some of them reduce or eliminate unpleasant feelings, some of which are produced by the drugs themselves. The immediate consequences of these drugs are more powerful than the realization that in the long term, bad things will happen.

What Is Addiction?

The term *addiction* derives from the Latin word *addicere,* "to sentence." Someone who is addicted to a drug is, in a way, sentenced to a term of involuntary servitude, being obliged to fulfill the demands of his or her drug dependency.

A Little Background

Long ago, people discovered that many substances found in nature—primarily, leaves, seeds, and roots of plants but also some animal products—had medicinal qualities. They discovered herbs that helped to prevent infections, that promoted healing, that calmed an upset stomach, that reduced pain, or that helped to provide a night's sleep. They also discovered "recreational drugs"—drugs that produced pleasurable effects when eaten, drunk, or smoked. The most universal recreational drug, and perhaps the first one that our ancestors discovered, is ethyl alcohol. Yeast spores are present everywhere, and these microorganisms can feed on sugar solutions and produce alcohol as a by-product. Undoubtedly, people in many different parts of the world discovered the pleasurable effects of drinking liquids that had been left alone for a while, such as the juice that had accumulated in the bottom of a container of fruit. The juice may have become sour and bad-tasting because of the action of bacteria, but the effects of the alcohol encouraged people to experiment, which led to the development of a wide variety of fermented beverages.

Our ancestors also discovered other recreational drugs. Some of them were consumed only locally; others became so popular that their cultivation as commercial crops spread throughout the world. For example, Asians discovered the effects of the sap of the opium poppy and the beverage made from the leaves of the tea plant, East Indians discovered the effects of the smoke of cannabis, South Americans discovered the effects of chewing coca leaves and making a drink from coffee beans, and North Americans discovered the effects of the smoke of the tobacco plant. Many of the drugs they discovered served to protect the plants from animals (primarily insects) that ate them. Although the drugs were toxic in sufficient quantities, our ancestors learned how to take these drugs in quantities that would not make them ill—at least, not right away. The effects of these drugs on their brains kept them coming back for more.

Table 16.1 lists the most important addictive drugs and indicates their sites of action.

Physical Versus Psychological Addiction

Some drugs have very potent reinforcing effects, which lead some people to abuse them or even to become addicted to them. Many people (psychologists, health professionals, and laypeople) believe that "true" addiction is caused by the unpleasant physiological effects that occur when an addict tries to stop taking the drug. For example, Eddy et al. (1965) defined *physical dependence* as "an adaptive state that manifests itself by intense physical disturbances when the administration of a drug is suspended" (p. 723). In contrast, they defined *psychic dependence* as a condition in which a drug produces "a feeling of satisfaction and a psychic drive that requires periodic or continuous administration of the drug to produce pleasure or to avoid discomfort" (p. 723). Most people regard the latter as less important than the former. But, as we shall see, the *reverse* is true.

For many years, heroin addiction has been considered as the prototype for all drug addictions. People who habitually take heroin become physically dependent on the drug; that is, they show *tolerance* and *withdrawal symptoms.* As we saw in Chapter 4, **tolerance** is the decreased sensitivity to a drug that comes from its continued use; the drug user must take larger and larger amounts of the drug for it to be effective. Once a person has taken an opiate regularly enough to develop tolerance, that person will suffer withdrawal symptoms if he or she stops taking the drug. **Withdrawal symptoms** are primarily the opposite of the effects of the drug itself. The effects of

tolerance The fact that increasingly large doses of drugs must be taken to achieve a particular effect; caused by compensatory mechanisms that oppose the effect of the drug.

withdrawal symptoms The appearance of symptoms opposite to those produced by a drug when the drug is suddenly no longer taken; caused by the presence of compensatory mechanisms.

Table 16.1

Addictive Drugs

Drug	Sites of Action
Ethyl alcohol	NMDA receptor (indirect antagonist); $GABA_A$ receptor (indirect agonist)
Barbiturates	$GABA_A$ receptor (indirect agonist)
Benzodiazepines (tranquilizers)	$GABA_A$ receptor (indirect agonist)
Cannabis (marijuana)	CB1 cannabinoid receptor (agonist)
Nicotine	Nicotinic ACh receptor (agonist)
Opiates (heroin, morphine, etc.)	μ and δ opioid receptor agonist
Phencyclidine (PCP) and ketamine	NMDA receptor (indirect antagonist)
Cocaine	Blocks reuptake of dopamine (and serotonin and norepinephrine)
Amphetamine	Causes release of dopamine (by running dopamine transporters in reverse)

Source: Adapted from Hyman, S. E., and Malenka, R. C. *Nature Reviews: Neuroscience,* 2001, *2,* 695–703.

heroin—euphoria, constipation, and relaxation—lead to the withdrawal effects of dysphoria, cramping and diarrhea, and agitation.

Most investigators believe that tolerance is produced by the body's attempt to compensate for the unusual condition of heroin intoxication—a hypothesis that was first proposed by Himmelsbach (1943). The drug disturbs normal homeostatic mechanisms in the brain, and in reaction these mechanisms begin to produce effects opposite to those of the drug, partially compensating for the disturbance (Trujillo and Akil, 1991; Zukin et al., 1993). Because of these compensatory mechanisms, the user must take increasing amounts of heroin to achieve the effects that were produced when he or she first started taking the drug. They also account for the symptoms of withdrawal: When the person stops taking the drug, the compensatory mechanisms make themselves felt, unopposed by the action of the drug.

Heroin addiction has provided such a striking example of drug dependence that some authorities have concluded that "real" addiction does not occur unless a drug causes tolerance and withdrawal. Without doubt, withdrawal symptoms make it difficult for a person to stop taking heroin: They help to keep the person hooked. But withdrawal symptoms do not explain why a person becomes a heroin addict in the first place; that fact is explained by the drug's reinforcing effect. Certainly, people do not start taking heroin so that they will become physically dependent on it and feel miserable when they go without it. Instead, they begin taking it because it makes them feel good.

Perhaps the best evidence that the tolerance and withdrawal are not the causes of addiction is the fact that prolonged use of some drugs—in particular, β-adrenergic agonists inhalers used to treat asthma, α-adrenergic agonists used as nasal decongestants, and several drugs used to treat hypertension and the pain of angina pectoris—leads to tolerance and withdrawal, but the drugs are not themselves addictive (Hyman and Malenka, 2001).

In the past, the preoccupation with "physical" drug dependence has led to the neglect of the addictive properties of some drugs. For example, some very potent drugs, including cocaine, do not produce physical dependency. That is, people who take the drug do not show tolerance; and if they stop, they do not show significant withdrawal symptoms. As a result, experts believed for many years that cocaine was a relatively innocuous drug, not in the same league as heroin. Obviously, they were wrong; cocaine is even more addictive than heroin.

Common Features of Addiction

What occurs physiologically to make a person dependent on a drug? This section describes some common features of addictive drugs—drugs that people often become dependent on. A later section describes the details of particular drugs.

Positive Reinforcement

Drugs that lead to dependency must first reinforce people's behavior. As we saw in Chapter 12, positive reinforcement refers to the effect that certain stimuli have on the behaviors that preceded them. If, in a particular situation, a behavior is regularly followed by an appetitive stimulus (one that the organism will tend to approach), then that behavior will become more frequent in that situation.

Role in Drug Abuse. The effectiveness of a reinforcing stimulus is greatest if it occurs immediately after a response occurs. If the reinforcing stimulus is delayed, it becomes considerably less effective. The reason for this is found by examining the function of instrumental conditioning: learning about the consequences of our own behavior. Normally, causes and effects are closely related in time; we do something, and something happens, good or bad. The consequences of the actions teach us whether to repeat that action, and events that follow a response by more than a few seconds were probably not caused by that response.

An experiment by Logan (1965) illustrates the importance of the immediacy of reinforcement. Logan trained hungry rats to run through a simple maze in which a single passage led to two corridors. At the end of one corridor the rats would find a small piece of food. At the end of the other corridor they would receive much more food, but it would be delivered only after a delay. Although the most intelligent strategy would be to enter the second corridor and wait for the larger amount of food, the rats chose to take the small amount of food that was delivered right away. Immediacy of reinforcement took precedence over quantity.

This phenomenon explains why the most addictive drugs are those that have immediate effects. As we saw in Chapter 4, drug users prefer heroin to morphine not because heroin has a *different* effect, but because it has a more *rapid* effect. In fact, heroin is converted to morphine as soon as it reaches the brain. But because heroin is more lipid soluble, it passes through the blood–brain barrier more rapidly, and its effects on the brain are felt sooner than those of morphine. The most potent reinforcement occurs when drugs produce sudden changes in the activity of the reinforcement mechanism; slow changes are much less reinforcing, and continuous activity may even be aversive. (As we will see later, the use of methadone for opiate addiction and the use of nicotine patches for tobacco addiction are based on this phenomenon.)

Neural Mechanisms. As we saw in Chapter 12, all natural reinforcers that have been studied so far (such as food for a hungry animal, water for a thirsty one, or sexual contact) have one physiological effect in common: They cause the release of dopamine in the nucleus accumbens (White, 1996). This effect is undoubtedly not the *only* effect of reinforcing stimuli, and even aversive stimuli can trigger the release of dopamine (Salamone, 1992). But even though there is much that we do not yet understand about the neural basis of reinforcement, the release of dopamine appears to be a *necessary* (but not *sufficient*) condition for reinforcement to take place.

Addictive drugs—including amphetamine, cocaine, opiates, nicotine, alcohol, PCP, and cannabis—trigger the release of dopamine in the nucleus accumbens, as measured by microdialysis (Di Chiara, 1995). Some drugs do so by increasing the activity of the dopaminergic neurons of the mesolimbic system, which originates in the ventral tegmental area and terminates in the nucleus accumbens (and some other forebrain regions). Other drugs inhibit the reuptake of dopamine by terminal buttons and hence facilitate the postsynaptic effects of dopamine. If the release of dopamine in the nucleus accumbens is prevented by damaging the mesolimbic neurons, most addictive drugs lose their reinforcing effects. The details of the ways in which particular drugs interact with the mesolimbic dopaminergic system are described later.

Negative Reinforcement

You probably have heard the old joke in which someone says that the reason he bangs his head against the wall is that "it feels so good when I stop." Of course, that joke is funny (well, mildly amusing) because we know that although no one would act that way, ceasing to bang our head against the wall is certainly better than continuing to do so. If someone else started hitting us on the head and we were able to do something to get them to stop, whatever it was that we did would certainly be reinforced.

A behavior that turns off (or reduces) an aversive stimulus will be reinforced. This phenomenon is known as **negative reinforcement,** and its usefulness is obvious. For example, consider the following scenario: A woman staying in a rented house cannot get to sleep because of the unpleasant screeching noise that the furnace makes. She goes to the basement to discover the source of the noise and finally kicks the side of the oil burner. The noise ceases. The next time the furnace screeches, she immediately goes to the basement and kicks the side of the oil burner. The unpleasant noise (the aversive stimulus) is terminated when the woman kicks the side of the oil burner (the response), so the response is reinforced.

It is worth pointing out that *negative reinforcement* should not be confused with *punishment.* Both phenomena involve aversive stimuli, but one makes a response more likely, while the other makes it less likely. For negative reinforcement to occur, the response must make the unpleasant stimulus end (or at least decrease). For punishment to occur, the response must *make the unpleasant stimulus occur.* For example, if a little boy touches a mousetrap and hurts his finger, he is unlikely to touch a mousetrap again. The painful stimulus *punishes* the behavior of touching the mousetrap.

As we saw earlier in this chapter, the withdrawal effects, which occur when a habitual user of a drug stops taking the drug, are unpleasant. Although positive reinforcement seems to be what provokes drug taking in the first place, reduction of withdrawal effects could certainly play a role in maintaining someone's drug addiction. The withdrawal effects are unpleasant, but as soon as the person takes some of the drug, these effects go away, producing negative reinforcement.

Negative reinforcement could also explain the acquisition of drug addictions under some conditions. If a person is suffering from some unpleasant feelings and then takes a drug that eliminates these feelings, the person's drug-taking behavior is likely to be reinforced. For example, alcohol can relieve feelings of anxiety. If a person finds herself in a situation that arouses anxiety, she may find that a drink or two makes her feel much better. In fact, people often anticipate this effect and begin drinking before the situation actually occurs.

Craving and Relapse

Why do drug addicts crave drugs? Why does this craving occur even after a long period of abstinence? Knowing the answers to these questions might help clinicians to devise therapies that will assist people in breaking their drug dependence once and for all.

negative reinforcement The removal or reduction of an aversive stimulus that is contingent on a particular response, with an attendant increase in the frequency of that response.

Figure 16.13

Cocaine craving. PET scans show activation of the orbitofrontal cortex (arrows) in abstinent cocaine abusers describing their own method of preparing cocaine.

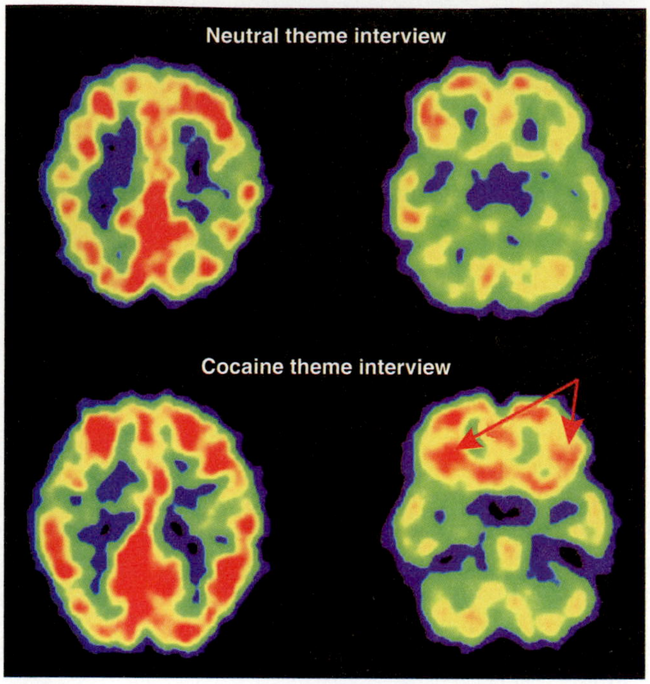

From Wang, Wang, G.-J., Volkow, N. D., Fowler, J. S., Cervany, P., Hitzemann, R. J., Pappas, N. R., Wong, C. T., and Felder, C. *Life Sciences,* 1999, *64,* 775–784.

Robinson and Berridge (1993) suggest that when an addictive drug activates the mesolimbic dopaminergic system, it gives *incentive salience* to stimuli present at that time. By this they mean that the stimuli associated with drug taking become exciting and motivating—a provocation to act. When a person with a history of drug abuse sees or thinks about these stimuli, he or she experiences craving—an impulsion to take the drug. Note that this hypothesis does not imply that the craving is caused solely by an unpleasant feeling.

Evidence obtained from both humans and laboratory animals indicates that long-term drug abuse does indeed produce long-term changes in the brain. Lets consider humans first. A review by Goldstein and Volkow (2002) reported that most functional imaging studies show activation of the orbitofrontal cortex and the anterior cingulate cortex when taking or craving an addictive drug. During withdrawal these regions generally show a decreased level of activation in drug abusers. For example, Wang et al. (1999) induced craving in cocaine abusers by having them describe their own method of preparing cocaine. As a control condition, they asked them to discuss their family tree. PET scanning revealed that the orbitofrontal cortex was activated while the subjects were craving cocaine. (See ***Figure 16.13.***)

In another PET study, Volkow et al. (1992) examined regional cerebral blood flow of cocaine abusers and control subjects during resting conditions. As Figure 16.14 shows, the activity of the prefrontal cortex and the anterior cingulate cortex of cocaine abusers was less active than that of normal subjects during abstinence. (See ***Figure 16.14.***)

Figure 16.14

Effects of prior cocaine abuse on resting cerebral blood flow. PET scans show higher activity of the prefrontal cortex and the anterior cingulate cortex in a normal subject than in an abstinent cocaine abuser.

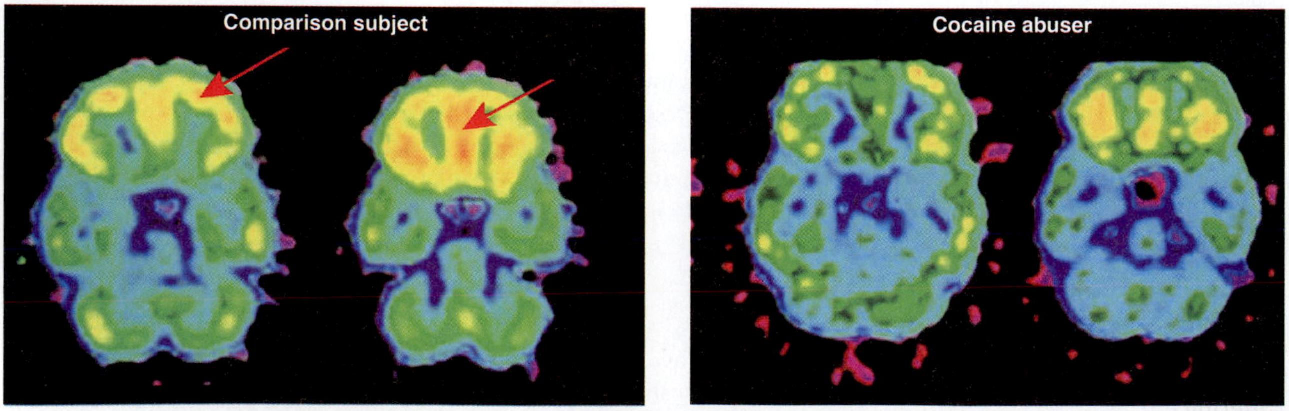

From Volkow, N. D., Hitzemann, R., Wang, G.-J., Fowler, J. S., Wolf, A. P., Dewey, S. L., and Handlesman, L. *Synapse,* 1992, *11,* 184–190.

Studies with laboratory animals have also shown changes in brain function after administration of addictive drugs. Some of these changes involve long-term potentiation or long-term depression—changes in synaptic strength that play a role in learning and memory. First, several studies have shown that NMDA receptor–dependent long-term potentiation and long-term depression can take place in the nucleus accumbens and ventral tegmental area. (See Hyman and Malenka, 2001, for a review.) Ungless et al. (2001) found that cocaine administration induces long-term potentiation in the ventral tegmental area by increasing the strength of synaptic transmission between glutamatergic synapses on dopaminergic neurons located there. Robinson et al. (2001) found increased dendritic branching and increased numbers of dendritic spines on neurons in the nucleus accumbens and the prefrontal cortex in rats that had previously self-administered cocaine one hour each day for one month. Finally, Vorel et al. (2001) stimulated glutamatergic axons in a portion of the hippocampal formation that projects to the ventral tegmental area. The stimulation produced long-lasting activation of neurons in the ventral tegmental area, increased the release of dopamine in the nucleus accumbens, and reinstated cocaine-seeking behavior.

Figure 16.15

Effects of social stress on cocaine intake. Mean cocaine intake of control rats and rats subjected to isolation stress early in life.

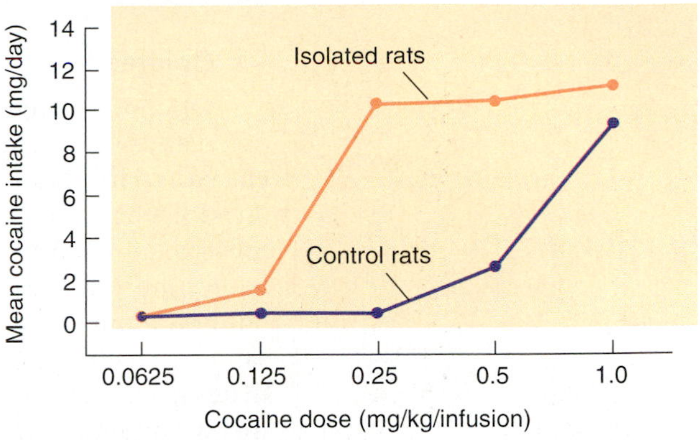

From Kosten, T. A., Miserendino, M. J. D., and Kehoe, P. *Brain Research,* 2000, *875,* 44–50.

Other stimuli can also trigger drug-seeking behavior. For example, clinicians have long observed that stressful situations can cause former drug addicts to relapse. Presumably, the intense, pleasurable effects of the drug help them to forget about their current difficulties. These effects have been observed in rats that had previously learned to self-administer cocaine or heroin. Covington and Miczek (2001) paired naïve rats with rats that had been trained to become dominant. After being defeated by the dominant rats, the socially stressed rats became more sensitive to the effects of cocaine and showed bingeing—self-administration of larger amounts of the drug. Kosten, Miserendino, and Kehoe (2000) showed that stress that occurs early in life can have long-lasting effects. They stressed infant rats by isolating them from their mother and littermates for one hour per day for eight days. When these rats were given the opportunity to inject themselves with cocaine, they readily acquired the habit and took more of the drugs than control rats that had not been stressed. (See ***Figure 16.15.***)

Commonly Abused Drugs

People have been known to abuse an enormous variety of drugs, including alcohol, barbiturates, opiates, tobacco, amphetamine, cocaine, cannabis, LSD, psilocybin, PCP, volatile solvents such as glues or even gasoline, ether, and nitrous oxide. The pleasure that children often derive from spinning themselves until they become dizzy may even be related to the effects of some of these drugs. Obviously, I cannot hope to discuss all these drugs in any depth and keep the chapter to a reasonable length, so I will restrict my discussion to the most important of them in terms of popularity and potential for addiction. Some drugs, such as caffeine, are both popular and addictive, but because they do not normally cause intoxication, impair health, or interfere with productivity, I will not discuss them here. (Chapter 4 did discuss the behavioral effects and site of action of caffeine.) I will also not discuss the wide variety of hallucinogenic drugs such as LSD or PCP. Although some people enjoy the mind-altering effects of LSD, many people simply find them frightening; in any event, LSD use does not normally lead to addiction. PCP (phencyclidine) acts as an indirect antagonist at the NMDA receptor, which means that its effects overlap with those of alcohol. Rather than devoting space to this drug, I have chosen to say more about alcohol, which is abused far more than any of the hallucinogenic drugs. If you would like to learn more about drugs other than the ones I discuss here, I suggest that you consult the books listed among the suggested readings at the end of this chapter.

Opiates

Opium, derived from a sticky resin produced by the opium poppy, has been eaten and smoked for centuries. Opiate addiction has several high personal and social costs. First, because heroin, the most commonly abused opiate, is an illegal drug, an addict becomes, by definition, a criminal. Second, because of tolerance, a person must take increasing amounts of the drug to achieve a "high." The habit thus becomes more and more expensive, and the person often turns to crime to obtain enough money to support his or her habit. Third, an opiate addict often uses unsanitary needles; at present, a substantial percentage of people who inject illicit drugs have been exposed in this way to hepatitis or the AIDS virus. Fourth, if the addict is a pregnant woman, her infant will also become dependent on the drug, which easily crosses the placental barrier. The infant must be given opiates right after being born and then weaned off the drug with gradually decreasing doses. Fifth, the uncertainty about the strength of a given batch of heroin makes it possible for a user to receive an unusually large dose of the drug, with possibly fatal consequences. In addition, dealers typically dilute pure heroin with various adulterants such as milk sugar, quinine, or talcum powder; and dealers are not known for taking scrupulous care with the quality and sterility of the substances they use. Some heroin-induced deaths have actually been reactions to the adulterants mixed with the drugs.

When an opiate is administered systemically, it stimulates opiate receptors located on neurons in various parts of the brain and produces a variety of effects, including analgesia, hypothermia (lowering of body temperature), sedation, and reinforcement. Opiate receptors in the periaqueductal gray matter are primarily responsible for the analgesia, those in the preoptic area are responsible for the hypothermia, those in the mesencephalic reticular formation are responsible for the sedation, and those in the ventral tegmental area and the nucleus accumbens are responsible for the reinforcing effects.

As we saw earlier, reinforcing stimuli cause the release of dopamine in the nucleus accumbens. Injections of opiates are no exception to this general rule; Wise et al. (1995) found that the level of dopamine in the nucleus accumbens increased by 150 to 300 percent while a rat was pressing a lever that delivered intravenous injections of heroin. Rats will also press a lever that delivers injections of an opiate directly into the ventral tegmental area (Devine and Wise, 1994) or the nucleus accumbens Goeders, Lane, and Smith (1984). In other words, injections of opiates into both ends of the mesolimbic dopaminergic system are reinforcing. These findings suggest that the reinforcing effects of opiates are produced by activation of neurons of the mesolimbic system and release of dopamine in the nucleus accumbens.

Figure 16.16

Cumulative fatalities in groups of rats self-administering cocaine or heroin.

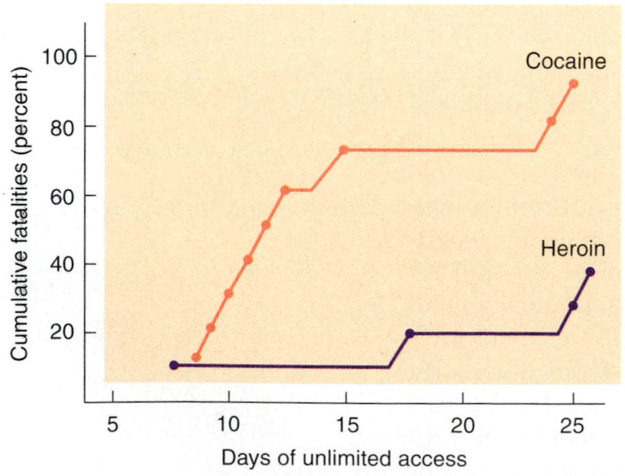

Adapted from Bozarth, M. A., and Wise, R. A. *Journal of the American Medical Association,* 1985, *254,* 81–83. Reprinted with permission.

Cocaine and Amphetamine

Cocaine and amphetamine have similar behavioral effects, because both act as potent dopamine agonists. Freebase cocaine ("crack"), a particularly potent form of the drug, is smoked and thus enters the blood supply of the lungs and reaches the brain very quickly. Because its effects are so potent and so rapid, it is probably the most effective reinforcer of all available drugs.

When people take cocaine, they become euphoric, active, and talkative. They say that they feel powerful and alert. Some of them become addicted to the drug, and obtaining it becomes an obsession to which they devote more and more time and money. Laboratory animals, who will quickly learn to self-administer cocaine intravenously. If rats or monkeys are given continuous access to a lever that permits them to self-administer cocaine, they often self-inject so much cocaine that they die. In fact, Bozarth and Wise (1985) found that rats that self-administered cocaine were almost three times more likely to die than rats that self-administered heroin. (See ***Figure 16.16.***)

Several studies have shown that intravenous injections of cocaine and amphetamine increase the concentration of dopamine in the nucleus accumbens, as measured by microdialysis (Petit and Justice, 1989; Di Ciano et al., 1995; Wise et al., 1995). For example, Figure 16.17 shows data collected from rats who learned to press a lever that delivered intravenous injections of cocaine. The colored bars at the base of the graphs indicate the animals' responses, and the line graphs indicate the level of dopamine in the nucleus accumbens. (See ***Figure 16.17.***)

Some evidence suggests that the use of stimulants such as cocaine and amphetamine may have adverse long-term effects on the brain. For example, a PET study by McCann et al. (1998) discovered that prior abusers of methamphetamine showed a decrease in the numbers of dopamine transporters in the caudate nucleus and putamen, despite the fact that they had abstained from the drug for approximately three years. The decreased number of dopamine transporters suggests that the number of dopaminergic terminals in these regions is diminished. As the authors note, these people might have an increased risk of Parkinson's disease as they get older. (See ***Figure 16.18.***)

Nicotine

Nicotine might seem rather tame in comparison to opiates, cocaine, and amphetamine. Nevertheless, nicotine is an addictive drug, and it undoubtedly accounts for more deaths than the so-called hard drugs. The combination of nicotine and other substances in tobacco smoke is carcinogenic and leads to cancer of the lungs, mouth, throat, and esophagus. Investigators estimate that by the year 2020, tobacco will be the largest single health problem worldwide, with 8.4 million deaths per year (Murray and Lopez, 1997). Smoking by pregnant women also has negative effects on the health of their fetuses—apparently worse than those of cocaine (Slotkin 1998). Unfortunately, approximately 25 percent of pregnant women in the United States expose their fetuses to nicotine.

Figure 16.17

Dopamine concentration in the nucleus accumbens, measured by microdialysis, during self-administration of intravenous cocaine by rats.

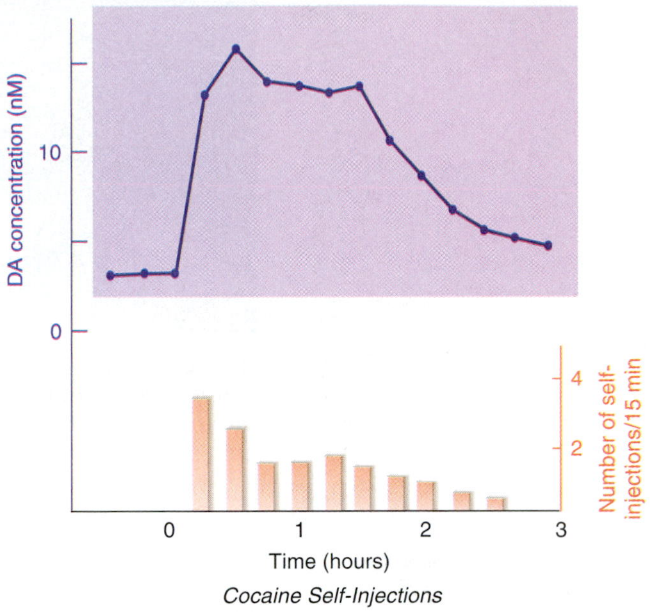

Adapted from Di Ciano, P., Coury, A., Depoortere, R. Y., Egilmez, Y., Lane, J. D., Emmett-Oglesby, M. W., Lepiane, F. G., Phillips, A. G., and Blaha, C. D. *Behavioural Pharmacology,* 1995, *6,* 311–322.

Figure 16.18

PET scans of the brain showing concentrations of dopamine transporters from a control subject, a subject who had previously abused methamphetamine, and a subject with Parkinson's disease. Decreased concentrations of dopamine transporters indicate loss of dopaminergic terminals.

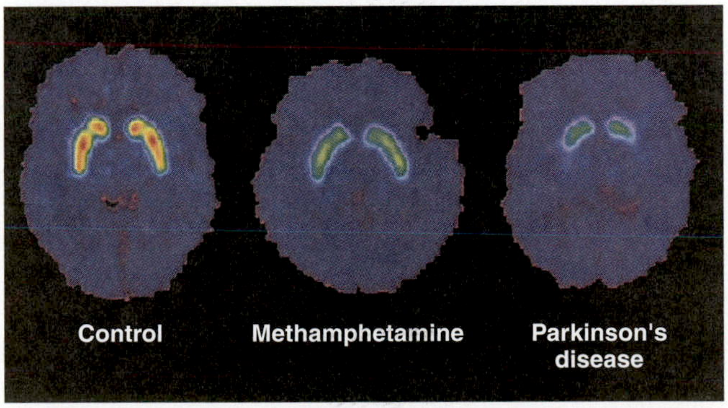

From McCann, U. D., Wong, D. F., Yokoi, F., Villemagne, V., Dannls, R. F., and Ricaurte, G. A. *Journal of Neuroscience,* 1998, *18,* 8417–8422. Copyright 1998 by the Society for Neuroscience.

Now that many employers prohibit smoking in the workplace, we have become accustomed to the sight of people outside a building, satisfying their nicotine addiction.

The addictive potential of nicotine should not be underestimated; many people continue to smoke even when doing so causes serious health problems. For example, Sigmund Freud, whose theory of psychoanalysis stressed the importance of insight in changing one's behavior, was unable to stop smoking even after most of his jaw had been removed because of the cancer that this habit had caused (Brecher, 1972). He suffered severe pain and, as a physician, realized that he should have stopped smoking. He did not, and his cancer finally killed him.

Although executives of tobacco companies and others whose economic welfare is linked to the production and sale of tobacco products argue that smoking is a "habit" rather than an "addiction," evidence suggests that the behavior of people who regularly use tobacco resembles that of compulsive drug users. In a review of the literature, Stolerman and Jarvis (1995) note that smokers tend to smoke regularly or not at all; few can smoke just a little. Males smoke an average of seventeen cigarettes per day, while females smoke an average of fourteen. Nineteen out of twenty smokers smoke every day, and only 60 out of 3500 smokers questioned smoke fewer than five cigarettes per day. Forty percent of people continue to smoke after having had a laryngectomy (which is usually performed to treat throat cancer), more than 50 percent of heart attack survivors continue to smoke, and about 50 percent of people continue to smoke after submitting to surgery for lung cancer. Of those who attempt to quit smoking by enrolling in a special program, 20 percent manage to abstain for one year. The record is much poorer for those who try to quit on their own: One-third manage to stop for one day, and one-fourth for one week, but only 4 percent manage to abstain for six months. It is difficult to reconcile these figures with the assertion that smoking is merely a "habit" that is pursued for the "pleasure" that it produces.

Ours is not the only species that is willing to self-administer nicotine; so will laboratory animals (Donny et al., 1995). Nicotine stimulates acetylcholine receptors, of course. It also increases the activity of dopaminergic neurons of the mesolimbic system, which contain these receptors (Mereu et al., 1987), and causes dopamine to be released in the nucleus accumbens (Damsma, Day, and Fibiger, 1989). Figure 16.19 shows the effects of two injections of nicotine or saline on the extracellular dopamine level of the nucleus accumbens, measured by microdialysis. (See ***Figure 16.19.***)

Alcohol

Alcohol has greater costs to society than any other drug. A large percentage of deaths and injuries caused by motor vehicle accidents are related to alcohol use, and alcohol contributes to violence and aggression. Chronic alcoholics often lose their jobs, their homes, and their families; and many die of cirrhosis of the liver, exposure, or diseases caused by poor living conditions and abuse of their bodies. As we saw in Chapter 14, women who drink during pregnancy run the risk of giving birth to babies with fetal alcohol syndrome, symptoms of which include malformation of the head and the brain. The leading cause of mental retardation in the Western world today is alcohol consumption by pregnant women (Abel and Sokol, 1986). Thus, understanding the physiological and behavioral effects of this drug is an important issue.

Figure 16.19

Changes in dopamine concentration in the nucleus accumbens, measured by microdialysis, in response to injections of nicotine or saline. The arrows indicate the time of the injections.

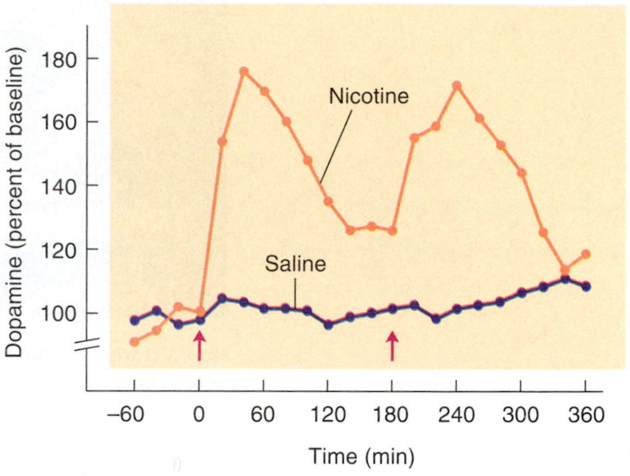

Adapted from Damsma, G., Day, J., and Fibiger, H. C. *European Journal of Pharmacology,* 1989, *168,* 363–368. Reprinted with permission.

At low doses alcohol produces mild euphoria and has an *anxiolytic* effect—that is, it reduces the discomfort of anxiety. At higher doses it produces incoordination and sedation. In studies with laboratory animals the anxiolytic effects manifest themselves as a release from the punishing effects of aversive stimuli. For example, if an animal is given electric shocks whenever it makes a particular response (say, one that obtains food or water), it will stop doing so. However, if it is then given some alcohol, it will begin making the response again (Koob et al., 1984). This phenomenon explains why people often do things they normally would not when they have had too much to drink; the alcohol removes the inhibitory effect of social controls on their behavior.

Alcohol produces both positive and negative reinforcement. The positive reinforcement manifests itself as mild euphoria. As we saw earlier, *negative* reinforcement is caused by the termination of an aversive stimulus. If a person feels anxious and uncomfortable, then an anxiolytic drug that relieves this discomfort provides at least a temporary escape from an unpleasant situation. It is probably the unique combination of stimulating and anxiolytic effects—of positive and negative reinforcement—that makes alcohol so difficult for some people to resist.

Alcohol, like other addictive drugs, increases the activity of the dopaminergic neurons of the mesolimbic system and increases the release of dopamine in the nucleus accumbens as measured by microdialysis (Gessa et al., 1985; Imperato and Di Chiara, 1986). The release of dopamine appears to be related to the positive reinforcement that alcohol can produce. An injection of a dopamine antagonist directly into the nucleus accumbens decreases alcohol intake (Samson et al., 1993), as does the injection of a drug into the ventral tegmental area that decreases the activity of the dopaminergic neurons there (Hodge et al., 1993).

What is responsible for the sedative and anxiolytic effects of alcohol? In low to moderate doses, alcohol appears to have two major sites of action in the nervous system: NMDA receptors and $GABA_A$ receptors. Alcohol acts as an indirect antagonist at NMDA receptors, interfering with the effects of glutamate. Like alcohol, NMDA antagonists produce sedative and anxiolytic effects and interfere with cognitive performance (Tabakoff and Hoffman, 1996). Also like alcohol, NMDA antagonists cause the release of dopamine in the nucleus accumbens (Imperato et al., 1990; Loscher, Annies, and Honack, 1991). Thus, NMDA receptors are at least partly responsible for both the positively and negatively reinforcing effects of alcohol.

As we saw in Chapter 12, NMDA receptors are involved in long-term potentiation, a phenomenon that plays an important role in learning. Thus, it will not surprise you to learn that alcohol, which antagonizes the action of glutamate at NMDA

In low doses, alcohol produces a mile euphoria and has an anxiolytic effect. For this reason, alcohol is part of social occasions in many cultures.

receptors, disrupts long-term potentiation and interferes with the spatial receptive fields of place cells in the hippocampus (Givens and McMahon, 1995; Matthews, Simson, and Best, 1996). Presumably, this effect at least partly accounts for the deleterious effects of alcohol on memory and other cognitive functions.

The second site of action of alcohol is the $GABA_A$ receptor. Alcohol acts as an indirect agonist at these receptors, binding with one of the many binding sites and increasing the effectiveness of GABA in opening the chloride channel and producing inhibitory postsynaptic potentials. Suzdak et al. (1986) discovered a drug (Ro15-4513) that reverses alcohol intoxication by blocking the alcohol binding site on the $GABA_A$ receptor. Figure 16.20 shows two rats that received injections of enough alcohol to make them pass out. The one facing us also received an injection of the alcohol antagonist and appears completely sober. (See ***Figure 16.20.***)

This wonder drug is not likely to reach the market. Although the behavioral effects of alcohol are mediated by their action on $GABA_A$ receptors and NMDA receptors, high doses of alcohol have other, potentially fatal effects on all cells of the body, including destabilization of cell membranes. Thus, people taking some of the alcohol antagonist could then go on to drink themselves to death without becoming drunk in the process. Drug companies naturally fear possible liability suits stemming from such occurrences.

Figure 16.20

Effects of Ro15-4513, an alcohol antagonist. Both rats received an injection of alcohol, but the one facing us also received an injection of the alcohol antagonist.

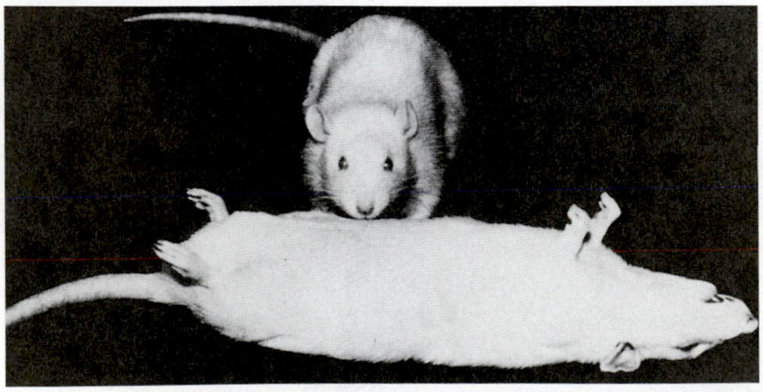

Photograph courtesy of Steven M. Paul, National Institute of Mental Health, Bethesda, Md.

Cannabis

Another drug that people regularly self-administer—almost exclusively by smoking—is THC, the active ingredient in marijuana. As you learned in Chapter 4, THC receptors have been discovered, and their distribution in the brain has been mapped. The endogenous ligand for these receptors, anandamide, is a lipid. But we still do not know what situations trigger the release of anandamide or what functions this chemical serves. Incidentally, di Tomaso, Beltramo, and Piomelli (1996) discovered that chocolate contains three anandamide-like chemicals. Whether the existence of these chemicals is related to the great appeal that chocolate has for many people is not yet known. (I suppose that this is the place for a chocoholic joke.)

One thing we do now know about THC is that it, like other drugs with abuse potential, has an effect on dopaminergic neurons. Chen et al. (1990) injected rats with low doses of THC and measured the release of dopamine in the nucleus accumbens by means of microdialysis. Sure enough, they found that the injections caused the release of dopamine. (See ***Figure 16.21.***)

As we saw in Chapter 4, the hippocampus contains a large concentration of THC receptors. Marijuana is known to affect people's memory. Specifically, it impairs their ability to keep track of a particular topic; they frequently lose the thread of a conversation if they are momentarily distracted. Perhaps the drug does so by disrupting the normal functions of the hippocampus, which plays such an important role in memory.

Figure 16.21

Changes in dopamine concentration in the nucleus accumbens, measured by microdialysis, in response to injections of THC or an inert placebo.

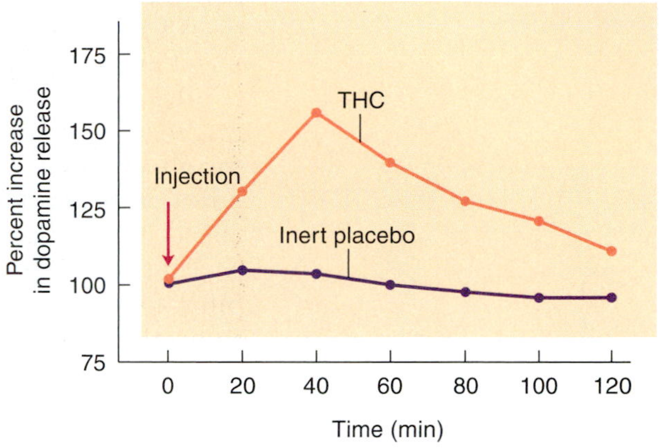

Adapted from Chen, J., Paredes, W., Li, J., Smith, D., Lowinson, J., and Gardner, E. L. *Psychopharmacology,* 1990, *102,* 156–162. Reprinted with permission.

Heredity and Drug Abuse

Not everyone is equally likely to become addicted to a drug. Many people manage to drink alcohol moderately, and even many users of potent drugs such as cocaine and heroin use them "recreationally" without becoming dependent on them. There are only two possible sources of individual differences in any characteristic: heredity and environment. Because this book considers the *physiology* of behavior, I will not discuss the role that environment plays in a person's susceptibility to the addicting effects of drugs. Obviously, environmental effects are important; people who are raised in a squalid environment without any real hope for a better life are more likely than other people to turn to drugs for some temporary euphoria and removal from the unpleasant world that surrounds them. But even in a given environment, poor or privileged, some people become addicts and some do not—and some of these behavioral differences are a result of genetic differences, as we will see in the following subsections.

Most of the research on the effects of heredity on addiction have been devoted to alcoholism. One of the reasons for this focus—aside from the importance of the problems caused by alcohol—is that almost everyone is exposed to alcohol. Most people drink alcohol sometime in their lives and thus have firsthand experience with its reinforcing effects. The same is not true for cocaine, heroin, and other drugs that have even more potent effects. In most countries alcohol is freely and legally available in local shops, whereas in purchasing cocaine and heroin, one runs the risk of being arrested, perhaps even imprisoned.

A few researchers have begun looking at the genetics of dependence on other drugs, such as cocaine, nicotine, and marijuana. In general, studies have found that the heritability of smoking is just as strong as that of alcoholism. Smoking has also been shown to be related to some personal characteristics, including neurosis, social alienation, impulsiveness, sensation seeking, low conscientiousness, low socioeconomic status, and low achievement (Gilbert and Gilbert, 1995; Heath et al., 1995). A twin study by True et al. (1999) found that alcoholism and nicotine dependence have genetic factors in common, which may explain why alcoholics are often addicted to nicotine. A family study comparing siblings (Bierut et al., 1998) suggests that both common and specific genetic factors are involved in addiction to alcohol, cocaine, nicotine, and marijuana. In other words, there appears to be a genetic trait that increases vulnerability to dependence on addictive substances in general and genetic traits associated with vulnerability to dependence on each of the particular drugs.

The Evidence

Alcohol consumption is not distributed equally across the population; in the United States, 10 percent of the people drink 50 percent of the alcohol (Heckler, 1983). The best evidence for an effect of heredity on susceptibility to alcoholism comes from two main sources: twin studies and cross-fostering studies. Monozygotic twins tend to resemble each other more closely than dizygotic twins in many ways, including the likelihood of alcohol abuse (Goodwin, 1979).

The second type of heritability study uses children who were adopted by nonrelatives when they were young. A study like this permits the investigator to estimate the effects of family environment as well as genetics. That is, one can examine the effects of being raised by an alcoholic parent, or having a biological parent who is an alcoholic, or both on the probability of becoming alcoholic. Such a study was carried out in Stockholm by Cloninger et al. (1981, 1985) and was replicated in Gothenburg, another Swedish city (Sigvardsson, Bohman, and Cloninger, 1996). Briefly, the studies found that heredity was much more important than family environment. But the story is not quite that simple.

In a review of the literature on alcohol abuse, Cloninger (1987) notes that many investigators have concluded that there are two principal types of alcoholics: those who cannot abstain but drink consistently and those who are able to go without drinking for long periods of time but are unable to control themselves once they start. (For convenience I will refer to these two groups as "steady drinkers" and "bingers.") Steady drinking is associated with antisocial personality disorder, which includes a lifelong history of impulsiveness, fighting, lying, and lack of remorse for antisocial acts. Binge drinking is associated with emotional dependence, behavioral rigidity, perfectionism, introversion, and guilt feelings about one's drinking behavior. Steady drinkers usually begin their alcohol consumption early in life, whereas binge drinkers begin much later. (See ***Table 16.2.***)

Steady drinking is strongly influenced by heredity. The Stockholm adoption study found that men with fathers who were steady drinkers were almost seven times more likely to become steady drinkers themselves than were men whose fathers did not abuse alcohol. Family environment had no measurable effect; the boys began

Table 16.2

Characteristic Features of Two Types of Alcoholism

Feature	TYPE OF ALCOHOLISM: Steady	Binge
Usual age of onset (years)	Before 25	After 25
Spontaneous alcohol seeking (inability to abstain)	Frequent	Infrequent
Fighting and arrests while drinking	Frequent	Infrequent
Psychological dependence (loss of control)	Infrequent	Frequent
Guilt and fear about alcohol dependence	Infrequent	Frequent
Novelty seeking	High	Low
Harm avoidance	Low	High
Reward dependence	Low	High

Source: From Cloninger, C. R. *Science,* 1987, *236,* 410–416. Copyright 1987 by the American Association for the Advancement of Science.

drinking whether or not the members of their adoptive family themselves drank heavily. Very few women become steady drinkers; the daughters of steady-drinking fathers instead tend to develop *somatization disorder.* People with this disorder chronically complain of symptoms for which no physiological cause can be found, leading them to seek medical care almost continuously. Thus, the genes that predispose a man to become a steady-drinking alcoholic (antisocial type) predispose a woman to develop somatization disorder. The reason for this interaction with gender is not known.

Binge drinking is influenced both by heredity and by environment. The Stockholm adoption study found that having a biological parent who was a binge drinker had little effect on the development of binge drinking unless the child was exposed to a family environment in which there was heavy drinking. The effect was seen in both males and females.

Therapy for Drug Abuse

There are many reasons for engaging in research on the physiology of drug abuse, including an academic interest in the nature of reinforcement and the pharmacology of psychoactive drugs. But most researchers entertain the hope that the results of their research will contribute to the development of ways to treat and (better yet) prevent drug abuse in members of our own species. As you well know, the incidence of drug abuse is far too high, so obviously, research has not yet solved the problem. However, real progress has been made.

The most common treatment for opiate addiction is methadone maintenance. Methadone is a potent opiate, just like morphine or heroin. If it were available in a form suitable for injection, it would be abused. (In fact, methadone clinics must control their stock of methadone carefully to prevent it from being stolen and sold to opiate abusers.) Methadone maintenance programs administer the drug to their patients in the form of a liquid, which they must drink in the presence of the personnel supervising this procedure. Because the oral route of administration increases the opiate level in the brain slowly, the drug does not produce a high, the way an injection of heroin will. In addition, because methadone is long-lasting, the patient's opiate receptors remain occupied for a long time, which means that an injection of heroin has little effect.

As we saw earlier, the reinforcing effects of cocaine and amphetamine are primarily a result of the sharply increased levels of dopamine that these drugs produce in the nucleus accumbens. Drugs that block dopamine receptors certainly block the reinforcing effects of cocaine and amphetamine, but they also produce dysphoria (an unpleasant feeling) and anhedonia (inability to experience pleasure). People will not tolerate the unpleasant feelings these drugs produce, so they are not useful treatments for cocaine and amphetamine abuse. Drugs that *stimulate* dopamine receptors can reduce a person's dependence on cocaine or amphetamine, but these drugs are just as addictive as the drugs they replace and have the same deleterious effects on health.

An interesting approach to cocaine addiction is suggested by a study by Carrera et al. (1995), who conjugated cocaine to a foreign protein and managed to stimulate rats' immune systems to develop antibodies to cocaine. These "cocaine-immunized" rats were less sensitive to the activating effects of cocaine, and brain levels of cocaine in these animals were lower after an injection of the drug. As Leshner (1996) suggests, it might someday be possible to vaccinate cocaine abusers (or perhaps inject them with an antibody developed by genetic engineering) so that an injection of cocaine will not produce reinforcing effects. This treatment would have many advantages, because (theoretically, at least) it would interfere only with the

Figure 16.22

Percentage of smokers chewing nicotine gum alone or in conjunction with counseling who abstained from smoking. S = start of treatment; E = end of treatment.

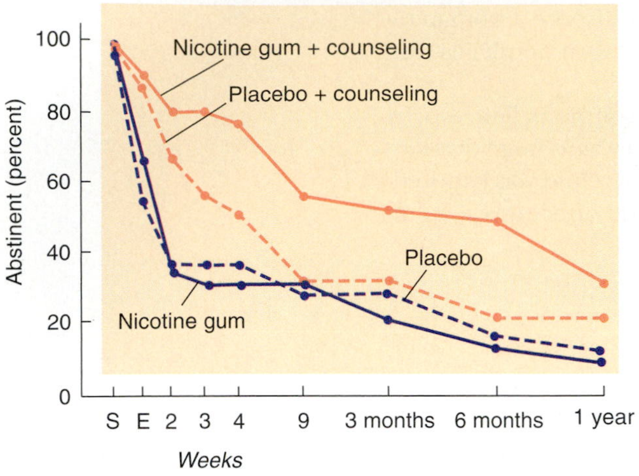

Adapted from Schneider, N. G., and Jarvik, M. E. *NIDA Research Monographs,* 1985, *53,* 83–101.

action of cocaine and not with the normal operations of people's reinforcement mechanisms. Thus, the treatment should not decrease their ability to experience normal pleasure.

A treatment similar to methadone maintenance has been used as an adjunct to treatment for nicotine addiction. For several years, chewing gum containing nicotine has been available, and more recently, transdermal patches that release nicotine through the skin have been marketed. Both methods maintain a sufficiently high level of nicotine in the brain to decrease a person's craving for nicotine. Once the habit of smoking has subsided, the dose of nicotine can be decreased to wean the person from the drug. Carefully controlled studies have shown that nicotine maintenance therapy, and not administration of a placebo, is useful in treatment for nicotine dependence (Stolerman and Jarvis, 1995). However, nicotine maintenance therapy is most effective if it is part of a counseling program. (See ***Figure 16.22.***)

As we saw in Chapter 15, serotonin agonists have proved themselves useful in treatment of panic disorder and obsessive-compulsive disorder (and related disorders such as hair pulling and nail biting). These drugs also appear to be useful in treating alcoholism; several double-blind studies have found that 5-HT reuptake blockers make it easier for alcoholics to abstain. For example, Naranjo et al. (1992) found that citalopram (a serotonin agonist) "decreased interest, desire, craving, and liking for alcohol" in alcoholics who were receiving treatment for their addiction. It appeared to do so by decreasing the reinforcing effects of alcohol.

Several studies have shown that opiate antagonists decrease the reinforcing value of alcohol in a variety of species, including our own (Altschuler, Phillips, and Feinhandler, 1980; Davidson, Swift, and Fitz, 1996; Reid, 1996). This finding suggests that the reinforcing effect of alcohol—at least in part—is produced by the secretion of endogenous opioids and the activation of opiate receptors in the brain. A study by Davidson, Swift, and Fitz (1996) clearly illustrates this effect. The investigators arranged a double-blind, placebo-controlled study with sixteen college-age men and women to investigate the effects of naltrexone on social drinkers. (**Naltrexone** is a drug that blocks opiate receptors.) None of the participants were alcohol abusers, and pregnancy tests ensured that the women were not pregnant. They gathered around a table in a local restaurant/bar for three two-hour drinking sessions, two weeks apart. For several days before the meeting, they swallowed capsules that contained either naltrexone or an inert placebo. The results showed that naltrexone increased the latency to take the first sip and to take a second drink and that the blood alcohol levels of the naltrexone-treated participants were lower at the end of the session. In general, the people who had taken naltrexone found that their drinks did not taste very good—in fact, some of them asked for a different drink after taking the first sip.

These results are consistent with reports of the effectiveness of naltrexone as an adjunct to programs designed to treat alcohol abuse. For example, O'Brien, Volpicelli, and Volpicelli (1996) reported the results of two long-term programs using naltrexone along with more traditional behavioral treatments. Both programs found that administration of naltrexone significantly increased the likelihood of success. As Figure 16.23 shows, naltrexone decreased the participants' craving for alcohol and increased the number of participants who managed to abstain from alcohol. (See ***Figure 16.23.***)

naltrexone A drug that blocks mu opiate receptors; antagonizes the reinforcing and sedative effects of opiates.

Figure 16.23

Mean craving score and proportion of patients who abstained from drinking while receiving naltrexone or a placebo.

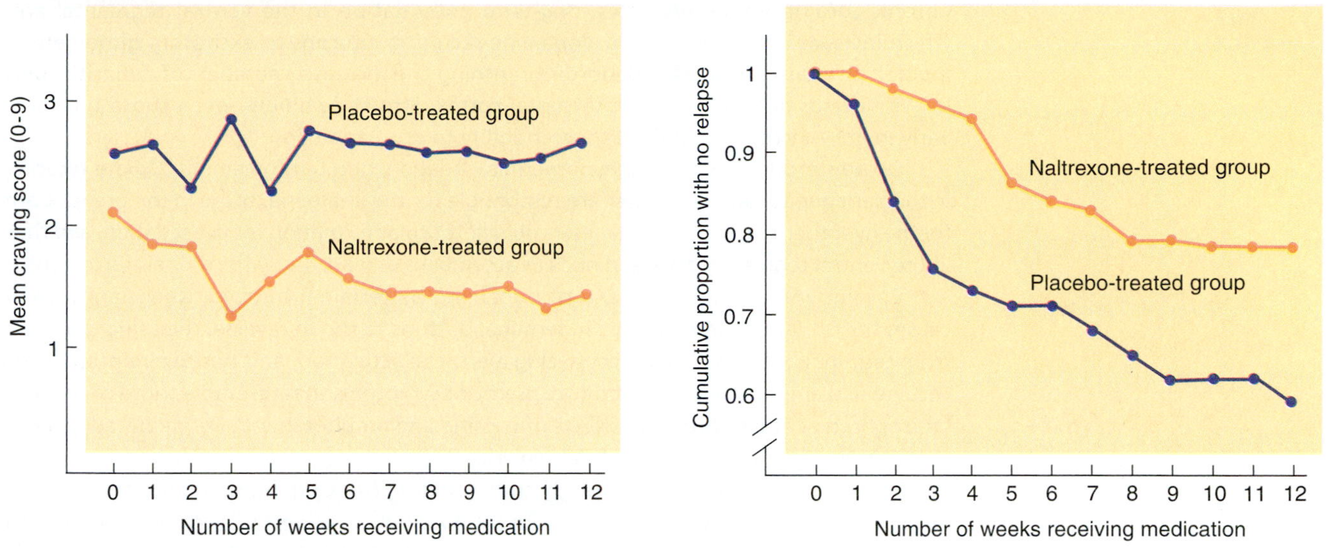

Adapted from O'Brien, C. P., Volpicelli, L. A., and Volpicelli, J. R. *Alcohol,* 1996, *13,* 35–39.

INTERIM SUMMARY

Drug Abuse

Addictive drugs are those whose reinforcing effects are so potent that some people who are exposed to them are unable to go for very long without taking them and whose lives become organized around taking them. Originally, addictive drugs came from plants, which used them as a defense against insects or other animals that otherwise would eat them, but chemists have synthesized many other drugs that have even more potent effects. If a person regularly takes some addictive drugs (most notably, the opiates), the effects of the drug show tolerance, and the person must take increasing doses to achieve the same effect. If the person then stops taking the drug, withdrawal effects, opposite to the primary effects of the drug, will occur. However, withdrawal effects are not the cause of addiction—the abuse potential of a drug is related to its ability to reinforce drug-taking behavior.

Positive reinforcement occurs when a behavior is regularly followed by an appetitive stimulus—one that an organism will approach. All addictive drugs produce positive reinforcement; they reinforce drug-taking behavior. The faster a drug produces its effects, the more quickly dependence will be established. All addictive drugs stimulate the release of dopamine in the nucleus accumbens, a structure that plays an important role in reinforcement.

Negative reinforcement occurs when a behavior is followed by the reduction or termination of an aversive stimulus. If, because of a person's social situation or personality characteristics, he or she feels unhappy or anxious, a drug that reduces these feelings can reinforce drug-taking behavior by means of negative reinforcement. Also, the reduction of unpleasant withdrawal symptoms by a dose of the drug undoubtedly plays a role in maintaining drug addictions, but it is not the sole cause of craving.

Craving—the urge to take a drug to which one has become addicted—cannot be completely explained by withdrawal symptoms, because it can occur even after an addict has refrained from taking the drug for a long time. In laboratory animals inactivation of the prefrontal cortex, ventral tegmental area, or nucleus accumbens prevents a "free" shot of cocaine from reinstating drug-seeking behavior; conversely, injection of cocaine into the prefrontal cortex or the nucleus accumbens causes reinstatement. Presentation of stimuli previously associated with cocaine also causes reinstatement but not if the basolateral amygdala is destroyed or inactivated. Functional imaging studies find that craving for cocaine increases the activity of the orbitofrontal prefrontal cortex and the anterior cingulate cortex. Chronic cocaine intake produces long-term potentiation in the ventral tegmental area, which increases the sensitivity of dopamine-secreting neurons to excitatory glutamatergic input; it also causes increased dendritic branching and increased numbers of dendritic spines in the nucleus accumbens and prefrontal cortex. Stressful stimuli—even those that occur early in life—increase an animal's susceptibility to drug addiction.

Opiates produce analgesia, hypothermia, sedation, and reinforcement. Opiate receptors in the periaqueductal gray matter are responsible for the analgesia, those in the preoptic area for the hypothermia, those in the mesencephalic reticular formation for the sedation, and those in the ventral tegmental area and nucleus accumbens at least partly for the reinforcement.

Cocaine inhibits the reuptake of dopamine by terminal buttons, and amphetamine causes the dopamine transporters in terminal buttons to run in reverse, releasing dopamine from terminal buttons. Besides producing alertness, activation, and positive reinforcement, cocaine and amphetamine can produce psychotic symptoms that resemble those of paranoid schizophrenia. The reinforcing effects of cocaine and amphetamine are mediated by an increase in dopamine in the nucleus accumbens.

The status of nicotine as a strongly addictive drug (for both humans and laboratory animals) was long ignored, primarily because it does not cause intoxication and because the ready availability of cigarettes and other tobacco products does not make it necessary for addicts to engage in illegal activities. However, the craving for nicotine is extremely motivating. Nicotine stimulates the release of mesolimbic dopaminergic neurons, and injection of nicotine into the ventral tegmental area is reinforcing.

Alcohol has positively reinforcing effects and, through its anxiolytic action, has negatively reinforcing effects as well. It serves as an indirect antagonist at NMDA receptors and an indirect agonist at $GABA_A$ receptors. It stimulates the release of dopamine in the nucleus accumbens.

The active ingredient in cannabis, THC, stimulates receptors whose natural ligand is anandamide. THC, like other addictive drugs, stimulates the release of dopamine in the nucleus accumbens.

Most people who are exposed to addictive drugs—even drugs with a high abuse potential—do not become addicts. Evidence suggests that the likelihood of addiction, especially to alcohol and nicotine, is strongly affected by heredity. There may be two types of alcoholism, one related to an antisocial, pleasure-seeking personality (steady drinkers) and another related to a repressed, anxiety-ridden personality (binge drinkers).

Although drug abuse is difficult to treat, researchers have developed several useful therapies. Methadone maintenance replaces addiction to heroin by addiction to an opiate that does not produce euphoric effects when administered orally. Similarly, nicotine-containing gum and transdermal patches help smokers combat their addiction. The development of antibodies to cocaine in rats holds out the possibility that people may some day be immunized against the drug. Serotonin agonists show promise in decreasing craving for alcohol. However, the most effective pharmacological adjunct to treatment for alcoholism appears to be the opiate antagonist naltrexone, which blocks some of the drug's reinforcing effects.

A personal note: You are now at the end of the book (as you well know), and you have spent a considerable amount of time reading my words. While working on this book, I have tried to imagine myself talking to someone who is interested in learning something about the physiology of behavior. As I mentioned in the preface, writing is often a lonely activity, and the imaginary audience helped keep me company. If you would like to turn this communication into a two-way conversation, write to me. My address is given at the end of the preface.

THOUGHT QUESTIONS

1. Although executives of tobacco companies used to insist that cigarettes were not addictive and asserted that people smoked simply because of the pleasure the act gave them, research indicates that nicotine is indeed a potent addictive drug. Why do you think it took so long to recognize this fact?

2. In most countries alcohol is legal and marijuana is not. In your opinion, why? What criteria would you use to decide whether a newly discovered drug should be legal or illegal? Danger to health? Effects on fetal development? Effects on behavior? Potential for dependence? If you applied these criteria to various substances in current use, would you have to change the legal status of any of them?

EPILOGUE

Classically Conditioned Craving

When a person takes heroin, the primary effects of the drug activate homeostatic compensatory mechanisms. These compensatory mechanisms are provided by neural circuits that oppose the effects of the drug. As Siegel (1978) has pointed out, the activation of these compensatory mechanisms is a response that can become classically conditioned to environmental stimuli that are present at the time the drug is taken. The stimuli associated with taking the drug—including the paraphernalia involved in preparing the solution of the drug, the syringe, the needle, the feel of the needle in a vein, and even the sight of companions who are usually present and the room in which the drug is taken serve as conditional stimuli. The homeostatic compensatory responses provoked by the effects of the drug—serve as the unconditional response, which becomes conditioned to the environmental stimuli. Thus, once classical conditioning has taken place, the sight of the conditional stimuli will activate the compensatory mechanisms.

When John, the former addict in the chapter prologue, saw the poster, the sight of the drug paraphernalia acted as a conditional stimulus and elicited the conditional response the compensatory mechanism. Because he had not taken the drug, he felt only the effect of the compensatory mechanism: dysphoria, agitation, and a strong urge to relieve these symptoms and replace them with feelings of euphoria. He found the urge irresistible.

Experiments with laboratory animals have confirmed that this explanation is correct. For example, Siegel et al. (1982) gave rats daily doses of heroin—always in the same chamber—long enough for tolerance to develop. Then, on the test day, the experimenters gave the rats a large dose of the drug. Some of the animals received the drug in the familiar chamber, while others received it in a new environment. The investigators predicted that the animals receiving the drug in the familiar environment would have some protection from the drug overdose because the stimuli in that environment would produce a classically conditioned compensatory response. Their prediction was correct; almost all of the rats who received the overdose in the new environment died, compared with slightly more than half of the rats injected in the familiar environment. Siegel and his colleagues suggest that when human heroin addicts take the drug in an unfamiliar environment, they too run the risk of death from a drug overdose.

By the way, the story of John that I recounted in the chapter prologue is unlikely to occur nowadays. Because so many heroin addicts trying to break their habit have reported that the sight of drug paraphernalia made it difficult for them to abstain, the agencies trying to combat drug addiction have stopped preparing posters that feature these items.

KEY CONCEPTS

AUTISTIC DISORDER

1. Autistic disorder is characterized by poor or absent social relations, communicative abilities, and imaginative abilities and the presence of repetitive, purposeless movements.
2. Although autism used to be blamed on poor parenting behavior, it is now recognized that the disorder is caused by hereditary factors or events that interfere with prenatal development.

ATTENTION-DEFICIT/HYPERACTIVITY DISORDER

3. Attention-deficit/hyperactivity disorder (ADHD) shows up in childhood, and is characterized by difficulty concentrating, remaining still, and working on a task. Children with ADHD also have difficulty withholding a response, act without reflecting, often show reckless and impetuous behavior, and let interfering activities intrude into ongoing tasks.
4. ADHD is treated by dopamine agonists such as methylphenidate (Ritalin). The disorder may be caused by abnormalities in the brain's reinforcement mechanisms, which result in a steeper delay of reinforcement gradient.

STRESS

5. The stress response consists of the physiological components of an emotional response to threatening stimuli. The long-term effects of these responses—

particularly of the secretion of the glucocorticoids—can damage a person's health. Stress-related secretion of catecholamines may be a factor in the development of cardiovascular disease.

6. The way people cope with stress can affect their physiological reaction and thus their health.
7. Stress can suppress the immune system, primarily through the secretion of glucocorticoids and therefore can make a person more susceptible to infections.

SUBSTANCE ABUSE DISORDERS

8. All addictive substances studied so far—including opiates, cocaine, amphetamine, nicotine, marijuana, and alcohol—have been shown to cause the release of dopamine in the nucleus accumbens.
9. Although chronic intake of opiates causes tolerance and leads to withdrawal symptoms, these phenomena are not responsible for addiction, which is caused by the ability of these drugs to activate dopaminergic mechanisms of reinforcement.
10. Alcohol has two sites of action: It serves as an indirect antagonist at the $GABA_A$ receptor and an indirect antagonist at the NMDA receptor.
11. Research indicates that the susceptibility to alcoholism is strongly influenced by heredity. Binging and steady drinking appear to caused by different mechanisms.
12. Physiological therapy for drug addiction includes methadone for opiate addiction, nicotine chewing gum or skin patches for addiction to nicotine, and serotonin agonists or naltrexone (an opiate receptor blocker) for alcoholism.

SUGGESTED READINGS

Ader, R., Felten, D. L., and Cohen, N. (eds.). *Psychoneuroimmunology,* 2nd ed. San Diego: Academic Press, 1991.

Bauman, M. L., and Kemper, T. L. *The Neurobiology of Autism.* Baltimore: Johns Hopkins University Press, 1994.

Brown, M. R., Koob, G. F., and Rivier, C. (eds.). *Stress: Neurobiology and Neuroendocrinology.* New York: Dekker, 1990.

Gershon, E. S., and Cloninger, C. R. *New Genetic Approaches to Mental Disorders.* Washington, DC: American Psychiatric Press, 1994.

Goodwin, D. W., and Guze, S. B. *Psychiatric Diagnosis,* 5th ed. New York: Oxford University Press, 1996.

Yudofsky, S. C., and Hales, R. E. *The American Psychiatric Press Textbook of Neuropsychiatry.* Washington, DC: American Psychiatric Press, 1997.

SUGGESTED WEB SITES

Facts on Post-Traumatic Stress Disorder (PTSD)
www.nimh.nig.gov/events/ptsdfact.htm

This NIH site discusses the causes and symptoms of PTSD and provides links to key sites on PTSD.

On-Line Anxiety Course
http://salmon.psy.plym.ac.uk/year2/anxiety.htm

This site provides access to a comprehensive set of materials relating to the pharmacology of anxiety.

The Emotional Brain
www.nimh.nih.gov/events/ledoux.htm

This site details the research of Dr. Joseph LeDoux relating the emotion of fear to mechanisms within the amygdala.

Anxiety Disorder Education Program
www.nimh.nih.gov/anxiety/news/index.htm

This NIMH site provides links to articles and fact sheets on anxiety disorders.

Generalized Anxiety Disorder
www.mentalhealth.com/dis/p20-an07.html

This site contains descriptions of diagnosis and treatment issues for generalized anxiety disorder

REFERENCES

Abe, M., Saito, M., and Shimazu, T. Neuropeptide Y and norepinephrine injected into the paraventricular nucleus of the hypothalamus activate endocrine pancreas. *Biomedical Research,* 1989, *10,* 431–436.

Abel, E. L., and Sokol, R. J. Fetal alcohol syndrome is now a leading cause of mental retardation. *Lancet,* 1986, *2,* 1222.

Abercrombie, H. C., Schaefer, S. M., Larson, C. L., Oakes, T. R., Lindgren, K. A., Holden, J. E., Perlman, S. B., Turski, P. A., Krahn, D. D., Benca, R. M., and Davidson, R. J. Metabolic rate in the right amygdala predicts negative affect in depressed patients. *Neuroreport,* 1998, *9,* 3301–3307.

Abrahamov, A., Abrahamov, A., and Mechoulam, R. An efficient new cannabinoid antiemetic in pediatric oncology. *Life Sciences,* 1995, *56,* 2097–2102.

Adams, D. B., Gold, A. R., and Burt, A. D. Rise in female-initiated sexual activity at ovulation and its suppression by oral contraceptives. *New England Journal of Medicine,* 1978, *299,* 1145–1150.

Adams, R. D., and Victor, M. *Principles of Neurology.* New York: McGraw-Hill, 1981.

Adey, W. R., Bors, E., and Porter, R. W. EEG sleep patterns after high cervical lesions in man. *Archives of Neurology,* 1968, *19,* 377–383.

Adieh, H. B., Mayer, A. D., and Rosenblatt, J. S. Effects of brain antiestrogen implants on maternal behavior and on postpartum estrus in pregnant rats. *Neuroendocrinology,* 1987, *46,* 522–531.

Adler, C. M., Malhotra, A. K., Elman, I., Goldberg, T., Egan, M., Pickar, D., and Breier, A. Comparison of ketamine-induced thought disorder in healthy volunteers and thought disorder in schizophrenia. *American Journal of Psychiatry,* 1999, *156,* 1646–1649.

Adler, C. M., Malhotra, A. K., Elman, I., Pickar, D., and Breier, A. Amphetamine-induced dopamine release and post-synaptic specific binding in patients with mild tardive dyskinesia. *Neuropsychopharmacology,* 2002, *26,* 295–300.

Adolphs, R., Damasio, H., Tranel, D., Cooper, G., and Damasio, A. R. A Role for somatosensory cortices in the visual recognition of emotion as revealed by three-dimensional lesion mapping. *Journal of Neuroscience,* 2000, *20,* 2683–2690.

Adolphs, R., and Tranel, D. Intact recognition of emotional prosody following amygdala damage. *Neuropsychologia,* 1999, *37,* 1285–1292.

Adolphs, R., Tranel, D., Damasio, H., and Damasio, A. Impaired recognition of emotion in facial expressions following bilateral damage to the human amygdala. *Nature,* 1994, *372,* 669–672.

Adolphs, R., Tranel, D., Damasio, H., and Damasio, A. Fear and the human amygdala. *Journal of Neuroscience,* 1995, *15,* 5879–5891.

Advokat, C., and Kutlesic, V. Pharmacotherapy of the eating disorders: A commentary. *Neuroscience and Biobehavioral Reviews,* 1995, *19,* 59–66.

Aharon, I., Etcoff, N., Ariely, D., Chabris, C. F., O'Connor, E., and Breiter, H. C. Beautiful faces have variable reward value: fMRI and behavioral evidence. *Neuron,* 2001, *32,* 537–551.

Akhtar, S., Wig, N., Pershad, D., and Varma, S. A phenomenological analysis of symptoms in obsessive compulsive disorder. *British Journal of Psychiatry,* 1975, *127,* 342–348.

Alain, C., Arnott, S. R., Hevenor, S., Graham, S., and Grady, C. L. "What" and "where" in the human auditory system. *Proceedings of the National Academy of Science,* USA, 2001, *98,* 12301–12306.

Alexander, M. P., Fischer, R. S., and Friedman, R. Lesion localization in apractic agraphia. *Archives of Neurology,* 1992, *49,* 246–251.

Allen, L. S., and Gorski, R. A. Sexual orientation and the size of the anterior commissure in the human brain. *Proceedings of the National Academy of Sciences,* 1992, *89,* 7199–7202.

Allison, D. B., Kaprio, J., Korkeila, M., Koskenvuo, M., Neale, M. C., and Hayakawa, K. The heritability of body mass index among an international sample of monozygotic twins reared apart. *International Journal of Obesity,* 1996, *20,* 501–506.

Altschuler, H. L., Phillips, P. E., and Feinhandler, D. A. Alterations of ethanol self-administration by naltrexone. *Life Sciences,* 1980, *26,* 679–688.

Amaral, D. G., Price, J. L., Pitkänen, A., and Carmichael, S. T. Anatomical organization of the primate amygdalid complex. In *The Amygdala: Neurobiological Aspects of Emotion, Memory, and Mental Dysfunction.* New York: Wiley-Liss, 1992.

Anand, B. K., and Brobeck, J. R. Hypothalamic control of food intake in rats and cats. *Yale Journal of Biology and Medicine,* 1951, *24,* 123–140.

Ancoli-Israel, S., and Roth, T. Characteristics of insomnia in the United States: Results of the 1991 National Sleep Foundation survey. *Sleep,* 1999, *22,* S347—S353.

Anderson, A. K., and Phelps, E. A. Expression without recognition: Contributions of the human amygdala to emotional communication. *Psychological Science,* 2000, *11,* 106–111.

Anderson, C. M., Polcari, A., Lowen, S. B., Renshaw, P. F., and Teicher, M. H. Effects of methylphenidate on functional magnetic resonance relaxometry of the cerebellar vermis in boys with ADHD. *American Journal of Psychiatry,* 2002, *159,* 1322–1328.

Andreasen, N. C. Symptoms, signs, and diagnosis of schizophrenia. *Lancet,* 1995, *346,* 477–481.

Andrews, N., Miller, E., Taylor, B., Lingam, R., Simmons, A., Stowe, J., and Waight, P. Recall bias, MMR, and autism. *Archives of Disease in Childhood,* 2002, *87,* 493–494.

Archer, J. Testosterone and aggression. *Journal of Offender Rehabilitation,* 1994, *5,* 3–25.

Arendt, J., Deacon, S., English, J., Hampton, S., and Morgan, L. Melatonin and adjustment to phase-shift. *Journal of Sleep Research,* 1995, *4,* 74–79.

Arnason, B. G. Immunologic therapy of multiple sclerosis. *Annual Review of Medicine,* 1999, *50,* 291–302.

Aronson, B. D., Bell-Pedersen, D., Block, G. D., Bos, N. P. A., Dunlap, J. C., Eskin, A., Garceau, N. Y., Geusz, M. E., Johnson, K. A., Khalsa, S. B. S., Koster-Van Hoffen, G. C., Koumenis, C., Lee, T. M., LeSauter, J., Lindgren, K. M., Liu, Q., Loros, J. J., Michel, S. H., Mirmiran, M., Moore, R. Y., Ruby, N. F., Silver, R., Turek, F. W., and Zatz, M. Circadian rhythms. *Brain Research Reviews,* 1993, *18,* 315–333.

Artmann, H., Grau, H., Adelman, M., and Schleiffer, R. Reversible and non-reversible enlargement of cerebrospinal fluid spaces in anorexia nervosa. *Neuroradiology,* 1985, *27,* 103–112.

Aschoff, J. Circadian rhythms: General features and endocrinological aspects. In *Endocrine Rhythms,* edited by D. T. Krieger. New York: Raven Press, 1979.

Asnis, G. M., Hameedi, F. A., Goddard, A. W., Potkin, S. G., Black, D., Jameel, M., Desagani, K., and Woods, S. W. Fluvoxamine in the treatment of panic disorder: A multicenter, double-blind, placebo-controlled study in outpatients. *Psychiatry Research,* 2001, *103,* 1–14.

Aston-Jones, G., and Bloom, F. E. Activity of norepinephrine-containing locus coeruleus neurons in behaving rats anticipates fluctuations in the sleep-waking cycle. *Journal of Neuroscience,* 1981a, *1,* 876–886.

Aston-Jones, G., Rajkowski, J., Kubiak, P., and Alexinsky, T. Locus coeruleus neurons in monkey are selectively activated by attended cues in a vigilance task. *Journal of Neuroscience,* 1994, *14,* 4467–4480.

Atack, J. R., Broughton, H. B., and Pollack, S. J. Inositol monophosphatase: A putative target for Li^+ in the treatment of bipolar disorder. *Trends in Neurosciences,* 1995, *18,* 343–349.

Attia, E., Haiman, C., Walsh, T., and Flater, S. T. Does fluoxetine augment the inpatient treatment of anorexia nervosa? *American Journal of Psychiatry,* 1998, *155,* 548–551.

Auer, R. N., Jensen, M. L., and Whishaw, I. Q. Neurobehavioral deficit due to ischemic brain damage limited to half of the CA1 section of the hippocampus. *Journal of Neuroscience,* 1989, *9,* 1641–1647.

Avenet, P., and Lindemann, B. Perspectives of taste reception. *Journal of Membrane Biology,* 1989, *112,* 1–8.

Avila, M. T., Weiler, M. A., Lahti, A. C., Tamminga, C. A., and Thaker, G. K. Effects of ketamine on leading saccades during smooth-pursuit eye movements may implicate cerebellar dysfunction in schizophrenia. *American Journal of Psychiatry,* 2002, *159,* 1490–1496.

Baddeley, A. D. Memory: Verbal and visual subsystems of working memory. *Current Biology,* 1993, *3,* 563–565.

Bagatell, C. J., Heiman, J. R., Rivier, J. E., and Bremner, W. J. Effects of endogenous testosterone and estradiol on sexual behavior in

normal young men. *Journal of Clinical Endocrinology and Metabolism,* 1994, *7,* 211–216.
Bai, F. L., Yamano, M., Shiotani, Y., Emson, P. C., Smith, A. D., Powell, J. F., and Tohyama, M. An arcuato-paraventricular and dorsomedial hypothalamic neuropeptide Y-containing system which lacks noradrenaline in the rat. *Brain Research,* 1985, *331,* 172–175.
Bailey, A. The biology of autism. *Psychological Medicine,* 1993, *23,* 7–11.
Bailey, A., Le Couteur, A., Gottesman, I., Bolton, P., Simonoff, E., Yuzda, E., and Rutter, M. Autism as a strongly genetic disorder: Evidence from a British twin study. *Psychological Medicine,* 1995, *25,* 63–77.
Bailey, A., Luthert, P., Dean, A., Harding, B., Janota, I., Montgomery, M., Rutter, M., and Lantos, P. A clinicopathological study of autism. *Brain,* 1998, *121,* 889–905.
Bailey, J. M., and Pillard, R. C. A genetic study of male sexual orientation. *Archives of General Psychiatry,* 1991, *48,* 1089–1096.
Bailey, J. M., Pillard, R. C., Neale, M. C., and Agyei, Y. Heritable factors influence sexual orientation in women. *Archives of General Psychiatry,* 1993, *50,* 217–223.
Baizer, J. S., Ungerleider, L. G., and Desimone, R. Organization of visual inputs to the inferior temporal and posterior parietal cortex in macaques. *Journal of Neuroscience,* 1991, *11,* 168–190.
Bak, T. H., O'Donovan, D. G., Xuereb, J. H., Boniface, S., and Hodges, J. R. Selective impairment of verb processing associated with pathological changes in Brodman areas 44 and 45 in the motor neurone disease-dementia-aphasia syndrome. *Brain,* 2001, *124,* 103–120.
Baker, D. G., West, S. A., Nicholson, W. E., Ekhator, N. N., Kasckow, J. W., Hill, K. K., Bruce, A. B., Orth, D. N., and Geracioti, T. D. Serial CSF corticotropin-releasing hormone levels and adrenocortical activity in combat veterans with posttraumatic stress disorder. *American Journal of Psychiatry,* 1999, *156,* 585–588.
Baldessarini, R. J. *Chemotherapy in Psychiatry.* Cambridge, Mass.: Harvard University Press, 1977.
Ballantine, H. T., Bouckoms, A. J., Thomas, E. K., and Giriunas, I. E. Treatment of psychiatric illness by stereotactic cingulotomy. *Biological Psychiatry,* 1987, *22,* 807–819.
Banks, W. A., Kastin, A. J., Huang, W. T., Jaspan, J. B., and Maness, L. M. Leptin enters the brain by a saturable system independent of insulin. *Peptides,* 1996, *17,* 305–311.
Barbazanges, A., Piazza, P. V., Le Moal, M., and Maccari, S. Maternal glucocorticoid secretion mediates long-term effects of prenatal stress. *Journal of Neuroscience,* 1996, *16,* 3943–3949.
Barber, T. X. Responding to "hypnotic" suggestions: An introspective report. *American Journal of Clinical Hypnosis,* 1975, *18,* 6–22.
Barclay, C. D., Cutting, J. E., and Kozlowski, L. T. Temporal and spatial factors in gait perception that influence gender recognition. *Perception and Psychophysics,* 1978, *23,* 145–152.
Bard, F., Cannon, C., Barbour, R., Burke, R. L., Games, D., Grajeda, H., Guido, T., Hu, K., Huang, J., Johnson-Wood, K., Khan, K., Kholodenko, D., Lee, M., Lieberburg, I., Motter, R., Nguyen, M., Soriano, F., Vasquez, N., Weiss, K., Welch, B., Seubert, P., Schenk, D., and Yednock, T. Peripherally administered antibodies against amyloid beta-peptide enter the central nervous system and reduce pathology in a mouse model of Alzheimer disease. *Nature Medicine,* 2000, *6,* 916–919.
Bartness, T. J., Powers, J. B., Hastings, M. H., Bittman, E. L., and Goldman, B. D. The timed infusion paradigm for melatonin delivery: What has it taught us about the melatonin signal, its reception, and the photoperiodic control of seasonal responses? *Journal of Pineal Research,* 1993, *15,* 161–190.
Batterham, R. L., and Bloom, S. R. The gut hormone peptide YY regulates appetite. *Annals of the New York Academy of Science,* 2003, *995,* 162–168.
Batterham, R. L., Cowley, M. A., Small, C. J., Herzog, H., Cohen, M. A., Dakin, C. L., Wren, A. M., Brynes, A. E., Low, M. J., Ghatei, M. A., Cone, R. D., and Bloom, S. R. Gut hormone PYY_{3-36} physiologically inhibits food intake. *Nature,* 2002, *418,* 650–654.
Baylis, G. C., Rolls, E. T., and Leonard, C. M. Selectivity between faces in the responses of a population of neurons in the cortex in the superior temporal sulcus of the monkey. *Brain Research,* 1985, *342,* 91–102.
Bean, N. J. Modulation of agonistic behavior by the dual olfactory system in male mice. *Physiology and Behavior,* 1982, *29,* 433–437.
Bean, N. J., and Conner, R. Central hormonal replacement and home-cage dominance in castrated rats. *Hormones and Behavior,* 1978, *11,* 100–109.
Bear, O., and Fedio, P. Qualitative analysis of interictal behavior in temporal lobe epilepsy. *Archives of Neurology,* 1977, *34,* 454–467.
Beauvois, M. F., and Dérouesné, J. Lexical or orthographic dysgraphia. *Brain,* 1981, *104,* 21–45.
Beauvois, M. F., and Dérouesné, J. Phonological alexia: Three dissociations. *Journal of Neurology, Neurosurgery and Psychiatry,* 1979, *42,* 1115–1124.
Bechara, A., Damasio, H., Tranel, D., and Anderson, S. W. Dissociation of working memory from decision making within the human prefrontal cortex. *Journal of Neuroscience,* 1998, *18,* 428–437.
Bechara, A., Tranel, D., Damasio, H., Adolphs, R., Rockland, C., and Damasio, A. R. Double dissociation of conditioning and declarative knowledge relative to the amygdala and hippocampus in humans. *Science,* 1995, *269,* 1115–1118.
Beckstead, R. M., Morse, J. R., and Norgren, R. The nucleus of the solitary tract in the monkey: Projections to the thalamus and brainstem nuclei. *Journal of Comparative Neurology,* 1980, *190,* 259–282.
Beeman, E. A. The effect of male hormone on aggressive behavior in mice. *Physiological Zoology,* 1947, *20,* 373–405.
Beidler, L. M. Physiological properties of mammalian taste receptors. In *Taste and Smell in Vertebrates,* edited by G. E. W. Wolstenholme. London: J. & A. Churchill, 1970.
Belin, P., Zatorre, R. J., Lafaille, P., Ahad, P., and Pike, B. Voice-selective areas in human auditory cortex. *Nature,* 2000, *403,* 309–312.
Bell, A. P., Weinberg, M. S., and Hammersmith, S. K. *Sexual Preference: Its Development in Men and Women.* Bloomington: Indiana University Press, 1981.
Benington, J. H., Kodali, S. K., and Heller, H. C. Monoaminergic and cholinergic modulation of REM-sleep timing in rats. *Brain Research,* 1995, *681,* 141–146.
Bermant, G., and Davidson, J. M. *Biological Bases of Sexual Behavior.* New York: Harper & Row, 1974.
Bernhardt, P. C., Dabbs, J. M., Fielden, J. A., and Lutter, C. D. Testosterone changes during vicarious experiences of winning and losing among fans at sporting events. *Physiology and Behavior,* 1998, *65,* 59–62.
Berson, D. M., Dunn, F. A., and Takao, M. Phototransduction by retinal ganglion cells that set the circadian clock. *Science,* 2002, *295,* 1070–1073.
Berthier, M., Kulisevsky, J., Gironell, A., and Heras, J. A. Obsessive-compulsive disorder associated with brain lesions: Clinical phenomenology, cognitive function, and anatomic correlates. *Neurology,* 1996, *47,* 353–361.
Best, P. J., White, A. M., and Minai, A. Spatial processing in the brain: The activity of hippocampal place cells. *Annual Review of Neuroscience,* 2001, *24,* 459–486.
Bettelheim, B. *The Empty Fortress.* New York: Free Press, 1967.
Bier, M. J., and McCarley, R. W. REM-enhancing effects of the adrenergic antagonist idazoxan infused into the medial pontine reticular formation of the freely moving cat. *Brain Research,* 1994, *634,* 333–338.
Bierut, L. J., Dinwiddie, S. H., Begliter, H., Crowe, R. R., Hesselbrock, V., Nurnberger, J. I., Porjexz, B., Schukit, M. A., and Reich, T. Familial transmission of substance dependence: Alcohol, Marijuana, cocaine, and habitual smoking. *Archives of General Psychiatry,* 1998, *55,* 982–988.
Bigiani, A., Delay, R. J., Chaudhair, N., Kinnamon, S. C., and Roper, S. D. Responses to glutamate in rat taste cells. *Journal of Neurophysiology,* 1997, *77,* 3048–3059.
Birch, L. L., McPhee, L., Shoba, B. C., Steinberg, L., and Krehbiel, R. "Clean up your plate": Effects of child feeding practices on the conditioning of meal size. *Learning and Motivation,* 1987, *18,* 301–317.
Bird, E., Cardone, C. C., and Contreras, R. J. Area postrema lesions disrupt food intake induced by cerebroventricular infusions of 5-thioglucose in the rat. *Brain Research,* 1983, *270,* 193–196.
Bisiach, E., and Luzzatti, C. Unilateral neglect of representational space. *Cortex,* 1978, *14,* 129–133.
Blaustein, J. D., and Feder, H. H. Cytoplasmic progestin receptors in guinea pig brain: Characteristics and relationship to the induction of sexual behavior. *Brain Research,* 1979, *169,* 481–497.
Blest, A. D. The function of eyespot patterns in insects. *Behaviour,* 1957, *11,* 209–256.
Bleuler, E. *Dementia Praecox of the Group of Schizophrenia, 1911.* Translated by J. Zinkin. New York: International Universities Press, 1911/1950.
Bliss, T. V. P., and Lømo, T. Long-lasting potentiation of synaptic transmission in the dentate area of the anaesthetized rabbit following stimulation of the perforant path. *Journal of Physiology (London),* 1973, *232,* 331–356.
Bloch, V., Hennevin, E., and Leconte, P. Interaction between post-trial reticular stimulation and subsequent paradoxical sleep in memory consolidation processes. In *Neurobi-*

ology of Sleep and Memory, edited by R. R. Drucker-Colín and J. L. McGaugh. New York: Academic Press, 1977.

Blonder, L. X., Bowers, D., and Heilman, K. M. The role of the right hemisphere in emotional communication. *Brain,* 1991, *114,* 1115–1127.

Blundell, J. E., and Halford, J. C. G. Serotonin and appetite regulation: Implications for the pharmacological treatment of obesity. *CNS Drugs,* 1998, *9,* 473–495.

Boatman, D., Gordon, B., Hart, J., Selnes, O., Miglioretti, D., and Lenz, F. Transcortical sensory aphasia: Revisited and revised. *Brain,* 2000, *123,* 1634–1642.

Bodner, S. M., Morshed, S. A., and Peterson, B. S. The question of PANDAS in adults. *Biological Psychiatry,* 2001, *49,* 807–810.

Boeve, B. F., Silber, M. H., Ferman, T. J., Lucas, J. A., and Parisi, J. E. Association of REM sleep behavior disorder and neurodegenerative disease may reflect an underlying synucleinopathy. *Movement Disorders,* 2001, *16,* 622–630.

Bon, C., Böhme, G. A., Doble, A., Stutzmann, J.-M., and Blanchard, J.-C. A role for nitric oxide in long-term potentiation. *European Journal of Neuroscience,* 1992, *4,* 420–424.

Born, R. T., and Tootell, R. B. H. Spatial frequency tuning of single units in macaque supragranular striate cortex. *Proceedings of the National Academy of Sciences,* 1991, *88,* 7066–7070.

Bornstein, B., Stroka, H., and Munitz, H. Prosopagnosia with animal face agnosia. *Cortex,* 1969, *5,* 164–169.

Borod, J. C., Koff, E., Yecker, S., Santschi, C., and Schmidt, J. M. Facial asymmetry during emotional expression: Gender, falence, and measurement technique. *Neuropsychologia,* 1998, *36,* 1209–1215.

Boulos, Z., Campbell, S. S., Lewy, A. J., Terman, M., Dijk, D. J., and Eastman, C. I. Light treatment for sleep disorders: Consensus report. 7: Jet-lag. *Journal of Biological Rhythms,* 1995, *10,* 167–176.

Bouwknecht, J. A., Hijzen, T. H., van der Gugten, J., Maes, R. A. A., Hen, R., and Olivier, B. Absence of 5-HT_{1B} receptors is associated with impaired impulse control in Male 5-HT_{1B} knockout mice. *Biological Psychiatry,* 2001, *49,* 557–568.

Bowers, D., and Heilman, K. M. A dissociation between the processing of affective and nonaffective faces. Paper presented at the meeting of the International Neuropsychological Society, Atlanta, 1981.

Bowersox, S. S., Kaitin, K. I., and Dement, W. C. EEG spindle activity as a function of age: Relationship to sleep continuity. *Brain Research,* 1985, *63,* 526–539.

Boynton, R. M. *Human Color Vision.* New York: Holt, Rinehart and Winston, 1979.

Bozarth, M. A., and Wise, R. A. Toxicity associated with long-term intravenous heroin and cocaine self-administration in the rat. *Journal of the American Medical Association,* 1985, *254,* 81–83.

Bradbury, M. W. B. *The Concept of a Blood-Brain Barrier.* New York: John Wiley & Sons, 1979.

Bradley, D. C., Maxwell, M., Andersen, R. A., Banks, M. S., and Shenoy, K. V. Mechanisms of heading perception in primate visual cortex. *Science,* 1996, *273,* 1544–1547.

Bradley, S. J., Oliver, G. D., Chernick, A. B., and Zucker, K. H. Experiment of nurture: Ablatio penis at 2 months, sex reassignment at 7 months, and a psychosexual follow-up in young adulthood. *Pediatrics,* 1998, *102,* E91-E95.

Braun, S. New experiments underscore warnings on maternal drinking. *Science,* 1996, *273,* 738–739.

Brecher, E. M. *Licit and Illicit Drugs.* Boston: Little, Brown & Co., 1972.

Breedlove, S. M. Sexual differentiation of the brain and behavior. In *Behavioral Endocrinology,* edited by J. B. Becker, S. M. Breedlove, and D. Crews. Cambridge, Mass.: MIT Press, 1992.

Breedlove, S. M. Sexual differentiation of the human nervous system. *Annual Review of Psychology,* 1994, *45,* 389–418.

Breier, A., Su, T.-P., Saunders, R., Carson, R. E., Kolachana, B. S., de Bartolemeis, A., Weinberger, D. R., Weisenfeld, N., Malhotra, A. K., Eckelman, W. C., and Pickar, D. Schizophrenia is associated with elevated amphetamine-induced synaptic dopamine concentrations: evidence from a novel positron emission tomography method. *Proceedings of the National Academy of Science, USA,* 1997, *94,* 2569–2574.

Breisch, S. T., Zemlan, F. P., and Hoebel, B. G. Hyperphagia and obesity following serotonin depletion by intraventricular *p*-chlorphenylalanine. *Science,* 1976, *192,* 382–384.

Bremner, J. D. Does stress damage the brain? *Biological Psychiatry,* 1999, *45,* 797–805.

Bremner, J. D., Innis, R. B., Salomon, R. M., Staib, L. H., Ng, C. K., Miller, H. L., Bronen, R. A., Krystal, J. H., Duncan, J., Rich, D., Price, L. H., Malison, R., Dey, H., Soufer, R., and Charney, D. S. Positron emission tomography measurement of cerebral metabolic correlates of tryptophan depletion-induced depressive relapse. *Archives of General Psychiatry,* 1997, *54,* 364–374.

Bremner, J. D., Randall, P., Scott, T. M., Bronen, R. A., Seibyl, J. P., Southwick, S. M., Delaney, R. C., McCarthy, G., Charney, D. S., and Innis, R. B. MRI-based measurement of hippocampal volume in patients with combat-related posttraumatic stress disorder. *American Journal of Psychiatry,* 1995, *152,* 973–981.

Bridges, R. S. A quantitative analysis of the roles of dosage, sequence and duration of estradiol and progesterone exposure in the regulation of maternal behavior in the rat. *Endocrinology,* 1984, *114,* 930–940.

Bridges, R. S., Numan, M., Ronsheim, P. M., Mann, P. E., and Lupini, C. E. Central prolactin infusions stimulate maternal behavior in steroid-treated, nulliparous female rats. *Proceedings of the National Academy of Sciences, USA,* 1990, *87,* 8003–8007.

Britten, K. H., and van Wezel, R. J. Electrical microstimulation of cortical area MST biases heading perception in monkeys. *Nature Neuroscience,* 1998, *1,* 59–63.

Britton, D. R., Koob, G. F., Rivier, J., and Vale, W. Intraventricular corticotropin-releasing factor enhances behavioral effects of novelty. *Life Sciences,* 1982, *31,* 363–367.

Broberg, D. J., and Bernstein, I. L. Cephalic insulin release in anorexic women. *Physiology and Behavior,* 1989, *45,* 871–874.

Broberger, C., de Lecea, L., Sutcliffe, J. G., and Hökfelt, T. Hypocretin/orexin- and melanin concentrating hormone-expressing cells form distinct populations in the rodent lateral hypothalamus: Relationship to the neuropeptide Y and agouti gene-related protein systems. *Journal of Comparative Neurology,* 1998, *402,* 460–474.

Broca, P. Remarques sur le siège de la faculté du langage articulé, suivies d'une observation d'aphemie (perte de la parole). *Bulletin de la Société Anatomique (Paris),* 1861, *36,* 330–357.

Brown, R. E., Stevens, D. R., and Haas, H. L. The physiology of brain histamine. *Progress in Neurobiology,* 2001, *63,* 637–672.

Brownell, W. E., Bader, C. R., Bertrand, D., and de-Ribaupierre, Y. Evoked mechanical responses of isolated cochlear outer hair cells. *Science,* 1985, *227,* 194–196.

Bruce, H. M. A block to pregnancy in the mouse caused by proximity of strange males. *Journal of Reproduction and Fertility,* 1960a, *1,* 96–103.

Bruce, H. M. Further observations of pregnancy block in mice caused by proximity of strange males. *Journal of Reproduction and Fertility,* 1960b, *2,* 311–312.

Brüning, J. C., Gautam, D., Burks, D. J., Gillette, J., Schubert, M., Orban, P. C., Klein, R., Krone, W., Muller-Wieland, D., and Kahn, C. R. Role of brain insulin receptor in control of body weight and reproduction. *Science,* 2000, *289,* 2122–2125.

Bryden, M. P., and Ley, R. G. Right-hemispheric involvement in the perception and expression of emotion in normal humans. In *Neuropsychology of Human Emotion,* edited by K. M. Heilman and P. Satz. New York: Guilford Press, 1983.

Buchs, P. A., and Muller, D. Induction of long-term potentiation is associated with major ultrastructural changes of activated synapses. *Proceedings of the National Academy of Sciences of the United States of America,* 1996, *93,* 8040–8045.

Buchsbaum, M. S., Gillin, J. C., Wu, J., Hazlett, E., Sicotte, N., Dupont, R. M., and Bunney, W. E. Regional cerebral glucose metabolic rate in human sleep assessed by positron emission tomography. *Life Sciences,* 1989, *45,* 1349–1356.

Buck, L. B. Information coding in the vertebrate olfactory system. *Annual Review of Neuroscience,* 1996, *19,* 517–544.

Buck, L., and Axel, R. A novel multigene family may encode odorant receptors: A molecular basis for odor recognition. *Cell,* 1991, *65,* 175–187.

Bueler, H., Aguzzi, A., Sailer, A., Grenier, R. A., Autenreid, P., Aguet, M., and Weissmann, C. Mice devoid of PrP are resistant to scrapie. *Cell,* 1993, *73,* 1339–1347.

Buggy, J., Hoffman, W. E., Phillips, M. I., Fisher, A. E., and Johnson, A. K. Osmosensitivity of rat third ventricle and interactions with angiotensin. *American Journal of Physiology,* 1979, *236,* R75–R82.

Bunyard, L. B., Katzel, L. I., Busby-Whitehead, M. J., Wu, Z., and Goldberg, A. P. Energy requirements of middle-aged men are modifiable by physical activity. *American Journal of Clinical Nutrition,* 1998, *68,* 1136–1142.

Burnstock, G., and Wood, J. N. Purinergic receptors: Their role in nociception and primary afferent neurotransmission. *Current Opinion in Neurobiology,* 1996, *6,* 526–532.

Burton, M. J., Rolls, E. T., and Mora, F. Effects of hunger on the responses of neurons in the lateral hypothalamus to the sight and taste of food. *Experimental Neurology,* 1976, *51,* 668–677.

Buxbaum, L. J., Glosser, G., and Coslett, H. B. Impaired face and word recognition without object agnosia. *Neuropsychologia,* 1999, *37,* 41–50.

Byne, W., Tobet, S., Mattiace, L. A., Lasco, M. S., Kemether, E., Edgar, M. A., Morgello, S., Buchsbaum, M. S., and Jones, L. B. The interstitial nucleus of the human anterior hypothalamus: An investigation of variation with sex, sexual orientation, and HIV status. *Hormones and Behavior,* 2001, *40,* 86–92.

Cador, M., Robbins, T. W., and Everitt, B. J. Involvement of the amygdala in stimulus-reward associations: Interaction with the ventral striatum. *Neuroscience,* 1989, *30,* 77–86.

Cahill, L., Haier, R. J., Fallon, J., Alkire, M. T., Tang, C., Keator, D., Wu, J., and McGaugh, J. L. Amygdala activity at encoding correlated with long-term, free recall of emotional information. *Proceedings of the National Academy of Sciences of the United States of America,* 1996, *93,* 8016–8021.

Cain, W. S. Olfaction. In Stevens' *Handbook of Experimental Psychology. Vol. 1: Perception and Motivation,* edited by R. C. Atkinson, R. J. Herrnstein, G. Lindzey, and R. D. Luce. New York: John Wiley & Sons, 1988.

Calder, A. J., Young, A. W., Rowland, D., Perrett, D. I., Hodges, J. R., and Etcoff, N. L. Facial emotion recognition after bilateral amygdala damage: Differentially severe impairment of fear. *Cognitive Neuropsychology,* 1996, *13,* 699–745.

Cameron, H. A., and McKay, R. D. G. Adult neurogenesis produces a large pool of new granule cells in the dentate gyrus. *Journal of Comparative Neurology,* 2001, *435,* 406–417.

Campeau, S., Hayward, M. D., Hope, B. T., Rosen, J. B., Nestler, E. J., and Davis, M. Induction of the c-fos proto-oncogene in rat amygdala during unconditioned and conditioned fear. *Brain Research,* 1991, *565,* 349–352.

Campeau, S., Miserendino, M. J. D., and Davis, M. Intra-amygdala infusion of the N-methyl-D-aspartate receptor antagonist AP5 blocks acquisition but not expression of fear-potentiated startle to an auditory conditioned stimulus. *Behavioral Neuroscience,* 1992, *106,* 569–574.

Campfield, L. A., Smith, F. J., Guisez, Y., Devos, R., and Burn, P. Recombinant mouse ob protein: Evidence for a peripheral signal linking adiposity and central neural networks. *Science,* 1995, *269,* 546–549.

Cannon, M., Jones, P. B., and Murray, R. M. Obstetric complications and schizophrenia: Historical and meta-analytic review. *American Journal of Psychiatry,* 2002, *159,* 1080–1092.

Cannon, M., Jones, P., Gilvarry, C., Rifkin, L., McKenzie, K., Foerster, A., and Murray, R. M. Premorbid social functioning in schizophrenia and bipolar disorder: Similarities and differences. *American Journal of Psychiatry,* 1997, *154,* 1544–1550.

Cannon, W. B. The James-Lange theory of emotions: A critical examination and an alternative. *American Journal of Psychology,* 1927, *39,* 106–124.

Card, J. P., Riley, J. N., and Moore, R. Y. The suprachiasmatic hypothalamic nucleus: Ultrastructure of relations to optic chiasm. *Neuroscience Abstracts,* 1980, *6,* 758.

Carew, T. J. Development assembly of learning in Aplysia. *Trends in Neuroscience,* 1989, *12,* 389–394.

Caro, J. F., Kolaczynski, J. W., Nyce, M. R., Ohannesian, J. P., Opentanova, I., Goldman, W. H., Lynn, R. B., Zhang, P. L., Sinha, M. K., and Consodine, R. V. Decreased cerebrospinal fluid/serum leptin ration in obesity: A possible mechanism for leptin resistance. *Lancet,* 1996, *348,* 159–161.

Carpenter, C. R. Sexual behavior of free ranging rhesus monkeys (*Macaca mulatta*). I. Specimens, procedures and behavioral characteristics of estrus. *Journal of Comparative Psychology,* 1942, *33,* 113–142.

Carr, D. B., and Sesack, S. R. Projections from the rat prefrontal cortex to the ventral tegmental area: Target specificity in the synaptic associations with mesoaccumbens and mesocortical neurons. *Journal of Neuroscience,* 2000, *20,* 3864–3873.

Carrera, M. R., Ashley, J. A., Parsons, L. H., Wirsching, P., Koob, G. F., and Janda, K. D. Suppression of psychoactive effects of cocaine by active immunization. *Nature,* 1995, *378,* 727–730.

Carroll, R. C., Lissin, D. V., von Zastrow, M., Nicolol, R. A., and Malenka, R. C. Rapid redistribution of glutamate receptors contributes to long-term depression in hippocampal cultures. *Nature Neuroscience,* 1999, *2,* 454–460.

Carter, C. S. Hormonal influences on human sexual behavior. In *Behavioral Endocrinology,* edited by J. B. Becker, S. M. Breedlove, and D. Crews. Cambridge, Mass.: MIT Press, 1992.

Castellanos, F. X., Lee, P. P., Sharp, W., Jeffries, N. O., Greenstein, D. K., Clasen, L. S., Blumenthal, J. D., James, R. S., Ebens, C. L., Walter, J. M., Zijdenbos, A., Evans, A. C., Giedd, J. N., Rappoport, J. L. Developmental trajectories of brain volume abnormalities in children and adolescents with attention-deficit/hyperactivity disorder. *Journal of the American Medical Association,* 2002, *288,* 1740–1748.

Castles, A., and Coltheart, M. Varieties of developmental dyslexia. *Cognition,* 1993, *47,* 149–180.

Caterina, M. J., Leffler, A., Malmberg, A. B., Martin, W. J., Trafton, J., Petersen-Zeitz, K. R., Koltzenburg, M., Basbaum, A. I., and Julius, D. Impaired nociception and pain sensation in mice lacking the capsaicin receptor. *Science,* 2000, *288,* 306–313.

Cenci, M. A., Kalen, P., Mandel, R. J., and Bjoerklund, A. Regional differences in the regulation of dopamine and noradrenaline release in medial frontal cortex, nucleus accumbens and caudate-putamen: A microdialysis study in the rat. *Brain Research,* 1992, *581,* 217–228.

Chaudhari, N., Yang, H., Lamp, C., Delay, E., Cartford, C., Than, T., and Roper, S. The taste of monosodium glutamate: Membrane receptors in taste buds. *Journal of Neuroscience,* 1996, *16,* 3817–3826.

Chemelli, R. M., Willie, J. T., Sinton, C. M., Elmquist, J. K., Scammell, T., Lee, C., Richardson, J. A., Williams, S. C., Xiong, Y., Kisanuki, Y., Fitch, T. E., Nakazato, M., Hammer, R. E., Saper, C. B., and Yanagisawa, M. Narcolepsy in orexin knockout mice: molecular genetics of sleep regulation. *Cell,* 1999, *98,* 437–451.

Chen, J., Paredes, W., Li, J., Smith, D., Lowinson, J., and Gardner, E. L. Delta^9-tetrahydrocannabinol produces naloxone-blockable enhancement of presynaptic basal dopamine efflux in nucleus accumbens of conscious, freely-moving rats as measured by intracerebral microdialysis. *Psychopharmacology,* 1990, *102,* 156–162.

Chen, Y. W., and Dilsaver, S. C. Lifetime rates of suicide attempts among subjects with bipolar and unipolar disorders relative to subjects with other axis I disorders. *Biological Psychiatry,* 1996, *39,* 896–899.

Chou, T. C., Bjorkum, A. A., Gaus, S. E., Lu, J., Scammell, T. E., and Saper, C. B. Afferents to the ventrolateral preoptic nucleus. *Journal of Neuroscience,* 2002, *22,* 977–990.

Clapham, J. C., Arch, J. R., Chapman, H., Haynes, A., Lister, C., Moore, G. B., Piercy, V., Carter, S. A., Lehner, I., Smith, S. A., Beeley, L. J., Godden, R. J., Herrity, N., Skehel, M., Changani, K. K., Hockings, P. D., Reid, D. G., Squires, S. M., Hatcher, J., Trail, B., Latcham, J., Rastan, S., Harper, A. J., Cadenas, S., Buckingham, J. A., Brand, M. D., Abuin, A. Mice overexpressing human uncoupling protein-3 in skeletal muscle are hyperphagic and lean. *Nature,* 2000, *406,* 415–418.

Clark, J. T., Kalra, P. S., Crowley, W. R., and Kalra, S. P. Neuropeptide Y and human pancreatic polypeptide stimulates feeding behavior in rats. *Endocrinology,* 1984, *115,* 427–429.

Clément, K., Vaisse, C., Lahlou, N., Cabrol, S., Pelloux, V., Cassuto, D., Gourmelen, M., Dina, C., Chambaz, J., Lacorte, J. M., Basdevant, A., Bougnères, P., Lebouc, Y., Froguel, P., Guy-Grand, B. A mutation in the human leptin receptor gene causes obesity and pituitary dysfunction. *Nature,* 1998, *392,* 398–401.

Cloninger, C. R. Neurogenetic adaptive mechanisms in alcoholism. *Science,* 1987, *236,* 410–416.

Cloninger, C. R., Bohman, M., and Sigvardsson, S. Inheritance of alcohol abuse: Cross-fostering analysis of adopted men. *Archives of General Psychiatry,* 1981, *38,* 861–868.

Cloninger, C. R., Bohman, M., Sigvardsson, S., and von Knorring, A.-L. Psychopathology in adopted-out children of alcoholics: The Stockholm Adoption Study. *Recent Developments in Alcoholism,* 1985, *3,* 37–51.

Cobb, S., and Rose, R. M. Hypertension, peptic ulcer, and diabetes in air traffic controllers. *Journal of the American Medical Association,* 1973, *224,* 489–492.

Coble, P. A., Scher, M. S., Reynolds, C. F., Day, N. L., and Kupfer, D. J. Preliminary findings on the neonatal sleep of offspring of women with and without a prior history of affective disorder. *Sleep Research,* 1988, *16,* 120.

Coccaro, E. F., and Kavoussi, R. J. Fluoxetine and impulsive aggressive behavior in personality-disordered subjects. *Archives of General Psychiatry,* 1997, *54,* 1081–1088.

Coccaro, E. F., Silverman, J. M., Klar, H. M., Horvath, T. B., and Siever, L. J. Familial correlates of reduced central serotonergic system function in patients with personality disorders. *Archives of General Psychiatry,* 1994, *51,* 318–324.

Cohen, E. A. *Human Behavior in the Concentration Camp.* New York: W. W. Norton, 1953.

Cohen, S., Tyrrell, D. A. J., and Smith, A. P. Psychological stress and susceptibility to the common cold. *New England Journal of Medicine,* 1991, *325,* 606–612.

Colapinto, J. *As Nature Made Him: The Boy Who Was Raised as a Girl.* New York: HarperCollins, 2000.

Cole, B. J., and Koob, G. F. Propranalol antagonizes the enhanced conditioned fear produced by corticotropin releasing factor. *Journal of Pharmacology and Experimental Therapeutics,* 1988, *247,* 901–910.

Collaborative Research Group. A novel gene containing a trinucleotide repeat that is expanded and unstable on Huntington's disease chromosomes. *Cell,* 1993, *72,* 971–983.

Comuzzie, A. G., and Allison, D. B. The search for human obesity genes. *Science,* 1998, *280,* 1374–1377.

Coolen, L. M., and Wood, R. I. Testosterone stimulation of the medial preoptic area and medial amygdala in the control of male hamster sexual behavior: Redundancy without amplification. *Behavioural Brain Research,* 1999, *98,* 143–153.

Coover, G. D., Murison, R., and Jellestad, F. K. Subtotal lesions of the amygdala: The rostral central nucleus in passive avoidance and ulceration. *Physiology and Behavior,* 1992, *51,* 795–803.

Corkin, S., Amaral, D. G., González, R. G., Johnson, K. A., and Hyman, B. R. H. M.'s medial temporal lobe lesion: Findings from magnetic resonance imaging. *Journal of Neuroscience,* 1997, *17,* 3964–3979.

Corkin, S., Sullivan, E. V., Twitchell, T. E., and Grove, E. The amnesic patient H. M.: Clinical observations and test performance 28 years after operation. *Society for Neuroscience Abstracts,* 1981, *7,* 235.

Cottingham, S. L., and Pfaff, D. Interconnectedness of steroid hormone-binding neurons: Existence and implications. *Current Topics in Neuroendocrinology,* 1986, *7,* 223–249.

Courchesne, E., Karns, C. M., Davis, H. R., Ziccardi, R., Carper, R. A., Tigue, Z. D., Chisum, H. J., Moses, P., Pierce, K., Lord, C., Lincoln, A. J., Pizzo, S., Schreibman, L., Hass, R. H., Akshoomoff, N. A., and Courchesne, R. Y. Unusual brain growth patterns in early life in patients with autistic disorder: an MRI study. *Neurology,* 2001, *57,* 245–254.

Covington, H. E., and Miczek, K. A. Repeated social-defeat stress, cocaine or morphine: Effects on behavioral sensitization and intravenous cocaine self-administration "binges." *Psychopharmacology,* 2001, *158,* 388–398.

Cox, A., Rutter, M., Newman, S., and Bartak, L. A comparative study of infantile autism and specific developmental language disorders. I. Parental characteristics. *British Journal of Psychiatry,* 1975, *126,* 146–159.

Crane, G. E. Iproniazid (Marsilid) phosphate, a therapeutic agent for mental disorders and debilitating diseases. *Psychiatry Research Reports,* 1957, *8,* 142–152.

Creese, I., Burt, D. R., and Snyder, S. H. Dopamine receptor binding predicts clinical and pharmacological potencies of antischizophrenic drugs. *Science,* 1976, *192,* 481–483.

Crick, F., and Mitchison, G. The function of dream sleep. *Nature,* 1983, *304,* 111–114.

Crick, F., and Mitchison, G. REM sleep and neural nets. *Behavioural Brain Research,* 1995, *69,* 147–155.

Crow, T. J. A map of the rat mesencephalon for electrical self-stimulation. *Brain Research,* 1972, *36,* 265–273.

Crow, T. J. Positive and negative schizophrenic symptoms and the role of dopamine. *British Journal of Psychiatry,* 1980, *137,* 383–386.

Cubelli, R. A selective deficit for writing vowels in acquired dysgraphia. *Nature,* 1991, *353,* 258–260.

Culotta, E., and Koshland, D. E. NO news is good news. *Science,* 1992, *258,* 1862–1865.

Cummings, D. E., Purnell, J. Q., Frayo, R. S., Schmidova, K., Wisse, B. E., and Weigle, D. S. A preprandial rise in plasma ghrelin levels suggests a role in meal initiation in humans. *Diabetes,* 2001, *50,* 1714–1719.

Currie, P. J., and Coscina, D. V. Regional hypothalamic differences in neuropeptide Y-induced feeding and energy substrate utilization. *Brain Research,* 1996, *737,* 238–242.

Dabbs, J. M., Frady, R. L., Carr, T. S., and Besch, N. F. Saliva testosterone and criminal violence in young adult prison inmates. *Psychosomatic Medicine,* 1987, *49,* 174–182.

Dabbs, J. M., and Morris, R. Testosterone, social class, and antisocial behavior in a sample of 4,462 men. *Psychological Science,* 1990, *1,* 209–211.

Dabbs, J. M., Ruback, J. M., Frady, R. L., and Hopper, C. H. Saliva testosterone and criminal violence among women. *Personality and Individual Differences,* 1988, *9,* 269–275.

Dallos, P. The active cochlea. *Journal of Neuroscience,* 1992, *12,* 4575–4585.

Damasio, A. R., Brandt, J. P., Tranel, D., and Damasio, H. Name dropping: Retrieval of proper or common nouns depends on different systems in left temporal cortex. *Society for Neuroscience Abstracts,* 1991, *17,* 4.

Damasio, A. R., and Damasio, H. The anatomic basis of pure alexia. *Neurology,* 1983, *33,* 1573–1583.

Damasio, A. R., and Damasio, H. Hemianopia, hemiachromatopsia, and the mechanisms of alexia. *Cortex,* 1986, *22,* 161–169.

Damasio, A. R., Damasio, H., and Van Hoesen, G. W. Prosopagnosia: Anatomic basis and behavioral mechanisms. *Neurology,* 1982, *32,* 331–341.

Damasio, A. R., and Tranel, D. Nouns and verbs are retrieved with differentially distributed neural systems. *Proceedings of the National Academy of Sciences, USA,* 1993, *90,* 4957–4960.

Damasio, A. R., Yamada, T., Damasio, H., Corbett, J., and McKee, J. Central achromatopsia: Behavioral, anatomic, and physiologic aspects. *Neurology,* 1980, *30,* 1064–1071.

Damasio, H. Neuroimaging contributions to the understanding of aphasia. In *Handbook of Neuropsychology, Vol. 2,* edited by F. Boller and J. Grafman. Amsterdam: Elsevier, 1989.

Damasio, H., and Damasio, A. R. The anatomical basis of conduction aphasia. *Brain,* 1980, *103,* 337–350.

Damasio, H., Eslinger, P., and Adams, H. P. Aphasia following basal ganglia lesions: New evidence. *Seminars in Neurology,* 1984, *4,* 151–161.

Damasio, H., Grabowski, T., Frank, R., Galaburda, A. M., and Damasio, A. R. The return of Phineas Gage: Clues about the brain from the skull of a famous patient. *Science,* 1994, *264,* 1102–1105.

Damsma, G., Day, J., and Fibiger, H. C. Lack of tolerance to nicotine-induced dopamine release in the nucleus accumbens. *European Journal of Pharmacology,* 1989, *168,* 363–368.

Daniele, A., Giustolisi, L., Silveri, M. C., Colosimo, C., and Gainotti, G. Evidence for a possible neuroanatomical basis for lexical processing of nouns and verbs. *Neuropsychologia,* 1994, *32,* 1325–1341.

Daniels, D., Miselis, R. R., and Flanagan-Cato, L. M. Central neuronal circuit innervating the lordosis-producing muscles defined by transneuronal transport of pseudorabies virus. *Journal of Neuroscience,* 1999, *19,* 2823–2833.

Darwin, C. *The Expression of the Emotions in Man and Animals.* Chicago: University of Chicago Press, 1872/1965.

Davidson, D., Swift, R., and Fitz, E. Naltrexone increases the latency to drink alcohol in social drinkers. *Alcoholism: Clinical and Experimental Research,* 1996, *20,* 732–739.

Davis, J. D., and Campbell, C. S. Peripheral control of meal size in the rat: Effect of sham feeding on meal size and drinking rate. *Journal of Comparative and Physiological Psychology,* 1973, *83,* 379–387.

Davis, J. O., Phelps, J. A., and Bracha, H. S. Prenatal development of monozygotic twins and concordance for schizophrenia. *Schizophrenia Bulletin,* 1995, *21,* 357–366.

Davis, M. The role of the amygdala in fear and anxiety. *Annual Review of Neuroscience,* 1992a, *15,* 353–375.

Davis, M. The role of the amygdala in fear-potentiated startle: Implications for animal models of anxiety. *Trends in Pharmacological Sciences,* 1992b, *13,* 35–41.

Davison, G. C., and Neale, J. M. *Abnormal Psychology: An Experimental Clinical Approach.* New York: John Wiley & Sons, 1974.

Daw, N. W. Colour-coded ganglion cells in the goldfish retina: Extension of their receptive fields by means of new stimuli. *Journal of Physiology (London),* 1968, *197,* 567–592.

Dawson, T. M., and Dawson, V. L. Molecular pathways of neurodegeneration in Parkinson's disease. *Science,* 2003, *302,* 819–822.

Day, J., Damsma, G., and Fibiger, H. C. Cholinergic activity in the rat hippocampus, cortex and striatum correlates with locomotor activity: An in vivo microdialysis study. *Pharmacology, Biochemistry, and Behavior,* 1991, *38,* 723–729.

Deacon, S., and Arendt, J. Adapting to phase shifts. I. An experimental model for jet lag and shift work. *Physiology and Behavior,* 1996, *59,* 665–673.

Dean, P. Effects of inferotemporal lesions on the behavior of monkeys. *Psychological Bulletin,* 1976, *83,* 41–71.

Debanne, D., Gähwiler, B. H., and Thompson, S. M. Asynchronous pre- and postsynaptic activity induces associative long-term depression in area CA1 of the rat hippocampus in vitro. *Proceedings of the National Academy of Sciences,* 1994, *91,* 1148–1152.

de Castro, J. M., McCormick, J., Pedersen, M., and Kreitzman, S. N. Spontaneous human meal patterns are related to preprandial factors regardless of natural environmental constraints. *Physiology and Behavior,* 1986, *38,* 25–29.

De Gennaro, L., Ferrara, M., and Bertini, M. The spontaneous K-complex during stage 2 sleep: Is it the "forerunner" of delta waves? *Neuroscience Letters,* 2000, *291,* 41–43.

Dejerine, J. Contribution à l'étude anatomo-pathologique et clinique des différentes variétés de cécité verbale. *Comptes Rendus des Séances de la Société de Biologie et de Ses Filiales,* 1892, *4,* 61–90.

De Jonge, F. H., Oldenburger, W. P., Louwerse, A. L., and van de Poll, N. E. Changes in male copulatory behavior after sexual exciting stimuli: Effects of medial amygdala lesions. *Physiology and Behavior,* 1992, *52,* 327–332.

Delgado, P. L., Charney, D. S., Price, L. H., Aghajanian, G. K., Landis, H., and Heninger, G. R. Serotonin function and the mechanism of antidepressant action: Reversal of antidepressant induced remission by rapid depletion of plasma tryptophan. *Archives of General Psychiatry,* 1990, *47,* 411–418.

DeLong, G. R. Autism: New data suggest a new hypothesis. *Neurology,* 1999, *52,* 911–916.

Dement, W. C. The effect of dream deprivation. *Science,* 1960, *131,* 1705–1707.

Deol, M. S., and Gluecksohn-Waelsch, S. The role of inner hair cells in hearing. *Nature,* 1979, *278,* 250–252.

Dérousné, J., and Beauvois, M.-F. Phonological processing in reading: Data from alexia. *Journal of Neurology, Neurosurgery, and Psychiatry,* 1979, *42,* 1125–1132.

Desimone, R., Albright, T. D., Gross, C. G., and Bruce, D. Stimulus-selective properties of inferior temporal neurons in the macaque. *Journal of Neuroscience,* 1984, *8,* 2051–2062.

Deutch, A. Y. The regulation of subcortical dopamine systems by the prefrontal cortex: Interactions of central dopamine systems and the pathogenesis of schizophrenia. *Journal of Neural Transmission,* 1992, *36,* 61–89.

Deutsch, J. A., and Gonzalez, M. F. Gastric nutrient content signals satiety. *Behavioral and Neural Biology,* 1980, *30,* 113–116.

De Valois, R. L., Albrecht, D. G., and Thorell, L. Cortical cells: Bar detectors or spatial frequency filters? *In Frontiers in Visual Science,* edited by S. J. Cool and E. L. Smith. Berlin: Springer-Verlag, 1978.

De Valois, R. L., and De Valois, K. K. *Spatial Vision.* New York: Oxford University Press, 1988.

Devane, W. A., Hanus, L., Breuer, A., Pertwee, R. G., Stevenson, L. A., Griffin, G., Gibson, D., Mandelbaum, A., Etinger, A., and Mechoulam, R. Isolation and structure of a brain constituent that binds to the cannabinoid receptor. *Science,* 1992, *258,* 1946–1949.

Devine, D. P., and Wise, R. A. Self-administration of morphine, DAMGO, and DPDPE into the ventral tegmental area of rats. *Journal of Neuroscience,* 1994, *14,* 1978–1984.

Diamond, D. M., Park, C. R., Heman, K. L., and Rose, G. M. Exposing rats to a predator impairs spatial working memory in the radial arm water maze. *Hippocampus,* 1999, *9,* 542–552.

Diamond, M., and Sigmundson, H. K. Sex reassignment at birth: Long-term review and clinical implications. *Archives of Pediatric and Adolescent Medicine,* 1997, *151,* 298–304.

Di Chiara, G. The role of dopamine in drug abuse viewed from the perspective of its role in motivation. *Drug and Alcohol Dependency,* 1995, *38,* 95–137.

Di Ciano, P., Coury, A., Depoortere, R. Y., Egilmez, Y., Lane, J. D., Emmett-Oglesby, M. W., Lepiane, F. G., Phillips, A. G., and Blaha, C. D. Comparison of changes in extracellular dopamine concentrations in the nucleus accumbens during intravenous self-administration of cocaine or d-amphetamine. *Behavioural Pharmacology,* 1995, *6,* 311–322.

Digiovanni, M., Dalessandro, G., Baldini, S., Cantalupi, D., and Bottacchi, E. Clinical and neuroradiological findings in a case of pure word deafness. *Italian Journal of Neurological Sciences,* 1992, *13,* 507–510.

Dijk, D. J., Boulos, Z., Eastman, C. I., Lewy, A. J., Campbell, S. S., and Terman, M. Light treatment for sleep disorders: Consensus report. 2. Basic properties of circadian physiology and sleep regulation. *Journal of Biological Rhythms,* 1995, *10,* 113–125.

di Tomaso, E., Beltramo, M., and Piomelli, D. Brain cannabinoids in chocolate. *Nature,* 1996, *382,* 677–678.

Dixon, A. K. The effect of olfactory stimuli upon the social behaviour of laboratory mice (*Mus musculus L*). Doctoral dissertation, Birmingham University, Birmingham, England, 1973.

Dixon, A. K., and Mackintosh, J. H. Effects of female urine upon the social behaviour of adult male mice. *Animal Behaviour,* 1971, *19,* 138–140.

Donny, E. C., Caggiula, A. R., Knopf, S., and Brown, C. Nicotine self-administration in rats. *Psychopharmacology,* 1995, *122,* 390–394.

Doty, R. L. Olfaction. *Annual Review of Psychology,* 2001, *52,* 423–452.

Dougherty, D. D., Baie, L., Gosgrove, G. R., Cassem, E. H., Price, B. H., Nierenberg, A. A., Jenike, M. A., and Rauch, S. L. Prospective long-term follow-up of 44 patients who received cingulotomy for treatment-refractory obsessive-compulsive disorder. *American Journal of Psychiatry,* 2002, *159,* 269–275.

Dougherty, D. D., Bonab, A. A., Spencer, T. J., Rauch, S. L., Madras, B. K., and Fischman, A. J. Dopamine transporter density in patients with attention deficit hyperactivity disorder. *Lancet,* 1999, *354,* 2132–2133.

Douglass, J., McKinzie, A. A., and Couceyro, P. PCR differential display identifies a rat brain mRNA that is transcriptionally regulated by cocaine and amphetamine. *Journal of Neuroscience,* 1995, *15,* 2471–2481.

Dovey, H. F., John, V., Anderson, J. P., Chen, L. Z., de Saint Andrieu, P., Fang, L. Y., Freedman, S. B., Folmer, B., Goldbach, E., Holsztynska, E. J., Hu, K. L., Johnson-Wood, K. L., Kennedy, S. L., Kholodenko, D., Knops, J. E., Latimer, L. H., Lee, M., Liao, Z., Lieberburg, I. M., Motter, R. N., Mutter, L. C., Nietz, J., Quinn, K. P., Sacchi, K. L., Seubert, P. A., Shopp, G. M., Thorsett, E. D., Tung, J. S., Wu, J., Yang, S., Yin, C. T., Schenk, D. B., May, P. C., Altstiel, L. D., Bender, M. H., Boggs, L. N., Britton, T. C., Clemens, J. C., Czilli, D. L., Dieckman-McGinty, D. K., Droste, J. J., Fuson, K. S., Gitter, B. D., Hyslop, P. A., Johnstone, E. M., Li, W. Y., Little, S. P., Mabry, T. E., Miller, F. D., Ni, B., Nissen, J. S., Porter, W. J., Potts, B. D., Reel, J. K., Stephenson, D., Su, Y., Shipley, L. A., Whitesitt, C. A., Yin, T., and Audia, J. E. Functional gamma-secretase inhibitors reduce beta-amyloid peptide levels in brain. *Journal of Neurochemistry,* 2001, *76,* 173–181.

Drevets, W. C. Neuroimaging studies of mood disorders. *Biological Psychiatry,* 2000a, *48,* 813–829.

Drevets, W. C. Functional anatomical abnormalities in limbic and prefrontal cortical structures in major depression. *Progress in Brain Research,* 2000b, *126,* 413–431.

Drevets, W. C. Neuroimaging and neuropathological studies of depression: Implications for the cognitive-emotional features of mood disorders. *Current Opinions in Neurobiology,* 2001, *11,* 240–249.

Drevets, W. C., Price, J. L., Simpson, J. R., Todd, R. D., Reich, T., Vannier, M., and Raichle, M. E. Subgenual prefrontal cortex abnormalities in mood disorders. *Nature,* 1997, *386,* 824–827.

Drevets, W. C., Videen, T. O., Price, J. L., Preskorn, S. H., Carmichael, S. T., and Raichle, M. E. A functional anatomical study of unipolar depression. *Journal of Neuroscience,* 1992, *12,* 3628–3641.

Dronkers, N. F. A new brain region for coordinating speech articulation. *Nature,* 1996, *384,* 159–161.

Dryden, S., Wang, Q., Frankish, H. M., Pickavance, L., and Williams, G. The serotonin (5-HT) antagonist methysergide increases neuropeptide-Y (NPY) synthesis and secretion in the hypothalamus of the rat. *Brain Research,* 1995, *699,* 12–18.

Dube, M. G., Kalra, S. P., and Kalra, P. S. Food intake elicited by central administration of orexins/hypocretins: Identification of hypothalamic sites of action. *Brain Research,* 1999, *842,* 473–477.

Duchenne, G.-B. *The Mechanism of Human Facial Expression* (translated by R. A. Cuthbertson). Cambridge, England: Cambridge University Press, 1990. (Original work published 1862.)

Dujardin, K., Guerrien, A., and Leconte, P. Sleep, brain activation and cognition. *Physiology and Behavior,* 1990, *47,* 1271–1278.

Dunnett, S. B., Lane, D. M., and Winn, P. Ibotenic acid lesions of the lateral hypothalamus: Comparison with 6-hydroxydopamine-induced sensorimotor deficits. *Neuroscience,* 1985, *14,* 509–518.

Durie, D. J. Sleep in animals. In *Psychopharmacology of Sleep,* edited by D. Wheatley. New York: Raven Press, 1981.

Duva, M. A., Tomkins, E. M., Moranda, L. M., Kaplan, R., Sukhaseum, A., Jimenez, A., and Stanley, B. G. Reverse microdialysis of N-methyl-D-aspartic acid into the lateral hypothalamus of rats: Effects on feeding and other behaviors. *Brain Research,* 2001, *921,* 122–132.

Eaton, W. W., Kessler, R. C., Wittchen, H. U., and Magee, W. J. Panic and panic disorder in the United States. *American Journal of Psychiatry,* 1994, *151,* 413–420.

Eaton, W. W., Mortensen, P. B., and Frydenberg, M. Obstetric factors, urbanization and psychosis. *Schizophrenia Research,* 2000, *43,* 117–123.

Eckel, L. S., Langhans, W., Kahler, A., Campfield, L. A., Smith, F. J., and Geary, N. Chronic administration of OB protein decreases food intake by selectively reducing meal size in female rats. *American Journal of Physiology,* 1998, *275,* R186—R193.

Eddy, N. B., Halbach, H., Isbell, H., and Seevers, M. H. Drug dependence: Its significance and characteristics. *Bulletin of the World Health Organization,* 1965, *32,* 721–733.

Eden, G. F., and Zeffiro, T. A. Neural systems affected in developmental dyslexia revealed by functional neuroimaging. *Neuron,* 1998, *21,* 279–282.

Edwards, D. P., Purpura, K. P., and Kaplan, E. Contrast sensitivity and spatial-frequency response of primate cortical neurons in and around the cytochrome oxidase blobs. *Vision Research,* 1995, *35,* 1501–1523.

Eichenbaum, H., Otto, T., and Cohen, N. J. The hippocampus: What does it do? *Behavioral and Neural Biology,* 1992, *57,* 2–36.

Eichenbaum, H., Stewart, C., and Morris, R. G. M. Hippocampal representation in spatial learning. *Journal of Neuroscience,* 1990, *10,* 331–339.

Ekman, P. *The Face of Man: Expressions of Universal Emotions in a New Guinea Village.* New York: Garland STPM Press, 1980.

Ekman, P. Facial expressions of emotion: An old controversy and new findings. *Philosophical Transactions of the Royal Society of London [B],* 1992, *335,* 63–69.

Ekman, P., and Davidson, R. J. Voluntary smiling changes regional brain activity. *Psychological Science,* 1993, *4,* 342–345.

Ekman, P., and Friesen, W. V. Constants across cultures in the face and emotion. *Journal of Personality and Social Psychology,* 1971, *17,* 124–129.

El Mansari, M., Sakai, K., and Jouvet, M. Unitary characteristics of presumptive cholinergic tegmental neurons during the sleep-waking cycle in freely moving cats. *Experimental Brain Research,* 1989, *76,* 519–529.

Elias, C. F., Lee, C., Kelly, J., Aschkenasi, C., Ahima, R. S., Couceyro, P., Kuhar, M. J., Saper, C. B., and Elmquist, J. K. Leptin activates hypothalamic CART neurons projecting to the spinal cord. *Neuron,* 1998b, *21,* 1375–1385.

Elias, C. F., Saper, C. B., Maratos-Flier, E., Tritos, N. A., Lee, C., Kelly, J., Tatro, J. B., Hoffman, G. E., Ollmann, M. M., Barsh, G. S., Sakurai, T., Yanagisawa, M., and Elmquist, J. K. Chemically defined projections linking the mediobasal hypothalamus and the lateral hypothalamic area. *Journal of Comparative Neurology,* 1998a, *402,* 442–459.

Elias, M. Serum cortisol, testosterone and testosterone binding globulin responses to competitive fighting in human males. *Aggressive Behavior,* 1981, *7,* 215–224.

Elkis, H., Friedman, L., Buckley, P. F., Lee, H. S., Lys, C., Kaufman, B., and Meltzer, H. Y. Increased prefrontal sulcal prominence in relatively young patients with unipolar major depression. *Psychiatry Research: Neuroimaging,* 1996, *67,* 123–134.

Elmquist, J. K., Elias, C. F., and Saper, C. B. From lesions to leptin: Hypothalamic control of food intake and body weight. *Neuron,* 1999, *22,* 221–232.

Ende, G., Braus, D. F., Walter, S., Weber-Fahr, W., and Henn, F. A. The hippocampus in patients treated with electroconvulsive therapy. *Archives of General Psychiatry,* 2000, *57,* 937–943.

Endoh, M., Maiese, K., and Wagner, J. A. Expression of the neural form of nitric oxide synthase by CA1 hippocampal neurons and other central nervous system neurons. *Neuroscience,* 1994, *63,* 679–689.

Ernst, M., Zametkin, A. J., Matochik, J. A., Jons, P. H., and Cohen, R. M. DOPA decarboxylase activity in attention deficit hyperactivity disorder adults: A [fluorine[18]] flurodopa positron emission tomographic study. *Journal of Neuroscience,* 1998, *18,* 5901–5907.

Ernulf, K. E., Innala, S. M., and Whitam, F. L. Biological explanation, psychological explanation, and tolerance of homosexuals: A cross-national analysis of beliefs and attitudes. *Psychological Reports,* 1989, *248,* 183–188.

Eslinger, P. J., and Damasio, A. R. Severe disturbance of higher cognition after bilateral frontal lobe ablation: Patient EVR. *Neurology,* 1985, *35,* 1731–1741.

Estabrooke, I. V., McCarthy, M. T., Ko, E., Chou, T. C., Chemelli, R. M., Yanagisawa, M., Saper, C. B., and Scammell, T. E. Fos expression in orexin neurons varies with behavioral state. *Journal of Neuroscience,* 2001, *21,* 1656–1662.

Everitt, B. J., Cador, M., and Robbins, T. W. Interactions between the amygdala and ventral striatum in stimulus-reward associations: Studies using a second-order schedule of sexual reinforcement. *Neuroscience,* 1989, *30,* 63–75.

Fabbro, F. The bilingual brain: Bilingual aphasia. *Brain and Language,* 2001a, *79,* 201–210.

Fabbro, F. The bilingual brain: Cerebral representation of languages. *Brain and Language,* 2001b, *79,* 211–222.

Fanselow, M. S., and Kim, J. J. Acquisition of contextual Pavlovian fear conditioning is blocked by application of an NMDA receptor antagonist, D,L-2-amino-5-phosphonovaleric acid to the basolateral amygdala. *Behavioral Neuroscience,* 1994, *108,* 210–212.

Faraone, S., and Biederman, J. Genetics of attention-deficit hyperactivity disorder. *Child and Adolescent Psychiatric Clinics of North America,* 1994, *3,* 285–302.

Farber, N. B., Wozniak, D. F., Price, M. T., Labruyere, J., Huss, J., St. Peter, H., and Olney, J. W. Age-specific neurotoxicity in the rat associated with NMDA receptor blockade: Potential relevance to schizophrenia? *Biological Psychiatry,* 1995, *38,* 788–796.

Farlow, M., Murrell, J., Ghetti, B., Unverzagt, F., Zeldenrust, S., and Benson, M. Clinical characteristics in a kindred with early-onset Alzheimers-disease and their linkage to a G/T change at position-2149 of amyloid precursor protein gene. *Neurology,* 1994, *44,* 105–111.

Farooqi, I. S., Keogh, J. M., Kamath, S., Jones, S., Gibson, W. T., Trussell, R., Jebb, S. A., Lip, G. Y. H., and O'Rahilly, S. Partial leptin deficiency and human adiposity. *Nature,* 2001, *414,* 34–35.

Farrington, C. P., Miller, E., and Taylor, B. MMR and autism: Further evidence against a causal association. *Vaccine,* 2001, *27,* 3632–3635.

Fava, M., Copeland, P. M., Schweiger, U., and Herzog, M. D. Neurochemical abnormalities of anorexia nervosa and bulimia nervosa. *American Journal of Psychiatry,* 1989, *146,* 963–971.

Feder, H. H. Estrous cyclicity in mammals. In *Neuroendocrinology of Reproduction,* edited by N. T. Adler. New York: Plenum Press, 1981.

Feigenbaum, S. L., Masi, A. T., and Kaplan, S. B. Prognosis in rheumatoid arthritis: A longitudinal study of newly diagnosed younger adult patients. *American Journal of Medicine,* 1979, *66,* 377–384.

Feinle, C., Grundy, D., and Read, N. W. Effects of duodenal nutrients on sensory and motor responses of the human stomach to distension. *American Journal of Physiology,* 1997, *273,* G721—G726.

Fernandez-Ruiz, J., Wang, J., Aigner, T. G., and Mishkin, M. Visual habit formation in monkeys with neurotoxic lesions of the ventrocaudal neostriatum. *Proceedings of the National Academy of Sciences, USA,* 2001, *98,* 4196–4201.

Fibiger, H. C. The dopamine hypothesis of schizophrenia and mood disorders: Contradictions and speculations. In *The Mesolimbic Dopamine System: From Motivation to Action,* edited by P. Willner and J. Scheel-Krüger. Chichester, England: John Wiley & Sons, 1991.

Fieve, R. R. The clinical effects of lithium treatment. *Trends in Neurosciences,* 1979, *2,* 66–68.

Fiez, J. A., and Petersen, S. E. Neuroimaging studies of word reading. *Proceedings of the National Academy of Science, USA,* 1998, *94,* 914–921.

Fiez, J. A., Balota, D. A., Raichle, M. E., and Petersen, S. E. Effects of lexicality, frequency, and spelling-to-sound consistency on the functional anatomy of reading. *Neuron,* 1999, *24,* 205–218.

Finger, S. *Origins of Neuroscience: A History of Explorations into Brain Function.* New York: Oxford University Press, 1994.

Firestein, S., Zufall, F., and Shepherd, G. M. Single odor-sensitive channels in olfactory receptor neurons are also gated by cyclic nucleotides. *Journal of Neuroscience,* 1991, *11,* 3565–3572.

Fisher, C., Gross, J., and Zuch, J. Cycle of penile erection synchronous with dreaming (REM) sleep: Preliminary report. *Archives of General Psychiatry,* 1965, *12,* 29–45.

Fisher, S. E., Marlow, A. J., Lamb, J., Maestrini, E., Williams, D. F., Richardson, A. J., Weeks, D. E., Stein, J. F. and Monaco, A. P. A quantitative-trait locus on chromosome 6p influences different aspects of developmental dyslexia. *American Journal of Human Genetics,* 1999, *4,* 146–156.

Fishman, P. S., and Oyler, G. A. Significance of the parkin gene and protein in understanding Parkinson's disease. *Current Neurology and Neuroscience Reports,* 2002, *2,* 296–302.

Fiske, A. P., and Haslam, N. Is obsessive-compulsive disorder a pathology of the human disposition to perform socially meaningful Rituals? Evidence of similar content. *Journal of Nervous and Mental Disease,* 1997, *185,* 211–222.

Fitzpatrick, D., Itoh, K., and Diamond, I. T. The laminar organization of the lateral geniculate body and the striate cortex in the squirrel monkey *(Saimiri sciureus). Journal of Neuroscience,* 1983, *3,* 673–702.

Fitzsimons, J. T., and Moore-Gillon, M. J. Drinking and antidiuresis in response to reductions in venous return in the dog: Neural and endocrine mechanisms. *Journal of Physiology (London),* 1980, *308,* 403–416.

Flaum, M., and Andreasen, N. C. Diagnostic criteria for schizophrenia and related disorders: Options for DNS-IV. *Schizophrenia Bulletin,* 1990, *17,* 27–49.

Fletcher, P. J., Currie, P. J., Chambers, J. W., and Coscina, D. V. Radiofrequency lesions of the PVN fail to modify the effects of serotonergic drugs on food intake. *Brain Research,* 1993, *630,* 1–9.

Flock, A. Physiological properties of sensory hairs in the ear. In *Psychophysics and Physiology of Hearing,* edited by E. F. Evans and J. P. Wilson. London: Academic Press, 1977.

Flood, J. F., and Morley, J. E. Increased food intake by neuropeptide Y is due to an increased motivation to eat. *Peptides,* 1991, *12,* 1329–1332.

Folstein, S. E., and Piven, J. Etiology of autism: Genetic influences. *Pediatrics,* 1991, *87,* 767–773.

Folstein, S. E., and Rosen-Sheidley, B. Genetics of autism: Complex aetiology for a heterogeneous disorder. *Nature Reviews: Genetics,* 2001, *2,* 943–955.

Fombonne, E. The epidemiology of autism: A review. *Psychological Medicine,* 1999, *29,* 769–786.

Forno, L. S. Neuropathology of Parkinson's disease. *Journal of Neuropathology and Experimental Neurology,* 1996, *55,* 259–272.

Foy, M. R., Stanton, M. E., Levine, S., and Thompson, R. F. Behavioral stress impairs long-term potentiation in rodent hippocampus. *Behavioral and Neural Biology,* 1987, *48,* 138–149.

Freed, C. R. Will embryonic stem cells be a useful source of dopamine neurons for transplant into patients with Parkinson's disease? *Proceedings of the National Academy of Science, USA.* 2002, *99,* 1755–1757.

Freed, C. R., Breeze, R. E., DeMasters, B. K., Galvin, J., Trojanowski, J. Q., Greene, P., Eidelberg, D., Fahn, S. Transplants of embryonic dopamine cells show progressive histologic maturation for at least 8 years and improve signs of Parkinsons up to the maximum benefit of L-DOPA preoperatively. *Annual Meeting, American Academy of Neurology,* Denver, CO, April 2002.

Freedman, M. S., Lucas, R. J., Soni, B., von Schantz, M., Muñoz, M., David-Gray, Z., and Foster, R. Regulation of mammalian circadian behavior by non-rod, non-cone, ocular photoreceptors. *Science,* 1999, *284,* 502–504.

Frey, U., and Morris, R. G. Synaptic tagging and long-term potentiation. *Nature,* 1997, *385,* 533–536.

Frey, U., Krug, M., Reymann, K. G., and Matthies, H. Anisomycin, an inhibitor of protein synthesis, blocks late phases of LTP phenomena in the hippocampal CA1 region in vitro. *Brain Research,* 1988, *452,* 57–65.

Fride, E., and Mechoulam, R. Ontogenetic development of the response to anandamide and D^9-tetrahydrocannabinol in mice. *Developmental Brain Research,* 1996, *95,* 131–134.

Friedman, M. I., and Bruno, J. P. Exchange of water during lactation. *Science,* 1976, *191,* 409–410.

Fry, J. M. Treatment modalities for narcolepsy. *Neurology,* 1998, *50,* S43-S48.

Fukuwatari, T., Kawada, T., Tsuruta, M., Hiraoka, T., Iwanaga, T., Sugimoto, E., and Fushiki, T. Expression of the putative membrane fatty acid transporter (FAT) in taste buds of the circumvallate papillae in rats. *FEBS Letters,* 1997, *414,* 461–464.

Fullerton, C. S., Ursano, R. J., Epstein, R. S., Crowley, B., Vance, K., Kao, T. C., Dougall, A., and Baum, A. Gender differences in posttraumatic stress disorder after motor vehicle accidents. *American Journal of Psychiatry,* 2001, *158,* 1485–1491.

Gaffan, D., Gaffan, E. A., and Harrison, S. Disconnection of the amygdala from visual association cortex impairs visual reward-association learning in monkeys. *Journal of Neuroscience,* 1988, *9,* 3144–3150.

Gagliardo, A., Ioalé, P., and Bingman, V. P. Homing in pigeons: The role of the hippocampal formation in the representation of landmarks used for navigation. *Journal of Neuroscience,* 1999, *19,* 311–315.

Gallassi, R., Morreale, A., Montagna, P., Cortelli, P., Avoni, P., Castellani, R., Gambetti, P., and Lugaresi, E. Fatal familial insomnia: Behavioral and Cognitive Features. *Neurology,* 1996, *46,* 935–939.

Garcia-Velasco, J., and Mondragon, M. The incidence of the vomeronasal organ in 1000 human subjects and its possible clinical significance. *Journal of Steroid Biochemistry and Molecular Biololgy,* 1991, *39,* 561–563.

Gardner, H., Brownell, H. H., Wapner, W., and Michelow, D. Missing the point: The role of the right hemisphere in the processing of complex linguistic materials. In *Cognitive Processing in the Right Hemisphere,* edited by E. Pericman. New York: Academic Press, 1983.

Gariano, R. F., and Groves, P. M. Burst firing induced in midbrain dopamine neurons by stimulation of the medial prefrontal and anterior cingulate cortices. *Brain Research,* 1988, *462,* 194–198.

Gatchel, R. J., Baum, A., and Krantz, D. S. *An Introduction to Health Psychology,* 2nd ed. New York: Newbery Award Records, 1989.

Gauthier, I., Skudlarski, P., Gore, J. C., and Anderson, A. W. Expertise for cars and birds recruits brain areas involved in face recognition. *Nature Neuroscience,* 2000, *3,* 191–197.

Gauthier, I., Tarr, M. J., Anderson, A. W., Skudlarski, P., and Gore, J. C. Activation of the middle fusiform "face area" increases with expertise in recognizing novel objects. *Nature Neuroscience,* 1999, *2,* 568–573.

Gayán, J., Smith, S. D., Cherny, S. S., Cardon, L. R., Fulker, D. W., Brower, A. M., Olson, R. K., Pennington, B. F., and DeFries, J. C. Quantative-trait locus for specific language and reading deficits on chromosome 6p. *American Journal of Human Genetics,* 1999, *4,* 157–164.

Gazzaniga, M. S. *The Bisected Brain.* New York: Appleton-Century-Crofts, 1970.

Gazzaniga, M. S., and LeDoux, J. E. *The Integrated Mind.* New York: Plenum Press, 1978.

Geinisman, Y., DeToledo-Morrell, L., and Morrell, F. Induction of long-term potentiation is associated with an increase in the number of axospinous synapses with segmented postsynaptic densities. *Brain Research,* 1991, *566,* 77–88.

Geinisman, Y., DeToledo-Morrell, L., Morrell, F., Persina, I. S., and Beatty, M. A. Synapse restructuring associated with the maintenance phase of hippocampal long-term potentiation. *Journal of Comparative Neurology,* 1996, *368,* 413–423.

George, M. S., Ketter, T. A., Parekh, P. I., Horwitz, B., Herscovitch, P., and Post, R. M. Brain activity during transient sadness and happiness in healthy women. *American Journal of Psychiatry,* 1995, *152,* 341–351.

George, M. S., Parekh, P. I., Rosinsky, N., Ketter, T. A., Kimbrell, T. A., Heilman, K. M., Herscovitch, P., and Post, R. M. Understanding emotional prosody activates right hemisphere regions. *Archives of Neurology,* 1996, *53,* 665–670.

Georges-François, P., Rolls, E. T., and Robertson, R. G. Spatial view cells in the primate hippocampus: Allocentric view not head direction or eye position or place. *Cerebral Cortex,* 1999, *9,* 197–212.

Gerbino, L., Oleshansky, M., and Gershon, S. Clinical use and mode of action of lithium. In *Psychopharmacology: A Generation of Progress,* edited by M. A. Lipton, A. DiMascio, and K. F. Killam. New York: Raven Press, 1978.

Gerhand, S. Routes to reading: A report of a non-semantic reader with equivalent performance on regular and exception words. *Neuropsychologia,* 2001, *39,* 1473–1484.

Gershon, E. S., Bunney, W. E., Leckman, J., Van Eerdewegh, M., and DeBauche, B. The inheritance of affective disorders: A review of data and hypotheses. *Behavior Genetics,* 1976, *6,* 227–261.

Geschwind, N., Quadfasel, F. A., and Segarra, J. M. Isolation of the speech area. *Neuropsychologia,* 1968, *6,* 327–340.

Gessa, G. L., Muntoni, F., Collu, M., Vargiu, L., and Mereu, G. Low doses of ethanol activate dopaminergic neurons in the ventral tegmental area. *Brain Research,* 1985, *348,* 201–204.

Gibbs, J., Young, R. C., and Smith, G. P. Cholecystokinin decreases food intake in rats. *Journal of Comparative and Physiological Psychology,* 1973, *84,* 488–495.

Giedd, J. N., Rapoport, J. L., Kruesi, M. J. P., Parker, C., Schapiro, M. B., Allen, A. J., Leonard, H. L., Kaysen, D., Dickstein, D. P., Marsh, W. L., Kozuch, P. L., Vaituzis, A. C., Hamburger, S. D., and Swedo, S. E. Sydenham's chorea: Magnetic resonance imaging of the basal ganglia. *Neurology,* 1995, *45,* 2199–2202.

Gilbert, D. G., and Gilbert, B. O. Personality, psychopathology, and nicotine response as mediators of the genetics of smoking. *Behavioral Genetics,* 1995, *25,* 133–148.

Gilbertson, T. A., Fontenot, D. T., Liu, L., Zhang, H., and Monroe, W. T. Fatty acid modulation of K+ channels in taste receptor cells: Gustatory cues for dietary fat. *American Journal of Physiology,* 1997, *272,* C1203—C1210.

Giles, D. E., Biggs, M. M., Rush, A. J., and Roffwarg, H. P. Risk factors in families of unipolar depression. I. Psychiatric illness and reduced REM latency. *Journal of Affective Disorders,* 1988, *14,* 51–59.

Giles, D. E., Roffwarg, H. P., and Rush, A. J. REM latency concordance in depressed family members. *Biological Psychiatry,* 1987, *22,* 910–924.

Gillespie, P. G. Molecular machinery of auditory and vestibular transduction. *Current Opinion in Neurobiology,* 1995, *5,* 449–455.

Gillette, M. U., and McArthur, A. J. Circadian actions of melatonin at the suprachiasmatic nucleus. *Behavioural Brain Research,* 1995, *73,* 135–139.

Giordano, A. L., Siegel, H. I., and Rosenblatt, J. S. Nuclear estrogen receptor binding in the preoptic area and hypothalamus of pregnancy-terminated rats: Correlation with the onset of maternal behavior. *Neuroendocrinology,* 1989, *50,* 248–258.

Givens, B., and McMahon, K. Ethanol suppresses the induction of long-term potentiation in vivo. *Brain Research,* 1995, *688,* 27–33.

Glaser, R., Rice, J., Sheridan, J., Post, A., Fertel, R., Stout, J., Speicher, C. E., Kotur, M., and Kiecolt-Glaser, J. K. Stress-related immune suppression: Health implications. *Brain, Behavior, and Immunity,* 1987, *1,* 7–20.

Glaum, S. R., Hara, M., Bindokas, V. P., Lee, C. C., Polonsky, K. S., Bell, G. I., and Miller, R. J. Leptin, the obese gene product, rapidly modulates synaptic transmission in the hypothalamus. *Molecular Pharmacology,* 1996, *50,* 230–235.

Gloor, P., Olivier, A., Quesney, L. F., Andermann, F., and Horowitz, S. The role of the limbic system in experiential phenomena of temporal lobe epilepsy. *Annals of Neurology,* 1982, *12,* 129–144.

Goate, A. M. Monogenetic determinants of Alzheimer's disease: APP mutations. *Cellular and Molecular Life Sciences,* 1998, *54,* 897–901.

Goddard, G. V. Development of epileptic seizures through brain stimulation at low intensity. *Nature,* 1967, *214,* 1020–1021.

Goeders, N. E., Lane, J. D., and Smith, J. E. Self-administration of methionine enkephalin into the nucleus accumbens. *Pharmacology, Biochemistry, and Behavior,* 1984, *20,* 451–455.

Goedert, M. Alpha-synuclein and neurodegenerative diseases. *Nature Review Neuroscience,* 2001, *2,* 492–501.

Goedert, M., and Spillantini, M. G. Tau mutations in frontotemporal dementia FTDP-17 and their relevance for Alzheimer's disease. *Biochimica et Biophysica Acta,* 2000, *1502,* 110–121.

Goff, D. C., Tsai, G., Levitt, J., Amico, E., Manoach, D., Schoenfeld, D. A., Hayden, D. L., McCarley, R., and Coyle, J. T. A placebo-controlled trial of D-cycloserine added to conventional neuroleptics in patients with schizophrenia. *Archives of General Psychiatry,* 1999, *56,* 21–27.

Golden, P. L., MacCagnan, T. J., and Pardridge, W. M. Human blood–brain barrier leptin receptor: Binding and endocytosis in isolated human brain microvessels. *Journal of Clinical Investigation,* 1997, *99,* 14–18.

Goldstein, R. Z., and Volkow, N. F. Drug addiction and its underlying neurological basis: Neuroimaging evidence for the involvement of the frontal cortex. *American Journal of Psychiatry,* 2002, *159,* 1642–1652.

Gonzales, R. A. NMDA receptors excite alcohol research. *Trends in Pharmacological Science,* 1990, *11,* 137–139.

Goodglass, H., and Kaplan, E. *Assessment of Aphasia and Related Disorders.* Philadelphia: Lea & Febiger, 1972.

Goodwin, D. W. Alcoholism and heredity: A review and hypothesis. *Archives of General Psychiatry,* 1979, *36,* 57–61.

Gordon, H. W., and Sperry, R. Lateralization of olfactory perception in the surgically separated hemispheres in man. *Neuropsychologia,* 1969, *7,* 111–120.

Gorski, R. A., Gordon, J. H., Shryne, J. E., and Southam, A. M. Evidence for a morphological sex difference within the medial preoptic area of the rat brain. *Brain Research,* 1978, *148,* 333–346.

Gottesman, I. I., and Shields, J. *Schizophrenia: The Epigenetic Puzzle.* New York: Cambridge University Press, 1982.

Gouras, P. Identification of cone mechanisms in monkey ganglion cells. *Journal of Physiology (London),* 1968, *199,* 533–538.

Grabowski, T. J., Damasio, H., Tranel, D., Ponto, L. L., Hichwa, R. D., and Damasio, A. R. A role for left temporal pole in the retrieval of words for unique entities. *Human Brain Mapping,* 2001, *13,* 199–212.

Grace, A. A. Phasic versus tonic dopamine release and the modulation of dopamine system responsivity: A hypothesis for the etiology of schizophrenia. *Neuroscience,* 1991, *41,* 1–24.

Graf, P., Squire, L. R., and Mandler, G. The information that amnesic patients do not forget. *Journal of Experimental Psychology: Learning, Memory, and Cognition,* 1984, *10,* 164–178.

Grafton, S. T., Waters, C., Sutton, J., Lew, M. F., and Couldwell, W. Pallidotomy increases activity of motor association cortex in Parkinson's disease: A positron emission tomographic study. *Annals of Neurology,* 1995, *37,* 776–783.

Gratacos, M., Nadal, M., Martin-Santos, R., Pijana, M. A. Gago, J., Peral, B., Armengol, L., Ponsa, I., Miro, R., Bulbena, A., and Estivill, X. A polymorphic genomic duplication on human chromosome 15 is a susceptibility factor for panic and phobic disorders. *Cell,* 2001, *106,* 367–379.

Grattan, D. R., Pi, X. J., Andrews, Z. B., Augustine, R. A., Kokay, I. C., Summerfield, M. R., Todd, B., and Bunn, S. J. Prolactin receptors in the brain during pregnancy and lactation: Implications for behavior. *Hormones and Behavior,* 2001, *40,* 115–124.

Graybiel, A. M. Basal ganglia: New therapeutic approaches to Parkinson's disease. *Current Biology,* 1996, *6,* 368–371.

Greenberg, R., and Pearlman, C. A. Cutting the REM nerve: An approach to the adaptive role of REM sleep. *Perspectives in Biology and Medicine,* 1974, *17,* 513–521.

Greene, J. D., Sommerville, R. B., Nystrom, L. E., Darley, J. M., and Cohen, J. D. An fMRI investigation of emotional engagement in moral judgment. *Science,* 2001, *293,* 2105–2108.

Grelotti, D. J., Gauthier, I., and Schultz, R. T. Social interest and the development of cortical face specialization: What autism teaches us about face processing. *Developmental Psychobiology,* 2002, *40,* 213–225.

Grigorenko, E. L., Wood, F. B., Meyer, M. S., Hart, L. A., Speed, W. C., Shuster, A., and Pauls, D. L. Susceptibility loci for distinct components of developmental dyslexia on chromosomes 6 and 15. *American Journal of Human Genetics,* 1997, *60,* 27–39.

Grill, H. J., and Kaplan, J. M. Caudal brainstem participates in the distributed neural control of feeding. In *Handbook of Behavioral Neurobiology. Vol. 10: Neurobiology of Food and Fluid Intake,* edited by E. Stricker. New York: Plenum Press, 1990.

Gross, C. G. Visual functions of inferotemporal cortex. In *Handbook of Sensory Physiology, Vol. 7: Central Processing of Visual Information,* edited by R. Jung. Berlin: Springer-Verlag, 1973.

Grossman, E. D., and Blake, R. Brain activity evoked by inverted and imagined biological motion. *Vision Research,* 2001, 41, 1475–1482.

Grossman, E. D., Donnelly, M., Price, R., Pickens, D., Morgan, V., Neighbor, G., and Blake R. Brain areas involved in perception of biological motion. *Journal of Cognitive Neuroscience,* 2000, *12,* 711–720.

Guerin, G. F., Goeders, N. E., Dworkin, S. I., and Smith, J. E. Intracranial self-administration of dopamine into the nucleus accumbens. *Society for Neuroscience Abstracts,* 1984, *10,* 1072.

Guilleminault, C., Wilson, R. A., and Dement, W. C. A study on cataplexy. *Archives of Neurology,* 1974, *31,* 255–261.

Gura, T. Obesity sheds its secrets. *Science,* 1997, *275,* 751–753.

Gurd, J. M., and Marshall, J. C. Cognition: Righting reading. *Current Biology,* 1993, *3,* 593–595.

Gurevich, E. V., Bordelon, Y., Shapiro, R. M., Arnold, S. E., Gur, R. E., and Joyce, J. N. Mesolimbic dopamine D_3 receptors and use of antipsychotics in patients with schizophrenia: A postmortem study. *Archives of General Psychiatry,* 1997, *54,* 225–232.

Guridi, J., and Obeso, J. A. The subthalamic nucleus, hemiballismus and Parkinson's disease: Reappraisal of a neurosurgical dogma. *Brain,* 2001, *124,* 5–19.

Gurvits, T. V., Shenton, M. E., Hokama, H., Ohta, H., Lasko, N. B., Gilbertson, M. W., Orr, S. P., Kikinis, R., Jolesz, F. A., McCarley, R. W., and Pitman, R. K. Magnetic resonance imaging study of hippocampal volume in chronic, combat-related posttraumatic stress disorder. *Biological Psychiatry,* 1996, *40,* 1091–1099.

Habib, M. The neurological basis of developmental dyslexia: An overview and working hypothesis. *Brain,* 2000, *123,* 2373–2399.

Hadjikhani, N., Liu, A. K., Dale, A. M., Cavanagh, P., and Tootell, R. B. H. Retinotopy and color sensitivity in human visual cortical area V8. *Nature Neuroscience,* 1998, *1,* 235–241.

Hahn, T. M., Breininger, J. F., Baskin, D. G., and Schwartz, M. W. Coexpression of Agrp and NPY in fasting-activated hypothalamic neurons. *Nature Neuroscience,* 1998, *1,* 271–272.

Hajak, G., Clarenbach, P., Fischer, W., Haase, W., Bandelow, B., Adler, L., and Ruther, E. Effects of hypnotics on sleep quality and daytime well-being: Data from a comparative multicentre study in outpatients with insomnia. *European Psychiatry,* 1995, *10* (Suppl. 3), 173S—179S.

Hakansson, M. L., Hulting, A. L., and Meister, B. Expression of leptin receptor messenger RNA in the hypothalamic arcuate nucleus: Relationship with NPY neurons. *Neuroreport,* 1996, *7,* 3087–3092.

Halaas, J. L., Gajiwala, K. D., Maffei, M., Cohen, S. L., Chait, B. T., Rabinowitz, D., Lallone, R. L., Burley, S. K., and Friedman, J. M. Weight-reducing effects of the plasma protein encoded by the obese gene. *Science,* 1995, *269,* 543–546.

Haley, J. E., Wilcox, G. L., and Chapman, P. F. The role of nitric oxide in hippocampal long-term potentiation. *Neuron,* 1992, *8,* 211–216.

Halgren, E. Walter, R. D., Cherlow, D. G., and Crandall, P. E. Mental phenomena evoked by electrical stimultion of the human hippocampal formation and amygdala. *Brain,* 1978, *101,* 83–117.

Halmi, K. A. Anorexia nervosa: Recent investigations. *Annual Review of Medicine,* 1978, *29,* 137–148.

Halmi, K. A., Eckert, E., LaDu, T. J., and Cohen, J. Anorexia nervose: Treatment efficacy of cyproheptadine and amitriptyline. *Archives of General Psychiatry,* 1986, *43,* 177–181.

Halpern, M. The organization and function of the vomeronasal system. *Annual Review of Neuroscience,* 1987, *10,* 325–362.

Hamberger, M. J., Goodman, R. R., Perrine, K., and Tamny, T. Anatomic dissociation of auditory and visual naming in the lateral temporal cortex. *Neurology,* 2001, *56,* 56–61.

Hamm, R. J., Temple, M. D., O'Dell, D. M., Pike, B. R., and Lyeth, B. G. Exposure to environmental complexity promotes recovery of cognitive function after traumatic brain injury. *Journal of Neurotrauma,* 1996, *13,* 41–47.

Hara, J., Beuckmann, C. T., Nambu, T., Willie, J. T., Chemelli, R. M., Sinton, C. M.,

Sugiyama, F., Yagami, K., Goto, K., Yanagisawa, M., and Sakurai, T. Genetic ablation of orexin neurons in mice results in narcolepsy, hypophagia, and obesity. *Neuron,* 2001, *30,* 345–354.

Hardy, J. Amyloid, the presinilins and Alzheimer's disease. *Trends in Neuroscience,* 1997, *4,* 154–159.

Harris, G. W., and Jacobsohn, D. Functional grafts of the anterior pituitary gland. *Proceedings of the Royal Society of London [B],* 1951–1952, *139,* 263–267.

Hartline, H. K. The response of single optic nerve fibers of the vertebrate eye to illumination of the retina. *American Journal of Physiology,* 1938, *121,* 400–415.

Harvey, S. M. Female sexual behavior: Fluctuations during the menstrual cycle. *Journal of Psychosomatic Research,* 1987, *31,* 101–110.

Hattar, S., Liao, H.-W., Takao, M., Berson, D. M., and Yau, K.-W. Melanopsin-containing retinal ganglion cells: Architecture, projections, and intrinsic photosensitivity. *Science,* 2002, *295,* 1065–1070.

Haug, H.-J. Prediction of sleep deprivation outcome by diurnal variation of mood. *Biological Psychiatry,* 1992, *31,* 271–278.

Havel, P. J., Townsend, R., Chaump, L., and Teff, K. High-fat meals reduce 24-h circulating leptin concentrations in women. *Diabetes,* 1999, *48,* 334–341.

Hawke, C. Castration and sex crimes. *American Journal of Mental Deficiency,* 1951, *55,* 220–226.

Haxby, J. V., Horwitz, B., Ungerleider, L. G., Maisog, J. M., Pietrini, P., and Grady, C. L. The functional organization of human extrastriate cortex: A PET-rCBF study of selective attention to faces and locations. *Journal of Neuroscience,* 1994, *14,* 6336–6353.

Heath, A. C., Madden, P. A. F., Slutske, W. S., and Martin, N. G. Personality and the inheritance of smoking behavior: A genetic perspective. *Behavioral Genetics,* 1995, *25,* 103–118.

Hebb, D. O. *The Organization of Behaviour.* New York: Wiley-Interscience, 1949.

Heckler, M. M. *Fifth Special Report to the U.S. Congress on Alcohol and Health.* Washington, DC: U.S. Government Printing Office, 1983.

Heffner, H. E., and Heffner, R. S. Role of primate auditory cortex in hearing. In *Comparative Perception. Vol. II: Complex Signals,* edited by W. C. Stebbins and M. A. Berkley. New York: John Wiley & Sons, 1990.

Heilman, K. M., Watson, R. T., and Bowers, D. Affective disorders associated with hemispheric disease. In *Neuropsychology of Human Emotion,* edited by K. M. Heilman and P. Satz. New York: Guilford Press, 1983.

Heimer, L., and Larsson, K. Impairment of mating behavior in male rats following lesions in the preoptic-anterior hypothalamic continuum. *Brain Research,* 1966/1967, *3,* 248–263.

Heinrichs, S. C., Menzaghi, F., Pich, E. M., Baldwin, H. A., Rassnick, S., Britton, K. T., and Koob, G. F. Anti-stress action of a corticotropin-releasing factor antagonist on behavioral reactivity to stressors of varying type and intensity. *Neuropsychopharmacology,* 1994, *11,* 179–186.

Helenius, P., Uutela, K., and Hari, R. Auditory stream segregation in dyslexic adults. *Brain,* 1999, *122,* 907–913.

Hellhammer, D. H., Hubert, W., and Schurmeyer, T. Changes in saliva testosterone after psychological stimulation in men. *Psychoneuroendocrinology,* 1985, *10,* 77–81.

Helmuth, L. Dyslexia: Same brains, different languages. *Science,* 2001, *291,* 2064–2065.

Henderson, W. W. The epidemiology of estrogen replacement therapy and Alzheimer's disease. *Neurology,* 1997, *48,* S27—S35.

Hendrickson, A. E., Wagoner, N., and Cowan, W. M. Autoradiographic and electron microscopic study of retino-hypothalamic connections. *Zeitschrift für Zellforschung und Mikroskopische Anatomie,* 1972, *125,* 1–26.

Hendry, S. H. C., and Yoshioka, T. A neurochemically distinct third channel in the cacaque dorsal lateral geniculare nucleus. *Science,* 1994, *264,* 575–577.

Henke, P. G. The telencephalic limbic system and experimental gastric pathology: A review. *Neuroscience and Biobehavioral Reviews,* 1982, *6,* 381–390.

Hennessey, A. C., Camak, L., Gordon, F., and Edwards, D. A. Connections between the pontine central gray and the ventromedial hypothalamus are essential for lordosis in female rats. *Behavioral Neuroscience,* 1990, *104,* 477–488.

Heresco-Levy, U., Javitt, D. C., Ermilov, M., Mordel, C., Silipo, G., and Lichtenstein, M. Efficacy of high-dose glycine in the treatment of enduring negative symptoms of schizophrenia. *Archives of General Psychiatry,* 1999, *56,* 29–36.

Herholz, K. Neuroimaging in anorexia nervosa. *Psychiatry Research,* 1996, *62,* 105–110.

Hertzmann, M., Reba, R. C., and Kotlyarov, E. V. Single photon emission computed tomography in phencyclidine and related drug abuse. *American Journal of Psychiatry,* 1990, *147,* 255–256.

Hetherington, A. W., and Ranson, S. W. Hypothalamic lesions and adiposity in the rat. *Anatomical Record,* 1942, *78,* 149–172.

Hettema, J. M., Neale, M. C., and Kendler, K. S. A review and meta-analysis of the genetic epidemiology of anxiety disorders. *American Journal of Psychiatry,* 2001, *158,* 1568–1578.

Hetz, C., Russelakis-Carneiro, M., Maundrell, K., Castilla, J., and Soto, C. Caspase-12 and endoplasmic reticulum stress mediate neurotoxicity of pathological prion protein. *The EMBO Journal,* 2003, *22,* 5435–5445.

Heuser, J. E. Synaptic vesicle exocytosis revealed in quick-frozen frog neuromuscular junctions treated with 4-aminopyridine and given a single electrical shock. In *Society for Neuroscience Symposia, Vol. II,* edited by W. M. Cowan and J. A. Ferrendelli. Bethesda, Md.: Society for Neuroscience, 1977.

Heuser, J. E., Reese, T. S., Dennis, M. J., Jan, Y., Jan, L., and Evans, L. Synaptic vesicle exocytosis captured by quick freezing and correlated with quantal transmitter release. *Journal of Cell Biology,* 1979, *81,* 275–300.

Heywood, C. A., Gaffan, D., and Cowey, A. Cerebral achromatopsia in monkeys. *European Journal of Neuroscience,* 1995, *7,* 1064–1073.

Higley, J. D., Mehlman, P. T., Higley, S. B., Fernald, B., Vickers, J., Lindell, S. G., Taub, D. M., Suomi, S. J., and Linnoila, M. Excessive mortality in young free-ranging male nonhuman primates with low cerebrospinal fluid 5-hydroxyindoleacetic acid concentrations. *Archives of General Psychiatry,* 1996a, *53,* 537–543.

Higley, J. D., Mehlman, P. T., Poland, R. E., Taub, D. M., Vickers, J., Suomi, S. J., and Linnoila, M. CSF testosterone and 5-HIAA correlate with different types of aggressive behaviors. *Biological Psychiatry,* 1996b, *40,* 1067–1082.

Hilditch-Maguire, P., Trettel, F., Passani, L. A., Auerbach, A., Persichetti, F., and MacDonald, M. E. Huntingtin: An iron-regulated protein essential for normal nuclear and perinuclear organelles. *Human Molecular Genetics,* 2000, *9,* 2789–2797.

Himmelsbach, C. K. Can the euphoric analgetic and physical dependence effects of drugs be separated? With reference to physical dependence. *Federation Proceedings,* 1943, *2,* 201–203.

Hines, M., Allen, L. S., and Gorski, R. A. Sex differences in subregions of the medial nucleus of the amygdala and the bed nucleus of the stria terminalis of the rat. *Brain Research,* 1992, *579,* 321–326.

Hinjo, S., Hirano, C., Murase, S., Kaneko, T., Sugiyama, T., Ohtaka, K., Aoyama, T., Takei, Y., Inoko, K., and Wakbayshai, S. Obsessive-compulsive symptoms in childhood and adolescence. *Acta Psychiatrica Scandanivica,* 1989, *80,* 83–91.

Hirsch, J. The search for new ways to treat obesity. *Proceedings of the National Academy of Science, USA,* 2002, *99,* 9096–9097.

Hobson, J. A. *The Dreaming Brain.* New York: Basic Books, 1988.

Hock, C., Konietzko, U., Streffer, J. R., Tracy, J., Signorell, A., Müller-Tillmans, B., Lemke, U., Henke, K., Moritz, E., Garcia, E., Wollmer, M. A., Umbricht, D., de Quervain, D. J. F., Hofmann, M., Maddalena, A., Papassotiropoulos, A., and Nitsch, R. M. Antibodies against ß-amyloid slow cognitive decline in Alzheimer's disease. *Neuron,* 2003, *38,* 547–554.

Hodge, C. W., Haraguchi, M., Erickson, H., and Samson, H. H. Ventral tegmental microinjections of quinpirole decrease ethanol and sucrose-reinforced responding. *Alcohol: Clinical and Experimental Research,* 1993, *17,* 370–375.

Hoebel, B. G., Monaco, A. P., Hernandez, L., Aulisi, E. F., Stanley, B. G., and Lenard, L. Self-injection of amphetamine directly into the brain. *Psychopharmacology,* 1983, *81,* 158–163.

Hohman, G. W. Some effects of spinal cord lesions on experienced emotional feelings. *Psychophysiology,* 1966, *3,* 143–156.

Holden, C. The violence of the lambs. *Science,* 2000, *289,* 580–581.

Hollander, E., DelGiudice-Asch, G., Simon, L., Schmeidler, J., Cartwright, C., DeCarla, C. M., Kwon, J., Cunningham-Rundles, C., Chapman, F., and Zabriskie, J. B. B lymphocyte antigen D8/17 and repetitive behaviors in autism. *American Journal of Psychiatry,* 1999, *156,* 317–320.

Hollander, E., Schiffman, E., Cohen, B., Rivera-Stein, M. A., Rosen, W., Gorman, J. M., Fyer, A. J., Papp, L., and Liebowitz, M. R. Signs of central nervous system dysfunction in obsessive-compulsive disorder. *Archives of General Psychiatry,* 1990, *47,* 27–32.

Hollister, J. M., Laing, P., and Mednick, S. A. Rhesus incompatibility as a risk factor for schizophrenia in male adults. *Archives of General Psychiatry,* 1996, *53,* 19–24.

Honda, T., and Semba, K. Serotonergic synaptic input to cholinergic neurons in the rat

mesopontine tegmentum. *Brain Research,* 1994, *647,* 299–306.
Hopf, H. C., Mueller-Forell, W., and Hopf, N. J. Localization of emotional and volitional facial paresis. *Neurology,* 1992, *42,* 1918–1923.
Horne, J. A. A review of the biological effects of total sleep deprivation in man. *Biological Psychology,* 1978, *7,* 55–102.
Horne, J. A., and Minard, A. Sleep and sleepiness following a behaviourally "active" day. *Ergonomics,* 1985, *28,* 567–575.
Horner, P. H., and Gage, F. H. Regenerating the damaged central nervous system. *Nature,* 2000, *407,* 963–970.
Horowitz, R. M., and Gentili, B. Dihydrochalcone sweeteners. In *Symposium: Sweeteners,* edited by G. E. Inglett. Westport, Conn.: Avi Publishing, 1974.
Horton, J. C., and Hubel, D. H. Cytochrome oxidase stain preferentially labels intersection of ocular dominance and vertical orientation columns in macaque striate cortex. *Society for Neuroscience Abstracts,* 1980, *6,* 315.
Houpt, T. A., Boulos, Z., and Moore-Ede, M. C. MidnightSun: Software for determining light exposure and phase-shifting schedules during global travel. *Physiology and Behavior,* 1996, *59,* 561–568.
Hubel, D. H., and Wiesel, T. N. Brain mechanisms of vision. *Scientific American,* 1979, *241,* 150–162.
Hubel, D. H., and Wiesel, T. N. Functional architecture of macaque monkey visual cortex. *Proceedings of the Royal Society of London,* 1977, *198,* 1–59.
Hublin, C. Narcolepsy: Current drug-treatment options. *CNS Drugs,* 1996, *5,* 426–436.
Hudspeth, A. J., and Gillespie, P. G. Pulling springs to tune transduction: Adaptation by hair cells. *Neuron,* 1994, *12,* 1–9.
Hughes, J., Smith, T. W., Kosterlitz, H. W., Fothergill, L. A., Morgan, B. A., and Moris, H. R. Identification of two related pentapeptides from the brain with potent opiate agonist activity. *Nature,* 1975, *258,* 577–579.
Hulshoff Pol, H. E., Schnack, H. G., Bertens, M. G. B. C., van Haren, N. E. M., Staal, W. G., Baaré, W. F. C., and Kahn, R. S. Volume changes in gray matter in patients with schizophrenia. *American Journal of Psychiatry,* 2002, *159,* 244–250.
Humphrey, A. L., and Hendrickson, A. E. Radial zones of high metabolic activity in squirrel monkey striate cortex. *Society for Neuroscience Abstracts,* 1980, *6,* 315.
Humphreys, G. W., Donnelly, N., and Riddoch, M. J. Expression is computed separately from facial identity, and it is computed separately for moving and static faces: Neuropsychological evidence. *Neuropsychologia,* 1993, *31,* 173–181.
Hungs, M., and Mignot, E. Hypocretin/orexin, sleep and narcolepsy. *Bioessays,* 2001, *23,* 397–408.
Hunt, D. M., Dulai, K. S., Cowing, J. A., Julliot, C., Mollon, J. D., Bowmaker, J. K., Li, W.-H., and Hewett-Emmett, D. Molecular evolution of trichromacy in primates. *Vision Research,* 1998, *38,* 3299–3306.
Huttunen, M. O., and Niskanen, P. Prenatal loss of father and psychiatric disorders. *Archives of General Psychiatry,* 1978, *35,* 429–431.
Hyman, S. E., and Malenka, R. C. Addiction and the brain: The neurobiology of compulsion and its persistence. *Nature Reviews: Neuroscience,* 2001, *2,* 695–703.
Ibuka, N., and Kawamura, H. Loss of circadian rhythm in sleep-wakefulness cycle in the rat by suprachiasmatic nucleus lesions. *Brain Research,* 1975, *96,* 76–81.
Iggo, A., and Andres, K. H. Morphology of cutaneous receptors. *Annual Review of Neuroscience,* 1982, *5,* 1–32.
Iijima, M., Arisaka, O., Minamoto, F., and Arai, Y. Sex differences in children's free drawings: A study on girls with congenital adrenal hyperplasia. *Hormones and Behavior,* 2001, *20,* 99–104.
Imaki, T., Shibasaki, T., Hotta, M., and Demura, H. Early induction of c-fos precedes increased expression of corticotropin-releasing factor messenger ribonucleic acid in the paraventricular nucleus after immobilization stress. *Endocrinology,* 1992, *131,* 240–246.
Imperato, A., and Di Chiara, G. Preferential stimulation of dopamine-release in the accumbens of freely moving rats by ethanol. *Journal of Pharmacology and Experimental Therapeutics,* 1986, *239,* 219–228.
Imperato, A., Scrocco, M. G., Bacchi, S., and Angelucci, L. NMDA receptors and in vivo dopamine release in the nucleus accumbens and caudatus. *European Journal of Pharmacology,* 1990, *187,* 555–556.
Ingelfinger, F. J. The late effects of total and subtotal gastrectomy. *New England Journal of Medicine,* 1944, *231,* 321–327.
Inoue, M., Koyanagi, T., Nakahara, H., Hara, K., Hori, E., and Nakano, H. Functional development of human eye movement in utero assessed quantitatively with real time ultrasound. *American Journal of Obstetrics and Gynecology,* 1986, *155,* 170–174.
Isenberg, N., Silbersweig, D., Engelien, A., Emmerich, S., Malavade, K., Beattie, B., Leon, A. C., and Stern, E. Linguistic threat activates the human amygdala. *Proceedings of the National Academy of Sciences, USA.,* 1999, *96,* 10456–10459.
Iwata, M. Kanji versus Kana: Neuropsychological correlates of the Japanese writing system. *Trends in Neurosciences,* 1984, *7,* 290–293.
Izard, C. E. *The Face of Emotion.* New York: Appleton-Century-Crofts, 1971.
Jackson, M. E., Frost, A. S., and Moghaddam, B. Stimulation of prefrontal cortex at physiologically relevant frequencies inhibits dopamine release in the nucleus accumbens. *Journal of Neurochemistry,* 2001, *78,* 920–923.
Jacob, S., and McClintock, M. K. Psychological state and mood effects of steroidal chemosignals in women and men. *Hormones and Behavior,* 2000, *37,* 57–78.
Jacobs, B. L., and McGinty, D. J. Participation of the amygdala in complex stimulus recognition and behavioral inhibition: Evidence from unit studies. *Brain Research,* 1972, *36,* 431–436.
Jacobs, G. H. Primate photopigments and primate color vision. *Proceedings of the National Academy of Sciences, USA,* 1996, *93,* 577–581.
James, W. What is an emotion? *Mind,* 1884, *9,* 188–205.
Jaramillo, F. Signal transduction in hair cells and its regulation by calcium. *Neuron,* 1995, *15,* 1227–1230.
Jasper, J. H., and Tessier, J. Acetylcholine liberation from cerebral cortex during paradoxical (REM) sleep. *Science,* 1969, *172,* 601–602.
Javitt, D. C., and Zukin, S. R. Recent advances in the phencyclidine model of schizophrenia. *American Journal of Psychiatry,* 1991, *148,* 1301–1308.
Jaynes, J. The problem of animate motion in the seventeenth century. *Journal of the History of Ideas,* 1970, *6,* 219–234.
Jensen, T., Genefke, I., and Hyldebrandt, N. Cerebral atrophy in young torture victims. *New England Journal of Medicine,* 1982, *307,* 1341.
Jentsch, J. D., Redmond, D. E., Elsworth, J. D., Taylor, J. R., Youngren, K. D., and Roth, R. H. Enduring cognitive deficits and cortical dopamine dysfunction in monkeys after long-term administration of phencyclidine. *Science,* 1997, *277,* 953–955.
Jentsch, J. D., Tran, A., Taylor, J. R., and Roth, R. H. Prefrontal cortical involvement in phencyclidine-induced activation of the mesolimbic dopamine system: Behavioral and neurochemical evidence. *Psychopharmacology,* 1998, *138,* 89–95.
Jeste, D. V., Del Carmen, R., Lohr, J. B., and Wyatt, R. J. Did schizophrenia exist before the eighteenth century? *Comprehensive Psychiatry,* 1985, *26,* 493–503.
Jewett, D. C., Cleary, J., Levine, A. S., Schaal, D. W., and Thompson, T. Effects of neuropeptide Y on food-reinforced behavior in satiated rats. *Pharmacology, Biochemistry, and Behavior,* 1992, *42,* 207–212.
Jiang, C. L., and Hunt, J. N. The relation between freely chosen meals and body habitus. *American Journal of Clinical Nutrition,* 1983, *38,* 32–40.
Johanson, A., Gustafson, L., Passant, U., Risberg, J., Smith, G., Warkentin, S., and Tucker, D. Brain function in spider phobia. *Psychiatry Research: Neuroimaging Section,* 1998, *84,* 101–111.
Johansson, G. Visual perception of biological motion and a model for its analysis. *Perception and Psychophysics,* 1973, *14,* 201–211.
Johnson, A. K., and Edwards, G. L. The neuroendocrinology of thirst: Afferent signaling and mechanisms of central integration. *Current Topics in Neuroendocrinology,* 1990, *10,* 149–190.
Johnson, M. K., Kim, J. K., and Risse, G. Do alcoholic Korsakoff's syndrome patients acquire affective reactions? *Journal of Experimental Psychology: Learning, Memory, and Cognition,* 1985, *11,* 22–36.
Jones, B. E. Influence of the brainstem reticular formation, including intrinsic monoaminergic and cholinergic neurons, on forebrain mechanisms of sleep and waking. In *The Diencephalon and Sleep,* edited by M. Mancia and G. Marini. New York: Raven Press, 1990.
Jones, B. E., and Beaudet, A. Distribution of acetylcholine and catecholamine neurons in the cat brain stem studied by choline acetyltransferase and tyrosine hydroxylase immunohistochemistry. *Journal of Comparative Neurology,* 1987, *261,* 15–32.
Jones, D. T., and Reed, R. R. G_{olf}: An olfactory neuron specific-G protein involved in odorant signal transduction. *Science,* 1989, *244,* 790–795.
Jones, M. B., and Szatmari, P. Stoppage rules and genetic studies of autism. *Journal of Autism and Developmental Disorders,* 1988, *18,* 31–40.
Jones, S. S., Collins, K., and Hong, H.-W. An audience effect on smile production in 10-

month-old infants. *Psychological Science,* 1991, *2,* 45–49.

Jope, R. S., Song, L., Li, P. P., Young, L. T., Kish, S. J., Pacheco, M. A., and Warsh, J. J. The phosphoinositide signal transduction system is impaired in bipolar affective disorder brain. *Journal of Neurochemistry,* 1996, *66,* 2402–2409.

Jornales, V. E., Jakob, M., Zamani, A., and Vaina, L. M. Deficits on complex motion perception, spatial discrimination and eye-movements in a patient with bilateral occipital-parietal lesions. *Investigative Opthalamolgy and Visual Science,* 1997, *38,* S72.

Jouvet, M. The role of monoamines and acetylcholine-containing neurons in the regulation of the sleep-waking cycle. *Ergebnisse der Physiologie,* 1972, *64,* 166–307.

Kahler, A., Geary, N., Eckel, L. A., Campfield, L. A., Smith, F. J., and Langhans, W. Chronic administration of OB protein decreases food intake by selectively reducing meal size in male rats. *American Journal of Physiology,* 1998, *275,* R180—R185.

Kales, A., Scharf, M. B., Kales, J. D., and Soldatos, C. R. Rebound insomnia: A potential hazard following withdrawal of certain benzodiazepines. *Journal of the American Medical Association,* 1979, *241,* 1692–1695.

Kalin, N. H., Sherman, J. E., and Takahashi, L. K. Antagonism of endogenous CRG systems attenuates stress-induced freezing behavior in rats. *Brain Research,* 1988, *457,* 130–135.

Kanner, L. Autistic disturbances of affective contact. *The Nervous Child,* 1943, *2,* 217–250.

Kanwisher, N., McDermott, J., and Chun, M. M. The fusiform face area: A module in human extrastriate cortex specialized for face perception. *Journal of Neuroscience,* 1997, *17,* 4302–4311.

Kapp, B. S., Frysinger, R. C., Gallagher, M., and Haselton, J. R. Amygdala central nucleus lesions: Effect on heart rate conditioning in the rabbit. *Physiology and Behavior,* 1979, *23,* 1109–1117.

Kapp, B. S., Gallagher, M., Applegate, C. D., and Frysinger, R. C. The amygdala central nucleus: Contributions to conditioned cardiovascular responding during aversive Pavlovian conditioning in the rabbit. In *Conditioning: Representation of Involved Neural Functions,* edited by C. D. Woody. New York: Plenum Press, 1982.

Karacan, I., Salis, P. J., and Williams, R. L. The role of the sleep laboratory in diagnosis and treatment of impotence. In *Sleep Disorders: Diagnosis and Treatment,* edited by R. J. Williams and I. Karacan. New York: John Wiley & Sons, 1978.

Karacan, I., Williams, R. L., Finley, W. W., and Hursch, C. J. The effects of naps on nocturnal sleep: Influence on the need for stage 1 REM and stage 4 sleep. *Biological Psychiatry,* 1970, *2,* 391–399.

Karlson, P., and Luscher, M. "Pheromones": A new term for a class of biologically active substances. *Nature,* 1959, *183,* 55–56.

Kartsounis, L. D., Rudge, P., and Stevens, J. M. Bilateral lesions of CA1 and CA2 fields of the hippocampus are sufficient to cause a severe amnesic syndrome in humans. *Journal of Neurology, Neurosurgery and Psychiatry,* 1995, *59,* 95–98.

Kattler, H., Dijk, D. J., and Borbély, A. A. Effect of unilateral somatosensory stimulation prior to sleep on the sleep EEG in humans. *Journal of Sleep Research,* 1994, *3,* 159–164.

Kawamura, M., Hirayama, K., and Yamamoto, H. Different interhemispheric transfer of kanji and kana writing evidenced by a case with left unilateral agraphia without apraxia. *Brain,* 1989, *112,* 1011–1018.

Kawauchi, H., Kawazoe, I., Tsubokawa, M., Kishida, M., and Baker, B. I. Characterization of melanin-concentrating hormone in chum salmon pituitaries. *Nature,* 1983, *305,* 321–323.

Kayama, Y., Ohta, M., and Jodo, E. Firing of "possibly" cholinergic neurons in the rat laterodorsal tegmental nucleus during sleep and wakefulness. *Brain Research,* 1992, *569,* 210–220.

Kaye, W. H. Neuropeptide abnormalities in anorexia nervosa. *Psychiatry Research,* 1996, *62,* 65–74.

Kaye, W. H., Berrettini, W., Gwirtsman, H., and George, D. T. Altered cerebrospinal fluid neuropeptide Y and peptide YY immunoreactivity in anorexia and bulimia nervosa. *Archives of General Psychiatry,* 1990, *47,* 548–556.

Kaye, W. H., Nagata, T., Weltzin, T. E., Hsu, G., Sokol, M. S., McConaha, C., Plotnicov, K. H., Weise, J., and Deep, D. Double-blind placebo-controlled administration of fluoxetine in restricting- and restricting-purging-type anorexia nervosa. *Biological Psychiatry,* 2001, *49,* 644–652.

Keller, S. E., Weiss, J. M., Schleifer, S. J., Miller, N. E., and Stein, M. Stress-induced suppression of immunity in adrenalectomized rats. *Science,* 1983, *221,* 1301–1304.

Kelso, S. R., Ganong, A. H., and Brown, T. H. Hebbian synapses in hippocampus. *Proceedings of the National Academy of Sciences, USA,* 1986, *83,* 5326–5330.

Kendell, R. E., and Adams, W. Unexplained fluctuations in the risk for schizophrenia by month and year of birth. *British Journal of Psychiatry,* 1991, *158,* 758–763.

Kennard, C., Lawden, M., Morland, A. B., and Ruddock, K. H. Colour identification and colour constancy are impaired in a patient with incomplete achromatopsia associated with prestriate cortical lesions. *Proceedings of the Royal Society of London (B),* 1995, *260,* 169–175.

Kertesz, A. Anatomy of jargon. In *Jargonaphasia,* edited by J. Brown. New York: Academic Press, 1981.

Kestler, L. P., Walker, E., and Vega, E. M. Dopamine receptors in the brains of schizophrenia patients: A meta-analysis of the findings. *Behavioral Pharmacology,* 2001, *12,* 355–371.

Kety, S. S., Rosenthal, D., Wender, P. H., and Schulsinger, K. F. The types and prevalence of mental illness in the biological and adoptive families of adopted schizophrenics. In *The Transmission of Schizophrenia,* edited by D. Rosenthal and S. S. Kety. New York: Pergamon Press, 1968.

Kety, S. S., Wender, P. H., Jacobsen, B., Ingraham, L. J., Jansson, L., Faber, B., and Kinney, D. K. Mental illness in the biological and adoptive relatives of schizophrenic adoptees: Replication of the Copenhagen Study in the rest of Denmark. *Archives of General Psychiatry,* 1994, *51,* 442–455.

Khanna, S., and Channabasavanna, S. Toward a classification of compulsions in obsessive compulsive neurosis. *Psychopathology,* 1987, *20,* 23–28.

Khateb, A., Fort, P., Pegna, A., Jones, B. E., and Muhlethaler, M. Cholinergic nucleus basalis neurons are excited by histamine in vitro. *Neuroscience,* 1995, *69,* 495–506.

Kiang, N. Y.-S. *Discharge Patterns of Single Fibers in the Cat's Auditory Nerve.* Cambridge, Mass.: MIT Press, 1965.

Kiecolt-Glaser, J. K., Marucha, P. T., Malarkey, W. B., Mercado, A. M., and Glaser, R. Slowing of wound healing by psychological stress. *Lancet,* 1995, *346,* 1194–1196.

Kihlstrom, J. F. Hypnosis. *Annual Review of Psychology,* 1985, *36,* 385–418.

King, G. A., Fitzhugh, E. C., Bassett, D. R., McLaughlin, J. E., Strath, S. J., Swartz, A. M., and Thompson, D. L. Relationship of leisure-time physical activity and occupational activity to the prevalence of obesity. *International Journal of Obesity,* 2001, *25,* 606–612.

Kingston, K., Szmukler, G., Andrewes, D., Tress, B., and Desmond, P. Neuropsychological and structural brain changes in anorexia nervosa before and after refeeding. *Psychological Medicine,* 1996, *26,* 15–28.

Kinnamon, S. C., and Cummings, T. A. Chemosensory transduction mechanisms in taste. *Annual Review of Physiology,* 1992, *54,* 715–731.

Kinnamon, S. C., Dionne, V. E., and Beam, K. G. Apical localization of K+ channels in taste cells provides the basis for sour taste transduction. *Proceedings of the National Academy of Sciences, USA,* 1988, *85,* 7023–7027.

Kinney, D. K., Yurgelun-Todd, D. A., Levy, D. L., Medoff, D., Lajonchere, C. M., and Radford-Paregol, M. Obstetrical complications in patients with bipolar disorder and their siblings. *Psychiatry Research,* 1993, *48,* 47–56.

Kinney, D. K., Yurgelun-Todd, D. A., Tohen, M., and Tramer, S. Pre- and perinatal complications and risk for bipolar disorder: A retrospective study. *Journal of Affective Disorders,* 1998, *50,* 117–124.

Kinon, B. J., and Lieberman, J. A. Mechanisms of action of atypical antipsychotic drugs: A critical analysis. *Psychopharmacology,* 1996, *124,* 2–34.

Kirkpatrick, B., Kim, J. W., and Insel, T. R. Limbic system fos expression associated with paternal behavior. *Brain Research,* 1994, *658,* 112–118.

Kitada, T., Asakawa, S., Hattori, N., Matsumine, H., Yamamura, Y., Minoshima, S., Yokochi, M., Mizuno, Y., and Shimizu, N. Mutations in the parkin gene cause autosomal recessive juvenile parkinsonism. *Nature,* 1998, *392,* 605–608.

Klein, E., Kreinin, I., Chistyakov, A., Koren, D., Mecz, L., Marmur, S., Ben-Shachar, D., and Feinsod, M. Therapeutic efficacy of right prefrontal slow repetitive transcranial magnetic stimulation in major depression: A double-blind controlled study. *Archives of General Psychiatry,* 1999, *56,* 315–320.

Kleitman, N. Basic rest-activity cycle—22 years later. *Sleep,* 1982, *4,* 311–317.

Kleitman, N. The nature of dreaming. In *The Nature of Sleep,* edited by G. E. W. Wolstenholme and M. O'Connor. London: J. & A. Churchill, 1961.

Knebelmann, B., Boussin, L., Guerrier, D., Legeai, L., Kahn, A., Josso, N., and Picard, J.-Y. Anti-Muellerian hormone Bruxelles: A nonsense mutation associated with the persistent Muellerian duct syndrome. *Proceedings of the National Academy of Sciences, USA,* 1991, *88,* 3767–3771.

Knecht, S., Drager, B., Deppe, M., Bobe, L., Lohmann, H. Floel, A., Ringelstein, R. B., and Henningsen, H. Handedness and hemispheric language dominance in healthy humans. *Brain,* 2000, *123,* 2512–2518.

Knutson, B., Adams, C. M., Fong, G. W., and Hommer, D. Anticipation of increasing monetary reward selectively recruits nucleus accumbens. *Journal of Neuroscience,* 2001, *21,* RC159 (1–5).

Kojima, M., Hosoda, H., Date, Y., Nakazato, M., Matsuo, H., and Kangawa, K. Ghrelin is a growth-hormone–releasing acylated peptide from stomach. *Nature,* 1999, *402,* 656–660.

Komatsu, H. Mechanisms of central color vision. *Current Opinion in Neurobiology,* 1998, *8,* 503–508.

Komisaruk, B. R., and Larsson, K. Suppression of a spinal and a cranial nerve reflex by vaginal or rectal probing in rats. *Brain Research,* 1971, *35,* 231–235.

Komisaruk, B. R., and Steinman, J. L. Genital stimulation as a trigger for neuroendocrine and behavioral control of reproduction. *Annals of the New York Academy of Sciences,* 1987, *474,* 64–75.

Koob, G. F., Thatcher-Britton, K., Britton, D., Roberts, D. C. S., and Bloom, F. E. Destruction of the locus coeruleus or the dorsal NE bundle does not alter the release of punished responding by ethanol and chlordiazepoxide. *Physiology and Behavior,* 1984, *33,* 479–485.

Koopman, P. Gonad development: Signals for sex. *Current Biology,* 2001, *11,* R481-R483.

Koroshetz, W. J., and Moskowitz, M. A. Emerging treatments for stroke in humans. *Trends in Pharmacological Sciences,* 1996, *17,* 227–233.

Kortegaard, L. S., Hoerder, K., Joergensen, J., Gillberg, C., and Kyvik, K. O. A preliminary population-based twin study of self-reported eating disorder. *Psychological Medicine,* 2001, *31,* 361–365.

Kosten, T. A., Miserendino, M. J. D., and Kehoe, P. Enhanced acquisition of cocaine self-administration in adult rats with neonatal isolation stress experience. *Brain Research,* 2000, *875,* 44–50.

Kourtzi, A., and Kanwisher, N. Activation in human MT/MST by static images with implied motion. *Journal of Cognitive Neuroscience,* 2000, *12,* 48–55.

Kovács, G., Vogels, R., and Orban, G. A. Selectivity of macaque inferior temporal neurons for partially occluded shapes. *Journal of Neuroscience,* 1995, *15,* 1984–1997.

Koylu, E. O., Couceyro, P. R., Lambert, P. D., and Kuhar, M. J. Cocaine- and amphetamine-regulated transcript peptide immunohistochemical localization in the rat brain. *Journal of Comparative Neurology,* 1998, *391,* 115–132.

Kozlowski, L. T., and Cutting, J. E. Recognizing the sex of a walker from a dynamic point-light display. *Perception and Psychophysics,* 1977, *21,* 575–580.

Kraut, R. E., and Johnston, R. Social and emotional messages of smiling: An ethological approach. *Journal of Personality and Social Psychology,* 1979, *37,* 1539–1553.

Kress, M., and Zeilhofer, H. U. Capsaicin, protons and heat: New excitement about nociceptors. *Trends in Pharmacological Science,* 1999, *20,* 112–118.

Kristensen, P., Judge, M. E., Thim, L. Ribel, U. Christjansen, K. N., Wulff, B. S., Clausen, J. T., Jensen, P. B., Madsen, O. D., Vrang, N., Larsen, P. J., and Hastrup, S. Hypothalamic CART is a new anorectic peptide regulated by leptin. *Nature,* 1998, *393,* 72–76.

Kuffler, S. W. Discharge patterns and functional organization of mammalian retina. *Journal of Neurophysiology,* 1953, *16,* 37–68.

Kuffler, S. W. Neurons in the retina: Organization, inhibition and excitation problems. *Cold Spring Harbor Symposium on Quantitative Biology,* 1952, *17,* 281–292.

Kunos, G., and Batkai, S. Novel physiologic functions of endocannabinoids as revealed through the use of mutant mice. *Neurochemical Research,* 2001, *26,* 1015–1021.

Kupfer, D. J. REM latency: A psychobiologic marker for primary depressive disease. *Biological Psychiatry,* 1976, *11,* 159–174.

Kupfer, D. J., Ehlers, C. L., Frank, E., Grochocinski, V. J., McEachran, A. B., and Buhari, A. Persistent effects of antidepressants: EEG sleep studies in depressed patients during maintenance treatment. *Biological Psychiatry,* 1994, *35,* 781–793.

Kurihara, K. Recent progress in taste receptor mechanisms. In *Umami: A Basic Taste,* edited by Y. Kawamura and M. R. Kare. New York: Dekker, 1987.

Kuriki, S., Mori, T., and Hirata, Y. Motor planning center for speech articulation in the normal human brain. *Neuroreport,* 1999, *10,* 765–769.

LaBar, K. S., LeDoux, J. E., Spencer, D. D., and Phelps, E. A. Impaired fear conditioning following unilateral temporal lobectomy in humans. *Journal of Neuroscience,* 1995, *15,* 6846–6855.

Lahti, A. C., Weiler, M. A., Michaelidis, T., Parwani, A., and Tamminga, C. A. Effects of ketamine in normal and schizophrenic volunteers. *Neuropsychopharmacology,* 2001, *25,* 455–467.

Lai, E. C., Jankovic, J., Krauss, J. K., Ondo, W. G., and Grossman, R. G. Long-term efficacy of posteroventral pallidotomy in the treatment of Parkinson's disease. *Neurology,* 2000, *55,* 1218–1222.

Laitinen, L. V., Bergenheim, A. T., and Hariz, M. I. Leksell's posteroventral pallidotomy in the treatment of Parkinson's disease. *Journal of Neurosurgery,* 1992, *76,* 53–61.

Lange, C. G. *Über Gemüthsbewegungen.* Leipzig, Germany: T. Thomas, 1887.

Langston, J. W., and Ballard, P. Parkinsonism induced by 1-methyl-4-phenyl-1,2,3,6-tetrahydropyridine (MPTP): Implications for treatment and the pathogenesis of Parkinson's disease. *Canadian Journal of Neurological Science,* 1984, *11*(1 Suppl), 160–165.

Langston, J. W., Ballard, P., Tetrud, J., and Irwin, I. Chronic parkinsonism in humans due to a product of meperidine-analog synthesis. *Science,* 1983, *219,* 979–980.

Langston, J. W., Irwin, I., Langston, E. B., and Forno, L. S. Pargyline prevents MPTP-induced parkinsonism in primates. *Science,* 1984, *225,* 1480–1482.

Laruelle, M., Abi-Dargham, A., Van Dyck, C. H., Gil, R., D'Souza, C. D., Erdos, J., McCance, E., Rosenblatt, W., Fingado, C., Zoghbi, S. S., Baldwin, R. M., Seibyl, J. P., Krystal, J. H., Charney, D. S., and Innis, R. B. Single photon emission computerized tomography imaging of amphetamine-induced dopamine release in drug-free schizophrenic subjects. *Proceedings of the National Academy of Sciences, USA,* 1996, *93,* 9235–9240.

Laschet, U. Antiandrogen in the treatment of sex offenders: Mode of action and therapeutic outcome. In *Contemporary Sexual Behavior: Critical Issues in the 1970's,* edited by J. Zubin and J. Money. Baltimore: Johns Hopkins University Press, 1973.

Lavond, D. G., Kim, J. J., and Thompson, R. F. Mammalian brain substrates of aversive classical conditioning. *Annual Review of Psychology,* 1993, *44,* 317–342.

LeDoux, J. E. Brain mechanisms of emotion and emotional learning. *Current Opinion in Neurobiology,* 1992, *2,* 191–197.

LeDoux, J. E. Emotion: Clues from the brain. *Annual Review of Psychology,* 1995, *46,* 209–235.

LeDoux, J. E., Iwata, J., Cicchetti, P., and Reis, D. J. Different projections of the central amygdaloid nucleus mediate autonomic and behavioral correlates of conditioned fear. *Journal of Neuroscience,* 1988, *8,* 2517–2529.

LeDoux, J. E., Sakaguchi, A., and Reis, D. J. Subcortical efferent projections of the medial geniculate nucleus mediate emotional responses conditioned to acoustic stimuli. *Journal of Neuroscience,* 1984, *4,* 683–698.

Lehman, M. N., and Winans, S. S. Vomeronasal and olfactory pathways to the amygdala controlling male hamster sexual behavior: Autoradiographic and behavioral analyses. *Brain Research,* 1982, *240,* 27–41.

Lehman, M. N., Silver, R., Gladstone, W. R., Kahn, R. M., Gibson, M., and Bittman, E. L. Circadian rhythmicity restored by neural transplant: Immunocytochemical characterization with the host brain. *Journal of Neuroscience,* 1987, *7,* 1626–1638.

Leibenluft, E., and Wehr, T. A. Is sleep deprivation useful in the treatment of depression? *American Journal of Psychiatry,* 1992, *149,* 159–168.

Leibowitz, S. F., Weiss, G. F., and Suh, J. S. Medial hypothalamic nuclei mediate serotonin's inhibitory effect on feeding behavior. *Pharmacology, Biochemistry, and Behavior,* 1990, *37,* 735–742.

Leonard, C. M., Rolls, E. T., Wilson, F. A. W., and Baylis, G. C. Neurons in the amygdala of the monkey with responses selective for faces. *Behavioral Brain Research,* 1985, *15,* 159–176.

Leonard, C. S., Kerman, I., Blaha, G., Taveras, E., and Taylor, B. Interdigitation of nitric oxide synthase-, tyrosine hydroxylase-, and serotonin-containing neurons in and around the laterodorsal and pedunculopontine tegmental nuclei of the guinea pig. *Journal of Comparative Neurology,* 1995, *362,* 411–432.

Leonard, H. L., Lenane, M. C., Swedo, S. E., Rettew, D. C., Gershon, E. S. and Rapoport, J. L. Tics and Tourette's disorder: a 2- to 7-year follow-up of 54 obsessive-compulsive children. *American Journal of Psychiatry,* 1992a, *149,* 1244–1251.

Leonard, H. L., Swedo, S. E., Rapoport, J. L., Koby, E. V., Lenane, M. C., Cheslow, D. L., and Hamburger, S. D. Treatment of obsessive-compulsive disorder with clomipramine and desipramine in children and adolescents: A double-blind crossover comparison. *Archives of General Psychiatry,* 1989, *46,* 1088–1092.

Leshner, A. I. Molecular mechanisms of cocaine addiction. *The New England Journal of Medicine,* 1996, *335,* 128–129.

Lesser, R. Selective preservation of oral spelling without semantics in a case of multi-infarct dementia. *Cortex,* 1989, *25,* 239–250.

LeVay, S. A difference in hypothalamic structure between heterosexual and homosexual men. *Science,* 1991, *253,* 1034–1037.

Levine, J. D., Gordon, N. C., and Fields, H. L. The role of endorphins in placebo analgesia. In *Advances in Pain Research and Therapy, Vol. 3,* edited by J. J. Bonica, J. C. Liebeskind, and D. Albe-Fessard. New York: Raven Press, 1979.

Levy, F., Hay, D. A., McStephen, M., Wood, C., and Waldman, I. Attention-deficit hyperactivity disorder: a category or a continuum? Genetic analysis of a large-scale twin study. *Journal of the American Academy of Child and Adolescent Psychiatry,* 1997, *36,* 737–744.

Levy, R. M., and Bredesen, D. E. Controversies in HIV-related central nervous system disease: Neuropsychological aspects of HIV-1 infection. In *AIDS Clinical Review 1989,* edited by P. Volberding, and M. A. Jacobson. New York: Marcel Dekker, 1989.

Lewin, R. Big first scored with nerve diseases. *Science,* 1989, *245,* 467–468.

Lewis, D. A., and Smith, R. E. Steroid-induced psychiatric syndromes. A report of 14 cases and a review of the literature. *Journal of the Affective Disorders,* 1983, *5,* 19–32.

Lewy, A. J., Bauer, V. K., Cutler, N. L., Sack, R. L., Ahmed, S., Thomas, K. H., Blood, M. L., Latham Jackson, J. M. Morning vs evening light treatment of patients with winter depression, *Archives of General Psychiatry,* 1998, *55,* 890–896.

Li, B.-H., and Rowland, N. E. Effects of vagotomy on cholecystokinin- and dexfenfluramine-induced fos-like immunoreactivity in the rat brain. *Brain Research Bulletin,* 1995, *37,* 589–593.

Li, B.-H., Spector, A. C., and Rowland, N. E. Reversal of dexfenfluramine-induced anorexia and c-Fos/c-Jun expression by lesion in the lateral parabrachial nucleus. *Brain Research,* 1994, *640,* 255–267.

Li, J. Y., Finniss, S., Yang, Y. K., Zeng, Q., Qu, S. Y., Barsh, G., Dickinson, C., and Gantz, I. Agouti-related protein-like immunoreactivity: characterization of release from hypothalamic tissue and presence in serum. *Endocrinology,* 2000, *141,* 1942–1950.

Lidberg, L., Asberg, M., and Sundqvist-Stensman, U. B. 5-Hydroxyindoleacetic acid levels in attempted suicides who have killed their children. *Lancet,* 1984, *2,* 928.

Lidberg, L., Tuck, J. R., Asberg, M., Scalia-Tomba, G. P., and Bertilsson, L. Homicide, suicide and CSF 5-HIAA. *Acta Psychiatrica Scandanavica,* 1985, *71,* 230–236.

Lin, J. S., Sakai, K., and Jouvet, M. Evidence for histaminergic arousal mechanisms in the hypothalamus of cat. *Neuropharmacology,* 1998, *27,* 111–122.

Lin, L., Faraco, J., Li, R., Kadotani, H., Rogers, W., Lin, X., Qiu, X., de Jong, P. J., Nishino, S., and Mignot, E. The sleep disorder canine narcolepsy is caused by a mutation in the hypocretin (orexin) receptor 2. *Cell,* 1999, *98,* 365–376.

Lindemann, B. Taste reception. *Physiological Reviews,* 1996, *76,* 719–766.

Links, J. M., Zubieta, J. K., Meltzer, C. G., Stumpf, M. J., and Frist, J. J. Influence of spatially heterogenous background activity on "hot object" quantitation in brain emission computed tomography. *Journal of Computer Assisted Tomography,* 1996, *20,* 680–687.

Liotti, M., Mayberg, H. S., McGinnis, S., Brannan, S. L., and Jerabek, P. Unmasking disease-specific cerebral blood flow abnormalities: Mood challenge in patients with remitted unipolar depression. *American Journal of Psychiatry,* 2002, *159,* 1830–1840.

Lipton, S. A. Neuropathogenesis of acquired immunodeficiency syndrome dementia. *Current Opinion in Neurology,* 1997, *10,* 247–253.

Lipton, S. A. Similarity of neuronal cell injury and death in AIDS dementia and focal cerebral ischemia: Potential treatment with NMDA open-channel blockers and nitric oxide-related species. *Brain Pathology,* 1996, *6,* 507–514.

Lipton, S. A., Dreyer, E. B., Kaiser, P. K., and Offermann, J. T. HIV-1 coat protein neurotoxicity prevented by calcium channel antagonists. *Science,* 1990, *248,* 364–367.

Lisk, R. D., Pretlow, R. A., and Friedman, S. Hormonal stimulation necessary for elicitation of maternal nest-building in the mouse *(Mus musculus). Animal Behaviour,* 1969, *17,* 730–737.

Lisman, J. E., and Zhabotinsky, A. M. A model of synaptic memory: a CaMKII/PP1 switch that potentiates transmission by organizing an AMPA receptor anchoring assembly. *Neuron,* 2001, *31,* 191–201.

Livingstone, M. S., and Hubel, D. H. Anatomy and physiology of a color system in the primate visual cortex. *Journal of Neuroscience,* 1984, *4,* 309–356.

Livingstone, M. S., and Hubel, D. Segregation of form, color, movement, and depth: Anatomy, physiology, and perception. *Science,* 1988, *240,* 740–749.

Lledo, P. M., Hjelmstad, G. O., Mukherji, S., Soderling, T. R., Malenka, R. C., and Nicoll, R. A. Calcium/calmodulin-dependent kinase II and long-term potentiation enhance synaptic transmission by the same mechanism. *Proceedings of the National Academy of Science, USA,* 1995, *92,* 11175–11179.

Llorca, P. M., Chereau, I., Bayle, F. J., and Lancon, C. Tardive dyskinesias and antipsychotics: A review. *European Psychiatry,* 2002, *17,* 129–138.

Loeb, G. E. Cochlear prosthetics. *Annual Review of Neuroscience,* 1990, *13,* 357–371.

Loewenstein, W. R., and Mendelson, M. Components of receptor adaptation in a Pacinian corpuscle. *Journal of Physiology (London),* 1965, *177,* 377–397.

Logan, F. A. Decision making by rats: Delay versus amount of reward. *Journal of Comparative and Physiological Psychology,* 1965, *59,* 1–12.

Lohr, J. B., Caligiuri, M. P., Edson, R., Lavori, P., Adler, L. A., Rotrosen, J., and Hitzemann, R. Treatment predictors of extrapyramidal side effects in patients with tardive dyskinesia: Results from Veterans Affairs Cooperative Study 394. *Journal of Clinical Psychopharmacology,* 2002, *22,* 196–200.

Lohse, P., Lohse, P., Chahrokh-Zadeh, S., and Seidel, D. The acid lipase family: Three enzymes, one highly conserved gene structure. *Journal of Lipid Research,* 1997, *38,* 880–891.

Lømo, T. Frequency potentiation of excitatory synaptic activity in the dentate area of the hippocampal formation. *Acta Physiologica Scandinavica,* 1966, *68* (Suppl. 227), 128.

Loscher, W., Annies, R., and Honack, D. The N-methyl-D-aspartate receptor antagonist MK-801 induces increases in dopamine and serotonin metabolism in several brain regions of rats. *Neuroscience Letters,* 1991, *128,* 191–194.

Lu, J., Greco, M. A., Shiromani, P., and Saper, C. B. Effect of lesions of the ventrolateral preoptic nucleus on NREM and REM sleep. *Journal of Neuroscience,* 2000, *20,* 3830–3842.

Lu, J., Zhang, Y.-H., Chou, T. C., Gaus, S. E., Elmquist, J. K., Shiromani, P., and Saper, C. B. Contrasting effects of ibotenate lesions of the paraventricular nucleus and subparaventricular zone on sleep-wake cycle and temperature regulation. *Journal of Neuroscience,* 2001, *21,* 4864–4874.

Lucas, B. K., Ormandy, C. J., Binart, N., Bridges, R. S., and Kelley, P. A. Null mutation of the prolactin receptor gene produces a defect in maternal behavior. *Endocrinology,* 1998, *139,* 4102–4107.

Lupien, S., Lecours, A. R., Schwartz, G., Sharma, S., Hauger, R. L., Meaney, M. J., and Nair, N. P. V. Longitudinal study of basal cortixol levels in healthy elderly subjects: Evidence for subgroups. *Neurobiology of Aging,* 1996, *17,* 95–105.

Lüscher, C., Xia, H., Beattie, E. C., Carroll, R. C., von Zastrow, M., Malenka, R. C., and Nicoll, R. A. Role of AMPA receptor cycling in synaptic transmission and plasticity. *Neuron,* 1999, *24,* 649–658.

Lutz, T. A., Diener, M., and Scharrer, E. Intraportal mercaptoacetate infusion increases afferent activity in the common hepatic vagus branch of the rat. *American Journal of Physiology,* 1997, *273,* R442—R445.

Luzzi, S., Pucci, E., Di Bella, P., and Piccirilli, M. Topographical disorientation consequent to amnesia of spatial location in a patient with right parahippocampal damage. *Cortex,* 2000, *36,* 427–434.

Lydic, R., Baghdoyan, H. A., Hibbard, L., Bonyak, E. V., DeJoseph, M. R., and Hawkins, R. A. Regional brain glucose metabolism is altered during rapid eye movement sleep in the cat: A preliminary study. *Journal of Comparative Neurology,* 1991, *304,* 517–529.

Lynch, G., Larson, J., Kelso, S., Barrionuevo, G., and Schottler, F. Intracellular injections of EGTA block induction of long-term potentiation. *Nature,* 1984, *305,* 719–721.

Lytton, W. W., and Brust, J. C. M. Direct dyslexia: Preserved oral reading of real words in Wernicke's aphasia. *Brain,* 1989, *112,* 583–594.

Ma, W., Miao, Z., and Novotny, M. Induction of estrus in grouped female mice (*Mus domesticus*) by synthetic analogs of preputial gland constituents. *Chemical Senses,* 1999, *24,* 289–293.

MacLean, H. E., Warne, G. L., and Zajac, J. D. Defects of androgen receptor function: From sex reversal to motor-neuron disease. *Molecular and cellular Endocrinology,* 1995, *112,* 133–141.

MacLean, P. D. Psychosomatic disease and the "visceral brain": Recent developments bearing on the Papez theory of emotion. *Psychosomatic Medicine,* 1949, *11,* 338–353.

Madden, P. A. F., Heath, A. C., Rosenthal, N. E., and Martin, N. G. Seasonal changes in mood and behavior: The role of genetic factors. *Archives of General Psychiatry,* 1996, *53,* 47–55.

Magistretti, P. J., Pellerin, L., Rothman, D. L., and Shulman, R. G. Energy on demand. *Science,* 1999, *283,* 496–497.

Maguire, E. A., Burgess, N., Donnett, J. G., Frackowiak, R. S. J., Frith, C. D., and O'-Keefe, J. Knowing where and getting there: A human navigation network. *Science,* 1998, *280,* 921–924.

Maguire, E. A., Frackowiak, R. S. J., and Frith, C. D. Recalling routes around London: Activation of the right hippocampus in taxi drivers. *Journal of Neuroscience,* 1997, *17,* 7103–7110.

Maguire, E. A., Gadian, D. G., Johnsrude, I. S., Good, C. D., Ashburner, J., Frackowiak, R. S. J., and Frith, C. D. Navigation-related structural change in the hippocampi of taxi drivers. *Proceedings of the National Academy of Science, USA,* 2000, *97,* 4398–4403.

Mahley, R. W., and Rall, S. C. Apolipoprotein E: Far more than a lipid transport protein. *Annual Review of Genomics and Human Genetics,* 2000, *1,* 507–537.

Maier, S. F., Drugan, R. C., and Grau, J. W. Controllability, coping behavior, and stress-induced analgesia in the rat. *Pain,* 1982, 12, 47–56.

Maj, M. Organic mental disorders in HIV-1 infection. *AIDS,* 1990, *4,* 831–840.

Malizia, A. L., Cunningham, V. J., Bell, C. J., Liddle, P. F., Jones, T., and Nutt, D. J. Decreased brain GABA(A)-benzodiazepine receptor binding in panic disorder: preliminary results from a quantitative PET study. *Archives of General Psychiatry,* 1998, *55,* 15–20.

Mallow, G. K. The relationship between aggression and cycle stage in adult female rhesus monkeys *(Macaca mulatta). Dissertation Abstracts,* 1979, *39,* 3194.

Mallucci, G., Dickinson, A., Linehan, J., Klöhn, P. C., Brandner, S., and Collinge, J. Depleting neuronal PrP in prion infections prevents disease and reverses spongiosis. *Science,* 2003, *302,* 871–874.

Malnic, B., Hirono, J, Sato, T., and Buck, L. B. Combinatorial receptor codes for odors. *Cell,* 1999, *96,* 713–723.

Malsbury, C. W. Facilitation of male rat copulatory behavior by electrical stimulation of the medial preoptic area. *Physiology and Behavior,* 1971, *7,* 797–805.

Manji, H. K., and Lenox, R. H. Lithium: A molecular transducer of mood-stabilization in the treatment of bipolar disorder. *Neuropsychopharmacology,* 1998, *19,* 161–166.

Manji, H. K., Moore, G. J., and Chen, G. Bipolar disorder: Leads from the molecular and cellular mechanisms of action of mood stabilisers. *British Journal of Psychiatry,* 2001, *178* (Suppl. 41), S107—S109.

Mann, J. J., Malone, K. M., Diehl, D. J., Perel, J., Nichols, T. E., and Mintun, M. A. Positron emission tomographic imaging of serotonin activation effects on prefrontal cortex in healthy volunteers. *Journal of Cerebral Blood Flow and Metabolism,* 1996, *16,* 418–426.

Manning, L., and Campbell, R. Optic aphasia with spared action naming: A description and possible loci of impairment. *Neuropsychologia,* 1992, *30,* 587–592.

Mantzoros, C., Flier, J. S., Lesem, M. D., Brewerton, T. D., and Jimerson, D. C. Cerebrospinal fluid leptin in anorexia nervosa: Correlation with nutritional status and potential role in resistance to weight gain. *Journal of Clinical Endocrinology and Metabolism,* 1997, *82,* 1845–1851.

Maquet, P. Sleep function(s) and cerebral metabolism. *Behavioural Brain Research,* 1995, *69,* 75–83.

Maquet, P., Dive, D., Salmon, E., Sadzot, B., Franco, G., Poirrier, R., Von Frenckell, R., and Franck, G. Cerebral glucose utilization during sleep-wake cycle in man determined by positron emission tomography and [18F]2-fluoro-2-deoxy-D-glucose method. *Brain Research,* 1990, *513,* 136–143.

Maren, S. Auditory fear conditioning increases CS-elicited spike firing in lateral amygdala neurons even after extensive overtraining. *European Journal of Neuroscience,* 2000, *12,* 4047–4054.

Maret, G., Testa, B., Jenner, P., el Tayar, N., and Carrupt, P. A. The MPTP story: MAO activates tetrahydropyridine derivatives to toxins causing parkinsonism. *Drug Metabolism Review,* 1990, *22,* 291–332.

Margolin, D. I., and Goodman-Schulman, R. Oral and written spelling impairments. In *Cognitive Neuropsychology in Clinical Practice,* edited by D. I. Margolin. New York: Oxford University Press, 1992.

Margolin, D. I., and Walker, J. A. Personal communication, 1981.

Margolin, D. I., Marcel, A. J., and Carlson, N. R. Common mechanisms in dysnomia and post-semantic surface dyslexia: Processing deficits and selective attention. In *Surface Dyslexia: Neuropsychological and Cognitive Studies of Phonological Reading,* edited by M. Coltheart. London: Lawrence Erlbaum Associates, 1985.

Marler, J. R., Tilley, B. C., Lu, M., Brott, T. G., Lyden, P. C., Grotta, J. C., Broderick, J. P., Levine, S. R., Frankel, M. P., Horowitz, S. H., Haley, E. C., Lewandowski, C. A., and Kwiatkowski, T. P. Early stroke treatment associated with better outcome: The NINDS rt-PA stroke study. *Neurology,* 2000, *55,* 1649–1655.

Marrocco, R. T., Witte, E. A., and Davidson, M. C. Arousal systems. *Current Opinion in Neurobiology,* 1994, *4,* 166–170.

Marshall, B. E., and Longnecker, D. E. General anesthetics. In *The Pharmacological Basis of Therapeutics,* edited by Goodman, L. S., Gilman, A., Rall, T. W., Nies, A. S., and Taylor, P. New York: Pergamon Press, 1990.

Marshall, J. C., and Newcombe, F. Patterns of paralexia: A psycholinguistic approach. *Journal of Psycholinguistic Research,* 1973, *2,* 175–199.

Marson, L. Central nervous system neurons identified after injection of pseudorabies virus into the rat clitoris. *Neuroscience Letters,* 1995, *190,* 41–44.

Marson, L., and McKenna, K. E. CNS cell groups involved in the control of the ishiocavernosus and bulbospongiosus muscles: A transneuronal tracing study using pseudorabies virus. *Journal of Comparative Neurology,* 1996, *374,* 161–179.

Martin, A., Wiggs, C. L., Ungerleider, L. G., and Haxby, J. V. Neural correlates of category-specific knowledge. *Nature,* 1996, *379,* 649–652.

Martin, P. R., White, A. J., Goodchild, A. K., Wilder, H. D., and Sefton, A. E. *European Journal of Neuroscience,* 1997, *9,* 1536–1541.

Martinez, M., Campion, D., Babron, M. C., and Clergetdarpous, F. Is a single mutation at the same locus responsible for all affected cases in a large Alzheimer pedigree (Fad4)? *Genetic Epidemiology,* 1993, *10,* 431–435.

Martin-Santos, R., Bulbena, A., Porta, M., Gago, J., Molina, L., and Duro, J. C. Association between joint hypermobility syndrome and panic disorder. *American Journal of Psychiatry,* 1998, *155,* 1578–1583.

Mas, M. Neurobiological correlates of masculine sexual behavior. *Neuroscience and Biobehavioral Reviews,* 1995, *19,* 261–277.

Masland, R. H. Neuronal diversity in the retina. *Current Opinion in Neurobiology,* 2001, *11,* 431–436.

Matsuda, L. A., Lolait, S. J., Brownstein, M. J., Young, A. C., and Bonner, T. I. Structure of a cannabinoid receptor and functional expression of the cloned cDNA. *Nature,* 1990, *346,* 561–564.

Matteo, S., and Rissman, E. F. Increased sexual activity during the midcycle portion of the human menstrual cycle. *Hormones and Behavior,* 1984, *18,* 249–255.

Matthews, D. B., Simson, P. E., and Best, P. J. Ethanol alters spatial processing of hippocampal place cells: A mechanism for impaired navigation when intoxicated. *Alcoholism: Clinical and Experimental Research,* 1996, *20,* 404–407.

Mawson, A. R. Anorexia nervosa and the regulation of intake: A review. *Psychological Medicine,* 1974, *4,* 289–308.

Mayer, D. J., Price, D. D., Rafii, A., and Barber, J. Acupuncture hypalgesia: Evidence for activation of a central control system as a mechanism of action. In *Advances in Pain Research and Therapy, Vol. 1,* edited by J. J. Bonica and D. Albe-Fessard. New York: Raven Press, 1976.

Mazur, A. Hormones, aggression, and dominance in humans. In *Hormones and Aggressive Behavior,* edited by B. B. Svare. New York: Plenum Press, 1983.

Mazur, A., and Lamb, T. Testosterone, status, and mood in human males. *Hormones and Behavior,* 1980, *14,* 236–246.

McCann, U. D., Wong, D. F., Yokoi, F., Villemagne, V., Dannls, R. F., and Ricaurte, G. A. Reduced striatal dopamine transporter density in abstinent methamphetamine and methcathinone users: Evidence from positron emission tomography studies with [^{11}C]WIN-35,428. *Journal of Neuroscience,* 1998, *18,* 8417–8422.

McCarley, R. W., and Hobson, J. A. The form of dreams and the biology of sleep. In *Handbook of Dreams: Research, Theory, and Applications,* edited by B. Wolman. New York: Van Nostrand Reinhold, 1979.

McCarthy, R. A., and Warrington, E. K. Evidence for modality-specific meaning systems in the brain. *Nature,* 1988, *334,* 428–435.

McCarthy, R. A., and Warrington, E. K. *Cognitive Neuropsychology: A Clinical Introduction.* San Diego: Academic Press, 1990.

McCaul, K. D., Gladue, B. A., and Joppa, M. Winning, losing, mood, and testosterone. *Hormones and Behavior,* 1992, *26,* 486–504.

McClintock, M. K. Menstrual synchrony and suppression. *Nature,* 1971, *229,* 244–245.

McClintock, M. K., and Adler, N. T. The role of the female during copulation in wild and domestic Norway rats *(Rattus norvegicus). Behaviour,* 1978, *67,* 67–96.

McCormick, D. A. Neurotransmitter actions in the thalamus and cerebral cortex. *Journal of Clinical Neurophysiology,* 1992, *9,* 212–223.

McEwen, B. S., and Sapolsky, R. M. Stress and cognitive function. *Current Biology,* 1995, *5,* 205–216.

McFarlane, A. C., Atchison, M., and Yehuda, R. The acute stress response following motor vehicle accidents and its relation to PTSD. *Annals of the New York Academy of Science,* 1997, *821,* 437–441.

McGinty, D. J., and Sterman, M. B. Sleep suppression after basal forebrain lesions in the cat. *Science,* 1968, *160,* 1253–1255.

McHugh, T. J., Blum, K. I., Tsien, J. Z., Tonegawa, S., and Wilson, M. A. Impaired hippocampal representation of space in CA1-specific NMDAR1 knockout mice. *Cell,* 1996, *87,* 1339–1349.

McIver, B., Connacher, A., Whittle, I., Baylis, P., and Thompson, C. Adipsic hypothalamic diabetes insipidus after clipping of anterior communicating artery aneurysm. *British Medical Journal,* 1991, *303,* 1465–1467.

McLaughlin, S. K., McKinnon, P. J., Robichon, A., Spickofsky, N., and Margolskee, R. F. Gustducin and transducin: A tale of 2 G-proteins. *CIBA Foundation Symposia,* 1993, *179,* 186–200.

Meesters, Y., Jansen, J. H. C., Beersma, D. G. M., Bouhuys, A. L., and Van den Hoofdakker, R. H. Light therapy for seasonal affective disorder. The effects of timing. *British Journal of Psychiatry,* 1995, *166,* 607–612.

Mehlman, P. T., Higley, J. D., Faucher, I., Lilly, A. A., Taub, D. M., Vickers, J., Suomi, S. J., and Linnoila, M. Correlation of CSF 5-HIAA concentration with sociality and the timing of emigration in free-ranging primates. *American Journal of Psychiatry,* 1995, *152,* 907–913.

Meijer, J. H., and Rietveld, W. J. Neurophysiology of the suprachiasmatic circadian pacemaker in rodents. *Physiological Reviews,* 1989, *69,* 671–707.

Mellet, E., Tzourio, N., Crivello, F., Jolio, M., Denis, M., and Mazoyer, B. Functional anatomy of spatial mental imagery generated from verbal instructions. *Journal of Neuroscience,* 1996, *16,* 6504–6512.

Melzak, R. Phantom limbs. *Scientific American,* 1992, *266(4),* 120–126.

Menco, B. P. M., Bruch, R. C., Dau, B., and Danho, W. Ultrastructural localization of olfactory transduction components: The G protein subunit G_{olf} and type III adenylyl cyclase. *Neuron,* 1992, *8,* 441–453.

Mercer, J. G., Hoggard, N., Williams, L. M., Lawrence, C. B., Hannah, L. T., Morgan, P. J., and Trayhurn, P. Coexpression of leptin receptor and preproneuropeptide Y mRNA in arcuate nucleus of mouse hypothalamus. *Journal of Neuroendocrinology,* 1996, *8,* 733–735.

Meredith, M. Chronic recording of vomeronasal pump activation in awake behaving hamsters. *Physiology and Behavior,* 1994, *56,* 345–354.

Meredith, M., and O'Connell, R. J. Efferent control of stimulus access to the hamster vomeronasal organ. *Journal of Physiology,* 1979, *286,* 301–316.

Mereu, G., Yoon, K.-W. P., Boi, V., Gessa, G. L., Naes, L., and Westfall, T. C. Preferential stimulation of ventral tegmental area dopaminergic neurons by nicotine. *European Journal of Pharmacology,* 1987, *141,* 395–400.

Mesches, M. H., Fleshner, M., Heman, K. L., Rose, G. M., and Diamond, D. M. Exposing rats to a predator blocks primed burst potentiation in the hippocampus *in vitro. Journal of Neuroscience,* 1999, *19,* RC18(1–5).

Mesulam, M.-M. Frontal cortex and behavior. *Annals of Neurology,* 1986, *19,* 320–325.

Meyer-Bahlburg, H. F. L. Psychoendocrine research on sexual orientation: Current status and future options. *Progress in Brain Research,* 1984, *63,* 375–398.

Mignot, E. Genetic and familial aspects of narcolepsy. *Neurology,* 1998, *50,* S16—S22.

Miller, M. T., and Strömland, K. Thalidomide embryopathy: An insight into autism. *Teratology,* 1993, *47,* 387–388.

Miller, N. E. Understanding the use of animals in behavioral research: Some critical issues. *Annals of the New York Academy of Sciences,* 1983, *406,* 113–118.

Milner, B. Memory and the temporal regions of the brain. In *Biology of Memory,* edited by K. H. Pribram and D. E. Broadbent. New York: Academic Press, 1970.

Milner, B., Corkin, S., and Teuber, H.-L. Further analysis of the hippocampal amnesic syndrome: 14-year follow-up study of H. M. *Neuropsychologia,* 1968, *6,* 317–338.

Mindus, P., Rasmussen, S. A., and Lindquist, C. Neurosurgical treatment for refractory obsessive-compulsive disorder: Implications for understanding frontal lobe function. *Journal of Neuropsychiatry and Clinical Neurosciences,* 1994, *6,* 467–477.

Mishkin, M. Visual mechanisms beyond the striate cortex. In *Frontiers in Physiological Psychology,* edited by R. W. Russell. New York: Academic Press, 1966.

Mitchell, J. E. Psychopharmacology of eating disorders. *Annals of the New York Academy of Sciences,* 1989, *575,* 41–49.

Mitler, M. M. Evaluation of treatment with stimulants in narcolepsy. *Sleep,* 1994, *17,* S103-S106.

Moghaddam, B., and Bunney, B. S. Differential effect of cocaine on extracellular dopamine levels in rat medial prefrontal cortex and nucleus accumbens: Comparison to amphetamine. *Synapse,* 1989, *4,* 156–161.

Moldin, S. O., Reich, T., and Rice, J. P. Current perspectives on the genetics of unipolar depression. *Behavioral Genetics,* 1991, *21,* 211–242.

Mollon, J. D. "Tho' she kneel'd in that place where they grew . . . ": The uses and origins of primate colour vision. *Journal of Experimental Biology,* 1989, *146,* 21–38.

Moltz, H., Lubin, M., Leon, M., and Numan, M. Hormonal induction of maternal behavior in the ovariectomized nulliparous rat. *Physiology and Behavior,* 1970, *5,* 1373–1377.

Mombaerts, P. Molecular biology of odorant receptors in vertebrates. *Annual Review of Neuroscience,* 1999, *22,* 487–510.

Money, J., and Ehrhardt, A. *Man & Woman, Boy & Girl.* Baltimore: Johns Hopkins University Press, 1972.

Money, J., Schwartz, M., and Lewis, V. G. Adult erotosexual status and fetal hormonal masculinization and demasculinization: 46,XX congenital virilizing adrenal hyperplasia and 46,XY androgen-insensitivity syndrome compared. *Psychoneuroendocrinology,* 1984, *9,* 405–414.

Monsonego, A., and Weiner, H. L. Immunotherapeutic approaches to Alzheimer's disease. *Science,* 2003, *302,* 834–838.

Montague, C. T., Farooqi, I. S., Whitehead, J. P., Soos, M. A., Rau, H., Wareham, N. J., Sewter, C. P., Digby, J. E., Mohammed, S. N., Hurst, J. A., Cheetham, C. H., Earley, A. R., Barnett, A. H., Prins, J. B., and O'Rahilly, S. Congenital leptin deficiency is associated with severe early-onset obesity in humans. *Nature,* 1997, *387,* 903–908.

Moore, G. J., Bebchuk, J. M., Wilds, I. B., Chen, G., and Manji, H. K. Lithium-induced increase in human brain grey matter. *Lancet,* 2000, *356,* 1241–1242.

Moore, R. Y. Neural control of the pineal gland. *Behavioural Brain Research,* 1995, *73,* 125–130.

Moore, R. Y., and Eichler, V. B. Loss of a circadian adrenal corticosterone rhythm following suprachiasmatic lesions in the rat. *Brain Research,* 1972, *42,* 201–206.

Moore, R. Y., Card, J. P., and Riley, J. N. The suprachiasmatic hypothalamic nucleus: Neuronal ultrastructure. *Neuroscience Abstracts,* 1980, *6,* 758.

Morales, F. R., Boxer, P. A., and Chase, M. H. Behavioral state-specific inhibitory postsynaptic potentials impinge on cat lumbar motoneurons during active sleep. *Experimental Neurology,* 1987, *98,* 418–435.

Moran, T. H., Shnayder, L., Hostetler, A. M., and McHugh, P. R. Pylorectomy reduces the satiety action of cholecystokinin. *American Journal of Physiology,* 1989, *255,* R1059—R1063.

Mori, E., Ikeda, M., Hirono, N., Kitagaki, H., Imamura, T., and Shimomura, T. Amygdalar volume and emotional memory in Alzheimer's disease. *American Journal of Psychiatry,* 1999, *156,* 216–222.

Morris, J. S., Frith, C. D., Perrett, D. I., Rowland, D., Young, A. W., Calder, A. J., and Dolan, R. J. A differential neural response in the human amygdala to fearful and happy facial expressions. *Nature,* 1996, *383,* 812–815.

Morris, N. M., Udry, J. R., Khan-Dawood, F., and Dawood, M. Y. Marital sex frequency and midcycle female testosterone. *Archives of Sexual Behavior,* 1987, *16,* 27–37.

Morris, R. G. M., Garrud, P., Rawlins, J. N. P., and O'Keefe, J. Place navigation impaired in rats with hippocampal lesions. *Nature,* 1982, *297,* 681–683.

Moscovitch, M., and Olds, J. Asymmetries in emotional facial expressions and their possible relation to hemispheric specialization. *Neuropsychologia,* 1982, *20,* 71–81.

Moscovitch, M., Kapur, S., Koehler, S., and Houle, S. Distinct neural correlates of visual long-term memory for spatial location and object identity: A positron emission tomography study in humans. *Proceedings of the National Academy of Sciences,* 1995, *92,* 3721–3725.

Moscovitch, M., Winocur, G., and Behrmann, M. What is special about face recognition? Nineteen experiments on a person with visual object agnosia and dyslexia but normal face recognition. *Journal of Cognitive Neuroscience,* 1997, *9,* 555–604.

Mukhametov, L. M. Sleep in marine mammals. In *Sleep Mechanisms,* edited by A. A. Borbély and J. L. Valatx. Munich: Springer-Verlag, 1984.

Munro, J. F., Stewart, I. C., Seidelin, P. H., Mackenzie, H. S., and Dewhurst, N. E. Mechanical treatment for obesity. *Annals of the New York Academy of Sciences,* 1987, *499,* 305–312.

Murphy, A. Z., and Hoffman, G. E. Distribution of gonadal steroid receptor-containing neurons in the preoptic-periaqueductal gray-brainstem pathway: A potential circuit for the initiation of male sexual behavior. *Journal of Comparative Neurology,* 2001, *438,* 191–212.

Murray, A. M., Hyde, T. M., Knable, M. B., Herman, M. M., Bigelow, L. B., Carter, J. M., Weinberger, D. R., and Kleinman, J. E. Distribution of putative D4 dopamine receptors in postmortem striatum from patients with schizophrenia. *Journal of Neuroscience,* 1995, *15,* 2186–2191.

Murray, A. M., Ryoo, H., Gurevich, E., and Joyce, J. N. Localization of dopamine D_3 receptors to mesolimbic and D_2 receptors to mesostriatal regions of human forebrain. *Proceedings of the National Academy of Sciences, USA,* 1994, *91,* 11271–11275.

Murray, C. J., and Lopez, A. D. Alternative projections of mortality and disability by cause 1990–2020: Global Burden of Disease Study. *Lancet,* 1997, *349,* 180–183.

Must, A., Spadano, J., Coakley, E. H., Field, A. E., Colditz, G., and Dietz, W. H. The disease burden associated with overweight and obesity. *Journal of the American Medical Association,* 1999, *282,* 1523–1529.

Myers, R. D., Wooten, M. H., Ames, C. D., and Nyce, J. W. Anorexic action of a new potential neuropeptide Y antagonist [D-Tyr27,36,D-Thr32]-NPY (27–36) infused into the hypothalamus of the rat. *Brain Research Bulletin,* 1995, *37,* 237–245.

Nadeau, S. E. Impaired grammar with normal fluency and phonology. *Brain,* 1988, *111,* 1111–1137.

Nader, K., Majidishad, P., Amorapanth, P., and LeDoux, J. E. Damage to the lateral and central, but not other, amygdaloid nuclei prevents the acquisition of auditory fear conditioning. *Learning and Memory,* 2001, *8,* 156–163.

Naeser, M. A., Palumbo, C. L., Helm-Estabrooks, N., Stiassny-Eder, D., and Albert, M. L. Severe nonfluency in aphasia: Role of the medial subcallosal fasciculus and other white matter pathways in recovery of spontaneous speech. *Brain,* 1989, *112,* 1–38.

Nafe, J. P., and Wagoner, K. S. The nature of pressure adaptation. *Journal of General Psychology,* 1941, *25,* 323–351.

Nakahara, D., Ozaki, N., Miura, Y., Miura, H., and Nagatsu, T. Increased dopamine and serotonin metabolism in rat nucleus accumbens produced by intracranial self-stimulation of medial forebrain bundle as measured by in vivo microdialysis. *Brain Research,* 1989, *495,* 178–181.

Nakamura, T., and Gold, G. A cyclic nucleotide-gated conductance in olfactory receptor cilia. *Nature,* 1987, *325,* 442–444.

Nakazato, M., Mauakami, N., Date, Y., Kojima, M., Matsuo, H., Kangawa, K., and Matsukura, S. A role for ghrelin in the central regulation of feeding. *Nature,* 2001, *409,* 194–198.

Nambu, T., Sakurai, T., Mizukami, K., Hosoya, Y., Yanagisawa, M., and Goto, K. Distribution of orexin neurons in the adult rat brain. *Brain Research,* 1999, *827,* 243–260.

Naranjo, C. A., Poulos, C. X., Bremner, K. E., and Lanctot, K. L. Citalopram decreases desirability, liking, and consumption of alcohol in alcohol-dependent drinkers. *Clinical Pharmacology and Therapeutics,* 1992, *51,* 729–739.

Nathans, J., Piantanida, T. P., Eddy, R. L., Shows, T. B., and Hogness, D. S. Molecular genetics of inherited variation in human color vision. Science, 1986, 232, 203–210.

Nauta, W. J. H. Hypothalamic regulation of sleep in rats: Experimental study. *Journal of Neurophysiology,* 1946, *9,* 285–316.

Nauta, W. J. H. Some efferent connections of the prefrontal cortex in the monkey. In *The Frontal Granular Cortex and Behavior,* edited by J. M. Warren and K. Akert. New York: McGraw-Hill, 1964.

Navia, B. A., Dafni, U., Simpson, D., Tucker, T., Singer, E., McArthur, J. C., Yiannoutsos, C., Zaborski, L., and Lipton, S. A. A phase I/II trial of nimodipine for HIV-related neurologic complications. *Neurology,* 1998, *51,* 221–228.

Nef, P., Hermansborgmeyer, I., Artierespin, H., Beasley, L., Dionne, V. E., and Heinemann, S. F. Spatial pattern of receptor expression in the olfactory epithelium. *Proceedings of the National Academy of Sciences (USA),* 1992, *89,* 8948–8952.

New, A. S., Hazlett, E. A., Buchsbaum, M. S., Goodman, M., Reynolds, D., Mitropoulou, V., Sprung, L., Shaw, R. B., Koenigsberg, H., Platholi, J., Silverman, J., and Siever, L. J. Blunted prefrontal cortical 18fluorodeoxyglucose positron emission tomography response to meta-chlorophenylpiperazine in impulsive aggression. *Archives of General Psychiatry,* 2002, *59,* 621–629.

Nicholl, C. S., and Russell, R. M. Analysis of animal rights literature reveals the underlying motives of the movement: Ammunition for counter offensive by scientists. *Endocrinology,* 1990, *127,* 985–989.

Nicholls, P., and Wenner, C. E. Release of respiratory control by uncouplers: the question of stoichiometry. *Archives of Biochemistry and Biophysics,* 1972, *151,* 206–215.

Nicolas, A., Petit, D., Rompre, S., and Montplaisir, J. Sleep spindle characteristics in healthy subjects of different age groups. *Clinical Neurophysiology,* 2001, *112,* 521–527.

Nicoll, J. A. R., Wilkinson, D., Holmes, C., Steart, P., Markham, H., and Weller, R. O. Neuropathology of human Alzheimer disease after immunization with amyloid-ß peptide: A case report. *Nature Medicine,* 2003, *9,* 448–452.

Nishino, S., Ripley, B., Overeem, S., Lammers, G. J., and Mignot, E. Hypocretin (orexin) deficiency in human narcolepsy. *Lancet,* 2000, *355,* 39–40.

Nonogaki, K., Strack, A. M., Dallman, M. F., and Tecott, L. H. Leptin-independent hyperphagia and type 2 diabetes in mice with a mutated serotonin 5-HT_{2C} receptor gene. *Nature Medicine,* 1998, *4,* 1152–1156.

Norgren, R., and Grill, H. Brain-stem control of ingestive behavior. In *The Physiological Mechanisms of Motivation,* edited by D. W. Pfaff. New York: Springer-Verlag, 1982.

Novin, D., VanderWeele, D. A., and Rezek, M. Hepatic-portal 2-deoxy-D-glucose infusion causes eating: Evidence for peripheral glucoreceptors. *Science,* 1973, *181,* 858–860.

Novotny, M. V., Ma, W., Wiesler, D., and Zidek, L. Positive identification of the puberty-accelerating pheromone of the house mouse: The volatile ligands associating with the major urinary protein. *Proceedings of the Royal Society of London [B],* 1999, *266,* 2017–2022.

Numan, M. Medial preoptic area and maternal behavior in the female rat. *Journal of Comparative and Physiological Psychology,* 1974, *87,* 746–759.

Numan, M., and Numan, M. J. Projection sites of medial preoptic area and ventral bed nucleus of the stria terminalis neurons that express Fos during maternal behavior in female rats. *Journal of Neuroendocrinology,* 1997, *9,* 369–384.

Numan, M., and Smith, H. G. Maternal behavior in rats: Evidence for the involvement of preoptic projections to the ventral tegmental area. *Behavioral Neuroscience,* 1984, *98,* 712–727.

Numan, M., Rosenblatt, J. S., and Komisaruk, B. R. Medial preoptic area and onset of maternal behavior in the rat. *Journal of Comparative and Physiological Psychology,* 1977, *91,* 146–164.

Nutt, D. J., Glue, P., Lawson, C. W., and Wilson, S. Flumazenil provocation of panic attacks: Evidence for altered benzodiazepine receptor sensitivity in panic disorders. *Archives of General Psychiatry,* 1990, *47,* 917–925.

Oaknin, S., Rodriguez del Castillo, A., Guerra, M., Battaner, E., and Mas, M. Change in forebrain Na,K-ATPase activity and serum hormone levels during sexual behavior in male rats. *Physiology and Behavior,* 1989, *45,* 407–410.

Obler, L. K., and Gjerlow, K. *Language and the Brain.* Cambridge, England: Cambridge University Press, 1999.

O'Brien, C. P., Volpicelli, L. A., and Volpicelli, J. R. Naltrexone in the treatment of alcoholism: A clinical review. *Alcohol,* 1996, *13,* 35–39.

O'Callaghan, E., Gibson, T., Colohan, H. A., Buckley, P., Walshe, D. G., Larkin, C., and Waddington, J. L. Risk of schizophrenia in adults born after obstetric complications and their association with early onset of illness: A controlled study. *British Medical Journal,* 1992, *305,* 1256–1259.

O'Carroll, R., Shapiro, C., and Bancroft, J. Androgens, behavior and nocturnal erection in hypogonadal men: The effects of varying the replacement dose. *Clinical Endocrinology,* 1985, *23,* 527–538.

O'Dell, T. J., Hawkins, R. D., Kandel, E. R., and Arancio, O. Tests of the roles of two diffusible substances in long-term potentiation: Evidence for nitric oxide as a possible early retrograde messenger. *Proceedings of the National Academy of Sciences, USA,* 1991, *88,* 11285–11289.

Ogawa, S., Olazabal, U. E., Parhar, I. S., and Pfaff, D. W. Effects of intrahypothalamic administration of antisense DNA for progesterone receptor mRNA on reproductive behavior and progesterone receptor immunoreactivity in female rat. *Journal of Neuroscience,* 1994, *14,* 1766–1774.

O'Keefe, J., and Bouma, H. Complex sensory properties of certain amygadala units in the freely moving cat. *Experimental Neurology,* 1969, *23,* 384–398.

O'Keefe, J., and Dostrovsky, T. The hippocampus as a spatial map: Preliminary evidence from unit activity in the freely moving rat. *Brain Research,* 1971, *34,* 171–175.

Olausson, H., Lamarre, Y., Backlund, H., Morin, C., Wallin, B. G., Starck, G., Ekholm, S., Strigo, I., Worsley, K., Vallbo, Å. B., Bushnell, M. C. Unmyelinated tactile afferents signal touch and project to insular cortex. *Nature Neuroscience,* 2002, *5,* 900–904.

Olds, M. E., and Fobes, J. L. The central basis of motivation: Intracranial self-stimulation studies. *Annual Review of Psychology,* 1981, *32,* 523–574.

Oleksenko, A. I., Mukhametov, L. M., Polyakova, I. G., Supin, A. Y., and Kovalzon, V. M. Unihemispheric sleep deprivation in bottlenose dolphins. *Journal of Sleep Research,* 1992, *1,* 40–44.

O'Mara, S. M., Rolls, E. T., Berthoz, A., and Kesner, R. P. Neurons responding to whole-body motion in the primate hippocampus. *Journal of Neuroscience,* 1994, *14,* 6511–6523.

Ossebaard, C. A., Polet, I. A., and Smith, D. V. Amiloride effects on taste quality: Comparison of single and multiple response category procedures. *Chemical Senses,* 1997, *22,* 267–275.

Otsuki, M., Soma, Y., Arihiro, S., Watanabe, Y., Moriwaki, H., and Naritomi, H. Dystypia: Isolated typing impairment without aphasia, apraxia or visuospatial impairment. *European Neurology,* 2002, *47,* 136–140.

Owen, A. M., James, M., Leigh, P. N., Summers, B. A., Marsden, C. D., Quinn, N. P., Lange, K. W., and Robbins, T. W. Frontostriatal cognitive deficits at different stages of Parkinson's disease. *Brain,* 1992, *115,* 1727–1751.

Ozata, M., Ozdemir, I. C., and Licinio, J. Human leptin deficiency caused by a missense mutation: Multiple endocrine defects, decreased sympathetic tone, and immune system dysfunction indicate new targets for leptin action, greater central than peripheral resistance to the effects of leptin, and spontaneous correction of leptin-mediated defects. *Journal of Clinical Endocrinology and Metabolism,* 1999, *84,* 3686–3695.

Packard, M. G., and Teather, L. A. Double dissociation of hippocampal and dorsal-striatal memory systems by posttraining intracerebral injections of 2-amino-5-phosphonopentanoic acid. *Behavioral Neuroscience,* 1997, *111,* 543–551.

Pallast, E. G. M., Jongbloet, P. H., Straatman, H. M., and Zeilhuis, G. A. Excess of seasonality of births among patients with schizophrenia and seasonal ovopathy. *Schizophrenia Bulletin,* 1994, *20,* 269–276.

Papadimitriou, G. N., Christodoulou, G. N., Katsouyanni, K., and Stefanis, C. N. Therapy and prevention of affective illness by total sleep deprivation. *Journal of the Affective Disorders,* 1993, *27,* 107–116.

Papez, J. W. A proposed mechanism of emotion. *Archives of Neurology and Psychiatry,* 1937, *38,* 725–744.

Pascoe, J. P., and Kapp, B. S. Electrophysiological characteristics of amygdaloid central nucleus neurons during Pavlovian fear conditioning in the rabbit. *Behavioural Brain Research,* 1985, *16,* 117–133.

Pattatucci, A. M. L., and Hamer, D. H. Development and familiality of sexual orientation in females. *Behavior Genetics,* 1995, *25,* 407–420.

Patterson, K., and Ralph, M. A. L. Selective disorders of reading? *Current Opinion in Neurobiology,* 1999, *9,* 235–239.

Paulesu, E., Démonet, J.-F., Fazio, F., McCrory, E., Chanoine, V., Brunswick, N., Cappa, S. F., Cossu, G., Habib, M., Frith, C. D., and Frith, U. *Science,* 2001, *291,* 2165–2167.

Pauls, D. L., and Leckman, J. F. The inheritance of Gilles de la Tourette's syndrome and associated behaviors. *New England Journal of Medicine,* 1986, *315,* 993–997.

Pauls, D. L., Towbin, K. E., Leckman, J. F., Zahner, G. E., and Cohen, D. J. Gilles de la Tourette's syndrome and obsessive-compulsive disorder. Evidence supporting a genetic relationship. *Archives of General Psychiatry,* 1986, *43,* 1180–1182.

Peck, B. K., and Vanderwolf, C. H. Effects of raphe stimulation on hippocampal and neocortical activity and behaviour. *Brain Research,* 1991, *568,* 244–252.

Pedersen-Bjergaard, U., Host, U., Kelbaek, H., Schifter, S., Rehfeld, J. F., Faber, J., and Christensen, N. J. Influence of meal composition on postprandial peripheral plasma concentrations of vasoactive peptides in man. *Scandanavian Journal of Clinical and Laboratory Investigation,* 1996, *56,* 497–503.

Pelleymounter, M. A., Cullen, M. J., Baker, M. B., Hecht, R., Winters, D., Boone, T., and Collins, F. Effects of the obese gene product on body weight regulation in ob/ob mice. *Science,* 1995, *269,* 540–543.

Penfield, W., and Perot, P. The brain's record of auditory and visual experience: A final summary and discussion. *Brain,* 1963, *86,* 595–697.

Pennington, B. F., Gilger, J. W., Pauls, D., Smith, S. A., Smith, S. D., and DeFries, J. C. Evidence for major gene transmission of developmental dyslexia. *Journal of the American Medical Association,* 1991, *266,* 1527–1534.

Perlmutter, S. J., Garvey, M. A., Castellanos, X., Mittleman, B. B., Giedd, J., Rapoport, J. L., and Swedo, S. E. A case of pediatric autoimmune neuropsychiatric disorders associated with streptococcal infections. *American Journal of Psychiatry,* 1998, *155,* 1592–1598.

Pert, C. B., Snowman, A. M., and Snyder, S. H. Localization of opiate receptor binding in presynaptic membranes of rat brain. *Brain Research,* 1974, *70,* 184–188.

Petersen, S. E., Fox, P. T., Snyder, A. Z., and Raichle, M. E. Activation of extrastriate and frontal cortical areas by visual words and word-like stimuli. *Science,* 1990, *249,* 1041–1044.

Petit, H. O., and Justice, J. B. Dopamine in the nucleus accumbens during cocaine self-administration as studied by in vivo microdialysis. *Pharmacology, Biochemistry and Behavior,* 1989, *23,* 899–904.

Petre-Quadens, O., and De Lee, C. Eye movement frequencies and related paradoxical sleep cycles: Developmental changes. *Chronobiologia,* 1974, *1,* 347–355.

Petryshen, T. L., Kaplan, B. J., Fu, L. M., de French, N. S., Tobias, R., Hughes, M., and Leigh, F. L. Evidence for a susceptibility locus on chromosome 6q influencing phonological coding dyslexia. *American Journal of Medical Genetics,* 2001, *105,* 507–517.

Peuskens, H., Sunaert, S., Dupont, P., Van Hecke, P., and Orban, G. A. Human brain regions involved in heading estimation. *Journal of Neuroscience,* 2001, *21,* 2451–2461.

Pfaff, D. W., and Keiner, M. Atlas of estradiol-concentrating cells in the central nervous system of the female rat. *Journal of Comparative Neurology,* 1973, *151,* 121–158.

Pfaff, D. W., and Sakuma, Y. Deficit in the lordosis reflex of female rats caused by lesions in the ventromedial nucleus of the hypothalamus. *Journal of Physiology,* 1979, *288,* 203–210.

Pfaus, J. G., Kleopoulos, S. P., Mobbs, C. V., Gibbs, R. B., and Pfaff, D. W. Sexual stimulation activates c-fos within estrogen-concentrating regions of the female rat forebrain. *Brain Research,* 1993, *624,* 253–267.

Phiel, C. J., and Klein, P. S. Molecular targets of lithium action. *Annual Review of Pharmacology and Toxicology,* 2001, *41,* 789–813.

Phillips, D. P., and Farmer, M. E. Acquired word deafness, and the temporal grain of sound representation in the primary auditory cortex. *Behavioural Brain Research,* 1990, *40,* 85–94.

Phillips, M. I., and Felix, D. Specific angiotensin II receptive neurons in the cat subfornical organ. *Brain Research,* 1976, *109,* 531–540.

Phillips, M. L., Young, A. W., Scott, S. K., Calder, A. J., Andrew, G., Giampietro, V., Williams, S. C. R., Bullmore, E. T., Brammer, M., and Gray, J. A. Neural responses to facial and vocal expressions of fear and disgust. *Proceedings of the Royal Society of London [B],* 1998, *265,* 1809–1817.

Phillips, R. G., and LeDoux, J. E. Differential contribution of amygdala and hippocampus to cued and contextual fear conditioning. *Behavioral Neuroscience,* 1992, *106,* 274–285.

Piccirillo, J. F., Duntley, S., and Schotland, H. Obstructive sleep apnea. *Journal of the American Medical Association,* 2000, *284,* 1492–1494.

Pickar, D. Prospects for pharmacotherapy of schizophrenia. *Lancet,* 1995, *345,* 557–562.

Pickles, J. O., and Corey, D. P. Mechanoelectrical transduction by hair cells. *Trends in Neuroscience,* 1992, *15,* 254–259.

Pierce, K., Müller, R.-A., Ambrose, J., Allen, G., and Courchesne, E. Face processing occurs outside the fusiform "face area" in autism: Evidence from functional MRI. *Brain,* 2001, *124,* 2059–2073.

Pijl, S., and Schwarz, D. W. F. Intonation of musical intervals by musical intervals by deaf subjects stimulated with single bipolar cochlear implant electrodes. *Hearing Research,* 1995a, *89,* 203–211.

Pijl, S., and Schwartz, D. W. F. Melody recognition and musical interval perception by deaf subjects stimulated with electrical pulse trains through single cochlear implant electrodes. *Journal of the Acoustical Society of America,* 1995b, *98,* 886–895.

Pilleri, G. The blind Indus dolphin, *Platanista indi. Endeavours,* 1979, *3,* 48–56.

Pitkänen, A., Savander, V., and LeDoux, J. E. Organization of intra-amygdaloid circuits: An emerging framework for understanding functions of the amygdala. *Trends in Neuroscience,* 1997, *20,* 517–523.

Pleim, E. T., and Barfield, R. J. Progesterone versus estrogen facilitation of female sexual behavior by intracranial administration to female rats. *Hormones and Behavior,* 1988, *22,* 150–159.

Poggio, G. F., and Poggio, T. The analysis of stereopsis. *Annual Review of Neuroscience,* 1984, *7,* 379–412.

Polymeropoulos, M. H., Higgins, J. J., Golbe, L. I., Johnson, W. G., Ide, S. E., Di Iorio, G., Sanges, G., Stenroos, E. S., Pho, L. T., Schaffer, A. A., Lazzarini, A. M., Nussbaum, R. L., and Duvoisin, R. C. Mapping of a gene for Parkinson's disease to chromosome 4q21-q23. *Science,* 1996, *274,* 1197–1199.

Pomp, D., and Nielsen, M. K. Quantitative genetics of energy balance: Lessons from animal models. *Obesity Research,* 1999, *7,* 106–110.

Porkka-Heiskanen, T., Strecker, R. E., and McCarley, R. W. Brain site-specificity of extracellular adenosine concentration changes during sleep deprivation and spontaneous sleep: An *in vivo* microdialysis study. *Neuroscience,* 2000, *99,* 507–517.

Portas, C. M., Thakkar, M., Rainnie, D., and McCarley, R. W. Microdialysis perfusion of 8-hydroxy-2-(di-n-propylamino)tetralin (8-OH-DPAT) in the dorsal raphe nucleus decreases serotonin release and increases rapid eye movement sleep in the freely moving cat. *Journal of Neuroscience,* 1996, *16,* 2820–2828.

Post, R. M., Ballenger, J. C., Uhde, T., and Bunney, W. Efficacy of carbamazepine in manic-depressive illness: Implications for underlying mechanisms. In *Neurobiology of Mood Disorders,* edited by R. M. Post and C. Ballenger. Baltimore, Md.: Williams and Wilkins, 1984.

Powers, J. B., and Winans, S. S. Vomeronasal organ: Critical role in mediating sexual behavior of the male hamster. *Science,* 1975, *187,* 961–963.

Price, C. The functional anatomy of word comprehension and production. *Trends in Cognitive Science,* 1998, *2,* 281–288.

Price, D. B. Psychological and neural mechanisms of the affective dimension of pain. *Science,* 2000, *288,* 1769–1772.

Price, D. L., and Sisodia, S. S. Mutant genes in familial Alzheimer's disease and transgenic models. *Annual Review of Neuroscience,* 1998, *21,* 479–505.

Price, L. H., and Heninger, G. R. Drug therapy: Lithium in the treatment of mood disorders. *New England Journal of Medicine,* 1994, *331,* 591–598.

Price, R. A., and Gottesman, I. I. Body fat in identical twins reared apart: Roles for genes and environment. *Behavioral Genetics,* 1991, *21,* 1–7.

Pritchard, T. C., Hamilton, R. B., Morse, J. R., and Norgren, R. Projections of thalamic gustatory and lingual areas in the monkey, *Macaca fascicularis. Journal of Comparative Neurology,* 1986, *244,* 213–228.

Provencio, I., Rodriguez, I. R., Jiang, G., Hayes, W. P., Moreira, E. F., and Rollag, M. D. A novel human opsin in the inner retinal *Journal of Neuroscience,* 2000, *20,* 600–605.

Proverbio, A. M., Lilli, S., Semenza, C., and Zani, A. ERP indexes of functional differences in brain activation during proper and common names retrieval. *Neuropsychologia,* 2001, *39,* 815–827.

Prusiner, S. B. Novel proteinaceous infectious particles cause scrapie. *Science,* 1982, *216,* 136–144.

Pulvermüller, F. Words in the brain's language. *Behavioral and Brain Sciences,* 1999, *22,* 253–279; Peer commentary and author's replies, pp. 280–336.

Pulvermüller, F., Harle, M., and Hummel, F. Neurophysiological distinction of verb categories. *Neuroreport,* 2000, *11,* 2789–2793.

Qu, D., Ludwig, D. S., Gammeltoft, S., Piper, M., Pelleymounter, M. A., Cullen, M. J., Mathes, W. F., Przypek, R., Kanarek, R., and Maratos-Flier, E. A role for melanin concentrating hormone in the central regulation of feeding behaviour. *Nature,* 1996, *380,* 243–247.

Quillen, E. W., Keil, L. C., and Reid, I. A. Effects of baroreceptor denervation on endocrine and drinking responses to caval constriction in dogs. *American Journal of Physiology,* 1990, *259,* R618-R626.

Quirk, G. J., Repa, J. C., and LeDoux, J. E. Fear conditioning enhances short-latency auditory responses of lateral amygdala neurons: Parallel recordings in the freely behaving rat. *Neuron,* 1995, *15,* 1029–1039.

Raine, A., Lencz, T., Bihrle, S., LaCasse, L., and Colletti, P. Reduced prefrontal gray matter volume and reduced autonomic activity in antisocial personality disorder. *Archives of General Psychiatry,* 2002, *57,* 119–127.

Raine, A., Meloy, J. R., Bihrle, S., Stoddard, J., LaCasse, L., and Buchsbaum, M. S. Reduced prefrontal and increased subcortical brain functioning assessed using positron emission tomography in predatory and affective murderers. *Behavioral Science and the Law,* 1998, *16,* 319–332.

Rainville, P., Duncan, G. H., Price, D. D., Carrier, B., and Bushnell, M. C. Pain affect encoded in human anterior cingulate but not somatosensory cortex. *Science,* 1997, *277,* 968–971.

Rakic, P. Mode of cell migration to the superficial layers of fetal monkey neocortex. *Journal of Comparative Neurology,* 1972, *145,* 61–83.

Rakic, P. Specification of cerebral cortical areas. *Science,* 1988, *241,* 170–176.

Raleigh, M. J., McGuire, M. T., Brammer, G. L., Pollack, D. B., and Yuwiler, A. Serotonergic mechanisms promote dominance acquisition in adult male vervet monkeys. *Brain Research,* 1991, *559,* 181–190.

Ralph, M. R., and Lehman, M. N. Transplantation: A new tool in the analysis of the mammalian hypothalamic circadian pacemaker. *Trends in Neuroscience,* 1991, *14,* 362–366.

Ramirez, I. Why do sugars taste good? *Neuroscience and Biobehavioral Reviews,* 1990, *14,* 125–134.

Rapin, I. Autistic regression and disintegrative disorder: How important the role of epilepsy? *Seminars in Pediatric Neurology,* 1995, *2,* 278–285.

Rapin, I. Autism in search of a home in the brain. *Neurology,* 1999, *52,* 902–904.

Rapoport, J. L. Recent advances in obsessive-compulsive disorder. *Neuropsychopharmacology,* 1991, *5,* 1–10.

Rapoport, J. L., Ryland, D. H., and Kriete, M. Drug treatment of canine acral lick: An animal model of obsessive-compulsive disorder. *Archives of General Psychiatry,* 1992, *49,* 517–521.

Rasmusson, D. D., Clow, K., and Szerb, J. C. Modification of neocortical acetylcholine release and electroencephalogram desynchronization due to brain stem stimulation by drugs applied to the basal forebrain. *Neuroscience,* 1994, *60,* 665–677.

Ratcliff, G., and Newcombe, F. Object recognition: Some deductions from the clinical evidence. In *Normality and Pathology in Cognitive Functions,* edited by A. W. Ellis. London: Academic Press, 1982.

Ratnasuriya, R. H., Eisler, I., Szmukler, G. I., and Russell, G. F. M. Anorexia nervosa: Outcome and prognostic factors after 20 years. *British Journal of Psychiatry,* 1991, *158,* 495–502.

Rauschecker, J. P., and Tian, B. Mechanisms and streams for processing of "what" and "where" in auditory cortex. *Proceedings of the National Academy of Science (USA),* 2000, *97,* 11800–11806.

Ravussin, E., Valencia, M. E., Esparza, J., Bennett, P. H., Schulz, L. O. Effects of a traditional lifestyle on obesity in Pima Indians. *Diabetes Care,* 1994, *17,* 1067–1074.

Reber, P. J., and Squire, L. R. Encapsulation of implicit and explicit memory in sequence learning. *Journal of Cognitive Neuroscience,* 1998, *10,* 248–263.

Recer, P. Study: English is a factor in dyslexia. Washington, DC: Associated Press, 16 March 2001.

Reed, C. L., Caselli, R. J., and Farah, M. J. Tactile agnosia: Underlying impairment and implications for normal tactile object recognition. *Brain,* 1996, *119,* 875–888.

Regan, B. C., Julliot, C., Simmen, B., Vienot, F., Charles-Dominique, P., and Mollon, J. D. Fruits, foliage and the evolution of primate colour vision. *Philosophical Transactions of the Royal Society of London [B],* 2001, *356,* 229–283.

Reid, L. D. Endogenous opioids and alcohol dependence: Opioid alkaloids and the propensity to drink alcoholic beverages. *Alcohol,* 1996, *13,* 5–11.

Rempel-Clower, N. L., Zola, S. M., Squire, L. R., and Amaral, D. G. Three cases of enduring memory impairment after bilateral damage limited to the hippocampal formation. *Journal of Neuroscience,* 1996, *16,* 5233–5255.

Reppert, S. M., and Weaver, D. R. Molecular analysis of mammalian circadian rhythms. *Annual Review of Physiology,* 2001, *63,* 647–676.

Resnick, H. S., Yehuda, R., Pitman, R. K., and Foy, D. W. Effect of previous trauma on acute plasma cortisol level following rape. *American Journal of Psychiatry,* 1995, *152,* 1675–1677.

Ressler, K. J., Sullivan, S. L., and Buck, L. A molecular dissection of spatial patterning in the olfactory system. *Current Opinion in Neurobiology,* 1994a, *4,* 588–596.

Ressler, K. J., Sullivan, S. L., and Buck, L. Information coding in the olfactory system: Evidence for a stereotyped and highly organized epitope map in the olfactory bulb. *Cell,* 1994b, *79,* 1245–1255.

Rhees, R. W., Shryne, J. E., and Gorski, R. A. Termination of the hormone-sensitive period for differentiation of the sexually dimorphic nucleus of the preoptic area in male and female rats. *Developmental Brain Research,* 1990, *52,* 17–23.

Riemann, D., Berger, M., and Voderholzer, U. Sleep and depression—Results from psychobiological studies: An overview. *Biological Psychiatry,* 2001, *57,* 67–103.

Riemann, D., König, A., Hohagen, F., Kiemen, A., Voderholzer, U., Backhaus, J., Bunz, J., Wesiak, B., Hermie, L., and Berger, M. How to preserve the antidepressive effect of sleep deprivation: A comparison of sleep phase advance and sleep phase delay. *European Archives of Psychiatry and Clinical Neuroscience,* 1999, *249,* 231–237.

Riemann, D., Wiegand, M., and Berger, M. Are there predictors for sleep deprivation response in depressive patients? *Biological Psychiatry,* 1991, *29,* 707–710.

Ritter, R. C., Brenner, L., and Yox, D. P. Participation of vagal sensory neurons in putative satiety signals from the upper gastrointestinal tract. In *Neuroanatomy and Physiology of Abdominal Vagal Afferents,* edited by S. Ritter, R. C. Ritter, and C. D. Barnes. Boca Raton, Fla.: CRC Press, 1992.

Ritter, R. C., Slusser, P. G., and Stone, S. Glucoreceptors controlling feeding and blood glucose: Location in the hindbrain. *Science,* 1981, *213,* 451–453.

Ritter, S., and Taylor, J. S. Vagal sensory neurons are required for lipoprivic but not glucoprivic feeding in rats. *American Journal of Physiology,* 1990, *258,* R1395-R1401.

Robbins, L. N., Helzer, J. E., Weissman, M. M., Orvaschel, H., Gruenberg, E., Burke, J. D., and Regier, D. A. Lifetime prevalence of specific psychiatric disorders in three sites. *Archives of General Psychiatry,* 1984, *41,* 949–958.

Robertson, G. S., Pfaus, J. G., Atkinson, L. J., Matsumura, H., Phillips, A. G., and Fibiger, H. C. Sexual behavior increases c-fos expression in the forebrain of the male rat. *Brain Research,* 1991, *564,* 352–357.

Robinson, T. E., and Berridge, K. C. The neural basis of drug craving: An incentive-sensitization theory of addiction. *Brain Research Reviews,* 1993, *18,* 247–291.

Robinson, T. E., Gorny, G., Mitton, E., and Kolb, B. Cocaine self-administration alters the morphology of dendrites and dendritic spines in the nucleus accumbens and neocortex. *Synapse,* 2001, *39,* 256–266.

Rodieck, R. W. *The First Steps in Seeing.* Sunderland, MA: Sinauer Associates, 1998.

Rodier, P. M., Ingram, J. L., Tisdale, B., Nelson, S., and Romano, J. Embryological origin for autism: Developmental anomalies of the cranial nerve motor nuclei. *Journal of Comparative Neurology,* 1996, *370,* 247–261.

Roeltgen, D. P., Rothi, L. H., and Heilman, K. M. Linguistic semantic apraphia: A dissociation of the lexical spelling system from semantics. *Brain and Language,* 1986, *27,* 257–280.

Roffwarg, H. P., Muzio, J. N., and Dement, W. C. Ontogenetic development of human sleep-dream cycle. *Science,* 1966, *152,* 604–619.

Rogan, M. T., and LeDoux, J. E. LTP is accompanied by commensurate enhancement of auditory-evoked responses in a fear conditioning circuit. *Neuron,* 1995, *15,* 127–136.

Rogers, J., Kirby, L. C., Hempelman, S. R., Beery, D. L., McGeer, P. L., Kaszniak, A. W., Zalinshi, J., Cofield, M., Mansukhani, L., Willson, P., and Kogan, F. Clinical trial of indomethacin in Alzheimer's disease. *Neurology,* 1993, *43,* 1609–1611.

Roland, P. E. Metabolic measurements of the working frontal cortex in man. *Trends in Neurosciences,* 1984, *7,* 430–435.

Rolls, E. T. Feeding and reward. In *The Neural Basis of Feeding and Reward,* edited by B. G. Hobel and D. Novin. Brunswick, Me.: Haer Institute, 1982.

Rolls, E. T. A theory of hippocampal function in memory. *Hippocampus,* 1996, *6,* 601–620.

Rolls, E. T., and Baylis, G. C. Size and contrast have only small effects on the responses to faces of neurons in the cortex of the superior temporal sulcus of the monkey. *Experimental Brain Research,* 1986, *65,* 38–48.

Rolls, E. T., Murzi, E., Yaxley, S., Thorpe, S. J., and Simpson, S. J. *Brain Research,* 1986, *368,* 79–86.

Rolls, E. T., Yaxley, S., and Sienkiewicz, Z. J. Gustatory responses of single neurons in the orbitofrontal cortex of the macaque monkey. *Journal of Neurophysiology,* 1990, *64,* 1055–1066.

Romanski, L. M., Tian, B., Fritz, J., Mishkin, M., Goldman-Rakic, P. S., and Rauschecker, J. P. Dual streams of auditory afferents target multiple domains in the primate prefrontal cortex. Nature Neuroscience, 1999, 12, 1131–1136.

Rose, J. D. Changes in hypothalamic neuronal function related to hormonal induction of lordosis in behaving hamsters. *Physiology and Behavior,* 1990, *47,* 1201–1212.

Rosenblatt, J. S., Hazelwood, S., and Poole, J. Maternal behavior in male rats: effects of medial preoptic area lesions and presence of maternal aggression. *Hormones and Behavior,* 1996, *30,* 201–215.

Rosenthal, D. A program of research on heredity in schizophrenia. *Behavioral Science,* 1971, *16,* 191–201.

Rosenthal, N. E., Sack, D. A., Gillin, C., Lewy, A. J., Goodwin, F. K., Davenport, Y., Mueller, P. S., Newsome, D. A., and Wehr, T. A. Seasonal affective disorder: A description of the syndrome and preliminary findings with light therapy. *Archives of General Psychiatry,* 1984, *41,* 72–80.

Rosenthal, N. E., Sack, D. A., James, S. P., Parry, B. L., Mendelson, W. B., Tamarkin, L., and Wehr, T. A. Seasonal affective disorder and phototherapy. *Annals of the New York Academy of Sciences,* 1985, *453,* 260–269.

Roses, A. D. A model for susceptibility polymorphisms for complex diseases: Apolipoprotein E and Alzheimer disease. *Neurogenetics,* 1997, *1,* 3–11.

Rothman, S. M., and Olney, J. W. Excitotoxicity and the NMDA receptor. *Trends in Neurosciences,* 1987, *10,* 299–302.

Routtenberg, A. "Self-starvation" of rats living in activity wheels: Adaptation effects. *Journal of Comparative Psychology,* 1968, *66,* 234–238.

Routtenberg, A., and Malsbury, C. Brainstem pathways of reward. *Journal of Comparative and Physiological Psychology,* 1969, *68,* 22–30.

Roy, A., De Jong, J., and Linnoila, M. Cerebrospinal fluid monoamine metabolites and suicidal behavior in depressed patients. *Archives of General Psychiatry,* 1989, *46,* 609–612.

Rubin, B. S., and Barfield, R. J. Priming of estrous responsiveness by implants of 17B-estradiol in the ventromedial hypothalamic nucleus of female rats. *Endocrinology,* 1980, *106,* 504–509.

Rubin, L. L., and Staddon, J. M. The cell biology of the blood–brain barrier. *Annual Review of Neuroscience,* 1999, *22,* 111–128.

Rusak, B., and Morin, L. P. Testicular responses to photoperiod are blocked by lesions of the suprachiasmatic nuclei in golden hamsters. *Biology of Reproduction,* 1976, *15,* 366–374.

Rusak, B., McNaughton, L., Robertson, H. A., and Hunt, S. P. Circadian variation in photic regulation of immediate-early gene mRNAs in rat suprachiasmatic nucleus cells. *Molecular Brain Research,* 1992, *14,* 124–130.

Rusak, B., Robertson, H. A., Wisden, W., and Hunt, S. P. Light pulses that shift rhythms induce gene expression in the suprachiasmatic nucleus. *Science,* 1990, *248,* 1237–1240.

Russchen, F. T., Amaral, D. G., and Price, J. L. The afferent connections of the substantia innominata in the monkey, *Macaca fascicularis. Journal of Comparative Neurology,* 1986, *242,* 1–27.

Russell, G. F. M., and Treasure, J. The modern history of anorexia nervosa: An interpretation of why the illness has changed. *Annals of the New York Academy of Sciences,* 1989, *575,* 13–30.

Russell, M. J. Human olfactory communication. *Nature,* 1976, *260,* 520–522.

Russell, M. J., Switz, G. M., and Thompson, K. Olfactory influences on the human menstrual cycle. Paper presented at the meeting of the American Association for the Advancement of Science, San Francisco, June 1977.

Ryback, R. S., and Lewis, O. F. Effects of prolonged bed rest on EEG sleep patterns in young, healthy volunteers. *Electroencephalography and Clinical Neurophysiology,* 1971, *31,* 395–399.

Saayman, G. S. Aggressive behaviour in free-ranging chacma baboons *(Papio ursinus). Journal of Behavioral Science,* 1971, *1,* 77–83.

Sackeim, H. A. Lateral asymmetry in bodily response to hypnotic suggestion. *Biological Psychiatry,* 1982, *17,* 437–447.

Sackeim, H. A., and Gur, R. C. Lateral asymmetry in intensity of emotional expression. *Neuropsychologia,* 1978, *16,* 473–482.

Sackeim, H. A., Paulus, D., and Weiman, A. L. Classroom seating and hypnotic susceptibility. *Journal of Abnormal Psychology,* 1979, *88,* 81–84.

Saffran, E. M., Marin, O. S. M., and Yeni-Komshian, G. H. An analysis of speech perception in word deafness. *Brain and Language,* 1976, *3,* 209–228.

Saffran, E. M., Schwartz, M. F., and Marin, O. S. M. Evidence from aphasia: Isolating the components of a production model. In *Language Production,* edited by B. Butterworth. London: Academic Press, 1980.

Sagvolden, T., Aase, H., Zeiner, P., and Berger, D. Altered reinforcement mechanisms in attention-deficit/hyperactivity disorder. *Behavioural Brain Research,* 1998, *94,* 61–71.

Sagvolden, T., and Sergeant, J. A. Attention deficit/hyperactivity disorder: From brain dysfunctions to behaviour. *Behavioural Brain Research,* 1998, *94,* 1–10.

Sahu, A., Kalra, P. S., and Kalra, S. P. Food deprivation and ingestion induce reciprocal changes in neuropeptide Y concentrations in the paraventricular nucleus. *Peptides,* 1988, *9,* 83–86.

Sakai, F., Meyer, J. S., Karacan, I., Derman, S., and Yamamoto, M. Normal human sleep: Regional cerebral haemodynamics. *Annals of Neurology,* 1979, *7,* 471–478.

Sakai, K. Some anatomical and physiological properties of pontomesencephalic tegmental neurons with special reference to the PGO waves and postural atonia during paradoxical sleep in the cat. In *The Reticular Formation Revisited,* edited by J. A. Hobson and M. A. Brazier. New York: Raven Press, 1980.

Sakai, K., and Jouvet, M. Brain stem PGO-on cells projecting directly to the cat dorsal lateral geniculate nucleus. *Brain Research,* 1980, *194,* 500–505.

Sakuma, Y., and Pfaff, D. W. Convergent effects of lordosis-relevant somatosensory and hypothalamic influences on central gray cells in the rat mesencephalon. *Experimental Neurology,* 1980a, *70,* 269–281.

Sakuma, Y., and Pfaff, D. W. Excitability of female rat central gray cells with medullary projections: Changes produced by hypothalamic stimulation and estrogen treatment. *Journal of Neurophysiology,* 1980b, *44,* 1012–1023.

Sakuma, Y., and Pfaff, D. W. Facilitation of female reproductive behavior from mesencephalic central grey in the rat. *American Journal of Physiology,* 1979a, *237,* R278–R284.

Sakuma, Y., and Pfaff, D. W. Mesencephalic mechanisms for integration of female reproductive behavior in the rat. *American Journal of Physiology,* 1979b, *237,* R285–R290.

Sakurai, T., Amemiya, A., Ishii, M., Matsuzaki, I., Chemelli, R. M., Tanaka, H., Williams, S. C., Richardson, J. A., Kozlowski, G. P., Wilson, S., Arch, J. R., Buckingham, R. E., Haynes, A. C., Carr, S. A., Annan, R. S., McNulty, D. E., Liu, W. S., Terrett, J. A., Elshourbagy, N. A., Bergsma, D. J., and Yanagisawa, M. Orexins and orexin receptors: A family of hypothalamic neuropeptides and G protein-coupled receptors that regulate feeding behavior. *Cell,* 1998, *20,* 573–585.

Sakurai, Y., Ichikawa, Y., and Mannen, T. Pure alexia from a posterior occipital lesion. *Neurology,* 2001, *56,* 778–781.

Sakurai, Y., Momose, T., Iwata, M., Sudo, Y., Ohtomo, K., and Kanazawa, I. Different cortical activity in reading of Kanji words, Kana words and Kana nonwords. *Cognitive Brain Research,* 2000, *9,* 111–115.

Sakurai, Y., Sakai, K., Sakuta, M., and Iwata, M. Naming difficulties in alexia with agraphia for kanji after a left posterior inferior temporal lesion. *Journal of Neurology, Neurosurgery, and Psychiatry,* 1994, *57,* 609–613.

Salamone, J. D. Complex motor and sensorimotor function of striatal and accumbens dopamine: Involvement in instrumental behavior processes. *Psychopharmacology,* 1992, *107,* 160–174.

Saller, C. F., and Stricker, E. M. Hyperphagia and increased growth in rats after intraventricular injection of 5,7-dihydroxytryptamine. *Science,* 1976, *192,* 385–387.

Samson, H. H., Hodge, C. W., Tolliver, G. A., and Haraguchi, M. Effect of dopamine agonists and antagonists on ethanol reinforced behavior: The involvement of the nucleus accumbens. *Brain Research Bulletin,* 1993, *30,* 133–141.

Sanders, S. K., and Shekhar, A. Anxiolytic effects of chlordiazepoxide blocked by injection of $GABA_A$ and benzodiazepine receptor antagonists in the region of the anterior basolateral amygdala of rats. *Biological Psychiatry,* 1995, *37,* 473–476.

Saper, C. B., Chou, T. C., and Scammell, T. E. The sleep switch: Hypothalamic control of sleep and wakefulness. *Trends in Neurosciences,* 2001, *24,* 726–731.

Sapolsky, R. *Stress, the Aging Brain and the Mechanisms of Neuron Death.* Cambridge, Mass.: MIT Press, 1992.

Sapolsky, R. M. Social subordinance as a marker of hypercortisolism: Some unexpected subtleties. *Annals of the New York Academy of Science,* 1995, *771,* 626–639.

Sassenrath, E. N., Powell, T. E., and Hendrickx, A. G. Perimenstrual aggression in groups of female rhesus monkeys. *Journal of Reproduction and Fertility,* 1973, *34,* 509–511.

Sastre, M., Dewachter, I., Landreth, G. E., Willson, T. M., Klockgether, T., van Leuven, F., and Heneka, M. T. Nonsteroidal anti-inflammatory drugs and peroxisome proliferators-activated receptor-gamma agonists modulate immunostimulated processing of amyloid precursor protein through regulation of beta-secretase. *Journal of Neuroscience,* 2003, *23,* 9796–9804.

Saudou, F., Amara, D. A., Dierich, A., Lemeur, M., Ramboz, S., Segu, L., Buhot, M. C., and Hen, R. Enhanced aggressive behavior in mice lacking $5\text{-}HT_{1B}$ receptor. *Science,* 1994, *265,* 1875–1878.

Savic, I., Berglund, H., Gulyas, B., and Roland, P. Smelling of odorous sex hormone-like compounds causes sex-differentiated hypothalamic activations in humans. *Neuron,* 2001, *31,* 661–668.

Sawchenko, P. E. Toward a new neurobiology of energy balance, appetite, and obesity: The anatomist weigh in. *Journal of Comparative Neurology,* 1998, *402,* 435–441.

Saxena, S., Brody, A. L., Schwartz, J. M., and Baxter, L. R. Neuroimaging and frontal-subcortical circuitry in obsessive-compulsive disorder. *British Journal of Psychiatry,* 1998, *173,* 26–37.

Scammell, T. E., Estabrooke, I. V., McCarthy, M. T., Chemelli, R. M., Yanagisawa, M., Miller, M. S., and Saper, C. B. Hypothalamic arousal regions are activated during modafinil-induced wakefulness. *Journal of Neuroscience,* 2000, *20,* 8620–8628.

Scammell, T. E., Gerashchenko, D. Y., Mochizuki, T., McCarthy, M. T., Estabrooke, I. V., Sears, C. A., Saper, C. B., Urade, Y., and Hayaishi, O. An adenosine A2a agonist increases sleep and induces Fos in ventrolateral preoptic neurons. *Neuroscience,* 2001, *107,* 653–663.

Scarpace, P. J., Matheny, M., and Tümer, N. Hypothalamic leptin resistance is associated with impaired leptin signal transduction in aged obese rats. *Neuroscience,* 2001, *104,* 1111–1117.

Schenck, C. H., and Mahowald, M. W. Motor dyscontrol in narcolepsy: Rapid-eye-movement (REM) sleep without atonia and REM sleep behavior disorder. *Annals of Neurology,* 1992, *32,* 3–10.

Schenck, C. H., Bundlie, S. R., Ettinger, M. G., and Mahowald, M. W. Chronic behavioral disorders of human REM sleep: A new category of parasomnia. *Sleep,* 1986, *9,* 293–308.

Schenck, C. H., Garcia-Rill, E., Segall, M., Noreen, H., and Mahowald, M. W. HLA class-II genes associated with REM-sleep behavior disorder. *Annals of Neurology,* 1996, *39,* 261–263.

Schenck, C. H., Hurwitz, T. D., and Mahowald, M. W. REM-sleep behavior disorder: An update on a series of 96 patients and a review of the world literature. *Journal of Sleep Research,* 1993, *2,* 224–231.

Schenk, D., Barbour, R., Dunn, W., Gordon, G., Grajeda, H., Guido, T., Hu, K., Huang, J., Johnson-Wood, K., Khan, K., Kholodenko, D., Lee, M., Liao, Z., Lieberburg, I., Motter, R., Mutter, L., Soriano, F., Shopp, G., Vasquez, N., Vandevert, C., Walker, S., Wogulis, M., Yednock, T., Games, D., Seubert, P. Immunization with amyloid-beta attenuates Alzheimer-disease-like pathology in the PDAPP mouse. *Nature,* 1999, *400,* 173–177.

Scherschlicht, R., Polc, P., Schneeberger, J., Steiner, M., and Haefely, W. Selective suppression of rapid eye movement sleep (REMS) in cats by typical and atypical antidepressants. In *Typical and Atypical Antidepressants: Molecular Mechanisms,* edited by E. Costa and G. Racagni. New York: Raven Press, 1982.

Schiffman, J., Ekstrom, M., LaBrie, J., Schulsinger, F., Sorensen, H., and Mednick, S. Minor physical anomalies and schizophrenia spectrum disorders: A prospective investigation. *American Journal of Psychiatry,* 2002, *159,* 238–243.

Schiffman, S. S., Lockhead, E., and Maes, F. W. Amiloride reduces the taste intensity of Na+ and Li+ salts and sweeteners. *Proceedings of the National Academy of Sciences, USA,* 1983, *80,* 6136–6140.

Schiller, P. H., and Malpeli, J. G. Properties and tectal projections of monkey retinal ganglion cells. *Journal of Neurophysiology,* 1977, *40,* 428–445.

Schiller, P. H., Sandell, J. H., and Maunsell, J. H. R. Functions of the ON and OFF channels of the visual system. *Nature,* 1986, *322,* 824–825.

Schmidt, M. H., Valatx, J.-L., Sakai, K., Fort, P., and Jouvet, M. Role of the lateral preoptic area in sleep-related erectile mechanisms and sleep generation in the rat. *Journal of Neuroscience,* 2000, *20,* 6640–6647.

Schnabel, J. New Alzheimer's therapy suggested. *Science,* 1993, *260,* 1719–1720.

Schneider, B., Muller, M. J., and Philipp, M. Mortality in affective disorders. *Journal of the Affective Disorders,* 2001, *65,* 263–274.

Schrauwen, P., Xia, J., Bogardus, C., Pratley, R. E., and Ravussin, E. Skeletal muscle uncoupling protein 3 expression is a determinant of energy expenditure in Pima Indians. *Diabetes,* 1999, *48,* 146–149.

Schuman, E. R., and Madison, D. V. A requirement for the intercellular messenger nitric oxide in long-term potentiation. *Science,* 1991, *254,* 1503–1506.

Schwartz, M. F., Marin, O. S. M., and Saffran, E. M. Dissociations of language function in dementia: A case study. *Brain and Language,* 1979, *7,* 277–306.

Schwartz, M. F., Saffran, E. M., and Marin, O. S. M. The word order problem in agrammatism. I. Comprehension. *Brain and Language,* 1980, *10,* 249–262.

Schwartz, M. W., Peskind, E., Raskind, M., Boyko, E. J., and Porte, D. Cerebrospinal fluid leptin levels: Relationship to plasma levels and to adiposity in humans. *Nature Medicine,* 1996, *2,* 589–593.

Schwartz, W. J., and Gainer, H. Suprachiasmatic nucleus: Use of ^{14}C-labelled deoxyglucose uptake as a functional marker. *Science,* 1977, *197,* 1089–1091.

Schwarzkopf, S. B., Nasrallah, H. A., Olson, S. C., Coffman, J. A., and McLaughlin, J. A. Perinatal complications and genetic loading in schizophrenia: Preliminary findings. *Psychiatry Research,* 1989, *27,* 233–239.

Scott, S. K., Blank, E. C., Rosen, S., and Wise, R. J. S. Identification of a pathway for intelligible speech in the left temporal lobe. *Brain,* 2000, *123,* 2400–2406.

Scott, T. R., and Plata-Salaman, C. R. Coding of taste quality. In *Smell and Taste in Health and Disease,* edited by T. N. Getchell. New York: Raven Press, 1991.

Scoville, W. B., and Milner, B. Loss of recent memory after bilateral hippocampal lesions. *Journal of Neurology, Neurosurgery and Psychiatry,* 1957, *20,* 11–21.

Sedvall, G., Fyrö, B., Gullberg, B., Nybäck, H., Wiesel, F.-A., and Wode-Helgodt, B. Relationship in healthy volunteers between concentrations of monoamine metabolites in cerebrospinal fluid and family history of psychiatric morbidity. *British Journal of Psychiatry,* 1980, *136,* 366–374.

Seidman, L. J., Biederman, J., Weber, W., Hatch, M., and Faraone, S. V. Neuropsychological function in adults with attention-deficit hyperactivity disorder. *Biological Psychiatry,* 1998, *44,* 260–268.

Selye, H. *The Stress of Life.* New York: McGraw-Hill, 1976.

Semenza, C., and Zettin, M. Evidence from aphasia for the role of proper names as pure referring expressions. *Nature,* 1989, *342,* 678–679.

Sforza, E., Montagna, P., Tinuper, P., Cortelli, P., Avoni, P., Ferrillo, F., Petersen, R., Gambetti, P., and Lagaresi, E. Sleep-wake cycle abnormalities in fatal familial insomnia: Evidence of the role of the thalamus in sleep regulation. *Electroencephalography and Clinical Neurophysiology,* 1995, *94,* 398–405.

Shallice, T. Phonological agraphia and the lexical route in writing. *Brain,* 1981, *104,* 413–429.

Sham, P. C., O'Callaghan, E., Takei, N., Murray, G. K., Hare, E. H., and Murray, R. M. Schizophrenia following pre-natal exposure to influenza epidemics between 1939 and 1960. *British Journal of Psychiatry,* 1992, *160,* 461–466.

Shapiro, L. E., Leonard, C. M., Sessions, C. E., Dewsbury, D. A., and Insel, T. R. Comparative neuroanatomy of the sexually dimorphic hypothalamus in monogamous and polygamous voles. *Brain Research,* 1991, *541,* 232–240.

Sharp, F. R., Sagar, S. M., Hicks, K., Lowenstein, D., and Hisanaga, K. C-fos mRNA, Fos, and Fos-related antigen induction by hypertonic saline and stress. *Journal of Neuroscience,* 1991, *11,* 2321–2331.

Shastry, B. S. Schizophrenia: A genetic perspective (review). *International Journal of Molecular Medicine,* 2002, *9,* 207–212.

Shaywitz, B. A., Shaywitz, S. E., Pugh, K. R., Mencl, W. E., Fulbright, R. K., Skudlarski P., Constable, R. T., Marchione, K. E., Fletcher, J. M., Lyon, G. R., and Gore, J. C. Disruption of posterior brain systems for reading in children with developmental dyslexia. *Biological Psychiatry,* 2002, *52,* 101–110.

Shearman, L. P., Sriram, S., Weaver, D. R., Maywood, E. S., Chaves, I., Zheng, B., Kume, K., Lee, C. C., van der Horst, G. T., Hastings, M. H., and Reppert, S. M. Interacting molecular loops in the mammalian circadian clock. *Science,* 2000, *288, 1013–1019.*

Shepherd, G. M. Discrimination of molecular signals by the olfactory receptor neuron. *Neuron,* 1994, *13,* 771–790.

Sher, A. E. Surgery for obstructive sleep apnea. *Progress in Clinical Biology Research,* 1990, *345,* 407–415.

Sher, L., Goldman, D., Ozaki, N., and Rosenthal, N. E. The role of genetic factors in the etiology of seasonal affective disorder and seasonality. *Journal of Affective Disorders,* 1999, *53,* 203–210.

Sherin, J. E., Elmquist, J. K., Torrealba, F., and Saper, C. B. Innervation of histaminergic tuberomammillary neurons by GABAergic and galaninergic neurons in the ventrolateral preoptic nucleus of the rat. *Journal of Neuroscience,* 1998, *18,* 4705–4721.

Sherin, J. E., Shiromani, P. J., McCarley, R. W., and Saper, C. B. Activation of ventrolateral preoptic neurons during sleep. *Science,* 1996, *271,* 216–219.

Sherry, D. F., Jacobs, L. F., and Gaulin, S. J. C. Spatial memory and adaptive specialization of the hippocampus. *Trends in Neuroscience,* 1992, *15,* 298–303.

Shi, S.-H., Hayashi, Y., Petralia, R. S., Zaman, S. H., Wenthold, R. J., Svoboda, K., and Malinow, R. Rapid spine delivery and redistribution of ampa receptors after synaptic NMDA receptor activation. *Science,* 1999, *284,* 1811–1816.

Shifren, J. L., Braunstein, G. D., Simon, J. A., Casson, P. R., Buster, J. E., Redmond, G. P., Burki, R. E., Ginsburg, E. S., Rosen, R. C., Leiblum, S. R., Caramelli, K. E., and Mazer, N. A. Transdermal testosterone treatment in women with impaired sexual function after oophorectomy. *New England Journal of Medicine,* 2000, *343,* 682–688.

Shimada, M., Tritos, N. A., Lowell, B. B., Flier, J. S., and Maratos-Flier, E. Mice lacking melanin-concentrating hormone are hypophagic and lean. *Nature,* 1998, *396,* 670–674.

Shimura, T., Yamamoto, T., and Shimokochi, M. The medial preoptic area is involved in both sexual arousal and performance in male rats: Re-evaluation of neuron activity in freely moving animals. *Brain Research,* 1994, *640,* 215–222.

Shinohara, K., Morofushi, M., Funabashi, T., and Kimura, F. Axillary pheromones modulate pulsatile LH secretion in humans. *Neuroreport,* 2001, *12,* 893–895.

Shipley, M. T., and Ennis, M. Functional organization of the olfactory system. *Journal of Neurobiology,* 1996, *30,* 123–176.

Shors, T. J., Seib, T. B., Levine, S., and Thompson, R. F. Inescapable versus escapable shock modulates long-term potentiation in the rat hippocampus. *Science,* 1989, *244,* 224–226.

Shoulson, I., Oakes, D., Fahn, S., Lang, A., Langston, J. W., LeWitt, P., Olanow, C. W., Penney, J. B., Tanner, C., Kieburtz, K., and Rudolph, A. Parkinson Study Group. Impact of sustained deprenyl (selegiline) in levodopa-treated Parkinson's disease: A randomized placebo-controlled extension of the deprenyl and tocopherol antioxidative therapy of parkinsonism trial. *Annals of Neurology,* 2002, *51,* 604–612.

Sidman, M., Stoddard, L. T., and Mohr, J. P. Some additional quantitative observations of immediate memory in a patient with bilateral hippocampal lesions. *Neuropsychologia,* 1968, *6,* 245–254.

Siegel, A., Roeling, T. A. P., Gregg, T. R., and Kruk, M. R. Neuropharmacology of brain-stimulation-evoked aggression. *Neuroscience and Biobehavioral Reviews,* 1999, *23,* 359–389.

Siegel, R. M., and Andersen, R. A. Motion perceptual deficits following ibotenic acid lesions of the middle temporal area (MT) in the behaving monkey. *Society for Neuroscience Abstracts,* 1986, *12,* 1183.

Siegel, S. A Pavlovian conditioning analysis of morphine tolerance. In *Behavioral Tolerance: Research and Treatment Implications,* edited by N. A. Krasnegor. Washington, DC: NIDA Research Monographs, 1978.

Siegel, S., Hinson, R. E., Krank, M. D., and McCully, J. Heroin "overdose" death: Contribution of drug-associated environmental cues. *Science,* 1982, *216,* 436–437.

Sigvardsson, S., Bohman, M., and Cloninger, R. Replication of the Stockholm adoption study of alcoholism. *Archives of General Psychiatry,* 1996, *53,* 681–687.

Silva, A. J., Stevens, C. F., Tonegawa, S., and Wang, Y. Deficient hippocampal long-term potentiation in α-calcium-calmodulin kinase II mutant mice. *Science,* 1992, *257,* 201–206.

Silver, J. M., Shin, C., and McNamara, J. O. Antiepileptogenic effects of conventional anticonvulsants in the kindling model of epilepsy. *Annals of Neurology,* 1991, *29,* 356–363.

Silver, R., LeSauter, J., Tresco, P. A., and Lehman, M. N. A diffusible coupling signal from the transplanted suprachiasmatic nucleus controlling circadian locomotor rhythms. *Nature,* 1996, *382,* 810–813.

Silveri, M. C. Peripheral aspects of writing can be differentially affected by sensorial and attentional defect: Evidence from a patient with afferent dysgraphia and case dissociation. *Cortex,* 1996, *32,* 155–172.

Simpson, J. B., Epstein, A. N., and Camardo, J. S. The localization of dipsogenic receptors for angiotensin II in the subfornical organ. *Journal of Comparative and Physiological Psychology,* 1978, *92,* 581–608.

Simuni, T., Jaggi, J. L., Mulholland, H., Hurtig, H. I., Colcher, A., Siderowf, A. D., Ravina, B., Skolnick, B. E., Goldstein, R., Stern, M. B., and Baltuch, G. H. Bilateral stimulation of the subthalamic nucleus in patients with Parkinson disease: A study of efficacy and safety. *Journal of Neurosurgery,* 2002, *96,* 666–672.

Sinclair, A. H., Berta, P., Palmer, M. S., Hawkins, J. R., Griffiths, B. L., Smith, M. J., Foster, J. W., Frischauf, A. M., Lovell-Badge, R., and Goodfellow, P. N. A gene frrom the human sex-determining region encodes a protein with homology to a conserved DNA-binding motif. *Nature,* 1990, *346,* 240–244.

Singer, C., and Weiner, W. J. Male sexual dysfunction. *Neurologist,* 1996, *2,* 119–129.

Singer, F., and Zumoff, B. Subnormal serum testosterone levels in male internal medicine residents. *Steroids,* 1992, *57,* 86–89.

Singh, N. A., Clements, K. M., and Fiatarone, M. A. Sleep, sleep deprivation, and daytime activities: A randomized controlled trial of the effect of exercise on sleep. *Sleep,* 1997, *20,* 95–101.

Sipos, M. L., and Nyby, J. G. Concurrent androgenic stimulation of the ventral tegmental area and medial preoptic area: Synergistic effects on male-typical reproductive behaviors in house mice. *Brain Research,* 1996, *729,* 29–44.

Sitaram, N., Moore, A. M., and Gillin, J. C. Experimental acceleration and slowing of REM ultradian rhythm by cholinergic agonist and antagonist. *Nature,* 1978, *274,* 490–492.

Skaggs, W. E., and McNaughton, B. L. Spatial firing properties of hippocampal CA1 populations in an environment containing two visually identical regions. *Journal of Neuroscience,* 1998, *18,* 8455–8466.

Skakkebaek, N. E., Bancroft, J., Davidson, D. W., and Warner, P. Androgen replacement with oral testosterone undecanoate in hypogonadal men: A double blind controlled study. *Clinical Endocrinology,* 1981, *14,* 49–61.

Skene, D. J., Lockley, S. W., and Arendt, J. Melatonin in circadian sleep disorders in the blind. *Biological Signals and Receptors,* 1999, *8,* 90–95.

Skutella, T., Criswell, H., Moy, S., Probst, J. C., Breese, G. R., Jirikowski, G. F., and Holsboer, F. Corticotropin-releasing hormone (CRH) antisense oligodeoxynucleotide induces anxiolytic effects in rat. *Neuroreport,* 1994, *5,* 2181–2185.

Slotkin, T. A. Fetal nicotine or cocaine exposure: Which one is worse? *Journal of Pharma-*

cology and Experimental Therapeutics, 1998, *22,* 521–527.

Smith, C. Sleep states, memory processes and synaptic plasticity. *Behavioural Brain Research,* 1996, *78,* 49–56.

Smith, C., and Lapp, L. Increased number of REMs following an intensive learning. *Sleep,* 1991, *14,* 325–330.

Smith, G. P., Gibbs, J., and Kulkosky, P. J. Relationships between brain-gut peptides and neurons in the control of food intake. In *The Neural Basis of Feeding and Reward,* edited by B. G. Hoebel and D. Novin. Brunswick, Me.: Haer Institute, 1982.

Smith, K. A., Morris, J. S., Friston, K. J., Cower, P. J., and Dolar, R. J. Brain mechanisms associated with depressive relapse and associated cognitive impairment following acute tryptophan depletion. *British Journal of Psychiatry,* 1999, *174,* 525–529.

Smith, M. J. Sex determination: Turning on sex. *Current Biology,* 1994, *4,* 1003–1005.

Snyder, S. H. *Madness and the Brain.* New York: McGraw-Hill, 1974.

Soares, J. C., and Gershon, S. The lithium ion: A foundation for psychopharmacological specificity. *Neuropsychopharmacology,* 1998, *19,* 167–182.

Solyom, L., Turnbull, I. M., and Wilensky, M. A case of self-inflicted leucotomy. *British Journal of Psychiatry,* 1987, *151,* 855–857.

Sørensen, T. I. A., Price, R. A., Stunkard, A. J., and Schulsinger, F. Genetics of obesity in adult adoptees and their biological siblings. *British Medical Journal,* 1989, *298,* 87–90.

Soto, C. Unfolding the role of protein misfolding in neurodegenerative diseases. *Nature Review Neuroscience,* 2003, *4,* 49–60.

Speelman, J. D., Schuurman, R., de Bie, R. M., Esselink, R. A., and Bosch, D. A. Stereotactic neurosurgery for tremor. *Movement Disorders,* 2002, *17,* S84—S88.

Sperry, R. W. Brain bisection and consciousness. In *Brain and Conscious Experience,* edited by J. Eccles. New York: Springer-Verlag, 1966.

Spiegler, B. J., and Mishkin, M. Evidence for the sequential participation of inferior temporal cortex and amygdala in the acquisition of stimulus-reward associations. *Behavioural Brain Research,* 1981, *3,* 303–317.

Spiers, H. J., Maguire, E. A., and Burgess, N. Hippocampal amnesia. *Neurocase,* 2001, *7,* 357–382.

Spray, D. C. Cutaneous temperature receptors. *Annual Review of Physiology,* 1986, *48,* 625–638.

Sprengelmeyer, R., Rausch, M., Eysel, U. T., and Przuntek, H. Neural structures associated with recognition of facial expressions of basic emotions. *Proceedings of the Royal Society of London [B],* 1998, *265,* 1927–1931.

Sprengelmeyer, R., Young, A. W., Calder, A. J., Karnat, A., Lange, H., Hömberg, V., Perrett, D. I., and Rowland, D. Loss of disgust: Perception of faces and emotions in Huntington's disease. *Brain.* 1996, *119,* 1647–1665.

Sprengelmeyer, R., Young, A. W., Pundt, I., Sprengelmeyer, A., Calder, A. J., Berrios, G., Winkel, R., Vollmöeller, W., Kuhn, W., Sartory, G., and Przuntek, H. Disgust implicated in obsessive-compulsive disorder. *Proceedings of the Royal Society of London [B],* 1997, *264,* 1767–1773.

Squire, L. R. Memory and the hippocampus: A synthesis from findings with rats, monkeys, and humans. *Psychological Review,* 1992, *99,* 195–231.

Squire, L. R. Stable impairment in remote memory following electroconvulsive therapy. *Neuropsychologia,* 1974, *13,* 51–58.

Squire, L. R., Shimamura, A. P., and Amaral, D. G. Memory and the hippocampus. In *Neural Models of Plasticity: Experimental and Theoretical Approaches,* edited by J. H. Byrne and W. O. Berry. San Diego: Academic Press, 1989.

St. George-Hyslop, P. H., Tanzi, R. E., Polinsky, R. J., Haines, J. L., Nee, L., Watkins, P. C., Myers, R. H., Feldman, R. G., Pollen, D., Drachman, D., Growdon, J., Bruni, A., Foncin, J.-F., Salmon, D., Frommelt, P., Amaducci, L., Sorbi, S., Piacentini, S., Stewart, G. D., Hobbs, W. J., Conneally, P. M., and Gusella, J. F. The genetic defect causing familial Alzheimer's disease maps on chromosome 21. *Science,* 1987, *235,* 885–890.

Stallone, D., and Nicolaïdis, S. Increased food intake and carbohydrate preference in the rat following treatment with the serotonin antagonist metergoline. *Neuroscience Letters,* 1989, *102,* 319–324.

Stanley, B. G., Willett V. L., Donias, H. W., Dee, M. G., and Duva, M. A. Lateral hypothalamic NMDA receptors and glutamate as physiological mediators of eating and weight control. *American Journal of Physiology: Regulatory, Integrative and Comparative Physiology,* 1996, *270,* R443–R449.

Stanley, B. G., Willett, V. L., Donias, H. W., Ha, L. H., and Spears, L. C. The lateral hypothalamus: A primary site mediating excitatory amino acid-elicited eating. *Brain Research,* 1993a, *630,* 41–44.

Stanton, P. K., and Sejnowski, T. J. Associative long-term depression in the hippocampus induced by Hebbian covariance. *Nature,* 1989, *339,* 215–218.

Starkey, S. J., Walker, M. P., Beresford, I. J. M., and Hagan, R. M. Modulation of the rat suprachiasmatic circadian clock by melatonin in-vitro. *Neuroreport,* 1995, *6,* 1947–1951.

Stein, M. B., Jang, K. L., Taylor, S., Vernon, P. A., and Livesley, W. J. Genetic and environmental influences on trauma exposure and posttraumatic stress disorder symptoms: A twin study. *American Journal of Psychiatry,* 2002, *159,* 1675–1681.

Steininger, R. L., Alam, M. N., Szymusiak, R., and McGinty, D. State dependent discharge of ruberomammillary neurons in the rat hypothalamus. *Sleep Research,* 1996, *25,* 28.

Stellar, J. R., Kelley, A. E., and Corbett, D. Effects of peripheral and central dopamine blockade on lateral hypothalamic self-stimulation: Evidence for both reward and motor deficits. *Pharmacology, Biochemistry, and Behavior,* 1983, *18,* 433–442.

Stephan, F. K., and Nuñez, A. A. Elimination of circadian rhythms in drinking activity, sleep, and temperature by isolation of the suprachiasmatic nuclei. *Behavioral Biology,* 1977, *20,* 1–16.

Stephan, F. K., and Zucker, I. Circadian rhythms in drinking behavior and locomotor activity of rats are eliminated by hypothalamic mic lesion. *Proceedings of the National Academy of Sciences, USA,* 1972, *69,* 1583–1586.

Steriade, M. Arousal: Revisiting the reticular activating system. *Science,* 1996, *272,* 225–226.

Steriade, M. Basic mechanisms of sleep generation. *Neurology,* 1992, *42* (Suppl. 6), 9–18.

Steriade, M., Paré, D., Datta, S., Oakson, G., and Curró Dossi, R. Different cellular types in mesopontine cholinergic nuclei related to ponto-geniculo-occipital waves. *Journal of Neuroscience,* 1990, *8,* 2560–2579.

Sterman, M. B., and Clemente, C. D. Forebrain inhibitory mechanisms: Cortical synchronization induced by basal forebrain stimulation. *Experimental Neurology,* 1962a, *6,* 91–102.

Sterman, M. B., and Clemente, C. D. Forebrain inhibitory mechanisms: Sleep patterns induced by basal forebrain stimulation in the behaving cat. *Experimental Neurology,* 1962b, *6,* 103–117.

Stern, K., and McClintock, M. K. Regulation of ovulation by human pheromones. *Nature,* 1998, *392,* 177–178.

Stevens, J. R. Neurology and neuropathology of schizophrenia. In *Schizophrenia as a Brain Disease,* edited by F. A. Henn and H. A. Nasrallah. New York: Oxford University Press, 1982.

Stinson, D., and Thompson, C. Clinical experience with phototherapy. *Journal of the Affective Disorders,* 1990, *18,* 129–135.

Stolerman, I. P., and Jarvis, M. J. The scientific case that nicotine is addictive. *Psychopharmacology,* 1995, *117,* 2–10.

Stone, A. A., Reed, B. R., and Neale, J. M. Changes in daily event frequency precede episodes of physical symptoms. *Journal of Human Stress,* 1987, *13,* 70–74.

Stowers, L., Holy, T. E., Meister, M., Dulac, C., and Koentges, G. Loss of sex discrimination of male-male aggression in mice deficient for TRP2. *Science,* 2002, *295,* 1493–1500.

Stoyva, J., and Metcalf, D. Sleep patterns following chronic exposure to cholinesterase-inhibiting organophosphate compounds. *Psychophysiology,* 1968, *5,* 206.

Strakowski, S. M., DelBello, M. P., Zimmerman, M. E., Getz, G. E., Mills, N. P., Ret, J., Shear, P., and Adler, C. M. Ventricular and periventricular structural volumes in first-versus multiple-episode bipolar disorder. *American Journal of Psychiatry,* 2002, *11,* 1841–1847.

Stricker, E. M., Swerdloff, A. F., and Zigmond, M. J. Intrahypothalamic injections of kainic acid produces feeding and drinking deficits in rats. *Brain Research,* 1978, *158,* 470–473.

Strobel, A., Issad, T., Camoin, L., Ozata, M., and Strosberg, A. D. A leptin missense mutation associated with hypogonadism and morbid obesity. *Nature Genetics,* 1998, *18,* 213–215.

Strömland, K., Nordin, V., Miller, M., Akerstrom, B., and Gillberg, C. Autism in thalidomide embryopathy: A population study. *Developmental Medicine and Child Neurology,* 1994, *36,* 351–356.

Stunkard, A. J., Sørensen, T. I. A., Harris, C., Teasdale, T. W., Chakraborty, R., Schull, W. J., and Schulsinger, F. An adoption study of human obesity. *New England Journal of Medicine,* 1986, *314,* 193–198.

Sturgis, J. D., and Bridges, R. S. N-methyl-DL-aspartic acid lesions of the medial preoptic area disrupt ongoing parental behavior in male rats. *Physiology and Behavior,* 1997, *62,* 305–310.

Sturup, G. K. Correctional treatment and the criminal sexual offender. *Canadian Journal of Correction,* 1961, *3,* 250–265.

Styron, W. *Darkness Visible: A Memoir of Madness.* New York: Random House, 1990.

Su, T.-P., Pagliaro, M., Schmidt, P. J., Pickar, D., Wolkowitz, O., and Rubinow, D. R. Neuropsychiatric effects of anabolic steroids in male normal volunteers. *Journal of the American Medical Association,* 1993, *269,* 2760–2764.

Sutherland, R. J., McDonald, R. J., and Savage, D. D. Prenatal exposure to moderate levels of ethanol can have long-lasting effects on hippocampal synaptic plasticity in adult offspring. *Hippocampus,* 1997, *7,* 232–238.

Suzdak, P. D., Glowa, J. R., Crawley, J. N., Schwartz, R. D., Skolnick, P., and Paul, S. M. A selective imidazobenzodiazepine antagonist of ethanol in the rat. *Science,* 1986, *234,* 1243–1247.

Svennilson, E., Torvik, A., Lowe, R., and Leksell, L. Treatment of Parkinsonism by stereotactic thermolesions in the pallidal region. *Neurologica Scandanavica,* 1960, *35,* 358–377.

Swaab, D. F., and Hofman, M. A. An enlarged suprachiasmatic nucleus in homosexual men. *Brain Research,* 1990, *537,* 141–148.

Swaab, D. F., Gooren, L. J. G., and Hofman, M. A. Brain research, gender, and sexual orientation. *Journal of Homosexuality,* 1995, *28,* 283–301.

Swanson, R. A. Physiologic coupling of glial glycogen metabolism to neuronal activity in brain. *Canadian Journal of Physiology and Pharmacology,* 1992, *70,* S138—S144.

Swanson, R. A., and Choi, D. W. Glial glycogen stores affect neuronal survival during glucose deprivation in vitro. *Journal of Cerebral Blood Flow and Metabolism,* 1993, *13,* 162–169.

Sweet, W. H. Participant in brain stimulation in behaving subjects. Neurosciences Research Program Workshop, 1966.

Swerdlow, N. R. Obsessive-compulsive disorder and tic syndromes. *Medical Clinics of North America,* 2001, *85,* 735–755.

Swerdlow, N. R., Geyer, M. A., Vale, W. W., and Koob, G. F. Corticotropin-releasing factor potentiates acoustic startle in rats: Blockade by chlordiazepoxide. *Psychopharmacology,* 1986, *88,* 147–152.

Szuba, M. P., Baxter, L. R., and Fairbanks, L. A. Effects of partial sleep deprivation on the diurnal variation of mood and motor activity in major depression. *Biological Psychiatry,* 1991, *30,* 817–829.

Szuba, M. P., O'Reardon, J. P., Rai, A. S., Snyder-Kastenberg, J., Amsterdam, J. D., Gettes, D. R., Wassermann, E., and Evans, D. L. Acute mood and thyroid stimulating hormone effects of transcranial magnetic stimulation in major depression. *Biological Psychiatry,* 2001, *50,* 22–27.

Szymusiak, R., Alam, N., Steininger, T. L., and McGinty, D. Sleep-waking discharge patterns of ventrolateral preoptic/anterior hypothalamic neurons in rats. *Brain Research,* 1998, *803,* 178–188.

Tabakoff, B., and Hoffman, P. L. Alcohol addiction: An enigma among us. *Neuron,* 1996, *16,* 909–912.

Taipale, N., Kaminen, N., Nopola-Hemmi, J., Haltia, T., Myllyluoma, B., Lyytinen, H., Muller, K., Kaaranen, M., Lindsberg, P. J., Hannula-Jouppi, K., and Kere, J. A candidate gene for developmental dyslexia encodes a nuclear tetratricopeptide repeat domain protein dynamically regulated in brain. *Proceedings of the National Academy of Science, USA,* 2003, *100,* 11553–11558.

Takahashi, L. K. Hormonal regulation of sociosexual behavior in female mammals. *Neuroscience and Biobehavioral Reviews,* 1990, *14,* 403–413.

Takahashi, L. K., Turner, J. G., and Kalin, N. H. Prenatal stress alters brain catecholaminergic activity and potentiates stress-induced behavior in adult rats. *Brain Research,* 1992, *574,* 131–137.

Tamminga, C. A., Burrows, G. H., Chase, T. N., Alphs, L. D., and Thaker, G. K. Dopamine neuronal tracts in schizophrenia: Their pharmacology and *in vivo* glucose metabolism. *Annals of the New York Academy of Sciences,* 1988, *537,* 443–450.

Tang, Y.-P., Shimizu, E., Dube, G. R., Rampon, C., Kerchner, G. A., Zhuo, M., Lium, G., and Tsien, J. Z. Genetic enhancement of learning and memory in mice. *Nature,* 1999, *401,* 63–69.

Tanner, C. M. The role of environmental toxins in the etiology of Parkinson's disease. *Trends in Neuroscience,* 1989, *12,* 49–54.

Tarsy, D., Baldessarini, R. J., and Tarazi, F. I. Effects of newer antipsychotics on extrapyramidal function. *CNS Drugs,* 2002, *16,* 23–45.

Taub, E., Miller, N. E., Novack, T. A., Cook, E. W., Fleming, W. C., Nepomuceno, C. S., Connell, J. S., and Crago, J. E. Technique to improve chronic motor deficit after stroke. *Archives of Physical Medicine and Rehabilitation,* 1993, *74,* 347–354.

Taylor, B., Miller, E., Lingam, R. Andrews, N., Simmons, A., and Stowe, J. Measles, mumps, and rubella vaccination and bowel problems or developmental regression in children with autism: Population study. *British Medical Journal,* 2002, *324,* 393–396.

Taylor, S. F. Cerebral blood flow activation and functional lesions in schizophrenia. *Schizophrenia Research,* 1996, *19,* 129–140.

Tei, H., Soma, Y., and Maruyama, S. Right unilateral agraphia following callosal infarction in a left-hander. *European Neurology,* 1994, *34,* 168–172.

Teicher, M. H., Anderson, C. M., Polcari, A., Glod, C. A., Maas, L. C., and Renshaw, P. F. Functional deficits in basal ganglia of children with attention-deficit/hyperactivity disorder shown with functional magnetic resonance imaging relaxometry. *Nature Medicine,* 2000, *6,* 470–473.

Teitelbaum, P., and Stellar, E. Recovery from the failure to eat produced by hypothalamic lesions. *Science,* 1954, *120,* 894–895.

Terenius, L., and Wahlström, A. Morphine-like ligand for opiate receptors in human CSF. *Life Sciences,* 1975, *16,* 1759–1764.

Terman, T., Terman, J. S., and Ross, D. C. A controlled trial of timed bright light and negative air ionization for treatment of winter depression, *Archives of General Psychiatry,* 1998, *55,* 875–882.

Terry, R. D., and Davies, P. Dementia of the Alzheimer type. *Annual Review of Neuroscience,* 1980, *3,* 77–96.

Tetel, M. J., Celentano, D. C., and Blaustein, J. D. Intraneuronal convergence of tactile and hormonal stimuli associated with female reproduction in rats. *Journal of Neuroendocrinology,* 1994, *6,* 211–216.

Tetel, M. J., Getzinger, M. J., and Blaustein, J. D. Fos expression in the rat brain following vaginal-cervical stimulation by mating and manual probing. *Journal of Neuroendocrinology,* 1993, *5,* 397–404.

Tetrud, J. W., and Langston, J. W. The effect of deprenyl (Selegiline) on the natural history of Parkinson's disease. *Science,* 1989, *245,* 519–522.

Thaker, G. K., and Carpenter, W. T. Advances in schizophrenia. *Nature Medicine,* 2001, *7,* 667–671.

Thakkar, M. M., Winston, S., and McCarley, R. W. Orexin neurons of the hypothalamus express adenosine A1 receptors. *Brain Research,* 2002, *944,* 190–194.

Theorell, T., Leymann, H., Jodko, M., Konarski, K., Norbeck, H. E., and Eneroth, P. "Person under train" incidents: Medical consequences for subway drivers. *Psychosomatic Medicine,* 1992, *54,* 480–488.

Thiels, E., Xie, X. P., Yeckel, M. F., Barrionuevo, G., and Berger, T. W. NMDA receptor-dependent LTD in different subfields of hippocampus in vivo and in vitro. *Hippocampus,* 1996, *6,* 43–51.

Thompson, P. M., Vidal, C., Giedd, J. N., Gochman, P., Blumenthal, J., Nicolson, R., Toga, A. W., and Rapoport, J. L. Mapping adolescent brain change reveals dynamic wave of accelerated gray matter loss in very early-onset schizophrenia. *Proceedings of the National Academy of Science, USA,* 2001, *98,* 11650–11655.

Thompson, S. M., Fortunato, C., McKinney, R. A., Müller, M., and Gähwiler, B. H. Mechanisms underlying the neuropathological consequences of epileptic activity in the rat hippocampus in vitro. *Journal of Comparative Neurology,* 1996, *372,* 515–528.

Thrasher, T. N. Role of forebrain circumventricular organs in body fluid balance. *Acta Physiologica Scandanavica,* 1989, *136* (Suppl. 583), 141–150.

Toni, N., Buchs, P.-A., Nikonenko, I., Bron, C. R., and Muller, D. LTP promotes formation of multiple spine synapses between a single axon terminal and a dendrite. *Nature,* 1999, *402,* 421–425.

Topper, R., Kosinski, C., and Mull, M. Volitional type of facial palsy associated with pontine ischemia. *Journal of Neurology, Neurosurgery, and Psychiatry,* 1995, *58,* 732–734.

Tordoff, M. G., and Friedman, M. I. Hepatic control of feeding: Effect of glucose, fructose, and mannitol. *American Journal of Physiology,* 1988, *254,* R969—R976.

Träskmann, L., Åsberg, M., Bertilsson, L., and Sjöstrand, L. Monoamine metabolites in CSF and suicidal behavior. *Archives of General Psychiatry,* 1981, *38,* 631–636.

True, W. R., Xian, H., Scherrer, J. F., Madden, P. A., Bucholz, K. K., Heath, A. C., Eisen, S. A., Lyons, M. J., Goldberg, J., and Tsuang, M. Common genetic vulnerability for nicotine and alcohol dependence in men. *Archives of General Psychiatry,* 1999, *56,* 655–661.

Trujillo, K. A., and Akil, H. Opiate tolerance and dependence: Recent findings and synthesis. *New Biologist,* 1991, *3,* 915–923.

Trulson, M. E., and Jacobs, B. L. Raphe unit activity in freely moving cats: Correlation with level of behavioral arousal. *Brain Research,* 1979, *163,* 135–150.

Tsacopoulos, M., and Magistretti, P. J. Metabolic coupling between glia and neurons. *Journal of Neuroscience,* 1996, *16,* 877–885.

Tsai, G., and Coyle, J. T. Glutamatergic mechanisms in schizophrenia. *Annual Review of Pharmacology and Toxicology,* 2002, *42,* 165–179.

Tschöp, M., Smiley, D. L., and Heiman, M. L. Ghrelin induces adiposity in rodents. *Nature,* 2000, *407,* 908–913.

Tsien, J. Z., Huerta, P. T., and Tonegawa, S. The essential role of hippocampal CA1 NMDA receptor-dependent synaptic plasticity in spatial memory. *Cell,* 1996, *87,* 1327–1338.

Tsuang, M. T., Gilbertson, M. W., and Faraone, S. V. The genetics of schizophrenia: Current knowledge and future directions. *Schizophrenia Research,* 1991, *4,* 157–171.

Turner, S. M., Beidel, D. C., and Nathan, R. S. Biological factors in obsessive-compulsive disorders. *Psychological Bulletin,* 1985, *97,* 430–450.

Turrone, P., Remington, G., and Nobrega, J. N. The vacuous chewing movement (VCM) model of tardive dyskinesia revisited: Is there a relationship to dopamine D_2 receptor occupancy? *Neuroscience and Biobehavioral Reviews,* 2002, *26,* 361–380.

Tyrell, J. B., and Baxter, J. D. Glucocorticoid therapy. In *Endocrinology and Metabolism,* edited by P. Felig, J. D. Baxter, A. E. Broadus, and L. A. Frohman. New York: McGraw-Hill, 1981.

Unger, J., McNeill, T. H., Moxley, R. T., White, M., Moss, A., and Livingston, J. N. Distribution of insulin receptor-like immunoreactivity in the rat forebrain. *Neuroscience,* 1989, *31,* 143–157.

Ungerleider, L. G., and Mishkin, M. Two cortical visual systems. In *Analysis of Visual Behavior,* edited by D. J. Ingle, M. A. Goodale, and R. J. W. Mansfield. Cambridge, Mass.: MIT Press, 1982.

Ungless, M. A., Whistler, J. L., Malenka, R. C., and Bonci, A. Single cocaine exposure in vivo induces long-term potentiation in dopamine neurons. *Nature,* 2001, *411,* 583–587.

Uno, H., Tarara, R., Else, J. G., Suleman, M. A., and Sapolsky, R. M. Hippocampal damage associated with prolonged and fatal stress in primates. *Journal of Neuroscience,* 1989, *9,* 1705–1711.

Urban, P. P., Wicht, S., Marx, J., Mitrovic, S., Fitzek, C., and Hopf, H. C. Isolated voluntary facial paresis due to pontine ischemia. *Neurology,* 1998, *50,* 1859–1862.

Vaina, L. M. Complex motion perception and its deficits. *Current Opinion in Neurobiology,* 1998, *8,* 494–502.

Valenza, N., Ptak, R., Zimine, I., Badan, M., Lazeyras, F., and Schnider, A. Dissociated active and passive tactile shape recognition: A case study of pure tactile apraxia. *Brain,* 2001, *124,* 2287–2298.

Van Bockstaele, E. J., Bajic, D., Proudfit, H., and Valentino, R. J. Topographic architecture of stress-related pathways targeting the noradrenergic locus coeruleus. *Physiology and Behavior,* 2001, *73,* 273–283.

Vandenbergh, J. G., Whitsett, J. M., and Lombardi, J. R. Partial isolation of a pheromone accelerating puberty in female mice. *Journal of Reproductive Fertility,* 1975, *43,* 515–523.

van de Poll, N. E., Taminiau, M. S., Endert, E., and Louwerse, A. L. Gonadal steroid influence upon sexual and aggressive behavior of female rats. *International Journal of Neuroscience,* 1988, *41,* 271–286.

van der Lee, S., and Boot, L. M. Spontaneous pseudopregnancy in mice. *Acta Physiologica et Pharmacologica Néerlandica,* 1955, *4,* 442–444.

Vanderwolf, C. H. The electrocorticogam in relation to physiology and behavior: A new analysis. *Electroencephalography and Clinical Neurophysiology,* 1992, *82,* 165–175.

Van Essen, D. C., Anderson, C. H., and Felleman, D. J. Information processing in the primate visual system: An integrated systems perspective. *Science,* 1992, *255,* 419–423.

Van Goozen, S., Wiegant, V., Endert, E., Helmond, F., and Van de Poll, N. Psychoendrocrinological assessments of the menstrual cycle: The relationship between hormones, sexuality, and mood. *Archives of Sexual Behavior,* 1997, *26,* 359–382.

Van Tol, H. H. M., Bunzow, J. R., Hong-Chang, G., Sunahara, R. K., Seeman, P., Niznik, H. B., and Civelli, O. Cloning of the gene for a human dopamine D4 receptor with high affinity for the antipsychotic clozapine. *Nature,* 1991, *350,* 614–619.

Vassar, R., Ngai, J., and Axel, R. Spatial segregation of odorant receptor expression in the mammalian olfactory epithelium. *Cell,* 1993, *74,* 309–318.

Veldman, B. A., Wijn, A. M., Knoers, N., Praamstra, P., and Horstink, M. W. Genetic and environmental risk factors in Parkinson's disease. *Clinical Neurology and Neurosurgery,* 1998, *100,* 15–26.

Vergnes, M., Depaulis, A., Boehrer, A., and Kempf, E. Selective increase of offensive behavior in the rat following intrahypothalamic 5,7-DHT-induced serotonin depletion. *Brain Research,* 1988, *29,* 85–91.

Verney, E. B. The antidiuretic hormone and the factors which determine its release. *Proceedings of the Royal Society of London [B],* 1947, *135,* 25–106.

Vgontzas, A. N., and Kales, A. Sleep and its disorders. *Annual Review of Medicine,* 1999, *50,* 387–400.

Victor, M., and Agamanolis, J. Amnesia due to lesions confined to the hippocampus: A clinical-pathological study. *Journal of Cognitive Neuroscience,* 1990, *2,* 246–257.

Vikingstad, E. M., Cao, Y., Thomas, A. J., Johnson, A. F., Malik, G. M., Welch, K. M. A. Language hemispheric dominance in patients with congenital lesions of eloquent brain. *Neurosurgery,* 2000, *47,* 562–570.

Virkkunen, M., De Jong, J., Bartko, J., and Linnoila, M. Psychobiological concomitants of history of suicide attempts among violent offenders and impulsive fire setters. *Archives of General Psychiatry,* 1989, *46,* 604–606.

Voci, V. E., and Carlson, N. R. Enhancement of maternal behavior and nest behavior following systemic and diencephalic administration of prolactin and progesterone in the mouse. *Journal of Comparative and Physiological Psychology,* 1973, *83,* 388–393.

Vogel, G. W., Buffenstein, A., Minter, K., and Hennessey, A. Drug effects on REM sleep and on endogenous depression. *Neuroscience and Biobehavioral Reviews,* 1990, *14,* 49–63.

Vogel, G. W., Thurmond, A., Gibbons, P., Sloan, K., Boyd, M., and Walker, M. REM sleep reduction effects on depression syndromes. *Archives of General Psychiatry,* 1975, *32,* 765–777.

Vogel, G. W., Vogel, F., McAbee, R. S., and Thurmond, A. J. Improvement of depression by REM sleep deprivation: New findings and a theory. *Archives of General Psychiatry,* 1980, *37,* 247–253.

Volkow, N. D., Hitzemann, R., Wang, G.-J., Fowler, J. S., Wolf, A. P., Dewey, S. L., and Handlesman, L. Long-term frontal brain metabolic changes in cocaine abusers. *Synapse,* 1992, *11,* 184–190.

Volpe, B. T., LeDoux, J. E., and Gazzaniga, M. S. Information processing of visual stimuli in an "extinguished" field. *Nature,* 1979, *282,* 722–724.

vom Saal, F. S. Models of early hormonal effects on intrasex aggression in mice. In *Hormones and Aggressive Behavior,* edited by B. B. Svare. New York: Plenum Press, 1983.

vom Saal, F. S., and Bronson, F. H. *In utero* proximity of female mouse fetuses to males: Effect on reproductive performance during later life. *Biology of Reproduction,* 1980, *22,* 777–780.

von Békésy, G. *Experiments in Hearing.* New York: McGraw-Hill, 1960.

Vorel, S. R., Liu, X., Hayes, R. J., Spector, J. A., and Gardner, E. L. Relapse to cocaine-seeking after hippocampal theta burst stimulation, *Science,* 2001, *292,* 1175–1178.

Wada, H., Inagaki, N., Itowi, N., and Yamatodani, A. Histaminergic neuron synstems in the brain: Distribution and possible functions. *Brain Research Bulletin,* 1991, *27,* 367–370.

Wahlestedt, C., Skagerberg, G., Edman, R., Heilig, M., Sundler, F., and Hakanson, R. Neuropeptide Y (NPY) in the area of the paraventricular nucleus activates the pituitary-adrenocortical axis in the rat. *Brain Research,* 1987, *417,* 33–38.

Walker, E. F., Lewine, R. R. J., and Neumann, C. Childhood behavioral characteristics and adult brain morphology in schizophrenia. *Schizophrenia Research,* 1996, *22,* 93–101.

Walker, E. F., Savoie, T., and Davis, D. Neuromotor precursors of schizophrenia. *Schizophrenia Bulletin,* 1994, *20,* 441–451.

Walker, P. A., and Meyer, W. J. Medroxyprogesterone acetate for paraphiliac sex offender. In *Violence and the Violent Individual,* edited by J. R. Hays, T. K. Roberts, and T. S. Solway. New York: SP Medical and Scientific Books, 1981.

Wallen, K. Desire and ability: Hormones and the regulation of female sexual behavior. *Neuroscience and Biobehavioral Reviews,* 1990, *14,* 233–241.

Wallen, K. Sex and context: Hormones and primate sexual motivation. *Hormones and Behavior,* 2001, *40,* 339–357.

Wallen, K., Eisler, J. A., Tannenbaum, P. L., Nagell, K. M., and Mann, D. R. Antide (Nal-Lys GnRH antagonist) suppression of pituitary-testicular function and sexual behavior in group-living rhesus monkeys. *Physiology and Behavior,* 1991, *50,* 429–435.

Walsh, B. T., and Devlin, M. J. Eating disorders: Progress and problems. *Science,* 1998, *280,* 1387–1390.

Walsh, V., Carden, D., Butler, S. R., and Kulikowski, J. J. The effects of V4 lesions on the visual abilities of macaques: Hue discrimination and color constancy. *Behavioural Brain Research,* 1993, *53,* 51–62.

Walters, E. E., and Kendler, K. S. Anorexia nervosa and anorexic-like syndromes in a population-based female twin sample. *American Journal of Psychiatry,* 1995, *152,* 64–71.

Wang, G.-J., Volkow, N. D., Fowler, J. S., Cervany, P., Hitzemann, R. J., Pappas, N. R., Wong, C. T., and Felder, C. Regional brain metabolic activation during craving elicited by recall of previous drug experiences. *Life Sciences,* 1999, *64,* 775–784.

Wang, Q., Bing, C., Al-Barazanji, K., Mossakowaska, D. E., Wang, X. M., McBay, D. L., Neville, W. A., Taddayon, M.,

Pickavance, L., Dryden, S. Thomas, M. E., McHale, M. T., Gloyer, I. S., Wilson, S., Buckingham, R., Arch, J. R., Trayhurn, P., and Williams, G. Interactions between leptin and hypothalamic neuropeptide Y neurons in the control of food intake and energy homeostasis in the rat. *Diabetes,* 1997, *46,* 335–341.

Warne, G. L., and Zajac, J. D. Disorders of sexual differentiation. *Endocrinology and Metabolism Clinics of North America,* 1998, *27,* 945–967.

Wassink, T. H., Piven, J., Vieland, V. J., Huang, J., Swiderski, R. E., Pietila, J., Braun, T., Beck, G., Folstein, S. E., Haines, J. L., and Sheffield, V. C. Evidence supporting WNT2 as an autism susceptibility gene. *American Journal of Medical Genetics,* 2001, *105,* 406–413.

Watkins, K. E., Dronkers, N. F., and Vargha-Khadem, F. Behavioural analysis of an inherited speech and language disorder: Comparison with acquired aphasia. *Brain,* 2002a, *125,* 452–464.

Watkins, K. E., Vargha-Khadem, F., Ashburner, J., Passingham, R. E., Connelly, A., Friston, K. J., Frackowiak, R. S. J., Mishkin, M., and Gadian, D. G. MRI analysis of an inherited speech and language disorder: Structural brain abnormalities. *Brain,* 2002b, *125,* 465–478.

Webster, H. H., and Jones, B. E. Neurotoxic lesions of the dorsolateral pontomesencephalic tegmentum-cholinergic cell area in the cat. II. Effects upon sleep-waking states. *Brain Research,* 1988, *458,* 285–302.

Weggen, S., Eriksen, J. L., Sagi, S. A., Pietrzik, C. U., Ozols, V., Fauq, A., Golde, T. E., and Koo, E. H. Evidence that nonsteroidal anti-inflammatory drugs decrease amyloid beta production by direct modulation of gamma-secretase activity. *Journal of Biological Chemistry,* 2003, *278,* 31831–31837.

Wehr, T. A. Improvement of depression and triggering of mania by sleep deprivation. *Journal of the American Medical Association,* 1992, *267,* 548–551.

Wehr, T. A., Giesen, H. A., Schulz, P. M., Anderson, J. L., Joseph-Vanderpool, J. R., Kelly, K., Kasper, S., and Rosenthal, N. E. Contrasts between symptoms of summer depression and winter depression. *Journal of the Affective Disorders,* 1991, *23,* 173–183.

Wehr, T. A., Sack, D. A., and Rosenthal, N. E. Seasonal affective disorder with summer depression and winter hypomania. *American Journal of Psychiatry,* 1987, *114,* 1602–1603.

Weinberger, D. R. Schizophrenia and the frontal lobe. *Trends in Neurosciences,* 1988, *11,* 367–370.

Weinberger, D. R., and Wyatt, R. J. Brain morphology in schizophrenia: *In vivo* studies. In *Schizophrenia as a Brain Disease,* edited by F. A. Henn and H. A. Nasrallah. New York: Oxford University Press, 1982.

Weiner, R. D., and Krystal, A. D. The present use of electroconvulsive therapy. *Annual Review of Medicine,* 1994, *45,* 273–281.

Weintraub, S., Mesulam, M.-M., and Kramer, L. Disturbances in prosody: A right-hemisphere contribution to language. *Archives of Neurology,* 1981, *38,* 742–744.

Weiss, J. M. Effects of coping response on stress. *Journal of Comparative and Physiological Psychology,* 1968, *65,* 251–260.

Weissman, M. M., Canino, G. J., Greenwald, S., Joyce, P. R., Karam, E. G., Lee, C. K., Rubio-Stipec, M., Wells, J. E., Wickramaratne, P. J., and Wittchen, H. U. Current rates and symptom profiles of panic disorder in six cross-national studies. *Clinical Neuropharmacology,* 1995, *18* (Suppl. 2), S1—S6.

Weitzman, E. D. Sleep and its disorders. *Annual Review of Neuroscience,* 1981, *4,* 381–418.

Welsh, D. K., Logothetis, D. E., Meister, M., and Reppert, S. M. Individual neurons dissociated from rat suprachiasmatic nucleus express independently phased circadian firing rhythms. *Neuron,* 1995, *14,* 697–706.

Weltzin, T. E., Hsu, L. K. G., Pollice, C., and Kaye, W. H. Feeding patterns in bulimia nervosa. *Biological Psychiatry,* 1991, *30,* 1093–1110.

Wernicke, C. *Der Aphasische Symptomenkomplex.* Breslau, Poland: Cohn & Weigert, 1874.

West, D. B., Fey, D., and Woods, S. C. Cholecystokinin persistently suppresses meal size but not food intake in free-feeding rats. *American Journal of Physiology,* 1984, *246,* R776-R787.

Whalen, P. J., Rauch, S. L., Etcoff, N. L., McInerney, S. C., Lee, M. B., and Jenike, M. A. Masked presentations of emotional facial expressions modulate amygdala activity without explicit knowledge. *Journal of Neuroscience,* 1998, *18,* 411–418.

Whipple, B., and Komisaruk, B. R. Analgesia produced in women by genital self-stimulation. *Journal of Sex Research,* 1988, *24,* 130–140.

White, F. J. Synaptic regulation of mesocorticolimbic dopamine neurons. *Annual Review of Neuroscience,* 1996, *19,* 405–436.

White, J. Autonomic discharge from stimulation of the hypothalamus in man. *Association for Research in Nervous and Mental Disorders,* 1940, *20,* 854–863.

Whitten, W. K. Occurrence of anestrus in mice caged in groups. *Journal of Endocrinology,* 1959, *18,* 102–107.

Wiesner, B. P., and Sheard, N. *Maternal Behaviour in the Rat.* London: Oliver and Brody, 1933.

Wilckens, T., Schweiger, U., and Pirke, K. M. Activation of 5-HT1C-receptors suppresses excessive wheel running induced by semi-starvation in the rat. *Psychopharmacology (Berlin),* 1992, *109,* 77–84.

Wilens, T. E., Biederman, J., and Spencer, T. J. Attention deficit/hyperactivity disorder across the lifespan. *Annual Review of Medicine,* 2002, *53,* 113–131.

Wilensky, A. E., Schafe, G. E., and LeDoux, J. E. Functional inactivation of the amygdala before but not after auditory fear conditioning prevents memory formation. *Journal of Neuroscience,* 1999, *19,* RC48 (1–5).

Willesen, M. G., Kristensen, P., and Romer, J. Co-localization of growth hormone secretagogue receptor and NPY mRNA in the arcuate nucleus of the rat. *Neuroendocrinology,* 1999, *70,* 306–316.

Willingham, D. G., and Koroshetz, W. J. Evidence for dossociable motor skills in Huntington's disease patients. *Psychobiology,* 1993, *21,* 173–182.

Wilson, B. E., Meyer, G. E., Cleveland, J. C., and Weigle, D. S. Identification of candidate genes for a factor regulating body weight in primates. *American Journal of Physiology,* 1990, *259,* R1148–R1155.

Winans, S. S., and Powers, J. B. Olfactory and vomeronasal deafferentation of male hamsters: Histological and behavioral analyses. *Brain Research,* 1977, *126,* 325–344.

Wirz-Justice, A., and Van den Hoofdakker, R. H. Sleep deprivation in depression: What do we know, where do we go? *Biological Psychiatry,* 1999, *46,* 445–453.

Wirz-Justice, A., Graw, P., Kraeuchi, K., Gisin, B., Jochum, A., Arendt, J., Fisch, H.-U., Buddeberg, C., and Poeldinger, W. Light therapy in seasonal affective disorder is independent of time of day or circadian phase. *Archives of General Psychiatry,* 1993, *50,* 929–937.

Wirz-Justice, A., Graw, P., Kraeuchi, K., Sarrafzadeh, A., English, J., Arendt, J., and Sand, L. "Natural" light treatment of seasonal affective disorder. *Journal of Affective Disorders,* 1996, *37,* 109–120.

Wise, R. A., Leone, P., Rivest, R., and Leeb, K. Elevations of nucleus accumbens dopamine and DOPAC levels during intravenous heroin self-administration. *Synapse,* 1995, *21,* 140–148.

Wise, R. J. S., Greene, J., Buchel, C., and Scott, S. K. Brain regions involved in articulation. *Lancet,* 1999, *353,* 1057–1061.

Wise, S. P., and Rapoport, J. L. Obsessive compulsive disorder: Is it a basal ganglia dysfunction? *Psychopharmacology Bulletin,* 1988, *24,* 380–384.

Wissinger, B., and Sharpe, L. T. New aspects of an old theme: The genetic basis of human color vision. *American Journal of Human Genetics,* 1998, *63,* 1257–1262.

Wolfe, P. A., Cobb, J. L., and D'Agostino, R. B. In *Stroke: Pathophysiology, Diagnosis, and Management,* edited by H. J. M. Barnett, B. M. Stein, J. P. Mohr, and F. M. Yatsu. New York: Churchill Livingstone, 1992.

Wolff, P. H., and Melngailis, I. Family patterns of developmental dyslexia: Clinical findings. *American Journal of Medical Genetics,* 1994, *54,* 122–131.

Wong, G. T., Gannon, K. S., and Margolskee, R. F. Transduction of bitter and sweet taste by gustducin. *Nature,* 1996, *381,* 796–800.

Wong-Riley, M. T. Personal communication, 1978. Cited by Livingstone, M. S., and Hubel, D. H. Thalamic inputs to cytochrome oxidase-rich regions in monkey visual cortex. *Proceedings of the National Academy of Sciences, USA,* 1982, *79,* 6098–6101.

Wood, R. I., and Newman, S. W. Mating activates androgen receptor-containing neurons in chemosensory pathways of the male Syrian hamster brain. *Brain Research,* 1993, *614,* 65–77.

Woodruff-Pak, D. S. Eyeblink classical conditioning in H. M.: Delay and trace paradigms. *Behavioral Neuroscience,* 1993, *107,* 911–925.

Woods, B. T. Is schizophrenia a progressive neurodevelopmental disorder? Toward a unitary pathogenetic mechanism. *American Journal of Psychiatry,* 1998, *155,* 1661–1670.

Woods, S. C., Lotter, E. C., McKay, L. D., and Porte, D. Chronic intracerebroventricular infusion of insulin reduces food intake and body weight of baboons. *Nature,* 1979, *282,* 503–505.

Woodworth, R. S., and Schlosberg, H. *Experimental Psychology.* New York: Holt, Rinehart and Winston, 1954.

Wu, J. C., and Bunney, W. E. The biological basis of an antidepressant response to sleep deprivation and relapse: Review and hypothesis. *American Journal of Psychiatry,* 1990, *147,* 14–21.

Wu, J. C., Buchsbaum, M. S., and Bunney, W. E. Positron emission tomography study

of phencyclidine users as a possible drug model of schizophrenia. *Yakubutsu Seishin Kodo,* 1991, *11,* 47–48
Wysocki, C. J. Neurobehavioral evidence for the involvement of the vomeronasal system in mammalian reproduction. *Neuroscience and Biobehavioral Reviews,* 1979, *3,* 301–341.
Yadin, E., Thomas, E., Strickland, C. E., and Grishkat, H. L. Anxiolytic effects of benzodiazepines in amygdala-lesioned rats. *Psychopharmacology,* 1991, *103,* 473–479.
Yanovski, J. A., and Yanovski, S. Z. Recent advances in basic obesity research. *Journal of the American Medical Association,* 1999, *282,* 1504–1506.
Yates, W. R., Perry, P., and Murray, S. Aggression and hostility in anabolic steroid users. *Biological Psychiatry,* 1992, *31,* 1232–1234.
Yatham, L. N., Liddle, P. F., Shiah, I. S., Scarrow, G., Lam, R. W., Adam, M. J., Zis, A. P., and Ruth, T. J. Brain serotonin-2 receptors in major depression: A positron emission tomography study. *Archives of General Psychiatry,* 2000, *57,* 850–858.
Yehuda, R. Are glucocorticoids responsible for putative hippocampal damage in PTSD? How and when to decide. *Hippocampus,* 2001, *11,* 85–90.
Yokoo, H., Tanaka, M., Yoshida, M., Tsuda, A., Tanaka, T., and Mizoguchi, K. Direct evidence of conditioned fear-elicited enhancement of noradrenaline release in the rat hypothalamus assessed by intracranial microdialysis. *Brain Research,* 1990, *536,* 305–308.
Yokota, T., Ishiai, S., Furukawa, T., and Tsukagoshi, H. Pure agraphia of kanji due to thrombosis of the Labbe vein. *Journal of Neurology, Neurosurgery, and Psychiatry,* 1990, *53,* 335–338.
Yost, W. A. Auditory image perception and analysis: The basis for hearing. *Hearing Research,* 1991, *56,* 8–18.
Young, A. W., Aggleton, J. P., Hellawell, D. J., Johnson, M., Broks, P., and Hanley, J. R. Face processing impairments after amygdalotomy. *Brain,* 1995, *118,* 15–24.
Zayfert, C., Dums, A. R., Ferguson, R. J., and Hegel, M. T. Health functioning impairments associated with posttraumatic stress disorder, anxiety disorders, and depression. *Journal of Nervous and Mental Disease,* 2002, *190,* 233–240.
Zeki, S. The representation of colours in the cerebral cortex. *Nature,* 1980, *284,* 412–418.
Zeki, S., Aglioti, S., McKeefry, D., and Berlucchi, G. The neurological basis of conscious color perception in a blind patient. *Proceedings of the National Academy of Science, USA,* 1999, *96,* 14124–14129.
Zeki, S., and Shipp, S. The functional logic of cortical connections. *Nature,* 1988, *335,* 311–317.
Zenner, H.-P., Zimmermann, U., and Schmitt, U. Reversible contraction of isolated mammalian cochlear hair cells. *Hearing Research,* 1985, *18,* 127–133.
Zhang, C. Y., and Wong-Riley, M. T. Do nitric oxide synthase, NMDA receptor subunit R1 and cytochrome oxidase co-localize in the rat central nervous system? *Brain Research,* 1996, *729,* 205–215.
Zihl, J., Von Cramon, D., Mai, N., and Schmid, C. Disturbance of movement vision after bilateral posterior brain damage: Further evidence and follow up observations. *Brain,* 1991, *114,* 2235–2252.
Zola-Morgan, S., Squire, L. R., and Amaral, D. G. Human amnesia and the medial temporal region: Enduring memory impairment following a bilateral lesion limited to field CA1 of the hippocampus. *Journal of Neuroscience,* 1986, *6,* 2950–2967.
Zola-Morgan, S., Squire, L., Rempel, N. L., Clower, R. P., and Amaral, D. G. Enduring memory impairment in monkeys after ischemic damage to the hippocampus. *Journal of Neuroscience,* 1992, *12,* 2582–2596.
Zou, Z., Horowitz, L. F., Montmayeur, J.-P., Snapper, S., and Buck, L. B. Genetic tracing reveals a stereotyped sensory map in the olfactory cortex. *Nature,* 2001, *414,* 173–179.
Zukin, S. R., Pellegrini-Giampietro, D. E., Knapp, C. M., and Tempel, A. Opioid receptor regulation. *Handbook of Experimental Pharmacology,* 1993, *104,* 107–123.
Zumpe, D., Bonsall, R. W., Kutner, M. H., and Michael, R. P. Medroxyprogesterone acetate, aggression, and sexual behavior in male cynomolgus monkeys (Macaca fascicularis). *Hormones and Behavior,* 1991, *25,* 394–409.

NAME INDEX

SUBJECT INDEX

Note: Boldfaced page numbers indicate pages where terms are defined. Page numbers followed by the letter *f* or *t* indicate figures or tables, respectively.